Antenna Topics

Cuttings from more than 40 years of the *Technical Topics* column
written by Pat Hawker, G3VA,
for the journal of the Radio Society of Great Britain

Chapter	*page*
1958 - 1969	**1**
1970 - 1979	**33**
1980 - 1989	**151**
1990 - 1999	**261**

Radio Society of Great Britain

Published by the Radio Society of Great Britain, Lambda House, Cranborne Road, Potters Bar, Herts EN6 3JE.

First published 2002

© Radio Society of Great Britain, 2002. All rights reserved. No part of this publication may be reproduced, stored in a retrieval system, or transmitted in any form, or by any means, electronic, mechanical, photocopying, recording or otherwise, without the prior written agreement of the Radio Society of Great Britain.

ISBN 1 872309 89 5

Publisher's note

The opinions expressed in this book are those of the authors and not necessarily those of the RSGB. While the information presented is believed to be correct, the authors, publisher and their agents cannot accept responsibility for consequences arising from any inaccuracies or omissions.

Antenna Topics has been compiled from the printed pages of the RSGB's journal, so its style, layout and typography reflects the changes made over more than 40 years. For the same reason, the early pages refer to 'aerials', not 'antennas', and even 'Mc/s' rather than 'MHz'. By publishing the items as they originally appeared and in chronological order, it is hoped that the reader will get a sense of the history of antennas used and developed by amateurs and professionals, and that this will assist in understanding the subject matter.

Cover design: Braden Threadgold Advertising

Typography: Mike Dennison, Emdee Publishing, Welwyn Garden City

Production: Mark Allgar

Printed in Great Britain by PWP Acrolith Ltd

Preface

WHEN I BEGAN compiling and writing the *Technical Topics* column over 40 years ago, in April 1958, amateur radio was still rooted in valve technology with a few experimental uses of germanium bipolar transistors just emerging. RF power transistors, integrated circuits and surface mount technology were still years away. Firms such as Eddystone, Hallicrafters, Hammarlund, National, Panda Radio, KW Electronics, Geloso, Minimitter were catering for the amateur market, although much surplus World War 2 equipment and many home-brew rigs were still to be heard. Racal had lately commenced production of their RA17 receiver. Collins were on the brink of marketing their S-line with the 75S-1.

Soon the first amateur SSB/CW transceiver (KWM-1) appeared from Collins and a trickle of Japanese communication receivers and then low-cost transceivers were marketed under Western brand names (Lafayette, Trio, Sommerkamp, etc). The epoch of home-construction continued to flourish, particularly for power supply units, ancillary and test units. Some decades of kit assembly brought Heathkit to the fore.

Much of '*TT*' was initially concerned with these valved units and related topics, but in addition to equipment, components, fault-finding etc, *TT* has always attempted to provide practical information, hints and tips, some basics and much comment on practical antennas for the many amateurs and short-wave listeners struggling to overcome restricted space, difficult environments and limited finances. It is not suggested that the HF antennas described in *TT* are likely to outperform a TH6 rotary beam mounted on a 20m tower! Nevertheless, I remain convinced that the LF, MF, HF and VHF/UHF antenna systems described in this compilation of items published in *TT* between 1958 and 1999 will provide an almost endless source of interest and experiment, capable of achieving a useful performance at an acceptable cost.

Even today, when so much depends on commercial products, antennas still remain the sector of our hobby in which home construction and experimentation play a significant role.

A major impact on the hobby, reflecting particularly on antenna systems, has resulted from the release of additional freq-uency bands. Whereas, in 1958, HF activity was confined to 3.5, 7, 14, 21 and 28MHz bands (all harmonically related) and VHF to 70 and 144MHz, the amateur today can make use also of the so-called 'WARC' bands at 10, 18 and 24MHz, temporary UK assignments at 5MHz, the important VHF band at 50MHz, and the LF band at 136kHz. This has brought about a revival in multiband and broadband antennas, open-wire transmission lines etc and these changes are well reflected in this unique compilation of *TT* items.

As with the earlier *Technical Topics Scrapbooks*, this is essentially an ideas book based on reprinted extracts from *TT*, but in this case devoted entirely to material relating to antenna systems and covering more than 40 years of the column. It is not another antenna textbook, but instead provides, in understandable and largely non-mathematical terms, a unique compendium of useful suggestions and advice contributed by several generations of RSGB members, both in the UK and overseas. This is supplemented by digests of articles that have appeared in amateur radio and professional journals and magazines, or presented at national or international conferences.

Unlike the major and continuous changes in equipment, the basics of antennas remain ageless. Antenna systems developed up to 100 years ago are as valid today as when they first emerged from such pioneers as Marconi, Levy, Franklin, Beverage, Uda-Yagi, George Brown of RCA, Kraus of Ohio State University and the Bell Laboratories' rhombic. Perhaps the single most significant development during the time that *TT* has been appearing is the development of computer-modelling and simulation of HF antennas. The Numerical Electromagnetic Code based on the Methods of Moments has made a significant impact on antenna design by both professionals and amateurs. Nevertheless, it is important to remember that the performance of simulated designs (and indeed of any antenna) may be greatly affected by the environments in which they are erected.

Unlike the professional broadcast or communications engineer, the radio amateur is seldom in a position to put up an antenna in an extensive, favourably-located site. It is usually a matter of a small (or no) garden, often in an urban area surrounded by large buildings, with grounds of poor electrical conductivity. It may be a matter of utilising a roof space, balcony or even an indoor room. This compilation is catholic, it discusses antennas for the favoured few with excellent sites through to indoor antennas that can be stuck to windows, draped round rooms or even where the RF output from the transmitter has to be coupled into metal drain pipes etc.

Particular attention has always been given to electrically-short 'loaded' antennas such as those used for mobile operation or in the most restricted of locations. *TT* was the first amateur radio column to draw attention to the development of compact, reasonably-efficient transmitting loops, initially developed by the US military for use in the jungles of Vietnam.

A few of the experimental designs presented in *TT* have proved controversial, with the resulting critical views presented in subsequent issues. A very few of the designs, not only those originated by amateurs, have proved fundamentally unsound; for some others the debate continues. Experimental antennas can generate heated controversy! We are fortunate that a number of professional antenna specialists are also radio amateurs and contribute to *TT*, though even these would admit that there is still much to learn about some aspects of antenna design!

It has been my good fortune in London to have access to several excellent technical libraries where copies of the journals of the IEE, IEEE, etc and magazines and books intended for professional engineers can be consulted. These include the British Library, the IEE Library and the Science Museum Library. Such access has enabled *TT* to keep abreast of some at least of the trends of current professional and academic Research & Development – and to survey this work in terms that can be grasped by radio amateurs with no professional connection with the subject. I acknowledge my great debt to these sources.

For some, the antenna is still a mixture of myth and magic. It defies the simple logic of direct current electricity. But in reality it an be explained in terms of alternating current theory, impedance, inductive and capacitive reactance, once it is recognised that *any piece of wire or conductive metal tubing will radiate a signal provided that one can couple RF energy into it*. Until this energy is radiated as an electromagnetic wave, it is in the form of an electrical alternating current in which the amplitude of the current and potential will be alternating between maximum positive and maximum negative values millions of times per second. Where current flows a small part of the power will be radiated in the form of an electromagnetic wave.

A short piece of wire radiates energy less readily than a longer wire with a physical length approaching one half-wavelength or more but this is primarily because it is more difficult to couple energy into and out of a short length of wire. There will also be an increase in energy losses (IR, 'current times resistance' losses) resulting in lower radiation efficiency, rather than any fundamental requirement that an antenna should always have a length of a half-wave or more. This is just as well since at the LF band of 136kHz, this would require a length of some 1100 metres! Part of the art of antenna design centres on the design and use of electrically-short antennas without too great a reduction in efficiency. Since an antenna radiates power when there is current flowing in it, it can be thought of as possessing *radiation resistance*. This should not be confused with its *feed-point impedance*, although in the case of a resonant half-wave dipole element, the values may be the same (73 ohms purely resistive) when the element is fed at its centre point. But in most cases, the feed-point impedance comprises a combination of capacitive or inductive reactance and resistance.

In practice an *antenna system* should always aim at being resonant at the frequency of operation. This does not imply that the radiating wire or element itself need always be resonant, since the system may be 'loaded' with lumped inductance (or unusually its electrical length made less than its physical length by series capacitors). The system may also be made 'resonant' by means of open-wire transmission lines and the 'tuning out' of reactance by means of a suitable antenna system tuning unit (ASTU, ATU). A 'dipole' type of balanced antenna operates without a requirement for a ground system; a 'monopole' antenna inherently depends on having an effective real or artificial (elevated radials) earth system. Ideally a radiating element should be well removed from any energy-absorbing materials, such as buildings, trees, metal fences, metal drainpipes, house electrical wiring etc. Its height above earth (which acts as both an absorber and reflector of radio waves) has an important bearing on its operation. For most practical purposes, the 'higher the better' applies, unless the antenna is primarily for 'short skip' (NVIS) contacts.

The *TT* items in this compilation include comments originating from Walter Maxwell, W2DU who has done much to counter the myths surrounding the interpretation of VSWR measurements that still cause some amateurs to believe that 'reflected power' is dissipated in the transmitter and not radiated. It is perhaps unfortunate that the myth has been reinforced by the fact that many of the early solid-state transmitters needed to be operated into a well-matched load.

It is my hope that such fundamentals will become clearer to newcomers to the hobby in the course of reading (or dipping into) this book and that it will succeed in de-mystifying for all the world of practical antennas!

Grateful acknowledgement is made to all the many radio amateurs, professional engineers and scientists worldwide, and to the amateur radio and professional engineering publications from which so much of the material was originally drawn or inspired. It is my policy always, wherever possible, to acknowledge fully the source of all abstracts and ideas and to credit the originators. Acknowledgement is also made to the editorial staff of the RSGB for their patience and encouragement over the years, not only during the publication of *TT* but in proposing and assembling this volume devoted to Antenna Topics. Finally, acknowledgement is also made to Derek Cole, who prepared the *TT* technical illustrations for some 30 years; more recently by Bob Ryan, 2E1EKS, the Society's technical illustrator since 1994.

Pat Hawker, G3VA

London, September 2002

1958 - 1969

Simple Aerials using 300-ohm Feeder

Extracted from 'Technical Topics',
RSGB Bulletin, July 1958

Aerials from Ribbon Feeder

Extracted from 'Technical Topics',
RSGB Bulletin, July 1959

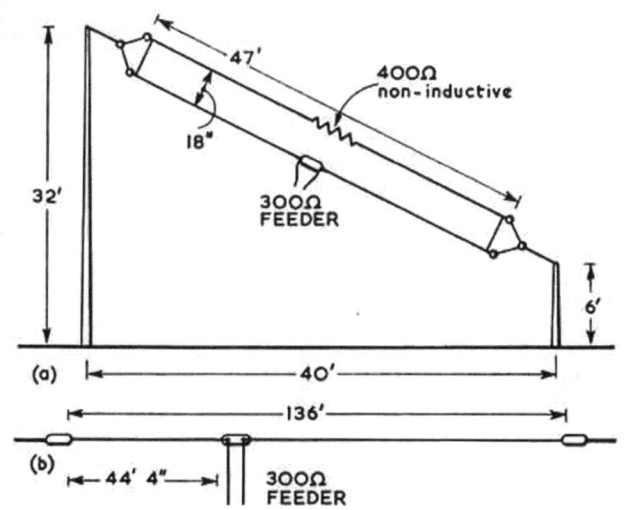

Fig. 3 (a) The "T2FD" aerial. (b) The twin feeder Windom.

Simple Aerials using 300-ohm Feeder

Despite the current popularity of co-axial feeders, many amateurs have a sneaking preference for 300 ohm ribbon feeder; one reason is the ease of checking for excessive standing waves by the well-known twin lamp system or by the even simpler method of running a neon bulb along the line. Then there are no "balun" difficulties at the aerial end of dipoles as the ribbon is a balanced feeder, and—a severely practical point—the flat type of ribbon feeder can usually be run out through windows or over doors to try out aerials without drilling.

Two simple multi-band aerials which use 300 ohm feeder and which, although not new, have not been featured previously in the BULLETIN are shown in Fig. 3. Fig. 3 (b) is a modern adaptation of the famous off-centre fed dipole or Windom aerial and with the dimensions given (taken from 1958 *A.R.R.L. Handbook*) is said to provide a reasonable match on 80, 40, 20 and 10 metres; the dimensions can be scaled down if the lower frequency bands are not required. Provided that there is no excessive radiation from the feeder, the radiation patterns will be those of any normal 136 ft. aerial. Fig. 3 (a) is the so-called "T2FD" (terminated tilted folded dipole) introduced some years ago in *CQ* (November 1951, February 1953, June 1957). With the dimensions given it is said to perform effectively on 3·5, 7 and 21 Mc/s as a more or less omni-directional aerial.

Aerials from Ribbon Feeder

Some months ago we described two aerials using 300 ohm feeders: the twin-feed Windom and the T2FD. This month we propose to include two aerials in which 300 ohm feeder is used for the dipole elements: see Fig. 4. The ribbon feeder folded dipole (Fig. 4(a)) has been with us for a long time now but the form shown (it appears in several editions of *The Radio Handbook*) takes into account the velocity factor of the ribbon feeder and gives a better match than the more usual system of just joining up the ends of a length of the feeder; the length ($462/f$ ft.) is also slightly modified from the standard dipole formula. Where a space-saving is required the end pieces can be dropped down symmetrically with very little lowering of efficiency. This system has given satisfactory service at G3VA and can be recommended to anyone looking for a simple non-critical single-band

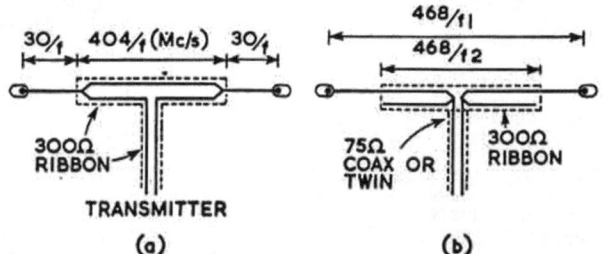

Fig. 4. Two aerials using 300 ohm ribbon: (a) The conventional ribbon folded dipole with modifications suggested by "The Radio Handbook"; (b) Paralleled dipoles made easy with 300 ohm ribbon, by making f_1 7 Mc/s and f_2 14 Mc/s. The aerial can be used on 7, 14 and 21 Mc/s.

aerial. The multi-band aerial of Fig. 4(b) has appeared in a number of publications, including *QST*, but may be new to some. In this aerial, the ribbon feeder is simply used as a very easy means of producing two paralleled dipoles, so that the actual feeder is a standard 70 ohm type. By erecting a 66 ft. span, and using 33 ft. of ribbon feeder plus two 16 ft. lengths of wire, the resulting aerial functions on 7 and 14 Mc/s as half-wave dipoles; on 21 Mc/s the 7 Mc/s section operates as a $\tfrac{3}{2}\lambda$ aerial; the dimensions could of course be scaled for any other combination of bands. But watch out for 42 Mc/s harmonic from your 21 Mc/s output since this will be radiated very nicely from the 33 ft. dipole section.

ANTENNA TOPICS

Broadband Aerials

Extracted from 'Technical Topics',
RSGB Bulletin, January 1960

Broadband Aerials

When we think of a multi-band aerial we normally think of one that resonates on a number of harmonically related bands. There is another approach to this problem: this is to devise an aerial which will operate over a continuous very wide band of frequencies. A good rhombic is one example; another is the "discone"—one practical design (*Radio Handbook*) covers 13-58 Mc/s with a standing wave ratio on 52 ohm feeder remaining below 1·5 throughout this range. Now a new name to conjure with is the "log periodic" aerial. In an article introducing this new family of aerials to the amateur, W1FVY (*QST*, November, 1959) explains how ten-to-one bandwidths can be obtained on one aerial (e.g. 14-144 Mc/s or 28-280 Mc/s) and gives some practical design data for fixed arrays, requiring two 30 ft., and one 15 ft., masts and without any major constructional problems. Although the main virtue of this type of aerial is its broadband feature, the design discussed provides a modest but useful 6db gain.

Vertical Aerials

Extracted from 'Technical Topics',
RSGB Bulletin, April 1960

Vertical Aerials

Paradoxically, the best way to improve a Top Band aerial system is to make a better earth connection. With the average short aerial providing a radiation resistance of only a few ohms, earth losses account for a substantial portion of the total power supplied to the aerial system. The earth is equally important for the multi-band vertical aerials now becoming popular on 14, 21 and 28 Mc/s. A booklet prepared by Mosley Electronics, with useful tips on installation of such aerials, was distributed at the R.S.G.B. Radio Hobbies Exhibition last November. Contrary to usual amateur practice the best place for the base of these aerials is at ground level, provided that a good network of radials is used. The B.B.C. uses up to 144 half-wave radials for some of its main medium wave stations, attached to a mesh of wires some 20 ft. square immediately under the mast, but Mosleys suggest that satisfactory results can be obtained with four radials about as long as the equivalent length of the aerial with an earth rod at the end of each radial, which can be left on the surface (the B.B.C. use mole ploughs for sinking their wires). An earth rod should also be fitted immediately under the aerial. It has been pointed out elsewhere (*Radio and Television Engineers' Reference Book*) that where a restricted earth system is used, all nearby metalwork should be connected to it. High losses can occur, for example, in fencing wires if they run close to a low vertical aerial.

W9KPD in *CQ* (November, 1959) suggests that an effective multiband vertical with a low angle of radiation and without traps consists of a ⅝-wavelength long rod or wire for the highest frequency required; this length will function well on lower but not on higher frequency bands. For example, a 41·5 ft. aerial should be good on 14, 7 and 3·5 Mc/s but could not be expected to do well on 21 and 28 Mc/s. His suggested matching unit for installation at the base of the mast is shown in Fig. 4.

G4ZU 'Birdcage' Aerial

Extracted from 'Technical Topics',
RSGB Bulletin, June 1960

Also Noted

G4ZU describes his happily-named "Birdcage" aerial in *CQ*, April, 1960. Strong claims are made for this interesting new array, including a 10db gain, a relatively simple mechanical structure (in effect two X's one above the other with the ends joined with wire) and only a limited space needed for erection and rotation. One-wavelength loop elements of the quad type are used as radiator and reflector and in appearance it is not unlike the traditional Bellini-Tosi d.f. aerial except that each loop, which may be square or circular, does not cross but is bent back in the form of two stacked V-dipoles. Single and multi-band versions using the same loops are described. Now it only remains for someone to come up with a modern radio-goniometer which would make it unnecessary to rotate the aerial

Inverted-V Dipoles

Extracted from 'Technical Topics',
RSGB Bulletin, October 1960

Inverted-V Dipoles

With sunspot activity—to quote—"on the skids" we can expect good DX on 3·5 and 7 Mc/s during the next few years. K7GCO in the August 1960 *QST* urges the use on these bands of the "inverted V-shaped dipole," claiming consistent out-performance of ground planes and horizontal and vertical dipoles. This aerial is simply a centre-fed dipole with a high centre and the two ends attached to much lower anchor posts, without any suggestion of there being any critical apex angle. Sloping the dipole elements shortens the electrical length and an extra 5 per cent or so should be added to their length; the centre impedance will also be lowered so that it presents a better match to 50-ohm than to 70-ohm coax. K7GCO suggests that band width can be increased—if necessary—by using three- or five-wire "cage" elements rather than a single wire, while two bands can be covered by running paralleled dipoles at right angles from the single high support point.

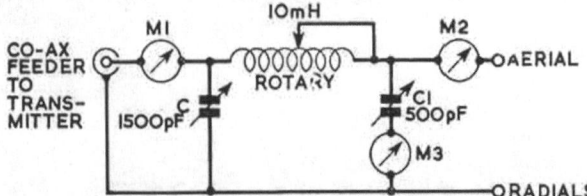

Fig. 4. W9KPD's suggested pi-coupler for matching to a 5/8 wavelength aerial. For high impedance aerial condition, C should be open, the coil adjusted and C1 tuned. For low impedance, C1 should be at minimum; tune C and the coil.

1958 - 1969

A Span of Aerials (or a 'Clutch of DX')

Extracted from 'Technical Topics', *RSGB Bulletin,* December 1960

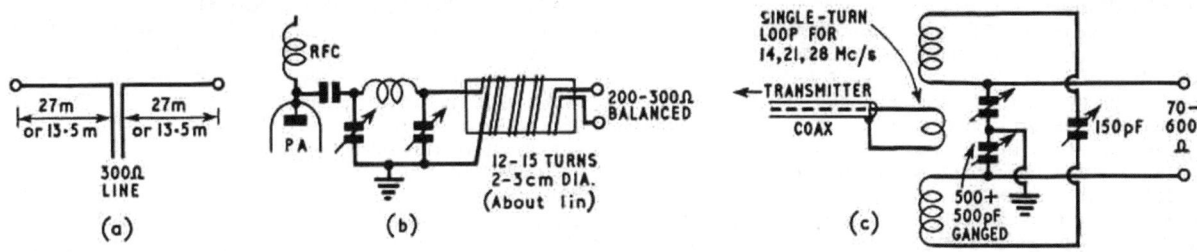

Fig. 1 (a) The DJ2ZF multi-band dipole; (b) Balun suggested by DJ2ZF; (c) Alternative pi-network type aerial tuning unit which provides balanced output.

A Span of Aerials (or should it be a "Clutch of DX"?)

From time to time, we have drawn attention to aerials which use 300 ohm ribbon feeder either as a transmission line or for the aerial itself. Recently several more have come to our notice. Admittedly, the evaluation of new amateur aerials is not always simplified by the "wash whiter" claims sometimes put forward on their behalf; it is as well to remember that, in the words of *CQ* Magazine, "everything is experimental and we guarantee nothing." So do not ask how, why or if they really work for everyone as well as apparently they do for their originators!

In *DL-QTC* (November, 1959) DJ2ZF described a new "all band doublet antenna" which consisted simply of a dipole of dimensions 2 × 27m (i.e. overall length about 167 ft.) fed at the centre by 300 ohm line: see Fig. 1(a). The author claimed—and provided mathematical analysis—that the centre impedance at least on the 3·5, 7 and 14 Mc/s bands falls within the range 240-300 ohms and thus presents an excellent match to ribbon feeder. A further article of his in the September 1960 issue suggests that the overall length can if necessary be scaled down to half the above figure (2 × 13·5m, or 83 ft. 6 in. overall) for 7, 14 and 28 Mc/s. The DJ2ZF aerial should preferably be fed from a balanced source and details of a simple balun were given in the original article though as a translation is not available Fig. 1 (b) represents the only information we have. An alternative matching unit, suitable for providing 50-600 ohms or so

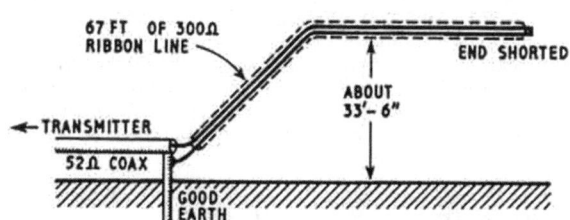

Fig. 3. The quarter-wave grounded Marconi for 3·5 Mc/s using 67 ft. of 300 ohm ribbon line.

said, the s.w.r. on 14 Mc/s can be as low as 2 : 1 and unity on the other bands. It is claimed that this beam can be used directly from an unbalanced pi-network without using a balun. (This incidentally seems in line with an article in *Proc. I.E.E.*, January 1960, giving detailed information on the performance of balanced aerials when connected directly to an unbalanced line and suggesting *inter alia* that the distortion of the radiation pattern is appreciably less for a Yagi array than for a simple dipole.)

The 3·5 Mc/s grounded quarter-wave Marconi aerial formed from 67 ft. of 300 ohm ribbon feeder shown in Fig. 3 is not new, and it has appeared in several editions of *Radio Handbook* but our excuse for including it this month is that it was reprinted recently in *Radio ZS* (September, 1960) on the recommendation of ZS6AUB. A good earth, such as a rising water pipe is needed. It could be scaled down for 7 Mc/s or the dimensions doubled for 1·8 Mc/s.

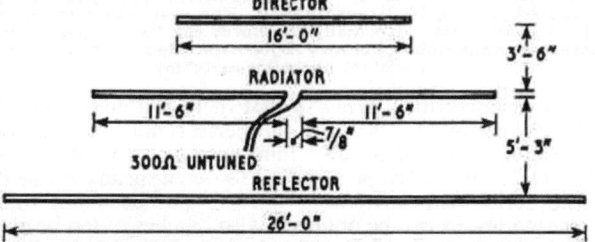

Fig. 2. Dimensions for the "ZE4JJ Special" three-band beam for 14, 21 and 28 Mc/s. Elements are made from ⅜ in. tubing and the radiator is mounted 2 in. above the plane of the other elements.

balanced output from a co-ax line is shown in Fig. 1 (c), this being a system which has proved satisfactory at G3VA for a number of years.

The lively *Journal of the Radio Society of East Africa* occasionally reprints items from this feature: now we are glad to return the compliment by showing (Fig. 2) details of the multi-band "ZE4JJ Special" described in the September 1960 issue by VQ2JV (ex-ZE4JJ). This is said to provide excellent results as a tri-band beam for 14, 21 and 28 Mc/s. No analysis of the mode of operation is given but it is stated that dimensions must be followed accurately. An unusual feature is that the driven element should be mounted 2 in. above the plane of the other elements; if this is done, it is

Multiband Aerial Using Stubs

Extracted from 'Technical Topics', *RSGB Bulletin,* February 1961

Multiband Aerials using Stubs

A clever way of using shorted quarter wave stubs for multiband aerials was patented some ten years ago by W4JRW, but received little publicity until details were given in *QST* (December 1960). An attractive feature of his system is the convenient form of construction, requiring simply the insertion of a section of 300 ohm twin feeder into the actual dipole (alternatively the entire dipole can be made from 300 ohm line by paralleling the wires where not needed for the stub). The idea is to separate off part of a dipole used on a lower frequency band by inserting the stub to form an electronic insulator on the higher frequency band only (as

ANTENNA TOPICS

Aerial Miscellany

Extracted from 'Technical Topics', *RSGB Bulletin,* October 1961

G4ZU's 'FB-5' Multiband Aerial

Extracted from 'Technical Topics', *RSGB Bulletin,* December 1961

Aerial Miscellany

Perhaps one reason why so many different types of aerials have been developed by amateurs is that site problems vary so much. It is often necessary to consider and reject countless good aerial systems before finding one that exactly fits all our particular requirements. Certainly there is no slowing down in new ideas—or in revivals of old ones.

For those with some spare 300 ohm cable, the "One-third Multiband" described by OH1NE (*CQ*, August) should be worth a try. Basically its operation depends upon the fact that at a point one-third along a 3·5 Mc/s quarter-wave open-ended stub section the impedance is close to 300 ohms and that the same point is also approximately one-third of a quarter-wave from a point of current maximum on 7, 14 and 28 Mc/s; and even on 21 Mc/s provides a workable match to 300 ohms. Details are given in Fig. 2 (a). A half-scale version is said to work on 7, 14, 21 and 28 Mc/s. OH1NE also suggests that the system could be used to feed a 33 ft. ground plane with a 29 ft. stub of 300 ohm line tapped one-third distance from the radiator and fed with 120 ohm co-ax.

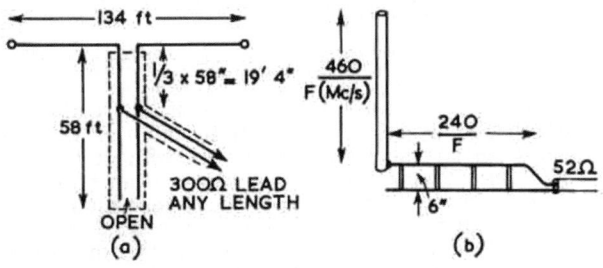

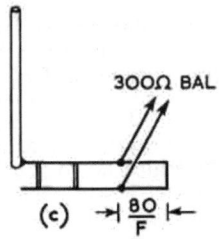

Fig. 2. (a) OH1NE's "one-third" multiband aerial for 3·5–28 Mc/s using 300 ohm feeder and stub. (b) Half-wave vertical aerial recommended by EL4A with 6 in. spaced stub section. (c) Aerial can alternatively be fed with 300 ohm feeder by using "one-third" tap.

Another vertical aerial with stub tuning (which can also make use of the one-third point) is recommended by EL4A. This is simply one form of the erstwhile popular half-wave vertical Zepp. In one version, see Fig. 2 (b), the end of the quarter-wave resonant feeder section is connected to an untuned transmission line of 52 ohm co-ax. When erecting the resonant point of the stub section alone, and subsequently the stub plus radiator, should be checked with a grid dip oscillator (short end of stub and couple this to g.d.o.) before connecting the co-ax. The other version, indicated in Fig. 2 (c), connects 300 ohm feeder at the one-third point; in this case it should be connected to the transmitter either through a balun or a tuning unit which serves the same purpose (for example, the one shown in *T.T.* December, 1960). This aerial was described in an article by K7GCO in *Western Radio Amateur* (May, 1958).

Many of us have at some time or another had to depend on indoor aerials. When sited low down in a large building results tend to be pretty poor, but a good loft or roof-space aerial can often give first-rate results. W2LCB (*CQ* August) gives some hints on "Indoor Antenna Farming" and in particular recommends the use of 300 ohm line type of folded dipoles which can easily be suspended from small hooks and eyes and rolled up when not in use.

G4ZU's "FB-5" Multiband Aerial

G4ZU certainly deserved the full house he had for his recent lecture at the I.E.E. By now details of his ingenious but basically simple new multiband array must have reached many members by the grapevine. Pending a full account by G4ZU here are the essentials, though as a reporter G3VA fell down on this occasion since two pens ran dry on him.

Briefly the heart of the system consists of using ferrite beads (see *T.T.*, August 1961) to lengthen electrically an aerial. Since these beads have a much greater loading effect at current maxima than at current minima, it is possible to use the same beads to provide different loading effects on various bands. An additional refinement is incorporated to overcome the pronounced radiation lobes of long wire aerials: this consists of a section of 300-ohm ribbon to adjust the phase of the radiating portion of the aerial.

Fig. 2(a) shows the basic aerial while Fig. 2(b) shows how G4ZU has combined two such elements into a fixed beam array providing really useful gains on 14, 21 and 28 Mc/s. On 3·5 and 7 Mc/s "at least up to dipole" results are claimed. The array is fed with 70 or (preferably) 50 ohm untuned feeder and no aerial tuning unit is needed; thus used with a bandswitched transmitter the array is instantly ready for operation on five bands.

With accurate adjustment of the number or position of the ferrite beads very low s.w.r. can be achieved, but this is

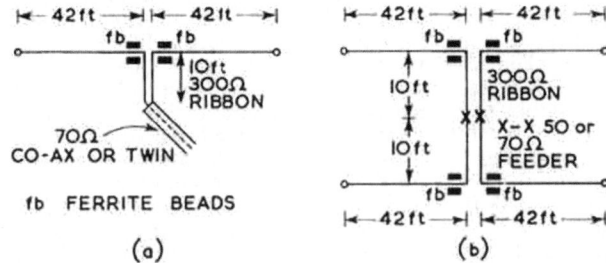

Fig. 2. (a) Basic multiband element for G4ZU's FB-5 array—could be used in this form for 3·5, 14, 21 and 28 Mc/s. (b) The full FB-5 array combines two elements, usually stacked one above the other. The lower element can be as low as about 5 ft. off the ground. Operates on all bands from 3·5 to 28 Mc/s without additional tuning, providing substantial gain on 14, 21 and 28 Mc/s. The radiation pattern on 14 Mc/s is broadside. Normally the beads can be up against the junction with the ribbon, but may require moving slightly along the aerial for optimum matching.

basically a non-critical array so that there is a good deal of tolerance all round, and only the perfectionists will strive for absolutely flat lines. For minimum s.w.r. G4ZU uses groups of 25 Mullard B4 pattern FX1300 ferrite beads threaded on the aerial wire (18 s.w.g. or less), but he states that acceptable results can be obtained with batches of ten beads.

The array resonates on 14 Mc/s without electrical loading, and the beads are thus at a low current point as seen by 14 Mc/s signals. The effect of this loading is to resonate the array on both 21 and 28 Mc/s. The 3·5 and 7 Mc/s bands pretty well look after themselves, although the loading probably helps.

This is clearly a highly practical use of electrical loading and it looks as though G4ZU has come up with another winner in the "ferrite-bead five-band" or "FB-5" aerial.

Condensed Rotary Dipole for 14MHz

Extracted from 'Technical Topics',
RSGB Bulletin, June 1962

Condensed Rotary Dipole for 14 Mc/s

The rotating dipole can still be a most useful aerial for those who want to radiate signals to all points of the compass without the constructional and adjustment problems of a multi-element beam. But for 14 Mc/s it is often difficult to fit a rotating 33 ft. element into the space available. In *CQ* (March 1962), K2EEE describes the construction of a mini-dipole (Fig. 4) of about 16 ft. overall length, using two 7·5 μH loading coils (approximately 11 turns on 2½ in. diameter former, 6 t.p.i. using U.S. No. 12 or 14 wire). Final adjustment is made by two end lengths (each 2 ft. long) of ⅝ in. tubing which slide into the main ¾ in. tubing. K2EEE's centre hardwood mounting is 28 in. by 2¾ in. by ¾ in., and at the two coil mounts, the ends of the ¾ in. tubing are flattened and sandwiched between two 6 in. by 2 in. polystyrene plates with the coils connected to the inner mounting screws. The dipole need be rotated by only 90°, or even less if necessary.

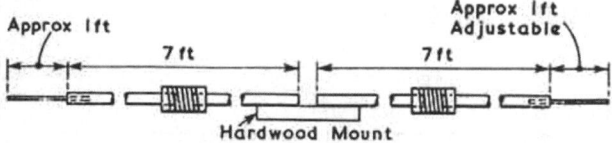

Fig. 4. K2EEE's mini-dipole for 14 Mc/s, fed with 70 or 50 ohm coax. (CQ).

VS1AA Multiband Aerial

Extracted from 'Technical Topics',
RSGB Bulletin, December 1962

VS1AA Multiband Aerial

Recently in *T.T.* we mentioned a number of popular multiband aerials: to these we could well add the VS1AA which seems to be staging quite a comeback these days—particularly on the Continent. For those who are unfamiliar with this compromise Windom we would refer them to the *Amateur Radio Handbook* and to Fig. 7 which shows dimensions given in DM2ABK's *Antennenbuch*. The old trick for tuning Windoms and VS1AAs was to run a neon along the feeder and adjust for minimum change in brightness but presumably these days one should insist on measuring the s.w.r. with a meter!

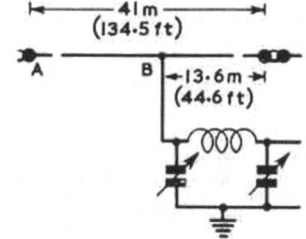

Fig. 7. The VS1AA multiband aerial: diameter of aerial wire about 2 mm. (say 14 s.w.g.); diameter of feeder wire (B) about 1 mm. (say 18–20 s.w.g.).

DL7AB Multiband Aerial

Extracted from 'Technical Topics',
RSGB Bulletin, August 1962

DL7AB Multiband Aerial

Multiband aerials are sometimes, by their very nature, susceptible to harmonic radiation; but to judge by the number of stations we work who give "G5RV," "W3DZZ" and "G8KW" as the aerial in use, they meet a real need. A simple all-band aerial which is not very well known in the U.K. is the DL7AB multiband; this is a modified form of Zepp aerial with electrical loading to bring a single 40-metre length of wire into resonance on all bands from 3·5 to 28 Mc/s. The loading, with varying effects on the different bands, uses a technique which is similar to that of G4ZU's FB5 but with a loading coil instead of ferrite beads. Fig. 3 shows the end-fed version with the coil placed two metres along the top. The coil consists of five turns of wire to a diameter of 50 mm. If space is available for two 40-metre spans, a centre-fed version can be made by connecting a duplicate aerial to the other Zepp feeder.

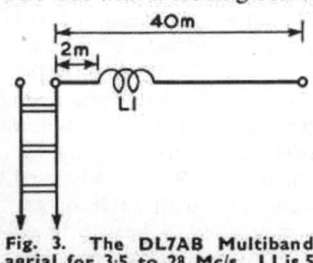

Fig. 3. The DL7AB Multiband aerial for 3·5 to 28 Mc/s. L1 is 5 turns, 50 mm. diameter.

A Breakthrough in Verticals?

Extracted from 'Technical Topics',
RSGB Bulletin, April 1963

A Breakthrough in Verticals?

Good DX aerials for the lower frequency bands are of increasing importance these days. If you doubt this then W3ASK's table of smoothed sunspot numbers (*CQ,* January, 1963) should remove all doubts. Taking the single month of April the recorded and predicted figures are: 1958 197; 1959 169; 1960 120; 1961 64; 1962 38; 1963 26; 1964 11; 1965 5. Each drop in value indicates a shortening of the time each day when the higher frequency bands are open to DX.

For those who can contemplate erecting a 50 ft. self-supporting vertical using 4 in. diameter aluminium pipe at the base, tapering to 1½ in. pipe at the top, with a co-axial stub sleeve section and different feedpoints for each band, an article by W3JHR in *CQ* (December, 1962) should be of interest since the result is a 3·5, 7, 14 and 21 Mc/s aerial with low angles of radiation on each band.

But a much more revolutionary approach which may allow us eventually to forget high masts or towers is foreshadowed in "Hula Hoop Antennas: A Coming Trend" by J. M. Boyer in *Electronics* (January 11, 1963), an article aimed primarily at commercial stations. It would take one of our aerial wizards to do real justice to this exciting new concept which suggests that an aerial only about *2 ft. high* can give a performance comparable to that of a full quarter-wave high 60 ft. aerial, a height saving of some 30 times. Imagine an effective DX aerial some 4 ft. high for 1·8 Mc/s, down to 3½ in. high for 28 Mc/s!

ANTENNA TOPICS

Most of us are likely to approach such claims a little sceptically, but the fact that the article appears in the highly respected *Electronics* suggests that here is something which should be investigated as soon as possible. In the past it has been shown that when vertical aerial height is reduced by electrically loading the element (as for example in mobile rigs) efficiency deteriorates pretty rapidly. But in this new system, which is termed a "leaky waveguide radiator," it is claimed that circumferential aperture is substituted for the lost height of the aerial.

This particular "hula hoop" has no connection with an earlier amateur aerial of the same name. In general appearance it resembles the popular halo but the loop extends right round (see Fig. 1) and the whole system is tuned against the

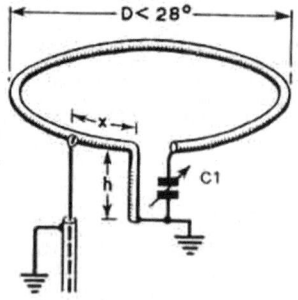

Fig. 1. The Hula Hoop Aerial: h = 2·5°, D is less than 28°, X is adjusted to match the feeder line. The capacitor is C1.

ground plane earth by C1 rather like a quarter-wave Marconi. Basically it is explained as "a circular array with a conductor one-quarter wavelength long conductively joined to the top of a 2·5° high vertical element and bent round in the horizontal plane at this height to form a circle."

In the article all dimensions are given in terms of electrical degrees (90° equals an electrical quarter wave). As stated the vertical section is only about 2·5°, and the circular conductor has a diameter less than 28°. The feedpoint dimension X depends upon the feeder impedance and it is stated that it can be adjusted for lines of 36-500 ohms. By varying C1 a given aerial can be tuned over a frequency range of 2:1 (thus in theory making possible use on two adjacent bands) without exceeding a feeder standing wave ratio of 2:1, although its efficiency would appear to fall off fairly sharply.

A 2 ft. high model at KM2XOP (an American experimental station) supported on a circular ring of insulators was tested against 110 ft. and 68 ft. high radiators all using the same ground plane. At 4 Mc/s (h = 2·88°, D = 26·28°) the loss compared with a 68 ft. tower was less than 3db (½ S point). At 2 Mc/s the same aerial was only 1·44° high, 12·9° diameter and compared with a 110 ft. tower represented a loss of about 2-2½ S points.

A mobile model for 26·5 to 31 Mc/s, 27 in. in diameter and only 3½ in. above the vehicle roof which formed the ground plane, is reported to have performed better than a quarter-wave whip.

The design is apparently patented in the United States but this does not prevent any amateur testing out the idea. Since it could represent a major breakthrough for low frequency and mobile operation, this is clearly a project of considerable potential value. We must stress however that our only source of information on this aerial is what is given in the *Electronics* article.

Correspondence: Birdcage & Hula Hoop

Extracted from 'Technical Topics', *RSGB Bulletin,* August 1963

In *73* (April, 1963) K3LNZ comes up with the idea of using the G4ZU "Birdcage" type aerial in a quarter-wave version instead of the original full-wave form, and calls this the "wee birdcage." In effect, this means simply using an array built for 14 Mc/s on 3·5 Mc/s, etc. Or, for a 14 Mc/s array, the element size would be only 2 ft. 2 in. instead of 8 ft. 8 in., thus simplifying construction. Performance of the quart-size array is well below that of the gallon model, but K3LNZ and W3CYT claim that the miniature model still gives appreciable gain over a dipole.

The 'Maria Maluca' Multiband Aerial

Extracted from 'Technical Topics', *RSGB Bulletin,* October 1963

The "Maria Maluca" Multiband Aerial

Aerials remain an endless topic of interest to amateurs, and we generally try to keep our eyes and ears open for news of developments in this field. But we must admit to never having heard of the intriguingly-named "Maria Maluca" multiband aerial developed by PY2BCD until we came across an article by F9VS in the combined August/September, 1963 issue of *Radio REF*, and we still remain

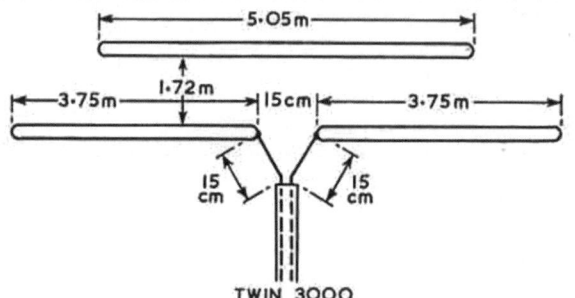

Fig. 5. The "Maria Maluca" multiband aerial devised by PY2BCD and as described by F9VS. Tuned 300-ohm feeder lengths either 10·07m, 18·06m or 23·40m for 0·9 velocity factor cable.

hazy as to the exact principles of operation which are not explained.

But F9VS writes with true Gallic enthusiasm of the results he has achieved with this system and we are therefore passing on the details he gives: see Fig. 5. Apparently the aerial works effectively on 28, 21, 14 and 7 Mc/s and even on 3·5 Mc/s if the 23·40-metre length of twin 300-ohm feeder is used. The resonant feeder dimensions are given for Amphenol line with a velocity factor of 0·9 as widely used in South America but F9VS states that with cable of say 0.86 velocity factor the length may have to be shortened slightly with the help of a grid dip meter. The coupling between the feeder line and the transmitter is given as two turns on the earthy side of the output coil with a 100 pF capacitor in parallel for tuning, but we are not certain whether this figure applies only to 21 Mc/s.

Two Metre Aerial

Extracted from 'Technical Topics',
RSGB Bulletin, December 1963

Two Metre Aerial

From WA6TGY and *The DX'er* comes a note on a useful and fairly easily constructed extended full-wave aerial for 144 Mc/s as used at W6WX: see Fig. 9. This provides a gain

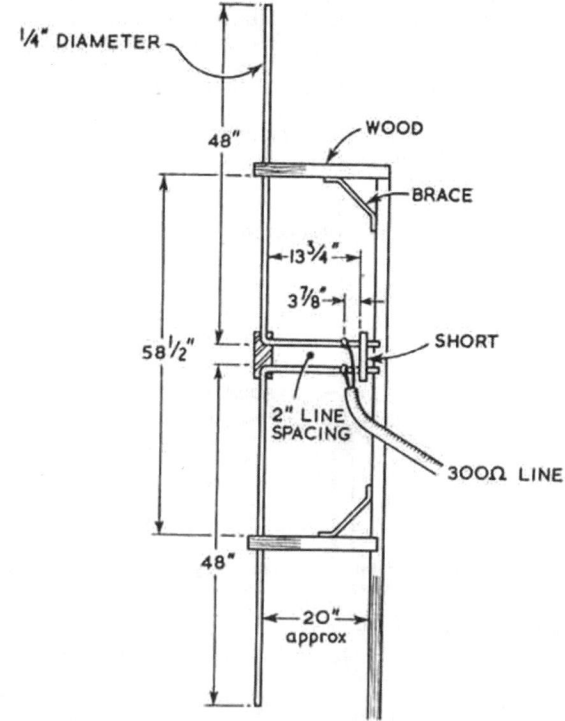

Fig. 9. Extended full-wave 144 Mc/s aerial designed by W6WX.

of about 3·2 db over a vertical dipole, has a low angle of radiation and reasonably good bandwidth. The aerial is omnidirectional but can be converted into a beam with about 10 db gain by adding directors about 40 in. in length spaced at 21 in. from the two radiating elements.

Although the aerial is shown with 300 ohm balanced feed, a coaxial balun (see *TT* August, 1963) could be used mounted at the phasing line feeder tap point. No insulation is required except between the two radiators. The 2 in. spaced phasing line is made of the same material as the radiators (¼ in. o.d. aluminium). If possible the feeder line should be extended horizontally some 40-50 in. before being brought downwards in order to minimize any interference with the radiation pattern. The wooden " C " frame can be made of any suitable, light wood.

The DDRR Hula-Hoop Aerial

Extracted from 'Technical Topics',
RSGB Bulletin, September 1964

The DDRR Hula-Hoop Aerial

Last year, *TT* (April, 1963) presented the first brief description in an amateur journal of the " hula-hoop " or DDRR (directional discontinuity ring radiator) aerial invented by Mr. J. M. Boyer, W6UYH, of Northrop Space Laboratories. Subsequently, several British amateurs are known to have carried out some experiments although results were generally rather disappointing. Later we worked YU3EM who told us that on 7 Mc/s he had worked some very good DX with a hula hoop aerial, although we are not certain if this was a true DDRR system.

Now, in *CQ* (June, 1964) W4MIP provides an extensive description of these aerials with dimensions for all bands: see Fig. 2.

He points out—as we indicated in *TT* (August, 1963)—that an extremely efficient ground plane is needed and recommends a solid copper or aluminium (provided this is prevented from becoming oxidized) sheet with a diameter about 25 per cent larger than the aerial ring.

By using a thick loop (as shown in the table) operation is possible, says W4MIP, on two bands; for single-band operation a much thinner loop is possible. He also points out that the tuning capacitor must have very high voltage rating—about 4 kV for 100 watts.

It is only fair to add that there is still some controversy over various points relating to the principles of the DDRR aerial, and an article in *Microwave Journal* (November, 1963) did not support the views of W6UYH, although the aerial then described did not have precisely the configuration of his ring aerial.

Early this year we wrote to W6UYH to ascertain whether any further articles had been published on this system, and he very kindly replied that although additional information was being prepared, most of the existing material is in the form of " classified " military reports.

The stringent requirements for the ground plane make the aerial rather attractive than at first sight for amateur operation on the low-frequency bands—but there is obviously a good deal of scope for further experimenting.

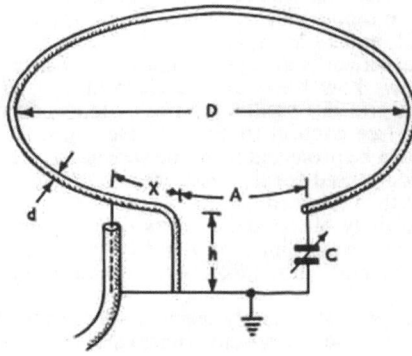

Fig. 2. Dimensions given by W4MIP for the W6UYH Northrop Hula-Hoop DDRR aerial.

Band	D	H	d	A	X	C1
160m	36 ft.	48 in.	5 in.	18 in.	12 in.	100 pF
80m	18 ft.	24 in.	5 in.	12 in.	6 in.	100 pF
40m	9 ft.	12 in.	2½ in.	6 in.	3 in.	75 pF
20m	4 ft. 6 in.	6 in.	1 in.	3 in.	1½ in.	50 pF
15m	3 ft. 4 in.	4½ in.	½ in.	2 in.	1 in.	35 pF
10m	2 ft. 3 in.	3 in.	½ in.	2 in.	¾ in.	25 pF

where D is diameter of loop, H is height above ground plane, d is tube diameter (two band), A is gap, X is feed-point.

ANTENNA TOPICS

Multiband Dipole

Extracted from 'Technical Topics', *RSGB Bulletin,* September 1964

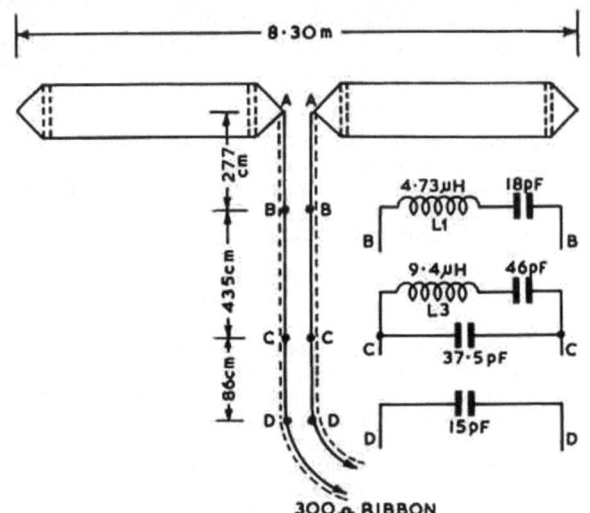

Fig. 3. F9GO's multi-band dipole for 7, 14, 21 and 28 Mc/s. Basically the aerial is a broadband doublet resonating on about 17 Mc/s and appears capacitive on 7 and 14 Mc/s and inductive on 21 and 28 Mc/s. Network for terminals B-B with leads shorted should resonate at 17·3 Mc/s. Network for C-C should resonate at 12 Mc/s with terminals open and 7·8 Mc/s with C-C short circuited. L1, 25 turns, 15 mm diam., 26 mm long. L3, 35·5 turns, 15 mm diam., 28 mm long. For adjustment of feeder, aerial at A-A can be replaced by 10 ohms in series with 29 pF (7·1 Mc/s); 51 ohms in series with 110 pF (14·2 Mc/s); 150 ohms in series with 1·8 μH inductor (21·3 Mc/s); and 310 ohms in series with 3·3 μH (28·4 Mc/s).

Multiband Dipole

An aerial matching technique of some interest is also described by F9GO in *Radio-REF* (June, 1964). This consists basically of a broadband dipole element about 25 ft. long fed by conventional 300 ohm balanced feeder with three compensating reactive networks connected across the feeder near the dipole feed point. The remaining portion of the feeder is then non-resonant and can be extended to any length. The dipole can be used without any modifications on 7, 14, 21, and 28 Mc/s, it is stated.

Reactive networks always present a bit of a problem but F9GO shows how these can be checked and adjusted by means of a grid dip oscillator before connection across the feeder line (see caption to Fig. 3). He suggests that these networks can be protected from the weather in the polythene bottles widely used for domestic cleaning fluids. These can be cut and then rejoined.

The directivity of the aerial is less pronounced than for a full length half-wave dipole on 7 and 14 Mc/s, a little sharper on 21 Mc/s, and rather like two half-waves in phase on 28 Mc/s.

The arrangement certainly seems to offer a versatile multiband aerial for use in restricted spaces and one which should prove fairly easy to transport for portable or /A operation.

Some methods of feeding 300 ohm balanced feeders from conventional pi-networks were described in *TT* (December, 1960).

14MHz Ground-Plane

Extracted from 'Technical Topics', *RSGB Bulletin,* March 1965

14 Mc/s Ground-Plane

Some time ago OZ5S in Copenhagen kindly sent along a note on the 14 Mc/s ground plane which he warmly recommends as a simple aerial particularly suitable for c.w. DX working and which he points out has never been mentioned in *TT*. This omission has been because this type of aerial can be found in the various handbooks including the RSGB *Amateur Radio Handbook*. However it is quite likely that there are some readers who are a bit hazy on constructional aspects so we are reproducing some points from OZ5S's letter.

The radiator is self-supporting and made from aluminium tubing, length 5·1 metres (16 ft. 11 in.) for 14 Mc/s. The four

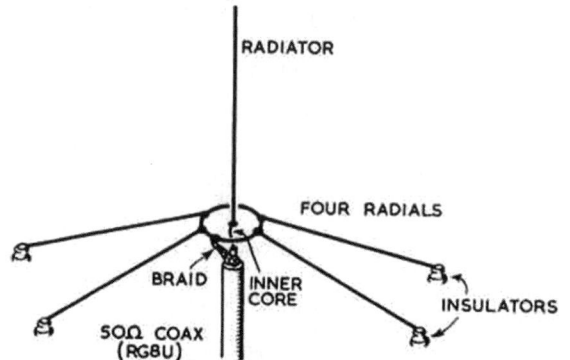

Fig. 8. Ground-plane aerial recommended by OZ5S. The radials are roughly at 90° spacing.

radials are made from hard drawn copper wire each 5·25 metres (17 ft. 2¼ in.) long, with insulators at the ends, and guy wires to support points. The radiator is insulated from the fixing mount with the inner core of the 50-ohm co-ax soldered or bolted to the end. The radials are soldered to a copper ring together with the braid of the co-ax and kept well apart from the vertical element and the inner core of the co-ax. Usually the vertical element is mounted on a chimney stack with the radials sloping down to the roof corners of the house, at a tilt depending upon the angle of the roof. However, it should be noted that the feedpoint impedance increases with the slope of the radials but matches 50 ohms very well when they are at an angle of about 120° to the radiator. If mounted on a flat roof, some matching device may be needed since the feedpoint impedance will be only about 20-30 ohms. Dimensions can be scaled up or down for other bands. OZ5S has worked over 150 countries using 100 watts with this type of aerial.

At G3VA we have always noticed that 14 Mc/s signals from European stations using ground planes come in during those hazy summer daytime weak-signal conditions with a much louder thump than other stations, although we use a horizontally polarized receiving aerial. One theory is that they have high angle radiation off the radials as well as low angle radiation off the element, but this theory is not altogether satisfying, since in that case why are they louder than stations using low horizontal dipoles—and why is the effect noticed only under certain conditions?

Broadband Dipoles

Extracted from 'Technical Topics',
RSGB Bulletin, November 1964

Broad-band Dipoles

In the course of scanning commercial as well as amateur literature, we constantly observe that new and revived ideas diffuse through both fields at much the same time. For example, an article "An Antenna System for the Entire H.F. Band" in *Electronic Industries* (August, 1964) describes the advantages of fan-type, 48 ft. or 64 ft. two-wire dipoles, with a 20 ft. length of two-wire balanced transmission line into a pi-network/balun aerial coupling unit to match it to 50 ohm co-ax. The 48 ft. broad-band dipole is claimed as suitable for use throughout the range 4-30 Mc/s and the 64 ft. version for 3-22·5 Mc/s, for military or commercial use.

We then remembered an article by W5VOH and WA5DEL "All Band Conical Antenna" in *73 Magazine*, which presented two examples of what were called "two horizontal Vs back to back, centre-fed with 450 ohm feed line matched to a low impedance line with a Johnson Matchbox coupler"—substantially the same arrangement as above. In this case the conical broad-band dipoles had an overall length of about 105 ft. with a spacing of about 25 ft. at the outer ends (see Fig. 4), and were said to provide an effective aerial for use throughout 3·5–30 Mc/s with unity s.w.r. in the co-ax section. The actual element can be flat-top, inverted-V (centre-support) or any other configuration provided that the system remains balanced to earth.

Old-timers may, of course, smile reflectively at the current interest in such aerials, recalling the many years in which the so-called centre-fed Zepps were one of the main weapons in the armoury of the DX-man—and even the spider-web broad-band dipole receiving system developed by RCA in the 'thirties.

But for more recent recruits, this could be a relatively simple yet effective answer to the problem of multi-band operation. For those interested in more advanced forms of broad-band aerials, and in particular the log-periodic, a review of recent developments in this field appears in *IEEE Spectrum* (April, 1964).

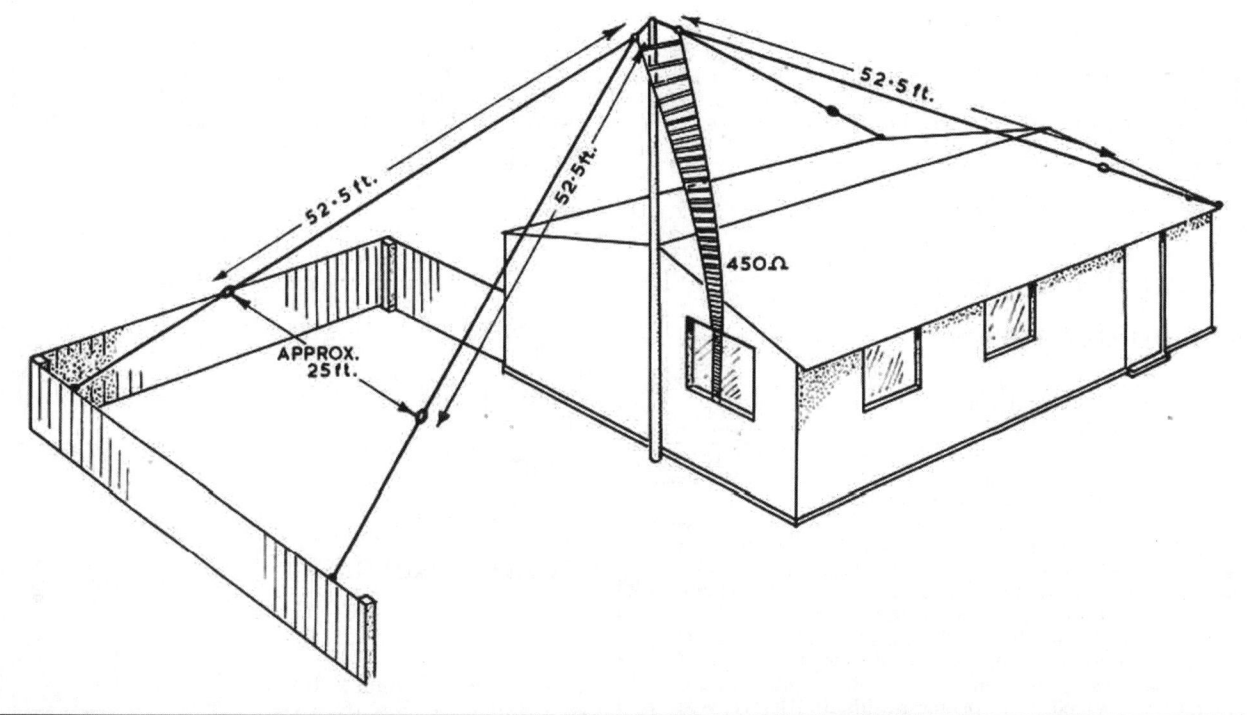

The W6BCX Multee

Extracted from 'Technical Topics',
RSGB Bulletin, May 1965

The W6BCX Multee

A two-band aerial with a top portion only 35 ft. long for use on 3·5/7 Mc/s, or 70 ft. for 1·8/3·5 Mc/s clearly has some attractions to those with restricted space. But rather surprisingly the "W6BCX Multee," although included in some editions of *The Radio Handbook* has never been widely used over here. We were therefore interested to note that this aerial turns up again in an article by W6WAW on short folded dipoles (*73*, December, 1964). Fig. 7(a) shows the usual arrangement with both horizontal and vertical sections formed from 300-ohm line.

On the higher of the two bands, the top section forms a quarter-wave folded dipole (feed impedance about 6000 ohms) with the vertical section forming a quarter-wave matching transformer. On the lower frequency band the

ANTENNA TOPICS

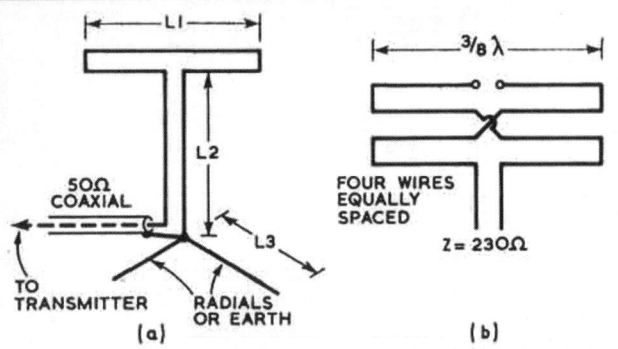

Fig. 7. (a) The Multee two-band aerial. L1 is ¼λ, and L2 is ¼λ times the velocity factor of the feeder.

	1·8/5·5 Mc/s	3·5/7 Mc/s	7/14 Mc/s
L1 (ft.)	65	33	17
L2 (ft.)	54	27	13·5
L3 (ft.)	50	25	12

(b) A basic ¾ folded dipole.

entire system forms a top loaded vertical. A very good earth system is recommended, preferably in the form of four or six radials buried just below the surface of the ground; but an ordinary water pipe earth will function with some decrease of efficiency.

For the lower band, where the vertical portion forms the radiator, this section should be as nearly vertical as possible, but if main operation is on the h.f. band this is less important.

W6WAW also describes the little known ¾ wavelength folded dipole arrangement (Fig. 7(b)) which can be used where space is insufficient for the usual half-wave span. In this case feedpoint impedance is roughly 230 ohms but this is close enough to 300 ohms to allow the use of ribbon or other 300 ohm line.

Ground Planes, Radials and Counterpoises

Extracted from 'Technical Topics', *RSGB Bulletin*, July 1965

Ground Planes, Radials and Counterpoises

The description (*TT*, March, 1965) of OZ5S's ground-plane has stirred John Farrar, ex-5B4JF, VS9SJF, to send along details of a modified form of ground plane, originally devised by 5B4IP (formerly G8IP) to overcome the problem of low feedpoint impedance when using horizontal radials.

In Cyprus, with many flat roofs, it is much easier to have the radials horizontal than sloping downwards, so that the impedance drops to around 20-30 ohms, presenting a mis-match to coax feeder. To overcome this, 5B4IP increased the length of the vertical radiator element from 90 electrical degrees (i.e. quarter-wavelength) to 113° and so raised the impedance to about 75 ohms. This results on 14·1 Mc/s in a radiator length of 22 ft. 6 in., still quite manageable. Since the aerial is not resonant, there is a reactive element at the feedpoint and this is tuned out by the insertion of a 60 pF variable capacitor in series with the inner core of the coax and the radiator: see Fig. 5. This capacitor must be capable of withstanding the high voltages developed at this point and should therefore be similar in spacing to that in the p.a. tank circuit. It should be mounted at the base of the radiator in a water-tight box. John Farrar states that with an s.w.r. bridge in the feeder line, unity s.w.r. can be obtained easily by adjusting the capacitor and also that the aerial works quite well on 21 Mc/s.

G5XD, on the subject of ground planes generally, mentions that after using a triband ground plane made from lighting flex taped to lashed together canes, with three sets of three radials and three radiators taped together, he came to

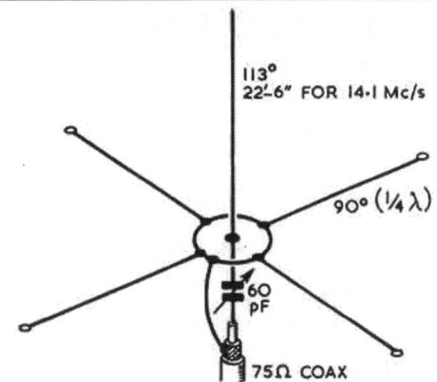

Fig. 5. Ground-plane for use with horizontal radials.

the conclusion that the close proximity of the radiators was not good, and now uses—with better results—two separate ground planes for 14 and 21 Mc/s about five yards apart and fed in parallel with 50-ohm coax. He still finds that cane rods lashed together, with plastic covered (single) lighting flex are satisfactory. G5XD is interested in obtaining user experience of verticals not using radials—from what one reads a good deal would seem to depend upon the effectiveness of the earth system so that results in an area of poor earth conductivity may not match up with those achieved elsewhere.

In this connection, we noted some interesting comments on the effects of "earths" on mobile operation by G6GR in a recent issue of *Mobile News*, the ARMS journal. He points out that, contrary to widely held views, optimum results on 1·8 Mc/s are more likely to be obtained from low lying, relatively marshy areas than from those super hills where the rocky soil usually forms a poor capacitance earth in conjunction with the car body.

The other day it came to us with something of a shock that one seldom sees much comment or even reference to the use of "counterpoise" earth systems for Top Band Marconi aerials. At one time counterpoises (often comprising just a single 66 ft. wire suspended a few feet above earth and running roughly beneath the main aerial) were held in high regard by those without a really good earth system—and our own recollections of using them in the 'thirties are distinctly favourable. Yet it now seems ages since we have seen any general description of them in the amateur literature. Any comments?

Backfire Aerials

Extracted from 'Technical Topics', *RSGB Bulletin*, September 1965

Backfire Aerials

A few years ago there was a flurry among some v.h.f. enthusiasts at a new concept in "backfire" aerials first put forward in 1960 by H. W. Ehrenspeck of the USAF Cambridge Research Laboratories. The basic idea was to direct, for example, a multielement Yagi in the opposite direction to that required into a plane reflector sheet or screen mounted on the end of the boom. The theory was that the wave would be reflected back through the array so that the directors would have a double effect. Originally it was claimed that up to 5-6db additional gain (above isotropic) could be attained compared with a conventional endfire array of equivalent length.

W1HDQ of ARRL HQ carried out some experiments using the technique and rather poured cold water on it by reporting (*QST*, February, 1961) that he had been unable to "get anything that looked even close to 6db" of extra gain, and surmised that there were more complications than was then apparent from the published information.

Later (*QST*, October, 1961) W1YLW and W1PYT, both at the USAF Cambridge Research Laboratory, came back with a description of a 220 Mc/s array giving an extra 4·5db gain with a simple reflector screen (now said to be suitable only for monopulse transmission).

There the matter seemed to rest. But now (*Proc. IEEE*, June, 1965) Ehrenspeck publishes a good deal of additional information on backfire systems using a rather more complicated reflector arrangement made up of several different reflectors of critical dimensions and with a smaller reflector at the " front " of the array—but still by no means an impossible structure for an amateur to build at v.h.f. He claims that experience has shown that far better pattern control than originally claimed has proved possible and quotes an additional gain of 8db, sidelobes 22db down and backlobe close to 30db down—desirable figures indeed!

He suggests that this technique should prove particularly attractive for v.h.f., u.h.f., and s.h.f. aerials with gains between 15—30db which would otherwise need impractically

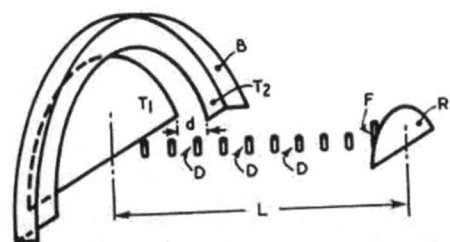

Fig. I. Model of a backfire aerial shown on a ground plane. In practice the semicircular reflectors, etc. would be circular. TI 2λ radius. T2 ring of 1λ width with an outside radius of 3λ. B, rim of about 0·25λ surrounding edges of T2. R reflector 0·51λ radius, spaced 0·2λ from driven element F. Spacing F to first director 0·2λ, all other directors 0·4λ spacing. Total length L 4λ. Distance D between TI and T2 adjusted experimentally to 0·25λ.

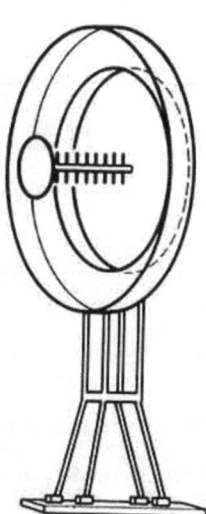

Fig. 2. Large backfire array with gain of 23·5db above an isotropic source.

long conventional arrays; particularly for applications where a paraboloid dish reflector is too costly. The technique is not confined to Yagi arrays but can be used with other slow wave structures.

Fairly detailed dimensions of a typical backfire system are given in his letter in *Proc. IEEE*.—see Figs. 1 and 2. Provided that reasonable performance is readily reproducible, backfire arrays could prove of considerable interest to amateurs. On the other hand the disappointing experiences of W1HDQ suggests that such work must be regarded as an advanced project. But may we suggest that some of our v.h.f. enthusiasts have a careful look into the whole idea, and see if they can come up with a surefire backfire design for amateur use?

Modified Birdcage Aerial

Extracted from 'Technical Topics', *RSGB Bulletin*, September 1965

Modified Birdcage Aerial

In *CQ* (June, 1965), W2EEY/DJ0BU describes a variation of the G4ZU Birdcage which appears to offer some constructional advantages. It is claimed to provide results comparable to those of a 14 Mc/s two-element close-spaced Yagi, but with the turning radius kept down to 12 ft.

Fig. 9 gives the basic information. The aerial can be fed

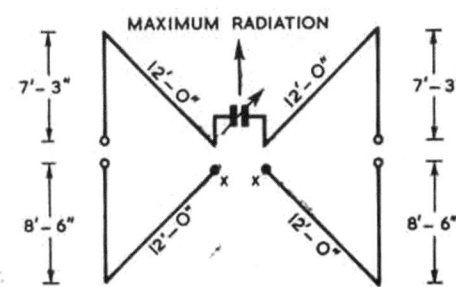

Fig. 9. Looking down on the W2EEY variation of the Birdcage aerial. The capacitor can be a 250 pF receiver type. Feedpoints X, X.

directly from 52 ohm co-ax at points X,X, or via a balun such as that described in the original article.

Vertical Two-Band Trap Aerial

Extracted from 'Technical Topics', *RSGB Bulletin*, September 1965

Vertical Two-Band Trap Aerial

A number of the overseas journals adopt a regular practice of making one particular town or district responsible for providing all technical features for an issue—rather as though we had Birmingham, Blackpool and then Bristol issues of the BULLETIN. It is surprising how often this trick produces good ideas.

We were reminded of this by the June, 1965 issue of *Radio-ZS* featuring articles by the Pretoria group, including a useful description by ZS6AOU of the construction and adjustment of a two band (14 and 21 Mc/s) vertical trap aerial. The bottom section is 11 ft. long, with a trap inductor parallel tuned to 21 Mc/s by the capacitance (about 20 pF) between the top and bottom tube sections with the polystyrene insulator as the dielectric.

The adjustment procedure recommended by ZS6AOU requires an s.w.r. bridge and a g.d.o. He believes that the trick in correctly tuning up is to grid-dip the trap without the top section of the aerial in position. To do this a short length of similar ¼-inch rod, just long enough to protrude out of the polystyrene insulator is inserted in its place. Using the g.d.o. the trap coil is then resonated by stretching or compression to 21 Mc/s (later with the true top in position it appeared to resonate on 15 Mc/s due to the extra capacitance between the rods).

ZS6AOU's adjustment procedure is then: erect bottom section, without trap, and check that s.w.r. is low on 21

ANTENNA TOPICS

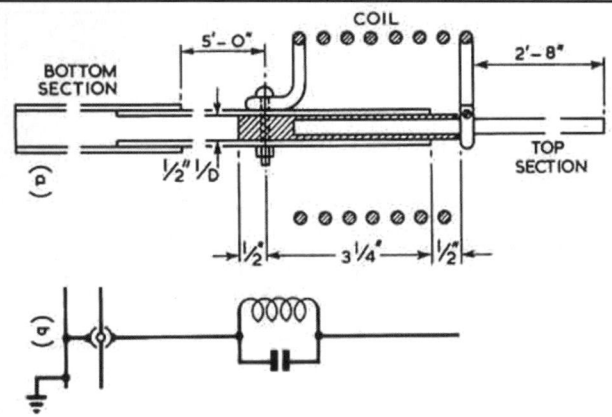

Fig. 10. ZS6AOU 21-14 Mc/s trap vertical. Bottom section ⅜ in. diameter aluminium tubing ¼ in. inside diameter inserted into 6 ft. section of ¾ in. diameter aluminium tubing. Top section is ¼ in. diameter aluminium rod. The trap coil is formed from 7½ turns of ¼ in. diameter aluminium wire, 3 in. inside diameter. The coil is 3½ in. long.

Mc/s, using a good earth, and adjusting if necessary at the joint. Then add trap and top section and recheck 21 Mc/s s.w.r., possibly adjusting trap for low s.w.r.

Once the s.w.r. is low on 21 Mc/s with the complete aerial erected, tune to 14 Mc/s, and trim for low s.w.r. by pruning top section. If the previous adjustments were correct the pruning adjustments should not interact with the 21 Mc/s settings.

ZS6AOU states that the vertical could be used with radials rather than true ground (or corrugated iron roofing) by using radials of different length to form a two-band ground plane.

Multi-band and Low-angle Ground Planes

Extracted from 'Technical Topics', *RSGB Bulletin,* November 1965

Multi-band and Low-angle Ground Planes

Another remarkably interesting letter, though again we shall not be able to do full justice to it here, has come along from George Barrett, ZD7IP (former G8IP, ZC4IP, 5B4IP) on St. Helena who for long has been a firm and most knowledgeable advocate of ground plane aerials as compared, for example, with trap verticals which he considers throw away power at low angles in the process of trapping off lumps of the radiating element.

He was stirred to write by finding himself credited (*TT*, July, 1965) as the originator of the "113°" ground-plane with series capacitor, and points out that most of the basic ideas stem from a study of Laporte's standard textbook on aerials. He refers in particular to the section on medium-wave vertical radiators which contains a series of charts on feed impedances and radiation patterns which he has found to give excellent results when applied to amateur-band ground planes. He has found it possible, by adopting these ideas, to design multi-band ground planes entirely devoid of traps. In fact with the aid of a relay-switched *L*-network at the base of the radiator and a wafer switch at the operating position he could put a vertical on 7, 14 or 21 Mc/s, operating on each band as a properly matched ground plane with all its built-in harmonic rejection and with every inch of the vertical radiator helping to form the lowest possible radiation angle on all bands.

Prime factor in the design procedure is to forget about "electrical length" of the radiator but rather to think of it in terms of physical lengths, on the basis that 984/*f* gives the length in feet of a 360° physical wavelength. The interesting point is that as the length of the radiator is increased the radiated power is concentrated more and more at low angles, up to a maximum of about 220-225° when secondary high angle lobes start to appear. With 220° gain at low angles is about 3db compared with the conventional electrical quarter-wave element.

For this reason George is convinced that the usual technique of shortening a quarter-wavelength radiator to obtain electrical resonance is the wrong approach. From Laporte it can be seen that at lengths of about 110° and 220° (figures quoted from memory), the resistive component of the feed impedance passes through 75 ohms; 110° having a series inductive reactance, and 220° having a series capacitive reactance. All that is needed to make the feed point purely resistive is to insert series capacitive reactance for around 110° (as in the May *TT*) or series inductance for 220°. A variable capacitor or inductor allows setting up to be done simply with an s.w.r. meter.

Furthermore since the physical lengths of these two arrangements are related by 2 : 1 a 28/14 Mc/s aerial can be made by adjusting for 220° at 28 Mc/s and having a relay-switched coil/capacitor at the base of the radiator.

Alternatively, for a 7/14/21 Mc/s ground plane, the element can be made 220° on 21·1 Mc/s and the radiator will then be about 147° on 14·1 Mc/s and 74° on 7·1 Mc/s, and all three lengths can be matched by means of relatively simple *L*-networks at the base of the radiator. George used a number of pre-set air-spaced Command capacitors and a surplus Ledex relay; after matching, the capacitor rotors were clamped. The result, "a lovely aerial for the experimentally minded amateur to tinker with and the reward of excellent results on DX." All those who heard George knocking them off from Cyprus will appreciate these remarks.

It would be good to see a full length article on these multi-band ground planes, though apparently the notes are in the UK. At least we hope this much abridged precis of the letter from ZD-land will result in even more interest in ground planes. It makes us feel decidedly humble to recall that when we started off this series of remarks on ground-planes (*TT* March, 1965 with the notes provided by OZ5S) we had the temerity to suggest that most of what needed to be known about them had already appeared in the *Handbooks*!

Aerial Topics

Extracted from 'Technical Topics', *RSGB Bulletin,* January 1966

Further information on the Ehrenspeck "backfire" aerial (*TT*, September, 1965) appears in the form of a letter in *Proc. IEEE* (August, 1965) including what promises to be a particularly useful form of "short-backfire aerial." In this there is only the large back saucepan lid reflection plate (2 λ diameter) and the small front disc reflector (0·4 λ diameter) plus the dipole, and the overall length of the structure is only 0·5 λ. Yet it is claimed that the array is capable of some 15db gain over isotropic or equivalent to a conventional Yagi of over 20 elements. The large reflector plate in fact has changed the overall shape of the Yagi so that its physical dimensions are much more like those of a parabolic dish aerial—but without the problem of obtaining an accurate parabola. In this form the array would clearly be of interest primarily to v.h.f. and u.h.f. operators.

We wonder how many of the users of Yagi aerials are aware that they have a much longer history than might be imagined—the aerial was developed originally by Professor Hidetsugu Yagi and S. Uda of Tokoku Imperial University in connection with original experiments on wavelengths of between 60 and 200cm, and first described by them in 1928! Dr Yagi was elected to the Japanese House of Councillors in 1953 and, in his old age, is still a much respected figure in Japan.

Another new variation of the Yagi, incorporating a built-in balun by the use of a ground-plane reflecting plate and with the excited element as a ¼ λ monopole conductively connected to the central boom with a gain over a frequency range of 30 per cent was described at the u.h.f. television conference already mentioned.

A further reference to the hula-hoop aerial but using a larger loop appears in the IEE's *Electronic Letters* (September 1965). This has been investigated in Italy and uses a ½ λ instead of the ¼ λ loop as in the original Boyer system described in *TT* and *TTftRA*. Again there is emphasis on the need for a good ground plane (in this case aluminium sheet some 3 λ diameter) but the system still seems to have practical value particularly for mobile operation.

G3TMA comments on the recent description of vertical ground plane aerials and sends along a description of a 40 ft. aerial he uses on 1·8, 7 and 14 Mc/s fed against ground with separate aerial tuning units on each band, relay switched from the shack. His earth system consists of four 40 ft. lengths of insulated wire laid on the ground, each at right angles to its neighbour. Details of his tuning arrangements are shown in Fig. 6.

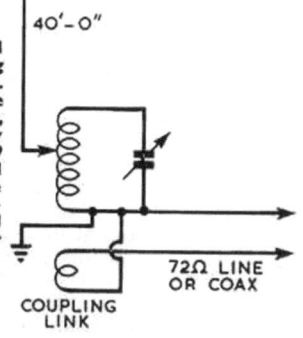

Fig. 6. G3TMA's 40 ft. vertical aerial. For 1·8 Mc/s, the tuning coil is 120 turns on a 2 in. diam. former, tapped every 5 turns. The link coil is 5 turns. 7 Mc/s: 25 turns, 1½ in. diam. former, tapped every turn, with 3 turn link. 14 Mc/s: 9 turns, 1½ in. diam. former, tapped every turn, with 3 turn link. The tap is adjusted with an r.f. ammeter in base of aerial or a field strength meter with transmitter on low power.

Most conventional ground plane aerials use four radials as above, and it may not be known generally that it is quite possible to use three radials spaced at 120° and sloping at about 60° (" the triple leg aerial "); this tends to give a radiation pattern with nulls along the line of the radials and maxima along the bisection of the angle between each pair of radials.

The aerial was built using a bamboo framework with a basic spider consisting of a 12 × 12 × ¼ in. square of aluminium with 8 ft. of 1 in. aluminium angle stock—but any of the usual quad constructional techniques could be used.

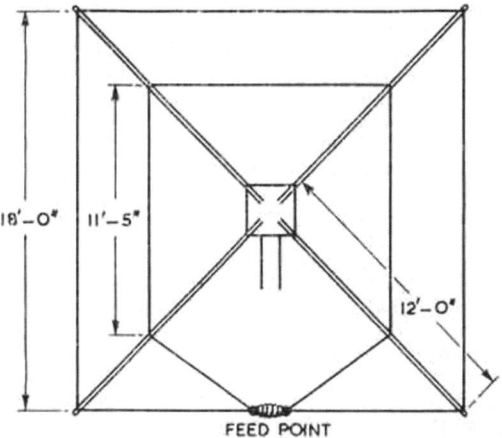

Fig. 5. W6WAW's simple DX aerial using a single quad element.

Single-loop Quad Aerial

Extracted from 'Technical Topics', *RSGB Bulletin,* March 1966

Single-loop Quad Aerial

Another of the *73* articles which attracted my notice was that by W6WAW (*73*, September 1965) on a single-loop quad aerial, with which he has been working DX out of North Fairfax Avenue in Hollywood—a busy street just under the Hollywood Hills which we well recall going along last year, and which is certainly far from an ideal QTH. (G3WW could probably also confirm this since he also made a trip to the land of the Californian kilowatts at around the same time.)

W6WAW built and put up this 14/21 Mc/s aerial " in less than two hours." It is simply a single quad loop which can later be converted to the more conventional two loop quad for greater gain: Fig. 5. Feed impedance is theoretically around 125 ohms but W6WAW has used it with RG59/U coax (75 ohms) quite effectively. He says that 7 Mc/s operation is possible by connecting a 28 ft. 9 in. length of 300 ohm twin lead, shorted at the far end, across the feed point, without affecting 14 and 21 Mc/s working.

Broadband Baluns

Extracted from 'Technical Topics', *RSGB Bulletin,* May 1966

Broadband Baluns

The problem of feeding a balanced aerial, such as a dipole, from unbalanced co-ax has long been recognized, and has led to the development of many types of balun (balanced-to-unbalanced) transformers. The basic problem was well put by G6CJ back in 1965 (BULLETIN, December 1955): " a centre fed dipole is a balanced circuit; a concentric cable is unbalanced, they cannot be joined directly without some trouble or other— the fact that this often goes undetected has only made it more difficult to understand what is happening when things go wrong."

G6CJ pointed out that this is the reason why it is sometimes impossible to get sensible results from impedance or polar diagram measurements, and can cause the shack to be alive with r.f. causing TVI; or the aerial fires in the wrong direction; or local electrical noise crawls up the outside of the line and back into the receiver. Because of the low impedances involved, multi-element Yagi arrays, he stressed, are particularly sensitive to unbalanced feed. Dipoles such as the W3DZZ multi-band units may also sometimes be improved with a balun.

The commercial people have been able to sew up this problem by developing weatherproof wideband ferrite transformers. These have ratings up to many kilowatts, and are used, for example, to feed wideband log-periodic arrays from transmitters with pi or pi-L output networks. But these users are often prepared to pay a price which would, so to speak, " unbalance " an amateur's budget rather more

ANTENNA TOPICS

There are, of course, various forms of standard coax baluns, some providing a 4 : 1 and others a 1 : 1 impedance transformation. Most of these tend to be frequency selective, and can add yet another critical dimension to aerial construction as well as posing problems for multi-band aerials.

Recently various forms of broadband baluns at more modest prices have been appearing in the United States. In a *QST* review (October 1965) several baluns priced between £3 10s. and around £5 were described. Two of these, including the W2AU balun and the lightweight Fungle balun, are based on toroid cores. In this country, KW Electronics manufacture a balun priced at 35/-. But the third family of devices were the Hy-gain 1 : 1 types using two tightly coupled coils of coax: Fig. 3.

Clearly, publication of this design has inspired a number of amateurs to try one for themselves, at costs of only a few shillings for the coax. Fuller descriptions have appeared in *CQ* (February 1966) by W6SAI, and in *DL-QTC* (March 1966) by DL1HM. The W6SAI article gives a very detailed description of the construction of one of these broadband lumped-constant baluns.

A 16 ft. 6 in. length of 50 ohm coax such as RG8/U or equivalent is tightly coiled to form a 9 turn coil with an inside diameter of 6¾ in. leaving an inch or two at either end. W6SAI uses a piece of p.v.c. plastic pipe as a former, but it is possible to form the coil without using a former.

When the centre-point of the coil has been carefully found, the outer coax plastic cover is trimmed back and the flexible screen, but not the inner lead, is broken; then a jumper short circuit is soldered across one section of the coax: see Fig. 3. A similar jumper is connected across one of the outer ends of the coax coil.

W6SAI describes in considerable detail the construction of the device and how he fastens the coax on to the former;

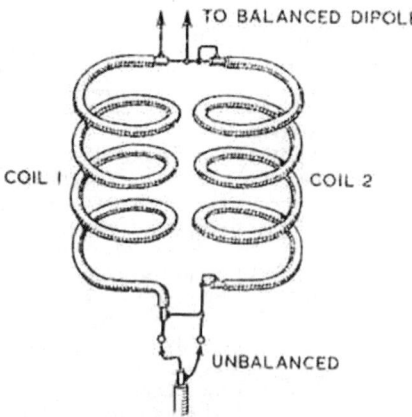

Fig. 3. A broad band balun with 1 : 1 impedance transformation. Although shown as two coils, a single length of co-ax may be used (see text).

but provided that it is remembered that the two sections of the coil should be electrically similar and tightly coupled together (preferably in a type of bifilar winding), there seems no reason why other forms of construction should not be used. The devices are broadband and it is claimed that a 9 turn unit will be effective over the range 6-32 Mc/s; by adding turns the lower limit can be extended, and a 13 turn balun is said to work down to about 1·5 Mc/s.

Broadband Biconicals

Extracted from 'Technical Topics', *RSGB Bulletin*, May 1966

Broadband Biconicals

Broadband vertical arrays also have a number of attractions, including the elimination of any switched networks such as those needed for multi-band verticals and ground planes as described in recent *TT*s. Unfortunately most of the broadband verticals tend to have rather complicated structures. Details of h.f. discones, for example, have been given in a number of amateur publications but have never proved very popular, one of the many problems being the " top hat " disc and the dimensions which in practice limit their use to 14 Mc/s and above.

An alternative, though related broad-band vertical is the biconical monopole. This is a form of aerial which has been used by the British and American services. In effect it replaces the disc of a discone with another conical arrangement, and brings the feedpoint down to the base. Constructional details of one form of this aerial is given by W5WEU/4, in *CQ* (January 1966), in which an effective bandwidth of 4 : 1 is claimed. The aerial takes the form of two cones, made from a skeleton of wires, one above the other. The *CQ* design has six-sided double wire cones with electrical connection at the interface between the two cones by means of the metal cross pieces: Fig. 6. While a 43 ft. structure is needed to cover 3·5-15 Mc/s; a 23 ft. high aerial will cover 7-28 Mc/s; and even a 12 ft. high one 14-56 Mc/s. W5WEU has been using a 12 ft. model with promising results and reports other amateurs using the 23 ft. version. Altogether there are 12 perimeter wires grouped in six double

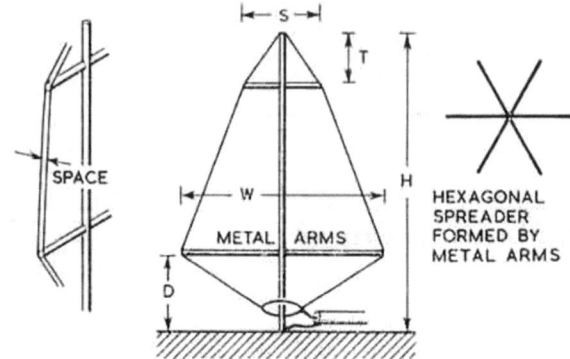

	H	W	D	T	S	SPACE	WIRE
3·5 – 15 Mc/s	43'	17'- 8"	16'-10"	2'- 2"	5'- 10"	3"	NR 8
7 – 28 Mc/s	23'	9'- 6"	9'	12"	3'- 2"	2"	NR 10
14 – 56 Mc/s	12'	5'	4'- 9"	8"	1'- 8"	1"	NR 12

Fig. 6. Constructional data for the W5WEU biconical aerial.

units. W5WEU suggests the smaller models work best higher off the ground with a good counterpoise earth.

Reading the *CQ* article, with its emphasis on amateur use of these aerials, reminded us that there was a useful description of a slightly different form of biconical monopole (plus a good deal of information on radiation patterns and design formulae) presented by Mr H. P. Mason of the Admiralty Surface Weapons Establishment at the 1963 IEE " Convention on H.F. Communication." His paper is printed in the Convention book which may be found in a number of technical and company libraries. His design (Fig. 7) uses some 12 single wires equally spaced around the central steel mast which is on an insulated base. The cone interfaces are joined together by wire, there being no cross-arms, but with external stays to keep the whole aerial in shape.

The ASWE paper claims a 2·6 : 1 bandwidth with low s.w.r. but this could almost certainly be extended for amateur use. Apparently three aerials covering 2-5 Mc/s, 4-11 Mc/s and 10-26 Mc/s have been designed for naval coast stations.

The paper indicates, most vividly, how important is the best possible ground plane if the aerial is to give optimum DX performance. A series of vertical radiation pattern diagrams show the great difference in the amount of low angle radiation when mounted above different ground planes. The paper recommended the use of 36 ground radials of about the lowest frequency.

Whereas there is plenty of radiation, even with an average ground system, at high angles, the vital low angle (0-15°) radiation largely disappears from those diagrams representing radiation with a less efficient ground system. This, of course, is true with all forms of vertical aerials fed against earth and emphasizes once again that the best way of improving such aerials almost always consists of providing a better earth system. What I have never yet found is any detailed comparison between the effectiveness of a ground radial system and that of the four- or three-wire up-in-the-air technique which we associate with " ground plane " aerials—and how much the ground conductivity below such sloping ground plane systems affects low angle radiation.

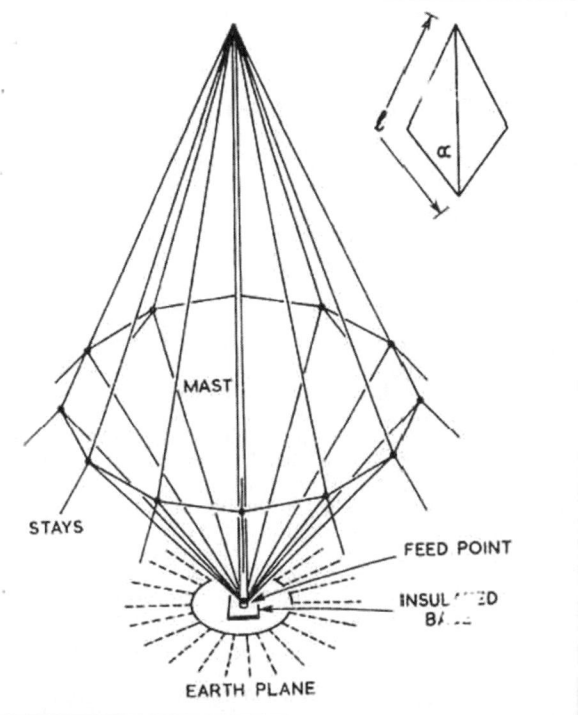

Fig. 7. The ASWE version of the broadband biconical aerial. With a lower cone half-angle (α) of 38·5° feed impedance is 50 ohms. If this is decreased to 23·2° impedance increases to 75 ohms. For the 50 ohm version, the length of each semi-perimeter wire (l) is equal to 0·269 to 0·735λ, and for the 75 ohm version the corresponding figures are 0·284-0·735λ. The earth plane comprises some 36 radials of 0·4λ.

Elevated Feed Verticals

Extracted from 'Technical Topics', *RSGB Bulletin*, July 1966

Elevated Feed Verticals

Just as the arrival of a letter describing a new type of oscillator can be quite an exciting moment, so scanning technical journals, even those which have no anticipated connection with Amateur Radio, from time to time produces a subject that seems to have considerable relevance to typical amateur operation. Such a moment came while reading an article in *The Marconi Review* (Vol XXIX, No. 160, First quarter 1966) on the new direction finder, type S480. For this contains a most interesting discussion on a type of elevated feed monopole due to W. Struszynski used in the eight element Adcock system; and from this it would seem that such a technique might provide an answer to a problem of particular importance to amateurs: how to get really good low angle radiation, without unwanted high-angle side lobes, from vertical aerials of appreciable electrical length.

In the particular application described, the elevated feed aerials are used to form a wide band (1·5-30 Mc/s) receiving system but, the same principles would apply to transmission. Admittedly the average amateur might not be able to reproduce such good low angle results as are indicated in

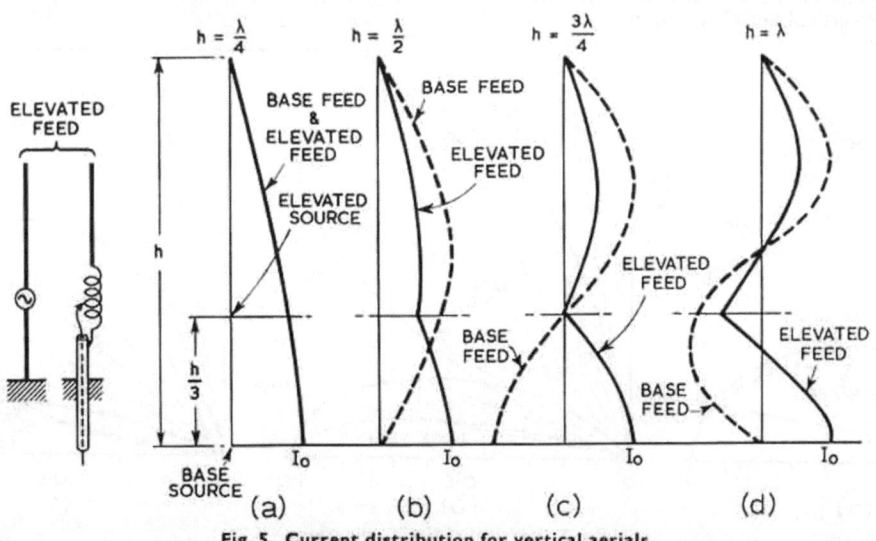

Fig. 5. Current distribution for vertical aerials.

ANTENNA TOPICS

the article, since for D/F installations considerable regard is paid nowadays to the ground plane in the form of large earth mats extending right around the multiple-element Adcock system (for the S480 a 2 ft. square copper wire mesh some 120 ft. in diameter elevated 1 ft. above the ground is recommended), and a more normal conventional earth system would undoubtedly degrade the vertical radiation patterns to some extent. The system increases earth currents and thus the need for good earth radials or mats (see G3HRH's article in the June issue).

The raising of the feed point up a vertical aerial has been done in the past for other reasons (for example in the "sleeve" aerials in which a low-impedance co-ax feeder is taken up through a sleeve) but this use of elevated feed to reduce vertical radiation angles seems to be relatively new. As shown in Fig. 5 the vertical aerial is earthed at its base, but at a point ⅓ of its height, an insulator is inserted to form a feed point. In the Marconi D/F system, each of the eight elevated feed aerials uses a triangular mast type of construction, and the top ⅔ of the height is supported on the insulators, with the co-ax feed line brought up inside the triangular mast and inner conductor connected to the top section either directly or through a suitable step-up matching transformer.

A form of elevated feed was used for a considerable time on the BBC anti-fading aerial for the Third Programme Daventry transmitter to optimise the vertical radiation pattern, and Telefunken are also believed to have done work with elevated feed systems.

The two sections of the aerial thus have a current distribution of the type we associate with "in-phase" aerials. Fig. 5 shows the current distribution for total heights of ¼, ½, ¾ and full-wave aerials, but the more interesting diagram is that of Fig. 6 showing computed vertical radiation patterns. It will be clear that there is no particular advantage over conventional base fed aerials until one gets to about ¾λ and full-wave, and this means that height limitations tend to rule out its use except on 14 Mc/s and above. The ¾λ system seems particularly attractive, though this results in high-impedance feed across the insulator; while this could be done with a step-up matching network, there might well be the possibility of using a tuned feeder run out for some distance horizontally from the vertical element, and then if required continued with a low-impedance feeder in the G5RV technique. One good point is that the two sections of the aerial form an in phase system and this tends to result in the reactance changing less rapidly than with equivalent base fed systems, so easing matching problems.

While it must be made clear that the concept of the elevated feed monopole for amateur operation (and the use of tuned feeders) has not yet been tried out, at least by G3VA, the information presented in the Marconi journal certainly makes the whole idea look very attractive, with its concentration of almost all radiation at low angles. We would be glad to pass on comments from anyone trying the system out for amateur operation, since it could well form a most useful addition to vertical aerial techniques.

Aerials for DX

Extracted from 'Technical Topics',
RSGB Bulletin, November 1966

Aerials for DX

Another new *QST* series, "Station design for DX" by W3AFM comes out firmly in favour of horizontally polarised h.f. aerials, basing his argument on the high ground losses of verticals. His estimate is that the radiation efficiency of a quarter-wave ground plane with the usual four earth radials is "probably less than 20 per cent" obtaining this figure by interpolation of figures given in 1939 by G. H. Brown of RCA (in fact this was an investigation into the direct ground wave of m.f. broadcast aerials and is probably not directly applicable to sky wave radiation). Certainly, the work by Brown did emphasize the tremendous importance of an extremely good earth system for vertical radiators, but we do not think that all users of ground planes will agree with W3AFM's views, though it must be admitted that verticals, even when correctly matched, can sometimes prove disappointing.

Less controversially, W3AFM draws attention to the many different ways in which manufacturers can state "aerial gain" (this subject is well covered in an article in *Wireless World*, October 1966). In an attempt to resolve some of these differences—which apply just as much to manufacturers of commercial transmitting aerials as to the firms catering for amateurs—the CCIR has recently proposed a new term e.i.r.p. instead of e.r.p.; this will stand for "effective isotropically radiated power" to clean up the ambiguity that arise since e.r.p. is sometimes with reference to a dipole and sometimes with reference to an isotropic aerial (the imaginary

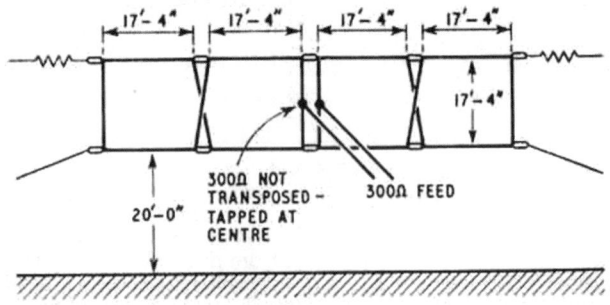

Fig. 6. 14 Mc/s Bruce array dimensions suggested by W2EEY (*73 Magazine*).

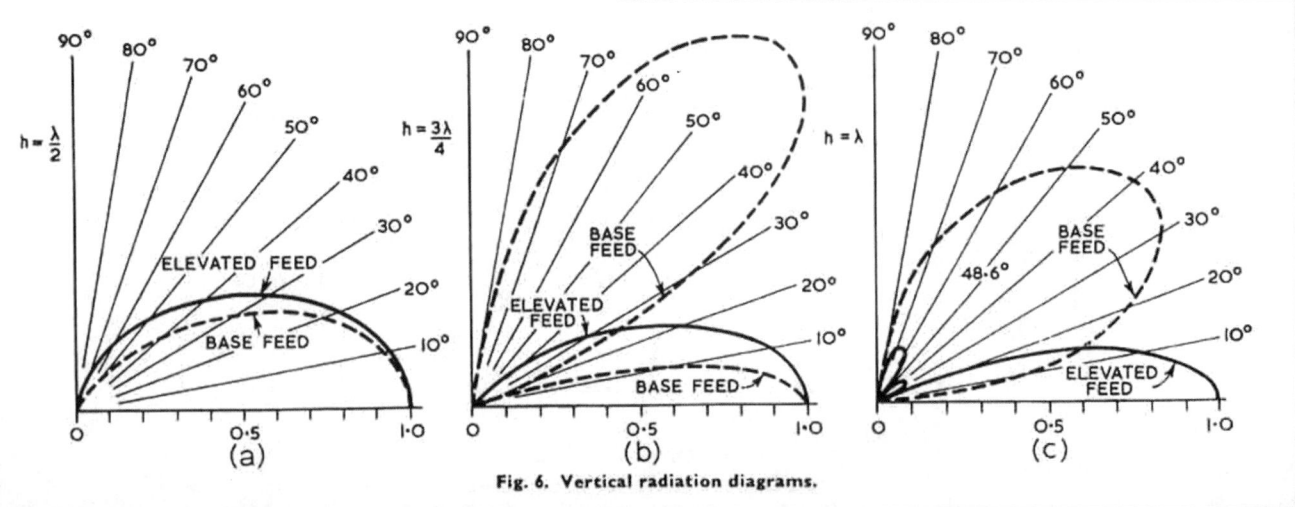

Fig. 6. Vertical radiation diagrams.

aerial which spreads its radiation out in all directions equally).

Sometimes one feels that the dominance of the directional aerial scene by Yagis and quads, good though they undoubtedly are, has tended to mean that to many newcomers the 8JK, Bruce, Sterba, etc., are little more than names dimly from the past. W2EEY/1 has some notes in *73* (August 1966) on curtain type aerials, which can make effective fixed beams, and makes the point that these are high-impedance arrays and so make the dimensions far less critical than, for example, with Yagi elements. This strikes a chord since for many years our own basic aerial has been the 300-ohm ribbon-type folded dipole (*TTftRA*, page 78) which is one of the least critical and most satisfactory forms of single-band dipole and capable of reasonable results when about 20 ft. above indifferent ground, or inside attics or jammed between buildings. Although most curtains tend to require a fair amount of real estate and high supports, the 20m array given by W2EEY (Fig. 6) is capable of fitting into many gardens and gives low angle radiation on either side of its axis.

A useful form of unidirectional aerial which has also been around a long time but has apparently never appeared in the BULLETIN is the " ZL-Special " which can be easily slung up as a fixed beam, or can be fashioned into a rotatable beam by using 1 in. tubing. Basically two folded dipole elements are driven with current 135° out of phase using transposed 300-ohm line as a $\frac{1}{8}$-wave phasing section. Figs. 7 and 8 show two slightly different forms of the ZL-Special, one from *Amateur Radio Antenna Handbook* (W6TYH) and the other from *Antennenbuch* (DM2ABK); the latter source also rpovides suggested dimensions for use where the spacing between the dipoles is reduced to about one-tenth wavelength.

Gain of this aerial is usually given as about 6 or 7db better than a dipole, with a very good back-to-front ratio to cut down reception from unwanted stations.

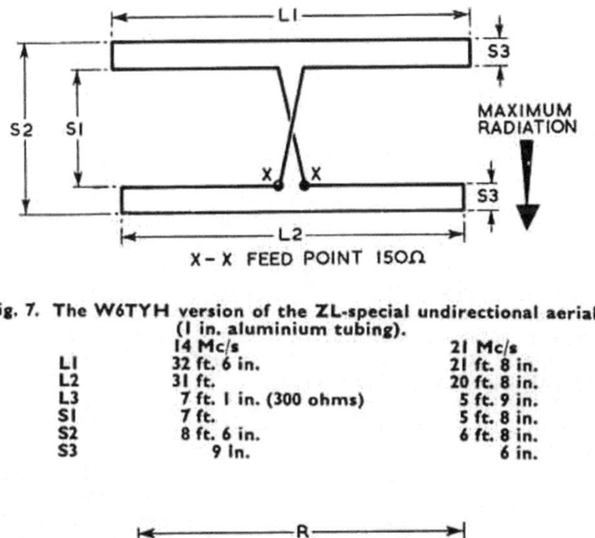

Fig. 7. The W6TYH version of the ZL-special undirectional aerial (1 in. aluminium tubing).

	14 Mc/s	21 Mc/s
L1	32 ft. 6 in.	21 ft. 8 in.
L2	31 ft.	20 ft. 8 in.
L3	7 ft. 1 in. (300 ohms)	5 ft. 9 in.
S1	7 ft.	5 ft. 8 in.
S2	8 ft. 6 in.	6 ft. 8 in.
S3	9 in.	6 in.

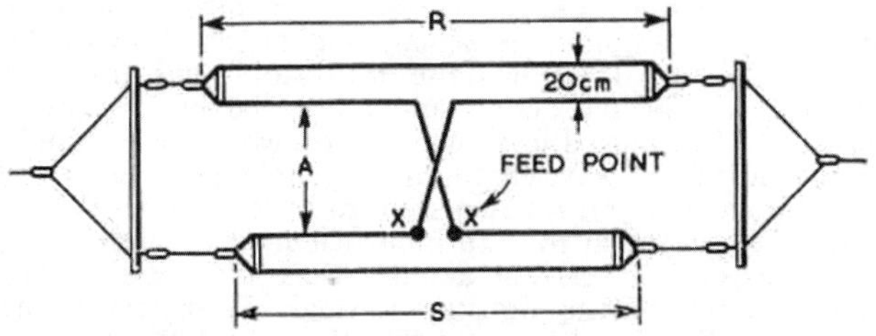

Fig. 8. DM2ABK's version of the ZL-Special (plan view). The feed impedance of 90 ohms is suitable for 70 ohm coax or 120 ohm balanced feeder.

	S	R	A	A
28 Mc/s	5·09m	5·39m	1·29m	$\frac{1}{8}\lambda$
	4·17m	4·42m	1·06m	$\frac{1}{10}\lambda$
21 Mc/s	6·85m	7·24m	1·72m	$\frac{1}{8}\lambda$
	5·62m	5·94m	1·41m	$\frac{1}{10}\lambda$
14 Mc/s	10·30m	10·85m	2·58m	$\frac{1}{8}\lambda$
	8·45m	8·90m	2·12m	$\frac{1}{10}\lambda$

More on Elevated Feed Verticals

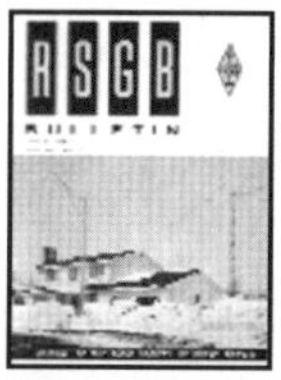

Extracted from 'Technical Topics', *RSGB Bulletin,* July 1967

More on Elevated Feed Verticals

In *TT* (July, 1966) we gave some details of the Marconi elevated feed aerials showing how the technique could apparently be used to lower the radiation angles of vertical aerials over $\frac{5}{8}$ λ long (though warning that full benefits were unlikely to be obtained without good earth conductivity, or alternatively a really effective ground plane). We had hoped to hear some practical work on their use for amateur band operation, but must admit that the response was not exactly overwhelming; at least we noted that the Japanese journal reprinted the item.

Further reference to this system, this time in the form of phased doublets for incorporation in large aperture " Wullenweber " electronically steerable receiving and D/F arrays appeared in *Marconi Review* (First Quarter, 1967), showing incidentally how quite an effective looking directional array can be formed using a pair of these elevated feed aerials. But a full Wullenweber ring is not the type of aerial you can put in a back garden.

But now has come a note from F8ZF on a multiband vertical aerial which he and F3YR (the leading French DXCC-er) have used to good effect at various times. This

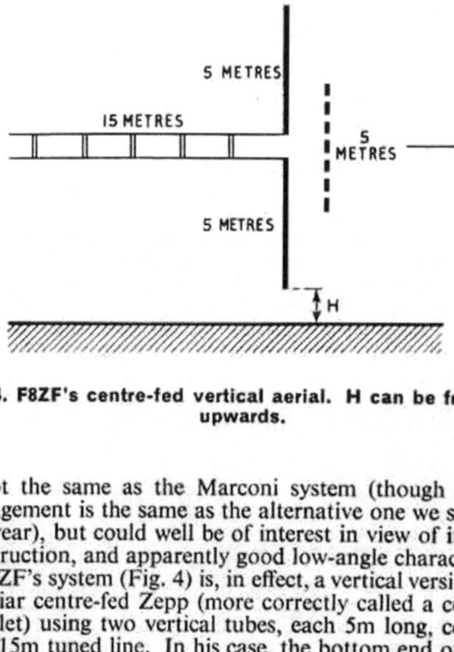

Fig. 4. F8ZF's centre-fed vertical aerial. H can be from 0·5m upwards.

is not the same as the Marconi system (though the feed arrangement is the same as the alternative one we suggested last year), but could well be of interest in view of its simple construction, and apparently good low-angle characteristics.

F8ZF's system (Fig. 4) is, in effect, a vertical version of the familiar centre-fed Zepp (more correctly called a centre-fed doublet) using two vertical tubes, each 5m long, centre-fed by a 15m tuned line. In his case, the bottom end of the rod is only about 0·5m above ground, but F3YR has the same aerial on the top of his house (F8ZF is not sure of the angle at which 'YR runs his feeder).

F8ZF says the aerial will of course tune from 10 to 20m and can also work on 40 and 80m (as a short dipole with aerial coupler, or with feeder wires connected together to form a voltage fed $\frac{1}{2}\lambda$ on 40m and $\frac{1}{4}\lambda$ on 80m).

For an ARRL contest some years ago, one of these aerials was used in conjunction with a very close spaced director on 28 Mc/s (about 90° phase difference which stops backward radiation) to produce a cardioid pattern. During the contest the main aerial was a 90m per leg rhombic beam but it was noted that whenever the band seemed to run out of stations a new crop would answer the vertical.

He points out that the radiator can be extended to 6·4m to form an extended double Zepp on 10m, and then a 10m long director can be used on 14 Mc/s (90° phase difference), though 'ZF feels that phased pairs might be better since the

ANTENNA TOPICS

Active Aerials

Extracted from 'Technical Topics',
RSGB Bulletin, July 1967

Active Aerials

On several occasions in the past, reference has been made in TT to "active aerials" and what are sometimes called integrated aerials, antennafiers, antennamitters, and antennaverters. Such concepts are currently the subject of a good deal of research, and appear to have definite possibilities in the amateur radio field.

The idea, basically, is to get away from the classic belief that an aerial is a linear, passive and reciprocal device designed independently of the transmitter and receiver packages. Put simply, many of the techniques are logical extensions to the development of mast-head pre-amplifiers. Several of the systems which have been described include a number of tunnel diodes in the aerial system itself. Related concepts were also described in a *Motorola Engineering Bulletin* some time ago, in order to integrate aerials in small hand-held two-way units with semiconductors, so as to avoid transmission-line losses and to eliminate the tank circuit. In effect, this is done by locating the r.f. power oscillator or p.a. within the aerial structure, and using the aerial itself as the tank circuit. In the examples given in the Motorola article, this is done by making use of the interesting DDRR form of low-profile aerials (i.e. "hula hoops" of the type described in *TTftRA*, page 85) resulting in what are called "amplifying aerials." In the terminology, an antennamitter is a complete transistor power oscillator in the aerial system; an antennafier places a p.a. in the aerial system, with conventional exciter; while antennaverter is the term given when a mixer diode is also incorporated to form a transceiver set-up.

The Motorola article, by Earl Murphy, outlines some examples of such devices, as applicable to small 300 Mc/s equipments. In the antennamitter the transistor is mounted directly in the ground plane, which thus also forms the heat sink. The transmission line aerial, itself, consists of a $\frac{1}{4} \lambda$ of wire formed into a figure of eight, mounted parallel to, and typically 2·5 electrical degrees above the small ground plane. The aerial is tuned to $\frac{1}{2} \lambda$ resonance by means of the capacitance reactance of the stub connected to the mid-point of the aerial, tuning being carried out by trimming the length of the stub.

This system, but in the form of an antennafier, is shown in Fig. 8. In this case the input power is matched to the base of the u.h.f. power transistor, and precautionary measures taken to prevent feedback (this can be done by using the ground plane as a screen).

The article emphasises that the examples shown are only a few of the many possible approaches to integrated aerial concepts: many different types of aerials could be used, in many ways and functions. Low profile ddrr hula hoop aerials, it says, can provide results comparable with $\frac{1}{4}\lambda$ whips, but since they are high Q structures they can also provide preselection and filtering functions on transmission and reception.

In general, and putting aside its use in this form of active aerial, one has the impression that the ddrr hula hoop, originally developed by W6UYH of Northrop, has not yet been fully exploited by amateurs. Admittedly, the h.f. problem of achieving a good enough ground plane is formidable, but this hardly applies to its use for mobile working on 28, 70 or 144 Mc/s. Recently, for instance, we read that communications engineers have been investigating it as a tunable v.h.f. aerial covering 30 to 76 Mc/s for use on aircraft, with a 5 ft. ground plane.

Fig. 8. One form of a 300 Mc/s "antennafier". It is claimed that average radiated power is 6 to 8db greater than from an equivalent non-integrated aerial and amplifier. Low-profile transmission-line aerials can be fabricated in many shapes, including circular and tight spirals.

Active Aerials

Extracted from 'Technical Topics',
RSGB Bulletin, September 1967

Active Aerials

In the July *TT* we included a section on "active aerials" suggesting that there were useful possibilities in including active devices, such as transistors or tunnel diodes, as part of the aerial structure. In fact this item was rather overtaken by events, and there has been a good deal of speculation in the United States and West Germany that active aerials could render obsolete almost all roof-top television aerials, etc.

This widespread interest arises primarily from the work— on behalf of the US Air Force—of Professor Meinke of Munich who has developed various forms of "subminiature integrated antennae." While the publicity has been directed mainly at the idea, feasible but not immediately likely, of developing these for television reception, much more important would seem to be that the work has shown that in future the "active aerial" concept is likely to become an increasingly powerful tool in the hands of the aerial designer, particularly for miniature receiving aerials of broadband or highly directional characteristics.

A 20 in. model, it is reported, has been shown to provide good broadcast reception throughout the range 500 kc/s to 100 Mc/s.

In one design, apparently for an omni-directional system, a small capacitance hat on a short rod is used in connection with four bent-down ground-plane type elements, with four transistors to amplify the signals and match them to the coaxial feeder. The low-noise transistors thus form an integral part of the aerial, and allow the basic element lengths to be reduced from one-quarter-wavelength to only about one-fiftieth wavelength, making a compact aerial.

But directional arrays also seem to have been developed, since it is suggested that an almost immediate application could be as a D/F aerial on about 5 Mc/s, with the ability to rotate the zero pick-up direction through 360 degrees (i.e. as with a unidirectional beam) rather than the 180° of loops. In amateur working one could well imagine that such a system could prove very effective in overcoming QRM from unwanted directions. While a certain amount of technical information has already appeared in various journals, nothing we have seen yet would show an amateur how to set about designing such an array—possibly because of the military implications of this work.

But it is becoming clear that this is a technique to keep an eye on.

Transmitting Loop Aerials

Extracted from 'Technical Topics', *RSGB Bulletin,* November 1967

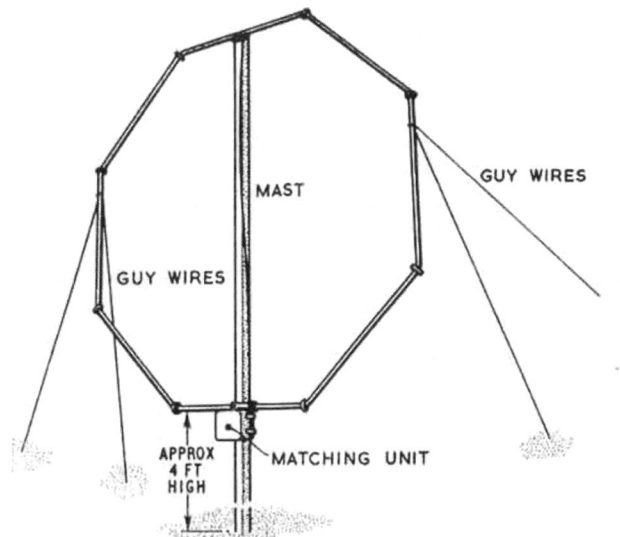

Fig. 1. Sketch of the octagon loop aerial with 5 ft. sides developed for the US Army. It is claimed that the performance matches that of half-wave dipoles up to 40 ft. high, but is easy to transport and to set up. In the balanced version it appears that an earth wire is taken up to the centre of the top horizontal bar from the matching unit.

DURING those now distant days before the coming of the Radio Amateurs' Examination, old timers may recall that it was necessary when applying for the British "experimental" licence to include in the application an outline of the proposed experiments for which (officially) the licence was required. Fortunately perhaps, this was never taken too seriously and, at least during the 'thirties, developed almost into a polite game of wits between the would-be amateur and the Post Office.

For instance, if one were unwise enough to say that the licence was needed to develop new techniques in transmitter design, this could be countered by the Post Office pointing out that such work could be carried out satisfactorily under the terms of an "artificial aerial" licence; it was even more foolhardy to indicate an interest in receiver design. Amateur radio operating, of course, was not then considered as any purpose of the licence.

The usual procedure was to concoct (often in collusion with someone who had succeeded in obtaining a licence) an impressive account of how a licence was essential in order to carry out experiments involving either aerials or propagation. I imagine that tucked away somewhere in the PO vaults must be some weird and wonderful experimental projects, few of which were really intended to be carried out. For, luckily, once the coveted licence was issued, the Post Office was discreet enough not to ask the embarrassing question of how the experiments were getting along.

There is a reason for recounting this fragment of pre-war lore. For if my memory serves me correctly one of the purposes for which "G3VA" was issued was to carry out experiments with compact transmitting loop aerials. Largely by coincidence, some 15 years later I did in fact get round to trying loop aerials in order to put out a 3·5 Mc/s signal from a Central London flat. To judge by the reports received, the loops could not be considered a shattering success.

Nevertheless, it has always seemed that eventually someone might come up with improved techniques for transmitting with loop aerials. And from an excellent account in *Electronics* (21 August 1967) of work by the US Army Limited War Laboratory, it seems that the required push in this direction has come from the tricky problem of operating portable military h.f. radios in the jungles of Vietnam. The article describes a compact octagonal loop (Fig. 1) having 5 ft. sides; this is seriously claimed as "usually doing as good a job as a full-length dipole (from 94 ft. long at 5 Mc/s to 234 ft. at 2 Mc/s) 40 ft. above the ground."

Recalling those 339 reports, this claim—in a journal not usually given to wildly extravagant claims—was enough to set us looking for some magic new approach. In fact, the article makes it clear that no really new principles are involved, but rather that very careful consideration has been given to means of simultaneously raising radiation resistance, and reducing to a minimum the inherent ohmic resistances in the loop and its aerial matching network.

The article points out that in the case of low horizontal dipoles (of a height less than about $0·12\lambda$, or say 30 ft. at 3·5 Mc/s) the reflected wave from the surface of the earth tends to have a cancelling effect on the incident wave (i.e. a dipole at zero height above a *perfectly conducting* earth would have zero radiation). This is because of the phase inversion on reflection.

Conversely, signals from vertically polarised systems (in this case loops but the argument applies to other vertical aerials) are reflected predominantly in phase with the incident wave so that there is no decrease of total radiation with decreasing height. For this reason, it is suggested that wherever an aerial must be severely limited in height, vertical polarization should give improved results. The loop approach was adopted in preference to vertical grounded whips, since the overall height can be much less, and there is no overhead null in its radiation pattern.

Furthermore, the loop does not depend on any artificial ground plane for its efficient operation. While its operation over a good earth would presumably be more efficient than over an extremely poor earth, this is a far less critical factor than with whips or vertical rods tuned against earth.

The author admits frankly that a compact loop is not being put forward " as the best design for every application." It will not, he stresses, " outperform the large rhombic in specific low angle unidirectional tasks. But the loop can do the job at installations where real estate is limited and a complex of high aerial masts is impracticable" (a situation possibly even more common among amateurs than in military communications). This viewpoint has been confirmed during extensive trials in the USA and in Vietnam, using frequencies between 2 and 5 Mc/s.

Fig. 2 shows the aerial matching network used to feed the loop from 50 or 70 ohm coaxial line throughout this frequency range: for use only on one or two amateur bands, the number of "coarse" impedance settings could be much reduced. This type of matching, it is claimed, keeps resistive power losses to a practical minimum, with no inductive taps or links, and using only air-dielectric and fixed micadielectric capacitors. The network shown is approximately balanced about earth (this reduces the peak voltages in the network) but it is said that for low power this is an unnecessary refinement. This matching unit is mounted immediately below the lower horizontal member of the octagonal loop.

The other major reduction in ohmic losses is achieved by using large surface tubing to form the single turn loop (which is shown to be generally preferable to using a smaller multi turn loop). Apparently the earlier models used $\frac{3}{4}$-in. tubing, but a change has been made to $1\frac{1}{2}$ in., and it is thought that in some cases it would be advantageous to increase this even to 3, 4 or 6 in. tubing!

The octagonal loop has its eight sides each 5 ft. long (chosen to allow dismantling and easy transport); this shape increases the area enclosed by 20 per cent beyond a square: even better in terms of area (and hence radiation resistance) would be a circle, but it is suggested that the straight tubes, with what are termed "els" (electricians?) corners, are more readily available.

Altogether, this type of approach to loops seems to offer the promise of efficient aerials for the lower frequency bands in sites where this would otherwise be almost impossible: their value for 1·8, 3·5 and possibly for 7 Mc/s would certainly seem to be well worth investigating if some large diameter alloy tubing is available! One further possibility is also hinted at: that of using the loop as the final output tank

ANTENNA TOPICS

circuit of a low power transmitter mounted in the position of the matching unit, so that in effect it forms an active aerial of the "antennafier" type mentioned in *TT* (July, 1967).

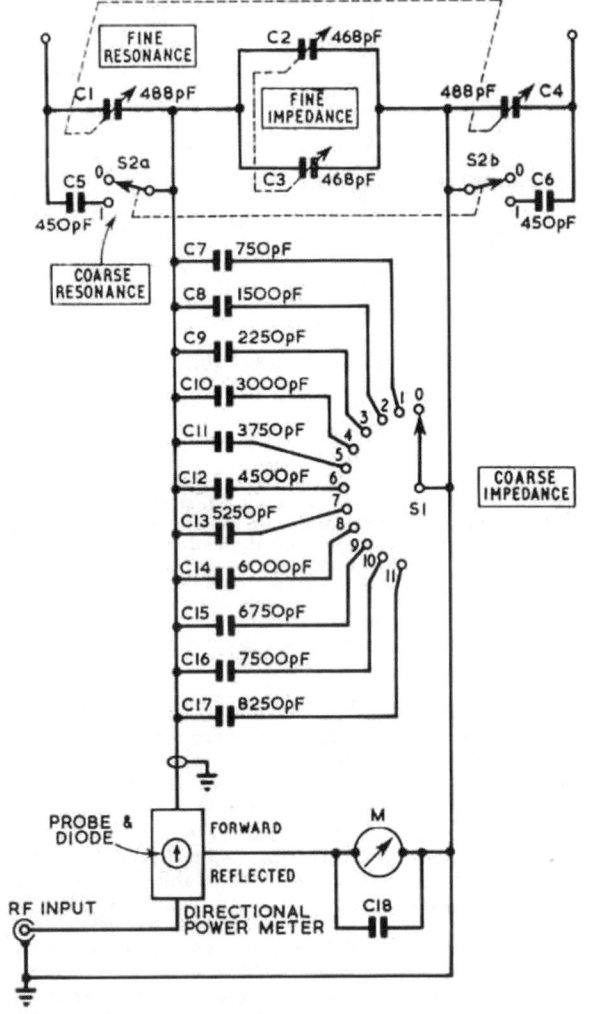

Fig. 2. The low-loss matching unit intended for use throughout the range 2 to 5 Mc/s, incorporating directional power meter to facilitate matching.

Loop and SIA Receiving Aerials

Extracted from 'Technical Topics', *Radio Communication*, January 1968

Loop and SIA Receiving Aerials

Some of the possibilities offered by low-loss transmitting loops were described in *TT* (November, 1967). A new wideband, directional receiving array with good front-to-back ratio, based on a series of small (one-metre diameter) loops a few feet above ground has been developed by the Canadian firm EMI-Cossor Electronics (*Electronics Weekly*, 29 November, 1967) as an alternative to log periodics or rhombics, and capable of being erected very quickly at an unprepared site.

This particular form of array, with its special wideband preamplifiers located immediately beneath each of eight pairs of balanced loops is perhaps not of immediate concern to amateurs. But a point of general interest is made strongly in the manufacturer's notes on this aerial: that an aerial may be inefficient for h.f. transmission but is not necessarily unsuitable for reception. This arises from the absence of a need in receiving aerials for efficient free space coupling.

At frequencies below about 30 MHz where atmospheric and galactic noise is the limiting factor, it is possible to use an aerial for receiving purposes which is electrically small and which thus has a poor free space coupling efficiency. It is this fact which also opens the way for the use of active subminiature integrated aerials (*TT*, September, 1967).

In *Electronics* (12 June, 1967), it is noted that the problem

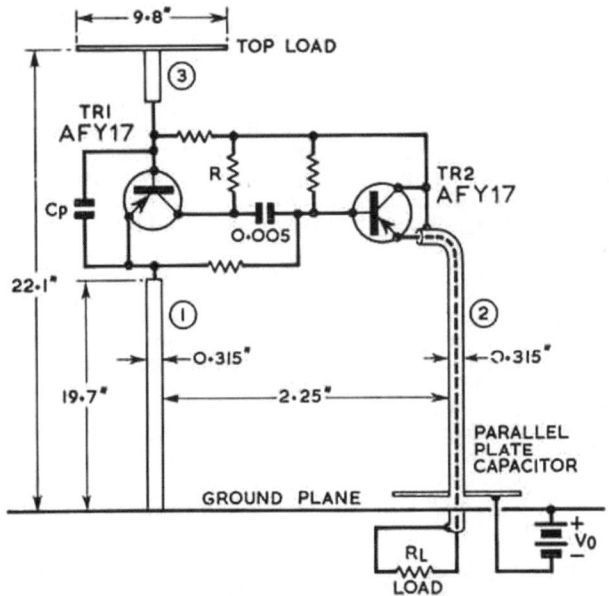

Fig. 9. One of the subminiature integrated aerials developed by Professor Meinke. This is a wideband omnidirectional aerial for use between 3 and 30 MHz. One transistor provides amplification, the second for matching. C_p prevents oscillation. The parallel plate capacitor provides an a.c. ground. Some component values not shown in the original diagram (*Electronics*, 12 June, 1967).

with electrically short aerials (less than $\tfrac{1}{8}\lambda$) arises from the difficulty in drawing maximum power from such an aerial without dissipating too much of it in the matching circuit. Such aerials usually act like a large capacitive reactance; this reactance can be tuned out with an inductance, but the problem of low loss broadband matching remains. This is where Professor H. Meinke's active devices come into the picture, as they can provide a wideband match without the use of tuning coils or transformers.

Fig. 9 shows one of his designs, in the form of a wideband 3–30 MHz omni-directional system only some 22 in. in height. As indicated in earlier *TT*, there is a good deal of controversy about these SIA systems, and there is no

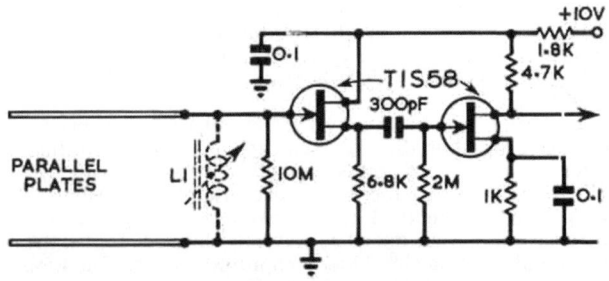

Fig. 10. One form of parallel plate capacitor proposed for the exalted carrier receiver of Fig. 7.

guarantee that the arrangement of Fig. 9 will live up to expectations.

Another compact " plate " aerial, taken from the paper on homodyne broadcast receivers by Dr Macario already referred to, is shown in Fig. 10. This uses two parallel copper laminated plates fitted in the upper and lower portions of the receiver cabinet; a tunable coil is placed across the plates and matching and amplification then achieved by means of two TIS58 field effect transistors.

Helicone Aerial

Extracted from 'Technical Topics',
Radio Communication, February 1968

Helicone Aerial

A letter in *Proc IEEE* (April 1967) from K. R. Carver reports that much improved sidelobe performance with circularly polarized helical aerials of the type used by a number of amateurs for space experiments and for receiving satellite cloud cover pictures can be achieved by mounting

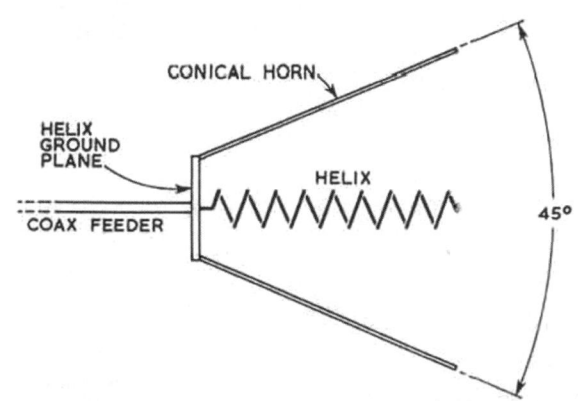

Fig. 3. Helicone aerial for reception of circularly polarized " space " signals. Typically cone mouth diameter is about 3 λ, the helix ground plane base plate 0·75 λ with a 10-turn helix, and cone angle of about 45°.

the helix within a conical horn structure. The axial length of the helix is approximately equal to the altitude of the truncated horn: see Fig. 3. Half-power beamwidth of the " helicone " is given as about 17° compared with 33° for a 10-turn helix, and first sidelobe is almost 20dB lower (from −14dB to −33dB).

Earth Conductivity and Vertical Aerials

Extracted from 'Technical Topics',
Radio Communication, March 1968

Earth Conductivity and Vertical Aerials

One of the recurrent themes of *TT* has been the effect of earth conductivity on vertically polarized aerials—and of the importance of a good low-ohmic earth connection when the aerial is tuned against earth. Much of the almost traditional belief that vertical aerials provide more effective low-angle radiation than horizontal ones is based on the theoretical vertical radiation pattern diagrams that appear in almost all of the Handbooks. Unfortunately, those patterns are the ones which would be obtained over a perfectly conductive ground-plane, and this fact is not always made clear. In practice, in many locations, far from the strong almost horizontal radiation, there is virtually a null. For reception purposes, a reasonably simple artificial ground plane or earth mat can help eliminate the null, but this is not so easily achieved for transmission. This is, in fact, a notable example of how the simplified approach so often adopted by those of us who put pen to paper can at times be positively misleading.

An illuminating paper on the improvement that can be obtained at m.f. when an aerial " looks out " over salt-water was included in a recent IEE conference on " m.f., l.f. and v.l.f. radio propagation." This was by P. Knight of the BBC research department and is believed to have resulted from studies made in connection with a proposed overseas m.f. relay station.

This paper points out that " if the Earth were a perfect conductor, the direct and ground-reflected waves for a vertical aerial would tend to add at very low angles, giving a large radiated field, the vertical radiation pattern having a maximum in the horizontal direction. With imperfectly conducting ground, however, the phase of the ground wave is reversed at low angles and the vertical radiation pattern has a zero in the horizontal direction."

The author points out that " the vertical radiation pattern for sea-water resembles those for perfectly-conducting ground down to angles very close to the horizontal, whereas those for imperfectly conducting ground start their downward trend at much higher angles." The observation is also made that " very large increases in signal strength might occur when propagation to the distant receiver takes place via a low-angle mode. These increases cannot often be realized (in broadcasting) because the contribution of higher angles modes—to which smaller increases apply—will usually predominate because receiving aerials on land discriminate against lower angle radiation by the same mechanism as that for transmitting aerials."

The paper indicates that increases in receiver input voltage of at least 6dB and may reach some 16dB if the transmitting aerial is sited near the sea instead of on ground of average conductivity. It suggests that the most important part of the ground plane is the first *50 wavelengths* in the direction towards the receiver.

These arguments would apply also on h.f. (although here a rough sea might have unfortunate results) and underline the importance of the ground conductivity extending well out beyond the aerial itself.

Fig. 6 gives a theoretical indication of the variation of low angle radiation of a 0·25 λ vertical aerial, calculated at 750 kHz.

Another paper at the conference gave a full list of ground conductivity constants of various soils, sea and fresh water,

ANTENNA TOPICS

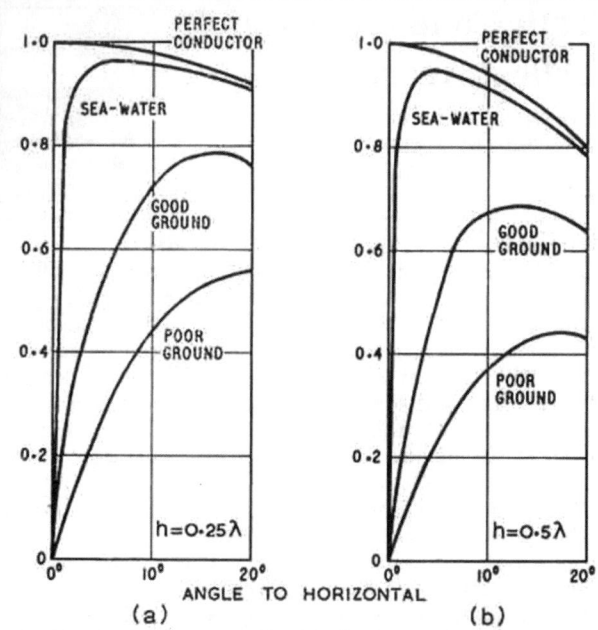

Fig. 6. Effect of the ground on the vertical radiation pattern of (a) ¼λ and (b) ½λ vertical aerials.

and of many types of rocks, sediments etc. This shows variations (in units of mho/m) from 4 to 5 for sea-water, 10^{-2} to 10^{-1} for good soil, 10^{-3} to 10^{-4} for poor soil and fresh water. There is a fascinating figure given for galena (PbS)—no less than 20 to 200. So perhaps when looking for a good site, it may be advisable to find out what is underneath. Anybody know a galena deposit extending out to 50 wavelengths in all directions?

to secure the octagon to the mast. I had to use heavy steel pipe to support the loop as aluminium pipe bent around freely. I use three about 500 pF variables (this may be 5500 pF variables—3VA) to tune the 'thing.'"

With the loop at a nominal height of 30 ft. mounted next to the aluminium siding of the house, and with the loop tuned for 7 MHz c.w. low-frequency end driven by a Swan 500 he has worked: IT1AGA (589), DM2BTO (579), YU3BUV (579), LZ2KLC (579), YO9APJ (559), G8AX (459), 7X2ED (569), VE6WG (579) and PY7AUU (559)—the signal reports indicating incoming report, from Rockville Centre, New York. He is hoping to try the aerial out soon on 3·5 MHz but seems already convinced that this is " a great low frequency aerial."

Looking back over the years, old timers may recall that a good deal of early v.h.f. (56 and 112 MHz) activity made use of the active type of loop aerial which also formed the p.a. tank coil. And checking through *Proc IRE* on this track recently, several articles on h.f. transmitting loops were found (typically January, 1934 and May, 1936).

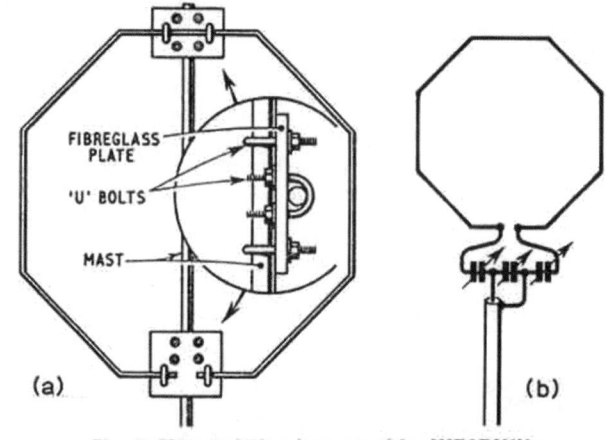

Fig. 7. Transmitting loop used by WB2PWU.

Those Transmitting Loops

Extracted from 'Technical Topics', *Radio Communication*, March 1968

Those Transmitting Loops

Last month, we noted (in anticipation of his full article) that work by G6NA on transmitting loops (*TT*, November, 1967) seems to confirm that this is an effective and thoroughly practical approach on 1·8 MHz; in his case with an ingenious alternative to large diameter copper tubing, and with a simple unbalanced matching network.

Since then an encouraging report on this technique has also come in from Ed Gerber (WB2PWU) who has been using an octagonal loop roughly of the type described in November to work some useful DX on 7 MHz. Like G6NA he is using a simple all-capacitor matching network, but in a balanced arrangement. He writes:

" I have had a sad dipole up on forty metres, the opposite of an inverted-vee, but could never work out locally very well. Though I did work 18 countries in the October, 1967, *CQ* WW test. But, in any case, this loop aerial interested me. So, with the help of W2GCX, I constructed one.

" I used ¾-in. (inner diameter) copper pipe and ' plumbers' 45s ' (they are actually 135° angle couplers), with regular plumbers' liquid solder to connect the pipes to the couplers. At the top and bottom of the loop I used a piece of about ¼-in. heavy fibreglass board with an oxen-yoke arrangement

Aerials - Good or Bad?

Extracted from 'Technical Topics', *Radio Communication*, June 1968

Aerials—good or bad?

Two types of aerials discussed in *TT* in recent months continue to be at the centre of some controversy—the Meinke SIA (subminiature integrated aerial) and the US Army transmitting loop.

Several attempts to build SIAs for such applications as broad-band v.h.f./f.m. reception have been reported in *Radio-Electronics*: so far with only limited success. My feeling now is that until more is disclosed on this type of aerial, nothing sensational is likely to be achieved in copying the designs so far published.

Meanwhile, *QST* set out to prove or disprove the transmitting loop, with W1ICP making a close copy of the original published design (*Electronics*, 21 August, 1967 and *TT*, November 1967) with 1½ in. aluminium tubing. He tested it against a number of conventional aerials (*QST*, March 1968) but obtained decidely disappointing results; so much so that he 'phoned the writer of the original article, K. Patterson, to ask for comments. The US Army Laboratory man pointed out that the loop has been used for two years in Vietnam, but added a little extra information which makes it clear that extreme care has been taken to minimize the ohmic losses; it was not revealed in the original article, for instance, that special jointing sleeves and gold plated joints have been used to keep resistance right down at the joints.

To achieve really good results, it rather looks as though one needs almost continuous copper tubing to meet that original claim of "full-dipole up 40 ft."—but then there are many situations where one would willingly settle for something less (for instance on 1·8 MHz where dipoles are few and far between). W1ICP seems to have concluded that a pukka loop could be an expensive project (his version cost almost £30), and that it might work out cheaper to put up a couple of masts. But it is possible that there are applications where the loop—and not necessarily one made of copper tubing—could be effective, once the point has been grasped that the total ohmic resistance at the transmitting frequency has just got to be brought down to a matter of milliohms—and the loop matching re-tuned up after every frequency shift of more than about 10 kHz.

regarded at most sites compared with the inevitable atmospheric and galactic noise, except possibly at the extreme h.f. end.

From an amateur viewpoint, the greatest drawback to these particular systems is that they are for receiving only; then again most amateurs are not primarily concerned with broadband coverage throughout the h.f. spectrum but only with amateur frequencies. Otherwise there would be a rush to develop simplified versions of these "rhombics in the back garden" systems. Certainly, the demonstrations left one with the feeling that the "active aerial" concept is one with a considerable future: good directivity in a mini-system.

Transmitting Loop Suggestions

Extracted from 'Technical Topics',
Radio Communication, August 1968

Transmitting Loop Suggestions

Interest continues high in transmitting loop aerials, and many comments and ideas are now appearing in *QST* and other US journals (e.g. "Ferris Wheel Antenna" in *73*, February 1968). K. Patterson, the designer of the original US Army loop has pointed out (*QST*, May 1968) that the *QST* version which produced disappointing results was by no means an exact copy, and that the matching constants seem wrong. Two other letters in the same issue suggest that loops can be made using the readily available 12 in. wide kitchen aluminium foil. In one case folded and Scotch-taped to the wall of an apartment with a minimum of folding; in another crumpled to form a rope-like conductor.

A note from R. L. Ames of Ingham suggests that a pipe loop aerial could be made up fairly easily using "Yorkshire" capillary (soldered) pipe fittings. He believes these would be simple to use, give a good soldered joint and could be disassembled; thus giving a low resistance joint without expensive equipment and possibly suitable for /A or /P with the help of ten minutes with a blowlamp. Am not sure what these fittings are made of—but willingly pass on the idea.

An 'Antennafier' in Operation

Extracted from 'Technical Topics',
Radio Communication, July 1968

An "Antennafier" in Operation

Having written in *TT* a good deal about various "active aerials" (i.e., aerials which depend on transistor or tunnel diode amplifiers for their correct operation) without ever having actually seen one in operation, I was particularly pleased to watch a practical demonstration. This was at the Diplomatic Wireless Service centre at Hanslope, and was of a new "aperiodic loop aerial array." This has been developed by EMI-Cossor in Canada—though it is rumoured that G6CJ was very much concerned with the original proposals.

This very unorthodox aerial (see *Electronics Weekly*, 29 November, 1967 and 12 June, 1968) basically consists of a series of eight small untuned double loops (each loop only one metre in diameter and mounted a few feet off the ground on tripods) extending in a line some 90 ft. long. Each group of two side-by-side loops (to achieve better balance) has its own transistor pre-amplifier mounted in the tubing below, and is spaced 13 ft. from the next pair. The entire system provides a broadband vertically polarized receiving array for use throughout the range 2 to 32 MHz with a directive gain (reference isotropic) of about 8dB at 5 MHz, 13dB at 30 MHz, and front-to-back ratios throughout the range better than 13dB (and considerably better at some specific frequencies). The array is thus comparable to a log periodic or even a rhombic, yet taking up only a fraction of the ground area. At DWS, the aerial was shown bringing in Canadian ionospheric sounder transmissions in direct comparison with an 80 ft. high rhombic, beamed in the same direction. It came out of this stiff test pretty well, though clearly to evaluate any aerial system one needs to note results over quite a period of time.

To "pay" for the small size one has to accept that there will be some noise contributed by the pre-amplifiers, even though they use low-noise transistors. However, a good case can be made to show that on h.f. this extra noise can be disregarded at most sites compared with the inevitable atmo-

144MHz DDRR Aerial

Extracted from 'Technical Topics',
Radio Communication, August 1968

144 MHz DDRR Aerial

A. F. Ward, 5Z4FB has reported building a 145 MHz version (Fig. 5) of the ddrr "hula-hoop" aerial and obtained a v.s.w.r. of less than 1·2 : 1 at this frequency. He also feels that it should be possible to make a beam with horizontal polarization by turning the aerial on its side and adding quarter-wave loops at 0·1 and 0·2 wavelength spacing from the radiator, gradually reducing the diameter as with a Yagi. This seems a little debatable because of the dual nature of radiation from a ddrr, and the added complexity compared with a Yagi, but 5Z4FB intends trying it. Unfortunately,

ANTENNA TOPICS

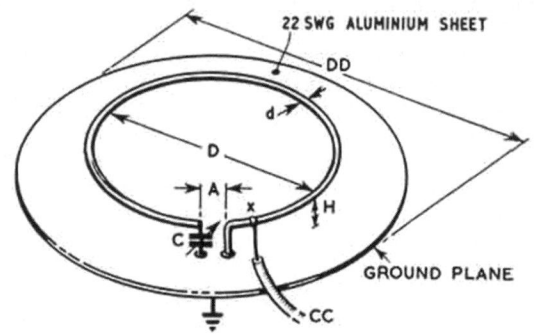

Fig. 5. 144 MHz DDRR Hula-hoop aerial by 5Z5FB. DD = 7 in. D = 5·4. H = 0·6. d = 0·1 (5Z4ZB used ⅛ in.). A = 0·3. X = 0·15 –1·0 in. (for best match to feeder). c = 1-15 pF. cc = 75 ohm semi-air spaced coax.

there is a shortage of 145 MHz operation in 5Z4!

Walkie-talkie Aerials

Extracted from 'Technical Topics', *Radio Communication*, September 1968

Walkie-talkie Aerials

Perhaps because of the influence of the 27 MHz CB units, amateur interest in compact, low-power, hand-held transmitter-receivers has waned—yet there are many "legal" uses for such equipment, and work to be done in improving range. One aspect of the subject that has not received as of short v.h.f. "whip" aerials. Some of those who helped develop equipment for police foot-patrol work, and I am thinking particularly of Ian Campbell-Bruce (G5IB) who was one of the first advocates of this type of equipment, have sometimes told me that a whip held up to speak into the microphone gives much better results than some of the various body and microphone-lead aerials. But few seem to have studied just why this should be so, apart that is from Zdeněk Krupa of the Czech Tesla-Popov research institute ("Effect of Human Body on Radiation Properties of Small-sized Communications Systems," *IEEE Translations on Antennas and Propagation*, March, 1968).

He has come up with some interesting observations and detailed measurement including an appraisal of the very considerable absorption of v.h.f. radiation (he has investigated from 30 to 150 MHz) when an aerial is close to the human body. His article provides plots of the change of impedance and radiation pattern when an aerial is held close to one side of the body (for example with the equipment in a bag or haversack suspended from the shoulder) compared with a whip held well up in front of the head.

He points out that, in effect, many of these aerial systems are really two-element arrays with the body forming a dissipative radiating element, and this results in appreciable variations in the horizontal radiation pattern (often far from the commonly accepted omni-directional pattern), with even a body resonance effect at some frequencies. Even more important is that he shows that the body may be absorbing up to 97 per cent of the transmitter power, leaving only a tiny 3 per cent actually radiating.

The conclusion that may be drawn from this article is that when using a short v.h.f. whip, it should give far better results when well up and clear of the user—otherwise you are likely to be forming a highly effective dummy load.

Hoop and Thin-wire Aerials

Extracted from 'Technical Topics', *Radio Communication*, October 1968

Hoop and Thin-wire Aerials

The September article by G6NA has shown clearly and expertly that low-resistance loops can be successfully used on 1·8, and probably on 3·5 MHz. But what of "thin-wire" loops and hoops for h.f. and v.h.f.? There seems increasing evidence—certainly enough to justify some further investigations—that there may be equally interesting possibilities that such loops could be used in a variety of ways, in situations where space and high supports are at a premium.

For instance, the description of the "2PL Special" (*TT* July, 1968—a normal quad operated with the reflector just off ground and shooting upwards) brought in a supporting comment from Ian Mitchell, G3MQY who notes that as VS1KY in Singapore in 1961 and using 60 watts series-gate a.m. the feedpoint of his 21MHz quad was normally only 3 ft. above ground (though providing good world-wide contacts), On one occasion, the rig was operated with the reflector actually on the ground and the radiator firing straight up. This arrangement, as for G2PL, resulted in useful contacts, in this case to JA6, JA4 and VS9. Admittedly, it is difficult to evaluate a 21 or 28 MHz aerial on the basis of a few contacts, since when conditions are good the proverbial "wet string" can produce good DX. Still, this is encouraging. It should be made clear that we are not suggesting that people with quads should normally operate them in this way—rather, as 2PL pointed out, that this might form the basis of a simply constructed aerial using four short posts to give results akin to a dipole at normal height.

The quad "hoop" is basically one wavelength in perimeter. The original Boyer (W6UYH) DDRR hula hoop was resonated to ¼-λ by the capacitor at the free end. This immediately suggests that there might be an intermediate ½-λ form of hoop—and sure enough some intensive delving into the literature has produced evidence (*Electronics Letters*, September, 1965) that this has indeed been recognized. A group of Italian research people then pointed out that, compared with the Boyer ¼-λ, "less known is the ½-λ closed-loop aerial which had a quite different and, in some ways, better performance." Fig. 1, derived from their letter shows the basic differences between the hula-hoop and the ½-λ closed

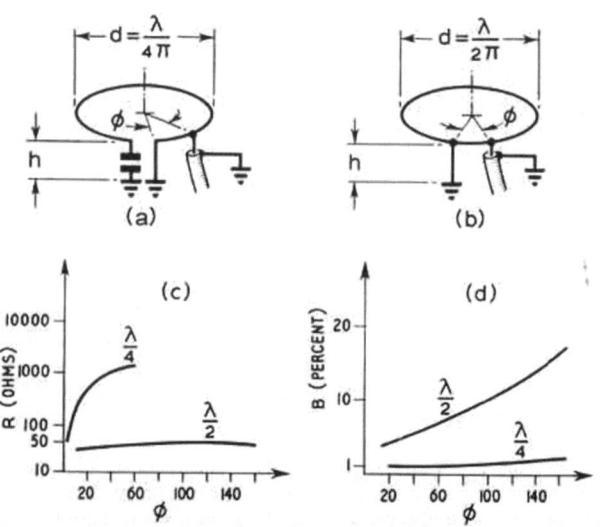

Fig. 1. (a) The ¼λ hula hoop DDRR aerial; (b) ½λ closed loop; (c) resonance impedance versus feed-point angle; (d) bandwidth versus feed-point angle.

loop.

The useful information given by the Italians (including various plots of impedance and radiation characteristics) all seems to indicate that the $\frac{1}{2}$-λ system may have considerable advantages for amateur experimentation: the bandwidth of the $\frac{1}{2}$-λ system can be up to ten times that of the $\frac{1}{4}$-λ system

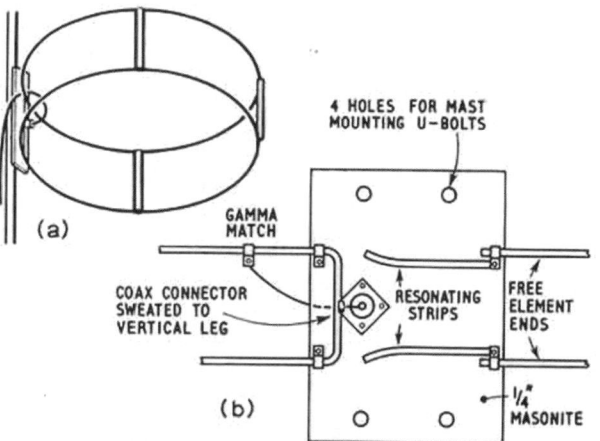

Fig. 2. Details of the K2ICF "double hula." (a) Complete vertical polarization system clamped on a vertical mast; (b) detail of mounting assembly and resonating strip "capacitors." Details of hula hoop dimensions (*TT*, September 1964, *TTftRA* or *Amateur Radio Techniques*), basically loop + height ($\frac{1}{2}$ of double hoop spacing) is $\frac{1}{4}\lambda$ at highest frequency.

thus allowing a band to be covered without retuning; the feedpoint impedance remains roughly 50 ohms for ϕ angles from about 20° to 160° (making for easy matching and providing a simple means of finally resonating the loop to the required centre frequency); feedpoint impedance and resonance frequency can also be varied by changing h.

Altogether one has the impression that the $\frac{1}{2}$-λ closed-loop should prove far less critical in adjustment, and—with a good ground plane—should give excellent omni-directional radiation at reasonable vertical angles. A suggested value for ϕ for 50-ohm coax would be roughly 100° and h/λ about 5 per cent. The letter suggests that there could be many applications, particularly for mobile work, of such loops (the original work appears to have been done at 400 MHz), but surprisingly, I have seen little subsequent reference to this system, though I seem to recall an article by an Italian amateur on the subject. There is obviously scope for further experimental work from h.f. to u.h.f. And, from the following section, arises the important question of whether this form of loop could be used in a double-loop arrangement to eliminate the need for an extensive ground plane. Those with very long memories may recall the Reinhartz $\frac{1}{2}$-λ double open-loop rotary beams that were used successfully in the 'thirties on 56 MHz (e.g. *T. & R. Bulletin*, September 1938, G5NG). Single $\frac{1}{2}$-λ open loops are also being currently offered by J-Beams for Band I television reception, and are claimed to facilitate nulling out "ghosts."

Balanced Double-hoops and Arrays

Extracted from 'Technical Topics', *Radio Communication,* October 1968

Balanced Double-hoops and Arrays

The note on 5Z4FB's 144 MHz DDRR (*TT*, August) resulted in correspondence from Brian Rose, G3ULR who has been doing a good deal of work on various forms of 21 MHz balanced loops turned on their side to give horizontal polarization. Among other points, he has come to the conclusion (hinted at in my note on 5Z4FB's planned Yagi-type loop array) that placing additional tuned loops parallel to one another is unlikely to result in high-gain beam arrays; but he is now looking into the question of using pairs of double loops in a form of "ZL-special" arrangement, with the loops spaced co-planar rather as in the EMI-Cossor "active" array of aperiodic loops for receiving (*TT*, July).

Soon afterwards, I came across an article (*73 Magazine*, April 1965) on the DDRR by Peter Lovelock, K2ICF/6. This pointed out that one of the main problems of the vertical polarization $\frac{1}{4}$-λ DDRR is the requirement for an extremely good ground plane. This led K2ICF to investigate a double hula in which the ground plane is replaced by a second "image" hula hoop to provide a complete "doublet" structure. This, he found, could be mounted parallel to ground for vertical polarization (Fig. 2) or turned on its side, like a thick wheel, to give horizontal polarization. There are some significant differences between the K2ICF and G3ULR double hoops; for example the 'ICF spacing is 5·6 electrical degrees (i.e. twice the original 2·8°) whereas 'ULR uses 2·8°. 'ICF uses resonating strips (in lieu of high voltage capacitors) tuned about the "earth" point represented by the coax feed outer, while 'ULR simply puts a ganged capacitor in series across his open ends, and he feeds with balanced 300 ohm line.

Both 'ICF and 'ULR note that results can be affected when loops are mounted on metal supports (a result to be expected with vertical polarization). Loops are high-Q and must be accurately tuned. 'ICF uses $\frac{5}{8}$-in. copper tubing. Although 'ICF had to abandon work before he could try out any ideas on double-loop arrays he felt that "at least it had been proved that vertical or horizontal, the double hula works and offers lots of opportunity for the experimentally minded, as well as practical joy for those who are underprivileged in space."

To sum up. At present all these hula-hoop-type systems still seem to be at the stage of being experimental concepts rather than cut and dried designs. But somewhere, still buried in this work, must surely be some really useful new aerials for those amateurs not blessed with acres of space, or tall masts. Remember, a good vertically polarized system benefits rather than the opposite from being close to its ground-plane.

Aerial Protection Against Metal Fatigue

Extracted from 'Technical Topics', *Radio Communication,* October 1968

Aerial Protection against Metal Fatigue

Metal fatigue is a term which has come to be associated with aircraft, but one has only to glance at the rooftops to spot that many television aerials have been damaged by the elements being flexed continually in resonant modes by wind vibration. This problem applies to any aerial array using rod-like elements, and can be serious in exposed areas or where winds are continuously blowing for a large part of the time.

A technique used to overcome this problem on Yagi and log-periodic h.f. arrays at Washington State University was put forward some time ago (*Electronic Design*, 2 August, 1966) but is likely to be new to many. This item suggested

ANTENNA TOPICS

that flat rubber sheets, or sheets fashioned by splitting a length of rubber garden hose, can be used as energy absorbers to prevent rupturing of aerial elements. It was pointed out that the mechanical impedance of any rod-like element is high at a free end, regardless of the number of modes along the elements. This means that placing an energy-absorbent device at the ends can reduce the amplitude of vibration and minimize the chance of breakage.

The protective device could be made from a short section of lightweight garden hose, split lengthwise every 90°, and held in place on the end of the elements by a hose clamp: Fig. 5. The writer pointed out that a more efficient and durable protection can be made from a sheet of flat rubber or pliable plastic material, ⅛ to ¼-in. thick by 5 to 6 in. long. If this is made just wide enough to wrap once round the element, the damping will be matched to the size of the element. The material is cut lengthwise to make four tabs. Ideally, they would be more effective if clamped at the very end, but in practice they are positioned so that the free ends of the tabs are about 2 in. from the ends, to prevent changes in the electrical length of the elements and impedance.

It was pointed out that the system had been used on Yagi and log-periodic aerials for over three years. Element diameters ranged from ⅜ to 1 in., and not a single breakage occurred.

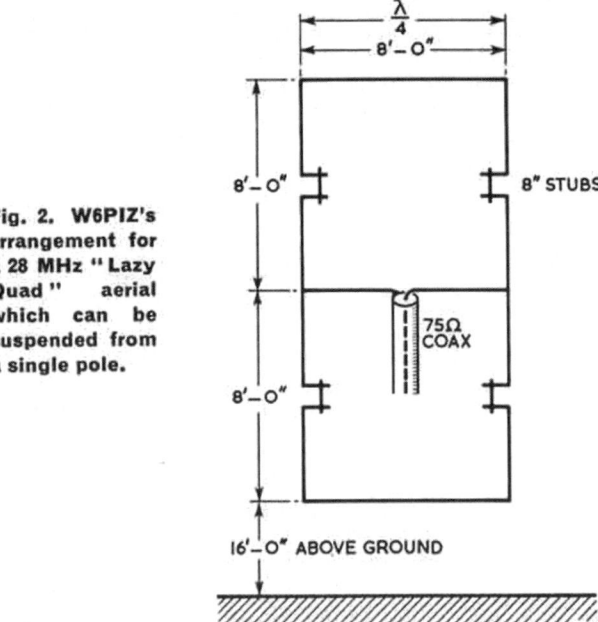

Fig. 2. W6PIZ's arrangement for a 28 MHz "Lazy Quad" aerial which can be suspended from a single pole.

sections mounted on 8 ft. lengths of 1 × 2 in. timber, and adjustable self-supporting stubs made of the same wire. Such construction is able to withstand high winds, and the system picks up less QRN than vertically polarized systems. The stubs are 8-in. and for peaking at 28,050 kHz for c.w. operation, he finds the setting is about 6 in.

W6PIZ makes the further suggestion that such an array could be backed by a reflector employing a similar configuration, though this has not been tried.

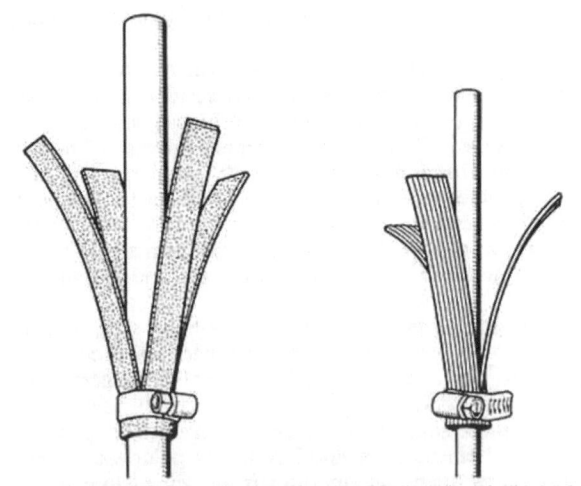

Fig. 5. Flat rubber sheets protect aerial elements by absorbing and dissipating mechanical energy due to wind.

W6PIZ's 'Lazy Quad'

Extracted from 'Technical Topics',
Radio Communication, November 1968

W6PIZ's "Lazy Quad"

A suggestion by W6PIZ (*QST*, September, 1968) is for a novel 28 MHz "Lazy Quad" which combines Lazy H and Quad techniques: Fig. 2. The idea is novel to me, but W6PIZ modestly admits that he adapted the arrangement from 21 MHz users. He considers that the array provides extreme simplicity and the feasibility of putting it up on a single 32 ft. unguyed pole, with particularly modest horizontal space requirements. The aerial, he reports, has given results "consistently better than with vertical or horizontal dipoles at the same location."

He uses loops made of No. 14 wire, with the horizontal

Capacitively Loaded Dipoles

Extracted from 'Technical Topics',
Radio Communication, December 1968

Capacitively Loaded Dipoles

Have you ever wanted a dipole element that could be used on 14, 21 and 28 MHz—or anywhere between—and possibly slung immediately below a 7 MHz dipole without any interaction? Or another covering both 70 and 144 MHz? Or in quarter-wave form as a grounded monopole or ground-plane in which ground losses are dramatically reduced? Or a "dipole" with a 3·2 dB gain over a dipole, though requiring more space?

The answer is hardly likely to be "no." Yet it seems quite possible that these and other benefits have been there for the asking for a number of years, certainly ever since Dud Charman, G6CJ wrote an article "Loaded Wire Dipoles" (*RSGB Bulletin*, July 1961). Surprisingly, we have never seen much evidence of any rush to take advantage of this interesting concept, which is not to be found in the handbooks.

G6CJ showed how capacitively loaded or "stretched" dipoles up to 100 ft. long for 14 MHz could be formed quite simply from overlapping sections of 80-ohm flat twin line.

My excuse for referring back to this neglected 1961 item is a recent article "Impedance properties of capacitively loaded dipoles" by T. S. M. Maclean of the University of

Birmingham (*Proc IEE*, October 1968) complete with some pretty ferocious-looking mathematical analyses. This reports experimental work at v.h.f. and u.h.f. using a ground plane monopole made of short brass rod elements of about 0·5 cm diameter fitting together by plugging them into perspex tubes which have a controlled gap between the rods. This technique was used to form a triply-loaded monopole providing a v.s.w.r. better than 2·5 in the 75-ohm feeder over a frequency range greater than 2·5:1. The article provides graphs comparing input resistance and reactance of unloaded, dual-loaded and triply-loaded monopoles.

The *Proc IEE* paper makes no reference to the G6CJ-type dipoles which stemmed from the work of E. C. Cork of EMI on the tilted wire TV aerial that never gained much popularity (despite its useful characteristics). Nevertheless, the principles seem to be the same. This new paper puts main emphasis on the broadband feature: the characteristic impedance increases progressively from the centre; thus the outgoing current waveform decreases, so that ideally at the end of the aerial there is virtually no current to be reflected, so that variation of input impedance with frequency is much reduced.

Probably, the *Proc IEE* paper is likely to appeal primarily to professional aerial people—but this seems an opportune time for suggesting that all of us could do worse than to re-read 6CJ's 1961 article, and perhaps be stirred into taking the capacitively loaded dipole much more seriously.

3.5MHz Mini-Antenna

Extracted from 'Technical Topics',
Radio Communication, January 1969

3·5 MHz Mini-Antenna

Folding back arrangements can, of course, often be adopted in order to radiate better signals on 1·8 or 3·5 MHz from sites where only a short span of aerial can be put up. As a rather novel arrangement of this type, R. A. Lowe, ZL1AYN describes a " Mini-Antenna" (*Break-in,* May, 1968) that he has been using on 3·5 MHz (Fig. 7) although he has only 30 ft available from his shack to his aerial support. The 60 ft or so of wire is simply doubled back, spaced about 6 in with Paxolin spacers and the free-end connected to

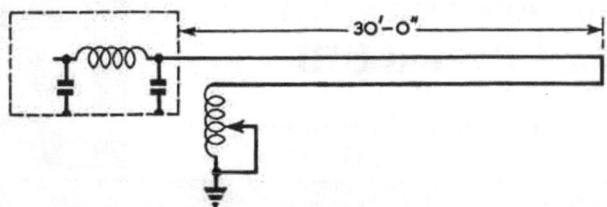

Fig. 7. The ZL1AYN "mini antenna" for 3·5 MHz.

earth via an ex-ZC1 variable inductor. He reports the system as far more effective than just a 30 ft wire, or a fold-back without the variable inductor.

Franklin Uniform Aerial

Extracted from 'Technical Topics',
Radio Communication, January 1969

Franklin Uniform Aerial

Over the years, fashions in aerials as well as in systems have changed; today those in widespread use tend to be derived from a relatively few basic types. Many other aerials, including some dating back well over 40 years (but none the worse for that), have become little more than names in old text books to many of the current generation of amateurs.

Recently, going through old *Bulletins*, I was interested in several early references to the Franklin Uniform aerial—one of the first designs to take practical advantage of the fact that, since most radiation takes place from current nodes, sections at high voltage can be folded back with relatively little loss of total radiation. This technique allows in-phase or collinear arrays to be erected in less space than would otherwise be needed, and without phasing stubs.

The original Franklin Uniform was invariably described as a vertical array, though this involved some problems since the sections were not equally balanced to earth, and dimensions were critical. The vertical form of the array has in fact been recently described in the October, 1968 section of a series of articles on vertical aerials in *CQ* by Paul Lee,

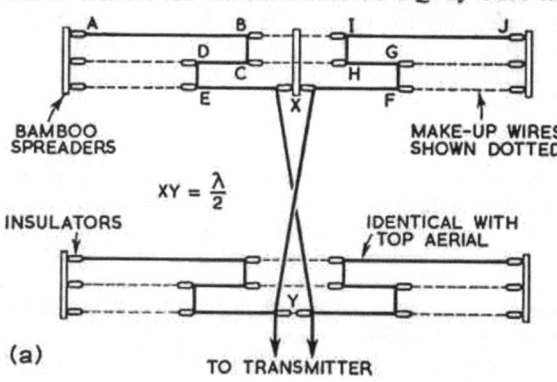

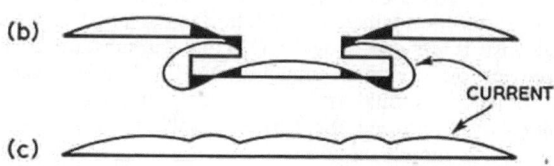

Fig. 6. (a) The 1938 bi-directional ZE1JA fixed beam array for 14 MHz, based on the Franklin Uniform aerial adapted for horizontal polarization. Dimensions (14 MHz)
AB = IJ = (⅜λ − 2·5%) − 1 foot = 0·609λ − 1 foot
CD = GH = (¼λ − 2·5%) − 2 feet = 0·244λ − 2 feet
EF = (¾λ − 2·5%) − 2 feet = 0·731 − 2 feet
BC, DE, FG, HI each 2 feet (λ in feet 984/MHz). Bamboo spreaders lying in the horizontal plane (shown in vertical plane for simplification). ¼λ spacing between X, Y.
(b) Current distribution in 3λ/2 Franklin uniform array. Radiation from shaded portions cancel.

W3JM. He points up the omnidirectional gain provided by its vertical radiation pattern, and puts forward the suggestion of making vhf and uhf versions by shaping the aerial in stiff wire. In practice, however, few vhf operators are interested in aerials for vertical polarization.

It may not be generally appreciated that this technique can equally be used to form horizontal arrays; indeed it was so used in an impressive fixed bidirectional Lazy-H for

ANTENNA TOPICS

14 MHz described by ZE1JA (*T & R Bulletin*, December, 1938). I seem to remember ZE1JA putting in a whale of a signal despite his location on the wrong side of a large Cable & Wireless point-to-point beam array. Fig 6 shows the array, as described then—a bulky beast on 14 MHz but it could still be attractive if scaled down for higher frequencies, or used without the second lower element. Correct feed-point impedance is not known, though ZE1JA fed it with 600-ohm line. This technique for putting out the maximum radiation from a given span seems too good to be forgotten entirely.

Mobile Loop Aerials

Extracted from 'Technical Topics', *Radio Communication*, February 1969

Mobile Loop Aerials

The controversy over the US Army "down-to-earth" loop aerial (*ART*, page 135) continues to simmer. A detailed account of commercial tests by HB9AGK with a large static aerial of this type while seeking an aerial without high angle nulls for working short distances out of deep valleys suggests that the loop is at least some 15 dB below an inverted vee dipole using a 40 ft mast in the range 2 to 3·5 MHz.

On the other hand, J. E. Taylor, W2OZH in the same issue of *QST* (November, 1968) describes a 3·5 MHz half-loop mobile aerial rising over the vehicle from front to rear bumper (some 30 ft of radiator) performed "better than all previous configurations tried." The aerial (using two vertical section and two whips bent over and joined with stout wire in low resistance joint) is fed by coax with a 2000 pF capacitor down to the front bumper, and resonated by a neutralizing type capacitor to the rear bumper.

It may be argued that it is the length of the radiator rather than the loop configuration that puts out the strong signal. But it can hardly be a coincidence that in *CQ* also of November, 1968 a basically similar arrangement using two 8 ft vertical section joined by a 17 ft horizontal length of heavy gauge wire is described by W2OZH as "a substantial improvement on previous configurations." All this suggests that somebody should try out a G6NA type coax loop (*Radio Communication*, September, 1968) as a Top-band or 3·5 MHz mobile aerial.

The Delta-Loop Beam

Extracted from 'Technical Topics', *Radio Communication*, May 1969

The Delta-Loop Beam

Two articles in the same issue of *QST* (January, 1969) sing the praises of a Quad-type configuration of loops that is claimed to offer considerable mechanical advantages over the normal Quad while retaining the performance. The idea stems from H. R. Habig, K8ANV but is also presented by ARRL-staffer W1ICP as being ideal for 21 MHz novice operation with its "plumber's delight" construction, good matching over a band, and effective performance, even when mounted only a few feet off the ground.

Basically, the aerial uses two triangular rather than square

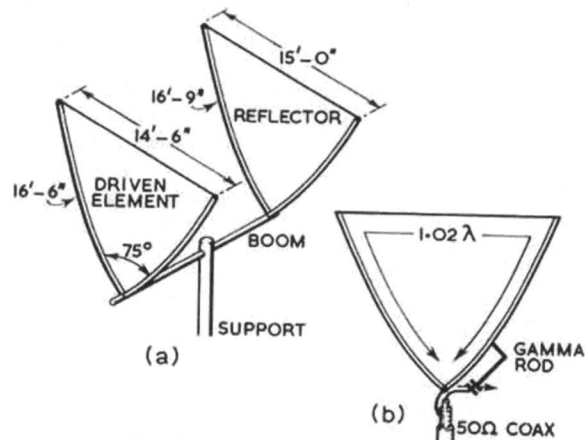

Fig 7. HRH Delta-loop beam. Main dimensions shown for 21 MHz, using 9 ft spacing and 3 ft gamma rod. For 28 MHz driven element 12 ft. sides, 11 ft top, 75° angle. 6 ft 6 in boom spacing to reflector having 12 ft sides, 11 ft 10 in top.

loops: 1005/MHz feet for the gamma-matched driven element, and 1030/MHz feet reflector, spaced 0·2-λ (6 ft 6 in for 28 MHz). The entire elements are above the boom which joins two points at electrically similar potentials, so that the boom need not be insulated from the loops (i.e. "plumber's delight"). Construction takes the form of two V's made of tubing, with the base of the V's solidly mounted on the boom, and then a top section to complete the loop using No 12 or 14 copper wire. The whole structure is made reasonably "solid", and there are no cross supports needed between reflector and driven elements at the top. The high-voltage 100 pF matching capacitor can be mounted in a plastic "freezer" box, and the gamma rod for the 21 MHz version fashioned from 36-inches of rod. The two *QST* articles give full constructional details for both 21 and 28 MHz versions, but it is hoped that Fig. 7 plus these brief notes will allow mechanically-minded readers to figure out their own approaches.

John Pegler, G3ENI has been using "double delta" loops on vhf for several years, and we hope to include his approach to this technique shortly.

'Double-Delta' Aerials for VHF and UHF

Extracted from 'Technical Topics', *Radio Communication*, June 1969

" Double-Delta " Aerials for VHF and UHF

The recent *QST* articles on delta-loop aerials (see *TT*, May 1969) have prompted John Pegler, G3ENI, chairman of the Royal Naval Amateur Radio Society, to pass along information on two and three element "double delta" aerials he has been using for some years on 70 and 144 MHz as well as an eight element version used for television reception on uhf Channel 24.

The radiator consists of two dural tubing triangles mounted vertically so that their apexes can be joined and earthed to the boom, in a "plumber's delight" configuration. These deltas are fed in phase by means of a double balanced gamma matching system: Fig. 4. Reflectors and directors have a similar configuration, and are mounted on the boom with a reflector spacing of 0·2 λ and a director spacing of 0·15 λ. This unequal spacing, G3ENI suggests, appears to provide optimum gain, and also has the advantage of keeping the radiator clear of the support mast. Overall lengths of each Delta can be calculated as follows:

Reflector 1078/(MHz) feet or 12936/(MHz) inches
Radiator 1007/(MHz) feet or 12084/(MHz) inches
Director 948/(MHz) feet or 11376/(MHz) inches.

These dimensions are very slightly longer than would be obtained using conventional formulae: actual dimensions for 70·250 MHz and 145 MHz are shown in Table 1. G3ENI says that if maximum front/back ratio is required the reflector length may be varied slightly as a result of listening tests. The radiator lengths are empirical ones arrived at by measuring with the aid of a gdo.

TABLE I

Element	70.25 MHz	145 MHz
Reflector	184 in.	89¼ in.
Radiator	172 in.	83¼ in.
Director	162 in.	78¼ in.

The radiating action of this aerial can be visualised as two one-third-λ horizontal radiators spaced broadside at just over ½-λ, with associated reflectors and directors: a horizontal component is also radiated from the central apexes.

G3ENI has obtained approximate figures for gains referred to a half-wave dipole, by means of listening tests in conjunction with a low-loss rf attenuator with constant S-meter reading. He lists these as: radiator alone 3–4dB; radiator plus reflector 8–9dB; reflector/radiator/director 10–11dB.

He considers that the additional gain which would be obtained using a second director in a four-element beam as hardly worth the added mechanical complexity. However, he puts the gain from an eight-element uhf aerial for Channel 24 (500 MHz) as about 15dB (reference dipole).

The 70 and 144 MHz arrays were made using ⅜-inch dural tubing; the 500 MHz array from 12 swg tinned copper wire using a wooden boom.

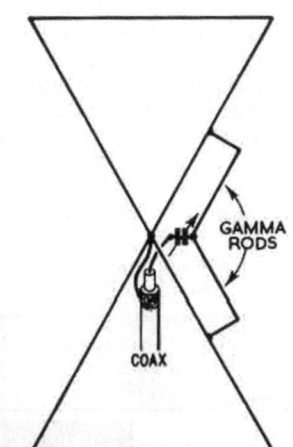

Fig 4. G3ENI "double delta" aerials for vhf— basic driven element.

HF 'Skeleton Slot'

Extracted from 'Technical Topics', *Radio Communication,* June 1969

HF "Skeleton Slot"

There have been many innovations which although originally adopted or intended for more than one region of the radio spectrum have subsequently tended to become associated with only one part of the spectrum. For example the cascode rf amplifier, originally described for hf, was for about a decade used almost exclusively at vhf. The Armstrong "super-regen" was initially intended for medium-wave broadcast reception!

Bill Capstick, G3JYP, points out that, when B. Sykes, G2HCG, first described the Skeleton Slot (*SWM*, January, 1955), his article underlined its possibilities for hf as well as vhf applications. Yet, although this aerial subsequently proved extremely popular on vhf, little attention has been given to it by hf operators despite the good results obtained by G2HCG with a multi-element 28MHz skeleton-slot beam.

G3JYP has been rectifying this omission by building a 21 MHz skeleton slot (9 ft by 27 ft) and finding to his delight that it also works well on 14 and 28 MHz, and has had some success even on 70 and 7 MHz, even though, with these slot dimensions, it is down on a 7 MHz dipole. He believes that a smaller version (7 ft by 21 ft) would be suitable for those not requiring a major 14 MHz capability. The close similarity to the "Lazy Quad" given in the November, 1968, *TT* is very evident from Fig. 5.

G3JYF's skeleton slot is made from 1¼-in dural tubing

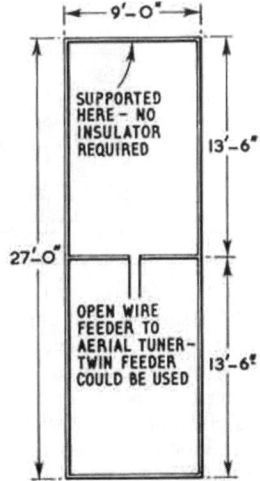

Fig 5. G3JYP's hf "skeleton slot" aerial.

(though only because G6VQ had denuded the local supplier of 1-in tubing). It is fed with open wire feeder via a Z-match in the shack, and the bottom of the slot is about 30 ft off ground, on a metal pole (no noticeable difference in performance noted with a similar aerial mounted on a wooden pole—presumably a result of the horizontal polarization).

Clearly, this form of array calls for relatively high supports, but G3JYP points out that, apart from the useful performance, its appearance is "reasonably tidy" against a backcloth of tall trees.

ANTENNA TOPICS

Simple Balun

Extracted from 'Technical Topics',
Radio Communication, July 1969

Simple Balun

In a letter to *QST* (April, 1969), old-timer Walter van Roberts, W2CHO/K4EA (whose part in the development of the Seiler oscillator we noted some years ago) draws attention to a neglected lumped-constant resonant balun—the Alford circuit. This he believes could usefully be revived to assist in changing from 50-ohm coax to open-wire or other balanced feeder lines.

The arrangement is shown in Fig 6 and consists of just one variable capacitor and a centre-tapped coil (or two equal inductively coupled coils). Since this is a fixed impedance arrangement, ideally it should be preceded by a matching network and swr meter, though one suspects that it might often be possible to use the Pi or Pi-L matching network built into the transmitter. The system is a bit more bother, in having to adjust for resonance and changing coils for different bands, than some of the wideband balun techniques, but it could still be a handy circuit to know.

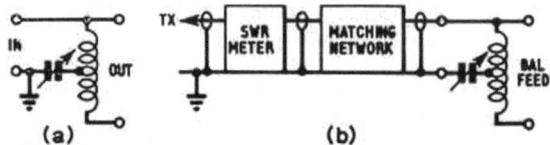

Fig 6. Resonant balun for feeding balanced feeders.

Low-loss Cubicle Quad

Extracted from 'Technical Topics',
Radio Communication, July 1969

Low-loss Cubicle Quad

Another article in the May, 1969 issue of *Old Man* (reprinted from *73 Magazine*) is one by H. A. Rideout, WA6IPD showing how lower losses in feeder lines to quads can often be achieved by using a folded driven element. This provides a feed point of 600 ohms impedance, which is reduced by the usual reflector loop to roughly 300 ohms, thus providing a good match to 300-ohm open wire transmission line having lower losses than the more usual coax feeder. In construction, 300-ohm open line is used not only for the feeder but also conveniently to form the double loop: Fig 7. WA6IPD notes that insulation will be required on the open wire line where it circumvents a rotator and also suggests that 300-ohm ribbon feeder should be avoided on account of its varying characteristics with weather, unless in a very dry site.

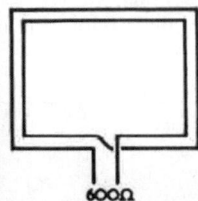

Fig 7. Folded driven element for quad aerials allows use of low-loss open line. Feed point impedance is reduced to about 300 ohms when a reflector loop is used.

Miniature Active Receiving Aerials

Extracted from 'Technical Topics',
Radio Communication, August 1969

Miniature Active Receiving Aerials

Quite a number of references have been made in recent years in *TT* to the miniature "active" or transistorised receiving aerial technique being developed in West Germany by Prof. Hans Meinke. This work has caused a lot of controversy, particularly in the United States, and some pretty bitter attacks on the concept have been published. At the recent Montreux international television symposium therefore, I was particularly interested to listen to Meinke and his colleague Dr H. Lindenmeier describe some of their latest results.

They showed how the combination of a transistor and compact dipole structure results not only in amplification of signals by the transistor (this can be done with a conventional mast-head amplifier) but also can result in considerable improvement in signal/noise ratio because of the very accurate noise match that can be achieved. They listed very low noise temperatures achieved with compact vhf aerials under a foot in length, and many slides were shown of various forms of compact active aerials, of which they have now built over 100. Many of these are for normal television reception on Bands I, III and IV/V in typical urban areas; easily mounted on a roof or balcony edge or in loft spaces, and claimed to be very effective in overcoming multipath ("ghost") problems.

Single-channel, wideband and wideband/bandstop (for instance to cover Band I and III but reject Band II signals) active aerials all appear to have been tested successfully. They could do much to eliminate the roof clutter (and inefficiency due to interaction) of television receiving aerials —though apparently there is still no immediate industry plans for marketing such aerials and the economics remain to be ascertained.

All the aerials use a single active arrangement and Dr Lindenmeier told me afterwards that he felt that this is the right approach to active aerials (ie one should not attempt to incorporate active devices in a whole series of separate elements).

Despite what some critics have suggested, the miniature arrays are claimed to have very good cross-modulation performance, partly because the actual signal pick-up on the compact elements is relatively small. Personally, I found the explanations pretty convincing, though I am not too sure whether the principles could be applied to benefit amateur radio, mainly because this is a receiving-only system. But certainly this is a fascinating subject, well worth keeping an eye on.

More on the T2FD Multiband Aerial

Extracted from 'Technical Topics',
Radio Communication, August 1969

More on the T2FD Multiband Aerial

Some 11 years ago (*TT*, July 1958) a few brief notes were given on the "T2FD" (terminated tilted folded dipole) multiband aerial originally described by G. L. Countryman, W3HH in *QST*, June 1949 with subsequent additional coverage in *CQ* (November 1951, February 1953, June 1957). This aerial, even from the beginning, was always a controversial design with sceptics and supporters coming forward in roughly equal numbers—and it never made the *Handbooks*. However, we felt it worth including in *TTftRA* and more recently in *Amateur Radio Techniques*, and as a result have received several requests for more details, particularly on the terminating resistor.

A dig back into the W3HH articles has resulted in some additional information on this aerial, although frankly I still find it difficult to decide from the available evidence whether to be a sceptic or a supporter.

The basic arrangement is shown in Fig. 4. With these dimensions it is claimed that the system is virtually aperiodic over about a 5 : 1 frequency span. The version with 47 ft. overall dimensions was claimed to be effective on 7, 14, 21 and 28 MHz (and according to some accounts not too bad on 3·5 MHz). The aerial can be fed by 600-ohm open line or 300 ohm twin feeder, but these different feeders require different terminating resistors, in each case somewhat greater than the feeder impedance (ie about 650 ohms for 600 ohm line; 390-400 ohms for 300-ohm ribbon feeder), and this value is stated to be fairly critical.

The wattage of this resistor was given as 35 per cent of the dc power input to the transmitter (i.e. dissipating about half the power output), though presumably an appreciably lower wattage might be suitable for the low duty cycle of ssb. W3HH stated that the aerial was virtually aperiodic if a non-inductive resistor (i.e. carbon or graphite rod or using a transmission line made of resistance wire) he also considered that conventional wire-wound resistors could be used—" the difference is that with a wire-wound resistor it will be necessary to use some form of aerial coupler depending on your installation, and the coupling will probably be different for different bands." However he also suggested that a wire-wound resistor with slider provided a convenient means of adjusting the terminating resistor for optimum radiation. Angles of tilt can be anywhere between about 20 to 40 degrees with a preferred value of 30 degrees.

So there we are. The aerial stemmed originally from the US Navy, although at least one theoretical study by the Navy reported against it. But at one time quite a few amateurs found the T2FD useful. After the 1958 *TT* item, N. P. Spooner, G2NS commented favourably on his results with the aerial, saying that the 47 ft version radiated on all bands from 3·5 to 28 MHz, while a 94 ft version having about 3 ft spacing would include Top Band; he also said the resistor could conveniently be of the wire-wound type. So if anyone is looking for a compact, omnidirectional, all-band aerial how about trying a T2FD—and letting us all know how well (or how badly) it works.

Fig 4. The T2FD (terminated tilted folded dipole) omni-directional multiband aerial as originally described in **1949** by W3HH. For details of R see text.

Multiband Stub Dipole

Extracted from 'Technical Topics', *Radio Communication*, October 1969

Multiband Stub Dipole

To judge by the popularity of the W3DZZ-type of trapped dipole, there is a continuing demand for fairly simple aerials that can work effectively on a number of hf bands. One should not, of course, forget the attractions of such " old-fashioned " aerials as the so-called " centre-fed Zepp " (more correctly a centre-fed dipole with resonant line feeders), despite the current disdain for resonant feeder systems.

In *CQ* (July, 1969), Cortland Richmond, W1CEJ, describes a multiband " portable dipole " for 7, 14, 21 and 28 MHz, although the system would seem to have advantages over the trapped dipole for fixed operation; maybe the Americans no longer dare to suggest anything less than a beam as suitable for home use! The W1CEJ aerial makes use of two techniques which have been previously described in *TT*, but the combination seems to be a novel one. These techniques are the well-known paralleled dipoles using 300 ohm line (*Amateur Radio Techniques*, page 121) and the use of 300 ohm stub sections as originally patented by W4JRW (*ART*, page 126).

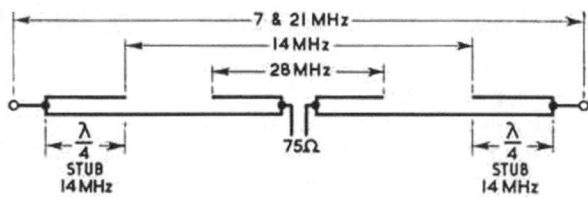

Fig 3. The W1CEJ multiband (7, 14, 21 and 28 MHz) "portable dipole."

The W1CEJ aerial (Fig 3) has an overall length of 67 ft which, when fed with 75-ohm line, results in a $\tfrac{1}{2}\lambda$ dipole for 7 MHz and a $\tfrac{3}{2}\lambda$ arrangement for 21 MHz. A 28 MHz paralleled dipole is formed from 300 ohm ribbon. To allow 14 MHz operation, a 14 MHz $\tfrac{1}{2}\lambda$ stub section is incorporated (we have made a slight modification on the original diagram to underline that the length of this stub section depends on the velocity factor of the 300-ohm ribbon) as in the W4JRW manner. Because of the interaction and the effect of the stub, the dimensions need to be adjusted by means of a grid dip oscillator for optimum performance on the various bands (there will be some compromise on either 7 or 21 MHz).

In practice, the whole top element can most conveniently be fashioned from 300-ohm twin feeder or 450-ohm open wire line; the lower velocity factor of the 300 ohm feeder might be found useful, since the inclusion of the stub section tends to shorten the overall length on the lower frequency band. It may be found worth looking up the earlier material on this use of stubs in this manner, either in *ART* or in the original *QST* article (December, 1960) which covered a 14 and 28 MHz arrangement. With some care in adjustment, the result should be a multiband system with appreciable advantages over the trap dipole.

ANTENNA TOPICS

Here and There: Delta Loop Beam

Extracted from 'Technical Topics', *Radio Communication*, November 1969

Harry R. Habig, K8ANV, the author of the article on the HRH-delta loop beam (*QST* January 1969 and *TT*, May 1969) writes to point out that the formulae for the dimensions of the G3ENI double-delta vhf aerials (*TT*, June 1969) appeared originally in the useful article by A. C. Doty, K8CEU, "Circular antennas for 10 metres" (*QST*, November 1958). K8ANV has been doing a lot of work on various delta loop systems (including double-delta configurations which he foresaw in his patent application), and on their mechanical aspects. He has been using a novel 2 delta loop for 28MHz (using a special 28MHz gamma matching system with 14MHz loop) to provide what he believes to be a very fine 28MHz beam. It is hoped that further details can be given later.

Multiband Stub Aerials

Extracted from 'Technical Topics', *Radio Communication*, December 1969

Multiband stub aerials

In view of the recent reference in *TT* (October) to the use by W1CEJ of stubs instead of traps to provide multiband operation of a dipole structure, we were interested to see at the RSGB Show the new J-beam tri-band for 14, 21 and 28MHz. This appears to make very effective use of concealed stubs, which are formed from 72Ω flat line wound internally on a former accommodated within the elements. A description of this sturdy-looking array by B. D. Sykes, G2HCG, appeared in the May 1969 issue of *SWM*. G2HCG drew attention to the dx gain of beam aerials which is derived from the angle of radiation and which can result in a practical gain appreciably better than the theoretical gain.

Active Car Radio Aerial

Extracted from 'Technical Topics', *Radio Communication*, December 1969

Active car radio aerial

In the August *TT* (and on several previous occasions) we reviewed briefly some of the fascinating work being done by Professor Hans Meinke on miniature active receiving aerials in which a transistor not only provides amplification but is also used to achieve an accurate noise match, thus preserving the good signal/noise ratio of signals picked up on a small structure. Since then at least two of his designs have appeared in actual commercial equipments.

Rohde and Schwarz have announced the use of active aerials for some specialized aviation applications. And "fuba" (Hans Kolbe and Co) have released information on their new Alpha 3 car radio aerial which is entirely incorporated within a compact wing mirror. Inside the housing is a printed-circuit panel containing aerial loops and two transistor amplifiers (see *Wireless World*, November 1969 or *Electronics*, 15 September). The aerial is intended for use throughout the range 150kHz to 25MHz and also on Band II (vhf/fm). While the price (about £9 in West Germany) is appreciably above that of a conventional telescopic rod, a number of useful advantages are being claimed—not least the reduced likelihood of accidental or deliberate damage often experienced with rod aerials. The aerial incorporates static protection diodes, and it is claimed that as a result of the band-pass characteristics and low signal pick-up, cross-modulation characteristics are very good. The aerial provides an input to the receiver claimed as better than the average telescopic rod. Altogether it is beginning to look as though our earlier guesses that more would be heard of active aerials (see for example *Amateur Radio Techniques*, pages 136-137) were not too far off the beam.

1970 - 1979

Quickies: Multi-band Trap Vertical

Extracted from 'Technical Topics',
Radio Communication, January 1970

J. R. King, G3TPG, reports a simple multi-band "trap" vertical (Fig 7) which seems to work out quite successfully on 3·5, 7, 14, 21 and 28MHz. The system has a reasonably high impedance feed thus resulting in lower earth resistance losses. Removing the high-Q loading or trap coil has no noticeable effect on the transmitter loading on 14, 21 and 28MHz, but its presence on 7MHz and lower seems to improve performance considerably, he finds.

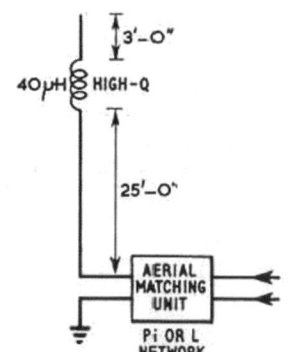

Fig 7. G3TPG's multi-band vertical

of the three bands (12 wires in all).
The approximate impedances at the base of the 22ft radiator are:

	Resistance	Reactance
14,250kHz	100Ω	200Ω
21,375kHz	1,200Ω	—500Ω
28,500kHz	60Ω	—220Ω

The effect of the matching section is to transform these to:

	Resistance	Reactance
14,250kHz	93Ω	177Ω
21,375kHz	63Ω	0
28,500kHz	75Ω	—282Ω

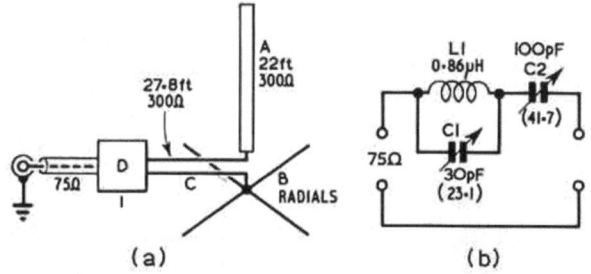

Fig 8. The OD5CG triband vertical aerial for 14, 21 and 28MHz. The radiator (A) comprises 22ft of 300 Ω feeder shorted at each end. The ground plane (B) comprises quarter-wave radials for each band (12 wires in all). The matching section (C) is 27·8ft of 300 Ω feeder. The reactance matching section (D) is shown in detail in (b), the coil L1 comprises 7 turns of No 16 wire 1in in diameter and 1in winding length

Triband Vertical

Extracted from 'Technical Topics',
Radio Communication, April 1970

Triband vertical

In *QST* (December 1969) Frank Regier, OD5CG, describes a simple triband vertical for 14, 21 and 28MHz avoiding the use of traps and providing the effective ⅝λ radiator (22ft) on 28MHz (Fig 8). A single matching section brings all the resistive impedances close enough to a 75Ω line, while a non-switched matching unit takes reasonable care of the reactive components which occur only on 14 and 28MHz.

OD5CG indicates that the reactance matching unit (Fig 8(b)) can be set up using only a grid dip oscillator. C1 is adjusted so that L1—C1 resonates to 35·85MHz. Then C2 is temporarily connected in parallel with L1—C1 and set so that the circuit now resonates at 21·37MHz.

The matching section comprises some 27·8ft of 300Ω twin feeder, with 22ft of this type of feeder also used for the radiator with the ends short-circuited. The matching section assumes a cable velocity factor of 0·82, and a slightly different length would be needed with cables having a significantly different velocity factor. The ground plane comprises four radials each consisting of ¼λ of wire for each

Variable Length Monopole

Extracted from 'Technical Topics',
Radio Communication, April 1970

Variable length monopole

Clearly, the problems of matching and the elimination of the reactive components would vanish if one had an effective means of varying as required the length of the radiating element. Such an approach can be found in a new medium power variable length monopole aerial (type AE3062) which is being introduced by Racal for commercial and military applications and which has been brought to my notice by D. G. Pinnock, G3HVA. In its most ambitious form (covering all frequencies from 2 to 30MHz) the mast (6in diameter glass-fibre sections) is 125ft high; for 4—30MHz the height becomes 65ft.

At the base are two motor-driven spools. On one spool is wound a flat silver-coated copper tape; on the other a flat melinex (insulator) tape. Both tapes are joined to form one complete tape running up the mast and through a spring-supported sheave at the top. This allows any required amount of the copper tape to be run up the mast. Various arrangements are used to adjust the tape to represent a quarter-wavelength at the desired frequency (in one version a

33

ANTENNA TOPICS

frequency discriminating bridge provides a sensor for an automatically tuned servo-system). The monopole thus operates against a ground screen as a ¼λ vertical. With 125ft available one wonders whether it might have been worth trying to utilize the radiator as ⅝λ or the useful 113°, but presumably a major part of the object was to achieve similar radiation characteristics at all frequencies. Some elements of the system might well be possible to duplicate more simply for amateur operation.

Another feature of this aerial is the emphasis placed on the ground screen. This consists of 60 radials either 120ft long for the 2—30MHz version or 60ft for the 4—30MHz unit. The radials are copper weld 12 gauge wire attached at one end to the base plate and at the other end to earth spikes at 12° intervals right round the mast.

Those interested in earths will find some useful notes in an article "The siting of earths for telecommunication installations" in *Point-to-Point Telecommunications* (January 1969). One hint is that at sites having such high earth-resistivity that even multiple electrode systems will not give low enough earth resistance, it may be necessary to reduce resistivity by adding salts to the soil in the vicinity of the earth spikes. Some of the salts commonly used for this purpose are sodium chloride, copper sulphate and calcium chloride, with a need to repeat treatments every one to four years. I seem to recall, in the 'thirties, that a proprietary radio earth consisted of a small copper cup in which salts were placed. The article also contains a table useful in appraising sites:

Soil type	Resistivity (ohm-cm)
Marsh	100 to 300
Loams	100 to 5,000
Clays	200 to 16,000
Peat	4,000 to 20,000
Chalk	5,000 to 15,000
Rock	10,000 upwards

G6XN on Low Angle Propagation

Extracted from 'Technical Topics', *Radio Communication*, May 1970

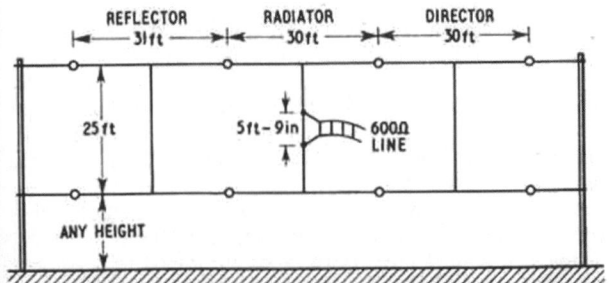

He also describes a fixed low-angle beam aerial for 7MHz (Fig 5) making use of vertical polarisation but reducing mast height requirements by using the horizontal supporting wires to provide end-loading of the shortened vertical elements.

Fig 5. G6XN's low radiation angle aerial for 7MHz. The reflector and director are tunable by adjusting the length of verticals or lower horizontal wires. (*Wireless World*)

The Vertical-Tee or Inverted Ground-Plane

Extracted from 'Technical Topics', *Radio Communication*, July 1970

The vertical-Tee or inverted ground-plane

For some years a simple 300Ω feeder type of 14MHz folded dipole only about 20-25ft high has been in use at G3VA. This has always brought plenty of contacts, although there have been some blind areas due to the dipole radiation pattern, screening from buildings, and the high-angle of radiation to be expected from a dipole little more than quarter-wave above earth.

We have often suggested in *TT* that it is a fallacy to believe that a vertically polarized aerial will automatically provide a much lower angle of radiation than a horizontal dipole; much depends upon the reflection coefficient resulting from the conductivity of the earth. Most tests have indicated that where a dipole can be at a good height it will have as effective a low-angle radiation as the average vertical. But the fact remains that, where aerial support height is extremely limited, vertical polarization has considerable attractions, even in "hostile" sites.

The quarter-wave (or 113°) ground plane aerial has for long upheld its reputation as an effective long-range aerial. But the physical requirements for putting up a ground plane can sometimes be daunting—and for this reason the quarter-wave vertical fed against ground has found considerable acceptance. This is fine, provided that the amateur is prepared to put in a really effective earth connection. I would strongly disagree with G3SAA's suggestion in the June issue that this is "not a dx transmitting aerial".

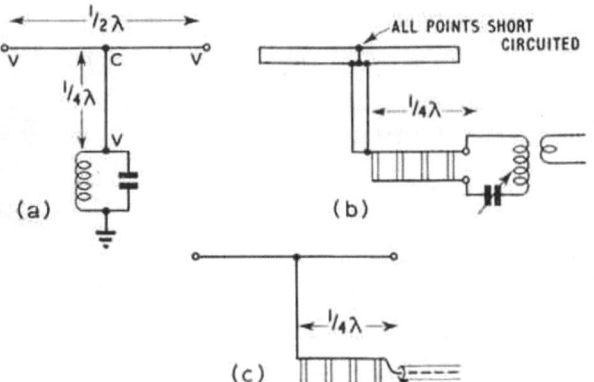

Fig 1. The basic arrangement of the vertical-Tee aerial. V are points of high voltage, C of high current. (b) Showing how the G3VA 300Ω feeder-type folded dipole has been converted by shorting across the two feeder wires to the mid-point of the dipole and adding a Zepp matching section. The use of feeder for the vertical section should help increase bandwidth. (c) Modified arrangements used by G3HQX eliminating the separate aerial tuner. Other possible feeder arrangements are suggested in the *ART* notes on vertical Zepp aerials. Typically for 14MHz vertical element 16ft 11in. Top section two times 17ft 2in

Looking around for a lazy man's way of simplifying the erection of a vertically polarized aerial suitable for use with the available 20-25ft supports, I began to ponder on the various ways in which verticals can be operated without good earth connections. One of the most effective (though today often overlooked) is the ½λ Zepp (see *ART*, section 8). But this requires a vertical height of some 35ft-plus. Why not top-load such a system, as in G6XN's centre-fed 7MHz aerial (*TT*, May 1970) or in the bobtail array (see later)?

This would result in a T aerial (Fig 1(a)), which seems to have been virtually forgotten for amateur applications, though various systems of this type were explored by C. A. Heathcote, G3JR, before the war (*T & R Bulletin*, March 1939). The T aerial has always been one of the classic mf broadcasting and marine aerials, and used to be popular for mf reception. Some extremely simple alterations to the existing folded dipole resulted in the arrangement shown in Fig 1 (b). Here, at least in theory, was an aerial in which radiation from the two top sections would approximately cancel out, leaving a voltage-fed ¼λ vertical radiator, but not dependent upon any earth connection, and requiring a minimum height of only about 20ft.

Tests with this system, which appears to be usefully non-critical in dimensions, have brought a pleasant improvement in 14MHz dx-effectiveness. During the month following its erection on 2 May (if the simple changes merit such a term) the 125 or so dx contacts represent a gratifying increase on the usual bag: plenty of west coast Americans and Canadians, JA, KL7, KH6, VU5, VU2, JT1 and a UA0 in zone 23, XE, ZE, ZS, ZM, AX, PY, YV, YA, 7Q7 etc. While some of these probably reflect the well-known "new aerial improvement factor", it remains a firm conviction that at distances over about 3,500 miles the aerial is laying down a more consistent signal than in its horizontal dipole form, and is omnidirectional.

This view is supported by John Brodzky, G3HQX, who has been trying some modified versions of the aerial with rather more care in comparison and swr checking than my own slapdash approach. He finds, for instance, that while east coast Americans are no better than with a low dipole, the advantage is clearly with the vertical-Tee as one goes towards the west coast; the vertical also brings in many weak extended ground-wave signals which are not audible on the dipole. He has also used a 28MHz version. Interestingly enough, he also finds his 14MHz vertical-Tee an improvement on 3·5MHz, although for that band we both agree that it must be acting as an "aog" aerial (and newcomers who do not know what an aog aerial is should enquire at their local club!). By adopting the established technique of joining a Zepp feeder directly to coaxial cable he eliminates the need for a separate aerial tuner. Like any other vertical aerial, the system needs to be erected clear of other aerials and can lose power to fencing etc—it also produces a strong ground wave which may not be advisable in tv fringe areas. Tvi should not be a problem in areas of BBC and ITA main uhf stations, however, all of which use horizontal polarization. G3HQX has also found that a 25ft top (ie two times 12·5ft) gives a good match, though we are not sure why.

Although it is always risky to attempt to assess a new hf aerial over a matter of a few weeks, it does already appear that this aerial (which is an amalgam of a number of well-established techniques) has a useful place in the amateur field. It may be noted that it is virtually a ground-plane aerial with two radials, but upside down and far easier for most amateurs to put up than the conventional ground-plane. The impedance matching also seems much less critical. We do not suggest that the vertical-Tee will outperform a good ground plane, but rather that one can achieve much the same results far more easily.

The Bobtail Curtain

Extracted from 'Technical Topics', *Radio Communication*, July 1970

The bobtail curtain

For those amateurs who want to put out a more dominating signal than is likely to be achieved with a simple vertical-Tee omnidirectional aerial, it has already been hinted that there is the bobtail. Although I cannot recall this being described

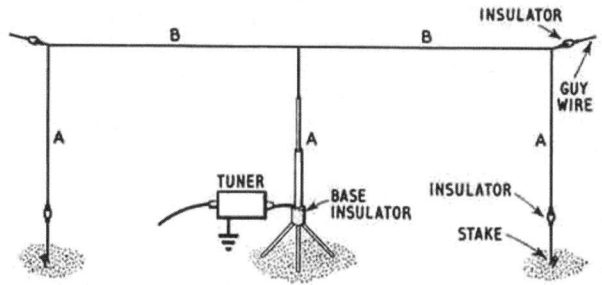

Fig 2. The bobtail-curtain aerial as described in *Radio Handbook* and by VE1TG. Dimensions:

	3·5MHz	7MHz	14MHz
A	66ft	33ft	16·5ft
B	132ft	66ft	33ft

in any RSGB publication, it has been included (as a low-frequency aerial) in many editions of the *Radio Handbook* and other "Editors and Engineers" publications; it also received attention in an article by George Cousins, VE1TG, "A 40-metre Bobtail Curtain Array" (*Ham Radio*, July 1969) who also included dimensions for 3·5 and 14MHz operation. He was enthusiastic about the results achieved on 7MHz contacts over distances exceeding 2,500 miles, though he warned that it is no use expecting much improvement in local signal reports. In all the accounts of the bobtail this is shown with an aerial tuner located at the base of the centre element to provide voltage feed, but it would seem possible to use one of the techniques already suggested for the vertical-Tee, without excessively distorting the radiation pattern.

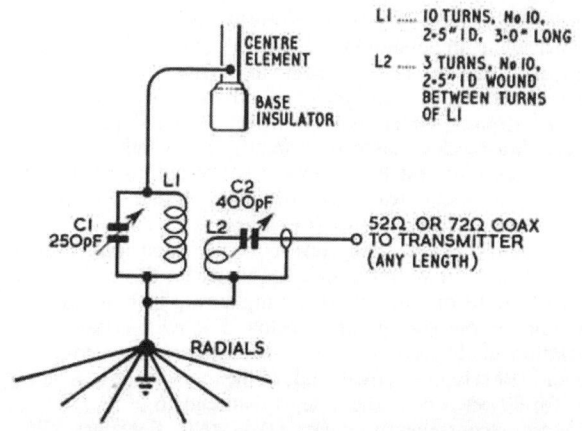

Fig 3. VE1TG's tuner for 7MHz bobtail. For 14MHz, L1 and C1 should be about one-half values shown, C2 about the same. L1 10 turns No 10, 2·5in inner diameter by 3in long. L2 3 turns No 10, 2·5in inner diameter wound between turns of L1

ANTENNA TOPICS

The *Radio Handbook* points out that the array can provide a practical signal gain averaging from 7 to 10dB over a horizontal half-wave dipole using the same pole height where the path length exceeds 2,500 miles. The horizontal directivity is only moderate, since the two outer radiators carry only about half as much current as the centre, driven element. It is noted that a moderate amount of sag can be tolerated at the centre of the flat top, but the vertical elements should be approximately vertical. Some high-angle radiation results from imperfect cancellation in the top section; it is also important to note that the lower ends of the vertical elements will be quite "hot" where appreciable power is involved.

VE1TG considers that the only major disadvantages of this aerial (which is an offshoot of the classical three-element vertical broadside array) are height and area requirements and the need for an aerial tuner: for 7MHz the aerial needs a 132ft span and about 35ft height—but on 14MHz this would reduce to 66ft and about 20ft height. Although he uses quite a good earth connection, it will be appreciated that with the voltage feed, earth currents will be relatively low compared with aerials tuned against earth.

angles below 20°.

If we could concentrate our entire power below 20°, and with a reasonable proportion below 5°, we would achieve the equivalent of a power gain of many times over the existing situation. This is one of the prime advantages of beam aerials mounted at a good height above ground; but even so, many amateurs do not appreciate just how high an aerial needs to be to achieve a really low take-off angle. Fig 7 indicates that even with rhombic aerials (well liked for their low angle radiation), a mast height of about $1 \cdot 5\lambda$ is needed to put the main lobe at 10°.

Les Moxon, G6XN, has pointed out (*Wireless World*, April 1970) that sloping ground can be effectively used to lower radiation angles. A similar point, but with artificial ground planes, is explored in an article "Enhancing hf received fields with large planar and cylindrical ground screens" (*IEEE Transactions on Antennas and Propagation*, November 1967) which shows that large ground planes can achieve substantial improvement of received signals, and that similar benefits can be achieved by much smaller ground screens if these are sloping. Unfortunately, even the smaller 10-λ sloping ground-planes suggested in this article are far too large for most amateurs, though not impossible at vhf. However, at vhf the problem of achieving very low radiation angles is by no means so acute.

Vertical Radiation Angles

Extracted from 'Technical Topics', *Radio Communication,* August 1970

Vertical radiation angles

From time to time everyone interested in long-distance hf operation pays lip-service to the benefits of good low-angle radiation (and increasingly to the even more spectacular benefits of extremely low-angle radiation). Yet only rarely do most of us stop to think quantitively what this is all about. One result is that most amateur dx contacts are being made with an effective power of just a few watts. It is almost certainly true to say that in many cases the vast majority of the power actually radiated from our aerials plays little or no part in the signal received in the distant country.

One of the basic problems about lowering vertical radiation patterns is the extreme difficulty of measuring these patterns; another is that above typical earth (particular urban and suburban earth) the real vrp is often very different from the theoretical patterns shown in the text books.

Just what angle should we aim to achieve? The answer, almost certainly, is the lower the better. Some figures derived from the commercial world of point-to-point are useful; though we should remember that the particularly interesting modes that exist primarily at twilight and dusk are of more interest to amateurs than to commercial traffic people. Vertical wave-arrival angles based on 30,000 measurements made in 1960–61 on signals arriving in the UK from Poona, Sydney and New York indicated that most of these signals arrived at angles less than 10°, often as low as 5° to 6° (and one doubts if the measuring techniques were capable of measuring much below 5°), with considerable variation at different seasons. In summary, between about 10 and 19MHz, the arrival angle of the main mode was below 15° for 90 per cent of the time, with a median of 8°.

More recent measurements (*Proc IEE*, February 1969) made only on *European* stations on frequencies from 5 to 12MHz, and including sporadic E, F1 and F2 modes, show a much greater spread; roughly from 7° to 43°, but even here with more than 50 per cent of the measurements indicating

Vertically Polarized Aerials

Extracted from 'Technical Topics', *Radio Communication,* September 1970

Vertically polarized aerials

The recent description (*TT*, July) of the simple vertical-Tee and the associated bobtail array has brought in quite a few comments, all of them indicative of considerable interest in the development of new or improved forms of vertically-polarized aerials.

John Crux, G3JAG, is a little concerned that readers may have gained the impression, from my use of the secondary title "inverted ground plane", that the two "radials" forming the top loading section of the vertical-Tee renders the aerial in any way independent of the ground conductivity beneath it. He considers that top-loading may actually increase losses in poor ground; further that the $\frac{1}{2}\lambda$ vertical dipole is recognized as being more affected by earth constants than a $\frac{1}{4}\lambda$ grounded radiator. Basically, I would not disagree with these views, though—for hemmed-in sites—there seem useful advantages in putting the radiating current up in the air. For more open sites, G3JAG is probably right in suggesting that a $\frac{1}{4}\lambda$ (or less) grounded radiator is more efficient with a few short radials than a $\frac{1}{2}\lambda$ over the same earth. However, I am still convinced that the vertical-Tee and bobtail can be useful in overcoming the very significant ohmic losses that often result from current feeding a vertical without installing a really low-resistance earth connection; this has always been one of the main attractions of the ground plane with drooping radials.

G3JAG takes the opportunity to draw attention to a number of useful short vertical aerials that were included in the series of *CQ* articles on vertical aerials by Paul Lee, W3JM; these began in June 1968 and continued over many months. W3JM, incidentally, was formerly W3JHR, the originator of the well-known Seiler "synthetic rock" transistor vfo.

In particular, G3JAG mentions the NOL folded unipole with shunt-feed, and has also tried successfully the NORD (see also US Patent No 3,386,098), while G3THA is planning a "UG". These unfamiliar sounding types and many other arrangements are all described by W3JM; some make use of top loading and allow multiband operation with quite low support height, since several were originally developed for mf broadcasting from ships, and make use of the guys as part of the top loading.

G3JAG considers that it is quite feasible to erect 40 and 50ft verticals single-handed, if you plan the operation. His record is 69ft, put up some five times without mishap, once in semi-darkness. His technique is based on pivoting the base of the pole in a squared U channel section screwed to a wooden stump, using a $\frac{5}{16}$in steel pin. A 21ft $1\frac{3}{4}$in steam-pipe mast is put up next to the stump, and guyed with $\frac{1}{2}$in diameter polypropylene caving (or yacht) rope. This has a block and tackle at the top, fitted with plastic clothes-line and gives a 2:1 mechanical advantage, a pulley being tied to the vertical 20ft from the pivot. He just hauls on the rope and "up she goes", the steam-pipe holding the pole (nearly) vertical until he walks round and fixes the guys. The guying of the steam-pipe is good enough to allow use of a ladder to detach the pulley when the guys for the pole are roughly adjusted to length. After taking down the steam-pipe, the vertical can be trued up as accurately as desired. Before finally tightening the guys he knocks out the steel pin and replaces it with a $\frac{1}{4}$in plastic-sheathed pin to provide an insulated base. The whole vertical weighs only about 20 to 30lb and is easily lifted with a car jack or by hand to exchange the pins. The verticals are guyed with braided nylon "boot-lace" type line, polyester ("Terylene") tyre cords and polypropylene garden twine.

An All-band Vertical

Extracted from 'Technical Topics',
Radio Communication, September 1970

An all-band vertical

Brian Rose, G3ULR, who—as reported in *TT*, October 1968—has been experimenting for some time with modified forms of ddrr aerials, mentions that recent American work (not yet published) indicates that directional arrays can be made using parasitic elements consisting of vertically polarized ddrr elements; there is hope of an article on this subject turning up before too long in *73 Magazine*.

Meanwhile during the past year G3ULR has been using an interesting all-band vertical which combines the well-established technique of a tri-band ground-plane (for 14, 21 and 28MHz) with unusual loading techniques to permit the effective use of the same structure on 1·8, 3·5 and 7MHz.

Although the overall height, with the tri-band ground plane mounted on top of a 25ft 2in dural pipe mast, is only about 40ft, it can be resonated, without loading coils, even on 1·8MHz, using only series tuning capacitors. The ground-plane, basically similar to a standard ARRL design, has drooping 0·3λ-trifilar radials connected to the pipe mast supporting the base of the ground plane; these radials provide top loading for the mast radiator on the lower-frequency bands. The dural mast is insulated at the base, and this is always a low impedance point. Originally an outrigger wire was run up the mast to allow shunt-feed tests; although this is no longer used for this purpose it still serves to increase self-capacitance by a small amount, see Fig 2. The $\frac{1}{4}λ$ self-resonance of the entire structure is roughly 4MHz due to the top loading, facilitating matching on 3·5MHz.

The key feature providing the 1·8MHz performance is that the coaxial feeder for the ground-plane is run down inside the dural mast; the coaxial braid is insulated from the mast except at the 25ft height where it connects the radials together. G3ULR has only a short run of 10ft from the base of the mast to bring the coaxial into his shack. Within the shack, on 1·8MHz, the coaxial cable inner and outer are connected together and to earth. This means that, on this band, there is virtually a wire running down the inside of the mast from the 25ft level to earth; since it is screened from the aerial currents on the outer skin of the dural pipe it does not carry much rf current, but it does have significant effect on the resonant frequency of the structure as "seen" at the base of the mast, due to the reactance of the coaxial stub formed between the coaxial braid and the inside of the dural pipe. This method of loading was described by Leonhard, Mattuck and Poté (*IRE Transactions on Antennas and Propagation,* July 1955, page 111) as an effective means of loading short vertical aerials. In their case, the arrangement was that of Fig 3, in which the inner wire is connected to earth via a loading inductance. For the G3ULR aerial it was found that a simpler system could be adopted, omitting the small inductor and tuning for resonance by means of a series tuning capacitor in lead A, resulting in an excellent match to 75Ω cable. This method of loading is versatile, and masts of various sizes could be used by adjusting the position of the cable connection inside the mast.

The same arrangement also happens to provide reasonable match on 3·5MHz (though resonance is not in the Leonhard mode) using more series capacitance (of the order of 800pF) than the 400pF for 1·8MHz. On 3·5MHz the aerial has quite low reactance and can also be fed directly or via a series capacitor when the ground-plane feeder coaxial is insulated from earth; it is also possible to use a pi-network atu on this

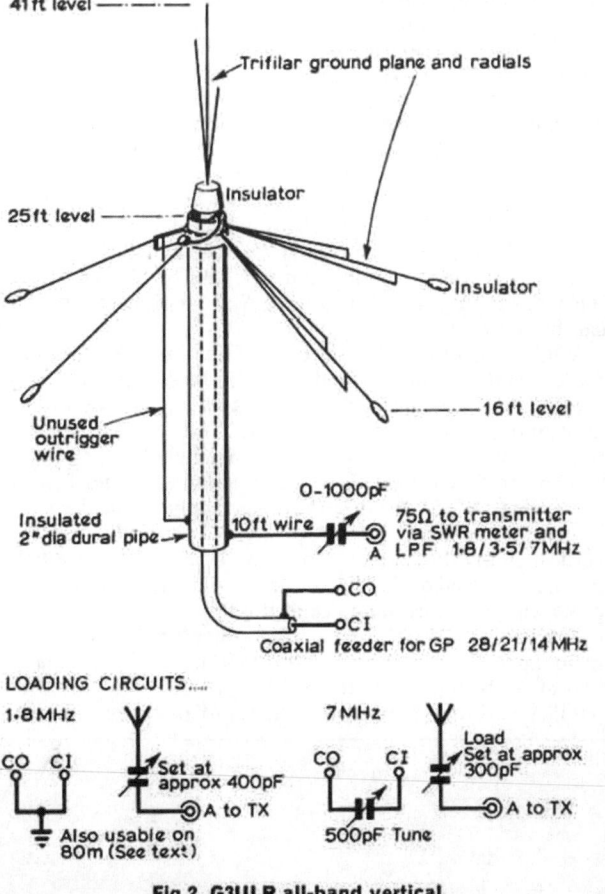

Fig 2. G3ULR all-band vertical

ANTENNA TOPICS

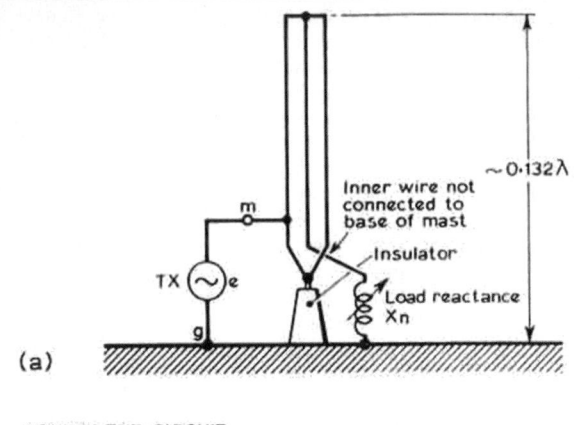

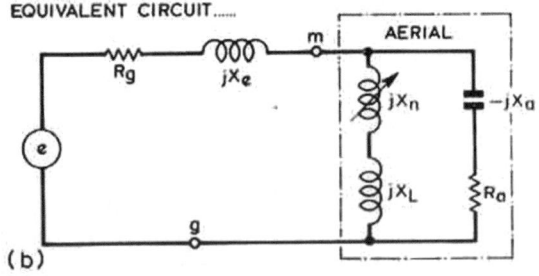

Fig 3. General technique for loading short vertical aerials (from Leonhard, Mattuck and Poté). (b) Equivalent circuit (though G3ULR suggests it is easier to cut and try). In the G3ULR aerial $jX_e = 0$, $jX_n = 0$ by use of suitable values of X_a, jX_L which depend on aerial height and capacitance

band. It should be recognized that the 3·5MHz dx performance depends to a considerable extent on the earthing system, and that vertical polarization is not really suitable for medium-distance 3·5MHz operation. However, the system has been found adequate for 3·5MHz at G3ULR.

On the other hand, most satisfactory results (S7 from ZS, Ws etc) are achieved on 7MHz, at which frequency the top-loaded vertical is non-resonant. Resonance is achieved by reactance transfer up the ground-plane feeder, which is insulated and short-circuited at the shack via a variable 500pF capacitor. Since the feeder is roughly ¼λ at 7MHz and about ⅛λ electrical length, this is equivalent to placing a variable capacitor across the base insulator of the ground plane, so that the vertical element acts as a base-loaded whip at the top of a top-loaded 25ft vertical; one position of the capacitor gives minimum swr, and by also adjusting the series tuning capacitor in lead A, a good match to 75Ω can be achieved.

Within this general framework different mast heights and feeder lengths could be used, possibly requiring a relay to short-circuit the coaxial feeder to earth at the base of the mast; if the feeder is near to ¼λ electrical on 7MHz, reactance transfer could be done using a variable inductor at the station end. At odd feeder lengths a combination of L and C may be needed. While these suggestions apply particularly to resonating existing ground planes, a specially erected vertical should be designed from the 1955 paper, since it is possible to make the mast match directly into coaxial cable without series tuning capacitors.

The earth at G3ULR is a solid connection to the water main, augmented by a 5ft rod driven in under the mast, and two 8ft rods about 10ft to each side of the mast, wired in parallel with stout copper wire, since radials cannot be used.

'30 Up and 30 Out'

Extracted from 'Technical Topics', *Radio Communication,* September 1970

"30 up and 30 out"

To continue this saga of verticals, E. J. Younge, G3IVH, mentions that a detailed description of a 7MHz bobtail array by Woodrow Smith, W6BCX, appeared in *CQ* in March 1948. This article also recalled from the 'twenties, a 7MHz aerial which was the forerunner of the ground-plane. This was the so-called "30 up and 30 out" and comprised a 30ft (or slightly longer) vertical radiator worked against a 30ft (or slightly shorter) horizontal counterpoise, usually suspended a few feet above earth, fed by means of a series tuned circuit: see Fig 5. W6BCX noted that, in its heyday, "the vertical element often was terminated with a copper toilet ball, which was supposed by the more superstitious to possess some magical dx raising power," (I suppose it helped flush out the rare ones).

by Woodrow Smith, W6BCX, appeared in *CQ* in March 1948. This article also recalled from the 'twenties, a 7MHz aerial which was the forerunner of the ground-plane. This was the so-called "30 up and 30 out" and comprised a 30ft (or slightly longer) vertical radiator worked against a 30ft (or slightly shorter) horizontal counterpoise, usually suspended a few feet above earth, fed by means of a series tuned circuit: see Fig 5. W6BCX noted that, in its heyday, "the vertical element often was terminated with a copper toilet ball, which was supposed by the more superstitious to possess some magical dx raising power," (I suppose it helped flush out the rare ones).

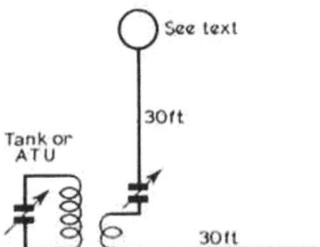

Fig 5. "30 up and 30 out" aerial for 7MHz

This same arrangement (without the copper ball) still turns up in military pack-set instruction books for use where only one support is available. For those who have no room for the full set of 7MHz ground-plane radials, the old omni-directional "30 up and 30 out" might still be well worth a try. Counterpoise techniques seem to have gone out of fashion except in the form of radials since the old days of using them on 1·8MHz or for the "all-purpose" W3EDP (an 84ft end-fed wire tuned against various counterpoises).

1970 - 1979

Directional Verticals

Extracted from 'Technical Topics',
Radio Communication, September 1970

Directional verticals

The usual method of obtaining directional effects with vertical radiators is to use two similar ¼λ verticals spaced apart, and fed with currents of different magnitudes and phases so as to produce a variety of non-uniform patterns, including cardiods (a classic paper on this is one by G. H. Brown—who is credited with the ground-plane—in *Proc IRE,* January 1937, and a well-known diagram from this paper, giving 40 patterns for two radiators spaced between ⅛λ and 1λ apart can be found in many standard textbooks, including *Radio & Television Engineers' Reference Book*). It is possible to use vertical radiators shorter than ¼λ in this application, although the resulting patterns may be affected by insulation and ground conductivity.

This technique need not be confined to fixed beams, provided that means are incorporated to vary the phase fed to one of the two radiators. Fig 4 shows an "electronic rotary" of this type from an article by G. Tomassetti, I1BER, reprinted in *Old Man* (July 1970). The article includes radiation patterns indicating that the five positions are capable of putting broad beams towards almost all points of the compass, though the pattern differs in each switch position. Typically, gains of about 5dB are possible, and the nulls can be used to reduce interference from unwanted medium-distance stations.

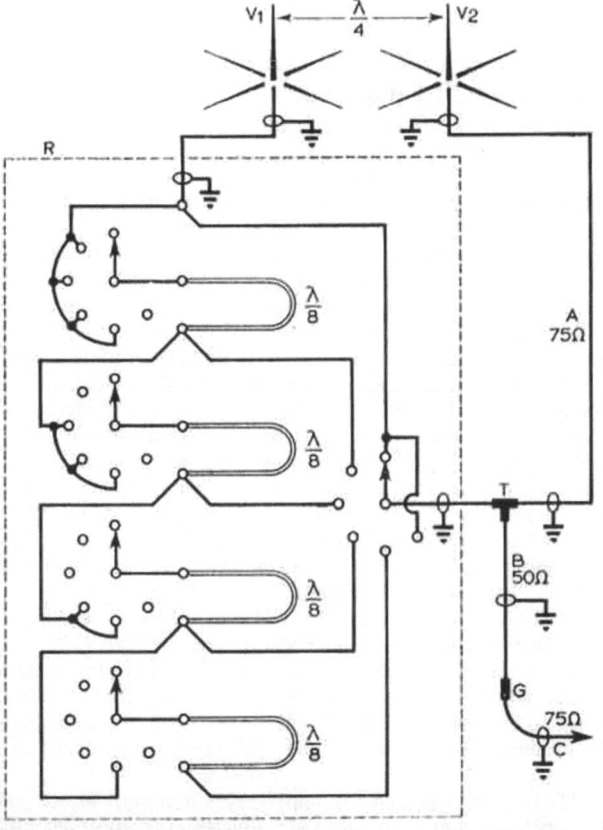

Fig 4. 7MHz directional providing five different radiation patterns. A is RG11 cable; B is ¼ of RG8 cable for impedance transformation; R, aluminium screening; G, cable connector; C, RG11 cable any length; V1 and V2, vertical aerials spaced ¼λ

L-Network for Voltage-Fed Aerials

Extracted from 'Technical Topics',
Radio Communication, September 1970

L-network for voltage-fed aerials

G3IVH also suggests that another method of voltage-feeding a vertical-Tee or bobtail aerial would be an L-network (*ART*, Section 8): see Fig 6. He has successfully used L-networks for ½λ end-fed aerials on 1·8 and 3·5MHz, using an swr bridge in the coaxial link to the transmitter. He finds that a tank circuit from a Collins TCS surplus unit (300pF high-voltage variable and 52-turn "roller coaster" variable inductor) makes a good L-network for 7 and 3·5MHz, while with additional outboard inductance it will cover 1·8MHz also.

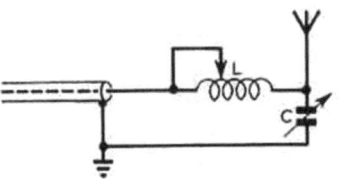

Fig 6. L-network for voltage-fed aerials

Beverage Aerials

Extracted from 'Technical Topics',
Radio Communication, October 1970

Beverage aerials

Top-band dx enthusiasts will probably need no reminding of the Beverage aerial which has recently been used on both sides of the Atlantic for the reception of 1·8MHz signals. Several references to these aerials have appeared in W1BB's *160-metre DX Bulletin*. But there must be quite a few *TT* readers who have only a hazy idea of this highly effective directional receiving aerial although it has been around for almost 50 years.

So, a few words of introduction. The Beverage aerial (originally called "The Wave Aerial") was developed by Harold Beverage (one-time W2BML), Chester Rice and Edward Kellogg in the early 'twenties for the reception of commercial long-distance stations operating on the very low frequencies. In its simplest form it consists of a very long straight wire, extending sometimes up to several miles in length, mounted on quite low poles, and correctly terminated at the far end to earth so as to prevent reflections. Not exactly an aerial for the amateur with only a short garden.

But a check with the original description of this aerial (*American IEE,* 1923) has brought to light several features which are seldom mentioned. For instance, the normal system on vlf was to use two wires with a reflecting transformer at the far end and the terminating impedance at the receiving end, making it possible accurately to null out interference. Then again, although one normally thinks of the Beverage as being many wavelengths long, this was always impossible at vlf, and the paper suggests that pronounced directional effects can be achieved with an electrical length of ½λ to 1λ—this puts a different order of magnitude on the real

ANTENNA TOPICS

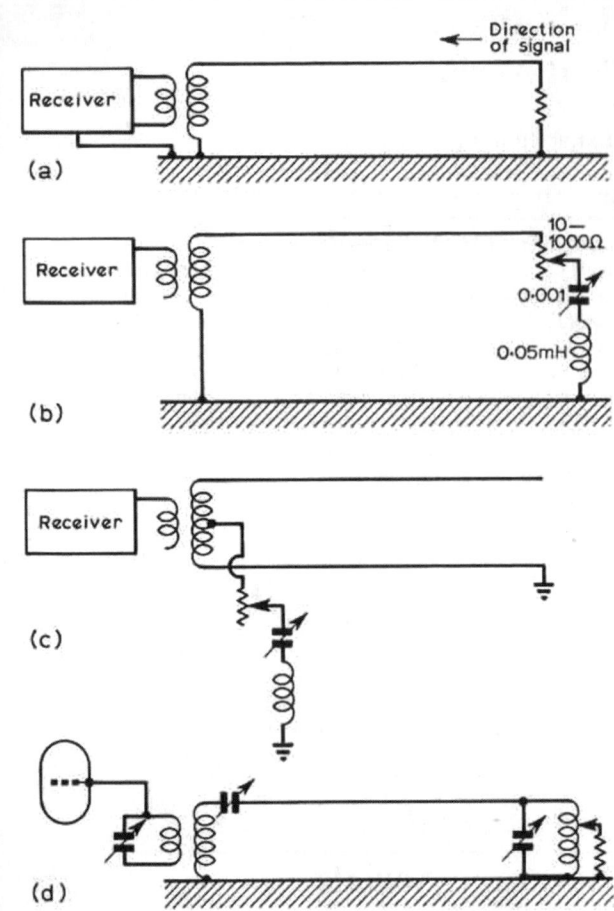

Fig 5. Some variations of the Beverage or wave aerial. (a) is the basic arrangement; (b) was suggested in 1923 for "short waves" (ie less than 450m); (c) is a variation of (b) enabling the termination to be at the receiving end; (d) from 1931 edition of the *Admiralty Handbook of Wireless Telegraphy*. Arrangements (a) to (c) come from the original 1923 paper

estate needed on hf! The Beverage is more or less related to the vee-beam and rhombic aerials, and is not limited to low frequencies. Very much to my surprise, I found that the original 1923 paper actually showed how the electrical length of the aerial could be reduced by "stretching" the wire by inserting a series of capacitors at intervals along its length (the basis of G6CJ's very interesting "Loaded wire dipoles" described in the *RSGB Bulletin*, July 1961).

One of the most famous early Beverage aerials was that erected by Paul Godley at Ardrossan in Scotland during the vital amateur transatlantic tests of 1922 when his 400-metre long wire collected signals from a number of American amateurs who (despite the classic phrase "200 metres and down") were using around 200 to 300 metres. I can recall using a wartime Beverage aerial about ½-mile or so long, on frequencies of the order of 3·5 to 9MHz; it was reckoned to be a very effective directional receiving aerial.

So far as signal *collecting* properties are concerned, there is little point in stringing this type of aerial higher than is required for ordinary security and to pass over obstructions. One of the organizations currently using Beverage aerials for the reception of overseas mf broadcasting stations has recently been carrying out some theoretical studies on optimum lengths and heights to see if any improvement could be obtained by raising the present aerials (from 1,000ft to 2,500ft long and about 10ft high) to a height of about 30ft. Generally, these studies indicate that the first effect of raising height is to *degrade* sidelobe performance: the only real advantage in raising height would seem to be where

extremely long aerials are possible, since additional height lowers the rate of attenuation. It is also shown that by connecting two Beverage aerials in parallel it is possible to slew the directivity over a useful angle. The study suggests that these aerials are useful for the reception of signals arriving at angles of, typically, about 5°.

Prof J. Brown of Imperial College has recently stated that a communications problem at present being investigated is the design of a single aerial system capable of receiving simultaneously many transmissions on different frequencies and from different directions. A proposed solution uses the Beverage aerial as the element of an array with combining networks, originally developed for microwave systems, as the means of providing simultaneous reception capability.

One way and another, it does seem as though we ought to be thinking rather more about the old Beverage, not only for 1·8MHz, where one needs some hundreds of feet of wire, but possibly also for hf (and even vhf?) bands, where the length of wire could be quite modest. It is worth remembering that some amateurs (and some of the early vhf radio link systems) have made very effective use of rhombics on vhf. And it is being increasingly recognized that there are advantages to be gained from using a different aerial for reception than for transmission.

K2QBW Multi-Band Vertical

Extracted from 'Technical Topics', *Radio Communication,* December 1970

K2QBW multi-band vertical

Many times in *TT*, the point has been made that while it is extremely helpful to know the theoretically ideal way of doing things, in amateur practice what is often needed is a working compromise that provides acceptable results. Particularly is this true of aerials where most of us are usually faced with the problem of choosing an aerial to fit a far from ideal site, rather than being able to seek out a site which would be capable of giving the optimum results.

A couple of years ago (*CQ*, October 1968) in W2AEF's *Q & A* column, Raphael Soifer, K2QBW, provided some details of an ingeniously simple multi-band vertical. It was made clear that the aerial was not proposed to replace, for example, a ground-mounted vertical system using two dozen radials under irrigated peat moss, but rather "because it does work and takes up virtually no space". Basically, the idea is to operate a trap-vertical (in K2QBW's case a three-band Hy-Gain 12AVQ) against a series of downward vertical monopoles. In effect, it is a combination of the "paralleled dipoles" technique and trapped quarter-wave verticals.

K2QBW's interest was sufficiently aroused by the discussion on the vertical-tee and bobtail type verticals (*TT*, July 1970) to feel that readers would be interested in his arrangement—and his reasoning behind its adoption. In fact, these views have relevance well beyond the question of this particular system, and seem well worth quoting in some detail. He writes:

"There has persisted for many years a canard about the ½λ vertical radiator operated at some distance above ground and without a ground connection. This maintains that such an aerial will never function properly owing to cancellation effects stemming from ground reflection. Having operated a special version of such an aerial since March 1968, I am convinced that this statement must have been originally perpetrated by someone living entirely in a world of perfectly reflecting grounds and unobstructed terrain. Although there are, of course, several qualifications, such an aerial can be a very practical dx-chaser under many unfavourable conditions.

"Operating independently of an earth system means that one must pay a price in efficiency owing to absorption effects. Depending upon the particular location, P. H. Lee, W3JM, ("Vertical antennas part XI" *CQ*, April 1969) estimates that between 40 and 80 per cent of the radiated energy from such an aerial is so lost. Putting this another way, the radiation resistance of a ½λ radiator may be taken as 73Ω, and taking these efficiency ratings in the form of effective earth resistance, the earth resistance exhibited by this "non-ground" ranges from 45Ω (60 per cent efficiency) to about 285Ω (20 per cent efficiency).

"These figures are obviously discouraging when compared with an extensive earth system. However, they are not at all discouraging when compared with the so-called "grounds" which many amateurs actually use. For example, Ray Hills, G3HRH, ("The ground beneath us", *RSGB Bulletin*, June 1966) observes that the common "ground plane" (¼λ radiator plus four ¼λ horizontal radials) often exhibits an effective earth resistance of 100Ω. When the radiation resistance of 35Ω is taken into account, the resulting efficiency is only about 27 per cent! Where a simple ground rod is substituted for the four radials, the earth resistance often reaches 200Ω, only 13½ per cent efficiency!

"The K2QBW antenna consists of a three-band trap vertical for 28, 21 and 14MHz, operated against a series of downward vertical monopoles, one for each band and each ¼λ long. These are cut from four-conductor rotor cable as indicated in Fig 1. The aerial is centre fed with 52Ω coaxial cable, and is mounted on a 10ft mast above the chimney. The centre-point of the ½λ radiator is thus always about 40ft above ground, regardless of band.

"In preparing the aerial, the rotor cable is shorted together at the top and fastened (soldered) to the usual ground terminal of the 12AVQ. Each conductor is cut to a ¼λ at one of the bands covered by the aerial, so that a series of parallel monopoles are formed. The cable thus prepared is run straight down the mast and chimney supporting the 12AVQ, using stand-off insulators. Both balanced and unbalanced feed has been tried, the better results being obtained with unbalanced feed, the centre conductor going to the trap vertical and the braid to the lower paralleled monopoles.

"This aerial naturally exhibits a current loop at the feed point. The fact that this is quite high above surrounding obstructions in my opinion gives this aerial a major advantage over a ground-mounted vertical, whose lower-angle radiation is often shielded by buildings, hills or other obstructions. Typically, at K2QBW, this relative freedom of the high-mounted aerial from obstructions more than makes up for the probable loss of radiation below about 10° resulting from the absence of an extensive ground system. Better a good lobe at 20° than a beautiful lobe at 5° elevation smack into a steel building!

"Although it could be argued that a horizontal dipole with the same feed-point height would give a lower radiation angle, this presupposes that a site is available with fairly uniformly level ground over the aerial's length. Again, in urban areas, often not realized in practice. In my own case, I have not even the room for a dipole, let alone the unobstructed site!

"Experience since March 1968 suggests this aerial to be a consistent dx performer. Well over 200 countries have been worked, including all 40 WAZ zones, BCRTA and DUF-4 certificates using a Collins KWM-2 running 180W cw and 200W p.e.p. ssb. Although performance may well not have been that of a grounded vertical above salt water or a four-element quad up 100ft, it has certainly succeeded in putting a workable signal into every area of the world from an otherwise difficult site."

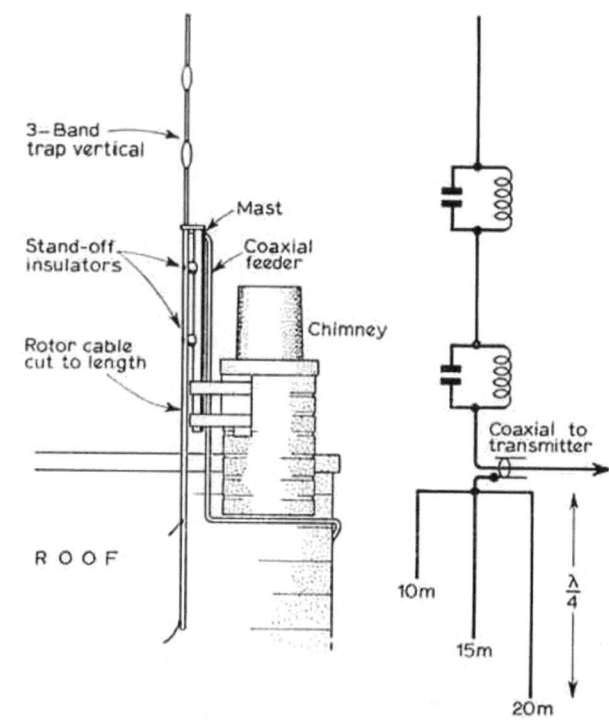

Fig 1. The K2QBW multi-band vertical using a trap vertical in conjunction with parallel monopoles

ANTENNA TOPICS

Base-fed Verticals

Extracted from 'Technical Topics',
Radio Communication, December 1970

Base-fed verticals

My own experiences with the simple vertical-tee have similarly convinced me that these various forms of ½λ verticals, raised ground-planes and the like can be extremely useful in overcoming site problems, despite the theoretical advantages of base-fed and elevated-feed verticals (see *ART* 2 & 3). However, for those blessed with suitable sites and space for good ground systems, interest will not unnaturally be directed towards the base-fed vertical.

A recent two-part article on this subject has appeared in *QST* (August/September, 1970) by Dr Yardley Beers, W0JF (who, if my memory serves me right, used to contribute occasional notes on the American amateur scene in the "Bull" over 35 years ago). In discussing short vertical aerials for the lower frequencies, he points out: "Experiments suggest that it is more important to have a large number of short radials than a smaller number of resonant ones." In practice, for near-ideal low-angle radiation, it is necessary for the earth screen to extend, in the target sector, out to almost 15λ—though few hf amateurs could hope to achieve such a massive system. However, W0JF also includes in his article a useful summary of matching techniques for single-band operation of base-fed verticals of various lengths. Fig 2 will serve as a reminder.

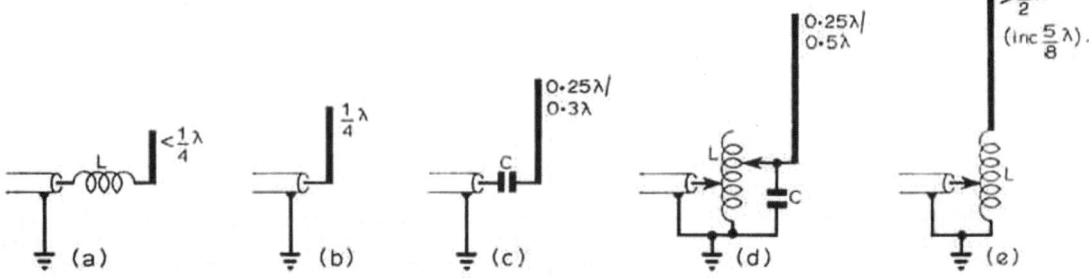

Fig 2. A summary of matching techniques for single-band base-fed verticals as suggested by W0JF. In the case of (d) and (e) these networks can be used with shorter aerials than those indicated where it is intended to match resistance as well as reactance

Loft Loop Aerial

Extracted from 'Technical Topics',
Radio Communication, December 1970

Loft loop aerial

Some time ago (*TT,* July 1968 and *ART* 3, p 180) we noted the "G2PL Special" which was virtually a quad aerial turned over on its side resting just above ground. This possibility of using a full-wave loop (ie as in the basic quad) as a loft aerial was mentioned briefly by GM4QK in his recent survey (*Radio Communication,* October 1970), and turns up again, in rather more detail, in *CQ* (September, 1970) by Malcolm Bibby, GW3NJY/W8, as "an efficient multiband loop antenna". He notes that if one takes one quad-type element, turns it horizontally, fed at the mid-point of one side with coaxial cable then this produces a simple aerial with "real and effective gain over a dipole". The aerial is horizontally polarized and GW3NJY/W8 manages to squeeze a 33ft by 33ft element into his roof space, fed with RG58/U coaxial cable, and this has provided him with many useful dx contacts on 7MHz. He provides detailed polar diagrams but, as someone who has occasionally made use of loft aerials, I would agree with GM4QK's remark that "directivity is largely determined by the house structure and not by the radiating system". However, since working a BV1 station, and some other useful dx, with a loft dipole, I have not been inclined to scoff at indoor transmitting aerials. But the GW3NJY work further implies that the full-wave loop and the "G2PL Special" are useful aerials to try either indoors or outside.

Triangular (Delta) Loops

Extracted from 'Technical Topics',
Radio Communication, February 1971

Triangular (delta) loops

A simple system that has received only limited attention, yet offers a degree of aerial gain and can fit into various types of locations, is the single-element triangular loop. The use of this configuration has been hinted at in the earlier references to triangular loop hf/vhf/uhf arrays (*TT* May-June 1969 and *ART*3). But just as the single-element "quad" full-wave loop is often overlooked, so equally is the triangular form. Basically the performance of these two configurations should be closely similar—but it is felt that the triangular loop is the easier to implement without a framework.

Two horizontally-polarized forms of this loop are shown in Fig 1. The single-support system of Fig 1(*a*) has been

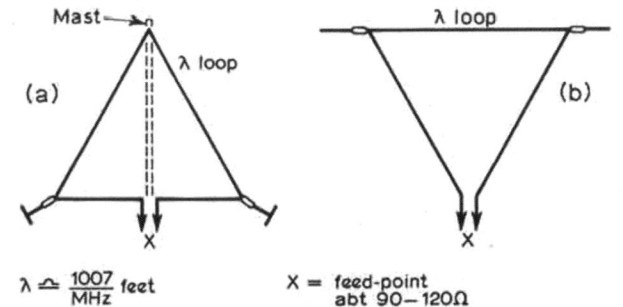

Fig 1. Two forms of the single-element triangular loop aerial. (a) Suitable for single support; (b) Simple twin-support system. Main lobe of radiation towards and away from reader

described by Edward Noll, W3FQJ, (*Radio-amatööri*, Nr 10, 1969) as an hf aerial not unlike the inverted-V but without the need to take the feeder up the mast. The twin-support system of Fig 1(b) is one of many other possible arrangements and also features a feed-point at the base of the aerial. Both K8ANV and G3ENI have indicated that further configurations could be devised. W3FQJ indicates how, by disconnecting the feeder and closing the loop with a small 1-2 turn coil, the length of the loop can be adjusted to resonance using a grid-dip oscillator. Theoretically, I suppose the feed-point impedance must be of the order of 100-120Ω or so, but in practice it should be possible to achieve a reasonably good match with 75Ω coaxial or twin feeder. It might also be possible to achieve 7MHz operation by connecting a 28ft 9in length of 300Ω twin lead, shorted at the far end across the feed point as suggested for the single-loop quad aerial (*ART2* and *3*).

full-size ¼λ vertical. Results include North and South America on 3·5MHz ssb, North America and Australia on 7MHz cw using a Swan 500C.

He points out that on 7MHz the low angle properties of the vertical can be "felt" by the improvement of dx/European signal ratio compared with a dipole. On 3·5MHz, the top-loading plus the vertical radiator gives a useful aerial, working well also for inter-G operation. It all fits into small gardens and should give good results to anyone prepared to take care to provide a really good earth system. G3VYF

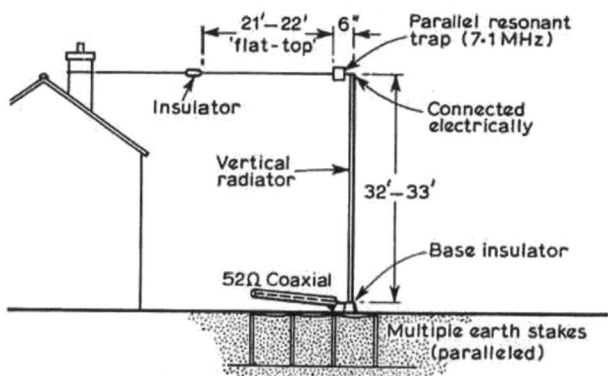

Fig 2. The G3VYF suggestions for the semi-vertical half-trap aerial. For optimum results a very good earth connection is needed

also suggests that this type of approach could be used to turn a trapped vertical such as the 12AVQ or similar chimney-mounted vertical into a useful five-band two-aerial system.

Inverted-L or Semi-Vertical Trap Aerials

Extracted from 'Technical Topics', *Radio Communication*, February 1971

Inverted-L or semi-vertical trap aerials

Another technique which seems to be attracting increased attention is the use of inverted-L aerials to provide mainly vertically-polarized radiation. By incorporating a resonant trap at the top of the vertical section, a multi-band system can be achieved. This arrangement was described (and its good performance on 7MHz emphasized) in an article by Brian Watling, G3RNL, "Which aerial?" (*Radio Communication*, March 1968) and a more recent note on the technique is given by G3BID in an article on portable operation for mobile operators in the current issue of *Mercury* (Journal of the Royal Signals ARS). We have also received recent letters from G3VYF and G3CDR describing related systems.

M. R. Lee, G3VYF, has been making very effective use of one of those half-trap dipole arrangements on 3·5 and 7MHz. In his case the 7MHz radiator is a guyed, surplus telescopic mast (this could equally be a dural self-supporting radiator): Fig 2. At the top of this 32ft section is placed the 7·1MHz trap, with a flat top wire section about 21ft long which, in conjunction with the trap, results in resonance on 3·5MHz, and providing a useful bandwidth of about 100kHz and minimum swr of about 1·2 : 1. The aerial is fed directly with 52Ω coaxial cable. He goes to some trouble to provide a good earth mat, using multiple parallel earth stakes over an area of about 20ft by 20ft. On 7MHz the vertical section forms a

G3CDR Inverted-L

Extracted from 'Technical Topics', *Radio Communication*, February 1971

G3CDR inverted-L

Geoff Scholey, G3CDR, has also been using an inverted-L aerial for about 2¼ years on 3·5MHz, and this has attracted sufficient interest to convince him that other readers may like details. He feels that the 25ft vertical section has been instrumental in putting good signals into ZL and elsewhere, while for short-haul work the aerial works as well as a dipole. The 25ft vertical "happened" when a 28MHz beam superseded an 0·78λ vertical though this length has since proved a happy proportion of the complete ¼λ. The top-loading section was adjusted with the help of a receiver and aerial noise bridge at the base of the aerial to achieve resonance at 3·75MHz (impedance turned out to be about 28–30Ω).

The base matching unit is simple and compact using a toroidal transformer as shown in Fig 3. The toroid material is unknown but is believed to be suitable for use up to 20MHz and measures about 1¼in with ½in cross-section. Starting at the common earthy end, the two wires are wound side by side (bifiliar fashion) both windings being tapped for experimental purposes. The wire is 16 gauge with 11 turns primary and 4 turns secondary to give an approximate 1 : 1 swr (he points out that a similar technique might be used with a trapped system for multi-band working). To prove that the coaxial line really was flat, he checked by varying its length with no change in swr. A different turns ratio would be used

ANTENNA TOPICS

for 52Ω coaxial cable.

G3CDR rightly again emphasizes the importance of the earth connection. In his case, various pieces of coaxial cable stripped to the braiding are buried, together with a couple of pieces of copper piping, around the foot of the aerial; four 30ft lengths of copper strip are also laid out beneath the turf. Some tests have been carried out on 7MHz by lengthening the loading wire to form a ¾λ without changing the transformer; this seemed to work fairly well but in his case was not required for long.

Both trapped and non-trapped versions of the inverted-L seem to fit well into typical garden spaces. Trap construction has been described in most of the journals. Fig 4 shows the suggestions made by G3BID in *Mercury* for a 7,100kHz trap:

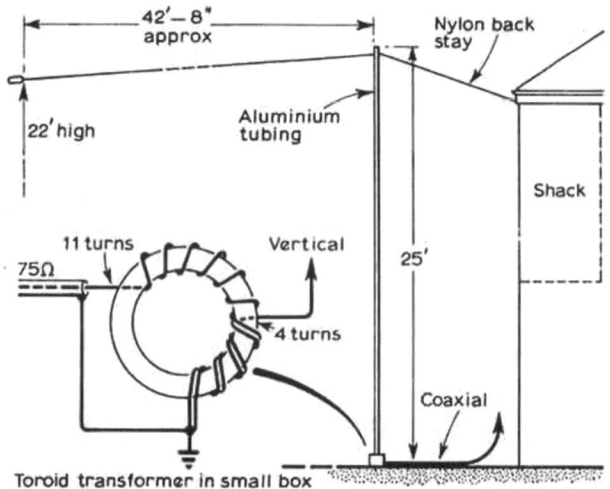

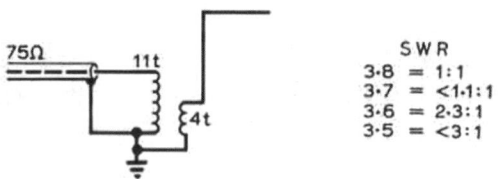

Fig 3. Single-band inverted-L aerial for 3·5MHz by G3CDR. Coaxial fed through a toroid matching transformer at base of radiator. Again, the better the earth connection, the better the results

the former is about 1¼in diameter, about 3in long and wound with about 23 turns of 18swg wire (adjusted to resonance using a grid-dip oscillator). The capacitor must have a high voltage rating suitable for the power used, and the 18swg wire should be sufficiently well spaced to avoid arcing. The whole unit, for a fixed aerial, can be contained in a sealed plastics container from domestic surplus.

HF Polarization Gains and Losses

Extracted from 'Technical Topics', *Radio Communication,* February 1971

HF polarization gains and losses

On vhf it has long been recognized that significant coupling losses occur in communications systems when attempts are made to receive vertically-polarized signals with horizontally-polarized aerials, or vice versa. Indeed this problem has led recently to the use, for some BBC local radio stations, of slant polarization, and in the USA of circular polarization; it has been found that such techniques improve pick-up on portable receivers using small telescopic aerials and also by car radio aerials.

Yet a very different situation is commonly considered to apply to hf ionospheric operation. We confidently use receiving aerials of either polarization to receive signals transmitted with either polarization. In doing so we rely on the firmly rooted belief that during the sojourn of the signals in the ionosphere they get so mixed up that they can be safely regarded as randomly or circularly polarized when they emerge.

A few years ago a rather different concept took root, once again helped along by the work of a number of amateurs. This was the principle of polarization diversity, based on the discovery that fading seldom coincided in time if signals were received with two aerials of different polarization without the requirement of physical separation. For example, George Messenger, K6CT, did a lot of work on a simple form of polarization diversity using crossed-dipole Yagi beams (which were later marketed by the Space Raider Antenna Company) for 28MHz. He reported his work in a number of journals, including the *RSGB Bulletin* (December 1962). Possibly because this was a time when sunspot numbers were declining, so that 28MHz was at a low ebb, and because such crossed-dipole arrays would be difficult to make on the lower frequency bands, the technique did not immediately attract much attention among amateurs (though a re-read of the article shows how impressive were his results).

However, the idea of polarization diversity was taken up by commercial companies, and certainly Granger Associates (large log-periodic arrays) and Rohde & Schwarz (simpler ground-plane-type monopoles) promoted this technique, and I do not think anyone today would seriously question the basic principles. A detailed explanation of these was published, for example, in Granger Associates' *Technical Bulletin No. 4* "Polarization diversity reception of high frequency signals" issued about 1965.

True diversity reception (involving two receivers and some form of switched combining) must always be very much of a luxury in the amateur field, and most proposals have involved the rather less elegant system of combining signals before they reach the input of a single receiver; one exception was a simplified diversity combiner described by P. Lee, W3JM, "Diversity reception made easy" *CQ* (May 1964) involving two receivers, one connected to a vertical dipole and the other to a horizontal dipole.

But certainly all the work of amateurs and professionals indicated that fading could be significantly reduced in this way; the K6CT work also indicated that his crossed-dipole beams extended the time when 28MHz was effectively open, presumably the result of the low angle of radiation of the vertically-polarized Yagi.

A recent paper in *Proc IEE* (January 1971) by P. A. Bradley of RSRS includes many measurements made at Slough of hf signals from transmitters in the Shetlands (operated by, among others, R. Flavell, G3LTP) and some interesting comments about polarization of signals, though this was not the primary purpose of the experiments which were to investigate the accuracy of two commonly-used techniques for calculating path-loss of hf signals. The work involved simultaneous measurements on different frequencies (3·2, 5·9, 7·9 and 11·2MHz) over this 960km path of signals radiated from horizontal half-wave dipoles. The receiving aerials were a horizontal dipole broadside-on to the incoming signals, a second end-on to the signals, and the third a vertical monopole with a vertical response nearly constant for signals at angles from 5° to 50° to the horizon.

For our purposes, one of the interesting conclusions

reached is that the results suggest that the downcoming waves were of *markedly elliptical polarization*, whereas the path-loss calculations assume that such signals are normally circularly polarized. It seems to me that this can be interpreted as confirming the value of being able to use both vertical and horizontal elements in any hf receiving (or transmitting) system even if one is not planning to attempt full polarization diversity. One notes, for example, the popularity of inverted-V dipoles (even though *QST* recently suggested that these have low-angle radiation only in a direction along the sloping ends), or the inverted-L as suggested in the February *TT* by G3VYF and G3CDR. The proportions of the G3CDR 3·5MHz aerial are such (25ft vertical, 42ft 8in horizontal) that very roughly half the radiation occurs in each section. By coincidence, just as the February issue was going through the press, I came across an article in *CQ* (December 1970) by the well-known *Radio Handbook* editor, William Orr, W6SAI, describing "an inexpensive utility antenna for 80 metres" with a configuration closely resembling that of G3CDR's quasi-vertical. While he commented that "old timers will scoff that this antenna is little more than a jazzed up version of the old Marconi", it seems well worth including his arrangement (Fig 3) which has no ferrite matching transformer but simply a series capacitor ("a bit of juggling with this value can move the resonant frequency several hundred kilohertz across the American 3·5MHz band"). And instead of the multiple earth spikes he runs out three 66ft insulated radials above ground. He does not propose this as a dx aerial but rather as giving good utility service out to a thousand miles or so. By disconnecting the series capacitor from the coaxial cable and inserting a two-turn coil from the capacitor down to the radials, the aerial can be adjusted to resonance by means of a dip oscillator.

But it does seem part of these general ideas that perhaps we should stop thinking that cross-polarization does not matter on hf and instead should start thinking more on how to take advantage of elliptical polarization and polarization diversity to avoid polarization coupling losses.

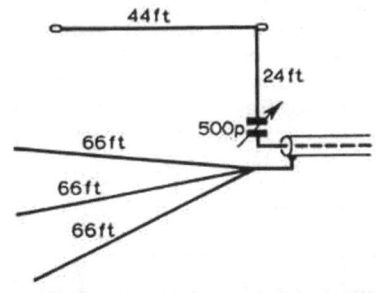

Fig 3. W6SAI's utility aerial for 3·5MHz

LA1EI Three-Band Vertical

Extracted from 'Technical Topics', *Radio Communication,* March 1971

LA1EI three-band vertical

I make no pretence of understanding the Norwegian text of an article by Petter Braekken, LA1EI, in the NRRL journal *Amator Radio* (Nr 9 1970) but his final diagram is reproduced here as Fig 4. This represents what appears to be a useful ⅝λ vertical monopole for 14MHz with ingenious use of RG8U coaxial matching sections to allow the same vertical to be used on 3·5 and 7MHz, and with a gamma-matching feed on 3·5MHz. It would seem that excellent matching can be achieved on 14 and 3·5MHz, with very usable results also on 7MHz.

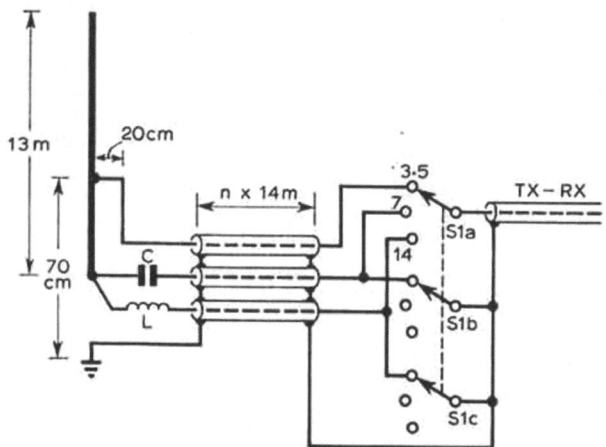

Fig 4. LA1EI's three-band vertical. C about 88pF. L about 2·8µH. If n is an odd number, then impedances are 3·5MHz 75Ω, 7MHz 140Ω, 14MHz 75Ω. If n is an even number, then impedance is 3·5MHz 75Ω, 7MHz 34Ω, 14MHz is 75Ω

Low-angle Operation

Extracted from 'Technical Topics', *Radio Communication,* April 1971

Low-angle operation

From time to time we have referred in *TT* and *ART* to the growing appreciation in recent years that useful hf communication modes exist which can be utilized by stations able to transmit and receive at extremely low angles to the horizon. These ionospheric propagation modes are often additional to the conventional single- and multi-hop modes which have for so long been used to good effect on hf. It seems an appropriate time to tie together some of the ideas which are now becoming established.

1. The bulk of wanted long-distance signals arrive at angles below 10° with a median value of around 7–8°. There is some variation of the angle with season.

2. Aerials which are effective at angles below 5° (and preferably below 2·5°) allow difficult dx paths to be maintained even during severe fade-out conditions (for example on the unreliable North Atlantic path).

3. Aerials which are effective at extremely low angles allow contacts to be made at times when, for those with more conventional aerials, the band has either not yet opened or has closed for the night. Such extended times of "openings" appear to be progressively more important on the lower frequency bands such as 3·5 and 7MHz and rather less significant on 21 and 28MHz (although the work on Oscar-5 shows that even on 28MHz it can be considerable).

If we accept these statements (and they are all based on solid experimental evidence in the literature), then we should be considering how amateurs can best exploit this new knowledge. Rather understandably, the commercial point-to-point people, although increasingly recognizing the validity of these low-angle modes, tend to be reluctant to do anything

ANTENNA TOPICS

very much about them, mainly on economic grounds (the cost of putting rhombics up a lot higher is not insignificant) but also because the alternative Intelsat space communications systems are confidently expected to take over more and more of the long-haul traffic in the coming decade.

How then can radiation and reception angles be forced down?

(a) By the use of beam aerials: the vertical radiation pattern of Yagi and quad aerials, for example, is concentrated in the vertical plane to much the same extent as in the horizontal plane (although the full benefit may be lost due to ground interference).

(b) By increasing the height of any horizontally-polarized aerial (but only a lucky few amateurs can reach the sort of heights which are really called for).

(c) By making use of the *theoretical* low angle of radiation of vertically polarized aerials and preferably by enhancing this by using array techniques (Dr John Kraus of W8JK fame recently described a versatile five-band vertically polarized rotary array—*QST*, July 1970—with 24ft elements and providing 3·4dB gain at 7MHz to 7·6dB at 28MHz.)

(d) By utilizing the benefits of real or induced good ground conductivity, remembering that ground conductivity right out to about 100λ in the target direction affects radiation angle.

(e) By utilizing ground slope towards the target area (see G6XN's article in *Wireless World*, (April 1970).

(f) By noting that very low take-off angles are more likely to be achieved from a very high site than a low one (one thinks of the good signals put out by stations in Nairobi and Asmara). An exception is the seaside site which can make use of nature's best ground-plane—the sea.

An interesting feature of this list is that it throws open again the old controversy of horizontal versus vertical polarization for hf aerials. This can be further complicated by our recent suggestion (*TT*, March) that polarization coupling losses may occur even on ionospheric communication, so that some of the benefits of using vertical polarization could be lost if the vast majority of stations use horizontal polarization.

Fig 5 indicates the theoretical vertical radiation patterns of a number of vertical aerials, and this highlights the usefulness of the $\tfrac{5}{8}\lambda$ aerial. Some years ago George Barrett, G8IP, ZC4IP etc, pointed out the value of vertical radiators 110° and 220° in length (in which 360° represents the *physical* wavelength of $984/f$ feet). He also gave what we believe is a most valuable hint: in designing hf vertical aerials a lot of valuable information can be gleaned from standard engineering texts (such as Laporte) on *broadcast-type medium-wave aerials*. It must be remembered that mf broadcast engineers regard any radiation above about 3° as useless for ground-wave service and make considerable use of T aerials and elevated feed aerials to increase ground-wave coverage. Unfortunately it seems a common fallacy to divide aerials quite arbitrarily into those suitable for mf, hf or vhf. Recent use of a T aerial not more than about 20ft high (see *TT*, July 1970) on 7MHz as well as on 14MHz has convinced me that such aerials have at least some application on hf.

In general we are coming to believe that many of the old arguments against vertical polarization were based, understandably enough, on the idea that the aerial which lays down the strongest dx signal under normal conditions is necessarily the best. A better yardstick would be the time during which it can maintain a difficult circuit, and we shall be discussing techniques for measuring aerial gain and performance down to small fractions of a decibel later. Meanwhile, we would suggest that for amateur operation there is a great deal to be said for using vertical (or mixed) polarization on 1·8, 3·5 and 7MHz if the aim is dx; on 14MHz there is probably not a lot in it, unless you only

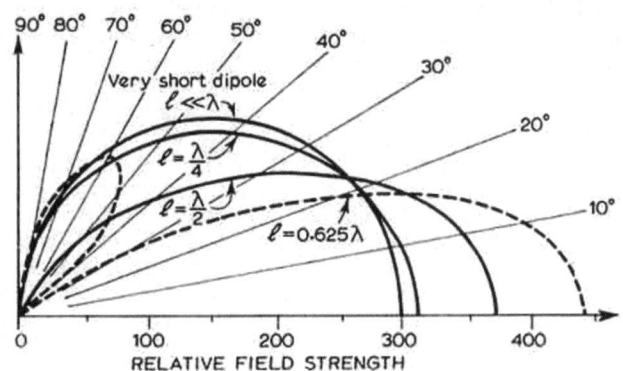

Fig 5. Theoretical vertical radiation patterns of vertical aerials of varying length indicating how, for base-fed systems, the 0.625λ aerial gives maximum low angle radiation. For some elevated-feed patterns see *ART2* or *3*

have low supports (under, say, 30ft) in which case the choice should again go to the vertical; on 21 and 28MHz a horizontally polarized beam is probably the most sensible choice, though vertical radiators can be very effective.

For horizontal polarization do not be misled by the fallacy that some types of arrays, for example the quad, perform so well at low heights that it is not worth worrying about extra height. An attempt to assess the effect of height on practical dx performance was reported recently in *QST* by Wayne Overbeck, K6YNB, who compared results from a quad at 72ft with one at 34ft; "every single dx station reported a substantially better signal from the high quad than the low one". On 14MHz dx contacts, the mean advantage was as much as 2·1 S units. Only a small percentage of us can hope to get 14MHz aerials up more than a wavelength, and this is perhaps the main reason for the renewed interest recently in vertically polarized aerials.

The use of a number of monopole vertical aerials to form arrays has been mentioned on a number of occasions (for example, the electronically switched system described in *TT*, September 1970). Almost all systems of this type have been based on the use of quarter-wave monopoles, but it is worth noting a letter from R. J. F. Guertler recently published in *Proc IREE Australia* (September 1970) which starts: "Directional mf broadcast antenna arrays consist usually of two masts operating as base-driven monopoles. High masts, of the order of $\tfrac{1}{2}\lambda$, compared with short masts, give

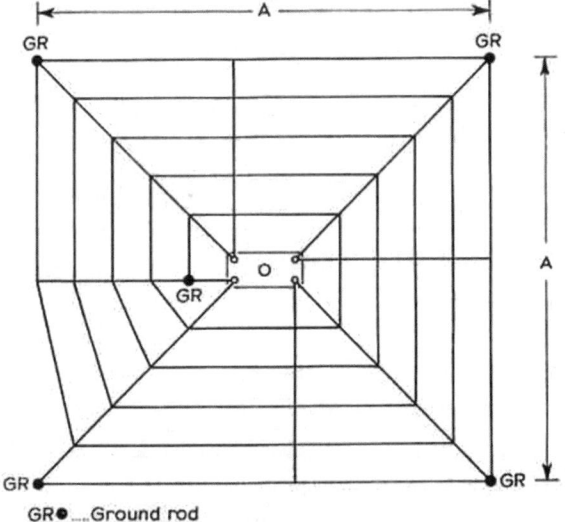

Fig 6. Where space is limited for full earth radials, this arrangement may be used. Dimension A should be not less than one-half the total aerial height. Solder or braze each junction. GR ground rods. Preferably, earth mats and radials should extend as far as possible, particularly towards main target areas

the advantage of increased gain and considerably reduced sky wave." However, he notes that the design of $\frac{1}{2}\lambda$ monopole arrays poses a number of problems.

Again, one must always emphasize that with any vertical radiator every effort should be made to improve the earth system. Multiple earth stakes and/or radials (even if not radial in shape) are always advisable: in effect use as much wire and as many earthstakes as possible, connecting them all together electrically. And if you have the ground available, run out some wires (which can be buried a few inches below the surface) as far as possible in the direction of the main dx target. Earth mats can be formed by the technique shown in Fig 6 (taken from a guide to vertical aerial installation issued some years ago by *Mosley Electronics*) provided that a good connection, soldered or brazed, is made at each junction. The same booklet points out that if it is not possible to form the earth system centrally about the aerial, it may be formed off-centre.

Sloping-V Aerials

Extracted from 'Technical Topics',
Radio Communication, April 1971

Sloping-V aerials

For those with space available, long-wire V beams have much to commend them, although these are often overlooked in favour of the rhombic. There is one form of V, however, that appears to be little known to amateurs, although a professional system of this type was used by Cove Radio at Farnborough for its share of the Arctic Trek communications in 1968–69. This is the sloping-V with a single aerial-support mast (for the ambitious a considerable number of directions are possible by selection of any two of a large number of wires to one central mast, as at Cove). Fig 7 indicates the basic arrangement although for dimensions etc reference should be made to any of the handbooks covering standard V beams (for example *Radio Communication Handbook*). This particular illustration is taken from the CCIR's *Handbook on high-frequency directional antennae,* published by ITU, where it is stated: "The sloping-V antenna has received little attention in comparison with that given to the rhombic antenna. As a receiving antenna, however, it has virtues which could commend it in many situations." The system, of course, can be used for transmitting provided that the terminating resistors are of appropriate rating. One wonders whether on *vhf* it would be possible to set up a Cove Radio system in a small space?

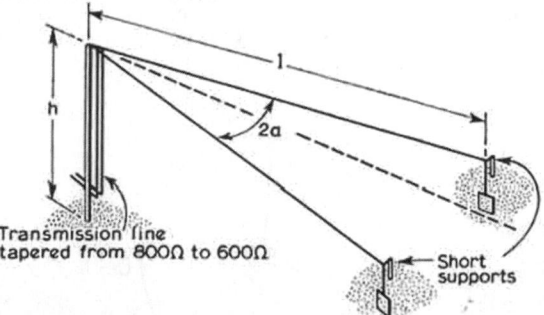

Fig 7. General arrangement of sloping-V aerial. The ends are connected to ground through 600Ω resistors. For transmission these resistors should be of suitable power rating (about one quarter transmitter power rating for a.m., but probably considerably lower rating will be satisfactory for ssb and cw). See also *Radio Communication Handbook,* page 13.61

Another Look at Transmitting Loops

Extracted from 'Technical Topics',
Radio Communication, June 1971

Another look at transmitting loops

In November 1967, *TT* became the first, in any amateur journal, to comment on the US Army octagon loop aerial, originally described in *Electronics* (31 August 1967). During the following months many further ideas were widely reported: these included simplification of the capacitive matching network which is possible when only single-band operation is required, and the use of loops for mobile operation (*QST*, November 1968). One of the most practical suggestions was that put forward by "Spenny" (G6NA) in the September 1968 *Radio Communication*; p. 576; this was to use "½in coaxial" as a convenient means of achieving the very necessary low resistive losses.

Recently, Jim Fisk, W1DTY, editor of *Ham Radio,* drew my attention to a "Designer's casebook" item in *Electronics,* April 12, 1971. This was by James Taylor, W2OZH, who had written the earlier *QST* piece on "The Mobiloop" referred to above.

In his latest work on transmitting loops, he claims that a very simply constructed low-frequency balanced dipole loop can provide reasonably efficient performance even when mounted close to ground; he suggests that with a maximum linear dimension of under 25ft, a 4MHz loop

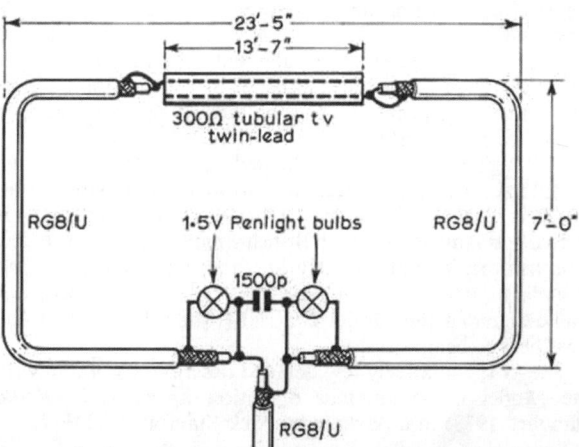

Fig 1. Low-cost balanced loop aerial. This is trimmed to resonance by symmetrically trimming open ends of the 300Ω twin lead. Flashlamp bulbs should indicate current balance at resonance. Dimensions shown are for 3,942kHz and should be scaled proportionately for other frequencies

aerial can provide signals only 5–10dB below those from a full-length, high dipole. Mounted on a wood-frame building, his loop has an input resistance of 59Ω, showed unity swr at 3·942MHz, and 1·5 : 1 swr at ± 50kHz.

The construction of the loop is indicated in Fig 1. It will be seen that, as in the Spenny loop, he uses coaxial cable (RG8/U) as a large diameter, low resistance conductor. An interesting further idea, however, is the use of 300Ω tubular twin lead cable to form a high-voltage capacitance which can readily be trimmed for resonance to form a balanced configuration. He also suggests that the impedance match at the feedpoint can be improved by adding a 1,500pF 500V capacitor (adequate for powers up to 500W) across the feedline as shown. The 1·5V flashlight bulbs are used as tuning indicators. The bulbs, which indicate current balance, are brightest when the aerial is at resonance.

ANTENNA TOPICS

His arrangement thus eliminates completely the need for any conventional high-voltage variable capacitors. The loop structure should be mounted vertically since horizontal placing will produce an overhead null. If near the ground it would be better to make the twin-lead member the lower one.

Taking radiation resistance as $3 \cdot 1 \times 10^4 \, (A^2/\lambda^4)\Omega$, then a loop enclosing 165ft yields (at 4MHz) an R_r of $0 \cdot 27\Omega$. Taking the rf resistance of the RG8/U cable as 3Ω, this would give an efficiency of 8 per cent or about 10dB below maximum efficiency. W2OZH considers this theoretical figure is borne out by results. Many amateurs may consider that 8 per cent efficiency sounds very low—but in practice many short aerials are in use which must be significantly less efficient than this. It does not depend on any earth connection or ground plane. As Spenny showed very clearly, this type of loop aerial has very practical uses where more conventional aerials cannot be accommodated.

The Echelon or Model C Aerial

Extracted from 'Technical Topics', *Radio Communication,* June 1971

The echelon or Model C aerial

It may seem a far, far cry from the small loop to a long wire aerial. But it seems an opportune time to focus a little attention on an interesting type of long wire aerial which is capable of providing two different bi-directional lobes and can be used to achieve either two- or four-point coverage, without physical rotation or the use of an excessively large area of real-estate.

Although the echelon is included in *The ARRL Antenna Handbook*, we suspect that this form of long-wire aerial, which is closely akin to the far better known Vee beam, is virtually unknown to most British amateurs. Yet, in a few months time, it will be exactly 40 years since it was described in a classic RCA paper in *Proc IRE* (October 1931) where it was designated the Model C aerial (Model D, incidentally, was the Vee-beam).

One of the relatively few detailed descriptions of applying the Model C to amateur operation appeared in *Radio* (January 1938) in an article by Nick Stavrou, W2DFN.

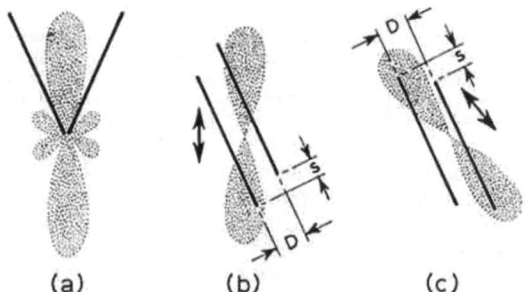

Fig 2. Comparison of the Vee and Model C (echelon) aerials. (a) the bi-directional Vee; (b) the Model C aerial; (c) Model C aerial showing how bi-directional lobes swing round when the stagger is reversed

Why is this aerial worth dragging out from obscurity? After all, the gain is slightly down on a Vee of equivalent leg length. And, more importantly, the Model C is essentially a single-band aerial. These are valid criticisms, but it must be remembered that both the Vee and the rhombic are not only long but also broad—and to provide on hf an equivalent number of lobes would fill up a great deal of space. And furthermore, although originally described for hf, there seems no reason why it should not be used at vhf where it could be fitted very conveniently into quite a modest garden.

For the Model C consists of just two long wire aerials, about a half-wave apart: Fig 2(b). On these wires, the phase is staggered in such a way as to result in two very pronounced major lobes, 180° apart. And, if the stagger is reversed, the two lobes swing round conveniently: see Fig 2(c). The *ARRL Antenna Handbook* indicates that this electronic beam steering can be done simply by changing the phasing of the signal fed to the two wires. Three ways of feeding the aerial are shown in Fig 3. In 1938, W2DFN actually moved one of his wires along by a simple but ingenious system using a counterbalance weight and a rope brought into the shack. He shifted the wire of one leg along by twice the stagger distance: Fig 4.

While, very roughly, the two wires are about $0 \cdot 5\lambda$ apart, and the stagger is of the order of $0 \cdot 25\lambda$, more exact figures (for optimum lobes) depend on the angle of radiation from the long wire, and this, in turn, depends on how long, in terms of wavelength, the long wire is. Table I, derived from W2DFN's 1938 article, gives typical figures. As with other long-wire aerials such as the Vee and rhombic, the power gain and width of the lobes depend on the length of wire.

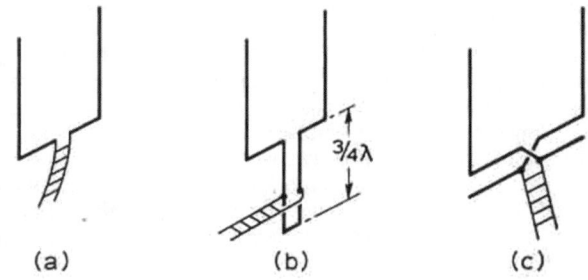

Fig 3. Three methods of feeding the Model C aerial. (a) Zepp feed; (b) stub matching to any impedance transmission line; (c) system shown in *The ARRL Antenna Book*

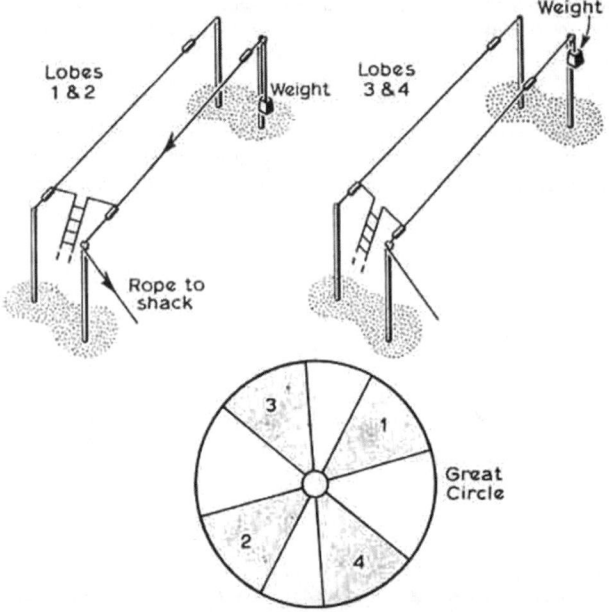

Fig 4. The 1938 arrangement described by W2DFN with directivity changed by hauling in or letting out rope

Apart from Model C, there was also a so-called Model B using sloping wires and a reflector, and producing vertically-polarized waves—this, however, appears to call for very high supports.

We should perhaps stress that while in the past we have been fortunate enough to use Vees and rhombics (although not for amateur operation), we have no personal experience of the Model C or echelon configuration. But it seems a pity if this system is entirely forgotten. We should be interested to learn of any current or past experimental work on this type of beam array.

Table I. Model C (echelon) aerial data

Length of radiators (L)	Lobe angle (α)	Spacing (D)	Stagger (S)
$1\frac{1}{2}\lambda$	42	$0{\cdot}746 \times \frac{1}{2}\lambda$	$0{\cdot}67 \times \frac{1}{2}\lambda$
2λ	36	$0{\cdot}85 \times \frac{1}{2}\lambda$	$0{\cdot}62 \times \frac{1}{2}\lambda$
3λ	29	$1{\cdot}03 \times \frac{1}{2}\lambda$	$0{\cdot}57 \times \frac{1}{2}\lambda$
4λ	25	$1{\cdot}18 \times \frac{1}{2}\lambda$	$0{\cdot}55 \times \frac{1}{2}\lambda$
5λ	22·5	$1{\cdot}3 \times \frac{1}{2}\lambda$	$0{\cdot}54 \times \frac{1}{2}\lambda$

Length of radiators $= \frac{984}{f(\text{MHz})} \times (k - 0{\cdot}025)$

where K is number of wavelengths.

$S = \frac{\sin \alpha}{\sin 2\alpha}$. $D = \frac{\cos \alpha}{\sin 2\alpha}$.

To convert to feet, multiply by 492/f(MHz).

Typical 2λ 14·2MHz system:

L = 136·2ft, D = 29·5ft, S = 21·5ft.

Aluminium Foil Dipoles

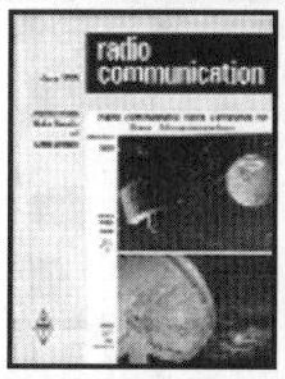

Extracted from ‘Technical Topics’, *Radio Communication,* June 1971

Aluminium foil dipoles

QTC (January 1971) publishes an item by SM5JV (with acknowledgements to earlier work reported by DJ7VYA in *DL-QTC* of March 1970). This shows how rolls of household aluminium foil can be used to form short wideband dipole aerials for lofts or for other indoor or wall mounting: see Fig 5. His suggested lengths of 45cm wide foil are:

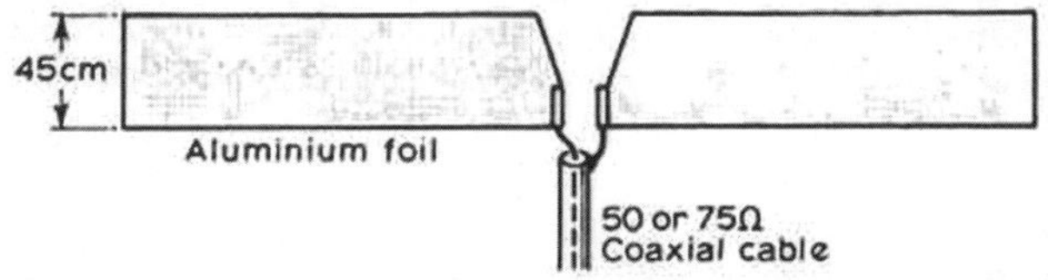

Fig 5. Broad-band aluminium foil aerial. For dimensions see text. Directivity patterns can be changed by having the two foil sections in the same or different planes (eg 180° or 90° or 45° angle between foils).

3·5MHz, 2 by 12m; 7MHz, 2 by 6·2m; 14MHz, 2 by 3·4m. The idea reminds one of the inbuilt vfm/fm aerials in some broadcast radio receivers. It is possible that this could be quite an effective method of constructing loft, room or wall aerials, with broad-band characteristics making it easier to achieve a good match than with most thin-wire indoor aerials. By having the foils at different angles (ie in the form of a short Vee) it should be possible to achieve near-omnidirectional radiation.

Reflectors Under Dipoles

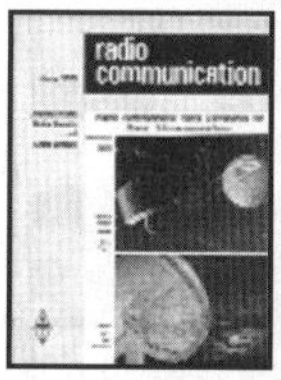

Extracted from ‘Technical Topics’, *Radio Communication,* June 1971

Reflectors under dipoles

Ted Cook, ZS6BT, wonders if anyone else has thought of hanging a parasitic reflector a half-wave below a conventional dipole. He has been experimenting with this idea with, as he puts it, “interesting results”.

He points out that the use of driven elements stacked a half-wave above one or another is accepted practice (Sterba curtain, Lazy-H etc). And, of course, the advantages accruing from mounting a dipole a multiple of a half-wave above ground have long been recognized. So why not use an artificial ground wire?

ZS6BT writes: “The rules say that if two elements are spaced a half-wave apart, the current in the interfering dipole will be in phase with the driving element and the pattern will be broadside. The rules also indicate that changing the phase slightly will cause the pattern to change from a right-angled broadside; the phase may be changed by varying the spacing or by varying the reactance of the reflector.

“Radiation from a dipole, if viewed from the end, may be represented by a dot in a circle. If a parasitic reflector is used at half-wave spacing the pattern looks more like a dumb-bell. If stacked horizontally, the elements would tend to minimize the up-and-down radiation and concentrate it forwards and backwards, with an increase in gain. I leave it to readers to consider all the implications !

“What goes for a dipole goes for a centre-fed co-linear or a multi-band G5RV with two or more in-line reflectors for each of several bands and each set of reflectors ‘doing its own thing’. The use of reflectors should not change the lobe pattern but only increase gain. However, the lobe pattern *might* be changed; for example, a $\frac{3}{2}\lambda$ dipole might have one central reflector or two (in-line) end reflectors, or three in-line reflectors; or two in-line reflectors might have inner ends close together or wide apart; on top of all this is possible change of phase.

“Basically, reflectors should not be shorter than 492/*f* feet (where *f* is in MHz), and the spacing should have a similar dimension. It would seem preferable to make each reflector a half-wave, rather than to hang (say) a $\frac{11}{2}\lambda$ wire below a $\frac{3}{2}\lambda$ top. Reflectors could be made physically shorter, and then fitted with tuning stubs for phase adjustment.”

One suspects that for maximum effect, the original height of the dipole would need to be fairly high, and that in such circumstances there is no reason why one should not opt for a Lazy-H. Nevertheless the whole idea seems well worth considering—and preferably investigating further: after all, as ZS6BT points out, “there are still many assorted types of dipoles in use—why not try and improve them.”

ANTENNA TOPICS

Broad-band Dipoles

Extracted from 'Technical Topics', *Radio Communication,* August 1971

Broad-band dipoles

While we were at ASWE, one of the items which came to our notice was the rigging of broadband dipoles for hf. These now often consist of about four or five spaced wires having an appearance very much like the traditional 600m mf shipborne T aerial. But we gathered that it has been found that the broadband characteristics of this type of aerial tend to vanish if the far ends of the dipole are joined together. Each wire is kept physically and electrically separate from the point it leaves the matching to the transmission line. It is thus significantly different from the more usual cage-type fat dipoles where all the wires come together again at the high-voltage ends.

So a few days later we were interested to find (*CQ* June 1971) an article "Broadband Antenna for Forty Metres" by Howard Phillips, WB5ACP, indicating somewhat similar ideas used to produce an aerial resonant across the entire American 7MHz band (7·0 right through to 7·3MHz, a spread that only pre-war British amateurs can still remember!). His design (Fig 3) uses four-wire tv rotor cable but with the last few feet separated and fanned out to enhance end effect and capacitance loading. One result is that the

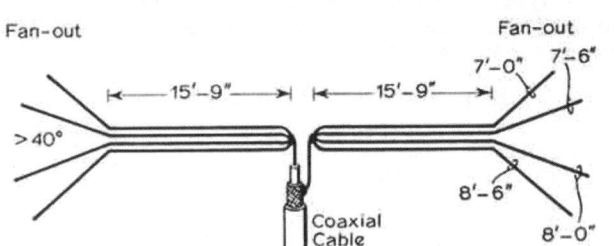

Fig 3. WB5ACP broadband 7MHz aerial using four-core cable with fan-out over last 7/8½ft

overall span of the dipole is about 48ft instead of the usual 66ft; another is a claimed swr of 1·3:1 or less (if that really means anything) across the full range. He points out that the aerial can be put up either in flat-top or inverted-V configuration. While few of us need such a broad-band aerial on 7MHz the idea is a useful one to know, apart from being handy if your garden span will not hold a conventional dipole span.

The 9M2CP Z-Beam

Extracted from 'Technical Topics', *Radio Communication,* August 1971

The 9M2CP Z-beam

A few days ago on 3·5MHz a British amateur gently chided me for admitting to using an end-fed long wire aerial. With all those exotic aerials in *TT*, he suggested, fancy using such an unexciting arrangement! The point was taken, though we have always stressed the value of the classic aerials, including the very ancient Zepp. Perhaps we should have claimed that the aerial was in accordance with the in-trend in American electronics—the "kiss" technique (for the uninitiated, "keep it simple stupid"). Fortunately, there are amateurs still prepared to tackle aerial configurations which would be difficult to erect in a small garden surrounded by anxious neighbours.

One of the most interesting of these to come along recently stems from Philip Zeid, 9M2CP, in Penang. This is a 14MHz Z-beam possessing good low-angle characteristics; he has combined this with a 21MHz double-delta beam.

9M2CP writes: "I have had the aerial in use for both 21 and 14MHz for about seven months. It is originally derived from the delta loop but has several advantages. The 21MHz section might be termed a double delta, whilst the 14MHz gradually developed from a quad: Fig 5. I tried double quad, phased arrays etc, and finally arrived at the present

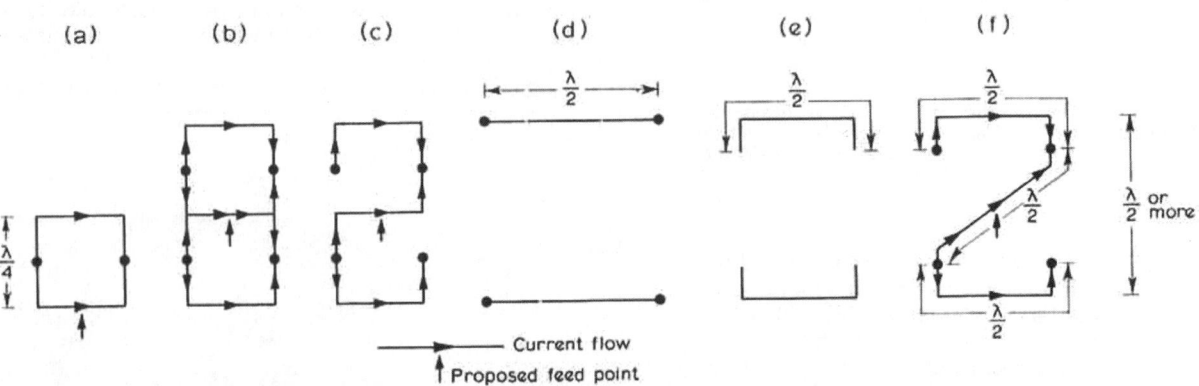

Fig 5. Development of the 9M2CP Z-beam: (a) conventional quad; (b) double quad—difficult to tune and little apparent advantage over (a); (c) open-ended double quad developed to eliminate possibility of double currents in centre element—it gave improved results over (b); (d) half-wave dipoles spaced about half-wavelength apart vertically; (e) as (d) but with ends bent inwards to permit joining diagonals with half-wave wire; (f) the 9M2CP Z-beam as now evolved

design which has proved better, so far, than any other beam I have had for this band.

"Both beams have optimum gain for the length of boom used, since both end-fire and broadside gain are used. The 14MHz beam has a portion having vertical polarization. Both beams, on the same boom, have excellent low-angle radiation, indicated by the vastly increased difference in signal strengths, compared to a standard dipole at 60ft, as dx signals start to come in. During the early mornings the difference is absolutely amazing.

"On 21MHz there is a standard delta loop, with a similar delta pair mounted below the boom, as a mirror image of the upper pair. A common gamma tuning capacitor is used and is better and easier to adjust than separate capacitors. The gamma arms are adjusted equally and matching is equal to that found with a single delta loop beam.

"For 14MHz, 5ft (or longer) wooden extensions are placed in the ends of the delta loop Vs to provide at least half-wavelength vertical spacing between upper and lower horizontals. The whole is laced round with nylon line, to form a framework for the 14MHz beam and also support for the lower Vs which tend to collapse inwards under their own weight. The radiator is made up of $1\frac{1}{2}\lambda$ of wire laced as shown in Fig 6, and fed with a gamma match at the centre. The length of wire is slightly shorter than $1\frac{1}{2}\lambda$ to account for two end effects only. A sliding loose noose of nylon is run round the vertical nylon and includes the radiator so that it can be adjusted to take up slack when in position. The reflector is cut to just under the full theoretical $1\frac{1}{2}\lambda$ and a tuning stub is put in the centre. This can readily be adjusted for maximum gain or best back-to-front ratio. The tuning is quite marked for best back-to-front ratio and also provides what appears to be best gain."

9M2CP adds that there is no reason why this system should not be extended to more than two elements (so long as they do not foul guy wires) or more than one vertical pair on higher frequencies. It would also appear quite feasible, he suggests, to put the tuning in the lower horizontal member if this provides easier access for tuning. Phasing is accomplished automatically.

Interestingly enough, the double delta configuration for hf was investigated by the originator of the delta aerial—H. R. Habig, K8ANV, and for vhf and uhf by John Pegler, G3ENI. (see *ART3* page 183). For 14MHz, 9M2CP has arrived, under his own steam, at a configuration which appears to resemble closely the Aerialite "Supreme" aerial for uhf television reception (see *TT* April 1970). Interestingly enough, the Supreme is generally regarded as a very high gain array, although some people appear to worry at the possibility of mixed polarization which could increase co-channel interference on television stations. On the other hand, as we suggested in *TT* recently, mixed polarization may be a positive advantage for hf operation.

A 14MHz 9M2CP array clearly needs a lot of height, but on 21 and 28MHz would be much less formidable to construct. It certainly seems to be an arrangement which deserves to be widely known.

Aerial Matching with Transmission Lines

Extracted from 'Technical Topics', *Radio Communication,* October 1971

Aerial matching with transmission line sections

Before describing several practical hf aerials this month, we would like to draw attention to what could be an important development in the use of transmission-line matching transformers. For many years, the quarter-wave transmission line transformer has been a known and useful method of matching a transmission line to an aerial of a different feed-point impedance. For example, we can match a 300Ω line to a 600Ω line or aerial by means of a quarter-wave line of $\sqrt{(300 \times 600)}$ or about 425Ω impedance. The same technique can be used with unbalanced coaxial lines.

But generally, this technique has been useful only when matching into purely resistive loads and with simple transformation ratios. Now, Frank Regier of the American University of Beirut (who as OD5CG was responsible for the tri-band vertical aerial given in *TT* April 1970 and in *ART3*) has presented in *Proc IEEE* (July 1971 pages 1,133-34) a generalization of this type of transmission line transformer, showing how its use can be extended to match complex loads and provide a wide range of impedance transformations with

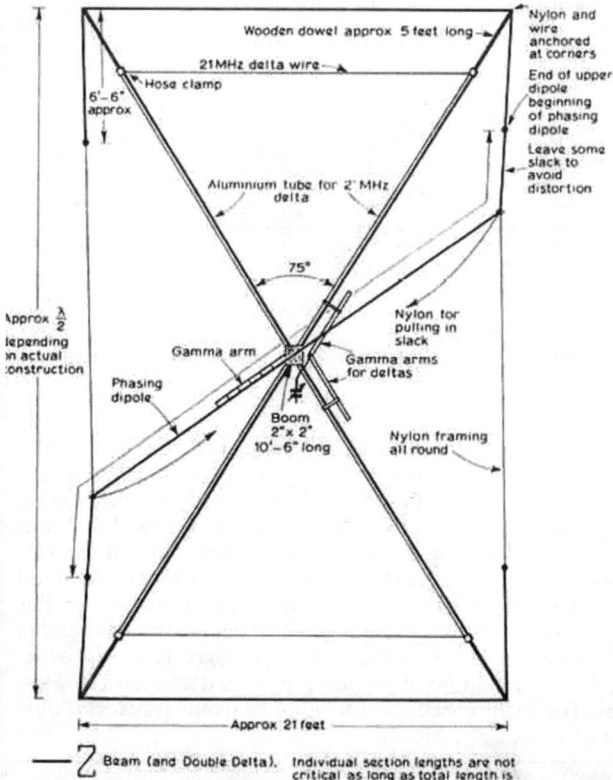

Fig 6. Constructional details of the 9M2CP 21 MHz double-delta and 14MHz Z-beam

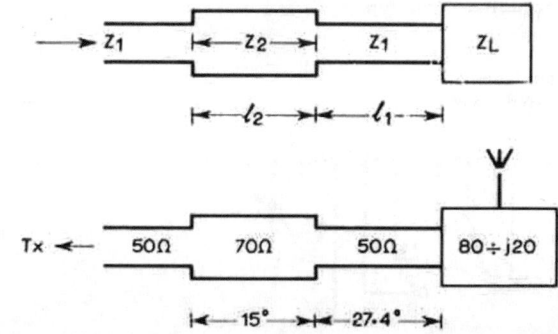

Fig 6. (a) Generalized form of the quarter-wave transmission line matching transformer. (b) Example of its use to match to a complex impedance, as described by **OD5CG** in "Proc IEEE"

ANTENNA TOPICS

a single combination of line impedances, when these differ significantly.

In effect, he shows that the electrical length of the matching section need not be restricted to 90°, provided that the section is placed at a specific electrical distance from the end of the line: see Fig 6. As an example of what can be done, he indicates how a 50Ω coaxial can be correctly matched to an aerial offering a feed-point impedance of 80 + 120Ω, by placing a section of 70Ω coaxial cable, with an electrical length of 15°, in the main cable at a distance of 27·4 electrical degrees from the aerial connection.

The use of this general theory for matching coaxial cable to vertical or whip aerials of non-resonant lengths—and indeed for any other aerial offering a complex load—could clearly be very attractive.

Frank Regier gives detailed information on how to use this general theory in the form of a series of formulae. We would suggest that one of our aerial wizards might look carefully into his presentation to see if some down-to-earth guidance could be given in a form rather more suitable for use by amateurs.

On the subject of transmission line transformers, Barry Priestley, G3JGO, drew our attention some time ago to a hint in a Texas handbook: 61Ω coaxial cable can be made by removing the No 20 centre conductor from RG58/U cable and substituting a No 21 conductor. At vhf or uhf, G3JGO suggests this could be a useful way of making up a quarter-wave transformer to match 50Ω line to 75Ω.

End-fed Multiband Aerial

Extracted from 'Technical Topics', *Radio Communication*, October 1971

End-fed multiband aerial

To judge from the stations we work, the two most popular simple multiband aerials these days are the W3DZZ trap dipole and the G5RV type of dipole. One of the reasons for their popularity is undoubted that they can be fed readily from coaxial cables without additional matching units. But both these are centre-fed systems, and the need quite often arises for an end-fed arrangement. In *Amateur Radio* (No 6, 1971), Tom Segalstad, LA4LN, reminds us that a simple but effective five-band aerial (offering 2dB gain on 21MHz and 3·5dB on 28MHz relative to a half-wave dipole) consists of a 132ft wire end-fed from coaxial line through a simple switched L-matching network: see Fig 7. The capacitor needs to be a high-voltage type.

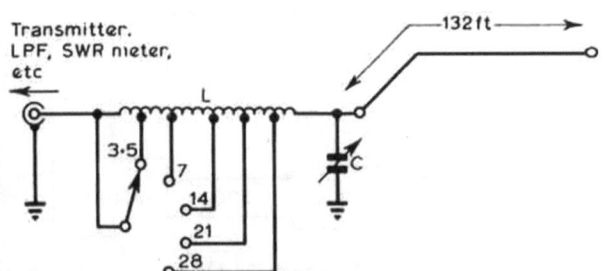

Fig 7. 132ft end-fed aerial used in conjunction with switched L-network matching unit. C is high-voltage 100pF capacitor. Diameter of L is uncertain but, typically, turns are 3·5MHz, 32; 7MHz, 15; 14MHz, 9; 21MHz, 4 and 28MHz, 3

Three-Eighth Wave Aerials

Extracted from 'Technical Topics', *Radio Communication*, October 1971

Three-eighth wave aerials

The folded ⅜λ vertical aerial described recently in *TT* (May 1971) reminded several readers of other uses of this length. For example, *The Radio Handbook* has long pointed out that a ⅜λ Marconi aerial can be operated on its harmonic frequency as a ¾λ, thus providing a useful dual-band aerial. Fig 8 shows the system described in this handbook using 180ft for 1·8/3·5MHz and 90ft for 3·5/7MHz. An interesting feature is that this aerial can be fed directly from a low-impedance pi-network transmitter output or as an end-fed from a coaxial cable since on both bands the feed impedance is of the order of 40 to 60Ω. The series capacitor is in circuit on the lower band but short-circuited on the higher

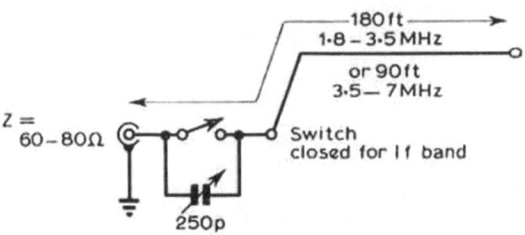

Fig 8. Two-band ⅜λ Marconi dual-band aerial. Typically 180ft for 1·8/3·5MHz or 90ft for 3·5/7MHz

band; the aerial can be adjusted for resonance on its harmonic frequency and then adjusted on the lower frequency using the capacitor. There also seems no reason why it should not be used on some other bands as a voltage fed aerial (for example a 90ft wire would represent a 1½λ aerial on 14MHz).

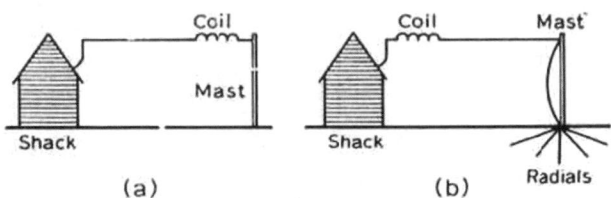

Fig 9. Use of electrical loading to provide ⅜λ Marconi on 1·8 MHz, (a) as used by GW3PJT, (b) preferred method

Dr R. C. Whelon, GW3PJT, comments that he and G3PLP have made effective use of a ⅜λ Marconi aerial on 1·8MHz, in the belief that this length should perform better than a ¼λ wire since the current maximum can be where it does most good, and the higher feed impedance can make it a lot easier to feed. The technique can be used at sites where a full physical length of ⅜λ is not practicable by using a loading coil; GW3PJT used a loading coil about 6ft from the end of the wire as shown in Fig 9 (a). He suggests that a better technique might be to ground the far end as shown in Fig 9 (b). The earth system (as for other Marconi systems) should be as good as possible.

Remotely Tuned Mobile Whip

Extracted from 'Technical Topics',
Radio Communication, October 1971

Remotely tuned mobile whip

After reading the interesting article on mobile aerials by E. L. Gardiner, G6GR, in the July issue of *Radio Communication,* Roy Eldridge, G3RAE, was prompted to describe his experiences in making a remotely tuned base-loaded whip for 1·8MHz mobile operation.

For some time he used a "Chinese copy" of a G3FIF-type whip, but tired of having to stop and get out of the car to extend or shorten the whip when changing frequency. In the end the following technique was developed to overcome this problem.

The whip is resonated in the normal manner to 2MHz, then to load the transmitter at any lower frequency a piece of B2 ferrite rod 10mm in diameter is pushed up inside the coil: see Fig 10. The rod can move upwards from the base a distance of 1in, sufficient to resonate the aerial anywhere in the band 1·8 to 2MHz, its position being controlled from the operating position by means of a length of Bowden cable.

Tests of this system over a period of some 18 months have shown that radiation is consistently good over the entire

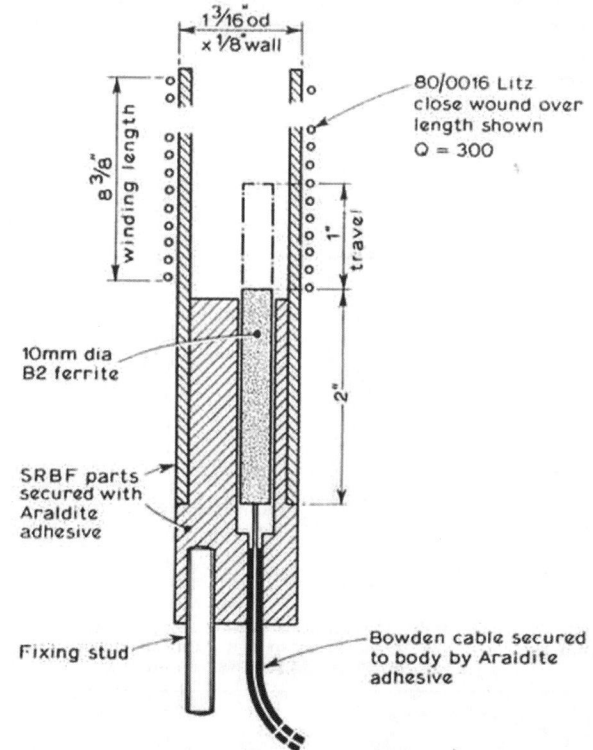

Fig 10. Remotely controlled 1·8MHz mobile as developed by G3RAE. The aerial is mounted on the vehicle 2ft forward of offside windscreen pillar

band with no difficulty in loading the all-transistor transmitter to the full 10W without a separate aerial tuning unit. The power is fed from the transmitter to the aerial using a short length of coaxial cable. With a fixed-length 4ft whip, good contacts have been made both locally and up to about 30 miles.

G3RAE admits that some difficulties may be experienced in duplicating his construction. The ferrite rod was cut with a diamond impregnated grinding wheel, and the hole required for fixing the operating cable was drilled by ultrasonic methods. For this reason no precise dimensions are given in Fig 10, as this is intended primarily to illustrate the principles involved rather than for exact duplication.

G3RAE also made good use of this aerial arrangement on a 30ft motor cruiser on the Norfolk Broads this summer.

Shortened Dipoles

Extracted from 'Technical Topics',
Radio Communication, November 1971

Shortened dipoles

It is always interesting to note how often the same idea seems to occur to several people at roughly the same time. One example of this is an inverted V-dipole with the size drastically reduced by inductive loading. A 3·5MHz design of this type was presented by Juergen Berger, DL7LJ, in *DL-QTC* (No 5, 1971); another has come along from A. J. Russell, BRS32857, who uses a rather similar arrangement for dx reception on 1·8, 3·5 and 7MHz, each requiring the use of only a short garden.

DL7LJ uses a coaxial balun between the coaxial feeder and the dipole, and his loading coils are wound on a 22mm former about 350mm long wound with 145 turns of aluminium wire 1·5mm in diameter. The swr curves indicate that resonance is fairly sharp, although the aerial should be satisfactory over at least 100kHz of the 3·5MHz band; one possible technique for lowering resonant frequency mentioned by DL7LJ is the use of two capacitance hats in the high-voltage sections using about eight radial wires.

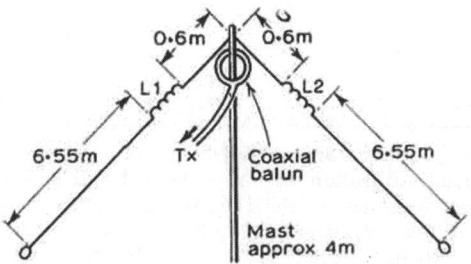

Fig 6. DL7LJ short dipole for 3·5MHz

A. J. Russell, BRS32857, has a roughly similar system except that his loading consists of two helically wound sections each 10ft long. He winds 56ft of 16swg wire on pvc tubing 10ft by 1¼in, with wood plugs at each end. He uses the aerial as a dipole on 3·5 and 7MHz and as a T on 1·8MHz. He would be interested to hear from anyone using the aerial for transmitting: his address is 90 Portland Road, Street, Somerset.

During the past few months we have had several contacts on 3·5MHz with "Spenny", G6NA, who is using a small 4W transistor transmitter. His aerial is, in effect, half of one of these loaded dipoles—about 30ft of wire running up and then along only about 9ft above ground and inductively loaded at the far end with some 5in of closewound 20swg on a 1¼in diameter former, the other end of the coil being connected to 3ft of ¼in copper tubing to provide a simple capacitance hat. He often works North America with this

ANTENNA TOPICS

set-up, though he experiences considerable variations in feed point impedance which he is still investigating.

There is, of course, a touch of the Joystick about all these short loaded aerials used as fixed-site systems, and we do not intend to enter into that particular controversy—although we should in fairness mention that we seem to work quite a few reasonable signals which turn out to be coming from Joysticks.

A further variation of the helically wound form of loading turns up in the October *SWM* in the form of a 1·8MHz vertical aerial comprising 250ft wire helically wound on a 15–20ft pole and fed from coaxial cable via a variable loading coil. Despite the use of about 1λ of wire, the aerial, it is said, appears to function more as a quarter-wave vertical.

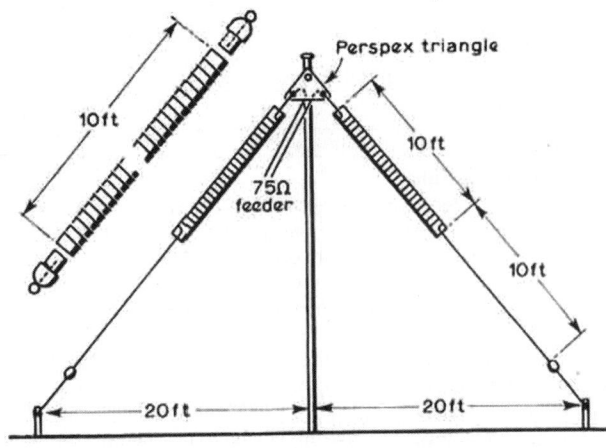

Fig 7. The BRS32857 version of the short dipole

operating from a location in a valley having very good earthing characteristics (G3TKN on a sandstone hill less than a quarter of a mile away generally had reports from North America about 10dB down). Clearly this is a useful configuration for the low-frequency bands, especially if you are fortunate enough to have ground of good conductivity below you.

Matching a Beam to a 300-ohm Feeder

Extracted from 'Technical Topics',
Radio Communication, November 1971

Matching a beam to 300Ω feeder

D. Boucheron, F2AI, in *Radio-REF* (No 7, 1971) describes a 14MHz two-element Yagi beam with a rather novel (at least to me) way of matching a feed point impedance of about 33Ω to 300Ω tubular feeder. He uses the well-known quarter-wave matching transformer, calling for a matching section of roughly 100Ω ($\sqrt{(33 \times 300)}$: Fig 8). The novelty is his use of two sections of RG8U 52Ω coaxial cable with the outer cables electrically wired together at the top and bottom, on the principle that this then forms a balanced 100Ω section. The use of two coaxial sections in parallel is fairly well-known, but I cannot recall seeing the series idea used before.

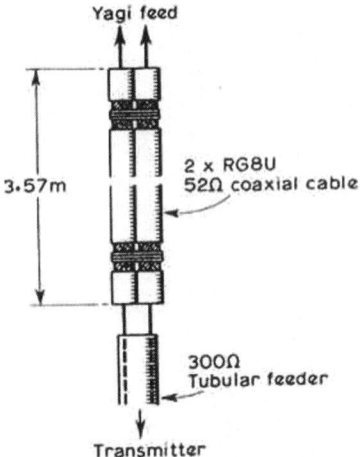

Fig 8. F2AI's method of feeding a 14MHz two-element beam using quarter-wave transformer of two coaxial cables. The length, 3·57m, is for 14,200kHz resonance

1.8MHz U-Type Marconi Aerial

Extracted from 'Technical Topics',
Radio Communication, November 1971

1·8MHz U-type Marconi aerial

A practical realization of the U-type 1·8MHz Marconi aerial recommended in the HF Aerials chapter of *Radio Communication Handbook* is warmly endorsed in a letter from Dr Michael Eccles, G3PPE/W6. He points out that this type of aerial provides the cross-polarization mentioned several times earlier this year in *TT*. Before he went to California, the aerial shown in Fig 9 plus a genuine 8W gave excellent results both on dx (W, OE, 9M4, 9V1 etc) and local stations. On dx he noticed far less fading than with either a horizontal wire or a loaded vertical while

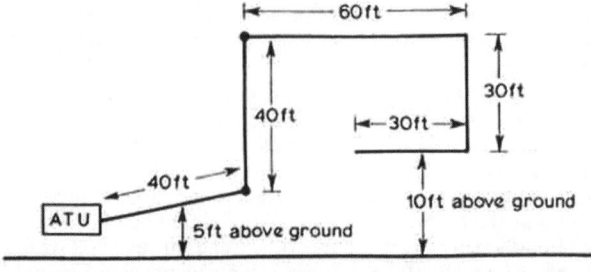

Fig 9. G3PPE's U-type 1·8MHz Marconi aerial

1970 - 1979

Maximum Gain of Yagi Aerials

Extracted from 'Technical Topics', *Radio Communication*, November 1971

Long Wires - and Upstairs Operation

Extracted from 'Technical Topics', *Radio Communication*, December 1971

Maximum gain of Yagi aerials

Although the Yagi-Uda aerial was first described over 40 years ago, there is still quite a bit of hit and miss in designing one—at least when compared with driven element arrays. In recent years there has emerged, for example, the Ehrenspeck backfire systems (see *ART*) though these have not been widely taken up by amateurs; this seems a pity as some time ago we heard about work on this system by one of the television receiving aerials firms which confirmed that useful extra gain can be achieved in this way, although it did not appear practicable to obtain the wide bandwidth needed for British four-channel uhf television.

Some recent work at the Danish Technical University at Lyngby (*Electronics Letters*, 9 September 1971) seems to open up further possibilities, though—to be frank—I find it difficult to fathom out exactly what the writers have in mind. What does emerge is that their work indicates that there is a further useful form of reflection-type Yagi, apart from the backfire. To quote the letter: "It appears that this reflection type Yagi-Uda antenna has, asymptotically, twice the gain of a conventional travelling-wave type or, expressed differently, for the same gain it needs half the length. This is somewhat similar to the backfire antenna which, however, requires a much larger extent traverse to the antenna axis."

As far as I can judge, they are proposing an array with maximized unequal spacing capable of giving an extra 3dB (double the power) of gain. The letter provides information on element lengths and spacing for 4, 5 and 6 element arrays, based on computer analyses; however, it is indicated that the results have been confirmed experimentally. What is needed is for someone to translate the graphs given in the letter into practical designs for amateur vhf operation.

On this question of achieving maximum gain with vhf parasitic arrays, it may be worth drawing attention to another recent item: an article on circular loop aerial arrays (*IEEE Trans. Ant. & Prop.* July 1971). While this is largely a theoretical study, the Japanese authors note that arrays using a driven loop in conjunction with parasitic loops can provide about 1·8dB more gain than a comparable conventional Yagi. Apparently this technique is used quite widely in a number of Japanese television receiving aerials. The following loop dimensions are suggested: a loop 1·1λ in circumference is said to work well as a reflector; 0·95λ a good director with 0·1λ~0·2λ spacing; it was found (and this seems an unexpected figure) that a driven element of 1·2λ ~ 1·3λ in circumference is desirable for high-gain and bandwidth.

A related form of aerial is the multi-element vhf quad; we recently noted in the Italian *Radio Rivista* (No 8, 1971) an 11-element quad for 144MHz with a claimed gain of 18–19dB! The elements are spaced along a 4·10m boom so that it is by no means an impossible size.

Long wires—and upstairs operation

The note in the October *TT* on the LA4LN arrangement for multiband operation of a 40m end-fed wire has reminded Dick Halls, G3EIW/ON8KM etc, of a useful tip on using long-wire aerials. As one of those amateurs who have operated in a number of different parts of the world, he has often found himself needing an aerial in a block of flats; quite often the only practical aerial is a long-wire strung out to a tree or other conveniently high point. In Singapore, for example, as 9V1LK, he used a 500ft wire and found this highly effective, particularly on 28MHz. But a common problem in such circumstances is that the earth lead on the transmitter and/or matching unit will often have standing waves with a voltage point where "earth" should be. This can frequently lead to excessive rf coupling into the mains supply, or result in hot points on the transmitter cabinet or on the atu, rf burns on the fingers, and bci/tvi in nearby sets in the

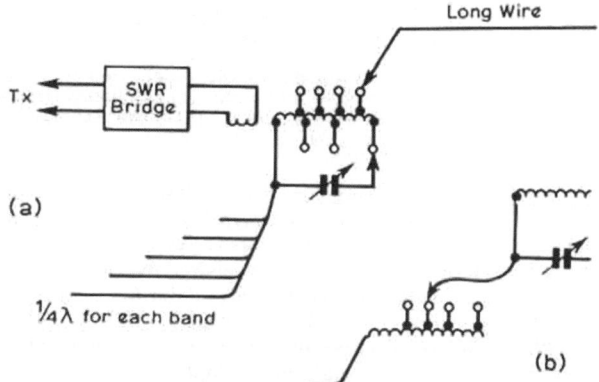

Fig 2. (a) ¼λ lengths of wire used to produce artificial earth for a multi-band long wire aerial; (b) alternative technique used tapped inductor with single wire. As recommended by G3EIW/ON8KM

same building. Dick Halls points out that if instead of trying to connect an earth to the atu/transmitter, one connects instead a ¼λ length of wire for the band in use, the rf hot point disappears, the other problems often vanish, and radiation and radiation patterns improve. For multiband operation a series of wires can be left permanently connected as in Fig 2(*a*); alternatively, instead of using several wires, it is possible to have a series-tapped or variable inductor which changes when the atu taps are changed: see Fig 2(*b*).

It so happened that a few days after receiving the note from Dick Halls we were using what was basically an LA4LN type of arrangement, with L-network matching, on 7MHz and the exact problem described by Dick Halls arose. Connecting a 33ft length of wire to the rotor spindle of the L-network capacitor completely cured the hot condition, even though this rotor was connected back to the transmitter earth through the feeder. So, this time, we can recommend this technique unreservedly!

ANTENNA TOPICS

All-band Double Dipole

Extracted from 'Technical Topics',
Radio Communication, December 1971

All-band double dipole
Now for another approach to a simple multi-band aerial. Many years ago we included in *TT* a DJ2ZF dipole for

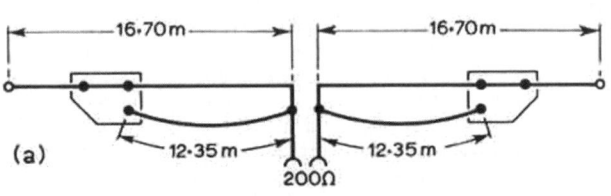

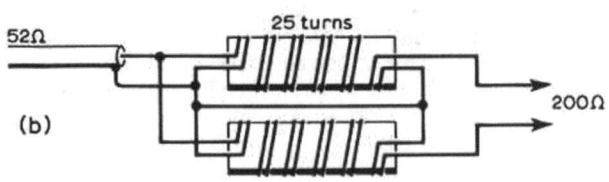

Fig 3. (a) The DJ4BQ five-band double dipole designed to provide 200Ω feed-point on all hf bands; (b) 4:1 balun transformer used with the double dipole to allow the use of 52Ω coaxial feeder

3·5, 7 and 14MHz having two 27m sections and fed with 300Ω line; this design appears in *ART* and has also been included in *Radio Communication Handbook.* However, neither this aerial, nor its half-scale version, made provision for 21MHz and neither was claimed as suitable for more than three bands. So we were interested to find in *DL-QTC* (No 10, 1971) a somewhat similar idea, but made suitable for all five hf bands by using a double dipole system having a shorter dipole suspended beneath the main wire, see Fig 3(*a*). The dimensions are such that the originator, Heinz Scheunemann, DJ4BQ, is able to show that the centre feedpoint impedance on all five hf bands (3·5, 7, 14, 21 and 28MHz) is approximately 200Ω; no traps or stubs are used. The aerial could be fed directly with 200Ω balanced line, but as this is not readily available, DJ4BQ shows how a 4:1 wideband balun transformer can be placed at the feed-point, so enabling the aerial to be fed from 52Ω coaxial cable (Fig 3(*b*)).

Aerial Feed Points and Radiation Patterns

Extracted from 'Technical Topics',
Radio Communication, December 1971

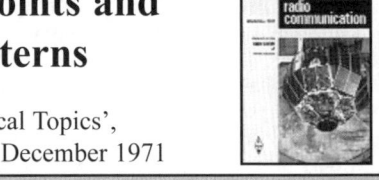

Aerial feed points and radiation patterns
In the early days of hf operation the average amateur often had very little idea indeed of the radiation patterns of different lengths of aerial wire. For this reason one of the articles which had a major impact on some of us was "DX to order" by Dud Charman, G6CJ, which appeared in the old *T & R Bulletin* back in January 1937. In that article he not only described the basic radiation patterns but also did so in relation to a great circle map. He succeeded in convincing at least one schoolboy reader that it really was possible to put signals out in the required directions! Of course that is now ancient history, and for many years radiation patterns have been such a standard feature of every amateur handbook that they are burned deeply into the consciousness of most hf operators.

But usually these patterns are shown as being symmetrical, and little or no indication is given that the position of the feedpoint can be used deliberately to distort the patterns and to put significantly more power into some of the lobes. Recently, John Brodzky, G3HQX, drew my attention to an idea by D. C. Cleckner in *Electronics Manual for Radio Engineers,* Zeluff & Markus, McGraw-Hill, 1949 (collected articles from *Electronics*). This article presented a number of patterns showing clearly the effect of changing the feed-point, and were based on work carried out on a scale-model, table-top aerial range. In practice, it must be pointed out, there may well be other distortions, and unless the aerial is well up and really in the clear it is usually over-optimistic to expect the pattern to be exactly according to the book.

It will be appreciated that there is a major difference in feeding an aerial at an internal voltage point rather than a current point in that this results in in-phase operation, but

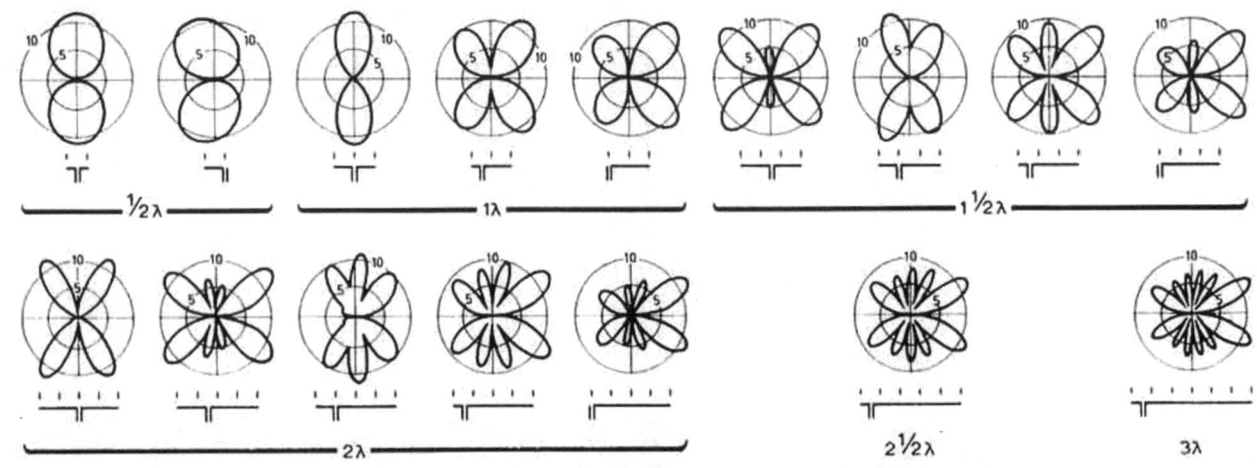

Fig 4. Horizontal radiation patterns of aerials indicating the effect of feed point. Based on model aerial range measurements by D. C. Cleckner (*Electronics Manual for Radio Engineers*)

the diagrams show that, apart from this, there are quite significant differences as one moves out from the centre point towards the end of the aerial. Generally an end-fed arrangement tends to put more pronounced lobes towards the free-end direction than backwards from the fed end. Fig 4 shows 16 of these patterns covering most of the possible arrangements for $\frac{1}{2}\lambda$, 1λ, $1\frac{1}{2}\lambda$, 2λ aerials, and examples of $2\frac{1}{2}\lambda$ and 3λ long wires.

One of the points which G3HQX noted, and which seems well worth emphasizing, was the very useful patterns of the little-used $1\frac{1}{2}\lambda$ aerial, which can be fed to produce either four or six main lobes in directions well suited to dx operation from the UK. And on this subject of $1\frac{1}{2}\lambda$ aerials, we noted in the October *TT* that the 90ft aerial described for 3·5/7MHz operation appeared to offer possibilities as a voltage-fed arrangement for 14MHz where it is roughly $1\frac{1}{2}\lambda$. Unfortunately, as L. F. Ivin, G5IC, noticed, the description of using the series tuning capacitor of this current-fed dual-band aerial suggested in the text that the capacitor is used on the *lf* band, whereas the circuit diagram showed it switched out of circuit on this band but used on the hf band. G5IC expounded an interesting theory on how a handwriting error could have caused this confusion. While agreeing that my handwriting could indeed cause such an error, reference back to the original source (*The Radio Handbook*) shows that the error crept in a long time ago, for the same mix up appears there. Personally, I suspect that the diagram, rather than the text, is correct, and that the capacitor is adjusted to accurate resonance on the hf band where the aerial functions as a $\frac{3}{4}\lambda$ wire; however, would-be users should be warned that it may be the other way round.

two cables concerned: see Fig 6. The original article provided fairly elaborate formulae for the construction of coaxial cable transformers. G3KYH suggests that, in practice, for this type of transformer a simplification will provide all the information that is necessary, viz

$$\cot^2\theta = \frac{Z_1}{Z_2} + \frac{Z_2}{Z_1} + 1$$

For a 50/75Ω transformer this works out to an electrical length of 29·3° for each section of cable; the physical length must take into account the velocity factor of the cable (typically for coaxial cable around 0·66).

Inverted-V W8JK

Extracted from 'Technical Topics',
Radio Communication, December 1971

Inverted-V W8JK

Two other aerials deserve brief mention this month. A note by Andrian Weiss, K8EEG/O in *CQ* (September 1971) indicates that a 70ft W8JK (Fig 5) aerial can form a potent bi-directional fixed beam when set up in "inverted-V" configuration. A roof top 10ft spacing boom mounted atop a short pole can readily provide about 40ft height at the centre, with the wires then sloping away to tree or other supports at about 20ft anchoring level. The array, it is claimed, still provides a useful 4·7dB gain on 7MHz and 6·2dB on 14MHz and can also form the basis of a top-loaded vertical for 1·8MHz (and presumably 3·5MHz). The W8JK configuration, of course, is well known, but I cannot recall having seen this type of mounting arrangement suggested before.

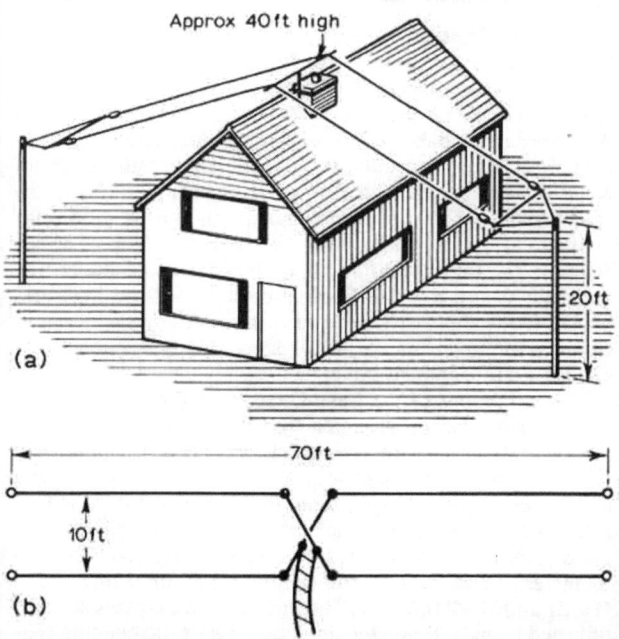

Fig 5. The K8EEG/O "optimum performance array for 1·8, 7 and 14MHz" aerial using the W8JK as an inverted-V fixed beam

Transmission Line Transformers

Extracted from 'Technical Topics',
Radio Communication, December 1971

Transmission line transformers

In the October *TT* a suggestion was included on how to modify a piece of RG58U coaxial cable in order to make-up a $\frac{1}{4}\lambda$ transmission-line transformer to match 50Ω coaxial cable to 75Ω coaxial. This had prompted J. A. Carter, G3KYH, and L. J. Rottier to point out that there is another rather more elegant (and simpler) solution to this problem, by using a relatively little known approach which also has other potential applications.

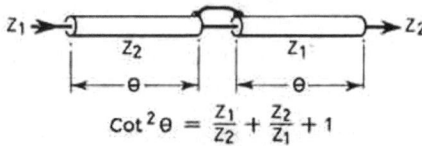

Fig 6. Transmission line transformer technique used to provide simple means of matching 50 to 75Ω coaxial cable

In an article "Wideband coaxial transformers using solid dielectric cables" (*Electronic Engineering* April 1962), two BBC engineers, A. B. Shone and W. Wharton, described a number of matching transformer techniques; one of these allows any two cables of different impedance to be matched together simply by using matching lengths made up of the

ANTENNA TOPICS

The DDRR as a 144MHz Mobile Aerial

Extracted from 'Technical Topics',
Radio Communication, December 1971

Also in the same issue John Schultz, W2EEY, explains in some detail the usefulness of a ½λ ddrr loop aerial which for 144MHz need be mounted only 1⅜in above a metal ground plane (thus making a very attractive mobile aerial). The configuration all seemed vaguely familiar until I remembered that the advantages of the half-wave form of ddrr appeared several years ago in *TT*, based on some work in Italy (see *Amateur Radio Techniques*, 3rd edition, page 184). Apparently a commercial model of this aerial has appeared in the USA. For 144MHz the loop is only about 11½in in diameter and is fed by coaxial cable between the grounded vertical radiator and a tap about ½ to ¾in along the circumference. It is claimed that with this type of aerial one can achieve low swr across the complete range of any vhf band. We should perhaps make it clear that the ddrr loop is not going to out-perform a simple dipole aerial, but on at least some bands overcomes the dipole length and directivity problems—it should also be noted that, if working correctly, the aerial is vertically polarized, which may or may not be an advantage when working mobile on vhf.

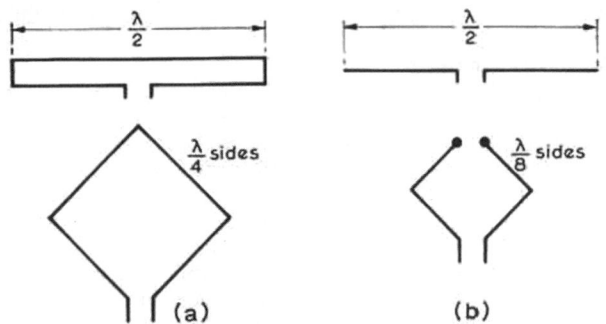

Fig 3. (a) Conventional quad based on folded-dipole; (b) Levy-Quad based on dipole reduces dimensions by one half with lower gain

The G8ON Multiband Aerial

Extracted from 'Technical Topics',
Radio Communication, January 1972

The G8ON multiband aerial

In *TT* (November 1971) a brief note was included on a 1·8MHz aerial used by G3PPE before he went to California; this was likened to the U-type, low-frequency aerial shown in *Radio Communication Handbook* (page 13.45). This led to correspondence with Harold Chadwick, G8ON, whose article ("The Top Band Special", *RSGB Bulletin*, September 1957) was the inspiration for the *RCH* notes. Later he showed ("The G8ON all-band aerial", *RSGB Bulletin*, June 1966) how this configuration could result in an effective multi-band aerial.

G8ON believes that the version built by G3PPE (and reported by him to be very effective but dependent on good earth conductivity) loses some of the basic advantages of the original; further he feels that the simplified diagram in *RCH* may mislead amateurs into thinking of the aerial as a current-fed Marconi. G8ON has been using and evaluating this type of aerial for 15 years; he considers it can perform well even over a poor sandy earth (some disappointments have been reported in areas of good earth conductivity). He also points out that the "in phaseability" between top and bottom wires is important, particularly when using it as a multiband aerial. Like G3PPE, he is convinced of its anti-fade properties, possibly the result of the mixed polarization. The main design aims are to achieve a current maximum at point X and voltage feed.

For those who do not have access to the earlier issues, the basic dimensions of both versions are given in Fig 4, although, if possible, reference should be made to the original articles which provide a good deal of additional information. G8ON has provided some information on 3·8MHz signal strengths during the early morning periods which appear to support his view that the angle of radiation is low. By using a loading coil on 1·8 and 3·5MHz (as described in his 1957 article), the aerial can be put up in less space than a trap-dipole or G5RV aerial, yet is resonant on one more band. But the main point on which G8ON insists is the need to bend the aerial "in the right places"; he thinks that because it is

The Levy Quad

Extracted from 'Technical Topics',
Radio Communication, January 1972

The Levy-Quad

The classic cubical quad, with full-wave loop, and sides of ¼λ makes—it is universally agreed—an extremely fine and effective dx aerial. But for 14MHz, it is big, oh so big! An alternative, half-size form, with some sacrifice of performance, has been around for some time, though we cannot recall it ever appearing in *Radio Communication*. This is the so-called Levy-Quad which is essentially just a ½λ dipole, bent round into a square, with ⅛λ sides and a gap of about 50cm at the top: see Fig 3. It is thus a cross between the usual quad and a Yagi. Feed impedance will be low, and probably the simplest way to feed it is to use a short length of resonant open line or 300Ω feeder with a Z-match or similar atu into coaxial cable.

The attractions of the Levy-Quad, as a simple directional aerial, have been set out again by J. P. Seuillot, F6AMA, in *Old-Man* (No 11, 1971)—the article was originally published in *Radio-REF*. This describes a two-element array, using a reflector slightly longer than the fed element, tuned by means of a stub section. The array uses a boom (2·5m) with cross-pieces formed of plastic tubes, 4m long and 32mm in diameter; these proved sufficiently rigid for a three-band (14, 21 and 28MHz) array. The three driven elements are best adjusted using a dip-meter since because of the bending they will be a little longer than the text-book figure for a dipole; it is also desirable for the current maxima to be in the element rather than in the feeder. For the reflector, the three wires are independent of each other.

F6AMA is apparently well satisfied with the results

easier to measure current than electrostatic potentials, the importance of the latter tends to be overlooked. Above all he is dismayed by some amateurs who have copied the "U" pattern in the horizontal plane (G8ON reckons this should be fine for satellite working but *not* for terrestrial dx!).

Another type of aerial which he finds effective, and again so often overlooked, is the sloping wire dipole, with the low

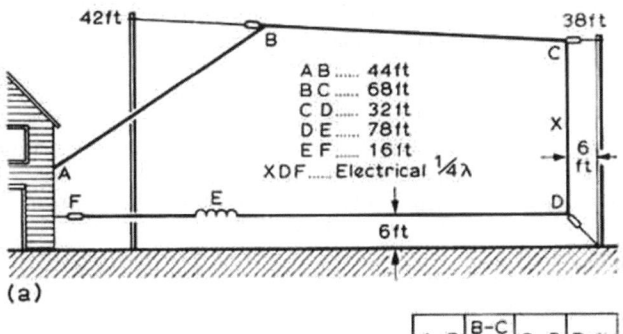

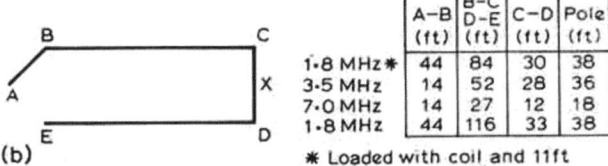

Fig 4. Diagrams reproduced from the original G8ON articles

end towards the target area; with one of these, with a 30° slope (but broadside to the USA with the high point to the south), he has kept an International Rotary Net schedule on 21MHz for 192 out of 204 Sundays in the past four years —more consistently than some members with beams.

Joost Berden, G3RND/G6AAR/T, is another reader who believes that for simplicity and efficiency there is still much to be said for long-wire aerials; he has a 240ft end-fed aerial, much of it at about 80ft thanks to a mast on an old railway bridge; on 3·5MHz he zepp feeds this with 600Ω open line from a Z-match atu or, alternatively, a Windom which provides a perfect match on 3·5, 7, 14 and 28MHz. He is thus a firm supporter of the theory that "old-fashioned" long-wire type aerials do work very well.

The Window-pane Simple Quad

Extracted from 'Technical Topics',
Radio Communication, January 1972

The window-pane simple quad

G8ON also mentions a subject which has long been a favourite theme of mine—that "textbook" aerials are not the only types that can be used, provided always that sound basic principles are followed. He uses no textbook types, even for Band I, III and IV television and Band II sound reception. For example his uhf television aerial is a coaxial-fed centre-tapped two-turn coil, 8in in diameter, indoors, 4ft above ground, yet 40 miles away from the new concrete aerial-support tower at Emley Moor. One day, he threatens, he will tune his dustbin as a cavity.

This brings us, conveniently, to what George Goldstone, W8AP, describes in *QST*'s Hints and Kinks (September 1971) as "a quickie quad for two". This is another aerial based on

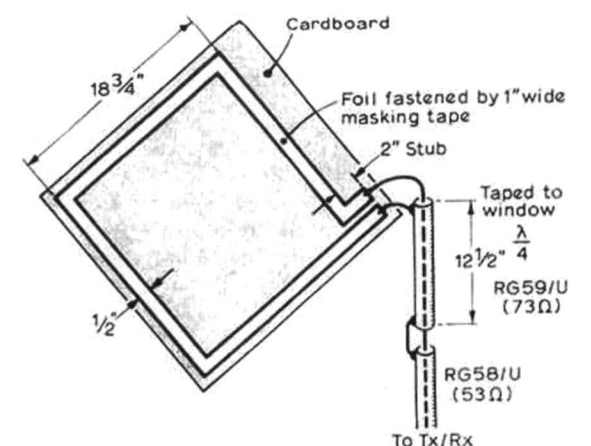

Fig 5. Window-pane single-element quad for 144 MHz operation using household aluminium foil mounted on cardboard

the use of household aluminium foil, mounted on a sheet of cardboard and taped to the inside of a window: see Fig 5. It looks as though it could form a useful travelling or alternative address aerial for local—and not so local—144MHz operation.

Construction is roughly as follows: Cut a piece of aluminium foil to the outside dimensions, and a piece of cardboard of the same size. With one-inch masking tape fasten the foil and cardboard sheets together on the window. Cut the inside of the foil out with a razor, taking care not to go through the cardboard and scratch the window. Then tape the inside edge of the foil to the cardboard, leaving the 2in slit free of tape. The $\frac{1}{4}\lambda$ matching transformer reduces the feed-point of about 100Ω to match the 50Ω coaxial. The aerial when arranged as shown results in vertically polarized signals: if it is moved around through 90° so that the feed point is at the bottom of the square, the signals will be horizontally polarized.

Log Periodic Dipoles

Extracted from 'Technical Topics',
Radio Communication, February 1972

Log periodic dipoles

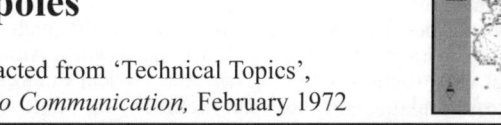

One of the very few basic new aerial structures to have been developed during the past 25 years is the log periodic. But generally amateurs have made relatively little use of this form of wideband aerial array—it is not, for example, even mentioned in *Radio Communication Handbook*. The reason for this lack of interest is not particularly difficult to discover: although the advantages of a non-critical wide-band aerial are well recognized, the gain/size ratio of a log periodic is usually well down on the more conventional Yagi-Uda arrays. But the log periodic—mostly in the form of the log periodic dipole (lpd) arrangement of Fig 1(a) has been widely used in hf communications where the ability to work on a number of different, non-harmonically related frequencies is often very important. More recently, it has come into considerable use for uhf (less frequently for vhf) television reception, particularly in tricky areas where its well-defined back-to-front ratio and smooth response patterns often prove very useful in eliminating ghosts and

ANTENNA TOPICS

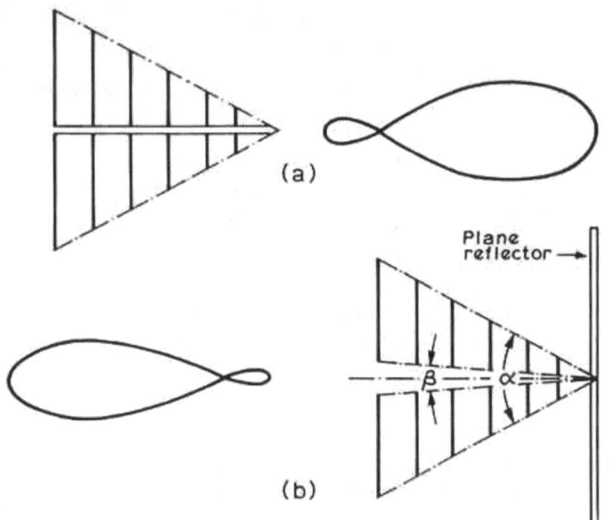

Fig 1 (a) Conventional form of a log periodic dipole array with its associated radiation pattern; (b) modified form of array showing axial displacement of elements and the plane reflector which increases gain and reverses the direction of fire; apex angle α and displacement angle β

the problem of different optimum pointing directions on different channels.

A few amateur hf designs have appeared from time to time: some years ago, for example, G3LQC described in the RSARS journal *Mercury* a practical 13 to 60MHz log periodic using a single pole, although needing a fairly large ground area (120ft by 50ft). This array was rather similar to the military aerials produced by Granger Associates. The G3LQC design provided a forward gain of about 6 to 8dB while providing a good match to 75Ω coaxial cable throughout the range 13 to 60MHz. For the current tv receiving aerials, a typical specification for a 21-element model covering all channels in Bands IV and V (470 to 850MHz) is a claimed 9·5dB forward gain (ref dipole) with about 30dB front/back ratio.

An interesting hf design using shortened dipoles only half the normal span was developed by Rohde and Schwarz—this had a capacitance hat in the form of a rhombic at the ends of the elements. At the other extreme, there is the large TCI array using stretched, capacitance-loaded elements (extended aperture) needing masts over 200ft high but providing gains of the order of 13dB (ref dipole). Another form of construction is the log periodic vertical monopoles with ground plane, and these can retain the desirable wideband characteristics. Another basic form is the log periodic Yagi (lpy), and an amateur lpy design for 50 to 52MHz appeared in *Ham Radio* (July 1969); this had five driven elements in conjunction with a further three parasitic elements and had an estimated gain of the order of 12dB.

In *73 Magazine* (October 1967) Hal Greenlee, K4GYO, provided information on designing vhf/uhf log periodics including a "log scan 420" array using four stacked log periodics to provide almost 15dB gain and 50MHz bandwidth. At that time, K4GYO suggested: "Soon vhf log-periodic antennas will be replacing Yagi arrays of practically all types, and also replacing old stand-bys such as the collinear, helix and corner reflector". He suggested that log periodics with small apex angles with a limited 1·5 : 1 bandwidth could deliver virtually as much gain as a Yagi of the same size and suitable for bandwidths of only a few per cent. But in practice the Yagi still seems the dominant structure.

But recently two new ideas for increasing the forward gain of log periodics have appeared, based on theoretical studies carried out at the Central Electronics Engineering Research Institute in India: see two papers by Murli Dhar Singh and Shiv Prasad Kosta in *International Journal of Electronics*, 1971, Vol 31, No 6. They point out that if the gain of the lpd can be increased without sacrificing the inherent bandwidth properties it would become a more useful device for long-distance communications. They suggest two modifications which together can provide a gain improvement of from 4 to 5dB, although it would appear that these figures have yet to be proved experimentally.

The first modification is to provide axial displacement of the dipole elements, the displacement increasing as the elements are lengthened: see Fig 1(b).

The second is a more fundamental change, reminiscent of Ehrenspeck's "backfire Yagi aerials" (see *Amateur Radio Techniques*), and consists of placing a large plane reflector at the apex of the log periodic, so that the beam is shot into the reflector and then back out in the opposite direction, and it is this which provides the bulk of the additional gain. It is suggested in the papers that by using a combination of these techniques, whereas a conventional lpd of practical size might have a gain of 8 to 9dB, the modified array would be capable of 13 to 14dB, which would clearly transform the system into a high-gain array.

Obviously the provision of a large plane reflector would not be easy for amateurs at hf, but should not be particularly difficult at vhf or uhf. It could well be that concealed in these new ideas is a most useful array for amateur operation—waiting to get out!

Wet-weather Ribbon Feeder

Extracted from 'Technical Topics', *Radio Communication*, February 1972

Wet-weather ribbon feeder

The 300Ω ribbon feeder remains a useful form of transmission line with a number of advantages over coaxial cable (and one or two disadvantages). One attractive feature is the easy check, with a neon, of standing waves; another is that short lengths can be used at high swr or as resonant sections

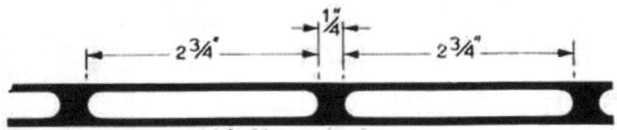

Fig 3. Modification of 300Ω flat ribbon feeder as suggested by G3WBT using a leatherpunch and fine scissors

without undue losses. A very common use is for the stub section of the popular G5RV multiband dipole.

Unfortunately, as is well known, the flat ribbon type of line undergoes significant changes during wet weather; the tubular form is much less affected but is also appreciably more expensive.

Quite a few years ago I recall an item in the *RSGB Bulletin* about cutting away a substantial part of the ribbon dielectric in order to reduce losses on vhf; in fact I spent some time converting a length of feeder in this way, although in the end too much of the ribbon got cut away with the result that the wire spacing tended to vary unless the entire feeder was kept under tension, thus defeating part of value of this type of cable.

Recently, Graham Thornburn, G3WBT, sent along a similar suggestion but with rather shorter slots, and it would seem this could make a very attractive modification. His reason for modifying the 300Ω ribbon was the change introduced in a G5RV not only by rain but also by sea spray at his site on the Cumberland coast.

He cut his ribbon rather like the well-known Dexion angle material; this was done quite easily with the aid of a leather-punch and fine scissors. With these aids, he was able to cut and pinch out slots 2¾in long, leaving ¼in ties between each slot, as in Fig 3. It took about an hour to modify 30ft.

The modified cable will, in theory, have a slightly different velocity factor, so that theoretically the stub section for a G5RV rises to about 29ft 6in or 30ft, though in practice he finds it will still usually work with about 29ft or so. Now he finds that neither rain, mist nor salt spray seem to have any effect on the aerial.

We suspect that cable modified in this way would also be useful low-loss vhf feeder. Back in January 1955, GM3BDA described how to make low-loss 360Ω balanced feeder for 144MHz using 18swg wire spaced ½in apart by means of ⅜in polythene tubing to form spacers every 9in or so, and the whole system kept under tension. The modified 300Ω cable should prove nearly as effective; it is often forgotten that at vhf and uhf even "low-loss" coaxial cable introduces quite significant losses.

readings reported by the German station may have been just "one of those miracles that make up the spice of the amateur's life". He thinks that DJ4BQ may have overlooked the basic fact that since the aerial element is not resonant, the feed-point impedance must comprise reactance as well as resistance, and reference to Jasik's *Antenna Engineering Handbook* suggests that on 3·5MHz this is going to make the feedpoint almost purely capacitive for the usual range of wire sizes. PA0SE puts forward the suggestion that, in DJ4BQ's case, it could be that his balun compensates for the "weird impedance" with which it is presented. Since we presented in *TT* only the aerial and not the technical commentary of DJ4BQ, we will restrict this comment to just these remarks, and thank PA0SE for his detailed analysis. But we would be interested to know if anyone tried one out and, if so, what results or swr readings they obtained.

Multi-element Dipoles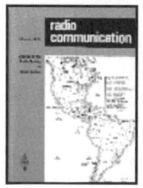

Extracted from 'Technical Topics',
Radio Communication, March 1972

Aerial Topics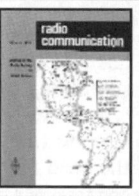

Extracted from 'Technical Topics',
Radio Communication, March 1972

Aerial topics
One subject affects all amateurs and listeners, whether phone or cw addicts, whether favouring commercial or home-brew gear: the perennial topic of aerials. This month the ideas are mostly follow-ups to types discussed over the past few months—but surely no less useful for that.

First a comment from Les Moxon on the "Levy-Quad" (*TT* January). He points out that it would be better when using this type of structure to turn the aerial upside down (electrically) and voltage feed at points a, b, of Fig 3. This places the maximum current section higher off the ground. But he warns that no matter which way round it is arranged, the radiation resistance will be down to about 5Ω; this in itself is feasible for single-element quad-type aerials but G6XN feels that it would be unsuitable for building into a beam array, since this will further lower the radiation resistance to around 2Ω. G6XN described a number of related aerials in an article in *CQ* (November 1962).

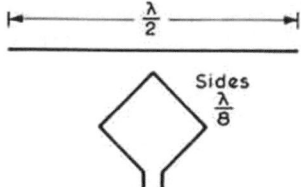

Fig 3. Preferred method of using the "Levy-Quad" element as suggested by G6XN. The aerial is voltage-fed at a,b.

Dick Rollema, PA0SE, is worried about the technical justification provided by DJ4BQ in his original description in *DL-QTC* (No 10, 1971) of the all-band double dipole (*TT* December 1971). He warns that the favourable swr readings reported by the German station may have been just "one of those miracles that make up the spice of the

Multi-element dipoles
In *TT* August 1971 we reported, from a visit to the Admiralty Surface Weapons Establishment (ASWE) that the British Navy uses a form of broadband hf dipole consisting of four or five spaced wires joined at the centre feed points but left disconnected at the far ends. At the same time we included a design of a 7MHz broadband dipole by WB5ACP comprising a four-wire dipole (using rotor cable) with the ends fanned out and the lengths staggered in increments of 6in.

It was, therefore, with something of a shock that we recently came across in *IEEE Transactions on Antennas and Propagation* (September 1971, pages 682-684) a letter from S. K. Chowdhury of Jadavpur University concluding as follows: "A new wide-band antenna has been developed from a very simple idea. Its impedance properties have been investigated both theoretically and experimentally. The results indicate that it can be used where the bandwidth requirement is less than a log-periodic array but much larger than a single dipole. It has the added advantage of light weight, and it can be fabricated very easily."

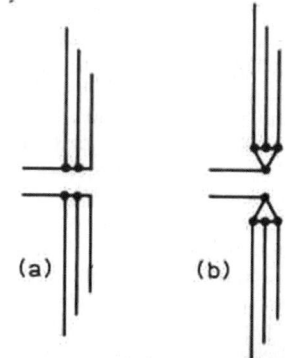

Fig 4. Chowdhury multi-element dipoles: (a) fed directly from two-wire transmission line: (b) via conical conductors

Reference to Fig 4 shows that this new aerial is, in effect, a cross between the ASWE and WB5ACP aerials and has the same basic ideas. We are not, of course, suggesting that someone is trying to claim credit to which they are not entitled: rather it is another example of how the same ideas and proposals tend to germinate at roughly the same time in many minds in many parts of the world.

ANTENNA TOPICS

The experimental trials in India were based on uhf models at about 85cm (350MHz) with a spacing between adjacent elements of 0·5cm and a preferred difference in length between adjacent elements of 0·25cm. It thus seems that this form of construction represents a useful approach for a non-critical single-band dipole at almost any frequency from hf to uhf. At hf an easy way of fabricating a dipole with two elements would be to use 300Ω ribbon, as is often done for two-band aerials, but with just a few inches difference in length; one application would be for portable operation to avoid having to trim to resonance when putting up the aerial at different heights.

So it really does look as though a valuable new idea has emerged from these Indian, British and American sources.

28 MHz 'Folded Stacked Dipoles'

Extracted from 'Technical Topics', *Radio Communication,* April 1972

28MHz "folded stacked dipoles"

From Ted Cook, ZS6BT, comes a further idea on folding aerials into loop-type aerials, stemming from a recent need to establish a 28·5MHz link over about five miles with 5W. A conventional dipole failed to produce sufficient signal and improvement was sought if this could be done without anything too fancy. So it was planned to try a pair of co-linear dipoles (Fig 3(a)) voltage-fed from coaxial cable by means of a lightweight matching unit suspended in the aerial, and the matching unit shown in Fig 3(b) was built. This has 10 turns on a ribbed and grooved former, ¾in diameter, as L1 with six turns overwound to form L2. C1 was a tiny 30 + 30pF air-spaced split-stator with C2 a 100pF mica compression trimmer, all mounted in a 4 by 4 by 3in plastics box with feed-throughs on top and a coaxial socket underneath, capable of being made fully waterproof after initial adjustment, and suitable for powers up to about 10W. But before the original plan was implemented another idea occurred to ZS6BT, why not bend round two full-wave wires to produce a loop ¾λ long with ¼λ spacing between them: Fig 3(c).

The system is brought to exact resonance by L1-C1, and L2-C2 tuned to series resonance. Once the transmitter has been tuned into a dummy load at the aerial end of the feeder, a reflectometer can be inserted between coaxial and matching unit and the unit tuned up until (a) the aerial draws the same load as the dummy load; and (b) zero swr on the feeder. The matching unit can then be sealed, and hangs from the centre of the lower element. A piece of vertical nylon cord between upper and lower elements keeps the spacing correct and helps take the small weight of the matching unit.

ZS6BT reports results as fantastic. Perfect aerial balance, perfect resonance, absence of standing waves and the gain of a two-over-two co-linear array—and judging from mobile checks with sharp beam focus.

ZS6BT puts forward a further possible application of this "double-quad loop"—this time for 144MHz. Two similar loops from small diameter tubing, both with L1-C1 and one driven by a coupling coil, spaced one-fifth wavelength apart. ZS6BT feels such an arrangement would form the basis of a double-quad rotatable array with the back-to-front ratio tunable by a capacitor; the loops would be only 5ft by about 20in but should represent something like eight half-waves in

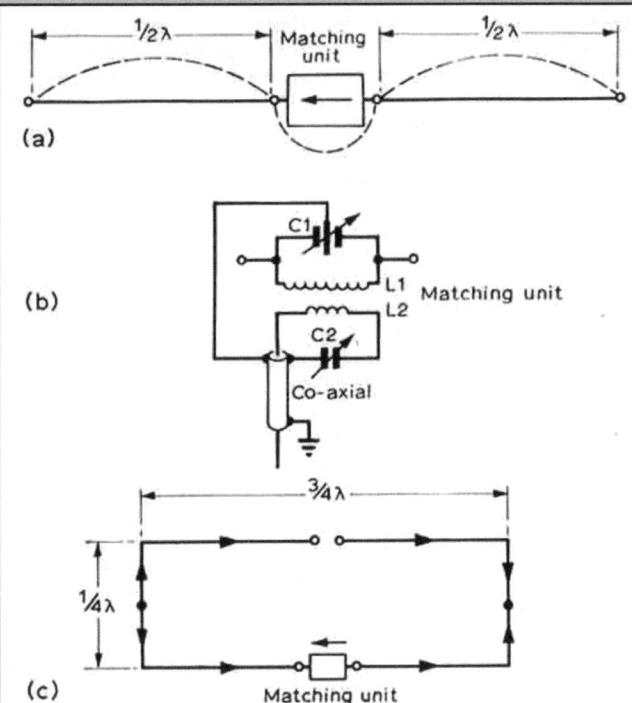

Fig 3. Development of ZS6BT's "double quad loop" or folded stacked dipole aerial for 28MHz

phase with the back-to-front ratio of a quad array. This idea has not been used in practice but might give vhf operators something to try.

Another possibility, it seems to me, would be to try feeding the aerial with open-wire zepp feeders to eliminate the need for a matching unit.

Short-Span 3.5MHz Dipole

Extracted from 'Technical Topics', *Radio Communication,* April 1972

Short-span 3·5MHz dipole

A frequent requirement in these days of low sunspot activity is for a 3·5MHz dipole that will fit into a small garden. Peter Waters, G3OJV, has been using the configuration shown in Fig 4 to good effect; although only 20ft high he has been getting useful reports on ssb from VE, KP4, VP2 etc.

Dimensions of the various sections are not important provided that the whole aerial is made to resonate. The simplest method is to make the dimensions roughly as above but

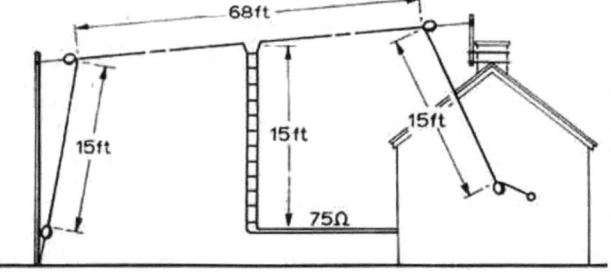

Fig 4. Short-span 3·5MHz dipole found effective by G3OJV, using section of open line or 300Ω feeder

with 18ft of 300Ω ribbon or open-wire feeder in the centre and then to trim this back for minimum swr at the transmitter end. The resonant feeder section can be fed by coaxial cable (preferably with a balun) or with 75Ω balanced twin. With a little care, the aerial will work usefully also on 14MHz. In this case, first disconnect the entire feeder and feed directly at the top with coaxial cable, adjust length for minimum swr which will indicate three half-waves on 14MHz. Then add 18ft feeder as before and adjust for minimum swr on 3·5MHz. G3OJV says the swr on 14MHz should not be affected.

Although the approach is akin to the G5RV, G3OJV considers that it provides vastly superior swr on 3·5MHz and makes feeding much easier.

Also in the aerial department are useful ideas from Dick Halls, G3EIW/ON8KM, (power meter/dummy load) and S. M. de Wet, ZS6AKA, (loop-type aerials) both of which we will try and squeeze in before long.

Of course, one must always remember that almost any wire provided it is correctly matched to the transmitter can perform well on hf in good conditons. But there is no doubt that it is useful to have a radiation pattern that puts signals where they do the most good.

Experiments with Multiband Loop Aerials

Extracted from 'Technical Topics', *Radio Communication,* June 1972

The One and a Half Wavelength Dipole

Extracted from 'Technical Topics', *Radio Communication,* May 1972

The 1½λ dipole

When various radiation patterns by D. C. Cleckner were reproduced in *TT* (December 1971), we reported that John Brodzky, G3HQX, had drawn particular attention to the useful pattern provided by the 1½λ wire (ie about 102ft on 14MHz, 67ft on 21MHz).

This has prompted Alf Bruce, G5BB, to mutter hear-hear, and to relate his experiences with the version shown in Fig 4. For a number of years he had used a ½λ dipole on 14MHz, until Percy Heston, G5HS, recommended him to try a 1½λ—"I took his advice and have never looked back". Total length is 102ft of 16swg hdc fed at the first ¼λ current lobe (17ft from the house end) with 75Ω flat twin feeder. This has brought plenty of useful dx, with a radiation pattern that appears to be closely akin to that shown in the December diagram. G5BB is now firmly convinced that, at least for a UK station, this provides good all-round coverage of the main dx areas.

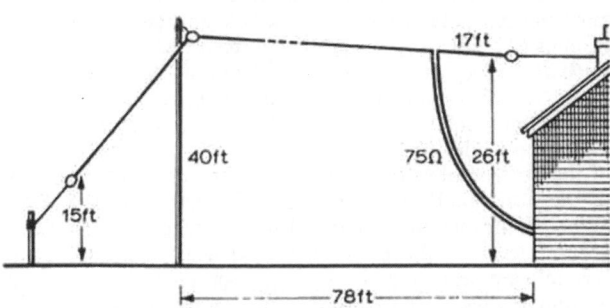

Fig 4. The 14MHz 1½λ aerial used at G5BB

Although essentially a single-band aerial, he has found it works quite well on 21MHz (though he has since put up a second 1½λ wire for this band) and by using one side of the feeder as a long wire also on 3·5MHz. Certainly the list of stations worked by G5BB on cw and ssb shows the day of simple wire aerials, even on highly competitive bands, is by no means over; particularly as they benefit from the beam receiving facilities so often used at the other end.

Experiments with multiband loop aerials

S. M. de Wet, ZS6AKA, recently sent along some most interesting notes on a series of experiments he carried out during the South African summer in the investigation of multiband loop-type wire aerials. He points out that the large "loop" configuration is consistently omitted from the standard engineering textbooks (possibly, he believes, because the mathematical analysis of practical harmonic loops would present a particularly sticky problem).

As noted on several occasions in *TT*, loop aerials made from a λ-length of wire (as in the standard quad) have some interesting properties, for example, the "G2PL Special" which emerged from operating a quad-on-its-back on the ground. ZS6AKA has taken this type of approach further in order to investigate loops suitable for multiband operation, in his firm belief that simple aerials can often prove surprisingly useful.

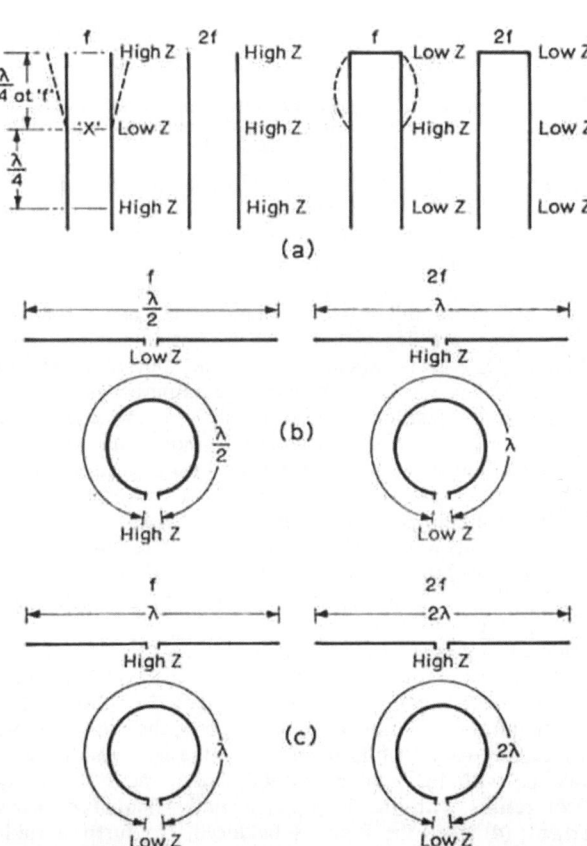

Fig 4. Principles of harmonic loop aerials with low-impedance feed point. (a) transmission line analogues; (b) half-wave on fundamental results in mixed impedances; (c) full-wave gives low-Z on fundamental and harmonics

ANTENNA TOPICS

ZS6AKA notes that a good insight into the impedance behaviour of aerials can be gained by considering them as a special kind of transmission line. The classical cases of transmission lines are: (*a*) terminated in their characteristic impedance; (*b*) end open-circuited; (*c*) end short-circuited. In Fig 4 (*a*) and (*b*) he shows the open- and short-circuited cases; the dotted lines indicate the transmission line being "opened" so that it begins to radiate: X indicates a physical spot on the line. It can be seen that if *f* is the lowest frequency then the impedance in the open-circuited condition is low for odd harmonics and high for even harmonics; the opposite applies for the short-circuited line.

If one starts with an aerial one-wavelength long or one-wavelength circumference at *f*, then the input impedance will be high for all harmonics in the case of the open aerial, and the impedance would be low for all harmonics of *f* in the case of the loop: see Fig 4(*c*). ZS6AKA considers that a high input impedance is awkward to handle, but that the low input impedance loop can be useful in a number of cases.

As with an open line aerial (for similar practical heights), the loop will give all-round radiation, mostly upwards, for the lower frequencies, but breaks up into a series of lobes when operated at higher frequencies. Fig 5 shows some of the practical configurations tried by ZS6AKA. The measuring instruments were crude but the 1λ loop test set up showed an input impedance of about 100Ω at 3·5MHz increasing to about 200Ω at 28MHz, though the 28MHz impedance proved difficult to measure.

Some other general observations were: (1) the loop tuned much more broadly than a dipole; (2) the voltages along the loop were much lower than a dipole; (3) although the loop requires a minimum of three supports, the extra support was usually easy to find in practice—the best results were obtained with the loop horizontal, but it did not greatly affect results with the loop horizontally slanted or even vertical; (4) when the input is balanced, the furthest mid-point may be earthed; (5) when the loop is fashioned in rhombic shape it does in fact become a rhombic directional aerial at the higher frequencies with a low input impedance; (6) if the shape of the loop is changed from circular to square, triangle, rectangle and the like, the radiation resistance decreases as the enclosed area decreases—this means that a shape may easily be found which has an input impedance of 50Ω; (7) and finally ZS6AKA notes that there are many shapes and mounting configurations which remain to be explored.

ZS6AKA (c/o Racal-SMD Electronics (Pty) Ltd, PO Box 60, Irene, Transvaal, South Africa) would be interested to hear from anybody who has better measuring equipment and is able to provide accurate figures for radiation resistance etc at various frequencies. He believes it would also be useful if someone could measure actual field patterns.

While a number of these configurations (for instance, the vertical triangular loop) are becoming quite widely known and used, it seems pretty clear that there is still useful experimental work to be done in collating and refining the principles and practice of wire loop aerials. ZS6AKA is to be congratulated on giving us all a useful shove in this direction.

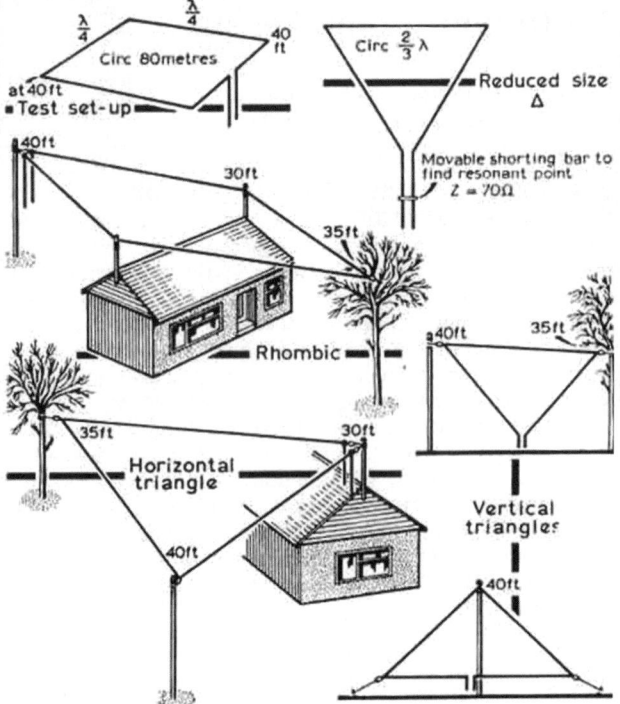

Fig 5. Some of the configurations tried by ZS6AKA. No unbalanced transmitter line currents detected with either twin or coaxial feeder

Vertically Phased Arrays

Extracted from 'Technical Topics', *Radio Communication,* July 1972

Vertically phased arrays

Suddenly all the amateur journals seem to be filled with articles on vertically-polarized phased arrays, either to form a fixed beam, or, as in the design given in *TT* (September 1970) using switched delay lines to provide electronic steering. It should not be forgotten that there are some alternatives to the grounded monopole approach: one is the Bobtail (*TT* July 1970); another is resurrected in PA0SE's *Reflecties* (*Electron* April 1972) from a 1934 design by PA0ZN. This is shown in Fig 6 and will be seen to have a close affinity to the Bobtail but is even simpler to try out. The Zepp feeder provides a voltage feed at the centre point of the horizontal span, with cancellation in some directions of the horizontally polarized radiation from the top span. Some people may not like the idea of voltage points down at ground level at the ends of the vertical sections, but it certainly amounts to an easily implemented design. It would presumably work, though rather differently, on all multiples of the fundamental frequency.

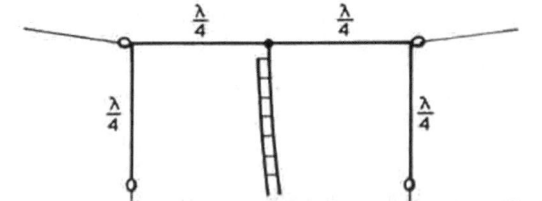

Fig 6. A 1934 aerial by PA0ZN as described by PA0SE in 1972

High-angle 'Super-gain' Dipole

Extracted from 'Technical Topics', *Radio Communication,* July 1972

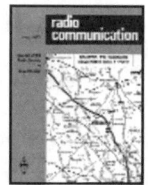

High-angle "super-gain" dipole

In most of what is written about amateur radio aerials, it is assumed that the prime object is to work long distances, calling for maximum low-angle radiation. But there are exceptions to this requirement: some amateurs want to maintain regular contact with stations at quite modest distances. For this, high-angle radiation and reception not only provides a useful boost to signals, but also discriminates against unwanted signals coming in at the lower angles. High-angle systems are widely used in tropical broadcasting stations, and Paul Sollom described a number of arrays based on this approach some years ago in the *RSGB Bulletin*.

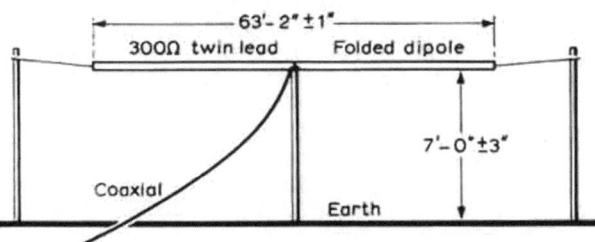

Fig 8. High angle "super-gain" dipole

Old Man (Nr 11/1971) reprints an article by Ed Dusena, W4NVK, on "A super-gain antenna for 40m". In effect this is a folded dipole slung just 7ft above ground and fed by 50Ω coaxial cable to take into account the low feed impedance resulting from the aerial's proximity to ground. The arrangement is intended for working over distances of about 50 to 200 miles, but is said to be reasonably effective at times up to about 1,000 miles. The ground effect is increased by placing three reflecting wires of non-critical length, 65 to 85ft, along the ground directly beneath the aerial.

In *TT* (March 1971) we reprinted the diagram of a three-band vertical aerial ($\frac{5}{8}\lambda$ on 14MHz but effective also on 7 and 3·5MHz) by Peter Brekken, LA1EI, from his original article in *Amator Radio*. At the time we admitted that there was a good deal more to his article than just the diagram. It was, therefore, interesting to find an English translation in the annual antenna issue of *Ham Radio* (May 1972) including a full discussion of the design principles, and adding further confirmation to the initial impression that this is a useful design for dx operation.

Matching Mobile Whip Aerials

Extracted from 'Technical Topics', *Radio Communication,* July 1972

Matching mobile whip aerials

Phil Zeid, 9M2CP, whose previous contribution to *TT* was the large Z-beam (August 1971), now comes up with a novel and apparently effective system of feeding mobile whip aerials—or indeed other short aerials. He uses a broad-band ferrite-core transformer, similar to the type found in 4 : 1 bifilar-wound baluns but having taps taken off one of the windings to provide a selection of matching ratios. No details are given of the actual core used, although clearly

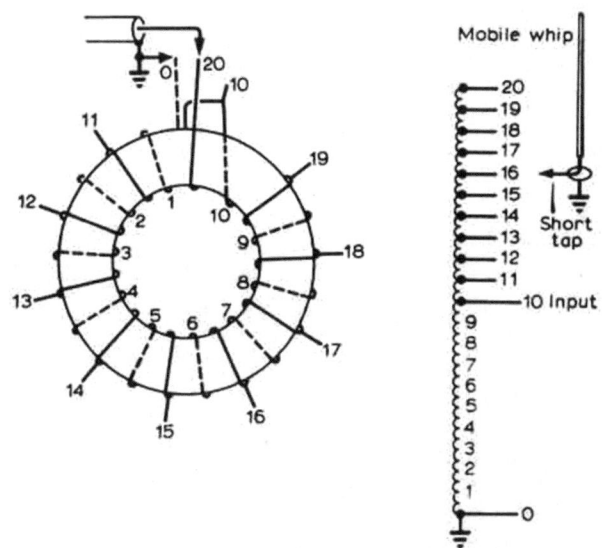

Fig 9. 9M2CP's ferrite broad-band bifilar-wound step-down rf transformer for use with mobile whip aerials. Approximate step-down ratios for the various tap positions: 20, 1·0; 19, 0·90; 18, 0·81; 17, 0·72; 16, 0·64; 15, 0·58; 14, 0·49; 13, 0·42; 12, 0·36; 11, 0·30; 10, 0·25

this could be similar to the type used by G3CDR in his inverted-L aerial (*TT* February 1971) or, of course, a ferrite-core type balun converted to this purpose.

The details given in Fig 9 are largely self-explanatory but 9M2CP adds the following notes: "Keep earth point of the coaxial shield near the base of the whip to a good chassis earth. A 1 : 1 swr can be obtained only at the resonant frequency of the aerial. Adjust aerial to the approximate frequency (or accurately with a noise bridge). Use tap giving lowest swr. Check the frequency giving lowest swr. Re-adjust length of aerial. Repeat if necessary. Tuning is very sharp on low-frequency bands."

Although the principle is a simple one, 9M2CP has not seen it described anywhere and has not come across anyone else using the technique. In practice he finds it gives outstanding results and considers: "It is comforting to ride along and, on your desired frequency, hardly see a movement on the swr meter when pushing out peak power!"

9M2CP does not indicate on which bands he uses the system and we suspect that this may be rather more on hf bands than is usual in mobile operation here; nevertheless the idea is well worth keeping in mind.

ANTENNA TOPICS

A W8JK in the Loft

Extracted from 'Technical Topics',

The Loop and Low-Frequency DX

Extracted from 'Technical Topics',

A W8JK in the loft

Quite a few hf amateurs depend on loft or roof-space aerials and most will have found that results are in line with those described by John Roscoe, GM4QK in *Radio Communication* October 1970. There is no doubt that one loses a good deal of power in absorption and reflections of the water tank and electric conduit; my own feeling is that these losses are more significant than the actual roof attenuation which can be quite low, at least in dry weather. But the loft aerial does make hf operation possible, and can give reasonable dx.

Recently, Brian Booth, G3SYC, noting the interest in "wire aerials", sent along details of the simple single-section, end-fed W8JK that he has been using on 21MHz. This fits quite conveniently into the average roof space as indicated in Fig. 4(a).

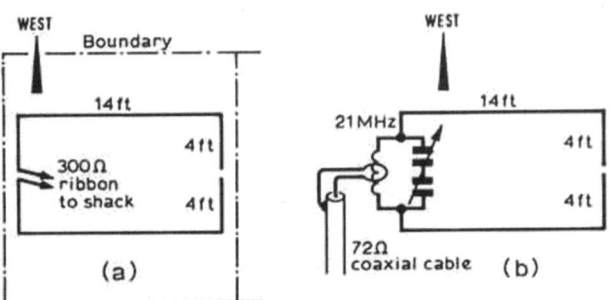

Fig 4. Simple single-section end-fed W8JK beam with "bent-in" ends favoured by G3SYC for loft use. (b) shows his proposed modifications

He writes: "It's simply voltage-fed and has really surprised me as to what an indoor aerial can do. I have used it in comparison with a 21MHz dipole and have never received reports other than that the beam was two S-points better. In bad conditions 4,000-6,000 mile dx cannot hear me on the dipole although my signals are workable on the W8JK. I know that this form of W8JK is not original, but I feel that the W8JK driven beam, in all its many forms, makes one of the best amateur radio antennas and is sadly neglected. After using them for a number of years I have great faith in them—particularly the low-angle benefits they give."

"This particular array is due for further development soon; the wire is being replaced by lightweight ⅜in aluminium conduit which should broaden bandwidth and improve efficiency. A tuning unit is going to be placed in the aerial (as in the ZS6BT aerial described in *TT*, April)."

Stirred by G3SYC's letter, I put up a simple wire aerial to these dimensions in the roof space (very much around the plumbing) using a half-wave of 300Ω line to provide a resonant feeder. It all worked "first go" and in a few days provided a reasonable selection of contacts with Europe, and North and South America, though perhaps a little less consistently than the comparison 132ft end-fed (of which about 35ft are indoors). Because of the low radiation resistance of the bent W8JK (and hence high currents and voltages) results could almost certainly have been improved by using better wire and insulation; but certainly the aerial itself seems virtually fool-proof even when entirely indoors.

For anyone with a much larger roof space, an extremely interesting technique would be to form one of these W8JK arrays using G6CJ's "stretched dipole" (capacitively loaded wires) technique, since this would not only raise the radiation resistance but should be significantly less influenced by the proximity of the water tank etc. Because of the difficulty that newer members may have in getting hold of G6CJ's original 1961 paper on this technique we have included the bare bones in *ART4* for easy reference.

The loop and low-frequency dx

Interest in dx on the 1·8, 3·5 and 7MHz bands has increased steadily in recent years, and with the current phase of the sunspot cycle it seems likely that even more effort will be concentrated on this subject this coming autumn and winter. From time to time, *TT* has drawn attention to the use of vertically or dual-polarized aerials for such operation (incidentally the advantages of dual-polarization for hf are again underlined in an article by Walter Stiles, W7NYO in *QST* March 1972). Another approach, a little neglected, is that of the advantages that can sometimes be achieved by using different aerials for transmission and reception. Amateurs with plenty of room have a "natural" in the Beverage *receiving* aerial (*TT* October, 1970 or *ART4*).

Some pertinent remarks about low-frequency dx aerials appear in *Ham Radio* (June 1972) in a letter from Harry Hyder, W7IV. He points out that while (with good earth systems) vertically polarized aerials usually radiate more at lower angles than the horizontally polarized aerials that are practicable at these frequencies, the vertically polarized aerials may result in up to 10dB more man-made noise. Because of this horizontally polarized aerials may be a better choice for *reception*.

Another reason for the use of separate aerials is the possibility of achieving good directivity on reception. Most of us have to write off any prospect of an efficient rotary beam for 1·8MHz! But in fact, for reception, this is entirely possible—in the form of the traditional loop or frame aerial, or its more modern equivalent the ferrite rod.

A recent contributor to *World Radio Club* described the reception of medium wave broadcast stations in the Far East and Pacific areas, in the West Coast of the United States and in South America with the aid of a frame aerial consisting of about seven turns of wire on a frame with (I think) 40in sides, tuned by a 500pF capacitor and with a single turn coupling coil connected to the dipole sockets of his receiver. This allowed him to null out interference from European stations while digging for the dx. I remember once using an almost identical system and finding to my great surprise that the Irish Radio Athlone programmes appeared to be transmitted (with commercials and all) from wartime England. At the time I almost convinced myself that this was due to some fundamental error in my amateur df—but years later read that this was actually done to prevent the Athlone signals providing a beacon for aircraft navigation!

So there might well be possibilities in using say a top-loaded omnidirectional vertical for transmission plus a loop for reception. And if you feel that "loops" are too old-hat, one could become trendy by designing this in the form of an "active" aerial by building in a transistor amplifier (see, for example, "Active loop-dipole aerials" by P. A. Ramsdale and T. S. M. MacLean in *Proc IEE*, Vol.118 No 12 December 1971.)

The Coaxial Collinear Array

Extracted from 'Technical Topics',
Radio Communication, September 1972

The coaxial collinear array

In searching through the professional journals for ideas that might offer something of real practical interest to amateurs, a phrase such as the following can be calculated to attract attention: "There are a variety of situations in present day hf or vhf radio/radar applications that require a directional antenna which is lightweight, portable, easily-erected and reasonably inexpensive." You can say that again!

And this, in fact, is the promising start of an item, "A portable coaxial collinear antenna", by B. B. Balsley and Warner Eckland in *IEEE Transactions on Antennas & Propagation* (July 1972, pp 513–516). Further reading revealed a down-to-earth description of the construction of a 26-element aerial for 49·8MHz having a half-power beamwidth of 5·6°, using a technique which could readily be applied to similar or much less ambitious arrays for amateur hf or vhf work: Fig 2. Basically the principle is very simple: it is to form a collinear array by connecting together a string of $\tfrac{1}{2}\lambda$ (electrical) sections of coaxial cable, interchanging the inner and outer conductors at each junction. In this way it is clearly possible to form a collinear array (because the "wrong-phase" sections are shielded within the cable) without any of the usual phasing sections. Further, since the velocity factor of the cable is about 0·67, each half-wave will be only about a third of a wavelength long physically.

Although the authors state frankly that the idea has been around for some time, and used before, it was new to me.

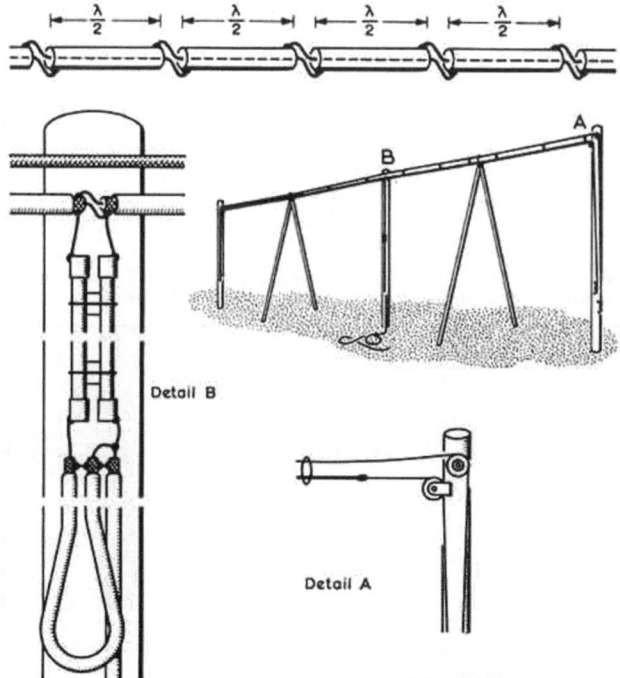

Fig 2. Basic principles of the coaxial collinear array and details of the 26-element array described in *IEEE Trans*, with coaxial aerial mounted on three poles. The nylon messenger line and polyethylene slip rings used to connect to the aerial are shown in inset A. Inset B shows feed arrangement consisting of balun and a quarter-wave matching transformer. All the electrical connections are waterproofed

However, a few days later, when talking to Vic Hartopp, G8COB, technical director of J-Beam, he immediately recognized the technique as having been used commercially in West Germany and also (for marine applications) by his own firm, though he agreed that little use appears to have been made of the principle for amateur operation.

The 49·8MHz aerial is formed from RG-8 coaxial cable (for use with radar peak powers up to over 100kW) with each junction carefully sealed and weatherproofed, and then suspended from three poles (plus guying between poles) using a series of slip rings and a $\tfrac{3}{8}$in nylon messenger line. The array is centre-fed from coaxial cable via a balun and quarter-wave matching section, although a balanced twin-line 300Ω feeder would probably be suitable where, as in this case, there are a considerable number of elements, with rather lower impedance for fewer elements. At the junctions the outer braid of the cable is peeled back about 1in from each cable end to expose the polyethylene insulation; the inner core is bound round and soldered to the outer braid of the next section. The weather sealing consists of first coating the entire connection with silicone sealant and then covering the joint with heat shrink tubing (such joints are claimed to withstand temporary tensions of over 300lb). The aerial is fed at the two outer (braid) conductors of the centre elements. (I am not sure from the diagram whether the inners are actually connected at this point, although from theoretical considerations this would appear to be immaterial).

The entire 26-element array, including messenger line, weighs less than 30lb and can be stored in a container 2ft by 2ft by 1ft; it is stated that total construction cost was about three times the cost of the coaxial cable; installation time (assuming the support poles are in place) less than one hour. Bandwidth to vswr of two is about 1MHz for the 49·8MHz array. The authors also indicate that by using four of these 26-element arrays (representing 104 elements), correctly phased, a half-power beamwidth of only 1·4° was achieved.

Probably few amateurs would aim even at 5° but with many less elements it should be quite easy to achieve, say, 15° in the two lobes (see *Radio Communication Handbook*, p13.56, Fig 13.96, for polar diagrams of collinear arrays with five elements and less). With two arrays and appropriate phasing, it would be possible to make a unidirectional aerial along the lines of the G8PO and ZL-special.

So, though we stress G8COB's comments that this is not a new idea and is not foolproof, it seems well worth bringing it to the attention of amateurs, for hf and vhf fixed beams, and for portable applications.

Polarization Switching Made Easy

Extracted from 'Technical Topics',
Radio Communication, September 1972

Polarization switching made easy

In *TT* (July 1970) when describing a vertical-T or inverted ground-plane aerial that I had been using on 14MHz, I stated: "The ease with which a dipole aerial can be converted to a vertical-T suggests that it should be relatively easy to develop an aerial which could be switched from horizontal to vertical polarization and vice versa". At the same time attention was drawn to a Telefunken mf broadcasting aerial which allows polarization to be changed at dusk to reduce interference.

ANTENNA TOPICS

Now in *CQ* (July 1972), Ken Glanzer, K7GCO, follows up this suggestion and describes "The 10°–90° antenna for

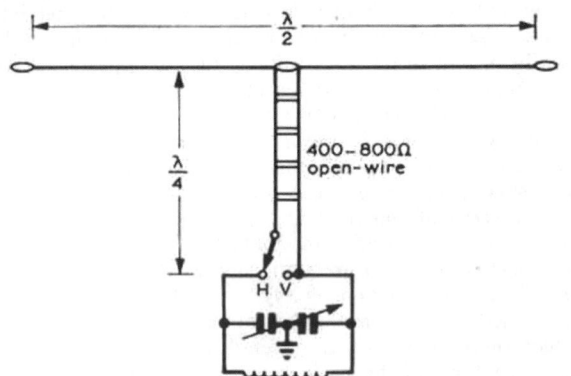

Fig 3. The K7GCO aerial for 3·5 and 7MHz can be switched from vertical to horizontal polarization using the inverted ground-plane or vertical-T principles described in *TT* (July 1970)

75 and 40 metres": the two angles referring to the predominant vertical radiation angle—90° with the fairly low horizontally polarized dipole and (hopefully) 10° with the aerial in its vertical-T configuration. Those who recall the original *TT* notes (also *ART3* and *4*) will have little difficulty in sorting out the K7GCO arrangement of Fig 3. The twin open-wire feed is used as such for horizontal polarization, but switched so that both wires go to the same side of the matching coil to form the voltage-fed ¼λ top-loaded vertical. In his implementation of this arrangement, K7GCO incorporates remote switching and remote (selsyn) tuning of the matching unit, in his belief that it is very useful to be able to switch rapidly between the two polarizations to take advantage of propagation quirks, noting that there may even be occasions when it is better to switch to a different polarization for reception than transmission—which is in line with our remarks in the August *TT*.

Five-band VS1AA / Windom

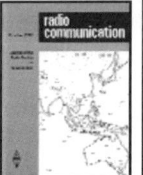

Extracted from 'Technical Topics', *Radio Communication*, October 1972

Five-band VS1AA/Windom

Some 43 years ago (*QST*, September 1929), L. Windom, W8GZ, described the original single-wire-feeder Windom aerial. This utilized the fact that when an aerial is resonant, the impedance at any point along its length is a pure resistance—which in practice varies from under 50Ω to about 5,000Ω. There is thus always some tapping point at which the radiator can be matched to a transmission line—which can take the form of a single wire. In these conditions the wire no longer radiates or has pronounced standing waves on it, but acts as though it were a conventional transmission line.

The original Windom was essentially a one-band aerial and sometimes proved pretty critical to adjust (usually by running a neon along the feeder to see if there were pronounced standing waves). Soon afterwards, G2BI showed that by cutting the feeder carefully so that the whole system provided resonance on a lower frequency band, it was possible to use a Windom quite effectively on, say, 7 and 14MHz. Then

Jim MacIntosh, VS1AA (now GM3IAA), in his classic "Some experimental work with aerials", (*The T & R Bulletin*, November 1936), introduced an important new idea—the "one-third" tap: "During the course of experiments with a 264ft Windom, it occurred to the writer that there must be an arithmetical relation between these somewhat mythical tapping points, and after a little juggling with pencil and paper, the fraction one-sixth was evolved" (ie one sixth from the centre). He added: "This one-sixth business sounds too good to be true, but it at least has the merit—if such it may be termed—of being geometrically correct." And so was born the multi-band VS1AA which is still going strong, particularly in some parts of Europe. Actually, since the original work was carried out by GM3IAA while he was VS2AF I suppose to be strictly accurate it should be known as the VS2AF. By using the one-third tap on a 138ft wire (and using thinner-gauge wire for the feeder) one still has a very useful four-band aerial for 3·5, 7, 14 and 28MHz.

In recent years, the VS1AA has been given a new lease of life in its twin-wire form, using a conventional 300Ω balanced feeder instead of the slightly more critical single-wire. Theoretically the impedance at the one-third tap is of the order of 500Ω (or rather less, due to the presence of ground etc) on 3·5, 7, 14 and 28MHz. Unfortunately this is not the case on 21MHz where the point is at high impedance. One method of coping with 21MHz, suggested some years ago by W9GJY, is to add two shorted quarter-wave stubs at 76ft and 38ft from the feed point—but stubs are never very popular.

An alternative technique is described by F. Spillner, DJ2KY, in *QRV Amateur Radio*, Nr 8, August 1972. He uses a 1:6 balun with 60Ω coaxial cable for the feeder, but 300Ω or open-wire line, or single wire feeder could be substituted. His basic idea is to make use of the well-known multi-wire dipole technique adding two wires, 4·5m and 2·25m as shown in Fig 1. This seems a usefully simple approach to five-band operation.

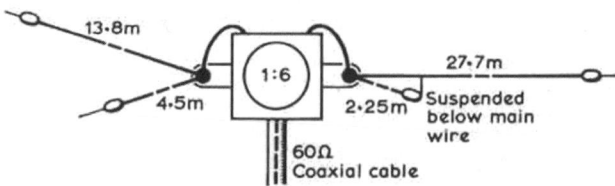

Fig 1. DJ2KY's five-band Windom. 300Ω twin line could be used instead of the coaxial cable plus 1 : 6 balun transformer

The DDRR Aerial Again

Extracted from 'Technical Topics', *Radio Communication*, October 1972

The ddrr aerial again

In *TT* (August 1971), John Pegler, G3ENI, questioned the results sometimes claimed for the ddrr low-profile aerial and called for comparative results. None came forward at the time but now in *QST* (July 1972), Robert Dome, W2WAM (of ssb phasing-rig fame), provides an interesting analysis of quarter-wave ddrr aerials. He suggests that efficiency will usually be very low compared with a half-wave dipole suspended well above earth, and bandwidth will be narrow.

These are because of the extremely low radiation resistance (typically 0·095Ω), so that (as in the small transmitting loop) conductor ohmic losses consume most of the power.

The original ddrr (as described by J. M. Boyer, W6UYH), had an electrical height of only 2·5°, representing about 1ft for a 7MHz aerial. Now W2WAM suggests that a modest increase in vertical height could improve the efficiency very appreciably because the radiation resistance for short vertical heights varies as the *square* of the height. He believes that increasing height to 3½ft instead of 1ft would raise the radiation resistance to 1·16Ω which, with typical conductors etc, would increase efficiency from around 2·75 per cent to 25·8 per cent, or a 9·8dB improvement—and a 25 per cent efficiency for a vertical radiator should give quite useful results. Of course, I suppose if one carried this to a logical conclusion one would be saying in effect that a top-loaded vertical can be very effective! But the W2WAM article clearly points the way to achieving a useful ddrr aerial provided one remembers the ohmic losses etc and avoids unsuitable thin wire construction. And may I put in a plea for more investigation into the ½-wave closed-loop version (*ART3* or *4*) which seems to have significant advantages?

voltage drops slightly. Most amateurs have long used bulbs and neons to check aerials but the novelty of G2ALM's arrangement is to have them both connected permanently and simultaneously.

Another Look at the Coaxial Collinear

Extracted from 'Technical Topics',
Radio Communication, November 1971

Another look at the coaxial collinear

Several comments have come in on the coaxial collinear array described in September *TT* (incidentally is it collinear or colinear—both spellings abound in the various text books?). John Roscoe, GM4QK, for example, suggests its value for amateurs who want to try an Indian rope trick by lifting one end with a model helicopter powered over the cable!

Pol Parrott, G3HAL, has come across a note in the vhf column of *QST* (August 1961) in which W6PIV briefly mentioned his use of a 144MHz vertical based on the same technique in conjunction with radials and a first element one quarter-wave long: see Fig 4. The only claims made for it were that it gave low-angle radiation and made use of odd pieces of coaxial cable. The dimensions shown are for a centre frequency of 147MHz (the American band extends from 144 to 148MHz) with a suggested change of 0·2in/MHz per half-wave section for shifting frequency.

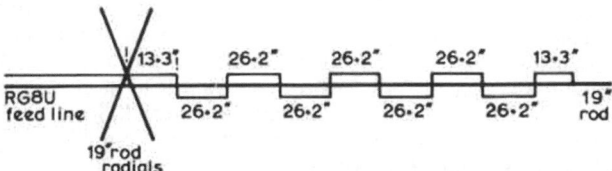

Fig 4. The W6PIV version of the coaxial collinear aerial for 144MHz (for convenience the aerial is shown horizontally but is of course mounted vertically)

Long Wires - Some Hints

Extracted from 'Technical Topics',
Radio Communication, October 1972

Long wires—some hints

The 132ft long-wire remains deservedly a popular multi-band aerial—but it can produce arguments about just how long it should be—132ft, 136ft, 138ft etc are all commonly recommended figures. The theoretical length (which can be affected by height above ground, "bends" and near-by objects) varies quite significantly with the bands, due to the "end-effect" which need be taken from only one half-wave.

Table 1—Resonant lengths

3,500kHz	133·7ft	14,300kHz	135·9ft
3,600kHz	130·0ft	21,000kHz	139·4ft
3,700kHz	126·5ft	21,450kHz	136·5ft
7,000kHz	137·0ft	28,000kHz	139·7ft
7,300kHz	131·0ft	29,700kHz	131·7ft
14,000kHz	138·8ft		

In *QST* (July 1972), Howard Hanson, W7MRX, lists the theoretical lengths for various frequencies (see Table 1) spanning from about 126 to 139·7ft. While we are not too sure that this matters much in practice, for those who like to feel their aerial really is resonant, he comes up with a solution: a "stretcher" comprising two No 12 copper wires running the length of a 7ft board, about 2½in apart, rather like the old Lecher wires, with a sliding short-circuit (see Fig 2(a)). The slider consists of two springy copper plates clamped centrally to a plastic pill bottle which acts as a handle. This can be readily moved along to provide up to 14ft of extra wire in the aerial (though because the wires are close together the effective length will be rather less).

This idea brings to mind another dodge intended to provide a clear visual indication of just what is happening to long-wire resonance. It stems from Roy Wilkins, G2ALM, and consists simply of connecting a small pilot bulb between tuner and aerial *and* a neon bulb through a suitable resistor down to earth, as in Fig 2(b). If the aerial is exactly resonant, there will be virtually no current to light the bulb, but as it goes off resonance the bulb will begin to light up and

But clearly the system did not catch on, and some of the reasons for this appear in some most interesting comments from "Dud" Charman, G6CJ. He recalls that the first references to this type of array date from 1935 but adds that he feels there must be something inherently amiss with the technique "or it would surely have been seen more often". He mentions that the redoubtable Alan Blumlein tried to use one as a television transmitting aerial in the early days of high-definition television, using 4in coaxial copper pipes! Sad to recount "it did not work—the reason may be that Blumlein was not an aerial man, and this was probably the only one he ever made—but there were engineers there who could have made it go it if were go-able."

Stirred by the revival of interest in this system, G6CJ has made a mathematical analysis of the array to try and reconcile the problems of some users (a fact underlined in our comments in September) with the results described in *IEEE Trans Ant & Prop*, July 1972. One conclusion he reaches is that when used as a transmitting aerial "half the power pumped into the system is cooking it" with the power reaching the outermost ends reduced. He adds: "I somehow do not think it will ever find a great use in the amateur field, partly because long lengths of coaxial cable are too expensive for most of us, but also because unless it is a fairly long array I do not think it will work properly". His analysis suggests that the fairly high attenuation in each

ANTENNA TOPICS

section actually contributes to the very good radiation pattern reported, as this means that large reflections will not be returned from the ends to disturb the critical distribution of current between inner and outer conductors; this taper contributing to the low side-lobe levels.

Of course with a large number of elements the 3dB waste of power would not necessarily rule the system out of court, but for fewer elements it would be a significant disadvantage compared with conventional arrays with stubs.

But if you do get one to work really well you will have achieved something that the great Blumlein never did!

A G6CJ Special

Extracted from 'Technical Topics',
Radio Communication, November 1972

A G6CJ special

In commenting on the coaxial collinear and the use of insides and outsides of coaxial cable, Dud Charman, G6CJ comes up with another system which is unlikely to be known by many amateurs. It was invented in the fifties and the patent has now expired—and G6CJ says it worked perfectly, and is one answer for the amateur who lives in an attic and can use only end-fed arrangements. He also believes that it would make a fine aerial for uhf television reception because it could be made of stiff rods (G6CJ once tried to interest one of the firms in this field "but they didn't bite"). The system is made as follows, he writes: "You take a length of coaxial cable; join a quarter-wave of wire to the inner conductor at the far end; at the other end put a quarter-wave rejector at the point where you want it to stop being an aerial. This is fine but somewhat mismatched. So take a quarter-wave of cable as a dummy and lay it alongside and adjust the spacing. That works.

"Now double it and make a half-rhombic. The two cables are bonded at the end of the rejector, so you have a very convenient place to put the termination resistor.

"This system was made to work at 400MHz, and we were able to terminate it and match it to provide an swr of 1·1. It needed special care with the resistor."

So that—plus Fig 5—forms the basis of what I have taken the liberty of calling a G6CJ special. It would be interesting to hear how it makes out on vhf or uhf! Incidentally, this adds further support to a long held belief that the various "long wire" rhombics and vee-beams are sadly neglected on vhf and uhf, the part of the spectrum where one does not need a field to put up a rhombic.

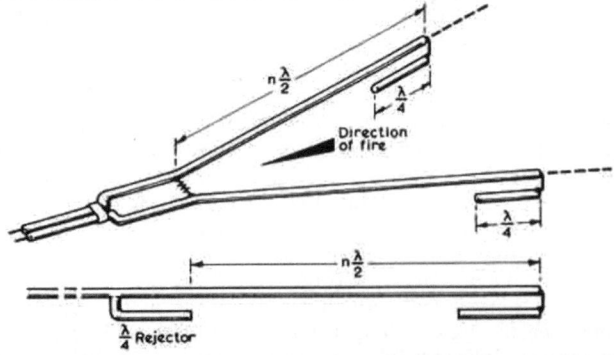

Fig 5. The G6CJ special based on coaxial cable, stubs and terminated half-rhombic configuration to provide directional beam for vhf and uhf applications

All-band Terminated Long-wire

Extracted from 'Technical Topics',
Radio Communication, November 1972

All-band terminated long-wire

From Richard White, G3SRO, comes a reminder that an all-band aerial that does not require an atu (at least for matching purposes), yet can give a satisfactorily low swr across all the hf bands, is the terminated long-wire. He uses one about 400ft long and 40ft high: see Fig 6. At the far end this is terminated with a non-inductive high-wattage 500Ω resistor earthed to an 8ft aluminium stake via a vertical down-lead. The transmitter feeds the aerial via a ferrite toroidal step-up transformer using a toroid of unknown origin about 1½in diameter. The transmitter feed goes to a three turn winding and the aerial to seven turns

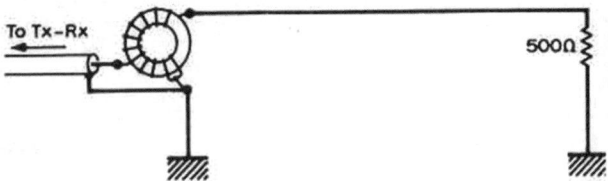

Fig 6. G3SRO's terminated long-wire aerial with ferrite broad-

bifiliar wound and spaced. This gives a worst swr on any band (3·5 to 28MHz) of only about 1·8 to 1. In practice the aerial has the two main lobes to be expected from the theory of non-resonant aerials, showing up well on 14MHz and above. By directing the aerial towards central America, G3SRO gets good coverage of North and South America.

Multi-band Verticals

Extracted from 'Technical Topics',
Radio Communication, December 1972

Multi-band verticals

Some 15 years ago, Hans Ruckert, VK2AOU, developed a multi-band aerial technique that had a good deal in common with the multi-resonance tuning circuits that at one time were quite popular for transmitters and aerial tuning units. The VK2AOU approach depends on the fact that a half-wave dipole with two parallel-tuned resonant circuits in series at the centre is resonant at three different frequencies, and no others. He exploited this technique to form tri-band

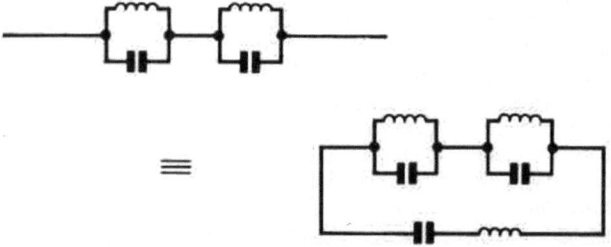

Fig 7. Basic principles of the VK2AOU three-band dipole element

beams, including a tri-band single loop quad element (published originally in *Amateur Radio*, April 1968).

For example, if two equal lengths of wire are strung up horizontally with two parallel resonant circuits inserted near the centre, investigation with a good grid dip meter coupled to either tuned circuit should indicate three resonances, not necessarily harmonically related, and no other pronounced dips: see Fig 7.

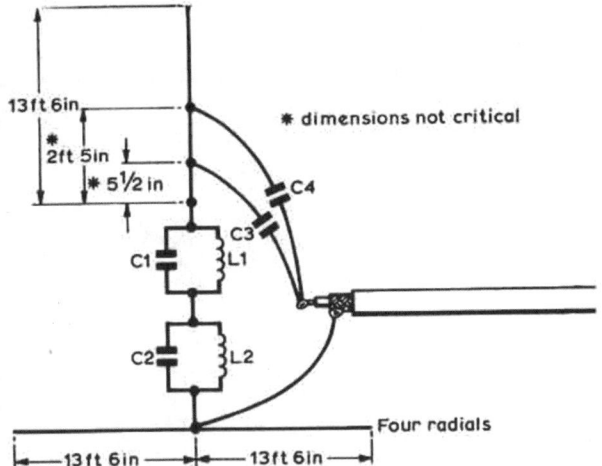

Fig 8. Ground-plane for 14, 21 and 28 MHz bands. L1 mainly affects 14 MHz, 6½in piece of 14 gauge wire bent into semicircle; L2 mainly affects 21 MHz, 2t No 14, 1⅛in dia, ½in long, leads 2in and 4in long. C1 mainly affects 21 MHz about 160pF; C2 mainly affects 28 MHz, 60pF; C3 mainly affects 28 MHz, 55pF (adjustment fairly critical); C4 mainly affects 14 and 21 MHz, 52pF (adjustment fairly broad). Space gamma section 2in from radiator to 2ft 5in tap, otherwise swr on 28 MHz may be seriously affected

Ian Pogson (VK2AZN/T and originator of the home-built Deltahet receivers) has recently described two multi-band verticals based on this three-resonance technique; one covers 14, 21 and 28 MHz; the other 3·5 and 7 MHz. He provides (*Electronics Australia*, August 1972) a four-page description of the construction and adjustment of this form of aerial, and some of the finer points must inevitably be lost in a brief summary. However, it is felt that at least some readers will be able to work out the essential data from the diagrams, once the basic principle has been grasped. We would not be inclined to recommend the multi-resonance technique to someone who is not armed with a good gdo or not prepared to take time to ensure that the system is really working as it should be. Of course this warning goes for most aerials—since dimensions and adjustments always tend to be affected by the environment, by the screening, and (particularly for verticals) by the ground conductivity and so on.

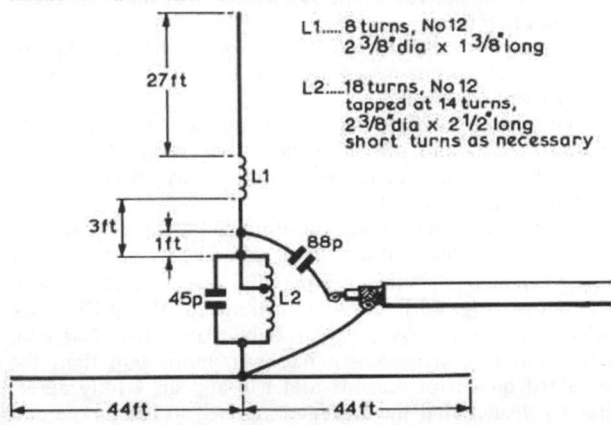

Fig 9. Ground plane system for 3·5 and 7 MHz

For the higher bands, the basic element lengths fall between those which would normally be used on 14 and 21 MHz: in other words the system is shortened for 14 MHz, somewhat lengthened for 21 MHz, and lengthened still further for 28 MHz. Ian Pogson suggests that the element dimensions given in Fig 8 are about the longest for the frequencies involved, and that it would be possible for rather lower efficiency to reduce the vertical radiator and radials to about 11ft; if this is done it will be necessary to set about finding the necessary values for L and C. The feedline is 75Ω coaxial cable, and it is stated that the whole system can be set up to provide "a low" swr on all bands, though no figures are quoted. All the capacitors were of the miniature variable type, each in a protective plastic container derived from pill boxes and other pharmaceutical products. L1 is just a semi-circle of a 6½in length of wire. C3 and C4 are mounted close to the end of the feedline; the lead from C3 should be a heavy gauge of wire run directly to the tap point 5½in up the vertical element. Greater care is needed with the lead from C4 to the tap 2ft 5in up the element—this must be run parallel with the vertical element starting from an inch or two of the bottom to form a gamma matching arrangement.

Ian Pogson describes a wooden base for mounting the vertical element and the four horizontal radials, all made from 1in od dural tubing, but presumably other forms of construction could be used, or the vertical element fed against a very good earth.

We are by no means certain from the description whether the main application of the original aerial has been as a receiving or transmitting aerial, although both uses are mentioned. So, for someone prepared to experiment, this technique looks interesting.

Unidirectional Dipoles?

Extracted from 'Technical Topics',
Radio Communication, December 1972

Unidirectional dipoles?

We have suggested before in *TT* that there is a place for receiving aerials that provide signals which may be weaker than those from a normal dipole but which possess desirable directional characteristics: for example frame aerials, found useful for mf and 1·8 MHz dx reception (*TT*, August 1972).

An interesting new concept has been reported recently (with detailed mathematical analysis) by Y. Mikuni and K. Nagai of the Toshiba Research Centre (*Electronics Letters*, Vol 8, No 19, 21 September 1972, p472-3). This consists of a unidirectional dipole aerial intended primarily for vhf television reception but which might well have amateur applications.

The aerial closely resembles a shortened folded dipole, but with the two connecting links at the ends made up of an impedance (capacitor in series with resistor) rather than just a short-circuit. It then acts rather like an extremely close-spaced two-element beam.

Fig 10 suggests that front-to-back ratios of up to 30dB have been achieved experimentally and closely conform to theoretical predictions (though there are still frequency differences between theoretical and experimental performance).

A warning to those who think this means that they can quickly convert a folded dipole into an effective beam aerial: the "gain" is given as about 13dB below a dipole—so it is not going to make an effective transmitting aerial. But it is

ANTENNA TOPICS

pointed out that in a high noise-temperature area, such as a city, the signal/noise ratio of a received signal may actually be higher than with a dipole, because of the directivity.

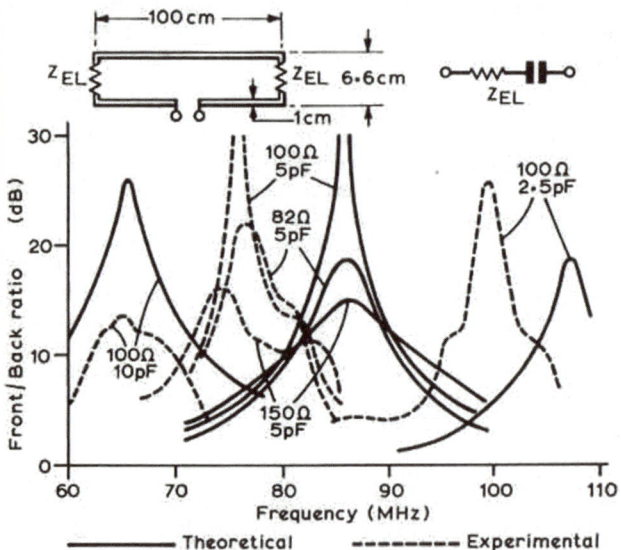

Fig 10. Details of the unidirectional dipole technique showing the front-to-back ratio at various frequencies and with various impedances, theoretical and experimental results

One suspects that for most amateur vhf applications, this arrangement would be less attractive than more conventional arrays: on the other hand the very high back-to-front ratio might make such an aerial a very good receiving system for hf, cutting down signals from the Continent, while open to North and South America.

On the subject of compact directional receiving aerials, we recall seeing in 1968 a demonstration at Hanslope of the EMI-Cossor series of active aperiodic loops (*TT*, July 1968) providing equivalent directivity to a full-scale rhombic. Current advertisements appearing for what looks like the same idea (but marketed by Hermes Electric) say that more than 53 government agencies are now using this form of broadband 2-32MHz receiving aerial; in rosette configuration such active loop systems can provide an omnidirectional "antenna farm" in only one-hundredth of the space needed for an equivalent configuration of rhombics!

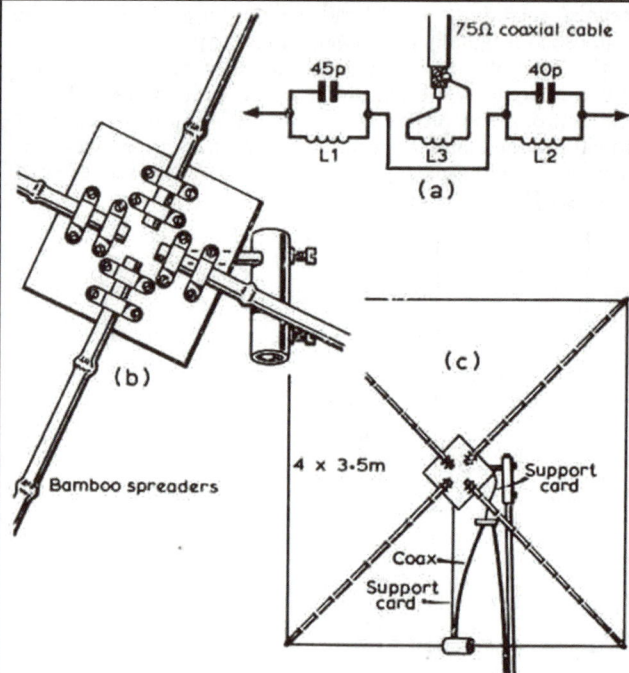

Fig 4. The three-band (14, 21 and 28MHz) single-element quad of PA0HTR based on the multi-resonance technique. The single trap inductor is wound on a former 8cm long with diameter of 3·7cm, L1 7 turns, 1·6cm long; L2 5 turns, 1·1cm long; L3 4 turns, 1cm long. L1 resonates at 17MHz, L2 on 23MHz. Constructional details show how the element is formed and supported

Three-band Single-element Quad

Extracted from 'Technical Topics', *Radio Communication*, January 1973

Three-band single-element quad

Last month we included some notes on multiband vertical aerials based on the multi-resonance technique where the traps are both at the centre of the aerial. Looking through some old copies of *Electron* recently, we came across (No 12 1968) an example of this technique in a single-element three-band (12, 21 and 28MHz) quad described by H. A. Kanon, PA0HTR.

L1, L2 and L3 are all wound on the same former, making the whole construction look quite simple: see Fig 4. Capacitors must be high-voltage types up to 10kV, and the trap-system waterproofed etc. Weight of the traps is supported from the centre board.

Multiband Loops and Quads

Extracted from 'Technical Topics', *Radio Communication*, February 1973

Multiband loops and quads

Recently we have included information in *TT* on multi-resonance quad and dipole elements incorporating traps (*TT* December 1972 and January 1973). But this is not the only approach. Just as, say, a 132ft long-wire aerial will resonate on all hf bands from 3·5 to 28MHz without any special loading, so can loops be used on more than one band without alteration.

A pioneer in this field was Les Moxon, G6XN, and before adding a few comments of my own, I want to reproduce a recent letter from him:

"You may remember the *TT* note on the 'Levy quad' (*TT* January 1972) and my subsequent suggestion (*TT* March 1972) that it should be turned the other way up in order to increase effective height.

"I have unearthed an odd variation on the same theme and feel the issues involved are important. The Levy quad used just $\frac{1}{2}\lambda$ of wire, but imagine building one with $1\frac{1}{2}\lambda$ wire in the loop: Fig 1(a). Now according to W6SAI's book (*Cubical quad antennas*, Radio Publications Inc, 2nd edn, page 105) this arrangement has even more gain than the standard quad; for reasons that will appear, I fully agree. But I consider that the argument applied to the Levy quad applies equally—turning the loop 'upside down' to put a voltage maximum point at the bottom increases the height of the current loops and hence the effective height of the aerial. Fig 1(b) shows the current distribution.

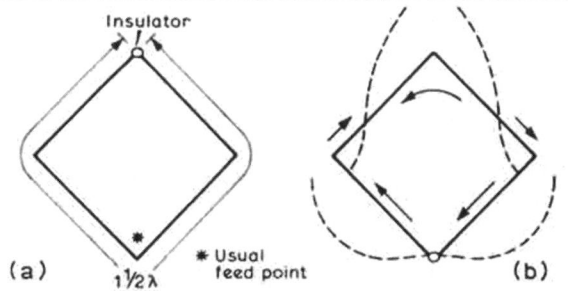

Fig 1. (a) 1½λ version of the "Levy Quad". (b) Current distribution of an inverted 1½λ element (current distribution shown dotted, direction indicated by arrows)

"However, W6SAI (caption to Fig 7, page 105) says that this is no good and that the insulator must go at the top, so if we follow his advice we would be stuck with Fig 1(a) for reasons which, to put it mildly, are less than obvious. Free space has no vertical reference and spinning a loop around on its axis should make no difference!

"The practical importance of getting this matter cleared up becomes rather more obvious when one appreciates that Fig 1(b) is in effect a 14MHz quad fed with 21MHz power—and if we wish to use it on 28MHz one needs only a trap at the top corner to turn it into a bi-square array (termed the X-Q array by W6SAI). Thus we now have all the ingredients for a triband quad but with *increased gain* on the higher frequencies and *without the usual spider's web* configuration to support three independent loops.

"This brings me to what I feel is a rather sad story. I have built several beams along these lines, including a 14/21MHz version in constant use since 1955. On 21MHz the front-back ratio is good and it outperforms more conventional aerials: on 14MHz it is, as might be expected, a conventional quad and performs as such.

"I first mentioned the idea in *Wireless World* (March 1959) and wrote it up in more detail and covering a lot of variations in *CQ* (November 1962). It was rediscovered a few years ago by others, but there seems to be no trace of it in current reference literature. Admittedly, by amalgamating pages 99 and 105 of the W6SAI handbook one could obtain a 'triband beam' identical with mine on 28 and 21MHz (except for being the other way up) but unless one is prepared to close the top of the loop or transfer the feeder to the top it would *not* (although W6SAI implies the contrary) work as a beam on 14MHz!

"Multiband operation requires resonant feeders which are perhaps a nuisance for rotary beams, but not too much of a problem if the beam is made reversible so that rotation can be restricted to say 120° or 150°.

"This brings me to another major advantage of quad loops for multiband operation. As shown in my 1962 *CQ* article, the loop arrangement shown in Fig 2 is simultaneously resonant (or nearly so) on all bands from 7 to 28MHz, though only suitable as a beam element on 14 and 21MHz. Even so, I have worked the USA on 28MHz with 0·5W ssb, and Australia on 7MHz ssb though this time with higher power.

"Yet another important property of quads has now apparently disappeared from the standard literature. Early descriptions of the quad aerial usually mentioned that considerably less gain resulted from tuning the parasitic element as a director rather than as a reflector. But both W6SAI's book and the current edition of ARRL's *The Radio Amateur's Handbook* suggest that either form can be used. From my own experience, I fail to see how anyone can tune up a quad without noticing the large decrease in front-to-back ratio when the parasitic element forms a director (unless of course the range of adjustment does not allow this possibility). This experience is readily explained theoretically by the relatively wide spacing between the top of the radiator and the bottom of the reflector, or vice versa, introducing a negative reactance term into the mutual impedance. By quite simple algebra, one can show that this increases the current in a reflector and decreases it in a

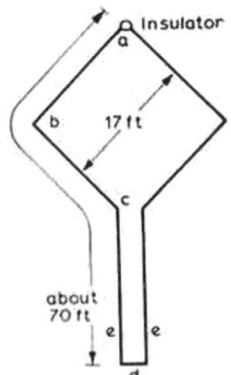

Fig 2. Multiband loop and stub arrangement that resonates at 7, 14, 21 and 28-MHz and suitable as a beam element for 14 and 21MHz. Can be fed with low-impedance feeders at point d, or with 600Ω-line at about point e

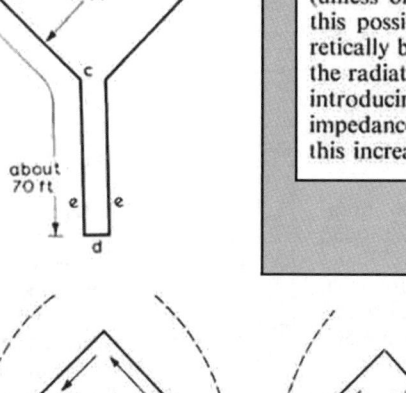

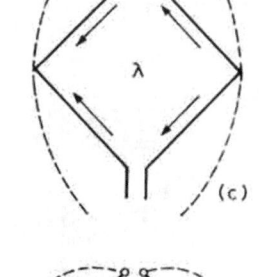

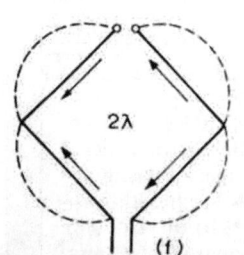

Fig 3. Current distribution in loops of various sizes at different frequencies. The arrow lengths represent different field strengths, the smallest being 8, the next 29 and the longest 92

ANTENNA TOPICS

W6SAI's book and the current edition of ARRL's *The Radio Amateur's Handbook* suggest that either form can be used. From my own experience, I fail to see how anyone can tune up a quad without noticing the large decrease in front-to-back ratio when the parasitic element forms a director (unless of course the range of adjustment does not allow this possibility). This experience is readily explained theoretically by the relatively wide spacing between the top of the radiator and the bottom of the reflector, or vice versa, introducing a negative reactance term into the mutual impedance. By quite simple algebra, one can show that this increases the current in a reflector and decreases it in a director. Working out a few examples, I find the calculated depth of nulls in the back direction is some 20–30dB for reflector operation but only 5–10dB for director operation.

"As pointed out in my article 'Supergain aerials' (*Radio Communication* September 1972) it is difficult to get extra gain out of additional elements, even without the 'negative reactance' handicap. I suspect that much money and effort is being wasted in the construction of 'monster' quads with one or more directors."

It seems to me well worth underlining one or two of the points made by G6XN, particularly the potential use of the 7–28MHz "loop plus stub" arrangement not only as part of a "driven element plus reflector" arrangement but as a multiband aerial in its own right, easily put up in "quad" or even more so in "triangular loop" form. And this brings me to yet another feature of the original article that was largely overlooked for a number of years until rediscovered and written up in many articles from 1969 onwards: the triangular loop. G6XN wrote in 1962: "We also discovered that loops can be distorted into a wide variety of shapes, such as triangular, without noticeably affecting their radiating properties."

John Brodzky, G3HQX, has brought to my attention the fact that G6XN's 1962 *CQ* article was later incorporated into *Antenna Roundup* (Vol 2) edited by Tom Kneitel, K2AES, (Cowan Publishing Corp), obtainable from RSGB at £1.65 inc p & p. Certainly it is well worth looking up in either publication since it contains a great deal of practical information on designing, constructing and tuning up various forms of multi-band quads all based on energizing the same loop on different bands. We have extracted a further diagram (Fig 3) providing a useful summary of current distribution in resonant loops.

It is thus a pertinent reflection on the information explosion that 14 years after G6XN showed clearly that quad and loop aerials can be used most effectively for multiband operation without reverting to individual loops for each band, the standard designs still ignore this and concentrate on the more mechanically complex arrangement which actually throws away available gain on the higher frequencies!

in having a voltage maximum point at the base of the vertical section, and thus had some affinity to a ground-plane turned through 180°: Fig 6.

G2BAB writes: "To me this is not a new type of aerial, although until you mentioned it in *TT* I had never seen any reference to it in amateur magazines. I first experimented with it in 1932, when it gave excellent results, but later I started work on compressed dipoles and other types for comparison and then for many years was unable to proceed with my experimental work.

"Now that I have retired to South Devon, with restricted aerial space, I have again put up a vertical-tee. The results are outstanding. On 7MHz I often hear American amateurs working each other obviously not knowing they are getting out; it works well on all bands but 'goes to town' on 14MHz.

"I find that the angle of radiation appears to be much lower than that of a single vertical, and the way that distant stations bounce in has to be heard to be believed. I use 110W coupled to the aerial with a modified Collins coupler and get unity vswr on all bands including 3·5MHz when used against ground.

"With a 66ft top it is fine on 3·5MHz but on 28MHz its resonant frequency came out at 30·5MHz. To correct this for 28MHz and all the other bands I have found that a small tapped coil in the vertical section at the shack end enables me to resonate the aerial on each band, with slightly better results. Altering the length of the vertical also puts the length of the top section right: this is far easier than attempting to alter both the top and vertical elements."

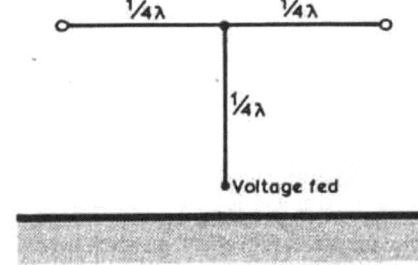

Fig 6. Basic arrangement of hf vertical-tee aerial as described in *TT* (July 1970) and *ART*

Even when not fed against ground the performance of this, like all other vertical radiators, is affected by the ground constants, and it is often well worth laying out some form of earth-mat all around the aerial. For anyone who is really prepared to put in an effective image plane of many, many wires, an interesting article on a three-element 14MHz vertical beam is the one by Jerry Sevick, W2FMI, in *QST* June 1972 or his earlier one on image planes (July 1971). The "beam" version of the vertical-tee is the Bobtail (*TT* July 1970, *ART4* or many other reference sources).

Comments on the 'Vertical-tee' Aerial

Extracted from 'Technical Topics', *Radio Communication,* March 1973

Comments on the "vertical-tee" aerial

An interesting letter from R. C. Harris, G2BAB, provides some further comments on an aerial technique in which I tried to rekindle interest a couple of years ago—not only for the lower frequency bands but also for 14MHz and above—the tee or "vertical-tee" aerial (*TT* July 1970 or *ART*3/4). My hf version differed from the conventional mf tee aerial

Multiband Loops

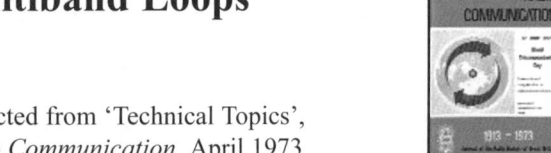

Extracted from 'Technical Topics', *Radio Communication,* April 1973

Multiband loops

Some follow-up notes on the G6XN multiband loop/quad techniques outlined in the February *TT*—and assuming you will have already noted last month's correction pointing out that there should be *no* insulator at the half-way point (unless of course one is needed for support).

One point I did not make clear: the total amount of wire in the loop plus stub is approximately 140ft, but the distribution between stub and loop can be varied (though clearly there will be advantages in having, say, 68-70ft in the loop); G6XN did describe a quad based on this technique having only 12ft sides, so making the construction a good deal less massive.

A. H. Mason, GM6MS, has successfully used a 140ft loop (ie all the wire in the loop and no stub). He fed this with 72Ω coaxial cable, though it should be noted that this is possibly not the ideal match. He found this system performed fairly well from 7 to 28MHz, and could be used also on 3·5MHz by open circuiting the loop at the half-way point, so turning it into an inverted Levy-quad element (Fig 2).

Another variation, which I have been trying, is a G6XN-type loop plus resonant feeders, twisted around through 90° to provide vertically-polarized signals. Initial results seem promising though I suspect that the closeness of one side of the square-loop to ground (maximum height is only

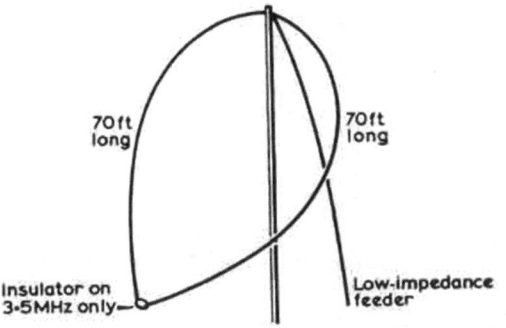

Fig 2. The 140ft multiband loop aerial used by **GM6MS** for 7 to 28MHz—for 3·5MHz operation the loop is open-circuited at its mid-point, 70ft from the feeder connection

24ft so that the lower wire is only 7ft above the ground) is causing some unbalance; still it has brought VK and W contacts on 7MHz. With points of maximum current halfway up each vertical leg, the astute may notice an affinity with the G8ON aerial (*TT*, January 1972 and *ART4*) which can be likened to a three-sided loop (if such a term is acceptable).

In his classic book *Antennas*, John D. Kraus, W8JK, shows another way in which vertical polarization can be achieved with square loops, though we have never heard of any amateur using this system. Fig 3(a) shows the conventional horizontally-polarized system, and (b) shows the system being tried at G3VA. In (c), the W8JK system, the loop is continuous and is fed by unbalanced line: the aerial currents flowing to the feed point are equal and in phase so that the current distribution changes to that indicated.

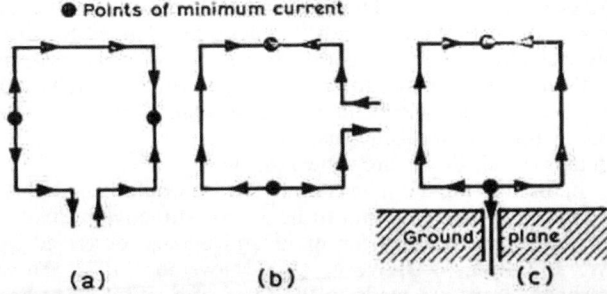

Fig 3. Current distribution in 1λ square-loop elements. (a) conventional horizontally-polarized element; (b) vertically-polarized system being tried at G3VA (but note unbalance to earth); (c) vertically-polarized voltage-fed element described by W8JK in *Antennas*

Although quad/loop aerials are most certainly better when hoisted well clear of the ground, it has often been observed that their performance at low heights is not at all bad. We were interested to note the following comment in *IEEE Trans on Ant & Prop* (January 1973): "it is known that the radiation characteristics of electric dipoles placed at or near ground level and operated at lf are strongly affected by the electrical properties of the soil and that magnetic dipoles or loop aerials are much less affected by comparison." It would be interesting to know if vertically-polarized loop aerials could help to overcome on hf the well-known hostile soil and surroundings of urban sites. Probably not—but one lives in hope! After all, the Beverage receiving aerial on lf and hf can pull in low-angle signals although very near the ground.

Delta-birdcage Aerials

Extracted from 'Technical Topics', *Radio Communication*, April 1973

Delta-birdcage aerials

Over the years there have been a number of techniques developed with the aim of simplifying the construction of quad-type aerials. Apart from the delta approach, one of the better known is the G4ZU birdcage, as described in *Radio Communication Handbook*.

An interesting combination of both these techniques is described in *QTC* No 1, 1973, by Kenneth Johansson, SM4EMO, though the idea stemmed from Yasuo Murai,

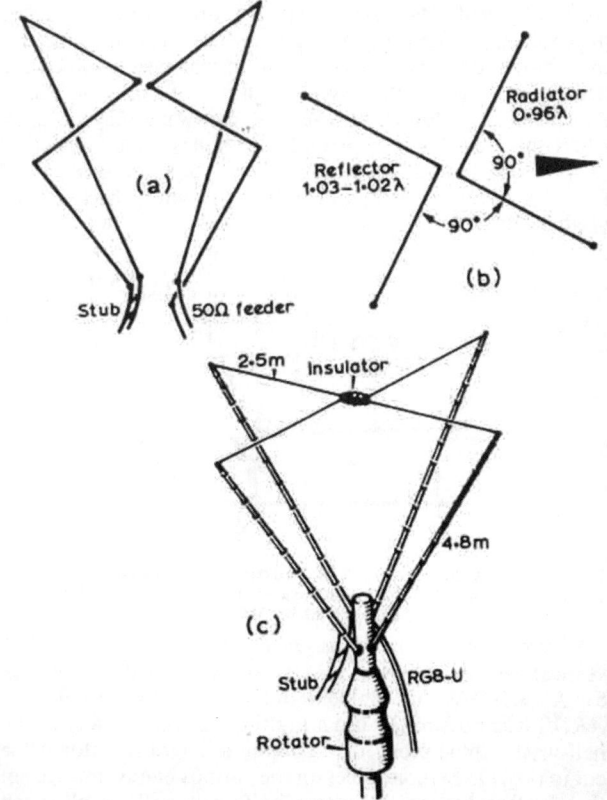

Fig 4. The delta-birdcage type of aerial described by **SM4EMO** based on a design by **JA5AO**. The dimensions shown are for a 21MHz array

ANTENNA TOPICS

JA5AO/7. This uses a triangular loop but distorted in the manner usually associated with the birdcage configuration at the top. Although the aerial requires quite long supports (4·5m for a 21MHz aerial) the arrangement is still probably a good deal simpler to build than a conventional quad. Each loop comprises approximately 2 by 0·15λ horizontal members and 2 by 0·3λ sloping members to make up the 1λ loop. The stub is adjusted to provide maximum front-to-back ratio; most of the mechanical details can be gathered from the 21MHz array shown in Fig 4.

Vertical Dipoles

Extracted from 'Technical Topics', *Radio Communication,* April 1973

Vertical dipoles

Every now and again somebody rediscovers the fact that a ½λ vertical dipole can be a very attractive alternative to the much better-known ¼λ grounded vertical or the ¼λ fed against an artificial wire ground plane. Latest to do so is B. H. Brunemeier, VO9N, who writes in *Ham Radio*, December 1972: "from personal observation the half-wave vertical is unknown around the world... I have never yet contacted another station using one... I can't help wondering why DXers around the world aren't using it."

Well, certainly we have long included some notes on the value of the vertical half-wave dipole in *ART* and can recall several amateurs writing over the years to point out (often with some evident surprise) that these aerials can and do work very well. The reason that they are largely ignored is probably the variability of results which depend markedly on ground conductivity. The position was well summed up many years ago in the original edition of *Amateur Radio Handbook* as follows: "the vertical half-wave may be used where the site is fairly open, and if the soil is a good reflector, as for example in damp country, it will be found very good for long distance work, but it has frequently been found disappointing."

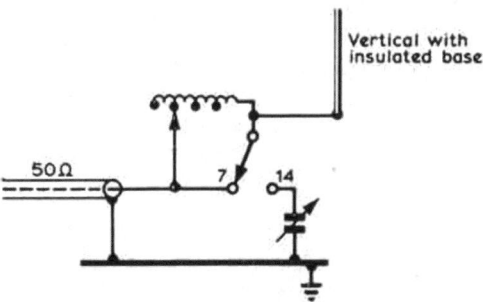

Fig 5. **Method of feeding a 34ft vertical as a half-wave dipole on 14MHz and as a quarter-wave monopole on 7MHz, as described by VO9N**

VO9N shows a useful suggestion for feeding a 31-34ft vertical element as ½λ on 14MHz and ¼λ on 7MHz, (see Fig 5). As K2QBW has pointed out (*TT,* December 1970 or *ART4*) it is possible to use a multi-band trap vertical in the half-wave dipole mode by attaching a length of rotor cable cut to provide ¼λ monopoles on the various bands; the system then in effect becomes a series of half-wave verticals, although some of those using the arrangement may not recognise that this is what they are using and continue to refer to the aerial simply as a "vertical".

The Short Backfire Again

Extracted from 'Technical Topics', *Radio Communication,* April 1973

The short backfire again

On several occasions we have referred in *TT* (and subsequently in *ART*) to the work of H. W. Ehrenspeck in developing high-gain "backfire" yagi aerials, including the so-called "short backfire" system in which a dipole is mounted between a reflector in front and a larger specially shaped reflector at the rear. Ehrenspeck has claimed that such an array can provide the equivalent gain of a conventional 20-element yagi, although it is fair to say that backfire systems have always been controversial—though I know of engineers who have been in touch with him and who are convinced that the

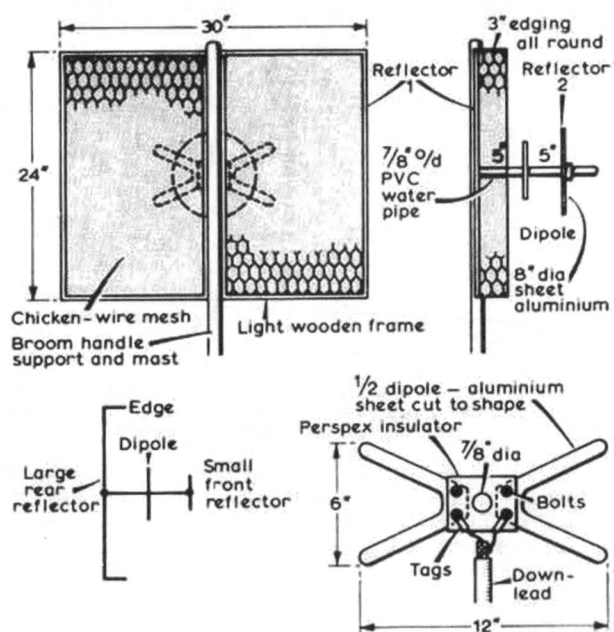

Fig 6. The *Television* design of a "short back-fire" aerial for uhf television reception. The dipole "arms" are about ⅜in wide. The pvc boom is mounted on the light wooden frame which is bolted to the broom handle mast using the type of metal bracket used to mount loft aerials, but other types could be used

system has merit, if not always suitable for the job they have in mind. There is, in fact, some evidence that properly designed short backfire aerials *do* work!

A practical design intended for uhf television reception appears in the February 1973 issue of the British magazine *Television*, though I am puzzled that the author has achieved good wideband performance (the design is claimed to work over channels 21 to 41, representing some 160MHz between 470 and 638MHz, and to provide a gain roughly equivalent to a 22-element wideband television yagi). This uses wire mesh for the specially shaped "saucepan lid" reflector: details of this design are shown in Fig 6.

Before leaving the subject of aerials we would like to draw attention to what appears to be a very attractive technique for constructing traps for multiband aerials, described by W. J. Lattin, W4JRW, in *QST*, November 1972. These resonant traps are made in the form of a spiral delay line and do not require any high-voltage capacitors; in effect they comprise a form of coaxial line with a helical inner conductor. He provides full constructional details and the resulting traps should prove of very high Q.

Building a Delta-loop Quad

Extracted from 'Technical Topics', *Radio Communication,* May 1973

Building a delta-loop quad

Harry R. Habig, K8ANV, who developed the HRH delta-loop beam, first described in *QST*, January 1969 (and see *ART3* or *4*), wrote last year to mention that he receives many letters from amateurs wondering how to get over the problem of putting up a 14MHz "plumber's delight" delta-loop beam, with their long V tubes which are joined at the top with wire.

Photo 1. Actual installation. The saddle mounting of the boom-to-mast fitting allows the boom to be rotated for easy work on the elements; the boom can also be lowered down parallel to the mast if necessary. In this instance the feed line runs up inside the 2in diameter mast. The rotator is located on the attic floor, and a 360° rotary coaxial fitting allows the aerial to be swung round and round

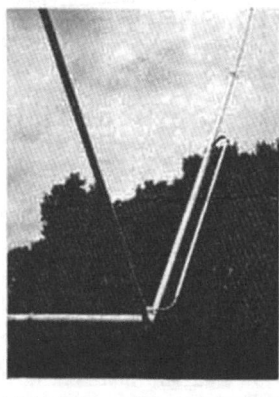

Photo 2. The gamma feed is spaced 4in from the element and on this 14MHz aerial has a total length of 46in

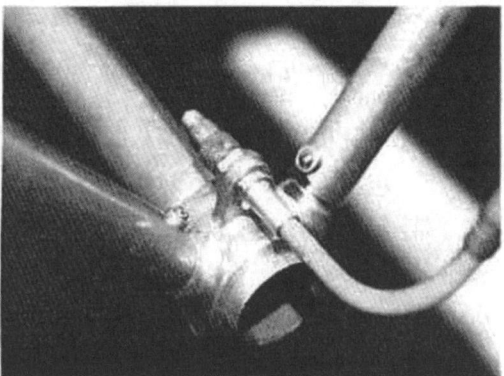

Photo 3. Element-to-boom fitting for 14MHz aerial. Tubing diameter at the base is 1¼in od 0·058in with a second inside tube od 1⅛in. The large tube is 6ft long and the 1⅛in tube 12ft with the 28MHz/12ft/1in tube added to the upper part, making the total element length 23½ft long. Note the earthing of the gamma feed to allow a truly flat line

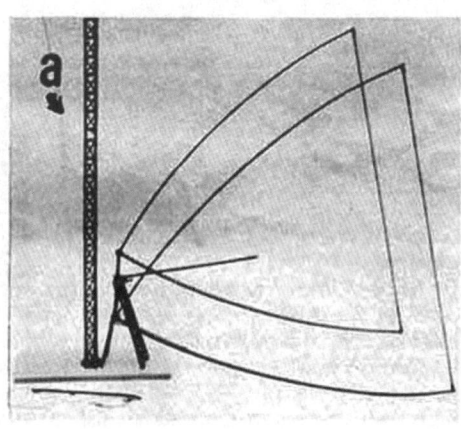

Photo a. Tools needed to instal the delta loop on the tower are: a stepladder; a gin pole with top pulley; a helper pole made from a 10ft length of 1¼in thinwall electrical conduit having two-screw split clamp on one end to fit the outer-diameter of the boom tube; and enough rope to reach from ground to tower top and back to ground. Assemble the beam on the ground with the mast-to-boom fitting in place. Mast stub facing towards the top centre of the elements; helper pole facing the same way and fastened opposite to the gamma-feed side in order to clear the tower side when the mast stub is installed in the rotor head. This means the helper pole will be facing downwards and close to the tower

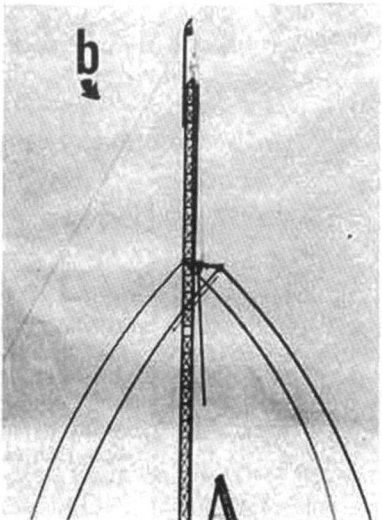

Photo b. At this stage the gin pole has been fastened in place and the rotor installed on the tower stub. The rope has been lowered and fastened to the centre of the boom ready for raising

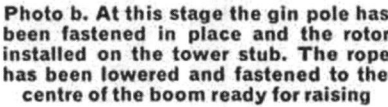

Step-by-step mounting procedure for the delta-loop quad

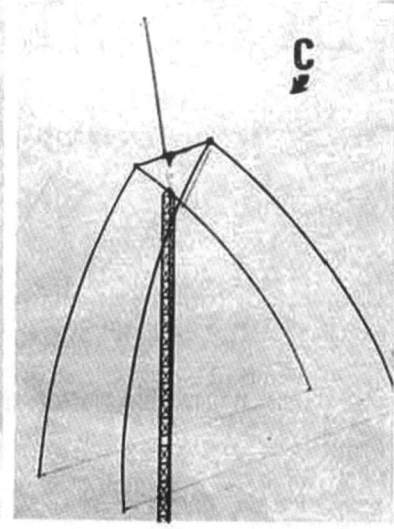

Photo c. The mast-to-boom fitting; mast stub has been lowered into the rotor head and fastened. The rope has been removed from the gin pole and lowered to the ground, and then the rope fastened to the helper pole. The screws on the helper pole are loosened and the pole swung to an "up" position and the screws tightened. The screws tightening the boom-to-mast fitting are then loosened just enough to allow the boom to rotate in the fitting. The helper on the ground then pulls on the rope and brings the beam into its correct "up" position, plumbing it at the same time. The screws on the mast-to-boom fitting are then tightened—and the beam is up

ANTENNA TOPICS

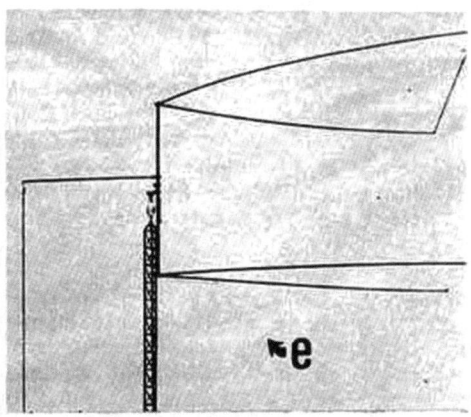
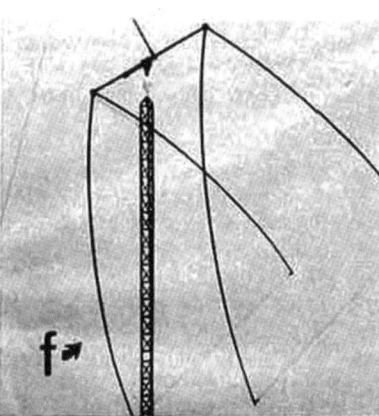

Photo d. Beam in "up" position with helper pole concealed on far side of mast. The helper pole can be used (in this position) to swing the gamma-feed side down parallel to the tower by pulling the heavy bolt on the reflector side and slightly loosening the other bolt. The helper on the ground can now hold the line in tension and the boom can be swung down parallel to the tower, so allowing work to be carried out on the gamma feed. Pulling the rope will bring the boom back into place

Photo b. At this stage the gin pole has been fastened in place and the rotor installed on the tower stub. The rope has been lowered and fastened to the centre of the boom ready for raising

Photo c. The mast-to-boom fitting; mast stub has been lowered into the rotor head and fastened. The rope has been removed from the gin pole and lowered to the ground, and then the rope fastened to the helper pole. The screws on the helper pole are loosened and the pole swung to an "up" position and the screws tightened. The screws tightening the boom-to-mast fitting are then loosened just enough to allow the boom to rotate in the fitting. The helper on the ground then pulls on the rope and brings the beam into its correct "up" position, plumbing it at the same time. The screws on the mast-to-boom fitting are then tightened—and the beam is up

As a result he made up a scale model of a lattice tower and rotator and arranged a series of photographs to show that with the proper aids it is relatively easy to get one up, even the large 14MHz types—but he advises the use of the mast-to-boom fitting and a "helper" tube. He also advises constructors to note the final location of the grounding on the gamma match. By having the coaxial braid connecting the elements at the apex of the elements he considers that it is possible to achieve a really flat line and cold braid. After many tries with a variety of tubing materials for the dielectric, he found ordinary pure laboratory gum rubber heavy tubing to be the most long lasting in bad weather.

The rubber tubing is unbroken, it runs from the top of the ¼in diameter solid aluminium rod (sealed at the upper end) through the gamma fitting at the boom and extends some 1/16in beyond the end of the fitting; by removing the two little bosses on the line fitting and drawing up the ferral, one then has an excellent "O" ring to effect a really good water seal. The aluminium rod is drilled and split at the coaxial end to receive the male stud on the line fitting; in this way there is no possible way for the weather to cause trouble. The hole in the gamma coaxial fitting is drilled smaller in diameter than the outside diameter of the rubber tubing, which is a snug fit on the ¼in rod; thus one stretches the rubber tubing and inserts it through the fitting, positioning the end of the centre rod with relation to the end of the fitting; then *releasing* the tension on the tubing and working it and the rod a little to allow it to set in the fitting, rather like the rubber fitting in the spring shackle of a car. The rubber tubing is then cut (square) about 1/16in longer from the end of the fitting to form the "O" ring.

This may seem a little confusing and probably anyone tackling a large delta-loop beam would be advised to consult also the original *QST* articles. But it is hoped that this extra information will be of interest even to those content with a less ambitious 21MHz aerial, or the delta-birdcage type of aerial. We are grateful to Harry Habig for supplying the details and photographs.

Vertically Polarized Loop Elements

Extracted from 'Technical Topics', *Radio Communication,* June 1973

Vertically polarized loop elements

L. V. Mayhead, G3AQC, was interested in the recent notes on vertically polarized loop elements (*TT* April) since he has been investigating various forms of loop aerials using scale models on 500 and 144MHz. Among many interesting items which this has shown up (and which G3AQC hopes to write up before long) is a delta loop which gives predominately vertical polarization with much the same current distribution as the Kraus arrangement given in Fig 3(c) in the

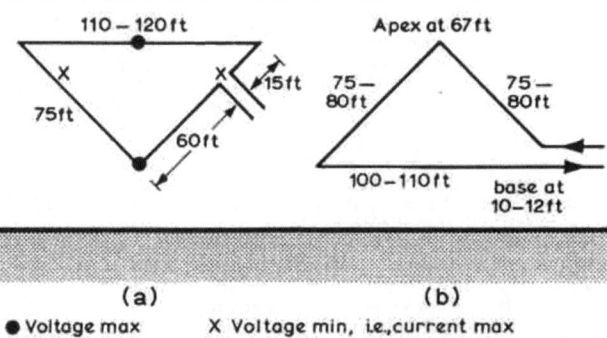

(a)   (b)

● Voltage max   X Voltage min, i.e., current max

Fig 5. Loop configurations providing predominantly vertical polarization: (a) arrangement used by G3AQC and (b) arrangement used by G3TZH. Dimensions refer to 3·5MHz but aerials are basically multi-band

April notes, yet with current feed which is usually more convenient for amateurs. The G3AQC arrangement is outlined in Fig 5(a) with the dimensions given for 3·5MHz operation where his supporting masts are 55 to 60ft high and the apex some 6ft from the ground: the aerial has an affinity to two sloping verticals in phase. His own location is not really suitable for low-angle propagation but he mentions that G3TZH, much more favourably located above more conductive earth, has had great success with the variant shown in Fig 5(b). As I do not want to pre-empt a chance of reading a full-length article on loop configurations—about which it is certain that there is a lot more to be found out—I will refrain from further details.

feed at points 1 and 4 to provide a broad-band dipole.
14MHz: Feed at points 2 and 3, leaving 1 and 4 open. Performance is then that of a 3 by ½λ.
28MHz: Feed at points 1 and 2, or alternatively 3 and 4, to provide a delta loop aerial.

This appears to be one of many possible forms making use of the loop and delta configuration; G4ABS does not give any indication of the swr he achieves on the low-impedance feeder.

G4ABS Multiband Aerial for Limited Spaces

Extracted from 'Technical Topics', *Radio Communication,* June 1973

Feeding Quad and Loop Elements

Extracted from 'Technical Topics', *Radio Communication,* July 1973

G4ABS multiband aerial for limited spaces
D. Bedford, G4ABS, sends along an ingenious multiband aerial which he says works "quite happily" in conjunction with an aerial tuning unit or Z-match. He reports that the performance is at least equal to half-wave dipoles for each band, and he believes that with further experimentation it might prove ideal for amateurs with limited space. Lowering the centre or raising the sides appeared to give broadside bi-directional properties, but this would require further investigation.

Feeding quad and loop elements
Two variations on the basic theme of matching coaxial feeders to loop and quad elements have been noted recently. Fig 4(a) shows the "X-ray delta match" of N. J. Sandbergen, PA0XD, as published in *Electron* (April 1972) and is interesting in that it appears to eliminate the need for the series capacitor of the usual gamma match system. The line is spaced about 5cm from the element wire and point P is respectively 110cm, 160cm and 220cm from the insulator on 28, 21 and 14MHz. For 28MHz he uses 60Ω coaxial, for the other bands 70Ω. It is claimed that an swr of virtually 1:1 can be achieved.

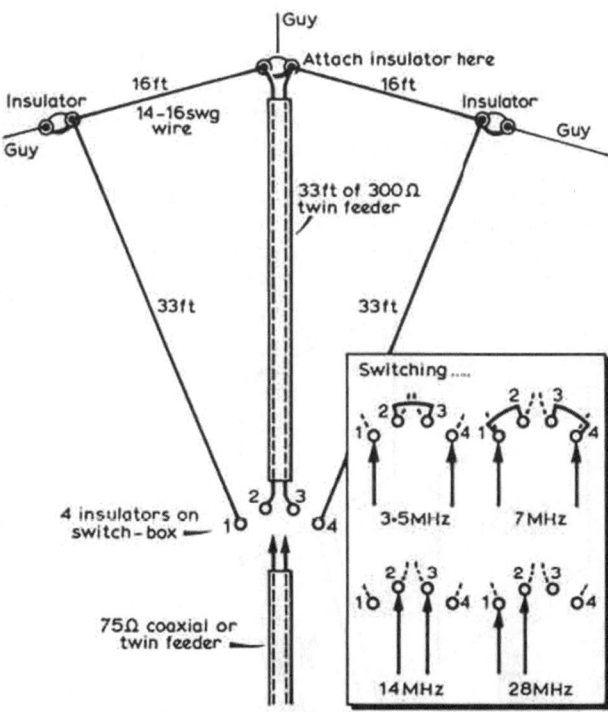

Fig 12. G4ABS multiband aerial for use in limited space

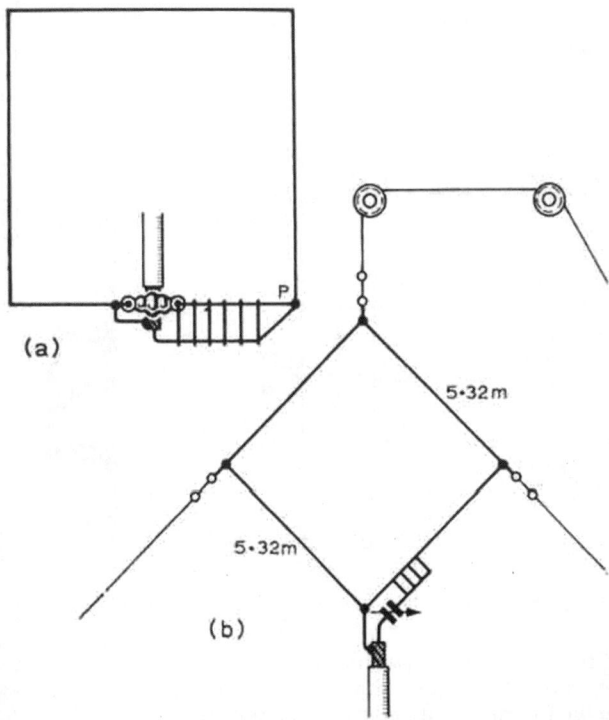

Fig 4. (a) X-ray delta match for loop or quad element described by PA0XD; (b) Gamma match arrangement from the Belgian journal CQ/QSO

He explains the operation of the aerial as follows:
3·5MHz: Switch-points 2 and 3 are shorted, and the aerial is fed via points 1 and 4. This provides a compressed form of delta loop containing 164ft of wire.
7MHz and 21MHz: Short points 1 and 2 and also 3 and 4,

Fig 4(b) shows an arrangement described in the Belgian journal *CQ/QSO* (May 1973) using the more orthodox gamma match. The element sides are given as 5·32m, 3·52m and 2·72m for 14, 21 and 28MHz respectively. The length of the gamma section (spaced off 10cm) and the capacitance is given as 1·30m (200pF), 1·10m (150pF) and 0·90m (100pF).

ANTENNA TOPICS

Tuning Quad Reflectors

Extracted from 'Technical Topics',
Radio Communication, July 1973

Tuning quad reflectors

In *Amateur Radio* (February 1973) S. E. Molen, VK2SG, writes a detailed article on "Tuning the quad—the easy way". He emphasizes that the reflector should be the first element to be tuned and outlines his method of doing this as follows; noting that it is not sufficiently accurate just to assume that this should be five per cent longer than the driven element:

"We set about tuning the reflector with a few very simple tools. If you take a lead from the S-meter of your receiver so that you can take the meter to the quad, you can tune the reflector on your own. The tools needed will be the extended S-meter, a long-shank screwdriver and a soldering iron— that is all. Of course you also need an external signal which must not be too strong as this could be misleading. It was found that a 12AT7 crystal oscillator with the second half as doubler, tripler or quadrupler, 120V ht, about 300ft from the reflector provided an adequate signal. Too much signal may give a false indication, for example two dips with a rise above normal between them. Keep the signal about 30dB above receiver noise, typically S7.

"Now to tune the reflector. Turn the back of the quad (reflector) on to the incoming signal, grasp the bottom of the stub in your hand and with the long shank screwdriver short out the stub at the top. Now watching your S-meter slide the screwdriver down the stub maintaining the short-circuit until the S-meter dips: see Fig 5. Carefully checking this point for minimum signal, put a wire link across the point, check it again to make sure you have the exact point, and solder it. Do the same for the other bands . . . it's as easy as that."

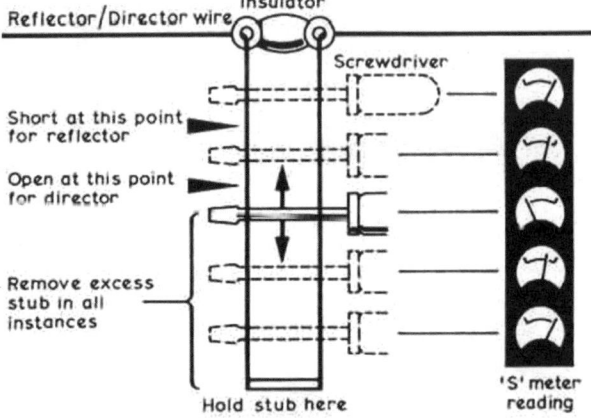

Fig 5. VK2SG's method of tuning quad reflector and director elements

It will be noted that this method assumes that maximum rejection of the signal will coincide with the required maximum forward gain—some might not agree that this will always be true.

Later in his article, VK2SG gives a useful rule of thumb for tuning quads when near the ground. He says allow 75kHz for the first 30ft rise and 25kHz for every 20ft above this—ie if tuning for 14,200kHz operational, tune for about 14,100kHz if the aerial is to be lifted to about 40–50ft.

Remote tuning quad reflectors

An ingenious alternative procedure to that outlined above has been brought to our notice by Pat King, G3PVA. It stems from an article by Peter Lovelock, W6AJZ, "Remote quad tuning" which appeared in *CQ Magazine* (November 1970).

W6AJZ points out that the adjustment of a quad reflector is quite critical if optimum performance is to be achieved; he suggests that a ½in adjustment to a shorting bar as used above can "make the difference between a directional quad and a bi-directional stacked dipole".

He notes that the three basic methods of tuning quad reflectors are those shown in Fig 6. His own remote tuning technique is an adaptation of the arrangement of Fig 6(b) and consists, in effect, of adding to the stub additional half-wavelength resonant stubs. He points out that the addition of a ½λ stub means that the inductive reactance across its far end will exactly reflect the inductive reactance across the near end. This means that the tuning capacitor can simply be transferred to the far end of the now long stub: Fig 7. By adding one or more half-wavelengths of transmission line, the capacitor can be brought into the operating shack, making it simple to set up or check the setting at any time, using the receiver S-meter. While ideally this stub would be open-wire transmission line, he points out that the standard American tv-type 300Ω flat line or tubular

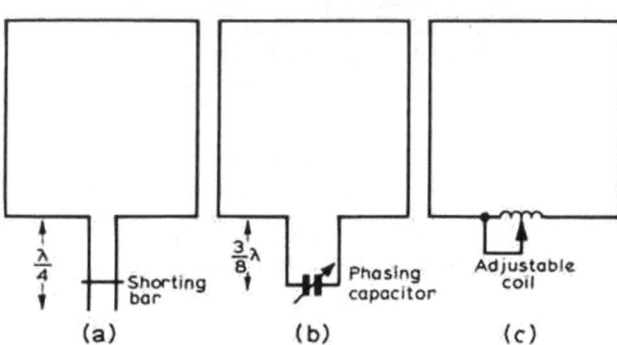

Fig 6. Basic methods of tuning quad reflectors

feeder will work almost as well provided the velocity factor is taken into account when calculating the electrical half-wavelengths (open wire about 0·975, flat or tubular 300Ω feeder about 0·82).

With the tuning capacitors mounted in a box at the operating position, it is claimed to be quite simple to tune up the reflector for maximum gain on any suitable ground-wave signal. In this case it is assumed that the driven

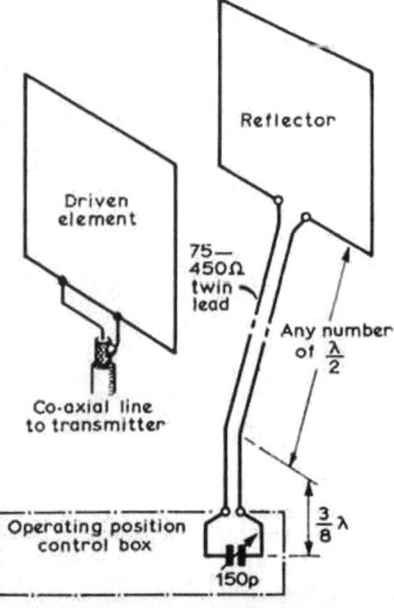

Fig 7. The W6AJZ technique for remote tuning of quad reflector allowing adjustment to be carried out from the shack

element has already been adjusted for resonance.

G3PVA reports that he has tried the system and adds, "Believe me it works and works very well indeed. When the object is maximum front/back ratio it is fascinating to hear signals disappear off the back when the optimum tune-point is reached. When the driven element is optimized for minimum swr with the reflector tuned for maximum f/b ratio, the swr is somewhat degraded when the reflector is tuned for optimum forward gain by this method—but this seems to be of no practical consequence."

G3PVA, after six years use of a two-element 14MHz quad, is hoping to replace this with a delta-loop arrangement. He has carried out many tests with VE1YY and VE1AEL, both of whom use the delta configuration, and he has been very impressed by the results; this he feels may be in part because of its unique construction that provides an extra 13ft or so of aerial height without an increase of mast height, providing additional low-angle radiation potential. He reports that Harry Habig, K8ANV, now suggests that the driven element of a triangular loop should be based on the formula $975/f$ feet rather than $1005/f$ as this has proven to be more accurate in practice.

with the ends hanging down in a restricted space. It is also very easy to check the state of any connections and joints by means of a simple continuity test. Both the element and the feeder can be conveniently made from 300Ω ribbon or tubular feeder.

For a number of years we used a version of the folded dipole which has long appeared in *Radio Handbook*—in which 300Ω line is used for the element but with account taken of the velocity factor of the ribbon: see Fig 4. This minor modification is always stated to allow a ribbon-type aerial to retain the good bandwidth characteristics of open-wire construction, and certainly we never found any reason to doubt the validity of the claim. The system was mentioned many years ago in *TT* (and can be found in *ART*) but there still seem to be many amateurs who are unaware of the system.

A further excuse for republishing this variation of the standard folded dipole is that it provides a useful introduction to yet another little-known variation: the "double coaxial" folded dipole.

Variations on Folded Dipoles

Extracted from 'Technical Topics',
Radio Communication, August 1973

Variations on folded dipoles

The hf folded dipole has lost a good deal of its former popularity since the advent of multiband dipoles. In some ways this is rather a pity since the folded dipole possesses a number of significant advantages over the higher-Q single-wire equivalent. Inherently it is a decidedly wider-band aerial and can almost always be depended upon to work efficiently when cut to formula dimensions without the need to trim to resonance in situ. This applies to a marked degree for different heights or in different conditions of screening, or where it is necessary to bend the aerial into odd shapes, or to operate it

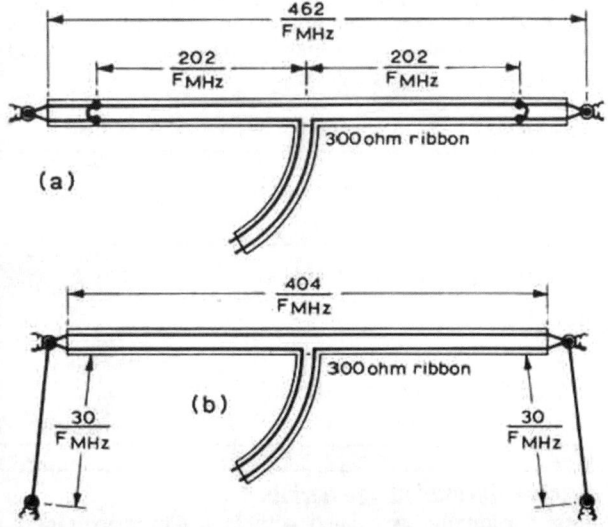

Fig 4. Use of shorting straps to improve match and bandwidth characteristics of folded dipole aerials made from 300Ω ribbon feeder. Shorting point represents the velocity factor times the dipole length from centre. (b) shows a basically similar system with ends bent downwards (*Radio Handbook*)

The Double-coaxial Folded Dipole

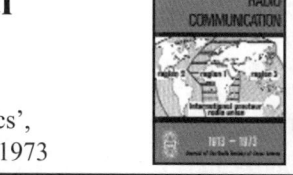

Extracted from 'Technical Topics',
Radio Communication, August 1973

The double-coaxial folded dipole

The double-coaxial aerial is not a new concept, but it is little known, and a timely reminder has recently been published in *73 Magazine* (May 1973) by John Schultz, W2EEY; and D. Ross Webster, K6WM, was kind enough to bring it to our attention. In this system, in effect, the 300Ω ribbon of Fig 4 is replaced by lengths of coaxial cable, and the velocity factor becomes 0·66 rather than 0·82: see Fig 5. There is also the difference that the inner and outer conductors are no longer the same, and this affects the feed impedance. It is claimed by W2EEY that this form of construction provides a good match to a 52Ω coaxial feeder, and further that because of the stub action of the lengths of coaxial in the aerial element there is no requirement for the use of a balun. In other words one finishes up with a dipole aerial that retains the advantages of a folded dipole but suitable for use with coaxial feeder. The

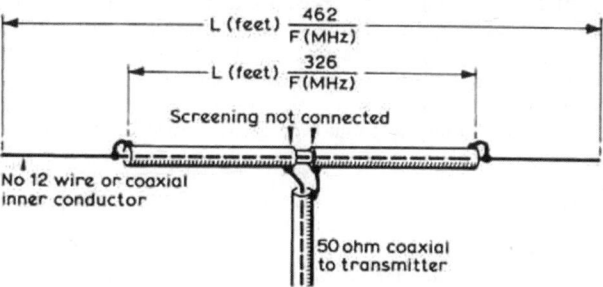

Fig 5. The basic dimensions and arrangement of the double-coaxial aerial (*73 Magazine*)

shield of each coaxial line section in the radiator is connected to the inner conductor only at the outer ends; the shield of each coaxial line section is not connected to the inner conductor at the centre of the aerial. The radiator sections can thus easily be formed from either a single piece of coaxial or, if required, by two pieces

In *73*, W2EEY provides a detailed account of why the aerial works and a good deal of advice on mechanical con-

ANTENNA TOPICS

struction, but the details given here should be sufficient for anyone to give the idea a try. It is stated that the swr should generally be less than 1·5:1 over all hf bands except the wide American 3·5MHz band (3·5 to 4MHz). For 3·5MHz it is pointed out that bandwidth can be widened if necessary by using, for the non-coaxial sections, twin or multiple wires of slightly different length, left unconnected at the far end, akin to the ideas discussed in *TT* of March 1972.

Conical Reflectors

Extracted from 'Technical Topics',
Radio Communication, September 1973

Conical reflectors

For the uhf and microwave operator the ultimate in high-gain aerials has for many years been the parabolic dish, the larger the better. But a true paraboloid is not an easy shape to come to terms with. The main reason for this is that the paraboloid is a doubly-curved surface: if constructed from flat sheets of material, part of the material needs to be either stretched or compressed or both. There is, I believe, an ingenious technique for moulding plastic reflectors which are then metallized—but even this is hardly a "one-off" procedure. Is there any alternative?

The answer, it would seem, is definitely yes—at least for vhf and uhf operation up to a few gigahertz. Recently Fred Brown, W6HPH/G5AWI, brought to my attention an approach which was new to me—and I suspect to many others. It was all explained in detail in an article he wrote in 1966 for *VHF'er* which I hope I am not denigrating by calling "little-known". This article shows that conical reflectors, constructed very easily from flat sheets of material, hardware cloth in his case, can provide an extremely useful substitute and give considerably more gain than would a corner reflector type of aerial, and is just as easy to build.

The shallow cone has the advantage of being a singly-curved surface and can, of course, be made from flat circular sheet by removing or overlapping a segment of the material. The conical reflector aerial makes use of the fact that it is not really vital for the surface of a parabolic reflector to be a true paraboloid. It is usually accepted, G5API points out, that there can be departures of up to $\frac{1}{16}$ of the wavelength concerned at any point on the surface without suffering any significant deterioration of gain and directivity. This $\frac{1}{16}\lambda$ figure may not sound very much but, in practice, it permits quite drastic changes in the overall shape. Up to a certain size, in terms of wavelength, it can be a shallow cone; up to an even greater diameter it can be

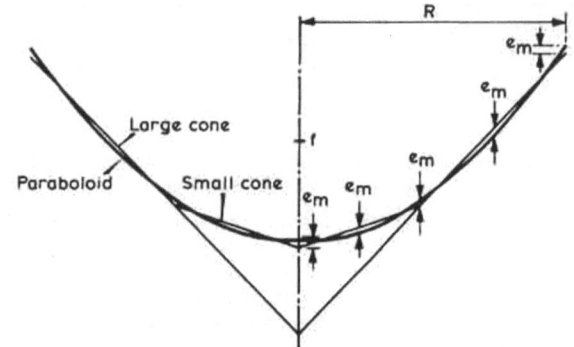

Fig 1. Principle of the polyconic reflector showing the small departures (m) from the true paraboloid

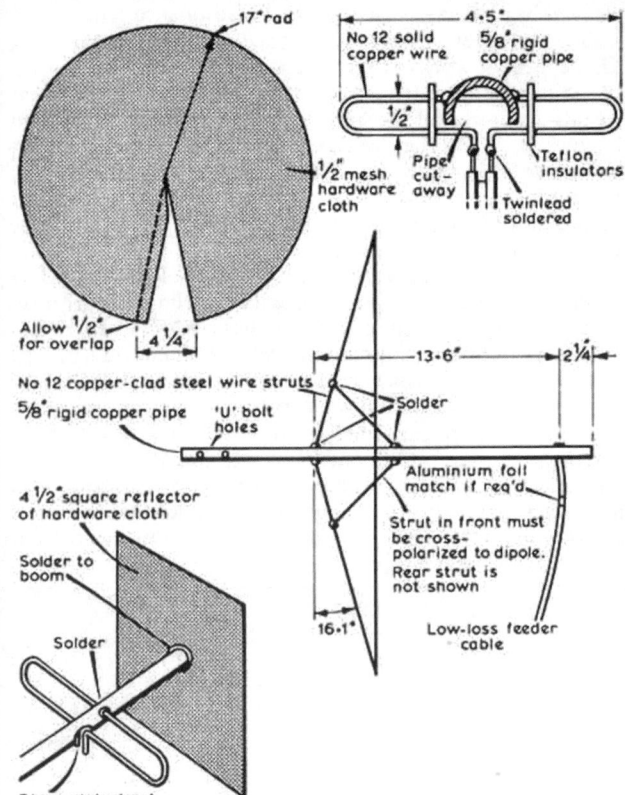

Fig 2. Details of a 1,296MHz single conical reflector aerial providing about 16dB gain

formed by fitting two shallow cones, one inside the other: Fig 1.

Fred Brown's original article shows that a two-cone reflector is entirely satisfactory up to 13·86 λ diameter in certain conditions. This means that one could build a reflector of 10¼ft diameter at 1,296MHz, or even 31·5ft at 432MHz, without having to worry about those doubly-curved surfaces. For single cones it is possible to go up to 3·46 λ, and details are given of a high-performance 1,296MHz aerial with a gain of just over 16dB "constructed in a few hours" for a cost of $1.50, the cone having a radius of 17in. Both the cone and the small 4½in square reflector for the folded dipole element are made from ½in mesh hardware cloth: Fig 2. In some ways the aerial is rather like the short backfire uhf aerial described in the April *TT*—and, of course, one of the possible applications of conical reflectors would be as high-gain television aerials.

One way and another it seems well worth considering the conical reflector as an alternative to the parabolic dish.

Capacitively Loaded Vee Aerials

Extracted from 'Technical Topics',
Radio Communication, October 1973

Capacitively-loaded vee aerials

Another technique associated with Dud Charman, G6CJ, is the capacitively-loaded aerial, described by him in the *RSGB Bulletin* as long ago as July 1961 (a summary is included in *ART4*) when he introduced a cheap method of making stretched dipoles by using overlapping lengths of cloth: Fig 2. In some ways the aerial is rather like the short backfire uhf aerial described in the April *TT*—and, of course, one of the possible applications of conical reflectors would be as high-gain television aerials.

One way and another it seems well worth considering the conical reflector as an alternative to the parabolic dish.

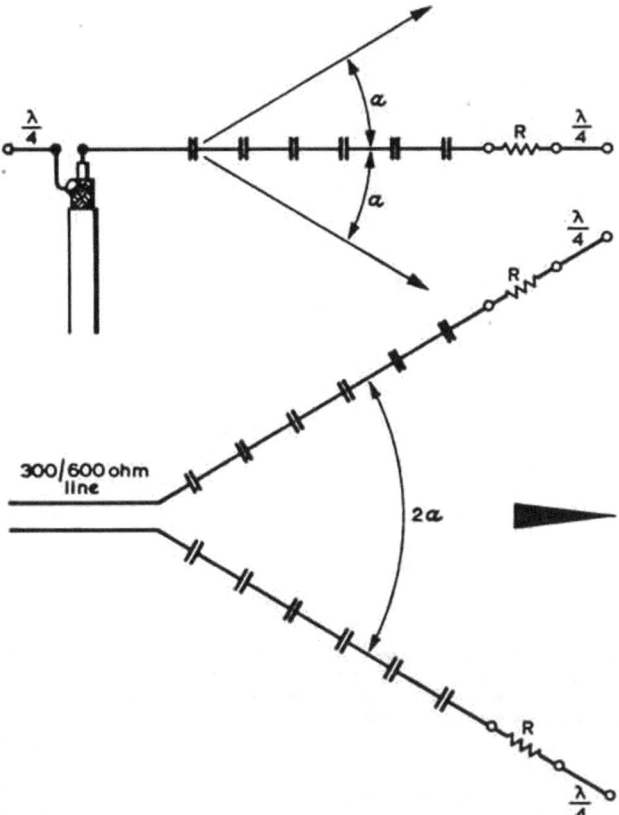

Fig 5. Terminated end-fire aerials using "stretched" (capacitively-loaded wires). The angle α depends only on the loading factor n; gain is proportional to length, with the following figures being typical (from G6CJ's 1961 article):

			Length	Gain
n = 2	α = 30°	R = 300Ω	1¼λ	5dB
n = 3	α = 20°	R = 200Ω	2λ	6dB
n = 4	α = 15°	R = 150Ω	3λ	10dB

But the point that seems worth stressing is the following quotation from this item:

"It is well known that an unloaded V antenna has a more directive radiation pattern than a straight dipole of the same dimensions. The properties of such antennas are, however, highly frequency dependent. This deficiency can be radically remedied by eliminating the reflected current wave from the antenna ends. As far as the authors are informed, previous attempts to eliminate this effect were made only using V antennas with resistive loading. Inherently, however, a resistively loaded antenna is a lossy structure, and a substantial part of the power delivered to the antenna is dissipated in the antenna itself.

"It has been shown that, for a straight cylindrical antenna, elimination of the reflected current wave can also be obtained by reactive loading along the antenna. If folded (ie bent round) to form a V antenna, this structure could be expected to continue to sustain travelling waves. In this manner a loss-less broadband V antenna might be obtained... this letter presents some experimental results for capacitively-loaded V antennas."

The published results show that a main lobe is maintained well over the range 1,800 to 2,400MHz. It should be appreciated that the form of aerial investigated in Yugoslavia was virtually a stretched dipole bent into a V (or, more strictly speaking, one leg of this against a ground plane) and not the long-wire type of vee. But these results support the view that capacitively loaded elements offer unique properties that deserve further investigation at hf and vhf.

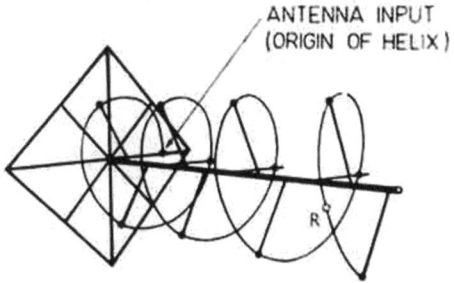

Fig 6. The 136MHz space telemetry helical aerial with optimized parameters as described in the Czech journal of *Tesla Electronics* (English language). Length (boom) 280cm; diameter 90cm; pitch angle 12°; reflector 116 by 116cm; input impedance 150Ω. Gain 12·7dB; beam width (−3dB) 43°, front-to-back ratio 15dB; maximum side-lobe level 11dB. This can also be used to form an array of four helical aerials

Another aspect of resistive loading in conjunction with a quarter-wave artificial ground wire was noted recently in *Tesla electronics* (No 2/72) in an article describing the optimization of parameters for a 136MHz helical aerial for the reception of space telemetry signals. This shows that in a helical aerial of moderate length improved overall results and reduced side lobes can be achieved by the insertion of a resistor a quarter-wave from the helix end. This is because a helical aerial of only a few turns does not radiate the entire energy propagating along the structure. The energy not radiated is reflected from the end and results in side-lobes and impairment of matching; it also impairs the polarization circularity. The article shows the improvement obtained with a 155Ω resistor in a four helix array having a gain of 16dB: Fig 6 shows the basic helical element with terminating resistor.

Capacitively Tuned Dipoles

Extracted from 'Technical Topics', *Radio Communication*, November 1973

Capacitively tuned dipoles

The usual approach to making an aerial effective over a wide band of frequencies is to adopt one of the various "broadband" approaches, as in the coaxial folded dipole. But would it be possible to develop a narrow-band dipole that could be electrically tuned over a wide-band of frequencies? Apparently so, to judge by some experimental work carried out at uhf at University College, London, and reported by D. Lamensdorf in *Electronics Letters*, Vol 9, No 13, 23 September 1973, pp445–6. This makes use of a configuration akin to a folded dipole but with the two sections capacitively coupled by means of capacitors. If these capacitors are fixed the dipole is resonant at one specific frequency; to make the system variably tuned, the capacitors are in the form of variable capacitance diodes. It is not intended here to attempt to reproduce the full design data given in the report. This makes it clear that there are limitations but shows that an experimental aerial operates successfully over the range 573 to 1,270MHz. In effect, the reactive component at the feed point is tuned out, leaving

ANTENNA TOPICS

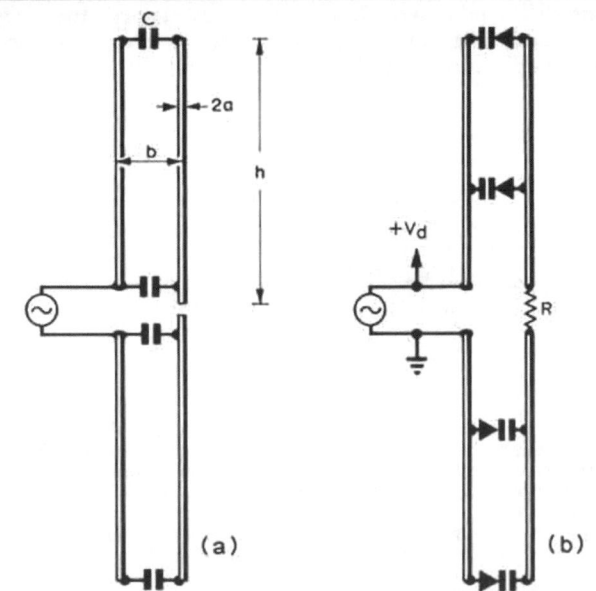

Fig 7. Capacitor tuned dipoles. (a) For single frequency (dimensions of experimental uhf model: a, 0·0794cm; b, 0·95cm; h, 7·5cm). (b) Variable capacitance diode tuned dipole covering wide band of frequencies (a, 0·0794cm; b, 0·95cm; h, 7·5cm).

reactive component at the feed point is tuned out, leaving only the resistive component; while the feed impedance varies to some extent with frequency it can be used over a wide band with a coaxial feeder and tuned for minimum swr.

which was also explored in the articles by G6XN to which we referred in the February *TT*). He notes that this can be done quite easily by using tuned feeders, although it is not a particularly efficient radiator on 7MHz since it forms, in effect, a Reinartz quarter-wave loop; radiating upwards or downwards depending on whether the loop is open or closed at the top. When open at the top the quad becomes what W6SAI calls the X-quad but in effect is a rediscovery of the old Chiriex-Mesny square of the 'twenties, which was also used with a reflector and made into arrays.

Eric Early mentions that at his suggestion F3EG has been using tuned lines to feed his quad for about five years and finds this an improvement; he himself has been using tuned lines on a 4-element 14MHz Yagi for over 15 years and on no account would ever go back to coaxial!

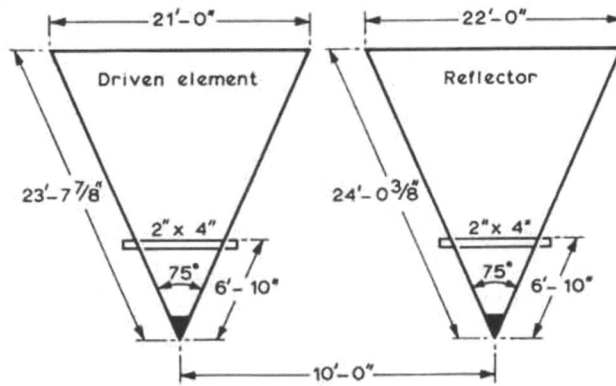

Fig 8. Dimensions of the W8PJ modified 14MHz delta-loop beam showing the use of the wooden spreaders which are then mounted on the main boom, with further struts from the apex of the loops to the boom near its central support, etc

Quad Loops and Feeders

Extracted from 'Technical Topics', *Radio Communication*, November 1973

Quads and loops and feeders

In *TT* (May 1973) we illustrated some of K8ANV's techniques for building and erecting 14MHz delta-loop beams. These showed a mechanically sound system when built with mechanical expertise, but one suspects that the amateur who owns a less perfect one is unlikely to sleep soundly during gales. This is because of the high torque which results from the high centre of gravity when the delta is mounted directly on to the boom. For those prepared to lose a little of the height advantage of the K8ANV form of mounting, Norman Fleming, W8PJ, (*QST* July 1973, pp24–27) suggests lowering the elements so that a significant part of the loop is below the boom. W8PJ says that supporting the elements by means of a wooden strut about 7ft up from the bottom takes a good deal of pressure off the boom, provides a better overall mechanical balance and keeps the elements from swinging wildly in a gale. Since the strength of the structure depends on the mechanical details, we suggest that the original article should be consulted, but Fig 8 gives some idea of the arrangement.

In his introductory notes to the 14MHz Zygi beam (*Radio Communication* July 1973), G3PTN mentions the use of a rotary half-wave loop. This has prompted Eric Early to comment on the use of 14MHz quads on 7MHz (a subject which was also explored in the articles by G6XN to which we referred in the February *TT*). He notes that this can be

Here and There: Delta-loop Quads

Extracted from 'Technical Topics', *Radio Communication*, December 1973

Here and there

In the May *TT* we included details of the method recommended by Harry Habig, K8ANV, for the building of delta loop quad aerials. During a recent 14MHz contact he passed along an important additional detail: "I was wondering why that rubber tubing was holding up so fine and then I found out it was silicon rubber. I am told that if ordinary rubber is used it is unlikely to stay put for more than a year's exposure to the sun's ultra-violet rays". The rubber tubing concerned is that used in the construction of the gamma match section. When the notes were originally prepared, K8ANV was under the impression that he was using ordinary pure laboratory gum rubber heavy tubing.

1970 - 1979

Aerials a la G6XN

Extracted from 'Technical Topics',
Radio Communication, January 1974

Aerials a la G6XN

All those who attended the recent London lecture on aerials by Les Moxon, G6XN, (a full house, but why so few younger members?) were rewarded with plenty to think about: a right royal evening of myth destruction and constructive hints. Looking through my notes I find such nuggets as:

"What's so important about front/back ratio if the beam has side lobes: tune for maximum gain".

"14MHz folded dipoles work very nicely on 21MHz" (the trick apparently is to use resonant feeders).

"There is no optimum height for horizontally-polarized aerials—get as much height as you possibly can" (even, apparently, if this means using a two-element rather than a three-element Yagi).

"Unless a low swr has been achieved after great care, this usually indicates *poor* performance."

"Interaction between different aerials is important" (and for the amateur who has everything, including *two* different beams, he can get an extra 3dB gain without difficulty).

"Loops are not single-band resonators" (see *TT* February 1973 for more G6XN views on this subject).

"Trees have a great effect on vertically polarized aerials".

"There is no limit to the possible errors when aerials are compared on the basis of ground-wave measurements".

Baluns in Reverse (Exit the Zepp)

Extracted from 'Technical Topics',
Radio Communication, January 1974

Baluns in reverse (exit the Zepp?)

G6XN also drew attention to the proportion of failures that can occur with aerials using the traditional Zepp feeder. Although the Zepp in its simplest form is still featured in almost every handbook, words of warning were published in the *RSGB Bulletin* as long ago as December 1955. Then G6CJ, in a survey of balun techniques, wrote:

"It is occasionally required to connect from an unbalanced aerial into a balanced line. The usual balun techniques can be used, but it is generally rather tricky to make all the currents keep to their correct paths when both ends of the cable are open. Fig 1 shows a good method. An aerial is connected to one side of a two-wire line. The earthed stub extension acts as a tuned centre-tapped transformer, so that the total impedance across the line is four times the aerial-earth impedance. The aerial may be moved along and a second stub added in the usual way if ratios other than 4 : 1 are needed. The earth may not be necessary but it is preferable. If a real earth is not readily available, an artificial earth can be provided in the form of a quarter-wave wire as shown: alternatively a ground plane of two or more such wires may be used.

"Simple connection of the aerial to one side of the line will not work—it is necessary to add the 'transformer winding' in the form of the stub to 'tell' the line it is balanced. *This is one reason why the old Zepp aerial was so uncertain in its behaviour*. On the other hand, two aerials, one either side and a half-wavelength apart, lazy-H style, would not need the addition of a transformer."

G6XN reported that he had made good use of the Fig 1 technique: once again pointing to the advantages of open wire feeders where no attempt need be made to keep the swr low.

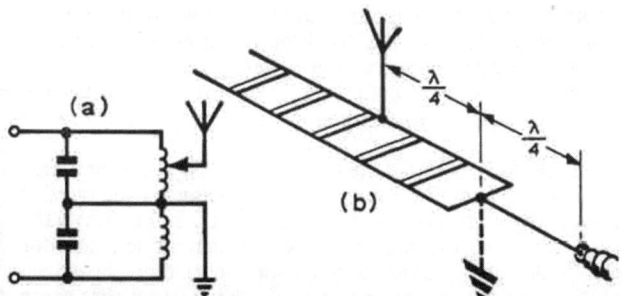

Fig 1. Technique for feeding unbalanced aerial from balanced line as originally recommended by G6CJ and found by G6XN to eliminate the proportion of failures involved in the traditional Zepp aerial while retaining the advantages of resonant feeder lines for multiband operation. Electrical equivalent is shown

Compact Beams

Extracted from 'Technical Topics',
Radio Communication, January 1974

Compact beams

One also came away from the lecture with a renewed belief in the value of the two-element beam (or rather a disbelief in the practical benefit of striving after more elements, at least

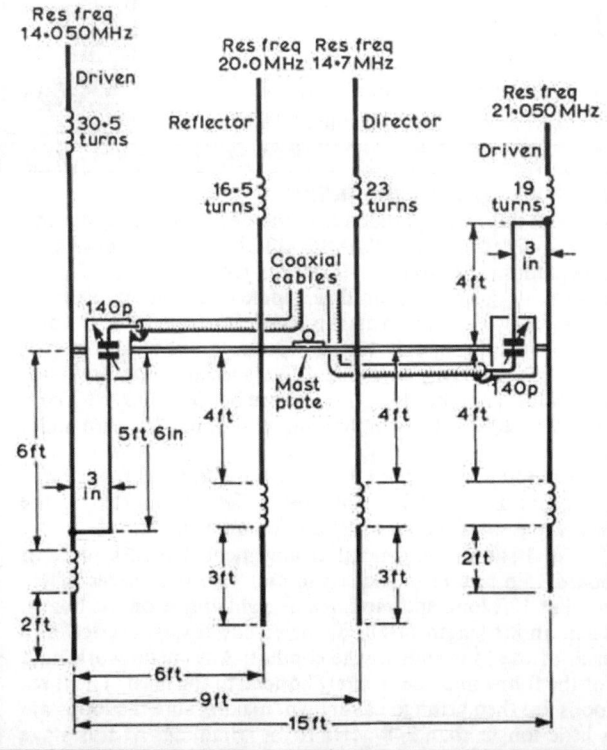

85

ANTENNA TOPICS

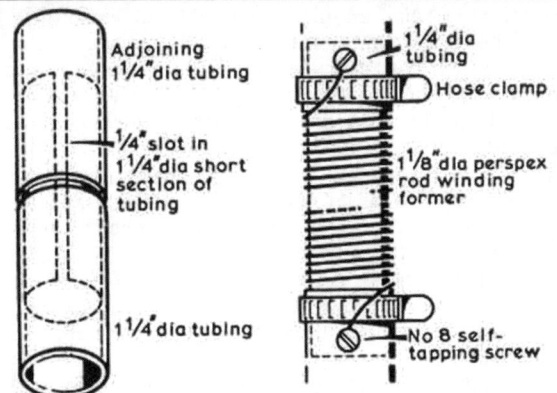

Fig 2. The compact 14/21MHz beam described by W1FBY and WA1JLD using inductance loaded elements and gamma matching

for hf). So this seems the right place to mention two recent designs.

In *QST* (September 1953) Robert Myers, W1FBY, and Clarke Green, WA1JLD, describe "A bite-size beam" for 14 and 21MHz. This is unusual in several respects, including the interleaving of two separate inductance-loaded, gamma-matched two-element Yagi beams: see Fig 2. For 14MHz this consists of a driven element plus director; for 21MHz driven element plus reflector with the direction of fire the same on both bands. The loading coils are wound on 1⅛in diameter Plexiglass rod slipped into the element tubing and held in place with compression clamps (be sure to split the ends of the aluminium tubing where the clamps are fitted). All elements and boom are in 1¼in aluminium tubing. In the original model the loading coils were wound with Teflon insulated miniature coaxial cable with shield braid and inner conductor shorted together, but a suitable substitute would be No 14 enam copper wire.

The VK2ABQ Triband Beam

Extracted from 'Technical Topics',
Radio Communication, January 1974

The VK2ABQ triband beam

A rather different approach has emerged from many months' work by Fred Caton, VK2ABQ/G3ONC, and his ideas have appeared in *Electronics Australia*, October 1973. This is shown in Fig 3 but it should be appreciated that this is drawn *looking down* on (or up at) the aerial. It has no traps or coils, a turning radius of only 12ft, no special 'blobs of electronics', and is mechanically convenient. No special claims are made for decibel gain, but the performance has left VK2ABQ convinced that "it is the simplest and best home-brew tribander yet".

In sending along the clipping from *Electronics Australia*, Fred Caton has added some extra details, inserted in the following notes on construction and adjustment.

"Fig 3 shows the general arrangement. I used a piece of board 15in square in the centre and then two pieces of ¾in conduit 10ft long and mounted at right angles on the board. Then an 8ft length of ⅝in diameter dowel was inserted into each of the four ends of the conduit. Any metal work used for the frame must be securely bonded to the mast. The three loops are then arranged as shown, making sure the loops are a little longer than 248/MHz ft for trimming. At this stage

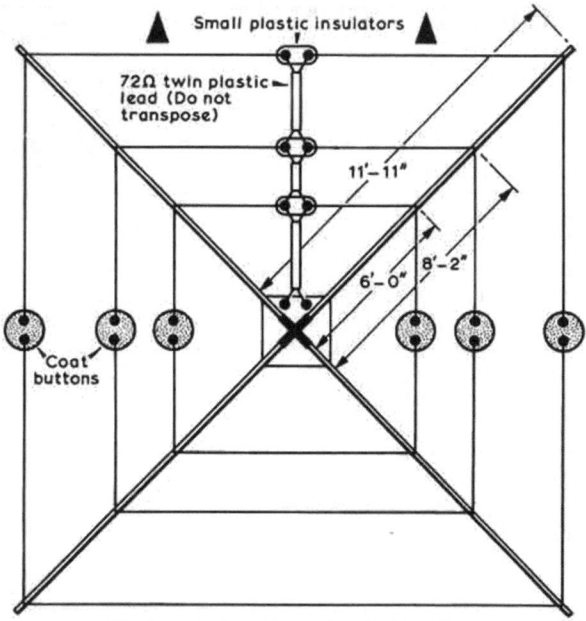

Fig 3. The VK2ABQ triband beam for 14/21/28MHz seen looking down on the aerial

leave the loops uncut, except for the interconnecting feeder: I used 72Ω twin feedline but 300Ω ribbon would probably be satisfactory, though this has not been tried.

"Adjustment is carried out with a gdo. Insert one- or two-turn link across the interconnecting feeder at the board end and check for resonance. When dipping to make sure that the dip really is of the loop of interest, grip the loop at a voltage point (eg where the button will be placed later on) and check that this affects the dip; if no change is observed grip the feeder to see if it is due to this. With adjustments made at about 4ft above ground, trim the loops to the low end of the band; this will then be about mid-band when the aerial is at normal height. At this stage the aerial takes the form of a "2PL Special" and provides a bi-directional array with relatively little radiation or pick-up off the sides.

"To make the beam uni-directional, cut the loops at exactly mid-point on each side, using coat buttons as insulators. Pass each lead through a hole in the button and tie a knot as close as possible to the wire end. This uses up very little of the loop length and resonance remains roughly as before. In this form the array should exhibit a good front-to-back ratio and forward gain.

"While adjusting, the loops are held in place by any temporary means; when trimmed, the loops can be held by open-ended screw eyes in the top of each rod. With the metal work of the conduits, VK2ABQ found the loops needed to be placed at 5ft 9in, 8ft 5in and 10ft 10in rather than as shown on the diagram.

"The impedance at the feed-point at the centre board is about 50Ω but 70Ω line can be used since the aerial exhibits a broad response. No balun has been found necessary and the radiation pattern appears to be symmetrical.

"Because of the small turning radius and lightweight construction it is easy to rotate on a pipe mast lashed to the house."

VK2BTS is reported to have duplicated the beam with equally good results. I must admit to being a little puzzled about the two sections of wire in each loop being exactly the same length, as I would have expected there to be a need for the "reflector" sections to be a little longer than the driven sections, and there are one or two other features that cause some slight qualms. But the general concept seems both interesting and a convenient way of constructing a compact tribander; so the information is presented as possibly experimental, but well worth investigating; certainly VK2ABQ/ G3ONC has had good results using such a beam.

Reducing Ground Losses with Verticals

Extracted from 'Technical Topics',
Radio Communication, March 1974

Reducing ground losses with verticals

In *QST* (December 1973) J. Sevick, W2FMI, returns to the subject of high performance vertical aerials and describes the use of top-loaded elements of about ¼λ in conjunction with an elaborate ground radial system (100 radials of No 15 aluminium wire each about 50ft long). For 3·5MHz he uses a 28ft vertical with top loading radials and base loading coil; for 14 and 7MHz a 16ft trap vertical with top and base loading. Both verticals are fed in parallel with a 4:1 matching transformer. From the illustrations it looks as though W2FMI has a site with reasonable ground conductivity and fairly open, although some trees are not far away. In his article W2FMI claims that similar good results could be achieved with a less complex ground system, but as with earlier articles on verticals by the same author it seems pretty evident that he owes a good deal to having achieved low earth losses.

Fine—but is there any practical way in which the ground losses of verticals can be reduced other than by extensive radials and favourable sites? Recent work at Fort Monmouth suggests that the answer may be "yes". The trick consists of using a number of driven verticals to form an array.

This approach is described in a paper by C. M. DeSantis, D. V. Campbell and F. Schwering in *IEEE Trans on Antennas and Propagation* Vol AP-21, No 6, November 1973, pp 769–773. This suggests that ground losses of hf aerials near ground are reduced if single aerials are replaced by arrays of, for example, two to four elements spaced by over 0·1λ apart. In the lower hf range (eg 3·5MHz) it is claimed that the achievable improvement closely approaches the theoretical limit. That is to say the use of n verticals would reduce ground losses by the factor 1/n and transmission efficiency would be raised by n^2. In practical terms this means that by using two whips one should achieve a 3dB gain, and with four verticals 6dB. This gain, it should be noted, is not the result of possible *directional* gain that can be achieved with multiple elements but is due to the reduction of ground losses—and amateurs know how much better it is to heat up the ionosphere than the soil.

The authors recall that the use of aerial arrays to reduce ground losses was suggested as long ago as 1920 and that this factor is made use of in Beverage aerials; nevertheless the principle has never been given the same attention as the use of extensive ground radials.

A number of computations at 3 and 6MHz and experimental results at 4·9MHz are presented and the idea looks decidedly promising. For the experiments the vertical radiators consisted of inductively loaded 4·9m whip aerials excited against a small 1·8 by 1·8m² wire mesh counterpoise (the whole assembly mounted on small wheels so that the radiators could easily be moved around). Special care was taken during the experiments to maintain currents of equal phase and amplitude in all array elements and to minimize undesired external feedline currents. Field strengths were measured at large distances from the array and compared to that generated by a single radiator fed with the same input as the array. Spacing of radiators was increased in steps of 0·1λ (two-element arrays show increasing gain up to about 0·4λ, broadside four-element arrays up to about 0·2λ, but in each case quite substantial gain is achieved with 0·1λ spacing).

The principle is that a substantial part of earth losses occurs in the immediate vicinity of the aerial. With an array, since ground losses are proportional to the electrical energy density in the earth, separation of the near fields results in a reduction of earth losses.

While at first sight it might appear that one is merely exchanging the need for a complex earth system for a more complex aerial array, there must be many situations in amateur operation where multiple verticals are more practical than big earth systems. So this concept seems to be an important one, and well worth following up.

PA0RCH Short Vertical for 1.8MHz

Extracted from 'Technical Topics',
Radio Communication, May 1974

PA0RCH short vertical for 1·8MHz

In *Electron* (February 1974)—and incidentally this is the journal of the Dutch society VERON and not the British publication of the same name—R. Cornet, PA0RCH, presents a detailed account of his development of a short vertical aerial suitable for 1·8MHz (and 3·5MHz). This started out, apparently, as a helix wound vertical using an 8m length of plastic drain pipe but subsequently developed into a vertical with top LC loading. He shows that this form of LC loading offers substantial advantages over an unloaded monopole of similar height and also has some advantage over the helical wound vertical, although the helix itself also gives substantially more power radiation than the plain monopole.

In effect the PA0RCH aerial provides a vertically polarized signal along the lines of the G8ON aerial where a maximum current section of a long wire aerial is arranged vertically. A basically similar effect is also achieved with the arrangement described recently by A. P. A. Ashton, G3XAP, in his "160m dx from suburban sites" article (*Radio Communication* December 1973, pp842–844). The difference with the PA0RCH is that the 130ft or so of loading wire of the G3XAP aerial is concentrated into an LC "top hat" mounted directly at the top of the vertical section. This would

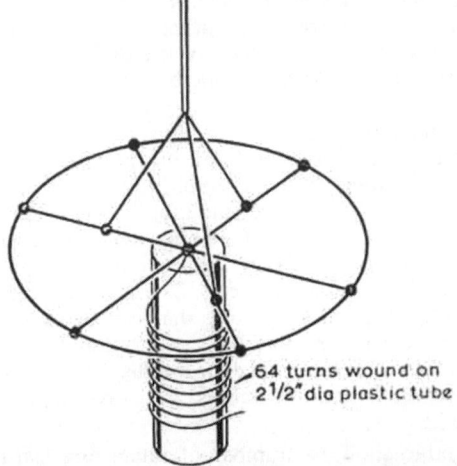

Fig 6. The top LC loading arrangements for the PA0RCH aerial. Diameter of the "wheel" is 110cm and the tripod is 1·5m high all formed with 6mm wire. Total capacitance is about 50pF and the resonate frequency of the LC is about 2·85MHz (for 3·5MHz this is made about 4MHz)

ANTENNA TOPICS

reduce the amount of horizontally polarized radiation but more importantly does not require the space needed for wire loading: the PA0RCH aerial could be erected on many sites where a G3XAP or G8ON type of aerial would be impossible.

The LC loading section consists of 64 turns of wire at the top of the 2½in diameter pipe (about 64µH) for the "L", with a capacitance hat in the form of a five-spoke wire "wheel" surmounted by a tripod wire structure: see Fig 6. The details given by PA0RCH indicate that such an aerial will tend to have a fairly narrow bandwidth (about 50kHz at 1,840kHz) for an swr of under 2.

TRANSITION LENGTHS

h/a	$Q^{\frac{1}{2}} \times h/\lambda$	h/λ Q = 300	h/λ Q = 100
50	0·307	0·046	0·066
500	0·379	0·057	0·082
5,000	0·435	0·065	0·094

26ft whereas 0·09λ is round about 47ft, it becomes clear that the use of a high quality loading coil and the form of the element have a very important bearing on the results likely to be achieved with an inductively loaded aerial.

On the general subject of short aerials, the February 1974 issue of *QST* has a clutch of articles on various forms of helical wound systems, including a 7MHz micro beam, with two 18ft elements and 15ft 8in spacing, an item on the construction and use of long helical coils for aerial loading and a review of the Teletron "Slinky Dipole" which can be stretched to between 12 and 35ft span for 7MHz and 24 to 70ft span for 3·5MHz (and which reminds me a bit of the old indoor broadcast aerials which used to be sold at Woolworth's for 6d in the 'thirties!).

Inductive Loading of Short Aerials

Extracted from 'Technical Topics', *Radio Communication*, May 1974

Inductive loading of short aerials

The PA0RCH aerial is an interesting example of how a short aerial can be improved by means of top loading, but it does appear that quite a number of amateurs are still a bit hazy about when and where it is possible to use the more conventional loading coils in conjunction with short aerials, despite the many designs, including mini-beams, that have been published. There is clearly rather more to this whole question than just sticking in an inductor of the right value and making sure with a gdo that the whole thing resonates.

Some of the important factors are well indicated in a contribution by R. C. Hansen, "Efficiency transition point for inductively loaded monopole" in *Electronic Letters* (Vol 9, No 5, 8 March 1973). The author notes that "whip or monopole antennas less than a quarter-wave long can be significantly improved through series inductive loading in the antenna wire provided that the coil losses are less than the improved radiation resistance ... however *if the antenna is too short or the coil too lossy the performance may degrade instead of improve* ... the combination of antenna length, radius, and coil Q for which the efficiency is 50 per cent is an important design guide ... this transition point varies as $Q^{\frac{1}{2}}$ and even more slowly with length to radius ratio. For Q equal to 300, the transition point occurs for monopole lengths between 0·05 and 0·07 wavelength."

Hansen refers to earlier work by Bulgerin and Walters which indicates that optimum efficiency is obtained with the loading inductor roughly *two-thirds* of the aerial length towards the end. This is in line with the positioning of the loading inductors in some mini-beams although rather different from normal practice in mobile operation.

He presents the results of a number of computer studies which give guidance on the various combinations of aerial length, aerial radius and coil Q for which the system efficiency is 50 per cent, noting that this figure is a useful guide since efficiency will fall away very rapidly below this.

In the following table, taken from this source, h and a are the monopole length and radius, λ is wavelength and Q is inductor Q.

This table shows a number of interesting features: for instance that inductive loading can be usefully employed with a thin-wire monopole (h/a = 5,000) when the monopole exceeds 0·09λ but with stubbier monopoles and higher-Q inductors the transition point is reduced to just below 0·05λ. Since, for example, at 1,900kHz, 0·05λ represents roughly

Multiband Dipoles

Extracted from 'Technical Topics', *Radio Communication,* June 1974

Multiband dipoles

An example of how an understanding of the correct handling of swr in transmission lines can be put to practical use appears in a beginner article by Ed Tilton, W1HDQ, (*QST,* reprinted *Old Man,* No 4, 1974). This is a "guy wire doublet" with a sloping 33ft top making use of an existing mast or

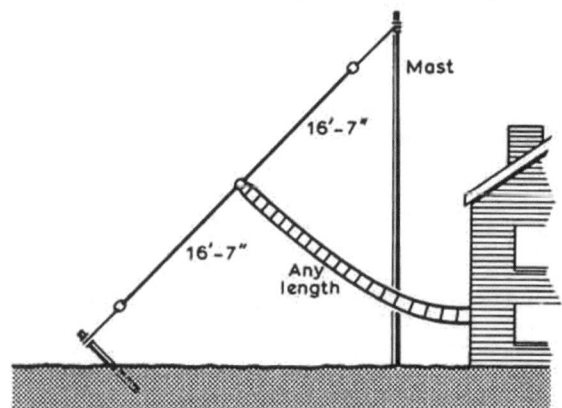

Fig 2. The simple "guy-wire doublet" which can make an effective aerial for 14, 21 and 28MHz. The balanced transmission line can either be a home-made spaced line or 300Ω feeder

tower, nothing fancy. But W1HDQ points out that with a suitable matching circuit at the transmitter end (eg Fig 3) it loads up nicely on 14, 21 and 28MHz: and if it loads up correctly it will radiate regardless of the swr and the conventional belief that the same dipole or doublet will not work on all these three bands.

Or again, the DJ2ZF multi-band dipole (included in *ART* and also *Radio Communication Handbook*) using a 2 × 13·5m element and fed with 300Ω line will work quite well on all

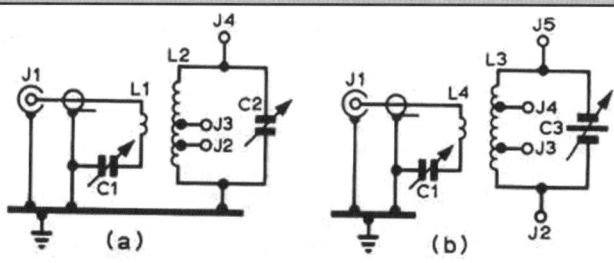

Fig 3. Typical atu or "transmatch" circuits. (a) for end-fed wires and (b) for either balanced feeders or end-fed wires, with balanced feed plugged into J2 and J5 or J3 and J4. The following values are those suggested by W1HDQ for 21 and 28MHz operation. C1 140pF, C2 as C1 but higher voltage type, C3 100pF per section split stator. J1 coaxial jack. J2-5 insulated tip jacks. L2 8 turns No 20 tinned 1¼in dia, 1¼in long, tap J2 at 2 turns, J3 at 4 turns and J4 at top end. L1 2 turns insulated hook-up wire, wound over bottom end of L2. L3 8 turns No 20 tinned, 1¼in dia, 1¼in long. Tap J2 and J5 at ends and J3 and J4 at 2 turns in from each end. L4 like L1 but wound over the middle of L3

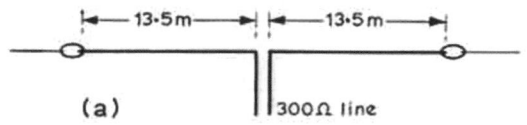

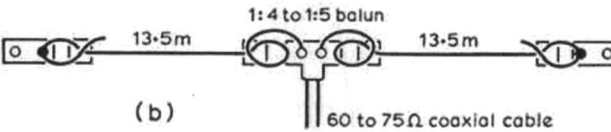

Fig 4. (a) The DL2ZF multiband dipole (element can alternatively be 2 × 27m). (b) The DJ4EL modification for use with coaxial feeder

bands from 3·5 to 28MHz (feed impedance is pretty near 300Ω on all bands from 7 to 28MHz, except for 21MHz where it is about 800Ω, but no matter). A recent version of this aerial but using 60–75Ω coaxial feeder with a 1 : 4 or 1 : 5 balun between feeder and element is described by DJ4EL in *Old Man* (No 3, 1974), see Fig 4.

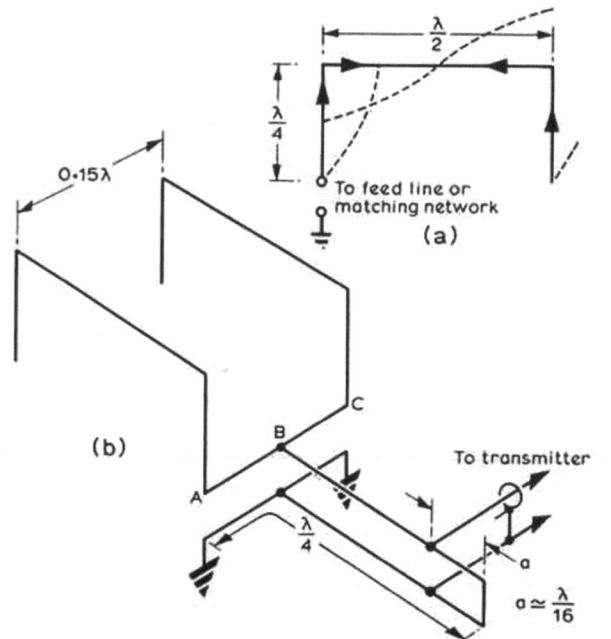

Fig 7. (a) The basic "half-square" element voltage fed at one end. (b) Two-element half-square with matching network giving greater gain and broader bandwidth

started using this arrangement when one section of his Bobtail (which once again is confirmed as a good dx aerial) had broken away without greatly affecting the feedpoint impedance and the remaining part was still giving good results.

Getting interested in this "half-square" configuration, K3BC then went further and added one (and then two) additional driven elements spaced about 0·15λ: see Fig 7(b). He found this gave consistently better results than the original Bobtail. This would seem to confirm the suggestion made by Fort Monmouth (*TT* March) that ground losses of vertically polarized aerials can be reduced by using additional elements. It would also be interesting to discover the relative proportions of vertical and horizontal polarization; in the Bobtail the horizontal radiation is partially cancelled out (at least in some directions). On the other hand, as we have noted before, there seems to be a lot to say for having dual polarized signals.

The Half-square Aerial

Extracted from 'Technical Topics', *Radio Communication,* June 1974

The half-square aerial
In *TT* (July 1972) we included an aerial that had originally been described by PA0ZN as long ago as 1934 consisting of a ½λ top section and two hanging-down ¼λ vertical sections. It was then pointed out that this arrangement had very close affinity to the Bobtail array (*ART* etc) with high-voltage points at the bottom of the two vertical sections. This particular design was voltage fed at the middle of the top section by means of the rather dubious unbalanced Zepp feeder arrangement.

It is rather interesting that this same configuration—now called a "half-square"—turns up in an article by Ben Vestler, K3BC, (*QST* March 1974) but with a different feed system and shown either by itself or with additional driven elements to form a very effective 3·5MHz dx aerial. K3BC started using this arrangement when one section of his Bob-

Broad Band Travelling Wave Dipole

Extracted from 'Technical Topics', *Radio Communication,* June 1974

Broad band travelling wave dipole
A new design for a dipole which when fed with 300Ω cable (or coaxial via a balun transformer as above) will maintain a vswr of less than 2 : 1 continuously from 3 to 15MHz and does not exceed 2·6 : 1 all the way from 2·3MHz to at least 30MHz was the subject of one of the papers at the Australian IREE Convention in Melbourne in August 1973 (an outline of some of the other papers was given in the April *TT*). This contribution was by Dr R. J. F. Guertler and G. E. Collyer and a digest has appeared in *Amateur Radio* (April 1974), the journal of the WIA. The aerial (Fig 5) consists of four sections: two 12·2m lengths of two wires spaced 1·8m apart by means of 25mm diameter aluminium tubes. A feedpoint

ANTENNA TOPICS

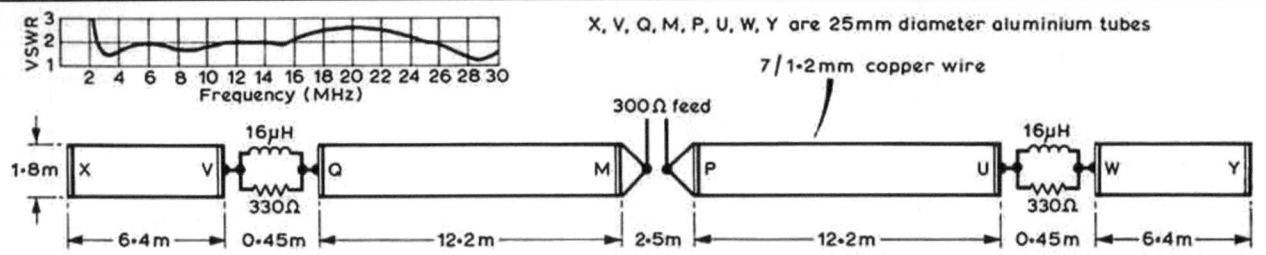

Fig 5. Broad-band travelling-wave dipole due to R. J. F. Guertler and G. E. Collyer showing magnitude of vswr over the range 2·3 to 30MHz

tapering section brings these two wires to the feedpoint. At the other end of these sections are inductor/resistor networks connected to another line section 6·4m long. The networks consist of 16μH inductors in parallel with 330Ω resistors. Overall length of the aerial is 40·6m.

It is stated that the value of neither the resistors nor the shunt inductors used in the networks is critical: the inductor has a small effect on swr at the lf end of the range; but reduction of resistor values to 150Ω caused the swr to fluctuate considerably with frequency. No indication is given in the paper of how the wattage of the resistors should relate to transmitted power, but since these are in shunt with 16μH this could be fairly modest. So if you are still worried about swr readings here is one design that keeps it below 2·5 on all bands from 3·5 to 28MHz; and should provide omni-directional radiation.

Folded Umbrella Aerials

Extracted from 'Technical Topics', *Radio Communication,* July 1974

Folded umbrella aerials

The use of guy wires to provide top loading for short vertical aerials has been described in a number of articles, but a variation is noted in an article by S. U. Nolan "Developments in mf radiator systems" in *Sound and Vision broadcasting,* Vol 15 No 1, Spring 1974.

This points out that many of the developments in mf aerials in recent years have been concerned with giving the users more for their money, both for broadcasting and maritime radio applications at 500kHz. A typical low-power umbrella aerial consists of a mast with a number of wires (typically nine) attached to the top and radiating outwards at an angle of about 45° to the horizontal.

The main limitations which arise from using a vertical radiator which is short in terms of wavelength are efficiency and bandwidth. It is stated that acceptable values of 90 per cent efficiency and 10kHz bandwidth with an swr less than 1·2 can be achieved with a mast height of only $\frac{1}{18}\lambda$ at frequencies down to about 500kHz (this ties up fairly closely with the figures we gave recently for inductively loaded monopoles for 1·8MHz). An umbrella aerial costs less than the conventional T-aerial in requiring only one mast.

It is claimed that a further simplification results from "folding" the vertical element to raise the impedance at the base to that of a coaxial feeder, so allowing the aerial to be fed directly without any matching network at the bottom of the mast, and also allowing the mast itself to be grounded for lightning protection.

The way this is done is to form a cage of wires running parallel to the mast and with all wires directly connected to the top of the mast and connected together at the base but insulated from ground and the mast: Fig 4.

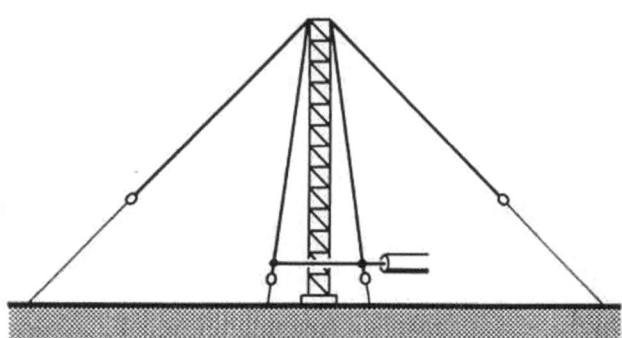

Fig 4. The folded umbrella aerial which allows mast radiators of $\frac{1}{18}\lambda$ or more to be fed directly from low-impedance coaxial feeder

The aerial is made self-resonant: that is to say, the inductance of the mast and cage of wires in parallel must tune with the "guy wire" top capacitance. The input impedance at the base of mast will be purely resistive and about 15Ω; this can be raised to the impedance of the coaxial feeder by the folding process and by adjusting the number of wires in the cage. A rather different way of loading short verticals by means of an inner wire was described some years ago by Brian Rose, G3ULR, (*ART*) but in this case the base of the mast radiator was insulated from ground. In fact the folded umbrella looks quite a useful approach for 1·8 and 3·5MHz, although to be most effective it needs either good ground conductivity or an effective earthing mat of radials.

ZS6BT Gamma-derived Stub Match

Extracted from 'Technical Topics', *Radio Communication,* August 1974

ZS6BT gamma-derived stub match

Ted Cook, ZS6BT, notes that among the various balun arrangements used to facilitate the feeding of balanced aerials from unbalanced coaxial line there is one omission. He has never seen a balun for matching coaxial to a quarter-wave closed stub, used in conjunction with a centre-fed

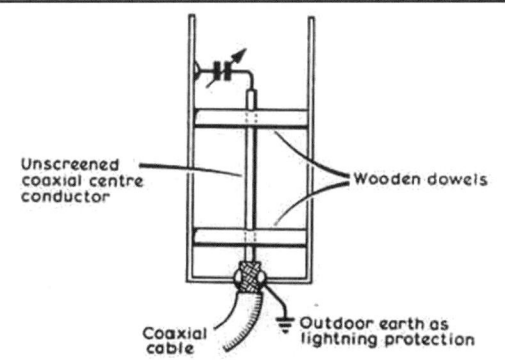

Fig 1. ZS6BT's arrangement for matching coaxial feeder to a short-circuited stub

ZS6BT gamma-derived stub match

Ted Cook, ZS6BT, notes that among the various balun arrangements used to facilitate the feeding of balanced aerials from unbalanced coaxial line there is one omission. He has never seen a balun for matching coaxial to a quarter-wave closed stub, used in conjunction with a centre-fed aerial. While I suppose it could be argued that the stub itself would represent a form of balun, this clearly does not satisfy ZS6BT. He is also keen (for lightning protection) to effectively earth down the aerial directly at the feedpoint.

Thinking the subject out, ZS6BT has come up with an ingenious solution to both his problems and he now regards the closed stub and coaxial as virtually made for each other. He simply takes over the principle of the gamma-match.

To quote ZS6BT: "Recently I erected a four-halfwave co-linear array for 21MHz using the traditional twin feeder. This meant that I had to use an atu to provide a connection to my reflectometer and transmitter via coaxial cable, and I wondered why I could not use coaxial all the way. Then the penny dropped: see Fig 1. The tapping-point is not critical (roughly one-fifth of the way up the stub). The capacitor setting is sharp but when adjusted will provide unity swr.

"The fact that the coaxial leaves the stub at the bottom point gives an excellent mechanical arrangement; as regards simplicity, it is better than using a twisted pair to feed a dipole.

"I feel that for those who used closed stubs and want to feed them—including vhf co-linear enthusiasts—this is a winner. For the inverted-V enthusiast who wishes to use half-wave legs, this is an almost ideal arrangement. Unless someone has beaten me to it, is this one for the book?"

More on the VK2ABQ Triband Beam

Extracted from 'Technical Topics', Radio Communication, September 1974

More on the VK2ABQ triband beam

January *TT* included a description of a triband hf beam which featured "no traps or coils, a turning radius of only 12ft, no special 'blobs of electronics' and mechanically simple". This design had emerged from a good deal of effort on the part of Fred Caton, VK2ABQ/G3ONC, although it was made clear in January that the dimensions suggested both on the diagram and in the text would almost certainly need a degree of cut and try and depended on such factors as the amount of metalwork used in its construction and at the top of the supporting mast or tower. In fact I was perhaps rather too cautious in adding that I had some slight qualms about the design and this may have put some readers off: this would be a pity since there are very few triband designs that can be claimed to be both suitable for home construction, easy on the pocket and offer the promise that once put up they have a good chance of staying up.

Fortunately at least one reader was not put off from trying out the idea. This was Phil Horwood, G3FRB, and his comments may well encourage others. He writes: "Results on the three bands have been very encouraging, particularly on 14MHz, where you have to be a big signal to work in the

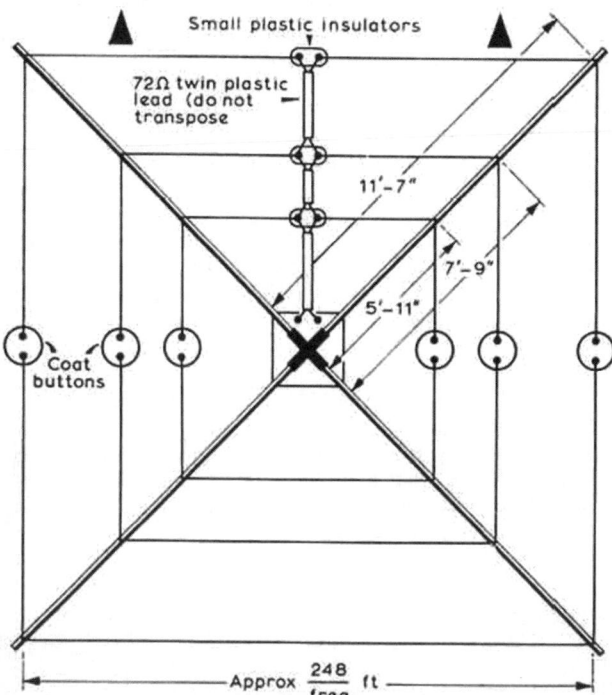

Fig 1. The VK2ABQ triband beam for 14/21/28MHz (seen looking down on the aerial) as published in the January issue but showing the final dimensions of G3FRB

American phone section. Although folded it is full-size on each band. 14MHz results are better than with a G4ZU Minibeam and comparable to the full-size 3-element Yagi previously used but which had to be taken down after neighbours had complained of a 4ft incursion into their airspace."

He adds: "On all bands front-to-back ratio is noticeably good, though not yet measured. At 55ft high I have regularly worked into VK and ZL at 2300 local time on 14MHz and during some recent unusual conditions worked W and VE east coast on 28MHz also at 2300. Even with my Versatower at minimum height, with the array just clearing the roof, I have had 59-plus reports from W and VE on 14MHz. I think this design deserves attention from amateurs who might otherwise spend £50-plus on a commercial trap beam. The cost of construction is minimal. I cut up my old Mini-beam (the victim of metal fatigue) to make the centre section, so it only cost me four 8ft bamboos and about 150ft of wire. It is very light and offers little wind resistance, and does not develop sympathetic mechanical resonances in a stiff breeze."

In fact it would seem that the only real snag is that of getting the dimensions correctly adjusted and this could be difficult without a fold-over tower or some easy way of putting the beam up and down; G3FRB found neither the dimensions given on the diagram nor those in the text were suitable in his case; 21 and 28MHz in particular varying considerably with the amount of metalwork inside the loops,

ANTENNA TOPICS

and it was also difficult to predict the change in frequency when adjusting 6ft off the ground and when finally at operating height; there was almost a 500kHz change on 14MHz in his case.

He adds to the comments of VK2ABQ on using a gdo to adjust the wires, saying: "When tuning with gdo coupled to the feed point and with the full loop uncut, gripping the voltage maxima will load the gdo and reduce the depth of dip. After the radiator is insulated from the reflector, gripping the end of the radiator increases the loading on the gdo, while gripping the end of the reflector *reduces* the load (presumably, he suggests, because this detunes the reflector and it absorbs less power from the radiator). It is useful to measure the gdo frequency on the shack receiver; he finds his gdo radiates well from the aerial over 100ft to receiver with 2ft of wire for aerial; the signal can be identified because of frequency modulation of the gdo at "wind" frequency. He feeds with 50Ω coaxial via a 1 : 1 balun at the boom, thence as suggested by VK2ABQ by flat twin, all radiators in parallel.

The final outcome of his adjustments (Fig 1) was resonance at the centre of each band, obtained with dimensions along the "booms" of 11ft 7in (14MHz), 7ft 9in (21MHz) and 5ft 11in (28MHz), but remember that these dimensions will not necessarily apply with a different amount of metalwork. Because the array is basically widespaced the bandwidth is sufficient to maintain a vswr of less than 1·5 : 1 over 14 and 21MHz and, if centred on 28·5MHz, ≤1·5 : 1 on 28–29MHz.

G3FRB also points out, to anyone still worried about my remark in January about expecting the reflector to be longer than the radiator, that at $\frac{1}{4}\lambda$ spacing a reflector is resonate at signal frequency (and similarly at $\frac{1}{10}\lambda$ the same length would be a director).

So there we are: confirmation that for the amateur prepared to do some cut and try the VK2ABQ really does represent a practical and useful approach to a triband beam.

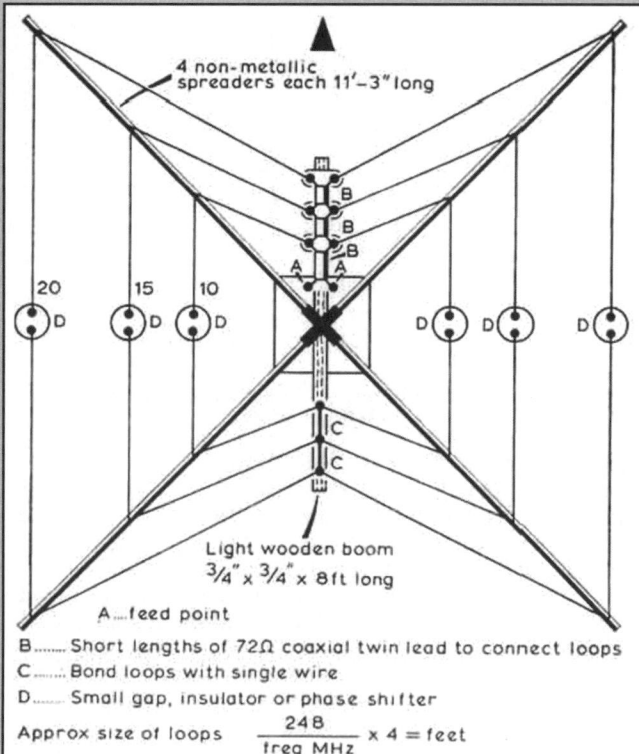

Fig 2. The modified form of VK2ABQ which by reducing the element spacing at the points of maximum current tends to produce an improved back to front ratio

that is to say the total length of wire in each initially uncut loop is about 4 by 248/f feet.

One can see both advantages and disadvantages in the modification, depending on the relative importance to the builder of front to back ratio or broader band operation and whether or not you want to avoid the extra wooden "boom".

A Modified VK2ABQ Tribander

Extracted from 'Technical Topics', *Radio Communication*, September 1974

A modified VK2ABQ tribander

Following up the original beam, as discussed above, another note from Fred Caton, VK2ABQ/G3ONC, provides two further ideas: one is a modification to the tribander, the second is a bow-tie monoband beam using rather similar mechanical concepts and which has also appeared in *Electronics Australia* (April 1974).

His modification to the triband array is basically by decreasing element spacing at the current maxima, resulting in greater front to back ratio and decreasing the turning radius to about 11ft 3in. As shown in Fig 2 he reduces spacing by means of a light wood boom (8ft by $\frac{3}{4}$in by $\frac{3}{4}$in) to which he bonds the loops with single wire. He also notes that the lengths of twin feeder between the loops does cause some capacitive loading on 28MHz and rather less so on 21MHz; these effects can be nullified by adjusting the total length of wire in the loops. Despite the change in shape, VK2ABQ finds the total length of wire in each loop remains roughly the same (but again he emphasizes the need to adjust using a gdo or swr bridge). He also clears up a point that caused some confusion in January: the suggested 248/f (MHz) represents the approximate side length of the loop in feet;

The Mono-band Bow-tie

Extracted from 'Technical Topics', *Radio Communication*, September 1974

The mono-band bow-tie

Fig 3 shows a design for a 14MHz bow-tie wire array with a turning radius of about 12ft which VK2ABQ suggests can provide a front to back ratio of the order of 20dB with forward gain of up to 6dB. It is built entirely with light timber, wire and nails. Without insulators (buttons) inserted at the extremities it will provide substantially bi-directional radiation; with the insulators it is uni-directional with up to 20–24dB front to back ratio.

The timber frame consists of one 12ft length of 2in by 1in timber, two 12ft lengths of 1in by 1in, and two 7ft lengths of 1in by 1in. Six feet in from each end of the main boom (24ft long) a 12ft cross-piece of 1in by 1in timber is fitted. Two lengths of insulated wire, each about 33ft 5in long are fitted with small close-spaced insulators at each end and with the driven element also broken in the centre with an insulator. The array can be fed with either 70 or 50Ω coaxial cable (a 1 : 1 balun would seem to be indicated but not essential).

I must admit to a feeling that if I made a framework to this

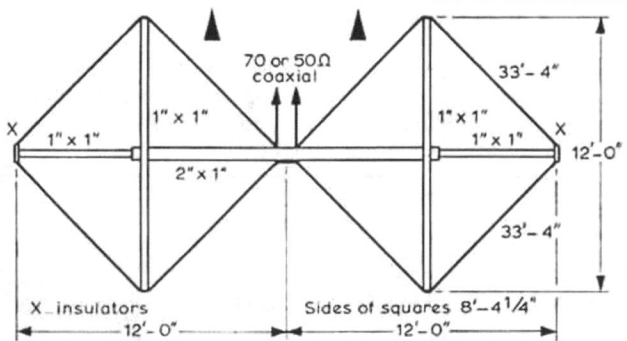

Fig 3. The VK2ABQ monoband bow-tie aerial showing dimensions for 14MHz

specification it would turn out to be rather unstable and less manageable than for the triband arrangement, but VK2ABQ states that a full scale unit has been built and fully tested at the home of a friend and that a model for reception on 144MHz has also been made. So here again is an idea for a rather out-of-the-ordinary aerial.

Some notes on recent progress of this work appear in *Electronics Letters*, 27 June 1974, in a letter from J. R. James, A. J. Schuler and R. F. Bingham. One technique which has been tried is a 3-element monopole Yagi at 1000MHz using barium-titanate powder dielectric packed between the elements; this permits their physical dimensions to be reduced by a factor of three. Tests have also been carried out using dielectric-loaded slot aerials suitable for aircraft applications: in this case the dielectric loading consisted of titanium-dioxide powder ($\epsilon_r \simeq 35$) held in position by a thin plastics skin: in this case slot lengths were reduced by about 20 per cent, the percentage bandwidth from 18 per cent to 10 per cent but the radiation resistance increased by 50 per cent. This experiment was repeated at 100MHz with ferrite loading with similar results and again with an increase in radiation resistance.

Ceramic coated monopoles at 100MHz can have a height reduction of the order of 10 times for a power loss in the material of about 2dB (but no indication is given of the maximum power that could be used).

So it is really beginning to look as though dielectric loading could prove an effective approach to miniaturized aerials, without having to put them in the sea!

Dielectric Loaded Aerials

Extracted from 'Technical Topics', *Radio Communication*, September 1974

Dielectric loaded aerials

I remember reading an article some years ago in one of the amateur journals which pointed out that if we all submerged our aerials in water it would be possible to reduce dimensions to an extent where 1·8MHz three-element beams would be all the rage. But fascinating though this seemed I was too dim-witted to see how the idea might have any real application to amateur radio. Fortunately this same concept has of late been attracting attention at the Royal Military College of Science and what is emerging (eg British Provisional Patent Application 27097 of 1973) is in a form where one can begin to see some very practical applications indeed, particularly for aerials where a degree of power loss can be tolerated in order to achieve dimensional reductions which may even be of the order of *10* times. Imagine a true $\tfrac{1}{4}\lambda$ vertical for 1·8MHz only 13ft high instead of 130ft! Though I hasten to add that I have no idea of the cost of the special ceramic material that would be needed to do this, or its power-handling capabilities.

This current work is based on the idea that if an aerial radiates into a dielectric-filled atmosphere the wavelength can be scaled down by a factor depending on the dielectric. If the relative permittivity is ϵ_r then the scaling down factor is $(\epsilon_r)^{\tfrac{1}{2}}$. The new twist is to question how much dielectric needs to surround the aerial elements. And the answer, apparently, is very little. In other words, if we have a suitable dielectric coating around the array we can achieve the reduced dimensions without affecting the radiation pattern as the waves diverge from the subsequent dielectric-air boundary.

Originally the Military College team used bulky coatings of powdered dielectric material, but more recently thinner coatings using a fired ceramic material of ϵ_r about 3,000 have been developed, allowing the overall diameter of the miniaturized element to be only a fraction of its reduced height.

Some notes on recent progress of this work appear in

Here and There: Verticals

Extracted from 'Technical Topics', *Radio Communication*, September 1974

Here and there

L. F. Ivin, G5IC, is puzzled at the value of 64µH given by PA0RCH. (*TT* May 1974) He calculates, from the details given, that the loading inductance of this short vertical aerial must be nearer 165µH. Incidentally, G5IC gets good results on 1·8MHz with a short T-aerial of which the vertical section consists of some 220 turns on 1½in tubing.

Spiral Top-loaded Aerial

Extracted from 'Technical Topics', *Radio Communication*, November 1974

Spiral top-loaded aerial

Another, but little-known, candidate for top-loaded aerials is the "spiral top-loaded aerial" (stla) which might be considered a special form of the inverted-L and which appears to offer several characteristics of particular interest to the amateur: Fig 5(a).

Basic information on the stla can be found in a paper "Spiral top-loaded antenna: characteristics and design" by H. R. Bhojwani & L. W. Zelby, *IEEE Transactions on Antennas & Propagation*, May 1973, pp 293–298. But this paper is concerned primarily with the use of such aerials for vlf operation, rather than mf or hf. More directly applicable to the amateur is an article "Experiments with two novel compact antennas for mf broadcasting" by J. L. Marshall of the Canadian Broadcasting Corporation in *CBC Engineer-*

ing Review, Vol 12, June 1974. This includes an account of the use of an stla and also a helical wound radiator: first experiments with the stla were in the form of a model aerial 0·1λ high at 30MHz; this led to a full-size aerial 65ft high and tested at frequencies between 990kHz and 1,400kHz and thus roughly equivalent to about 30ft high for 1·8MHz. Comparison tests were made with an inverted-L aerial 55ft high and with the tapered helical-wound monopole having a conductor embedded in the wall of a tubular fibre-glass mast 80ft high, with a thin whip section at the top.

The basic difference between the stla and the inverted-L is that the top wire of the stla is wound as a single unbroken wire in a spiral, in this case using insulated "X" booms at the top: Fig 5(b). It differs from the normal cartwheel type of "top hat" loading which has a series of spokes which may or may not be joined at their extremities.

In practice the Canadian mf stla took the form of a mast with total height of 63ft fed 8ft above ground, but the vertical radiator was lengthened from 55ft to 68ft by winding the

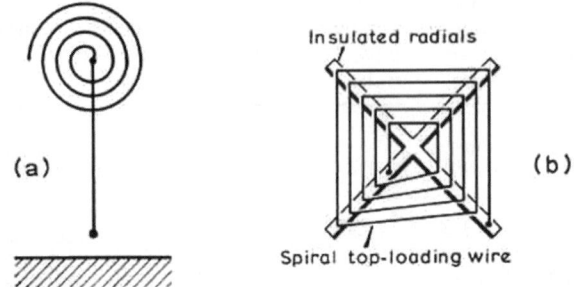

Fig 5. (a) Basic configuration of the spiral top-loaded aerial. (b) Practical arrangement of loading using insulated booms

down-lead around the wooden supporting pole in a helix, supported on small insulators. The top X structure was made of four 3in vinyl pipes, each pipe 8ft long. The top loading was then formed as a "pancake" type square-sided coil with an outer diameter of about 16ft and consisting of 135ft of wire.

The test site was on a dry sandy plateau with a few earth radials and an estimated ground resistance as high as 16Ω (ground conductivity estimated at 1mmho/m).

Various measurements made at a distance of one mile from the aerial showed that the spiral top-loaded aerial was a practical substitute for the helical-wound monopole although this was about 27 per cent higher, and was about 80 per cent as effective as the original (slightly lower) inverted-L. The author believes that if the ground resistance had been lower, the performance of the monopole and inverted-L would have improved more than the stla. On the other hand the relatively high radiation resistance of the stla is a feature of particular appeal to amateurs for whom extensive earth mats or radials are a major problem.

These practical results seem to bear out the conclusions of the *IEEE Trans* paper which suggests that the most efficient form of top loading is still the classic T or inverted-L, particularly if multiple-wire top sections are used, but that both these types require two supports and a fair amount of space. Next in order of efficiency is probably the umbrella-loaded aerial (see for example *TT* July 1974); and then the stla, which shows an improvement over the cart-wheel form of top loading and (for equivalent height) the helical-wound vertical element. The stla also seems suited to poor-earth locations.

Bhojwani and Zelby say: "The stla provides a welcome addition to the vlf antenna family with some desirable characteristics of relatively small size, low feed voltage and absence of tuning inductor."

So there we are. For the low-frequency bands, put up, if possible, a full ¼λ monopole; if this is impossible, go back to the age-old inverted-L or T using two or more spaced wires to form the top section. But if a single-mast form of construction is wanted, consider the folded umbrella or the spiral-top loaded systems as both being rather more efficient than the cartwheel top-hat. Thus, the stla is not a revolutionary breakthrough, but it does seem to provide another useful trick in the armoury of the aerial designer.

Conicals, Discones and Inverted Ground-planes

Extracted from 'Technical Topics',
Radio Communication, January 1975

Conicals, discones and inverted ground-planes

Quite a long time ago we included in *TT* (and subsequently *ART*) details of a couple of broad-band biconical aerials, including the pretty massive units developed for the Royal Navy at ASWE. A related form of broadband vertical is the discone of which, at the time, we wrote: "Details of hf discones have been given in a number of amateur publications but have never proved very popular, one of the many problems being the "top hat" disc and the dimensions which in practice limit their use to 14MHz and above". One of the standard sources on amateur discones was the 14th (and possibly other) editions of *The Radio Handbook*; the aerial was first described by Kandoian (*Proc IRE*, February 1946).

So it was with some interest that recently we received two letters about this family of aerials. One, from David Ellenberg, WA2KWP, drew attention to the article by W5WEU in *CQ* (January 1966). In fact this design of conical monopole was reproduced in *TT* (May 1966) and in all recent editions of *ART*. WA2KWP feels that this approach "represents the logical ultimate extension of the concept of top loading of the folded umbrella aerial" (*TT* July 1974).

The other letter was from Michael O'Beirne, BRS33172, and brought to attention the recent article by Mike Wintzer, DJ4GA, in *QST* (October 1974) "Dipole passé?—some experiments on discone arrangements".

This new article outlines the problems of using dipoles and ground-planes particularly for temporary locations, saying of vertical monopole aerials: "The obvious goal is to move the current maximum upwards and at the same time eliminate

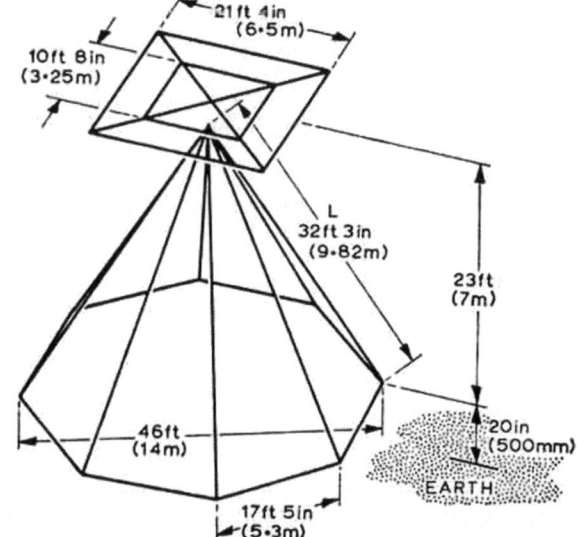

Fig 3. The simulated discone aerial investigated by DJ4GA for use between 7 and 29MHz

the necessity of a ground reference. It is also desirable to keep the magnitude of the vertical component of current high compared to any horizontal components. A first attempt in this direction would be to turn the ground plane upside down. While not very practical in most cases the principle is right!"

(This gives me an opportunity to do a little trumpet blowing in pointing out that the term "inverted ground plane" was used to describe a vertical-T aerial with two top radials used by G3VA and published in *TT*, July 1970. To the best of my knowledge this was the first advocacy in any amateur journal of this approach).

DJ4GA goes on to suggest that an aerial that satisfies these goals is the discone in which the top radials are in effect replaced by a disc (which may be simulated at hf by wires) and having a vertical radiator made broadband by the use of the conical principle of multiple wires gradually spreading out. He built a simulated discone using a "top cap" of wires about 6·5m square: Fig 3. However (to cut short the interesting description in the *QST* article) in his final form he eliminates the multiple wires and reduces the whole structure

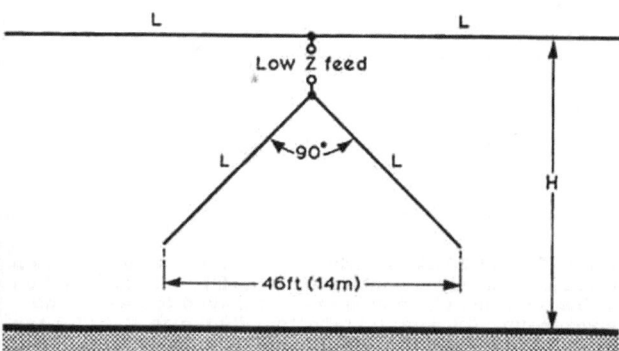

Fig 4. One version of the DJ4GA aerial as used on 7MHz. 2L is equal to 64ft 5in and all four wires are the same length L (32ft 2½in). The height H is 25ft 1in. Bandwidth for an swr of less than 2:1 was 550kHz

to two top radials (which may be in-line or at 90°) and two vertical wires: Fig 4. We are now back essentially to the G3VA vertical-T/inverted ground plane of 1970 except that the single vertical wire has been replaced by two sloping wires (and the aerial is top fed from coaxial rather than voltage-fed at the base) and this should improve bandwidth. Fig 4 shows a 7MHz version of which it is claimed that it produced significantly better results at dx and on ground-wave than a comparison dipole, but noticeably weaker signals on short skip. Altogether a very interesting aerial that can be constructed easily, though we would hesitate to call it a discone.

Low-cost Mini-quad

Extracted from 'Technical Topics',
Radio Communication, January 1975

Low-cost mini-quad

A recent newsletter of the Association of Sheffield Amateur Radio Clubs includes details of a useful-looking quad-type 14MHz beam aerial which has the elements little more than half normal size: Fig 5. It is described by P. E. H. Day, G3PHO, who, as ZL2BDA, used one most successfully during 1966-68. It has been published in a number of journals, including most recently the Russian *Radio*.

Among the attractions are that it can quite easily be made by one person, is much less conspicuous than a full-size quad, has a performance at long-distances which is claimed to be distinctly better than verticals and dipoles and, indeed, as good as the 14MHz performance of most of the popular triband beams. On the other hand it is admitted that the

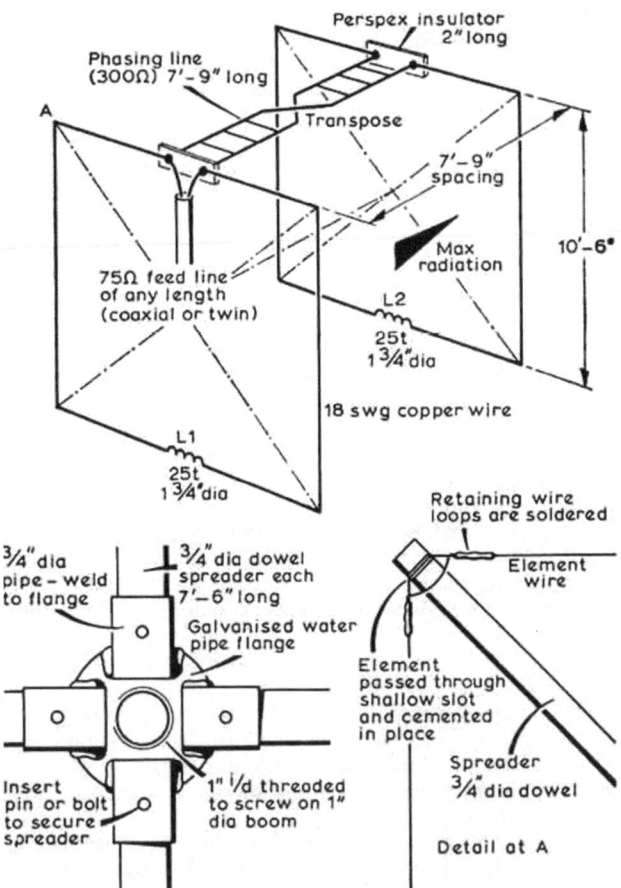

Fig 5. The mini-quad beam for 14MHz used by G3PHO/ZL2BDA as described in the newsletter of the Association of Sheffield Amateur Radio Clubs

front-to-back ratio will be less than for a full-size quad (typically 18 to 20dB at low angles, less at higher angles). It should also be noted that as for all compromise and loaded aerials it is necessary to tune and adjust the aerial carefully for optimum performance.

The following constructional hints are taken from G3PHO's notes:

(1) Spider. Cross-arms and boom assembly should be as strong as possible and able to withstand high winds. But do not use metal arms, since metal in the field of the loops can cause undesirable effects.

(2) Loading coils can be wound on pvc tubing (from builders merchants) preferably threaded on a lathe for 12 tpi. After final adjustments spray them with Holts Dampstart to keep out moisture.

(3) Tuning with swr indicator and gdo. Connect 75Ω feedline to beam and erect aerial as high as possible consistent with easy access to the coils. Preen the coils until gdo indicates resonance at 14MHz for forward element and 14·250MHz for rear element without adding or removing turns, by using 3in lengths of ferrite rod dipped in Bostik and sliding the rods in until the correct resonances are achieved, then leave well alone until the glue sticks firmly.

ANTENNA TOPICS

Aerial Miscellany

Extracted from 'Technical Topics',
Radio Communication, January 1975

Aerial miscellany

Writing from North Ryde, New South Wales, Denzil Roden, VK2BXF/G3KXF, raises some interesting points in connection with W2DU's check list on swr (*TT* June 1974) as he feels that some of these, while all true, can confuse newcomers. For instance where power is radiated from feeders it may be wasted by absorption by buildings or the ground, and such radiation can affect the directional properties of beams (but does an open wire feeder with a high swr lose power in this way to nearby objects or not?).

While he agrees that efforts to reduce swr below 2:1 on any coaxial line generally represents wasted effort from the viewpoint of increasing the radiation from the aerial, there are an increasing number of transistor output stages which have to be derated by about 3dB at this swr and should provide full power output only to an swr approaching unity.

Generally VK2BXF feels that too many amateurs (and professionals) are willing to spend much money on good transmitters and receivers while largely disregarding the inefficiency of aerials, insisting on trying and re-trying types that have been fully documented virtually since radio began, or using compromise aerials intended as a solution to space and cost limitations where these restrictions do not really apply. He writes:

"Wide-band aerials are often used where only two channels spaced less than 100kHz are used; yet such aerials require expensive heavy-duty supports and cannot easily be adjusted. In such circumstances a simple single-wire dipole would win hands down. I think that wideband aerials only have applications with the military and should be avoided where possible otherwise.

"I have come across commercial transmitters churning out 10kW via coaxial into balun-fed aerials with good swr and no indication that the aerial had collapsed and was draped across other radiators. It only goes to prove 100W erp is probably enough for a 2,000-mile path! And if one were cynical one might wonder why commercial baluns have large cooling fins!

"These are greatly over-rated for transmitting purposes and usually offer no improvement in radiation efficiency. The most they do is to cause dipoles etc to fire at right angles to the run of the wire and in practice this makes only marginal improvement. Commercial baluns often exhibit high losses at certain frequencies within the span of frequencies advertised as flat. A great awakening is taking place as users begin to look for the most efficient aerial for a particular situation."

The VK2ABQ Pseudo-quad

Extracted from 'Technical Topics',
Radio Communication, February 1975

The VK2ABQ pseudo-quad

Fred Caton, VK2ABQ/G3ONC, has already chalked up several useful contributions to *TT* aerial lore—but he has now come up with another novel idea for a mini-beam that has no traps or loading coils and looks like a quad but is not. Following evaluation of the design at vhf he has built and tried a 14MHz model and also proffers the (untried) suggestion that a 7MHz model would come out smaller than a conventional 14MHz quad. Like all miniaturized and loaded aerials one inevitably loses some gain and increases the need for careful adjustment, but VK2ABQ reports achieving about 18dB front-to-back ratio which in the real world of interference is often as useful operationally as striving after more forward gain.

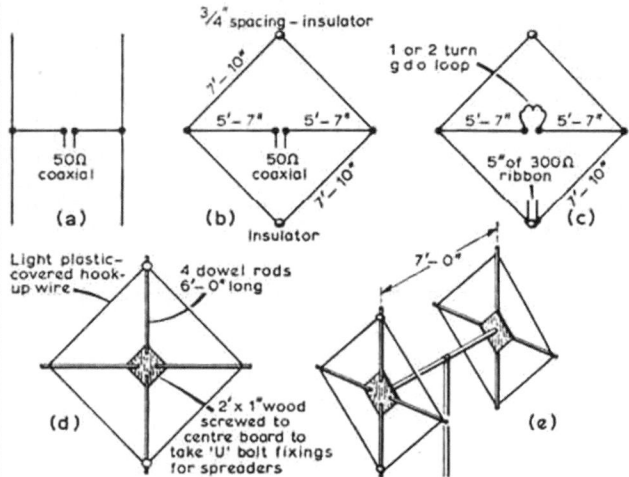

Fig 3. The VK2ABQ pseudo-quad (actually a form of Yagi using end-loaded horizontal elements): (a) basic configuration of the element; (b) formed into a diamond to provide more manageable structure; (c) reflector with tuning stub; (d) and (e) basic construction of the framework

The aerial is based on the relative high efficiency of a heavily end-loaded element. In practice the basic horizontal diagonal of a 14MHz element is about 11ft 4in and the boom about 7ft. As VK2ABQ puts it, with a touch of nostalgia, "this beam would fit into small but beautiful English gardens very nicely".

In effect an end-loaded dipole in the form of an H-element is bent into a more manageable diamond shape to make the driven element: Fig 3. In doing this the radiation pattern of the H element with its deep nulls off the ends is but little affected. The dimensions given in Fig 3 were those found by VK2ABQ to resonate at 14·2MHz with the bottom apex about 9ft off ground.

In practice simple and extremely light frames were made using ⅝in dowel rod with a wood plate 9in by 9in at the centre and with a piece of 2in by 1in wood for the U-bolt which attaches the element to the boom, for which he uses a 7ft length of light tubing of about 1¼in diameter. Both the frames for the driven element and the reflector are identical but the reflector includes about 5in of 300Ω ribbon feeder which is trimmed to resonate the reflector to 13·3MHz using a one- or two-turn gdo loop as shown, and which is then left *in situ* (or the two halves joined).

It would be possible to rotate the loops by 90° if vertical polarization were required, and a tri-band beam could be formed by interlacing the 21 and 28MHz elements in the usual way, and all fed at the same point; short horizontal wire sections are spaced equal distances along the dowel rod and taped in place. The reflector stubs are tacked on to the dowel rod and each reflector loop resonated at a frequency 5 per cent lower than the driven element.

Saucepan-lid Reflectors for UHF?

Extracted from 'Technical Topics',
Radio Communication, February 1975

Saucepan-lid reflectors for uhf?

On several occasions reference has been made in *TT* and *ART* to the development by H. W. Ehrenspeck at the USAF Research Laboratories of various forms of vhf/uhf "backfire" aerials and his use for this purpose of large planar

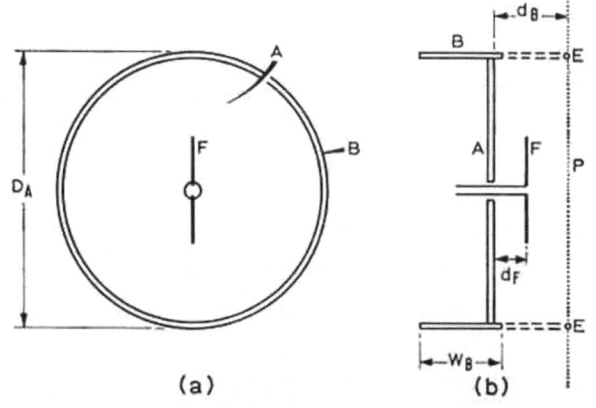

Fig 5. Sketch of the experimental aerial system used by Ehrenspeck to investigate effect of varying the rim depth on gain

reflectors having a saucepan-like lip or rim (Fig 5). He has now suggested that this type of reflector has a special value when the dimensions of the lip are carefully adjusted and can then give significantly greater gain than would be possible when using an equivalent area of plane reflector (*IEEE Trans Ant & Prop,* March 1974, pp329-332).

In one of a series of examples, Ehrenspeck uses a reflector with a diameter of less than 2.35λ having an adjustable depth of rim. His results indicate that gain is optimized when the rim in the forward direction is 0.6λ, at which point the directive gain of the aerial is 14·2dB or 5·2dB better than would be achieved with a rimless reflector: Fig 6. On the other hand increasing the rim beyond this depth causes the gain to fall off again until at 1.5λ it is actually below that of a rimless reflector.

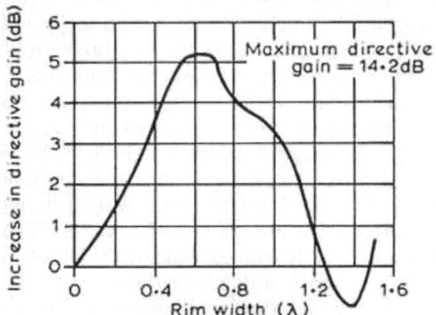

Fig 6. How rim width was found to effect the directive gain of the saucepan lid aerial

The short paper gives a detailed account of his series of experiments on various sizes of reflector (if beyond a specified diameter these need to be illuminated by a Yagi type of array as in his backward-firing aerials).

This approach could clearly be of interest at uhf as an alternative to conical or paraboloidal reflectors, or even G3RPE's microwave dustbin lids, though it must be admitted that relatively few amateurs appear to have followed up his earlier work on various backfire techniques.

Trees as Aerials

Extracted from 'Technical Topics',
Radio Communication, April 1975

Trees as aerials

In *TT* (April 1974) attention was drawn to work by the US Army in using trees as hf aerials with encouraging results, particularly in conjunction with hf pack sets under jungle conditions. Several readers have recently drawn attention to a more detailed account of this investigation in *IEEE Trans on Ant & Prop,* January 1975, pp137-39. For example, rather more details are given on the "hemac" (hybrid electromagnetic coupler) which is fastened to the tree to provide coupling to the transmitter.

To quote the paper: "The tree trunk was used as a single-turn secondary winding in a resonant toroid-type transformer, wherein the primary winding was a flexible toroidal spiral wrapped around the tree trunk. When stretched out completely, the toroid becomes a 24ft long electrical wire antenna; when pushed together it becomes a coiled magnetic loop antenna of about 8in diameter". In other words one has a large floppy coil fastened around the trunk with a matching unit between the coil and the coaxial feeder to the transmitter.

It is shown in the paper how trees were tested on a 12W pack set on 4·65MHz over distances of a few miles in various conditions, including damp jungle conditions in the Panama Canal Zone. The various combinations such as whip-to-whip, tree-to-whip, tree-to-tree of transmitting and receiving aerials were tried. In addition some tests were made with 35W at mf, between 425 to 460kHz, over distances of 30 to 35 miles using very large oak trees.

The various results do seem to indicate quite clearly that trees can provide considerably better performance (by up to 20dB) than short whip aerials used in jungle conditions. The authors (Ikrath, Kennebeck and Hoverter) suggest that the superior performance of the trees is in a large part due to their ability to produce and to sense the dominant horizontal polarization, ie horizontal polarization has the greater survival role in the dominant vertically-structured roughness of terrain and vegetation.

So this is yet another indication that for communication in jungle or even wooded areas, vertical polarization is something to be avoided—a point that has been made a number of times in connection with hf and vhf operation and which turns up again in the next item. This conclusion may in the long term prove more useful than the information on the use of trees as aerials, fascinating though it would be to have a whole new family of certificates and awards for "Worked all British deciduous trees" or perhaps "The Oak and the Ash and the Bonny Ivy Tree Award".

ANTENNA TOPICS

All-band Composite 'T' Aerials

Extracted from 'Technical Topics', *Radio Communication,* May 1975

All-band composite "T" aerials

Not a lot of space for aerial topics this month, but we will try and squeeze in a couple of ideas for multiband hf aerials, both drawing on the "T" principle.

Necessity led Bob Roberts, G2RO, to develop the composite, cut-and-try compact all-band (1·8 to 28MHz) arrangment shown in Fig 6, and applicable where there is a single high support point near the shack.

ABC, with an included angle as large as possible and with AB equal to BC, is resonated with a gdo as an independent $\lambda/2$ on 3·5MHz. DE is separately resonated as an earthed $\lambda/4$ to the same frequency. B and D are then permanently joined and the aerial is complete.

The matching arrangements are conveniently selected by a two-band, six-way switch. On 1·8MHz, E is connected to the inner conductor of the coaxial cable through a series capacitor. On the other bands, E and the coaxial cable inner conductor are connected to coil taps on a switch-selected tuned circuit. The cut-and-try of the taps is adjusted for maximum current or voltage on the aerial and for minimum swr, simply as an indication that the system is working as planned.

On 1·8MHz the aerial forms a long $\lambda/4$ matched directly to the coaxial feeder by the series capacitor of a non-critical value—around 680pF for 50Ω cable. Being top loaded, it has high current at the high point. On 3·5MHz the aerial couples like a $\lambda/2$ but has a vertical $\lambda/4$ component coupled to a $\lambda/2$ inverted V, both with maximum current at the high point. On 7MHz it again couples as a high impedance, representing a $\lambda/2$ vertical coupled to a co-linear pair of sloping $\lambda/2$ sections. On 14, 21 and 28MHz it couples as an odd or even number of approximately $\lambda/4$ sections.

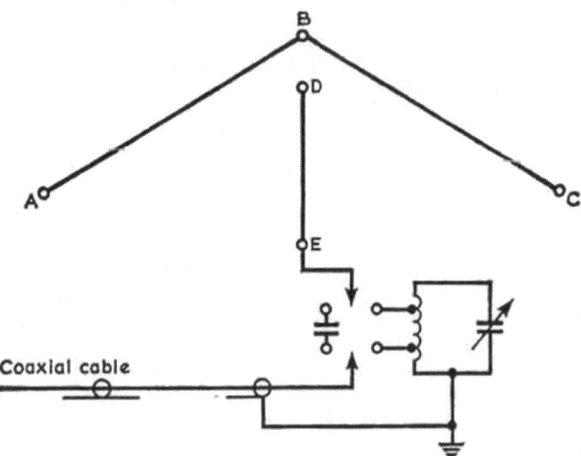

Fig 6. G2RO multiband aerial for all bands from 1·8MHz to 28MHz. For dimensions see text. After adjustment with gdo points B and D are permanently joined

On 1·8MHz it takes G2RO's 10W signals across the Atlantic. On 3·5 and 7MHz it forms a markedly competitive dx aerial. On 14, 21 and 28MHz it resonates tidily and radiates sufficiently.

The other system (Fig 7) comes from an article on L and T aerials by Hans-Joachim Brandt, DJ1ZB, in *QRV* Nr 2, 1975, and is based on a system used by DL2EO for 7 to 28MHz operation.

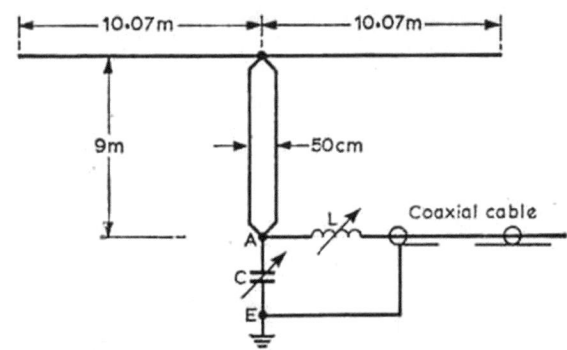

Fig 7. "T" aerial used by DL2EO for 7, 14, 21 and 28MHz. The feed impedance (A-E) is given by DJ1ZB as: 7MHz 1,500Ω; 14MHz 800Ω; 21MHz 700Ω; 28MHz 600Ω. Suitable values for L and C are given as follows:

Band(MHz)	7	14	21	28
L(µH)	6	2·3	1·4	1·0
C(pF)	80	50	40	30

Shoulder-mounted VHF Loop Aerial

Extracted from 'Technical Topics', *Radio Communication,* June 1975

Shoulder-mounted vhf loop aerial

The low-weight "personal" vhf/uhf transceiver is capable of providing a valuable and convenient communications facility—as witness its use by the police. I well remember the considerable struggle that took place some 10 years ago to convince the authorities that the policeman on the beat could really be provided with workable and reliable equipment that would keep him in touch with the station sergeant (one of the earliest and most fervent advocates was Ian Campbell-Bruce, G5IB). The amateur in many areas now has the further incentive of having repeater systems to extend the range.

Most of the British police adopted uhf rather than vhf; this gave the advantage that signals reflected well into built-up areas and also resulted in very short aerials that could be retracted into the body of the unit. But in many countries police personal radios operate in the range 150 to 170MHz and are thus directly comparable with 144MHz practice. This had led to considerable investigation into compact vhf aerials—and how these can be placed so as to minimize absorption losses of the human body.

In *TT* (September 1968) we referred to a classic paper on this subject by Krupa who recognized the very considerable losses that occur when the aerial is in close proximity to the operator's body. This was confirmed more recently in the UK by R. W. Smith, who showed that when an aerial is close to the body or limbs of an operator up to 90 per cent of the signal may be lost. Dr D. A. Tong, G8ENN, in a full-length article in *Radio Communication* (July 1974) drew attention to the normal-mode helical aerial which allows a 144MHz hand-portable aerial to be reduced in length to

1970 - 1979

a 144MHz hand-portable aerial to be reduced in length to about 6in (a technique commonly used by the American police) although he did not go into the question of body losses.

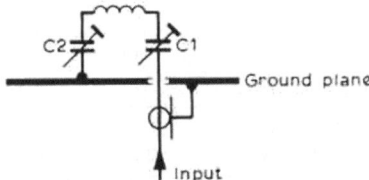

Fig 1. Arrangement of the multi-turn vhf loop aerial. C1 is 0·35 to 3·5pF to establish the correct impedance matching; C2 is 0·8 to 10pF for tuning to resonance. For 150 to 170MHz the loop consists of 3·5 turns of ⅜in wide copper foil wound on a styrofoam form 2·7 by 2·7 by 0·7in high

A novel idea for personal radio aerials is described by H. E. King in *IEEE Transactions on Antennas & Propagation*, March 1975, pp 242-245. This provides a very compact low-profile aerial for shoulder mounting that is only just over half-an-inch high, basically weighs under 3oz, (or a little more when used with a shaped "ground plane" that improves efficiency). The aerial, as described, is tunable over the range 150 to 170MHz with a bandwidth of 1·4MHz for a 3:1 swr; it would thus seem well suited for adaptation to 144MHz operation. The aerial is worn continuously on the shoulder and connected via coaxial cable to the equipment which may be carried in a pocket or waist pouch etc; it is possible to wear a jacket or coat *over* the shoulder aerial with only a little loss of efficiency, or of course the aerial can be worn outside a coat; with a microphone head-set and vox it could provide completely hands-free operation.

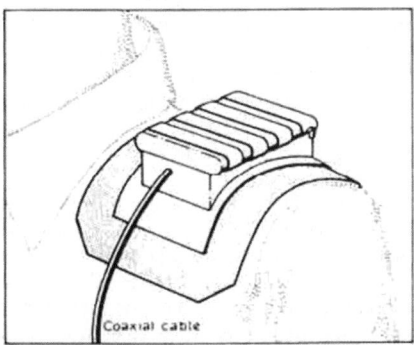

Fig 2. Sketch of shoulder-mounted multi-turn loop with 4·5 by 6·5in metal counterpoise

The aerial consists of a multi-turn loop wound on a styrofoam form 2·7 by 2·7 by 0·7in; the coil itself comprising 3·5 turns of ⅜in-wide copper foil: Fig 1. The coaxial cable and tuning and impedance matching capacitors are assembled on a metallic ground plane which is extended by a 4·5in by 6·5in (minimum) "counterpoise" shaped to fit round the shoulder. Detailed radiation patterns in the *IEEE Trans* paper show that this unit had an average gain of 3·8dB over a shoulder-mounted 6·6in helical-wound whip, which itself is roughly 5dB down on a full-size ¼λ monopole whip. A disadvantage compared with the helical aerial is the restricted bandwith, which calls for fairly careful tuning. This should be done with the aerial in position on the shoulder (requiring an assistant or a contortionist!) though there is little change in tuning adjustment from person to person so it can be tuned safely on someone else. It is also shown that better average results are achieved with the loop axis running fore and aft (Fig 2) rather than directed sideways along the shoulder. It is predominantly vertically polarized.

Altogether this multi-turn loop aerial looks well worth investigating for 144MHz use.

The Very Low Aerial

Extracted from 'Technical Topics', *Radio Communication,* August 1975

The very low aerial

What may turn out to be yet another version of this theory—the lower the better—seems to be rapidly gaining ground among military communicators. There is of course a solid basis for the idea that a very low dipole, a few feet above ground, radiates mostly at a very high angle of radiation and can thus be used effectively in the 50 to 200-mile range. An aerial between 7 and 20ft high can be very useful and can often be superior to whip aerials for medium distance working from sites among trees and buildings. For portable operation it is much easier to carry supports for a low dipole than a high one; as G6XN has shown convincingly you can, if you want to, also get good low-angle radiation from such an aerial by making use of ground slope. So far so good, but increasingly one finds writers going even further and making a positive virtue out of necessity and claiming that low aerials will give you *better* results in the 50–200-mile range than a higher dipole, ignoring the fact that a low aerial is likely to waste more power in heating up the ground (dielectric losses) or from absorption generally.

A recent article by Ross Bell of Collins Radio (*Telecommunications*, March 1975) along these lines, and advocating dipoles of less than 0·35λ above ground, has been

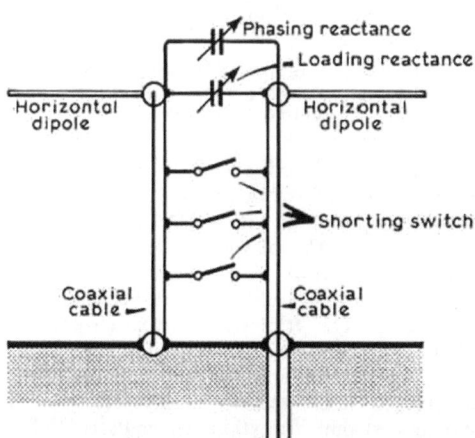

Fig 1. Low horizontal dipole with an outline of the coupler which is used to provide automatic frequency tuning throughout the hf band. The shorting switches in effect vary the inductance provided in the balun; the inductance is fine-tuned using the shunt capacitor. Typically the coupler efficiency is about 50 per cent at 2MHz and 80 per cent at 4MHz. Collins Radio have a 3kW coupler of this type, tuning any frequency in the 2 to 30MHz band in a matter of seconds

brought to my notice by R. Skelton, 6Y5SR. However, it includes a rather interesting form of balun and tunable coupling technique: Fig 1. The tuning components consist of a series capacitor (phasing reactance), a shunt capacitor, and a shunt inductor made from a two-wire line shorted at the base (ground), and with the inductance varied in steps by adjusting the length of the line by shorting switches across it. The inductance is fine-tuned using the shunt capacitor. Typically the aerial is 20ft above ground and is intended for operation throughout the range of 2 to 15 or even 30MHz. In military operation the coupler is fully automatically tuned to any frequency in a matter of seconds. But I would still like to know if it really gives better results than a similar aerial at say 30 or 40ft!

ANTENNA TOPICS

A Low Trapped Aerial

Extracted from 'Technical Topics', *Radio Communication,* August 1975

Changing Polarization

Extracted from 'Technical Topics', *Radio Communication,* August 1975

A low trapped aerial

But one useful outcome of this present interest in very low aerials is that it shows that, *when necessary,* acceptable results can be achieved with hf aerials only a few feet above deck (sometimes even when laid along dry earth).

For example, S. Beauchamp, G3SYD, wonders whether the idea shown in Fig 2 may be of interest to others who, like himself, have insufficient space to erect a full-sized aerial or a local authority refusal of permission to put up *any* aerial in the garden. Basically it is half a trapped dipole, with the radiator running along the side of the house only 6ft from the ground and only 3ft from the 7ft-high garden wall. It cannot be seen from the road. Without any atu it provides acceptable results on 3·5, 7 and 21MHz, with an swr of no more than 3:1 on 14 and 28MHz.

The requirements include a very good earth stake (G3SYD

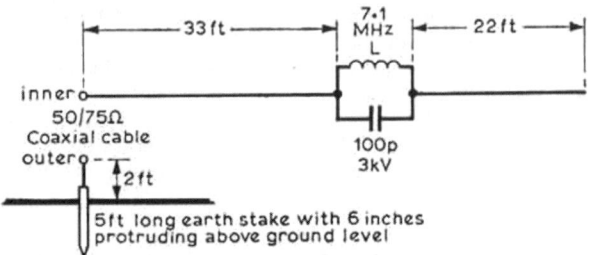

Fig 2. G3SYD's "invisible" aerial about 6ft from the ground and running alongside a 7ft garden wall gives him a 3·5 to 30MHz capability

uses a 5ft length of ½in copper pipe) and a 7·1MHz trap made from 12 turns of 16swg wire on a 1½in former (wire-diameter spaced) and tuned with a 100pF 3kV wkg capacitor, about 56ft of 28/0·0076 plastic-covered wire (or 14 swg hard drawn copper wire). Feeder length should of course not be critical, though G3SYD mentions that he avoids equal ¼λ lengths. The trap coil is weather-proofed with polyurethane varnish (well coated) and the connections between the aerial wire and the trap coil are made with connectors from "chocolate strip" connectors.

I would suggest that if anything other than QRP is used with these very low aerials, some thought should be given to ensuring that nobody gets rf burns off the wires, and that there is the usual rf choke as part of the pi-coupler to ensure that even under fault conditions no ht can possibly reach the aerial.

Incidentally, in *QST* (May 1975) Don Walters, WA8FCA, points out that inexpensive high-voltage capacitors for aerial traps can be made very simply from short lengths of coaxial cable which can then conveniently be bent around the inductor. He suggests that, for example, RG58/U cable will handle all the voltage likely to be encountered at operating powers up to about 100W.

Changing polarization

With the present mixture of vertically- and horizontally-polarized aerials for vhf fixed and mobile operation, the question of polarization coupling loss (ie the loss that occurs when receiving vertically polarized signals on a horizontally

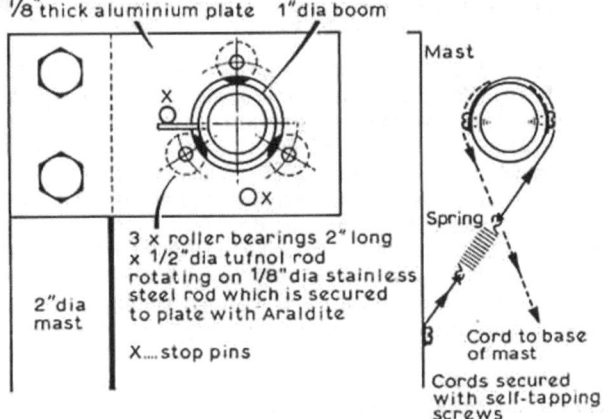

Fig 3. GW8JOJ avoids polarization coupling losses by swinging his 144MHz beam aerial through 90° to give him vertical or horizontal polarization

polarized aerial and vice versa) can loom very large. Mike Cooper, GW8JOJ, in some experiments with GW8GPX over a distance of 10 miles on 144MHz using a 10-element transmitting aerial and a dipole receiving aerial, measured an average coupling loss of 17dB with losses sometimes being as high as 30dB. These figures are in line with those found in vhf and uhf television practice.

So, he wondered, how should he mount his domestic beam? On 144MHz, horizontal polarization has the edge for dx operation, but vertical polarization is customary for mobiles and repeaters. The possibility of 45° slant polarization presents the problem that some stations may slant the other way. Circular polarization is attractive, though involving a 3dB power loss when received with linear polarization. His solution is shown in Fig 3 and consists of the ability to rotate his Yagi beam through 90°. The boom is held to the mast by two plates supporting three roller bearings. The boom is held horizontally by the tension of a spring. By pulling a cord at the base of the mast the boom is pulled against the spring to the vertical plane and the cord tied at the base of the mast to hold it in this position. Stops are fitted to ensure 90° rotation. Exit polarization coupling loss.

Ground Planes - Pros and Cons

Extracted from 'Technical Topics', *Radio Communication,* August 1975

Ground planes—pros and cons

Recently out of interest we counted up the totals of the various types of aerials reported in use by stations contacted on 14MHz over a few weeks and found that the ground plane emerged as a clear winner; twice as many stations gave it as their aerial as gave "dipole", and many more than most other types. Even if one counted the W3DZZ trap dipole and other variants as dipoles, the difference became less pronounced, but nevertheless the ground plane still led the field.

The reason is probably the mechanical simplicity of the ground plane and its suitability for use in limited space. One also suspects that there is a widespread belief that a vertical aerial results in low-angle radiation (a belief that can be justified only in conditions of good earth conductivity).

This brings us to a report from Ted Burgis, G6FB, who has carried out over a fairly long period on 14 and 21MHz a comparison between a dipole 22ft high and a conventional four-radial ground plane with the feed-point also about 22ft above ground.

He finds: (1) the dipole always gives an S-point advantage in the broad directions of its lobes, though the ground plane scores off the ends of the dipole; (2) the swr on the dipole changes after rain and it is possible (by assuming that wet grassy earth is a good conductor) to estimate fairly well the electrical height of the dipole by reference to the standard feed-point resistance versus height curves in the handbooks. Very little variation of the swr occurs with the ground plane.

This has led G6FB to question the efficiency of the four-radial system and he wonders if it would be better to use more, noting that up to 120 ground radials are used by the BBC and IBA for medium-wave operation. While it is true that the four-radial system is of limited efficiency, I suspect that on 14MHz and above it would not make a very significant difference to add radials to a raised ground plane, although certainly the creation of really good earth mats is important on the lower frequency bands and where using several verticals to form an array.

The very strong signals from East European stations using ground-plane aerials also suggest that in many cases they radiate a good deal of the energy at high angles.

Elastic Aerial Supports

Extracted from 'Technical Topics', *Radio Communication*, September 1975

Elastic aerial supports

Those of us who use trees as aerial supports know the problems only too well. I once virtually wrecked a window frame that was less strong than the aerial wire. The counterweight technique still leaves the branch constantly rubbing the support wire. For a time I used a metal spring that I believe had come originally from one of those old chest expanders, but they do corrode.

Brian Castle, G4DYF, has been using a piece of heavy-gauge elastic between the nylon lanyard and the aerial. By means of a spring balance with the wire temporarily rigged at ground level he found the tension in a total span of about 170ft was of the order of 25lb when the wire was pulled really tight. This tension can be sustained by minimal extension of a double length of the heaviest gauge of readily available elastic (about ⅜in diameter, nylon braided, as sold by builders merchants and ship chandlers). The length required can be estimated by watching the sway of the selected tree and then allowing a further margin for safety and checking that the elastic can provide this. A loose loop of rope between the ends will keep the aerial up when finally the elastic breaks, as it is sure to do eventually. By putting the elastic in the horizontal span one avoids the constant sawing of the rope through the pulley.

Low Aerials

Extracted from 'Technical Topics', *Radio Communication*, November 1975

Low aerials

Bob Eldridge, VE7BS, writes from British Columbia to challenge the view that there is no merit in purposely placing a dipole at a relatively low height for short-distance ionospheric communication. He writes:

"Surely you are not challenging the whole cos ($H \sin \phi \pm 90°$) thing? This is not just an idea, it is the basis for a lot of practical working short-distance circuits.

"I do not know whether Ross Bell mentioned the significance of the $0·35\lambda$ height in his article, but it makes sense to use this as the limiting height—at $0·4\lambda$ cancellation becomes marked in the straight-up direction, and by $0·5\lambda$ it is complete. To fire straight up, $0·25\lambda$ or some odd multiple would obviously be the best height but, since the gain straight up is as good at $0·25\lambda$ as at $0·75\lambda$ or $1·25\lambda$, why bother to go higher?

"These writers are not ignoring the possibility of dielectric losses in the ground—they are making the judgment that the reflective help from the ground is more beneficial than the possible losses are harmful. It is no myth that there is an optimum height for a specific vertical polar angle. This 'theory' tempted me to lower my 3·5MHz aerial to put a better signal into Seattle in order to run a chess match one Sunday, and I was rewarded with a continuous E-layer contact for more than 7h; I assure you that at its normal height the signal was several S-points lower. I adjusted it by successively lowering each end while checking signal reports, praying that it would not rain. After all, would you place the reflector of a beam as far back as possible rather than $0·25\lambda$ or less?"

On this one I still feel that much depends on the conductivity of the soil; my own argument was rather with those writers who suggest we must strive to put a dipole an exact $\lambda/2$ above ground to get the lowest possible angle of radiation due to cancellation. But clearly there can be two views!

DL2EO T-aerial on 3.5MHz

Extracted from 'Technical Topics', *Radio Communication*, November 1975

DL2EO T-aerial on 3·5MHz

In the May *TT* attention was drawn to a multi-band T-aerial as used by DL2EO and described by Hans-Joachim Brandt, DJ1ZB, in *QRV* No 2 1975. It was then indicated that the aerial could be used on 7, 14, 21 and 28MHz, but DJ1ZB noticed that no mention was made of its use on 3·5MHz as details of this had been contained in the German text. He has

ANTENNA TOPICS

details of this had been contained in the German text. He has kindly sent along the following additional notes on this aerial:

"It should be mentioned that this aerial can also be operated on 3·5MHz. DL2EO noticed that the 14MHz L-network component values also provided a low swr on 3·5MHz. Further investigations showed that the natural resonance of the T-aerial was about 3·2MHz, with a calculated feed-point resistance of about 25Ω. On 3·5MHz, therefore, the aerial must be inductive and higher in resistance. The inductance is thus compensated by the 'C' of the 14MHz impedance matching network, with the series 'L' for 14MHz having little effect on 3·5MHz.

"The aerial could also be tuned up on 3·5MHz by means of a series capacitor, in the manner used by G2RO in his 'double-size' 1·8MHz aerial (also described in the May *TT*).

"As the feed-point resistance of the DL2EO T-aerial is rather high on 7 to 30MHz, a relatively simple ground rod will usually prove sufficient; for optimum efficiency on 3·5MHz, however, where the feed-point resistance is low, five ground radials each ¼λ long are recommended by DL2EO."

This aerial can thus provide an effective five-band aerial despite the restriction of the "top" to just over 20m, at a height of 9m. Details are given in Fig 7, page 332 of the May issue.

Funkschau (No 17, 1975). This is shown in Fig 7 together with metric dimensions for 14, 21 and 28MHz operation. The variable capacitor at the base of the tall, central radiator element is adjusted for minimum swr on the 52Ω coaxial cable; HB9RU indicates that this can usually be adjusted to give an swr of the order of 1·3 or better. Gain is stated in the article as being 7dB, which seems a bit optimistic but, nevertheless suggests that the system is capable of giving excellent performance as a single-band aerial, particularly when over a good earth or a good earth mat. The boom should be a minimum of 1m above ground and this allows the array to be used without a mast or tower, and yet to be quite easily rotatable. It would be interesting to hear from anybody who gives this novel aerial a try.

Directional Vertical Arrays

Extracted from 'Technical Topics',
Radio Communication, November 1975

Directional vertical arrays

This mention of directional vertically-polarized arrays is a reminder that we owe much of the early work in this field (and also the concept of the ground-plane aerial) to Dr G. H. Brown of RCA. While very much of a professional aerial expert, George Brown supplied some interesting reminiscences of early amateur radio in a Marconi memorial speech last year. He said, for instance:

"I was bitten by the wireless bug when I was twelve years old. I had read all that the local library could provide concerning the adventures of an almost mythical person known as Marconi. My crystal detector was the result of a five-mile bicycle ride from Portage, Wisconsin, to a cluster of houses in a settlement named Galena. Here products of a lead mine were being loaded into railroad gondolas. I returned home with a brown paper bag filled with hundreds of shiny nuggets, one or two of which allowed me to receive code signals from some now-forgotten amateur station."

He also recalled how it was that, as a result of discussions between Godley and Beverage during his crossing to the UK in 1921, Godley erected one of the then-new Beverage aerials at Ardrossan, Scotland, for the historic reception of trans-atlantic amateur signals. Incidentally, Beverage was a pioneer amateur himself: W2BML.

To return, however, to directional arrays: in *Proc IRE*, January 1937, a paper by George Brown included a diagram that has since become the classic source of information on this subject, though curiously enough it is only very infrequently reproduced in amateur publications. It shows the horizontal radiation patterns for two vertical radiators fed with currents of equal magnitudes, and indicates how the patterns vary with the spacing of the two elements and the phase differences. In the original diagram, which is often reproduced in professional textbooks, the aerial spacings varied from λ/8 to 1λ, but for most amateur applications the spacing is unlikely to exceed λ/2. The relevant half of the original diagram is shown in Fig 8, from which it will be noted that cardioid (heart-shaped) patterns are relatively easily obtained, with a fairly sharp null in the backward direction—a characteristic which can be very useful in restricting pick-up of European signals when trying for North America on 7MHz and below. For any given mast spacing it is possible to obtain from the same array each of the patterns indicated by the different phases. For example,

Double Tuning-fork Beam

Extracted from 'Technical Topics',
Radio Communication, November 1975

Double tuning-fork beam

Vertically-polarized beams are fairly uncommon among amateurs, although directional arrays for mf broadcasting are in use in many countries and at a number of the IBA's independent local radio stations in the UK. These range from several four-mast arrays designed to provide very deep nulls in unwanted directions to the simple one-mast-plus-sloping-wire technique. In the latter, the parasitic reflector element is a wire sloping up to the top of the single radiator mast, from which it is insulated (a system that might well have possibilities for amateur operation on 1·8, 3·5 and 7MHz).

For the higher-frequency bands a novel array based on three boom-mounted vertical elements has been described by Erwin Schlatter, HB9RU, in the German periodical,

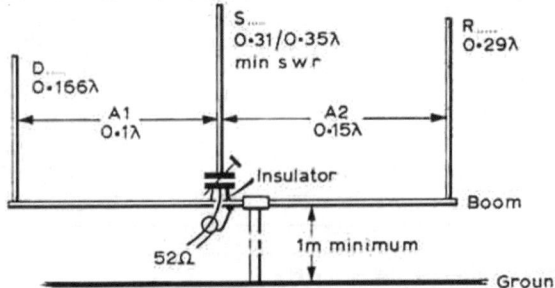

Fig 7. HB9RU's "double tuning fork" array (zwei stimmgabel beam)

Band	D (cm)	S (cm)	R (cm)	A1 (cm)	A2 (cm)	C for min swr (pF)
28MHz	174·5	347	302	105	158	approx 90
21MHz	235	467	410	142	212	approx 80
14MHz	356	698	612	211	317	approx 70

this can be done by switching in additional lengths of coaxial cable, as in the "electronic rotary" originally described by I1BER (*Amateur Radio Techniques*) and using λ/4 mast spacing.

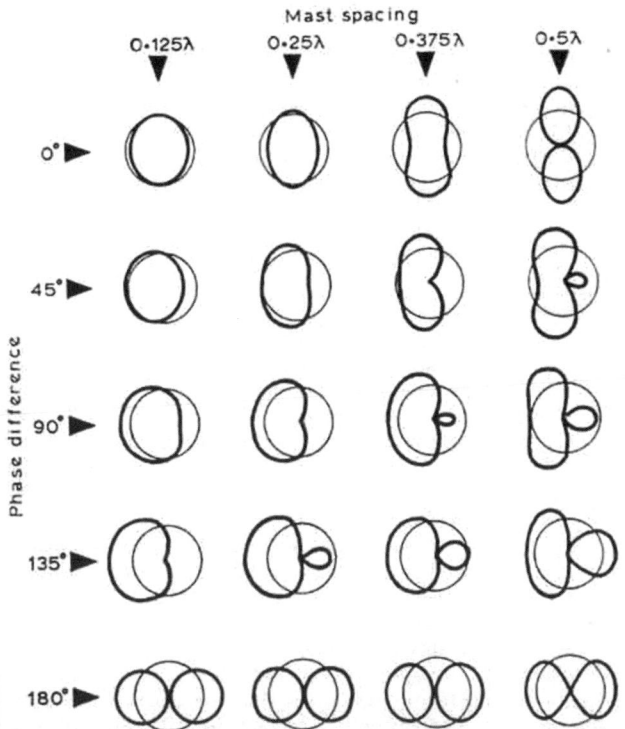

Fig 8. Part of the classic 1937 diagram by G. H. Brown showing horizontal radiation patterns for an array of two vertical aerials (such as monopoles) fed with current of equal magnitudes but varying phases.

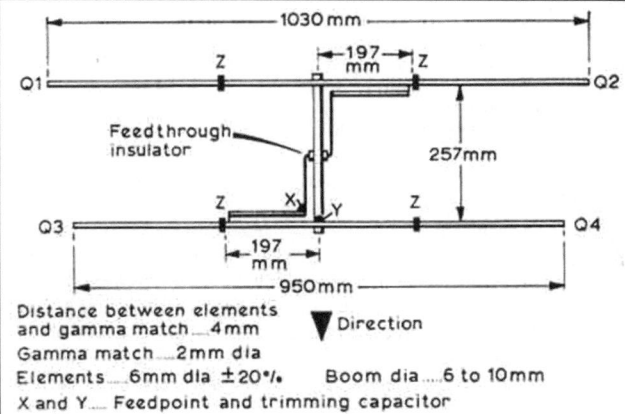

Fig 9. Details of the mobile 144MHz HB9CV two-element array used by PA0TBE/G5ASD

the same value. The coaxial cable can be 50, 60 or 70Ω impedance.

A 1·296GHz HB9CV-type two-element array enclosed in a glass-reinforced plastic sphere is used at the GB3DD beacon, and this type of aerial is equally effective on hf. Perhaps this item will help to get it better known.

144MHz HB9CV Portable Beam

Extracted from 'Technical Topics', *Radio Communication,* November 1975

144MHz HB9CV portable beam

Since 1972 Jan Jager, PA0TBE, has often operated in the UK as G5ASD/M on 144MHz, generally using a Trio 7200 with 5λ/8 whip but always taking with him an HB9CV-type beam to help with dx while static on hilltops. He finds that relatively few 144MHz enthusiasts know about the attractions of the HB9CV array, which is a development of the ZL-Special and has been known and used (mostly on hf) for many years. It provides some 5dB gain and is very much easier to carry around than a three- or five-element Yagi or quad arrays for 144MHz. A broomstick attached to the roof-rack serves as a convenient mast. "It will," he writes, "almost fit into a briefcase—what more do we want?" Details are shown in Fig 9.

He uses 6mm diameter tubing for the centre parts of the elements (ie between points Z-Z which are approximately 400mm apart). Bolts that will take 4mm tubing are soldered at points Z; the four sections shown as Q1, Q2, Q3 and Q4 are then made of 4mm tubing threaded at one end to fit the bolts. A 30pF trimmer is connected between points X and Y and adjusted for optimum swr; for convenience this trimmer can then be replaced by a fixed capacitor of approximately

G6XN Multiband Elements

Extracted from 'Technical Topics', *Radio Communication,* January 1976

G6XN multiband elements

Apart from straightforward harmonic resonances, several forms of multiband elements have been described over the years, including several in *TT*. But none has achieved widespread use, and most amateurs continue to put up hf arrays that squander precious decibels of gain by the restriction of "aperture" (ie by not making full use of the total length of the element on the higher frequency bands), by accepting the losses that occur with traps or those that arise from the interaction of "nested" elements as in the conventional two- or three-band quads and some Yagi beams. It is still widely believed that any multiband beam is bound to be a compromise and that for ultimate gain it is necessary to use monobanders.

Now Les Moxon introduces a new concept—though anticipating that it may suffer the same fate as previous multibanding techniques—that has the advantage of offering simpler and probably lower-cost arrays. It has something in common with G6CJ's "stretched dipoles", although again that technique (*Amateur Radio Techniques*) has been much undervalued; but it also exploits novel ideas including the mystery of the disappearing inductance.

Fig 1 shows three elements of different physical lengths but which, as is well known, can be made to resonate at the same frequency: the conventional dipole element; the inductively-loaded short dipole; and the capacitively stretched dipole. Fig 2 shows how a 14MHz element can be resonated at 21MHz (a) or 28MHz (b).

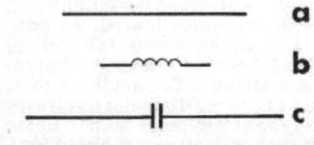

Fig 1. Three aerial elements of physically different length but which may all resonate at the same frequency.

ANTENNA TOPICS

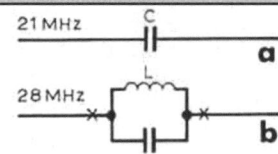

Fig 2. A 14MHz element can be resonated at 21MHz by capacitive loading and at 28MHz by a combination of L and C. To convert (b) into (a) C can be increased so that it tunes out L in addition to the inductive reactance of the dipole. However, the presence of L has considerable effect on the fundamental 14MHz resonance and this must be compensated by series capacitance at points X,X or by shortening the dipole. The new approach results in the mystery of the disappearing inductance L

But now, with these basics in mind, let us look at the end product of the new approach: Fig 3, an element that can simultaneously have two resonant frequencies. It looks a bit like a gamma-feed arrangement but the "short-circuited" C has nothing to do with matching. Instead it forms an element which uses all of its length on two frequencies which can include 14MHz and span 21 to 28MHz by adjustment of C. The element is resonated at its higher frequency by the capacitor acting in conjunction with the distributed inductance L represented by the section of the element across which C is connected. Matching to a driven element is no great problem, G6XN reports, since the radiation resistance of the dual-frequency element, when expressed as a resistance in parallel with L, has (or can easily be arranged to have) comparable values at each of the operating frequencies. The feed resistance between any two points along L *tends* to be independent of frequency. The beauty of the system is that the capacitor has virtually no effect on the basic dipole resonance (say 14MHz) except for a slight, and potentially useful, shift in band-centre frequency of the order of 1 per cent when a 14MHz element is being used and C is given the appropriate value for 21MHz. Since the full aperture of the element is used on all frequencies this means that a 14MHz element can itself give up to 2dB gain at 28MHz and up to 1dB at 21MHz. There are, of course, no traps to incur losses or to require supporting in the elements, so simplifying construction. When applied to a quad, as much as 3dB extra gain may be achieved at 28MHz, plus freedom from the interacting effects of "nested" elements. There is the problem of using the same element spacing on different bands, and this will be considered later.

It should be stressed that this novel technique would seem to be equally suitable for many types of arrays or even for simple wire aerials. In fact G6XN puts forward a new general theorem for aerials as follows:

Any aerial may be operated at its fundamental resonance and simultaneously at any frequency within a range from less than half to more than one octave above the fundamental resonance, by connecting capacitance across the central portion of each current loop (or in the case of a monopole from one side to ground). The direction of the main lobes is the same, and the full aperture is utilized at each frequency. The added capacitance has, at least to a first order of approximation, no effect at the fundamental resonance.

This approach opens the way, without any major problems, to dual-frequency operation: eg 14 and 21MHz, or 21 and 28MHz, or 14 and 28MHz aerials of many types. But what about triband operation? Here there exists the problem that the value of C has to be changed on the two higher frequency bands. This problem can be solved by a relay or possibly by using various forms of 28MHz traps or phasing stubs as a passive switch, although up to the present G6XN has only fully developed the relay method. But at least it has already been shown that triband operation is practicable.

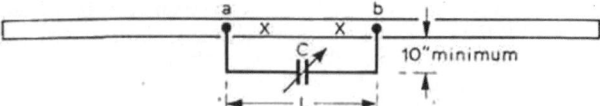

Fig 3. A typical half-wave dipole or driven or parasitic beam element designed for two-frequency operation. C, in conjunction with the inductance L between points (a) and (b) provides a resonance from 0·5 to 1·0 octave above the fundamental frequency without phase change. Connections to C are preferably made from tubing of ¼ to ⅜in diameter but 12swg wire has been used successfully. For a typical 14MHz beam the distance (a)–(b) is about 7ft (not critical) and C about 90pF

It will thus be seen that (at least for two-band operation) the key feature of the system is its stunning simplicity which will make readers say to themselves "Why didn't I think of that?", but it is worth mentioning that this arrangement was arrived at by what G6XN terms "a set of curious chances", evolving from what in itself was an ingenious system but using standard theory. It is not possible at this time to present all the fascinating twists to the story, and we have concentrated here on the stage this project has now reached.

His present work is based on what is in fact a standard three-element "plumber's-delight" Yagi designed *a la Handbook*, and it seems likely that most 14MHz monoband beams could be converted for dual-band operation very easily indeed by simply stringing a capacitor on each element as in Fig 3. These capacitors (for legal limit operation) should be rated at least 2kV and 5A with short stubs for fine tuning*. The effect on 14MHz mid-band resonance should not be more than about one per cent. When a monobander is converted in this way no guarantee can be given of achieving low swr at the higher frequency (although by now, perhaps, readers will no longer worry too much about this) and preferably a balanced feed should be used as in Fig 4.

G6XN anticipates that some readers will query whether the fixed element spacing of a monobander is likely to prove equally suitable for use on two or three bands. It is true that for a two-element array with about 8ft spacing there will be a gain penalty of roughly 0·5dB for driven arrays and 1dB for parasitic arrays plus deterioration of back-to-front ratio, but he considers that with three or more elements the wider electrical spacing at the higher frequencies is a positive advantage.

Balanced feed and plumbers-delight construction play a

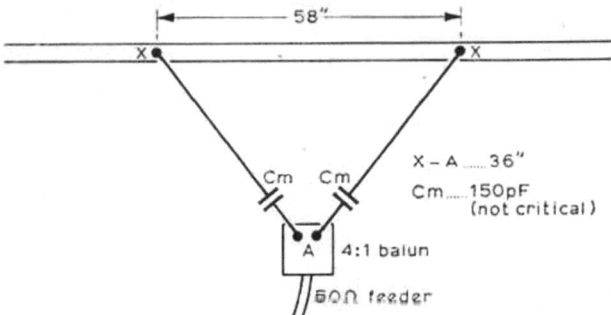

Fig 4. Typical balanced feed system for a G6XN driven element

useful role in avoiding skewing and narrow bandwidth. In his prototype three-element array G6XN achieves less than 2:1 swr over a bandwidth of 1MHz centred on 28·5MHz though he points out that bandwidth will be reduced, as might be expected, by tuning for maximum gain.

In selecting from G6XN's notes I hope that I have managed to pick out the salient points, although it is appreciated that there are some features of this new approach that have been rather glossed over. For instance, that the length of aerial that forms L when tuned by C disappears back into its normal function as the middle bit of the aerial when C is removed. But you may be saying C is not removed, it is still there. G6XN explains this by pointing out that C can be considered "removed" when the current in it is small com-

* G6XN suggests that it may be advisable to start off using small variable capacitors using low power and choosing dry weather. It is then not difficult to replace the variables by combinations of fixed capacitors with a short stub for fine tuning. Problems were experienced in wet weather when attempting to use a 300Ω feeder stub to provide the whole of the capacitance.

pared with the element current, and this comes about rather rapidly as the frequency is reduced, partly because, at the higher frequency, the value of C is artificially increased by the approach to series resonance. So you have an element that behaves differently when fed with rf at different frequencies. It seems simple when put like this but it took a long time for the full explanation to emerge and a new twist to be given to the search for multiband aerials of high performance. There is indeed *no* finality in any branch of amateur radio experimentation!

The AZ-Special Multiband Aerial

Extracted from 'Technical Topics',
Radio Communication, January 1976

The AZ-Special multiband aerial

The wish to make full use of the length of an aerial is not of course confined to beam elements. There is still a demand for simple multiband hf aerials that, unlike the popular W3DZZ aerial, do not depend on traps, such as the end-fed "long wire" or the centre-fed G5RV-type dipole.

A 3·5 to 21MHz aerial with centre-fed configuration requiring only an 88ft top but which should provide some gain on all bands above 3·5MHz (though with different lobe directions) is described by L. W. Aurick, K3AZ, in *CQ* September 1975. It uses λ/4 phasing sections on 21MHz to form a four-section colinear array; on all other bands, the phasing sections simply form folded portions of the radiating elements, but without being at current maxima on any band, so that the aerial resembles a centre-fed radiator, electrically equivalent to a top of 132ft.

The aerial (Fig 5) works on the various bands as follows:
3·5MHz: Half-wave dipole.
7MHz: Two half-wave dipoles in phase, providing roughly 2dB gain in the broadside lobes.
14MHz: Two-wave centre-fed aerial, resulting in four lobes (at about 54° to wire).
21MHz: Four-section colinear array with broadside gain of about 4dB.

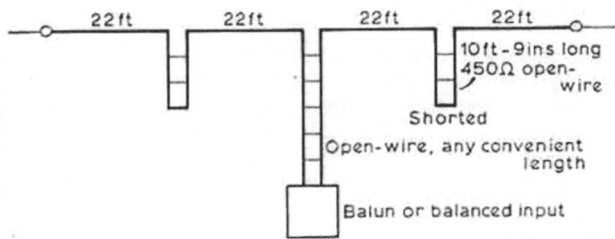

Fig 5. Multiband aerial for 3·5, 7, 14 and 21MHz—the "AZ-Special"

K3AZ makes his phasing sections and also the centre feeder from 450Ω open-wire transmission line, and then at a convenient distance from the feed point uses a balun to transform down to 50Ω coaxial, etc. It would, however, be possible, and in some ways preferable, to extend the balanced feeder through to the transmitter and then to interpose the simple bifilar inductor type of balun suggested some years ago by DJ2ZF: see Fig 6. It will be noted that the aerial is voltage-fed on 14MHz so that in effect one is using the open-wire line with high swr, and some lengths may be found easier to match than others. The aerial should preferably be mounted horizontally rather than in the inverted-V high-centre-point mode if full gain is to be obtained.

Portable Helical-mode HF Aerial

Extracted from 'Technical Topics',
Radio Communication, February 1976

Portable helical-mode hf aerial

Recently (*TT* November 1975) a design stemming from PA0TBE was presented of a 144MHz "HB9CV" beam based on a number of tubular elements that can be readily dismantled and then "almost fits a briefcase". One of those who have since made up this design and found it very satisfactory is Bill Scarr, G2WS.

This month we reproduce an hf design by J. Seakins, ZL1BDY (*Break-in* September 1975) which is similarly capable of being carried in a briefcase, yet when put together provides an effective low-cost vertical for 3·5MHz and other bands, using the well-established principle of a short helical-mode whip. Work previously reported on this type of aerial for vhf suggests that the effective radiation can approach to within 5 or 6dB of a full-size quarter-wave vertical provided that a really good earth is used.

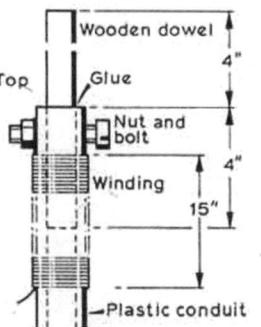

Fig 2. One section of ZL1BDY's portable hf helical-mode aerial wound on short sections of ¾in electrician's plastic conduit which can be readily assembled by means of the dowel joints

The aerial is wound on a series of five 16in lengths of ¾in plastic conduit as used by electricians: Figs 2 and 3. Into one end of each length of tubing is inserted an 8in length of wooden dowel, glued into position with 4in lengths protruding, and with a hole drilled for a nut and bolt to strengthen the joint and to provide tie points or terminals for one end of each winding. The top section has only a 4in length of dowelling, mounted flush with the top, and to this is mounted a standard 3ft telescopic whip aerial to provide fine tuning. Finally each section is finished with a covering of plastic tape.

Then to assemble, the top section is pushed on to the dowel of the next section and the lead from the bottom of the winding attached to the nut and bolt, and so on until the aerial is complete, representing for 3·5MHz an overall length of 6ft 3in of conduit plus the 3ft telescopic whip. Weight is about 2lb.

Fig 3. The assembled 3·5 MHz helical-mode quarter-wave aerial consisting of five 15in sections of conduit plus a 3ft telescopic whip section for fine tuning. Note that the aerial must be used with the *best-possible* earth connection

ANTENNA TOPICS

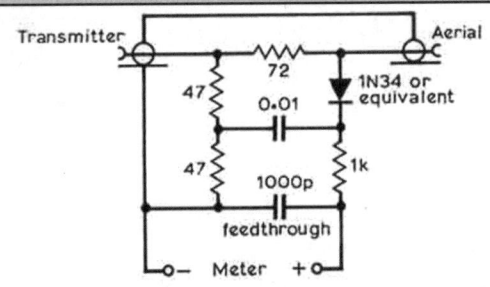

Fig 4. Resistance-type swr bridge suitable for adjusting a ZL1BDY or other aerials when required for low-power operation. The external multimeter should have a sensitivity of at least 1,000 Ω/V with an fsd range of 5 to 10V. Full details of this type of swr meter appeared in *The Radio Amateur's Handbook*, circa 1961

ZL1BDY points out that it may often be required to operate such an aerial at low power for portable work and in such circumstances a conventional coaxial swr bridge is likely to prove too insensitive and he therefore uses a resistance bridge unit (former *ARRL Handbook* design) constructed in a wedding cake tin: Fig 4.

Then, to tune the aerial, mount the bridge in the feeder, attach any pocket multimeter to the meter terminals, and with the transmitter on the desired operating frequency adjust the whip section for minimum meter reading. Finally, as ZL1BDY puts it, "remove the bridge from the feeder and begin the serious job of working the dx".

DL1FK and the G6XN Multiband Element

Extracted from 'Technical Topics', *Radio Communication*, March 1976

DL1FK and the G6XN multiband element

To know or find out just when you have discovered something that is completely novel is an extremely difficult problem. It is not made any easier by the fact that many very good ideas remain little used for several years, or by the "information explosion" that makes it virtually impossible to search *all* the literature on any given subject. I often wonder how Patent Office examiners can ever really be sure that patent applications are not invalidated by prior publication.

All this leads to an apology for what was a completely unintended breach of our "fair play to inventors" code by claiming (*TT* January) that the G6XN technique of adding capacitors across current modes to form multiband aerial elements was not only an important development (which we feel it is) but also as something completely new. B. Bossert, HB9QO, recalled that the basic technique had been described as long ago as July 1960 in *DL-QTC* by Richard Auerbach, DL1FK, following work in 1958 which led to the issue of a German patent (DBPa Nr A 30652–A12438 Gm). DL1FK in fact used the technique in a miniature three-element, three-band Yagi beam (maximum element length 7·4m with inductive loading) which was subsequently included in the German *Antennenbuch* by Karl Rothammel, DM2ABK, and has achieved some popularity among German amateurs, though I cannot trace it as having crossed the English Channel.

The work which led Leslie Moxon, G6XN, to this rediscovery was, of course, entirely independent of the German design and would seem to exploit the principle rather differently and more comprehensively; but there is no doubt that credit for first discovering this idea belongs to Richard Auerbach—a view with which G6XN fully concurs.

In fact G6XN is particularly impressed by the fact that

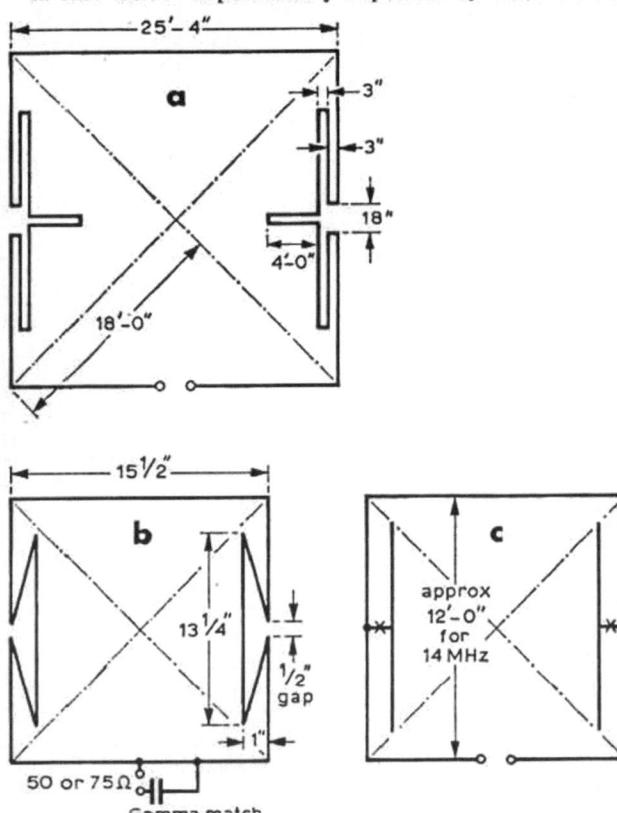

Fig 3. Three techniques for reducing the size of quad-loop elements: (a) system developed for 7MHz operation by G3FPQ; (b) G3MWV's scaled down quad element as tested on 144MHz consists of a 15½in square compared with a full-sized 144MHz quad which would have 21¼in sides. Wire used was 18swg tcw. Loop dimension is 34 per cent longer than that given by standard 1,005/f (MHz) length; (c) use of capacitive end loading results in high values of radiation resistance—this arrangement was originally described in a patent application by G3IMX who also uses traps at points X to provide two-band operation, although other techniques might be used for this purpose

DL1FK was able to use the idea in compact beams where one might have expected the high circulating currents that result from the lower radiation resistance to have presented particular problems. On the other hand it would appear that DL1FK thought that the idea could not be used successfully for a full-sized 14/21/28MHz beam; nor did he use it for his driven element which he simply fed with resonant lines. The DL1FK compact beam, in effect, uses this approach only for the parasitic elements and only for two of the three bands, although his text outlines a possible three-band element that uses two capacitors but requires no other form of switching.

It would thus seem that G6XN's work has already significantly advanced knowledge of how this system can be applied to a very much wider range of circumstances than was originally supposed, offering:

(1) non-resonant feeding of the driven element, a problem not solved in the DL1FK or in the G4ZU multiband designs;

(2) true triband operation with full-sized elements and without any lumped circuit components;

(3) possibly a rather better understanding of some of the physical processes involved, including the "disappearing inductance" concept.

So the discovery of DL1FK's work only reinforces the view that this type of multiband element has a very great deal to offer the amateur—and possibly also to the professional for certain applications.

One of the additional possibilities offered by the use of distributed resonant circuits of this type, G6XN suggests, is to replace the usual traps in multiband dipoles. Losses should be considerably reduced (though this may not be of great practical significance); the main advantages would be negligible cost, less weight to be supported by the dipole and no weatherproofing problems. G6XN has in fact made some preliminary tests of such an arrangement, quite successfully. But here again it should be stressed that this seems to be the only one of many applications of this technique of hanging a capacitor across part or parts of an aerial.

measured (and calculated) a radiation resistance of 75Ω which makes this approach a sound basis for essentially a "no compromise" mini-quad.

Trimming Aerials for Resonance

Extracted from 'Technical Topics',
Radio Communication, April 1976

Miniaturized Quad Elements

Extracted from 'Technical Topics',
Radio Communication, March 1976

Miniaturized quad elements
A number of ideas have been floating around during the past few years on the miniaturizing of quad elements which are often considered completely unmanageable on 7MHz and rather too large even on 14MHz. For example there is the technique described by D. L. Courtier-Dutton, G3FPQ, some years ago in *QST* (and included in some recent editions of the ARRL's *Radio Amateur's Handbook*): see Fig 3(a). This is designed to provide linear loading and allows a 7MHz element to have 25ft 4in sides (still big enough but a lot smaller than a full-sized 7MHz quad element).

Recently, seeking a replacement for a gale-written-off full-sized 14/21MHz quad, Dave Blake, G3MWV, has been investigating several forms of mini-quad arrangements and has come up with a system having some similarities to the G3FPQ element. While he intends soon to try this on hf, he has been conducting tests of a scaled-down element on 144MHz: Fig 3(b). To provide reference information he has used this two-thirds-sized loop as a single-element aerial, a similar but full-sized element and a reference dipole, put at the same height of 30ft. The feed impedance of a full-sized element was approximately 140Ω; the folded, two-thirds-sized element 75Ω. Tests were carried out over a 50-mile path to G2FT, and on both transmission and reception indicate only a very slight drop of signal strength when the folded element is compared with the standard element; both loops show a marked improvement over the reference dipole.

As a result of these tests G3MWV is now building a 14/21MHz version, adding a reflector element of the same configuration.

G6XN also recently commented on the use of miniaturized quad elements. In his estimation there is one arrangement, permitting 12ft sides for 14MHz, which he considers superior to all others that he has tried: Fig 3(c). This arrangement does not appear to be widely known although in fact it is described in a system patented by E. G. Jolliffe, G3IMX, also utilizing traps to form a two-band quad.

The "top hats" (if one can call these "sideburns" this) provide the equivalent of capacitive end-loading and this technique results in much higher values of radiation resistance than most other commonly-used arrangements; it also avoids the use of lossy components such as the loading coils used in a number of the miniature quads. G6XN has

Trimming aerials for resonance
Ted Cook, ZS6BT, was interested in the suggestion (*TT* January) that some of the older techniques used for matching transmitters to aerials possessed some useful virtues. He recalls a method commonly used in the 'thirties, in the "pre-gdo days", to adjust aerial systems—not just nostalgically but in the belief that the system can be updated and put to extremely good use. He writes:

"In my youth the method for finding aerial resonance was to disconnect the aerial from the feedline, insert an rf ammeter, then excite the aerial remotely from another temporary aerial some distance away, adjusting the transmitter and trimming the aerial while observing the rf meter through a pair of binoculars.

"Today we can still make use of this system but we no longer need to disconnect the feeders nor use binoculars; we can do the job from inside the shack by making use of the station's reflectometer.

"We still excite the aerial remotely but we *reverse* the reflectometer and connect the feedline to a matching dummy load (ie aerial to input of the reflectometer, dummy load to output). Then set the reflectometer to read a forward power of about 10W and vary the exciting frequency until the reflectometer peaks, indicating resonance.

"The explanation is that the aerial has now become the 'source of rf' and the power flowing down the feedline will deflect the reflectometer. But if we remember the rule that 'the coupling between transmitter and feedline cannot affect the match between aerial and feedline' but merely affects the amount of power transferred from the transmitter we find that we now have the power-transfer point at the aerial! The resistive feedline cannot affect the aerial and the aerial cannot react upon the resistive feedline. This means that a reflectometer peak indicates true aerial resonance.

"Imagine setting up and adjusting a tri-band trapped ground-plane by this method, adjusting for each band in turn. But what about the radials? Of course we can plot the bandwidth of an aerial but what about the matching, especially of those radials?

"The answer is beautifully simple. If the radiation resistance does not match the (resistive) feedline we cannot transfer all the power induced. The reflectometer peak still indicates resonance, but the reading will be below maximum. So if we can find and hold the transmitter at the resonant frequency, we can then adjust the matching if this is a practical proposition. In the case of a ground-plane with radials we can alter radial length and compensate by re-resonating the aerial (as one possible approach). All the rest follows.

"An important warning, of course, is not to attempt to do these adjustments when the band is 'open' or is busy, or you will not be popular! Normally about 100W in the exciting aerial is needed to produce an induced power of about 10W.

"For an experiment, I took my multi-band double-zepp (open-wire feedline down to a Z-match aerial tuning unit) and excited it at 21MHz. Then I tuned it up for resonance and loading into the dummy. The transmitter was next tuned up

ANTENNA TOPICS

on the dummy, and the double-zepp thereafter connected to the transmitter. It was so exact that I could not improve either resonance or loading.

"Adjusting a delta- or gamma-match by this technique is easy. It is an ideal way of ensuring that the aerial gets the maximum rf out of the transmitter, always provided that you are not using up lots of rf to heat up a ferrite balun."

A Dual-band Matching Technique

Extracted from 'Technical Topics', *Radio Communication,* April 1976

A dual-band matching technique

W. A. Roberts, G2RO, has come across a simple but useful aerial matching technique which seems capable of a more general application than in the particular circumstances for which it was used. He has a buried 50Ω coaxial feeder which goes to the bottom of his garden and there connects directly to a grounded 7MHz aerial which is five quarter-waves long (about 165ft) and which has been carefully pruned to resonance so that it provides an excellent match to the feeder.

The availability of a long aerial which is high over most of its length seemed to invite its use on 1·8MHz but, being on this band a quarter-wave plus about one-sixteenth wave, it provides only a poor match to the feeder. However, it occurred to G2RO that if he used a series capacitor to "shorten" the electrical length of the wire to one quarter-wave on 1·8MHz, then the series capacitance likely to be needed would be of a value large enough to make its effect at 7MHz trivial. So it has proved.

The series capacitance turned out to be about 600pF. The match at 1·8MHz became virtually perfect while the difference in the already excellent match at 7MHz was barely discernible. The result is that G2RO now has a dual-band aerial consisting of a single grounded wire correctly and resonantly matched at both 7MHz and 1·8MHz from a single 50Ω feeder.

This dual-band principle, he feels, might be applied to any pair of frequencies separated by a ratio of four or more; examples would be 1·8/7, 3·5/14 and 7/28MHz bands. The same technique could also be equally well applied to centre-fed aerials if the matching capacitor is repeated on each side of the feeder connection.

Feedpoint Impedance

Extracted from 'Technical Topics', *Radio Communication,* July 1976

Feedpoint impedance

Carl C. Drumeller, W5JJ, very rightly takes me to task for letting slip through in a recent *TT* a statement that clearly confused "radiation resistance" with "feedpoint resistance" or more correctly "feedpoint impedance" (in excuse, it did not affect the idea under discussion). As he points out: radiation resistance is the convenient fiction to describe the loss of power to space; it is determined by the configuration of the radiating device and by its environment. Feedpoint impedance is quite another matter. A half-wave antenna at a certain height above ground may have a feedpoint impedance of 73Ω at its centre. But that same antenna, with nothing done to affect its interface with space, can be delta fed from 600Ω open-wire feeders with a perfect match.

"There is no reason," he adds, "to confuse the two, yet often no distinction is made. It is no wonder that so many amateurs have such a hazy, even fuzzy, concept of antennas, feedlines, the junction between those two, and the effect of impedance mismatch at that junction upon the sending end impedance of the transmission line."

My apologies for adding to the fuzziness and I have humbly written out "radiation resistance is not feedpoint impedance" one hundred times. I feel almost as bad as I did at seeing that confounded 1971 April Fool joke of *Radio-REF* (the "NASA" audio filter for male and female voices) solemnly turn up once again in the June 1976 issue of *Ham Radio*! Luckily it was ascribed to NASA and not to *TT* or *Radio-REF*.

Active Loop Aerials

Extracted from 'Technical Topics', *Radio Communication,* August 1976

Active loop aerials

It seems a long time (*TT* July 1968) since I saw at Hanslope Park a demonstration of the low profile "aperiodic loop antenna array" developed by EMI-Cossor. This system was subsequently taken over and continues to be marketed by Hermes Electronics who currently claim that more than 53 different government agencies are using this type of array to provide roughly the equivalent of a large rhombic aerial. Each loop forms an "active" aerial by means of a matching amplifier, designed to provide low-noise and a wide dynamic range. Since then there has been a growing practical interest in various forms of active aerials, although from an amateur viewpoint a possible snag is that they are suitable for reception only.

However, in recent years a lot of people have come round to the view that there is much to be said for using different aerials for reception and transmission, if this means that you can obtain good directivity which is often more important than high signal levels. For instance, on several occasions we have pointed out the value of a good frame aerial (or even a good ferrite-rod system using multiple rods) for 1·8MHz reception to obtain excellent null directivity to minimize interference. In *TT* (August 1972) we drew attention to the value of a 1·8MHz loop consisting of about seven turns of wire on a frame with 40in sides and tuned with a 500pF capacitor.

At the "Communications 76" conference a description was given of a British low profile log periodic array based on a series of loop elements, developed by C & S Antennas. This uses a *terminated* single-turn loop element which, unlike the usual continuous loop, has a unidirectional cardioid type of response pattern (typically giving a 12dB front-to-back ratio): see Fig 1. The loop is made from aluminium strip embedded in glassfibre, giving a light but rigid construction with low series inductance and shunt capacitance. The matching amplifier is in a cast box at the base of the loop and the terminating components are in a recess at the top. B. S. Collins, in the first description of this aerial element

(*Comms* 74), warned against comparing active loops with monopoles on the basis of signal output, but showed that the performance of an active loop, on the basis of signal/noise performance on weak signals under normal noise-limited conditions, could be virtually the equivalent of a quarter-wave monopole.

In the latest, 1976, paper on this system, the question of forming log-periodic type arrays is further discussed, based on aperiodic loops 1m in diameter mounted 1·5m above ground in arrays covering various ranges such as 5·3 to 27MHz, 9 to 21MHz and 3·2 to 12MHz. It should be noted that although you can compress each element into miniature form, the spacing between the elements cannot similarly be reduced.

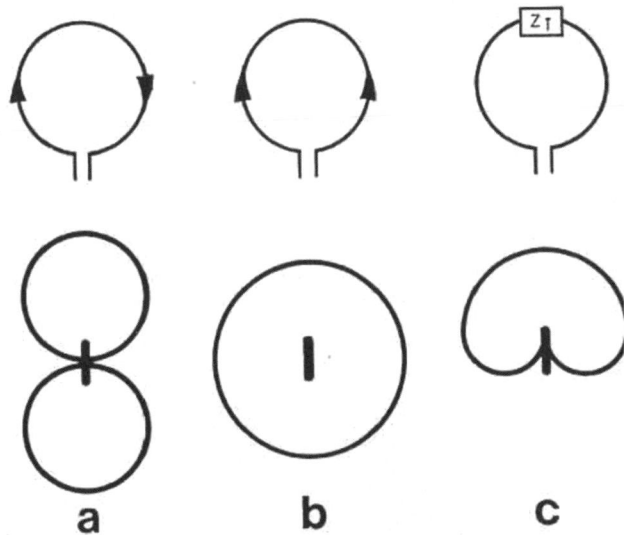

Fig 1. (*a*) Response of a conventional aperiodic loop aerial (zero-order mode). (*b*) Current-mode response. (*c*) Cardioid response to vertically polarized signals achieved by adjusting amplitude of the two modes by inserting a suitable impedance in series with the loop at a point diametrically opposite the 50Ω feedpoint. (B. S. Collins, *C & S Antennas*)

effective height in metres; N is the number of turns on the loop; A is the area enclosed by the frame in square metres; and Q is the usual goodness factor of the tuned circuit formed by the frame aerial and its associated tuning capacitor; and λ is the wavelength in metres.

From this expression it is clear that if any or all of the three factors N, A and Q can be increased, so will be the effective height and hence the signal provided by the system. N is limited by the need to tune the frame to the wavelength required; A is limited by the need to fit the frame into a room or loft where it can be easily rotated.

Q is affected by two factors: (1) the rf resistance of the conductor; and (2) the degree of loading imposed on the tuned circuit by the coupling to the receiver.

All these factors have been dealt with by BRS35518. He uses three turns, tuned by a 100pF capacitor; the frame is 5ft square, felt to be the largest suitable for indoor use. To improve Q he uses the outer conducting sheath of the largest size of domestic tv coaxial cable. Second, in order to reduce the loading, a fet amplifier is used in a source follower arrangement. This provides a very high input resistance and very low output resistance as with a cathode-follower valve: see Fig 2.

His checks have been carried out using a Galaxy R-1530 receiver which has an S-meter calibrated in decibels. The frame aerial is indoors adjacent to the receiver and with its lowest point some 2ft above the concrete floor of a ground

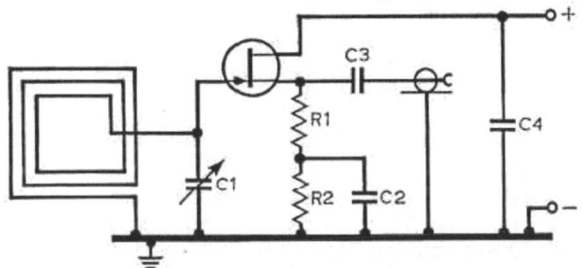

Fig 2. Optimized or active tuned frame aerial. C1 tuning capacitor (eg 100pF). C2, C4 by-pass capacitors (eg 0·01). C3 coupling capacitor (eg 0·01). R1 value equal to input impedance of receiver, usually 50Ω. R2 bias resistor to suit fet device used

floor room. As already stated, when the frame is correctly orientated for maximum signals, these are about 10dB up on the comparison aerial. BRS35518, pointing out that the source follower provides matching but no voltage amplification, is a little uncertain whether his design is an optimized frame aerial or really represents an "active aerial".

A 1.8MHz Active Frame Aerial

Extracted from 'Technical Topics', *Radio Communication,* August 1976

A 1·8MHz active frame aerial
This brings me to an interesting letter from P. L. Stiles, BRS35518 (formerly G2BHR). He has been conducting experiments with an active frame aerial covering from around 1·8 to 2·25MHz. His motivation was the usual one of local authorities who dislike outside aerials but his results are of general interest. His main concern has been to optimize the output from a frame aerial so that this now provides up to about 10dB more signal than his comparison aerial which is an inverted-L 15ft high and 60ft long used with a pi-coupler matching unit and an extensive ground system. As noted above, output level is not the only (or indeed even the most important) test of a receiving aerial, and sometimes it may be an advantage deliberately to keep output low and provide low-noise gain in the receiver proper. However, there must be plenty of people using 1·8MHz receivers which need a reasonably strong signal. BRS35518 optimized his effective height from the expression $h = 2\pi NAQ/\lambda$ where h is

Broadband Double-bazooka Dipole

Extracted from 'Technical Topics', *Radio Communication,* August 1976

Broadband double-bazooka dipole
It has often been stressed in these columns that the bandwidth of a conventional dipole is sufficiently broad for effective transmissions throughout any amateur band (including even the full American 3·5–4MHz band). In fact a wire dipole accurately cut for 3,750kHz may be expected to have an swr of around 5 : 1 at 3,500kHz and 4,000kHz, but with normal lengths of coaxial cable there should still be substantially the same power radiated at the ends of the band as at the middle. However, there is little doubt that many

ANTENNA TOPICS

amateurs still get worried when they see the swr creeping upwards with a change of frequency and, as W1ICP put it recently: "If you have confidence in your antenna it will work better than if you don't."

A more tangible advantage of an aerial specially designed to have a broader bandwidth is that it will usually be less critical to put up and less likely to be adversely affected by nearby objects.

There is one form of broadband dipole (or dipole element for a beam) that has been around many years and which I described briefly in *TT* (August 1973) based on the design by W2EEY, it also appears in some recent editions of the ARRL *Handbook*: it is known by various names including "a double bazooka".

Advantages for this approach have been claimed by F. Jennings, ZL1BET, in *Break-in* (July 1973) as a 3·5MHz aerial; and now recently in a letter from Cyprus by Gordon Thomas (5B4CA, G4AWJ) who has been using them on 14, 21 and 28MHz. In the ARRL version the two outer sections of the dipole are formed from twin open-wire or 300Ω line short-circuited at both ends; however, neither ZL1BET nor 5B4CA use this refinement, adopting simply single-wire sections.

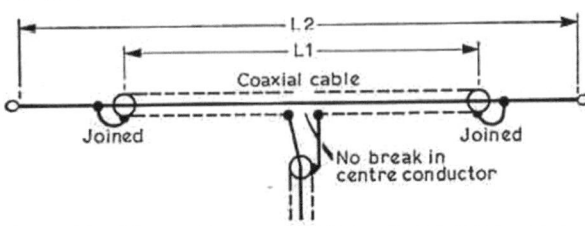

Fig 3. "Double-bazooka" form of broadband dipole element. For dimensions see text

Basically the double-bazooka (Fig 3) is an electrical half-wave of coaxial feeder (taking into account the typically 0·66 velocity factor) and thus a good deal shorter than a half-wave dipole, to which its length is extended by wire sections. The inner conductor of the feeder section is continuous but the braid is broken at the centre to provide a feedpoint.

The braid of the coaxial cable plus the extensions act as a conventional dipole; the inner conductor of the cable does not radiate but forms two quarter-wave short-circuited stubs. At exact dipole resonance these stubs represent infinitive resistive impedance at the feedpoint and have no effect; but as the system departs from resonance, the stubs represent reactive elements as seen at the feedpoint, opposite to the reactance of the dipole element. The result is that over an appreciable bandwidth the feedpoint impedance is mainly resistive. In other words the double-bazooka has a largely resistive feedpoint impedance over a greater bandwidth than would be the case for a conventional dipole.

ZL1BET suggests it is a constructional advantage, particularly for 3·5MHz, to clamp the centre junction and the ends of the coaxial sections firmly in phenolic or perspex clamps to prevent twisting and breaking of the cable, and clamps of this type are illustrated in the ARRL *Handbook*.

The main bone of contention are the length formulas: ARRL give $460/f$ for overall length, $325/f$ for the cable section; W2EEY gives $462/f$ and $372/f$; ZL1BET gives $468/f$ and $325/f$; 5B4CA after a good deal of cut and try found it desirable for an inverted-V form of construction to use different correction factors on the various bands: $475/f$ and $336/f$ on 14MHz; $490/f$ and $347/f$ on 21MHz; $495/f$ and $351/f$ on 28MHz. With these dimensions 5B4CA had no swr problems, and useful reports when using a 20ft bamboo as the centre support. In all these cases f represents centre frequency in megahertz.

Thoughts on Inverted-Vs

Extracted from 'Technical Topics', *Radio Communication*, September 1976

Thoughts on inverted-Vs

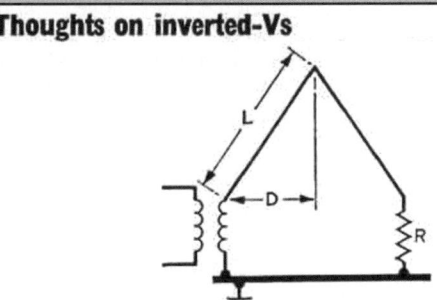

Fig 7. The original form of Bruce or "inverted-V" aerial as described in early editions of *The Amateur Radio Handbook*. When L is one half-wave greater than D, signals in the horizontal direction and in the plane of the "V" add up. When used without the terminating resistor R (about 400Ω) it is bi-directional; with R unidirectional and basically vertically polarized. Modern versions are often called side-terminated half-rhombics and design information for rhombics can be adapted

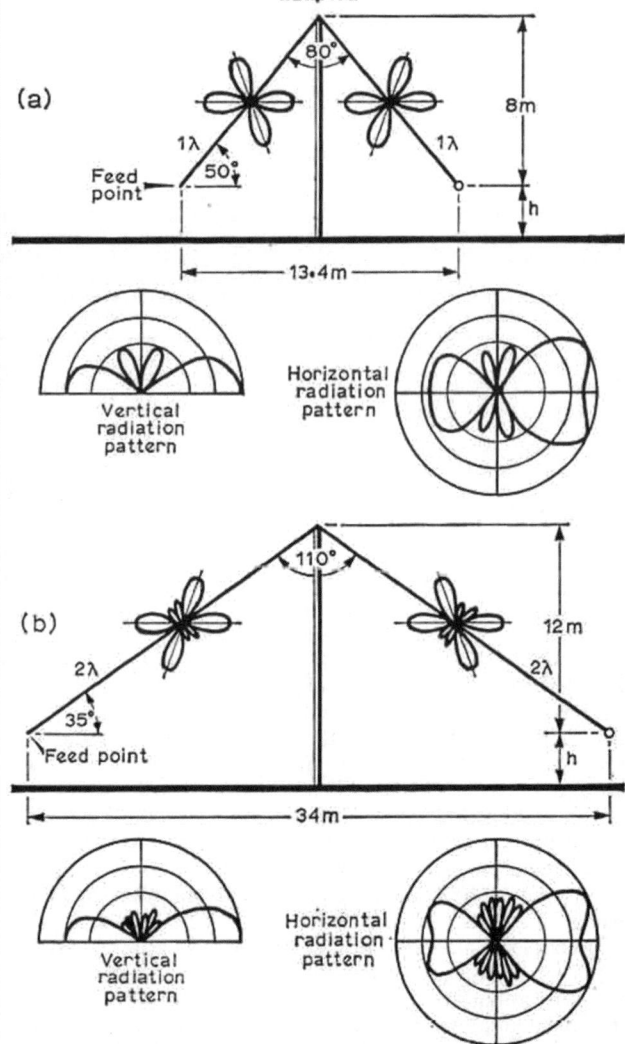

Fig 8. Two unterminated end-fed inverted-V aerials described by ZS6U showing polar diagrams for 28MHz operation. The aerials are voltage-fed from 50–75Ω coaxial cable via an L-network as shown in Fig 9

In the radio communication business it is easy to get left behind in changes of terminology. I do not mean just that we tend to go on measuring "condensers" in "jars" (we don't) or go on talking (as we do) of megacycles and not megahertz. But look at the "inverted-V". Early amateurs knew this in the form of the Bruce end-fed terminated design (one of the first fixed beams) and not in the modern form of almost any centre-fed "drooping" dipole.

It was the Bruce terminated design that was described in the first editions of *The Amateur Radio Handbook* as the inverted-V, yet few amateurs today remember this unidirectional, vertically-polarized, high-gain aerial (Fig 7). The old handbook used to add the warning that it needed a high mast and because of variable ground losses tended to be more suitable for reception than transmission. In this form, L should be one half-wave longer than D so that the signals in the horizontal direction in the plane of the inverted-V add up.

Nowadays this form of aerial may be implemented in a rather squatter form (ie without a particularly high support) and is generally called a "half-rhombic" since it is in effect half of a rhombic turned on its side. Despite the very high gain that is possible it is little known to many amateurs. For hf it does require a lot of space, but this does not apply to vhf —and indeed it is no disadvantage in such applications as portable field day operation where space usually *is* available.

Just as the rhombic can be used as a terminated or non-terminated configuration (the non-terminated system providing bi-directional characteristics) so can the half-rhombic or end-fed inverted-V, and interesting examples of both these designs have been noted recently.

The unterminated inverted-V

One of the few published references to a long-wire end-fed inverted-V is by Colin Dickson, ZS6U, ("More about the Minishack Special" *Radio-ZS*, August 1975, a follow-up to an earlier article in January 1973). This shows that the end-fed long-wire erected as a multiband hf aerial to specific slope angles can provide useful gain on the higher frequency bands: about 6dB on 28MHz with 34m ground space and single 12m-plus support, representing a $2 + 2\lambda$ aerial which can be fed on any hf band by means of a switched L-network aerial coupler. Because of radiation loss, the maximum gain is towards the *free* end of the aerial (as for all unterminated long-wire systems). Remember that there will be high rf voltages at each end so that safety precautions may be needed if the low-ends are within reach. Two designs are shown in Fig 8.

Where space is limited a "half inverted-V" can be used with same tilt and height; this is then in effect simply a sloping long-wire, and often useful to those operating in high buildings who feed the system at the high end.

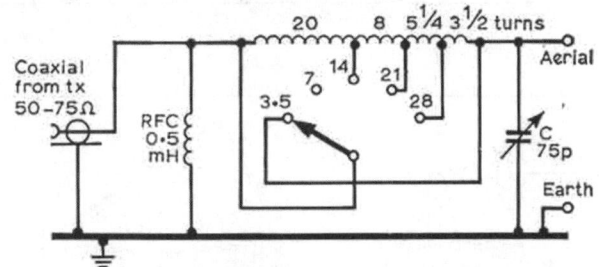

Fig 9. Matching network used by ZS6U with his end-fed inverted-V aerials

Coil diameter	Coil length	Wire diameter
35mm (1·375in)	38mm (1·5in)	0·95mm (0·0375in)
38mm (1·5in)	47mm (1·84in)	1·17mm (0·046in)
41·3mm (1·625in)	56mm (2·22in)	1·4mm (0·055in)
44·5mm (1·75in)	66mm (2·62in)	1·65mm (0·066in)
47·6mm (1·875in)	77mm (3·0in)	1·9mm (0·075in)
50·8mm (2·0in)	88mm (3·5in)	2·2mm (0·87in)

Terminated inverted-Vs

When the far end of an inverted-V long-wire aerial is correctly terminated to ground (or to a quarter-wavelength of wire forming an artificial ground) the current flowing in the wire is virtually a travelling wave. The absence of any reflected waves means that the whole thing becomes a unidirectional broadband array. The terminating resistor, which should be non-inductive, is usually described for transmission as requiring a power rating of one third of the output power, though for ssb average output is very much less than p.e.p. rating.

Some idea of the effectiveness of such arrays can be gleaned from a description of a massive array of half-rhombics built on San Clemente Island, off the coast of California, to monitor by means of hf doppler radar, the direction and magnitude of sea waves in the Gulf of Alaska: "A broadband antenna array for sea scatter measurements" by M. T. Ma and L. H. Tveten, (*IEEE Transactions on Antennas and Propagation*, May 1976, pp340–346). This system is built out over the sea so that it provides an excellent ground-plane and provides maximum gain at extremely low angles to the horizon (of the order of 2°–3°).

Basically, it shows that a single half-rhombic with a total length of 240m can provide a power gain of some 16·7dB at 10MHz—a power multiplication of over 45 times! Or some 10dB above what Les Moxon, G6XN, once described as the gain-barrier for Yagi-type hf beams. Admittedly, not many of us could run out 600ft of wire over the sea but it shows

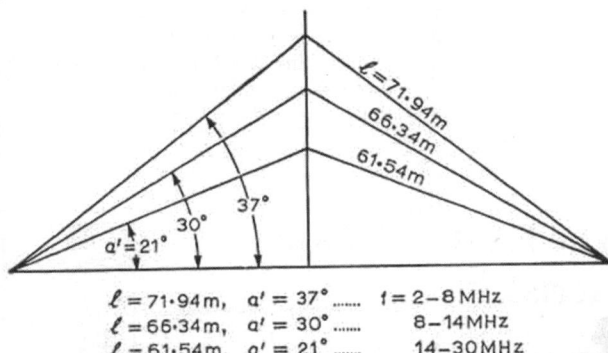

$\ell = 71·94m$, $a' = 37°$ .... $f = 2-8$ MHz
$\ell = 66·34m$, $a' = 30°$ .... $8-14$ MHz
$\ell = 61·54m$, $a' = 21°$ .... $14-30$ MHz

Fig 10. Showing how three side-terminated half-rhombics are used with single support to form the basic elements of a 2–30MHz high-gain hf radar array (terminating resistors not shown)

what can be done—and dimensions can be scaled down at vhf. Incidentally the power gain of the complete system of 25 of these half-rhombics for transmission and reception (taken together as it is a radar system) is around 55dB at 11MHz.

Fig 10 shows how three of these side-terminated inverted-Vs are arranged on a single mast to provide coverage from 2 to 30MHz, although most amateurs would be happy enough with the 14–30MHz section with 60 + 60m wires and a mast height of about 20m.

Inverted-Vs and Rhombics on VHF

Extracted from 'Technical Topics', *Radio Communication,* September 1976

Inverted-Vs and rhombics on vhf

The half-rhombic paper set me thinking once again about the curious lack of interest among vhf/uhf operators in all these

ANTENNA TOPICS

long-wire techniques. Recently, as a result of some articles I wrote in *Television*, I received a letter from a New Zealand tv-dx enthusiast who has been experimenting with vhf rhombics to receive 190MHz transmissions regularly over a 65-mile path and who is also interested in Australian tv transmissions. He mentions the improved performance achieved by adding two more wires to the sides of the rhombic, adding that when this was done: "no commercial tv aerial could match the gain and performance of this aerial". He sent along a copy of an item in *Radio & Electrical Review* (NZ) giving details of a Channel 2 (about 50MHz) rhombic with an overall length of 26ft providing some 10–12dB of gain.

The value of rhombics for uhf tv reception—together with the design of a simple tapered impedance matching device to allow the 600Ω balanced feed-point of a rhombic to be connected to 70Ω coaxial cable was described by A. B. Starks-Field, formerly G6YG, in *Wireless World*, December 1974. His loft rhombic with six-lambda legs had a theoretical gain of 19dB.

To anyone who has ever had access—if only for non-amateur purposes—to an aerial-farm of hf rhombics and Vs, and heard the magical way in which weak signals emerge from the noise, such long-wire aerials remain etched into the mind as the standard of comparison for all others. Admittedly these are *fixed* beams but we suspect that for vhf/uhf operation a few fairly compact high-gain fixed beams could prove extremely useful. It was while researching for these notes that we discovered with a shock that all mention of rhombic aerials has now disappeared from *The Radio Amateur's Handbook* while the latest RSGB *VHF/UHF Manual* makes no reference to *any* form of long-wire systems!

an array of two to four (or even more) elements spaced about 0·1λ apart. For example, at low hf, two driven elements will provide nearly 3dB (four elements nearly 6dB) more radiation than a single element, quite apart from any possible directional gain resulting from the use of an array.

Very little feedback was ever received on this item (although discussions with Ron Glaisher, G6LX, suggested that his experiences with multiple element verticals were in line with the Fort Monmouth experiments). It was not until glancing through the August 1976 issue of *Electron* that we have seen an aerial design specifically based on this technique.

This is the PA0RCH twin aerial developed by R. Cornet, PA0RCH, using as his basic structure two of his LC loaded short verticals for 1·8MHz using plastic drain pipes and "top hat" loading (*TT* May 1974). He shows how a "half-quad" arrangement can be used to take advantage of twin verticals as shown in Fig 3(a) with two λ/8 verticals and λ/4 joining section, current fed from coaxial cable at the base of one vertical. He then uses two of his short verticals to reduce the physical dimensions of this arrangement (Fig 3(b)), joining these together over the top of his house where voltage-feeding is convenient from a transmitter in the attic or upper storey (Fig 3(c)).

But do not forget that even with a twin system ground losses still need to be kept as low as possible by using extensive earth systems around each vertical. The idea could, of course, be extended to three or four short verticals spaced around the four sides of a building.

The PA0RCH Twin Aerial

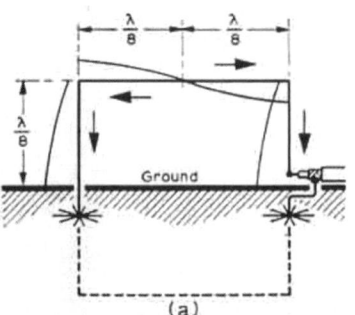

Extracted from 'Technical Topics', *Radio Communication*, October 1976

The PA0RCH twin aerial

A little more than two years ago (*TT* March 1974) attention was drawn to what seemed a very useful technique for reducing ground losses of short vertical aerials, such as whips or top-loaded monopoles, particularly those used on the lower hf bands such as 1·8 and 3·5MHz. This was achieved by the use of multiple elements, a revival by Fort Monmouth of an idea first put forward in 1920.

This item noted that ground losses of hf aerials near ground are reduced if the conventional single element is replaced by

The 'Double-bazooka' Knocked

Extracted from 'Technical Topics', *Radio Communication*, October 1976

The "double-bazooka" knocked

The double-bazooka or double-coaxial dipole described in August *TT* was introduced in a low-key manner which I hope made clear that I felt some of the claims made for this aerial should not be taken too seriously. By coincidence this point was made strongly in the August issue of *Ham Radio* in a 14-page article by Walt Maxwell, W2DU, "A revealing analysis of the coaxial dipole antenna". In effect, like *Punch* on marriage, the 14 pages add up to the single word "don't". Perhaps not quite "don't ever" since W2DU admits that it

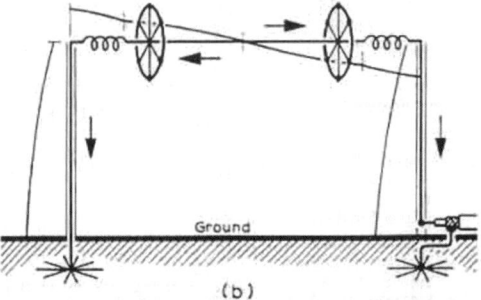

Fig 3. The development of the PA0RCH twin-vertical or shortened half-quad. (a) Basic half-quad element arrangement using one half-wavelength of wire. (b) As (a) but with physical dimensions reduced by LC loading as in the original PA0RCH vertical described in *TT* March 1974. (c) Voltage-fed version useful where transmitter is on upper storey and the aerial reaches over the house

can increase bandwidth moderately (though not if fed with 50Ω cable), but he seems to feel that the improvement is almost never worth the cost of the extra coaxial cable (though of course many amateurs have odd lengths around without having to buy any specially) and could be achieved more effectively at lower cost in other ways: eg the fan-shaped bow-tie arrangement using gradually diverging wire elements.

Incidentally, due to a last-minute proof correction that went wrong the dimension of the W2EEY coaxial section was given in August *TT* as 372/f when the figure should have been 326/f. Kris Partridge, G8AUU, points out that I did not make it clear that this gives the dimensions in *feet*

More on G3LHZ IP Quad

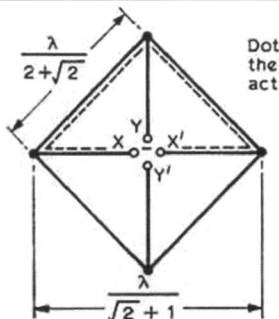

Extracted from 'Technical Topics', *Radio Communication,* November 1976

More on G3LHZ ip quad

In the September issue of *Radio Communication,* Mike Underhill, G3LHZ, presented a full description of his interesting ip quad element (ie *i*ndependent *p*olarized or *i*solated *p*ort) which was developed from the Tsukiji "centre-line-driven loop antenna" (cldla). As a result of publication several additional points have emerged and G3LHZ feels these will be of interest to anyone contemplating experimenting with this aerial, which is suitable for linear or circular polarization.

In fact within a week of the article appearing, Dennis Walker, G3OLM, had built and demonstrated to the UK FM Group a miniature 3·6GHz model. This led to the discovery that the ip quad element can be used also as a reflector by increasing its size by five per cent over the basic λ/3 sides normally used for narrow-band operation of the driven element and by short-circuiting the feed points.

G3LHZ considers this to be rather surprising since the measured reactance given in the original Tsukiji paper on the cldla indicates that this did not become inductive at any time; normally it might be expected that a reflector, in order to function correctly, would have to show an inductive reactance. Possibly, he feels, the current in the ip quad reflector element *does* lag sufficiently in phase, even though the effect is not observable at the feedpoint. The practical importance of this discovery is significant and further experimental and theoretical work is clearly needed.

Secondly, G3LHZ has found an alternative form of the ip quad element, possessing the same basic properties, yet rather easier to construct (particularly at hf). This form (Fig 4) can be considered as a "diamond" or "diagonal" ip quad element with the feed lines forming diagonals, and he tentatively proposes this form be called a *d*ip quad element. Here again the size of the active loops adds up to 1 λ: for example $\lambda/(2+\sqrt{2}) + \lambda/(2+\sqrt{2}) + \lambda/(\sqrt{2}+1) = 1\lambda$. In fact the 1λ dimensions appears to be the important common feature of all such structures. A few preliminary experiments by G3LHZ on 144MHz indicate that this modified structure gives a slightly lower impedance across its terminals than the original ip quad (perhaps about 0·8 times). A *d*ip quad element would clearly be easy to implement using the wire and bamboo approach commonly employed at hf. The bamboo spreaders can have the feed lines, XX' and YY' taped along them. Another advantage is that the overall element size is reduced from 0·333λ

Fig 4. Modified form of ip quad element developed by G3LHZ and termed a dip quad

to 0·293λ per side; a 12 per cent reduction bringing the structure to only 17 per cent larger than a conventional quad-driven element.

Thirdly, either the original ip quad of the *d*ip quad can be rotated by 45° and both input ports fed together: Fig 5. This still gives the choice of horizontal or vertical polarization at the cost of extra (relay?) switching at the feed points. The impedance as "seen" is almost halved and G3LHZ found this to be getting too low to be matched directly, through a 4 : 1 impedance balun into a 50Ω line when the element was used as the driven element of a multi-element quad. However, when used on its own with a 4 : 1 balun as described in the September article a good 50Ω match was easy to achieve.

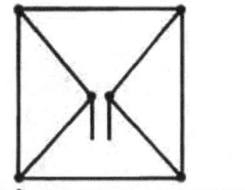 or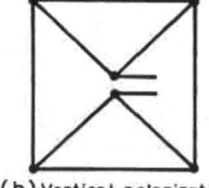

(a) Horizontal polarization   (b) Vertical polarization

Fig 5. Showing how either ip quad or dip quad elements can be rotated through 45° and both input ports fed together. This provides choice of horizontal or vertical polarization (as in original element) if switching at the feed points is used

Fourthly, John Roberts, G8FDJ, has made a 22-element, 432MHz version of the G3LHZ 144MHz design and is using it in a circularly-polarized mode fed with 4W of rf to work through Oscar 7, reporting very good results and a very marked improvement over an 8-over-8 conventional stacked Yagi array.

Fifthly, both G8FDJ and G3LHZ have found from their experiments how important it is to decouple the aerial from its supporting structure. This cannot be overstressed. Many amateurs have found how disappointing results can be when using any vertically-polarized beam mounted on a metal mast. Metal masts have even more disastrous effects on circularly-polarized aerials. Not only is the beam pattern distorted but the circularity of polarization is lost (this is recognized as a real problem in vhf/fm broadcasting practice and much has been said and written about this in the USA). G3LHZ believes that the only practical solution for amateurs is to use a *non-conducting* mast and to position the feeders very carefully. It also helps, he finds, to use λ/4 baluns on the outside of the feeders or to coil these to act as chokes at the operating frequency.

ANTENNA TOPICS

Mother Earth – Supergain or Attenuator

Extracted from 'Technical Topics', *Radio Communication,* November 1976

Mother earth—supergain or attenuator?

One of the fascinating aspects of amateur hf aerials is the difference between what we expect before we put them up and what we actually achieve. Those theoretical radiation patterns —even those based on model aerial ranges—never seem quite to tie up with the stations we actually work or do not work. There are several reasons for this (including radiation from what we fondly call transmission lines) and one prime cause is the effect of the environment—buildings, trees (with their particular ability to absorb vertically-polarized signals), wire fences, metal drain pipes and guttering, and of course the real earth below. Hands up those amateurs in typical urban areas who still believe that a vertical monopole aerial has extremely good low-angle radiation: yet such statements introduce almost every article ever written on vertically-polarized systems for amateurs. With poorly-conducting ground the amount of low-angle radiation is very small indeed unless extreme steps are taken to instal effective earth radials or earth mats.

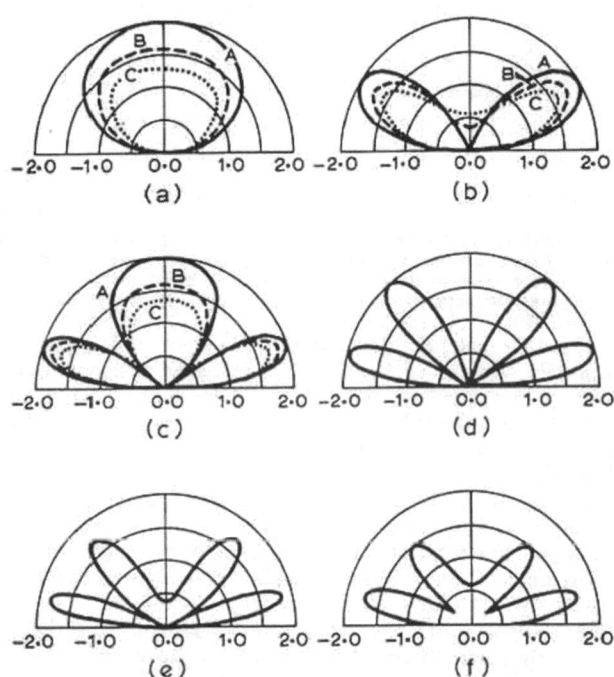

Fig 8. Computer diagrams showing effects on low horizontal aerials of different ground conductivities. (a) Height one-quarter wavelength, curve a perfect ground, curve b moist ground, curve c arid ground. (b) Height one-half wavelength, curves as for (a). (c) Height three-quarter wavelength, curves as for (a). (d) Height one-wavelength, perfect ground. (e) Height one-wavelength, moist ground. (f) Height one-wavelength, arid ground. Note how the lobes representing power gain tend to reduce over poor ground and the nulls begin to fill in. All diagrams represent vertical radiation patterns

One of the few attempts to present pattern factors for horizontally-polarized aerials over real earth is that by Hardy Landskov, W7KAR (*QST*, November 1975, pp19-21), though he also draws attention to a professional source of information: Ma and Waters, *ESSA Technical Report, ERL 104-ITS 74*, "Power gains for antennas over lossy plane ground", April 1969, from Supt of Documents, Washington DC, 20402, USA, 65c. W7KAR provides many pattern factors, based on computer analyses, as well as a table that summarizes the results. He concludes that:

(1) Low heights should be avoided with all horizontal aerials, because their gain suffers badly at elevations under one wavelength above ground.

(2) Aerials located one wavelength or more above ground have gains within a few tenths of a decibel of the perfect-earth case, *regardless of soil conditions*.

(3) High-angle radiation (above 45°) suffers as much as 3dB for aerials over poor earth, regardless of aerial height. This is an important consideration on 3·5 and 1·8MHz where few aerials exceed or even reach a quarter-wave above earth.

GAIN OF ½λ DIPOLE AS FUNCTION OF HEIGHT AND GROUND PARAMETERS, USING LOWEST LOBE

Height λ	Approx gain, dB/isotropic			Direction of gain, above horizontal		
	A	B	C	A	B	C
¼	8·14	6·28	5·14	90°	90°	90°
½	8·14	7·16	6·60	30°	29°	29°
1	8·14	7·64	7·30	15°	14·5°	14·5°
2	8·14	7·90	7·72	7·5°	7°	7°
4	8·14	8·03	7·94	3·75°	3·5°	3·5°

A—perfect ground; B—moist soil; C—dry soil

These are perhaps rather idealistic conclusions, since, as we have noted on other occasions, the low horizontal dipole may be very useful in practice. The fact that gain may fall by only 3dB in coming down (as W7KAR shows) from 4λ to ¼λ above ground shows that the low dipole can be used effectively, if it has to be, on short- and medium-distance paths.

W7KAR's diagrams (for example those in Fig 8) indicate well that the main effect of a poor earth on low aerials is to blur the theoretical vertical radiation pattern, reducing the lobes and partly filling in the nulls.

Miniature VK2ABQ 'X' Beams

Extracted from 'Technical Topics', *Radio Communication,* December 1976

Miniature VK2ABQ "X" beams

A previous item (*TT* January 1974) has reported on a low-cost wire-type triband "X" beam developed by Fred Caton,

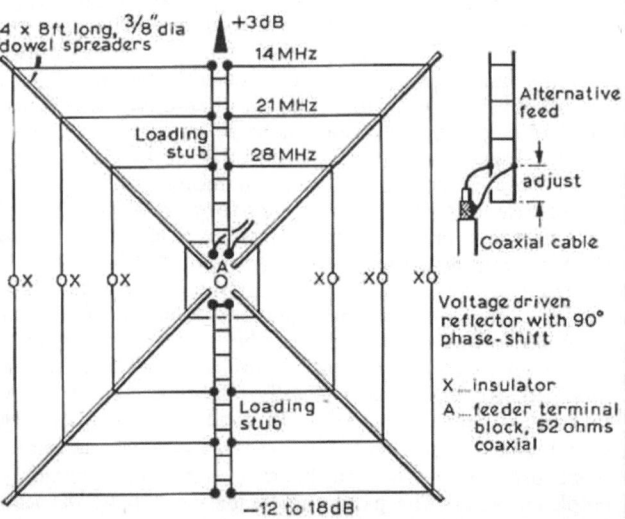

Fig 5. VK2ABQ's voltage-driven phased array minibeam with loading stubs

1970 - 1979

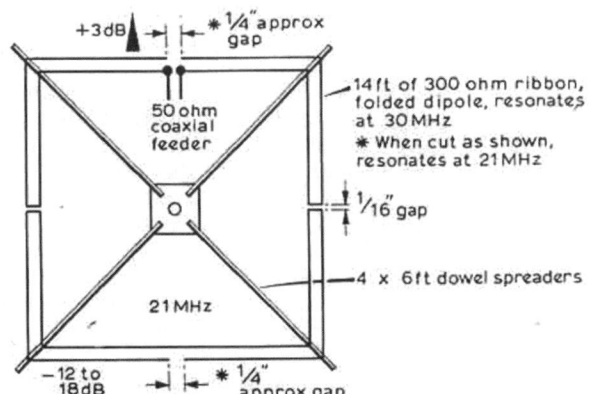

Fig 6. VK2ABQ's 21MHz beam using two 300Ω flat ribbon folded dipoles (about 14ft long). The dowel rods should be 4ft for 28MHz, 8ft for 14MHz

Inverted-Vs, Diversity, Long Wires and VHF

Extracted from 'Technical Topics', *Radio Communication,* December 1976

VK2ABQ (formerly G3ONC). Recently, two techniques for reducing the dimensions have been brought to my notice by VK2ABQ and a design for a reasonably compact 7MHz beam (usable also on 14MHz) has been published in *Amateur Radio* (August 1976) by David Down, VK5HP.

VK2ABQ suggests that his designs should provide about 3dB forward gain (reference dipole) but about −12 to −15dB in the backward direction.

The first of these designs (Fig 5) shows how the elements can be shortened by using "loading stubs" rather than lossy inductors. These stubs are made of a length of 2in (not less) spaced home-made line, permitting a 14/21/28MHz beam to be made with a turning radius of about 8ft. With the aid of a gdo the correct tapping points for the 21 and 28MHz can be found using crocodile clips, afterwards soldering them. The 2in spreaders were made from plastic ice-cream holders.

Fig 6 shows another technique for compact single-band beams, the "X" spreaders being dowel rods 4ft long for 28MHz, 6ft for 21MHz and 8ft for 14MHz, using 300Ω ribbon feeder to form the folded elements with small cut-out "gaps".

Fig 7 shows a version using 300Ω line (without gaps) described by VK5HP for a 7MHz beam with a turning radius of about 12ft 6in. He claims he built the entire beam for $A13: "It took two hours to build and can be turned by hand or by rotators such as the Stolle and has proved very effective with low power." The bamboos (Rangoon canes) are

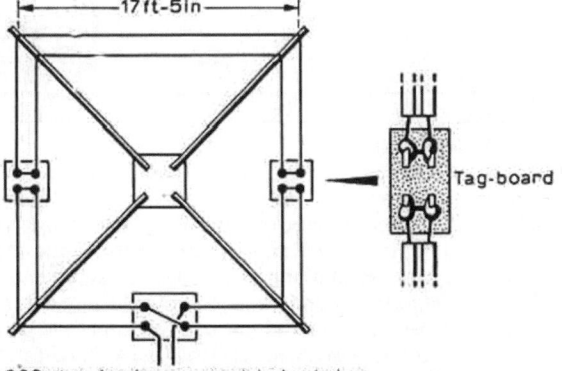

Fig 7. VK5HP's 7MHz beam based on the VK2ABQ approach

fixed by U bolts to the 15 by 15in square of ¾in marine plywood. Elements are adjusted by gdo and VK5HP states that it also works on 14MHz. It should be noted that all these beams need a "correction factor" when gdo-resonated at a low height as the resonant frequency will increase by a few hundred kilohertz at full height. The original full-sized VK2ABQ triband remains one of the few designs for a simple home-made aerial that does not involve the constructional problems of the quad.

Inverted-Vs, diversity and vhf

Several follow-up comments have been received on the September notes on inverted-V aerials and the general question of using long-wire techniques on vhf. First, to clear up one point, I have come to the conclusion that the gain comparisons between the half-rhombic (terminated inverted-V) and Yagi arrays were rather misleading and unfair to the hf Yagi. Although the power gains reported by Ma and Tveten included the figure of 16·7dB at low angles, this extremely high gain is not representative of what an amateur is likely to achieve at normal dx angles over normal ground. As a more direct comparison with the Yagi "gain barrier" of about 6dB, a more typical figure for a half-rhombic would be of the order of perhaps 4 to 8dB, although it should be stressed that large commercial rhombics can have true power gains (reference dipole) up to and beyond the figure of 16·7dB.

Owen Jackson, A9XU/G3LKZ, is in the fortunate position of being able to comment on a recent evaluation of a half-rhombic used at a professional receiving station in Bahrain. He writes:

"This aerial was erected as an experiment in compressing our site size due to encroaching housing developments, although to amateur eyes it could not be considered a backyard effort. It consisted of a single wire with a terminating resistor, the apex at 150ft and the total ground length about 900ft. It was deliberately erected alongside a full-sized rhombic in order to use this as a comparison. As indicated in Fig 8 the inverted-V used one of the masts of the rhombic. Initially I had doubts as to the wisdom of using a vertically-polarized aerial over such an apparently poor ground as the desert of Bahrain, and ground mats about 100ft by 50ft made

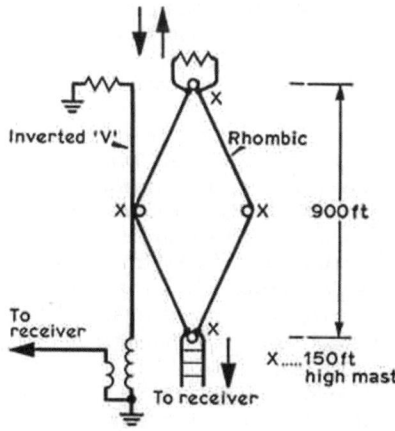

Fig 8. The experimental "half-rhombic" inverted-V erected alongside a rhombic in the system investigated by A9XU/G3LKZ and found to provide excellent polarization diversity reception

up of a grid of wires about 2-3ft apart were used under the terminated end and the feed end.

"The first results were so poor as to be unbelievable. This was fortunate since it led to the discovery of a faulty terminating transformer at the feed point. With this replaced the subsequent tests showed that it was a very encouraging aerial considering its simplicity. The rhombic had a known gain of between 14 and 18dB depending on frequency; the average gain of the inverted-V was some 10dB less. But this meant that we were achieving gains of almost up to 10dB

115

ANTENNA TOPICS

over poor ground, over the range 8 to 18MHz. In fact it performed as well as a commercial log-periodic costing about £9,000, although the log periodic could be rotated.

"However, the most interesting part of the experiment came when we used the two aerials as a diversity reception system. While I naturally hoped to achieve some benefit from polarization diversity between the rhombic and half-rhombic, the results were beyond expectation. It was quite normal to see 20dB or even up to 30dB difference between the two aerials (paths were balanced for this test by attenuating the rhombic so that these figures are true differences in the fading pattern). The combination meant that in practice it was impossible to tell if the receivers were operating in normal space diversity using two full-sized rhombics 500 yards apart or the rhombic and adjacent inverted-V.

"I am now firmly convinced that much of the fading we know so well in amateur operation arises more from polarization coupling losses brought about by the constantly changing polarization of the incoming signals than most of us realize. The experiment convinced us that we could dispense with one of the rhombics and still achieve the required diversity reception at a lot less cost.

"All this points to aerials having mixed polarization offering a definite advantage over those confined strictly to one linear plane, as is normal practice in amateur hf and vhf installations.

"It will be appreciated that these tests were for reception only and it was not possible to try the half-rhombic for transmission. However, it could well be that the usual warning about poor ground conductivity may be no more serious than in the case of the common vertical ground plane or monopole."

Long-wires on vhf

Owen Jackson also reports on the use of rhombics at vhf, based on some experiments carried out in conjunction with a friend while at Benghazi, Libya. He comments:

"At that time Libya had no national tv service and many attempts were made to achieve reception of stations in Malta or even in Rome, at distances up to 800 miles. To cut a long story short, the finest aerial proved to be a rhombic array which outperformed the best Yagi aerials used (up to four bays of 10 vhf elements). It is indeed a pity that information on long-wire systems for hf and vhf is disappearing from the handbooks—presumably reflecting the increasingly limited space available to most of us."

To add to this saga, W. D. Kidd, who is the IBA's engineer-in-charge of the television stations on the Channel Islands, has kindly sent me some background information on long-wire arrays used until recently for the reception of mainland transmissions. Since these signals have to be rebroadcast, very high orders of signal/noise and reliability are sought, despite the difficult long sea paths (this has now led to the development by the IBA of a null-steerable adaptive aerial for 625-line uhf colour signals, but that is another story). He writes:

"The story goes back to 1954-5 when I was associated with the setting up of a BBC Band 1 receiving station at Torteval, Guernsey. Initially the system was based on double Yagi arrays directed towards both Wenvoe and Alexandra Palace (130 and 190 miles respectively). Results, despite the use of masthead amplifiers, offered little encouragement. However, about this time the Channel 2 station at North Hessary Tor opened and it became possible to receive signals with a simple Yagi. As a result a system was built with diversity on North Hessary Tor (Cornwall) and Wenvoe (South Wales).

"However, this was not a complete answer since there was a 60dB variation in signal strength under varying propagation conditions, and rather severe precipitation static on the Yagi aerials. So as an alternative we experimented with the EMI type of sloping wire (this was a long-wire 'quarter rhombic' or 'tilted wire' system using capacitance loading as in the G6CJ 'stretched dipole' approach). Our early experiments aimed at establishing direction and vertical angles were carried out in the foulest possible weather. However, subsequently we used banks of these stretched quarter rhombics with 12 wires in the North Hessary Tor array and 16 on Wenvoe. The forward ends were terminated and supported about 6ft above ground level; the top ends, matching sections and head amplifiers were supported on a catenary slung between 110ft masts, ropes being used to keep the whole structure rigid. These long-wire arrays, together with the Yagis, allowed the BBC to start its service in 1956. However, the sloping wires proved mechanically weak and were replaced not long after I left the BBC.

"The inverted-V array which was installed by the British Post Office for the IBA service was erected at Alderney and consisted of a bank of 12 continuous lengths of solid copper arranged as half-rhombics. This array was directed on Caradon Hill, Cornwall, and was intended for use as an alternative to Stockland Hill, South Devon, which was the main source and for which two large 10m dish aerials were used. The half-rhombic, however, was needed since there were occasions, particularly during the summer months, when deterioration of the Stockland Hill–Alderney path was found to coincide with an improvement in the Caradon Hill–Alderney path. In practice, little or no signals of rebroadcastable quality were received from Caradon Hill between the autumnal and spring equinoxes, so that the half-rhombic was used only at times during the summer. The half-rhombic array is no longer in existence, having been taken down quite recently as part of the re-engineering of the link to allow the 625-line colour service to be started by ITV last summer. At the same time we also removed some 'bedstead' arrays directed on Chillerton Down, Isle of Wight. The uhf link is now based solely on Stockland Hill using the 10m dishes and the special adaptive aerial ("SABRE") which at present uses only half the number of elements of the final design."

Antenna Round-up

Extracted from 'Technical Topics',
Radio Communication, January 1977

Antenna round-up

Both G. R. Thomas, 5B4CA, and Gian Moda, I2SWX, were rather surprised at the comments on the double-bazooka/coaxial dipole based on the long article by Walt Maxwell, W2DU, in *Ham Radio* (August 1976). Both these users of this system send along notes, swr measurements or Smith Chart diagrams to underline their own feeling that this is a useful approach that should not be condemned. My own feeling is that probably everyone is right: the W2DU article, as I read it, reflects a concern that there have been some over-strong claims made for this system (not, I hasten to say, by 5B4CA in the August *TT* item) and that the extra bandwidth can be achieved in other ways rather more cheaply and with fewer problems. Certainly I hope that my facetious "don't" comment is not taken as suggesting that the double-bazooka does not work: there is plenty of evidence that it can result in a somewhat broader bandwidth—the argument is whether there are not simpler ways of doing this.

Bernard Howlett, G3JAM, was interested to see the antenna "shaped like a football goal" (*TT* October 1976,

Fig 3(a)) although he is not entirely happy at it being called a "half quad". He recalls that he tested a similar configuration on a 600MHz model table as long ago as 1950, and subsequently used one on 3·5MHz when he obtained his licence: two earthed 30ft vertical sections and a 60ft horizontal section running over the house, windom fed. However, he soon found that due to electrolytic action causing rapidly increasing earth resistance it worked better without the earthing, with voltage points at the ends. On 1·8MHz the wire was earthed at one end and shunt fed one third from this end. By changing the earthed end, reversible directivity could be obtained and the system proved very satisfactory. His original experiments had been to show that a normal dipole with current at the centre could be successfully "inverted" to have the voltage at the centre.

Incidentally the "normal" rather than the "inverse" configuration turned up recently in a note by C. M. Wintzner, F0AXP in the German magazine *QRV* (No 9, September 1976); Fig 4.

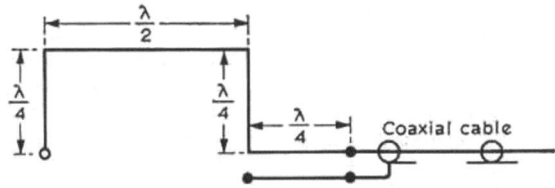

Fig 4. An "up-over-and-down" antenna described by F0AXP in *QRV* and representing the "inverse" of the grounded system mentioned in the October 1976 *TT*

Inverted-V and Chireix-Mesny

Extracted from 'Technical Topics',
Radio Communication, January 1977

Inverted-V and Chireix-Mesny

This conveniently brings us to another form of "long-wire" antenna that is closely related to the Bruce form of inverted-V but has been largely forgotten: the Chireix-Mesny antenna. This was developed originally as an alternative to the Marconi-Franklin beam arrays made up of large numbers of vertical dipoles, parallel to one another. In the Chireix-Mesny array the ½λ dipoles are disposed in the form of saw-teeth, rather like a series of 2λ quad elements. This has the advantage over the Franklin that each dipole element may be driven directly by the one preceding it. Fig 5(a) shows a large Chireix-Mesny array which would require vast space for hf but might well be worth investigating for vhf or uhf. From the point of view of the radiated field, such a sawtooth network is equivalent to an array of parallel dipoles. Fig 5 (b) forms the basis of the "zig-zag" antennas used at vhf/uhf for television broadcasting.

Ted Cook, ZS6BT, points out that a 90° inverted-V (Fig 5(c)) consisting of two ¼λ elements is, in effect, an elementary form of Chireix-Mesny array and can be fed as in the up-over-and-down configuration of Fig 4 to form a vertically-polarized monobander (the system would work on the harmonic bands when voltage fed but it would no longer be a Chireix-Mesny arrangement).

He has been using two such arrays: one on 14MHz and the other (with a V reflector spaced 0·1λ) on 28MHz. The performance of the 14MHz antenna, he finds, is roughly similar to a *half-wave* vertical, but appears to be less noisy

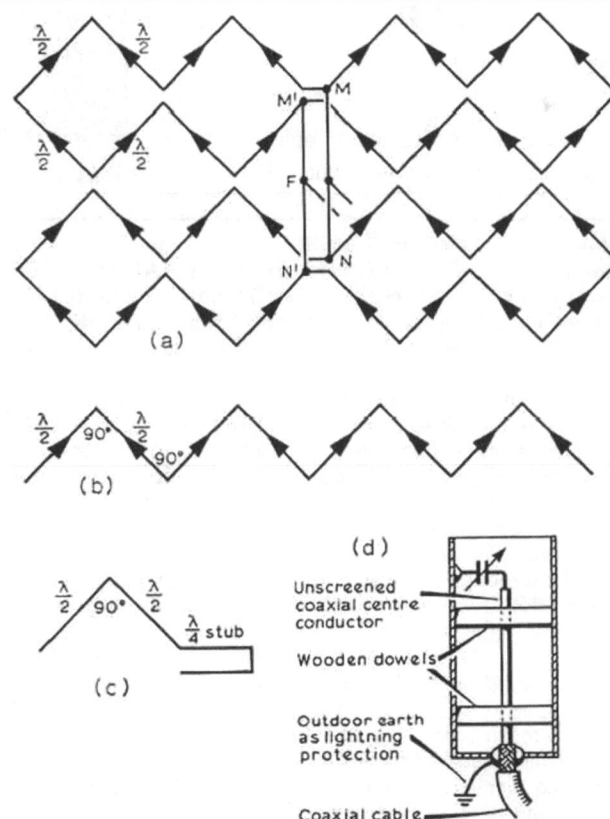

Fig 5. (a) A large Chireix-Mesny array of half-wave dipoles arranged in saw-tooth configuration and providing vertically-polarized signals with broadside directivity. Such an array might have applications at vhf or uhf. (b) Simplified Chireix-Mesny array which can be end fed. (c) Showing how the saw-tooth configuration reduces to a 90° inverted-V as used by ZS6BT. (d) The ZS6BT gamma-derived stub match (*TT* August 1974) provides a convenient means of connecting a coaxial-cable to the quarter-wave stub (it would also be suitable for use with the antenna of Fig 4)

and less prone to fading. On 28MHz his system forms a vertically-polarized broadside beam. The wires can be supported by a single mast (preferably not a metal one) or hung below a horizontal wire antenna.

By using his "stub match" (*TT* August 1974) he achieves perfect matching without disturbance of the phase.

In all end-fed "long-wire" arrays, the dipole sections closest to the feed-point radiate rather more power than those farthest away, leading to a degree of asymmetry in the radiation patterns. This is well illustrated in *ART* where a considerable number of long-wire patterns are presented showing the effect of feedpoint on radiation—a factor (as Hector Cole, G3OHK, has recently pointed out to me) often ignored in the standard radiation patterns shown in the handbooks. It is the reason why really long "long wires", such as the Beverage, do not need a terminating resistor since by the time the wave reaches the far end virtually all the power has been radiated. It also means that the impedance at the end of a multi-band long wire reduces at the higher frequencies, although this can be taken care of in most matching networks.

ANTENNA TOPICS

Duo-band 'Bow-tie' Beam

Extracted from 'Technical Topics',
Radio Communication, January 1977

Duo-band "bow-tie" beam

Ken A. Taylor, G4EEC (who passed his RAE in his 70th year and his morse test in his 71st!) sends along details of a duo-band system for 14 and 21MHz based on the VK2ABQ mono-band "bow-tie" described in *TT* September 1974. He comments:

"For an old man, the VK2ABQ X-type tribander seemed a bit too difficult to construct and handle on my own, but it seemed within my powers to make a bow-tie for two bands as shown in Fig 9. It performs very well despite adverse conditions here.

"The location is surrounded by parkland with huge beech and redwood and other forest trees all within about 100 yards, although there is a small gap to the west. Though about 150ft above sea level, it is not possible to hoist the antenna higher than 16ft but it has given good results into the USA and Canada on both bands with 200W p.e.p. ssb. It has stood up to some high winds and the cost was very low as befits an 'oap'. I avoided the original 'wood and nails' construction outlined by Fred Caton and used six varnished canes for spreaders clamped to the 2 by 1in timber by vee clamps of dural sheet with rustless screws (two 1½in long clamps per cane)". Other construction details will be found in the caption to Fig 9.

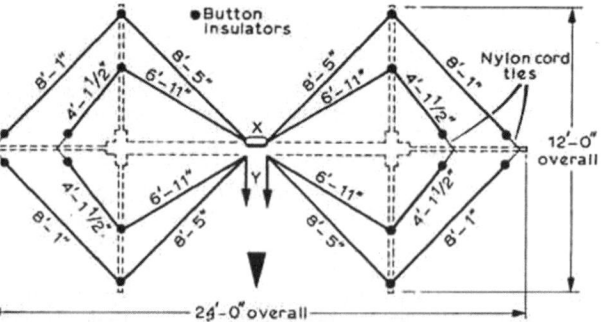

Fig 9. Two-band (14 and 21MHz) "bow-tie" antenna built by G4EEC and based on the VK2ABQ mono-band design (*TT* September 1974). Main support beam is 2 by 1in varnished softwood with 18 by 2 by 1in crosspieces and spreaders of 6ft varnished canes. Note that the loops were tuned with a single turn coil at Y against a gdo by folding back the wires where the nylon ties are indicated and altering the tie lengths to suit. Wire size is 18swg enam for outer loop, insulated pvc flex for inner loop. Point X egg insulator as anchor point for centre of loop. Point Y feed point for 50Ω coaxial feeder (no balun was used). Length of loop for 14MHz 33ft (swr 1·2:1, 14·15 to 14·275); 21MHz 22ft 1in (swr 1·15:1 for 21·2 to 21·3MHz). Height of antenna at G4EEC is only 16ft

Another "two-element" technique that makes use of the "phase centre" concept rather than fixed spacing is the use of a vertical mast radiator with a sloping wire running up to the top of the same mast but insulated from it. While such a system does not give very high forward gain it can put a useful notch in the backward direction. Such a system is used by the IBA for the Pennine Radio station (1,277kHz) at Bradford and also as a reserve antenna for the London stations, which normally use a four-mast directional array simultaneously on 1,151kHz and 1,546kHz.

Mini-beam Ideas

Extracted from 'Technical Topics',
Radio Communication, February 1977

Mini-beam ideas

In *TT* (December 1976) several ideas were presented on adapting the VK2ABQ X-beam principle to form mini-beams; and indeed even the full-sized VK2ABQ tri-band X-beam can be thought of as a form of compact beam with its turning radius of only 12ft. By coincidence, just before the December issue reached your letter boxes, a note was received from Les Moxon, G6XN, describing some recent investigations into mini-beams using the basic VK2ABQ approach, but in a rather different way. Subsequent correspondence has also highlighted his firm belief that it should be possible to develop "no-compromise" mini-beams that need be at no real disadvantage to full-sized units; and indeed, since they may often be raised to a greater height without becoming a major engineering operation, should often be capable in practice of out-performing their bigger but less tall brothers.

G6XN writes: "I am now confirmed in my belief that a mini-beam does not have to be a 'compromise', and this is very important if I am also right in thinking that many amateurs have lost interest in dx operation (or never acquired it) because they believe that without a big beam they cannot be competitive."

G6XN admits that hitherto two-element mini-beams have not given too good an account of themselves; yet he points out that it should not be necessary to lose *more than 2dB compared with a quad or 3-element full-sized Yagi at the same height*. This basic 2dB is made up of 1dB loss due to the use of two rather than three elements (and if this seems very little to lose refer to G6XN's excellent analysis of "Gains and losses in hf aerials", *Radio Communication* December 1973 and January 1974), and 1dB from tuning the beam for maximum (nominal) front-to-back ratio rather than (as should be done for a full-sized beam) for maximum gain (this is necessary to avoid paying too heavy a price in terms of bandwidth).

The gains from consideration of environment and height (ie getting the antenna well up in the clear) can more than compensate for this modest loss of 2dB. G6XN suggests that we must all be extremely careful in accepting any trade-off of fundamental gain for practical advantages, since otherwise one could end up with no real performance at all; and he urges that —2dB (compared with a properly designed and adjusted full-sized array) should be considered as about the right place to draw the line if top dx performance is to be achieved. But note that this implies that *it should be possible to obtain approximately 4dB forward gain from a light-weight mini-beam*, compared with the 6dB "gain barrier" for most rotary hf beams.

Then again most people using big beams insist on feeding them with coaxial cable. G6XN writes: "There is an average of 1dB (and a lot of money) to be saved by *not* using coaxial cable feeders. Again, with a mini or any other two-element beam, there is also a lot to be gained by driving both elements in a way which allows fine tuning to be carried out in the shack. This overcomes the problem of reduced bandwidth, although it requires two feeders and some skill on the part of the user."

Two open-wire feeders, brought into the shack, can offer the following advantages:

(1) Instantaneous beam reversal (a very useful operational feature that also more than halves the average time spent in

beam turning).

(2) Beam becomes tunable from the shack and the beam reversal feature makes tuning very easy: one tunes for null on the receiver and then operates the reversing switch.

(3) Instantaneous reversal also provides a simple check on beam performance.

(4) Less than 180° rotation is needed and this allows simpler and cheaper methods of beam rotation.

(5) Interference can be nulled out.

A further very important practical advantage is that it no longer becomes necessary to "tune up" the beam with the elements close to the ground, with the problem of having to allow correctly for the effect of raising the antenna. Some ideas for remote tuning of quad antennas, based on an article by W6AJZ, were given in *TT* (July 1973, reprinted in *ART5*), although in this case only one element was so tuned.

Although G6XN has not yet applied the full two-feeder tuning system to a mini-beam he feels it could represent perhaps the single most important step towards the production of a real competitor to the big beams.

A 'Neutralized' VK2ABQ Mini-beam

Extracted from 'Technical Topics',
Radio Communication, February 1977

A "neutralized" VK2ABQ mini-beam

In his own approach to the VK2ABQ mini-beam, G6XN has adopted a novel "neutralizing" technique to overcome the "double-humped" response brought about by what in effect is a pair of high-Q circuits tightly coupled by end capacitances, making it very difficult to obtain anything like equal element currents at the same time as correct phasing. It is not intended, this month, to explain this system in detail as it is still in process of being tested; however, the basic arrangement is shown in Fig 1. Preliminary trials on 14MHz are most promising and appear to open up other applications for antenna-element neutralizing.

In adopting the VK2ABQ approach, G6XN is convinced that to make an element as small as possible without adding lossy components (eg the loss resistance of loading coils) one *must* "end load" and the end-loading *must* be confined within the space enclosed by the radiating elements (as for example in the capacity hat loaded mini-quad described by G3YDX in *Radio Communication*, October 1976) and that this can

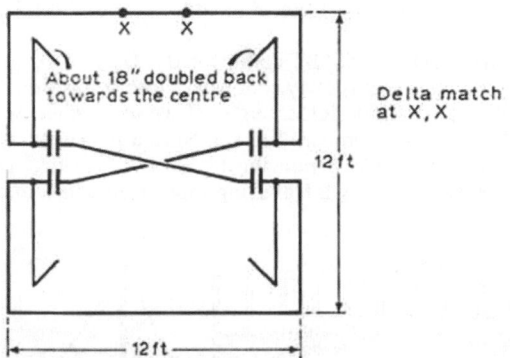

Fig 1. G6XN's neutralized form of the VK2ABQ mini-beam for 14MHz which has been tested at a height of 55ft with highly promising results as a "no compromise" mini-beam fully competitive with full-sized arrays at rather lower heights

G6XN considers the VK2ABQ tri-band mini-beam (Fig 5 of December 1976 *TT*) could be a serious contender in the search for high-performance mini-beams. While this might seem deliberately to *increase* (rather than neutralize) the capacitive coupling between the elements, nevertheless both techniques appear to be making deliberate use of capacitive coupling to create the "equal current" situation required to achieve good back : front ratio. On the other hand, the VK2ABQ approach will have a lower radiation resistance than the G6XN neutralizing technique and this means either less bandwidth *or* some sacrifice of gain (consistent with VK2ABQ's claimed 3dB forward gain), and greater wire diameter to achieve similar efficiency. Conversely, for similar results it should be possible to reduce the dimensions of the G6XN beam still further.

Clearly there is still a good deal of room for further investigations involving the use of two separate feeders to provide remote tuning, and in these notes I am briefly outlining only some of the many interesting points made by G6XN, although I hope to return to this subject before long.

One point made by G6XN is that he cannot believe that VK5HP's 7MHz version of the VK2ABQ beam (Fig 7 of December 1976 *TT*) can possibly resonate at 7MHz since the two 300Ω wires will tend to resonate as a single conductor and not as $(2 \times 17\text{ft } 5\text{in}) + (4 \times 8\text{ft } 8\text{in})$, ie 69ft 6in of wire. This might be worth checking since, rather curiously, in a subsequent issue of *Amateur Radio* VK5HP has described in detail a quad antenna based on the same form of folded element, so somehow he seems to have found the technique workable. I wonder if any reader has tried the idea and would care to comment.

Before leaving this fascinating subject of getting quarts out of pint bottles, one further general point made by G6XN: the importance of *not* securing wires directly to bamboo spreaders. Since such elements have low radiation resistances, they will have very strong electrostatic fields, and bamboo is a very bad insulator when wet. He uses polythene line (as thin as possible) exclusively for antenna insulation, and the corners of his elements are secured to radial ties, the spider being bowed to provide tension and clearance.

Frame Receiving Antenna

Extracted from 'Technical Topics',
Radio Communication, February 1977

Frame receiving antenna

On several occasions we have mentioned briefly the use of simple frame antennas, with single-turn coupling coils, for dx reception of medium-wave broadcast or 1·8MHz stations. Each time enquiries have been received seeking further constructional details, although these are not particularly critical. As such a design has recently appeared in *Electronics Australia* (October 1976) the opportunity is taken of reproducing it: Fig 5.

About 100ft of plastic-covered wire (about 22swg) should be used for the main winding and this should be wound to a whole number of turns; if it will not tune to 2MHz with seven turns, take one off and try again. Seventy-ohm coaxial cable can be used instead of 300Ω balanced feeder to the receiver, but aim at making the windings and general construction as symmetrical as possible since the depth of the rejection null depends on the electrical balance. Tune in signals on the receiver, peaking the antenna tuning control

ANTENNA TOPICS

and adjusting direction of loop for maximum pick-up or for maximum rejection of interference.

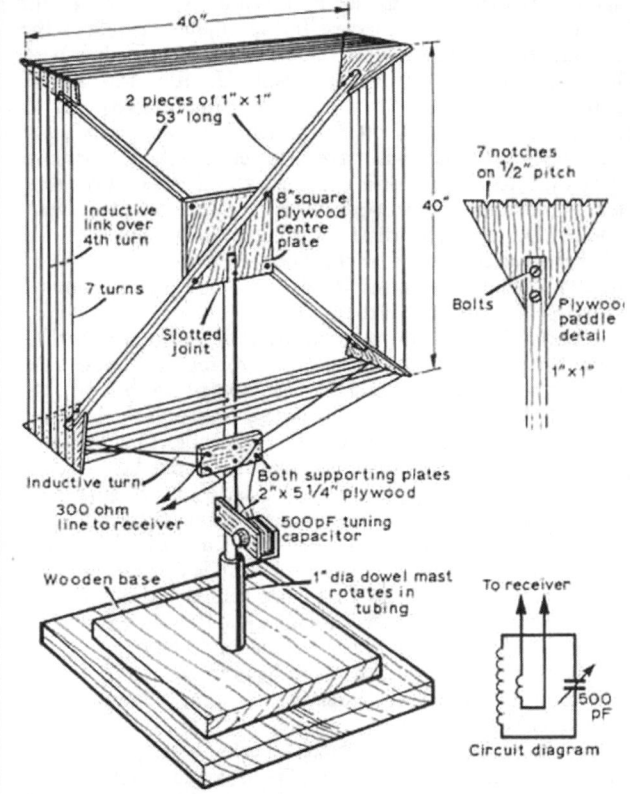

Fig 5. Constructional details of loop antenna for operation on medium waves and/or 1·8MHz and capable of providing deep null on interfering signals (*Electronics Australia*)

The Series-Phase Antenna

Extracted from 'Technical Topics', *Radio Communication,* April 1977

The series-phase antenna

During recent months a recurring topic in *TT* has been the potential value of traditional "long-wire" antennas not only for hf but also for vhf/uhf where the space problems are far less daunting: the long-wire terminated inverted-V ("Bruce"); the Chireix-Mesny zig-zag array; possibly the Beverage which works at hf but is virtually an unknown quantity at vhf; and above all that "queen" of antennas, the ever-attractive bi-directional or the terminated uni-directional rhombic which is known to be an excellent performer well up into the uhf range.

One "long-wire" antenna that was developed in the 'thirties (or possibly the 'twenties) and enjoyed some years of popularity both as an hf and as a vhf fixed beam antenna, but has long disappeared from the textbooks, is the Marconi-Franklin series-phase array. That indefatigable antenna experimenter, Ted Cook, ZS6BT, recently brought this array to my notice and a little library research soon brought out a number of additional reasons why it might be worth joining him in looking a little more closely into this system. ZS6BT has already developed a novel form of this array for use as a 144MHz antenna for working through Oscar.

Among the pre-war references to this array is its use for an early Marconi air-navigation aid working on about 33MHz (*Wireless Direction Finding*, by R. Keen, 3rd edition) and its use for hf communications ("The series phase aerial array" by N. Wells, *Wireless World,* 15 October 1937), although I should point out that ZS6BT disputes certain features of the description by N. Wells as to the way in which the system works, and has developed a rather different *balanced* form of the array suitable for either vertical or horizontal polarization. The original antennas comprised terminated unbalanced systems with vertical polarization (and which were sometimes made to reverse the direction of fire by transposing the terminating resistor and feed point): Fig 5.

While it could be argued that the gain for a given array size is unlikely to be as great as for a Yagi, there are some features of the system which would seem to make it attractive even today. Since basically it is a long-wire terminated array without parasitically excited elements it should not be difficult to achieve reasonable bandwidth; this is further underlined by the high radiation resistance which is specifically mentioned by N. Wells as one of the main attractions.

The main snag would be the large amount of ground needed for an hf array, which would limit the scope for achieving other than perhaps a moderately sharp reversible lobe, and on vhf the mechanical problems of forming each "element" of two separate wires rather than a solid element.

In the 1937 article it was shown that, by using up to four parallel "17-loop" arrays, forward gains of the order of 12-15dB (reference a vertical dipole) could be achieved in practice and that "theoretical gains are higher and, as a matter of fact, are often attained in practice". More realistically, an amateur hf array would be considerably lower in gain, but at vhf high gains are by no means out of the question. At this stage, ZS6BT is not prepared to estimate what gain he is achieving on 144MHz although he has an excellent front-to-back ratio, an apparently sharp lobe and adds: "Let's say that the array shows the sort of promise I had hoped for." But he stresses that he still has a good deal more work to do on the system. I have a few doubts as to whether his balanced form of array works in precisely the same way as the original series-phase and this may well account for the differences in the way that ZS6BT says it works and the diagrams in the 1937 *Wireless World* article. But does that really matter? Either way this could be a useful form (or two useful forms) of antenna.

In his original note, ZS6BT commented: "On first examination the phasing seems awry, but after close inspection the beauty of Franklin's design emerges. If we see five elements (ie five 'loops') then numbers 1, 3 and 5 are a half-wave part and 180° out of phase, producing the classic 'end-fire' pattern; however, assuming a travelling wave, elements 2 and 4

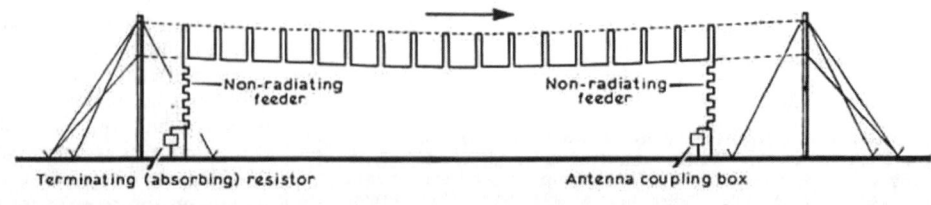

Fig 5. The original Marconi-Franklin hf series-phase "in-line" antenna of the form described in *Wireless World* 15 October 1937. This vertically-polarized antenna has 17 λ/4 "loops" spaced at λ/4 intervals. 36 λ/2 earth radials were placed below each end. Note that the line of fire is *away* from the termination

That Medium-wave Loop

Extracted from 'Technical Topics', *Radio Communication,* May 1977

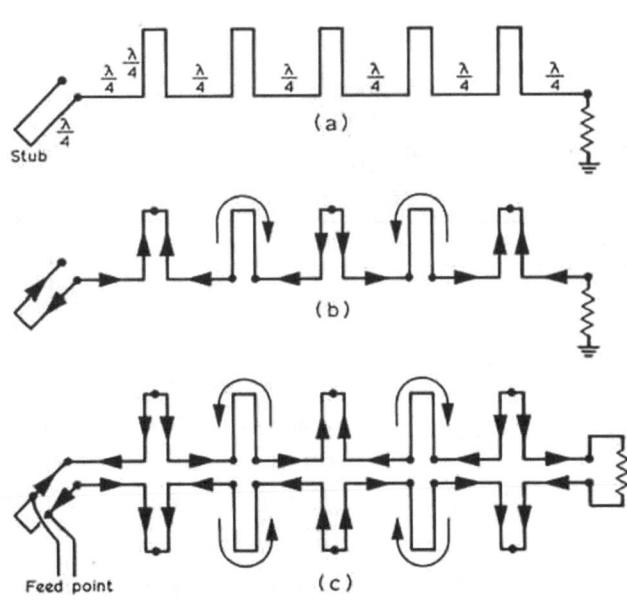

Fig 6. (a) ZS6BT's series-phase antenna showing the $\lambda/4$ loops. (b) Current distribution suggested by ZS6BT. (c) Balanced form of vhf array suitable for 144MHz with either horizontal or vertical polarization as being developed by ZS6BT

are 90° out of phase with 1, 3, 5 and are mutually a half-wave apart and 180° out of phase. Thus 90° after 1, 3 and 5 'fire', 2 and 4 take over."

To form the balanced array, ZS6BT simply stacks an inverted array under the first one, and the whole structure begins to look a bit like a Yagi but of course consists of long wires: ZS6BT in effect forms a wooden boom with dowel crosspieces and then tapes the wire to the structure.

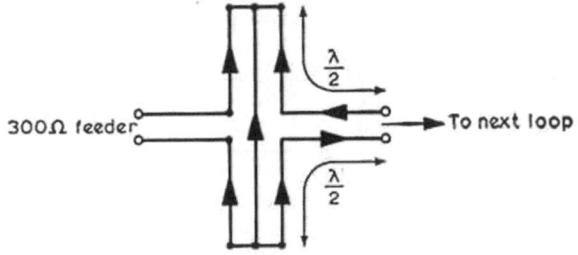

Fig 7. More recent technique used by ZS6BT for feeding his 144MHz series-phase antenna

Fig 7 shows the technique that ZS6BT uses to feed the first "loop".

Clearly the balanced vhf series-phase array is an idea for experimenters and not presented as a fully-fledged design; nevertheless it seems most interesting.

That medium-wave loop

In the February *TT* we included an illustration of a seven-turn large frame antenna which seems particularly useful for nulling out interference when chasing dx on mf or 1·8MHz. This illustration was redrawn from one that was published recently in *Electronics Australia*. Eric Dowdeswell, G4AR, has drawn my attention to an article by Charles Molloy on "Medium-wave dxing" which appeared in *Practical Wireless*, April 1970, and it is clear that this was the original source of this particular design about which the author wrote: "No one should be deterred from dxing on the medium waves through lack of an outside aerial.... No serious mw dxer would be without a loop ... frequently it is possible to null-out different stations on the same frequency, eg on 1,070kHz CBA in Canada can sometimes be heard free of interference if the null is pointing towards LR1 in Buenos Aires and similarly LR1 can be heard with CBA nulled out. There are additional benefits to be had from a loop. Static is reduced; in early summer when much of it comes from thunderstorms to the south, it can be eliminated when listening to the west ...". It all sounds pretty good going and a useful reminder of what can be done at mf.

Jan Martin Noding, LA8AK, writing from Bergen, Norway, also mentions that he has tried this type of frame receiving antenna on 3·5MHz and reports "the results were quite surprising, several W stations were heard above 3·8MHz".

ANTENNA TOPICS

Medium-sized Loop Antennas

Extracted from 'Technical Topics', *Radio Communication*, June 1977

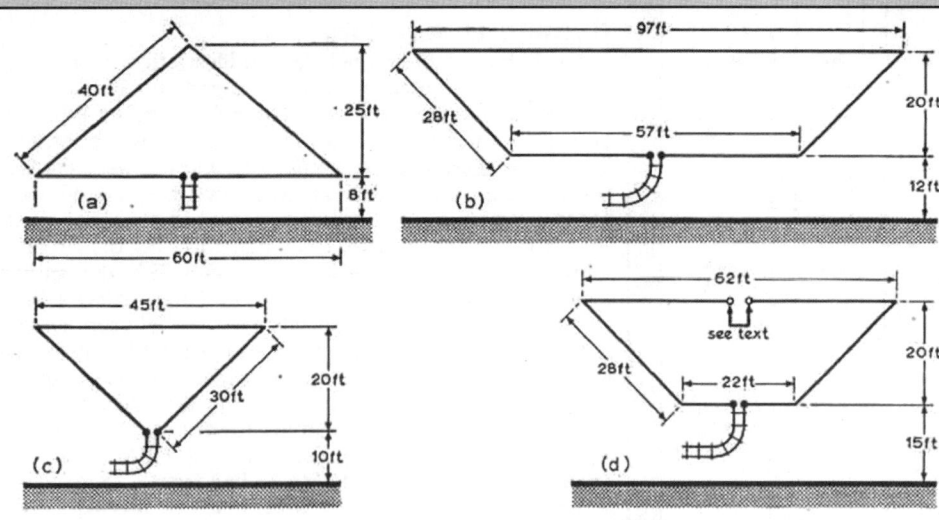

Fig 9. Some experimental loop antennas tried by GI3XZM. (a) 140ft loop to provide ½λ loop on 3·5MHz (open feeder about 15ft long with atu). (b) 210ft loop to provide ¾λ loop on 3·5MHz (open feeder about 80ft and also used with G5RV-type feed with open-feeders connected to 75Ω cable at suitable resonant point, permitting operation without balun or atu). (c) 105ft loop to provide ⅜λ on 3·5MHz (not recommended unless low-loss construction). (d) 140ft loop giving ½λ on 3·5-MHz and suitable also for 7 and 21MHz with link shorted and 14 and 28MHz with link open

Medium-sized loop antennas

In 1972 (*TT* January and March) attention was drawn to the use of small quad-type loop elements which totalled ½λ in perimeter or circumference rather than the conventional 1λ. The suggestion arose from a "Levy-Quad" (dipole-quad) beam with low-impedance feed described in *Radio-REF* by F6AMA; subsequently Les Moxon, G6XN, suggested that better results could be achieved by "inverting" the design, leaving no centre-point "gap" and providing a high-impedance feed from resonant feeders. But he also pointed out that such an element would have a radiation resistance of not more than about 5Ω. While such an element might well be attractive as a single-element loop, its use as part of a two-element quad beam, where radiation resistance would be forced down to a couple of ohms or so, was not really to be recommended.

Since then a short paper by A. Richtscheid in *IEEE Trans on Ant & Prop*, November 1976, pp 889–891 ("Calculation of the radiation resistance of loop antennas with sinusoidal current distribution") has presented a computer analysis of the radiation resistance of loop antennas having circumferences up to 2½λ: Fig 8. This provides further confirmation that the radiation resistance of a ½λ loop is bound to be less than 5Ω, compared with about 150Ω for a 1λ loop. Nevertheless it again indicates that ½λ loops *are* usable, even when constructed with wire of normal dimensions, but again emphasizes that loop dimensions less than ½λ call for very low-loss construction of the loop; for example using tubing or the outer conductor of ½in coaxial cable etc.

Someone who has been experimenting with loops of various shapes and of modest dimensions for QRP work on 3·5MHz is Des H. Vance, GI3XZM. It will be appreciated that non-circular loops (eg triangles and trapeziums) enclose less area than a circular loop of the same circumference and so further reduce the radiation resistance. Nevertheless his experiences indicates that in practice such systems, when fed with open-wire resonant feeders, can achieve better efficiency than some of the "bent" dipoles and squashed Marconi-type systems fed against doubtful earths. He believes that medium-sized loop systems have been needlessly neglected in the past.

Fig 9 shows some examples of loops tried by GI3XZM. He has recently estimated typical radiation resistances as about 1Ω for a 0·375λ loop; 3·5Ω for an 0·5λ loop; and 12Ω for an 0·75λ loop. Clearly a 0·375λ loop calls for low-loss construction, but 0·5λ or 0·75λ can be fashioned with wire and yet give a good account of themselves in locations where space is restricted or really good earths not possible. If fed with open-wire feeders it is, of course, possible to use such loops effectively on higher frequency bands, as has been indicated in the past by G6XN. GI3XZM reports effective use of ¾λ loops during 3·5MHz club activity periods.

Double-delta Array

Extracted from 'Technical Topics', *Radio Communication*, July 1977

Double-delta array

The April 1977 issue of *Old Man* reprints from *CQ Magazine* a short note by J. B. W. Jackman, ZF1MA, on a "ZF1MA Special" or double-delta beam. The antenna consists of two similar triangular loops each 69ft 9in in overall length: see Fig 8. It is stated that "both loops are coupled very closely by passing the loop of the driven side through the undriven side... The support boom can be made from any type of material: wood, bamboo, aluminium, pvc tubing etc. Nylon fishline was used for guying... On 28, 21 and 14MHz 75Ω cable provides a good match; however, on 7 and 3·5MHz a 'transmatch' is recommended."

ZF1MA makes strong claims for the effectiveness of this system. However, I am a little puzzled at his "boom" dimension of 20ft, as with the other dimensions indicated one would expect this to be 25ft, as shown in the redrawn diagram.

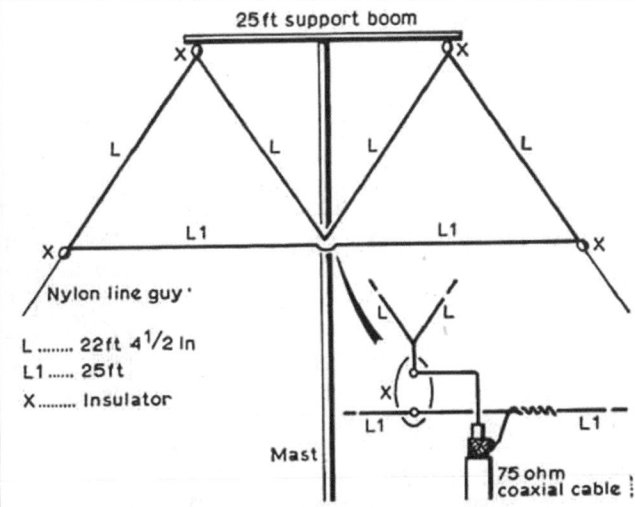

Fig 8. The "ZF Special"—a double-delta arrangement used by ZF1MA. See note in text on boom dimensions.

The G4BWE 'Titfer' Antenna

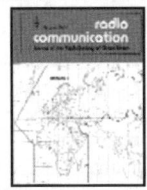

Extracted from 'Technical Topics', *Radio Communication*, August 1977

The G4BWE "titfer" antenna

Stephen Price, G4BWE, has come up with a vhf/uhf antenna for use with such rigs as the TR2200G or TR3200 that is not only good fun and convenient to use but also makes sense technically since it minimizes body absorption and body screening as well as putting the radiator as high as possible above ground. It could well start a "fashion" trend.

In essence he uses, see Fig 8, a sturdy leather hat, with "cowboy" brim, adapted to carry a λ/4 whip (19·2in for 144MHz) made from thin coat-hanger wire. This is attached to a wander plug with the join strengthened by sealing the plug top with Araldite and the element made visually less obtrusive by applying a coat of matt black paint. The centre conductor of a light and flexible coaxial feeder (eg UR43) is attached to the plug, and the braid is connected to the ground-plane formed by an aluminium foil lining inside the domed crown of the hat. It is difficult to solder the braid directly to this foil but G4BWE points out that if individual strands of the braid are spread out flat on the surface, a covering of adhesive tape should produce an acceptable join. The ground-plane can be extended as shown by weaving a length of pvc-covered wire through a pattern of small holes around the perimeter of the brim; this wire is of course also connected to the braiding of the coaxial feeder.

A chin strap is useful, and although G4BWE's prototype is for 144MHz it would be even more suitable for 432MHz operation with a need for an element only 6in long. He also points out that if you are a little coy about appearing in public in a cowboy style hat, other styles offer possibilities. We can imagine a fashion parade contest at some future mobile rally complete with toppers, bowlers etc. And taking a leaf from embassy antennas concealed in flag poles—why not an Austrian feather with the radiating element carefully threaded through it?

But do not use this approach for high power! G4BWE suggests a maximum of 3W—and of course avoid putting your head down and catching your neighbour in the eye. As shown, the tip of the wire element is bent round.

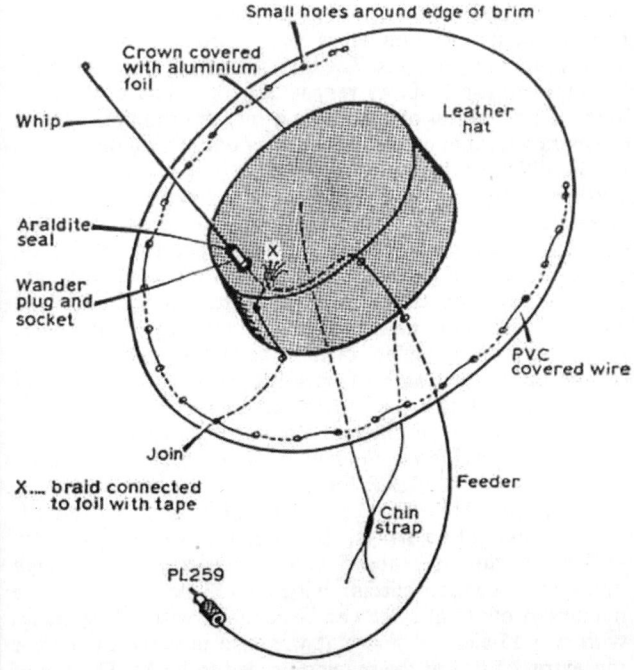

Fig 8. The G4BWE "titfer" or vhf/uhf hat antenna for portable low-power operation

The Classic Inverted-L Antenna

Extracted from 'Technical Topics', *Radio Communication*, October 1977

The classic inverted-L antenna

In February 1971 we included a couple of items in *TT* about end-fed and quarter-wave inverted-L antennas, one of which had then been used for about 2½ years on 3·5MHz by Geoff Scholey, G3CDR; a trial that had convinced him that this classic arrangement still possesses a number of useful features. In fact several other mentions were made of the dual- or cross-polarization feature of the inverted-L and similar forms of antennas, and the apparent benefits this could provide.

It was therefore enlightening, if a little *deja-vu*, to find (*QST* April 1977) a full length article by Richard A. Lodwig, W2KK, on the inverted-L antenna. In his case he uses a coaxial-fed dipole bent at 90° so that there is a λ/4 vertical section and, at the top, a λ/4 horizontal leg. Rather optimistically the author suggests this is a "novel" arrangement.

Signal levels received from 7MHz stations by W2KK

Antenna type	Local stations (less than 1,000 miles)	Distant stations (over 2,000 miles)
Horizontal dipole (λ/4 high)	"Reference"	"Reference"
λ/4-monopole (12 λ/4 radials)	−8dB	+2dB
(no radials)	−10dB	−4dB
λ/2-vertical dipole	−15dB	+9dB
Inverted-V (0·2λ-vertex height)	−3dB	+3dB
Inverted-L	−2dB	+6dB

On 7MHz, averaging out a considerable number of tests

ANTENNA TOPICS

on incoming a.m. (broadcast?) signals he tabulates the results as shown, though it should not be too readily assumed (reciprocal theory notwithstanding) that the results would equally hold good for transmission. For instance the λ/2 vertical (which shows up very well in his results) *can* be good on transmission when erected over highly conductive soil and well clear of nearby vertical "conductors" such as trees, metal drain pipes, etc but is recognized as being rather temperamental in other circumstances.

RMCS Compact VHF Antenna

Extracted from 'Technical Topics',
Radio Communication, December 1977

RMCS compact vhf antenna

Alan Williams, G3KSU, draws attention to an information sheet issued by the National Research Development Corporation about a new compact ferrite vhf antenna, for walkie-talkie transceivers or domestic portable radios, devised by R. J. Drewett of the Antennas and Propagation Research Group, Royal Military College of Science, Shrivenham.

This notes that the conventional ferrite-rod antenna is considered unsuitable for use at vhf (but see the November *TT* for mention of the BBC "active" ferrite-rod antenna). Portable units use whip or rod antennas which have a number of disadvantages: (1) they can be inconveniently long; (2) when used without ground planes they become highly directional, sometimes requiring awkward positioning for good reception; and (3) they are vulnerable to accidental or deliberate damage.

The RMCS antenna consists basically of a ferrite rod on to which a wire is wound in groups of turns in alternately a left-hand and right-hand sense (see Fig 5) so that it forms a λ/4 resonator. The antenna is tuned to the required frequency by winding excess turns and then successively clipping them off from the open-circuit end. Similar antennas, it is stated, can be made with dielectric or with conducting cores.

An antenna using a ferrite rod 200mm long has been tested by RMCS at 79MHz (bandwidth 5MHz) with a portable transceiver, and a 130mm antenna with similar

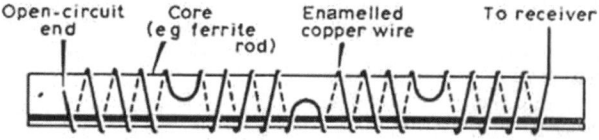

Fig 5. Basic design of the compact λ/4 vhf antenna developed at the Royal Military College of Science

bandwidth has been used for broadcast reception at 94MHz. In laboratory conditions with a large ground plane (eg vehicle roof) the gain of the RMCS antenna is markedly less than that of a whip antenna at the same frequency. However, in tests without the ground plane the performance of the compact antenna approaches that of a whip antenna except that it is less directional.

The performance, it is stated, is influenced both by wire geometry and the shape, size and material of the central rod.

The shortened helical-wound vhf/hf antenna is of course well-established but I have not previously seen reference to the idea of reversing the sense of the windings every few turns, and the idea might well prove worth investigating for amateur applications. The antenna is the subject of a patent application and the purpose of the NRDC information sheet was to bring it to the notice of manufacturers with a view to licensing agreements.

Gain of Yagi Arrays

Extracted from 'Technical Topics',
Radio Communication, January 1978

Gain of Yagi arrays

It is well known that many amateurs nourish an exaggerated view of the forward power gain they achieve with multi-element Yagi arrays on hf, vhf and uhf. This optimism is partly because it is much easier to achieve (and measure) high front-to-back ratios than forward power gain. In general terms, G6XN has shown how difficult it is to realize much more than 6dB from a single hf Yagi. The "antenna gain contests" popular in the USA and New Zealand suggest that 16-17dB represents very good going on 432MHz, which is probably the amateur band on which the highest gains are likely to be achieved with Yagi arrays. Above 1GHz, where very many elements can be used without the array becoming too massive, it seems to be extremely difficult to realize very high gains, even by carefully duplicating a "proven" design, and the parabolic reflector tends to reign supreme.

At the heart of the problem are the many variables that affect the gain of a Yagi array: element lengths, rod diameters, element spacing, etc. Despite the 50-year history of the Yagi, one suspects that the vast majority of the more successful designs continue to be based as much on pragmatic "trial and error" as upon precise design formulas.

However, a recent publication of the US Department of Commerce and National Bureau of Standards (*Yagi Antenna Design* by Peter P. Viezbicke) provides very detailed information in about 20 or so pages, based on experimental measurements made on 400MHz at a model antenna range while optimizing designs. The information, presented largely in graphical form, shows very vividly the effect of different antenna parameters on realizable gain. For example, it shows the extra gain that can be achieved by optimizing the lengths of the different directors, rather than making them all of uniform length; it also shows just what extra gain can be achieved by stacking two elements, or from a two-over-two array. In fact it shows: (a) the effect of reflector spacing on the gain of a dipole; (b) effect of different equal-length directors, their spacing and number on realizable gain; (c) effect of different diameters and lengths of directors on realizable gain; (d) effect of the size of a supporting boom on the optimum length of parasitic elements; (e) effect of spacing and stacking of antennas on gain; (f) measured radiation patterns of different Yagi configurations.

In very general terms, the highest gain reported for a single boom structure is 14·2dB for a 15-element array (4·2λ long, reflector spaced at 0·2λ, 13 graduated directors): see Table 1. When stacking two arrays, the author shows that the extra achievable gain is reduced at close spacing due to high mutual impedance effects: with two 7-element arrays a maximum of about 2·5dB can be achieved with 1·6λ spacing; with two 15-element arrays it was also possible to achieve the extra 2·5dB but the spacing needed to be 2λ. The use of four arrays, in correctly phased two-over-two systems, can

Table 1 — Optimized lengths of parasitic elements for Yagi antennas of six different lengths

	Length of Yagi in wavelengths					
	0·4	0·8	1·20	2·2	3·2	4·2
Length of reflector (λ)	0·482	0·482	0·482	0·482	0·482	0·475
Length of directors (λ)						
1st	0·424	0·428	0·428	0·432	0·428	0·424
2nd	—	0·424	0·420	0·415	0·420	0·424
3rd	—	0·428	0·420	0·407	0·407	0·420
4th	—	—	0·428	0·398	0·398	0·407
5th	—	—	—	0·390	0·394	0·403
6th	—	—	—	0·390	0·390	0·398
7th	—	—	—	0·390	0·386	0·394
8th	—	—	—	0·390	0·386	0·390
9th	—	—	—	0·398	0·386	0·390
10th	—	—	—	0·407	0·386	0·390
11th	—	—	—	—	0·386	0·390
12th	—	—	—	—	0·386	0·390
13th	—	—	—	—	0·386	0·390
14th	—	—	—	—	0·386	—
15th	—	—	—	—	0·386	—
Spacing (directors) in λ	0·20	0·20	0·25	0·20	0·20	0·308
Gain (ref dipole) in dB	7·1	9·2	10·2	12·25	13·4	14·2

Element diameter 0·0085λ. Reflectors spaced 0·2λ behind driven element. Measurements at 400MHz.

(Due to P. P. Viezbicke)

increase the realizable gain by about 5·2dB (one using 7-element units yielded a gain of 14·2dB; one with 15-element optimized units achieved 19·6dB, the highest gain measured during these experiments).

Since one British uhf tv antenna (Antiference XG21), consisting of a single-boom, multi-structure array, claims 21dB gain on Band 5, it is interesting to speculate what could be achieved with a two-over-two stack of these: possibly 25dB or so, which would be a truly remarkable figure for Yagi-type structures. Similarly it would be very interesting to know the maximum gain that might be achieved in practice by using a 432MHz rhombic. On 1·3GHz some 25dB has been realized in antenna contests using a homemade 7ft diameter dish.

Gain of Yagi Antennas - Another View

Extracted from 'Technical Topics', *Radio Communication*, April 1978

Gain of Yagi antennas—another view

Les Moxon, G6XN, has been reading the NBS publication *Yagi Antenna Design* from which some data were reproduced in *TT* January 1978, page 43. He notes that all the detailed information on optimizing the gain of multi-element Yagi arrays obviously represents a lot of hard work and that NBS publications tend to be regarded as impeccable sources. For these reasons he is reluctant to criticise the findings, but he cannot help feeling that the author, Peter Viezbicke, has failed to ask himself the two basic questions that should always be considered when presenting such findings: (1) do the results make sense?; and (2) are they consistent with previous work, and if not, why not?

G6XN is concerned about two of the basic findings of this investigation based on 400MHz model antennas: for a dipole with simple single-rod-type reflector, Viezbicke puts the optimum gain as only 2·6dB (increased by an extra 0·75dB to 3·35dB with a considerably more elaborate trigonal reflector). Then with the addition of just one director (using the trigonal reflector) *wham* the gain shoots up to 7·1dB. The third element thus appears to be capable of providing an extra 3·75dB of forward gain!

If this could be substantiated in normal practice it would, of course, be extremely important, particularly for hf operators, since it would make an overwhelmingly strong argument in favour of using three-element rather than two-element Yagi beams.

But, as G6XN points out. "Real life just isn't like this. Curves in the *ARRL Antenna Book* and elsewhere, based on the classic 1937 paper by G. H. Brown, show gains in excess of 5dB for a dipole plus reflector, and I have repeated the calculations myself many times, obtaining figures in the region of 5·2 to 5·4dB depending on the particular source from which one obtains one's data on mutual impedance."

G6XN continues: "It is true, as stated in the *ARRL Antenna Book*, that in practical antennas the gain is less than the calculated figure but, since the radiation resistance is relatively large compared with typical loss resistances, the theoretical gain is *nearly* all realizable in practice."

This, of course—as G6XN has previously pointed out for example in *TT* February 1977—makes a powerful case for using the lighter two-element arrays (which can be more readily raised to a good height) and encouraging further development of no-compromise *miniature* arrays with gains of up to 4dB or so. G6XN has shown on various occasions, as mentioned in my January notes, that a gain of 6dB is, in practice, the limit for a *three*-element array, only about 1dB more than what can be achieved with two full-sized elements.

In further support of his figure, G6XN quotes H. P. Williams who in *Antenna Theory and Design*, Vol 2, page 145, states that he had found it "never possible to obtain gain of more than 5·8dB over a half-wave dipole, but little difficulty in getting 5dB". If, in fact, one can get around 5dB from two-elements but less than 6dB from three, the natural choice for amateurs would be to settle for two and put the array up as high as possible.

Now it would seem that Peter Viezbicke has added to the confusion. Certainly there are a number of professional engineers who appear to be convinced that in doubling the number of elements from one to two it is impossible to achieve more than 3dB gain (double the effective radiated power), and this misleading idea can be found in a number of textbooks!

Again, a number of respectable sources suggest that it is possible to obtain more gain (about 0·5dB more) by using the second element as a director rather than as a reflector, but G6XN is unable to find any basis for this widespread belief and feels it may be just another of the many myths that still surround the Yagi. It is also worth stressing that while all this may seem to be just a mathematical debate about fractions of a decibel, it really is important to the amateur operator when translated into terms of cost-effectiveness, throwing into doubt the wisdom of both the large three-element Yagi and the large two-element quad, and opening the way to the high-performance mini-beam.

ANTENNA TOPICS

Low-noise 1.8/3.5MHz Receiving Antennas

Extracted from 'Technical Topics', *Radio Communication,* April 1978

Low-noise 1·8/3·5MHz receiving antennas

It is generally recognized that for good dx reception on the lower amateur frequencies, a vertically-polarized antenna (usually, of course, loaded into quarter-wave form) should provide the strongest long-haul signals; but in practice such antennas when used in the normal urban or suburban environment are also likely, unfortunately, to provide the most intense electrical noise. For dx *reception* it may be much better to use an antenna (eg frame or even ferrite-rod antenna) that provides much less signal, but may sometimes provide a better signal-to-noise ratio because of its directional properties.

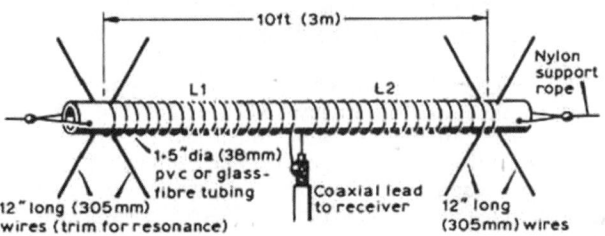

Fig 5. A 10ft helically wound 3·5MHz receiving dipole described by W1FB. The antenna is wound on pvc tubing and the capacitance hats at the ends of the element permit frequency adjustment and help to lower the Q of the antenna

In *QST* December 1977, Doug De Maw, W1FB, of ARRL, looks into this subject, although he recognizes that even after quite a lot of practical experiments he has "only agitated the surface". The classic Beverage wave antenna can give excellent results, but not everyone can run out some 560ft or more of straight wire, even if it only needs to be supported some 7 to 10ft above ground. W1FB describes a number of alternatives, including a shorter 200ft low wire used with the far end either open or grounded, and a 10ft helically-wound dipole for 3·5MHz (see Fig 5) with capacitance hats at the outer ends. This short dipole, he reports, appears to have low susceptibility to tv time-base radiation, but tends to be very narrow band.

A system which W1FB finds particularly effective is a half-wave open-loop antenna for 1·8MHz, again only 7ft high, but not requiring such extensive real-estate as the long wires: Fig 6. This is used in conjunction with a pre-amplifier, since the signal output is fairly low and some care needs to be given to avoiding pick-up from one's transmitting antenna, which can easily destroy pre-amplifier transistors and may even overwhelm protective diodes in the main equipment. The large, low loop can be set up in woodland, using trees for supports, without loss of effectiveness.

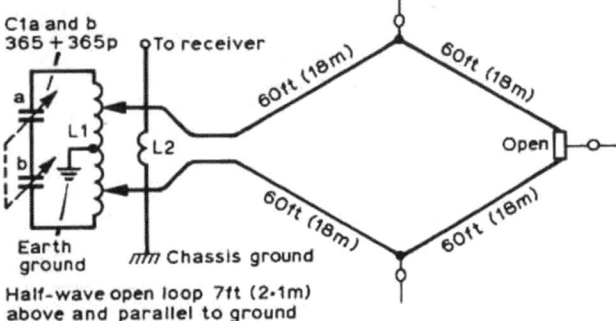

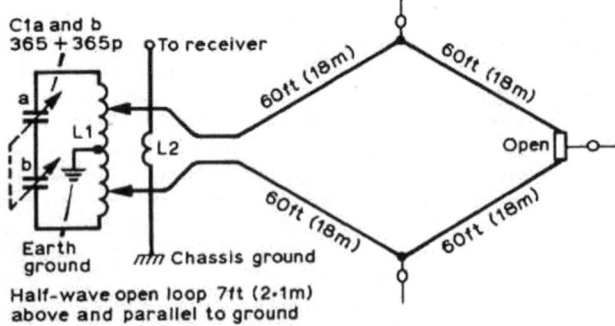

Fig 6. W1FB's half-wave open-loop low-noise receiving antenna for 1·8MHz. The antenna is parallel to the earth and at a height of 7ft. C1 is a two-gang broadcast-receiver tuning capacitor. L1 should have an inductance of 50μH and the feeders are tapped on L1 so as to obtain an swr close to unity

The Multiband 'Rhombiquad'

Extracted from 'Technical Topics', *Radio Communication,* April 1978

The multiband "rhombiquad"

Several years ago, ZS6AKA reported on various ways of using large horizontal loops to form multiband antennas; a recent reflection of this approach can be found in the "rhombiquad" which is attracting considerable attention in West Germany (*CQ-DL* No 9/77 by DF3FU and *CQ-DL* No 1/78 by Karl Hille, DL1VU). This square rhombic (Fig 7) can form an effective multiband system that can include switching techniques to allow it to be used in several different configurations; including an open type of loop, a terminated loop, a ring antenna, and as a loaded vertical for 1·8MHz dx operation. With 20·8m sides and a height of about 20m it will not go into many small gardens but is by no means impossible for those with rather more space, and it can provide an effective dx transmitting antenna on all bands from 1·8 to 30MHz.

A good deal of information on the various radiation patterns in different configurations is given by DL1VU, but here we have only space to bring out the main details

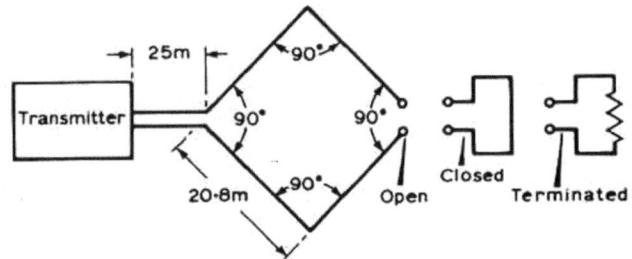

Fig 7. Basic details of the multi-band rhombiquad which can be used as an open loop, closed loop or as a terminated square rhombic. On 1·8MHz the feeders can be used as a vertical antenna, with top loading

and the way in which he matches his transmitter to the 450Ω open-wire feeder. The terminating resistor should be non-inductive and should be capable of dissipating at least five per cent of the dc p.e.p. input to the transmitter for cw or ssb operation, and provided that the key is not held down for long. Although capable of providing considerable gain in a number of directions, the rhombiquad is relatively easy to construct or modify, if one has sufficient space and some suitable supports.

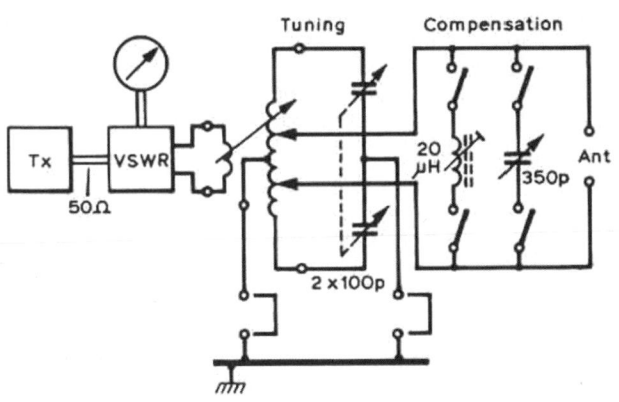

Fig 8. Matching arrangement used by DL1VU with the rhombiquad

Zig-zag Sloper

Extracted from 'Technical Topics', *Radio Communication*, April 1978

Zig-zag sloper
Bob Eldridge, VE7BS (8386 McGregor Avenue, Burnaby BC, V5J 4H9, Canada), mentions that he would be interested to hear from anyone using a zig-zag sloper antenna. For some time he used an end-fed inverted-V on 1·8MHz, and then improved the operation on long paths (1,000 to 6,000 miles) by dropping the far end vertically. He has now changed this to a sloping dipole centre fed and with both ends vertical, based on the theory that the current flowing in the same direction in each vertical section should make the antenna work like a pair of phased verticals. These arrangements are indicated in Fig 9. The basic idea is to try to avoid having to install masses of radials. Certainly the zig-zag sloper of Fig 9 (c) does not require radials as part of the antenna system, since it is a dipole rather than a Marconi form of antenna, but I suspect that earth conductivity may be an important element in achieving good results.

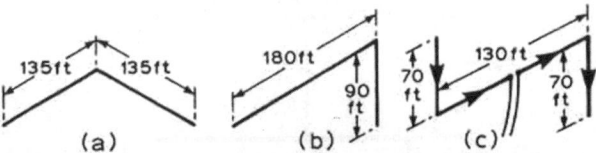

Fig 9. Arrangements used by VE7BS for dx operation on 1·8MHz showing the progressive modifications into the "zig-zag sloper" shown in (c)

Gain of Yagi Antennas - Continued

Extracted from 'Technical Topics', *Radio Communication*, May 1978

Gain of Yagi antennas—continued
Among the more revealing forms of amateur radio contests are those devoted to measuring the gain of the competitors' vhf antennas. Such contests involve a good deal of preparation, a suitable site, and trusted equipment and measuring techniques, but nevertheless are held occasionally in the USA and in New Zealand. Over the years the results suggest a steady improvement in antennas, but they still show that, in practice, forward gain often bears little relationship to the number of elements or theoretical considerations.

For example, a recent 144MHz contest of the Christchurch branch of NZART, held in an almost ideal location, showed that one 8-element log-Yagi had only 1dB forward gain (reference dipole) compared with 7dB for a 4-element Yagi (while another 4-element Yagi was only 1·5dB up on the dipole); in fact 4-element Yagis varied from 1·5 to 7dB; one 5-element Yagi registered −10·5dB; the highest recorded gain was 10dB for a 13-element Yagi; 3·5dB gains were registered by a 6-element log-Yagi and a 3-element Yagi. Beamwidth of most of the antennas exceeded 40° although front:side ratios commonly exceeded 30dB. Height gain is significant between 10 and 27ft, and all antennas were measured at 18 ft. It is noted that "the majority of antennas had gain over the reference dipole, although some antennas, considering their size, gave very poor results, which in some cases could be put down to poor matching". In a few instances the antennas included a length of coaxial feeder which in effect reduced the measured gain.

By comparison, collinear verticals produced some unexpectedly large gains (from 6 to 9dB reference λ/4 whip) suggesting that high-gain omni-directional antennas might prove as effective and far less expensive than rotary beams in applications where vertical polarization is acceptable. ZL3ABJ concludes the report by commenting: "Perhaps the moral of the story is, for dx work, use a whip antenna instead of a beam."

Reducing the Size of Antennas

Extracted from 'Technical Topics', *Radio Communication*, June 1978

Reducing the size of antennas
For many amateurs who are interested in operation at hf, or even 70MHz, one of the perennial problems is the basic size of the dipole element. It would be so much easier in many locations if a 3·5MHz monopole (ie λ/4 vertical in which the earth provides the missing half of the dipole) did not need a 66ft element, or if a 14MHz dipole needed only about the same span as one for the 21MHz band.

Over the years, of course, many antennas have been developed that provide the basic requirement of any effective antenna system (ie that it should represent a

ANTENNA TOPICS

series-resonant circuit at the operating frequency) with elements physically smaller than a standard λ/2 dipole or λ/4 monopole. The use of loading coils, helically wound radiators, tuning and matching units, capacitance hats of various forms etc, are all tried and tested methods of achieving series resonance; then there are such space saving techniques as dropping down the high-voltage ends of dipoles or folding parts of the element in the form of loading stubs etc, including those formed within quad loops. More recently, there has been considerable work, particularly for military communications, on various forms of dielectric loading, including coating the element with a high-permittivity (ferrite) material.

Some 30 years ago, Harold Wheeler wrote a paper "Fundamental limitations of small antennas" (*Proc IRE*, 1947, Vol 35, pp1479–84) which although concerned specifically with receiving antennas still remains one of the classic references on this subject. He wrote, for instance:

"It has occasionally been pointed out that a small antenna free of dissipation could take from a radio wave and deliver to a load *an amount of power independent of the size of the antenna*. This would be true at one frequency if the antenna could be resonated at that frequency without adding dissipation. It results from the fact that a smaller antenna delivers its lesser voltage from a lower resistance such that the available power remains the same."

However, Wheeler also noted: "While the radiation pattern and, hence, the directive gain of a small antenna remain the same for a smaller size, the radiation resistance decreases relative to the other resistance in the coupling circuit. *The resulting reduction in coupling efficiency is one of the principal limitations of the smaller antenna.* Another aspect of the same limitation relates to the frequency bandwidth of operation with fixed values of the circuit element. A smaller antenna with the same reactance and radiation resistance must be more sharply tuned to deliver its available power. Therefore, the *reduction of size imposes a fundamental limitation on the bandwidth.* If the bandwidth so limited is insufficient, further damping must be added at the expense of coupling inefficiency.

"The limitations verify the experience that larger antennas are generally more efficient, especially for wideband operation."

Since 1947 the development of the *active* antenna has shown that for reception it *is* possible to match a short antenna effectively over a wide bandwidth, although this does not mean that a short active antenna erected inside a building (and thus close to sources of electrical interference) should be expected to provide the same signal-to-noise ratios as an antenna out in the clear and having the benefit of height gain. Except at the very lowest powers, however, there has so far been little development of active antennas for amateur transmission.

Two recent articles provide useful surveys of techniques and characteristics of loaded short antennas: "Signal/noise performance of loaded wire antennas" by Dr P. A. Ramsdale (*Proc IEE*, Vol 124, No 10, October 1977, pp840–843) and "Properties of dielectrically loaded antennas" in the same journal (pp837–839). The former covers a number of different forms of loading, including the trap loading commonly used by amateurs and less well-known resistive and travelling-wave loading techniques where the object is to obtain directivity with relatively short antennas (though it is shown that these should include at least a λ/4 monopole section). This paper also brings out a point that has puzzled amateurs for a number of years: the difficulty of getting a good vertical collinear array simply by using a succession of resonant circuits (LC or stub) to provide 180° phase reversals.

D. L. Smith (*IEEE Trans Ant & Prop* AP-23, 1975

pp20–27) studied such antennas and found that a 180° phase shift was not achieved in this way but discovered that a collinear pattern was set up at *a lower frequency* (about 0.8 times the design frequency). In the equivalent monopole case such an antenna will act as a 0.6λ inductive-loaded element with the load 0.2λ from the end; its gain, however, is slightly less than an unloaded antenna of the same height. This could be the explanation of the problem noted by G6CJ in making the coaxial collinear antenna work (*TT* November, September 1972) although 144MHz versions of this antenna still turn up in the amateur journals from time to time, and an apparently successful large hf array was described in *IEEE Trans Ant & Prop* July 1972, pp513-516.

Doubly-fed Coaxial Antennas

Extracted from 'Technical Topics', *Radio Communication*, June 1978

Doubly-fed coaxial antennas

In *Electronics Letters*, 16 March 1978, Vol 14, No 6, pp178–9) F. Rahman and T. S. M. MacLean of the University of Birmingham describe a new form of dipole antenna which, in its monopole form, is claimed to have useful height reduction properties and which it would seem could also be developed as a vertically-polarized directive array of modest height. In monopole or dipole form it provides a purely resistive feedpoint.

Two different forms have been investigated at Birming-

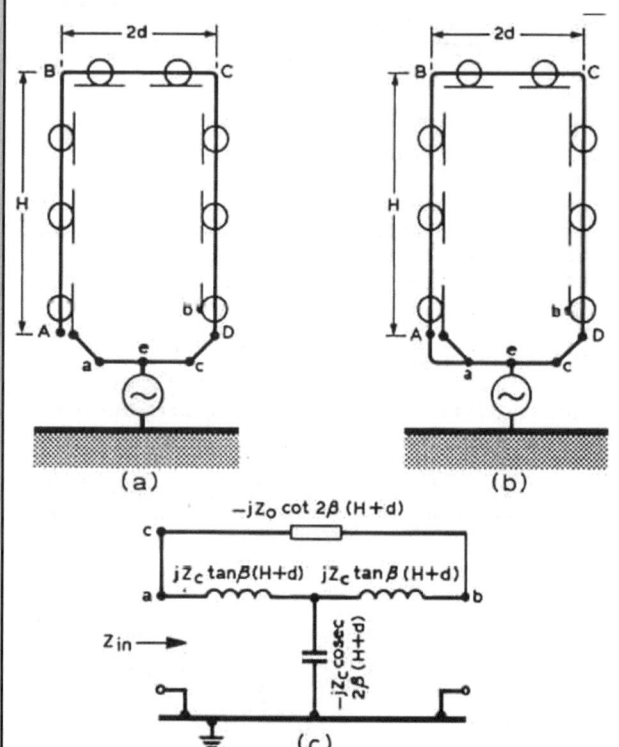

Fig 1. (a) The open-circuited form of doubly-fed coaxial monopole. (b) The short-circuited form that provides rather greater height reduction, even when the two branches are closely spaced, but of rather narrower bandwidth. (c) Equivalent circuit for the mathematically inclined

ham with self-resonant heights (dipole) of λ/3 and λ/4 respectively (ie about λ/6 and λ/8 monopole heights). The first type, it is stated, can also be made self-resonant at much lower heights and can then form a directive array.

Basically these antennas are made by using doubly-fed, air-cored coaxial line, folded back on itself so as to allow double feeding: see Figs 1 (a) and (b).

Operation of the antenna shown in Fig 1 (a) is described roughly as follows:

Let the spacing 2d be considered negligible initially, so that the electrical distance between e and the feed-points a and c can be ignored. When the coaxial cable length ABCD is λ/4, the input impedance between c and earth is equal to the input impedance between the coaxial outer conductor b and earth also. Hence equal voltages are applied to the outer surfaces of both radiating arms. Consequently the current distribution along AB and CD is the same as that along two monopoles connected in parallel, since the current will fall to zero at the midpoint of BC, which has been assumed to be of negligible length.

The input impedance in this case is that of these two λ/8 monopoles connected in parallel, and is thus capacitive. To eliminate this reactance the length of the coaxial cable ABCD must be increased (it will be assumed without increasing the spacing 2d). When ABCD is made equal to λ/3, for example, it can be shown that the antenna behaves as a series rather than a parallel resonant circuit, and thus fulfils the requirement for any useful wire antenna.

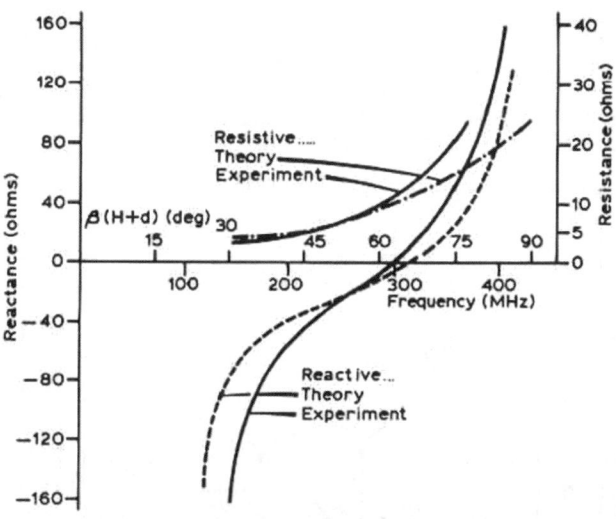

Fig 2. Input impedance of the open-circuited doubly-fed coaxial dipole plotted against frequency. Based on model antenna at 300MHz with dimensions of 2H 14cm and 2d 7cm using 1·6cm diameter coaxial cable. The graph shows both resistive and reactive components of the input impedance, theoretical and measured. The reactive component, of course, is zero at resonance, leaving a purely resistive impedance of over 10Ω

Fig 2 shows measurements made on a model antenna designed for 300MHz. Although the currents in the two monopoles are no longer equal, radiation patterns in both E and H planes were indistinguishable from those of a conventional dipole, it is stated. Further experiments with increasing separation between the vertical arms, but the same height H, gave increased height reduction factors up to over 3 (spacing said to be 27cm) with radiation pattern then showing array type characteristics. Input resistance is approximately that of a single monopole of height H when the spacing 2d is small, as indicated in Fig 2. The short-circuited form of this antenna, shown in Fig 1 (b), appears to be rather less attractive as the bandwidth is reduced, although of lower self-resonant height.

Although shown in monopole form, the antenna could, of course, be used in dipole form.

The experimental results would seem to be very promising and yet still leave plenty of scope for further development and evaluation as an antenna for amateur applications by anyone with some suitable spare cable.

G6XN Miniature and Compact Beams

Extracted from 'Technical Topics', *Radio Communication*, June 1978

G6XN miniature and compact beams

The February 1977 *TT* included the powerful arguments of Les Moxon, G6XN, in favour of further development of effective, lightweight two-element minibeams capable of about 4dB forward gain, achievable over restricted but practical bandwidths. One of the principal tools in achieving such results, G6XN then suggested, was the use of two open-wire feeders, one to each element, to allow fine tuning from within the shack and to permit just 180° rotation. The beam itself was loosely based on a form of "neutralized" VK2ABQ. Now, in a letter written at the end of January, G6XN reports further on this project. He writes:

"This development is going well, with dimensions (for 14MHz) now reduced to 10ft square, using all-metal construction. Vertical rods, each 2ft long, support zig-zag wire loading as roughly indicated in Fig 3. Two open-wire feeders are used and this is proving absolutely essential because the operational bandwidth for a better-than-20dB front-to-back ratio is only 65kHz; for better-than-10dB f:b ratio and less than 1dB drop in gain it is still only about 130–200kHz.

"Before putting this up in the air, in its new form, I have a few more measurements to make, including some experiments with a view to eventual multi-banding. Feasibility of this is already proved, but not the best method."

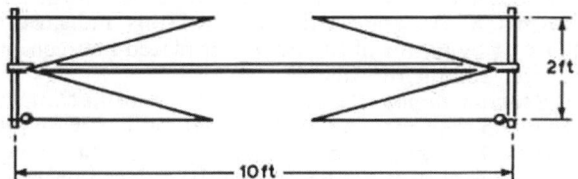

Fig 3. Use of vertical rods to support zig-zag wire loading in the latest version of G6XN's two-element 14MHz minibeam (see also *TT* February 1977)

G6XN has also been working on another form of compact VK2ABQ wire-loaded beam, improved by the addition of a third element, with boom lengths of 11ft, 12ft and 13ft, element lengths of the order of 24ft, and with a performance "indistinguishable from that of big beams" over a restricted range of frequencies. This beam incorporates the "disappearing inductance" form of multi-banding and has already been pretty thoroughly tested at 14MHz; it has also proved itself on 28MHz, even at low height.

ANTENNA TOPICS

All-band Trapless Vertical

Extracted from 'Technical Topics',
Radio Communication, June 1978

All-band trapless vertical

On previous occasions attention has been drawn to an important characteristic of any length of transmission line that is one or more exact electrical half-wavelengths long: the impedance at the far end of the line will be precisely duplicated at the near end, whether or not there are pronounced standing waves along the line. This property can be used, for example, as a means of tuning quad or beam reflector elements from within the shack (*TT* July 1973, *ART*, and also utilized in the G6XN twin feeders). Another application of this appears in *Zero Beat* (the lively monthly publication of the Victoria, BC,

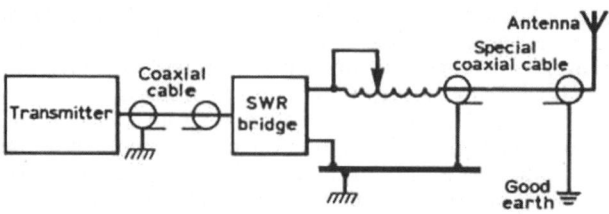

Fig 4. All-band trapless vertical antenna, described by VE3FHS, in which the base impedance of the vertical element is transferred into the shack by means of a length of transmission line that is an exact multiple of an electrical half-wave. The base matching network can thus be adjusted from the operating position

shortwave club) in an article by Rick Murphy, VE3FHS, reprinted from *The Canadian Amateur* of unknown date: see Fig 4.

This idea provides a means of matching, within the shack, the base impedance (which may be resistive or reactive) of a fixed-length vertical rod antenna, making it possible to use the element on different bands without any adjustment of matching networks located at the base of the antenna. The resonant length of transmission line simply transfers the base impedance into the shack where it can be matched to the transmitter: for example, by a roller-coaster series-inductor or by other forms of transmatch. Accurate adjustment of this inductor is indicated by means of the swr meter placed between the inductor and the transmitter.

The actual impedance of the resonant transmission line is of no consequence: VE3FHS suggests either 50 or 75Ω coaxial cable, although presumably the losses (due to high swr on this part of the line) would be reduced by using open-wire or 300Ω line. The matching inductor is tuned for minimum swr at the usual operating frequency, and VE3FHS reports that bandwidth for an swr of under about 1·7 is roughly 150kHz on all bands.

The system, it is stated, was tested with a 22ft vertical element working as $5\lambda/8$ on 28MHz, $\lambda/2$ on 21MHz, extended $\lambda/4$ on 14MHz and as a base-loaded $\lambda/4$ on 7 and 3·5MHz. It is claimed to provide a better performance than is usually achieved with the shorter trap-vertical rod antennas. VE3FHS recommends the use of a small loading coil at the base of the antenna to resonate it accurately at the highest frequency band (eg 28MHz), since this enables the shack tuning inductor to be smaller and more easily tuned, with wider bandwidth at all frequencies.

He used (for the cw ends of the bands) a 92ft length of unspecified coaxial cable (presumably having a velocity factor of the order of 0·7) to form an electrical $\lambda/2$ at 3·5MHz, λ at 7MHz, 2λ at 14MHz, 3λ at 21MHz and 4λ at 28MHz. To operate on 1·8MHz would require double the length of cable; for use only on 7MHz upwards, 46ft would suffice. Note that the feeder lengths will vary with the velocity factor of the cable. The length is fairly critical (within, say, 1ft) and this can be checked by obtaining unity swr at the required frequency. If the lowest swr dip is at a higher than required frequency, the cable needs lengthening. VE3FHS found 92ft satisfactory for all bands, except 14MHz where he connects in an extra 2ft length. Clearly some experimentation may be required—but then that is what amateur radio is all about.

Compact Quad-loop for 14 and 21MHz

Extracted from 'Technical Topics',
Radio Communication, July 1978

Compact quad-loop for 14 and 21MHz

Over 10 years ago W6WAW described in *73* a single quad-type loop antenna for 14 and 21MHz which he had built and put up in less than two hours (see *ART*). Although it gave only a modest gain over a dipole, it had proved capable of good dx performance and could be made rotatable more readily than a dipole element. However, the W6WAW, like a full-size quad, requires a bamboo framework capable of supporting the 18ft square loop.

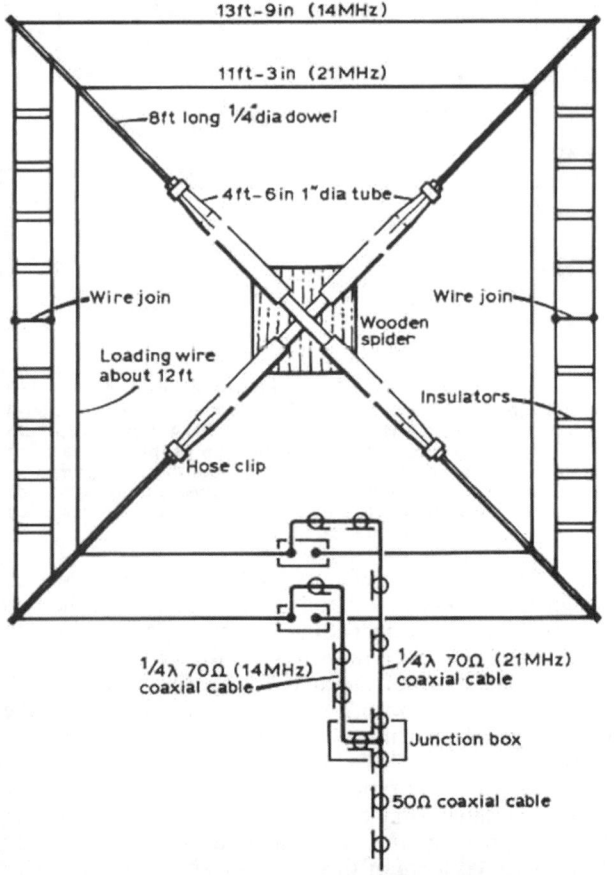

Fig 5. ZL1OI's compact 14/21MHz quad-loop antenna using linear loading of the 14MHz loop

In *CQ* (March 1978) Harry K. Bourne, ZL1OI (and presumably former G2AH), shows how the "linear loading" technique that has been advocated for compact quad antennas by G3IMX, G6XN and G3YDX (see for example "Practical design for a capacity hat loaded 14MHz mini-quad" *Radio Communication* October 1976, pp755-6) can be equally useful in the single element form. This allows the side length for 14MHz readily to be reduced to under 14ft while also providing a support for a full-size 21MHz loop: see Fig 5.

The feedpoint impedance for a full-size single loop is roughly 120Ω and, although a 70Ω feeder would possibly prove satisfactory, ZL1OI uses 70Ω λ/4 transmission line transformers to provide a good match to 50Ω coaxial cable, the joints being made in a weather-proof junction box.

He states that the antenna will also work on 28MHz but for low-angle radiation he recommends the use of a third (full-size) loop if one wants to make regular use of this band.

The 14MHz loop can be trimmed by adjusting the capacity-loading wires. This can be done with the antenna about 10ft high, provided a small allowance is made for an *increase* in resonant frequency when the antenna is raised to full height.

The coaxial or sleeve dipole has a long history as an effective form of dipole radiator, and I have been meaning for some time to include in *TT* an idea from H. R. Skelhorn (G6SOG/T, G8BPU) for a simple-to-make, vertically-polarized, omni-directional 144MHz antenna for working to mobiles directly, or via repeaters, using baked-bean tins. The diagram (Fig 6) gives all the necessary constructional information, but for the benefit of overseas readers "Araldite" is an epoxy-resin adhesive.

Improving the T Antenna

Extracted from 'Technical Topics',
Radio Communication, September 1978

Improving the T antenna

Back in July 1970 I introduced in *TT* a modified form of hf T antenna (inspired by the Bobtail), sometimes known as the "inverted ground plane". By top-loading a vertical λ/4 element with a λ/2 horizontal section, as in Fig 1(d), one achieves a structure with the maximum current at the high rather than the low end. It is also a form of "vertical" which can readily function also as a horizontal dipole (by using switched open-wire feeders for the vertical section), as suggested in 1972 by Ken Glanzer, K7GCO (*ART*).

It can be argued that raising the high current up an antenna structure can, in some circumstances, increase the theoretical effects of poor earth conductivity; nevertheless, in practice, this form of simple T antenna (which can easily be made from wire rather than tubing) does offer useful practical advantages in many typical locations, and does *not* depend upon a good earth connection. Although influenced by earth conductivity, this technique avoids the ohmic losses of the conventional monopole.

Beanz Meanz QSOz

Extracted from 'Technical Topics',
Radio Communication, July 1978

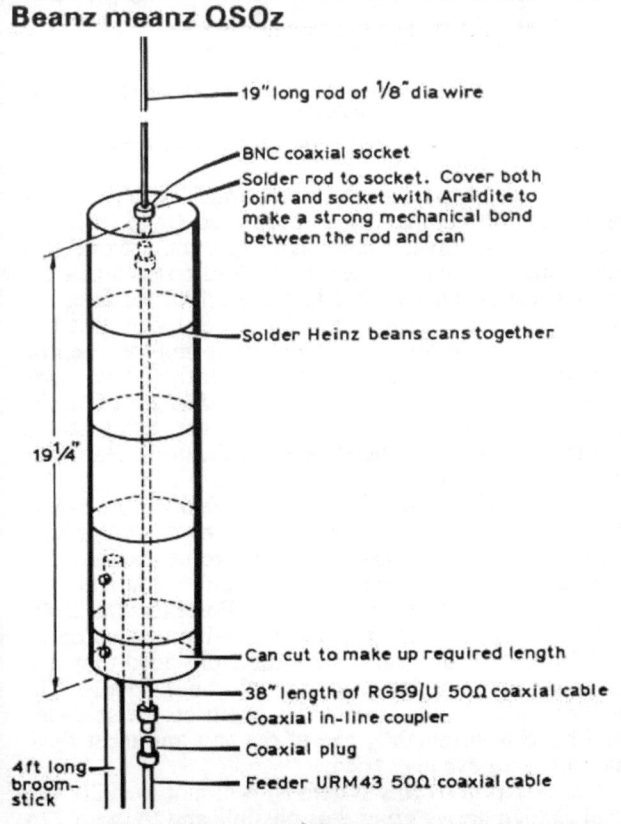

Fig 6. G8BPU's bean-can 144MHz sleeve dipole antenna mounted at 25ft brings in GB3MP (55 miles) at 59+ and has an swr of about 1·1:1 on transmission

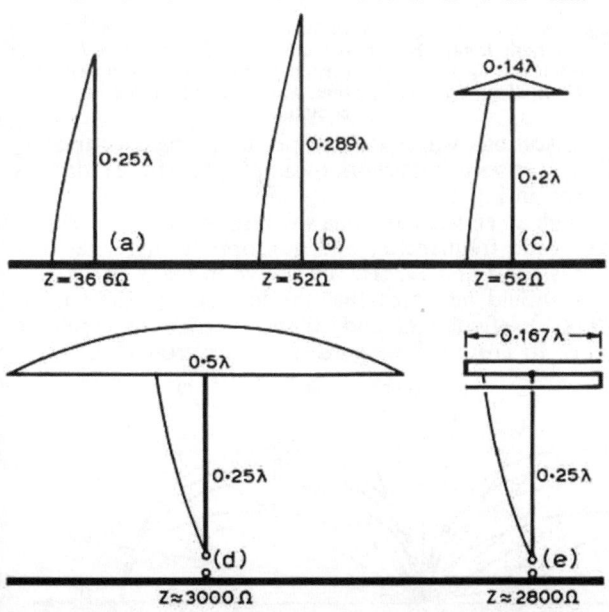

Fig 1. Vertical antennas showing feed point impedances: (a) standard 0·25λ monopole; (b) extended 0·289λ monopole; (c) typical T antenna as used on mf; (d) the inverted ground-plane form of hf T antenna as described in *TT* July 1970; (e) the DL1VU "improved T antenna", with better cancellation of horizontally polarized radiation

ANTENNA TOPICS

In *CQ-DL* (No 6, 1978, pp246–9) Karl H. Hille, DL1VU (9A1VU), provides a further study of this form of T antenna, and comes up with a modification which is claimed to reduce the radiation (and reception) of horizontally polarized signals from the top $\lambda/2$ section. This is accomplished by folding back the wire to form a triple wire, in appearance like one of the old short "caged dipoles": Fig 2. The radiation from the outermost $\lambda/6$ sections balances out the radiation from the inner

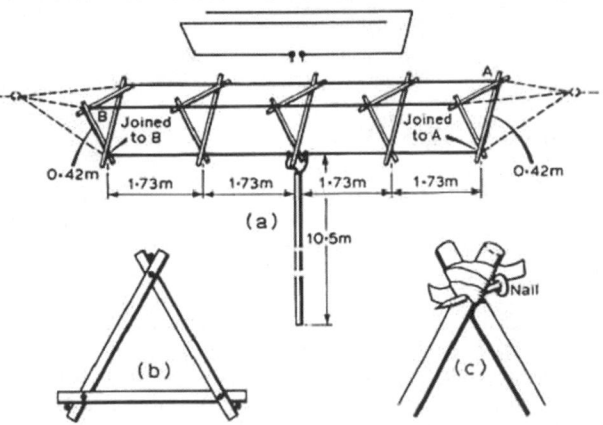

Fig 2. Practical implementation of DL1VU antenna intended for use on 7 and 14MHz, and showing some details of how the cage is made from glass-fibre rods

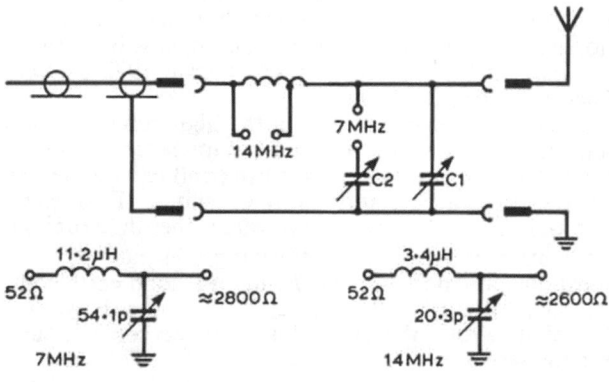

Fig 3. Base matching network for 7 and 14MHz. Typically C1 and C2 are high-voltage 50pF maximum. The inductor has a diameter of 6·6cm, length 8cm, 16 turns copper wire 2·7–3mm diameter, with windings spaced by 5mm. For 14MHz 9½ turns are short-circuited

$\lambda/12$ sections where current per unit length is greater. DL1VU uses a framework of simple glass-fibre struts, as shown in Fig 2.

Such an end-fed antenna will also work effectively on harmonic frequencies, and appropriate matching networks for 7 and 14MHz are shown in Fig 3.

It should be noted that the low end of the wire is "hot" to rf voltages, and suitable precautions should be taken to protect those gardening, etc, around the wire.

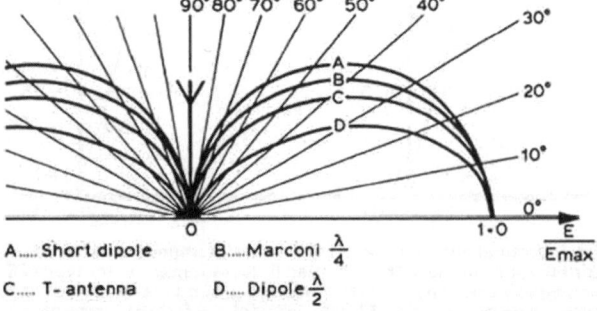

Fig 4. Vertical radiation patterns of vertically polarized antennas over perfect earth

Fig 4 shows how the vertical radiation angle of a vertical antenna varies according to the length of the radiator, although increasing the length may result in high angle lobes. It should also be appreciated that such diagrams are theoretical rather than practical, in that they ignore the very significant effects on the vertical angle of poor ground conductivity.

More on the Trapless Vertical

Extracted from 'Technical Topics', *Radio Communication*, September 1978

More on the trapless vertical

The June *TT* included an arrangement by VE3FHS for a 22ft vertical with the matching network "transferred" into the shack by means of a feeder an exact number of electrical half-waves long. This has reminded Cyril Mountjoy, GW3ASW, that a basically similar system was published in the 'forties in (probably) *QST*. This resulted in his using such a system from about 1947 to 1952 on 7, 14 and 28MHz, although with rather different feeder arrangements. Following the loss of his

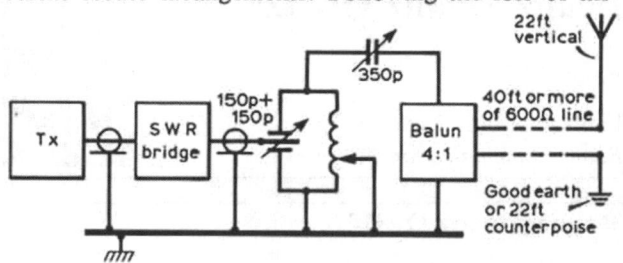

Fig 5. GW3ASW's all-band transmatch unit and open-wire feeder for trapless vertical

mast in last winter's gales, he reverted to a version of this system. He writes:

"With good coaxial cable at around 50–65p per metre one does *not* feel inclined to chop it about to reach the electrical half-wave, simple as it appears. I agree that 600Ω open line can reduce losses (and cost), and I use such a feeder. Originally I had some 100ft of line, but subsequently a change in garden layout meant this had to be reduced to about 60ft, but performance, even on 3·5MHz, was unaffected. More recently I have used 57ft and find that, as long as the *total* length of feeder *plus* the vertical element is slightly longer than a $\lambda/4$ on the lowest frequency band, it will operate as readily as with the longer length.

"It appears that the art of using 400–600Ω open-lines has been lost for many amateurs, many of whom have grown up on coaxial cable. It seems to be thought that they are tricky to tune and feed, but I contend that nothing is farther from the truth. For example, a 4:1 balun on the *output* of any atu capable of feeding an end-fed wire is all that is necessary, provided that it is preceded by a series capacitor of about 350pF. The system I use, shown in Fig 5, is based on the so-called "all-band transmatch", one of the best and most flexible tuners I have ever tried.

"A variation of this system is to mount the 22ft vertical as high above ground as possible and to use a 22ft counterpoise attached to the other end of the feeder, insulated from ground."

The 'Butterfly' Monoband Beam

Extracted from 'Technical Topics', *Radio Communication*, September 1978

The "butterfly" monoband beam

For home-construction of compact mono- and multi-band hf beams, one of the more successful family of designs has proved to be those proposed by VK2ABQ, described on several occasions in *TT* and *ART*. One advantage is that these can be constructed entirely from wire, using simple wooden frameworks. This, however, is not the only useful approach, as Tom Higginson, GW3AHN, reminds us. He is a long-time enthusiast for the "butterfly" design which, in effect, is a shortened X array and linked with the series of designs put forward some 20 years ago by "Dicky" Bird, G4ZU. This design does not use a wooden framework but is formed by self-supporting tubing, loaded by wire sections.

GW3AHN first built a "butterfly" array in 1962, and since then has worked over 350 countries using a 14MHz monobeam version with power input of some 25W cw and 66W p.e.p. output on ssb. He claims for the "butterfly" array:

(1) Physical size (turning radius) significantly less than that of a conventional 2-element array (17ft square on 14MHz).

(2) Requires no boom, no framework and less tubing than a conventional array.

(3) Higher gain and better front-to-back ratios than for a conventional 2-element Yagi due to V-shaped elements (this claim is open to debate!–*G3VA*).

(4) Easy to construct from readily available materials at a small fraction of the cost of a comparable commercial beam.

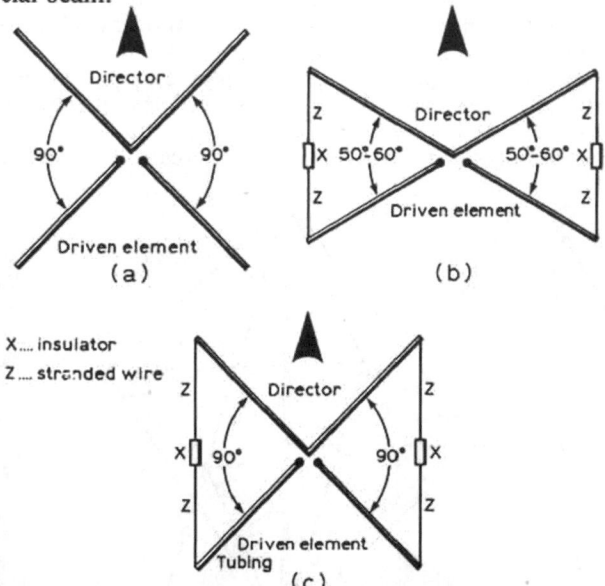

Fig 6. Variations of X and "butterfly" 14MHz arrays as investigated by GW3AHN: (a) all tubular X antenna with director 2 by 17ft 5in (34ft 10in), driven element 2 by 18ft 2in (36ft 4in); provides roughly 4dB forward gain and 12-15dB f:b ratio (according to height)–disadvantages include large size and significant side lobes; (b) Narrow "butterfly" with director 2 by 14ft plus 2 by 4ft 3in (36ft 6in); driven element 2 by 14ft plus 2 by 5ft 6in (39ft)–elements partly 1in tubing plus stranded wire, forward gain roughly 4-5dB (estd), f:b ratio 8-10dB, structure is still large and f:b ratio poor although side lobes reduced; (c) preferred "butterfly" with director 2 by 12ft plus 2 by 7ft (38ft), driven element 2 by 12ft plus 2 by 8ft 8in (41ft), gain estimated by GW3AHN up to 6dB, f:b ratio 15-20dB (estd) according to height

(5) Can be made very rugged by self-bracing, using nylon or polythene cord across the open ends.

Fig 6 shows that the "butterfly" is a development of the full-size X-beam (widely used at one time as a vhf tv receiving antenna). It is recommended that a gdo be used to tune the array. Typically for 14MHz, an array tuned at a height of 8-10ft should be tuned about 250kHz *lower* than the required frequency to allow for the change when raised to full height. 21 and 28MHz versions have been successfully built by scaling the dimensions indicated. A 3-element version has been developed and used successfully by W1BTU (Fig 7): this does require a boom, and I suspect that in practice the forward gain is likely to prove some 2dB or so less than the claimed 8dB. A triband version (using stacked separate elements) was commercially produced in Italy some years ago but is not thought to be still available; however, GW3AHN does not recommend such multiple

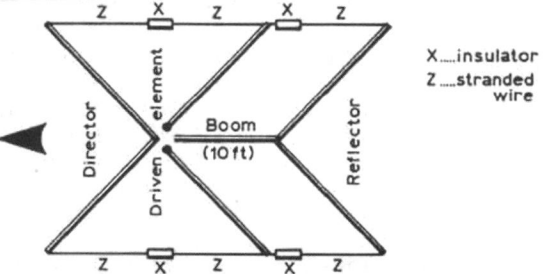

Fig 7. Three-element form of "butterfly" array used by W1BTU. Director 2 by 12ft plus 2 by 7ft; driven element 2 by 12ft plus 2 by 8ft 6in; reflector 2 by 12ft 6in plus 2 by 9ft. Although gain has been estimated as high as 8dB over dipole, a maximum of 6dB seems more probable; f:b ratio given as 20 to 30dB

arrays as these usually present severe problems of interaction and detuning.

The following details of constructional techniques are taken directly from GW3AHN's notes:

"There are many ways of constructing the basic "butterfly" (Fig 6c). One of the easiest is to obtain a steel or aluminium plate about 12in square and of suitable thickness, and then to mount the tubing portion of the elements (usually 1in od) on to the plate with suitable U-bolts, the director elements directly and the driven element insulated from the plate with plastic tube type insulation (plastic hosepipe has proved satisfactory). The outer ends of the tubing are flattened and drilled, and the end wires are attached with suitable bolts, washers and nuts. The two insulators between element end wires can be of plastic or Perspex strip, approximately 9in long. The end wires should be stranded wire (copper, aluminium or galvanized iron appear to be equally suitable), and the length required is dependent on the diameter of the wire. As an example of the effect of wire diameter on frequency, it was found that on 14MHz equal lengths of 7/0·029in and 7/0·036in resulted in a difference of approximately 250kHz (underlining the need to use a gdo to tune the array).

"The 12in square plate can be attached to the supporting mast with angle brackets. The feed point resistance is approximately 30Ω but a reasonably good match can be obtained by feeding the element with 50Ω coaxial cable. It is recommended that the cable be routed down the inside of the supporting mast (if metal) for at least a quarter of a wavelength in order to achieve good balun action. A better match can be obtained by using a λ/4 Q section of 50Ω cable followed by 75Ω cable to the transmitter."

Both the "butterfly" and the VK2ABQ 2-element arrays are particularly useful for amateurs having only small areas available for antennas, as the full-size Yagi beams have a turning radius too great for many gardens and the full-size quad is a fairly formidable structure.

ANTENNA TOPICS

Long-Yagi Antennas

Extracted from 'Technical Topics',
Radio Communication, September 1978

Long-Yagi antennas
Several vhf enthusiasts are concerned that the comments on the NBS booklet "Yagi Antenna Design" by Peter Viezbicke in the April *TT* (which were a follow up to the earlier notes in January) may have left readers feeling that there is little to be gained from studying this work. Although I stand firmly by the criticisms voiced by G6XN on the apparently misleading results with two or three elements (and there are some other points of debatable validity), there is equally little doubt that this work (which was apparently carried out in the 'fifties but published only in December 1976) does provide at least a working basis for the design of high-gain long-Yagi antennas. The report was surveyed in some detail by Joseph Reisert, W1JR (*Ham Radio* August 1977, pp22-31), and he pointed out that the information formed the basis of the 15-element Yagi by W0EYE (*QST* January 1972 and the ARRL *Handbook*) which has proved one of the more repeatable designs. The full report is available from Superintendent of Documents, US Printing Office, Washington DC, 20402, USA, order SD Catalog No. C13 46:688. The price is 65 cents, but add 25 per cent for other than USA mainland.

At the moment there appears to be a lot of interest in loop-Yagi antennas, now often known as "quagi" antennas. Chris Barthram, G4DGU, has sent along the details put out by K2UYH on the 432MHz Antenna Measurement Event at the 1978 West Coast VHF Conference. Seven designs achieved measured gains in excess of 13dB: a 21-element F9FT-design by WA6OIL and WB6OKK came top with 15·6dB; K6MBE's 16-element "KLM" came next with 15·2dB; then two 15-element quagi antennas with 14·8 and 14·2dB; a 13-element K2RIW with 13·7db; a 19-element F9FT with 13·6dB; and a 17-element Yagi by W7LUX and based on the NBS data with trigonal reflector with 13·4dB. Once again this contest does emphasize how difficult it is to reach or beat 15dB forward gain, even on 432MHz.

Beanz Meanz QSOz: Correction

Extracted from 'Technical Topics',
Radio Communication, September 1978

Incidentally, the 144MHz bean-can sleeve dipole in the July *TT* (Fig 6) showed a 38in length of RG59/U, incorrectly stated to be of 50Ω impedance. In fact, RG59/U is the correct cable but this is 75Ω impedance.

The UA3IAR Switch-rotatable Quad

Extracted from 'Technical Topics',
Radio Communication, October 1978

The UA3IAR switch-rotatable quad
For many years a two-element rotatable quad has been high on the list of what most members of the hf dx fraternity would like to own. But the quad imposes problems that too often lead ultimately to disaster. A few years ago, commuting into Victoria station, I noticed that a new 14MHz quad had appeared above the rooftops in the Brixton area; but came the first real gale of winter and it was gone, never to reappear. I could not help reflecting on all the effort that had gone into the project and its short effective life.

In truth, many quads suffer from lack of mechanical robustness, represent quite a difficult constructional project even if a suitable "spider" is available, while during operation the time taken to swing a large beam around to a required direction is often a considerable disadvantage. A full-size quad, particularly for 14MHz, is undoubtedly difficult to put up and difficult to keep up, especially in an urban environment where roof-top mounting may be required. Yet listening on the bands shows that the stations using quads often appear to have an edge over the others.

In *Radio* (Moscow), No 6, 1978, pp18-19, L. Vsevolzhskii, UA3IAR, has come up with an ingenious, though basically simple, arrangement that appears to overcome most of the usual problems in putting a quad on a rooftop. In effect, he has evolved a quad-type antenna that is *fixed*, requires *no framework* or self-supporting tubular elements, yet can be instantly switched (remotely) so that its main lobe is in any one of the four quadrants. Since the uni-directional beamwidth (to −3dB points) is roughly 90°, this means that such an array should provide an acceptable performance throughout the 360° with no turning delay (it may be recalled that bi-directional switching of hf arrays has been advocated by G6XN for this very reason). Indeed it

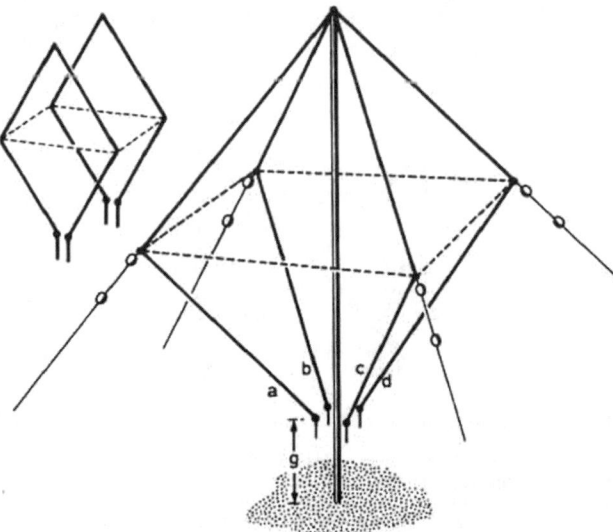

Fig 1. The UA3IAR switchable quad, showing its development from a conventional array. The four half-loops *abcd* are electrically joined at the top, and pairs of half-loops are used to form the full-wave loops which function either as radiator or, with the additional phasing extensions, as driven reflectors

would seem that the UA3IAR array combines much of the mechanical ruggedness and simplicity of a roof-mounted ground-plane antenna with a useful performance approaching that of a conventional full-size quad, although possibly of limited gain.

In providing notes on the UA3IAR design I am particularly indebted to Sid Dunn, who once again has provided me with a full translation of the Russian text from which I am quoting extensively.

The array is, in effect, a two-element array with actively fed reflector. The array is formed from four half-loops which can be so selected that, at any one time, two half-loops form the radiator and the other two the reflector; four-position switching provides the four-basic configurations of uni-directional beams. In each position, two half-loops form the radiator, while the other two form the reflector with its phasing section. Fig 1 gives an indication of the general configuration and how this is comparable with a conventional two-element quad. The upper vertices of the separate loops are joined together, while the lower vertices form the feed points; the middle portions of the loops are in effect pulled a little outwards. All wires are held in place by guying rather than any framework, noting that the four wires at the top are electrically joined.

The technique used by UA3IAR to switch his polar diagram is shown in Fig 2. To form a uni-directional radiation pattern it is necessary to provide a suitable phase difference between the currents flowing in the two loops, or rather more than 180°. The exact value of phase shift depends on the effective spacing between the loops, with an initial phase difference of 180° obtained by suitable connection to the appropriate windings of the ferrite-ring transformer T1.

Extra phasing elements are connected into the loop forming the reflector elements, with all switching provided by relays RLA and RLB. The switching sequence depends on the position of the selector switch S1, and this is best understood by considering just one example. In switch position 1, both relays are energized; winding L3 of T1 is connected directly to half-loops *c* and *d* through normally closed contacts RLA.2 and RLB.2. Winding L2 of T1 is connected to half loops *a* and *b* through the phasing extension elements. In this way, two full-loops (*ab* and *cd*) are formed, with *ab* acting as a reflector. In these circumstances the beam direction is that indicated by arrow 1. Arrows 2, 3 and 4 correspond to beam directions of the three other switch positions. Four hermetically-sealed relays connected in pairs are used by UA3IAR. Their contacts are rated at comparatively low power provided that all antenna beam switching takes place with no rf power applied to the array.

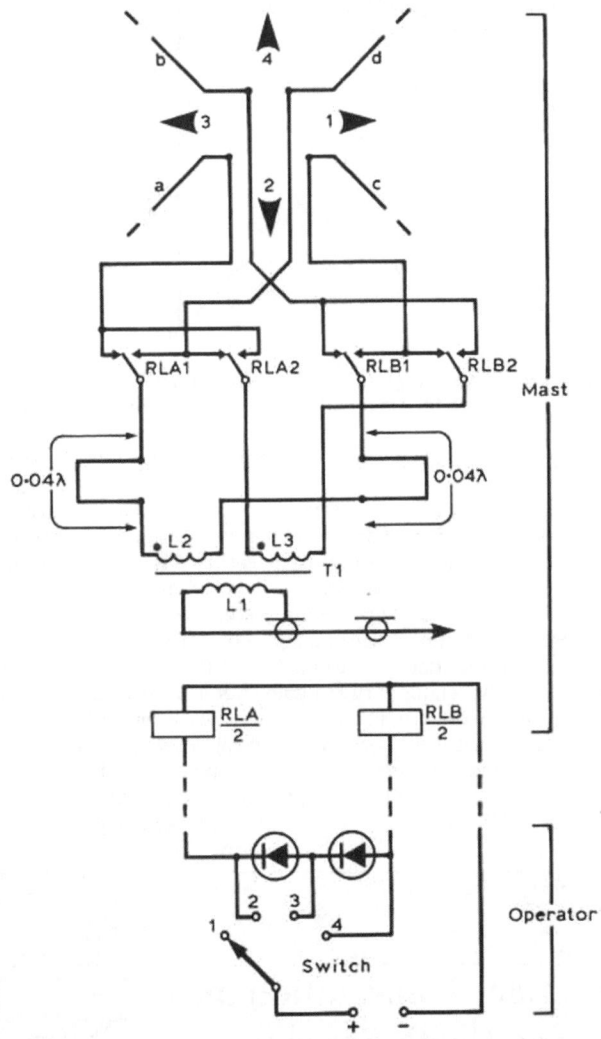

Fig 2. The control and switching system used by UA3IAR. The two 0·04λ extensions are used to provide an 0·08λ phasing section to convert the appropriate loop into a reflector. T1 is based on two ferrite ring cores with a Russian reference K32 × 16 × 8 but could be similar to the fairly substantial cores used to form transmitting baluns, though care should be taken that rf power loss in this component is not excessive. The "sense" of windings L2, L3 must be correct in order to provide the initial 180° phase difference between radiator and driven reflector. Control voltage and current steering silicon diodes as required by the relays. In the absence of any energizing voltage the beam will always be automatically set in Direction 1

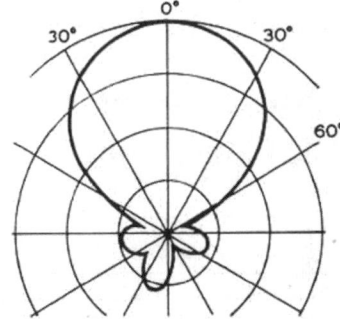

Fig 3. Polar diagram of UA3IAR array using optimized 0·53λ half-loops and a total phasing extension of 0·08λ (2 × 0·04λ)

T1 is described as based on two ferrite ring cores placed side by side, with windings made from 10 parallel strands of wire. Winding L1 has 10 turns; windings L2 and L3 have eight turns each. The antenna is fed with 75Ω coaxial cable, and it is stated that the swr does not exceed 1·4. Large toroidal cores similar to those used for baluns should prove suitable for the transformer.

The switching equipment is secured to the steel mast (20mm diameter steel tube) with the aid of four welded triangular steel plates. To these are also secured the insulators for bracing the half-loop wires. Special care was taken to see that wires joining corresponding circuits had equal and minimum lengths.

For 14·0 to 14·3MHz the mast is 9m high, with the point "g" 1·5m above the roof. The length of each half loop wire is 10·95m using copper wire of 2·5mm diameter; this wire is also used for the "extension" elements (total length 1m).

UA3IAR states that tests on 144–146MHz versions have shown that the optimum length of the half-loops is 0·53λ, and the optimum total length of extension phasing elements is 0·08λ. The polar diagram in one quadrant of an antenna of such dimensions is shown in Fig 3.

ANTENNA TOPICS

The system has been described here in some detail since it would seem to represent an extremely practical approach to the home-construction of a switched directional antenna array of good performance. Even if the full quadrant switching is not implemented it would seem possible to use such an arrangement of loops to provide fixed or reversible arrays based on a single support mast and no framework. For instance, the technique of using two (or even four) open-wire feeders brought into the shack, in the G6XN approach, might be worth considering. The basic arrangement might also be applied to 7MHz, where a mast or tower exceeding about 18–20m high is available, or less if capacity-hat loading is used. Again, an automatically switched array might prove a useful arrangement for an hf or vhf beacon station providing a sequence of transmissions directed in the four quadrants. There is also scope for the development of multi-band systems.

As UA3IAR points out in the original article: "Time and time again amateurs have set themselves the task of creating antennas with switchable polar diagrams, but up to the present time such antennas have not gained wide acceptance." In this system, UA3IAR appears to have at last come up with a thoroughly practical way of avoiding the disadvantages of mechanically rotating beams, while preserving most of the basic merits of the long-established cubical-quad array. A 14MHz array of this type has been in operation at UA3IAR at Kalinin City since 1973 and has proved "highly reliable and convenient". However, UA3IAR makes no claims as to forward gain, and G6XN thinks this may be under 4dB.

UA3IAR Switch-rotatable Quad: Correction

Extracted from 'Technical Topics',
Radio Communication, November 1978

UA3IAR switch-rotatable quad
In the circuit diagram published with this item in the October *Technical Topics* (Fig 2, page 861), the current steering diode between switch positions 3 and 4, is shown the wrong way round.

Another VK2ABQ Mini-beam

Extracted from 'Technical Topics',
Radio Communication, December 1978

Another VK2ABQ mini-beam
Over several years a number of designs for compact, lightweight mono- and multi-band hf beam arrays have been presented in *TT*, originated by Fred Caton, VK2ABQ (former G3ONC). These have been based on wooden, horizontal "X" frameworks, using wire elements. A new variation, reducing the size still further, has been developed by VK2ABQ and is shown in Fig 5. This takes the form of a compact 28MHz array, with a turning radius of only 4ft, although of course it could be scaled up for 14 or 21MHz.

The unusual form of cross-over folding of each element means that a similar amount of wire to a full-size dipole and reflector can be accommodated on this small structure, two-thirds the size of the original VK2ABQ design.

The main effect of reducing the size is to increase the Q of the array, and in turn this implies a reduction of effective bandwidth. This makes it essential to check carefully with a gdo at the feedpoint before cutting the side wires, as suggested for previous designs. It is possible to lower the resonant frequency by lengthening the bases of the overlapping "pyramid" sections, but this is not recommended unless it is necessary in order to reduce the size of the framework beyond that shown. The total length of wire for 28MHz is about 35ft.

Normally, points Y and Z should be half-way along the 4ft wooden dowels. Where the wires cross over, a small insulator should be used to keep the wires apart; otherwise when power

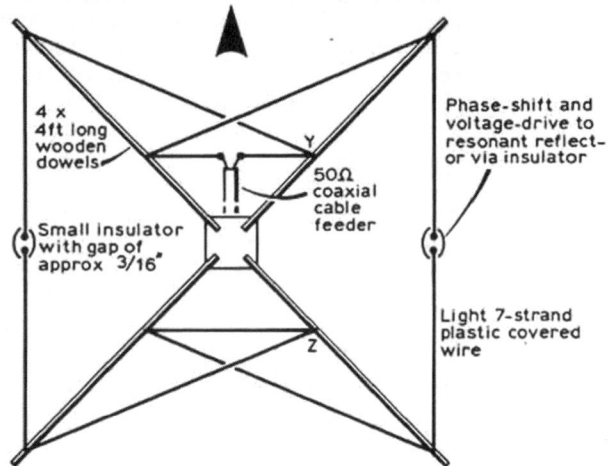

Fig 5. VK2ABQ's miniature 28MHz beam with 4ft turning radius. It can be scaled up for other bands. Note that accurate tuning up is needed

is applied there may be a tendency for the wires to weld together.

The "pyramids" can be thought of as a relatively efficient form of inductive loading, while the end sections continue to represent capacitive loading as in earlier VK2ABQ designs. When fed with 50Ω coaxial cable, an swr of less than 1·5 could be achieved around the correct operating frequency.

Despite the compact size and high-Q construction, VK2ABQ reports a substantial front-to-back ratio (of the order of three S-points), respectable forward gain over a full-size dipole and "excellent" side rejection (which had not been anticipated). Using a converted 8W citizen's band rig, many American stations and other dx have been worked from West Merrylands, New South Wales. Incidentally, in regard to the Australian cb situation, VK2ABQ contrasts the moronic chaos of 27MHz with the very successful Australian *novice* licence.

Vertical Polarization and Large Earth Screens

Extracted from 'Technical Topics',
Radio Communication, December 1978

Vertical polarization and large earth screens
The performance of vertically-polarized hf antennas is very significantly affected by earth conductivity. This is now widely recognized, although few amateurs are aware just how much

1970 - 1979

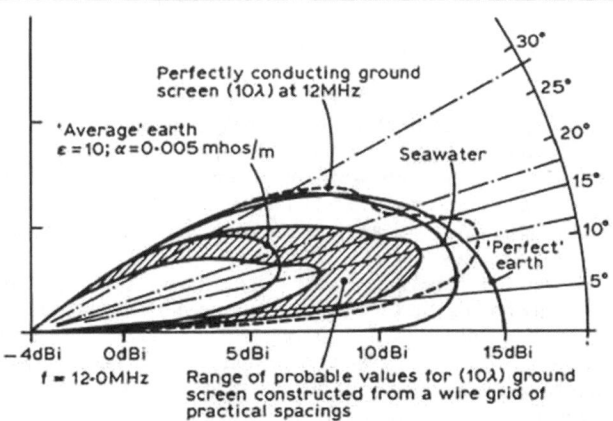

Fig 6. Vertical radiation patterns in boresight direction of a large extended aperture vertically-polarized log-periodic array showing how gain and radiation angle are improved by using extremely large earth screens. Note that for most urban and residential areas the earth conductivity is likely to be appreciably worse than the "average" indicated

additional low-angle radiation can be achieved when very large earth screens are used *extending out as far as possible* in the direction of the main target area.

The ideal vertical antenna is one sited *directly* at the edge of the sea (or better still, directly over a salt-water lagoon). Not many of us can do this; and unfortunately the sheer size of an earth screen needed to approach anywhere near the same performance is almost always out of the question: see Fig 6.

A recent article by TCI (an American firm making hf antennas for communications and broadcasting) in *ABU Technical Review* (September 1978, pp26–29) shows that the difference in power gain of a vertical antenna over perfect earth and one erected over good "average" earth can be as much as 9dBi. Poor earth conductivity virtually wipes out the low-angle radiation that we often hopefully associate with vertical polarization. Even with a screen some 1,000ft long and 400ft wide and the vertical antenna at one end, this may mean that the improved results in the target direction fall off quite rapidly in directions other than along the boresight (ie along the 1,000ft screen).

Here again it is important to note that directivity and power gain are not the same thing. For reception, it is seldom necessary to use earth screens with vertically polarized dipoles (radials are of course needed on vertical monopoles for purposes of impedance matching). In other words, it is not safe to assume that a vertically polarized antenna that brings in real dx well will necessarily be anything like as good on transmission as this might lead one to expect.

monopole over *perfect* ground achieves "omni-directional gain"). Les Moxon, G6XN, has considerable reservations about the results likely to be achieved with the UA3IAR form of quad, which he considers may be likened, alternatively, to two stacked X-type antennas, and which results in much reduced radiation resistance compared with the conventionally

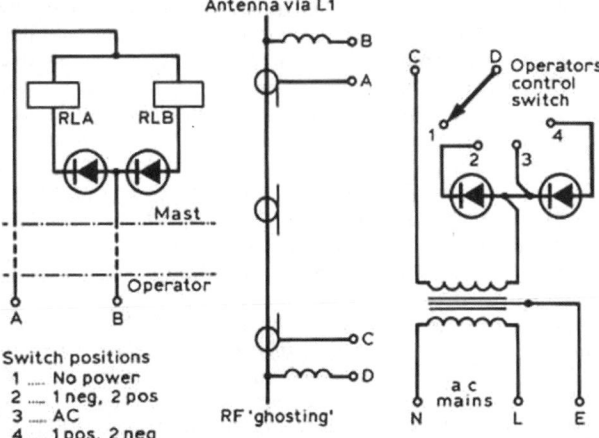

Fig 7. G8ABZ's suggested methods for using two-core or "ghost" (along the rf feeder) in the control system for the UA3IAR switchable quad as described in October *TT*

shaped quad and delta loops; possibly by a factor of eight. He notes the use of an actively fed reflector, which again is indicative of low radiation resistance and can also result in problems of sidelobe performance.

Nevertheless this interesting and novel design may well stir others into coming up with improvements while retaining the benefits of simple switching of the polar diagram. G6XN, for instance, has for some time had thoughts of using "slopers" in a similar type of arrangement, although he has yet to prove it in practice. This should not dissuade people from experimenting along the UA3IAR lines; indeed, Frank Emery, G3ZMF, has already reported achieving satisfactory results using the basic design on 28MHz.

The error in the diagram of the current-steering diodes was noted last month, and it should also be mentioned that there was an error in the text description. As made clear in the caption to Fig 2 (October), both relays are *un*energized in Position 1.

A. Tinsley, G8ABZ, has also pointed out that by using two more diodes it is possible to use a two-core control cable or even to "ghost" the control functions over the main coaxial cable, as shown in Fig 7.

More on the Switchable Quad

Extracted from 'Technical Topics', *Radio Communication,* December 1978

More on the switchable quad

The UA3IAR quad seems to have succeeded at least in arousing considerable interest in the concept of switched rather than mechanically-rotated beams. Not everybody, of course, accepts that UA3IAR has really solved all the problems of this approach. In the first place, a design intended to provide a 90° beamwidth is almost inevitably going to result in low forward power gain, unless this could be achieved by restricting still further the vertical radiation pattern (the way in which a

The Roberts / Brown / Yagi Array

Extracted from 'Technical Topics', *Radio Communication,* January 1979

UNTIL recently, if anyone had asked me who was responsible for the development of the two-element hf close-spaced Yagi array, I would have replied that presumably its development could be traced back directly to the late Professor Yagi or his student-associate Uda. In fact, as I discovered by accident recently, the correct answer is probably "Walter Van Roberts, W3CHO", and his ideas were the outcome of the work of Dr George Brown of RCA, who is more widely recognized as the father of vertically-polarized directional mf broadcast antennas.

137

ANTENNA TOPICS

The Roberts/Brown/Yagi array

The case for Roberts rests on a 41-year-old issue of *Radio* (January 1938) a, then, highly-regarded American west coast amateur radio magazine. This has a featured article, "The compact uni-directional array", by Van Roberts, the opening paragraph of which runs as follows:

"While the title of this article is too brief to indicate it, the antenna system to be described is believed to be not only just about the easiest rotatable beam to construct, but also the one that probably gives more power gain and useful directivity 'per unit of building trouble' than any of the more complicated structures. To be specific, the system may be adjusted to put out a signal equivalent to that from a simple dipole using 3·6 times as much power; in other words, the power gain of the system is about 5·5dB. Furthermore, at a sacrifice of less than 1dB in gain, the system may be adjusted to have a signal in the backward direction that is about 17dB 'down' with respect to the forward signal."

A series of statements, it may be observed with respect and humility, that have stood the test of 41 years! Hardly a word would need to be changed today, and the figures only slightly.

His basic ideas and his calculated performance figures, as he acknowledged, were derived from a portion (pages 103–8) of the paper "Directional antennas" by G. H. Brown (*Proc IRE* January 1937), a classic paper which has often been referred to in *TT* in connection with phased verticals. Neither Brown nor Roberts makes any reference to Yagi who had, some 10 years earlier, described directional arrays using parasitic elements. By 1937 this was a widely accepted form of array, but—to the best of my belief—normally with the reflector spaced exactly λ/4 from the driven element. In the mid-'thirties quite a few amateurs had developed Yagi antennas, usually vertically polarized, but based solidly on the idea that the correct spacing of the elements was λ/4.

The tremendous importance of the Brown/Roberts contribution was that they destroyed for ever this myth of λ/4 spacing, and so made possible a far more practical form of horizontal array. A single quotation from Brown shows this with devastating clarity: "In the case of a single parasitic reflector, it is found that the mysterious something that is supposed to happen when the spacing is one-quarter wavelength fails to materialize. Close spacings are found to be desirable in both the transmitting and receiving case." Brown also showed that it makes relatively little difference whether the parasitic element is used as a reflector or as a director.

Early in 1937 Roberts took the Brown monopoles; turned them into horizontal dipole elements using aluminium tubular elements, and put up on his house a rotatable two-element 14MHz beam with λ/10 spacing, fed with open-wire line and a simple matching section. It was a basic, practical design that could hardly be improved upon today. With 25W carrier input he was soon achieving his first European contacts.

Without having undertaken a detailed search of the literature, I am in no position to state *positively* that W3CHO was the first person ever to publish details of a close-spaced uni-directional rotary "Yagi" array. The circumstantial evidence, however, makes this a strong possibility. Roberts worked in the patent department of RCA and would have been well aware of Brown's work in advance of the *Proc IRE* publication. *Radio* was then at the height of its fame as the great rival of *QST*, with a reputation for being first with important technical developments.

So, without diminishing in any respect the work of Yagi and Uda, why not also just for once pay the credit long overdue to Walter Van Roberts, W3CHO (or perhaps someone who may have just pipped him to the post in some other magazine), for what has proved to be one of the most important developments ever made in the design of antennas for amateur radio; still, 41 years later, one of the best possible approaches in terms of results per unit of building cost and trouble. It will be observed, from Fig 1, that Van Roberts immediately recognized that it was unnecessary to insulate the elements and so, it would seem, may have to be credited also with developing the "plumber's delight" form of beam construction.

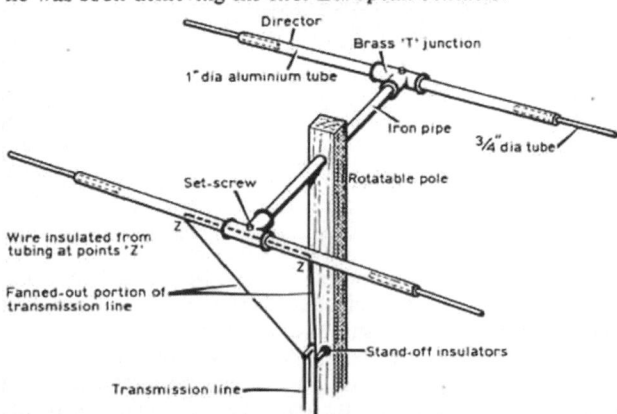

Fig 1. The W3CHO compact, unidirectional array as described in "Radio" in January 1938. Was this the first close-spaced plumber's delight rotary Yagi?

The Switchable Bi-square Antenna

Extracted from 'Technical Topics',
Radio Communication, January 1979

The switchable bi-square antenna

When the UA3IAR switchable quad was published in *TT* (October 1978 *et seq*) Eric McFarland, G3GMM, was firmly convinced that somewhere, sometime he had seen a description of a similar looking arrangement. After a search through his information store, he ultimately found what he was looking for: "A full coverage bi-square beam" in an early *Radio Antenna Handbook* (2nd edition, published in February 1938 at the incredible price of 75 cents). As may be seen from Fig 2, this looks, at first glance, the spitting image of the UA3IAR arrangement.

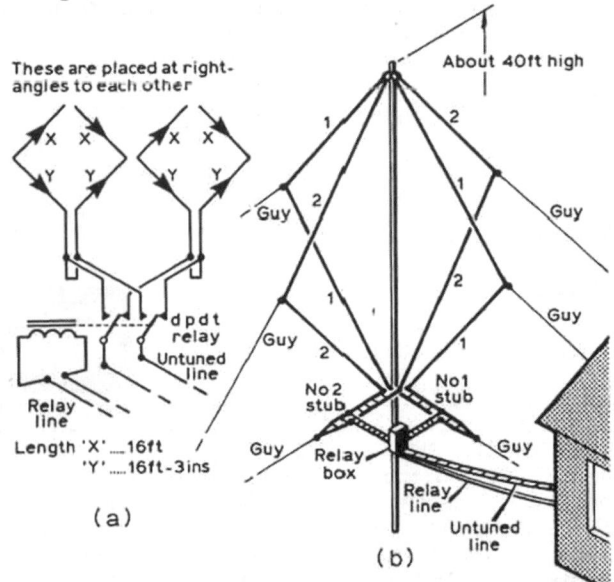

Fig 2. The switched dual bi-square antenna that looks like the UA3IAR but is a very different beast. The matching stubs are quarter-wave

However, a closer scrutiny will reveal a number of important differences: each loop is operated independently and each constitutes an "open" loop (no electrical join at the top) with a perimeter of 2λ, or double the size of the UA3IAR loops. And then again, whereas this bi-square system is essentially bi-directional (the two loops providing coverage of all four quadrants), the UA3IAR, despite its possibly modest power gain, is a true uni-directional beam array.

So, despite the remarkable resemblance, the Russian antenna is by no means just a revival of a 40-year-old design, though I share with G3GMM the view that many excellent systems have been invented in the past and then discarded and forgotten in the search for "progress", and then may suddenly reappear. They say a lot of people re-invented the wheel.

But what of this switched bi-square buried away in the old handbooks? It would seem, if you are prepared to accept its bi-directional characteristics, to have attractions of its own, particularly for 21MHz and above, where the support mast need not be more than about 30ft high. This form of 2λ loop gives a modest but useful power gain (and is claimed to provide good low-angle vertical directivity). Equally interesting is that, unlike the UA3IAR, the radiation resistance is high, leading not only to good bandwidth, but also making the construction and adjustment less critical, and with fewer worries about the efficiency of the insulators. The low-loss open line and stub matching transmission line techniques were deservedly popular at the time when the system was first published, but could easily be replaced by coaxial cable if you must.

There is also another reason for drawing attention to the bi-square loop: by incorporating a means of remotely connecting or disconnecting the vertices of the UA3IAR half-loops, it might prove relatively easy to develop a two- or multi-band system which would be a combination of switchable quad and bi-square techniques. This is a suggestion only, as no attempt has been made to test out the idea in practice.

and consisted of two 70ft vertical sections and a centre-fed 130ft sloping section, thus looking to the transmitter much like a common or garden half-wave dipole. For 1·8MHz such an antenna needs high masts and a fair amount of space.

Ray Fowell, G4GMX, has recently been trying a variation of this antenna, but scaled down for 7MHz. This has been proved to work well not only on 7MHz but also 21MHz in a very cramped location and with the two low points only a few feet above ground: see Fig 3.

On 7MHz this configuration represents a half-wave element, as in the VE7BS antenna, but voltage-fed from the base of the appropriate vertical element by means of a standard "L" matching network (one inductor, one capacitor). On 21MHz the antenna forms a 3λ/2 system, the phasing in the elements, together with their spacing, being such as to give the antenna good broadside directivity.

The Zig-zag Sloper Again

Extracted from 'Technical Topics',
Radio Communication, January 1979

The zig-zag sloper again

In *TT* (April 1978, page 327) brief reference was made to the 1·8MHz zig-zag sloper antenna used by Bob Eldridge, VE7BS. The basic idea of this type of antenna is to use a long dipole or end-fed wire with the two end sections forming vertical elements arranged so that the current flowing in the same direction in each vertical section makes them function as a pair of phased verticals, although not requiring any ground radials to achieve the impedance match.

The VE7BS zig-zag sloper was for top band dx operation,

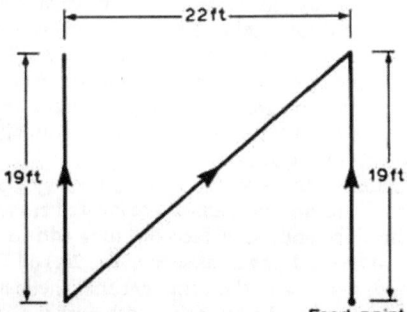

Fig 3. G4GMX's compact zig-zag sloper antenna for 7 and 21MHz

Superdirective Receiving Arrays

Extracted from 'Technical Topics',
Radio Communication, January 1979

Superdirective receiving arrays

In *TT* June 1978, the fundamental limitations involved in reducing the size of antennas were discussed; it was then indicated that miniaturizing an antenna imposes limitations on coupling efficiency and bandwidth.

There is a further important aspect to this general question: for many years it has been recognized that conventional array design practices do not result in arrays that, for a given size, provide the maximum possible theoretical gain. Any attempt to achieve maximum gain results in impossibly narrow bandwidth and impracticable mechanical tolerances, and has given rise to the term "superdirectivity" representing the missing directive gain of practical designs. There is a considerable body of published material relating to this "superdirectivity", although most writers have concluded by emphasizing that this is unlikely ever to be achieved in practice. Although the term "superdirectivity" turns up from time to time in amateur journals, it has had little impact on practical work.

However, recent work in the USA suggests that the concept of superdirectivity could, in fact, be usefully applied to compact *receiving* arrays in those cases where it is meaningful to think in terms of directivity gain, without relating this to efficiency and, hence, power gain.

Power gain can be defined as the product of directive gain times antenna efficiency. For *reception* at mf or hf, where external noise is dominant, antenna *efficiency* may be of only secondary importance; although directive gain is still valuable in order to reduce the strength of interfering signals coming from directions other than that of the wanted signals. A well-known example of such thinking is the compact mf frame antenna, which is often hopelessly inefficient as a transmitting antenna and yet can be extremely useful as a directional receiving antenna.

In a recent article "Superdirective receiving arrays" by E. H. Newman, J. H. Richmond and C. H. Walter *(IEEE Trans on Ant & Prop* Vol AP-26, No 5, September 1978, pp629–635) it is shown that superdirective principles can be usefully applied to compact hf receiving arrays, with experimental results (at 750MHz) in reasonably good agreement with theoretical predictions, although it is indicated that further work could be usefully carried out.

The key to this new breakthrough into superdirectivity is the

ANTENNA TOPICS

introduction into the design procedures of a tolerance constraint. What this seems to mean in practice is that instead of designing for the absolutely highest possible directivity (leading to impossibly low tolerances) the designer accepts some trade-offs between the various factors, including array size, directive gain, snr, efficiency, bandwidth, tolerances and far field patterns. The sort of results that seem to be feasible are directive gains of the order of 14dB with four close-spaced elements, and over 20dB with 10 close-spaced elements: the close spacing means that boom length is short and the whole array occupies very little space.

It is, however, important to keep firmly in mind that these are directive receiving gains *not* power gains.

Radiation Resistance of Medium Loops

Extracted from 'Technical Topics',
Radio Communication, February 1979

Radiation resistance of medium loops

Some time ago (June 1977) the question was raised in *TT* of the radiation resistance of medium-sized loop-type antennas, using material from A. Richtscheid (*IEEE Trans on Ant & Prop*), Des Vance, GI3XZM and Les Moxon, G6XN. This led to correspondence in which certain features of the computer calculations of A. Richtscheid were questioned both by GI3XZM and G6XN as not being borne out by practical experience. Somehow, at the time, this further material got squeezed out and one result is that readers may have been left with a misleading impression of the radiation resistance of non-circular medium-sized loop antennas.

So belatedly I am including this month some estimates made in 1977 by GI3XZM, based on what he described as a "pick and shovel method" (that is in relation to the use of a computer). In fact he integrated a sine current curve around the loop and compared this with the corresponding integral for a dipole, assuming its radiation resistance to be 72Ω. Although these represent "un-proven" calculations, the results seem to constitute a useful guide to this class of antenna, as well as overcoming some of the anomalies of the computer analysis: see Fig 6.

Shape	Wire length	Name	Radiation resistance (R_R)
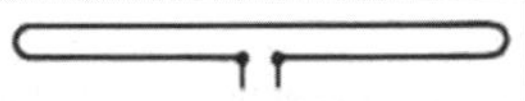 (elongated loop)	1λ	Folded dipole, half-wave	288Ω
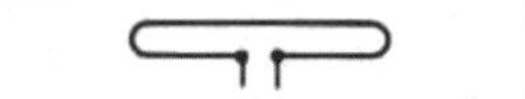 (elongated loop)	½λ	Folded dipole, quarter-wave	12·7Ω
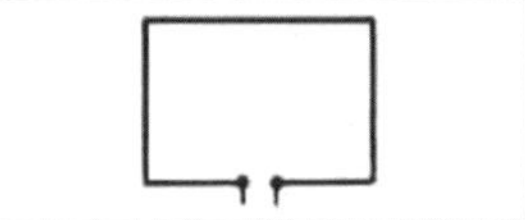 (square)	1λ	Quad (single element)	145Ω
 (square)	½λ	½ wave quad, side-fed	7Ω
 (diamond)	½λ	Levy quad, G6XN	6Ω
 (triangle up)	⅜λ	⅜ wave delta, equilateral, side-fed	1·4Ω
 (triangle down)	⅜λ	⅜ wave delta, equilateral, apex-fed	0·87Ω
 (right triangle up)	½λ	½ wave delta, right-angled, side-fed	10Ω
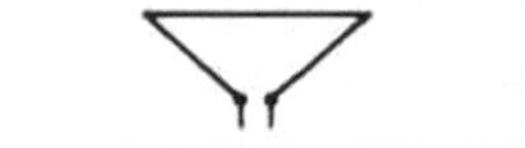 (right triangle down)	½λ	½ wave delta, right-angled, apex-fed	7·5Ω
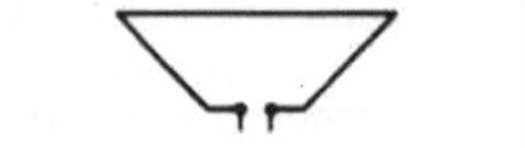 (trapezium)	½λ	½ wave, trapezium, GI3XZM	10Ω
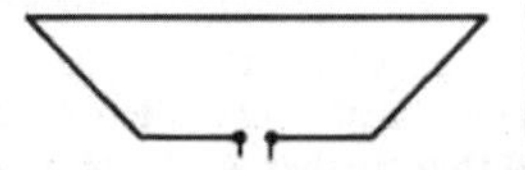 (trapezium)	¾λ	¾ wave, trapezium, GI3XZM	85Ω

Fig 6. Estimated radiation resistances of loop-type antennas as calculated by GI3XZM using "pick and shovel" technique

G3ZHL's Switched Octahedral Array

Extracted from 'Technical Topics',
Radio Communication, April 1979

G3ZHL's switched octahedral array

Guy Morgan, G3ZHL, is one of a number of amateurs who have indicated considerable interest in the UA3IAR switched "rotary" wire beam in octahedral form (*TT* October 1978 *et seq*) but who feel it should be possible to squeeze out rather more gain and/or bandwidth. In his case this has resulted in a design study for a double-sized array (similar in size to the old bi-square design unearthed by G3GMM, but with unidirectional characteristics) providing a calculated forward gain of 6·7dBi (ie just over 4·5dB reference dipole). Although G3ZHL has had to postpone putting his ideas into practice until the summer, he feels they may be of interest to others as a further contribution to the search for an effective switched rather than mechanically rotating low-cost beam. He writes:

"The radiation from an antenna is produced by the *current* flowing in it. Thus the properties of an array are determined by the location and relative phases of the current maxima in its various elements. In the UA3IAR antenna the current maxima occur at the top and bottom vertices, where all four wires are close together. This seems to indicate that the array should have a gain not too different from that of a single, one-wavelength loop. A possible disadvantage of the design is that one current maximum is at the lowest point, closest to any clutter on the ground.

"The use of a high impedance feed and isolated wires at the top vertex of the array moves the current maxima to where they do more to contribute gain. Splitting a one-wave loop at opposite corners and feeding at high impedance will not work. An extra 180° phase shift is introduced at the feed point and the two current maxima are out of phase when the loop is viewed face on. Note the difference from a conventionally current-fed loop as used in a quad.

"The situation with 2λ loops, as described by G3GMM, is very different. The current maxima are located at the four mid-points of the sides and, seen face on, they add to produce a horizontally-polarized signal, as seen in Fig 2(a) of *TT* January 1979. I cannot agree with the comment that the insulators are then less critical; quite the opposite, each corner of the loop is now at a voltage maximum so that the support wires need to be

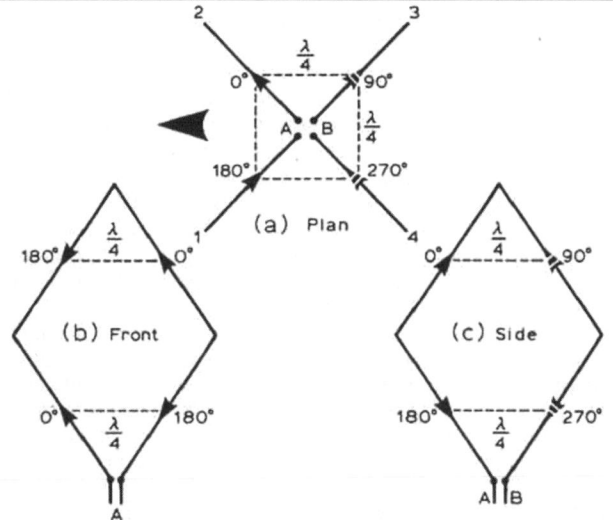

Fig 4. Single-pole switched octahedral quad array proposed by G3ZHL using "bi-square" (2λ) elements with high-impedance feed points (horizontal polarization)

insulated from high rf voltages.

"The 1938 bi-square design used only one loop at a time and was bi-directional. The following proposed design uses the same bi-square concept, with insulated wires at the top vertex, but with a different feed arrangement so as to make use of both loops simultaneously in order to produce some gain. A little geometry shows that the centres of the sides lie at the corners of horizontal λ/4 squares. Consider the antenna as consisting of two flat loops that have been folded about a vertical line. One of these can be fed at high impedance to produce a current pattern similar to a flat loop (see Fig 2(a) TT January 1979). If the other folded loop were to be fed in phase with this the signals would not add to best advantage because of the 90° phase shift introduced by the λ/4 spacing. The antenna would also be directional.

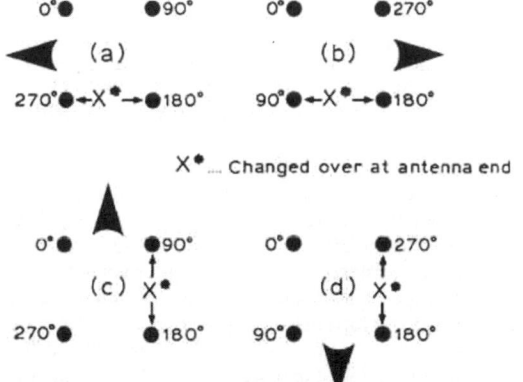

Fig 5. Phasing situations with G3ZHL array using "four-wire" open line feeder with switching arrangements at the antenna end of the line

"The spacing can be used to produce a better gain and a unidirectional radiation pattern by feeding the second loop 90° out of phase. This is shown in Fig 4, which represents a plan of the antenna. The relative phases of the currents are shown for the bottom half of the antenna. Half-loops 1 and 2 are fed from open-wire line A, and half-loops 3 and 4 (advanced 90° in phase from line A) are fed via line B. The phase shift, combined with the spacing, makes signals to the left add in-phase, while signals to the right cancel. The currents in the top legs are 180° out-of-phase with respect to the corresponding currents in the lower legs, but the bends in the wires make the horizontally-polarized signals add, and the vertically-polarized signals cancel. The direction of maximum radiation can be selected by switching phases at the feed point in a similar manner to the previous designs.

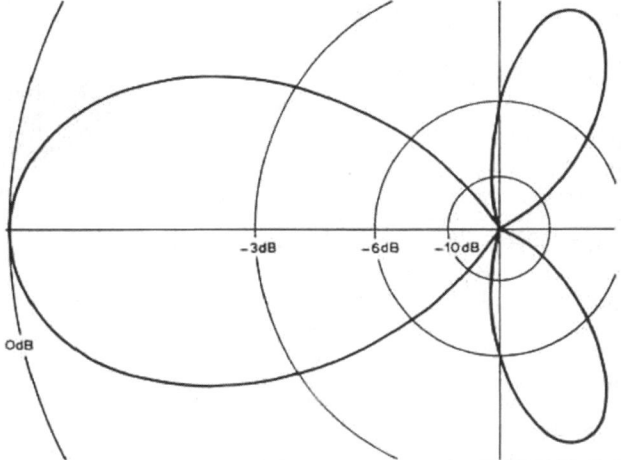

Fig 6. Polar diagram in the horizontal plane for the G3ZHL array

"The high impedance feed can be matched to a low impedance coaxial cable (or twin line) by means of two λ/4 transformers of open wire line which can be combined into a square four-wire arrangement. The diagonally opposite wires then form independent open-wire lines. Each pair lies in the zero equipotential plane of the other so the two pairs should have little interaction. The phasing for Fig 4 is produced by inserting an extra λ/4 (electrical) length of low-impedance feeder at the base of one open-wire transformer to give the required 90° phase shift, and swapping the 180° and 270° wires at the base of the antenna. The arrangements needed to give the four possible directions are indicated in Fig 5. The direction is reversed by interchanging the 90° and 270° wires at the low-impedance end of the open-wire transformer. The other two directions require switching at the antenna end. A three-pole changeover relay would be needed and should have widely-spaced contacts to cope with the high rf voltages at the antenna feed point."

G3ZHL considers that he can back-up the basic idea with the results of some calculations. He has computed the polar diagram of the array, approximating actual current distribution with Hertzian dipoles located at the midpoints of the sides (representing a reasonable approximation). The resulting pattern gives a gain of 6·7dBi, with the main lobe in the expected direction and a null in the opposite direction. In the horizontal plane (Fig 6) the main lobe has a half-power beam width of 68°. The reverse null is more than 20dB down for a width of 34°, and more than 10dB down for 66°. The bad news is that there are side lobes situated 112° either side of the main lobe, only 3dB down! The side lobes have 6dB points (relative to the main lobe) 45° apart. The nulls between the main and side lobes are more than 10dB down for angles of 53° to 80° off the main lobe.

Although G3ZHL recognizes that the side lobes could be annoying (particularly when trying to work South America from the UK) he feels that the design represents a significant improvement over the two previous single-pole, octahedral wire arrays. It is basically a monoband design, but if it were built for 21MHz with 3λ/4 matching lines then it would present a low impedance to the transmitter also on 7, 14 and 28MHz, although radiation patterns for such operation have not been calculated and the impedance match would not be very good on these additional bands.

ANTENNA TOPICS

G6XN 'Heath Robinson' Switched Quad

Extracted from 'Technical Topics', *Radio Communication,* April 1979

The G6XN "Heath Robinson" switched quad

In *Wireless World,* commenting on the UA3IAR design, I wrote: "It will be interesting to see who will be the first to come up with a low-cost switch-rotatable beam with a forward gain exceeding, say, 5dB." The G3ZHL entry is only one of a number of responses to this challenge.

Les Moxon, G6XN (who had actually been experimenting with switched beams *before* the publication of the UA3IAR design) reports: "I *think* I have now got the answer to the problem of all-round switchable arrays *without* the disadvantages of the UA3IAR version, and *plus* multiband operation." His array remains the same size and octahedral shape as the UA3IAR single-pole design, but (like G3ZHL) he makes some ingenious transpositions of current distribution to overcome the snags of X-type elements (looking down on a UA3IAR it can be thought of as two stacked X antennas) and the multiband feature can be achieved by an extension of the "linear

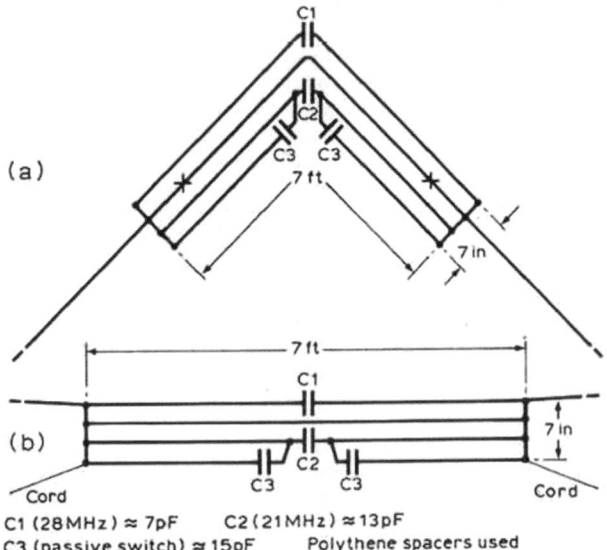

Fig 7. Linear resonators used by G6XN for triband quad elements. Loop circumference 66ft (1λ on 14MHz). The arrangement (a) is that used in practice by G6XN, but the arrangement (b) should also prove satisfactory

resonator" (disappearing inductance) technique (*Radio Communication* April 1977) and by the use of "counterpoise" elements. The following account reports progress (up to last December) on both mechanically rotated and switched versions of his multiband quad. It should be remembered that for many years G6XN has been a firm (if unheeded) advocate of using single large loops in quads rather than the conventional "nested" family of 1λ loops.

The latest version of his quad uses triband linear resonators (Fig 7). In effect, three elements on 14MHz become 12 on 28MHz, giving significant extra gain (G6XN sees this extra gain at higher frequencies as the main argument in favour of big beams as opposed to mini-beams, and he considers that it also resolves the quad versus Yagi debate in favour of the quad since this yields twice as many 28MHz elements). The quad forms a "bi-square" on 28MHz and "something in between" on 21MHz. For a rotary beam one needs resonators at the top and bottom of each loop. G6XN's original experimental fixed version had resonant stubs for the parasitic elements so that they could be adjusted at ground level as reflectors or directors an any band. But, as a result of gale damage, the driven element developed an unexplained fault on 21MHz. To try and get some clues as to the fault (without lowering the antenna) the lower resonator was scrapped and replaced with a stub, resulting in the current distribution slipping round by 90° and vertically-polarized radiation (parasitic elements becoming inactive). Although this was not of interest in itself, it started G6XN thinking and led to what may well prove to be a practical answer to the switched array problem. This train of thought was reinforced by his pondering on the basic evils of X-beams. G6XN writes:

"If taking a pair of parallel elements (Fig 8(a)) and bending them into X shape (Fig 8(b)) makes such a mess of things (low radiation resistance, nulls at 45° forward, large side and back lobes) why not try the opposite kind of bending: Fig 8(c). Notice that, as with standard elements, spacing S1 for the 45° direction is 0·707 of the maximum spacing S2 *but* in this case, allowing for the current distribution, the effective *mean* spacing for the beam direction is going to be a lot less than S2; in fact, not much greater than S1 (ie as the beam is rotated there is at first relatively *little* change in *effective* spacing. Thus, instead of being narrower, the beam will be broader than with normal elements, side lobes are almost suppressed and back lobes greatly reduced.

"But how, one might ask, do we go from Fig 8(b) to Fig 8(c)? The trick is simple and there is no basic structural change from the UA3IAR arrangement: we merely shift the feedpoint to the *middle* of a *side* of the quad loop; this switches the polarization from horizontal to vertical and pushes the current

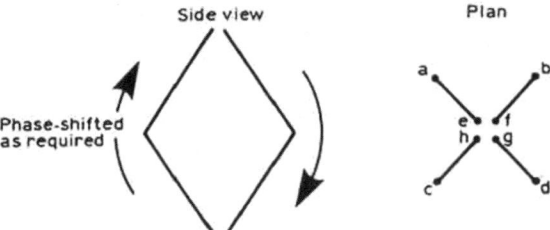

Fig 9. By shifting the feedpoint of a UA3IAR array it becomes vertically polarized with the current maxima at the corners instead of at the pinched-in top and bottom vertices

maxima out to the corners instead of the pinched-in top and bottom vertices!

"Looking from the side (Fig 9), we see current maxima at a, b, c and d, whereas for the UA3IAR quad the maxima are at e, f, g and h. By the nature of things there *is* a snag. Feeding at the corners is not nearly as convenient *and* we are going to have to feed all four corners, or two corners plus some tricky switching at the upper and lower high voltage points, *or* (having open-circuited the top) use a zepp feed at the bottom (with the G6CJ balun modification—see *ART5, 6* etc) plus a two-pole, four-position switch at the lower high-voltage point. I propose to try this first, using crocodile clips. I feel sure the switching problem is solvable, although the zepp feed may restrict bandwidth and there could be a multibanding problem at 28MHz because of a tendency to excite the full-wave mode; this can probably be overcome by using short counterpoises, so that we have an element looking like Fig 10 (for simplicity this is shown for two-band operation and it should be noted that counterpoises are needed only on 28MHz and are not needed with corner feeds). The four half-elements are paired, as required, for 90° switching of beam direction. For monoband operation one could use a single pair, and the array then, in effect, becomes a vertical VK2ABQ array! However, the full quad configuration should give slightly more gain and better back-to-front ratio, mainly because of the closer effective spacing, and it also cancels unwanted horizontal components.

"The multiband four half-element version suffers from excessive spacing on the higher frequency bands and might be better with one pair unused. Or one could pinch the corners

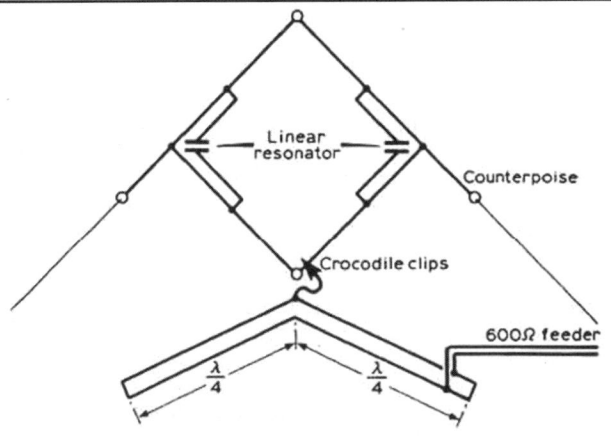

Fig 10. Multiband form of the basic vertically-polarized element, showing method of feeding and use of counterpoise on 28MHz. Note that two crocodile clips are required in order to drive two adjacent vertical members in phase

together by an arrangement of cords (plan view shown in Fig 11) to become what I have termed the 'Heath Robinson' quad. Pinching-in of the quad (at top and bottom) so that it can be supported from a single pole results in a tendency for spurious modes which are suppressed (in free space) *provided* that the current distribution is symmetrical; in contrast, an ordinary quad is remarkably tolerant of variations in the position of current nodes, etc.

"Another problem concerns the proximity of the high-voltage points to the supporting structure. Metal masts and guys would have to be non-resonant, but one could use an extension of, say, plastic tube, to take care of the top corners. The bottom corners are more of a problem and converting crocodile clips into a switched system may require ingenuity. In my case this represents a height of 25ft and can be reached by ladder for experimental purposes."

G6XN has also provided some notes on the adjustment of linear resonators for the triband and quad element (Fig 7) as follows:

"I set up the loops first of all in a horizontal position, about 6ft high. Walking round them with a current probe one can easily determine the points of zero current, which should be in the middle of the sides. C1 and C2 are adjusted to achieve this on 28MHz and 21MHz respectively. C3 is not critical but, at 28MHz, current through it should be equal to or rather less than that in the adjacent wire, and C1 and C2 should be re-checked after any adjustment of C3.

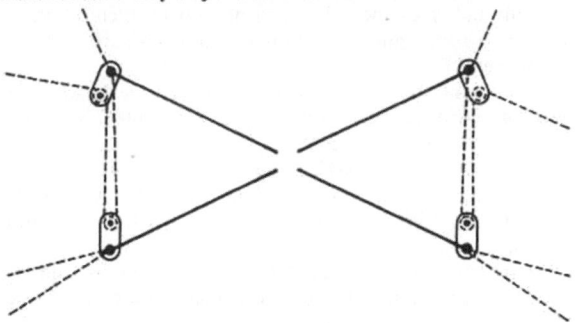

Fig 11. The G6XN "HR" (Heath Robinson) quad arrangement using cords and pulleys to pinch the corners together on the higher frequency bands

"*Lower* resonators need to be adjusted *in situ* (at low enough height for access) for best matching in the case of the driven element, and for maximum gain or f-b in the case of parasitic elements. For non-rotary operation, resonant stubs can be used with shorting bars (roughly 40 or 18ft for 21MHz, 25 or 42ft for 28MHz, 35ft for 14MHz) in place of the lower resonators."

Although it may be argued that considerable space has been devoted this month to what are still experimental or unproven design concepts by G3ZHL and G6XN, no apology is made since switched and multiband quads currently represent one of the most significant areas in amateur radio for serious and useful development work.

Beam with Multi-band Element

Extracted from 'Technical Topics', *Radio Communication*, May 1979

Beam with multi-band element

It is still not universally recognized that a plain and simple dipole element (no traps) can be used effectively on, say, 14, 21 and 28MHz provided that the transmission line is tuned and able to withstand a high swr without undue losses. The technique is to use a centre-fed element with the whole antenna/feeder system brought into resonance by means of a suitable antenna tuning unit. For example, some years ago Ed Tilton, W1HDQ, described a 33ft 2in "guy-wire doublet" for 14/21/28MHz using any convenient length of open-wire transmission line (*ART5/6*).

In *Amateur Radio* February 1979, Steve Bushell, VK3BHQ, uses this approach for a low-cost hf beam: Fig 4. This started off as a 14MHz monoband but he soon discovered the driven element could be used effectively on 21MHz (extended Zepp)

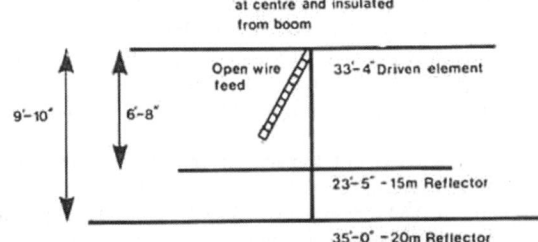

Fig 4. VK3BHQ's multi-band Yagi antenna using open-wire feeders to allow use of 33ft driven element on 14, 21 and 28MHz

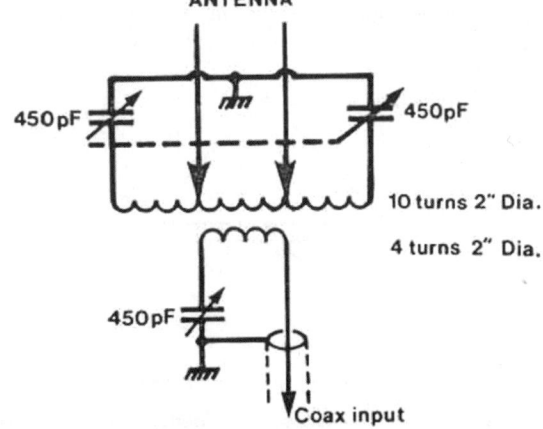

Fig 5. Antenna tuning unit to provide balanced output to the open-wire feeders of the VK3BHQ array. Taps are adjusted to provide correct matching and should be an equal number of turns from the centre of the inductor

and 28MHz (two $\lambda/2$ in phase). He added a $\lambda/2$ reflector for 21MHz but considers that even without a further 28MHz element the system also provides good forward gain on that band. Total cost was around $A45. One form of suitable atu is shown in Fig 5.

ANTENNA TOPICS

More on the Vertically-polarized UA3IAR Quad

Extracted from 'Technical Topics', *Radio Communication*, June 1979

More on the vertically-polarized UA3IAR quad

In the April *TT*, Les Moxon, G6XN, indicated that he believed that the gain and performance of UA3IAR-type one-pole octahedral wire arrays could be significantly improved by re-arranging the feed to provide vertical rather than horizontal polarization, so putting the current maxima where they do the most good. At the time those notes were compiled, however, he had not actually tried out the idea in practice. His latest report, based on experimental work, does in fact confirm that a very significant improvement *can* be achieved in this way. There still remains experimental work to be done on the question of switching the feed to "turn" the beam to each of the four quadrants, but it is becoming ever more clear that this basic "one-pole quad", which does not require any tubing, framework, boom or spider, really does seem to be the answer to the amateur who is looking for a low-cost and effective "fixed", "reversible" or "switch-rotatable" array which can be supported from a single wooden pole, garden or roof-mounted—always provided that there is sufficient area for the four "guy wires" that are needed to keep the array in shape.

In implementing the vertically-polarized array, Les Moxon has incorporated a number of ideas that were put forward some 10 years ago by Dr Werner Boldt, DJ4VM ("A new multiband quad antenna" initially in *DL-QTC* but in an English version in *Ham Radio* August 1969, pp41–45). This is an article which is still well worth studying in its own right, as DJ4VM, like G6XN, is a firm advocate of multiband loops rather than nested separate loops. In reporting his work on the octahedral array, G6XN writes:

"I have now tried out the use of vertical polarization to achieve the objectives, but with none of the disadvantages, of the original UA3IAR arrangement. The array I am using at the moment provides triband operation of 17ft square loops along the lines of the DJ4VM quad which is derived from the Lazy-H array. Fig 4 shows what each loop looks like when shifted round to provide vertical-polarized signals. The ends could be joined, but in principle this makes no difference electrically, and leaving them unjoined is easier and may slightly reduce

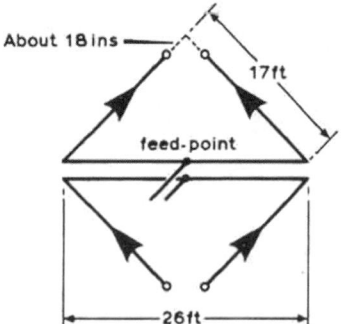

Fig 4. Basic vertically-polarized loop derived from DJ4VM's "Lazy-H" form of multiband quad antenna. Current direction arrows are valid for 14, 21 and 28MHz. Resonant open-wire stub connected to feed-point

dielectric losses in the mast. I have brought the ends of the two loops close together, top and bottom, so that the top half of the quad serves also as the top part of the guy-wire system. Except for the different method of feeding, the arrangement *looks* very much like the bi-square antenna shown in Fig 2 of the January *TT*. The important difference is that the array is tri-band and unidirectional! Unfortunately for full quadrant switching to provide omnidirectional operation, one needs a much more complicated switching arrangement, or two beams at right-angles on the same mast.

"With a 17ft loop, one has on 28MHz the full gain of a bi-square plus reflector (some 7–8dB), and on 14MHz one approaches normal quad performance (around 6dB reference dipole) although this will be slightly degraded unless one takes steps to equalize the currents. I have in fact come up against the overcoupling problem (see "A neutralized VK2ABQ mini-beam" in *TT* February 1977, pp 126–7) albeit in a much less extreme form. This is capable of being corrected by driving both elements, though neutralization also works. By adjusting the angle between guy wires one can have any desired spacing, but a very interesting point is the way the effective spacing automatically decreases with increasing frequency, without one having to do anything about it, such as using 'Heath Robinson' pulleys (*TT* April). On 28MHz the centres of the current loops move to the centres of the sides so that the mean spacing is exactly *half* the spacing between the corners. Admittedly the effective mean spacing on 14MHz is less than the spacing of the

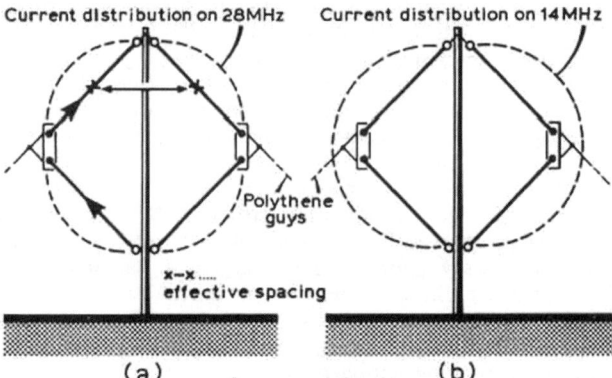

Fig 5. Loop erected in the single-pole form showing current distribution on 28 and 14MHz and indicating how the effective spacing is automatically reduced on 28MHz. Feeder arrangement not shown

corners so that the compensation is not perfect, but it is good enough.

"Fig 5 shows the array end-on but with the feeder omitted. With 50° between the loops the current ratio in dry weather is 1·6 on 14MHz, 1·0 on 21MHz and about 0·8 to 0·9 on 28MHz, but on 14MHz there is a drop to 1·1 in wet weather, accompanied by a change of some 10in in the required stub length; this indicates there is an insulation problem which I shall need to investigate later and which I am sure will not prove insuperable.

"The resonant stub reaches down to ground level where it could be matched into any kind of feeder. I use 600Ω line, and the length from the feed-point to shorting-bar works out at about 46ft for 21 and 28MHz, and 56ft for 14MHz. With a lower antenna, 23ft for 14 and 21MHz, and 31ft for 28MHz, would represent a better option where these points are within easy reach.

"If beam rotation is to be achieved by using two quads mounted at right angles, it will be necessary to throw the one

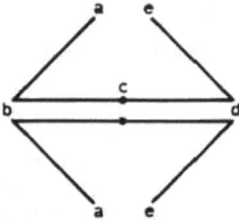

Fig 6. A problem may arise if *abcde* adds up to an odd number of half-waves, since it remains resonant whatever one does at the lower end of a stub connected to *c*

not in use out of resonance by means of suitable stub short-circuiting. The loop size is not critical, and I believe that anything from about 15ft to 21ft sides would be suitable for tri-band operation, but there is one important point that needs watching for the 'two at right-angles' case. In Fig 6, if the electrical length *abcde* is an odd number of half-wavelengths it remains resonant whatever one does at the lower end of the stub which is connected to *c*. Even with my dimensions there just *might* be trouble on 21MHz. This could probably be overcome by series capacitors at *c*, these would have little effect on 14 or 28MHz since *c* is a low-current point on these bands.

"Lots of other options remain to be investigated. I would like to try Zepp feed at the lower ends (Fig 7) rather as suggested in the April *TT*. Again, multibanding is feasible with linear resonators *if* one can alter the stub length. Structurally this should be easier, lighter and neater, but I am not sure if it would be possible to achieve multi-directional (as opposed to bi-directional) switching, since the switching has to be done at a point of high voltage which must be well-insulated and kept well away from any wet wood.

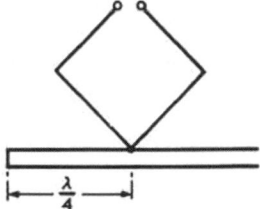

Fig 7. Balun-type Zepp feed is a possibility not yet tried by G6XN

"I am indebted to VK4TM for making the Lazy-H suggestion, but this 'rang a bell' and caused me to unearth the 1969 article by DJ4VM who has clearly got in first with the idea. A reversible beam for 7 to 21MHz would be an obvious possibility using a loop size of about 26ft. Bandwidth would be narrow on 7MHz, but then 7MHz is a narrow band! Extension to 28MHz could be achieved with the help of linear resonators, although performance would be degraded by non-optimum spacing, unless one added a third element which could be used for 14 to 28MHz. There are lots of other possibilities for us all to pursue."

Ferrite-clad Mini-antennas

Extracted from 'Technical Topics',
Radio Communication, July 1979

Ferrite-clad mini-antennas

In *TT*, back in September 1974 (pp602-3) attention was drawn to work then being carried out at the Royal Military College of Science on dielectric loading of antennas using ceramic (ferrite) powders. The aim was to reduce substantially the height of quarter-wave hf and vhf whips and monopoles.

Dick Biddulph, G8DPS, has now drawn attention to a recent *Interlab* bulletin (No 29) issued by the Department of Industry and based on this patented work by Professor J. R. James and Dr A. Henderson. This confirms that a thin cladding of ferrite material can be as effective as a thicker cladding of pure dielectric material in reducing the height of such antennas and offers the additional advantage of increased input impedance. It is indicated that with suitable ferrites a height reduction of no less than 7 or 8 times can be achieved. The ferrite cladding can be a coating formed *in situ* on the antenna tubing or can be achieved by sliding ferrite beads on to the conductor. One end of the antenna can be left bare to permit final trimming to a desired resonant frequency; additional support and protection can be provided by a sheath of insulating material.

Input impedances are appreciably higher than those generally associated with dielectric-clad antennas, and this can be further increased by feeding the monopole at an intermediate point along its length rather than its base, facilitating the design of matching arrangements.

Practical considerations put limits of 5 to 100MHz on the use of this technique, but the idea of an effective 7MHz vertical monopole only about 4 to 5ft in length is clearly attractive; less clear at the moment is what would be the cost and whether there would be a power limitation imposed by the ferrite material. These points are not made clear in the bulletin, which is intended to bring this work to the notice of manufacturers with a view to their taking out licences from NRDC.

It is pointed out that "Although the major application of ferrite cladding is expected to be in monopole whip antennas, it may well prove useful in other antenna configurations such as dipoles, Yagi arrays or wire-grid wideband structures, perhaps with different elements clad in different materials".

Quad Versus Yagi

Extracted from 'Technical Topics',
Radio Communication, August 1979

Quad versus Yagi

Two detailed articles in *Ham Radio* have raised again the long-standing controversy of quad versus Yagi, and have cast considerable doubt on the validity of some of the pro-quad arguments that have held sway during the past decade. In summary they provide convincing support for the view that a two-element quad can be roughly the equivalent of a three-element Yagi (both in practice providing up to about 6dB forward gain), but suggest there is little or no basis for the belief that three- and four-element quads are correspondingly superior to a Yagi array, or that the quad form of structure automatically provides an additional 2dB forward gain. Nor, it would seem, is it true, as so often stated, that quad arrays provide better low-height performance than Yagi arrays.

In *Ham Radio* March 1979 (pp12-24) Les Moxon, G6XN, provides what could be the definitive article on "high performance small beams" bringing together much advice on the question of element loading; correctly phasing element currents and the use of neutralizing wires; a three-element miniature beam design based on the VK2ABQ principle; and the use of linear resonators.

His article includes a realistic discussion of array gain and, for example, he comments: "It is unfortunate that many wild claims have been made for the quad, some of them involving professional journals and computer studies. It needs to be stressed that measurements are very difficult and computers need to be asked the right questions. The habit of accepting figures without checking them against ordinary common sense is not confined to the novice! In fact, as I have found, *better low-angle gain is obtained by omitting the lower halves of quad loops and using the upper halves as inverted V or U elements.* This increases the mean height by 2·4m (8ft) at 14MHz; low-angle gain for a flat unobstructed site being proportional to antenna height; this more than offsets any slight loss of free-space gain for heights up to about 21m (70ft)!

"The real advantage of the quad is the large amount of extra gain (3-4dB) obtainable by using the 14MHz elements at

ANTENNA TOPICS

28MHz with resonators so that they become a bi-square, but this is rarely exploited." (See *TT* April 1979.)

In "Quads versus Yagis revisited", *(Ham Radio* May 1979, pp 12-21) Wayne Overbeck, N6NB, reports on an extensive series of measurements of the gain of large hf beams. While it must be stressed that accurate gain measurements are extremely difficult to make on full-scale beams, it is interesting that N6NB comes to many of the same conclusions as G6XN, as the following extracts indicate:

"Cubical quads do *not* 'come into their own' at low heights. At any given height the vertical angle of radiation of quads and Yagis is virtually identical. The old idea of better low-height performance should be recognized as the myth that it is."

"In the uhf region, the performance of quads and Yagis may not deteriorate at the same rate."

"The data would support the conclusion that a two-element quad is superior to a two-element Yagi, but that larger-size quads are inferior to comparably-sized Yagis."

"If your quad really delivers 2dB more than my Yagi, I'll publicly recant the conclusions presented in this article."

All of this adds up to advice already given in *TT,* but not yet widely followed in practice: height gain is often the critical factor in performance—and this is achieved more easily with a lightweight two-element array, whether Yagi or quad; "nesting" elements affects performance much more than many people believe, and throws away, for example, the extra gain of a bi-square loop; and, finally, forget about that three- or four-element quad that you have always dreamed of putting up one day.

Fig 10. Electrician's knot prevents a zip-cord antenna from unzipping under tension

antennas of this type, with a dipole length of 5ft, are quite often used for Band 2 vhf/fm broadcast reception.

G3DMC reports that the transparent zip-cord available from Currys and Woolworth stores is effective when used as a four-wire feeder to a low-slung 3·5MHz vee antenna. He writes:

"Opposites are commoned at either end, the two lengths being taped in a neat square with plumbers' thin ptfe tape that clings without adhesive. The vee from eaves to fence has a very low impedance, which I would put at about 20Ω. Coupling to the transmitter coaxial cable output is via a ferrite ring balun in the shack (an old RSGB *Handbook* design modified by peeling back turns to achieve a correct match). The result is virtually unity swr when driven with a low-power (7W) transmitter, and brings in contacts with Sweden and Finland since erected three years ago."

Incidentally it should be remembered that with a high-loss feeder the swr at the transmitter end may appear deceptively low.

More on Zip-cord Antenna

Extracted from 'Technical Topics',
Radio Communication, August 1979

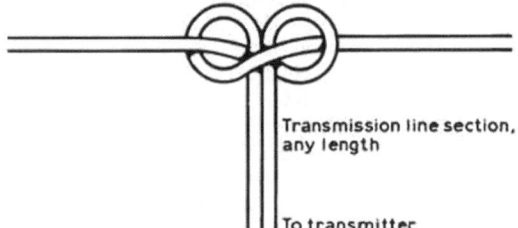

More on zip-cord antennas

Since preparing the item about the use of zip-cord electric cable (*TT* May 1979) some further information has appeared. Jerry Hall, K1TD, *QST*'s technical editor, asks in his March issue: "Zip-cord antennas—do they work?" The main attraction of this approach is the low-cost (about 6c/ft for twin-cable in the USA). In view of the opposing views on the use of such cable as a replacement for coaxial cable, K1TD bought a 100ft roll and tested it in the ARRL laboratories. Characteristic impedance of his sample proved quite close to the 100Ω suggested by ex-G3VBZ although differing slightly with frequency: 107Ω at 10MHz; 105Ω at 15MHz; and slightly less at 29MHz. Velocity factor proved to be 69·5 per cent.

The "bad news" proved to be appreciable attenuation when checked under correctly matched conditions: an estimated under 1dB at 3·5MHz; about 1·7dB at 7MHz; measured 4dB at 15MHz; and measured 7·5dB at 28MHz. Based on additional attenuation due to the mismatch (and consequent increase in swr) when used to power a dipole whose feedpoint impedance at low heights may be under the nominal 73Ω, K1TD feels that up to 100ft of zip cord could prove acceptable on 3·5MHz; up to about 50ft acceptable on 7MHz; but for longer lengths of feeder and/or higher frequencies his verdict is "look out".

However, K1TD sees no objection to using zip cord for the radiating element, and draws attention to the "electrician's knot" that prevents a zip-cord antenna from further unzipping itself under the tension of suspension: Fig 10. To tie the knot, first use the right-hand conductor to form a loop, passing the wire behind the unseparated zip cord and off to the left. Then, adds K1TD, pass the left-hand wire of the pair behind the wire extending off to the left, in front of the unseparated pair, and thread it through the loop already formed. Adjust the knot for symmetry while pulling on the two dipole wires. Incidentally,

The Bi-band Dipole Antenna

Extracted from 'Technical Topics',
Radio Communication, October 1979

The bi-band dipole antenna

Although it has been pointed out in the past that, provided open-wire feeders and an atu are used, a dipole antenna cut for 14MHz can be used quite successfully on 14, 21 and 28MHz (and even reasonably effectively on 7MHz) many amateurs still prefer untuned feeders. Multiband dipoles with coaxial feeders can be built by using the paralleled dipole technique (see *Radio Communication* June 1979, p527), but an alternative technique providing a 300Ω feedpoint on adjacent, harmonically related bands has been described by Ron May, VK1PM (*Amateur*

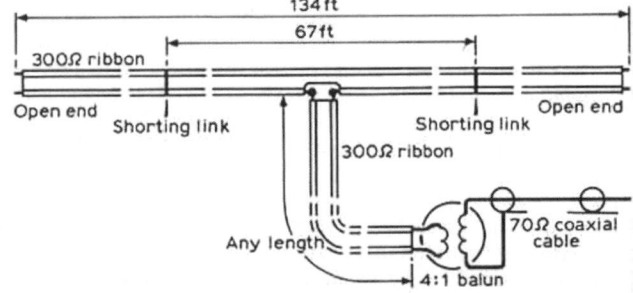

Fig 9. Bi-band dipole provides resistive match to 300Ω line on two adjacent harmonically related bands

146

Radio July 1979).

This antenna (Fig 9) uses the properties of a λ/4 stub to provide an approximate 300Ω resistive feedpoint on the two bands. The dimensions given are for 3·5MHz and 7MHz but these could be scaled for other bands. On the higher frequency band the centre section of the antenna acts as a folded dipole and so provides the 300Ω impedance. The end sections being each λ/4 long do not introduce reactance, and in effect are disconnected from the folded dipole section due to the impedance mismatch. On the lower frequency band the full length of the antenna element forms a λ/2 radiator, with a T-match section to the 300Ω line. For those who do not want to take the 300Ω balanced feeder into the shack, it is possible at any point to insert a 4:1 balun transformer and then use 70Ω coaxial cable.

Balanced Dipoles and Coaxial Cable

Extracted from 'Technical Topics',
Radio Communication, October 1979

Balanced dipoles and coaxial cable
From time to time we have commented rather coolly on the virtues and vices of balun transformers used between a coaxial feeder and a dipole element. However, a novel, virtually no-cost technique that appears to offer useful advantages has been described by Robert B. Dome, W2WAM, in *QST* May 1979, page 43.

He notes that, ordinarily, when a balanced dipole element is fed from coaxial cable an unwanted current flows down the outside conductor jacket of the cable. While such an arrangement may have a total radiated power equal to that when the element is fed from a balanced feeder, the radiation pattern may be distorted and the radiation from the feeder may contribute to tvi.

W2WAM shows (with mathematical justification) how the simple expedient of connecting the shield (outer conductor) of the cable to earth at a point λ/4 from the antenna feedpoint results in a minimum diversion of transmitter power on to the outside conductor of the cable.

Clearly this technique would be easy to implement on single-band dipole-type antennas or beams for the lower-frequency amateur bands. There could, of course, be problems for multi-band operation or where the antenna is more than λ/4 above earth (could a 3λ/4 section be equally effective?). A possibility worth investigating would be the use of an "artificial earth" consisting of one or more λ/4 wires, insulated at the far end, attached to the cable. It has been noted before that the use of artificial earths of this type can very effectively eliminate the problem of the "hot" earth point that often occurs when a long-wire antenna is used from an upstairs operating position. Altogether this could prove a powerful new technique for minimizing an old problem.

Practical Antenna Guidance

Extracted from 'Technical Topics',
Radio Communication, October 1979

Practical antenna guidance
For many months, Les Moxon, G6XN, has been carrying out a series of detailed investigations into hf antenna performance in support of a book which he is preparing for the RSGB. The aim is to provide amateurs with practical guidance that should enable more of us to achieve optimum results *in sites typical of those available to many amateurs*. While there are of course a number of mostly excellent books that outline antenna fundamentals and provide representative designs, almost everybody who has ever sought antenna information from them will have come rapidly to the conclusion that there are still many unresolved questions that often underline the difference between the professional situation (with tall masts and plenty of space) and the situations with which most of us have to contend. There are, as we have frequently noted in *TT*, many myths and ambiguities when it comes to such questions as miniature arrays, choice of array and the actual (as opposed to the theoretical) gain that is likely to be achieved, choice of polarization and the effects of poor ground conductivity, the effects of bending and folding elements in various ways, the question of proximity to houses, roofs and trees, trade-offs between gain, side-lobes, bandwidth, influence of nearby resonant and non-resonant elements, etc.

The projects which G6XN has been tackling recently have shown how many gaps there are in our knowledge when it comes to these practical questions, and together they look like forming an ambitious and almost certainly unique book. But before completing the manuscript, G6XN would be interested to receive suggestions and comments on just what questions readers would like to see answered in such a book. So if readers have come up against problems caused by sites or by apparent contradictions and ambiguities in existing sources of antenna information, please drop a line to Les Moxon, G6XN (1 Stoner Hill House, Froxfield, Petersfield, Hants GU32 1DX).

But could I make a suggestion? Do not divert G6XN from the task at hand: ie let him have comments but please do not bombard him with urgent antenna queries. His own investigations have already shown that there is considerable room for improvement in hf antenna design for those of us with restricted sites, so it is important not to delay the good work.

Dipole Insulators

Extracted from 'Technical Topics',
Radio Communication, October 1979

Dipole insulators
From V. J. Ludlow, G3JLZ, comes the suggestion that when erecting wire dipoles a reasonably effective set of insulators may be to hand in the form of three sections of those "chocolate blocks" used by electricians when jointing cables. Fig 12 shows how a two-section piece can be used for the dipole feed-point, with the dipole inner ends anchored under one screw in each metal insert, and the coaxial cable or twin balanced feeder ends fixed under the remaining screws. As outer insulators, again using a two-section block, the dipole wire

ANTENNA TOPICS

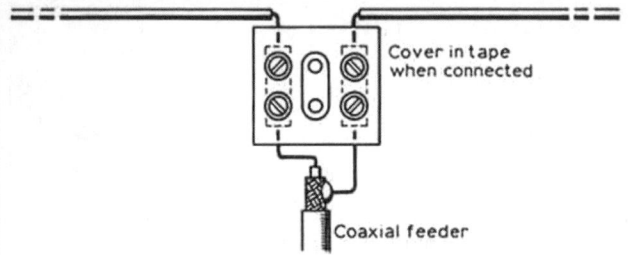

Fig 12. Use of electrician's "chocolate block" connectors to form centre insulator for wire dipole

ends can be taken right through the metal inserts and then twisted round, before the two screws are tightened down; a similar approach can be used for the anchor guys/halyards, using the second insert in each block. Nylon monofilament rated at 50 to 80lb breaking strain makes useful insulated guys without being too obtrusive, he adds.

G3JLZ wonders whether there is likely to be any difference in the performance of the clear as opposed to the chocolate-coloured versions.

28MHz element could be made 2 by 25ft, and the radiation pattern on that band would then line up with that on 21MHz.

He adds: "Where a top span of $\lambda/2$ on 3·5MHz can be erected, then the possibilities are even greater with $3\lambda/2$ on 14MHz, $5\lambda/2$ on 21MHz and $7\lambda/2$ on 28MHz, all accommodated within the 135ft or so span. Lengths of the parallelled elements could be chosen to provide the most desirable radiation pattern in the particular circumstances; it might also be feasible to use 'even' numbers of $\lambda/2$ elements provided there were an odd number of quarter-wavelengths on each side of the feedpoint, though this might tend to unbalance the system. Possibly the radiation patterns of the parallelled elements might be more affected than with the standard design, due to the increased coupling between the various wires resulting from the greater lengths of the higher-frequency elements, but even so the idea seems worth considering."

G6AU can only manage a 68ft span (and that with difficulty) but he has been trying a multiband system with 7/21MHz, 14MHz and 28MHz ($3\lambda/2$) wires. Meter indications suggest a reasonable match on all bands, although it still remains to be seen whether the results will show the anticipated radiation patterns on the various bands over a period of time.

Variation on Multiband Dipoles

Extracted from 'Technical Topics', *Radio Communication,* November 1979

144MHz Collinear Vertical Array

Extracted from 'Technical Topics', *Radio Communication,* December 1979

Variation on multiband dipoles

C. C. Alger, G6AU, raises an interesting point about the design of parallel multiband dipoles, and in so doing draws attention to the attractive radiation patterns of centre-fed long-wire antennas with radiating elements $3\lambda/2$, $5\lambda/2$, etc, long.

Fig 9 shows the significant differences between the standard

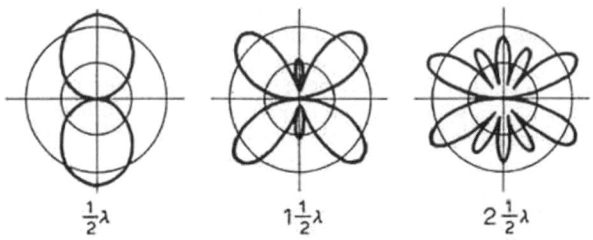

Fig 9. Horizontal radiation patterns of centre-fed antennas with $\lambda/2$, $3\lambda/2$ and $5\lambda/2$ elements

radiation patterns of centre-fed $\lambda/2$, $3\lambda/2$ and $5\lambda/2$ horizontal dipoles erected well clear of the ground. It should be noted that any dipole close to the ground in terms of wavelength (as most amateur antennas tend to be on 7MHz and below) will have a virtually omnidirectional radiation pattern. The useful feature of the longer dipole radiators is that the four major lobes (not unlike those of a full-wave radiator) enable UK amateurs to put signals towards all the main dx areas from antennas running either east-west or north-south, with, in addition, minor broadside lobes that roughly match the pattern from the standard $\lambda/2$ element.

G6AU notes that he has never seen a reference in any of the handbooks to the fact that when erecting parallel multiband dipoles it may well be advantageous to consider using longer elements on several of the higher frequency bands, since these can be accommodated within the span of the lower-frequency elements. It is, of course, common practice already to use a 2 by 33ft span on both 7MHz and 21MHz, but he notes that the

144MHz colinear vertical array

The attractions of a vertical, omni-directional colinear array for vhf or uhf operation become steadily more apparent as the use of vertically-polarized signals increases. But the colinear has to be approached with some caution; it is not a system that lends itself readily to fancy variations. One recalls, for example, the ingenious cross-over technique using lengths of coaxial cable to avoid the use of external phasing stubs; this looked better on paper than it ever seems to have worked out in practice (although one still sees glowing references to it occasionally in print, which leave one very puzzled). Just recently there has been quite a rash of new designs that claim to achieve colinear gain, but which seem to have overlooked the dangers and problems involved in bending elements so that they are quite close together and then expecting them to behave in true colinear fashion. There seems to be a whole set of new colinear myths in the making.

Nevertheless the traditional colinear design is still a very practical and useful arrangement. In *Amateur Radio* June 1979, VK2AXZ recalls the 144MHz array fashioned from stiff

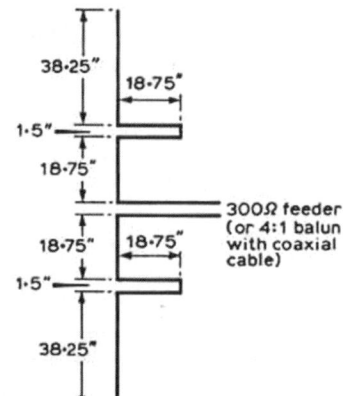

Fig 2. 144MHz colinear vertically-polarized array as used by VK2AXZ based on a classic ARRL handbook design. It can be used horizontally to provide a bi-directional broadside array

aluminium wire that used to appear in several editions of the ARRL handbook. Fig 2 shows his version, although I note that the original design had the phasing loops spaced 1in and that each comprised a 40in "hairpin" loop with 19in centre sections. The array can be made out of two 96-97in lengths of stiff ⅛in aluminium wire (ARRL used to suggest "aluminium clothesline wire") and is fed with 300Ω balanced feeder or from either 52 or 75Ω coaxial cable through a 4:1 coaxial balun.

The elements are mounted on small ceramic pillars on a wooden pole (using small clamps of sheet aluminium wrapped around the wire and screwed to the stand-offs). The array concentrates radiation in the horizontal plane to provide omni-directional gain—very useful for working to mobiles etc.

1980-1989

The VK2ABQ Antenna Again

Extracted from 'Technical Topics', *Radio Communication,* March 1980

The VK2ABQ antenna again

Of the many published proposals for new forms of amateur antennas, relatively few appear to be taken up by substantial numbers of amateurs; one reason for this is that many designs are evolved to meet specific requirements or to make use of existing facilities or materials. Then again, it is not always realized that many amateurs are more concerned to find a design that can be built and adjusted very simply, and is not liable to fall down in the first gale, than necessarily with achieving the ultimate in performance.

One design, however, that has rapidly established itself and has been widely used during the past six years is the compact VK2ABQ triband wire beam array which, for 14, 21 and 28MHz, requires only a modest support structure and has only a 12ft turning radius. When first introduced in the UK (*TT* January 1974), I quoted Fred Caton, VK2ABQ (G3ONC), as saying "It is the simplest and best homebrew tribander yet". The intervening years have done nothing to undermine this view, even if it can be argued that it is unlikely to quite reach or outperform a good conventional full-size Yagi or quad array.

Fig 1. Constructional details of the VK2ABQ triband beam as erected by G3LZR

The real attraction is the low cost, the minimum constructional problems and the light weight.

When Fred Caton was back in the UK during 1978 he persuaded (and then assisted) E. J. ("Ted") Womack, G3LZR, to build one. At a height of 30ft this has enabled G3LZR to keep in touch with VK2ABQ (now back in Australia) as well as a good number of other VK and ZL stations on 14MHz. While G3LZR's antenna (Fig 1) basically follows the modified VK2ABQ design described in *TT* (September 1974, Fig 2), there are a number of interesting constructional differences which could well prove useful to other constructors.

Phantom Stub Quad/Loop Element

Extracted from 'Technical Topics', *Radio Communication,* March 1980

Phantom stub quad/loop element

On several occasions last year (eg *TT* April 1979) we discussed the use of bisquare elements in which the perimeter is 2λ rather than the 1λ of conventional quad, delta and loop elements. It was pointed out by Les Moxon, G6XN, that multiband operation of a bisquare element is possible using his linear resonators; while the use of a conventional LC tuned circuit for this purpose is noted in *Radio Communication Handbook* (5th edition, Vol 2, pp12.86-7 and Fig 12.126(d)).

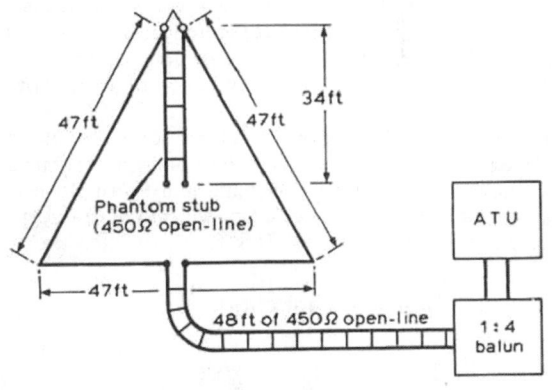

Fig 2. "Phantom stub" delta loop element as described by W7AAK. The dimensions shown are for 14, 7 and 3·5MHz but can be scaled for higher bands as noted in the text

In *QST* (December 1979, pp37-9) Harold E. Gullstad, W7AAK, uses a bisquare element to form a multiband delta single- or two-element beam, but replaces the LC circuit by what he calls a "phantom stub". By using an open λ/2 stub (and open-wire transmission line), he indicates how the 2λ element can be used effectively at f, $\frac{1}{2}f$ and $\frac{1}{4}f$ to form a multiband system with non-critical dimensions. With a 47ft (14·33m)-sided delta loop and 34ft (10·3m) stub, the element can be used on 14, 7 and 3·5MHz; W7AAK also claims that a half-size element will work satisfactorily on 28, 21, 14 and 7MHz. He describes his use of a two-element array based on this approach, but the article does not discuss the question of

ANTENNA TOPICS

element spacing or whether this can be optimized for more than one band. Nevertheless the idea would seem worth investigating, if only as a simple delta loop antenna: Fig 2.

The subject of multiband hf arrays is clearly going to become of increasing concern as the new 10, 18 and 24MHz bands become available (due to the new "transfer" procedure, however, it may well be quite a long time before the 18 and 24MHz bands are released to us). Rhombics, vees, log-periodics, long-wires and other broadband designs, such as centre-fed doublets with open-wire feeder, should be able to take the extra bands in their stride, but the many popular designs based on trapped elements, nested elements, stubs and other frequency-conscious elements seem bound to raise problems. The attractions of open-wire feeders in conjunction with flexible antenna matching units will become even more evident than at present. The departure from harmonically related hf bands will present hf operators with some new problems to solve, particularly if they are keen on atu-less coaxial cable feeders.

Optimizing Yagi Gain

Extracted from 'Technical Topics',
Radio Communication, March 1980

Optimizing Yagi gain

The publication in *TT* (January 1978) and *ART6* of some of the findings reported in "Yagi Antenna Design" by Peter P. Viezbicke, the subsequent debate in which G6XN pointed out the inconsistencies in those results for two- and three-element arrays, while other members defended them on the basis that they at least provided a helpful guide for the construction of long arrays for vhf/uhf, all showed once again how difficult it is to produce a set of practical, universal design parameters for Yagi antennas even after extensive theoretical and experimental studies. Indeed the optimization of Yagi designs, with so many possible variants, continues to be the subject of many papers in the professional journals.

Bill Pechey, G4CUE, brings a further source to attention: "A design of Yagi-Uda antennas by nonlinear optimization techniques" by Masanobu Kominami and Katsu Rokushima (English text in *Electronics and Communications in Japan*, Vol 61-B, No 1, 1978, pp47-54). This seems to introduce some potentially-useful new ideas, although the paper is highly mathematical and (even disregarding the maths) by no means easy to follow. As G4CUE points out:

"The paper deals with various criteria for optimization, including sidelobe suppression and broadbanding, so that arrays providing, for example, a gain of 7.7 ± 0.3dB over the range 260-340MHz with six elements, can be specified. In the various tables the optimization assumes an element diameter of 0.00337λ. This is reasonable for 144MHz (0.7cm) but would represent 7cm on 14MHz!

"I was confused at first by the difference between actual gain and directive gain as used in the paper, but I feel that by directive gain the authors imply the gain over isotropic, assuming perfect power transfer from the feeder (ie with matching network at the antenna), whereas actual gain takes account of the mismatch loss at the antenna assuming a 50Ω feeder directly connected. In some of the calculations the input impedance turns out to be $12.48 + j98.46$, or an swr of 19.74, suggesting that some pretty good matching will be needed to obtain the 13.51dB directive gain!"

I have simplified the authors' Table 1 which represents 3-, 4-, 5- and 6-element arrays optimized for maximum actual gain, although the original table has some features that I find confusing. I have also added information showing a modified six-element design optimized for minimum sidelobe level rather than maximum actual gain. Inspection of the table suggests that the results are likely to prove more applicable to vhf than hf, but it is interesting to note the appreciably lower gain likely to be achieved when an array is optimized for maximum sidelobe suppression.

Multiband Dipole with Coaxial Stubs

Extracted from 'Technical Topics',
Radio Communication, April 1980

Multiband dipole with coaxial stubs

About 1950, W4JRW patented a method of making multiband (14/28MHz) dipoles by using decoupling stubs formed from tubular 300Ω twin feeder with the stub forming part of the dipole element on the lower-frequency band: Fig 8(a). This design has been included in all editions of *ART* but has never attracted (to my knowledge) much attention; possibly because of the relatively little use made in the UK of balanced feeders with their susceptibility (more especially the flat "ribbon-type" of feeder) to a change of characteristics in wet weather conditions. An alternative form of dual-band dipole, again using twin feeder but in a folded dipole configuration, was reported more recently by VK1PM (*TT* October 1979, p939).

Now Vincent C. Lear, G3TKN, has come up with a three-band (7, 14, 21MHz) version of the W4JRW dipole but using coaxial cable to form the stubs: Fig 8(b). He writes:

"It appears that W4JRW recommended tubular 300Ω line for the stubs. However, I have found this difficult to obtain, while in my experience the flat 300Ω ribbon can be affected by rain and damp. I decided to try the W4JRW principle, but using 75Ω semi-airspaced uhf tv coaxial cable for the stubs.

"I have found this works well, provided that the cable is accurately trimmed to $\lambda/4$ resonance using a gdo or noise bridge, and that the ends are suitably sealed to prevent moisture from entering the cable. Fig 8(b) shows the dimensions of my antenna, but it is strongly advised that the stubs should be carefully resonated; since manufacturing differences in the cable can result in slightly different velocity factors, and hence different lengths for accurate resonance.

Table 1—Yagi antenna design

	3-el	4-el	5-el	6-el	6-el (min side lobe)
h1	0.238	0.240	0.243	0.238	0.242
h2	0.222	0.225	0.230	0.231	0.245
h3	0.218	0.219	0.221	0.223	0.231
h4	—	0.221	0.218	0.218	0.216
h5	—	—	0.216	0.218	0.202
h6	—	—	—	0.217	0.191
d1	0	0	0	0	0
d2	0.264	0.275	0.268	0.270	0.340
d3	0.538	0.589	0.555	0.544	0.448
d4	—	0.851	0.856	0.858	0.771
d5	—	—	1.183	1.196	1.200
d6	—	—	—	1.522	1.552
Directive gain (dB)	9.25	11.06	12.09	12.74	12.16
Input impedance (Ω)	31.03 + j2.68	28.90 + j2.50	30.46 + j4.84	36.04 + j1.37	9.49 + j9.92
SWR (Z = 50Ω)	1.62	1.74	1.67	1.39	5.49
Actual gain (dB)	9.01	10.73	11.81	12.63	9.34

Where h1, h2 etc are half-element lengths (h1 reflector, h2 driven element etc) in terms of λ, and d1, d2 etc are element spacings from h1 in terms of λ. All element radii assumed to be 0.00337λ. Gain figures are reference isotropic.

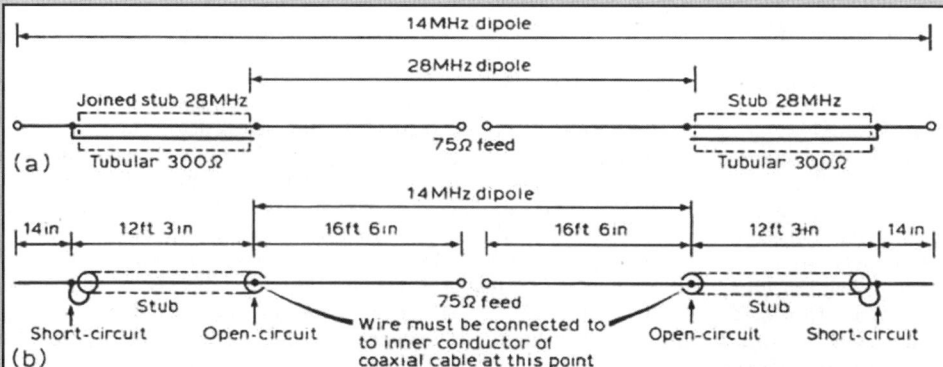

Fig 8. Multiband dipoles using stubs which also form part of the lower frequency radiating element. (a) W4JRW's original design for 14 and 28MHz using stubs made from 300Ω tubular cable; (b) G3TKN's 7/14/21MHz version with stubs using semi-airspaced uhf tv cable. The stubs should be carefully resonated at 14·2MHz

"The λ/4 stubs act in the same way as parallel LC traps; the antenna functions as a λ/2 dipole on 14MHz. On 7MHz the stubs present an inductive reactance and, together with the end wires, resonate the system on that band; virtually unity swr can be achieved on both these bands. Although the stubs offer some capacitive reactance at 21MHz, the antenna operates satisfactorily as a 3λ/2 element on that band, with an swr of about 1·4:1 achieved when using 75Ω feeder.

"I have run the antenna with 400W p.e.p. without observing any arcing at the open-circuit ends of the coaxial stub, where high voltage exists on 14MHz. However, if other types of coaxial cable were used this might be a point worth watching.

"With the help of G3FJ, some three miles away, I have carried out ground-wave tests. It was not possible to detect any noticeable drop in signal strength on either 7 or 14MHz when the antenna was restored to a normal dipole on either of these bands; so it seems reasonable to assume that this method of multibanding does not involve much 'compromise'. Because of the extra weight in the antenna element, such a system would be better suited to the 'inverted-V' configuration with centre support.

"I am hoping soon to experiment further with the system; for instance by attaching a pair of 7MHz stubs together with outer end wires and so resonate the system on 3·5MHz. The 7MHz stub should not only act as an isolator on 7MHz but also on 21MHz, so providing a 3·5/7/14/21MHz system.

Making Antennas Work

Extracted from 'Technical Topics', *Radio Communication*, May 1980

Making antennas work

Over the years it has become increasingly evident that different amateurs, when attempting to reproduce established designs of beam antennas (or even when using factory-built beams), often end up with very different results. Similarly it also seems that the use of model vhf/uhf antenna ranges to evaluate hf designs is far more difficult, and calls for more care, than many people realize. The vhf antenna gain contests that are held in the USA and New Zealand always produce an extremely wide spread of results, even though the entries are often based on a restricted number of types and designs. There is some evidence that operators often tend to judge the "goodness" of antennas by straightforward measurement of front-to-back ratio rather than by forward power gain or the precise position of the deepest nulls (indeed, for reception, the nulls are often operationally *more* important than forward gain). The very large number of variables (element lengths, element spacings, element diameters, coupling between elements, the degree of balance or unbalance of the currents, and the height and environment of the array) all combine to produce this very considerable spread of results, which have little to do with the theoretical analysis of an optimized design. For example, over the past few weeks a number of comments have been received from those who have used, or considered using, the VK2ABQ triband array (*TT* March 1980); while most of these have been extremely favourable, some have complained of lack of gain.

This is why the work carried out over many months and years by Les Moxon, G6XN, is particularly valuable: unlike most of us he evaluates a design carefully both in theory and practice, and is never satisfied until he can explain fully the

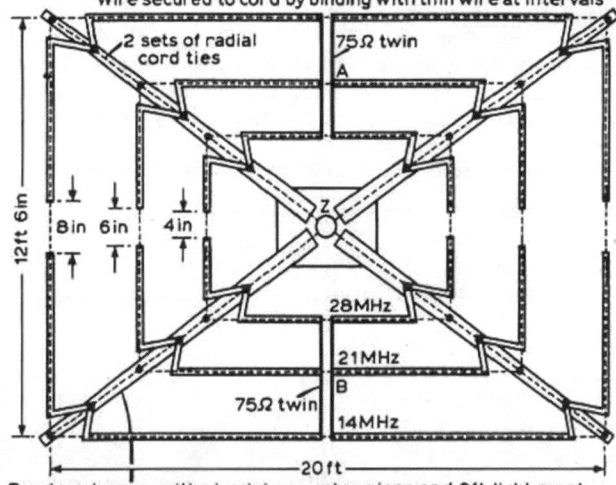

Fig 2. G6XN's suggestions for evolving a VK2ABQ beam into an antenna that should be "good by any standards" and seen as a step towards the ideal antenna. Transformers at A, B are either 1:1 baluns into 50Ω unbalanced feeders or 1:4 bal-bal units to give 200Ω for a 3:1 mismatch into open 600Ω line. Radial cord ties go to mast extension. Corners of elements are tucked in and hitched up onto the cord ties, thus keeping the wire elements clear of the bamboo spreaders

difference between what he achieves and what he feels should be possible. In doing so, he seems constantly to cut right across commonly-held beliefs about many forms of full-size and miniature arrays, as we have noted on previous occasions.

Arising out of recent comments on the VK2ABQ beam, G6XN has now put forward a number of points which have far-reaching implications, especially for those who may still dismiss the VK2ABQ approach as only to be commended on the grounds of being "simple and cheap" rather than "good by any standards".

To summarize briefly a number of his views:

ANTENNA TOPICS

(1) G6XN is coming to the view that if there is one shape for an element that is definitely *wrong*, it is "straight".

(2) VK2ABQ believes his design can outperform a good conventional full-size Yagi or quad. G6XN reckons that it *should*, though adding: "I am dashed if I can see *how* unless the ends are separated more, the shape made more rectangular, and each element given its own feeder." (*Note*: Peter Dodd, G3LDO, has developed an interesting variation called the "Double D" which it is hoped will form the subject of a forthcoming *Radio Communication* article—*G3VA*).

(3) G6XN stresses that of two-element designs published so far (including quads), the VK2ABQ is the *only* one to permit (at least in theory) adjustment of the critical distance between the *ends* of the elements, adding: "As I see it the correct operation of *any* two-element beam is a matter of achieving correct phase and amplitude balance, so that nulls are obtained in directions chosen to give the best compromise between gain and rejection of unwanted signals; the operation is just like balancing an ac bridge, with amplitude balance demanding slightly more than 'critical coupling' between the two elements. One needs the coupling that gives equal currents when the relative phase is adjusted to put nulls on bearings of about 140° (see "Supergain aerials" *Radio Communication* September 1972). This gives null depths above 23dB over a span of 110°, compared with 90° for a null in the back direction (ie 180°), and 4·6dB forward gain as against 4·2dB.

(4) It is a great advantage to be able to put the null where one wants it (not necessarily in the same place for transmission and reception). This need not be particularly difficult to achieve, as indicated by the "antenna vector processor" developed by Ken Franklin, G3JKF, (see below) which provides independent adjustment of phase and amplitude.

(5) The "standard" VK2ABQ has wire elements fixed to bamboo (when wet, bamboo becomes a very poor insulator) with very small "button" plastic insulators which provide no scope for adjustment. Fig 2 shows one way of killing all these birds with one stone.

(6) The highly reactive nature of the coupling in the VK2ABQ has the important bonus of providing most of the required phase shift. If two feeders are provided, as in Fig 2, one is more or less idling, although available for immediate beam reversal (another *very* important bonus) and for fine tuning.

G6XN compares these useful characteristics of the VK2ABQ approach with those of using just two straight elements in the conventional manner, much to the disadvantage of the latter! He points out that "the VK2ABQ is unique in offering also no difficulties when it comes to adding elements to cover the new bands (18 and 24MHz)". However, he warns that: "I consider a balun is *essential* if this beam (or any other) is fed from coaxial feeder". In the past it has been noted in *TT* that there are serious doubts as to whether balun transformers are really useful for dipole-type antennas, and that (for beam arrays) there is much to be said in favour of using balanced feeders with a balun arrangement at the transmitter end; the point that G6XN is making is for the many who use coaxial feeders with beam arrays.

With a reversible beam, G6XN comments, why go to the expense, slow turning motion and unreliability of beam rotators? Two cords and ±60° rotation is enough. Another major mechanical simplification is also possible: a light spreader is needed, but two of the spider arms can be disregarded by adopting an inverted-V approach: Fig 3. Theoretical forward gain, compared with a full-size quad, is only down 0·5dB, and this could easily be made up by a relatively insignificant amount of "height gain" (eg at 42ft such a VK2ABQ array should equal the gain of a quad at 40ft!).

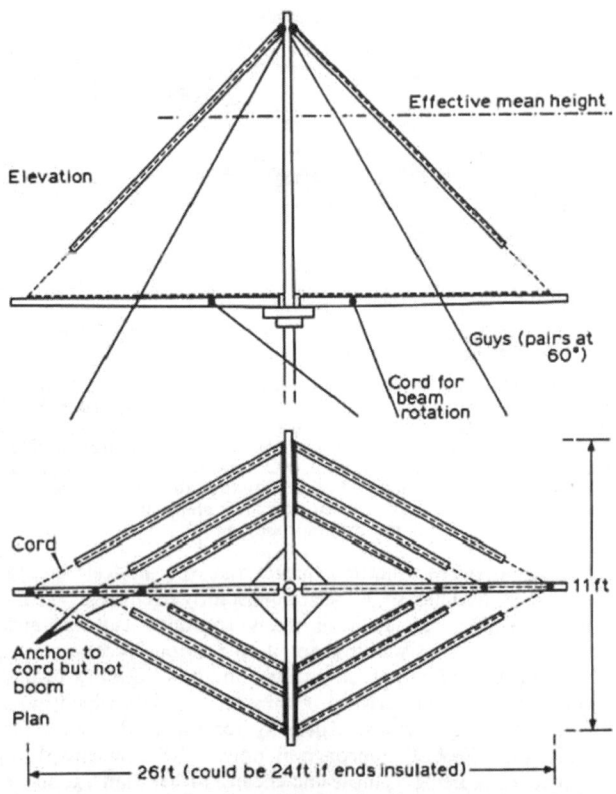

Fig 3. Inverted-V form of VK2ABQ array as suggested by G6XN. It is electrically almost equivalent to the standard VK2ABQ array

The 'Ideal' VK2ABQ?

Extracted from 'Technical Topics', *Radio Communication,* May 1980

The "ideal" VK2ABQ?

The above comments and suggestions have been rather ruthlessly extracted from G6XN's letter, but lead directly to a summary of his recommendations on how one could go about evolving an "ideal" antenna using the VK2ABQ as a starting point.

(1) Alter shape to rectangular to obtain a slight improvement in gain/directivity (recommended dimensions 20 by 12·5ft with same shape on all bands, but this is not critical).

(2) Use polythene cord-braced construction, partly to allow further reduction in weight and windage, but mainly to allow the wires to be routed clear of bamboos and to permit easy adjustment of element lengths, and especially adjustment of the spacing between adjacent ends as required for (3).

(3) Adjust reflector length and coupling (controlled by the end spacings) to obtain "infinite" rejection on bearings of 140° relative to the beam heading. This gives best rejection of signals off the back (more than 23dB over a total arc of 110°) and a possible gain of 4·6dB (only 0·5dB down on a quad at the same height and identically tuned).

(4) Use two feeders to allow instantaneous beam reversal and fine tuning from the shack. Consequential advantages include separate optimization of transmitting and receiving properties and more effective monitoring of performance.

(5) Taking advantage of (4), eliminate the beam rotator. This is a big cost saver which results in more rapid change of beam direction (use two cords to give at least ±60° rotation), less weight to be supported and greater reliability.

(6) Use a balun into 50Ω (balun vital *as an insurance policy*) or use 4:1 bal-bal and work with 600Ω line at an swr of about 3·0.

For long feeder runs use open wire line in multiples of 20m (1λ at 14MHz), then a 4:1 balun into less than 20m of 50Ω coaxial cable (this is a good idea for any beam as it avoids losses without much inconvenience. Balun transformer losses need not be more than 0·2dB).

(7) Do not bring the centres of the elements together. Join them with short lengths of low-impedance twin feeder. This has negligible effect on the tuning and makes it unnecessary to resort to undesirable (eg square) shapes.

(8) Use the device of Fig 4 to kill any 28MHz current flowing in the 21MHz element. Note that this technique will allow operation to be extended to new bands in due course and confers a unique advantage on this type of antenna.

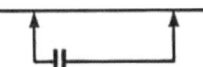

Fig 4. Traps used to kill any 28MHz current flowing in the 21MHz elements. A technique that allows operation to be extended to the new hf bands in due course and confers a unique advantage on this type of antenna

(9) Separate the transmitting and receiving functions, providing in the shack: *(a)* remote tuning of the reflector on transmit; and *(b)* separate phase and amplitude adjustments for receive, possibly on the lines of the G3JKF processor. This, incidentally, should make possible up to 0·5dB more gain on transmit.

(10) Take further advantage of item (4) by considering the alternative inverted-V configuration which is electrically almost identical although mechanically different. This eliminates two of the spider arms, the other two acting as a boom and supported at a relatively low height, thus helping with the mast. It requires the addition of an 11ft spreader.

(11) As an alternative to (10) consider the use of a third element, but not recommended to the novice.

'Hula-hoop' (DDRR) for 144MHz Mobile

Extracted from 'Technical Topics',
Radio Communication, June/July 1980*

"Hula hoop" (ddrr) for 144MHz mobile

In most, but not all, circumstances, the standard 144MHz λ/4 (19in) whip can be readily accommodated for mobile installations. Faced with a need to reduce still further the vertical dimension of a λ/4 roof-mounted whip on a Bedford van, in order that it could be garaged with minimum inconvenience, D. A. Bundey, G3JQQ, recalled the original "directional discontinuity ring radiator" (ddrr) or "leaky waveguide radiator" antenna (more popularly known as the "hula hoop") devised in 1962 by J. M. Boyer, W6UYH, for Northrop, and the later Italian-developed "half-wave" version (*Electronic Letters* September 1965, and subsequently in *TT, ART* and, in an article by I1MK, in *CQ* September 1967). G3JQQ examined the I1MK version, slightly modified and simplified it, and successfully installed this antenna (Fig 1) as a low-profile replacement for the whip. He writes:

"Performance has been somewhat better than the original whip, with the added advantage of much reduced own-ignition pick-up. The base is 18-gauge brass sheet, edge-angled to increase rigidity. The radiating element is 6mm microbore copper tubing, supported at one end by 0·25in perspex, at the other by a vertical copper stub, close to the feedpoint and soldered to both base and ring. The ring dimension was carefully adjusted for resonance within the band, using a gdo placed close to the stub support.

"Measured vswr is not worse than 1·3 over the band; the actual value is slightly affected by the positioning of the two magnets acting as clamps. The feed is 52Ω coaxial cable."

G3JQQ notes that the ddrr can be considered as basically a

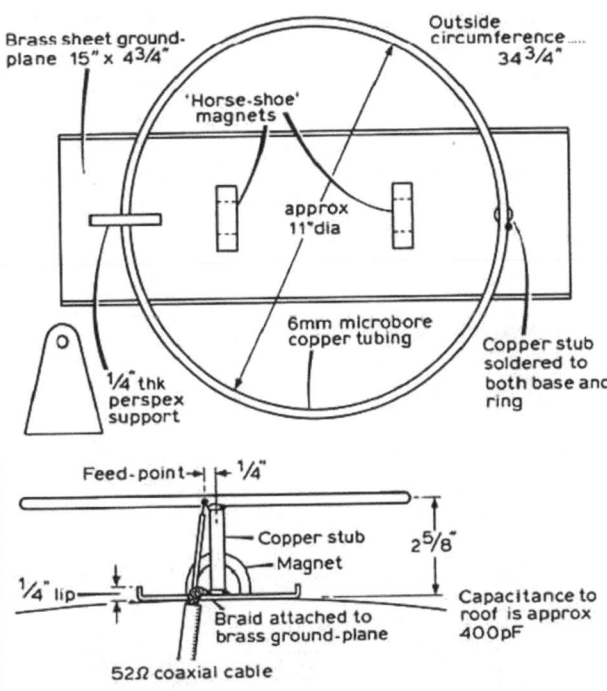

Fig 1. 144MHz λ/2 "hula hoop" ddrr mobile antenna as used by G3JQQ

"tortuous derivation of the well-known principle of the slot antenna" (this is supported, to some extent, by W6UYH's original description of the system as a "leaky waveguide radiator"). Although the "hoop" is horizontal, the signals are of course vertically polarized. It is interesting to recall that the original tests of the λ/4 ddrr included its use as a 28MHz mobile antenna making good use of the "ground plane" provided by the roof of the vehicle.

The All-band Dipole

Extracted from 'Technical Topics',
Radio Communication, June/July 1980*

The all-band dipole

A familiar, though frequently disregarded, theme emerges in a letter from Bill Stocking, W0VM, in the April *QST*: "I often wonder", he writes, "why most antennas described in books and articles use coaxial cable feeders when tuned feeders of parallel-conductor line work so much better. They permit the use of an antenna system on several bands, with the added benefit of gain (reference to a λ/2 dipole) on the higher-frequency bands. . . . Since low swr has become somewhat of a fetish among amateurs, many of them are using coaxial-to-coaxial antenna tuners to reduce the swr 'seen' by the transmitter. They do not seem to mind the extra knob required. If they used balanced open-wire twin feeders they could enjoy the ad-

ANTENNA TOPICS

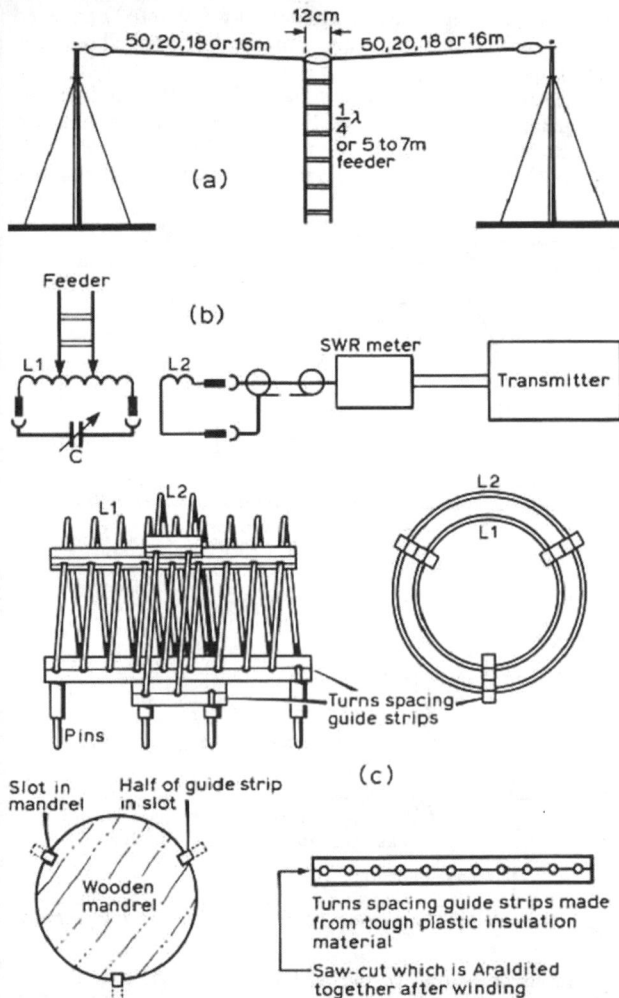

Fig 2. (a) The "Levy" centre-fed dipole antenna with resonant feeders; (b) how the antenna is connected to the unbalanced output of the transmitter; and (c) F8OP's suggested method of making self-supporting plug-in coils for the antenna tuning unit. Typically C is a 150 or 200pF(maximum) high-voltage tuning capacitor. L1 35t spaced 8mm, 8cm diameter for 3·5MHz; 14t similar for 7MHz; 7t spaced 10mm, 5cm diameter for 14MHz; 5t spaced 20mm, 4cm diameter for 21MHz; 3t spaced 30mm, 3cm diameter for 28MHz. L2 consists of 2t wound outside of L1 for 3·5/7/14MHz; 1t for 21/28MHz. Use suitable wire gauges, typically 2mm for 3·5/7MHz; 3mm for 21MHz; and 4mm for 28MHz Feeder tapping will depend on the impedance presented by the feeder and should be adjusted for unity swr (3·5MHz typically start with 4t and then increase gradually, adjusting C)

A printers' strike led to the June 1980 edition of Radio Communication being combined with July's.

full width of 3·5MHz, as well as on all bands;
(6) minimum disturbance to nearby television receivers, since the whole system (antenna, feeder, atu and transmitter) can be brought into perfect tune—a factor that is often overlooked by those who claim that open-wire feeders are not "screened" like coaxial cable, forgetting the currents that often flow back down the braid.

The length of the "top" radiating element is preferably $\lambda/2$ (or longer) on the lowest frequency band (although this is not essential) and again preferably with $\lambda/2$ resonant feeders on this band. Examples suggested by F8OP included 2 by 20m "top" with 2 by 20m parellel wire feeder; 2 by 18·5m "top" and 2 by 21·5m feed; or 2 by 16m "top" with 2 by 24m feed; although, with a suitable atu, virtually any lengths are reasonably effective, including shorter feeders of 5 to 7m. Fig 2 shows F8OP's suggestions, including an atu using plug-in coils. Most of his suggestions (except the inclusion of an swr meter) could have come straight out of almost any 'thirties handbook, but by no means the worse for that!

For those wondering how to make low-cost open-wire feeders, it may be worth recalling a tip given by Roger Wheeler, G3MGW, in *TT* November 1977: "Plastic plant labels can be drilled and make good spreaders for open-wire feeders, being low-loss and weather resistant".

vantages of a truly efficient multi-band antenna system. A coaxial-to-coaxial antenna tuner can easily be adapted for use with balanced feeders by adding a 4:1 balun. . . ."

As though "on cue" F8OP in *Radio-REF* (No 2, 1980) provides a full treatment of "L'antenne Levy", a design familiar to those with long memories as the "centre-fed dipole", "centre-fed zepp" or "centre-fed doublet". F8OP's enthusiasm for this system is based on his use of it over a period of some 20 years. He lists as useful advantages:
(1) the ability to work effectively on five bands, presenting (to the transmitter) an swr of 1:1 on each (an ability that will also extend to 10, 18 and 24MHz in due course);
(2) the ability to adapt the length to individual circumstances;
(3) the ability to radiate well even in an under-roof space (or inverted-V configuration), though of course height-gain is always useful;
(4) there should be only about 2 or 3 per cent of the power lost in the transmission line etc compared with possibly 20 to 30 per cent in typical coaxial cable systems;
(5) the ability to present unity swr to the transmitter over the

Switched Phased Verticals

Extracted from 'Technical Topics', *Radio Communication,* June/July 1980*

Switched phased verticals

E. J. Wellman, G2HJT, notes that it has been some time since there has been any mention in *TT* of the attractions of the use of phased verticals to provide hf directional arrays. He feels that for people in sites where it may be difficult to install rotary beams, this approach "seems the next best thing—the elements take up little room and are not overprominent". He has been using the system for two years and is well satisfied with its performance, even in dx pile-ups.

Recently, on behalf of VP8PP, he has put together the notes summarized below, although he points out that, apart from the phase-switching, it is all basically as per the *ARRL Antenna Handbook*. The usual warning needs to be given of the vital importance with any system based on monopoles that the best possible earthing system should be used (earthing mats, buried radials, or radials laid on the ground). The radiating elements can be made from aluminium or copper tubing, or heavy gauge wire taped to poles.

The basic configuration is shown in Fig 3(a) with dimensions for 14MHz. The array can be fed either at point "X" or "Y" depending on the required line of fire (including the possibility of manual changeover if two connectors are fitted with all inners and outers joined). The physical length of the electrical $\lambda/4$ phasing sections will depend on the velocity factor of the cable, and it will be advisable to check (eg with gdo). At the feedpoint(s) coaxial Tee-junctions or wire equivalents can be used.

Low-profile 1.8 and 3.5MHz Antennas

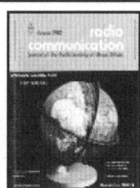

Extracted from 'Technical Topics', *Radio Communication,* August 1980

Low-profile 1·8 and 3·5MHz antennas

For extended ground-wave coverage and for low-angle dx operation on 1·8 and 3·5MHz it is desirable to transmit vertically-polarized signals; however, since a λ/4 monopole on 1·8MHz requires a mast some 130ft (40m) high, most amateurs need to adopt some form of loading to bring the height down to manageable dimensions. The extreme would be a ddrr "hula hoop" which would need a height of only about 1·5m (but would require a large "low-resistance" ring and a very good earth plane); more practical alternatives include various forms of "umbrella", "Nord" and "UG" top-loaded antennas. While these have appeared in various anthologies etc, they have received comparatively little attention from amateurs.

The Marconi "folded-umbrella" antenna was noted in *TT*

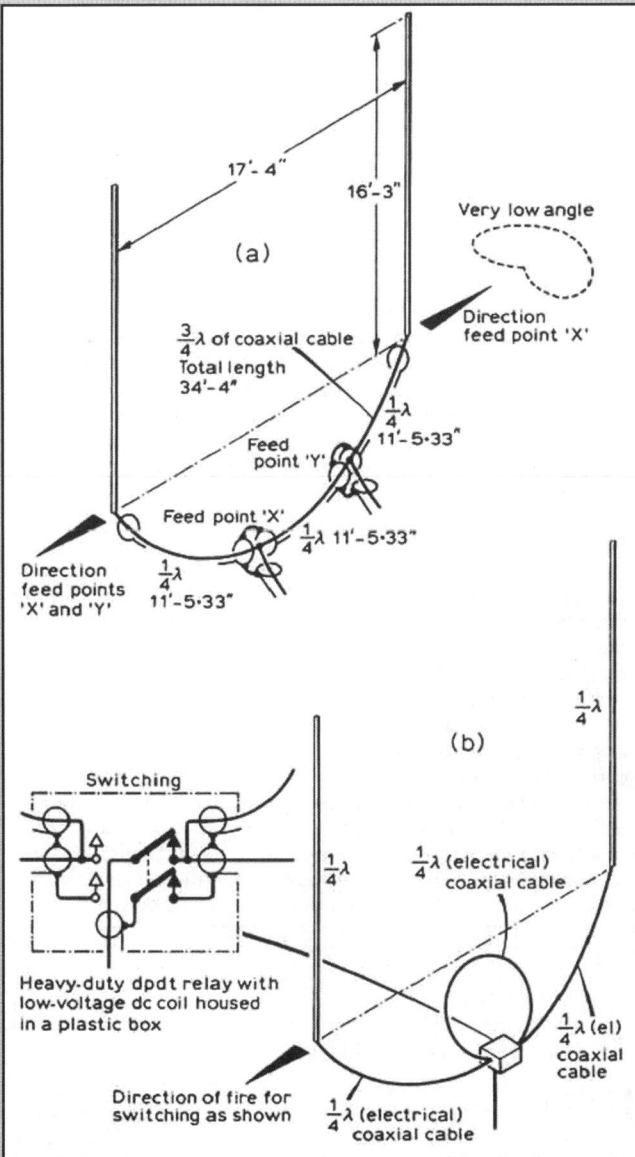

Fig 3(a). Reversible phased vertical array for 14MHz with manual change of direction; (b) System for switched reversal of beam direction

Approximate dimensions are:

Band	Verticals	Radials	Spacing	λ/4 sections (elec)
14MHz	16ft 3in	16ft 6in	17ft 4in	11ft 5·3in
21MHz	11ft 0in	11ft 4in	11ft 6in	7ft 7·3in
28MHz	8ft 2in	8ft 4in	8ft 6in	5ft 8·5in

G2HJT writes: "Switching to reverse the firing direction can be easily arranged in either of two ways. One is a dpdt relay in a weatherproof box between the verticals, controlled by a cable tape to the main feeder. The second is to use two exactly equal lengths of feeder to each vertical plus a λ/4 section of feeder situated near the transmitter that can be arranged to make either feeder λ/4 longer, so providing the necessary phase difference. With no 'turning lag' of the conventional beam, one can switch immediately between 'short' and 'long' paths, often with beneficial effects".

Another way of beam-switching is shown in Fig 3(b) with the extra phasing section coiled and secured to the weatherproof box, but it is regarded as essential in this case to replace the relay with medium-duty dpdt switch, contactor or relay. At G2HJT the relay switch is wall-mounted in a small metal box with amber indicator lights showing direction of fire. In his case he finds his "long path" position to be the most used, since it takes in VK, ZL, ZS, PY, VP8, Central America, Middle East and the long path to JA, VS6 etc.

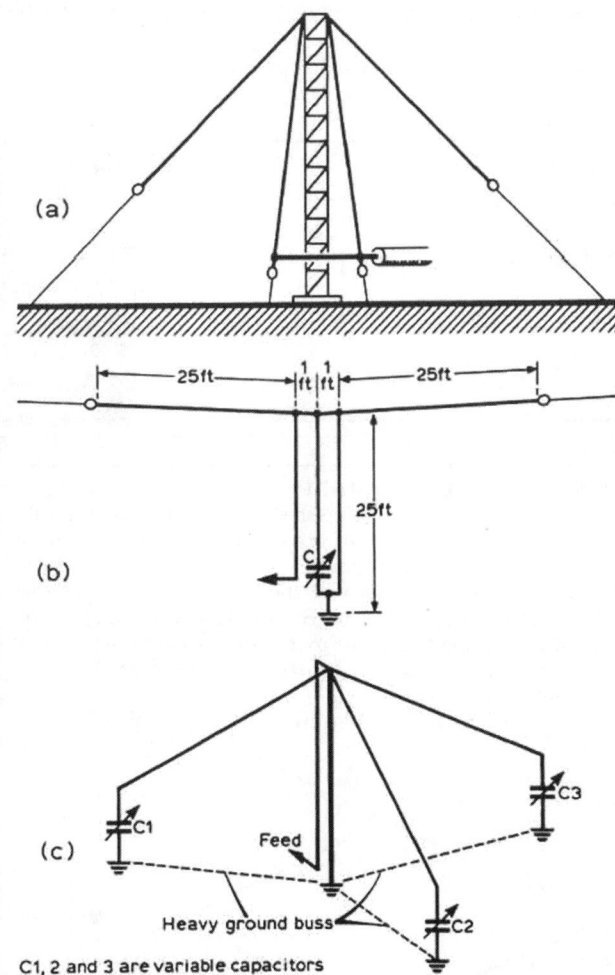

Fig 5. Low-profile short vertical antennas. (a) "Folded umbrella" antenna as developed by The Marconi Company can provide a resistive match directly to low-impedance coaxial cable with a grounded λ/10 mast. The folding "element" consists of a cage of wires running parallel to the mast with the wires connected together near its base; matching can then be adjusted by altering number and spacing of wires forming this cage. Top loading consists of a number of sloping "guy wires" with the whole system resonated to the transmission frequency. (b) "UG" antenna showing typical dimensions for 2MHz. (c) Nord antenna. For all short vertical antennas a good earthing system is essential. Bandwidth will be narrow so systems should be resonated to the required "dx" frequency in the 1·8 or 3·5MHz bands

ANTENNA TOPICS

July 1974, pp445-6, and is shown again in Fig 5 (a). The technique permits mast radiators of down to λ/10 to be fed directly from low-impedance coaxial feeder, with a resistive feed achieved by making the inductance of the mast and cage of "guy wire" loading wires tune to the transmission frequency. The same top-loading technique can be used without "folding" the radiator, in which case the base impedance is about 15Ω resistive.

A number of folded umbrella mf antennas are being installed by the IBA for the current extension of independent local radio services, and the first of these came into use at Cardiff last April. The station operates on 1,359kHz (221m) with a mast height of only 22m (72ft). This would be equivalent to under 50ft on 1·8MHz and 25ft on 3·5MHz.

The "UG" and "Nord" antennas were included in a comprehensive survey of vertically-polarized antennas in a series of articles in *CQ* in 1968 and again, recently, in *rf design* March 1980, pp16, 19.

The UG antenna is a variation of the well-known T top-loaded antenna, and the dimensions shown in Fig 5 (b) are for 2MHz operation. The only information given on matching is that "capacitor C is varied until a favourable feedpoint impedance is developed". Information on the Nord antenna is even more sparse, the recent article stating only that: "The Nord is a short vertical antenna used at lf and mf. It has a sufficiently high bandwidth and radiation efficiency for its intended use. It is basically three over-coupled tuned circuits. A centre tower is used as a common element."

cantly more than 20dB (ref dipole), ie a power gain of well over 100 times and very low transmission-line losses. Very few Yagi-type antennas can provide a gain of more than about 13dB on 144MHz and about 16dB on 432MHz. My reply, I seem to recall, was that a rhombic fixed array, with open-wire (cut-out 300Ω line) feeders, was by no means impossible on 144MHz or 432MHz, and should be capable of bringing erp at least close to the 100kW figure, even without one of those special 1kW permits that are (sometimes) issued for moonbounce and similar experiments. But I do not think either side truly convinced the other!

Since then I have noticed a Russian design for a *rotary* uhf rhombic for tv reception, though the size was probably not sufficient to provide very high gain (one British tv antenna firm claims a 21dB gain on Band 5 for one of the Continental-type complex Yagi structures). And recently, among the antennas in the series of *r.f. design* articles referred to in *TT* (August 1980), there was included the nested-rhombic design shown in Fig 6. It is claimed that this design, essentially a pair of staggered coplanar rhombics with a common feedpoint, has a gain on 144MHz of 27dB (ref dipole) or, in other words, a power gain of 500 times! The design is stated to be broadband, to have low vertical angle radiation, and with lower sidelobes than a conventional rhombic. Unfortunately very little practical information is given other than that it is fed by 300Ω balanced line, is mounted "12·29ft" above ground, and has vertical and horizontal beamwidths of 5·5° and 8·5° respectively. Although the articles include an extensive list of references, the original source of this particular design is not obvious; and the curious height dimension of "12·29ft" looks like a literal conversion from a metric dimension of 3·7m, since I cannot believe that the height is critical, certainly not to one hundredth of a foot! I seem to recall that an Australian amateur did a lot of experimental work on 144MHz moonbounce using rhombics, and this may have been the source of this design.

144MHz Nested Rhombic

Extracted from 'Technical Topics',
Radio Communication, September 1980

The HB9 Multiband Delta Loop

Extracted from 'Technical Topics',
Radio Communication, September 1980

144MHz nested rhombic
Several years ago I got into something of an argument with some of our leading vhf/uhf exponents by suggesting in print that effective radiated powers approaching 100kW were becoming feasible for amateur stations even when operating fully within the terms of the British licence. The opposition claimed that a limit of a little over 10kW, as then being achieved by a number of British amateurs, was an altogether more realistic figure.

To reach 100kW would involve an antenna gain of signifi-

The HB9 multiband delta loop
An easily-built delta loop antenna of modest dimensions which puts maximum current along the highest span, requires no tuning or switching for operation on any of the existing bands from 7 to 28MHz, and which has no traps or stubs etc, clearly adds up to an attractive proposition. All these features appear to be offered by a design by Willi Richartz, HB9ADQ, which has been published in *cq-DL* and also in the Swiss *Old Man* No 5, 1980: Fig 4. In effect the wire delta loop comprises an 8m top, with two sloping 6m sides (ie 20m perimeter) and is fed from a 10·5 to 11·5m length of 600Ω open-wire feeder that presents a compromise 200Ω impedance to a 1:4 balun transformer into 50Ω coaxial feeder, with a 20pF capacitor formed from twin-feeder to compensate for the inductive component on some bands. Constructional details of the broadband, air-cored balun are given in the German text: it appears to consist of two lengths of 7·5m of twin-feeder wound to form bifilar coils on two 30cm pvc formers with a diameter of 6cm held together with plastic strips.

For those who may not be keen on this type of balun, it should prove possible to feed the open-wire line directly from any suitable atu that provides balanced output of between about 100Ω and 600Ω. An arrangement which I have used successfully for conventional folded-dipoles with 300Ω feeder

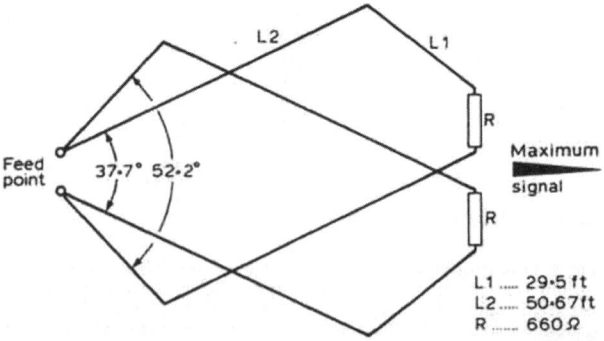

Fig 6. 144MHz nested rhombic antenna briefly noted in *r.f. design* and claimed to be capable of 27dB (ref dipole) gain. For transmission the non-inductive resistors must together be capable of dissipating about one third of the total output power (appreciably less for ssb and other low duty-cycle modes). A form of non-inductive resistor sometimes used for rhombics consists of a length of "lossy" 600Ω feeder (resistance wire) terminated by a low-wattage 600Ω resistor

is shown in Fig 5, and this will also reduce harmonic output etc, particularly if the coupling coil is made in the form of the coaxial-type Faraday screen.

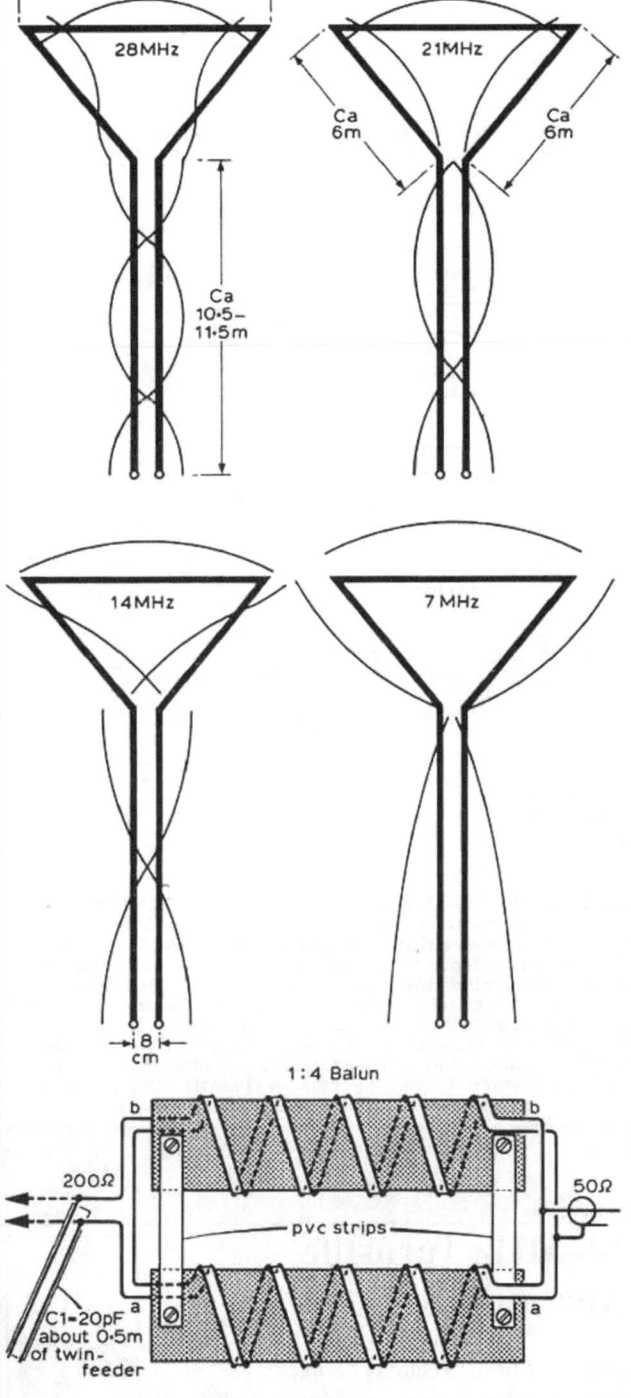

Fig 4. The HB9 multiband delta loop antenna for 7 to 28MHz operation, showing current distribution and suitable balun transformer

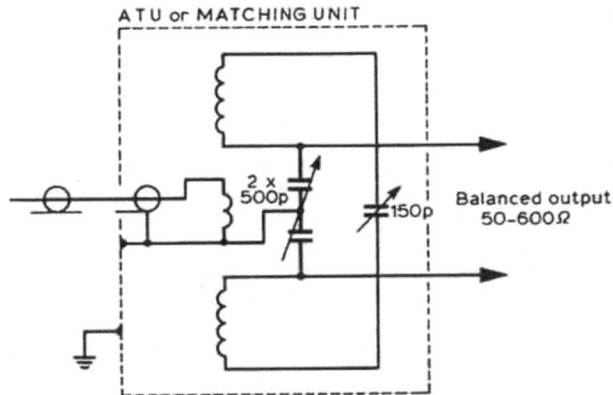

Fig 5. A pi-type atu providing balanced output suitable for the HB9 loop antenna in place of the wideband balun. Ganged-capacitor setting determines output impedance as in conventional unbalanced pi-network

DX and the Simple Antenna

Extracted from 'Technical Topics', *Radio Communication,* September 1980

DX and the simple antenna

In *TT* September 1979, pp831–2, it was noted that the long path between the UK and Australia remains extremely reliable throughout the sunspot cycle and, because it is mainly a "darkness" route, almost independent of the day-to-day variations in hf propagation conditions. Further, it was suggested that the chordal hop signals involved can be launched satisfactorily at such (morning) times even from antennas providing a *high angle of radiation*.

I was reminded of these comments by receiving a most interesting letter from Ron Fisher, VK3OM, a regular contributor to *Amateur Radio,* who writes:

"Over the past three years or so, I have worked nearly 500 different British stations on 14MHz ssb. About a year ago I got the idea that some data on the antennas used by these stations might prove interesting, and I began noting in my check list the type being used. Below are the results summarized from the 147 new stations contacted since then, divided into eight general types:

Antenna type	Total No	Percentage
Dipoles (incl G5RV, trap dipoles, Zepps and five indoor dipoles)	55	37·5
Ground planes and trap verticals	32	21·7
Three-el or larger tri-band beams (only two larger)	30	20·4
Two-el tribanders (incl five minibeams)	10	6·8
Wire beams (mostly two-el incl delta loops and one VK2ABQ)	6	4·1
Monoband beams (three and four-el)	5	3·4
Quads (Four two-el, one three-el)	5	3·4
Mobile whips	4	2·7

"Apart from a few skeds kept with regular stations, my contacts with British stations are quite at random, but all on long path. It is interesting to observe that some of the more consistent stations use dipoles; these are not necessarily the strongest signals, but often the difference between them and the strongest G signals heard at the same time is small, perhaps 1 to 1½S-points. The indoor dipoles were usually S5–6, but a couple managed S7. All my contacts are of reasonable length as I like to find out something about the fellow to whom I am speaking.

ANTENNA TOPICS

My own equipment is a TS820S transceiver with FL-2100 linear and three-element monoband beam at about 50ft with a good location for the long path to the UK."

These results thus provide further confirmation of the view that on long-path chordal hop transmissions the angle of radiation is not of prime importance; in such conditions the benefits of a beam array tend to be limited to the forward power gain, which is seldom, in practice, more than about 4-5·5dB. The fact that some 60 per cent of VK3OM's ssb contacts were with British stations using simple antennas, including indoor dipoles and mobile whips, should encourage more amateurs to feel that a beam array is not an absolutely indispensable adjunct to a modern hf station!

More on Low-profile Vertical Antennas

Extracted from 'Technical Topics', *Radio Communication,* November 1980

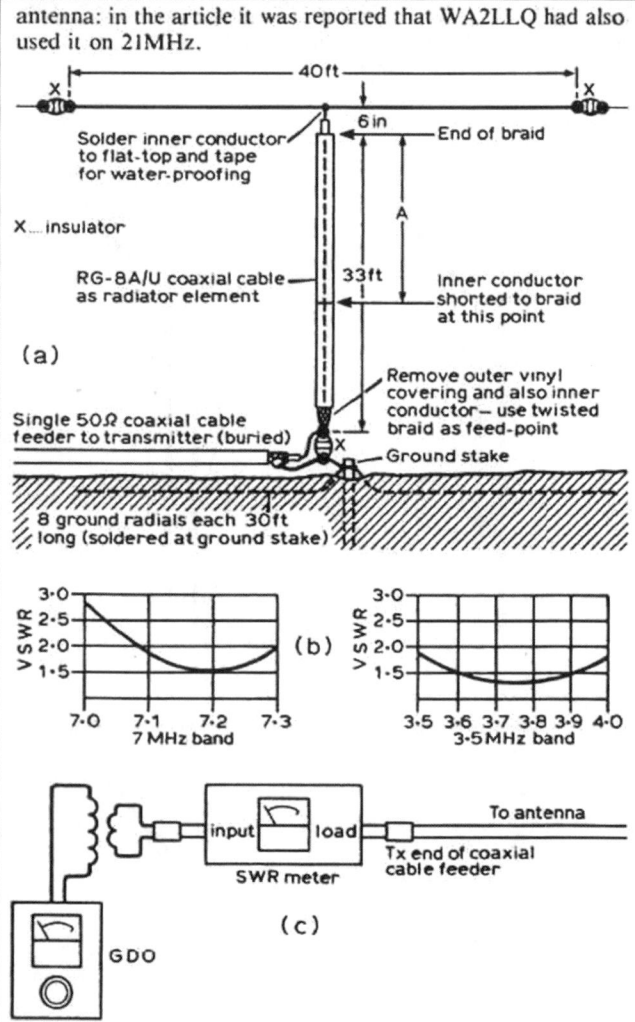

Fig 3. The 1961 "Ver-Tee" antenna suitable for 3·5 and 7MHz with a vertical height of 33ft. It could be used also on 21MHz. Dimension "A" is an electrical quarter-wave at the median operating frequency and depends on velocity factor of the cable (162/MHz gives approximate length in feet for cable indicated which is a solid-dielectric coaxial cable). W2JTJ found optimum lengths to be 23ft 2in for 7·1MHz and 22ft 10in for 7·2MHz. Note that his lengths were intended for the wider American 7 and 3·5MHz bands. (c) shows the method of adjusting lengths of "A" on 7MHz and the flat-top loading section on 3·5MHz. Output from a transmitter could be substituted for the gdo

More on low-profile vertical antennas

Brief notes on three low-profile top-loaded antennas ("Umbrella", "Nord" and "UG") suitable for 1·8MHz and 3·5MHz were given in the August *TT*. Although only about λ/10 high, these can be adjusted to provide a resistive match to coaxial cable over a fairly narrow bandwidth; and this type of approach is described in some detail in the book *Vertical antennas* based on articles which appeared in *CQ* some years ago.

John A. Crux, G3JAG, mentions that the Nord antenna was originally patented in 1968 (US patent 3,386,098) by John H. Mullaney on behalf of Multronics as "an electrically short tower antenna with controlled base impedance" capable of providing vertically polarized signals with mast heights equivalent to 5-20°. G3JAG notes that the umbrella information given in the *CQ* publication is sufficient to enable a satisfactory antenna to be built. He built one for 3·5MHz and "it was excellent". He points out that it is possible to make such an antenna work on 1·8MHz without *any* loading coils. "The bandwidth is narrow, but the efficiency is extremely high."

Charles Moizeau, ex-WB2URU, now living in France, was also interested in these low-profile designs. He draws attention to a "Vertee" design, intended for 3·5 and 7MHz, which was described by Pete Czerwinski, W2JTJ, in *QST* (December 1961, pp18-19): Fig 3. On 3·5MHz this works as a "T" with 40ft single-wire top loading (but WB2URU sees no reason why other forms of capacitive loading should not be used). On 7MHz this top loading is automatically "disconnected" from the vertical radiator, consisting of a length of coaxial cable, as a result of the shorted λ/4 transformer formed by the inner surface of the braid and the inner conductor: length "A" forming an electrical λ/4 dependent on the velocity factor of the cable (resonated by short-circuiting inner to outer by means of a needle). Thus on 7MHz the antenna works as a conventional monopole. On 3·5MHz "A" acts as a series inductance, reducing the amount of top loading to 40ft. On both bands the base impedance is resistive, and roughly about 30-35Ω, thus providing a reasonable match for 50Ω coaxial cable. Fine adjustments for optimum vswr on 3·5MHz can be made by pruning the flat-top loading without affecting 7MHz operation. Similarly, fine adjustments on 7MHz need not materially affect 3·5MHz operation. For the decoupling stub, once the optimum distance "A" has been established using a needle, it is possible to make a more permanent connection if required. Fig 3(c) shows the arrangement used by W2JTJ for adjusting the antenna: in the article it was reported that WA2LLQ had also used it on 21MHz.

144MHz Turnstile Antenna

Extracted from 'Technical Topics', *Radio Communication,* November 1980

144MHz tiltable turnstile antenna

Dave Gordon-Smith, G3UUR, points out that the simple reactive dipole technique for producing elliptically polarized signals (*TT* September 1980) extends back well before the 1979 *Radio* article. It is mentioned in the classic work by Kraus (*Antennas*, p427) who in turn credits G. H. Brown and J. Epstein of RCA (*Electronics* 18, June 1945). G3UUR used this idea in a 144MHz tiltable turnstile some years ago; this produced omnidirectional coverage in both horizontal and vertical modes which could be selected by pulling a rope. In the vertical mode

1980 - 1989

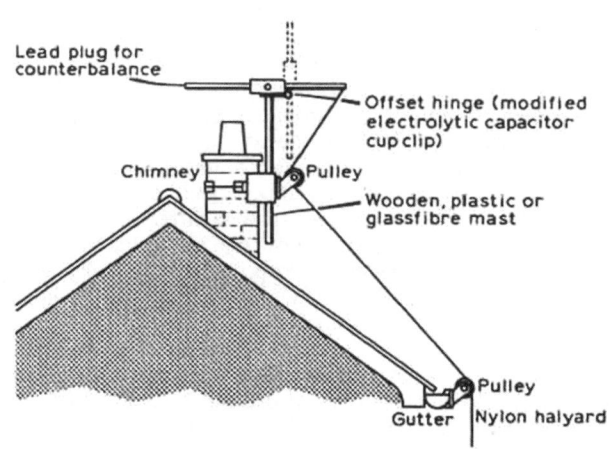

Fig 4. G3UUR's 144MHz omnidirectional "tiltable turnstile" providing horizontally-polarized signals when in the horizontal position, and elliptically-polarized signals (in some directions) when pulled into the vertical position

it provided some elliptical and some vertical-only polarization depending upon direction. At the time, G3UUR was concerned more with the ability to work both fm and ssb, mobile and fixed stations, rather than on securing the now-recognized advantages of circular polarization. He writes:

"The technique is a bit of a compromise since the resistance of the feed impedance changes as the length of the dipole is varied. Below the resonant length the feed impedance has a resistive portion nearer 50Ω and above it 80Ω. The actual lengths I ended up using were 34·7in and 41in. The power sharing is better than 0·5dB, and the phase greater than 80°. The feed impedance is near 50Ω if the residual capacitive reactance is cancelled with a 0·25µH coil (six turns of 20swg, 0·5in long and 0·375in id). This I think is the best compromise that can be obtained without special techniques to keep the radiation resistance constant at 65–70Ω. The coil also provides a dc short-circuit to guard against static."

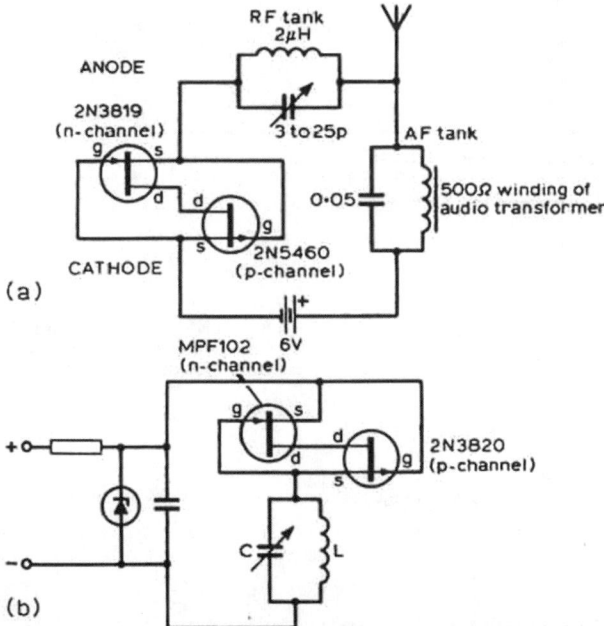

Fig 5. Negative resistance oscillator using n-channel and p-channel fets ("lambda diode oscillator"). (a) The *Electronics* signal source design; (b) G3MYM's 14MHz direct-conversion oscillator

The Flexible Dipole

Extracted from 'Technical Topics', *Radio Communication,* November 1980

The flexible dipole

The description of F8OP's classic centre-fed dipole (or "centre-fed zepp") in *TT* (June/July, p637) has brought several comments from other devotees of this flexible approach. For example, Stan Cook, G5XB, writes:

"I have been using this method of feed in various forms for close on 50 years and often wonder why other types of multi-band antennas are used. I have come to realize that the best rule is to make this form of antenna fit the space available, while avoiding, if possible, total λ/2 resonance. Even this resonance is not too troublesome if the so-called 'Z-match atu' is used in place of the more conventional tapped coil and series/parallel capacitor. At the heights normally used by amateurs, say 30 to 40ft, such an antenna on the lower bands

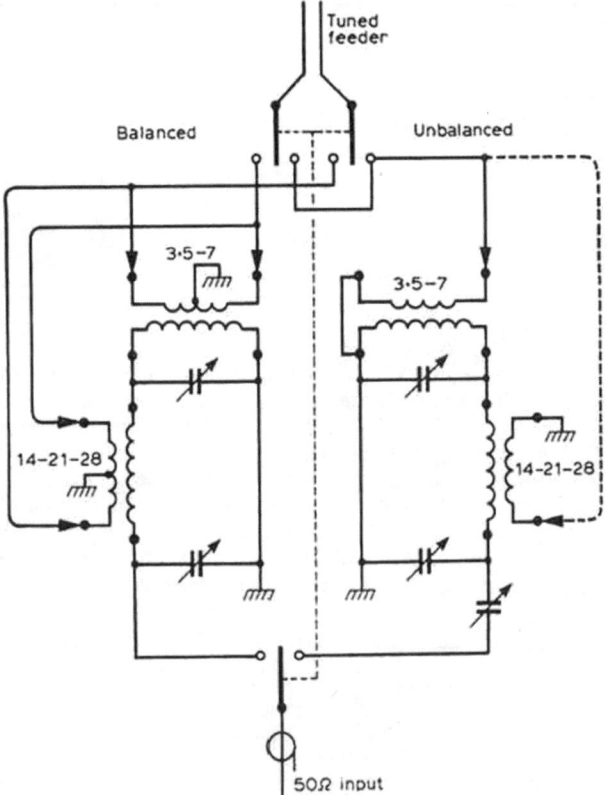

Fig 7. Antenna tuning arrangement used by G5XB with centre-fed multiband dipole to provide vertical or horizontal polarization

tends to be omni-directional, particularly for high-angle radiation, and only directional with lobes nearly in line with the wire; ie similar to the properties of a 'long wire'. There appears to be considerable advantage in symmetry, that is to say, the top should be as nearly level as possible, with the feeder vertical.

"It is not always realized that this type of antenna has a useful 'spin-off' in that it easily converts to a top-loaded vertical by strapping the feeders and exciting it against earth. The antenna then becomes a useful low-angle vertical radiator, being in effect a scaled-down version of the commonly-used broadcast-type 'T' antenna. In this condition it produces a high-intensity ground-wave beneficial to local working on 1·8 and 3·5MHz in addition to its low-angle dx-raising properties.

ANTENNA TOPICS

A 'T' antenna produces very little high-angle radiation, the discrimination being often in excess of 40dB at critical distances. The system in use at G5XB for the past 20 years has a 168ft 'top', is nearly 50ft high with 40ft of 3·5in-spaced open-wire feeder that requires only six spreaders. Two separate Z-match types of atu are used for quick switching between horizontal and vertical polarization, often with impressive results."

G5XB mentions that last June it was possible with this antenna to maintain communication with F0EWZ/G2HOP in the south of France during daylight on 3,677kHz at times when no other G signals were audible in that area (F0EWZ was using a loaded λ/4 vertical). Notable benefits also accrue for morning dx on 7MHz when the vertical polarization takes the sting out of the powerful and "over-driven" local stations which, G5XB claims, "inhabit the band mid-morning".

G5XB emphasizes that the advantages of this form of switched polarization feed can be achieved with a conventional feed arrangement if the coupling coil is screened, or electrically balanced to earth, to prevent capacitance coupling. An earthed centre tap on the coupling coil is usually sufficient, in lieu of a Faraday screen which can be rather cumbersome to accommodate. Fig 7 shows the arrangement used at G5XB.

Tony Preedy, G3LNP, has a 41m top centre-fed dipole and this does tend to have, as might be expected, negligible broadside radiation on 28MHz. He overcomes this problem by using a pair of high-voltage sealed relays to shorten the dipole span into the length required to form a double extended Zepp on this band. Normally the relays are closed, providing the traditionally good performance on all bands; however, when broadside radiation is required the relays are energized and an improvement of up to 10dB is achieved in some directions.

G3LNP points out that in situations where the antenna is easily raised and lowered it is quite possible to use links instead of relays for this purpose. I remember that at one time home-made mercury switches, opened by pulling a cord, were sometimes used to alter the length of antennas.

To power his relays G3LNP uses 600Ω feeder made of miniature coaxial cable. This also means that the feeder requires less tension than thin solid wire of the same effective diameter, and fewer spacers to keep it in shape.

The 44ft section of the dipole is made of twin flex, and the dc for the relays is introduced at the balun by means of 1mH rf chokes; 10nF capacitors ensure that only the relay voltage appears on the inner core of the miniature coaxial cable.

The Switched Dipole

Extracted from 'Technical Topics',
Radio Communication, November 1980

The switched dipole

As indicated by G5XB, a dipole at a height low in terms of wavelength has virtually an omni-directional radiation pattern (regardless of the advice frequently given to short-wave listeners to line up their dipoles carefully to be broadside on to the required stations on the 49, 41 and 31m broadcast bands!). But above about 14MHz the radiation pattern of an antenna at about 25ft or above does begin to resemble the text-book diagrams (though often still distorted by nearby objects, off-centre feeding, absence of balun transformer etc).

Loop Transmitting Antennas Again

Extracted from 'Technical Topics',
Radio Communication, December 1980

Loop transmitting antennas again

D. J. Reynolds, G3ZPF, has drawn attention to a low-profile transmitting loop antenna (Model 629) now being marketed by Technology for Communications International (TCI) and intended for professional communications, including embassy radio systems, at transmitter powers of up to 1kW.

However, the claims made on behalf of this antenna in some of the trade journals would appear to be misleading, since they

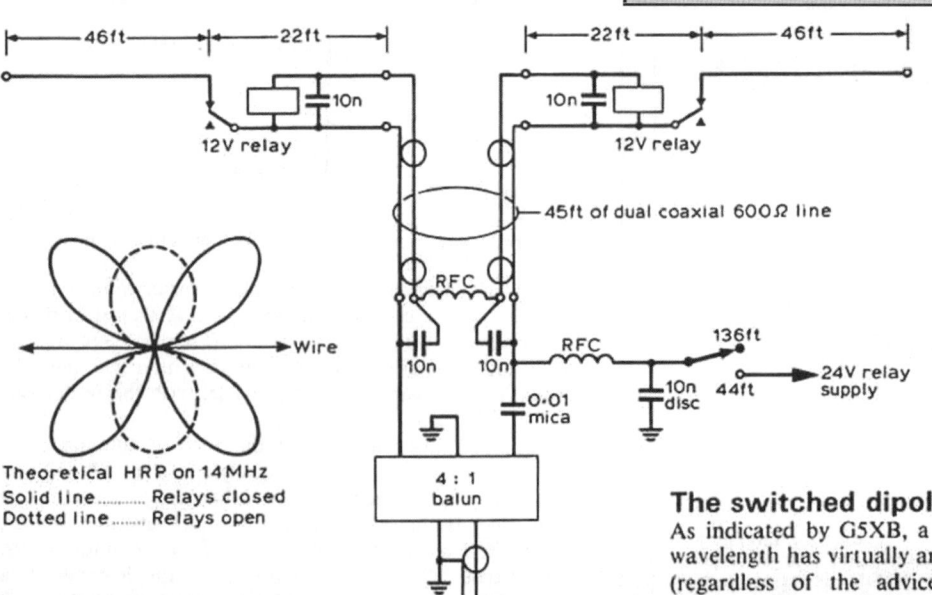

Fig 8. G3LNP's centre-fed dipole with relay switching in order to provide broadside radiation on 14MHz

The switched dipole

As indicated by G5XB, a dipole at a height low in terms of wavelength has virtually an omni-directional radiation pattern (regardless of the advice frequently given to short-wave listeners to line up their dipoles carefully to be broadside on to the required stations on the 49, 41 and 31m broadcast bands!).

suggest that compact loop antennas for hf transmission represent an entirely new development. Readers with long memories (or copies of *ART*) will recall the ingenious octahedral, low-resistance hf transmitter loops developed by the US Army for use in Vietnam jungles (*TT* November 1967 and *ART*) which sparked off quite a lot of amateur interest in this technique, including the use of coaxial cable braid to form the low-resistance loop as successfully developed by G6NA (*Radio Communication* September 1968).

From the illustrations, the TCI Model 629 appears to use large diameter (several inches) tubing formed into a squat "loop" only a few feet high with a microprocessor-controlled automatic tuning unit which appears to be housed in "bulges" on the main structure. It is claimed to be considerably more effective than vertical rod or whip antennas at low frequencies, and to provide more high-angle radiation for medium- and short-distance hf communication. The US State Department is said to have ordered a number of loops for embassies and consulates, and that low-profile loops are unlikely to attract attention from hostile political groups or environmentalists. I believe the British FCO favours vertical antennas made unobtrusive by concealing them in those dignified flag poles so beloved by the diplomatic community!

A detailed article on this antenna has appeared in *Communications International* (March 1980). TCI's data sheet reveals that the loop of copper tubing is some 70in (178cm) long by 39in (99cm) high, with a copper ground screen comprising eight 2·5 by 10ft sheets which form a rectangular ground screen 10 by 19ft (3 by 5·8m). Weight is about 550lb (250kg). Efficiency is claimed as five per cent at 3MHz; 21 per cent at 6MHz; 52 per cent at 10MHz; and 97 per cent at 18MHz, suggesting that such a loop would give useful results on all hf bands from 3·5MHz upwards.

The commercial unit, with its microprocessor atu etc, is presumably at a "professional" price, but for those with plenty of really hefty copper tubing and ground-plane sheets, such a transmitting loop would provide an unobtrusive, roof-top antenna: but be warned, the current price of copper is around £900/tonne!

Coplanar 144MHz Rhombic: Update

Extracted from 'Technical Topics',
Radio Communication, December 1980

Coplanar 144MHz rhombic
A number of useful comments have been received on the 144MHz coplanar rhombic (*TT* September) from Chris Bartram, G4DGU; Fred Brown, G5AWI/W6HPH; and "Pol" Parrott, G3HAL. The source was "Improved antennas of the rhombic class" by E. A. Laport and A. C. Veldhurs (*RCA Review* March 1960, pp117-25). But unfortunately although this paper *did* give a gain figure of 27dB it appears that the authors later agreed this had been wrongly calculated: in fact free-space gain is about 15dB, or (with 6dB earth gain) 21dB. This is about the same as for a conventional rhombic, although the sidelobes *are* considerably reduced; it is not enough gain for moonbounce. But there is still a lot to be said for vhf/uhf rhombics, and I hope to return to the subject later. The attraction of the rhombic is simplicity.

More on the Flexible All-band Dipole

Extracted from 'Technical Topics',
Radio Communication, December 1980

More on the flexible all-band dipole
Comments continue to arrive stressing the value of the flexible, multiband, centre-fed dipole (*TT* June/July, p637, and November, p1157). Ray Griese, K6FD, believes there are many features in this type of antenna that make it attractive for amateur operation, including both mechanical and electrical considerations, although some of these are seldom mentioned in print. He writes:

"Antennas of this type radiate best when the ends of the element are insulated with the usual glass or porcelain insulators *plus* nylon cord or rope to the supporting structure. It should be remembered that the glass insulators are dc insulators only, the capacitance effect between the high-voltage end of the antenna and a wire support is large enough effectively to couple the antenna into the supporting structure. A test for this is the null that should exist in the direction of the antenna but seldom does; the lack of a null is partly caused by ground reflection when the antenna is low in respect of wavelength but partly due to radiation from the supporting structures. To check this point, try erecting a self-supporting one-element rotary dipole; on the higher frequency bands the pattern becomes the familiar figure-of-8, and in a fairly clear location the nulls will be found to be deep and very sharp.

"It is desirable in many instances, however, to operate amateur stations with omni-directional antenna patterns. This can be done very simply and conveniently with this form of dipole, by bending in the form of a 'U', as originally noted by Dr G. H. Brown of RCA. An even simpler method is to support the antenna with three poles and to have the antennas separated by an angle of from 15-20° to 45-60°, forming what can be termed a "Lazy Vee" but providing virtually an omni-directional radiation pattern, depending on the circumstances. The departure from a true circular pattern should normally be only a few decibels at the most, representing one, or possibly two, S-points at the receiving end.

"The radiation is horizontally polarized, and maximum radiation, with low antenna height, will be straight up. However, this is very effective on 7 and 3·5MHz in daytime and early evening, although disappointing for dx during periods of low-angle signal propagation."

Polygonal Loop Antennas

Extracted from 'Technical Topics',
Radio Communication, February 1981

Polygonal loop antennas
Although the term "polygonal loop" may not immediately strike many amateurs as familiar, it is the generic term covering a number of popular and practical antennas of increasing importance to amateurs. These include, for example, the apex-fed or base-fed triangular ("delta") loops, either as single-element antennas or as part of arrays (a design first made familiar by H. R. Halig, K8ANV, in *QST* January 1969); it also includes the traditional square quad element and the various rectangular loops etc.

A recent paper by two Japanese engineers, Takehiko Tsukiji and Shigehumi Tou of Fukuoka University (*IEEE Trans on Ant & Prop*, Vol AP-28, No 4, July 1980, pp571-4) provides some new insight into the way

ANTENNA TOPICS

the basic characteristics of such loops depend on the shape of the loop. They show, for example, that some configurations are appreciably more broadband than others, a factor that can be useful to an amateur since it means that the adjustment becomes appreciably less critical. They also indicate that, for most polygon loops, the first resonance of a 1λ loop occurs when the perimeter is *greater* than the physical wavelength by 10 to 20 per cent, a factor that sometimes gets overlooked.

Of considerable interest is their conclusion that two particular configurations have unusually interesting and attractive properties. Both have

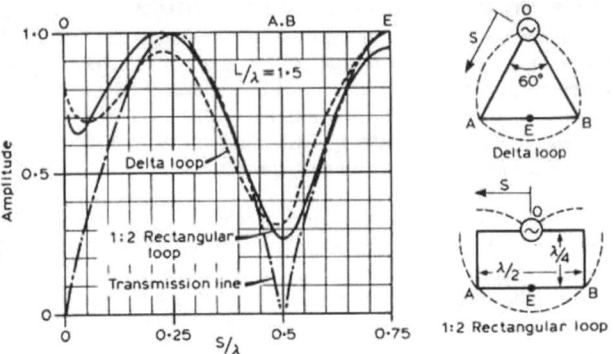

Fig 5. Current distribution of 1·5λ (voltage-fed) delta and rectangular loop antennas showing "fill-in" of voltage nulls that results from these being located at the corners and provides broadband characteristics

a total perimeter of 1·5λ and are operated in their "anti-resonance" mode (by which I take it to mean they are voltage rather than current fed, as for example when a 14MHz (1λ) loop is used at 21MHz, as can be done by using open-wire resonant feeders).

These are the top-driven delta loop with an apex angle of 60° and a rectangular loop in which the two vertical sides are λ/4 and the top and (centre-fed) lower elements are both λ/2: Fig 5. In both cases it is claimed that broadband characteristics result from having current nulls located at the corners of a loop, the sharp anti-resonance current distribution being damped by the presence of the corner. The authors state: "This is just like the travelling wave linear dipole antenna where its anti-resonance is damped by impedances loaded on the antenna element to realize broadband impedance characteristics."

They also indicate that delta loop antennas fed at the apex have rather different directivity characteristics to a similar loop fed at the centre of the base: Fig 6.

Another point is that a single loop 1λ element with an apex angle of about 40° provides a more accurate match to 50–70Ω coaxial cable than an equilateral loop with an apex angle of 60°.

'Trimming' Antennas

Extracted from 'Technical Topics',
Radio Communication, February 1981

"Trimming" antennas

Sometimes it is difficult for those of us who have been amateurs for longer than we care to remember to appreciate that newcomers often puzzle over those odd little bits of antenna lore that never seem to get into print. For example, in *Ham Radio Report* October 1980, one finds an American newcomer seeking advice on how to go about trimming a wire antenna. In other words should he cut the wire to the calculated length or should he add on an extra length for attaching the wire to the insulator?

The answer of course is that wire folded back on itself in close proximity to the element proper does *not* count as part of the resonant length: Fig 7. The usual procedure is to measure the correct length, making a kink in the wire to show where it should be bent round the insulator, and then leave initially not only enough wire to wrap round but also an extra amount in case it subsequently turns out that the antenna resonates at too high a frequency. In fact "trimming" the length of wire antennas need not involve any snipping off or (more difficult) adding on lengths of wire. Remember calculated lengths cannot be relied upon in all cases, since surrounding objects etc may lower the frequency of resonance, while "bends" in the element will raise it.

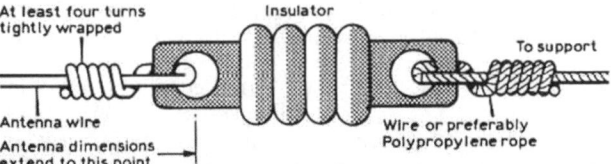

Fig 7. The resonant "length" of a wire antenna does *not* include the length of wire looped back through the insulator to form the wrap. This length can be dimensioned initially to provide a means of "trimming" the antenna to resonance without snipping the wire (*Ham Radio Horizons*)

It may also be worth remembering, particularly on the higher frequency bands, that a single insulator tends to look like a low-value capacitor to rf so that the "support wire" should either be broken up by further insulators or, preferably, consist of polypropylene rope—as recommended in the classic article by Michael Gale, G3JMG, "Ropes and rigging for amateurs—a professional approach" (*Rad Com* March 1970, pp144-52).

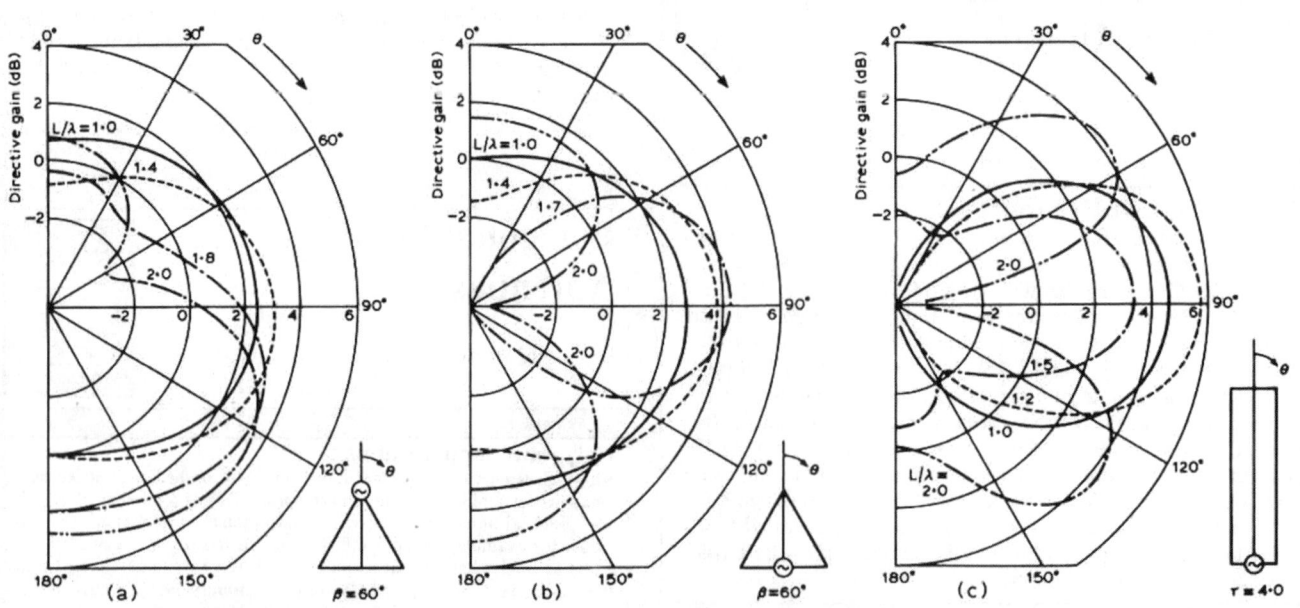

Fig 6. Radiation patterns of: (a) top-driven delta loops; (b) base-driven delta loops; and (c) rectangular loops for various ratios of perimeter length/wavelength (L/λ) (after Takehiko Tsukiji and Shigehumi Tou, *IEEE Trans on Ant & Prop*)

Vertical Polarization on HF

Extracted from 'Technical Topics', *Radio Communication,* March 1981

Vertical polarization on hf

HF directional arrays based on vertically-polarized dipole or monopole elements (see for example *TT* June/July 1980, pp637–8) are not as widely used as one might expect in view of the considerable attractions. These include the absence of any requirement for high (and costly) masts or tilt-over towers, etc; the unobtrusive way in which they can be fitted into an average garden or on a flat roof; the way in which, with the aid of phasing sections, they can be electronically "rotated" etc.

The analysis of British antennas by Ron Fisher, VK3OM (*TT* September 1980, p906) indicates that at present the use made of such arrays is minimal. On the other hand the single-element vertical monopole or ground-plane is much more popular than its performance really merits. What is it that puts so many people off the monopole array?

Several answers could be suggested. In the first place in an era of commercially manufactured beams nobody aggressively markets such a system. In the second place there is the important question of the earth system. Most of us have come to associate monopoles (particularly in arrays) with very extensive earth systems, influenced perhaps by the 120 radials used by mf broadcasters, involving much "buried treasure" in the form of copper, not to mention the sheer hard work of digging suitable trenches without the aid of a mole-plough. There are also questions relating to earth conductivity, which varies considerably and tends to be poor in urban areas. There is also the belief that the largest possible earth

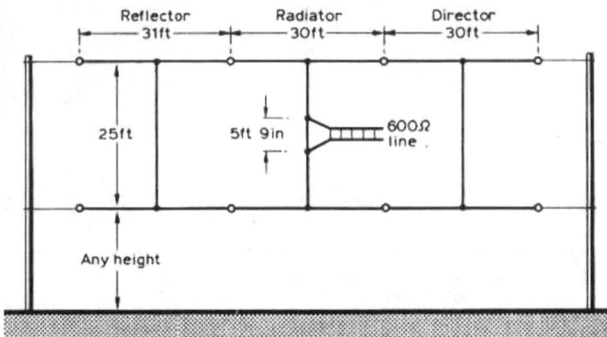

Fig 4. G6XN's 1970 design for vertically-polarized three-element fixed Yagi 7MHz array not requiring high poles. Reflector and director elements are tunable by adjusting the length of either vertical or lower horizontal end-loading wires

system is an absolute "must" if any attempt is to be made to shorten the height of a monopole by capacitive loading.

But what about the "old-fashioned" technique of using a counterpoise to turn an earthed Marconi antenna into a Hertz or resonant antenna? Buried away in old journals can be found plenty of evidence that the counterpoise can be an effective technique—and it can be applied just as easily to vertical monopoles as to λ/4 Marconi inverted-L antennas. In a 1970 article in *Wireless World* (see also many editions of *ART*), Les Moxon, G6XN, described a fixed 7MHz three-element beam based on top and bottom loading of each element: see Fig 4.

Recently, G6XN has again turned his powerful thoughts towards this subject, including the development of a new non-earthed monopole element that could be used either as a single-element vertical or more effectively for a vertically polarized array.

The Vertical Array

Extracted from 'Technical Topics', *Radio Communication,* March 1981

The vertical array

Last September, Les Moxon was struck particularly by the apparent complete absence from VK3OM's statistical table of any vertical beams. He promptly contacted VK3OM to verify that this was indeed the case; in the process using the vertically-polarized switched array outlined in *TT* April 1979, Fig 10, and so in fact adding a new category to VK3OM's list!

The original objective of G6XN's 1979 design was to provide a convenient all-round switched-beam system, and stemmed from his work in endeavouring to increase the gain of the UA3IAR switched-quad. This objective was achieved and the work showed the array had a useful dx capability. But G6XN found that the vertical array: (a) was not *quite* good enough to justify using it to replace his *high* horizontally-polarized beam arrays; and (b) it seemed to work just as well at ground level as when raised to the top of the mast. Item (b) struck G6XN as very important since it provided solid grounds for thinking that it *is* possible (on 14MHz and above) to put out a hefty dx signal without incurring the usual hassle of masts, towers, planning permissions *et al*. G6XN believes the results were not unduly influenced by his location, which he regards as "average" (though some might dispute that!).

These findings encouraged G6XN to investigate other vertical arrays. He has now achieved results comparable with those of his 1979 array using Yagi designs based on a simple, but ingenious, form of non-earthed monopole element. Further, he believes, though this has not yet been confirmed, that the λ/4 height of the element could be reduced on 14MHz by top loading, etc to about only 8ft (under 3m) or so.

Among the reasons for non-use of vertical arrays, G6XN points to the obsession of the *ARRL Antenna Book* and others (*mea culpa*) with elaborate systems of buried radials—often impossible for those unable to buy up the neighbouring properties or find the energy to dig hundreds of metres of trenches, and then afford the copper to fill them. The standard ground-plane, he feels, is too much of a compromise (although 3dB gain has been reported from two elements having a common ground-plane).

There are other, seldom mentioned, serious objections to the ground-plane in its usual form: the *ARRL Antenna Book* insists on λ/4 radials, yet, G6XN believes, this is the one length which should at all costs be avoided! The reason is that near resonance the impedance of each radial changes very rapidly with frequency; if there is a finite difference in lengths there will also be a finite range of frequencies over which one radial is *capacitive* and another *inductive*, ie a phase-reversal situation. This will tend to generate earth currents and large losses (though in turn the losses oppose the phase reversal). As G6XN puts it: "Precisely what happens is anybody's guess".

G6XN surmises that one way of getting around this would be by using a number of non-resonant radials connected in parallel and (with the monopole) brought to resonance by a common impedance. But this immediately invites further questions: To what extent can one shorten radials? Why not replace the monopole by a short end-loaded dipole of the type shown in Fig 4, as this is known to be an effective radiator? Or why not use an "earth connection" like that shown in Fig 5?

It can be argued that there is also the important question of radiation losses with vertical antennas caused by the circulating currents induced in a non-perfect earth; but if, for the moment, one ignores this, then the *only* loss in an arrangement such as Fig 5 is that due to the rf resistance of the coil. With a 6ft-or-so rod at 14MHz and linear loading this need be only a

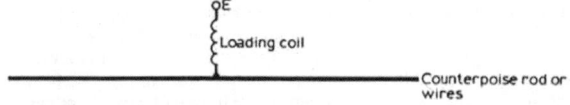

Fig 5. One form of counterpoise "earth connection" for use with vertical λ/4 monopole antennas. G6XN considers it as good as using buried radials—and much less work

small fraction of an ohm: G6XN is convinced that such an "earth" can be vastly more efficient than any conceivable arrangement of buried radials, yet allows the whole antenna to be readily moved.

But what about the induced ground losses? The literature yields little in the way of firm figures applicable to average sites, though there is some evidence to suggest that the contribution due to using such a counterpoise earth system rather than buried radials is negligible, provided that the horizontal rod (or wires) is more than a few millimetres above earth. Experiments with various counterpoise lengths at heights between 2 and 5ft have yielded *no* differences whatsoever.

ANTENNA TOPICS

A Basic No-radial Monopole Element

Extracted from 'Technical Topics', *Radio Communication,* March 1981

A basic no-radial monopole element

Fig 5 shows the final form of G6XN's monopole element, requiring no buried radials. Dimensions are not critical, except that, when used as a driven element, the feeder *must* be connected at a point of minimum rf voltage to ground, and it may be necessary to adjust the relative lengths of radiator and counterpoise to achieve this. G6XN emphasizes that vertical antennas near ground are inherently asymmetrical and that it is almost always difficult to ensure that no common-mode current flows on the outer screen of the coaxial feeder. This, he notes, may be one reason why dx signals from ground-plane antennas tend to be weaker than might reasonably be expected, and may also contribute to their "noisiness" when used for reception.

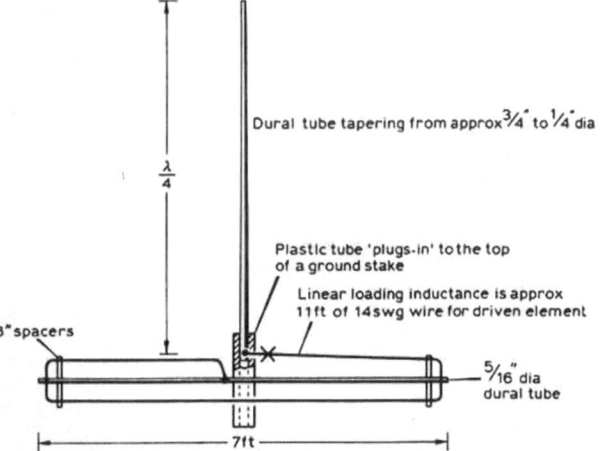

Fig 6. Final form of the G6XN 14MHz monopole element with counterpoise earth. Suitable for use in multi-element arrays or as a simple vertical. The driven element should be fed at point X using a 1:1 balun with coaxial feeder, but do not expect an swr of less than about two with 50Ω coaxial feeder unless additional impedance transformation is used

G6XN does not claim basic originality for the type of element shown in Fig 6. Military manuals often show pack sets working into a dipole in which one arm is run just above the ground; *TT* has included notes on using trap verticals by converting them into dipoles, and in particular VK3AM has been using a basically similar idea (often using small helices as counterpoises to short, loaded-verticals) in a successful project aimed at developing efficient antennas for use in confined spaces, including small boats.

Is the element shown in Fig 6 a monopole or a dipole? G6XN is convinced such a debate has little practical significance. He points out that of the three antennas in Fig 7, not only (a) but also (b) and (c) result (where the height is low) in "images" in the ground and so are, in effect equivalent to a dipole; above ground the vertical radiation patterns are all given by cosθ and so, in terms of performance, are *identical*. But (a) and (b) share the important practical advantage that the low-impedance point is accessible at ground level for adjustment, beam switching, multibanding etc—and the elements are normally self-supporting!

Also, as already noted, (b) avoids the IR ground losses of (a). It thus seems appropriate to refer to (b) as a monopole when it is close to earth. In fact (b) and (c) have the advantage of not being *tied* to ground level, with the possibility of the 3dB colinear gain when they are at an effective mean height of just over λ/4; in such circumstance it might be more appropriate to regard (b) as a dipole none the worse for being asymmetrical, although G6XN feels that in raising (b) well above ground it loses many of its practical advantages.

He has used the "low" monopole element of Fig 6 in an array that shows only the expected 2-3dB reduction on the results achieved with the 1979 type of vertical array, though very much simpler to implement. The difference could be removed by raising the elements, although if one has the space it is easier simply to put up a few extra (wide-spaced) elements as directors; and indeed this has been shown to work successfully in practice. The signals on the 14MHz path to Australia using three monopole elements have proved to be well up on those of other British stations using conventional ground-plane antennas. G6XN admits that an equivalent horizontally-polarized beam at a height of about 20ft would be marginally better, but points to the many practical and economic advantages of using monopole elements. These include portability, which allows the beam to be "swung" in any direction in about the same time as it takes to rotate a horizontal beam. Elements can be quickly taken down and stored away when not in use. G6XN uses short lengths of plastic pipe as base insulators, with sockets made from larger-diameter pipe which can be attached to wooden stakes in prepared positions.

There remains the disadvantage, when such a beam is erected near a house, of the considerable attenuation of signals "firing through" the building (a bungalow might not present much of an obstruction).

As with his 1979 modified-VK2ABQ antenna, G6XN finds it useful to increase the coupling between driven element and reflector (particularly important if only two elements are used). This can be done, as indicated in Fig 8, by increasing counterpoise lengths to about 10ft, assuming 8ft spacing between elements. Element currents should be equal when one element is driven. Note that, with two elements, the second *must* be tuned as a reflector (typical element resonances, when checking with a gdo, are 14MHz for reflector, 15MHz for directors).

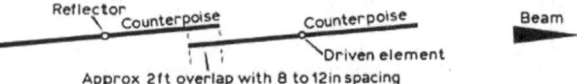

Fig 8. Arrangement used by G6XN to increase coupling between driven element and reflector (in plan view)

Some further recent work by G6XN will be reported later, but it is felt this detailed account of this novel monopole element will be of considerable interest to those seeking low-cost, easy-to-erect dx arrays, even though they should not be expected to outperform high horizontal beams. It would also seem to me that even the single-element form of this type of antenna would be well worthy of further investigation as an alternative to the usual vertical and ground-plane antennas.

Improved Active Antennas

Extracted from 'Technical Topics', *Radio Communication,* April 1981

Improved active antennas

The folding active loops of the novel C & S Antennas directional receiving array permit easy transportation. Intended for military and professional applications

1980 - 1989

Over a decade ago, I was fortunate enough to attend lectures at which Professor H. H. Meinke and Dr H. Lindenmeier of the Munich Technical High School described some of their pioneering work on miniature active antennas, with the result that *TT* was probably the first column in any amateur radio journal to mention this important development, since increasingly used in professional communications etc.

Although the principle is now well known, that of using just a very short antenna element over a very wide range of frequencies by incorporating into the antenna system a wideband low-noise amplifier designed to provide a suitable match at all frequencies, its use by transmitting amateurs (who normally wish to use a single antenna for both transmission and reception) is clearly limited. Nevertheless the active antenna deserves to be considered by those who are interested in receiving only, or those who wish to use separate antennas for receiving and transmitting. Several designs have been published for amateur use, although mostly these tend to be of limited dynamic range and subject to such problems as static damage unless intended for indoor use (which cannot be recommended).

In *IEEE Transaction on Ant & Prop* (Vol AP-28, No 6, November 1980, pp904-910) Ernst H. Nordholt and Durk Van Willigen, of the Delft University of Technology in The Netherlands, present "a new approach to active antenna design". This provides full design details for a novel family of amplifiers suitable for use with broadband active antennas covering 10kHz to 30MHz and using antenna rod elements having physical lengths less than 0·5m (diameter 30mm). The authors claim that "the resulting configurations have significantly better properties than those reported until now". The high performance amplifiers break with the "current prejudice that implies the input impedance of the active-antenna amplifier should be high for optimum performance". The Dutch system involves a large amount of negative feedback around several cascaded stages, and results in a virtual grounding of the gate of the E212 first-stage fet; the amplifier can be used with single elements or as part of an array; full details of one of the Dutch designs are given in Fig 6. The amplifiers will function in the presence of very strong local signals (up to about 10V/m) and are claimed to outperform most professional-class communication receivers in respect of dynamic range and noise. An active antenna of this class provides a signal-to-noise ratio fully equivalent to that of a good conventional antenna because of the inherent limitations of atmospheric, galactic and man-made (quiet location) noise. It should be mentioned that for optimum results the short antenna should preferably be out-of-doors and well clear of mains-borne interference; one sometimes sees the inference that because an active antenna can deliver as much signal to the receiver as a full-size antenna it can be placed on top of the receiver etc. Well it can, but the signals in your operating room are certain to be contaminated by local electrical noise.

The use of active loop antennas to form directional receiving arrays was pioneered by EMI-Cossor in the late sixties, using lines of about eight fixed double loops (*TT* July 1968). The British firm of C & S Antennas subsequently developed a unidirectional terminated loop (*TT* August 1976) intended for this type of application. They have recently redesigned this to form what they claim to be "the world's first portable hf antenna" (surely a remarkable claim!). However, what they have done (in more realistic terms) is to devise a novel form of folding loop, so that each array element packs down rather like a flat deck-chair so that up to four loops can be readily carried in a military vehicle. Despite their rather fulsome press release, which gives remarkably little information on actual performance and directivity etc, this is clearly a mechanically-cunning idea (see photograph).

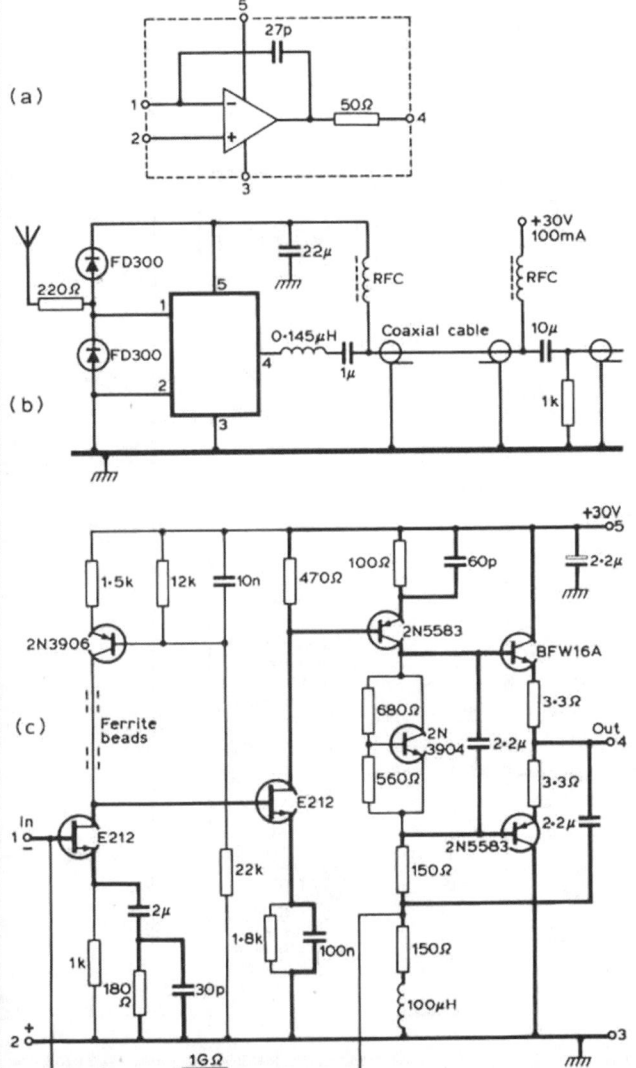

Fig 6. Details of the Dutch active antenna system. (a) One of the two basic configurations used to provide heavy negative feedback. (b) Overall scheme showing protective diodes, method of powering over the feeder cable etc. (c) Internal amplifier as used in the two different configurations, including that shown in (a). Numbers 1 to 5 correspond to those shown in (b)

Stretched VHF / UHF Antennas

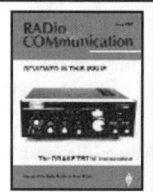

Extracted from 'Technical Topics', *Radio Communication*, June 1981

Stretched vhf/hf antennas

In the *RSGB Bulletin* of July 1961, F. J. ("Dud") Charman, G6CJ, described an important, though very little used, fundamental principle of antennas that can offer some significant advantages: this was the principle of capacitively-loaded or "stretched" antennas. Because most amateur hf stations suffer from space limitations, it has always been difficult to persuade many people that the unique properties of stretched elements make this sometimes a worthwhile and valuable approach. For the stretched element, which may be several times the length of a conventional wire element for the same band, has not only considerably increased radiation resistance, resulting in broadband operation and minimizing earth losses when used as a monopole, but also is hardly affected by the close proximity of normal (unloaded) wires.

G6CJ showed that it is possible to make hf elements stretched by a factor of from two to four times by using low-impedance balanced twin feeder, with loading capacitors formed from overlapping sections of the feeder. His information relating to these antennas has been reproduced in a number of editions of *Amateur Radio Techniques* (eg 7th edn, pp 303-5). Capacitively-loaded elements have been used in recent years in large commercial point-to-point/broadcasting arrays, and experimental work has been reported on several occasions on uhf and microwave antennas, but little evidence has come my way of this principle being used by amateurs; as far as is known *ART* remains the only book seeking to keep this idea going.

It was therefore particularly interesting to receive a letter from Phil Williams, VK5NN, indicating that he has been doing a lot of good work investigating the use of this technique at 144MHz (and hf) and that it has yielded "remarkably good results". VK5NN gave a lecture/demonstration of his work in Adelaide in September 1980, and the following notes are partly based on an account of this lecture published in the "VK5" journal. His work has aroused the interest of a number of local amateurs, particularly those concerned with the development of low-cost verticals and ground-plane antennas for 144MHz fm and repeater operation. One local amateur is using a stretched element concealed in a pvc sewer pipe in an

ANTENNA TOPICS

"antenna-sensitive" housing estate. VK5NN is now extending his work to hf, using, for example, "two × unipole" antennas for single-hop work on 3·5/7/14MHz, while operating portable and stationary-mobile in remote parts of Australia; in this case using loading capacitors moulded in hard-setting epoxy putty in a shape that allows the antenna to be readily pulled up through trees. He has also used stretched elements in vhf tv Band 3 antennas.

144MHz Stretched Antennas

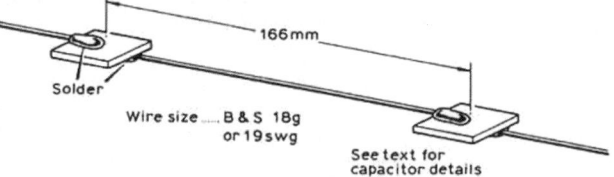

Extracted from 'Technical Topics', *Radio Communication,* June 1981

144MHz stretched antennas

VK5NN has developed a family of stretched dipoles and unipoles for 144MHz based on inserting small capacitors every 30° of length (every λ/12, ie every 166mm); this form of loading neutralizes a proportion of the inductance of the antenna element and so extends its resonant length (Fig 1). This has the effect of increasing the aperture and input impedance of the element and reduces the Q and the angle between the 3dB points on the polar diagram. A vertical element of this type radiates strongly broadside (in the horizontal plane), and is less affected by surrounding metal wires or metal poles. Because of their higher input impedance the effectiveness of the ground plane becomes less important, the bandwidth is increased and all dimensions become more tolerant etc.

The elements may be stretched to 2, 3 or 4 times the length of a resonant wire dipole or unipole: Fig 2. For a centre-fed dipole using 50Ω coaxial cable, a λ/2 section (26·5in or 673mm) of RG58-U or RG-174 cable is needed to reverse the phase of the lower section, and a small pi-network to match the coaxial cable. The 2× dipole does not need the pi-network and is easy to make at a first attempt. Fig 2(c) shows a 2m-high centre-fed dipole that can form an excellent vertically-polarized or horizontally-polarized indoor antenna for flat dwellers.

The 4× dipole, Fig 2(d) provides an even more satisfactory antenna which, for best results, should be erected as high as possible: it will work well even when spaced only 6in (152mm) from a vertical pipe mast, with the pi-network adjusted for minimum swr when the antenna is in position. The coaxial feeder cable can be brought down inside the pipe mast. Because of the strong broadside radiation, care should be taken to erect the element vertically.

Table 1 shows the dimensions, sizes of capacitors and approximate input impedances; capacitors can be made from 0·062in (1·588mm) double-sided glass-fibre printed circuit board which has a capacitance of 3pF/cm² etc. Capacitors should be cut rather longer than required and then filed down to the correct size (check with vernier calipers or by other means to ensure that they are of the correct capacitance). The element is made from 1mm diameter wire (or 18BS) with each 30° section 166mm in length.

The whole antenna, plus the λ/2 phasing section where appropriate, can be mounted inside electricians' plastic conduit (20mm) or pvc water pipe (15mm), the latter being more rigid, with "T" fittings and junction boxes as required. This is an inexpensive form of construction; ends can be pulled tight on fishing line through corks in the top and bottom of the conduit or pipe. Very thin RG174 cable is useful for forming the λ/2 phasing sections.

While the above dimensions will enable stretched antennas to be constructed without the need for design calculations, VK5NN provides the following notes for those wishing to calculate suitable capacitance values etc.
(1) For 1mm diameter wire L/4D = 1016 for a 144MHz dipole.
(2) The characteristic impedance of this wire is then:
$(Z_a = 120 (\ln L/4D - 2·55) = 525Ω)$ derived from *ARRL Antenna Handbook* with ln being the natural log, as explained in calculator instruction manuals.
(3) Z_a is predominantly inductive, so for a 166mm wire $X_L = 525 \tan 30° = 300Ω$.
(4) For a 2× stretch, half of this, or in other words 150Ω of capacitive reactance is required (ie 7·2pF as shown in Table 1).
(5) Similarly, for a 4× stretch, 0·75 of the reactance is neutralized; that is, 225Ω or 4·8pF.

With a handheld scientific calculator you can play with these figures and come up with your own design. But VK5NN adds the warning to use thin wires or you may run out of reactance; the designs will then not work out (ie avoid metal rods and tubes unless you are quite sure you know all about their impedances).

The pi-networks can be made from small plastic or ceramic trimmers. Use 4–15pF on the antenna side and 5–30pF on the 50Ω cable side. The coil can be made with about three or four turns of 18g wire about 0·25in (6·3mm) diameter. These parts will all mount on a small piece of pcb

Fig 1. Showing how home-made pcb capacitors are inserted at 166mm intervals to form a "stretched" 144MHz unipole or dipole antenna

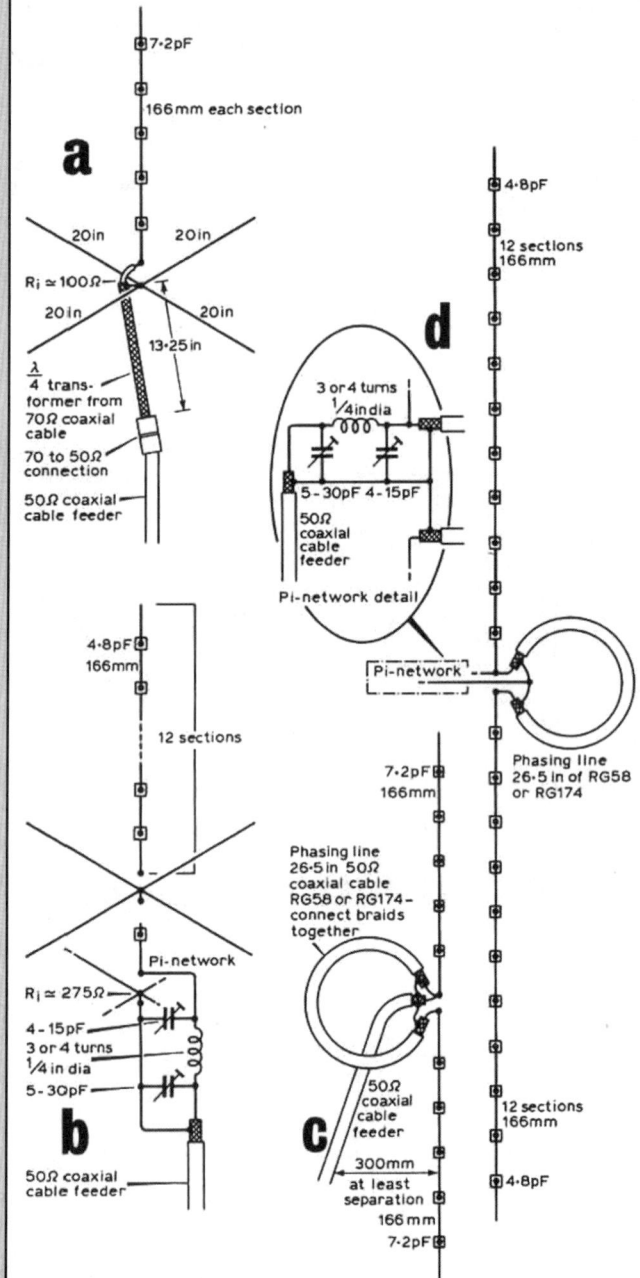

Fig 2. Realization of various "stretched" 144MHz antennas. (a) 2× unipole (ground plane); (b) 4× unipole; (c) 2× dipole; and (d) 4× dipole

Table 1. Dimensions, capacitances and approximate input impedances

Stretch factor	Reactance (Xc) (Ω)	C (pF)	PCB capacitor (cm²)	Input impedance		No of capacitors	
				Dipole (Ω)	Unipole (Ω)	Dipole	Unipole
2×	150	7·2	2·4	200	100	10	5
3×	200	5·4	1·8	400	200	16	8
4×	225	4·8	1·6	550	275	22	11

about 15mm wide inside the plastic pipe or junction box, with small holes for adjustment. Try different coil sizes until you can trim the swr down to near unity using the two capacitors; if you cannot achieve unity swr or one trimmer is at the limit of adjustment, try a larger or smaller coil until you get the result you want.

VK5NN briefly mentions his hf antennas. He has a 66ft (20·11m) 7MHz unipole with six sections each 11ft (3·35m) long and five 138pF loading capacitors. Used horizontally about 8ft (2·43m) above ground, it can be end fed as a portable antenna from equipment such as the TS-120V, using the vehicle as a counterpoise earth.

The Story of the Ground-plane

Extracted from 'Technical Topics', *Radio Communication,* July 1981

The story of the ground-plane

The recent work by Les Moxon, G6XN, on the use of counterpoise-type vertical antennas (*TT* March) suggested that large earth mats of buried radials etc may not be necessary for effective operation of vertical antennas. But, of course, very many of the vertically-polarized antenna systems currently used by amateurs do not use *any* buried radials: instead they use the artificial ground-plane technique with the antenna mounted well above earth so that the signals are not absorbed so much by surrounding trees and houses.

Conventional wisdom (eg *The ARRL Antenna Handbook*) claims that: "Instead of being actually grounded, a λ/4 antenna can work against a simulated ground . . . formed from wires λ/4 long radiating from the base of the antenna . . . However, with only one radial the directive pattern would be that of a λ/2 antenna bent into a right angle at the centre . . . this would result in equal components of horizontal and vertical polarization and a non-uniform pattern in the horizontal plane. This can be overcome by using a disk with a λ/4 radius. The effect of the disk can be simulated, with simpler construction, by using *at least four straight radials* equally spaced around the circle" (my italics).

The implication is that, as with buried radials for a monopole, the more ground-plane (insulated) radials the better, and that such an antenna cannot be expected to function efficiently, with an omnidirectional radiation pattern, with only two or three radials.

In a comprehensive article "The ground beneath us" (*RSGB Bulletin* June 1966, pp375–85), R. C. Hills, G3HRH, also considers that four radials represent an inefficient minimum. He wrote: "What then of the ground-plane? Let no one be deceived that the conventional four radials take care of the Brewster effect! The radial system of the normal elevated ground-plane does little more than provide a convenient connection for the unbalanced side of the feeder. It is electrically very transparent and the ground below the radials is well illuminated by the vertical radiator, so the presence of a good earth system is just as important as if the antenna were fed against ground." Here again the casual reader would assume that the use of four or more radials *plus* an extensive earth system buried in ground of good electrical conductivity was advisable to obtain optimum results.

But one needs to be careful what one reads into this. Certainly the effectiveness of any vertical antenna in providing low-angle radiation depends to a very marked extent upon earth conductivity; but an earth system that really meets this requirement cannot use a normal buried earth system, since it should extend many wavelengths around the antenna in all directions. The efficiency at low angles of either a vertical monopole or a ground-plane (gp) antenna increases enormously when, for example, you can use the sea for this purpose. John Roscoe, G4QK, recalls what happens when one *does* have a good earth: "One remembers tales 24 years ago of a gp on the flight deck of an aircraft carrier; or 12 years ago, when warships were larger than they are now, the 500W of illicit naval rf applied to a 50ft vertical, with impressive results. My office is on a site where some attention has been given to earthing, as there are over 1,500MW of electricity sculling around: a 7ft (indoor) vertical loaded against the ring-main earth gets out unexpectedly well."

So, one would not wish in any way to disparage the importance of earth conductivity, but what about that minimum of four radials for an elevated gp antenna? As G3HRH pointed out, their *prime* job is to provide a convenient connection for the feeder by bringing the antenna to resonance (just like the G6XN counterpoise). So why *four*? As noted by ARRL, *one* would result in radiation of a horizontally-polarized component and would not provide an omnidirectional pattern (although it can provide quite an effective general purpose antenna). So what about *two* spaced 180°? In other words an inverted-T with three λ/4 sections. Some years ago (*TT* July 1970, and all subsequent editions of *ART*) I described an "inverted ground-plane" antenna which was in the form of the classic "T" antenna except that the dimensions were all λ/4. I had taken the idea from the old "bobtail" antenna. Certainly my "inverted ground-plane" worked quite effectively from a poor site, and the system has since been further developed by several other amateurs, including K7GCO who implemented my suggestion that one could use this system as the basis for an antenna which could be switched to form a dipole with horizontal polarization as an immediately-available alternative to the vertical polarization of the "T" antenna.

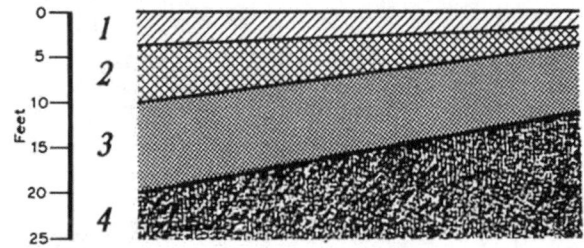

Fig 2. Typical section of earth's crust showing geological strata with several layers of different electrical conductivity. (1) Alluvial soil having relatively good conductivity (about 20×10^{-14} emu). (2) Sandy soil (about 4×10^{-14} emu). (3) Chalk (about 10×10^{-14} emu). (4) Young rock (1×10^{-14} emu). Sea water has conductivity of about 4×10^{-11} emu (ie $4,000 \times 10^{-14}$ emu). In practice effective conductivity depends upon depth of penetration of the earth currents and is thus a function of frequency (as frequency is raised more current will be concentrated in the uppermost layers). *(From "The ground beneath us", G3HRH, 1966)*

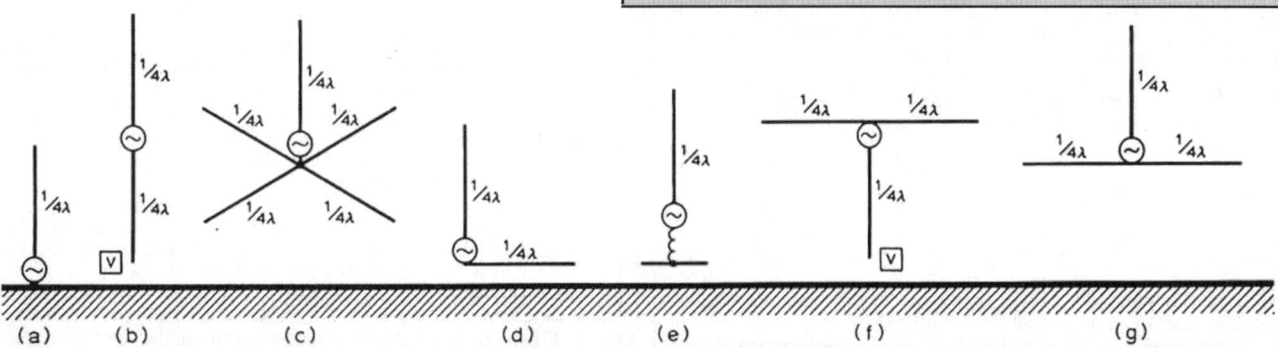

Fig 1. The family of verticals. (a) Standard monopole (unipole) antenna fed against earth. Any significant resistance in the earth connection will dissipate a substantial amount of the transmitter power so that good earthing systems (stakes, radials, mats etc) are most important. (b) The λ/2 vertical dipole requires no direct earth connection but has both high and low angle lobes of radiation. As for all vertical antennas the earth conductivity is important because of the large induced currents. Without very extensive earth mats only limited improvement is likely from any buried radials etc. The antenna can be voltage-fed at V with the current feed-point short-circuited. (c) Conventional four radial ground plane (radials usually slope downwards to facilitate impedance matching). The artificial earth formed by the four radials does not prevent large currents being induced in the real earth. (d) The "bent" dipole (ie single-radial ground plane) results in mixed polarization and is unlikely to provide true omnidirectional horizontal radiation pattern. Nevertheless it can form an effective general purpose antenna, particularly if the earth conductivity is good. (e) G6XN's inductively loaded counterpoise form of monopole/dipole as described in March *TT*. In practice the "coil" can be in the form of distributed inductance. (f) G3VA's 1970 "inverted ground plane" or "λ/4 T" raises the current maximum in cluttered sites. It can be voltage-fed at V if the current feed-point is short circuited. (g) The "original" two radial ground plane as developed by Dr George Brown of RCA (additional radials added later to meet customers' wishes!)

ANTENNA TOPICS

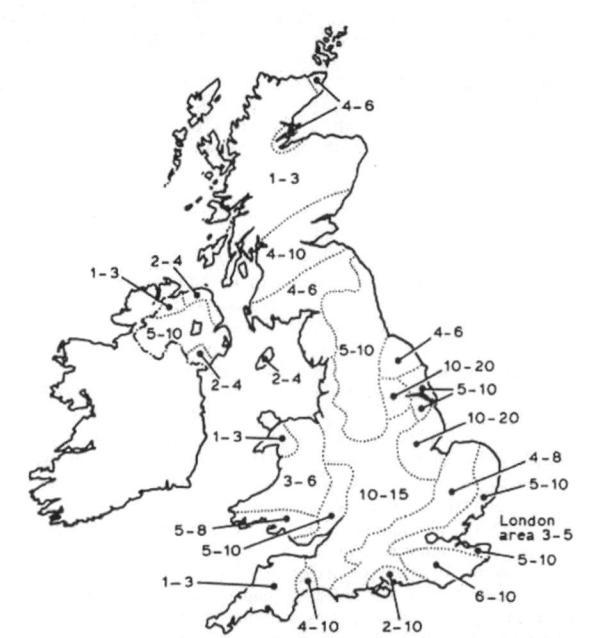

Fig 3. A rough ground conductivity map of the UK. Figures quoted are for 1·5MHz but the same general pattern can be assumed at higher frequencies. Conductivity is moderate to good in central and south-east England; poor to moderate in the west and north-west; and very variable in Scotland and Northern Ireland. Urban areas will tend to be poorer than farmland and rural areas. *(G3HRH, 1966)*

More Thoughts on Verticals

Extracted from 'Technical Topics',
Radio Communication, July 1981

More thoughts on verticals

Vertically-polarized antennas close, or reasonably close, to ground put one in mind of that nursery rhyme little girl who, when she was good, was very very good, but when she was bad she was horrid. The reason for this is primarily the very significant differences that are encountered at different sites, both in terms of earth conductivity and/or absorption and screening by any surrounding trees and man-made structures. It should also be appreciated that different systems, particularly different earthing arrangements (real or artificial) result in considerable differences in feed-point impedances: Phil Horwood, G3FRB, has carried out a valuable series of measurements on feed-point impedances, and it is hoped that his report will be published soon in *Rad Com*.

There is, of course, a fundamental difference between vertically- and horizontally-polarized antennas close to ground: they differ in the effects of the reversal of electric charges in the "image" antenna. Vertically-polarized waves are reflected with no change in phase: horizontally-polarized waves have their phase shifted 180° on reflection. This results in profound differences in the radiation patterns of the two types of antennas and the total radiated power.

Many amateurs still tend to visualize the vertical radiation pattern of a vertical antenna in the form in which it is usually presented in the various handbooks: that is to say, maximum radiation towards the horizon. In reality this is only (nearly) achieved over salt water. As earth conductivity decreases, not only does the total radiated power fall, but it virtually vanishes at low angles: see Fig 4. This effect occurs pretty well regardless

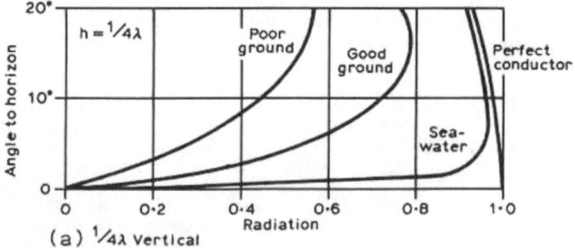

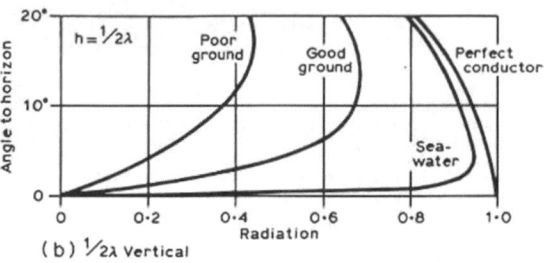

Fig 4. How the low-angle radiation of a vertical antenna differs from the theoretical vrp diagrams when a "real" earth is substituted for an "ideal" earth. Only with salt water do the vrp characteristics approach those of the theoretical text book patterns. (a) λ/4 vertical. (b) λ/2 vertical dipole

of which type of vertical antenna is being used, and is only moderately affected by man-made buried radials unless these are in the form of a truly massive earth mat. What many buried radials do, of course, is to reduce power losses in antennas fed against earth (ie, as in Fig 1 (a)). Earth conductivity depends primarily on location and "the ground beneath us" as described in great detail in G3HRH's 1966 paper; it also depends on frequency so that figures quoted for mf propagation have to be treated with some caution at hf although they provide a valuable guide.

There is another tantalizing question: to what extent is the vertical radiation pattern of a vertical antenna the same on transmit and receive? It is very difficult to find any clear indication of this in the text books. Yet it has certainly been my observation, when working medium-distance (say, East European) stations on hf that the signal reports I receive from stations which themselves have very strong incoming signals tend to be significantly lower from stations using vertically-polarized antennas, than from those (like myself) using fairly low horizontally-polarized antennas. The verticals appear to discriminate well *against* high-angle incoming signals but often radiate well at those same high angles. In other words, "real" earths appear to blur the nulls in the vrp on transmit more than on receive, just as, even over a poor earth, a vertical receiving antenna may

In the Beginning

Extracted from 'Technical Topics',
Radio Communication, July 1981

In the beginning

Now the man who, more than any other, was responsible for the development of the ground-plane antenna (not to mention also the vertical monopole arrays from which were developed both the close-spaced Yagi and the W8JK driven array) was the redoubtable Dr George Brown of RCA. Recently, it was my great pleasure to meet Dr Brown, now retired, and his wife Elizabeth, on one of their frequent visits to the UK. In the course of conversation I happened to mention that of all his many antenna developments it was for the ground-plane that he was perhaps most widely known to radio amateurs. He then related an interesting little anecdote which (if I understood it correctly) has an important bearing on the question of how many radials are really necessary.

He told me that the (elevated) ground-plane antenna was first devised in the 'thirties to meet an early requirement for police communications (American police mobiles then used to work around 30 to 45MHz). Its success was immediately evident when, at the first demonstration, the transmissions reached well beyond their anticipated service area. Now the important point was that the original design had only *two* radials; however, when it came to marketing the design the sales engineers reported that they could not persuade potential users that a two-radial antenna, with the two radials looking like a half-wave dipole, could possibly have an omnidirectional radiation pattern. On the classic principle that the customer is always right, George Brown and his colleagues simply added two more radials—and everybody was satisfied.

In other words, all that is required for a ground-plane antenna to function effectively is that the bulk of the "horizontal" radiation from the radials cancels out: and this happens with two radials. Now, of course, this anecdote does not *prove* that four may not be better than two; but at least it is an indication that an antenna using two radials or a G6XN-type counterpoise serves the purpose that the inventor had in mind! This is very different from the question of buried earth systems for monopoles where the lowest possible earth resistance is undoubtedly advisable to minimize the power losses.

perform well at low angles.

One of a number of interesting comments on the notes on G6XN's work in the March *TT* has come from Peter Pitts, G3GYE/A4XGC/VP8JP, who has always been far from satisfied with the treatment of vertical antennas in the text books which seem to concentrate on 120-buried-radial-type systems for broadcasting. He raises several points which I hope are partially answered in these notes. He is firmly in favour of the use of verticals mounted at least a few feet above ground to allow the use of sloping (insulated) resonant radials to avoid the power losses of antennas fed directly against poor earths and to provide a good match to 50Ω cable. His experiences also seem to bear out the view that the number of radials can be reduced with remarkably little effect on signal strengths. In tests from Oman to Cornwall using a 12AVQ vertical with sloping radials, he successively rolled up all the radials except one, with no adverse effect on the signals received in Cornwall.

The Modified VK2ABQ Antenna

Extracted from 'Technical Topics', *Radio Communication,* July 1981

The modified VK2ABQ antenna

Les Moxon, G6XN, mentions that for the modified VK2ABQ array (*TT* May 1980) even the spacings quoted there, though much greater than used originally by VK2ABQ, are on the low side. He has since found that about 20-24in (50-61cm) seems to be about right for 14MHz, but the interactions between elements for different bands can take subtle forms (eg affecting the coupling). He considers it best, if possible, to use relays to disable any element that has an observable effect on the current flowing in elements for other bands.

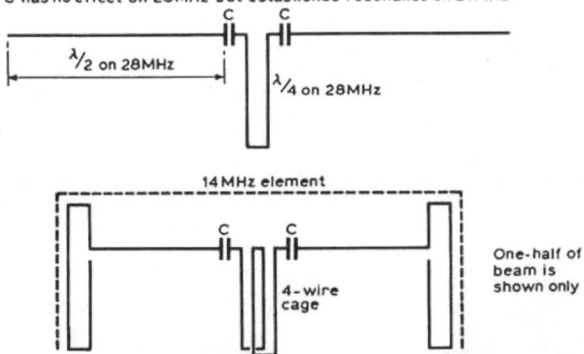

Fig 9. Use of combined 21/28MHz elements in G6XN's modified VK2ABQ three-band beam antenna

However, G6XN finds that he can get away with using two-band elements for 28/21MHz based on a 28MHz collinear pair, concertinaed to fit the space formed by the 14MHz elements, roughly as shown in Fig 9. Very tight coupling (*à la* VK2ABQ) is needed between these elements. In his experimental arrangement, G6XN uses two 600Ω open-wire feeders with passive switching between the 28/21 and 14MHz elements.

Twin-delta Loop Antenna Arrays

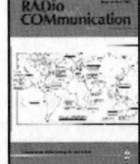

Extracted from 'Technical Topics', *Radio Communication,* September 1981

Twin-delta loop antenna arrays

In *TT* (March 1981) attention was drawn to the work of Takehiko Tsukiji and Shigehumi Tou of Fukuoka University on the analysis of delta-loop antenna elements, and their conclusion that triangular elements can result in very useful broadband characteristics. John Brodzky, G3HQX, has drawn attention to a later paper by the same authors: "High gain and broadband Yagi-Uda array antenna composed of twin-delta loops" (*IEE Conference Publication No 195 Part 1*—2nd International Conference on Antennas & Propagation, April 1981).

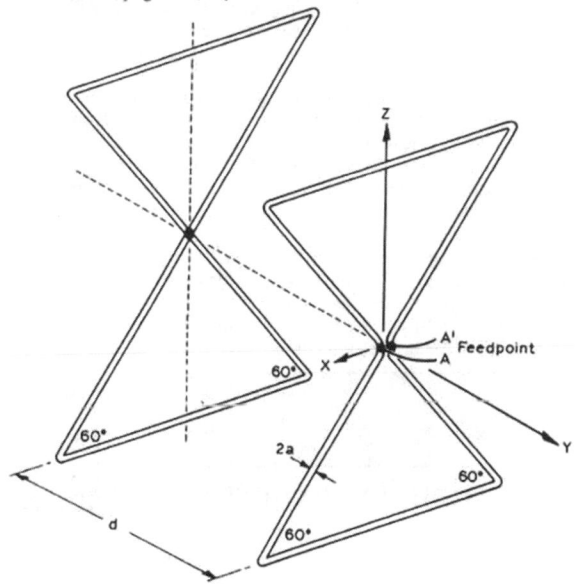

Fig 6. Twin-delta loop array providing wideband characteristics

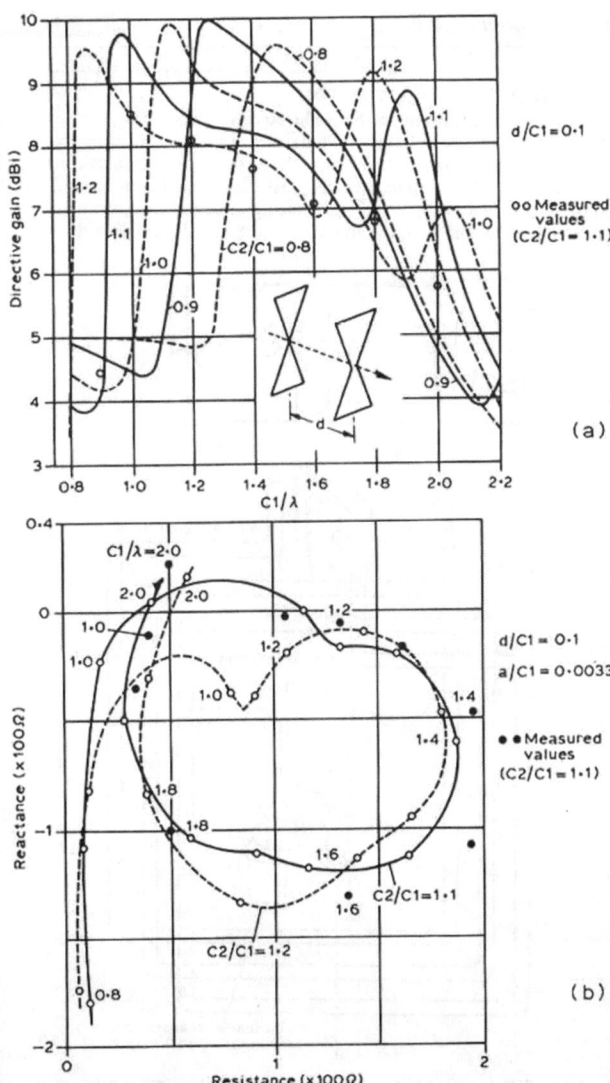

Fig 7. Directive gain and frequency characteristics of input impedance of twin-delta loop array where parasitic element is used as a reflector

ANTENNA TOPICS

The paper describes twin-delta loop arrays having maximum directive gain of about 9·8dBi (ie about 9·8-2·1 = 7·7dB gain ref dipole) but providing a gain of more than 7dBi over almost an octave frequency span. The broadband characteristics arise from the apex-driven triangular loop configuration. The authors claim that the broadband characteristics mean that it becomes very easy to form a high-gain array without critical dimensions of loop perimeter or element spacing. The paper shows that there are significant advantages in using the parasitic loop as a reflector rather than as a director.

As indicated in Fig 6 the shape of each loop is an equilateral triangle, and the perimeter of the driven and parasitic loop is C1 and C2. The perimeter of the loop is in the range 1-2; C2/C1 for a reflector is 1·1; and the spacing d can be as little as $d/C1 = 0·1$. Clearly the array would be easier to implement on vhf or uhf than hf, although presumably an hf version could be made to work well on 14, 18, 21, 24 and 28MHz with the same elements!

Rather interestingly, a similar double-delta loop configuration for 144MHz (and also uhf television) was described many years ago in *TT* by John Pegler, G3ENI, and has appeared in many editions of *ART*. However, although he reported it as a very useful array, G3ENI made no particular claims for broadband characteristics.

Multi-turn Transmitting Loop

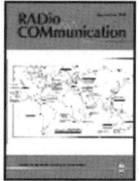

Extracted from 'Technical Topics',
Radio Communication, September 1981

Multi-turn transmitting loop

One of the contributions to the Radio Receivers and Associated Systems Conference directly relating to amateur radio was a paper by Sven Ramstrom, an SM-amateur, on "HF loop for transmitting and receiving". His SV1 antenna was originally developed at home and tested on the 3·5, 7 and 14MHz amateur bands, although since then it has been subjected to extensive tests and trials by Swedish and British defence establishments, and by Rediffusion Radio Systems Ltd (formerly Redifon Ltd).

The advantages and disadvantages of compact transmitting loop antennas have been the subject of a good deal of investigation both by professionals and amateurs in recent years, particularly since the development in the mid-'sixties at the US Army limited warfare laboratories of the single-turn octagonal loop antenna (5ft sides) as described in *ART*. More recently there has been the TCI Model 629 low-profile loop for diplomatic communications etc (*TT* December 1980, p1296). The trick in both these designs was to use large diameter copper tubing to reduce the power loss brought about by the very low radiation resistance of a small loop.

The Swedish SV1, which has been tested in fixed and marine mobile applications with transmitter powers up to 1kW, is much smaller in overall size, the whole antenna fitting into a cylindrical plastics cover some 0·8m (high) by 0·4m (wide) by 0·7m (deep). Basically it consists of three square turns tuned by a 30-100pF capacitor (vacuum type for high powers) to which a broadband single-turn square loop (each side 500mm) is inductively-coupled (with adjustable coupling): Fig 8. The feed to the single-turn loop is via a 1:4 balun (50-200Ω). From the illustrations the material used to form the main loop appears to be silver-plated (copper?) tubing, roughly about 0·5in diameter for the main loop and about 0·25in diameter for the single-turn loop. No ground plane is used. The final version uses motorized control of the vacuum capacitor and for adjusting the feed loop, and is clearly intended to be mounted at some distance from the transmitter.

The antenna is tunable about 1·9 to 16MHz, but the bandwidth at any given frequency is quite narrow, reflecting the high-Q design (from about 2·4kHz at 3MHz to about 13·2kHz at 10MHz). When tuned, the swr is a maximum of about 1·27 at 2MHz, less than 1·1:1 from 3·5 to 13MHz.

What about performance? In any consideration of small loops one has to accept that radiated power is likely to be significantly below what would be possible with a conventional dipole, and this unit is no exception. However, it is claimed that for high-angle radiation the system compares favourably with a 12m vertical whip antenna, and that the efficiency of both loop and whip antennas increases considerably with frequency. Although the near-field shows sharp nulls, in effect radiation from the loop is omnidirectional with an even vertical radiation pattern from horizon to zenith. From the information in the paper, it would appear that at 8MHz the loop is about -8dB ref dipole; at 4, 6 and 10MHz about -20dB, and at 2·6MHz about -25dB.

The paper includes a list of over 50 contacts made on the amateur bands, mostly between Sweden and other European countries but also including a few dx contacts on 14MHz. The transmitter power used is not stated, but the signal reports are reasonable on both ssb and cw. It is claimed that on reception the loop tends to provide clearer signals than the whip. The interest shown by the defence establishments etc would indicate that the results are sufficiently encouraging to suggest that such loop antennas may well find application in circumstances where only limited space is available, and where the smooth vrp makes it more suitable than a whip for medium-distance contacts. But don't expect it to work as well as a good dipole!

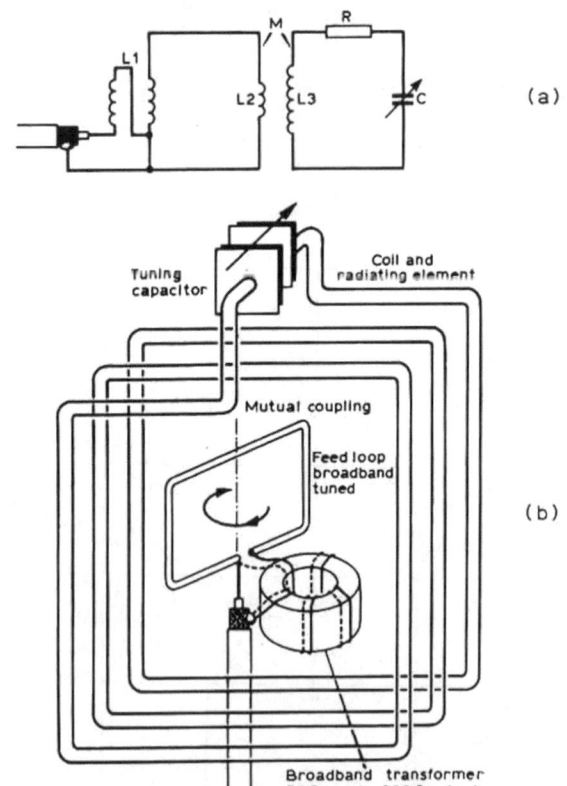

Fig 8. The SV1 compact hf tunable loop antenna for transmitting and receiving with top-driven square loop: (a) equivalent circuit; (b) basic arrangement of the SV1 loop antenna

A New Look at the W8JK

Extracted from 'Technical Topics',
Radio Communication, October 1981

A new look at the W8JK

For many years the W8JK, first of the "flat-topped" close-spaced arrays, has suffered a decline in popularity when compared with the uni-directional Yagi and the various unidirectional driven arrays discussed below. All close-spaced arrays, driven and parasitic, unidirectional and bidirectional arrays derive from the basic work at RCA of Dr G. H. Brown (*Proc IRE* January 1937, pp78-145). Historically, the driven bidirectional arrays of Dr John Kraus, W8JK, of Ohio State University, were the first flat-top arrays to become popular on the amateur hf bands from 1937-8 onwards, both for rotary and fixed arrays.

In *Ham Radio* (July 1981, pp60-3) Frank Regier, OD5CG, of the American University of Beirut, takes "A new look at the W8JK antenna". He goes right back to the original design based on two close-spaced transposed dipoles centre-fed 180° out of phase with balanced line: Fig 3. He shows that despite the disadvantages of bidirectivity for reception, lower gain (at resonance) than an equivalent Yagi and its low radiation

1980 - 1989

resistance, the W8JK does possess some useful advantages.

He draws particular attention to the fact that, as with the centre-fed dipole, it will operate reasonably satisfactorily over something like a 2·5:1 frequency span, with gain increasing on the higher-frequency bands. Theoretical free-space gain with $\lambda/2$ elements is about 4-4·5dB, but this increases to about 6dB at twice resonant frequency, and up to 7dB at 2·5 times resonant frequency. In practice rather lower gains can be expected. Element spacing is relatively uncritical and $\lambda/8$ spacing at the design frequency remains satisfactory throughout the frequency span. Finally, he claims that such an array will work surprisingly well at low heights where it does not suffer from the detuning effect of earth which tends to degrade Yagi performance.

OD5CG in fact claims that the W8JK array can outperform an equivalent three-element Yagi array when the height is less than about $\lambda/2$ above ground, provided that the symmetry of the W8JK array is maintained (ie it is all sufficiently far away from nearby structures, trees etc). He suggests that an array with an overall length of 40ft (11ft element spacing) would give good results on every band from 10 to 28MHz (including good reception on the various broadcast bands) though his own array is smaller: 30ft long, 8ft spacing, and is for 14 to 28MHz. He uses 300Ω balanced twin feeder; which is convenient except when it rains, when the impedance tends to become erratic (open-wire line avoids this problem).

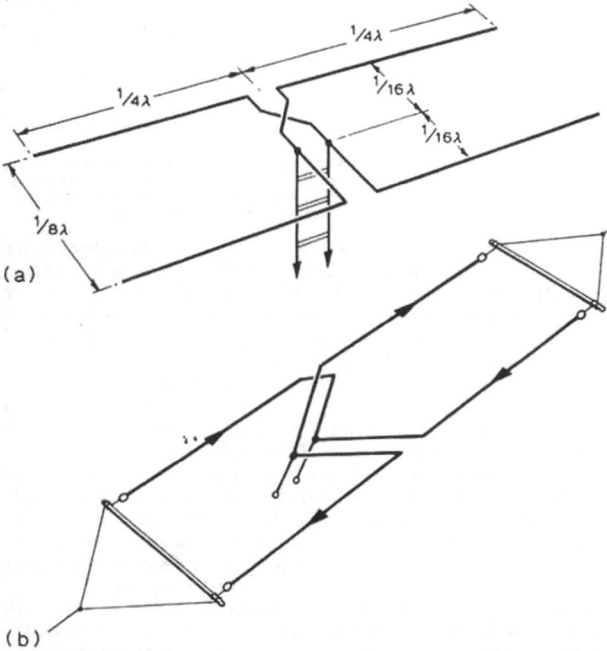

Fig 3. (a) Basic single-section centre-fed W8JK bidirectional array. With a 14MHz design frequency it should work well (and with some extra gain) at all frequencies to 28MHz. It consists of two closely-spaced dipoles fed out of phase. Spacing is non-critical but symmetry should be preserved and the array fed from balanced line through suitable atu. (b) W8JK implemented in wire form as fixed array, but note that the low radiation resistance calls for good insulation and minimum coupling off the ends into supports (use nylon or plastic rope etc rather than support wires)

Unidirectional Driven Arrays (monoband)

Extracted from 'Technical Topics', *Radio Communication*, October 1981

Unidirectional driven arrays (monoband)

George Brown showed that when two elements are fed 135° out-of-phase with equal amplitudes a cardioid-type pattern results. Over the past 45 years various ways of implementing such arrays as flat-top beams have been devised, of which the "HB9CV" and "ZL-Special" are among the better known, although the "G8PO" enjoyed a brief spell of popularity for fixed arrays because it was readily reversible.

The ZL-Special was so named and first described in print by Fred Judd, G2BCX. Although the design is often also credited to G2BCX, his original article in *Short Wave Magazine* (July 1950, pp337-9) made the position clear: "Data on the aerial to be described came to the writer from New Zealand, hence the name ZL-Special. Little is known of its origin save that it was designed in the USA, just prior to the late war, for commercial purposes. Since the war it has been modified and developed for amateur use by W5LHI, W0GZR and ZL3MH. Further tests and measurements made by the writer may be of interest". A later writer confirmed that in 1949 ZL3MH was using the system on 14 and 28MHz "with outstanding results".

The ZL-Special, of which there are several slightly different versions, basically consists of two close-spaced dipole elements, both of which are driven (preferably with near equal amplitudes) with a phase difference of approximately 135°: Fig 4. The 135° difference is achieved by using $\lambda/4$ (45°) phasing section which is transposed so that 180° − 45° = 135°. The elements may be folded-wire dipoles or rod elements; one version uses 300Ω twin cable throughout, another uses coaxial feeder and rod elements.

A more sophisticated version of what is essentially the same form of antenna was developed by Rudolf Baumgartner, HB9CV. In this case, self-supporting rod elements are normally used with T-match or gamma-match sections between the transposed phasing section and the driven

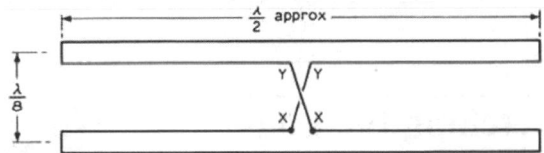

Fig 4. Basic arrangement of ZL-Special unidirectional driven array (monoband) using open-wire line or 300Ω feeder for the folded elements. Usually fed with low-impedance 120-150Ω twin line or, less correctly, 75Ω coaxial cable at points XX. Other variations include use of unequal lengths for elements

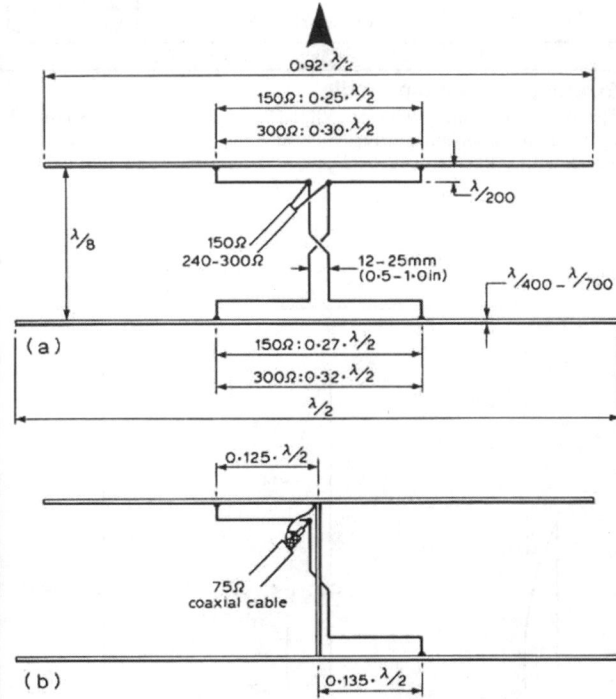

Fig 5. Basic arrangements of the HB9CV unidirectional array showing use of (a) T-match; and (b) gamma-match sections

elements; Fig 5. The array is suitable for use with either 75Ω coaxial cable or balanced feeders of from about 150 to 300Ω. A long, detailed account of the origin and principles of the HB9CV array has been published quite recently in *Radio-REF* (March 1981, pp155-71) although the antenna itself has been quite widely used for over 20 years (a 144MHz HB9CV portable array was published some years ago in *TT* and appears in recent editions of *ART*).

Les Moxon, G6XN, in "Gains and losses in hf aerials—Part 1" (*Rad Com* December 1973) noted: "There are several popular designs of two-element beams in which both elements are driven. In principle the advantage of driving is that phase and amplitude can be adjusted independently so that spacing is less critical and deep nulls are obtainable in back directions even with dipole elements. Unfortunately the usual methods of phasing are based on the false assumption that 'one eighth-wavelength of line equals 45° of phase shift' which is true only if a perfect match exists *at the elements*, whereas phasing, matching and current ratio are all critically interdependent. Since the radiation resistance is in the

ANTENNA TOPICS

region of 15Ω, for maximum gain with dipole elements a matching device (eg T or gamma match) is essential, and this is usually not provided."

Judged on this basis the HB9CV emerges rather better than the ZL-Special, although it should be appreciated that the latter design is to some extent self-compensating and can provide a good front-to-back ratio in many cases. G6XN noted that while a good two-element Yagi can approach the theoretical maximum forward gain of 5·2dB reference dipole, a ZL-Special is unlikely to exceed 3-4dB gain. This figure is nowadays generally accepted, although originally optimistic claims of 6-7dB were commonly made.

It will thus be clear that the gain of a bidirectional W8JK (4-4·5dB) may well exceed that of a unidirectional monoband driven array. One does, of course, lose the advantage of the good cardioid-type back-to-front ratio when receiving, but instead one finds quite deep nulls at 90° and 270°.

It is true that amateurs often judge the performance of an array on the basis of front-to-back ratio and frequently adjust the arrays on this basis (in the case of a Yagi or quad, losing about 1dB or so of forward gain in the process). But then in practice in some circumstances the receiving front-to-back ratio may prove as operationally important as additional forward gain.

Stretching the Log-periodic

Extracted from 'Technical Topics', *Radio Communication*, October 1981

Stretching the log-periodic

The notes (*TT* June 1981) on VK5NN's experiments with stretched 144MHz and hf antennas attracted the attention of a number of readers, including "Dud" Charman, G6CJ, whose article in the July 1961 issue of

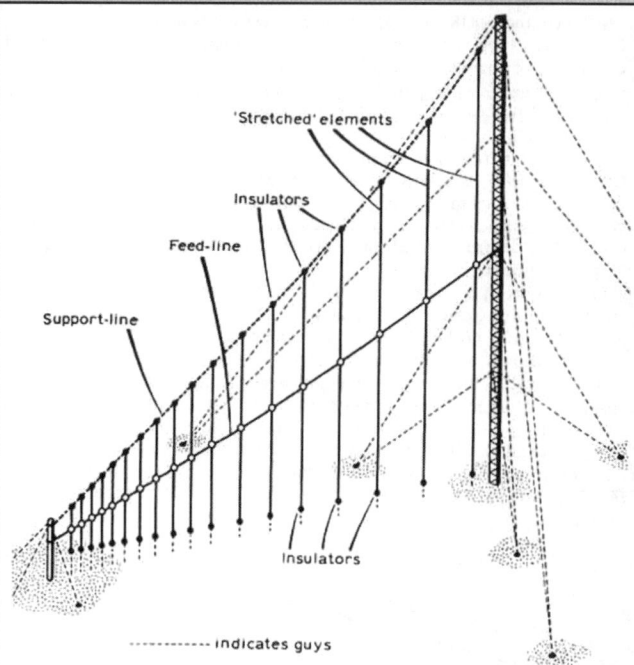

Fig 7. The TCI Model 510 professional "extended aperture" (stretched) vertically-polarized log periodic array. Very high gains can be achieved in this way but the system does require very high supports to achieve good low-frequency performance (over 200ft at about 7MHz)

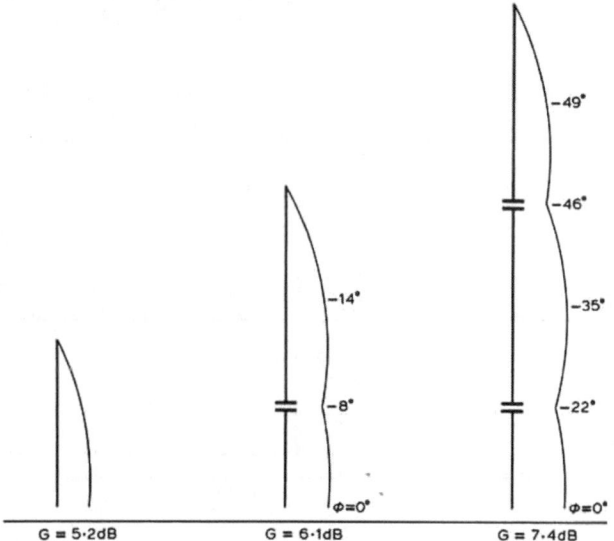

Fig 6. Use of stretched elements in vertical monopoles. The omnidirectional low-angle gain figures are relative to isotropic, and in practice the basic $\lambda/4$ monopole in amateur use seldom achieves the theoretical vertical-radiation pattern directivity gain due to site conditions (*TT* July)

RSGB Bulletin remains the basic source of information on this technique. G6CJ drew on the EMI work on this type of loaded wire antenna which began with E. C. Cork's formulation of the principles in 1938 and included the effective but "unfashionable" EMI tilted-wire Band 1 television receiving antenna of the early 'fifties. In the mid-'fifties, in his professional capacity, G6CJ developed a Band 3 array based on this technique, and went on from there to adapt the system for hf bands as described in his 1961 article.

G6CJ pointed out that stretched antennas have enhanced directivity and provide inherent gain over conventional dipoles or monopoles (for a multiplication factor of two you get an extra 1dB, for n=3, 2·1dB; and for n=4, 3·2dB); Fig 6. The system is particularly attractive as a monopole or ground plane antenna for low-angle radiation, not only because of the sharpened-up vertical radiation pattern but also because the increased radiation resistance reduces ground losses and increases bandwidth. The system is also of considerable interest in the long wire form since radiation is concentrated into a single (or bidirectional if unterminated) lobe rather than the conventional beam splitting and sidelobe radiation pattern of long wire antennas.

But the principle is now being exploited professionally in a manner not mentioned in G6CJ's 1961 article. This is in the form of high-gain extended aperture log periodic arrays. While the commercial models made by TCI use one or two masts some 210ft high, it would be possible for an amateur to erect a fixed vertically-polarized log-periodic array of this type covering, say, 18 to 70MHz with a stretch factor of two, using a single mast or support about 55ft or so high. Patents on this form of stretched antenna are held by TCI, and it would be an infringement of these to manufacture such arrays for sale; but this, of course, does not prevent amateurs from erecting a homebuilt array for their own use.

Gordon Sinclair, G4BWH/W6, who is a senior antenna engineer with TCI, has sent details of the large point-to-point arrays (TCI Models 510 (Fig 7) and 512 series) together with technical notes by Dr Robert L. Tanner, president and technical director of TCI.

These antennas, occupying relatively compact areas by professional standards, provide the high gains more usually associated with very large rhombics with an overall span of some 1,700ft. Traditionally, log-periodic arrays of dipoles or monopoles have been regarded as useful broadband arrays for medium-distance point-to-point or hf broadcasting operation, but are seldom considered as having high gain in relation to their size. This is because in the log-periodic form of array only those elements fairly close to resonance at the operating frequency are "active", the rest are virtually passengers. To quote the TCI technical notes:

"Conventional log periodics consist of arrays of dipole elements of progressively increasing length. At any particular frequency almost all the radiation from the antenna comes from a small number of elements adjacent to each other, which is known as the 'active region' of the antenna . . . This sets a clear limit to the broadside gain in the E-plane dimension that can be achieved with conventional log-periodic antennas. The practical effect is that most log-periodics have been used where moderate gains (10 to 14dBi) are required. Where gains of the order of 18dBi were desired, users generally settled for rhombics or very large log-periodics. The extended aperture antenna brings the desired broadside action into play, resulting in very directive, compact (relatively) antennas with great material and land savings and greater structural reliability." In effect at any given frequency more of the stretched elements are in the "active region" of the array, due to the lower Q of the elements.

It would be equally interesting from an amateur point of view to find out what sort of results would be achieved using stretched elements in a bidirectional W8JK fixed array!

A more conventional (non-stretched) but conveniently lightweight broadband log-periodic antenna is described in *QST* (July 1981) and we may return to this subject later.

Stretching and the Slotted Cylinder Antenna

Extracted from 'Technical Topics', *Radio Communication,* October 1981

Stretching and the slotted cylinder antenna

Ivan James, G5IJ, who recalls that the basic principle of stretched loading of antenna elements was noted by Beverage in 1923 in connection with his very long wire antennas, points out that there are alternative methods of stretching an element: instead of series-capacitance loading, shunt inductance loading can be used, provided that two (or more) terminals are readily available to shunt the inductance(s) across. Apart from applications of such a technique to the Beverage antenna, what he has in mind is the "slotted cylinder antenna" as disclosed by Alan D. Blumlein of EMI (who established a historic name in television, stereo records etc before his tragic wartime death while flight-testing H2S radar) in British patent 515684, applied for on 7 March 1938, although the antenna is often ascribed to Alford.

G5IJ shows that, mathematically, the slotted cylinder antenna element (as used, for example, by the BBC in many of their vhf/fm broadcasting installations) can be represented as a transmission line of series inductances, shunt inductances and capacitors forming the equivalent of a bandpass filter with stretched waves. He mentions that G3JVL has done some excellent work in adapting the slotted cylinder for GB3IOW, and has also developed a centre-fed 2λ-high slot, only 1·5in in diameter, in which the standing wave is increased by four times, providing a 1,296MHz horizontally polarized antenna for mobile operation, based on the so-called Alford slot.

G5IJ believes there is increasing interest among amateurs in the slotted cylinder for 432MHz and above: some basic references to such antennas include: "Long slot antennas" by Andrew Alford, *Proc National Electronics Conference*, 1946, pp143–5; "Slotted cylinder antennas", by Jordan & Miller, *Electronics*, February 1947, **20**, pp90–3; and *VHF-UHF Manual*, by D. S. Evans, G3RPE, and G. R. Jessop, G6JP (3rd edition pp727–8).

Three-wire 14MHz Ground-plane

Extracted from 'Technical Topics', *Radio Communication,* October 1981

Three-wire 14MHz ground-plane

G. V. Entwhistle, G3MXT, is one of a number of readers who have contributed to the discussion on vertical antennas (*TT* July etc). He writes:

"It seems to me that the great advantage of verticals over horizontals in many average locations is that they are less affected by the modern profusion of parasitic horizontal wires such as overhead telephone lines etc.

"Fig 8 shows a 14MHz groundplane antenna which has been in use at G3MXT since 1964. It was found by practical experiment that the optimum number of radials, in this case, was three; it would work well with four or two radials but, according to the swr indicator, three sloping radials provided a near 'perfect' match.

"Under short-skip conditions, comparing this antenna with a horizontal $\lambda/2$ folded dipole, the differences are very noticeable. It is rarely possible to maintain a European contact for more than about 10min with the groundplane, yet it appears to be omnidirectional as far as low-angle dx is concerned, in spite of numerous local telephone wires.

"To anyone who has never tried a groundplane antenna before, or who has been disappointed with a conventional coaxial-fed type, I can recommend this one."

The antenna uses a three-wire folded $\lambda/4$ element with three sloping radials. The feeder is ribbon-type 300Ω twin using the technique described in *TT* several years ago (*ART*7, p313) of removing "window slots" from the ribbon dielectric to reduce losses but primarily to minimize wet-weather changes.

Multiband Groundplane

Extracted from 'Technical Topics', *Radio Communication,* October 1981

Multiband groundplane

Bert Whatley, G2BY, has for several years been using a multiband form of the inverted-T groundplane (see July *TT*) with two in-line radials (ie 180° spaced) and finds it gives "really excellent results, seemingly with no preferred directions". He has tried adding additional elevated radials but find these make virtually no difference except in so far as they may either assist or hinder the impedance matching on the various bands.

In his case he uses a 26ft vertical element in a Butternut differential reactance vertical well suited to limited-space conditions. There are no traps, the whole 26ft being used on all bands from 3·5 to 28MHz, except on 21MHz where the $\lambda/4$ is terminated by a linear decoupler. Separate pairs of radials are used on the bands, with the exception that the 7MHz radials also serve as $3\lambda/4$ radials on 21MHz.

G2BY has the vertical element mounted on the top of a 17ft wooden mast (using 3 by 3in timber) standing out from the rear wall of his bungalow by about 18in. Since this is at the gable end, the sloping radials go nicely down the sloping gables on tall stand-off insulators. The 7/21MHz radials go to short posts mounted on the garden fences on each side of the bungalow (presumably he does not have any 3·5MHz radials). The antenna is "grounded" at the feed point via a heavy wire running

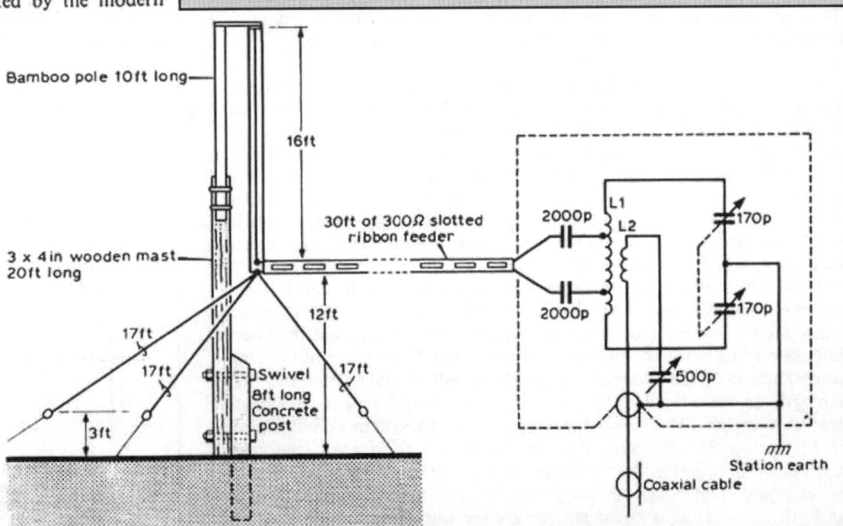

Fig 8. G3MXT's 14MHz three-wire (folded) groundplane using 7/029 pvc cable for vertical element with wires 1in apart with paxolin clamps every 3ft. The atu consists of L1 10t, 14swg. L2 4t, 16swg enam wound over centre of L1 with internal diameter 1·5in, 2·5in overall length, feeder taps 2·5t from each end. Feeder is 300Ω ribbon with "window" slots

ANTENNA TOPICS

down the mast to two buried stages as a protective measure. The wooden mast is hinged to a U-bracket at the lower end, so that to lower the mast and antenna it is necessary only to release the mast from the stand-off wall bracket and "walk" it back, having first released the radials from their stand-off insulators; a single-handed job!

This antenna convinces G2BY that Dr George Brown was right in originally specifying just two in-line radials for his original ground-plane antennas; incidentally he recalls hearing strong signals from the American police between 30 and 45MHz during the 1937–8 sunspot maximum period.

Groundplanes

Extracted from 'Technical Topics', *Radio Communication*, November 1981

Groundplanes

There is probably no such thing as a "simple" antenna. Indeed if one glances through the pages of, for example, *IEEE Trans Ant & Prop* (the prime source of information on what professional antenna research engineers and mathematicians are up to) one might be excused for thinking that only Senior Wranglers have any chance of understanding what happens when a piece of wire is fastened to the branch of a convenient tree or you hook up a tranny to the bed springs!

Perhaps, in spite of the various discussions recently in *TT* on vertical antennas, you still think of a groundplane antenna (gpa) or monopole as a basically simple and easily understood antenna. If so it is worth considering some comments that have come from Fred Brown, W6HPH/G5AWI, and John Wilson, G8KIS. W6HPH writes:

"I was intrigued by the dissertation on the groundplane antenna in July *TT*. Theoretical analysis of the gpa is perhaps as useful for illustrating certain antenna theorems as for understanding the groundplane itself. For instance, it can be shown that the gpa exhibits 3dB *gain* over a dipole. It is also possible to prove that the gpa in free space has 3dB *less gain* than a dipole. Both proofs are valid and do not contradict each other!

"It is quite easy to show that a $\lambda/4$ monopole over a perfectly conducting earth has 3dB of gain over a dipole in free space. This is simply a consequence of the fact that the monopole is radiating into a hemisphere rather than into a sphere; its three-dimensional directive pattern is identical to a dipole except sliced in half. Hence it is radiating into half the angular volume, and therefore exhibits 3dB of directive gain.

"What is not so well known is that at 0° elevation angle a gpa in free space is 3dB *worse* than a dipole in free space. At first this might seem to contradict the above paragraph, which could lead one to believe that an elevated gpa is 3dB better than a $\lambda/2$ dipole at the same height.

"The principle of symmetry permits us to insert a thin conducting sheet into the H-plane of any symmetric antenna without affecting the electromagnetic fields. This is shown in Fig 4 (a) for a $\lambda/4$ dipole.

"In Fig 4(b) the voltage generator has been split into two generators of half voltage so that connections can be made to the conducting plane. This, of course, makes it possible to split the antenna into two identical monopoles, each completely shielded from the other, and so one monopole can be considered by itself.

"Current into the monopole will remain exactly as it was for the dipole, but since the voltage generator is now $E/2$, we have the well-known result that the impedance of the monopole is exactly one-half that of the equivalent dipole. Although this analysis has assumed an infinite conducting plane, it also obviously holds true for a finite but large groundplane since the edge of any large plane will be too far from the feedpoint to affect impedance. It also has been shown experimentally to be valid for a groundplane of only $\lambda/4$ radius, as well as the more common configuration of four $\lambda/4$ radials.

"The field strength, e, at a distant point on the horizontal plane is found by integrating the current Idl over the length of the monopole. There are other factors involving distance and phase in the integral, but they need not concern us here. The important point is that if we carry out the same integration over the original $\lambda/2$ dipole, it will produce twice the field strength, $2e$, since the integration is over twice as much length. This might lead us to expect that a monopole would be 6dB worse than a dipole since e is 6dB below $2e$. But remember the dipole was fed from a generator voltage of E, whereas the monopole had a voltage of $E/2$. So twice as much power (3dB more) was going into the dipole since current is the same in both cases. Thus if equal *powers* are fed into the two antennas, the monopole will be 3dB worse in producing distant field strength. Hence its gain is −3dBd at zero elevation angle.

"The E-plane pattern of the gpa vs the dipole is shown in Fig 5. Note that regardless of the size of the conducting plane the gpa is always 3dB worse than the $\lambda/2$ dipole at zero elevation angle. Of course, this is virtually the only angle of interest in vhf propagation. At sufficiently high elevation angles, the gpa can actually show a gain over a $\lambda/2$ dipole, a result consistent with the analysis of my second paragraph. A larger conducting plane will bring down the elevation angle where maximum gain occurs; but at 0° the dipole will *always* be 3dB better than the groundplane, no matter how large a conducting plane is used.

"In view of these facts it is surprising that groundplanes are so widely used for vhf omnidirectional coverage. Not only do they throw away 3dB, both receiving and transmitting, they exhibit a difficult feed impedance of about 35Ω. Both feed impedance and gain can be improved by drooping the radials down to 60° or more below horizontal. This simple expedient will raise the feed impedance to the standard 50Ω and increase the gain to almost that of a dipole."

John Wilson, G8KIS, who is a member of the Science Unit at BBC Bush House, draws attention to a detailed letter from M.S. Smith and Gaelle de

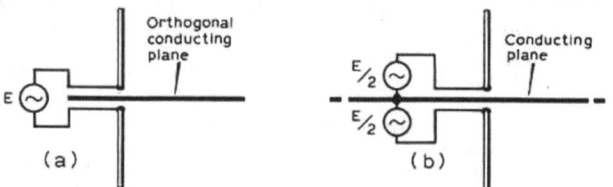

Fig 4. (a) Dipole element into which a thin conducting sheet has been inserted. (b) Showing how a voltage generator can be split into two so that connection can be made to the conducting plate (groundplane) to form two identical and separate monopoles each having a feedpoint impedance half that of a dipole

Prunelé, of University College London, published in *Electronics Letters* (3 September, 1981, Vol 17, No 18, pp 653–6). This shows that the size and nature of the "groundplane" of a monopole antenna also has a considerable effect on the amount of cross-polarized radiation, ie the extent of the horizontally-polarized component radiated from or received on this "vertically-polarized" antenna. G8KIS points out that this letter has practical consequences on the debate regarding polarization that is currently being conducted in both broadcasting and amateur mobile circles.

The writers point out in their introduction that "a monopole antenna equal or less than $\lambda/4$ long, on a groundplane whose dimensions are large compared to the operating wavelength, has an image due to induced currents in the groundplane, and the radiation pattern is principally vertically polarized. For groundplanes with dimensions of about one or two wavelengths (typical dimensions with a 144MHz antenna mounted on the roof of a car—*G3VA*) *the induced currents do not form a complete image* and this has several effects: (a) the vertically-polarized pattern is modified; (b) the input impedance is modified; and (c) *some horizontally-polarized radiation can occur, depending on the shape of the finite groundplane.*" It is also suggested that non-central monopoles, as commonly used on car roofs and boots (particularly for vhf/fm broadcast reception) and often with rectangular groundplanes tend to have a cross-polarized element independent of monopole length but which varies with the size of the groundplane in terms of the size/wavelength ratio.

G8KIS points out that such findings have a significant bearing on the question of using mixed polarization (circular or slant) for broadcasting and mobile operation. He also feels that this effect may explain why a 144MHz or 432MHz handy-talkie often works just as well (or better) when held horizontally while working a vertically-polarized distant station. He wonders whether amateur repeaters ought to be equipped with antennas providing mixed polarization as an experiment.

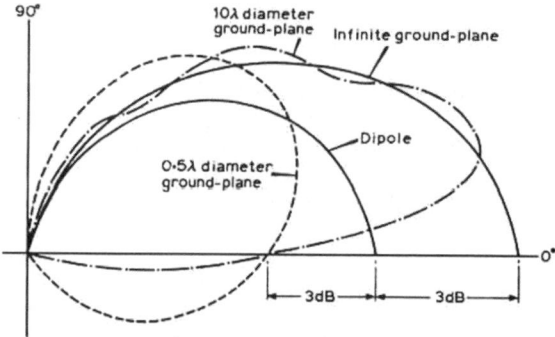

Fig 5. Free space radiation patterns of $\lambda/4$ monopoles over perfectly conducting groundplanes of various diameters. The infinite groundplane shows a 3dB gain over a dipole at 0° elevation angle, but any finite groundplane will exhibit a 3dB loss

Antenna Radiation Patterns

Extracted from 'Technical Topics', *Radio Communication,* November 1981

Antenna radiation patterns

Many of the antennas used by radio amateurs are (and have to be) located in far from ideal sites. It is extremely difficult to assess accurately the extent to which a particular site is likely to affect results. It is worth remembering that one of the most common problems is that nearby structures tend to blur and fill in the nulls that look so impressive in the theoretical radiation patterns, and which one hopes will reduce interference from short-skip signals.

Recently, for example, in discussing the ZL-Special and HB9CV unidirectional driven arrays (*TT* October) I mentioned the good back-to-front ratio associated with the cardioid radiation patterns. It is, however, worth noting that *Ham Radio* (October 1980) reported a professional investigation into the ZL-Special indicating that it can yield a power gain of about 4dB (reference dipole) and a front-to-back ratio of about 36dB with a deep null off the back of the beam. However, it then added: "the deep null directly off the back, shown in theory, is usually unobtainable because of reflection from nearby metallic objects or buildings". Any conductive object (including trees) in the plane of polarization of a transmitting antenna tends to pick up and re-radiate energy and so forms an extra (usually unwanted) element in the array.

This point is brought out in *IBA Technical Review No 14* in a section discussing the four-mast directional mf antenna with vertical polarization at Saffron Green, near Barnet, North London, where the primary object is to obtain deep rejection nulls in specific directions in order to prevent co-channel interference with other stations using the same channels (the antenna radiates simultaneously on two frequencies). Despite a long and intensive search, it was necessary to accept that any site in the London area was likely to be less than ideal—with the following results:

"At London, the site was adjacent to two lines of electricity pylons to the north and east, the pylons being of various heights between 27m and 32m and about 500m distant at their closest approach. The situation was complicated by the presence of a 24m steel tower at a distance of 700m in front of the antenna in the main lobe.

"The effect of these structures is to form a complex antenna of 32 radiating elements, tending to provide radiation patterns in which the broad nulls are broken by as many as a dozen small lobes, though in practice the antenna achieves the desired nulls in the critical directions."

The pylons and towers were a good deal shorter than the four radiating elements (each 71m high) and the closest was 0·5km distant (at the frequencies concerned this represents about 2λ or more). By comparison, most amateur antennas are positively hemmed in by metal gutters, fences, roof spaces containing water pipes etc, etc. It is no wonder that antennas so often have radiation patterns that differ from those in the handbooks!

Beverages and Rhombics

Extracted from 'Technical Topics', *Radio Communication,* December 1981

Beverage and rhombics

For those with plenty of space, long-wire antennas such as the Beverage and rhombic can still exert considerable fascination. There is also the point that for vhf and uhf the rhombic fits conveniently into an average back garden or even a loft-space. In *QST* (September 1981, p51) John S. Belrose provides some basic information on the long-wire, low Beverage antenna:

(1) For frequencies around 2MHz a Beverage antenna has *better* performance when the ground conductivity is *poor*.

(2) Gain and directivity increase with length of antenna.

(3) Gain increases with height of the antenna above ground but the difference is not large.

(4) For a 100m-long antenna only 1m above ground, the azimuthal bandwidth on about 2MHz is about 77°, vertical beamwidth about 60°, and take-off angle about 42°.

The characteristic impedance of a Beverage antenna is about 500Ω, and this is the value for both the terminating resistor and the antenna matching impedance. It should be appreciated that the main attraction of a Beverage antenna is the good signal-to-noise ratio when used as a receiving antenna; for transmission, radiation from a low Beverage will tend to be less than from a dipole.

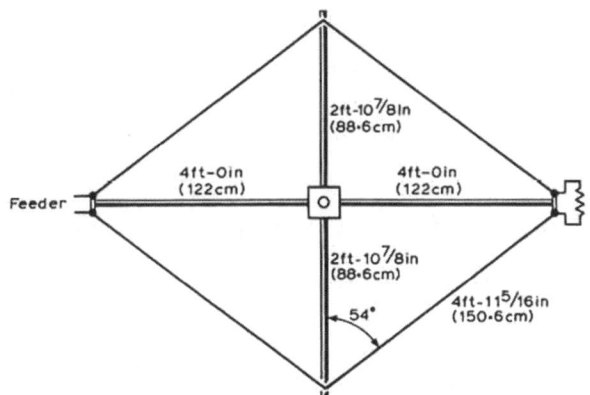

Fig. 4. N3AWE's 432MHz rhombic antenna only 8ft in overall length yet capable of gains of the order of 18dB. Terminating and input impedances about 300Ω

On uhf the dimensions of a rhombic become very attractive, and it is even possible to think in terms of a rotary system. From *Old Man* (no 9/81, p21) comes a 432MHz rhombic only 8ft overall length yet claimed to provide a gain of about 18dB: Fig 4. The design is credited to N3AWE and *CQ Magazine* of unknown date. The non-inductive terminating resistor is 300Ω, and the array can be fed directly with 300Ω balanced feeder. Without the terminating resistor, the array will be bidirectional; wattage of this resistor depends upon the duty cycle of the transmitter, but even for fm should not need to be more than about one-third of the output wattage of the transmitter, and less for low-duty-cycle transmissions.

Antenna Table

Extracted from 'Technical Topics', *Radio Communication,* January 1982

Antenna table

Most of the published tables of antenna element lengths do not include the new hf bands. To save pressing the keys on a pocket calculator, Table 1 shows lengths for selected frequencies for wire antennas erected well clear of the ground and away from other large objects; bends in the antenna may also increase the length required, and it is advisable to check elements with a gdo or noise bridge. In the table the second column represents the physical length of λ/2; the next column shows the usual end correction of roughly 5 per cent; the final column shows the correction deducted to the nearest inch. For antennas more than λ/2 long only one end correction should be deducted: for example, a full-wave antenna for 14,100kHz would be about 2 by 34ft 11in, less 1ft 9in, ie 68ft 1in, so that a given long-wire antenna will not resonate precisely on harmonic-related frequencies, although this is usually not of great practical consequence.

Table 1 — Antenna resonant lengths

Frequency (MHz)	λ/2 (492/f)	End correction approx 5%	λ/2 resonant length (468/f)
1·825	269ft 7in	13ft 2in	256ft 5in (78·21m)
1·900	258ft 11in	12ft 6in	246ft 4in (75·12m)
3·525	139ft 7in	6ft 11in	132ft 9in (40·5m)
3·650	134ft 9in	6ft 6in	128ft 3in (39·11m)
7·020	70ft 1in	3ft 6in	66ft 8in (20·33m)
10·125	48ft 7in	2ft 5in	46ft 3in (14·1m)
14·050	35ft 0in	1ft 9in	33ft 4in (10·16m)
14·200	34ft 8in	1ft 9in	32ft 11in (10·05m)
18·100	27ft 2in	1ft 4in	25ft 10in (7·89m)
21·050	23ft 4in	1ft 1in	22ft 3in (6·78m)
21·200	23ft 3in	1ft 2in	22ft 1in (6·73m)
21·300	23ft 1in	1ft 2in	22ft 0in (6·7m)
24·940	19ft 9in	1ft 0in	18ft 9in (5·72m)
28·050	17ft 6in	0ft 11in	16ft 8in (5·09m)
28·400	17ft 4in	0ft 10in	16ft 6in (5·03m)
29·500	16ft 8in	0ft 10in	15ft 10in (4·84m)

ANTENNA TOPICS

There is an interesting possibility for 10·1MHz operation that has been brought to my attention by an unknown reader. The use of the same 67ft or so dipole for both 7 and 21MHz is well known, the antenna working as a useful 3λ/2 dipole on 21MHz with its very attractive radiation pattern. A less precise, but roughly similar relationship exists between 10·1MHz and the cw end of 3·5MHz. The reader has checked his 3·5MHz antenna with a noise bridge and it looks quite good at 10·1MHz. If one takes 3 × 48ft 7in − 2ft 5in, it turns out to be about 143ft, a shade long for 3·5MHz but certainly very usable! This also raises the possibility that antennas such as the G5RV may turn out to be quite efficient antennas for 10·1MHz without modification.

Elevated-feed Multiband Vertical

Extracted from 'Technical Topics', *Radio Communication,* January 1982

Elevated-feed multiband vertical

Some 15 years ago, I reported in *TT* that a vertical antenna offering the low-angle radiation characteristics of a vertical colinear array could be achieved by feeding a vertical element across an insulator placed one-third of the way up the element. This idea was derived from a Marconi hf direction-finder where, of course, it was used only in the receive mode, so that little practical experience could be quoted for its use as a transmitting antenna. The principle of elevated feed has been used in the broadcast field to provide anti-fading characteristics for vertically polarized ground-wave signals.

The elevated-feed principle was described in some detail, and this information, together with current distribution and vertical radiation pattern diagrams for antennas having a total height of from λ/4 to 1λ and showing a significant reduction of high-angle radiation, has since appeared in many editions of *Amateur Radio Techniques.* However, I must confess that this has, until now, been one of those items on which no feedback has ever been received.

However, Paul Pauliukonis, WD9AHH, in *CQ Magazine* (August 1981, pp94–6) describes "The better vertical-elevated feed means low angle of radiation" which he acknowledges is based on the *ART* information. His article includes a detailed account of his construction of such an antenna having an overall height of 34ft 4in and with a small "top hat" loading element: Fig 3(a). He uses the lower end of the 1in pipe as an earth spike, and also has earth radials—because for this type of antenna a good earth system is clearly necessary when used for transmission.

He comments: "I feel the elevated-feed principle has much to offer to the amateur radio operator. In fact I like this antenna so much that I am planning to optimize performance on 14 and 7MHz by designing and building one which will be 66ft tall." With the dimensions shown in Fig 3(a) he claims good dx performance on 21 and 28MHz, reasonable results on 14MHz, and useful performance on 3·5 and 7MHz.

Elevated-feed antennas do pose some practical problems: the insulator up the mast, and the requirement for voltage rather than current feed. WD9AHH avoids the need to have a matching network at the feed point by using a length of coaxial cable to the matching network shown in Fig 3(b) located at the base of the mast, the high swr on the short length of foam cable having little practical effect on results. The components in his matching unit were taken from an army surplus tuning unit. The system involves a rather complex matching arrangement, and I would stress that the system is recommended only where the earth conductivity is reasonably good.

Half-square and G5RV-type Antennas

Extracted from 'Technical Topics', *Radio Communication,* February 1982

Half-square and G5RV-type antennas

The half-square antenna (Fig 7) has figured previously in *TT,* as indeed has the bobtail curtain which is in effect a "double half-square" (though this is not as one might suppose a "square" antenna!) and both designs in several versions can be found in *ART.* Nevertheless, it is worth noting that in *Ham Radio* December 1981, Robert "Hasan" Schiers, N0AN, writes with great enthusiasm of the results he achieves on a number of hf bands with a simple, low-cost 7MHz half-square antenna, voltage-fed in the manner more usually advocated for the bobtail. He finds this configuration functions well as a λ/4 Marconi on 1·8MHz (current fed), a λ/2 end-fed on 3·5MHz, a

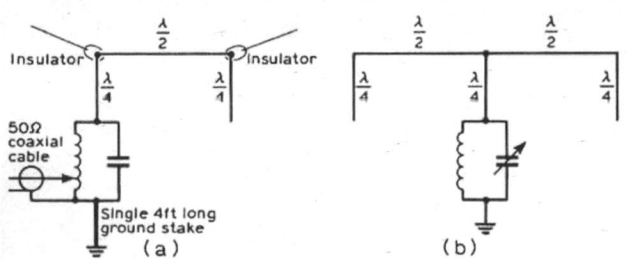

Fig 7. (a) The half-square antenna (mixed polarization) with the voltage-fed arrangement used by N0AN. This also provides an effective antenna on other hf bands. (b) The classic "bobtail" array in which the horizontally-polarized component is partially cancelled out to provide a three-element vertically-polarized array

half-square array on 7MHz, a pair of λ/2 verticals, space 1λ, on 14MHz, and a pair of 1λ verticals spaced 2λ on 28MHz. However, he does not mention that polarization (unlike the bobtail) is mixed, as there will be a horizontal component which is not cancelled out. We suspect this is no disadvantage when used for a general purpose or dx antenna.

This is another article in which it is suggested that a length of RG-8/U coaxial cable forms an effective high-voltage, low-cost capacitor of required value. This particular cable has a capacitance of 30pF/ft, and N0AN obtains a value of about 38pF using a 15·2in length.

The practical snag with voltage-fed bobtail or half-square antennas is the need to change the resonant matching circuit which will normally be located outside the house. This is why antennas such as trapped dipoles and the G5RV multiband antennas are still so popular. In the past few years the convenience of the G5RV technique has crossed the Atlantic, and several

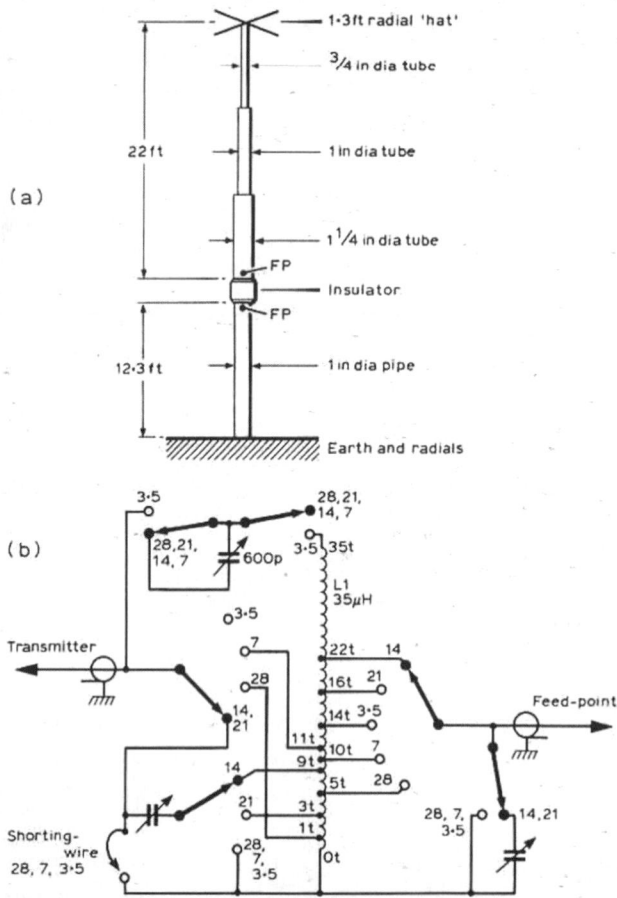

Fig 3. Practical realization of an elevated-fed multiband vertical antenna together with details of a matching unit located at the base of the antenna. Note that a very good earth is an important requirement, but the system provides colinear gain and concentrates more power at low angles of elevation. The 600pF variable capacitor can be low-voltage receiving type

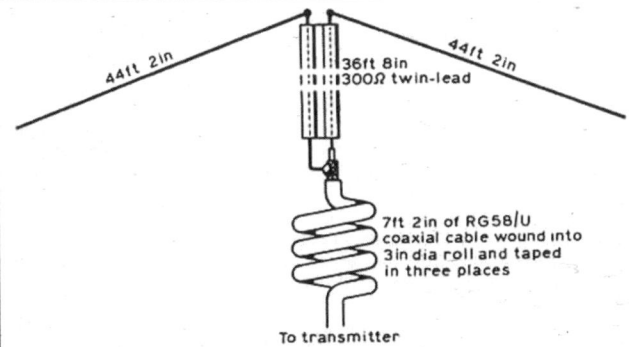

Fig 8. W5ANB's multiband antenna or "first cousin of the G5RV". With dimensions shown it is stated that it can be used without an atu on 7, 14 and 28MHz (and more critically on 21MHz, provided the transmitter will work satisfactorily with swr of about 3:1 or so

convenience of the G5RV technique has crossed the Atlantic, and several articles have appeared in *QST* etc. The latest version, described as a first cousin of the G5RV antenna, is by Taft Nicholson, W5ANB ("Compact multiband antenna without traps" *QST* November 1981, pp26–27): Fig 8. This is claimed to need no atu when used with a transmitter having a valve output stage, and to work with some transmitters in this way on 21MHz "but tuning is quite critical". It all adds up to an antenna claimed to be easy to pack, carry, erect and use.

Groundplanes Again

Extracted from 'Technical Topics',
Radio Communication, April 1982

Groundplanes again
Alan Boswell, G3NOQ, suggests that some readers may have been unnecessarily put off using vhf groundplane antennas by W6HPH's analysis in *TT* November 1981; this warned of a "3dB loss" compared with a vertical dipole. They may have gained the impression that half the total radiation is "lost" when a λ/4 radiator mounted over non-infinite radials is used. He stresses that dipoles and monopoles both radiate virtually all the energy fed to them, and to believe otherwise would contradict the fundamental laws of conservation of energy. Only a small part of the total energy would be accounted for by the cross-polarized radiation over a small groundplane, as mentioned by John Wilson, G8KIS.

G3NOQ considers that the λ/4 monopole with vehicle-roof groundplane forms an excellent omni-directional antenna ideally suited to vhf mobile operation. Although a vertical dipole theoretically is the better antenna (since it combines with its "image" in the ground to form a colinear array having a narrower beam in the vertical plane), for most mobile work this would be an impractical, unduly expensive, system. Though he admits to being surprised that the fixed vertical trap dipole has not found more favour among hf operators, as the full feed current does not flow into lossy earth (a point made last year in the earlier discussions on vertical antennas).

I hope I do nobody an injustice, but I have a sneaking feeling that G3NOQ may have rather misinterpreted W6HPH's analysis of the 3dB loss, or else that I have misunderstood G3NOQ's comments. The 3dB loss occurs only for radiation in the horizontal plane, and is made up for by additional radiation at higher vertical angles. Omnidirectional antennas frequently have appreciable gains or losses in specific planes by virtue of their vertical radiation pattern. This is seldom taken into account at hf, where the useful vertical angle radiation varies with height of the ionospheric layer etc. But, for example, vhf/uhf omnidirectional broadcasting antennas may have a colinear gain of over 10dB towards the horizon (or tilted slightly downwards). A uhf television station can have 1,000kW effective radiated power from transmitters providing only, say, 50kW peak output power.

One must, however, agree with G3NOQ that the whole subject of antenna gains and losses offers enormous scope for "sophistry, semantics and what is known in the trade as 'specmanship'—ie why say your antenna has a gain of 12dB when with some subtle redefinition you can say the gain is 18dB?"

It is all too true that the gain of any antenna depends on how you define gain—one reason why *QST* never allows advertisers to publish even a "claimed gain" figure for antennas!

Controlled-current-distribution Antennas

Extracted from 'Technical Topics',
Radio Communication, April 1982

Controlled-current-distribution antennas
Last year in *TT* June and October, an account was given of VK5NN's recent work on capacitively-loaded ("stretched") antennas for hf and vhf, exploiting the advantage of this technique as first described in detail in 1961 by "Dud" Charman, G6CJ (*ART*).

Harry A. Mills, W4FD, and Gene Brizendinge, W4ATE, have sent me extracts from two articles they wrote on hf "ccd" (controlled-current-distribution) antennas in *73 Magazine* (October 1978 and July 1981). The ccd antenna is basically a capacitively-loaded antenna stretched by a factor of two, as in the original EMI/G6CJ system, but with the addition of some capacitive end-loading (US patent 3,564,551 granted to W4FD). The use of

Table 1 — CCD (stretched) antenna dimensions

Band (MHz)	Length (ft)	(m)	Section (in)	(cm)	No of sections	Capacitors (pF)	No of capacitors
1·8	560	(170·7)	140	(356)	48	1,560	46
3·5	280	(85·4)	70	(178)	48	780	46
7	140	(42·7)	35	(89)	48	390	46
14	70	(21·3)	17·5	(44·5)	48	195	46
21	46·5	(14·2)	11·5	(29)	48	130	46
28	35	(10·6)	8·75	(22)	48	97·5	46

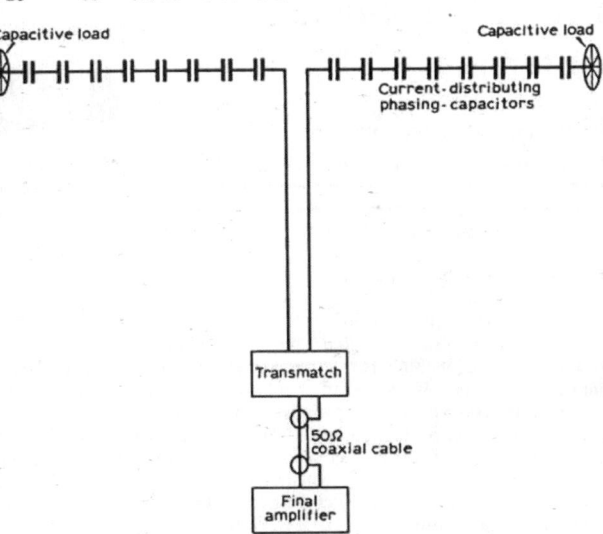

Fig 1. The "controlled-current distribution" antenna (stretched dipole) as described by W4FD and W4ATE. It seems likely that the end capacitive loading could be dispensed with without seriously affecting results

end-loading is claimed to further reduce dielectric and ground losses and lower the vertical angle of radiation while retaining the many advantages of stretched elements. It is felt that the following notes on the construction of such elements will prove useful to those whose interest in this system has been aroused and have the space to allow its exploitation.

Fig 1. shows a typical dipole element loaded in accordance with Table 1. For other capacitor values or frequencies the authors give:

Number of capacitors = f(MHz) × C(pF)/59·35
Number of wire sections(S) = number of capacitors plus two
Overall length (L) in inches = 984 × 12/f(MHz)
Length of wire sections = L/S

Twelve constructional hints were given, as follows:

(1) Select wire section lengths and capacitor values from Table 2 for the required band (measure to centre of insulators).

(2) Saw small insulators (0·6 by 1·75in, 15·8 by 44·5mm) from 0·13in (3·2mm) sheet plastic (or alternatively use 0·5in, 12·7mm plastic waterpipe both for insulation and to protect the capacitor).

(3) Match capacitors to within five per cent using only polystyrene, silver mica, mica or mylar (100V rating is adequate for 1kW).

(4) Connect the wire sections to the insulators, ensuring section lengths are accurate between centres of adjacent insulators.

(5) Scrape wire ends clean and solder well the capacitors across the insulators, omitting capacitor at the centre feedpoint.

(6) Build two simple end-loading 24in (61cm) diameter "wheels" of copper wire using for example No 10 stripped house wire for the rim and No 14 to 18 bare copper wire for eight "spokes". Carefully solder all joining

ANTENNA TOPICS

wires.

(7) Carefully solder the centre of the wheels to the ends of the ccd element.

(8) Suspend the antenna (without feeder) about 6ft (1·83m) high, for resonating and testing.

(9) Connect a one-to-two-turn coil to centre feedpoint and couple a dip meter, vswr or noise bridge, and adjust the ccd length to resonate at the *low* frequency end of the band, removing or adding an equal number of complete wire/capacitor sections from each end as necessary.

(10) Remove test instrument and connect a 300Ω line between the ccd element and the antenna tuning unit (alternatively use coaxial cable with 4:1 balun at the ccd centre).

(11) Apply reduced power, and test to ensure that power is distributed to ends of antenna by using a small neon lamp or other rf indicator against the antenna. Start at the antenna centre and explore all sections towards each end (if rf voltage indication is lost, it is probable that the last capacitor is poorly soldered or defective and needs to be replaced by another matched capacitor.

(12) Contact several stations with full power, before raising the ccd element to its final height. Note that the resonant frequency of the element will change by only an insignificant amount as the antenna is raised (one of the features of a capacitively-loaded element). If space is limited, erect as inverted-V dipole, or let antenna ends hang down etc. W4FD and W4ATE consider that such a λ/2 dipole (physically 1λ long) can form a very effective antenna, but point out that many other configurations are possible.

"Some two years ago I resumed operation from Hendon, NW4—a very ordinary London suburban location—after a year off the air. Previously I had worked from Essex using a TH6 beam, 60ft high, to compile a dx score over the years of 330-plus countries.

"Lack of space (and cash) dictated an altogether less ambitious antenna system. I use three separate dipoles, within a couple of feet of each other, for 14, 21 and 28MHz. These are about 25ft high, slung between the roof guttering and a convenient tree. For 7MHz I have an upside-down delta-loop with the apex at about 30ft (Fig 3). My rig is Heathkit SB401-200-303.

"I was apprehensive about the dx possibilities of such modest antennas, so different from the TH6 set-up. I need not have worried. In almost exactly two years I've worked 270 countries, entirely on ssb, including 115 countries on 7MHz. Only about half-a-dozen countries have been heard but not raised; S9-plus reports from every part of the globe; most dxpeditions worked; only in really horrendous pile-ups have my calls been wasted. With such an antenna farm it has all been totally surprising—and terrific fun.

"To those wanting to work dx in such circumstances, I would offer the following advice: *(1)* use as much power as money and licence regulations permit; *(2)* use resonant single-band antennas that do not require an atu; *(3)* make maximum use of dx nets, lists and helpful locals (and ensure they remain helpful by not making a nuisance of yourself); and *(4)* take care when setting up simple antennas, and make sure your measurements are correct (though mine are fashioned from 1943-vintage Army-surplus antennas fed with brown television-type coaxial cable!).

"The 7MHz antenna of Fig 3 (suggested to me by GW3AX) has an swr of less than 1·5:1 (if I dare mention that in *TT*!). Pruning is very easy because of the accessibility of the feedpoint. Very little directivity has been noted, and signals seem about level with those of G stations using wire or vertical antennas and about 2–3dB down on those with 7MHz beams. It makes a good receiving antenna on any band, mf or hf, it takes up less horizontal space than a dipole and needs less feeder. The formula 1007/MHz (ft) proved slightly long but readily pruned. It would make a cheap and simple antenna for any band."

DX and the Simple Antenna

Extracted from 'Technical Topics',
Radio Communication, May 1982

DX and the simple antenna

From time to time it has been noted in *TT* that simple hf antennas, including long wires, large loops, dipoles and verticals, are well capable of providing worldwide contacts, including (reasonably often) those with the type of dx rarity that attracts the notorious pile-ups. This view has recently been receiving support also in the *Rad Com* "Your opinion" column. But it would be a brave (or foolhardy) writer who would normally suggest that a simple antenna, in difficult urban or suburban conditions, can still yield very high dx scores over short periods of time. Yet a score of some 270 countries, and over a hundred on 7MHz, has recently been achieved by Laurie Margolis, G3UML, using simple tree-supported antennas. While there are many who are coming to believe that amateur radio has become rather too obsessed with country-chasing for its own good, this feat merits serious technical consideration. G3UML writes:

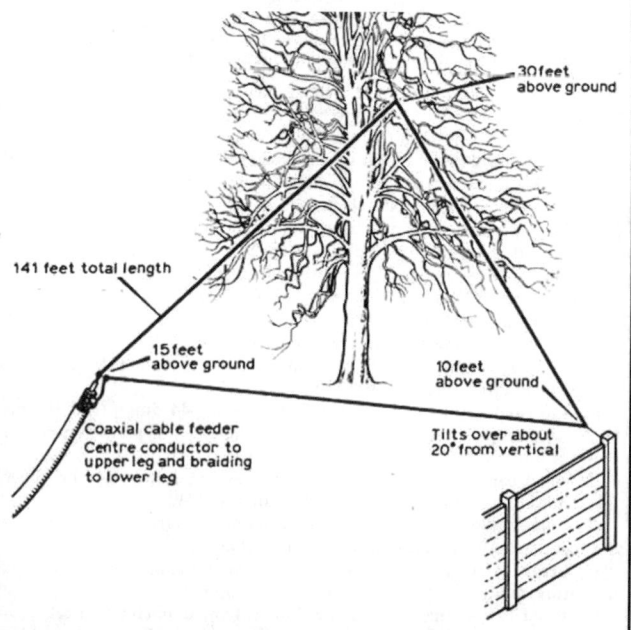

Fig 3. The inverted tree-supported delta loop that has brought G3UML some 115 "countries-worked" on 7MHz ssb in the past couple of years

Potential of the G5RV Antenna

Extracted from 'Technical Topics',
Radio Communication, May 1982

Potential of the G5RV antenna

B. A. Austin, ZS6BKW, and senior lecturer at the University of the Witwatersrand, Johannesburg, is in the fortunate position of being able to carry out professional research into ideas that come from his hobby. Recent mention in *TT* of the use of the G5RV centre-fed antenna on 10·1MHz encourages ZS6BKW to make a preliminary report on some computer investigations that he has been carrying out that underline the still unexplored potential of this antenna (Fig 4). He writes:

"I have used a G5RV antenna at home in an inverted-V configuration for many years, and its basic effectiveness is beyond doubt. My approach has been the standard one: approximately 31·1m (102ft) top, fed at the centre by an electrical λ/2 of 300Ω ribbon feeder (approximately 10·4m multiplied by the velocity factor of the cable for 14MHz) and then any convenient length of 72Ω balanced twin line.

"The G5RV represents a clever idea and has, I feel, some unexplored potential. To investigate it further I wrote a program in Basic for the Data General Eclipse machine in the department. The input data required are the values of the top section (the "antenna") for any given length, L1, and operating frequency. Such information is available in the literature (my source was Appendix 4 in *Antennas and Waves—A Modern Approach* by R. W. P. King and C. W. Harrison, published by the MIT Press, 1969). This provides free-space data but is a good point at which to start. The effects of

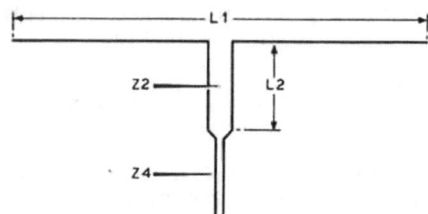

Fig 4. The basic G5RV-type antenna arrangement for which the dimensions L1 and L2 and balanced feeder impedances Z3 and Z4 have been subjected to computer analysis by ZS6BKW for all hf bands, including 10, 18 and 24MHz

The Short Vertical

Extracted from 'Technical Topics',
Radio Communication, August 1982

'real' earth below an antenna are very well documented in the literature, and use of that data plus some 'in situ' measurements of my own will form a further part of the research programme.

"First of all the results so far obtained show conclusively that Louis Varney's initial dimensions were not far off the mark! Fig 4 shows the theoretical antenna used for the computer results, together with some computer print-out.

Print-out No 1
Computer listing of vswr versus frequency for G5RV-type antenna of following specification: L1, 31·1m; L2, 10·366m; Z2 300Ω; Z4, 72Ω.

Frequency (MHz)	VSWR	Frequency (MHz)	VSWR
3·65	6·3286415	18·1	24·420945
7·05	5·825977	21·2	4·7205896
10·13	37·072547	24·9	1·3276165
14·2	1·9552423	28·5	38·633995

Print-out No 2
Specification: L1, 32·737m; L2, 10·366m; Z2, 300Ω; Z4, 72Ω.

Frequency (MHz)	VSWR	Frequency (MHz)	VSWR
3·65	3·5608961	18·1	23·268652
7·05	5·1625437	21·2	7·92111
10·13	41·554876	24·9	6·2673029
14·2	5·6544082		

Print-out No 3
Specification: L1, 27·9m; L2, 13·6m; Z2, 400Ω; Z4, 50Ω.

Frequency (MHz)	VSWR	Frequency (MHz)	VSWR
3·65	11·779485	24·9	1·869093
7·05	1·8361328	28·0	10·239141
10·13	88·172538	28·5	4·1535267
14·2	1·2883087	29·0	1·8422786
18·1	1·6040507	29·5	4·9340089
21·2	67·694191		

"I have considered eight frequencies covering the amateur hf allocations (in South Africa *all three* new bands were released to us from 18 January 1982). The specific frequencies examined were: 3·65, 7·05, 10·13, 14·2, 18·1, 21·2, 24·9 and 28·5MHz.

"The results of the first print-out show that the G5RV, as designed, will work 'well' on 14 and 24MHz when the matching section is 300Ω and the feedline is 72Ω. On the 10 and 28MHz bands the swr rises very rapidly (37 and 39). On the other frequencies the swr is quite manageable; on both 3·5 and 7MHz the swr is around six.

"The criterion used here for judging relative performance is 'swr' simply because this is an easily-measured parameter and indicates the range of load impedances presented by the antenna system to the transmitter. The frequent references in *TT* to the unwarranted reverence with which low swr is often treated are wholeheartedly supported!

"However, if an 'end-effect' connection of about five per cent is made, and the electrical length *increased* to 32·737m (as in the second print-out), the system becomes much less attractive. For example, on 14MHz the swr rises to 5·65. This suggests that a shorter antenna top (L1) would be better. The computer program allowed L1, L2, Z2 and Z4 all to be changed, and all combinations to be tested. The third print-out is interesting because it shows that a *theoretically* improved system would result with: L1, 27·9m (note *no* end-effect connection); L2, 13·6m (electrical length); Z2, 400Ω; and Z4, 50Ω.

"Then if one takes an swr criterion of less than or equal to 2:1, such an antenna should provide a very good match on 7, 14, 18, 24 and 29MHz (rather than 28·5MHz). In arriving at these results, I limited the options for Z4 to 50Ω and 72Ω for obvious reasons; I allowed Z2 to vary in 50Ω steps from 300 to 600Ω.

"I would stress these are preliminary results only, and the work is continuing, but I do believe that they give some useful idea as to how a G5RV-type antenna should behave over the hf spectrum. There are obviously applications other than amateur radio for such types of 'multi-frequency' (but not 'broadband') antennas, and the work will look at all possibilities with the aim of a detailed article if results should justify this. In the meanwhile the preliminary results may be of interest to members."

It is perhaps relevant to note that *QST* recently contained a suggestion that a somewhat similar form of antenna was in fact recommended for commercial communications applications in the 'thirties by Collins Radio, but no reference was given.

One point brought out by ZS6BKW is that the 3λ/2 relationship (third harmonic) between 7 and 21MHz can be upset in a G5RV antenna by the effect of the matching stub, L2. A low vswr on 7MHz does *not* imply that a low value will be achieved on 21MHz, and similarly with 3·35MHz or (in this case) 3·65MHz and 10·13MHz. In all three calculated examples the vswr on 10·1MHz is very high; this does not mean that the G5RV cannot be used on 10·1MHz, but it does suggest strongly that it requires an effective antenna matching unit. With recent solidstate transmitters (particularly with broadband power amplifiers) the vswr needs to remain below 2:1 over the bands (or sections of the band) in use.

The short vertical

Electrically short hf vertical transmitting antennas remain a tantalizing but important subject for further experimental work. In theory, even an almost infinitesimally short antenna, if matched and loaded correctly, should be capable of radiating a far field almost as strong as a conventional resonant λ/4 monopole over a narrow bandwidth. In practice, in a real situation, this is never achieved due to the rapid increase of losses in the impedance matching network and the earth losses etc. Nevertheless it is possible to achieve useful results with helically-wound elements such as the popular "rubber duck" type of vhf antennas etc.

On hf an interesting attempt to provide an efficient antenna only 2ft high (2·8 electrical degrees at 4MHz) almost as effective as a 60ft-high monopole was described some 20 years ago by J. M. Boyer, W6UYH, of Northrop Corporation (the hula hoop or ddrr antenna, see *ART*). The snag with the hula hoop was the need for high conductivity copper pipe in the large circular "top loading" section, and the need for an extremely good earth plane. More recently, the continuing requirement for antennas suitable for tactical defence applications with high-angle radiation has led to ferrite-loaded elements and to various forms of transmitting loop antennas.

Dr Martin Sweeting, G3YJO, of UoSAT fame, has noted the resurgence of interest in *Rad Com* in ground-based hf systems and the attempts to assess the various forms of earthing systems, including radials. He has sent along a paper presented a few years ago at an AGARD conference (NATO Advisory Group for Aerospace Research & Development, Conference Proceedings No 263, "Electrically short hf aerial systems" by M. N. Sweeting and Q. V. Davis); this paper was based on his doctorate thesis and explored the use of a standard 4m vertical whip antenna at frequencies in the range 1 to 20MHz in conjunction with a wide variety of earthing systems. No attempt was made to "load" the whip element, and the frequency range included its use as a resonant λ/4 whip.

At the lower frequencies, well below λ/4 resonance, radiation resistance of such an element decreases rapidly and reactance increases correspondingly. It was shown in the paper that an effective measure of the efficiency of such an antenna can be made by a study of the base impedance measurements.

G3YJO's detailed study covered a considerable number of earthing systems, including earth spikes, earth plates, radials along the ground, and elevated radials. These ranged from a simple 12in, 0·5in diameter earth spike to systems using aluminium discs of 3ft and 6ft diameter placed on the ground beneath the antenna, and on to radial systems with the antenna element at a height of 5ft above ground and radials up to 150ft long. The paper provides over 40 diagrams showing the results of this investigation. The following conclusions were reached:

"This practical study of electrically short hf antennas has provided fresh insight into their behaviour in a field environment, and has demonstrated that:

(1) Antenna base impedance measurements appear to provide a straightforward and rapid means of evaluating symmetrical antenna systems.

(2) Small ground systems can provide a significant improvement over a simple earth spike, and are competitive with larger radial systems when wideband operation is required.

(3) Larger ground systems may provide improved narrow-band performances; however, radial resonances at previously unexpected frequencies can give rise to substantial losses of efficiency.

(4) If narrow-band operation is desired then the radials should be designed to be nλ/4 resonant, taking into account the phase velocity reduction due to the proximity of the earth.

(5) Small elevated radial systems appeared to exhibit a 2 to 7dB groundwave advantage over the same system on the ground.

(6) Radial resonance frequencies can be predicted easily from a knowledge of the effective dielectric constant of the ground and the system geometry.

(7) A straightforward measurement of the nλ/2 resonant frequency of a shallow buried radial wire can be used to determine the effective dielectric constant of the ground at radio frequencies with minimal mathematics."

ANTENNA TOPICS

Three-band Short Vertical Antenna

Extracted from 'Technical Topics', *Radio Communication,* August 1982

Three-band short vertical antenna

A coaxial-fed three-band top-loaded vertical antenna for 14, 21 and 28MHz (but which could probably be modified to cover also 18 and 24MHz) has been described by PA3AFZ and summarized in *Amateur Radio* (April 1982) by VK4QA. The idea is apparently based on a concept by Fred Brown, W6PHP/G5AWI, although the original article has escaped my notice.

The system is intended for use with λ/4 radials (at least one and preferably two or more for each band) as a top-loaded groundplane, although it could also be fed against earth if you have a really good earthing system. It is claimed by PA3AFZ that construction of a considerable number of such antennas has shown that the design is readily reproducible and capable of excellent performance on all the bands, provided that the original dimensions are retained and the adjustments correctly carried out.

The antenna (Fig 6) forms a λ/4 vertical on 28MHz (fine adjustment of resonance using the top section), and the system is brought into resonance on 21 and 14MHz by the two LC loading sections, one coil being adjusted for resonance on each band. The loading coils are wound on the horizontal rod, this crossmember being made from weatherproof pvc tubing having a diameter of 22mm and total length 305mm. The main vertical section consists of two short aluminium pipes sliding into each other to permit adjustment of length, with a hose clamp used to secure them. The coils are close-wound using 1mm diameter enamelled copper wire from 1·96m of wire for the 21MHz coil and 4·33m of wire for the 14MHz coil. The coils should be wound so that they can be moved as necessary to provide fine adjustment (coil details apply only if tubing is 22mm diameter), and it is claimed that the adjustments do not need to be carried out with the rod at its final height. The summary provided by VK4QA leaves a good deal of the detailed implementation of this antenna to the individual reader, but the following is a summary of the suggested adjustment procedure:

(1) Adjust length of radials for minimum swr on each band in turn.
(2) Adjust length of lower radiator section until resonance is obtained on 21MHz.
(3) Adjust 14MHz loading coil for resonance on 14MHz.
(4) Adjust top section of radiator for resonance on 28MHz.

Repeat the sequence of adjustments several times since there will be some interaction between the band resonances. Finally, if necessary, readjust radials which tend to be rather shorter than λ/4.

It is interesting to speculate whether this short antenna system could be extended to provide satisfactory results also on 18 and 24MHz, when these bands become available in the UK, simply by adding a second horizontal pvc rod at 90° to the existing crossmember, with two more capacitance hats and loading coils to resonate the system on these bands. If this were done it would require some re-adjustment on the existing bands, and there might be some unwanted resonances, but the idea would certainly seem to be feasible. Another possibility would be to add a degree of broadbanding to the antenna, for example by bringing wires down from the inner connection of the loading coils to the base of the vertical element (while retaining the existing connections to the top of the main pipe). This is based on pure speculation, but the result, once adjusted correctly, might well prove to be quite an effective five-band antenna with the radiating element less than 3m in total height. The *Amateur Radio* summary showed that the system, although of narrower bandwidth than a full-sized groundplane antenna, is not unduly so.

The Absorbing Yagi

Extracted from 'Technical Topics', *Radio Communication,* November 1982

The absorbing Yagi

It is well known that parasitically-excited antenna arrays such as the Yagi and cubical quad have a lobe pattern that restricts the front-to-back ratio when compared to the deepest nulls towards the sides. This significantly reduces the value of such arrays for some applications including the 144MHz df "fox-hunts" popular in Europe, or for rejecting unwanted noise or interference from the back.

John Beech, G8SEQ, has spent considerable time experimenting with Yagi arrays, and has developed what appears to be an important new technique that can be used to clean up the side-lobe pattern of a Yagi and produce very high f/b ratios—for example, around an astonishing 75dB for his 13-element array. While it is much to be hoped that he will produce a full length article for *Rad Com* on his work, the following notes explain the basic idea and indicate strongly that this technique seems worthy of further investigation. As far as I and G8SEQ are aware this is a completely new technique—although when one says that it is not unusual to find that somewhere in the literature similar proposals have appeared before, but failed to make an impact.

John Beech points out that the typical Yagi array is made up of a driven element, a reflector, a number of directors and sometimes launch directors. For his new element he has coined the term *absorber element*. He writes: "What does the absorber do? Exactly what the name implies. It absorbs rf energy. At first sight that may seem a contradiction to what an antenna element should do. But there are many occasions when what we really need is a deep null in a particular direction or a much improved f/b ratio to reduce pick-up, local electrical interference or ignition interference from passing cars etc.

"The absorber element is strategically placed to knock out a side lobe. I think this could be any side lobe, although so far I have used one only to improve the f/b ratio of arrays by placing the absorber element behind the

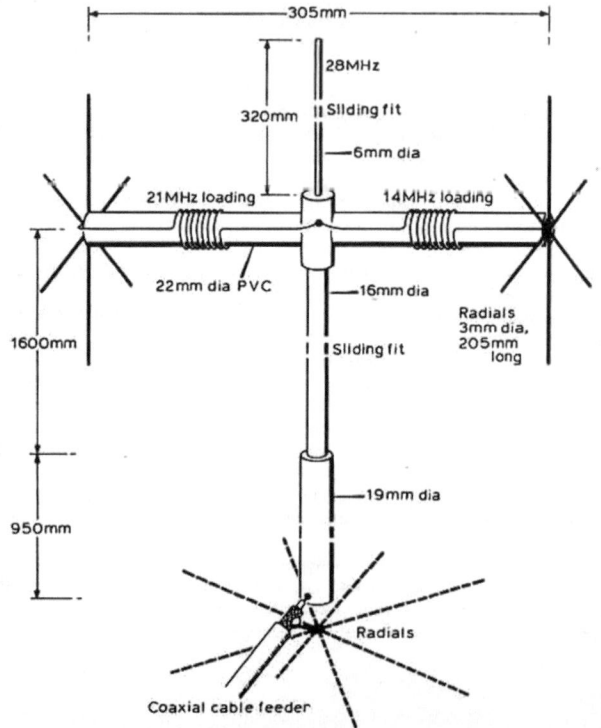

Fig 6. A three-band (14, 21 and 28MHz) short vertical antenna using top loading on 14 and 21MHz. The possibility of an additional crossmember carrying loading for 18 and 24MHz might be worth investigating

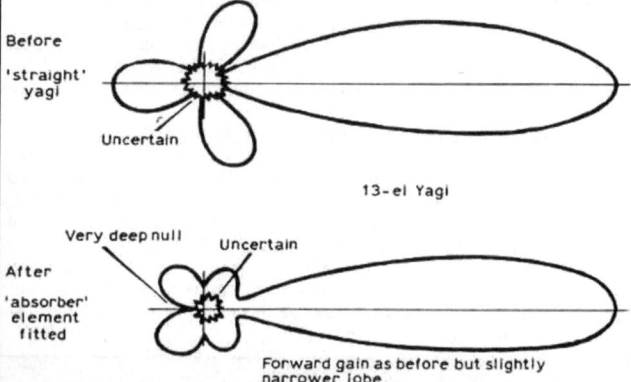

Fig 1. The effect of adding a G8SEQ "absorber element" to a 13-element 144MHz Yagi antenna. Power radiated in the backward direction is absorbed, creating a deep null that can be adjusted by "fine tuning" the absorber element

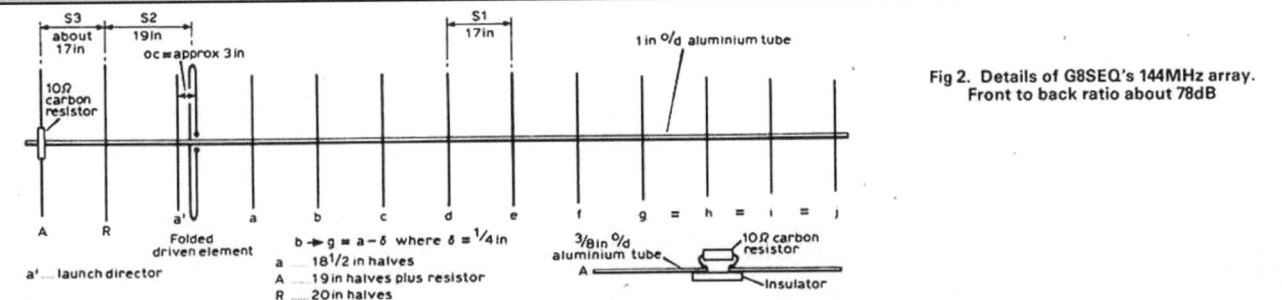

Fig 2. Details of G8SEQ's 144MHz array. Front to back ratio about 78dB

reflector. This is mechanically much simpler than for other lobes. For a 144MHz compact df antenna I have used an absorber *instead* of a reflector.

"So what does the absorber element consist of ? It is simply a dipole element at the array frequency (two 19in rods for 144MHz) with a chunky carbon resistor in the centre. The resistor should be equal in value to the centre impedance of the element when this is mounted in position on the array, and is best found by experiment using low power (ideally about 1W but less than 10W) in the transmit mode, aided by someone carefully monitoring your signal at a distance of more than about five miles. A small 100Ω slider pot or other preset resistor can be used for the initial setting up, although it is possible to "guestimate" the impedance and then simply use a carbon resistor near to this value. Final tuning is done by moving the absorber element towards or away from the reflector until optimum results are achieved. If the array is to be used for high power, a suitably-rated resistor must be used but, provided the antenna already has a reasonable f/b ratio, this is unlikely to be more than 25W even for the full legal power.

"To some extent the absorber element can be adjusted to give you the pattern you require. If you want to block out electrical interference or ignition noise from behind the antenna, first find the position giving the optimum f/b ratio and then 'detune' it slightly as this will broaden the null. On the other hand, for a df antenna you need the deepest, sharpest possible null to provide the most accurate bearing plus 'sense' . . . be adventurous, fit a 'radio black hole' to your antenna."

John Beech believes that the absorber technique could have a number of other applications. For example, on a sensitive eme array much of the "noise" comes from directions other than the moon. For domestic or professional television reception one could conceive this as a valuable technique for reducing co-channel interference; for rebroadcast (rbr) links, as widely used in the UK, it is generally felt that a 30dB null is about the limit for fixed arrays (one problem with narrow deep nulls on a high structure is mechanical rigidity). G8SEQ suggests that one can regard the Yagi array as a directional bandpass filter, and that the absorber is the element that has been missing for years. With the same thinking which is now sometimes being applied to absorptive low-pass tvi filters, the unwanted rf is safely dissipated in a dummy load rather than attempting merely to "short-circuit" it with a reflector. There is good reason to believe the absorptive ("hybrid") filter offers the better approach—it seems equally possible that "absorber elements" may come to play an important role in antenna design.

surprise when George Twist, EI5CF (G3LWH), drew my attention to an article by Dr Richard L. Schatz, WA3GWY, in *73 Magazine* May 1982, entitled "Americanizing the German Quad—the world's best antenna". Sure enough the "German Quad" (described by WD4CPK/DF3TJ in *73*

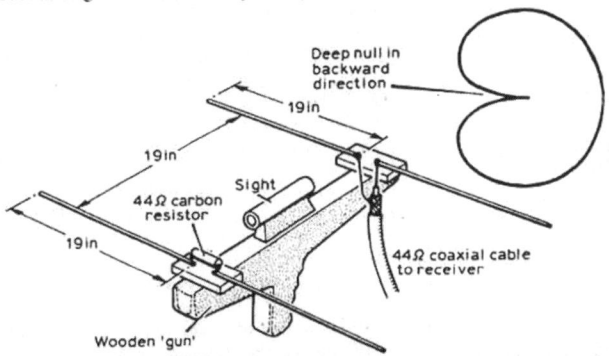

Fig 3. The compact 144MHz two-element df antenna mounted in wooden "gun" assembly with "sight" and adjusted to provide very deep null in backward direction

Magazine June 1978) turned out to be our friend "The G2PL Special" in the ZS6AKA form, although decked out with some stubs whose presence seems to be superfluous to the design. This article is a "rave" account of what the author claims to be "the best and probably the least-expensive antenna one can use". Perhaps we should all have taken more notice of the G2PL Special before it was first Germanized and now Americanized!

EI5CF clearly did not recall the G2PL/ZS6AKA notes, and has been testing the system as described in *73 Magazine*. With tuned feeder, a 69ft per side element at about 25ft above ground, he has at least confirmed that, even if not "the world's best antenna", it does form a useful and effective antenna suitable for all seven bands from 3·5MHz to 28MHz, though on a few bands he has had some difficulty in getting the final swr presented to his TR7 down to the 2:1 needed to prevent the protection circuits from reducing output power. But altogether a useful approach to a simple antenna providing virtually omni-directional coverage, and which one could possibly convince the authorities falls within the restrictions applied to 18 and 24MHz!

'German Quad' or 'G2PL Special'

Extracted from 'Technical Topics', *Radio Communication,* November 1982

"German quad" or "G2PL Special"?

Many years ago the late Peter Pennell, G2PL, discovered during a series of gales that his two-element quad operated unexpectedly well as an omni-directional antenna when his tilt-over mast was in the "down" position with the quad reflector virtually on the ground. So was born "The G2PL Special" (*TT* July 1968 and many editions of *ART*). A few years later S. M. de Wet, ZS6AKA (*TT* June 1972) showed that large horizontal loops of many shapes, including the quad square, formed useful, non-critical, multiband systems. A practical snag is that square loops normally require four support masts or poles, although it may be possible to make use of buildings, trees etc. Loops less than a wavelength in circumference can also be used (for example, on 3·5MHz) although the radiation resistance falls fairly rapidly.

The horizontal square loop or horizontal quad thus has a respectable history as a practical and useful antenna. But I must admit to a degree of

18 and 24MHz and the W8JK

Extracted from 'Technical Topics', *Radio Communication,* November 1982

18 and 24MHz and the W8JK

With the release, albeit with severe restrictions, of the 18 and 24MHz bands for low-power cw operation, it is appropriate to think again about suitable antennas and equipment modifications. For the time being, the antenna restriction of zero gain relative to a dipole, rules out some of the suggestions made earlier such as the classic 14MHz W8JK driven-array (*TT* October 1981 "A new look at the W8JK"). If fed with twin-line or open-wire feeders via an atu, a W8JK acts as a bi-directional array on *all* bands from 14MHz to 28MHz (and rather less efficiently on 10MHz).

No less an authority than John Kraus, W8JK, has recently restated (*QST* June 1982, pp11–4, "The W8JK antenna: recap and update") the very real attractions of this 45-year-old design when it comes to multi-band use.

ANTENNA TOPICS

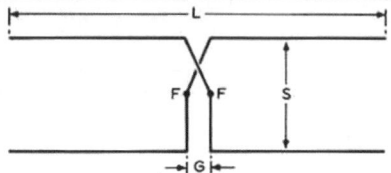

Fig 11. The basic centre-fed W8JK antenna. Typically spacing S is about λ/8 on the lowest frequency used. L can range from less than λ/2 to more than 3λ/2. For 14MHz and above L can be 7·3m, S 2·6m. Centre-gap G forms part of measurement L. *Gain:* 14MHz 5·7dBi, 21MHz 6·7dBi, 28MHz 7·7dBi, 50MHz 8·2dBi. Values for 18 and 24MHz bands can be interpolated

Among its plus points he lists: *(1)* continuous frequency span of more than 3 to 1; *(2)* no traps or loading coils; *(3)* no critical dimensions, as the entire antenna and feed system is resonated; *(4)* it can be used horizontally or vertically for optimum radiation angle; *(5)* it is ideal for finding round-the-world (long path) openings; *(6)* it has theoretically zero radiation off the ends of the elements; *(7)* it can be fed with low-loss, inexpensive twin-line (or very low-loss cut-away 300Ω line or open-wire line); and *(8)* a compact single-array with 7·3m elements can cover 14, 18, 21, 24, 28 and 50MHz bands. Minuses, I suppose, are that the bi-directional pattern does not give protection against continental European signals when the array is used in the UK and the gain tends to be lower than a good Yagi array; it should also be remembered that the low radiation resistance does not make this a good antenna system for installing in a roof space, although this applies also to a Yagi array.

W8JK provides a useful table of the performance characteristics of a W8JK array, with 7·3m elements spaced 2·6m, of the form shown in Fig 11. Values for the 18 and 24MHz bands can be interpolated. Remember that to convert dBi gain into gain reference to a dipole you have to subtract 2·1dB. Although it is important not to confuse these two different ways of expressing antenna gain, it is becoming clear that there are merits in using dBi in this connection. Gain in dBi is the gain of an antenna over an isotropic radiator; that is, an imaginary antenna that radiates equally well in all directions.

The antenna described by W8JK includes an elaborate balance-to-unbalance matching unit with a movable "trombone" formed by sliding aluminium tubes to provide an effective junction to 50Ω coaxial cable. This is an elegant arrangement, but would appear to require different dimensions on different bands. However, it should be appreciated that this refinement is not essential in circumstances where the twin-feeder can be brought all the way down to a flexible atu providing balanced output. The only disadvantage is that the line will be voltage-fed on some bands.

One must stress that the present restrictions rule out the use of a W8JK array on 18 and 24MHz in the UK, though of course these are temporary restrictions, and the design is entirely suitable for the other bands. Furthermore some, at least, of the plus points apply equally to a simple flex or rotary 14MHz dipole fed with balanced twin line, forming the mis-named centre-fed zepp (in other words a centre-fed doublet or dipole). It might also be possible to devise a system with remote switching that would remove drive from the second element on the new bands only.

A possible problem with 18MHz operation that I have not seen mentioned elsewhere is that the second harmonic falls around 36·2MHz. This is slap in the middle of the standard vision i.f. used in all British and European television receivers (a frequency that was chosen in part to avoid harmonic relationship with the amateur bands!). This should not present any great problem with a "clean" 10W of carrier power but may prove quite a tvi hazard when the power restrictions are lifted. Again, it is necessary to stress that it is the responsibility of the amateur to effect a cure when tvi can be traced to harmonic radiation, even though it could be argued that susceptibility to i.f. breakthrough is a function of the tv receiver design.

measurement of the forward gain. Ten 144MHz antennas were entered, ranging from 16-element Tonna Yagi arrays with a boom length of 21ft, to a five-element homebrew ZL-Special with a 3ft boom.

In no case did the forward gain (dBd) quite measure up to the maker's claimed figures, although several came fairly near, and it should be appreciated that antennas deteriorate over a period of time. One 10-element array modified to have an extra four elements did achieve 1·5dB more gain than the original specification.

Two of the long Tonna 16-element arrays were measured at 13·6 and 12·1dBd (specification 13·9dBd). Two 14-element Parabeams came out at 13·2 and 11·1dBd (specification 13·7dBd). A homebrew long Yagi with 19 elements and 19·6ft boom chalked up a disappointing 5·35dBd. Two Jaybeam six-element quads measured 9·4 and 9·0dBd (specification 12dBd). The five-element homebrew ZL-Special achieved only 3·6dBd and had virtually bi-directional characteristics. The beamwidths of the main lobes were on the whole very close to the claimed figures, but sidelobes and front-to-back ratios proved a very mixed bag.

The four 432MHz factory-made antennas were all between 2·5 and 4·8dB less than the expected figures. One of the best gain/element ratios was achieved with the homebrew loop Yagi of G3ZWM: with 22 elements and a boom length of 16ft this measured 12·1dBd and had a horizontal beamwidth of only 17°. An 88-element Multibeam bettered this with 13·9dBd, but this represents only an extra 1·8dB for 66 more elements.

It should be stressed that compared with the results of some of the antenna gain tests carried out in other countries, the standard achieved is reasonably good. It does emphasize, however, that an antenna gain of much more than about 11dBd (13dBi) is not readily achieved at vhf or even at uhf. Some allowance has to be made for measurement errors, though in this case these are not believed to be significant.

The horizontal radiation patterns are noticeably different from those usually shown in the text books, with some of the sidelobes tending to make a rotator almost a redundant luxury except along the directions of the deeper nulls. It should also be appreciated that when arrays are mounted in a typical residential array, at around roof-top height, the radiation patterns are likely to become even more distorted. TV antenna manufacturers sometimes make their patterns look quite respectable by presenting the results on linear rather than logarithmic scales! In not a few cases, much of the antenna gain can be eaten up by the feeder losses.

One way of overcoming this problem was noted at the recent International Broadcasting Convention at Brighton. A new ITN communications link vehicle has a 20W microwave (2·3GHz) solidstate amplifier mounted at the top of the telescopic mast; no feeder losses, but it does require quite a substantial mast.

Optimum-shaped Antennas

Extracted from 'Technical Topics', *Radio Communication,* December 1982

Optimum-shaped antennas

For many years it was generally assumed that the basic building block of an effective single-element or beam-array type of antenna should consist of straight elements approximately λ/2 long; indeed the term "dipole" has usually come to mean a λ/2 element, although more correctly it can mean any centre-fed and symmetrical system. A few years ago this idea began to break down with the development of simple, space-saving antennas that had the ends hanging down or turned inwards; most notably in the form of the VK2ABQ two-element beam in which the bent elements form, as G6XN has pointed out, a convenient means of adjusting the mutual coupling and also providing "neutralization".

An even more radical attack on the straight-line form of element has been mounted over the past few years by F. M. Landstorfer of the Technical University of Munich, which has been at the heart of the development of "active" receiving antennas. In a series of professional papers he has been advocating the use of 3λ/2 elements curved in a specific manner that provides forward gain and directivity. Most of the practical work has involved frequencies within the range 30MHz to 1GHz. The technique could also be used at hf although it would clearly be quite difficult to implement. Optimum-shaped self-supporting wire elements could be readily investigated at, say, 435MHz, possibly by modifying a conventional array designed for 144MHz.

Landstorfer's new type of shaped wire 3λ/2 element can, by itself, give a forward gain of up to 7 to 7·8dBi (that is to say, about 5 to 5·5dB gain with reference to a straight λ/2 dipole element). An experimental three-element

Antenna Gain: Theory and Practice

Extracted from 'Technical Topics', *Radio Communication,* December 1982

Antenna gain: theory and practice

Ken Franklin, G3JFK, recently provided me with the results of an antenna gain test held in May 1982 by the Crawley ARC on a number of factory-made and homebrew 144 and 432MHz antennas as part of an inter-club competition. This test was carefully carried out and included the production of the horizontal radiation patterns of the various antennas, as well as

Yagi-type array for 200MHz, reported in 1979, yielded a measured gain of 11·5dBi (9·4dBd).

My attention (and that of G3ZAY) was drawn to this work by a report in *Electronics Letters* Vol 18, No 19, 16 September 1982, by D. K. Cheng and C. H. Liang of Syracuse University, which provides a mathematical procedure for calculating the optimum shape of wire elements. However, a less formidable and more illuminating explanation of this new class of antenna element can be found in a paper presented by F. M. Landstorfer at the International Conference on Antennas and Propagation in London during November 1979, and published in *IEE Conference Publication No 169*, pp132-141. This book can be found in some technical reference libraries. The following notes are based on this conference paper.

Landstorfer notes that basically there is no real limitation to the maximization of the directivity or gain of an antenna as long as no further restrictions, such as size, costs or bandwidth have to be considered: indeed it could be said that on hf the 50-year-old rhombic remains supreme, and on shf the large dish parabolic reflector cannot be bettered.

For the amateur, of course, antenna size, or the size of the necessary real estate, both of which are to some degree equivalent to cost, is the main restriction.

The paper notes that the usual Yagi array at vhf/uhf consists of a number of straight-lined single dipoles with lengths roughly $\lambda/2$ but phase-adjusted to form radiators, reflectors and directors. Any improvement, Landstorfer argues, needs to start with the optimization of a single radiator. To do this we need to think in terms of elements longer than λ. However, if such elements are straight (with no phase-reversal stubs) then the phase reversal within the current distribution means that radiation normal to the dipole axis is poor. On the other hand, if the element is shaped in such a way as to *compensate for the phase differences* it is possible to make a long element that can be a very efficient radiator in the required direction. This can be done by suitable shaping of a long element such as a $3\lambda/2$ element. In effect a shaped $3\lambda/2$ element can be made roughly equivalent to a colinear array of three $\lambda/2$ elements in phase, but with no requirement for phase-reversing stubs or resonant circuit elements, and with unidirectional, rather than bidirectional, characteristics—and roughly 2dB more gain.

This all sounds fantastically attractive in theory, but what about in practice? For an amateur the main disadvantage of a $3\lambda/2$-element array is simply the larger size of the basic element, compensated for by the fact that far fewer elements are needed to obtain equivalent gain. It is also claimed that with optimum-shaped elements side-lobes can be reduced and the radiation pattern generally cleaned up.

Fig 1 shows the current distribution of a straight $3\lambda/2$ dipole and that of a similar element in gain-optimized shape. Fig 2 shows a Yagi array with three gain-optimized elements which, it is claimed, apart from 11·5dBi forward gain can have better than 20dB sidelobe attenuation and a front-to-back ratio of about 26dB. The 1979 paper states: "Field tests over more than three years confirmed the theoretical results in practice". The paper also shows that arrays of large bandwidth suitable for tv reception can be produced, and that this type of shaped element can be built into log-periodic arrays and also backfire structures.

As shown in the recent item in *Electronics Letters*, precise calculation of the optimized shape, which is to some degree related to wire diameter etc, involves complex mathematics. However, a practical start to investigating this type of array for amateur applications could be made by copying the shapes shown in Figs 1 and 2.

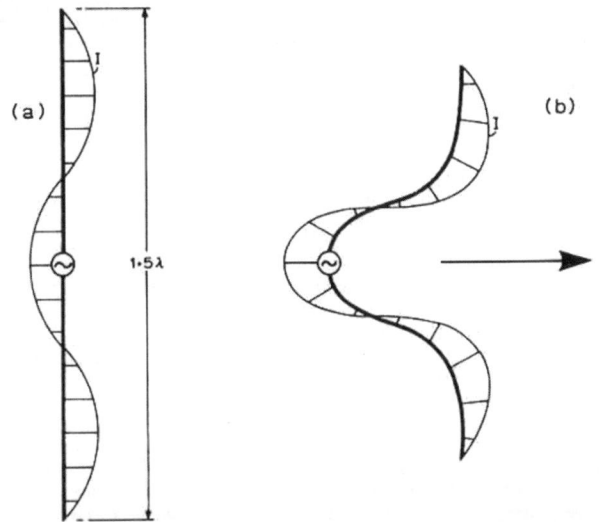

Fig 1. Showing the current distribution on: (a) a straight $3\lambda/2$ dipole where the phase reversal reduces radiation normal to the axis of the dipole; and (b) a $3\lambda/2$ dipole with a gain-optimized shape which causes radiation to increase greatly in the forward direction. (F. M. Landstorfer)

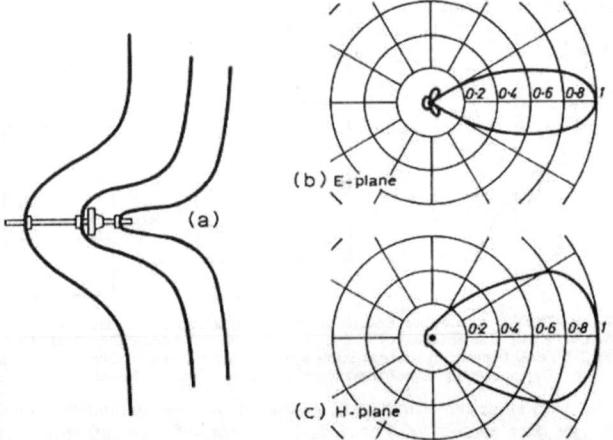

Fig 2. A Yagi-array using three gain-optimized elements each approximately $3\lambda/2$ long. A vhf array of this type has been shown to provide a gain of 11·5dBi, sidelobe attenuation better than 20dB and a front-to-back ratio of 26dB. (F. M. Landstorfer)

Travelling-wave Rectangular Antennas

Extracted from 'Technical Topics', *Radio Communication*, December 1982

Travelling-wave rectangular antennas

Another potentially-useful report on antenna developments appears in *IEEE Transactions on Antennas and Propagation* Vol AP-30, No 4, July 1982. This is a note "Unidirectional patterns of travelling-wave rectangular antenna" by Isamu Matsuzuka and Koji Nagasawa of Nihon University, Tokusada. In effect this describes a rectangular form of loop antenna, fed at the centre of one side and with a resistor placed in the opposite side: Fig 3. It is thus not unlike the small loops used in the active receiving arrays described in the November 1982 issue of *Rad Com* by J. A. Lambert, G3FNZ. This form of terminated rectangular antenna provides a backfire uni-directional pattern if the dimensions are small compared with a wavelength; but if the dimensions are comparable with a wavelength it gives an endfire uni-directional pattern. The notes in *IEEE Trans* are concerned

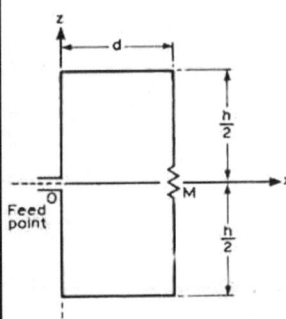

Fig 3. Basic geometry of a terminated, travelling-wave rectangular antenna as described by Isamu Matsuzuka and Koji Nagasawa

mainly with physically small antennas, but some details are given of a 200MHz model antenna where $h = \lambda$ and $d = \lambda/4$ and the matching resistor is 493Ω. This is shown to be capable of providing very high front-to-back ratios over a significant bandwidth. It would appear that both the dimensions and the resistor value are relatively non-critical, as might be expected from a travelling-wave antenna that has a family connection with long-wire rhombic and V-beams, where rf energy reaching the far end is dissipated in the terminating resistor rather than being reflected back to the feedpoint. Implementation of a rectangular array of this type would probably be easier than for a terminated circular loop antenna for physically large antennas.

ANTENNA TOPICS

Horizontal 'Circular' Loops

Extracted from 'Technical Topics', *Radio Communication,* December 1982

Horizontal "circular" loops

The November 1982 *TT* included some comments on horizontal quad antennas such as the "G2PL Special" and attention was drawn to the work of ZS6AKA, some years ago, on a wide variety of horizontal loop type antennas in various shapes and sizes (*ART7*, p306, Fig 100). Some useful constructional ideas and an indication that a simple horizontal loop antenna can "surpass all expectations" has come from Andy Churchley, G4EAQ, though I should make it clear that his notes arrived well before the publication of the November issue. He has been using two circular loop antennas in conjunction with a KW107 "Supermatch" atu for multiband hf operation. His loops have been made roughly circular, although perhaps more accurately described as a complex polygon enclosing as much area as conveniently possible.

As noted some time ago in connection with a *QST* article on rhombics,

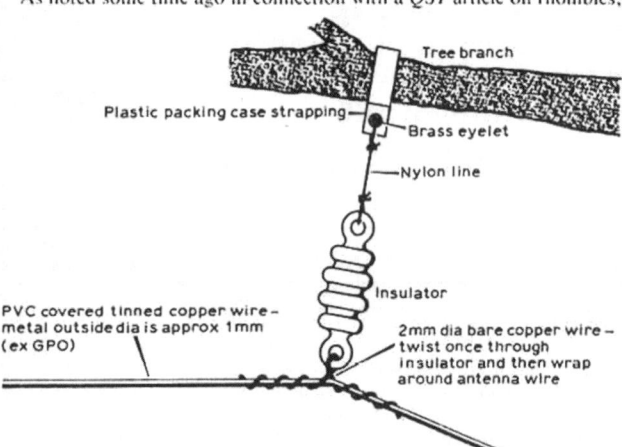

Fig 4. How G4EAQ fastens his circular loop antennas to the branches of trees without passing the antenna wire through the eye of the insulator, a technique adapted from British Telecom practice. The bare copper wire used to secure the antenna to the insulator is annealed at red heat and allowed to cool. This softens it considerably and makes it easy to wrap around the antenna wire

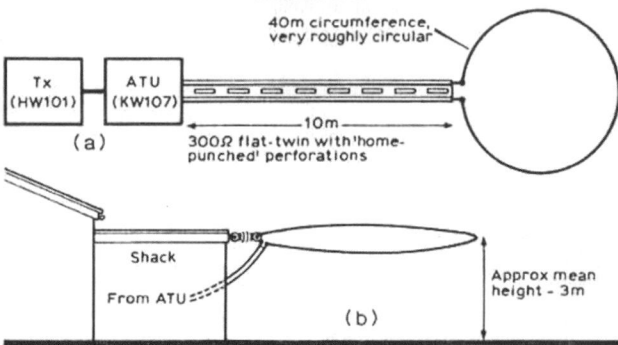

Fig 5. The first of G4EAQ's low horizontal loop antennas

these horizontal loop type antennas seem to work well even when slung among trees, which can provide some of the necessary skyhooks. G4EAQ believes in good insulation, using a technique adapted from British Telecom that avoids having to pass the antenna wire through the eye of the insulator: Fig 4. This makes it easy to change or adjust the antenna or to distribute the tension around the loop.

G4EAQ originally tried a low loop (Fig 5) and then, encouraged by the results, replaced it with a rather higher and larger loop: Fig 6. Both gave most satisfactory results, and indeed his fourth contact with the low loop gave him an unexpected VK contact. G4EAQ makes no claim to being a dyed-in-the-wool dx man, but is well satisfied with the results on all bands, including 3·5MHz. He notes a marked improvement over the results he achieved with a G5RV-type dipole.

SWR indications suggest that the antenna is reasonably broadband; with his matching unit he has no difficulty in achieving unity swr at the transmitter output.

G4EAQ was seemingly unaware of the previous work on large horizontal loop antennas, and I cannot recall any previous account of the results achieved with near circular loops. As noted in the November *TT*, there is growing evidence of the value of square, rectangular and now circular loops to form general-purpose, horizontally-polarized, multiband hf antennas.

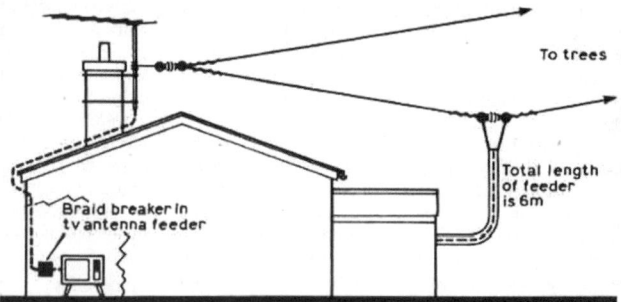

Fig 6. The second larger and rather higher horizontal loop antenna. It is at a mean height of about 5m and total circumference about 60m. The diameter is roughly 62ft, which can be fitted into some medium-sized gardens.

The Counterpoise Investigated

Extracted from 'Technical Topics', *Radio Communication,* February 1983

The counterpoise investigated

During the past few years three former professional engineers, led by Archibald Doty, K8CFU, have been enlivening their retirement by investigating this question of the relative efficiency of buried radials, groundscreens both on the surface and elevated, and elevated counterpoises. After making many *thousands* of measurements they have just presented to an IEEE meeting a paper "Characteristics of the counterpoise and the elevated groundscreen" (A. C. Doty with J. A. Frey and H. J. Mills) and a short version of this paper is due to appear in *QST* this month.

A privately-funded research project of such a magnitude, undertaken by three elderly engineers with an aggregate age of 203 years, setting out and succeeding in showing that a good deal of what has appeared in the professional antenna literature during the past 60 years on this subject is in error, or at least seriously flawed, is remarkable. That the project succeeds in pinpointing how the errors occurred and in resurrecting the importance of the counterpoise is even more remarkable!

This ambitious project has unearthed (if I dare use that word) several important new facts; in particular it shows that the currents flowing in buried radials of the conventional type are *not*, as usually postulated, uniform, but depend upon ground conductivity in the immediate vicinity of the individual wires. It indicates that there can be unexpectedly large variations in surface ground conductivity within the area covered by the ground system of a typical vertical antenna. But the tests further show that the distribution of return currents collected by wires elevated by 6 to 8ft is distinctly different from that found in buried radials. Lossy ground between the antenna and the radials reduces their efficiency in providing return currents. All the initial indications are that elevated ground systems (whether counterpoise or elevated but earthed groundscreens) as in Fig 2,

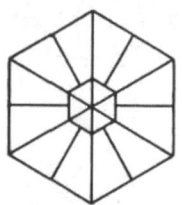 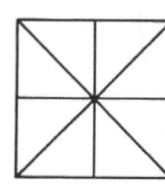 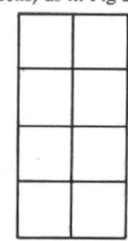

Fig 2. Typical multi-wire counterpoise or groundscreen system mounted below a vertical antenna. Recent intensive investigations by Arch Doty, K8CFU, and friends show that such systems are more efficient than *buried* systems of comparable size. (Doty, Frey and Mills)

used with electrically-short vertical antennas *require substantially fewer radials than needed by a buried wire system of equal efficiency.* A conclusion calculated to upset conventional thinking of the past 40 years!

This does not mean that buried radials do not make good earth systems, but it does suggest that elevated systems are more efficient.

Electrically Short Antennas

Extracted from 'Technical Topics', *Radio Communication,* February 1983

Electrically short antennas

One of the significant differences between operation on hf and vhf is that on some of the lower hf bands it is usually necessary to use antennas physically shorter than the $\lambda/2$ needed to achieve resonance and with the element relatively close to the ground. Even on the higher hf bands this will also usually be true of mobile or "balcony" antennas. Such antenna systems are made resonant by inductive or capacitive loading and/or by working in monopole rather than dipole fashion against earth.

Theoretically, it must be emphasized, a correctly-designed short vertical antenna can provide a very efficient system; unfortunately it is only in exceptional circumstances (for example, a ship-board installation with its salt-water "earth") that anything like the theoretical efficiency can be achieved, even when the ohmic losses are reduced by using large-diameter highly-conductive elements and capacitive rather than inductive loading. This is because the radiation resistance will normally be considerably lower than the total loss resistance, so that most of the rf energy fed to the antenna is dissipated as heat in the earth: Fig 1. The true radiation efficiency may be only a few per cent; for example, if this is five per cent (by no means untypical) then from every 100W of expensively-generated rf safely delivered to the element only 5W will radiate, most of it in every direction and at every vertical radiation angle other than those needed to take the signal towards the dx station.

Stan Gibilisco, W1GV/4, in "Efficiency of short antennas" (*Ham Radio* September 1982, pp18–21) shows that the radiation resistance of a $\lambda/10$ vertical rod is roughly 4Ω, whereas the total loss resistance of such a system may easily be 50Ω or more, representing an efficiency of less than eight per cent. In these circumstances, incidentally, a low swr is often a sure sign of *inefficiency*!

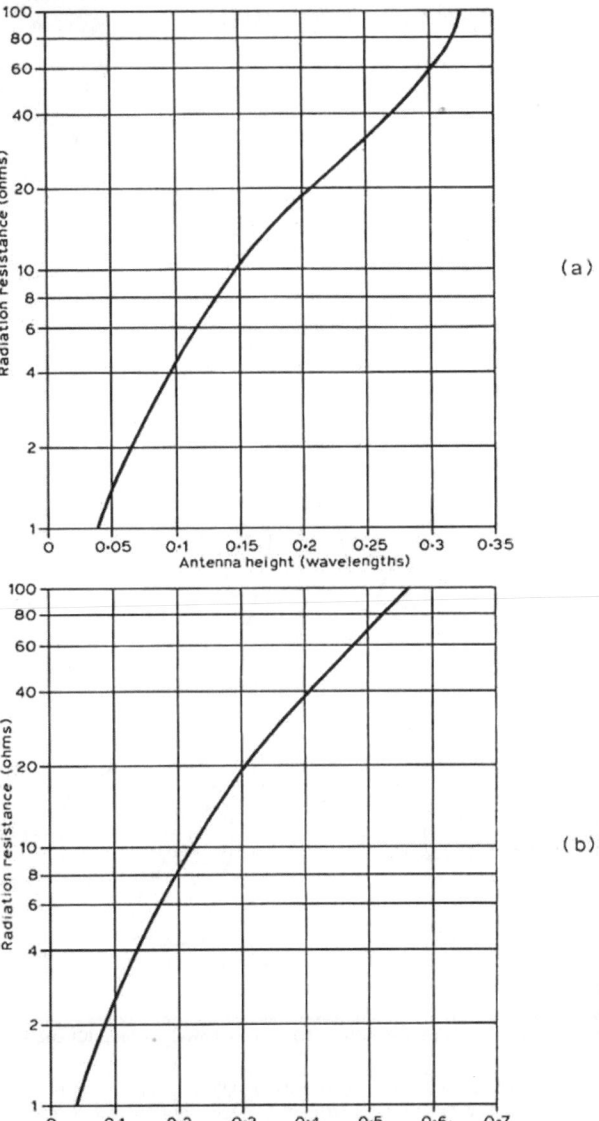

Fig 1. (a) Radio resistance of a short vertical antenna in terms of its height. Note this graph applies only to single-element radiators without parasitic or phased elements. (b) Similar curve for short centre-fed dipole elements. (Stan Gibilisco, W1GV/4)

The effect of the Earth

Extracted from 'Technical Topics', *Radio Communication,* February 1983

The effect of the earth

It has to be admitted that in our approach to antenna planning we tend to over-simplify and think in terms of text-book, two-dimensional radiation-pattern diagrams. It is not easy to think three-dimensionally except in terms of "free-space", even though we may be well aware of the basic fact that in practice the spherical shape of "free space" has to be cut in two by the ground beneath us with all the further complications of "image" elements. Nor do we usually worry unduly about the lobes and nulls in the vertical radiation pattern when we think in terms of directivity.

Table 1, derived from the Rockwell International (Collins) *HF Communication Data Book,* shows simple hf antennas in unfamiliar guise, suddenly endowed with "gains" that might appear to put a three-element beam to shame (although we should remember that an antenna array is equally not located in free space). The table assumes that the antenna is above a perfect earth. But if the figures show anything it is that they should bring home to us the extent of the losses brought about by less than a perfect earth.

Ever since the classic work by Dr George Brown and his RCA colleagues in the 'thirties, the preferred form of earth system for mf broadcasting monopole antennas has comprised 120 long buried radials. Indeed this can be shown to provide an extremely efficient earth, but it has meant that for over 40 years very little attention has been given to the use of elevated "counterpoise" systems that were widely used and popular in the 'twenties and 'thirties.

Thus for many years the very term "counterpoise" has been slipping out of use, at least until its recent revival as a result of the work of Les Moxon,

TABLE 1—Gain of simple antennas above perfect ground

Antenna type	How located	Max gain (dBi)	Direction of maximum gain
Short dipole	Free space	1·76	Plane perpendicular to axis
$\lambda/2$ dipole	Free space	2·15	Plane perpendicular to axis
Short vertical monopole	Over perfect ground	4·76	Towards horizon
$\lambda/4$ vertical monopole	Over perfect ground	5·15	Towards horizon
$\lambda/2$ horizontal dipole	Close to perfect ground	9·1	Straight upwards
	$\lambda/4$ above perfect ground	7·4	Straight upwards
	$\lambda/2$ above perfect ground	8·2	Plane perpendicular to axis, 30° above horizon
	$5\lambda/8$ above perfect ground	9·2	Plane perpendicular to axis, 24·6° above horizon
$\lambda/2$ vertical dipole	$\lambda/2$* above perfect ground	8·2	Towards horizon

*Height from ground to centre of antenna

(*Source HF Communication Data Book* by Collins/Rockwell International)

ANTENNA TOPICS

G6XN, *(TT* and *HF Antennas for all locations)*. Yet parallel work by Phil Horwood, G3FRB *(Rad Com* November 1981) and Dr Martin Sweeting, G3YJO, as reported in *TT* August 1982, shows that an elevated groundplane, groundscreen or counterpoise are systems *more* not *less* efficient than an equivalent number of buried radials.

Directivity of Optimum-shaped Antennas

Extracted from 'Technical Topics', *Radio Communication,* February 1983

Directivity of optimum-shaped antennas

Landstorfer's optimum-shaped 3λ/2 antenna element, described in the December 1982 *TT,* has attracted comment from readers who are puzzled by the single-headed arrow shown in Fig 1 that month and by my use of the term "unidirectional". It has been pointed out that the element can be *approximated* to a short unterminated long-wire V-beam or to a set of three dipoles in a W8JK-type of driven array. In both cases these approximations result in *bi-directional* radiation patterns. Jim Watt, G6ZC, has provided a careful vector analysis to support this view.

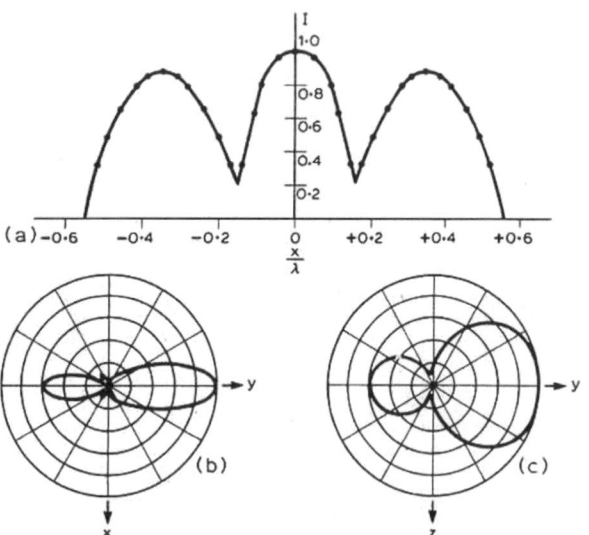

Fig 3. (a) Normalized current distribution on an optimum-shaped 3λ/2 element. (b) E-plane power pattern. (c) H-plane power pattern. (Cheng and Liang)

In fact, these readers are *approximately* right. Fig 3 shows the current distribution and radiation patterns of a *single* 3λ/2 shaped element as calculated by D. K. Cheng and C. H. Liang of Syracuse University (*Electronics Letters* 16 September 1982). These show an *approximately* bi-directional pattern, but with pronounced major and minor lobes that represent forward gain, though with a relatively poor front-to-back ratio. The forward lobe, however, is sufficiently pronounced to justify Landstorfer's single-headed arrow and (perhaps less excusably) my use of the term "unidirectional", even though from an operating viewpoint it would work well in both directions. To quote from Landstorfer's 1979 explanation: "If properly shaped a 3λ/2 dipole can be a very efficient radiator, which is superior in gain to conventional straight-lined dipoles. The basic idea is to compensate the phase differences within the current distribution by time delays. Due to a special shaping, waves originating from various sections of the antenna arrive at different times at a far-off point in the direction of main radiation (parallel to the plane of symmetry). The time delays correspond to phase shifts. For optimum shape of the antenna structure the resulting phase shifts will approximately compensate the phase reversals within the current distribution, and the field strength phasors in the far-field will add almost *in* phase. *This is only true, however, in the deliberate direction of main radiation*—but will in general not hold for other directions. As a consequence, relatively high values of directivity can be expected with such an antenna." (my italics). Of course when combined with other elements, as indicated in December, true unidirectional patterns with good front-to-back ratios can be expected.

Low Loop Antennas

Extracted from 'Technical Topics', *Radio Communication,* April 1983

Low loop antennas

TT, November and December 1982, raised once again the question of horizontal loop antennas such as the rectangular "G2PL Special" (turned-over quad) and G4EAQ's circular loops, as well as the variety of horizontal loop systems investigated some years ago by ZS6AKA. These systems all seem to indicate that a horizontal loop antenna can provide effective low-angle, dx-working, omnidirectional radiation, even when the wire is only a few feet above ground. It must be emphasized that it is always difficult to assess the dx performance of an hf antenna, and I sometimes suspect that it would be almost impossible to devise any piece of wire that would *never* result in dx when conditions were very good. I also subscribe to the theory that when an amateur first puts up a new antenna he tends to become more active, and this results in more and better dx until at least the first flush of enthusiasm has worn off.

But the evidence does suggest there may really be some basis for the idea that a loop performs very well at low height; although the theory that this applies also to conventional upright quad antennas, widely held for many years, is now largely discredited.

James H. Gray, W1XU, advertisements manager of *73 Magazine,* adds his support to the theory. He writes:

"For many years I have been 'playing around' with low horizontal loops, and have had some startling results. Initially, I used an 80m loop, coaxial fed through a λ/4 (electrical) of 75Ω coaxial cable as a matching transformer. The nominal impedance at the input end was close enough to 50Ω to make my transmitter completely happy. The nominal loop height was about 28ft, and results on 3·9MHz phone and 3·5MHz cw were gratifying.

"Then, upon moving to a new location, I decided to try a 40m loop. This was at only 10ft above ground, and used trees as supports. Again, the matching system of an electrical λ/4 impedance transformer was employed with success. I did do a fair amount of loop-length pruning to achieve exact resonance.

"Much dx was worked with this 40m loop. Then, along came 10MHz, so I cut the loop from 40 to 30m . . . again, with success.

"Finally, I put up an 80m loop once more, this time only 10ft high. I used the nominal formula of 1,005/f(MHz) but found it much too long! This was apparently due to the capacitance to ground making the electrical length longer than for a high loop. I cut 25ft out of the perimeter, making the overall length about 260ft. It resonates at the low end of 3·5MHz but, come spring, will need still more trimming.

"By accident I discovered a 1·8MHz resonance. This is how it happened: my wife had asked me to put up a wire dog-run in the back yard. The only place with sufficient room and clearance was in the middle of the loop, between two conveniently-located trees about 75ft apart, and with the wire at about the height of the loop antenna. When I tried to operate on 3·5MHz that evening, I had a vswr more than 3:1. Clearly the cable of the dog-run, roughly λ/4 at 3·5MHz, was detuning the loop.

"Rather than tear everything apart for a new start, I decided, just for fun, to see if there was a usable lower-frequency resonance. There was—on the 1·8MHz band! Serendipity had struck again. It's not a perfect match on 1·8MHz but is 2:1, low enough to permit operation without having to resort to using an antenna tuning unit.

"All of this strikes me as being useful, in the sense that it offers the possibility of fine-tuning a loop by erecting a nearby wire in the plane of the loop and then moving it slightly up or down—or back and forth with respect to one segment of the loop periphery. I feel reasonably confident that I shall be able to cut loops to formula, and 'tweak' them to the operating frequency by using this capacitance-loading technique. It might also provide a viable method of obtaining a 2:1, or possibly more, frequency range with a basic horizontal loop antenna. But further experimentation awaits the return of spring."

Two-band Groundplane

Extracted from 'Technical Topics', *Radio Communication*, May 1983

Two-band groundplane

Les Moxon, G6XN, moved QTH some months ago and, while further investigating the optimum design of multiband beam arrays, as a temporary measure for 7MHz put up an inverted groundplane. He writes:

"Have you noticed that this also makes an excellent dx antenna of the groundplane type for 3·5MHz? Mine *ought* not to be much good on 3·5MHz because the height is low (30ft) and the top is an inverted-V with the ends trailing down to about 8ft. The vertical portion is about 28ft of light-duty 75Ω twin feeder (ie the wire is much too thin). The 'earth' is one of my inductively-loaded counterpoises, see Fig 2. I made this much larger than would normally be required because of the extremely low estimated value of radiation resistance, and the need to keep loading coil relatively low. All of this results in very narrow bandwidth, about 40kHz, but then the ssb dx segment of 3·5MHz is only 20kHz wide. I have, in fact, only tried the system on 3·5MHz on three mornings, but reports have included RS54 from ZL, and RS46 from W0.

"Basically the antenna is a straightforward centre-fed, inverted-V dipole for 7MHz, although I have not used it for transmission in this mode yet. I have, however, fitted a switch so that it works *either* as an inverted-V dipole or as an inverted groundplane. Reception of dx signals, as expected, is better in the groundplane mode, though a CQ call resulted only in contacts with two Portuguese stations. Thin flex is used for the top. It has been up three months, blown down once, and it is time I overcame my dislike of 7MHz and tried it out properly.

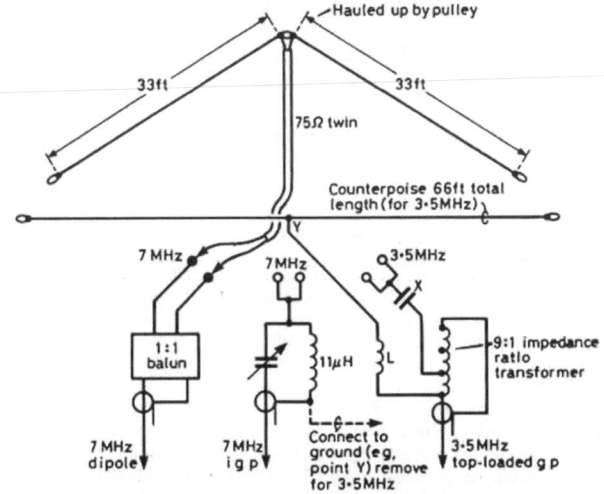

Fig 2. G6XN's 3·5/7MHz antenna, which can function as dipole or igp on 7MHz and as a top-loaded gp-type antenna on 3·5MHz

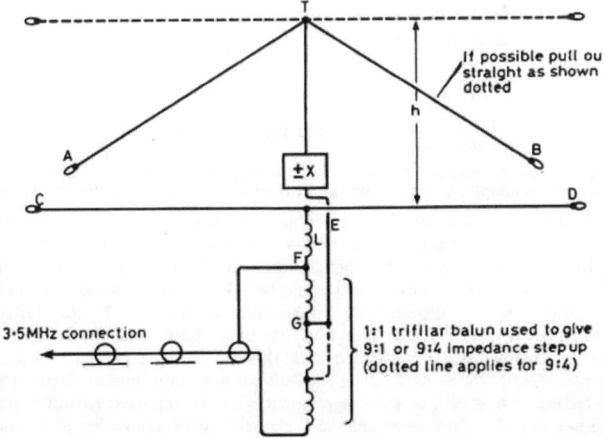

Fig 3. The antenna of Fig 2 re-drawn to show mode of operation on 3·5MHz

"To show the mode of operation on 3·5MHz more clearly, the antenna can be represented as in Fig 3. Note that the reactance 'x' depends on the height 'h'. I use a 250pF capacitor, though for greater height this would have to be reduced; for slightly less 'h', 'x' would equal zero, and for even less height a loading coil would be required. Point F must be as close as possible to ground potential. I used a temporary λ/4 wire, and adjusted 'x' to resonate the portion ET+ATB of the antenna against the temporary wire, using a gdo. Then one resonates CED, via inductor L, against the temporary wire in the same way. Connect as shown, with FG short-circuited. Resonance should then be at the required frequency, but may be slightly higher, depending on the layout. If necessary lengthen both the antenna and the counterpoise connections slightly.

"For an 'h' of about 40ft, with AB straight, the need for the matching transformer should disappear; for substantially greater heights a step-down transformer may be needed, ie as the radiation resistance increases.

"In my case L was a tapped coil. After adjustment the calculated inductance was about 13μH. However, as the radiation resistance increases one can shorten CD and increase L. As described, the loss resistance is probably about 3Ω and the radiation resistance not more than 4Ω. Straightening the top section could be expected to increase the radiation resistance to about 12Ω and reduce the loss from 2–3dB to about 1dB. Thicker wire should help a lot and losses should also disappear rapidly as the height increases.

"The 7MHz igp tuning arrangements can take care of length errors up to a few feet. For much larger values of 'h' alternative tuning arrangements could be worked out as for any 'random length' wire antenna."

The Inverted Groundplane Family

Extracted from 'Technical Topics', *Radio Communication*, May 1983

The inverted groundplane family

Almost 13 years ago, in *TT* (July 1970) I described an antenna that I called "the vertical-T or inverted groundplane". This was a simple antenna that I, and then John Brodzky, G3HQX, had tried out with reasonable success on 14MHz and other hf bands. It was a concept based partly on the traditional mf T-antenna, in which the top section provides electrical loading of a shortened λ/4 vertical radiator, and partly on a simplification of the "bobtail curtain" array originally described by Woodrow Smith, W6BCX, in 1947, as an outstandingly successful form of three-element vertically-polarized fixed array with low-angle radiation. An even earlier version of the same concept, but with two elements, is the "half-square" array, and such a system was described by PA0ZN as early as 1934.

Although the inverted groundplane antenna looks similar to the classical T-antenna there is a voltage node rather than a current-node at the base of the radiating element. Each of the three antennas in which the horizontal span is used as a matching element rather than as a radiating element has survived the test of time. My 1970 notes also suggested that it would be very easy to adapt the inverted groundplane into an antenna that could be readily switched to form either a horizontally-polarized dipole or the vertically-polarized igp. This idea was subsequently implemented and described by Ken Glanzer, K7GCO (*CQ* June 1972 and *ART*) simply by using an open-wire transmission line to provide a centre-fed dipole; then switching, when vertical polarization was required, so that the two ends of the transmission line were joined together.

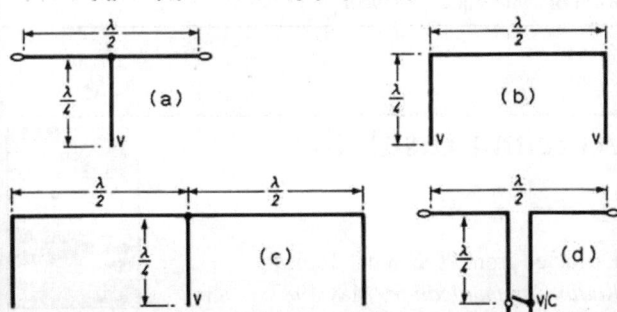

Fig 1. The inverted groundplane family. (a) Basic inverted groundplane antenna, voltage-fed at base. (b) Half-square two-element array. (c) The classic bobtail three-element array. (d) Combination dipole/igp formed by switching feeder at base, voltage fed as igp, matched impedance fed as dipole

ANTENNA TOPICS

I have followed the progress of the inverted groundplane with some interest, as to the best of my knowledge the notes in the July 1970 *TT* represent the first published discussion of this type of antenna. However, it is clear from W6BCX's articles that the technique had been used for 7MHz dx operation many years earlier, initially the result of serendipity when one of his friends discovered that an off-centre-fed Windom actually worked better when the tap was made to the centre of the top section; this in turn led to the development of the bobtail array that later was to be the starting point for my own work!

My excuse for bringing up this topic again is indeed partly the two-part article by Woodrow Smith, W6BCX, "The bobtail curtain and inverted groundplane" (*Ham Radio*, Part 1, February 1983, pp82–6, and Part 2, March 1983, pp 28-30) in which he discusses in some detail the history of this whole class of antenna, including the early "30-up and 30-out" (vertical plus single-wire counterpoise with top-loading provided by a copper toilet-ball (*ART*)), the inverted groundplane, the half-square and the full bobtail with its three vertical sections: Fig 1. But also it is partly because Les Moxon, G6XN, in the course of a long and interesting letter (including an important discussion on the optimum design of multiband beams that I shall refer to on another occasion), mentioned that he has been investigating how a 7MHz inv-gp can also provide an excellent dx antenna for 3·5MHz.

Groundplane Antennas

Extracted from 'Technical Topics', *Radio Communication,* May 1983

Groundplane antennas
On a slightly different, but related, topic, Les Moxon, G6XN, disagrees strongly with the suggestion by Fred Brown, W6HPH (*TT* November 1981) that a groundplane antenna *in free space* is 3dB worse than a dipole. He points out that, in free space, or even at quite a modest height above ground, the orthogonal conducting plane does not exist. He considers that the right way to tackle this question is to realise that the groundplane antenna, like a dipole, is virtually a point-source of radiation, and both have a cos θ radiation pattern; so there can be no difference in gain between the two, other than a small correction analogous to the "short dipole" effect, ie less than 0·4dB.

It is important to realize, adds G6XN, that the groundplane is merely a matching device, not something in which an "image" can exist. If it were so it would also act as a screen, and in that case the inverted groundplane antenna would not work!

As we do not get the 3dB loss, the radiation resistance of the groundplane in free space *must* be 18Ω and *not* 36Ω. There was, recalls G6XN, an early *Proc IRE* paper which presented sets of measured figures hovering just above the 18Ω mark. The slight increase above 18Ω would reflect the "short dipole" effect mentioned above. The figures were based on an elevated groundplane, as is usual for the majority of groundplane antennas used by radio amateurs. Yet virtually all subsequent papers take the incorrect 36Ω figure for granted—though G6XN mentions that nobody so far has queried the figure of 18Ω given in his book *HF antennas for all locations*. The figure of "about 18Ω" also applies to the loaded-counterpoise arrangements devised by G6XN and to the "asymmetrical dipoles" of VK3AM, provided that in all cases the antenna is at an effective mean height of about a quarter-wavelength or more.

Antenna Insulation

Extracted from 'Technical Topics', *Radio Communication,* May 1983

Antenna insulation
In his articles on the igp and bobtail, W6BCX underlines the importance, in any voltage-fed antenna, of using good insulation and providing sufficient spacing to avoid flash-over etc when running high power. For a bobtail, he counsels, always feed the centre element; he is not in favour of using a Zepp-type system as suggested in the original PA0ZN half-square, and as one of the possibilities in my notes on the igp. He points out that no antenna fed via an asymmetrical feed system can be completely ground-independent.

On the question of antenna insulation, some readers may have been following the correspondence over the past couple of years in *Wireless World* that has revealed the extent of the problem that can arise from the deposit of salt on insulators when transmitting on 500kHz with a relatively short whip or similar voltage-fed arrangement. Admittedly, this is usually far less of a problem at hf. However, it is worth considering some notes in *Amateur Radio (Australia)* February 1983, taken originally from an *ARNS Bulletin*:

"Aside from physical damage, the most common fault in an antenna system is low resistance to ground. Moisture in the system (impedance matching networks, coaxial cables etc), dirty insulators and coaxial-cable dielectric breakdown all cause varying degrees of shunting resistance. Changes in weather, high humidity, or other natural causes mean that "infinite" resistance is seldom found. Tests with (preferably) a megger, but even with a simple ohmmeter, can be useful; insulation of transmission lines should be tested. Often resistance can be increased by cleaning the insulators (particularly in salt-laden or industrial atmospheres).

The following values are suggested:
(1) 200MΩ or more to ground indicates antenna system in good condition.
(2) 5–200MΩ suggests insulators need cleaning or that coaxial cable may be contaminated with moisture.
(3) Less than 5MΩ suggests the antenna system is in bad shape and that there is urgent need to locate the reason for the low resistance path and to correct it.

Antenna systems isolated from ground from an rf viewpoint may, of course, have a dc leakage path to ground for static, and this has to be taken into account when taking measurements.

Optimum-shaped and Absorbing Elements

Extracted from 'Technical Topics', *Radio Communication,* June 1983

Optimum-shaped and absorbing elements
The Landstorfer concept of "optimum-shaped" antenna elements (*TT* December 1982, pp 1054–5; February 1983, pp131–2) continues to attract interest. Les Moxon, G6XN, confesses he is rather puzzled at the emphasis given in *Electronics Letters* to the wire diameter and the rather precise shape. He feels that, at least for hf, roughly the same useful characteristics could be achieved with a simpler, though related, structure consisting of a colinear pair with optimum spacing (3dB gain) in conjunction with a relatively inefficient reflector spaced 0·25λ behind, the whole constituting a driven array with a phasing line (Fig 5). This is not entirely unlike the suggestion made by Jim Watt, G6ZC, except that unquestionably it would provide a "unidirectional" pattern.

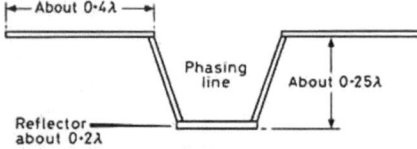

Fig 5. G6XN's suggested version of the "optimum shaped" element that would be simpler to implement on hf than the original Landstorfer shape

G6XN believes it should be possible to achieve a front/back ratio of about 1·0/0·6V, that is to say, about 4·5dB, which would be significantly better than that indicated by Cheng and Liang (*TT* February 1983, Fig 3). The reason for this improvement could be, G6XN suggests, because their "phasing line" is mismatched; "inspection of their Fig 3", he writes, "allowing for beamwidths, suggests that only about a third of the total power is being radiated backwards, and this should give a gain of 1·5 times in power, ie 1·76dB. Add to this the 3dB colinear gain, and one arrives at 4·76dBd or 6·91dBi, in good agreement with the reported forward gain figures for the "optimum-shaped" element, with an easier to realise structure."

However, he does not expect these systems to have a major impact on hf antenna design, although he admits that he cannot think of any other instance of a unidirectional radiation pattern being obtained using a single instance of a unidirectional radiation pattern being obtained using a single wire without a resistive termination; he feels that, if only for this reason, the Landstorfer concept is worthy of study.

Les Moxon also comments on G8SEQ's "absorber" elements (*TT* November 1982, pp959–60). Although he accepts the basic principle as implemented in the multi-element beam, he is not happy with the explanation given for the simpler two-element array developed for 144MHz df applications (Fig 3 of p960). He writes: "I fear this cannot be! In proof whereof, consider the 44Ω resistor short-circuited. We still have 73Ω radiation resistance of the reflector element and, even with optimum tuning of the array, rather poor null depth, since the current in the reflector is too low (ie lower than with an optimum close-spaced two-element Yagi array). Connecting additional resistance in series can only reduce the current in the reflector element still further; it cannot invoke any new principle. Knowing current and phase, both gain and radiation pattern can be precisely specified along the lines of Dr George Brown's original 1937 *Proc IRE* paper, ie as also indicated in my *HF Antennas for All Locations*."

G6XN in fact feels that the cardioid with a very deep null as indicated by G8SEQ defies any simple explanation but, in the absence of a balun, the outer braid of the coaxial feeder could be acting as part of the antenna system; the transmitted signal may also have had cross-polarization effects arising from the same cause. All this suggests that for 144MHz, df results with the arrangement developed by G8SEQ might well not prove reproducible.

This does not imply that the basic idea of an extra "absorbing" element such as the reflector shown in G8SEQ's multi-element array (Fig 2, p959) is not without interest. G6XN writes: "Without departing from the principles outlined above, one can perhaps envisage the second reflector of Fig 2 cleaning up the sidelobes of the array as suggested."

Concealment, however, may come to naught if the transmitter causes tvi, bci or the many other forms of present-day rfi—and this indeed can be a major problem when using older "suitcase" transmitters.

Indoor Antennas

Extracted from 'Technical Topics', *Radio Communication,* July 1983

Indoor antennas

Quite a large number of European amateurs successfully use "indoor" antennas even for their main installation, and there have been quite a few articles in *Radio Communication* in recent years giving useful advice.

In *ART* it is noted that rolls of household aluminium foil can be used to form short wideband hf dipole antennas suitable for use in lofts or for mounting on indoor walls: Fig 1. Suggested lengths for 3·5MHz are two by 12m; 7MHz two by 6·2m; 10·1MHz two by 4·4m; 14MHz two by 3·4m etc.

Fig 1. Indoor broadband dipole antenna using aluminium foil

For vhf operation, particularly from a high apartment or hotel room, a surprisingly effective antenna can take the form of a single-element "quad loop". A 1971 design by W8AP for 144MHz is shown in Fig 2 and can also be found in *ART*. This is another antenna based on the use of aluminium foil, mounted on a sheet of cardboard and taped to the inside of a window. In Canada some experiments have been reported on receiving 12GHz direct-broadcast-satellite signals with indoor dish antennas. Provided that the dish can be placed looking towards the satellite through a window-pane, satisfactory results can be expected. However, pictures were *not* received when the dish was put in a roof-space without a suitable window. It is worth remembering that some types of glass offer relatively little attenuation even to microwave signals. At low frequencies roofs often offer little attenuation but there is the problem of water-tanks, electric conduits, water-pipes etc.

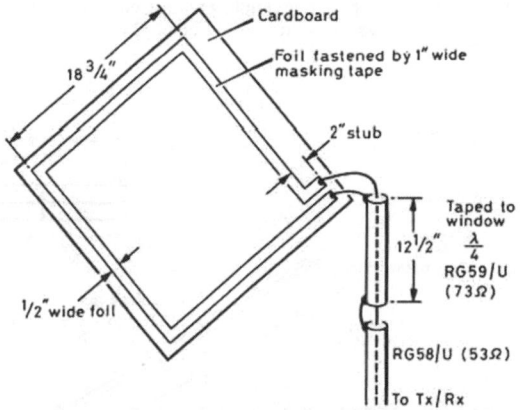

Fig 2. 144MHz single-element quad suitable for use on windows and made from household aluminium foil mounted on cardboard

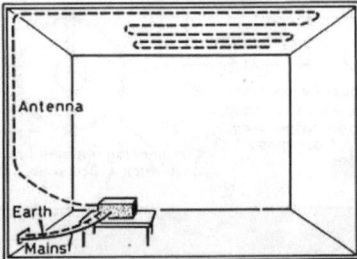

Fig 3. Random-length Marconi antenna in a room preferably high in the building using "mains earth"

Unobtrusive Antennas

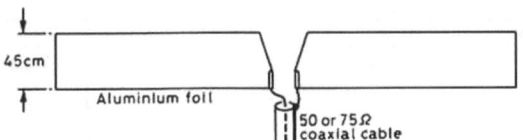

Extracted from 'Technical Topics', *Radio Communication,* July 1983

Unobtrusive antennas

An amateur operating from his home station, or as a well-equipped portable field-day station from a carefully selected site, can usually erect a good antenna. The travelling amateur or the amateur operating under contractual or local-authority restrictions, or from sites where it is virtually impossible to put a decent antenna, often has to make do with indoor, roof-space or "invisible" antennas.

I can still recall an account in the *RSGB Bulletin* in the post-war period by Eric Cole, G2EC (incidentally the only British amateur to have held a two-letter callsign containing an "E"), of how, when living in a Mayfair flat, he had to creep out, under the cover of darkness, on the flat-roof of the high seven-storey building in order to put up his antennas before he could begin to operate. Objections had been made to his antennas by his landlords, so General Cole devised three systems, including a 28MHz rotary beam, that could all be erected and dismantled in a few minutes during darkness or when he was unlikely to be observed by censorious eyes. At other times all poles and wires were dismantled and could not be seen from the ground 80ft below. In this case, ingenuity was rewarded by excellent antennas!

In the USA many radio amateurs are finding their activities increasingly restricted by local statutes, zoning restrictions etc, that seek to forbid the erection of antennas. *QST* has recently reviewed some techniques that can be used by those seeking "hidden" or "invisible" antennas, and some of which can also provide unobtrusive "temporary" antennas for the traveller.

A well-tested technique is to use a fixed outdoor long-wire antenna using very thin enamelled wire (24 or 26 gauge) supported by nylon kite string. Such an antenna can be efficient yet almost impossible to spot from a distance. Provided that it is fixed to an end support that does not move with the wind, it should last a reasonably long time, unless broken by an unwary bird to whom, it must be admitted, such antennas do represent a hazard, and *vice versa*. Another traditional technique is to use an aluminium-wire "clothesline" or to conceal a wire in a cord clothesline, or indeed in any form of rope or cord that does not look out-of-place. Wires can also be concealed in flagpoles or similar structures; then again it is possible to use the braid of the feeder cable of a television or vhf/fm broadcast antenna. Metal gutterings or drainpipes are rather more difficult since they tend to be less conveniently reached, may not be easy to make good conductive contact with, and are tending to disappear in favour of plastics.

ANTENNA TOPICS

In the manual for the para-military Mark 123 transmitter/receiver (see *TT* June 1983)—originally a "confidential" document but now "unclassified"—it is stressed that the efficiency of any antenna, particularly within buildings, depends on many factors not easily measured or described, and that the greatest efficiency is obtained from an antenna of adequate length installed out of doors away from buildings or other tall objects. Few would disagree, but the manual does go on to illustrate various ways in which random-length wire antennas can be installed in quite small rooms (provided always that these are not basement rooms) or in a roof space; Figs 3 to 5 are derived from the manual.

Fig 3 shows an antenna mostly draped under the ceiling and using a "mains socket" earth, suitable for use in the highest available room and stated to provide reasonably low angle radiation.

Fig 4 shows an alternative arrangement of an antenna plus counterpoise, providing rather more high-angle radiation than the previous example. Fig 5 shows an antenna in a loft or roof space, usually capable of considerably better performance than room antennas. in this case the earth consists of a connection to the radiator of a central-heating system.

All such systems should prove capable of providing medium-distance contacts on, say, 3·5, 7 or 10·1MHz. Many newcomers wrongly believe that antenna elements *must* be resonate, forgetting that it is the whole antenna system that matters. Random lengths of wire can be effectively tuned as a classic Marconi antenna against an earth or counterpoise, provided that you can cope with voltage (parallel tuned) or current (series tuned) situations, or, for example, use a pi-network or z-match.

For several years I operated from a first-floor flat (what Americans and others would call a second-floor flat!) in Central London using initially a wire draped around the room, though afterwards achieving much improved results when I managed to get a dipole out on to the balcony.

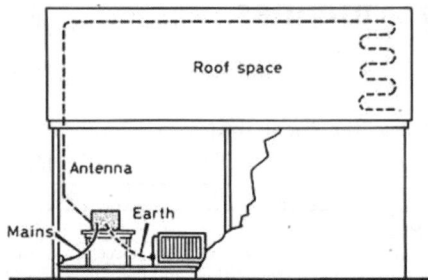

Fig 5. Antenna in roof space with central-heating radiator used as "earth"

Balcony Dipole

Extracted from 'Technical Topics', *Radio Communication,* July 1983

Balcony dipole

My balcony dipole was of the folded variety made from 300Ω line with the ends hanging down. However, in *cq-DL* (1/82, pp18-20) Helmut Spieler, DL6FY, describes what is claimed as "a highly efficient balcony mini-dipole for 7MHz" effective over a bandwidth of some 50kHz and of relatively simple construction. An unusual feature is the method of end-feeding the inductance-loaded element through a capacitance built into the system. He uses an L-network between the coupling "capacitor" and the 50Ω coaxial cable connected to his transceiver.

Fig 6 shows the principle of his dipole and how this can be adjusted for resonance by means of capacitive coupling plate. Constructional details are shown in Fig 7, though the system could be implemented in other ways

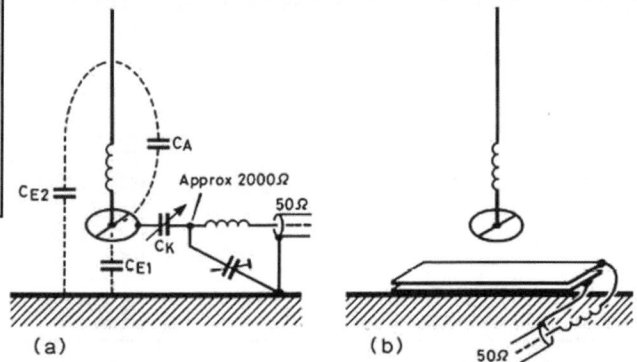

Fig 6. (a) Principle of the 7MHz mini-dipole used by DL6FY. (b) Test-rig used to adjust loaded dipole for resonance

Fig 6 shows the principle of his dipole and how this can be adjusted for resonance by means of capacitive coupling plate. Constructional details are shown in Fig 7, though the system could be implemented in other ways

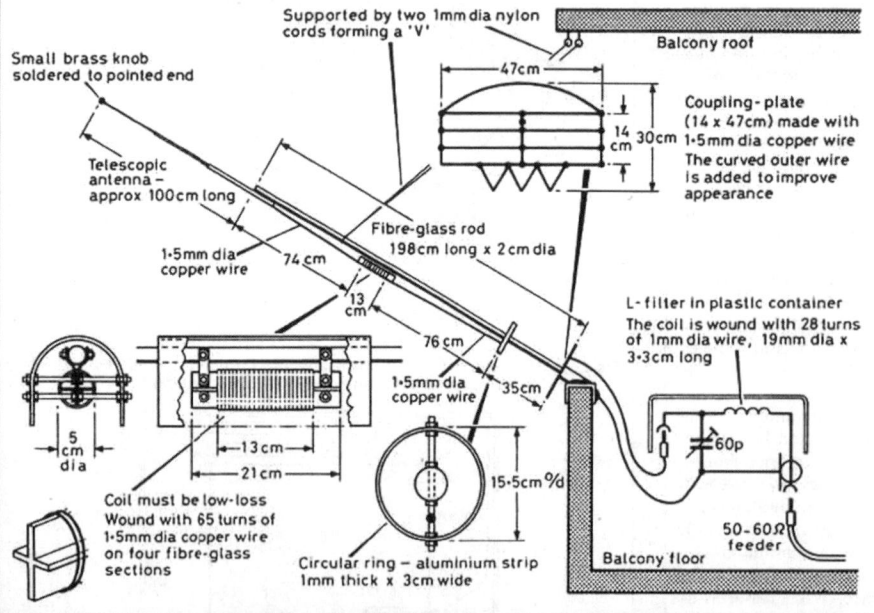

Fig 7. Constructional details of the DL6FY balcony-mounted mini-dipole

Multiband Arrays with 'KISS'

Extracted from 'Technical Topics', *Radio Communication,* August 1983

Multiband arrays with "kiss"

As mentioned recently, Les Moxen, G6XN, moved house soon after the publication of his excellent *HF Antennas for All Locations* with the result that he needed to concentrate for a time on his own antennas for the new location. He decided that he not only wanted one (or possibly two) "ideal" antennas, but also the opportunity of tidying up several loose ends left over from all his previous work, with the aim of shedding still more light on the general concept of basic multiband beam arrays, including compact arrays of less than full size.

After an abortive effort involved, as he puts it, in trying to be too clever, he fell back on "kiss" techniques. When later, during a contact with an American station, he described his "kiss" approach, the American suggested the G6XN had basically re-invented the "G5RV" and could not be persuaded otherwise.

In a sense, G6XN feels that the link with a G5RV multiband dipole is a good introduction, since if one starts from a G5RV all one has to do is to add the requirements for beam operation, such as having at least two elements, keeping within certain limits of length and spacing, and taking appropriate steps to ensure correct coupling. At the practical level, and paying due regard to radiation resistance, required bandwidth etc, there would seem to be distinct advantages in feeding elements across the *ends* instead of the conventional centre-fed approach. With this approach, after suitably disposing of the feeders, one ends up with what looks like a *triangular* version of G6XN's earlier multiband loop antenna, as in Fig 1 (Fig 107, *Amateur Radio Techniques*, 7th edn, p308). With some additional guidelines the end result is a beam array able to compete with full-sized monobanders, yet extremely light, low cost and easy to build, since dimensions are non-critical and no adjustments are needed before erection. Thereafter everything can be done at ground level or even, in some cases, from inside the shack. As the beam is electronically reversible there is no need for heavy, bulky and expensive rotators; sufficient rotation can be obtained from two cords which can often be brought into and operated from the shack.

So far this may seem "kiss" all the way. However, there remain a few problem areas that will irk some users more than others. In particular *narrow bandwidth*. This can be overcome by building additional complications into the system, so letting in the usual compromises; however, since there is a wide range of options open to the user, the amount of extra bandwidth can be tailored to suit individual needs. For example, a cw operator will usually be far less concerned with antenna bandwidth than, say, someone wishing to make full use of all bands. It is also worth remembering an earlier G6XN precept: a lightweight two-element array at a good height is usually as good as or better than more elements nearer the ground.

G6XN has provided two practical examples of arrays based on these principles, and some general notes on the use of open-wire transmission lines etc.

(1) Modified VK2ABQ all-wire beam

The first example (Fig 2) is a two-element wire beam using G6XN's modified form of the VK2ABQ compact array. The centrepiece is formed from one of those rotating "washing line" appliances with its four arms extended by 8ft bamboo garden canes (see photograph on p174 of *HF Antennas for All Locations*) supporting a pair of 19ft elements (14swg) spaced 10ft. Wires (19swg) are dropped down from the ends of the 19ft elements to form right-angled delta loops with their lower corners about 5ft apart. From these corners open-wire line is dropped down to ground level (line formed from 16swg but heavier gauge wire would be preferable). Height of the

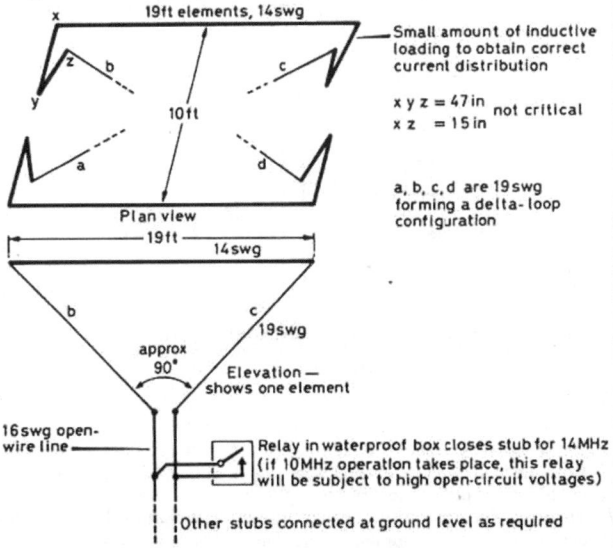

Fig 2. An example of the latest form of compact G6XN multiband all-wire beam based on the VK2ABQ form of construction. Main constructional details are similar to the photograph on page 174 of *HF Antennas for All Locations*

array is 42ft, and the two open-wire lines (about 110ft or 21swg) are taken back to the shack, one from each element.

For bypassing the rotating joint, line spacing is reduced to about 1·5in, with plenty of ceramic spacers over about 15in or so. Since the beam is reversible, rotation is limited to about 120°.

The elements are loaded by folds at the top corners so that *the current on 14MHz is zero at the centre of the sides of the loop*. This ensures that the sides do *not* radiate and *all radiation comes from the highest part of the system*.

Radiation resistance on 14MHz is about 44Ω for one element. This is a reasonable compromise, although difficulties could be expected to escalate fairly rapidly if the radiation resistance were further lowered by reducing the basic size of the elements.

The concentration of radiation from the highest part of the system is a major feature of this new beam *and applies to all versions*. Half of each side can be regarded as providing an inherent form of end loading.

On the adjustment and multiband use of this array, G6XN writes:

"Initially, stubs are connected at ground level so that resonances occur towards the lower end of each band, in the case of both elements. On 14MHz there is then a total of about 2λ of wire in the resonant loops, 3λ on 21MHz and 4λ on 28MHz. Operation is also possible on 10MHz with about 1λ of wire in the loop, some loss of effective gain and rather narrow bandwidth (not important on the narrow 10·1MHz band). Unfortunately for operation on 10MHz I had to climb a ladder to attach (and remove) the stubs; however, excellent signal reports were obtained from Australia, and about 12 to 15dB front/back ratio.

"The appropriate stubs can be selected by relays or manually. However, relay capacitance is not negligible, and I chose to restrict the use of relays to 14 and 21MHz only. This brings us to another very important point: as thus far described the design for 14MHz is marginal. By accepting this we reduce the weight, windage, visual impact and cost of the beam, and we are enabled to cover the widest possible range of frequencies with good gain on 28MHz and very useful performance on 10MHz. Unfortunately the useful bandwidth (without readjustment of stubs or by accepting losses) on 14MHz is not more than about 100kHz, and wet-weather effects can prove a nuisance.

"It is therefore important to use relays, at least for the 14MHz stubs; these can then be moved up the mast, exactly 0·5λ from their initial position. I found this had little effect on signal strength reports but null depths were greatly increased, eg from 15dB to over 30dB; adjustments became less critical and more stable, and the roughly doubled bandwidth proved a major asset. Null depths could have been increased equally well

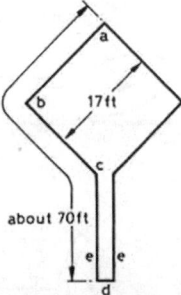

Fig 1. Multiband loop and stub element first described by G6XN in *Wireless World*, 1959. It resonates at 7, 14, 21 and 28MHz and is suitable as a quad-beam element on 14 and 21MHz. It can be fed with low impedance feeders at point d, or with 600Ω open line at about point e. A more detailed description can be found in all recent editions of *Amateur Radio Techniques*

ANTENNA TOPICS

by increasing coupling (ie bringing the lower corners of the loops closer together), but with the resulting very narrow bandwidth, tuning would then be too critical for the extra null depth to have much practical value."

(2) An alternative array design
As mentioned earlier, there are a number of different options possible within the same basic concept. Les Moxen has also checked-out an end-fed

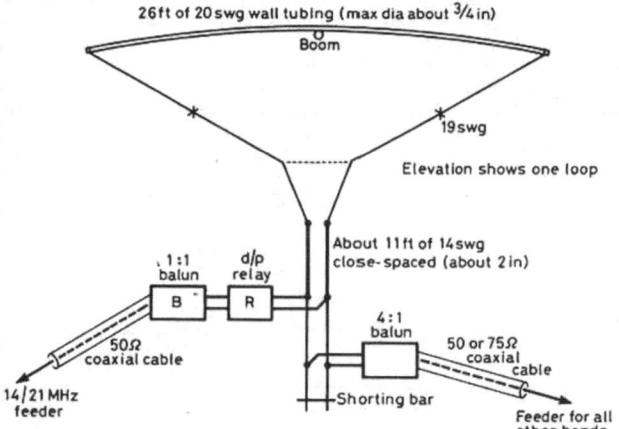

Fig 3. Another option for the G6XN multiband beam. This uses 26ft of tubing as the radiating element. On 14MHz all radiation is from the tubing forming the highest part of the system

beam using aluminium tubing for the horizontal span of the radiating element: Fig 3. Dimensions are chosen so that on 14MHz the current zeros occur at points X. There is then no radiation from the sides, all radiation is from the highest point in the system which in effect is the equivalent of two end-loaded dipoles spaced about 9ft.

The lower corners of the loops are brought in to about half this spacing, which provides extra coupling needed on all bands and also reduces the effective spacing at higher frequencies where the elements operate as loops.

The various changes of gauge shown in the diagram have the effect of bringing the first and second resonances closer together, so that in effect 21MHz becomes the second harmonic of 14MHz and the two resonances coincide when the relay contacts are made. The lower part of the system being high, impedance on these bands remains dead, and a reasonably good match is presented on both bands to the 50Ω coaxial cable. Either element can be driven, the other (also self-resonant) being correctly tuned to act as a reflector (the phase shift being provided by the additional coupling, not by detuning). However, fine tuning for the reflector is provided at the shack end of the feed lines.

With a height of 30ft the lower part of the feeder system can be reached from the ground for making small adjustments, resonances for 10, 18 and 28MHz being nearly coincident. Though designed primarily for 14 to 29MHz operation, fairly efficient operation is achieved on 10MHz with the bandwidth being just adequate for this 50kHz-wide band. It is important to note that because of the much higher radiation resistance on 25 to 28MHz (and in the case of 10 and 18MHz the narrow widths of the band) the additional length of feeder is not a disadvantage for these bands.

For 14MHz the length of the resonant part of the system should be kept as short as possible, since it is the ratio of radiation resistance to total length of conductor within the resonant loops which determines (approximately) the bandwidth and the extent of any losses. The higher this ratio, the smaller the antenna can be made for a given performance. Bandwidth can be expected to be about half that for a full-size monoband element on 14MHz. This should be adequate, although an atu and remote tuning of the reflector are desirable. For coverage of the whole of the 28MHz band some retuning is necessary.

General notes on multiband beams
G6XN has also put together some additional notes on the more general question of compact multiband beams, stemming partly from the response of readers of his *HF Antennas for All Locations*:

(a) Use of open-wire line. There is still a lot of resistance to this highly-effective system in the case of beam antennas, other than for some miniature beams; this opposition seems always to be directed against open-wire line as such but notably missing in the case of the G5RV dipole antenna which is very popular. It is to be hoped that this indulgence may be extended to beams based on the G5RV philosophy! The absurdity of much of the opposition to open-wire line is perhaps best illustrated by its apparent acceptability for minibeams (G4ZU, DL1FK) where there can be predictable swr values of 100 or more. G6XN is far from fussy about achieving low values of swr, but he feels this is ridiculous!

(b) Use of coaxial feeders. Advantageous or even essential in some cases. Using relays to switch stubs, G6XN notes that these could all be moved up the mast as close as possible to the elements and then switch into or across these stubs with the coaxial. Example (2) above has shown how two- or possibly three-band operation can be combined by using carefully-engineered multiple resonances, thus greatly simplifying the switching.

**(c) There remains a lot of opposition to the use of an atu, possibly due to "fantastic" prices, but a simple pi-network for this type of application can be improvised easily and cheaply; using the new automatic swr meters, adjustment is very easy and quickly carried out.

(d) 14MHz quad loops with $0 \cdot 5\lambda$ resonant feeders are quite easy to tune to 10MHz with series capacitors. In effect this invokes the same basic principles, with current zeros occurring in the middle of the lower sides. G6XN has found this works well and gain should be fully maintained at 10MHz (apart from the two small beams described earlier, G6XN has such a quad completely buried in a large beech tree.)

(e) Starting out from the arrangement of Example **(1)**, it is possible in principle to continue reducing the size but, as noted earlier, this leads to a rapid escalation of problems and should be kept as a last resort. Antenna "neutralization" soon becomes necessary, and although this presents few worries for monoband operation it would be difficult (if not impossible) to do this for five-band operation.

(f) There can be problems with loops fouling guy wires, but the situation is much the same as for the lower half of a quad. The use of reversible beams not requiring full rotation also helps. Currently, G6XN is adopting the same general principle but with folded dipole elements in planning a three-element "flat" design.

(g) With this approach relatively thin wire construction is acceptable for the loop sides, since current is low on 14MHz and radiation resistance high at the higher frequencies. Thick wire (requiring stronger construction) would be preferable for 10MHz.

It should be recognized that these notes cover only a few of the many possible options: for example, the entire system of Example **(1)** can be excited as a vertically-polarized antenna for operation on the lower frequencies.

The Groundplane Loop

Extracted from 'Technical Topics',
Radio Communication, August 1983

The groundplane loop
In *cq-DL*, the monthly journal of the German DARC, Hans Wuertz, DL2FA, has been presenting a long series of articles on "The dx antenna

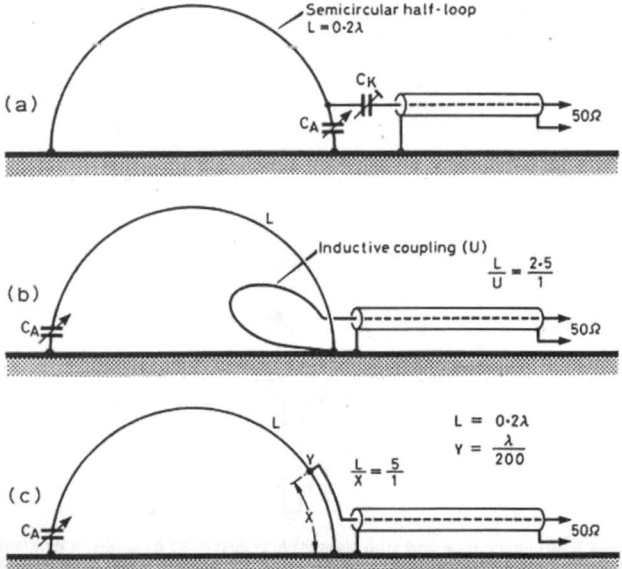

Fig 4. Various methods of feeding an emgi half-loop antenna: (a) capacitive coupling voltage fed; (b) inductive coupling; (c) tapped impedance matching

Table 1. Data for the semi-circular emgl antenna of Fig 5

Bands (MHz)	Semicircle length (l)	Coupling turn (U)	End capacitance (CA)	Bandwidth (—3dB points)		Efficiency (%)	Comparison with λ/4 monopole
3·5/7	8·4m	1·68m	332pF	3·5MHz 7MHz	5·7kHz 67kHz	70 96	—1·91dB —0·55dB
7/14	4·2m	0·84m	184pF	7MHz 14MHz	11·55kHz 147kHz	77 97	—1·52dB —0·50dB
14/28	2·1m	0·42m	102pF	14MHz 28MHz	24kHz 323kHz	83 98	—1·22dB —0·47dB

and its image". Part 13, *cq-DL* No 5/83, pp224–5, is devoted to an antenna that I cannot recall having been described in British amateur radio journals: the electro-magnetic groundplane loop (emgl). In effect this is half of a full-wave loop antenna with the other half formed by the ground image. With a 0·2λ semi-circular half-loop for the lowest frequency, it is claimed that the antenna can be tuned effectively to cover a 2:1 frequency range (eg 3·5/7MHz) although it should be noted that the bandwidth, without retuning the loop, is very narrow. DL2FA presents information showing that the efficiency of the antenna, despite its reduced dimensions, is relatively high —and even on 3·5MHz can be less than 2dB down on a full-size λ/4 monopole, and only about 0·5dB down on the higher frequency band. Fig 4 shows several basic versions, featuring different forms of coupling.

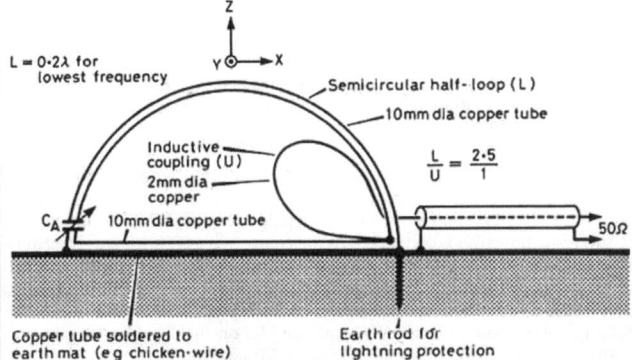

Fig 5. Practical example of an emgl half-loop antenna as described by DL2FA. Data is given in Table 1

Fig 5 is a practical design for which the data given in Table 1 applies, although the figures appear to be based on calculation. In practice, the groundplane is augmented by the 10mm diameter tubing, although radiation efficiency and vertical radiation pattern will presumably be affected by ground conductivity over the surrounding area.

More on Groundplanes

Extracted from 'Technical Topics',
Radio Communication, September 1983

More on groundplanes

One of the more surprising aspects of reporting the antenna scene is the degree of uncertainty—and controversy—that can still surround simple antenna systems that have been with us for 40, 50 or even 60 years. For example, the "zepp" technique of end-feeding a resonant element from a nominally "balanced" open-wire feeder, without any attempt to use a stub balun (*Amateur Radio Techniques, HF Antennas for All Locations* etc) is still regarded as an "acceptable" technique, although G6CJ drew attention to "the proportion of failures" that this involves as long ago as 1955.

More recently there has been the dispute over the basic feedpoint impedance and radiation resistance of an elevated groundplane antenna with horizontal wire radials: 36 or 19Ω? Fred Brown, W6HPH, noting G6XN's comments (*TT* May 1983), waxes indignantly, claiming "the 36Ω impedance of a groundplane has been well established, both theoretically and experimentally, for well over a quarter of a century", quoting such eminent sources as Kraus, *Proc IRE,* Jordan etc.

How come then that Les Moxon, with powerful support from Dave Gordon-Smith, G3UUR/W3, still has no doubt whatsoever that, whatever others may say, the correct figure is around 18–19Ω, that the dipole has no gain over the groundplane antenna in free space; and that this can readily be proved theoretically?

The confusion, G3UUR suggests, arose from the original use of vertical monopoles mainly by mf broadcasters; in other words as a λ/4 vertical with the earth theoretically providing an infinite, perfectly conducting "groundplane". In these circumstances the radiation resistance *is* 36Ω. But, as G3UUR puts it:

"The subsequent use of the elevated λ/4 groundplane at higher frequencies reflected practical rather than theoretical work, and the difference between the effect of the (wire radial) groundplane and an infinite, perfectly conducting ground. I agree with G6XN that radials by no means form a 'screen'. Provided that the radials are symmetrically placed about the base of the radiating element, the radiation pattern is essentially $\cos\theta$, though *not* a point-source. Only a hypothetical isotropic radiator can be considered, as G6XN suggests, 'merely a matching device'. The inherent radiation resistance of the groundplane element is determined by the current distribution on it. This is not altered by the existence of the radials. They provide only a return path for the E-field and current. A better description, I feel, would be to say that the radials act as a coupling device, since they are not transforming the feed impedance to some other value.

"Some years ago, while still at school, I derived a simple formula that has

Table 1

1. Radiation resistance of short dipoles ($l = \frac{\lambda}{2}$ or less)

$$R_{RAD} = 72 \left[\frac{1 - \cos\left(\pi \frac{l}{\lambda}\right)}{\sin\left(\pi \frac{l}{\lambda}\right)} \right]^2 \text{ ohms}$$

where l = length of dipole as proportion of wavelength, λ.

2. Radiation resistance of ground-mounted monopole ($l = \frac{\lambda}{4}$ or less)

$$R_{RAD} = 36 \left[\frac{1 - \cos\left(2\pi \frac{l}{\lambda}\right)}{\sin\left(2\pi \frac{l}{\lambda}\right)} \right]^2 \text{ ohms}$$

where l = length of vertical radiator proportion of wavelength, λ.

3. Radiation resistance of elevated groundplane with horizontal radials ($l = \frac{\lambda}{4}$ or less)

$$R_{RAD} = 18 \left[\frac{1 - \cos\left(2\pi \frac{l}{\lambda}\right)}{\sin\left(2\pi \frac{l}{\lambda}\right)} \right]^2 \text{ ohms}$$

where l = length of vertical radiator
l = length of radials as well in terms of λ.

4. Radiation resistance of elevated groundplane with 55° drooping radials ($l = \frac{\lambda}{4}$ or less)

$$R_{RAD} = 50 \left[\frac{1 - \cos\left(2\pi \frac{l}{\lambda}\right)}{\sin\left(2\pi \frac{l}{\lambda}\right)} \right]^2 \text{ ohms}$$

where l = length of vertical radiator
l = length of radials in terms of λ.

Note: It is interesting to note that the rate of change of radiation resistance vs horizontal droop angle is maximum at about 53° when the radiation resistance is 49Ω.

ANTENNA TOPICS

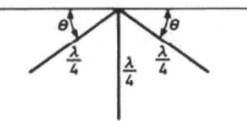

5. Radiation resistance of inverted groundplane with radials sloping downwards.

For $\theta = 45°$ $R_{RAD} = 4 \cdot 5\Omega$!
$\theta = 30°$ $R_{RAD} = 10 \cdot 1\Omega$

With 45° droop, the ohmic losses in an 18–20swg antenna could cause up to 2dB loss at hf

given good results. This relates the radiation resistance of an elevated groundplane, a ground-mounted λ/4 vertical monopole, or a dipole, to the radiation resistance of their shortened forms by using a correction factor: Table 1. In practice, as is well known, the radiation resistance of an elevated gpa can be increased by dropping the radials downwards. For resonant antennas Table 1 shows the radiation resistance of a dipole to be about 72Ω, a ground-mounted monopole about 36Ω; an elevated groundplane about 18Ω; and an elevated groundplane with 55° drooping radials about 50Ω."

IGP, T and M Antennas

Extracted from 'Technical Topics',
Radio Communication, September 1983

IGP, T and M antennas

TT (May 1983 pp424–5) attempted to trace briefly the history of "the inverted groundplane family", in so far as it was known to me. I suggested then that the first published discussion of the igp was my *TT* July 1970, though I recognized that the technique was not new but a re-invented wheel.

This led to an interesting letter from an old friend, George Proctor, GM8SQ, who recalled that "as far back as 1937 I experimented with a "T" antenna (Fig 1(a)) which then appeared to be called the "G5GQ" antenna. In June 1939 I concocted what I called the "M" antenna (Fig 1(c)) which although only about 15ft above ground was reasonably effective . . ." He later used the arrangment of Fig 1(d) which has appeared in American publications as a "novice" antenna. This information set me thinking: if the igp of Fig 1 (a) had been known to GM8SQ as a "G5GQ" antenna, it must surely have come from a published article—and I felt it would be valuable to track this down since 1937 was *before* the usual-way-up

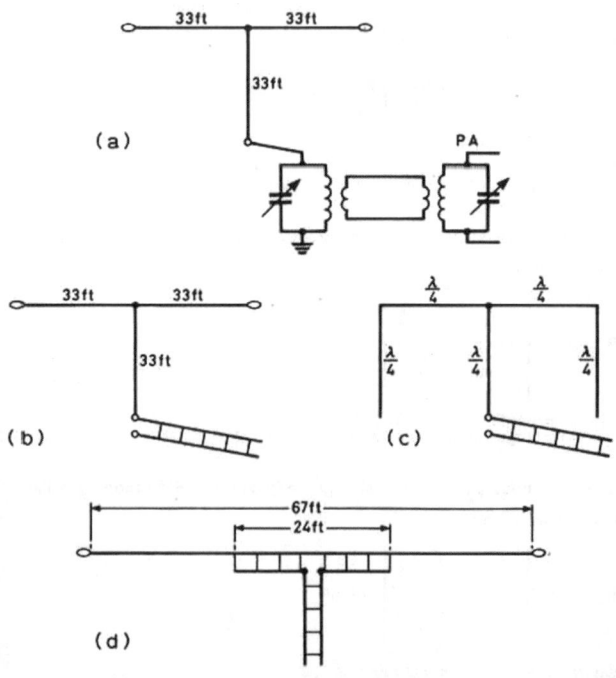

Fig 1. Ideas from GM8SQ's notes. (a) The "G5GQ" used pre-war; (b) alternative arrangement for "zepp feeding" the "G5GQ"; (c) GM8SQ's "M" antenna; (d) a useful multiband antenna GM8SQ used and later noted being recommended in American publications as a "novice" antenna

groundplane, developed by Dr George Brown of RCA, had become established!

The clue was G5GQ. This was the call of the late Basil Wardman—the original editor of *Short Wave Magazine,* though he soon handed the journal over to the late Austin Forsyth, G6FO.

A visit to the Science Museum Library brought confirmation of this hunch. The very first issue of *SWM* (March 1937, pp22–3) included an article "A new 'dx' aerial—for multiband operation" which described an antenna (Fig 2) used by G5GQ on 7, 14 and 28MHz, and which, sure enough—at least on 7MHz—was a genuine inverted groundplane! The description of its operation however, was somewhat incorrect in suggesting that "the horizontal section, radiates horizontally, the combined radiation of the aerial being at a far lower angle to the ground than that of a vertical aerial alone." G5GQ clearly did not appreciate that radiation in the horizontal span, as in the radials of a groundplane, is largely self-cancelling.

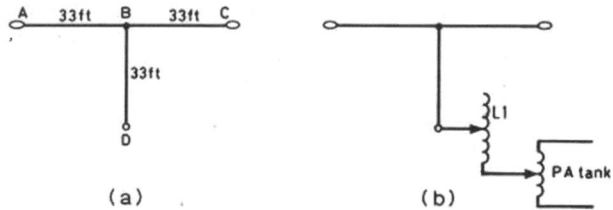

Fig 2. The "G5GQ" antenna as described in the very first issue of *Short Wave Magazine* in 1937. Intended for multiband use it is undoubtedly on 7MHz an inverted groundplane antenna, in the days before anyone was using the groundplane the usual way up!

Nevertheless G5GQ made a strong case for this antenna, including (*1*) multiband operation; (*2*) equal radiation in all directions; and (*3*) ease of operation. G5GQ pointed out that "the half-wave (on 14MHz) vertical (or semi-vertical) section is connected to the centre of a 66ft horizontal section. It looks like a single-wire-fed type (ie Windom) but the 33ft vertical section is not a feeder; it is intended to radiate". On 14MHz his dx results 45 years ago would still be entirely acceptable, including low-power tests achieving R8 on 14MHz from W2 with 3W input, and R7 on 7MHz with 6W, plus (on higher power) Japan, Philippines, South Africa, Brazil etc.

Apart from its historic interest, the G5GQ "T" antenna has value in underlining that this configuration provides useful *multiband* operation —both harmonic and sub-harmonic bands, as with the classic mf broadcast "T" antenna.

T With Sloping Radials

Extracted from 'Technical Topics',
Radio Communication, September 1983

T with sloping radials

The advantage of a single main support combined with the concentration of maximum radiation from the highest section of the element has made the inverted-V dipole or multiband dipole one of the most popular approaches to simple wire antennas. In the May 1983 *TT,* G6XN noted that the top non-radiating section of a T or inverted groundplane can slope downwards, though this does tend to reduce the effective bandwidth. The vertical radiating section can also slope.

Steve Ireland, G3ZZD, mentions that in January this year he enjoyed considerable success using a variant of the λ/4 T antenna. In his case he used

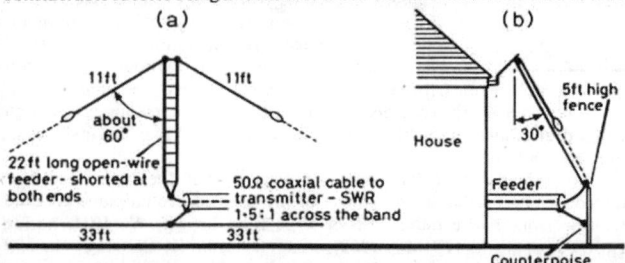

Fig 3. G3ZZD's T antenna with sloping T element. (b) Implementation using bamboo supported antenna with sloping "vertical" element

the vertical section of the open-wire feeder of a G5RV antenna to form the vertical radiating element: Fig 3 (a). He writes: "The vertical section of my antenna was supported by a 5ft bamboo cane wedged in the downpipe of the house guttering. The base of the 'semi-vertical' (about 30° true vertical) was secured to the garden fencing. The two λ/4 radials were run out horizontally along the garden fencing as a counterpoise. Despite the proximity of the house and guttering, results were excellent . . ."

Fig 4. How G3ZZD turns his antenna into a two-band antenna

The antenna can be very easily made into a two-band system (7/10MHz or 7/14MHz) by the addition of a parallel λ/4 vertical section and attachment of another pair of λ/4 radials: Fig 4. The additional vertical should be spaced about 6–12in from the 7MHz vertical section. This produces excellent results on both 7 and 14MHz.

Antenna Round-up

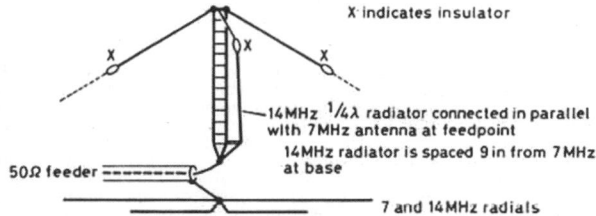

Extracted from 'Technical Topics', *Radio Communication,* September 1983

Antenna round-up

Follow-up notes on various hf antenna ideas that have appeared previously in *TT* underline the value of simple wire-loop systems.

Laurie Margolis, G3UML, mentions that the simple loop system described in *TT* (May 1982, Fig 3) has now accounted for 280 countries, all ssb except BY1PK. He has replaced the original wire, but otherwise found no reason to change it!

Tom Higginson, GW3AHN, notes that despite all that has been said against (and for) various forms of X arrays, he and other enthusiasts continue to find his Butterfly array (*TT* September 1978) performs very effectively. He draws attention to an article by Brice Anderson, W9PNE, "Horizontal X Beams for 15 and 20 metres" *QST* March 1983. GW3AHN remains convinced by his own experience and that of others that the "Butterfly" array is capable of good forward gain with much reduced sidelobes, compared with the full-sized X beams. A 220MHz model version by VE3BUP appears to confirm W9PNE's figures of about 6dBd forward gain, half-power beamwidth 60°, front/back ratio 15–18dB and negligible side lobes. Diligent readers will be aware of G6XN's disapproval of X-type arrays. GW3AHN feels that the experience and satisfaction of users deserves to be recorded, whatever the books may say.

Dr Guy Fletcher, VK2BBF (ex-G3LNX, FK0TAG), notes a reprint in *Amateur Radio* June 1983, p11, of an article he wrote for a local newsletter *QUA* "Another useful multiband antenna—the Delta loop". He mentions that this was based on notes by HB9ADQ (*TT* September 1980, pp904–5) and has proved a very effective "limited space" antenna on bands as low as 3·5MHz: Fig 5.

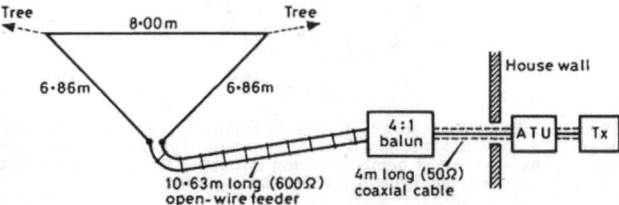

Fig 5. VK2BBF's version of the HB9ADQ triangular multiband loop antenna

Doubts on the value of the "absorber elements" proposed by G8SEQ (*TT* November 1982, pp959–60) last year continue to grow. G3UUR writes: "The idea intrigued me but, like G6XN, I find it hard to believe that it works! The "absorber element" can at most absorb only half the power that it gathers; the other half is always re-radiated in all directions . . . the only way a null can be produced without it being filled in by diffraction is through the destructive interference of two fields. The current in the "absorber element" is not sufficient to provide the second field, as pointed out by G6XN. I would be very wary of this technique, it sounds suspiciously like a hoax! It may improve the sidelobe situation, but my response to that is 'use a better design to begin with and you won't suffer from poor sidelobes!' As far as front/back ratio is concerned I would suggest using trigonal reflectors since they improve the f/b marginally as well as giving another 0·5dB forward gain." Perhaps G8SEQ would like to comment?

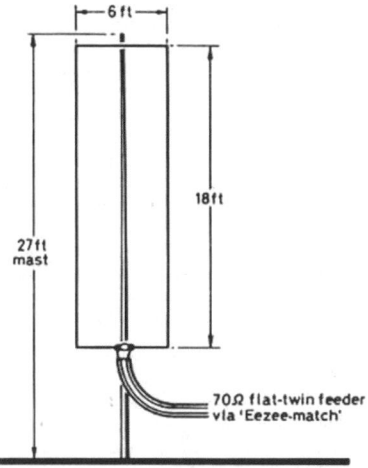

Fig 6. Vertically-elongated (3:1) loop antenna used by GM6RI and GM3VNW on 21MHz

Jim Macphee, GM3VNW, in collaboration with Walter Robertson, GM6RI, has been trying out a vertically-elongated (3:1) loop antenna on 21MHz, using ideas from the article "The gain of a quad" by F. Rasvall, SM5AGM, in *Rad Com* August 1980. SM5AGM provided theoretical computer calculations of a large number of loop shapes, including a horizontally-elongated element that should give a small (0·21dBd) gain relative to a dipole (2·3dBi). This was implemented (Fig 6) by GM6RI using a 27ft mast, with 48ft of wire trimmed to resonance using a grid dip oscillator. The vertical sides were 18ft, horizontal sides 6ft, with the lower horizontal section fed from 70Ω flat-twin feeder connected to a TS530S via an "Eezee Match" unit. An identical arrangement was set up at GM3VNW using a KW2000B. Over two years, results in both cases have proved encouraging, out-performing horizontal dipoles. The system takes up little space and is easy to erect. GM3VNW points out that he has never found any other stations using this configuration, and he would be interested to hear from anyone who gives it a try. Presumably it radiates with mixed polarization.

Miniature Antenna Elements

Extracted from 'Technical Topics', *Radio Communication,* October 1983

Miniature antenna elements

The search for antenna elements significantly shorter than a resonant half-wavelength has occupied the attention of many people over many years. For 144MHz vhf hand-portables the short "normal-mode helix" provides a reasonably effective system, well suited for use with repeaters; the normal-mode helix can also be used at hf for portable operation (*ART7* p324, ZL1BDY). At hf, the single-turn or multi-turn transmitting loop has found increasing use for Defence and diplomatic communications (a low-profile loop can be seen edging above the roof of the American embassy in Grosvenor Square, London) but unfortunately such systems require the use of conductors of exceptionally low ohmic losses and sometimes large

ANTENNA TOPICS

In theory, even a miniature dipole element radiates all the rf power that is fed to it; in reality there is a rapid escalation of losses in the coupling network and great difficulty in feeding all the available transmitter power into such an element, basically due to its low radiation resistance. A further practical drawback that arises with any high-Q system is the narrow bandwidth over which the antenna radiates effectively unless retuned.

Any practical antenna structure has losses due to its finite ohmic resistance (remembering that rf resistance is likely to be much higher than dc resistance), imperfect insulation, moisture and physical environment. The special problem of short voltage-fed ship antennas used on the 500kHz calling and distress frequency has been highlighted in a number of articles in recent years in *Wireless World* (for example August 1983, pp29–31).

The ratio of radiated power to the total input power fed to an antenna structure is termed the "antenna efficiency" where: Efficiency (%) = Radiation resistance/(Radiation resistance + antenna loss resistance) × 100.

Clearly if the loss resistance of an antenna structure could be reduced to zero, antenna efficiency would be 100 per cent; however, since it would presumably need a superconductive element at or near absolute zero temperature to do this, the next best thing is usually to seek to increase the ratio of radiation resistance to loss resistance, for example by using large copper or even silver-plated tubes for small transmitting loops.

The Toroidal Helix Antenna

Extracted from 'Technical Topics', *Radio Communication,* October 1983

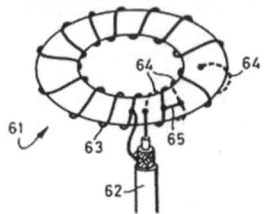

The toroidal helix antenna

Alec Clelland, DJ0FL/G3UUQ, who is an examiner in the European Patent Office, keeps an eye open for new ideas of potential use in amateur radio. Once a patent application has been published it passes into the public domain and it becomes possible for any amateur to use the information as the basis of further experimental work. It would, of course, be an infringement of a patent to use the disclosed information for commercial purposes. In other words, you can always build and try out a patented antenna or circuit device in your own station; but you cannot make such devices for sale without negotiating a licence with the patent holder or applicant.

Recently, DJ0FL/G3UUQ has drawn my attention to European Patent Application EP 0 043 591 A1, for which the applicant and inventor is James F. Corum (Route 9, Box 207-B, Morgantown, West Virginia 26505, USA). This patent application is for "an antenna for transmitting or receiving electromagnetic radiation, comprising a conductor configured to establish a closed standing-wave path, and to inhibit the velocity of propagation and support a standing-wave electromagnetic wave. One embodiment of the antenna (Fig 1) shows a toroidal helix antenna (61) which is adapted for unbalanced feed from transmission line (62). A sliding tap (65) is moved to a point for proper impedance matching".

In effect, as Alec Clelland notes, the basic idea is extremely simple: the reduction of the dimensions of a full-wave circular (or square) loop by winding it helically. The inventor claims that various implementations of this basic principle "possess greater radiation resistance and radiation efficiency than loop antennas of similar size". He also claims that such elements "radiate controllable mixtures of vertically, horizontally and elliptically polarized electromagnetic waves, and possess radiation power patterns different from those produced by small loop antennas." He claims that these toroidal loop antennas can be used to form both driven and parasitic arrays. It should be appreciated that although such elements are similar in form to a toroidal inductor, they are essentially *not* perfect

Fig 1. One simple form of the toroidal helix antenna as patented by James F. Corum. Isometric representation of the antenna (61) and transmission line (62). The main conductor (63) is continuous. In addition there is a shorter inductor (64) helically wound around the toroidal support between some of the turns of the main conductor (63). A sliding tap (65) connects the two conductors 63, 64. One side of the transmission line is connected to one end of the shorter conductor (64) and the other side attached to the main winding 63. The sliding tap (65) is moved to provide proper impedance matching. This point is found empirically at the operating frequency by moving the sliding tap to the optimum position

toroidal inductors which would have zero radiation efficiency.

James Corum, who, from the examples given in his patent application, would appear to be an active radio amateur, sets out eight design examples, some, but not all, of which appear to have been built and tested. These cover frequencies as low as 200kHz and as high as 450MHz. The design examples are: (1) vhf toroidal loop; (2) vhf vertically-polarized toroidal loop; (3) omnidirectional vhf array; (4) hf toroidal loop; (5) mf vertically-polarized toroidal loop; (6) hf rectangular toroidal loop; (7) uhf parasitic array; and (8) contrawound vhf toroidal loop. Examples which appear to be most relevant to amateur radio are shown in Table 1.

I should perhaps emphasize that it is difficult to determine readily from the 70-page patent application just what degree of improvement in efficiency is obtained over more conventional short elements and transmitting loops by adopting helical toroidal winding. It appears entirely possible, however, to obtain the advantages of resistive feedpoints at resonance, and that, as with a full-sized quad loop, harmonic resonances are usable, as in example 4. The inventor admits that "one does not get

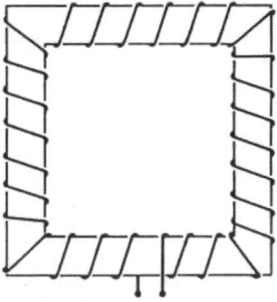

Fig 2. An hf rectangular toroidal loop antenna for 27MHz on 2·5in (63·5mm) od plastic pipe form 27in (68·58cm) by 27in. Measured feedpoint impedance about 2,600Ω resistive at resonant frequency with antenna comprising 115 equally-spaced turns of 18-gauge wire

something for nothing. The price one pays with the toroidal helix is that it is a narrowband (high-Q) structure and inherently not a broadband device". However, he adds: "These antennas by virtue of their construction possess a greater radiation resistance than known antennas of similar electrical size not having the slow-wave winding features . . . the helix

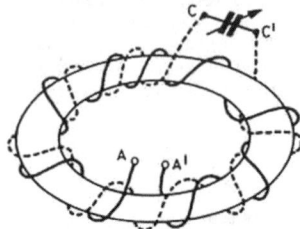

Fig 3. Use of a variable capacitor to vary the resonant frequency of a toroidal helix antenna without changing the number of turns. The antenna comprises two helices, one fed at points AA' and the other at CC'. The variable capacitor is connected across feedpoints CC'

Table 1. Simple toroidal loop antennas, design examples from patent application

	Frequency	Turns	Wire	Velocity factor	a	b	s
1 Toroidal loop for domestic vhf/fm receiver	100MHz (n = 1)	70	16g	0·332	6·25in	0·5in	0·56in
4 HF toroidal loop fed through 4:1 balun and 50Ω coaxial feeder	3·6MHz (n = 1) 7·2MHz (n = 2)	1,000	18g	—	2·74ft	0·925in	0·2in
6 HF rectangular toroidal loop (Fig 2)	27·42MHz (n = 1)	116	18g	—	2·5in od plastic pipe form (27 × 27in)		

where a = radius of torus (to centre of torus), b = radius of torus (ie 2b = minor diameter of the antenna), s = uniform turn-to-turn spacing of turns. n = 1 represents fundamental resonance, n = 2 harmonic resonance.

permits the formation of a resonant antenna current standing wave in a region of electrically small dimensions, and it permits the controlled variation of antenna currents, resonant frequency, impedance, polarization and antenna pattern."

The resonant frequency of the toroidal loop can be varied without changing the number of turns by using a variable capacitor, as shown in Fig 3. The antenna comprises two toroidal helices, one fed at points AA', the other at CC'. The capacitor is then connected across CC'.

whole 21MHz band."

Such an antenna system, ZL4DP points out, can be useful for portable work as it will all fit into the back boot of any car and still leave room for luggage etc. With low-power ssb, using this antenna, ZL4DP received Q5 from VK6PS (Perth) and N6NDA (Los Angeles), and Q3 from GI3OQR.

21MHz on 32in

Extracted from 'Technical Topics',
Radio Communication, October 1983

Broadband Dipoles

Extracted from 'Technical Topics',
Radio Communication, October 1983

21MHz on 32in

Short dipoles can be made from helical-wound elements without the toroid-loop configuration described above. In *Break-in* (March 1983, p16), Bill Evans, ZL4DP, describes making and using a 21MHz dipole antenna having an element length of only 2ft 8in (803mm) by winding two 22ft (6·7m) lengths of 24-gauge enamelled wire on to two 1·25in (32mm) diameter, 16in (406mm) long plastic tubes: Fig 4. ZL4DP describes construction and adjustment of this miniature dipole as follows:

"The wire is wound onto the plastic tubes evenly spaced, taking about 71 turns, and leaving enough at the ends for soldering the feeders and series capacitor into place. The two tubes are held end-to-end by joining them with a short length of smaller-diameter plastic tube; the top part of the mast should also be insulated from the metal support. The tuning capacitors can be mounted in any way that suits the particular circumstances, as the method of mounting should not make much difference to the tuning. The coaxial cable should be made long enough so that no trimming is needed when the antenna is finally mounted in position.

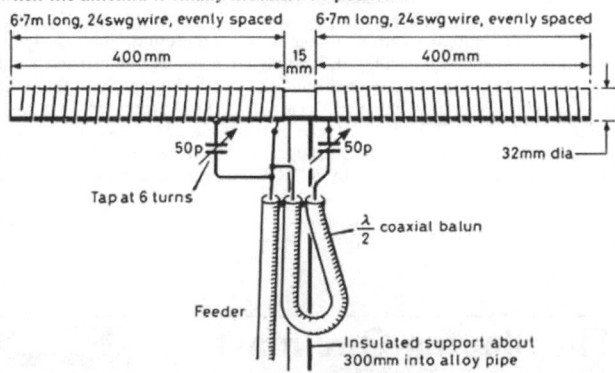

Fig 4. Short helical-wound 21MHz dipole built by ZL4DP with element length of 2ft 8in by winding two 22ft lengths of wire on two 1·25in diameter, 16in long plastic tubes

"The tuning should be undertaken out in the open away from metal objects such as roofs, other antennas etc. The top of a stepladder is ideal and an insulated tuning tool is essential. I tuned my dipole at about 21,250kHz and found that the swr was also unity at 21,100kHz so it would seem that it would be better to tune slightly high. The swr is 1·1:1 at 21,000kHz and 1·5:1 at 21,450kHz so that it is reasonably flat over the

Broadband dipoles

The much more generous spectrum allocation at 3·5MHz (3,500 to 4,000kHz) to radio amateurs in IARU Region 2 (North and South America) presents an antenna design problem appreciably more challenging than any that arises in Europe. This is to achieve on a simple antenna a vswr of under 2:1 right across the band without having to retune an atu. I should perhaps stress that the need to achieve a low vswr arises less from questions of antenna efficiency than the fact that modern solidstate broadband power amplifiers have protection circuits that automatically reduce transmitter output if the vswr exceeds about 2:1. A centre-fed dipole cut for 3,750kHz will radiate effectively on 3,999kHz and 3,501kHz, although at these extremities the swr of a wire antenna is likely to be about 5:1. With a suitable atu there is no real problem except the requirement to retune when shifting right across the band. These days such a requirement is becoming unacceptable to those who feel that the only operational adjustment to a transmitter should be turning the bandswitch and vfo control knobs to the desired frequency.

For many years there has been a succession of dipole antenna designs claimed to provide low swr over a greater bandwidth than a simple resonant length of wire. These have included the folded dipole, the double-bazooka (using elements made from coaxial cable), "hairpin" stubs etc. Jerry Hall, K1TD, of the ARRL technical staff, has recently been investigating many of these systems using computer analysis: "The search for a simple, broadband 3·5MHz dipole", *QST* April 1983, pp22–7. Although few of us on this side of the Atlantic need to worry about a bandwidth of 500kHz on 3·5MHz, his article gives some useful insights into antenna impedance calculations—and may also serve to destroy long-held beliefs about some designs.

What emerges from his work (Table 2), admittedly theoretical and with several simplifications such as omission of ground effects, is that most of the techniques normally advocated on the grounds of increased bandwidth do indeed show some improvement over a thin single-wire dipole, but *none* of them seems capable of achieving the full 500kHz without exceeding 2:1 swr. The *only* approach fed into the computer by K1TD that does do this is a very old friend indeed, long discarded and forgotten by most of us. It is the cage-dipole, an antenna system that dates back to the earliest days and adapted from non-resonant low-frequency antennas where the requirement was to increase the capacitance of the system. In the 'thirties and 'forties, however, dipoles formed from two sausage-shaped or "bird-cage" multiple wires kept apart by wooden spreaders were popular for commercial receiving and transmitting applications. When used with open-wire feeders they could be used over frequency spans of at least two-to-one.

K1TD's computer shows that with a four-wire radiating element 121·5ft (37·03m) long (note the reduction in resonant length brought about by the increased diameter/length ratio) and 3ft (91·5cm) cage, such a system when fed with 75Ω coaxial cable should maintain a less than 2:1 swr over the full 500kHz. Unfortunately, as K1TD points out, it needs some 486ft (148·13m) of wire, a couple of dozen spreaders and antenna supports that will take the weight without undue sagging, so that the cage-dipole only barely comes within the category of a "simple wire antenna".

Table 2. Examples of K1TD's computer-study of 3·5MHz antennas

Antenna	Radiator diameter (in)	Radiator diameter (mm)	Feeder impedance (Ω)	Bandwidth* (kHz)
Single-wire dipole	0·08	2·0	50	152
Double bazooka	0·38	9·6	50	190
Single-wire dipole	0·08	2·0	75	208
Single-wired dipole with 52·5ft hairpin (300Ω)	0·08	2·0	75	211
Single-wire dipole	0·5	12·7	75	252
Folded dipole of 300Ω cable, short-circuit 100ft apart	0·5	12·7	300	261
Folded dipole of 300Ω cable, shorted at ends	0·5	12·7	300	265
Double bazooka, 75Ω feeder	0·5	12·7	75	268
Single wire with coil and capacitor at feedpoint	0·5	12·7	75	375
Cage dipole	36	914·4	75	500

* between 2:1 swr points

ANTENNA TOPICS

The Quadplane

Extracted from 'Technical Topics',
Radio Communication, October 1983

The quadplane
In *cq-DL* No6, 1983, pp264-6, Siegfried Hari, DK9FN, provides information on yet another variation of the quad-loop antenna, in this case to provide vertically-polarized signals from masts of modest height. In effect the quadplane is a half-quad loop element suitable for use with either a single support pole or alternatively with a compact horizontal λ/4 "top", with the λ/2 bent element working against resonant λ/4 radials elevated a little above ground on short poles. Fig 5 shows the basic principles, while Fig 6 shows how the system can be implemented in practice. While DK9FN considers that his antenna has a feedpoint impedance of 60Ω (ie half the 120Ω of a full-wave quad-loop element) the recent discussion in *TT* of the impedance of groundplane antennas with elevated, horizontal radials (18-19Ω and not 36Ω as usually suggested) makes one wonder whether the figure for the DK9FN configuration may not be nearer to 30Ω in a correctly adjusted system when the radials are appreciably above ground. However, DK9FN claims an swr of 1·2:1 for a 7MHz quadplane of the type shown in Fig 6(a) when the element is fed with 50Ω coaxial cable (RG213U) with radials 0·5m above ground. DK9FN stresses the critical importance of the radials in such antennas. For example, one suspects that (as in conventional groundplanes) it is important to ensure that each radial is exactly the same electrical length. DK9FN also describes a two-band version using two separate loops one inside the other.

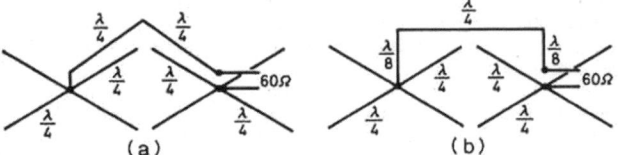

Fig 5. Basic principle of DK9FN's "quadplane" antenna

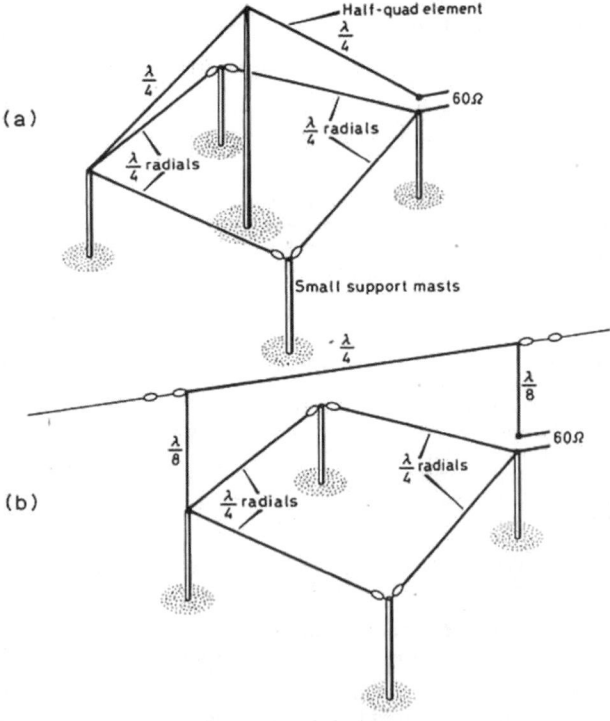

Fig 6. Two implementations of the quadplane. (a) Single pole support, with small masts supporting the radials a little above ground. (b) Implementation where two supports are available, though these can be shorter than for (a)

Half-delta Loop

Extracted from 'Technical Topics',
Radio Communication, October 1983

Half-delta loop
John S. Belrose, VE2CV (*Ham Radio* May 1983, pp37-9) has described what is, in effect, a variation of the quadplane: the half-delta loop: Fig 7. This has a mast radiator, height h, and a sloping wire, preferably 2h, and where h + 2h represents an electrical half-wave. An example would be a 25ft (7·62m) mast plus 52ft (15·85m) of sloping wire fed at ground-level from 50Ω coaxial cable. This antenna could be used on 7, 14, 21 and 28MHz since, unlike dipoles which resonate only at f, $3f$ and $5f$, the half-delta loop is resonant on all harmonics of the fundamental frequency (f, $2f$, $3f$, $4f$ etc).

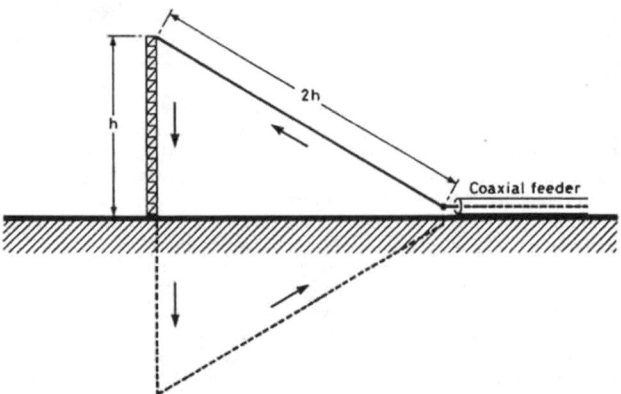

Fig 7. VE2CV's half-delta loop basically similar to the quadplane configuration but using the earth as a groundplane. Provides mainly vertically-polarized signals

Since this is an antenna with its image in the real ground, good earthing, preferably using a large earth mat, is needed to achieve good efficiency. At the very least a buried thick wire should connect the base of the mast to the shield of the coaxial feed cable, with two 6ft (1·82m) ground rods to earth the mast radiator and the outer screen of the feeder. The possibility exists, presumably, of using elevated, insulated λ/4 radials as for the quadplane, although this is not mentioned by VE2CV. Signals are similarly basically vertically polarized.

The Sloping One-mast Yagi

Extracted from 'Technical Topics',
Radio Communication, October 1983

The sloping one-mast Yagi
In recent years there has been growing interest in various forms of "slopers"—mostly in the form of antennas in which a λ/4 sloping wire element is top-fed against a grounded tower, which acts as the groundplane. One of the attractions of such a system is that the tower can be used also to support an independent Yagi antenna for the higher-frequency bands: Fig 8 shows a sloper antenna for 1·8, 3·5 or 7MHz bands as described in the *Radio Handbook* (22nd edn, pp27.18-19). Among the useful features of this arrangement is that (as for an inverted-V dipole) maximum current in the radiating element is at maximum height above ground. Polarization is mixed, with both vertical and horizontal components. There is only modest directivity, and such an antenna provides a virtually omni-directional pattern somewhat distorted by the presence of the grounded tower.

A different form of "sloper" has been used during recent years by the IBA for some of its mf local radio transmitting stations, either as the main antenna or a stand-by system for use while maintaining or repairing multimast directional antennas. In essence these antennas are basically a

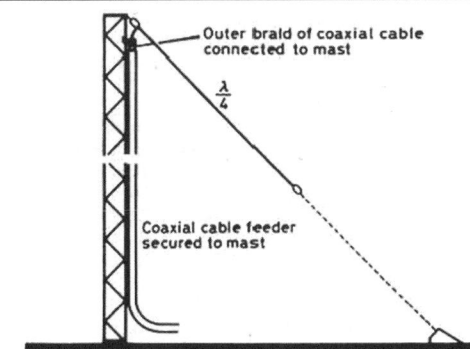

Fig 8. Usual form of λ/4 "sloper" with mast used as a groundplane

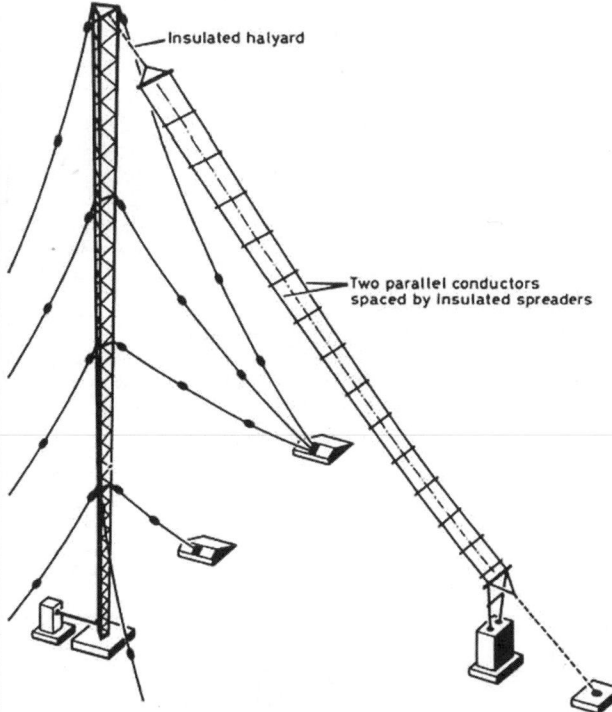

Fig 9. Directional mf two-element Yagi-type antenna with sloping reflector permitting the use of a single mast. Often used with electrically short mast primarily to obtain null, but can provide significant gain if the mast is λ/4 or λ/2 high

to support an independent Yagi antenna for the higher-frequency bands: Fig 8 shows a sloper antenna for 1·8, 3·5 or 7MHz bands as described in the *Radio Handbook* (22nd edn, pp27.18–19). Among the useful features of this arrangement is that (as for an inverted-V dipole) maximum current in the radiating element is at maximum height above ground. Polarization is mixed, with both vertical and horizontal components. There is only modest directivity, and such an antenna provides a virtually omnidirectional pattern somewhat distorted by the presence of the grounded tower.

A different form of "sloper" has been used during recent years by the IBA for some of its mf local radio transmitting stations, either as the main antenna or a stand-by system for use while maintaining or repairing multimast directional antennas. In essence these antennas are basically a pair of phased-verticals with one element used as a Yagi-type (parasitic) reflector. However, only one tower is used with a wire-element (twin or triple wires) connected to the top of (but insulated from) the tower: Fig 9.

Such an array provides the cardioid pattern of phased-verticals, with a useful front-to-back ratio; the amount of forward gain that can be realized depends on the height of the tower; many antennas for local radio need to be of modest height, often providing a radiating element of only about 67° rather than the 90° of a true λ/4 monopole. The efficiency of electrically short antennas, as we have often noted in *TT*, depends primarily on the efficiency with which power can be fed into it. A shortened element, of course, decreases the effective bandwidth of the antenna unless arrangements are incorporated for retuning the whole system when changing frequency.

Results achieved with nine Yagi-type sloping-wire antennas designed for frequencies from 774 to 1,359kHz, using towers of electrical heights from 60° to 93°, were described at ICAP83 by E. T. Ford. All provide an f/b ratio in operation between 5–17dB (up to 22dB achieved under test conditions). Absolute forward gain compared with a monopole reference is usually modest with 60° height (in this application the main consideration is often the need for a null to minimize interference to other co-channel services) but the Coventry installation, with a λ/4 58m mast, has 2·2dB gain on 1,359kHz. Bedford on 792kHz with a 73m mast provides 2·4dB gain.

Such a system would appear to offer a practical degree of directivity with reasonable mast heights for 7 or 3·5MHz operation, and would also be useful at higher frequencies where it is required to use only a single mast for a vertically polarized array. At the higher frequencies λ/2 elements would also be possible, giving an easy means of changing direction of the null by swinging round the sloping wire element.

Impedance of vertical Antennas

Extracted from 'Technical Topics',
Radio Communication, November 1983

Impedance of vertical antennas

Dave Gordon-Smith, G3UUR/W3, in a follow-up letter to his remarks in the September 1983 *TT*, writes:

"After some deliberation, I decided that I ought to calculate the radiation resistance of the λ/2 dipole from basics; I had previously taken it for granted that it was somewhere in the 72–73Ω region. My calculation shows it should be 73·13Ω. The elevated groundplane radiation resistance should thus be 18·28Ω and the ground-mounted λ/4 vertical 36·56Ω. These figures should be substituted for those given in Table 1, page 799, in the shortened formulas. This also affects the optimum angle of droop for the radials of an elevated gp antenna to obtain a match to 50Ω; this angle now becomes 54° rather than 55°.

"Another point worth mentioning is the effect of dropping the radials of the inverted-gp. The figures I gave for 45° and 30° drooping radials were for free space. In practice the igp is tuned against ground, and therefore the radiation resistance may be as low as half the figures given. This will result in a very low efficiency system if thin wire is used for the antenna and radials".

G3UUR also comments on several other myths concerning antennas, including the question of quad versus Yagi gain. These will have to wait for another time, although it is clear that he believes that the gain claims of some quad enthusiasts continue to be doubtful, if not "fraudulent". He believes that the extra gain of the quad, often claimed, can only be achieved at vhf and uhf where round rather than square loops can be used.

VK2ABQ's Hibernating Dipole

Extracted from 'Technical Topics',
Radio Communication, December 1983

VK2ABQ's hibernating dipole

Fred Cator, VK2ABQ/G3ONC, whose well-known bamboo wire beam first saw light of day in *Electronics Australia* just 10 years ago (October 1973, and then *TT* in January 1974) continues to experiment with compact antenna elements that depend on bends rather than using the less-effective loading coils. He calls his latest idea the "hibernating dipole". The 14MHz version can be built on a framework of four 6ft (1·82m) wooden dowels: Fig 2. When erected as shown (bird's eye view) it provides horizontally-polarised signals, but it can equally well be mounted, quad fashion, to provide vertical polarization. With the element about 3ft (0·91m) above ground, VK2ABQ carefully resonated it to 14MHz; when elevated it resonates about 14·15MHz. As would be expected, such an element is of higher Q and lower radiation resistance than a straight wire dipole, so that the bandwidth for a given change in swr is reduced. He warns that no attempt should be made to correct for the imbalance that appears at the

ANTENNA TOPICS

feedpoint, since this results in some directivity and a noticeable front-to-back ratio even on a single-element system. He has also found it possible to use the 14MHz element as an extended dipole on 21MHz, when the centre impedance rises. He has also used two 0·62in (15·87mm) aluminium tubes for the centre section, then requiring only two wood dowels. He has also investigated an elongated bent dipole of this type as the driven element of a Yagi array.

VK2ABQ refers to the shape of the structure as a "right-angle diamond shape" but his sketch looked like a square. However, if it were a square the total element length on 14MHz would be roughly 46ft (14·02m) whereas his notes indicate a length of 36ft (10·47m) (trimmed down for resonance) on 14MHz, and 24ft (7·31m) on 21MHz, which seems about right in view of the bends. I therefore assume that the sides are separated by rather less than the full 6ft (1·82m) lengths of the dowels.

VK2ABQ makes no strong claims for performance although he admits to working into Europe with the element only 12ft (3·65m) above ground.

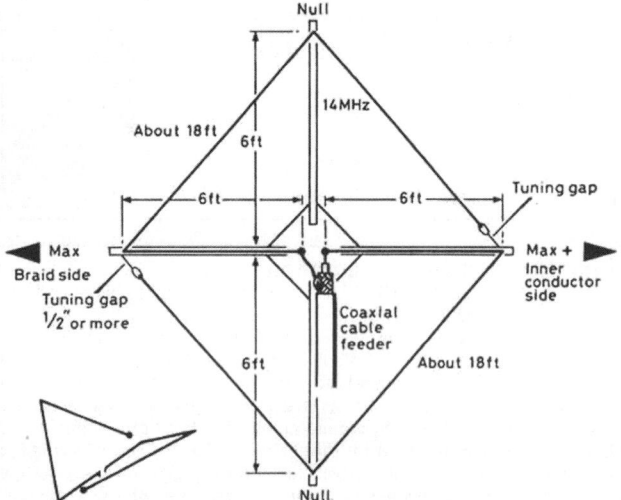

Fig 2. VK2ABQ's compact "hibernating dipole" providing some directivity with only a 6ft turning radius on 14MHz. On 14MHz total element length about 36ft trimmed accurately down to resonance (bent element will be longer than a straight one)

Its main virtues, he believes, are small size, turning radius only 6ft (1·82m) on 14MHz, and full resonance without traps or loading coils. It would be interesting to compare results with the helical-wound compact dipole as described in the October 1983 *TT*.

The Absorbing Yagi Element Again

Extracted from 'Technical Topics',
Radio Communication, December 1983

The absorbing Yagi element again

TT (November 1982) presented the novel ideas of John Beech, G8SEQ, on the use of strategically-placed resistor-loaded antenna elements intended to absorb rather than radiate, in order to reduce sidelobes or, more specifically, to improve significantly the front-to-back ratio of Yagi and other antenna arrays. One of his two designs was for a portable dipole-plus-absorber element intended for 144MHz df applications.

Since then two other contributors to *TT* have questioned the technical basis of this idea on theoretical grounds. Another possible problem in using absorber elements for such specialized applications as moonbounce (eme) was raised by Pat Gowen, G3IOR, who noted that if the absorbing resistor dissipated appreciable power during transmission it would heat up and act as a blackbody radiator during reception, and so could limit receiver sensitivity.

In *TT* (June 1983) Les Moxon, G6XN, was particularly worried about the two-element df array, while in August Dave Gordon-Brown, G3UUR/W, suggested the whole idea might even be a hoax. Both of these writers made it clear that although they had found the idea intriguing they had not attempted to try it out in practice.

John Beech, G8SEQ, has since replied to their criticisms. It is not intended this month to present his arguments in detail, but simply to re-iterate that he remains entirely convinced that the absorbing element really works; that it absorbs *all* the signal power it receives, re-radiating it only in the form of heat (infra-red radiation, but mostly the heat is simply convected away).

He maintains that results on the simple df antenna are reproducible without using a balun, though he does add a new warning to anyone building a similar antenna for serious df work: "It gives very good results on distant stations, but recent experiences have shown that it gives very poor nulls on local signals. This is (apparently) because modern vhf receivers are so sensitive (or possibly, without a balun, due to pick-up on the outer-braid of the coaxial cable?—*G3VA*). I could not get a null when closer than about one mile from a 2·5W transmitter using a 5λ/8 whip on a car roof, even when cross-polarizing the signal."

While refraining from entering into this debate on the absorbing element, I must admit that I still find G8SEQ's original claim of a 75dB f/b ratio with his 13-element array an astonishingly high figure, although not queried by the critics.

The Electromagnetic Groundplane Antenna

Extracted from 'Technical Topics',
Radio Communication, December 1983

The electromagnetic groundplane antenna

TT August 1983 provided some information on the electromagnetic groundplane loop (emgl) antenna as described by Hans Wuertz, DL2FA, in his *cq-DL* series "The dx antenna and its image". A subsequent article

Table 1—EMGA dimensions

Band (MHz)	a (m)	b (m)	x (m)	y (m)
3·5	13·16	6·58	3·55	0·42
7	7·04	3·52	1·90	0·21
14	3·48	1·74	0·94	0·10
21	2·33	1·17	0·62	0·07
28	1·68	0·84	0·46	0·05

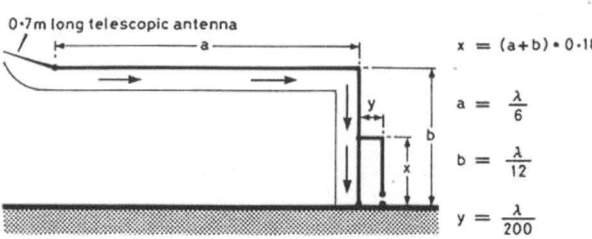

Fig 7. The low-profile electromagnetic groundplane antenna (emga) as described by DL2FA. Element and matching section uses 4mm diameter copper wire

$x = (a+b) \cdot 0.18$

$a = \frac{\lambda}{6}$

$b = \frac{\lambda}{12}$

$y = \frac{\lambda}{200}$

in this series (*cq-DL* No 6/83 pp 278–9) dealt with the related but open-ended electromagnetic groundplane antenna (emga). This forms a single-band antenna requiring a support height only λ/12 above ground, yet claimed to come close to the effectiveness of the conventional λ/4 monopole vertical antenna. The emga consists simply of a λ/4 element bent over so that it has a λ/6 horizontal span and λ/12 vertical section. At the end of the element, formed from 4mm diameter copper wire, is a short telescopic car radio antenna, extending to 0·7m, to permit trimming to resonance. As for the emgl, the matching section shown in Fig 7 can be replaced by an inductive coupling loop. DL2FA's dimensions for the traditional hf bands are given in Table 1. It should be stressed that since the impedance of such an element is roughly about 12Ω, it is highly advisable to use a good earthing system (eg earthing mat plus radials). No information is given by DL2FA on its use with elevated radials, or with a counterpoise.

1980 - 1989

Impedance and the Groundplane

Extracted from 'Technical Topics',
Radio Communication, December 1983

Impedance and the groundplane

Over the past few years there has been a growing tendency among scientists to challenge some important aspects of Einstein's theories of relativity and Darwin's theory of evolution; controversies that may never be resolved to everyone's satisfaction. There has also been the introduction of a "chaos concept" that postulates that some problems are too complex ever to be solved. *TT* is more fortunate; some of our debates tend to come to acceptable conclusions!

For instance, there has been the simmering question of the impedance of a $\lambda/4$ vertical radiator when used with elevated radials, and when used with an extensive set of buried radials, large earth spikes or an earth mat. Fred Brown, W6HPN, whose remarks in *TT* November 1981, p1033, threw doubt on the basic efficiency of groundplane antennas, has now conceded that the elevated gpa has a radiation resistance of around 19Ω, whereas for a $\lambda/4$ monopole mounted on a large ground system the figure is 36Ω. However, while now accepting that his earlier notes unfairly maligned the elevated gpa, he still feels that this should not obscure the fact that, as he indicated in 1981, a $\lambda/4$ radiator over a *large* conducting ground plane, with its 36Ω impedance, does have −3dB gain (ie 3dB loss) at zero elevation angle. And he notes that this includes the important practical case of a $\lambda/4$ vhf radiator mounted on a car roof.

Dud Charman, G6CJ, also makes a valuable contribution to this discussion. He agrees that in the past a number of professional antenna experts have mistakenly concluded that there is a 3dB loss between an ideal vertical, with extensive ground system, and the elevated gpa, as the result of overlooking the basic fact that all the power in a radiating element *must* radiate. A fallacy resulting from the fact that none of the experts appear to have actually checked their theoretical calculations. G6CJ writes:

"I did, many years ago, at vhf. The result was a radiation resistance of 'less than 20Ω' as I duly noted in the *RSGB Handbook*, along with a gpa having a folded radiating element to match 70Ω feeder. Also a design with sloping radials to match 50Ω with roughly 45° depression."

G6CJ explains the significance, in this connection, of the radiation resistance as follows:

"In the ideal grounded monopole the electric field and its return current in the ground is symmetrical about the antenna, giving the well-known value of R = 36Ω. With insulated radials the field is not symmetrical, but must 'close-in' on the radials and thus reduce the coupling between the antenna and whatever it is that the waves travel in: down goes R. The radials (if they are tuned and equal) provide only a point of zero potential against which to drive the radiator. There is a little leakage from the radials, but only from pairs of opposing currents at an average small spacing, and this can be neglected in a simple analysis. An antenna system puts out 72W of power with 1A in a dipole, 1·4A in the 'ideal' $\lambda/4$ vertical and 2A into the 18Ω gpa. Perhaps the past confusion has arisen by writing I for current and then forgetting that its value changes when going from 36 to 18Ω radiation resistance.

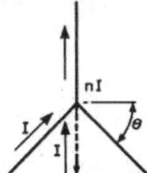

Fig 11. Drooping radials and groundplane antenna basics

"When the radials are sloped downwards they form a virtual extension of the $\lambda/4$ radiator (Fig 11) carrying the same current, I, at the feedpoint. This leads to a simple formula R = 18(1 + sin θ)² that seems to work pretty well. If θ is 90° we have a $\lambda/2$ dipole and R becomes 72Ω. The solution for 50Ω is θ = 42°."

G6CJ and several other readers have pointed out that in G3UUR's Table 1 the bracketed expression involving electrical angular lengths, say x, is in fact more simply put as tan (x/2). It may also be worth noting that in Table 1 it is the factor l/λ and not just *l* that is the "proportion of the wavelength" factor.

G6CJ adds that with a radiation resistance of 18Ω, a typical Zo of 500Ω, the end impedance will be about 14,000Ω: "You cannot run coaxial cable to the centre of an underground plane, and it is difficult to step 14,000Ω down to 50Ω in a damp matching box in the garden without heavy losses. One could halve the value by using two wires spaced about 1ft apart. But it is much better to extend the radiator to about $5\lambda/16$ and retune in the box. The impedance would then be much lower but still high enough to lose most of the effect of a 50Ω spike connection!"

Broadband Double Loops

Extracted from 'Technical Topics',
Radio Communication, January 1984

Broadband double loops

Mike Stringfellow, ZS6BUF, has been experimenting over several years with a number of loop and half-loop antennas for both hf and vhf, including single and twin loops that give exceptional broadband performance on vhf, and the DJ4VM loop on hf. He has also investigated a 28MHz six-element log-Yagi and the half-square form of inverted groundplane. I hope to refer on another occasion to all this work, but this month will confine myself to his broadband loops.

Incidentally, ZS6BUF acknowledges that he has received much moral and physical support for his antenna work from a number of other amateurs in the Johannesburg area, and mentions particularly Ted Cook, ZS6BT, no stranger to *TT*, who despite having just passed his 80th birthday is still active on the air and busy constructing antennas. Subsequent to the development of his broadband twin-square antenna, ZS6BUF's attention was drawn to earlier work by Japanese engineers (Matsumoto *et al*) who used a similar twin-square element but with director elements for broadband uhf tv antennas.

Dr Stringfellow presented a paper "A broadband high-gain antenna for

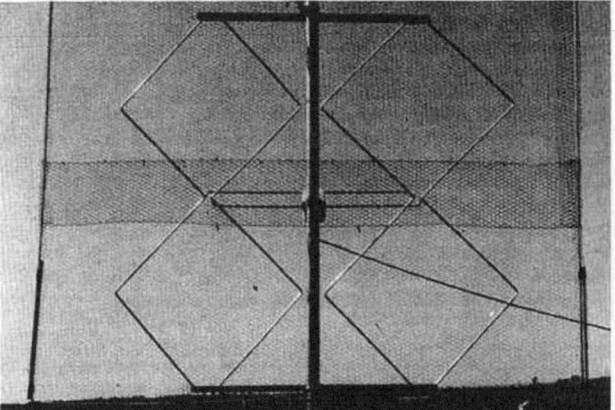

ZS6BUF's twin-square with mesh reflector vhf antenna with broadband characteristics. Design frequency 150MHz but covers 100-200MHz

vhf/uhf" at a symposium on antennas and propagation organized by the South African Institute of Electrical Engineers during May 1983, from which some of these notes are drawn. These vhf/uhf arrays were based on a broadside array of driven loops (single and dual) in front of a screen mesh reflector (examples of single loops are shown in Fig 6). ZS6BUF noted that "vhf/uhf antennas of high gain are generally achieved by using end-fire arrays of parasitically-excited dipoles or loops (Yagi array). Such antennas can provide very high gain, but this is at the expense of critical element dimensions and narrow operating bandwidth (typically a few percent)." Yagi antennas, such as those used for four-channel tv reception, can be adjusted to give useful gain over a larger bandwidth (up to ±15 per cent but exceptionally more) but the broadband gain is usually much lower than is possible on narrowband designs.

Over the restricted spectrum of single vhf/uhf amateur bands extended antenna bandwidth is perhaps less important than the advantages that broadbanding gives in overcoming the need for critical dimensions and adjustments. There are very few published designs for conventional vhf/uhf or even vhf antennas that can be relied upon to provide anywhere near optimum results without adjustments. A broadband approach, even at the cost of a little forward gain, is inherently more suited to home brewing!

The ZS6BUF 145MHz array combines reasonable gain with operation over a full 2:1 frequency span, ie in this case roughly 100 to 200MHz. The original experimental array using two square loops each of circumference of 1·05λ to 1·2λ depending on the element thickness was adopted after a series of trials of other loop configurations. The first trials used a single

ANTENNA TOPICS

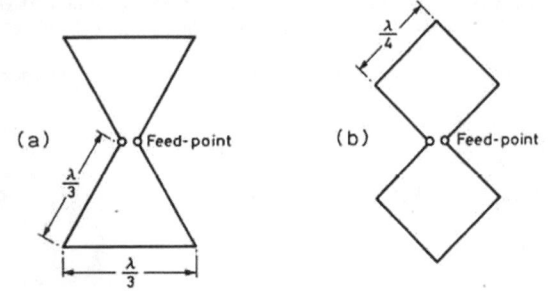

Fig 6. Experimental twin-loop antenna elements (a) twin delta (b) twin-square

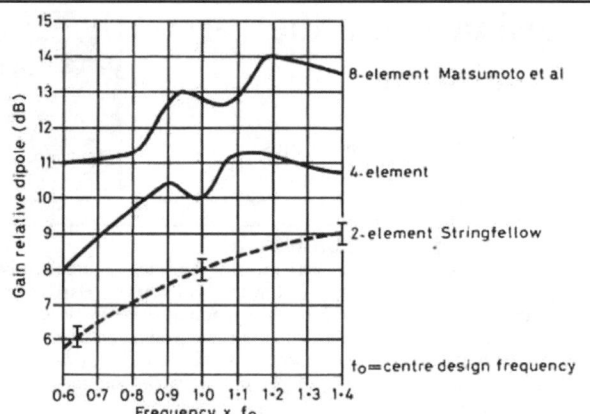

Fig 8. Measured gains of 2, 4 and 8-element twin-square antennas as a function (to centre design frequency is 150MHz)

driven twin-square loop mounted in front of a mesh reflector screen. The screen can be replaced by a pair of parasitic stacked dipole reflectors without loss of gain but again with a narrower bandwidth. Yagi directors can be used to increase gain but again introducing resonant effects. In this single twin-square loop estimated gain (based on use of test antennas) was 6 to 7dB at loop resonance, but making good use of the additional aperture at the higher frequencies.

His subsequent array used two broadside twin-square elements, also in front of a plane screen reflector with the centres of the two elements 0·5λ apart at centre frequency. A parallel tubular feedline connecting the elements was arranged so that its spacing could be adjusted (impedance variable between about 50 to 500Ω) to facilitate matching. The elements were fed in phase with 50Ω feedline via a 4:1 broadband balun to the centre point of the tubular feedline. See photograph and Fig 7. The matching arrangements proved capable of providing a perfect match over a small

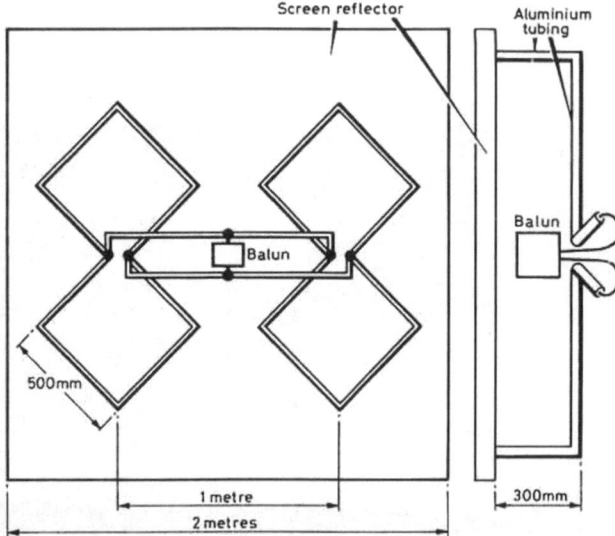

Fig 7. Constructional details of ZS6BUF's twin-square broadband antenna

frequency range but a compromise spacing could give an acceptable match (vswr less than 2:1) over the full 2:1 frequency span without adjustment. With some feeder adjustment this vswr could be achieved over the range 80 to 250MHz.

Gain at centre frequency showed a dip but generally was about 2-3dB above the single dual-loop. Front-to-back ratio was about 25dB with no major sidelobes identified. It can thus be assumed that doubling the size of the array will result in about 2dB or so of extra gain. Fig 8 shows the gain figures for the two ZS6BUF arrays and also an eight-element Matsumoto array.

Although not described in the conference paper, ZS6BUF has also constructed a number of the single 2λ loops for hf bands. A twin-delta loop designed for 21MHz was found to be effective on 28MHz as well, but would not quite stretch down to 14MHz. A 14MHz twin-square loop worked well on both 14 and 21MHz but no better than a dipole on 28MHz. Both these arrays were fed by 600Ω open line to a link-coupled tuner.

ZS6BUF believes that the broadband characteristics of these hf loops are limited to about 1·5:1 frequency span rather than 2:1 primarily by the relatively thin elements. However, the 14MHz twin-square array was successfully turned into a most effective tri-band antenna by adding 0·25λ open stubs at its top and bottom points. The stubs acted as frequency switches to close the loops on 14MHz and open them on 28MHz, turning the antenna into twin bi-squares on the higher frequency. The antenna was constructed from 16-gauge copper wire and suspended from an 18m-high lightweight dural mast. Nylon line was used to form the loops in place of spreaders making the whole assembly, including mast, only about 50lb. However, this particular antenna was later destroyed during a violent storm and in his subsequent hf experiments ZS6BUF used the DJ4VM form of loop which will have to wait for another issue.

Horizontally-elongated Quad Loop

Extracted from 'Technical Topics', *Radio Communication,* March 1984

Horizontally-elongated quad loop

The vertically-elongated quad loop antenna with an aspect ratio of 1:3 by GM6RI/GM3VNW (*TT* September, p800, with further note November, p998) caught the eye of Dave Gordon-Smith, G3UUR, as he had never come across a quad-loop extended in this way before. On the other hand, roughly 10 years ago, he used a horizontally-distended loop with an aspect ratio of about 2:1. He emphasizes that the crucial point to be observed if optimum performance is to be obtained it that, as in the Scottish version, the quad-loop is fed in the middle of one of the *short* sides. His loop (Fig 3(a)) had 48ft horizontal span and 24ft vertical sides conveniently fed from an upstairs shack. On 7MHz the feed impedance was approximately 50Ω. He feeds the antenna via the combined balun/atu shown in Fig 3(b). The transformer-type balun has an impedance ratio of 1:4 on 7MHz switched to provide 1:1 on 1·8 and 3·5MHz. Such loops can also be used on harmonic frequencies, though G3UUR does not mention whether he used his on bands above 7MHz.

On 1·8MHz the radiation resistance of a loop with these dimensions is only about 1Ω, but despite this he found that with 14swg wire the radiation efficiency was reasonable. No deep broadside nulls exist on 1·8/3·5MHz since the vertical sections do not carry equal currents. On the other hand, on these bands, the two horizontal wires do carry equal and opposite currents, and this, in conjunction with the relatively close spacing, means that the antenna radiates less power directly upwards, tending to result in desirable low-angle radiation for long-distance working.

On 7MHz the loop behaves in much the same fashion as a conventional quad loop. When fed as shown it provides *vertical* polarization and slightly more gain, 2dB rather than 1·2dB (see below), with reference to a dipole. The maximum lobe produced by the "long" sides carrying the out-of-phase components can be expected to be over 20dB down and of opposite polarization to the main lobe from the "short" sides. Like all loops, the average height above ground is reduced from that of a single wire type of antenna, but with vertical polarization this is less important than the effects of the conductivity of the ground.

G3UUR has recently calculated the gain and feed impedance of the conventional quad loop using what he feels is a rigorous approach. He finds that this gives a theoretical gain (ref dipole) of 1·2dB and an input impedance of 110·7Ω. An interesting point is that the gain is slightly higher than usually suggested. On the other hand the impedance is significantly lower than the figure of 120 to 140Ω usually quoted in amateur radio publications. While the actual impedance will be affected to some degree by ground proximity, this will tend to *decrease* the figure to below rather than above 110Ω. G3UUR has reasonable confidence that his calculations are correct, so that it may well be that the handbooks have got it wrong.

Fig 3. Horizontally-elongated vertically-polarized quad-loop antenna used by G3UUR on 7, 3·5 and 1·8MHz: (a) antenna with open-wire balanced feeders (b) atu with switched-ratio balun used to convert the unbalanced 50Ω transmitter output

Another Long Loop

Extracted from 'Technical Topics', *Radio Communication,* March 1984

Another long loop

By coincidence, G. E. Cripps, G3DWW, has recently sent in a note on an antenna of roughly similar shape and size to that described by G3UUR above, although his version does not tie up with the guidelines given above, and he incorporates a switch to open the loop on 3·5MHz: Fig 4.

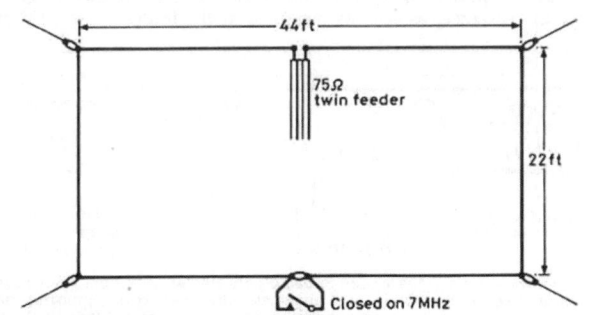

Fig 4. G3DWW's switched loop/dipole multiband antenna (horizontally polarized)

G3DWW writes: "The span available for wire antennas at this location is limited to 45ft in a straight line. A simple antenna for 3·5MHz and 7MHz was constructed in the form of an elongated quad loop with two horizontal sides of 44ft and two vertical 22ft sections. This is fed at top centre with 80Ω balanced twin feeder. On 7MHz the loop is continuous, but on 3·5MHz the lower horizontal limb is opened at the centre to form a folded form of "bent dipole". Since the antenna is of balanced form it discriminates well against the high level of tv timebase radiation at this location. As is normal with quad loops, the closed loop also radiates on harmonically-related frequencies."

The G3DWW antenna, of course, provides *horizontally*-polarized signals on 3·5/7MHz.

Multiband Trapped Dipoles

Extracted from 'Technical Topics', *Radio Communication,* March 1984

Multiband trapped dipoles

Although, today, many amateurs recognize that the use of traps to form multiband antennas is far from an ideal system, and that there are better techniques, the trap has become firmly established. The simplified form of multiband dipole, using just two 7MHz traps, as originally proposed by W3DZZ, is undoubtedly one of the most widely used of all "wire" hf antennas, though now tending to give way in the popularity stakes to such alternatives as the trapless G5RV and the multiband loop (quad or delta).

The way in which many trapped dipoles work is less simple than it may appear at first glance, yet relatively few of the usual handbooks other than the *ARRL Antenna Book* explain the principles in any detail. It is easy to see that on 7MHz the traps inserted in the wire at 33ft either side of centre act virtually as insulators, isolating the 66ft span from the outer section, and so forming an λ/2 dipole. Further it can be appreciated that both these traps need to be of high-Q construction and well protected against the effects of weather and ageing if performance on 7MHz is to remain good.

But just what do the traps do on the other bands, and why is it necessary to specify carefully the LC ratio of the traps in a W3DZZ-type antenna? Would not any trap tuned to 7,050kHz work just as well? The answer to this second question is that it would on 7MHz but not necessarily on the other bands. Remember that the W3DZZ with a 102ft span and two 7MHz traps is intended to work on all five of the pre-WARC hf bands from 3·5 to 28MHz without necessarily requiring an atu.

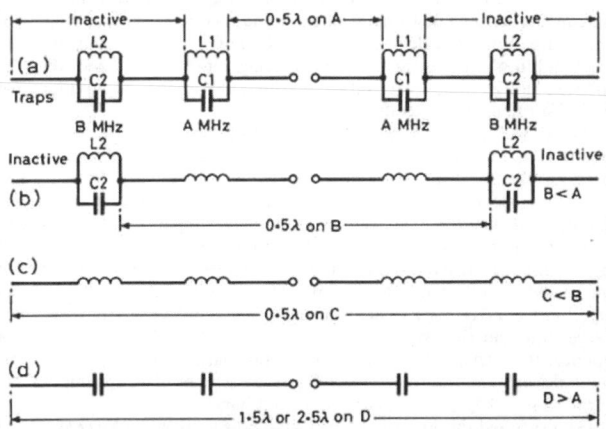

Fig 5. Showing the basic principles of the multi-band trap dipole antenna indicating the mode of operation on different frequency bands. The traps provide a very high isolating impedance on the band to which they are tuned; provide inductive (loading) reactance on lower frequency bands; and capacitive (stretching) reactance on bands of higher frequency

Fig 5 shows the principles of operation of a four-trap antenna on different bands. At lower frequencies than that to which it is tuned, the trap looks like an inductive reactance and so provides inductive loading thereby decreasing the span required for λ/2 resonance on the lower-frequency bands. At higher frequencies than that to which the trap is tuned, it acts as a capacitive reactance tending to "stretch" the element, although clearly, because of the length of the initial span, it cannot do this to the extent that the antenna forms a "stretched" λ/2 dipole; however, if the design figures are correct the whole span forms a resonant 3λ/2 or 5λ/2 centre-fed dipole, though the radiation pattern will not be the same as for the bands on which the antenna forms a λ/2 system. This is not necessarily a disadvantage, since there will be some power gain in the lobes of a 3λ/2 or 5λ/2 antenna.

It needs to be appreciated also that on the higher frequency bands, resonance for a given overall span will depend on such factors as the LC ratio of the trap, so that for a W3DZZ trap the capacitors should be within the span 50–60pF as well as being high-voltage, high-current types. The design of an antenna such as the W3DZZ, which depends on both inductive loading and capacitive stretching, is quite tricky unless, as most people do, you simply follow the original W3DZZ dimensions and values: Fig 6. Though it should be noted that these were intended for the wider American 3·5 to 4MHz and 7 to 7·2MHz bands.

Trapped-beam arrays tend not to use the capacitive/inductive reactance feature of the W3DZZ design, using "insulator-type" resonant traps for each band to maintain the λ/2 feature on each band: a three element array for 14/21/28MHz may thus use 12 traps.

ANTENNA TOPICS

The two-trap W3DZZ antenna at a reasonable height above ground, free of unbalancing features such as a slope over the entire span or proximity to other structures, should be capable of providing an swr ratio (without an

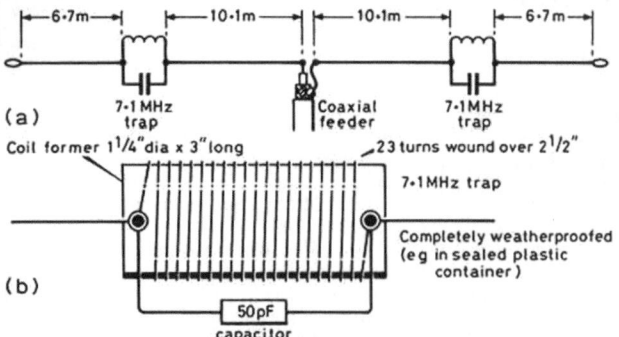

Fig 6. The original W3DZZ multiband trap dipole using only two 7·1MHz traps but designed to provide low-impedance centre feedpoint on 3·5/7/14/21/28MHz with an swr not greater than about 2·5:1. The whole system should be symmetrical about the feedpoint, with the top span either horizontal or in inverted-V form but not as a continuously-sloping wire. The new G3OSS modification consists of connecting the traps some feet into the central span, letting a few feet of wire hang down, and adjusting the outer span as necessary

atu) at the transmitter of less than about 2·5:1 on all five bands. Even this figure may require the use of an atu with some all-solidstate transmitters that automatically begin to reduce output with an swr above about 1·8:1, though it should be appreciated that the use of an atu in this way does not alter the swr of the coaxial feeder (in practice unless there is a *very* long feeder there will be virtually no loss of efficiency with an swr of around 2·5:1).

Traps have the disadvantage of introducing extra weight into a wire antenna, requiring additional strength in the supports to reduce sagging of the centre part of the element; they are also very frequency-conscious. On the band in which they are used as isolating "insulators", since they are inserted at high-impedance voltage maxima, any leakage or misalignment will affect the system significantly.

Angus McKenzie, G3OSS, in "Trapped dipoles—back to the drawing board?" (*Amateur Radio* (UK) December 1983, pp56-8) argues persuasively that a simple modification in design can result in better and more consistent performance, reflected in an swr that is much less frequency-dependent. His idea is stunningly simple. Why, he argues, connect traps at the most critical points, ie at the high-impedance end-point of the antenna when it is used on the "trap band"? We have all known for many years that the outer few feet of a dipole can hang downwards without significantly affecting its performance; a technique generally used when faced with a site that will not support a full-length dipole span. So why not connect the trap a few feet into the central span, letting the last few feet hang down? The trap is then connected at a point of lower impedance. Hence less leakage, and less change over a band.

G3OSS tested this idea on a four-trap dipole used on 1·8MHz as well as on the higher-frequency bands; he found the swr flattened out significantly. Results, particularly on 1·8 and 3·5MHz "improved dramatically". He is convinced that this simple modification, if carried out correctly and the outer span dimensions optimized, represents a significant advance on the conventional W3DZZ approach; it also means that a 1·8MHz antenna can be fitted into a little less space. Trapped dipoles to this modified design are likely to be marketed by G2DYM, but it should not be difficult to adapt an existing W3DZZ antenna. It might well be worth trying!

Antennas That Slow the Wave

Extracted from 'Technical Topics', *Radio Communication,* April 1984

Antennas that slow the wave

Last summer, Les Moxon, G6XN, outlined a series of antenna experiments based on the use of triangular loop elements for multiband arrays (*TT* August 1983, pp705-7). At that time a very brief mention was made of some investigations he was also making into "flat" reversible beams based on folded dipole elements, utilizing some of the same principles as the loop elements.

This further project subsequently developed into an interesting exercise in the use of slow-wave structures, a topic which he believes has come to the fore quite suddenly. W6QYT, for example, has drawn G6XN's attention to an mf broadcast antenna only 35ft high, though details of this interesting structure have not been fully disclosed. In the UK some limited use has been made of mf "umbrella" antennas about 90ft high, but most mf broadcast antennas, even for local radio, use mast-radiators or T-antennas at least 150ft high. G6XN also noted the short helix antenna described in *TT* October 1983, p890, Fig 6. He considers the simple helical-wound-element approach is much inferior to end-loading or its equivalent, although admitting that it is vastly better than the more common centre-loaded short antenna. He writes:

"If we compare centre loading, a resonant helix and end-loading, the current distributions are respectively triangular, sine-wave and square-wave. The sine-wave doubles the radiation resistance compared with triangular; the square-wave more than doubles it again. But it must be recognized that there are also major repercussions on loss resistance which will always tend to be rather large in the case of a small diameter helix because of the need to use relatively thin wire.

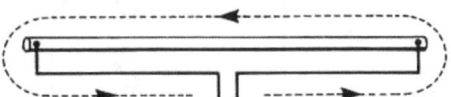

Fig 6. Basic form of G6XN's multiband folded dipole showing current distribution when the element is short

"To arrive at my form of short, multiband folded dipole one starts from the arrangement of Fig 6. From basic principles this element, with unequal diameter conductors, provides a large and useful impedance step-up, but such an element deteriorates in performance very rapidly if the physical length is reduced below the λ/2 electrically resonant length. The current flowing in the wrong direction brings the radiation resistance down with a bump. Also, as the current starting from the centre turns the corners at the end, it encounters a change in impedance. By reference to a Smith Chart it can be seen that since this change is occurring too soon, the step-up vanishes very quickly as overall length of the element is reduced.

"My first objective was to try to keep the impedance constant as the corner is turned, but without having to support a lot of additional metal. This can be done by *capacitive* loading, using only thin wire. L is large because the wire is thin, C is made large by attaching a lot of 'whiskers'. Zo = √(L/C) and therefore Zo *tends* to stay constant; on the other hand the velocity of the wave, which is given by √[1/(LC)] is greatly reduced. Thus one arrives fairly quickly at the point of minimum current. Provided that this point is substantially less than about half-way in to the centre, the radiation resistance, referred to the centre of the thick part of the element, is at least equal to that of the thick element, considering it to be end-loaded; ie to have a rectangular current distribution. By changing from capacitive to inductive loading at the point of zero current, Zo is increased but the velocity (measured axially) stays low. This transforms the radiation resistance to a relatively high value at the feedpoint. Note that one must allow for a corresponding drop in current as the current zeros must be pushed outwards towards the ends, hence the word 'substantially' above.

"What the element now looks like (electrically) is shown in Fig 7. Radiation resistance, as actually measured at the feedpoint, is 200Ω at

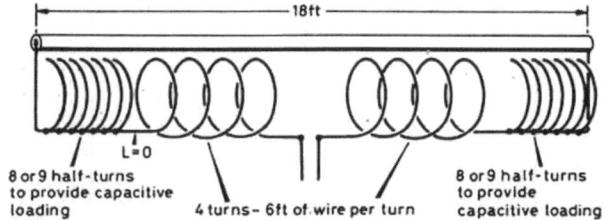

Fig 7. Electrical form of the loaded folded dipole element, including inductive and capacitive loading. Note that physically the loading is supported on nylon fishing line that runs outside of the tubular element (see text)

14MHz, 70Ω at 21MHz and 200Ω at 28MHz. The loading looks like a helix surrounding the 18ft tubular sections, although only the inner half is a true helix. I used 21swg wire, the supporting 'former' consisting of four lengths of nylon fishing line stretched between the tips of vertical T-pieces attached to the ends of the central tubular elements, and the line is routed via anchoring points on the boom, together with a boom extension; in cross-section this resembles a sort of twisted rectangular 'former' virtually impossible to illustrate clearly.

"Thinking it was going to be difficult to obtain enough loading, I overdid this originally to the extent of having just over one inductive turn too many, but this proved all to the good, the two elements worked on 10MHz with about 9dB front-to-back ratio, calculated losses roughly equal to the forward gain and, at 30ft, the array put a good signal into Australia although this was not part of the original plan!

"The design, looked at from a 'sales appeal' angle, is rather mind-boggling, and I am not expecting that anyone else will rush to copy it, despite its interesting exploitation of slow-wave techniques. Incredibly, however, the second element took only one day to construct. Compared with the first it was electrically spot on, and both elements seemed well balanced (I abandoned my original idea of a three-element array). On-the-air performance was at least as good as the beam it replaced (Fig 3 of *TT* August 1983) at the same height. There were also a number of surprises.

(a) Nothing had been done to increase coupling between the elements, and I had therefore expected unequal currents and poor nulls as normally experienced with conventional two-element arrays. In practice the nulls off the back were the most impressive I have ever had!

(b) Disappointingly, there was *no* improvement in effective bandwidth, which proved to be *identical* on 14 and 21MHz with the modified VK2ABQ array shown in Fig 2 of *TT* August 1983, the smaller of the triangular arrays.

(c) Unlike the triangular arrays, it was found possible to feed the flat array with some 24ft of open-wire line without degrading the bandwidth on 14MHz, a completely unforeseen and very valuable practical advantage, since it allowed all tuning and matching adjustments to be carried out at ground level. The low value of radiation resistance on 21MHz was tiresome,

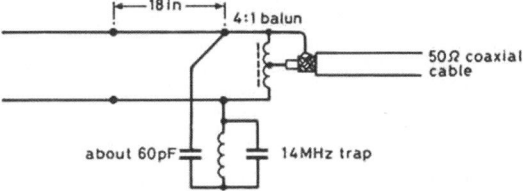

Fig 8. G6XN's feed arrangements with open-wire line transformed to 50Ω coaxial cable and designed for element feed impedances of about 200Ω on 14 and 28MHz, and about 70Ω on 21MHz. The 50Ω cable goes to an atu or to a series-tuned circuit to permit reflector tuning from the shack

but tuning on 14MHz provided about 18in of excess length at 21MHz, and this was used as a transformer to bring the impedance up to 200Ω with the help of a capacitor which then had to be removed at 14MHz by means of a trap: Fig 8.

"After taking a lot of measurements and giving the design a good try-out on the air, I finally decided that it must be regarded as one eyesore too many. I replaced it by an 'invisible array'."

It is hoped to include details of this later work in a future *TT*. G6XN has also been tackling the problem of building the "smallest possible" efficient dipole, starting out from the folded-dipole elements discussed above and using as a basis for comparison the helix design of ZL4DP (*TT* October 1983, p890).

End-fed Vertical Dipoles

Extracted from 'Technical Topics', *Radio Communication,* June 1984

End-fed vertical dipoles

In the December 1983 *TT* (p1085) I was rash enough to suggest that the intermittent debate in *TT* from November 1981 onwards concerning the impedance and vertical radiation patterns of grounded monopoles and groundplane antennas had come to an "acceptable conclusion" in printing some comments by G6CJ.

What a hope! Several readers, among them acknowledged experts on antenna theory, strongly disagree. They feel there are still misconceptions and fallacies that need to be cleared up. G6CJ himself appreciated that his

Table 1. Summary of end-fed antenna parameters

Antenna	Height (h/λ)	Gain ref Half-wave dipole	Impedance (ohms)
Quarter-wave monopole	0·23	−1·55	36
Quarter-wave extended	0·25	−1·55	50 + j50
Half-wave	0·45	1·67	900
Five-eighths-wave	0·6	3·02	108 − j280
Half-wave with centre λ/2 above ground plane	—	3·26	—
Two end-on half-waves in phase	—	4·67	—

A rubber flexible antenna has gain of about −6dBd (even less if inside vehicle) (VE2CV)

earlier brief note may have been misinterpreted to imply that it is only with elevated radials that the lower part of the field is dragged in towards the "ground" element, whereas in fact the same situation applies to the earthed monopole with a finite groundplane, so that over a real earth it also sends its strongest radiation at an upward angle and not in the horizontal direction shown in many textbooks in relation to "perfect" earth, a subject that has arisen before in*TT*.

G6CJ has contributed some further notes on this subject but, for the moment, I am holding these over while checking to what extent they overlap with the other comments that have come in.

Among the correspondents is Dr John S. Belrose, VE2CV, well known for his conference papers and articles on antennas on both sides of the Atlantic. He finds some of the comments "provocative, misleading or wrong". He has sent along a mass of detailed notes and reference material that I hope can be published in due course as a full-length article. But a few notes, here and now, will serve to introduce his belief in the value of the end-fed vertical λ/2 dipole as a preferred alternative to λ/4 radiators, particularly where effective earthing or a groundplane of radials is not available.

He writes: "In the professional literature a clear understanding has been reached about the upward tilting of the beam for monopole antennas on finite flat groundplanes, and the corresponding loss of field on the horizon; theory has been validated by experiment. It is also important to point out that the input impedance at the end of a λ/2 dipole is very much lower than the 14,000Ω suggested by G6CJ. In fact for a typical 144MHz rod antenna this impedance can be as low as 500Ω; 1,000Ω is typical for a 144MHz whip; and even for thin-wire hf antennas typically 2,000 to 4,000Ω. Table 1. An end-fed λ/2 is a very efficient radiator. It can be readily matched at vhf or hf: Fig 6."

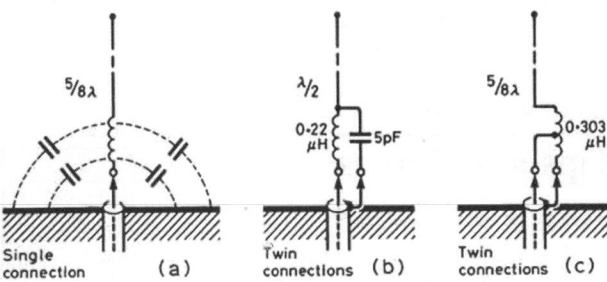

Fig 6. Methods of matching into the base of λ/2 and 5λ/8 144MHz whip antennas

In his notes he describes the significant advantages of λ/2 verticals, adding: "End-fed λ/2 dipoles are available for mobile or handheld portable use. An L-section match is employed and, while the antenna is not so well decoupled from the feeder as for a coaxial dipole, nevertheless the antenna outperforms other antennas (such as a λ/4) when no groundplane or radial

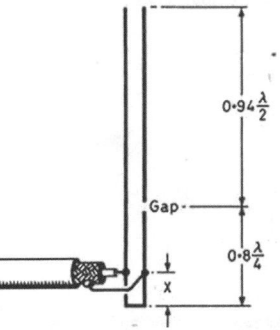

Fig 7. A roll-up J-antenna formed from 300Ω transmission line. The impedance matching distance X is best found by experiments but is about 0·0134λ from the shorted end. VE2CV used a 3·5MHz version of this antenna during experiments on kite and balloon supported antennas as described in QST March 1981

rods are used. For example, λ/2 will provide an "effective gain" of 5dB or more for a transceiver held in the hand of a man. A number of commercial models are available . . . . . including a Larsen base-loaded steel flexible radiating element; this can be rolled up for easy carrying and hung from a tree branch, a hook in the hotel room etc. A roll-up and put in your pocket ribbon J-antenna (Fig 7) can also be easily constructed for portable operation."

The topic of base impedance of long elements is also raised in a note from G. E. Cripps, G3DWW, although this was not intended specifically to deal with the groundplane controversy, but shows well the effect of "fat" elements on impedance. He writes:

"In the course of re-reading *Wireless Direction Finding* by Richard Keen, (4th edn, p274) I found an interesting graph of the base impedance of a 10m high, 1m diameter, six-wire "cage" antenna, of the type used as a sense antenna in some df stations of that period: Fig 8. This showed that over the 2–20MHz range the base impedance was between 60 and 360Ω with only a very gradual variation over the entire range. This compares with a variation over the same frequency range for a single wire given as 60–3,000Ω, and

ANTENNA TOPICS

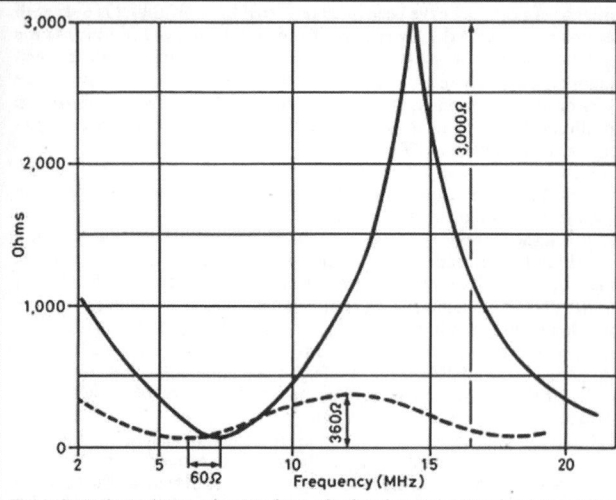

Fig 8. Base impedance of a 10m-long single wire and a 10m long "cage" of six wires with 1m diameter showing the lower and more constant impedance with the "fatter" element. From Dick Keen's *Wireless Direction Finding*, a classic text book of the 'thirties and 'forties. Vertical cages were used as the "sense" antenna in some df stations

could form a relatively easily matched transmitting antenna. The resonant length is also seen to be significantly decreased with the cage, the 10m wire antenna showing λ/4 resonance at 7·3MHz compared with the 10m cage at 6MHz due to the increased value of the phase constant."

Tips and Topics: Staggered Yagis

Extracted from 'Technical Topics', *Radio Communication,* June 1984

Tips and topics

W6SAI has drawn attention (*Ham Radio,* February 1984) to experiments by G. J. McDonald, VK2ZAB, which suggested that an improved front-to-back ratio of stacked Yagi antennas can be obtained by staggering the two arrays by a quarter-wave and adding an extra quarter-wave to the phasing

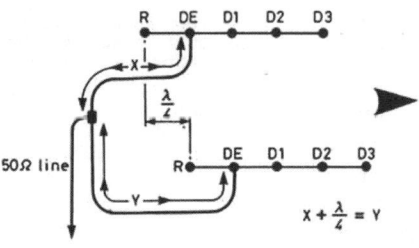

Fig 9. A staggered VK2ZAB stacked antenna array providing improved front-to-back ratio. The lower Yagi is advanced by a quarter-wave in front of the upper array and an extra quarter-wave (electrical) is added to the phasing line

line, Fig 9. In his experiments, VK2ZAB increased the measured 12·5dB fb ratio to 24dB with the staggered arrays. He also found that the staggered arrays had slightly more forward gain (about 0·25dB) and the sidelobes were reduced to some extent.

Tree-supported DX Antennas

Extracted from 'Technical Topics', *Radio Communication,* July 1984

Tree-supported dx antennas

A massive beam array is undoubtedly an aid for long-distance hf operation but, as suggested frequently in *TT*, it is surprising what can be done with unobtrusive wire antennas supported by trees or attached to convenient buildings. Laurie Margolis, G3UML, who figures prominently in the DXCC Honor Roll, recently erected what he calls a 3·5MHz top-loaded vertical after reading an article by G3ZZD in *Ham Radio Today* and discussing his site problems with G4GED. The antenna shown in Fig 5 was the result. This has a 45ft vertical section using fairly heavy gauge wire supported from the branch of a tree, with a 16ft bent-back section at an angle of about 45° to the horizontal eventually tied off to his house with a light nylon cord. The antenna is fed with about 60ft of RG8U coaxial cable, and there are two bent λ/4 radials about 1ft off the ground, stapled to the garden fence and each making a 90° turn about a third of the way round.

At resonance (3,775kHz) swr is virtually unity, and it remains below 1·8:1 to the lower band edge. According to G3UML it provides "terrific" performance on 3·5MHz dx, putting good signals into VK, ZL, AP, Caribbean area, North America etc.

G3UML describes his technique for getting lines over high branches as follows: "There is a public park backing my garden, so bow-and-arrow or throwing rocks are not on. I took a tennis ball and screwed into it a toggle screw; this is a Rawlplug-type device for fixing things to thin surfaces and has a form of alligator clip on the end of the screw. These can be bought

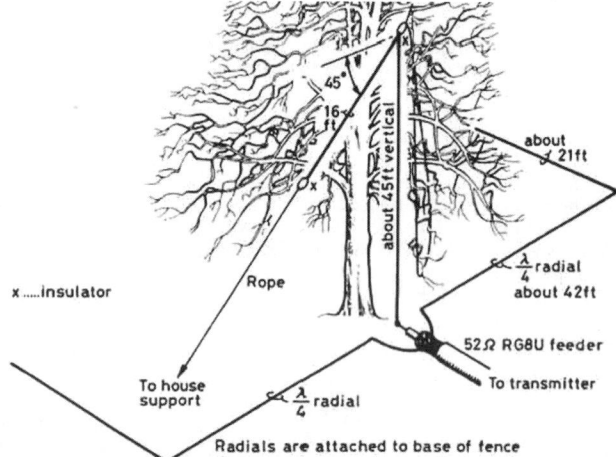

Fig 5. G3UML's tree-aided 3·5MHz "top-loaded" vertical with two bent radials —an exercise in fitting relatively inconspicuous antennas into available spaces with existing supports. Described by G3UML as "simple, old-fashioned and very effective!"

at almost any hardware shop. To the protruding screw I tied about 150ft of fishing line which is unrolled and left loose and untangled (fortunately the line tends not to tangle) at the feet of the server, with the far end tied firmly to a suitable mooring.

"With the tennis racket, the ball with line attached is simply clouted as high and as hard as possible. I managed my 45ft high branch at only the third attempt. Provided the ball returns obediently to ground level a more substantial rope can be hauled up and turned into a continuous loop so that any antenna can be raised: in my case both the 3·5MHz vertical and the 7MHz delta loop described in *TT* May 1982."

In those locations where it is quite safe to use a bow and arrow to put a line over a high branch, heights of up to 60ft were achieved by G. I. Turner, G3DGN, who reported his experiences of this technique in the *RSGB Bulletin* November 1965. He used a 38lb, 59in wooden bow with a 27in wooden arrow which he described as standard archery equipment for beginners. G3DGN warned that "inexperienced archers should be very cautious, as even blunt arrows can break windows, bruise people and disturb neighbours". The arrow *must* have a blunted arrow-head, not only for safety reasons but also to prevent the arrow from entering a branch etc, and thus failing to return to earth. He also suggested that local archery club members might be willing to exercise their skills when the antenna is needed for temporary outside events such as NFD. However, many of us would be very happy with a line over a 60ft high branch to provide an antenna support for fixed operation!

1980 - 1989

'Invisible' Two-element Array

Extracted from 'Technical Topics', *Radio Communication,* July 1984

"Invisible" two-element array

As mentioned in the April *TT*, Les Moxon, G6XN, has been trying out an "invisible" two-element fixed hf array for 14/21/28MHz based on his delta folded elements. His array, Fig 6, comprises a pair of the 14MHz elements moored for the north–south direction, and made from 21swg wire. The boom is 0·5in diameter tubing that could easily be replaced by a conventional tv antenna to provide a near-perfect "disguise".

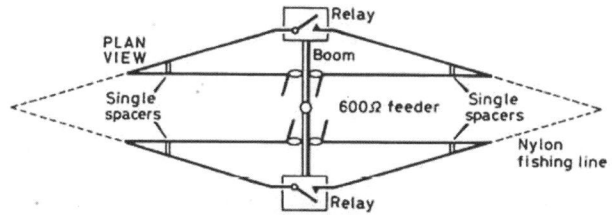

Fig 6. G6XN's inconspicuous two-element fixed array for 14/21/28MHz using thin wire elements and a boom that can be provided by a normal tv antenna when put up across a roof

The front–back ratio is very good on 14MHz but rather poor on 21MHz (about 7dB). On 28MHz, relays are used to open-circuit the elements. G6XN suspects that better results might be achieved on 21MHz with the elements in the 28MHz open-circuit condition, but feels his relays might not stand this.

More Compact Transmitting Loops

Extracted from 'Technical Topics', *Radio Communication,* July 1984

More compact transmitting loops

A few years ago the firm Technology for Communications International (TCI) marketed a Model 629 professional loop transmitting antenna intended to provide an unobtrusive hf system for such applications as diplomatic communications. In fact, one of these can be seen edging above the parapet of the roof of the US Embassy in Grosvenor Square, London. Like most other compact transmitting loops, this is made from large diameter copper pipe and requires a substantial copper ground screen. A motorized vacuum-type capacitor in the centre of the upper member of the trapezium-shaped loop is used to remote-tune the antenna over the range 3 to 24MHz. It is claimed to provide a directive gain, both vertically overhead and in the horizontal plane, of the order of 5dBi; making it suitable for short-, medium- and long-distance paths. However, it should be noted that "directive gain" is not necessarily the same thing as "power gain", and the efficiency of compact loops inevitably falls off at the lower end of the frequency range. The TCI loop is about 70in long by 39in high.

Ron Row, G3HAZ, has noted a brief description in *Microwaves & RF* March 1984 of a "Miniloop" antenna system made by Antenna Research Associates. This is a pedestal-mounted loop 5ft high by 7ft wide (12ft high with pedestal mast and rotator) covering either 2·3 to 16MHz, 1·8 to 14·5MHz or 3 to 24MHz. It has a fat section at the centre of the top section that, presumably like the TCI model, contains a tuning capacitor. At 14MHz, efficiency is claimed as 98 per cent.

All compact transmitting loops depend on achieving reasonable efficiency by using materials presenting very little rf ohmic resistance. As J. R. Killeen, G3KPV, indicated in *Radio Communication* September 1983, pp796–7, it is possible for amateurs to make transmitting loops of reasonable efficiency both for base or portable operation. His unit covered 3·4 to 15·2MHz, although he stressed that one should not expect to obtain equivalent performance to a dipole mounted at 60ft. Radiation resistance of a loop increases very rapidly as the circumference approaches a wavelength and one enters the familiar territory of the quad and delta loop antenna.

More Optimum-shaped Elements

Extracted from 'Technical Topics', *Radio Communication,* September 1984

More optimum-shaped elements

TT December 1982, pp1054-5, and June 1983, pp513-4, discussed the possibilities offered by the Landstorfer concept of curved $3\lambda/2$ dipole elements that provide gain and directivity, including a modest front-to-back ratio with a single element not resistively terminated; it was also indicated that such elements can be used to form high-performance vhf arrays. In the June notes, Les Moxon, G6XN, came up with a novel version of this idea based on the use of five straight segments that he felt would be much simpler to implement on hf than the curved Landstorfer shapes.

A similar concept, but using six straight segments, is published in *Electronics Letters* 24 May 1984, pp468-9) stemming from Du Jia-Cong and Zhang Zhong-Pei of the Guilin Institute of Electronic Technology, China. Their "tribroken-line dipole" element is a closer approximation to the shapes proposed for curved optimum-shaped elements, though one suspects that their shape would not be as simple to implement on hf as that

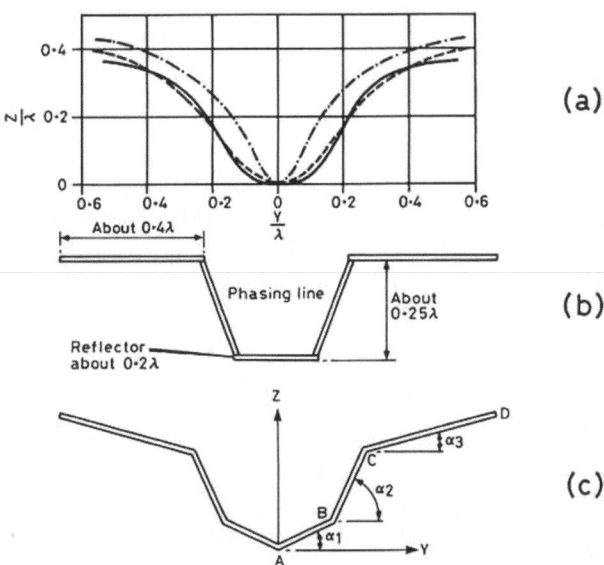

Fig 2. Optimum-shaped $3\lambda/2$ dipole wire antennas with maximum directivity (a) some suggested curves mathematically described as (1) Piecewise parabolic model; (2) Gaussian lineshape model; and (3) Witch of Agnes model. (b) The simplified shape suggested by G6XN; and (c) Chinese tribroken-line dipole shape

of G6XN. Directivity of the $3\lambda/2$ tribroken shape is about 6·6dB (this is presumably directivity gain in dBi *not* dBd). An experimental antenna for 203MHz is reported to have achieved 6·6dB with half-power bandwidths in the E-plane and H-plane about 37·5° and 110° respectively; input impedance is given as $118·64 + j15·7\Omega$. The various shapes are outlined in Fig 2.

The Chinese engineers conclude: "This type of dipole with higher gain and simpler construction, which can even be folded up, is being used as a receiving antenna for uhf and vhf television channels."

The Quarter-wave Sloper Again

Extracted from 'Technical Topics', *Radio Communication,* September 1984

The $\lambda/4$ sloper again

Vincent C. Lear, G3TKN, writes in praise of the $\lambda/4$ sloper antenna but points out that it is possible to encounter unexpected problems. He writes:

209

ANTENNA TOPICS

"A brief note on λ/4 sloper antenna, including a diagram (Fig 8) appeared recently in *TT* (October 1983) but this antenna does not appear to have enjoyed the same popularity in this country as in the USA, and very little has been written about it in British journals.

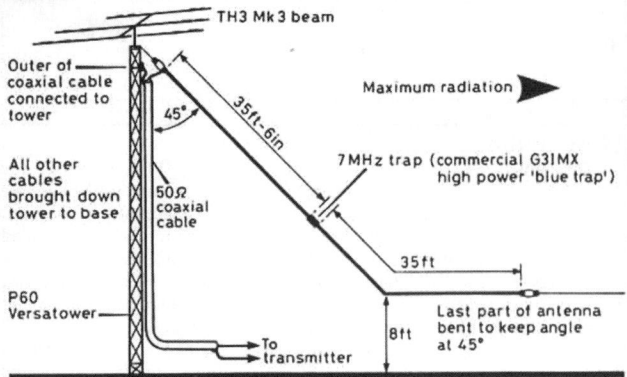

Fig 3. Dual-band λ/4 sloper antenna for 3·5 and 7MHz as used by G3TKN

"I have recently been experimenting with the system and have found it a very effective dx antenna for 7 and 3·5MHz: Fig 3. There are, however, some points that need to be considered when using one.

"My original 7MHz sloper was fed off the top of a 45ft tower, which also carries a Hygain TH3 Mk3 beam. The wire sloped at 45°. I found the length had to be increased to 35ft 6in to obtain resonance, and other users have confirmed the need to increase the length slightly compared with a conventional λ/4 element.

"I found, moreover, that when I removed the beam from the top of the tower the antenna would no longer resonate at 7MHz. This result is consistent with the findings of Doug De Maw, W1FB (*QST* October 1981) when he modelled his sloper and tower/beam combination at 144MHz. VE2CV (*QST* May 1980) modelled a sloper at 200MHz, but without having a scaled-down beam on the top of the structure supporting the sloper. His tests revealed that it was not possible to resonate the antenna despite adjustments of tower height and wire length.

"From all this, it does appear that for a λ/4 sloper to work correctly, it must be fed off a mask/tower that also carries an hf beam or similar amount of metalwork. It would appear that the array acts as a form of "inverted ground", raised groundplane or counterpoise.

"My tower is earthed automatically via its ground post, but the addition of a large number of radials at this level did not appear to improve the performance. However, some amateurs to whom I have spoken have reported improvement when extra radials were connected to the tower.

"In a series of tests on 7MHz both on ground wave and on contacts with VK/ZL via long path, the antenna showed a front-to-back ratio of approximately 10dB, which agrees with W1FB's 144MHz scale model. At high radiation angles, the antenna does not appear to show any directivity and, on average, signals from it are about +6dB compared to a horizontal dipole for UK and European contacts.

"As shown in Fig 3, I have trapped the sloper for operation on both 7 and 3·5MHz. However, I found the tower height had to be increased to 60ft to obtain a reasonable match on 3·5MHz. Results on this band have been very good, including contacts with VK2 and VK7 on short path with the antenna element sloping north-east. With the antenna sloping south-west I have received good reports from ZL, PY, LU and FM7."

Short Helical Circularly-polarized Antennas

Extracted from 'Technical Topics', *Radio Communication,* September 1984

Short helical circularly-polarized antennas

It has been shown in the past that axial-mode helical antennas for vhf omni-directional radiation should have only about one turn if they are to provide a broad radiation beam. Recent work by three Japanese engineers—H. Nakano, N. Asaka and J. Yamauchi—has shown that a two-turn helix fed at its periphery exceptionally radiates a circularly-polarized wave in spite of its short axial length. More recently (see *Electronics Letters* 1 March 1984, pp202-3) they have reported that circular polarization is also possible with a 1·5-turn short helix in which the feedpoint is located on the helical axis. Fig 6 shows the balanced and "monopole" versions of their configuration. The circumference of the helical cylinder C and the pitch angle are chosen to be, respectively, C = 1λ (λ = free space wavelength) and α = 12·5° which are common in a conventional axial-mode helical antenna. The wire radius is taken to be 0·005λ. The feedpoint is located on the helical axis, and a short wire inserted between the feedpoint and the beginning of the helix proper. This allows the rotation of the helix about the helical axis, with the feedpoint being fixed.

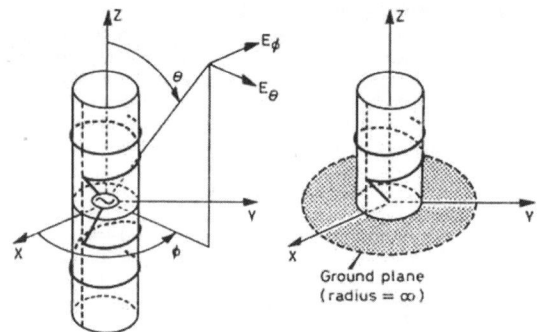

Fig 6. Configuration and co-ordinate system of circularly polarized 1·5 turn axial-mode helical antenna

They also show that a pair of identical 1·5-turn helixes wound in the same sense can form an array in which the mutual coupling can be reduced by rotating one helix with respect to the other; minimum coupling is when the rotation angle is about 180°.

Circularly-polarized Antennas

Extracted from 'Technical Topics', *Radio Communication,* September 1984

Circular-polarized antennas

For over a decade, the trend in vhf/fm/stereo broadcasting on Band 2 (gradually being extended in Europe up to 108MHz) has been firmly towards the use of circular (ie mixed) polarization. The prime reason for this has been the wish to improve reception on car radios, which usually have a vertical whip antenna, and also on portable receivers operated out of doors with telescopic whip antennas, while at the same time retaining the ability to provide good reception on horizontally-polarized dipoles or arrays usually favoured for domestic receivers.

Circular polarization is not without its problems. Because of the proximity of the metal tower or mast it is virtually impossible to obtain perfect circularity in all directions, which is why the term "mixed" polarization is preferred. Imbalance between the vertical and horizontal components can also arise from the receiving environment, including the effects of wooded areas, tall buildings, etc. For the broadcaster there is also the disadvantage that the vertical component is more subject to multipath reflections, at least in some

Stack of six circularly-polarized Band 2 elements forming the broadcasting antenna used by the IBA at Croydon for Capital Radio and LBC

environments, than a horizontally-polarized signal, resulting in more multipath distortion that can be very disturbing to those seeking really high-quality reception. Since power is shared between the vertical and horizontal components it also means that for a fixed transmitter output, a plane-polarized receiving antenna suffers a 3dB loss.

Nevertheless it is generally held that the advantages significantly outweigh the disadvantages, and the BBC is currently in the process of introducing mixed polarization on its high-power national networks; the IBA's independent local radio transmitters have used mixed (circular) polarization from the outset in 1973.

It could well be argued that vhf and uhf repeater stations should radiate signals of mixed polarity, permitting the users to have either horizontally or vertically-polarized antennas. Circular-polarized receiving antennas are virtually essential for many satellite applications.

B. Sykes, G2HCG, reports finding a solution to some long-standing problems affecting the use of circular polarization, including the development of a new phasing device he calls a "Polaplex". Since he hopes to market this device he is not prepared to release constructional details at this stage. For reception only, one could imagine the use, with crossed arrays, of the type of null-steering phasing techniques that have been developed for electronic-counter-counter-measures (*TT* August 1982).

G2HCG writes: "Operation through Oscar 10 on 144MHz has highlighted the need for a means of varying the antenna polarization to optimize signals. Helicals produce circular polarization but cannot be switched to the optimum direction of rotation which is dependent on the attitude of the 'bird' and whether it is coming or going. Crossed Yagis can be switched to any type of polarization but with some difficulty, involving much cutting and trying of coaxial cable to equalize the feeder lengths and to provide the appropriate phasing lengths. Also, when conventionally mounted, the vertical-element performance is invariably inhibited by the presence of the mast and feeders, resulting in elliptical polarization. This mast effect problem was of course fundamental to my 'Jaybeam' outlook resulting in the 'end-fed' systems.

"Now if a crossed Yagi is mounted with the elements at 45° to the mast, its detrimental effect is minimized or eliminated and there is no loss of circularity. At first sight there is no vertical or horizontal polarization, but these can be generated electrically by suitable phasing of the feeders, although, as noted above, this is a difficult and tedious task.

"I have at last produced a device, christened a 'Polaplex', which matches two feeders and gives variation of the phasing over 360°. Obviously with this available individual feeder length becomes irrelevant; horizontal, vertical, circular clockwise, circular anticlockwise, together with any elliptical modes in between, are all obtainable by the turn of a knob in the shack, even while transmitting high power.

"Other uses of the device have shown up while in operation; one in particular being the ability to take advantage of the seldom-appreciated fact that the designed polarization of an antenna applies only in the main beam. Thus with the Polaplex an interfering station, even of the same polarization, can be phased out provided that the signals are not arriving from the same direction. Further uses come to mind which have not yet been tried in practice, such as the electrical rotation of the radiation from crossed dipoles or turnstiles. Swinging the radiation up and down from a pair of stacked dipoles is also an interesting thought. Taking this to its logical conclusion, it should be possible to produce a satellite antenna with no moving parts; both bearing and elevation being controlled electrically from the shack. The Polaplex technique will cost a lot less than one rotator, let alone two.

"So far I have confined my attention to 144MHz, but 430MHz should not be impossible, though obviously needing careful attention to impedance discontinuities, and could prove costly."

Australian Broadband Sloper

Extracted from 'Technical Topics', *Radio Communication,* September 1984

Australian broadband sloper

A special form of broadband cage-dipole incorporating matching networks that covers much of the hf spectrum without matching adjustments has become known as the "Australian dipole". The original version, using just two wires, was described many years ago in *TT* (June 1974, p379): Fig 4.

Bill Orr, W6SAI (*Ham Radio* April 1984), reports that VK6IM and VK6YX have found that a grounded version of half this element functions effectively as a vertical monopole or sloper antenna over the range 1·8 to 14·34MHz with a measured swr on the feedline of only about 1·2 throughout the frequency range, and a feed impedance that remains roughly 154Ω: Fig 5.

Basically the VK6 version is a fat half-element about 75ft long with an impedance matching network placed about one-third in from the free end (ie high end of a vertical, low-end of a sloper). The antenna is fed against counterpoise earth (presumably attached at the top of the tower) through a simple broadband matching transformer (Fig 6 (b)). The element is 75ft long and requires a pretty high support, but presumably it might be possible to devise a scaled-down version where 1·8MHz operation is not essential.

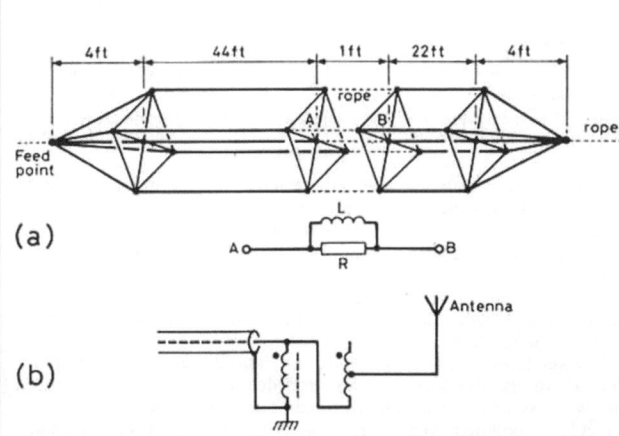

Fig 5. VK6 broadband cage antenna element used as a sloper or a vertical monopole. Spreaders are 6ft long. All five wires are bonded together at each spreader as shown. Connecting ropes join the antenna sections. The matching network is placed between points A and B of the cages. The antenna is fed at the left side using the matching transformer shown in (b) wound on an Amidon T200T powdered iron core. 24 bifilar turns are used. One winding is tapped for the antenna connection 18 turns from ground. Note that the tap is on the winding, not connected to the coaxial line

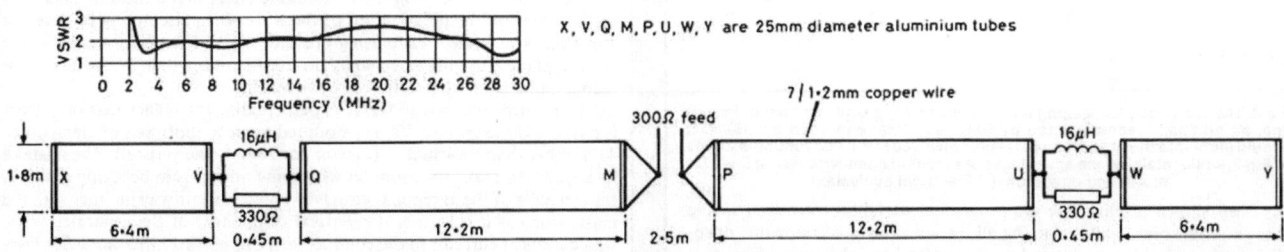

Fig 4. The original Australian broadband travelling-wave dipole as developed by R.J.F. Guertier and G.E. Collyer, showing magnitude of vswr over the range 2·3 to 30MHz. Later versions have used wire cages. (*TT* June 1974)

ANTENNA TOPICS

Wire Antennas for HF

Extracted from 'Technical Topics',
Radio Communication, November 1984

Wire antennas for hf

Rob Gurr, VK5RQ, has sent along a copy of his six-page article "Wire antennas" published in *Amateur Radio* (Australia) September 1984, pp12–8. This provides an excellent survey not only of a large number of hf antennas that can be implemented without the use of rod elements, together with notes on open-wire feeders and a Z-match atu, but also provides a general survey of the components used in the construction of wire antennas; including wire, connectors, masts, guy wires, transmission lines, earthing systems etc.

He discusses dipoles, colinear arrays, broadside arrays, end-fire arrays, noting that variations of these basic types are known in amateur circles under such names as G5RV, ZL-Special, G8PO, W8JK, Lazy-H, Sterba curtain, end-fed Zepp, double-Zepp, extended-Zepp, phased arrays, Franklin, four halfwaves in phase, etc. Undoubtedly many of those who have come into amateur radio with a professional background find the titles given to antennas rather confusing, though of course most are fully explained and described in the various handbooks.

For the moment, it is worth emphasizing VK5RQ's introductory notes: "A large number of recent entrants into the hobby of amateur radio have been indoctrinated with the belief that unless an antenna is made of aluminium tubing, has coaxial cable feedlines, and a popular brand name or type number, it is not worth considering. Regrettably also, they may come to believe that the only useful 'wire antennas' are the rhombic, vee beam and long wires which could not be considered for the average suburban backyard.

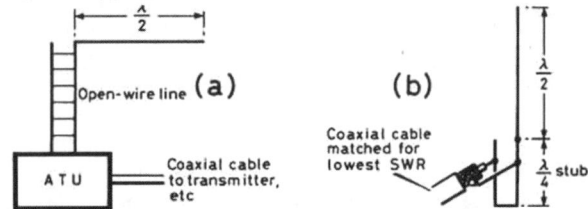

Fig 2. The classical form of Zepp antenna, one of many types discussed by VK5RQ in "Wire antennas". (a) HF version, (b) vhf version for vertical polarization

"Most of the popular commercial antennas have some limiting factor for today's amateur—they cover only one or at the most three narrow frequency bands (ie have low swr over small segments of the spectrum), require good groundplane radial systems, are difficult to tune to alternative frequencies, and in some cases are costly.

"The wire antennas discussed are those which, when erected in a suburban backyard, will give equal or better facilities than an equivalent commercial installation."

The antennas discussed by VK5RG are basically similar to those to be found in the handbooks, though his survey does underline the large number of "wire" systems that are relatively simple to construct and adjust yet are capable of good performance. The purist might have wished to see a faint question mark put against the traditional form of end-fed Zepp, nowadays regarded with some doubt in the absence of a G6CJ-type balun (Fig 3). This

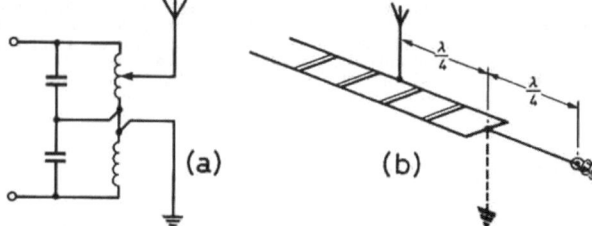

Fig 3. The technique for feeding an unbalanced Zepp antenna from balanced line, as originally recommended by G6CJ and later endorsed by G6XN. It should eliminate the proportion of failures involved in the conventional Zepps of Fig 2, while retaining the advantages of resonant open-wire feeder lines for multiband operation. (a) Electrical equivalent

has been shown to eliminate the proportion of failures involved in the conventional form, while retaining all the advantages of resonant, open-wire feeder lines for multiband operation. I have the impression that various forms of Zepp and centre-fed dipoles with open-wire resonant feeders are currently enjoying a fresh wave of popularity among those who have not fallen for the aluminium-tubing syndrome.

Multiband Loops

Extracted from 'Technical Topics',
Radio Communication, November 1984

Multiband loops

A further note from Laurie Margolis, G3UML, praises the multiband dx performance of large wire loop antennas. He writes:

"You have mentioned the 141ft delta loop which I use on 7MHz. This has now accounted for 175 countries on 7MHz ssb, and deserves to be considered seriously as a dx antenna. Initially, however, I did not realize how useful it could be as a multiband system. The loop, fed with tv-style brown 75Ω coaxial cable, loads beautifully on 21 and 14MHz without a tuner and is useful on parts of 28MHz.

"What I find fairly critical is the shape of the loop. I originally tended towards an equilateral loop requiring a top support about 45ft high, more because it looked right than for any other reason. However, matching appears better if the loop is flattened out a bit, though clearly for most people the shape depends more on the available supports than anything else.

"When using the loop multiband, a precise length of loop will be perfect for only one band, so some compromise is needed to give reasonable match on whatever bands are required. My arrangement gives me an swr of about 1·5 on 7,080kHz, 2 on 14·2MHz, 1·6 on 21·2MHz, a not-so-good 2·8 on 28·6MHz, and dropping to 1·8 at 29·1MHz . . . my feeder is about 30ft long and I have found that shorter lengths can prove a little naughty on one or more bands.

"1·8MHz operation is interesting. Again by accident I discovered that if the outer sleeve of the coaxial connector is disconnected at the rig end (so that just the centre pin is touching) there was a near perfect match at 1,940kHz, dropping to an swr of about 2 at 1,835kHz. This could be brought down simply by adding an extra 5ft of wire between the centre pin of the downlead and the connector at the equipment end . . . it has worked out to EA9 and UB5 on 1·8MHz ssb."

The use of loops for multiband operation can be facilitated by using open-wire feeders and an atu providing balanced output, as previously described in *TT*.

Circular Polarization and Crossed Yagis

Extracted from 'Technical Topics',
Radio Communication, November 1984

Circular polarization and crossed Yagis

The September *TT* included a note from G2HCG on his "Polaplex" device that he believes will provide complete and convenient control of polarization of the wave from crossed-Yagi arrays.

In the course of this note, G2HCG suggested that a conventionally-mounted crossed-Yagi array (ie +) is invariably inhibited by the presence of the mast and feeders, resulting in elliptically-polarized waves. He considered that these effects can be minimized or even eliminated by mounting the elements at 45° to the mast (ie ×).

This viewpoint is strongly challenged by Dr Neill Taylor, G4HLX, who writes:

"You quote G2HCG on the undesirable effect that a metallic mast and feeders have on the polarization of the wave when attempting to generate a circularly-polarized wave using crossed Yagis. The performance in the vertical plane is usually affected by the mast far more than in the horizontal plane, and a somewhat elliptical wave results.

"I was surprised to read G2HCG perpetuating the fallacy that this effect is reduced if the crossed-Yagi is mounted as an × (both sets of elements at 45°) rather than the usual + (one set horizontal, one vertical). The mistake he appears to make (in common with some others) is in believing that it is the elements of the antenna themselves which in some way interact with the mast, whereas it is in fact the vertical component of the generated wave which induces currents in the conductive mast, *however that wave has been produced*. The effect on a circular wave of a vertical mast is the same whether that wave is generated by Yagi arrays in a + or × formation.

"There is a good practical reason for wanting to mount crossed-Yagis in a + formation; namely that when, say, pure horizontal polarization is desired, the feeder to that array can be used alone, bypassing any type of switching or phasing unit that may be employed. No matter how well designed and constructed, this unit is bound to introduce a little loss into the system, and since this inevitably comes before the receiver front-end, *it adds to the noise figure*, where every 0·1dB counts!

"A crossed-Yagi is a popular choice with 144MHz enthusiasts who want to dabble in a number of activities. By mounting it in + formation they can get the best possible performance for tropo dx work by using the horizontal section alone, connecting both feeders with a phasing section when they want circular polarization for satellites etc. The point is that they are *not* compromising the performance as a circularly-polarized antenna by mounting it in this way, but do risk loss of performance for linear polarization by mounting it as G2HCG suggests and using a phasing unit, unless this is 'ideal' and completely 'loss-free'."

Shortening a Dipole Antenna

Extracted from 'Technical Topics', *Radio Communication,* November 1984

Shortening a dipole antenna

As noted last month, KA7QZK, for his low-budget station, put up a 3λ/2 wire dipole for 3·5MHz, some 390ft span for 3·5MHz, and suspended about 20ft off the ground. Fine for the mountains of Montana but most of us have far less room. For many even a resonant λ/2 dipole is too long on at least some hf bands. The usual trick is to shorten the overall span by letting the last few feet of wire on either side hang or slope downwards, though I have never seen any professional analyses of such dipoles.

Two alternative ways of shortening a dipole element without significantly reducing its performance have been investigated by a team of Japanese engineers at Hosei University, Tokyo: see "Shortening ratios of modified dipole antennas" by Hisamatsu Nakano, Hitoyaki Tagami, Ajihiro Yoshizawa and Junji Yamuchi (IEEE *Trans on Antennas and Propagation,* Vol AP-32, No 4, April 1984, pp385-6). This work apparently follows earlier investigation of bent-arm dipoles and the effects of asymmetric feeding, though the results were published in a journal to which I have no immediate access.

The team points out that there have been a number of attempts to make compact resonant antennas that do not use loading coils or similar lumped loading that inevitably reduces efficiency. They have examined two specific forms of element: the zig-zag dipole and the meander-line dipole (Fig 6).

Briefly, they show that a zigzag element with a wire length of 0·58λ results in a shortening ratio of the span of some 24 per cent yet provides a resonant resistance of 46Ω, entirely suitable for the usual coaxial-cable feed, and with a radiation pattern and efficiency virtually identical with a conventional half-wave (electrical) straight element. The 0·58λ factor is to take account of the many bends, just as the resonance of an inverted-V dipole is normally at a higher frequency than when suspended between two poles.

For the meander-line dipole, using 0·70λ of wire, the shortening ratio can be 30 per cent with a radiation resistance still as high as 43Ω at resonance.

In other words, both these structures can shorten the span by a useful 24 to 30 per cent without significantly degrading efficiency and directivity, but requiring, because of the bends, appreciably more wire to achieve resonance, and undoubtedly imposing more problems in implementing than a straight wire, though one could use two parallel nylon lines as a structure.

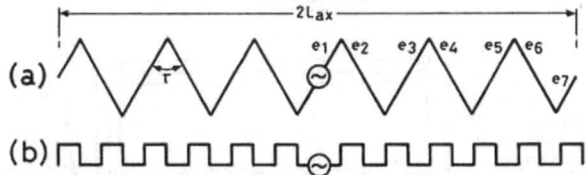

Fig 6. Significant shortening of the overall span of an λ/2 dipole can be achieved without significant loss of efficiency or directivity: (a) zigzag element (e1 = e7 = 0·208λ, e2 = e3 = e4 etc = 0·0416λ); (b) meander line element

The Ageless W3EDP Antenna

Extracted from 'Technical Topics', *Radio Communication,* January 1985

The ageless W3EDP antenna

In a recent "first steps in radio" article on "Radio antennas and how they operate" (*QST* September 1984, pp30–4), Doug DeMaw, W1FB, comments: "I've known a number of new hams (*sic*) who thought they could get on the air with a random length of wire at whatever height they could manage. Grave disappointment often follows . . . the amateurs received no responses to the CQs because they had ineffective antennas, and thereby were transmitting weak signals."

This discouraging and only partly valid observation can be justified only because W1FB makes it clear later in his useful article that the newcomers' problems were primarily because, in the absence of effective matching of the transmitter into a reactive impedance, very little power was being radiated. In other words, it was the *antenna system* and not necessarily the use of a random length of wire at uncertain height that made the antennas ineffective. In practice, as many amateurs have discovered, a random length of wire even a few feet off the ground *can* bring plenty of contacts, even though nobody should expect it to outperform a TH7DXX at 60ft.

The secret, if there is one, is simply to ensure that the whole antenna system is brought into a conjugate match with the aid of a very good earth, radials or, usually better still, a counterpoise insulated from ground, using an effective transmitter-antenna matching arrangement, and avoiding very heavy circulating currents.

About the mid-'thirties there appeared on the scene an antenna system designed by W3EDP that exploited this very effectively, though the length of the antenna wire (84ft) was not entirely random but chosen so that a simple parallel-tuned circuit inductively coupled to the transmitter tank coil, plus a short counterpoise of length suitable for the band in use, was all that was needed to bring the antenna system into resonance. Basically it is a simple "Marconi" antenna, and any other reasonable length of wire can be substituted for the 84ft length but may require a somewhat more flexible transmatch and different lengths of counterpoise. I recall using a W3EDP in 1939 for my 10W on 7 and 14MHz, and being reasonably happy with the results, which were roughly the same as with a 66ft end-fed wire that I also favoured.

Les Parnell, G8PP, still uses a W3EDP antenna on all pre-WARC bands from 3·5 to 28MHz, and reports receiving on ssb such comments as "this is a new one on me. If it is a new type of Yagi let me know how long the elements are, as my yard is very small and any rotatable thing with less than

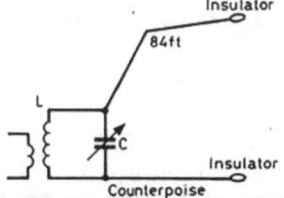

Fig 6. The traditional W3EDP 84ft end-fed antenna. L was often inductively coupled directly to the pa tank coil, but modern practice would be to use a low-impedance link winding on L. C is 250pF. L wound on 2in diameter former would be as follows:
 3.5MHz 21 turns, 16swg spaced one diameter. 17ft counterpoise
 7 MHz 7 turns, 16swg spaced one diameter. 17ft counterpoise
 14MHz 5 turns 16swg spaced one diameter. 6·5ft counterpoise
 28MHz 3 turns, 16swg 0·5in diameter. No counterpoise
Other bands will require some experimentation. G8PP uses a 3ft 4in counterpoise on 21MHz

12ft span would be more than welcome," and, again, "Is it omni-directional? You're coming in here 5 and 9 so I take it you've a reflector of some sort. If this is so, how do you radiate the other way? I'm using a three-element beam some 60ft high, and your W3EDP, as you call it, might have potential as you say it is only 21ft above ground."

G8PP comments: "These two quotes are not unusual responses to my saying that I'm using a W3EDP. So I explain that it is simply an end-fed wire some 84ft long with a short counterpoise that varies in length with the band in use: Fig 6. I first used this system in 1938–9, before we had access to 21MHz. I have since found that a counterpoise about 3ft 4in long gives the best results on that band."

It would be interesting to discover how well the basic W3EDP arrangement loads on 10, 18 and 24MHz (but remember, UK amateurs are not yet permitted to radiate a vertical component on 18 and 24MHz) and the optimum counterpoise lengths for these bands. It could prove necessary to use series tuning on one or more of the non-harmonically related bands.

Although it is unusual these days to hear anyone claiming to be using a

ANTENNA TOPICS

W3EDP, the basic design remains in the hf antennas chapter of the *Radio Communication Handbook*. It is described in the current edition as "an excellent solution for 'awkward locations' where an antenna of orthodox type cannot be made to fit in". Although most diagrams still show the W3EDP coil as inductively coupled to the pa tank coil, in 'thirties style, the current edition of the handbook makes it clear that there is no basic reason why it should not be link-coupled to the transmitter, directly or via a lowpass filter, swr meter etc. It is also pointed out that "there is scope for much experimental work with alternative lengths of antenna and counterpoise". It also stresses that, in general, it is much easier to achieve efficient radiation with systems of this type (ie not grounded, but with a counterpoise) than those relying on earth connections (ie Marconi-type end-fed antennas).

The Flexible Centre-fed Dipole

Extracted from 'Technical Topics', *Radio Communication,* January 1985

The flexible centre-fed dipole
In his "First steps in radio" article, Doug DeMaw, W1FB, pays tribute not only to the basic single-band half-wave resonant dipole with coaxial feeder, but also to the much more flexible centre-fed multiband dipole or doublet with open-wire or 300Ω resonant feeders.

Surprisingly, however, he does not mention one of the most important advantages of the multiband version: the top span does *not* necessarily have to be, as W1FB suggests, 468/f(MHz)ft, ie an electrical half-wave, "at the lowest operating frequency" with all the real-estate problems this involves for 1·8MHz (250ft), 3·5MHz (132ft) and even 7MHz (66ft) operation. Provided the whole system, top/feeders/atu can be brought into resonance, a "top" span of only about half this figure (λ/4), or even less at the lowest band, will radiate quite effectively. Remember that any antenna system radiates all the power that is fed into it, less that dissipated in losses. Although losses tend to rise with a short top span, even a 66ft span can prove quite effective on 3·5 and 1·8MHz.

The Flexible Centre-fed Dipole

Extracted from 'Technical Topics', *Radio Communication,* February 1985

Circular polarization and crossed-Yagi antennas
The notes in *TT*, September and November 1984, on circular polarization continue to attract comment. Not surprisingly, Bill Sykes, G2HCG, does not accept the views of Dr Neill Taylor, G4HLX, as altogether valid, at least from a practical point of view. Although this is a debate unlikely to be readily settled one way or the other, it is only fair to provide space for G2HCG's reply:

"The radio amateur is noted for considering the practicalities of a situation, but G4HLX asks us to accept that the losses inherent in any method of phasing two feeders are unacceptable... Altering the phase of two feeders requires that their difference in electrical length be changed by a maximum of λ/2 to achieve 360° phase change. Surely the addition (or even subtraction) of this length to the total feeder length is hardly a measurable quantity and would not affect the noise factor of the system.

"On mast effect, G4HLX states that the reduction of vertical radiation from a + mounted crossed-Yagi is the result of currents induced in the conductive mast. True, but one should consider other factors that are involved. An important effect, especially on phased systems, is the mismatch caused by the presence of the mast in the plane of the elements. Unbalance in the matching of two antennas fed in quadrature to produce circular polarization means that in addition to correct phasing of the feeds, the power levels in each antenna must also be controlled, a much more difficult proposition. Mounting the antennas in the 45° × configuration, instead of +, ensures that the effect of the mast on matching is equal, this virtually ensuring equal power distribution to each antenna.

"The question of which mast effect is the most important, especially as currents induced in the mast would be dependent on the length and type of material used, can be answered only by practical tests. Signal strength measurements over a short path with × mounted Yagis show no measurable difference between vertical and horizontal components, indicating that the theoretical mast currents in this configuration have little or no measurable effect.

"A daily 'sked' over a 130-mile path between the south coast and Northampton has been carried out for more than 30 years with 100 per cent contact on fm with only occasional necessity to use ssb. Noise figures are obviously of first importance, but complete control of polarization has proved particularly interesting. On this long path horizontal polarization is, as theory predicts, better than vertical. There is, however, a quite consistent polarization shift of some 45° with a total loss of polarization in the troughs of fades. Circular polarization has always been the optimum on this path, and the recent discovery of the 45° shift explains why, since the use of circular polarization means that signals remain unaffected by the shift.

"Reception of Oscar 10 on 144MHz is also interesting. Those familiar with the reception of this satellite will be aware of the regular fading caused by its rotation. Turning the knob of the "Polarphaser" (as I now call the device outlined in the September *TT*) alters the signal strength and the apparent speed of rotation, sometimes virtually eliminating the QSB, as the varying polarization lobes of the satellite antenna are explored."

A Poor-man's Log-periodic?

Extracted from 'Technical Topics', *Radio Communication,* March 1985

A poor man's log-periodic?
TT (April 1984, pp316–7) under the heading "Antennas that slow the wave" provided detailed information on a novel form of loaded folded dipole element developed by G6XN. Though, as he pointed out, the design lacked "sales appeal" it had the remarkable property that, despite its small size and multiband properties, it could be fed with any length of open-wire feeder without degrading its 14MHz bandwidth. This, G6XN reported, was in marked contrast to his experience with other multiband systems based on the use of open-wire lines which tend to involve fairly critical adjustment of the atu. G6XN admitted that this characteristic had been completely unexpected and was, in effect, yet another case of the serendipity that from time to time comes to the rescue—the obverse of Murphy's Law.

Fortunately, G6XN is of a disposition that does not just accept an apparent anomaly but seeks to find out just why it occurs and then to investigate whether it might provide a clue to further useful developments. In this instance, he confesses that it took him quite a long time to arrive at the explanation and to appreciate fully its practical significance. He writes:

"What has now emerged is, I believe, an entirely new and (potentially) very important family of multiband beam antennas. These can include many different forms of construction and a wide range of options. The earlier "loaded folded dipole" owes its membership of this family to the fact that, at the lowest frequency of operation, although physically reduced in size, it is electrically a full wavelength loop *with the two half-wavelengths having different values of Z_0 so that they act as quarter-wave transformers providing an impedance step-up equal to the square of the Z_0 ratio.* The

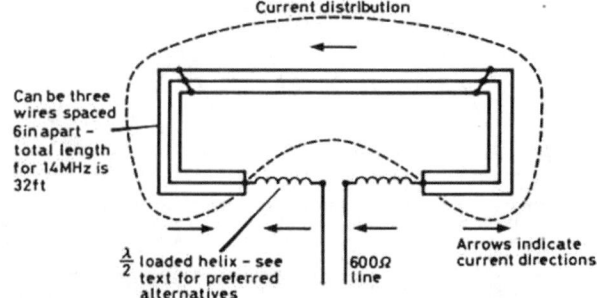

Fig 1. Basic concept of the reduced-size multiband folded-dipole element. The 600Ω feeder can be any length but, if long or thin, matching stubs switched in at ground level are an improvement and may be essential at the highest frequencies

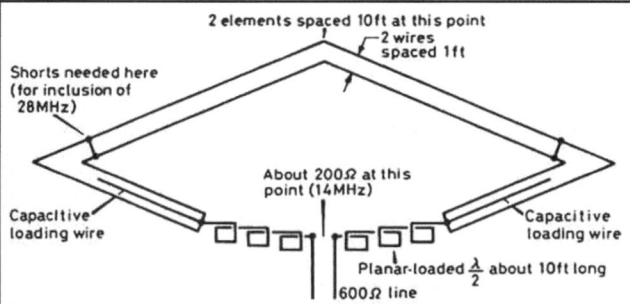

Fig 2. Practical implementation of arrays using multiband folded-dipole elements. This is G6XN's Mark 1 design. With 6ft spacing at the bottom, and 2ft at the ends between the two sections, there was severe overcoupling on 14MHz, cured by neutralization. Total span about 20ft

current is stepped *down* by the Z_o ratio, so that in the case of, say, a quad or delta loop having low Z_o at the top, *most of the radiation comes from the top of the loop, thus increasing the effective height*. This effect tends to be greatly augmented in practical designs which in most cases lead to relatively short lengths and less uniform current distributions for the high-Z_o portions of the loops.

"Fig 1 best illustrates the principle; Fig 2 shows the first version of the new beam to be tried in practice. The helix loading of Fig 1 has been

Fig 3. (a) VK5HA-type planar loading is preferable to helix loading and is a near optimum solution. (b) Meander-line loading is another alternative. (c) Triangular configuration for three parallel wires

replaced by 'planar loading', an idea for which I am indebted to VK5HA. This involves a string of one-turn loops as in Fig 3 (a). For these I have used three cords arranged as in Fig 3 (c), with appropriate spacers, instead of a solid former. With three loops each side of centre, I was able to fold a half-wave dipole element into about one-third of its normal length, at the cost of an increase of only some 15-20 per cent in total wire length. This is a big improvement over a helix or another alternative such as a form of the 'meader' system shown recently in *TT* (November 1984 Fig 6 (b)) as a means of reducing the overall span of a dipole element and which can be implemented as in Fig 3 (b).

"A Mark 2 version, dubbed by others 'The Claw', shown in Fig 4, has been my main antenna for several months, but has not been without problems due to a number of mechanical design errors. Planar loading, unfortunately, is ideally suitable for getting caught up in bushes etc, and the antenna sustained considerable damage en route from the lawn to the mast.

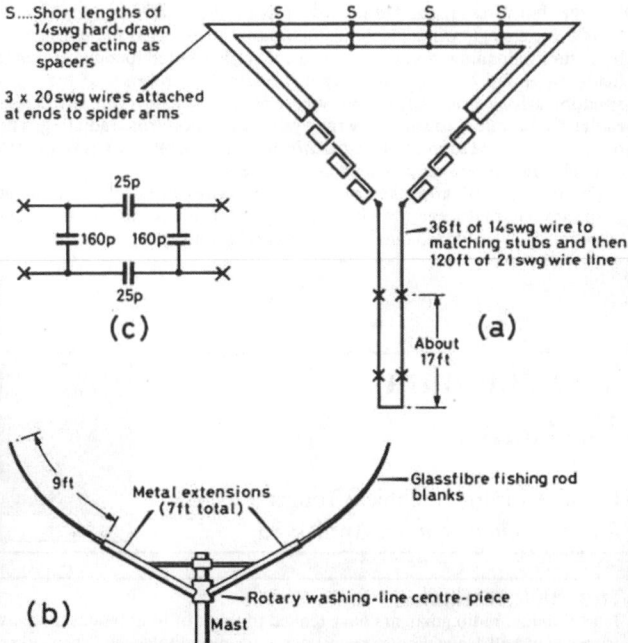

Fig 4. "The Claw" or Mark 2 design. (a) Basic shape of elements; (b) construction of supporting arms; and (c) matching/coupling network for 10MHz switched in by relays at point X in the feeders

Flimsy construction, relying partly on nylon fishing line ties, plus bending the top section down along thin glass-fibre arms, meant that the whole thing is top heavy and (the nylon line being elastic) wobbles like a jelly! Almost unbelievably, it survived the severe gales of December 1984.

"Worse problems have arisen from the resulting asymmetry (one arm broke in transit) in conjunction with a resonant mast which, on 10MHz, caused the current in the reflector to be either normal or zero depending on whether I was holding on to the wooden or metal part of the mast! Confusion abounded. Erratic results on 21 and 28MHz can be attributed partly to this and partly to other factors which came to light during development of the Mark 3 array, shown in Fig 5.

"This has now been completed and is being evaluated at relatively low height pending the advent of better weather (G6XN's letter was written in January). This is a relatively neat and clean arrangement and so far appears to have no vices. Inductive loading has been avoided by going to a larger loop size, and it has been found just possible to achieve this without pattern break-up at 28MHz, where the current zeros occur in the exact centre of the

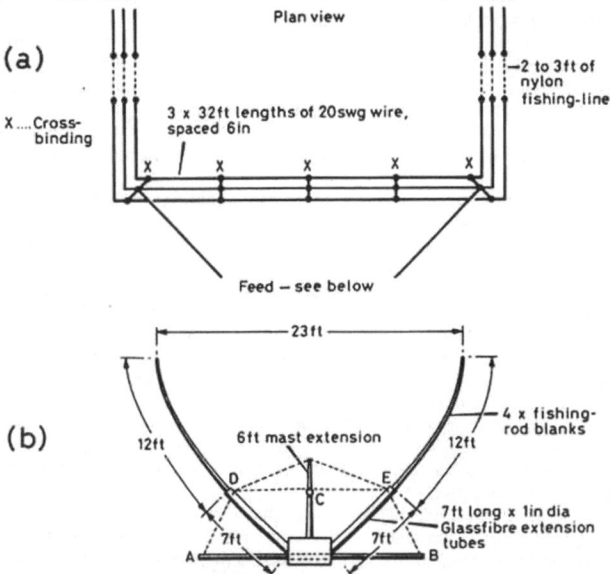

Fig 5. G6XN's latest Mark 3 design. (a) Shows basic shape, but when erected the elements are almost invisible. The arrangement is similar to the VK2ABQ flat array, and only one element is shown here in full. The feeders are single 20swg wires dropped down through the spider arms, then open-wire resonant lines (40ft) to the transmitter. (b) Shows supporting structure using fishing-rod blanks and glass-fibre extension tubes. AB is a 6ft dural tube and there is a short transverse tube at C, the arms being guyed back to the ends of these tubes which are insulated from the mast. The spacing rods (6ft of tube, 0.5in od, with insulated end pieces) are located at the glass-fibre rod junctions. Horizontal metal rods, if used, must not exceed about 8-10ft. The metal extensions almost certainly causing problems even though the elements in Fig 4 are are held clear of them

sides, which should therefore not radiate. This should maximize the effective height, but there is a bandwidth penalty unless one is prepared to retune; this can be done in the shack provided the feeders are not too long.

"The larger loops mean increased effective height at the lower frequencies, though this is largely offset by radiation from the sides, and the main incentive for the larger loops has been an improvement in gain, as predicted, of about 2dB at 10MHz. The Mark 2 design (Fig 4) has a predicted gain of only 2 to 3dB at 10MHz, after allowing for losses (and curing the mast resonance), but has given a pretty good account of itself over the long path to Australia.

"So far I have used only two elements, and this inevitably involves compromises at the extremes of the frequency range because of non-optimum spacings. With three elements a spacing of 8ft would be consistent with optimum performance all the way from 14 to 28MHz. The use of the outer two elements would give improved performance (due to the wider spacing) on 10MHz. However, for feeder lengths in excess of about 30ft it is essential to use some form of switched matching at 10MHz; this also provides independent control of coupling between the elements, as shown in Fig 4.

"This introduces yet another valuable feature of the new system: the ability to control coupling by the connection of small capacitors between the feedlines in a readily accessible position. The array of Fig 2 was so badly overcoupled that at 14MHz there was no f:b ratio at all, but neutralization produced (at the first attempt) 38dB of rejection! The array of Fig 4 was badly *undercoupled*, giving at first only 10dB f:b ratio, but with the in-phase connection of a pair of 5pF capacitors about 8ft from a current maximum I am getting 20-30dB of rejection. The null can be set for any frequency or back direction with a single knob at the operating position, controlling the resonant frequency of the reflector.

"The design of Fig 5 resembles very closely the well-known VK2ABQ

ANTENNA TOPICS

design. Drawing on past experience (as reflected in *TT* items and in *HF antennas for all locations*), the coupling has turned out to be very nearly optimum on all three bands (14/21/28MHz) without further adjustment."

Comparison with Log-periodic Arrays

Extracted from 'Technical Topics', *Radio Communication,* March 1985

Comparison with log periodic arrays

It will be appreciated that the object of this new family of designs is to provide a rotatable, directional antenna that can be used on 10MHz and on any frequency between 14 and 28MHz without the radiation pattern breaking up, characteristics normally associated with large and heavy log-periodic arrays whose use is virtually confined to professional communications and hf broadcasting. G6XN continues his explanatory notes as follows:

"With three elements one can expect a gain of 6dBd from 14 to 28MHz, plus 4dB at a spot frequency of 10·1MHz. This is directly comparable to what can be achieved with the size of log periodic arrays practicable for amateur radio. The log periodics have the advantage that there is no tuning operation needed and no theoretical limit to the frequency range. Nevertheless with the new array the tuning could be preset. Similarly, extending the coverage of a log-periodic to cover 7MHz would require an extremely large structure unlikely to be within the means of many amateurs. The new family of beams, on the other hand, offers the possibility of achieving the ultimate in lightness, low cost, low windage and miniaturization. They could be designed to 'look good', although it must be admitted that supplies of glass-fibre rods are difficult to find and it may be necessary to settle for compromises that would make it look less aesthetically attractive.

"The arrays have the big advantage that they can be made instantly reversible from the shack so that sufficient rotation can be achieved using two cords from a single position, so eliminating the need for a beam rotator. No adjustment is needed before erection, and dimensions become critical only when the operating range is being pushed to its limit. The need for symmetry, noted earlier, applies to *all* horizontal beams (lack of it may well account for the disappointing results of, for example, the TET antenna based on the principles formulated by VK2AOU). Mast resonances are probably the cause of much confusion. In this respect, serious problems arose on 21 and 28MHz due to resonances of metal struts used to reinforce the Fig 5 design at its centre, leading to considerable mechanical redesign. A slight tendency to overcoupling (rather than the anticipated undercoupling) at 21MHz is believed to be due to two short spacing rods, the ends of which are insulated but come close to points of high voltage."

Wires in Parallel

Extracted from 'Technical Topics', *Radio Communication,* March 1985

Wires in parallel

The use of parallel wires rather than tubular elements in the new arrays has brought to light an important finding that would seem to apply to virtually any use of this technique for multiband systems. This is the need to make *several* cross connections between the wires. G6XN identifies a link between this and his experiences with groundplane antennas (*TT* March 1981). It may be recalled that G6XN then noted that the *one* length of radial which should be avoided is the *usual* quarter-wave. This is because the impedance of a quarter-wave radial changes very rapidly near resonance; phase reversals could thus occur were it not for losses which have never been specified or investigated! Unfortunately this message, expressed both in *TT* and in G6XN's book, has failed to get through with the use of λ/4 radials still apparently universal.

This rapid change of impedance near resonance turns up in other guises.

G6XN himself was caught out twice in quick succession. In one case he had a vertical monopole with three thin wires joined in parallel at the base, but operation was haywire until the wires were joined also at a point some 2 to 3ft up from the base: Fig 6. With the beam of Fig 2, care was taken to put the short-circuit at a voltage point (14MHz). Nevertheless a big difference in wire currents resulted at 28MHz because the points of maximum voltage on 14MHz were current points on 28MHz.

G6XN therefore postulates, *as an axiom*, that wires in parallel must *never* be connected *only* at points of current maximum. This axiom clearly condemns virtually all conventional groundplane antennas (I shudder to think of the irate letters this statement may attract!). G6XN points out that the cure is trivial; it remains the fact that there is no *need* for long radials, and only a single radial is needed provided that it is short enough not to upset the radiation pattern. Planar loading in the VK5HA style (Fig 3 (b)) should prove a good way to construct such radials. Fig 6 shows one of G6XN's recommended forms of helix-loaded "counterpoise" type of radial for a groundplane antenna as discussed in *TT* (March 1981, pp 235–6) and *HFAfal*.

Fig 6. Multi-wire vertical groundplane antennas should always have the wires linked 2–3ft above the base. The diagram shows the use of G6XN's preferred form of artificial earthplane using a single-loaded counterpoise "radial"

Fig 7. Current distribution of loaded elements: (a) distributed loading results in sinusoidal current distribution; (b) centre loading gives triangular current distribution

The basic principle of the short multiband folded dipole element, such as those shown in Figs 4 and 5, can provide other options. For example, single-elements or arrays could be suspended between two masts or trees, using spreaders for the arrays. Similar principles can be applied to any shape or size of loop provided that it is small enough not to result in pattern break-up at the highest frequency. As a challenge, G6XN has considered trying to build an antenna with flat folded-dipole elements and a 12ft diameter turning circle, yet providing a gain approaching that of full-size performance. This would require either helical or, probably better, multi-turn planar loading.

Finally, G6XN adds a note on the impedance of multi-wire elements: "Three thin wires spaced 6in provide a Z_o of about 600Ω compared with 1,100Ω for a single wire. The latter figure can be expected to be increased by inductive loading, and one can use either distributed loading *or* centre loading (see Fig 7). The latter may be preferable, a reversal of the usual situation arising from the fact that we are not in this case trying to *increase* radiation but rather to *stop* the wrong part of the loop from radiating. The top portion of the loop can be *capacitively* loaded (stretched) as is done to a small extent in the arrangement shown in Fig 2."

For this type of array he considers three wires in parallel are about optimum. Beyond three, one is in the region of diminishing returns, but with only two the impedance ratio is reduced significantly.

The 200-ohm Vertical

Extracted from 'Technical Topics', *Radio Communication,* April 1985

The 200Ω vertical

Traditionally, radio amateurs have tended to think of hf antennas in terms of resonant half-wave dipoles or quarter-wave monopoles, and then either accepting these as single-band systems or alternatively taking advantage of the harmonic relationship of the pre-WARC bands. Admittedly, on 144MHz the 5λ/8 element has achieved some popularity as a mobile whip despite the tendency for the longer elements to flex during motion.

Yet, for military and professional communication, a single hf vertical whip antenna is normally used over a wide range of frequencies, emphasising once again that there is nothing magical about element resonance other than that it tends to make it easier to feed in rf energy without having to worry about a reactive feed impedance.

Over 20 years ago in *TT* I included some items based on the experiences of George Barratt (ex-G8IP, 5B4IP and ZD7IP) and later F. Regier (ex-OD5CG, who made the news media last year when he was kidnapped and held hostage for several weeks in Beirut). These reports showed how a 22ft vertical element (about 113° physical, 110° electrical on 14MHz) could be used effectively with horizontal radials or an earth mat, with the aid of quite simple matching networks, indeed on 14MHz all that is necessary is to insert a series capacitor between the element and the inner conductor of a 75Ω coaxial feeder. OD5CG provided information on a matching network for 14, 21 and 28MHz. ZD7IP quoted the classic antenna textbook by Laporte to show that at electrical lengths of 110° and 220° the resistive component of the feed impedance passes through 75Ω, with 110° having a series inductive reactance and 220° a series capacitive reactance.

John Share, GW3OKA, revives interest in this work in writing: "Last summer I was messing around with my antenna and came to the conclusion that the mast might prove more effective than some of the wires it was supporting. The mast is 25ft high and made from 1·5in aluminium tubing —my immediate impression was that this would not prove of much use for 14 or 21MHz, though I decided to work out the feed impedances. Here comes the surprise! On both 14 and 21MHz it proves to be about 200Ω (see Table 1 and Fig 1).

"These feedpoint impedances are of course reactive, but I remembered the comments on the 5B4IP vertical and also the 4:1 ferrite transformer and it proved all too easy. Connect the transformer to the 50Ω feeder and *voila* 50Ω becomes 200Ω! Series connect a capacitor to the antenna and tune for minimum swr. For the other band replace capacitor with an old rollercoaster and again adjust for minimum swr. Band change? A lead and a crocodile clip.

"When fed against an earth mat comprising lots of odd-length radials the system performed very well, working as a 3λ/8 vertical on 14MHz and 5λ/8 (well almost) on 21MHz, on both bands giving good low angle radiation and all round coverage: Fig 2. The arrival of winter stopped me 'messing around' further with the design for other bands: Fig 3. Later, the arrival of planning permission and a new tower to support an hf beam stopped work on this promising 200Ω vertical altogether. By the way, my definition of 'messing around' is what I do for free: 'research' is much the same, but done for payment!''

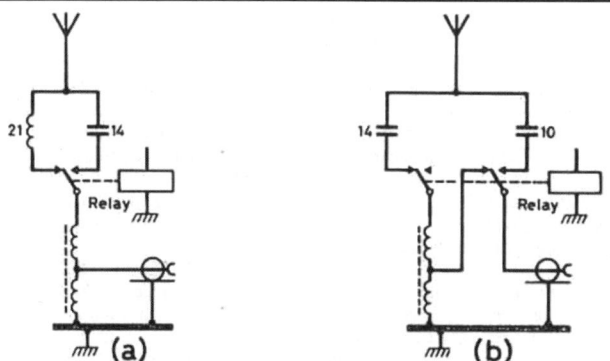

Fig 2. Dual-band operation of a 25·5ft vertical using a remotely-controlled relay rather than crocodile clips

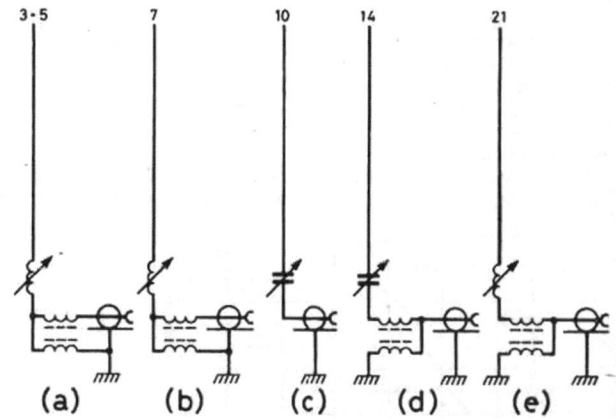

Fig 3. Suggested matching for five-band operation. Use on 28MHz not recommended

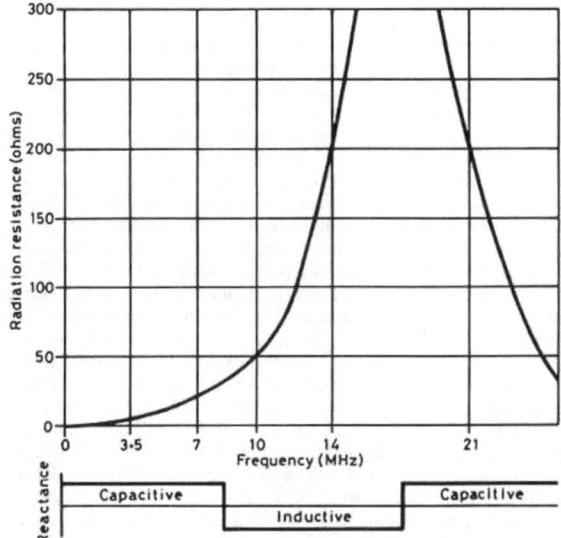

Fig 1. Feedpoint values for a 25·5ft vertical as plotted by GW3OKA

Table 1—Feedpoint values of 25·5ft vertical

MHz	a(°)	b(Ω)	c(X) (pF)	Feed	SWR
3·5	34·37	4		4:1 down	High
3·7	37·31	5			
7·0	68·74	18	120	4:1 down	1·5:1
10·0	98·20	46		1:1	2:1
10·2	100·16	50	75	1:1	1:1
14·0	137·48	200	300	1:4 up	1:1
14·3	140·00	208			
21·0	206·22	198		1:4 up	1:1
21·5	211·13	190		1:4 up	—
28·0	274·90	Much too long		Not suitable	

SWR readings may vary from those indicated according to individual circumstances

How High the Antenna?

Extracted from 'Technical Topics', *Radio Communication*, April 1985

How high the antenna?

When it comes to horizontally-polarized antenna systems there is an old adage that says "if it stays up it's too low"—at least for the dyed-in-the-wool dx operator. On several occasions it has been pointed out in *TT* that it may be preferable to use a lightweight two-element hf Yagi rather than a heavier three-element beam if this means that the bigger array has to be lower. Similarly, because the "average height above ground level" of a quad is lower than its top wire, this form of antenna is at a *disadvantage* to a Yagi. Believe it or not, there is no real basis for the long-standing myth of superior performance of quad antennas at low heights. It has, conversely, been stressed that in good propagation conditions, chordal-hop and grey-line dx is entirely possible on simple antennas only a few feet above ground. It is for *consistent* dx performance that height really comes into its own.

Yet it has to be recognized that the provision of really high masts or towers is usually expensive and can involve difficult neighbour/local-authority problems. It is for these reasons that the question of "how high is high enough?" arises, even for those whose bank manager does not blanche at the idea of 60ft-plus tiltover towers etc.

First one must stress the general truth of "the higher the better" and attempt to kill the myth that certain critical heights (multiples of λ/2)

ANTENNA TOPICS

significantly improve matters by reducing the vertical radiation angle.

It is, unfortunately, extremely difficult to measure "height gain" on hf, though rather more straightforward on vhf/uhf, since so much depends on site factors, ground conductivity etc. There is also the problem, when making measurements or contacts, of the constantly-changing band conditions and the tendency of all hf signals to fade quite rapidly.

An attempt to obtain meaningful results based on the reception of 14, 21 and 28MHz signals over paths exceeding 5,000km, and 145 and 435MHz signals over a path of about 20km, was made several years ago by a German antenna manufacturer, H. A. Rohrbacher, DJ2NN, from a reasonably good and uncluttered site. His results were published initially in *QRV* and then in English (translation by H. M. Lillienthal, F6DYG/DL7AH) in *Short Wave Magazine* (December 1981) and more recently in *Break-in* (June 1984). His measurement techniques and instrumentation are set out fully in his article and show that he went to considerable trouble to eliminate most of the usual problems, though it could be argued that any receiver measurements assume the "reciprocity theory" that equates the receiving and transmitting characteristics of a given antenna. This is by no means always true where radiation resistance is involved. Compare, for example, the performance of a small frame or ferrite-rod antenna on 1·8MHz for reception to that achievable when it is used for transmitting. Nevertheless this would not have been a problem in DJ2NN's project. He indicates once again, how misleading can be any attempt to access hf antenna performance on the basis of near-field signal-strength measurements.

DJ2NN measured incoming dx signals on an hf array which could be rapidly raised from about 2·5 to some 20m above ground, recognizing the problems of element detuning at very low heights.

His measurements (Fig 4) show that received signal strength increases continuously with height; but the increase is, as might be expected, greater at the lower levels above ground. On 14MHz, lowering the height of an array from, say, 25 to 12·5m reduces incoming signals by only one genuine S-point (6dB). Yet curiously, there is much less flattening of the height gain as the frequency increases.

DL2NN concludes on the basis of cost-effectiveness that an overall height for an hf array of about 17m (56ft) is about optimum, any additional height

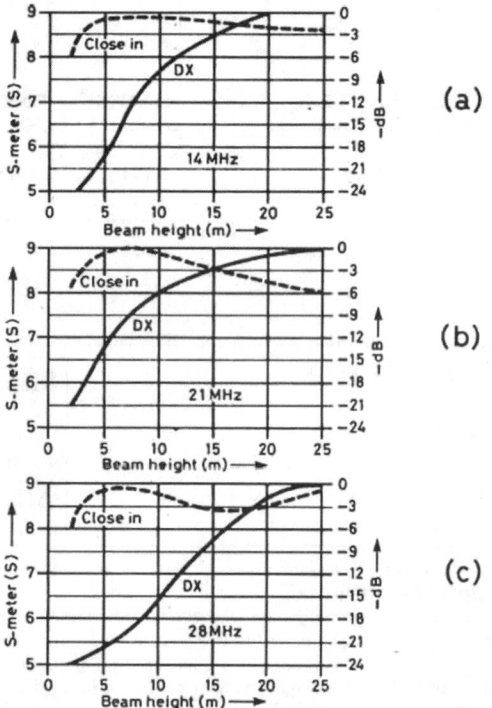

Fig 4. DJ2NN's antenna height-gain measurements. (a) 14MHz; (b) 21MHz; and (c) 28MHz. Note that increasing the height above about 15m shows relatively little improvement on 14 and 21MHz

adding much more to cost than to performance. For many of us, 17m is an impossible dream, and perhaps the more important finding is that between 2·5 and 10m an almost logarithmic increase of signal voltage occurs. An array height of less than 10m above ground, even on a clear site, is definitely disadvantageous. At 10m an array should be capable of putting up a good performance on 14, 21 and 28MHz, at least when the site is reasonably uncluttered, though the presence of trees usually has relatively little effect on a horizontally-polarized array.

On vhf/uhf, useful height-gain continues to be obtained even above 25m, and DJ2NN recommends that on a shared tower the vhf/uhf antennas should always be mounted *above* the hf array: Fig 5. He admits that his investigation left open some questions, including vertical radiation patterns

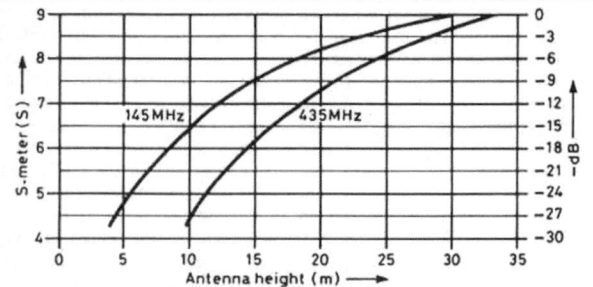

Fig 5. Antenna height-gain measurements on 145 and 435MHz

(which really require an aircraft as a measuring tool). Nevertheless his results do appear to provide some useful practical guidance, including the unanticipated conclusion that extreme height is less valuable on 14MHz than on higher-frequency bands.

More on the W3EDP Antenna

Extracted from 'Technical Topics', *Radio Communication,* April 1985

More on the W3EDP antenna

The January *TT* (p35) item on "the ageless W3EDP antenna" brought comments from readers with long memories. Brian Bower, G3COJ, recalls, while operating the BBC club station G3AYC in 1975, having a contact with W4AG in Florida who mentioned that it was he who had been W3EDP and had devised this simple multiband antenna. As W4AG is not listed in the 1985 Callbook, and as Florida is the retirement centre of the USA, it may well be that he is now operating only from that great shack in the sky. G3COJ also mentions that another antenna man from the 'fifties— "Dickie" Bird, G4ZU, of Mini-Beam fame—now hides under the callsign F6IDC, having retired to southwest France where he has been busy working on a new form of miniature beam.

Charles Bryant, G3SB, comments on the suggestion in *TT*, quoting the current *Radio Communication Handbook*, that it is unnecessary to inductively couple the W3EDP loading coil directly to the pa tank coil, as it can be link coupled—directly or via a lowpass filter, swr meter etc—to the normal low-impedance output socket of a transmitter. He recalls that early descriptions of the W3EDP suggested that direct inductive coupling was necessary in order to provide also a degree of capacitive coupling.

G3SB's memory is good. A check with the first (pre-war) edition of the RSGB's *The Amateur Radio Handbook* shows the counterpoise end of the coupling coil coupled to the "hot" (anode) end of the tank coil with the following text note: "The counterpoise, which is 17ft or 6·5ft long according to frequency, is taken away at right angles to the aerial, and may also be bent to fit the space available. The counterpoise is connected to the end of the coupling coil nearest the pa coil, because a certain amount of capacitance coupling to this part is necessary for correct working. For the same reason it is necessary to have the coupling coil proportioned correctly. The coupling coils should be made of the plug-in type, arranged to swing against the pa tank. It should be possible to tune up the coupler and then swing up until the pa is fully loaded. If the aerial current falls off, before what is considered correct load is obtained, the balance between capacitive and inductive coupling is not quite right, and this is best adjusted by trimming the length of the aerial a few inches at a time, up to a possible total of 2ft."

I cannot help feeling that this procedure is based on what W3EDP actually did in the 'thirties, rather than theoretical considerations. Such a procedure would be ruled out today except at the very lowest powers, since it would appear to be an almost ideal way of ensuring maximum harmonic radiation. I suspect that W3EDP's procedure was based on the problem that (except on 7MHz) both ends of the coupling/loading coil are "hot" to rf, and this can complicate the use of a link winding. It would, of course, be possible to incorporate an additional "tank" circuit, link coupling this to the transmitter, but I would expect the reassuring comment in the current edition of *RCH* to be valid.

A problem with any form of coupling to this antenna, as with most long-wire antennas operated in an upstairs shack with a long earth-lead, is the tendency for the transmitter chassis to become "hot" to rf. G3SB experiences a form of this problem when using 66 or 132ft antennas with a pi-coupler on mains-operated transmitters, finding that rf is injected into the mains earth-lead, causing various difficulties. In my experience an almost sure-fire cure for a "hot" chassis is to attach to it a quarter-wave wire (or several for different bands), and there would seem to be no reason why this should not be done when using a W3EDP provided that no direct connection is made to the short counterpoise.

Trigonal Reflectors

Extracted from 'Technical Topics', *Radio Communication,* May 1985

Trigonal reflectors

For most vhf arrays, operators accept the backward-looking lobes of Yagi antennas as an inevitable fact of life. In *TT*, November 1982, pp959–60, G8SEQ proposed the use of a second resistive-loaded reflector as a means of improving the back-to-front ratio of a 144MHz Yagi array, though subsequently theoretical considerations showed that even with an accurately-matched load in the centre of the second reflector half the energy in this element would inevitably be re-radiated, thus somewhat limiting the effectiveness of this approach.

It is perhaps surprising that more attention has not been paid to the use of trigonal reflectors—a technique first described (for a 120MHz array) by A Wheeler Nagy in 1936 and analysed by Dr George Brown in his definitive study of directional antennas (*Proc IRE*, Vol 28, No 1, January 1937, pp120–2).

In the UK the value of trigonal reflectors has perhaps been under-estimated due to what appears to have been a long-standing error in several

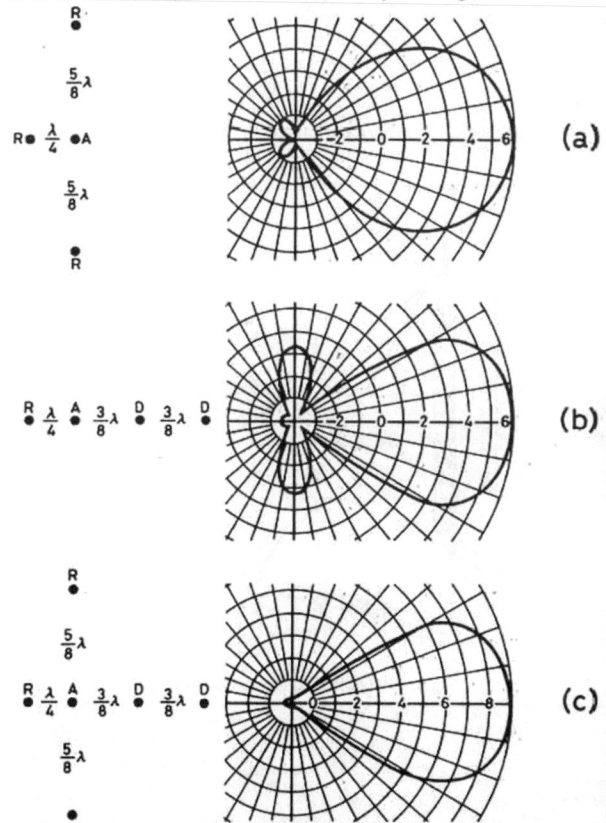

Fig 1. Use of trigonal reflectors compared with the single reflector of (a) shows the improved side and back lobe performance. But note that the diagrams originally used in *Radio Handbook* of 1938 are drawn to a line rather than a logarithmic scale as would be done today. A logarithmic scale would make the side lobes more prominent on all diagrams. Note also the element spacings are those that were commonly used in the 'thirties, with the reflector a full quarter-wave behind the driven element

editions of the RSGB's handbook where what purports to be a "Yagi array with trigonal reflectors" (Fig 13.19 in *Radio Communication Handbook,* 5th edn) shows the three reflectors mounted in a flat plane.

In *Break-in* (September 1984, pp10–11), Rex Cassey, ZL2IQ, reproduces some diagrams from the *Jones Radio Handbook* of 1938 which show (Fig 2) that the three reflectors should be located on a parabolic curve which has the feedpoint of the driven element as its focus.

He provides the following up-dated design criteria:
(a) the added reflectors should all be the same length as the normal reflectors;
(b) the three reflectors should lie on a parabolic curve, $y^2 = 4ax$ (Fig 2) but note that in modern practice a is usually much less than the $\lambda/4$ of the pre-George Brown era or Yagi antennas;
(c) if the added elements are directly above and below F, their distance away will be $2a$. However, they can be placed anywhere on the parabola. For example, if $x = a/2$, then y will be $\sqrt{2}a$.

It seems worth adding that there is no reason why more than three reflectors should not be used provided that they all lie on the parabola and are symmetrical (ie 3, 5, 7 reflectors).

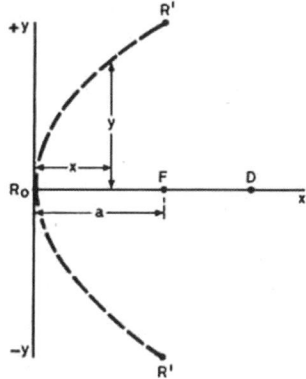

Fig 2. Trigonal reflectors should be located on the parabola having its focal point at F where the driven element is located

Delightful Dipoles?

Extracted from 'Technical Topics', *Radio Communication,* June 1985

Delightful dipoles?

One of several papers presented by well-known radio amateurs (though usually in the professional *alter ego* guise) at the hf conference was one by Maurice Hately, GM3HAT, on the multiband dipole which he is currently marketing as a "dipole of delight". This antenna is based on a UK patent application made in September 1981 on his behalf by the National Research Development Corporation (UK Patent Application GB 2112579, published 20 July 1983).

In effect, GM3HAT claims that by inserting suitable-value capacitors at

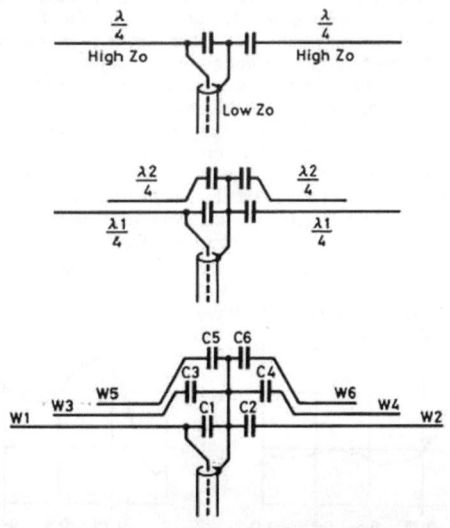

Fig 5. GM3HAT's patented "dipoles of delight" which use capacitors to improve the match between unbalanced coaxial feeders and the balanced elements. The capacitances should have a reactance at the frequency concerned equal to the impedance of the feeder. The incorporation of the capacitors "stretches" the element and at resonance the electrical length is roughly the same as the physical length

ANTENNA TOPICS

the feedpoint of a dipole element fed from coaxial cable, he achieves an efficient form of matching/balun that significantly reduces the effect of pick-up on the outer braid of the coaxial cable and thus provides not only an efficient radiator but also a receiving antenna that is much less susceptible to local rfi from tv sets, home computers, electrical appliances and the like. The insertion of capacitors involves a phase-shift that "stretches" the element so that its half-wave electrical resonance approximately equals a physical half-wave; in other words the usual five per cent end-correction does not apply.

The insertion of two capacitors in the element creates an electrical centre-point to which the braid of the coaxial feeder is connected, with also a low-impedance feedpoint (whose impedance can be made to match the cable) on the outer side of either of the two capacitors, and it is to one of these two points that the inner conductor of the cable is connected. It appears to me that this arrangement provides a form of gamma match that minimizes the age-old problem of joining an unbalanced feeder to a balanced element. In practice, GM3HAT then forms a multiband antenna by a series of resonant parallel wires in the accepted manner: Fig 5.

Provided that the capacitors are of the correct value for the frequency involved, the GM3HAT principle would seem to offer useful advantages in achieving a good match on each band over a reasonable bandwidth, and also minimizing pick-up of stray electrical interference on the feeder. Whether all of the advantages claimed by GM3HAT can be fully justified on theoretical grounds is a little more difficult to assess. As I mentioned at the conference, his paper seems to assume that the outer braid of a coaxial cable feeder, regardless of its length, represents an "electrical earth" point. To my mind, it doesn't.

this advantage is not observed in practice, it is almost certainly due to incorrect matching of the antennas, and to different power levels delivered to each by the transmitter."

For hf operators who cannot reach 5λ/8 (225°) it is worth mentioning that the 110° vertical mentioned in the April *TT* (200Ω vertical) does show a useful sharpening of the vertical radiation pattern, though less than the optimum 5λ/8.

Fig 11. G3SEK's method of trimming coaxial cable to length

Monopoles, Vertical Dipoles & the 5/8 Vertical

Extracted from 'Technical Topics', *Radio Communication*, June 1985

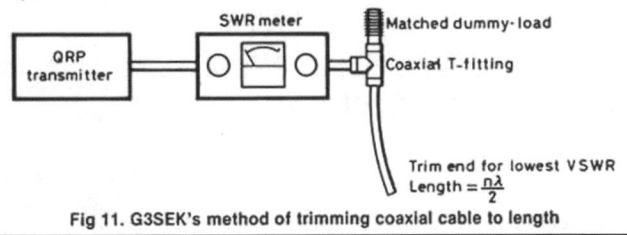

Monopoles, vertical dipoles and the five-eighths vertical

A three-part article "The feed impedance of an elevated vertical antenna" by Guy Fletcher, VK2BBF, in *Amateur Radio* (VK) of August, September and October 1984, explores in some depth the facts and fallacies surrounding the effect on vertical antennas of its elevation above ground and its effect on antenna gain. While there are several nuggets of useful information (eg Fig 10) in all three parts, there is space here only to quote some of the points made in the final part:

"It should be clearly understood that the ground-level monopole, an elevated monopole and an elevated half-wave vertical dipole should all have approximately the same gain over an *unobstructed, good ground*. The magic 3dB gain sometimes claimed for a λ/4 monopole over a dipole never existed. The argument for it is based, I think, on the fact that the same power is radiated into only half of all space (above ground level) so the signal should be doubled. This is not a fair comparison, since a vertical dipole over a ground has exactly the same advantage, and in free space (interplanetary) neither antenna has this advantage.

"Finally the 5λ/8 monopole. It can be shown that over a perfect ground and for the same total radiated power, the field strength due to an antenna of height 0·64λ (which is close enough to 5λ/8) exceeds that due to a λ/4 monopole by a factor 1·43 due to the sharpening of the radiation pattern; 0·64λ is the optimum length, and the field falls quickly for longer monopoles. This corresponds to a power gain of $1·43^2 = 2·03$ or 3dB.

"Thus a vertical 5λ/8 antenna, whether elevated or not, has a built-in advantage for low-angle radiation of 3·07dB over a vertical λ/4 antenna, and presumably $3·07 - 0·26 = 2·81$dB over a vertical half-wave dipole. If

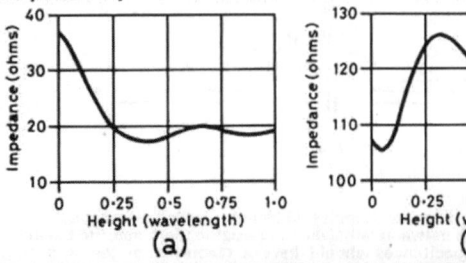

Fig 10. Base feed impedance of (a) λ/4 vertical monopole antenna; (b) base feed impedance (reactive) of 5λ/8 vertical monopole. Both as functions of height above ground

7MHz Sloping Delta Loop Antenna

Extracted from 'Technical Topics', *Radio Communication*, September 1985

7MHz sloping delta loop antenna

The full-wave 7MHz loop antenna has been shown by G3UML and others to be an effective dx antenna but tends to require a fairly high support in the form of a tree, pole or building. From Kjell Norlich, SM6CTQ, in his Swedish dx column in *QTC* (Nr 3, 1985, p112) comes the sloping form of delta loop shown in Fig 4 that he reports to be a useful dx performer and with a more modest height requirement. The impedance match is improved by the quarter-wave transformer (though this will tend to make such an antenna a one-band antenna). The formulas used were: loop (1,005 × 0·305)/f where the length is in metres and *f* in megahertz, and for the transformer (246 × 0·305)/f multiplied by the velocity factor of the cable (0·66 for RG59/U). Omission of the 0·305 factor gives the result in feet.

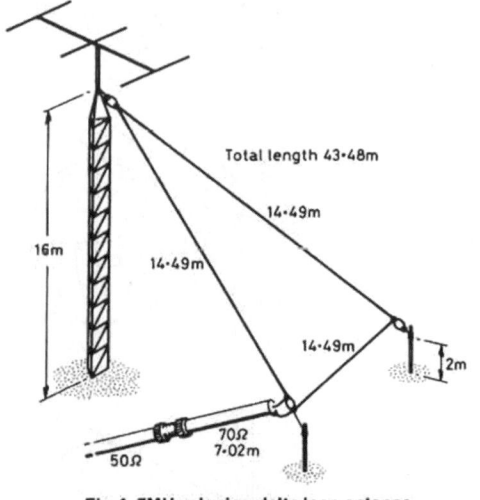

Fig 4. 7MHz sloping delta-loop antenna

1980 - 1989

Window-pane 144MHz Antenna

Extracted from 'Technical Topics',
Radio Communication, October 1985

Window-pane 144MHz antenna

Many broadcast engineers responsible for advising viewers on the reception of uhf television seem to be besotted with the idea that outdoor antennas are *always* essential in order to obtain good quality pictures. While I recognize that for very many viewers this is indeed the case, on occasions I find myself in disagreement with my colleagues since I remain convinced that, in some circumstances, perfectly good pictures, free of multipath "ghosting" and the effects of local movement *can* be achieved with window-pane loop antennas—provided of course that the window is looking roughly in the right direction and the local signal is reasonably strong and clean of multipath.

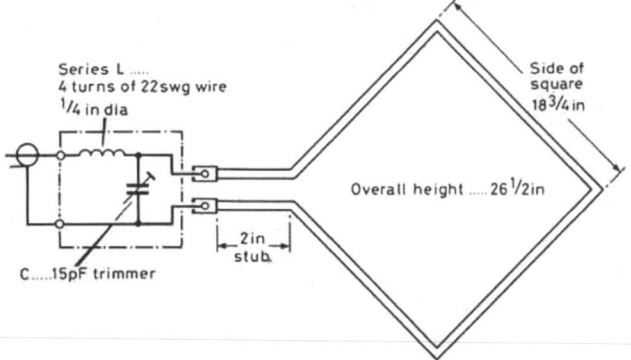

Fig 4. The aluminium-tape 144MHz "window pane" antenna used by G4WEA/A. This can be fed either side of the loop, as convenient, providing vertical polarization. For horizontal polarization feed at bottom corner. Mark the window with a felt-tip pen and then stick down the tape. The spacing of the stub was governed by the "burglar alarm" connectors which came as a pair, about an inch apart between centres

I was reminded of this ongoing debate by a note from John Wells, G4WEA, who has for several years used very successfully a 144MHz "quad loop" antenna formed from self-adhesive aluminium foil tape (see G3DQL's notes in the August *TT*) while operating /A with about 1·5W from an IC2E at the Medical Physics and Clinical Engineering laboratories of Barnsley District General Hospital. His antenna (Fig 4) uses burglar-alarm tape (readily obtainable from RS Components, Farnell etc) stuck on to the metal-framed laboratory window. A 2in (5cm) stub at one corner is fed with 50Ω coaxial cable via a simple matching network mounted on plain Veroboard, which is fastened to the tape's connectors with 4BA solder tags.

G4WEA acknowledges that the idea came from G6IDL, and reports that performance has been excellent—including even a contact with Holland under "lift" conditions. He points out that an added advantage is that, even at work, it does not have to be put away after every session, as it takes up virtually no room space!

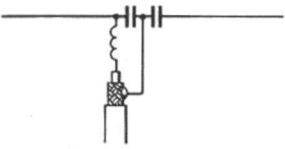

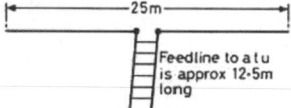

Fig 9. GM3HAT's monoband "dipole of delight" showing improved form with an inductor. Both capacitors and inductor have reactances numerically equal to the cable impedance at the frequency of operation

His Fig 2 is here reproduced as Fig 9, about which he explained: "The tuning problem can be alternatively cured if a series inductor is connected between the coaxial feeder and the capacitive balun. While a half-wave dipole constructed in this way is only a singly resonant device, it is nevertheless attractive in view of the accurately resistive input impedance over a wide bandwidth (some six per cent before the swr exceeds 1·5:1), minimal received interference and preclusion of overtone radiation."

Brian Bower, G3COJ, noted the 7MHz sloping delta loop antenna of SM6CTQ (*TT* September, Fig 4, p708) which adopts the ideas of W1FB and W1SE in their *QST* article of October 1984: "The full-wave delta loop at low height". However, he feels that the dimensions given by SM6CTQ are unduly pessimistic in suggesting that the support mast or tower needs to be 16m high. If the centre of the base of the antenna is spaced out at, say, 5m from the base of the tower, and the wire 2m above the ground, the apex would not reach the top of a 16m mast but would be some 13·5m above ground. However, this is only about 1m less than with the loop in the vertical plane. On the other hand, G3COJ suggests, if the plane of the loop slopes at 45°, then its apex would be at 10·88m, representing a worthwhile saving in mast height. Alternatively, for a given apex height, moving the loop out from the mast and raising it more than 2m above ground would raise the average height of the antenna. "It would be interesting to know whether this height improvement would be cancelled by the loop becoming less vertical", G3COJ writes.

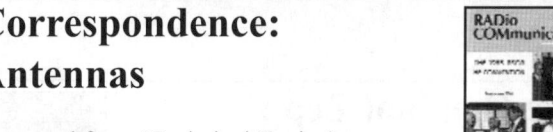

Fig 10. All-band centre-fed doublet antenna as recommended by VK5RG, for use on all hf bands from 1·8 to 28MHz

As *TT* has frequently noted the attractions of a centre-fed doublet antenna using open-wire feeder, it may be appropriate to reproduce from Rob Gurr, VK5RG's "Wire antennas" (*Amateur Radio (VK)* September 1984) an antenna he recommends as a flexible all-band system: Fig 10. He writes:

"This multiband general purpose system has the following radiation properties:
1·8MHz (with feeders tied together and tuned against earth) omnidirectional;
3·5MHz as a shortened dipole, excellent general coverage;
7MHz as an extended dipole, some bidirectional gain at right angles to the wire;
10MHz as shortened two halfwaves in phase, some bidirectional gain (1·8dBd);
14MHz as two extended halfwaves in phase, 3dBd gain;
18, 21 and 28MHz as a general-purpose centre-fed "long wire" with multiple lobes, some providing useful gain (eg 2·5-waves long on 28MHz for gain of 2dBd in each of four lobes at 30° with respect to the wire).

For this type of system one does need a flexible astu with balanced output that can be varied from high to low impedance.

Correspondence: Antennas

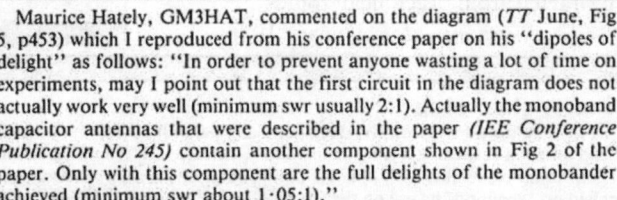

Extracted from 'Technical Topics',
Radio Communication, December 1985

Maurice Hately, GM3HAT, commented on the diagram (*TT* June, Fig 5, p453) which I reproduced from his conference paper on his "dipoles of delight" as follows: "In order to prevent anyone wasting a lot of time on experiments, may I point out that the first circuit in the diagram does not actually work very well (minimum swr usually 2:1). Actually the monoband capacitor antennas that were described in the paper *(IEE Conference Publication No 245)* contain another component shown in Fig 2 of the paper. Only with this component are the full delights of the monobander achieved (minimum swr about 1·05:1)."

WARC-bands Trapped Dipole

Extracted from 'Technical Topics',
Radio Communication, January 1986

WARC-bands trapped dipole

Although not everyone favours the use of traps, the trapped dipole does have the useful feature that it is possible to achieve a sufficiently low swr on each band to make it unnecessary to use an atu with most transmitters, unless any solidstate protective circuits have a low threshold. But few designs of trapped dipoles cover 3·5, 7, 10, 18 and 24MHz using eight traps constructed from coaxial cable. Such an antenna has been described by

ANTENNA TOPICS

Brian J Warman, VK5BI, in *Electronics Australia* June 1985, pp100–1. He has not attempted to cover 14, 21 or 28MHz for which bands he uses a triband beam array. The total span of the dipole is about 25m and could thus fit many gardens, yet providing a resonant antenna for 3·5MHz: Fig 1(a).

The traps comprise RG-58U cable wound on formers cut from a 1m length of 32mm polypipe; VK5BI suggests checking its rf properties by putting a bit in a microwave oven for 1min: there should be no reaction. Ten metres of RG-58U are used (Fig 1(b)) to the following dimensions:

7MHz trap	1,800mm of cable	110mm of pipe
10MHz trap	1,330mm of cable	90mm of pipe
18MHz trap	830mm of cable	70mm of pipe
24MHz trap	710mm of cable	70mm of pipe

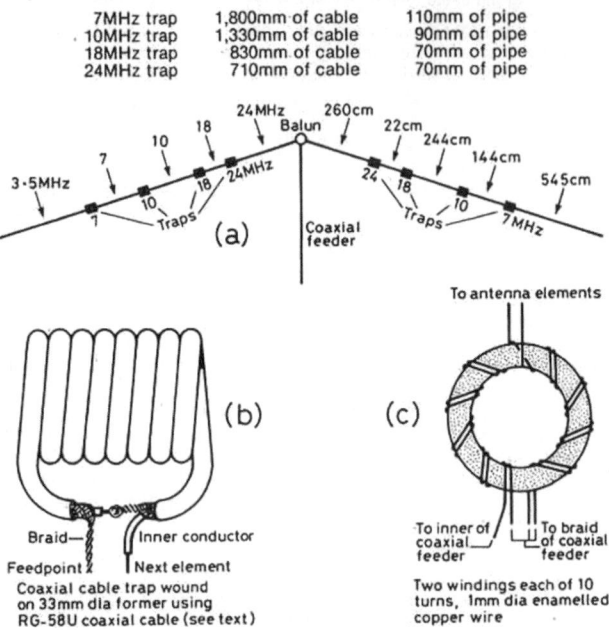

Fig 1. "WARC-bands" trapped dipole by VK5BI covers 3·5, 7, 10, 18 and 24MHz. Element lengths shown on the right, while the corresponding bands are shown on the left. (b) Details of coaxial cable traps. (c) Winding details for optional balun

The pipe is first drilled with three holes: one 5mm hole, 25mm from one end to secure the beginning of the coil; two 2mm holes 10mm from each end to attach the antenna wire. He proceeds as follows:

"Strip 75mm of jacket off each end of the length of coaxial cable followed by 50mm off the centre conductor. I have found the neatest way of finishing off the braid is to part the strands near the jacket and then fish the centre conductor out through this hole. In this way the weaving remains intact and makes for a very neat finish. Push one end of the cable through the 5mm hole at the end of the former until 5mm of the jacket is inside. Wind the cable to form a coil on the former, then mark a hole at the finish to allow 5mm of jacket to be pushed inside to finish the coil. Pull the remaining cable through this hole. You will now have approximately 70mm of cable inside the former at each end.

"Solder the centre conductor from one end of the coil to the braid at the other end. Fig 1(b) shows the general idea, but note that the connection will be inside the former, not on the outside as shown. (The figure has been drawn this way for clarity.) The remaining braid connects to the element coming from the feedpoint (centre) of the antenna, while the remaining inner conductor goes to the next element."

VK5BI used a ferrite-ring balun (Fig 1(c)) between the feeder and the element, primarily to reduce current flowing on the outer conductor of the cable to minimize tvi on vhf tv channels. It would probably have little effect in the UK, but be sure to seal the end of the cable to prevent moisture ingress.

The antenna sections comprise:

24MHz	2 × 260cm
18MHz	2 × 22cm
10MHz	2 × 244cm
7MHz	2 × 144cm
3·5MHz	2 × 545cm

plus in each case allowance for terminating the wire to the trap (about 30mm extra).

VK5BI stresses that trap dimensions are correct only for RG-58U cable, although even in this case it would be advisable to check resonance with a gdo, before drilling the second 5mm hole in the former, by temporarily connecting the inner conductor at one end to the braid at the other end. Resonance points to aim at are: 7·1, 10·1, 18·1 and 24·9MHz. Similarly, it is advisable to gdo-check element lengths as they are assembled progressively from 24MHz.

Loops and Dipoles

Extracted from 'Technical Topics', *Radio Communication,* January 1986

Loops and dipoles

Few authors ever seem to agree on the theoretical gain, radiation resistance etc of full-wave loop, quad and delta antenna elements. Since, for real antennas, the characteristics will be affected by such questions as height above ground etc, it could be argued that the published variations are of limited practical significance. However, James L Dietrich, WA0RDX, with the support of Walter Maxwell, W2DU, has tackled this problem once more, and has come up with a useful tabulation of four basic loops as a basis for the determination by trial and error of characteristics in a real situation.

Table 1—Summary of loop and dipole characteristics

		Gain over isotropic (dB)	Gain over dipole (dB)	Radiation resistance (Ω)	Rel level at vertical (dB)
λ/2	Dipole	2·15	0	73	0
1λ	Square loop	3·14	0·99	117	−3·01
1λ	Circular loop	3·49	1·34	133	−3·74
1λ	Diamond loop	3·14	0·99	117	−2·70
1λ	Delta loop	2·82	0·67	106	−2·09

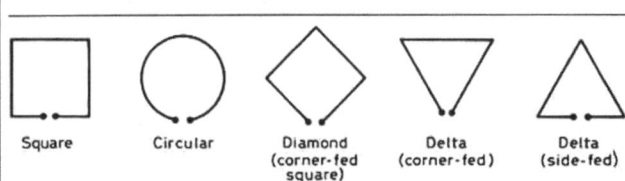

Fig 2. Five full-wave loop shapes. The delta loop is an equilateral triangle, each side one-third of a wavelength (from QST)

In general, it will be noted from Table 1 and Fig 2 that the greater the area enclosed by the loop, the greater the gain. Unfortunately, at least for hf, the large circular loop is the most difficult form to construct. Loops with a perimeter greater than 1λ will show more gain, just as a 3λ/2 dipole has gain over the conventional λ/2 dipole: Fig. 3.

It is worth stressing that the "gain" of an antenna derives from its directivity in the horizontal and vertical planes. An isotropic antenna is an imaginary antenna that radiates equal power in all directions. In practice

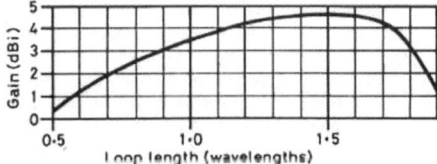

Fig 3. Computer gain versus length of a circular loop in the direction broadside to the loop. In practice, loops less than a full wave in circumference will have increased losses due to low radiation resistance

radiation patterns and "gain", as well as radiation resistance etc, are affected by height and ground conductivity, and also by nearby buildings, structures, trees etc.

The Original Zepp

Extracted from 'Technical Topics', *Radio Communication,* January 1986

The original zepp

An interesting sidelight on the once-popular (and still occasionally used) zepp antenna is shed by a letter from Alois Krischke, DT0TR/OE8AK, in *Ham Radio* November 1985, p8. He points out that the zepp antenna, so-called on account of its use on the German Zeppelin airships, is now more than 75 years old, having been patented by Dr Hans Beggerow in Germany as early as 1908. Its classical form is a full-wave, current-fed antenna with a λ/4 section folded back on itself to form a λ/2 radiator with a quarter-wave matching transformer.

The usual form in the 'thirties was to have the λ/2 radiator as a horizontal element (Fig 4(b)), but it is interesting to note that in the original patent it was shown as a vertical radiator suspended from a balloon, just like an inverted J-pole or Slim-Jim antenna: Fig 4(a). DJ8TR suggests that the design had a particular value for use in balloons and airships: the current-fed matching section was a big improvement over the dangerous practice of using a high-voltage feed in close proximity to the oxyhydrogen gas with which balloons were often filled. The zepp radiator was essentially fed from one end of the radiating section and poses the problem of a "balanced" transformer feeding an unbalanced radiator, though it has to be admitted that the system usually works quite well.

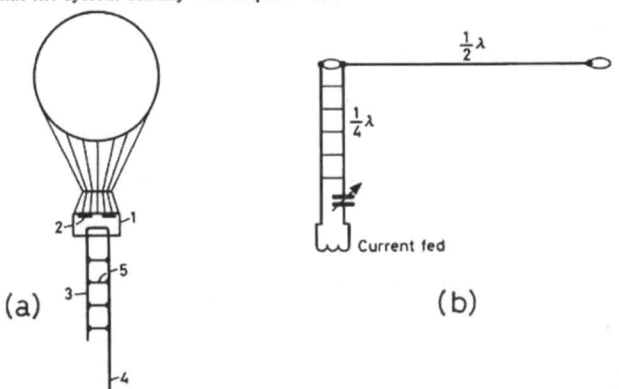

Fig 4. (a) The original zepp antenna as patented in 1909 by Dr Hans Beggerow for suspension from a balloon or airship. (b) Commonly used form of zepp in the 'thirties

Antennas where open-wire tuned feeders are connected to the centre of a dipole antenna were in the past often (and sometimes still are) incorrectly referred to as "centre-fed zepps". They constitute dipole or multi-band doublet antennas and are, as noted frequently in *TT*, highly reliable antennas. In this connection John Tuke, GM3BST writes: "I don't have room for a centre-fed doublet where I live now (I use an HF5 vertical), but in the past I have used large centre-feds, and they all seem to work well. I think dimensions are really quite unimportant unless you are stringing them between 100ft-high masts where one can get true radiation patterns because the antenna is well in the clear. But for the average location, directivity means little because of the low elevation and interference from surrounding objects. If I had room, I would be back with a centre-fed antenna with open-wire feeders—you can't beat them!"

Elements of Non-uniform Cross-section

Extracted from 'Technical Topics', *Radio Communication,* January 1986

Elements of non-uniform cross-section

Some 50 years ago mf broadcast antennas moved away from T designs supported by two high masts and tended to become mast-radiator designs. Some of the more ambitious stations used masts that tended to start thin, become wider at the centre and then taper off in the top section: rather like a squeezed diamond, though usually termed a "vertical guyed-cantilever antenna": Fig 5 (a). Alternatively tapered self-supporting towers were used.

It was left to the redoubtable Dr George Brown and Herman Gihring of RCA to show that the vertical radiation pattern of a typical 5λ/8 antenna of this type, a 500ft high installation at WCAU in Philadelphia, differed significantly from that of a 5λ/8 mast-radiator of uniform cross-section, with the result that its coverage area was well below expectations. In the course of this work the RCA engineers built an hf model antenna 7ft 10in high (1:64 scale) as a result of which the WCAU antenna was successfully modified (Fig 5 (c)). Since the results of the investigation were published in April 1935, mf tower antennas have been either structural steel towers of uniform cross-section or guyed flagpoles. The story is told in George Brown's very entertaining and outspoken autobiography *and part of which I was—recollections of a research engineer.*

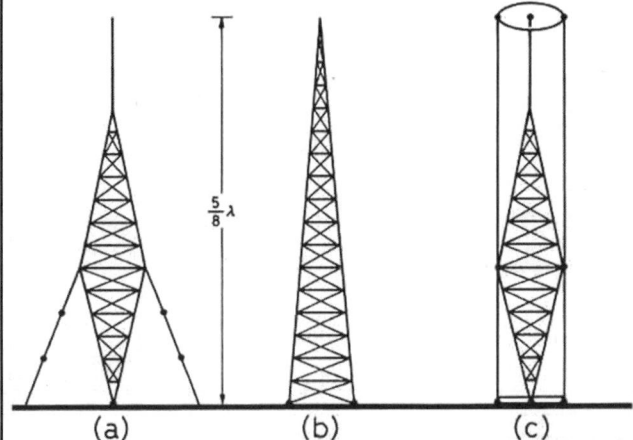

Fig 5. (a) Form of broadcast antenna tower promoted by Blaw Knox in the early 'thirties and used in a number of American stations until the problems were realized. (b) Another form of tower with non-uniform cross-section occasionally used in early 'thirties. (c) How wires were suspended at WCAU to restore proper current distribution

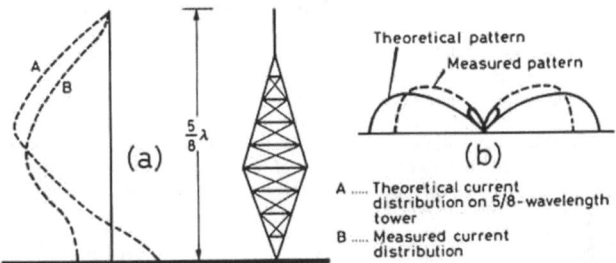

Fig 6. (a) Showing the non-sinusoidal current distribution that was found to occur with towers of non-uniform cross-section. (b) Field strength measurements made on WABC from aircraft that showed how vertical radiation pattern differed from theory

become wider at the centre and then taper off in the top section: rather like a squeezed diamond, though usually termed a "vertical guyed-cantilever antenna": Fig 5 (a). Alternatively tapered self-supporting towers were used.

It was left to the redoubtable Dr George Brown and Herman Gihring of RCA to show that the vertical radiation pattern of a typical 5λ/8 antenna of this type, a 500ft high installation at WCAU in Philadelphia, differed significantly from that of a 5λ/8 mast-radiator of uniform cross-section, with the result that its coverage area was well below expectations. In the course of this work the RCA engineers built an hf model antenna 7ft 10in high (1:64 scale) as a result of which the WCAU antenna was successfully modified (Fig 5 c). Since the results of the investigation were published in April 1935, mf tower antennas have been either structural steel towers of uniform cross-section or guyed flagpoles. The story is told in George Brown's very entertaining and outspoken autobiography *and part of which I was—recollections of a research engineer.*

I was reminded of this work by finding a detailed reference to it in the monthly "Techniques" column by Bill Orr, W6SAI, *Ham Radio* November 1985. He points out that the RCA work proved that the current distribution along a non-uniform cross-section element is non-sinusoidal, and that the theory governing the design of elements of constant cross-section does not apply. (W6SAI notes that the unexpected characteristics of a tapered element, although discovered from an hf model, escaped the notice of radio amateurs for many years.) This does not imply that an hf or vhf horizontal antenna element should never be tapered, but it does mean that you cannot use the conventional formulas for physical length etc, or assume that the vertical radiation pattern of a monopole will be exactly the same as for a uniform thin mast radiator.

W6SAI states that, for resonance, a tapered element, surprisingly, tends to be *longer* than for uniform cross-section. It was left to the late Jim Lawson, W2PV, to come up with computer programs that can be used to calculate the resonant lengths of tapered elements, but this can be done by trial-and-error provided that you recognize beforehand that its trimmed length may be longer than that given by the usual formulas.

In his refreshingly blunt manner, George Brown has written of this incident: "The vertical guyed-cantilever antenna promoted by Blaw-Knox was no doubt a mechanical marvel, but it was an outstanding example of the arrogance of ignorance. Apparently no consideration was given to the electrical performance of the structure before inflicting it upon a number of broadcasting stations who accepted the design in good faith . . . we all expended thousands of hours of engineering time to achieve a result which now comes routinely by using towers of uniform cross-section."

ANTENNA TOPICS

On the other hand, it provided an outstanding example of the value of using small model antennas at a correspondingly higher frequency, a technique that had been suggested by Professor Tykociner of the University of Illinois in 1925.

Antennas for Long, Long Waves

Extracted from 'Technical Topics', *Radio Communication,* January 1986

Antennas for long, long waves

Around the turn of the century, when radio communication was in its infancy, Marconi and his associates moved away from the ultra short wavelengths used for the earliest experiments by Heinrich Hertz, Lodge, Marconi and Chandra Bose to the lf and vlf spectrum with wavelengths of several thousand metres. Soon the "short waves" of 200m and down were declared useless and, in the USA, given to the newly-licensed "amateurs" in 1912.

To radiate signals on vlf/lf it was soon found that the more wire you could put up in the air the more power you could radiate. Antennas similar to those in Figs 7 and 8 were used. Even so the antennas were short in terms of wavelength. In the late 'twenties the most powerful transmitter in the world was Rugby Radio, GBR, on 16kHz (wavelength 18,750m) which could be relied upon to reach all parts of the globe due to the propagation of the signals via the earth–ionosphere waveguide. Such signals even

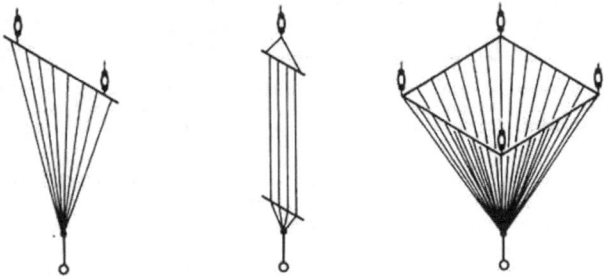

Fig 7. Fan, grid and square cone antennas popular at the turn of the century for long-wave transmissions

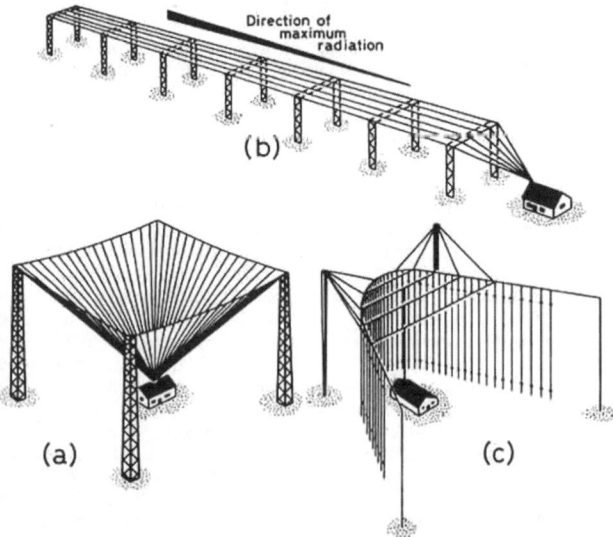

Fig 8. (a) The Poldhu antenna of 1901. (b) Inverted-L antenna of 1905. (c) Early hf directional antenna with parabolic reflector at Poldhu, 1923

penetrated some distance below the surface of the sea, permitting vlf to be used to broadcast messages to submarines.

However, vlf signals have a limited penetration in salt water, and for the past 20 years or so there has been work going on to exploit the elf spectrum below 3,000 hertz, including, for example, Project Sanguine (*TT* July, 1974) using frequencies as low as 45Hz. To radiate electromagnetic waves at such frequencies you need to send enormous power along many miles of wire—and then you are lucky to radiate, say, 1W! But the attenuation is so low (down to about 1·5dB per 1000km) that such signals can be picked up (even well below the sea's surface) on quite compact loop antennas. The snag is that you can send data only at about 1bit/s or less.

Ivan James, G5IJ, recently drew my attention to some fascinating work in northern Norway to use the hf "ionospheric heating" transmitter at Ramfjord to "modulate" the enormous natural currents in the polar electrojet. This then forms an extremely long antenna radiating up to about 1W in the frequency range 1 to 1·5kHz for hf effective radiated powers of

Fig 9. Map of Northern Scandinavia showing the location of the hf ionospheric heating transmitter at Ramfjord and the elf receiving sites at Kiruna and Lycksele

270MW (*Nature* 12 September 1985, p114 and pp155–6). This may not seem a highly efficient system but it avoids the problems of having to erect antennas up to a hundred miles or so long! The prime purpose of hf ionospheric heaters is to produce field-aligned scatter of vhf signals based on the non-linearity of the ionosphere producing cross-modulation (first observed in the 'thirties as the "Luxembourg effect"). Ionospheric heaters provide a practical way of extending the range of vhf transmissions. During the tests the hf transmitter was modulated at 1 and 1·5kHz and the ionospheric "mixing" resulted in elf signals being received at Kiruna and Lycksele: Fig 9.

Vertical Antennas and Real Earth

Extracted from 'Technical Topics', *Radio Communication,* February 1986

Vertical antennas and real earth

How many times have you read articles that start off by emphasizing that vertical antennas provide omni-directional low angle radiation and are therefore ideally suitable in the absence of a beam array for dx operation. Indeed if you listen with a good vertically-polarized antenna you can be reasonably sure of hearing any good dx that's going. It's only when, too often, the dx fails to come back to you and instead works someone with a horizontally-polarized dipole that doubts begin to creep in.

There's nothing basically wrong with a quarter-wave monopole, a half-wave vertical dipole or a $\tfrac{5}{8}\lambda$ vertical etc. With radials, earth mats or

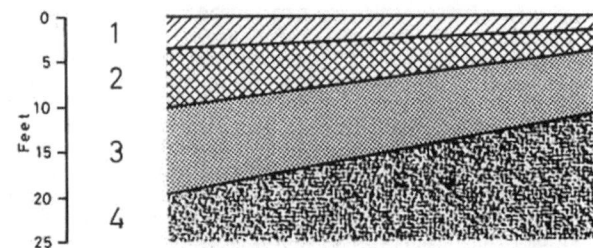

Fig 5. Typical section of earth's crust showing geological strata with several layers of different electrical conductivity. (1) Alluvial soil having relatively good conductivity (about 20×10^{-14} emu. (2) Sandy soil about 4×10^{-14} emu. (3) Chalk about 10×10^{-14} emu. (4) Young rock about 1×10^{-14}. Sea water has conductivity about 4×10^{-11}, ie about $4,000 \times 10^{-14}$. Effective conductivity depends upon depth of penetration of the earth currents and is thus a function of frequency: the higher the frequency the more the current will be concentrated in the uppermost levels. (From "The ground beneath us" G3HRH, 1966.)

counterpoises there is no reason why it should not put out most of the power you feed into it. Often the ground plane proves a really excellent medium-distance antenna and gives you the added bonus that the reports you are given are often two or three S-points above those you hand out to the stations you contact.

If you operate maritime mobile you are likely to find that a 30-ft all-band vertical really does live up to the claims of excellent dx performance. By now the penny will have dropped. With a ground plane consisting of conductive salt water you can confidently expect to achieve excellent low-angle radiation. In country areas in those parts of the UK that have good earth conductivity, or for the chap who can establish an earth mat stretching out for several wavelengths towards a desired direction, the 14/21/28MHz vertical is an excellent dx performer. See Fig 5 and Fig 6.

It is for the many of us who live in urban areas, or areas of poorish earth conductivity that the low angles are not achievable on transmission, though remaining reasonably unaffected on reception—a notable exception to the theory of reciprocity of antennas that seldom gets mentioned.

It is difficult, of course, to find out (except by frustration) the vertical

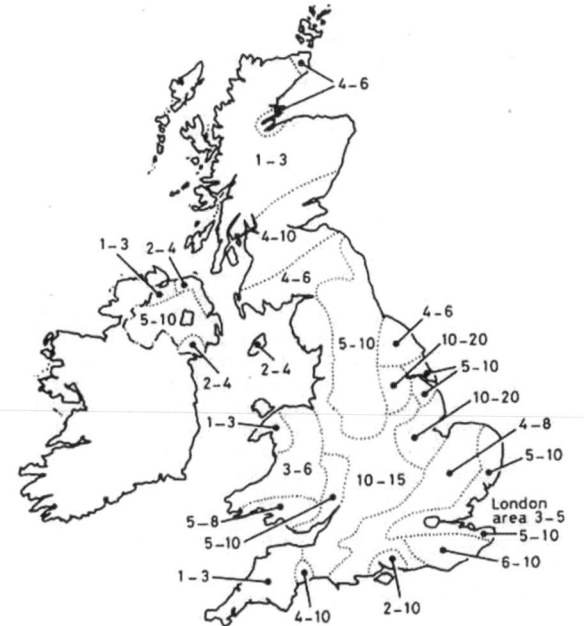

Fig 6. Rough ground conductivity map of the UK (figures quoted are for 1·5MHz). Conductivity is moderate to good in central and southeast England, poor in London, west and northwest. Urban areas tend to be of lower conductivity than farmland and rural areas

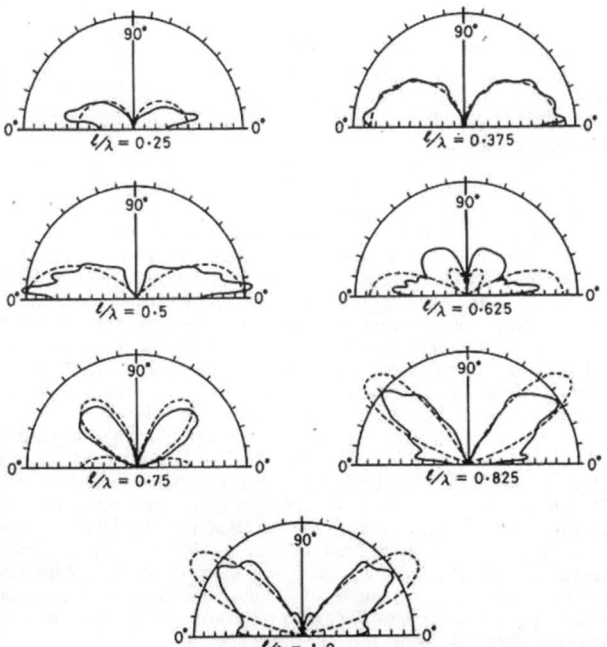

Fig 7. Vertical plane radiation characteristics of small-scale model antenna with effective groundplane

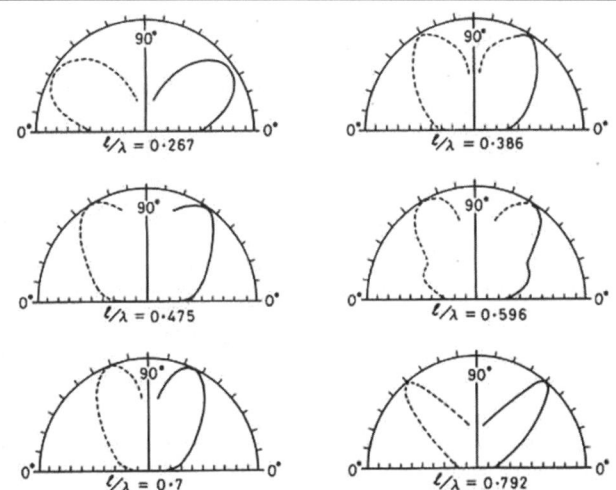

Fig 8. Vertical plane radiation characteristics of full-scale model of the biconical monopole antenna of Fig 10. Ground conductivity 8×10^{-3} mho/m. Note the much higher angle of maximum radiation

radiation pattern of an antenna above "real earth". The professionals who measure such patterns by flying aircraft around the area take care not to locate their vertical antennas for long-distance working in areas of poor conductivity or where the signals are likely to be affected by the many vertical structures that clutter our sites (trees, houses, electricity pylons etc).

On 14MHz and above, provided you can get a horizontal dipole 25ft or more above ground and in the clear, it will generally out-perform a vertical antenna unless you live in an area of extremely good earth conductivity or, conversely, in an area of extremely poor earth conductivity (where effectively the supergain "image" is not formed). This can apply also to antennas for 1·8 to 7MHz. Peter Chadwick, G3RZP has pointed out that his late father's "G8ON" antenna tends to perform better in areas of very poor conductivity, than in more conductive areas. The problem with verticals is mainly in areas of medium or poorish ground conductivity or where there are trees and other vertical structures.

Digging back in the literature to 1963, before the days of computer simulations, I found a set of diagrams relating to a broadband hf biconical

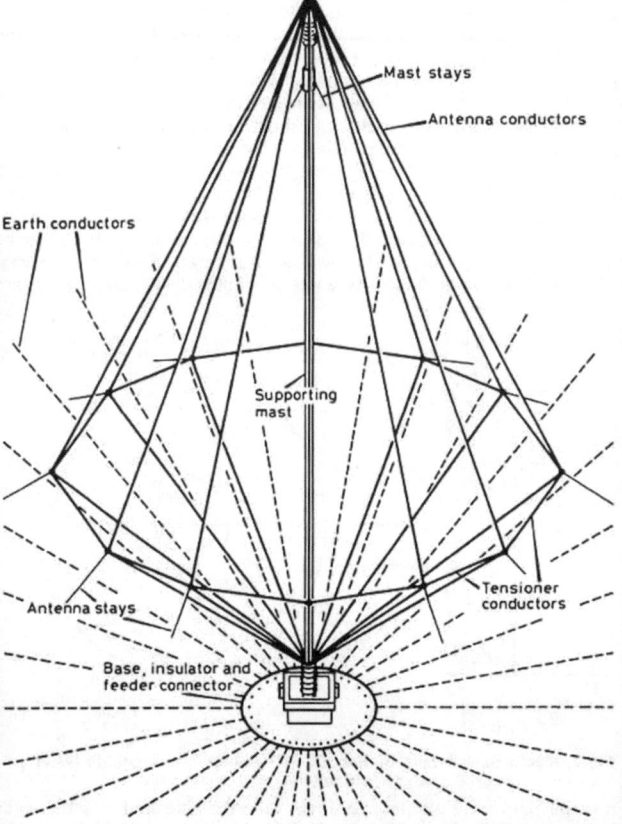

Fig 9. General arrangement of biconical monopole antenna designed for broadband operation

ANTENNA TOPICS

monopole developed for the Royal Navy that does show very clearly that low-angle radiation is not an inherent feature of vertically polarized antennas: compare Figs 7 and 8.

This design, and the associated vertical radiation patterns, come from "Some factors influencing the design of broadband hf monopole aerials" presented by H P Mason at the 1963 IEE Convention on hf communication (*IEE publication ED4*, pp114–20). This antenna was designed to cover the range 10 to 26MHz with a support pole of the order of 25ft and 36 ground radials: Fig 9.

The conductors were 7/19swg cadmium copper wire to a total semi-perimeter length of 25ft 10in, including the terminating sections. The wires were spaced equidistant around a concentric steel supporting mast of 1in radius . . . for structural reasons it was found to be of advantage to make the height of the lower cone less than the upper, in this instance the slant height ratio of the upper to lower cones was 2·6:1. Added rigidity was given to the conductors by fitting horizontal wires at the point of maximum diameter and maintaining the correct section by the use of insulated radial stays. The whole structure was supported upon a special low-loss insulator and base-plate assembly, designed to produce minimum discontinuity to the terminal characteristic. Connection to the feeder was made by means of a conductor, mounted concentrically within the insulator. The associated ground conductor system consisted of 36 equally spaced radial wires of 7/19swg. It was claimed the system could be designed to match either 50Ω (lower cone half-angle 38·5°) or 75Ω (lower cone half-angle 23·2°) to cover bandwidths of the order of 2·6:1 without any matching or tuning units with swr not exceeding 2:1. Operational designs covering also 4 to 11MHz and 2 to 5MHz were developed.

Short Backfire Antennas

Extracted from 'Technical Topics', *Radio Communication,* April 1986

Short backfire antennas

Many years ago in *TT* and *ART*, I drew attention to the backfire vhf/uhf antennas originally developed about 1960 by H W Ehrenspeck.

The basic principle was to mount a multi-element Yagi looking in the opposite direction to the target area, with the signal directed into a large plane reflector screen with a rim (rather like a large saucepan lid).

The theory was that the signals would be reflected back through the Yagi array so that the elements would, in effect, act twice. Attempts by amateurs to achieve similar results were not altogether successful.

However, one form of this antenna, known as a short backfire antenna (sba) dispensed with the line of Yagi director elements and comprised simply the large back "saucepan-lid" reflector plate (about 2λ diameter), the small front disc reflector (0·4λ diameter), plus the dipole. In this form, the backfire antenna has become well known among professional designers. The overall length of the structure was only about 0·5λ, and the structure

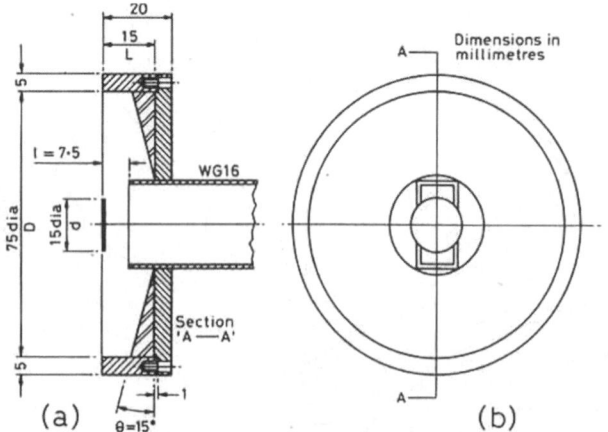

Fig 7. Mechanical details of the 10GHz rectangular waveguide (WG16)— excited short-back antenna with a conical rim

was not unlike a Cassegrain parabolic-reflector antenna but without the production difficulties of the parabolic shape. It was claimed that an sba could give up to 15dBi gain, equivalent to a much longer Yagi of over 20 elements.

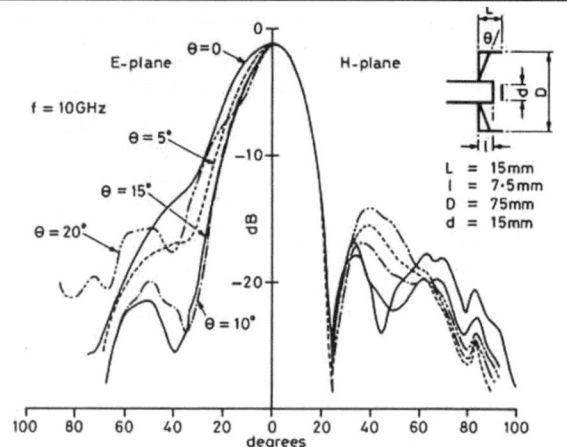

Fig 8. Measured E- and H-plane radiation patterns with conical main reflectors of slant angles (θ) of 0, 5, 10, 15 and 20°. 10 or 15° provides optimum pattern

More recently various improvements to the basic sba have been reported both at vhf/uhf (L-band) and at 10GHz (X-band). It was found (*IEEE Trans* AP-31, pp644–6) that significantly improved bandwidth could be obtained by replacing the large plane reflector by a curved surface. Later it was reported by M S Leong and P S Kooi (National University of Singapore) in *Electronics Letters*, Vol 20, No 18, 30 August 1984, pp749–51, that a conical main reflector can lead to a compact antenna having a directive gain of 16·7 to 18·3dB, sidelobe level below 13·8dB, and input vswr better than 2·5 over a 20 per cent bandwidth. The experimental model (Figs 7, 8) was, in this case, a waveguide-excited sba covering 9 to 11GHz, and thus suitable for the amateur 10GHz band. At this frequency the beamwidth and sidelobe level of the antenna was optimum at 10GHz when the slant angle of the conical surface is around 10–15°. Construction is simplified by the fact that the main reflector is a separate unit as a plane surface, with the conical surface in the form of an attachment to this main reflector plate. The sub-reflector disc is positioned by means of a thin low-permittivity plastic support. At lower frequencies the same basic technique could presumably be used with a coaxial fed dipole element rather than wave guide excited.

Antenna Basics

Extracted from 'Technical Topics', *Radio Communication,* April 1986

Antenna basics

At virtually any frequency, hf to microwave, physical size is important, and it becomes difficult to use short elements, particularly in close-spaced arrays. As pointed out recently by Clifford H Freeman (Hazeltine Corporation) in "Wideband matching of a small disk-loaded monopole" (*IEEE Trans* AP-33, No 10, October 1985) electrically small antennas pose a major problem with respect to their electrical performance. He writes: "These types of antenna have radiation resistances which decrease rapidly with size. As a consequence, tuning and matching become very difficult to compute. With these concepts in mind, the antenna efficiency deteriorates and performance parameters, such as bandwidth, tend to decrease to unacceptable levels. Therefore, designing compact antennas which are efficient in spite of their electrical size is a very difficult task."

For microwave antennas, physical size is less a problem than the need for mechanical precision. For this reason alone, an antenna having a large effective bandwidth, relatively straightforward mechanics, and without the difficult doubly-curved parabolic shape, should prove attractive. The parabolic dish has many good points, including the potential of very high gain. The Yagi array gives excellent gain in relation to its size, but is frequency sensitive and by no means fool-proof in practice. With care, stacked Yagis can give even higher gain, though one should not expect that, for example, four stacked similar arrays will give more than some 5dB extra gain, and often less, rather than the theoretical 6dB.

There is, indeed, often so great a difference between free-space theory and practice when it comes to questions of antenna characteristics, that many amateurs have come to rely on commercial designs even though this is still no guarantee that their performance will meet fully the claims made for them. It is a pity that no matter how logical technically, the 50MHz power limits have been based on effective radiated power (erp), an entity that none of us can measure directly. I have for many years argued that even professional broadcasters are stretching credibility to the limit by listing transmitter powers in terms of kilowatts erp or emrp (effective monopole radiated power) to three places of decimals. The answer I am usually given is that this is the figure that comes out of the computer based on the requisite coverage area!

current nodes occur in their centres. This increases the effective height, which may often be increased still further by taking advantage of smaller size and lower windage.

"Returning to the January *TT*, I am quite happy with Table 1, less so with Fig 3 in view of the misleading conclusions which appear to have been drawn from it. It may be no more than a coincidence that the gain for $3\lambda/2$ *exactly* equals the stacking gain for dipoles spaced by the width of a $3\lambda/2$ square loop, and it may be that the circular shape does provide extra gain equal to the 'mode loss'. Application of my square-counting methods to circular loops is extremely laborious and I have not attempted it."

Loops and Dipoles

Extracted from 'Technical Topics',
Radio Communication, April 1986

Increasing Antenna Bandwidth

Extracted from 'Technical Topics',
Radio Communication, June 1986

Loops and dipoles
A short note in January *TT* (p 35) commented on loop and dipole antennas from a *QST* article by J L Dietrich, WA0RDX. This has prompted Les Moxon, G6XN, to comment as follows, as he feels that readers could have been misled into attempting to put up some enormous loops as soon as the weather turned more spring-like.

"It is good to come across some recognition at last for the fact that 14MHz (1λ) quad loops work well on 21MHz. Unfortunately the claims made for larger loops generally based on computer studies appear to go well beyond the no-penalty multiband operation of loops featured hitherto.

"On theoretical grounds, as well as practical experience over many years covering this particular area, I find there is no substance in the suggestion that larger loops provide appreciably more gain or smaller loops less gain, nor is there any validity in the comparison, in this respect, with dipoles—though these do not show any significant gain variation with size either. The reference to a $3\lambda/2$ dipole is presumably a misprint for $3\lambda/4$, in which case the gain is 0·6dB over a λ/2 dipole, or 1dB over a very short dipole.

"What appears to have been overlooked is the strong vertically-polarized signal in the plane of the loop which results when the loop size is increased. For a $3\lambda/2$ loop, ignoring ground effects, we have the following field strength ratios:

$$\frac{\text{vertical in plane of loop}}{\text{horizontal at right angles}} = \begin{array}{l} 0\cdot 79 \text{ (square loop)} \\ 0\cdot 61 \text{ (delta loop)} \end{array}$$

"This does not help with the QRM situation, but fortunately there is less energy wasted in the unwanted mode than these figures might suggest, since it is produced by an "8JK-pair" having a gain of 3 to 4dB. On this basis the losses due to the unwanted mode come to 1·17dB and 0·67dB respectively, and these must be deducted from the 'stacking gain' obtained by considering the loops as a pair of dipoles having the appropriate spacing. Another small correction arises because the length (or width) of the antenna affects the width of the forward lobe; this is the 'short dipole' effect mentioned above about which there is little published information. I have derived some very rough estimates by finding the centres of gravity of the current distribution of each half of the radiator and then treating it as a colinear pair having very close spacing. This can be done by using the mutual impedance data available in the handbooks. This gives a somewhat too low figure in the case of a λ/2 dipole (0·25 instead of 0·4dB) but this is to be expected in view of the unsymmetrical nature of a λ/4 current distribution, and the extra weight which should be given to contributions from near the ends. On this basis I feel that the method is basically sound and the other corrections unlikely to be in error by more than 0·1dB. This results in Table 2.

Table 2. Dipole and loop performance

Type of element	Stacking gain (dB)	Unwanted mode loss (dB)	"Length" correction (dB)	Gain (dB) dBd	dBi
λ/2 dipole	—	—	—	0	2·15
λ/4 dipole, end-loaded*	—	Up to 0·2	−0·25	−0·45	1·7
1λ square loop	1·12	Very small	−0·32	0·8	2·95
3λ/2 square loop	2·5	1·17	−0·1	1·25	3·4
3λ delta loop	0·75	0·67	0	0·08	2·23
3λ/4 delta loop	0	0 (approx)	−0·25	−0·25	1·9

*eg, bent ends as in VK2ABQ antenna.
Note: Stacking gain for the 3λ/2 square loop assumes equal currents in the "dipoles". The actual ratio is 0·67 but it is very difficult to allow for this. The true gain figure could be as low as 3dBi.

"Note that the differences are in the main trivial, and single-element gain figures tend to disappear in the case of arrays, in line with normal stacking principles. In practice one is much better off with the *smaller* loops, since one can prevent sides or lower portions from radiating by arranging that

Increasing antenna bandwidth
As we have noted before, the wider 3·5MHz band (3,500 to 4,000kHz) available in some regions has encouraged the development of techniques that extend the bandwidth over which a dipole element and coaxial cable feeder results in an swr of less than, say, 2:1. A wire element will normally not do this over more than five per cent of its resonant frequency. Fatter elements, including the folded dipole element, have a lower *Q* and hence rather greater bandwidth. Bent and loaded elements tend to have higher *Q* and hence less bandwidth for a given swr ratio.

Bill McLeod, VK3MI, has tackled this problem in a novel way. In a recent article "Mis-matching for extended bandwidth", *Amateur Radio (VK)* April 1986, pp18–9, he shows how by the use of a quarter-wave impedance transformer and a compensating capacitance (which can be constructed from a length of feeder), an antenna element that is deliberately slightly mismatched at its resonate frequency can provide an extended bandwidth over which the swr remains below 2:1. Instead of about five per cent, which is, say, 180kHz at 3,600kHz with a conventional dipole, this technique can result in better than 10 per cent bandwidth for an swr of less than 2:1. This would enable a Region 1 operator to cover the entire 3·5MHz band with a wire dipole without an atu, yet without exceeding an swr of 2:1.

In practice, VK3MI has taken this technique to its extreme by using it in connection also with a "thick" dipole element made from a 15cm (6in)-wide ribbon of hot-dip galvanized wire mesh. This has a normal low-swr bandwidth of 300kHz, but his mis-matching technique extends this to 580kHz, thus covering the whole of the Region 2 and Region 3 band. To quote the introductory paragraphs to his article:

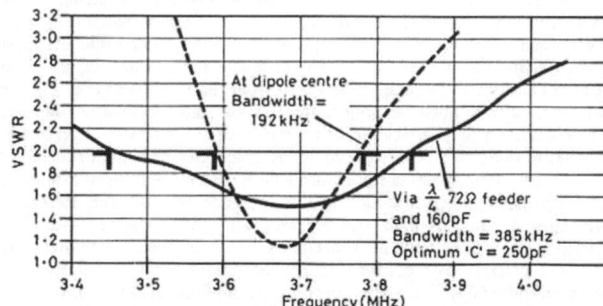

Fig 5. Showing how VK3MI finds that the bandwidth of a dipole can be increased by deliberately mis-matching a 50Ω dipole by feeding it with 72Ω cable and then providing capacitance compensation. In the example shown, the minimum vswr is about 1·5:1 but the bandwidth for which the vswr remains below 2:1 is increased from 192kHz to 385kHz

"The finicky transmitter that requires no greater than a 2:1 vswr from its nominal 50Ω implies that any load impedance from 25 to 100Ω would be satisfactory. There, matching it to a 50Ω load (in the conventional manner), that rises in a complex manner on either side of resonance, allows only half of the available range to be used.

"*Why not match it to 25Ω at antenna resonance for a rising characteristic, or alternatively to 100Ω with an inverted impedance characteristic?* Then, look at the hf coaxial feeder which is almost never a 'flat' 50Ω . . . The antenna, particularly for 3·5MHz, is usually a half-wave dipole of low height (10m or less), with a bandwidth around five per cent of resonant frequency (for 2:1 vswr), and a mid-band impedance about 55Ω. Only at the mid-band frequencies can a random length of 50Ω cable be successful.

"Now consider the quarter-wave transformer: *(a)* it transforms the load

ANTENNA TOPICS

impedance across its Zo by the square of the ratio between the two; (b) it inverts the load impedance characteristic over the bandwidth from a u shape to an n shape; (c) it transposes inductive reactance to capacitive reactance and vice versa; and (d) only half of the total load/source vswr shows at each end (more accurately the root of the ratio).

"With an electrical quarter-wavelength of 72Ω coaxial cable (eg UR70) between the element and the transmitter, a 55Ω element impedance can be inverted and transformed for the transmitter to "see" 94Ω at mid-band, falling away each side down through the nominal transmitter output impedance of 50Ω for the bandwidth to increase by a useful factor of 1·5. This can be further increased to a factor of 2 by compensating the capacitance mis-match at the antenna junction: Fig 5.

"The compensation required for the quoted example of 55/72Ω is 300pF at 3·65MHz, consisting of the difference between the total capacitance of the quarter wavelength of cable actually used (920pF for UR70 at 69pF/m), and that for a similar notional cable matching the antenna (1,220pF for 55Ω). This value is not critical and can be varied by 30 per cent or more to adjust the lowest vswr point two or three per cent for convenient system corrections.

"The capacitor can consist of an open stub of the same cable, cut for the required capacitance (eg 4·5m of UR70 taped to the feeder, or a fixed mica capacitor of suitable voltage rating (250V or higher), depending on arrangements for waterproofing at the element feedpoint.

"For those with a transmitter sited more than 13m from the antenna feedpoint, there are two alternatives. One is to use a three-quarter wavelength of 72Ω cable, with any excess stored in the rafters or attic. The other is to extend the antenna centre for the first quarter-wave using a matching cable (eg UR43 52Ω cable), then transform with a further quarterwave of 37Ω cable."

Compact Transmitting Loop Antennas

Extracted from 'Technical Topics', *Radio Communication,* June 1986

Compact transmitting loop antennas

From time to time, ever since the publication in the mid-'sixties of the details of an octagonal loop antenna made up from six straight 5ft tubes and developed by the US Army Limited War Laboratory (see most editions of *ART*), references have been made in *TT* to electrically-small transmitting loops both for amateur and professional radio communications. The key features are that the loop *must* have extremely low ohmic rf impedance and that there must be no undue losses in the matching arrangements. These basic essentials point to the use of copper- or even silver-plated tubing of several inches diameter for the loop—although the outer braid of good quality 0·5in coaxial cable has been used with reasonable success—and the use of a capacitive matching network rather than having any coils in the matching unit. It must be appreciated that a small loop used on say, 3·5MHz is likely to have a radiation resistance of only a tiny fraction of 1Ω, and that in these circumstances ohmic losses assume great importance.

In *TT* July 1984, p580, a note from Ron Rew, G3HAZ, drew attention to a professional pedestal-mounted loop made by Antenna Research Associates. It was 5ft high and 7ft wide and had a claimed radiation efficiency of 98 per cent at 14MHz. A basically similar product was marketed several years before this by Technology for Communications International (TCI) for such purposes as diplomatic communications networks operated from embassies etc. These antennas used remote-controlled motorized vacuum-type capacitors to tune the loop to the operating frequency, offering a tuning range of several octaves.

It was pointed out that although manufacturers may claim a "directive gain" of around 5dBi, this should not be confused with "power gain"—particularly at the lower end of the tuning range where the radiation efficiency inevitably drops due to the progressive reduction of radiation resistance as the loop becomes increasingly small in relation to the wavelength.

The original claim for the US military loop was that it could perform almost as well as a dipole at a height of 40ft. It is a pity that some articles in amateur radio journals have made excessive claims based on the theoretical gain at low vertical radiation angles of short vertically-polarized antennas over perfect earth. Such claims lead only to disappointment and ultimate rejection of the whole concept. Nevertheless, a small transmitting loop, provided the losses can be kept low, does offer scope for use in some awkward locations. It is, for example, well suited for use in buildings having a small flat roof that would not permit the erection of a conventional dipole.

A contribution to this technique stems from J H Dunlavy, who obtained a US Patent 3,588,905 (28 June 1971), for a "wide range tunable transmitting antenna" based on a configuration that has become known as a "miniloop". In this antenna an electrically small, capacitively-tuned outer loop is excited by an even smaller inner loop that can be fed directly by the coaxial cable feeder. A technique that also forms the basis of A R Carr's US Patent 4,433,336 of 21 February, 1984 for a "three-element antenna".

Fig 6 shows the "miniloop" principle, together with equivalent circuits for both inductively-fed and directly-fed loops. In effect, inductive feeding of a high-Q resonant loop antenna is simply a version of the once popular "link coupling" between resonant circuits with the aid of a low-impedance line.

Operation and equivalent circuits are discussed in a paper by Donald E Barrick (Ocean Surface Research) in *IEEE Transactions on Antennas & Propagation*, Vol AP-34, No 1, January 1986, pp111–4. Although his paper points out that this technique is not suitable for hf radars designed to measure ocean currents and waves, since the Q is so high that it stretches and delays short pulses, he does point out its advantages over systems using the outer loop alone, fed directly, for communications applications. He writes:

"It's main features (and differences in operation from the outer loop fed along) are: (*1*) the input resistance to the inner loop can be large (eg 50Ω), although the input (radiation) resistance when the outer loop alone is fed

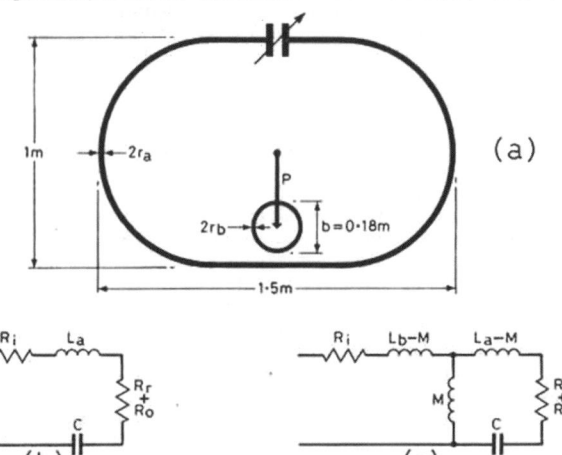

Fig 6. (a) Configuration of a typical miniloop structure designed as a transmitting loop from 3 to 24MHz. The outer loop is capacitively tuned to the frequency of operation. In this example the outer loop tubing has a radius of 0·04m and the coupling loop radius 0·006m, using copper tubing for both loops. (b) shows the equivalent circuit for an outer loop fed directly, while (c) represents the miniloop system with the inner loop fed and inductively coupled to the outer loop; in both cases, Ri represents the internal resistances of the source and transmission line

is generally a fraction of an ohm (decreasing as f_o^{-4}; hence feeding is easier for the miniloop; and (*2*) a fairly good match to the line can be maintained over nearly a decade bandwidth as long as the outer loop is tuned to the desired operating frequency and is electrically small at the upper end of the band."

Inductive coupling to a resonant loop was also used in the professional Swedish design that was tested initially on the 3·5, 7 and 14MHz amateur bands and described at an IERE conference in 1981 (*TT* September 1981, p821). This comprised a three-turn silver-plated radiating square loop with 500mm sides and using a ferrite balun to match a 52Ω coaxial cable to a 200Ω feedpoint of the coupling loop.

There is no longer any doubt that compact hf transmitting loops can be made to work efficiently provided that great care is taken to minimize losses and to tune it accurately to the operating frequency.

1980 - 1989

HF Active Receiving Loop Antenna

Extracted from 'Technical Topics',
Radio Communication, June 1986

HF active receiving loop antenna

While transmitting loops are still unfamiliar and rather strange beasts, simple loop receiving antennas date back to the earliest days. However, they are coming back into favour as the basic element of compact "active" antennas. John Hawes, G4UAZ, has drawn my attention to a design for a matching amplifier that he published in the *CARA Newsletter* (December 1984), of the Cheltenham Amateur Radio Association. He writes:

"Several active antennas have already been featured in *TT*, but I believe mine has the virtue of great simplicity yet seems to have good signal-handling capabilities, despite being essentially a broadband, untuned antenna."

The following notes are extracted from the original article:

"Small antennas (compared with the wavelength) are dogged with the problem of low radiation resistance. This means that an incoming signal must be transformed to the impedance of the receiver input with low loss. Conventionally this implies a narrow bandwidth, and matching difficulties. An answer is the so-called 'active' antenna with a small passive antenna element directly coupled to an impedance-transforming amplifier. Most commercial models use a small rod element and high input-impedance amplifier. Bipolar transistors do not lend themselves to this type of amplifier, and even fet devices have a large input capacitance.

"It seems more feasible to use a small loop antenna with a low input impedance. Such systems have been described before in *TT* but I wanted a simple amplifier that could be built in an evening or two: see Fig 7. I used BFW17A transistors, but any general-purpose rf type should work.

"The design uses a push-pull (long-tailed pair) configuration, presenting a balanced input to the loop. Shunt voltage-feedback is used to reduce the input impedance as well as to linearize the amplifier. Used with a square loop with 2m sides made from 16swg enamelled copper wire, it received

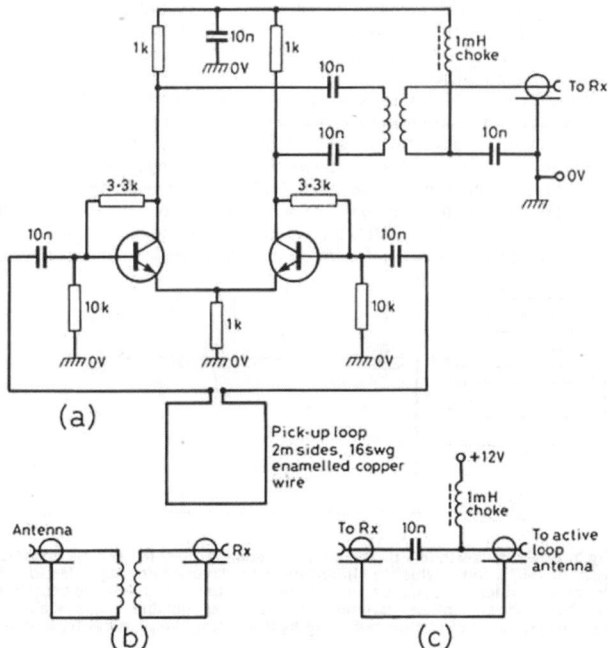

Fig 7. G4UAZ's active loop receiving antenna for use throughout the hf range. (b) Broadband toroidal coupling coil at receiver input. (c) Method of feeding active antenna over the coaxial cable transmission line

signals on 7MHz equivalent to my full-sized G5RV (with loop in vertical plane), and works over the full hf range. My amplifier was built on Veroboard with "ugly" wiring. The only difficult component is the 1:1 rf transformer for which I used a toroidal core from the junk box. Several turns of twisted bifilar wire were wound on the core, and checked as follows: First, one of the windings should be wired across the input of a receiver tuned to the lowest band of interest. The other winding must be open-circuit, and little reduction in signal should be noted provided the primary inductance is adequate. Then wire in receiver as in Fig 7(b). Before trying the amplifier, a dc check is worthwhile, about 10·5V on the collectors

and about 3V on emitters should be found with a 12V supply. I power my amplifier through the coaxial feeder with the circuit of Fig 7(c), but if you do not wish to spend money on 1mH chokes, running a separate supply wire would be entirely satisfactory. It makes an interesting constructional project."

Top Band Antenna and ATU

Extracted from 'Technical Topics',
Radio Communication, June 1986

Top band antenna and atu

Dr Constantion Feruglio, IV3VS, uses a "double Zepp" (centre-fed dipole with balanced 300Ω ribbon feeder) plus atu. This works well on 3·5 to 28MHz, with the antenna having a horizontal span of 40m. However, he found that results were "only middling" on 1·8MHz, and has lengthened the top section by folding in extra wire as shown in Fig 8(b). While the folding results in a lower radiation resistance than had the "top" being in a straight line, the antenna works reasonably well on all bands from 1·8 to 30MHz and permits working "all over Europe" on 1·8MHz. Marconi "end-fed" antennas are ruled out on the grounds of tvi, IV3VS being a "third-floor" dweller.

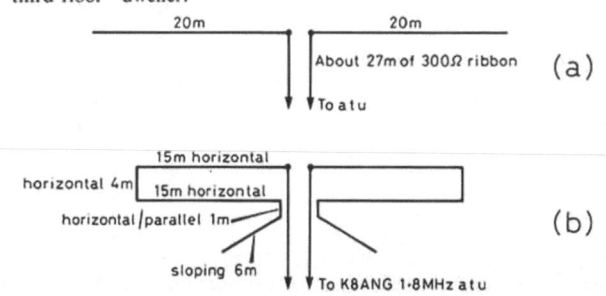

Fig. 8. (a) Centre-fed dipole as used by IV3VS but providing only marginal results on 1·8MHz. (b) Additional wire loading to improve results on 1·8MHz

As a flexible 1·8MHz atu he uses an arrangement described by John Skubick, K8ANG, in *73 Magazine* (date unknown): Fig 9(b). This is a variation of an atu that similarly delivers a balanced output based on pi-networks that has previously been described in *TT* and other RSGB publications (I used this arrangement for a number of years on 14 and 21MHz for feeding a folded dipole made from 300Ω line): Fig 9(a).

IV3VS constructed L1 and L2 using two perspex (lucite) pipes. L2 comprises 50 plus 50 turns on 56mm diameter pipe using 1mm diameter

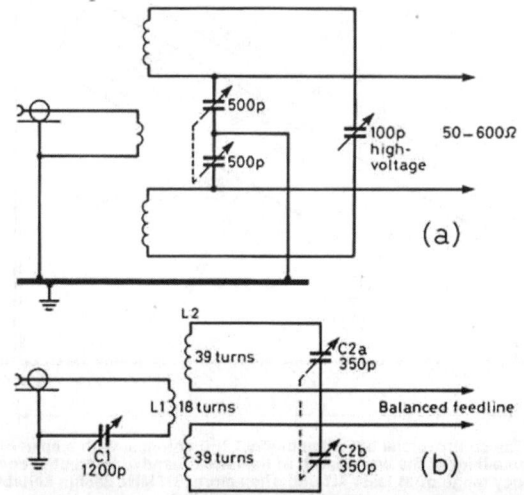

Fig. 9. Antenna matching units that provide balanced output suitable for open-wire or 300Ω balanced feeders. (a) System used at G3VA for 14 and 21MHz for a number of years. (b) The K8ANG arrangement used by IV3VS and suitable for 1·8MHz

enamelled copper wire, winding length about 110 plus 110mm. L1 on 70mm diameter pipe comprises 20 turns of 1mm diameter enamelled copper wire,

ANTENNA TOPICS

winding length 50mm and positioned over the centre of L2. C1 can be made from a three-section broadcast-type ganged capacitor. K8ANG advises not to earth any portion of L2 or C2 but leave them "floating" above earth on insulators.

T2FD Antenna Still Has Supporters

Extracted from 'Technical Topics', *Radio Communication,* July 1986

T2FD antenna still has supporters

One of the very first unconventional and "experimental" antennas ever to be described in *TT* more than 25 years ago was the so-called "T2FD" derived from "terminated titled folded dipole", and the basic details have appeared in every edition of *ART*, although usually accompanied by a warning that its performance as an aperiodic multiband antenna may leave something to be desired, particularly on some bands where an appreciable proportion of the transmitter output power is wasted in the "terminating" resistor.

This antenna stemmed from a development by the US Navy as a technique for broadening the bandwidth of a folded dipole to a reasonable degree. However, it was, and still is, being publicized in the amateur radio journals as suitable for use on all bands from 3·5 to 28MHz.

Since the terminating resistor is usually specified as having a wattage for cw of about one-third or one-quarter of the input power of the transmitter, this suggests that, at least on some frequencies, a very large amount of power is being dissipated in the resistor. Unlike the terminating resistors used in rhombics, long-wire vee beams, etc. there is no compensating directivity gain. *Ipso facto,* there must be frequencies on which the aperiodic T2FD radiates a lot less power than a resonant dipole.

Having said that, one has to admit that the T2FD has always found supporters who consider that the advantages of omni-directional, multiband, mixed (slant) polarization etc compensates for the lower efficiency on some bands. John Heys, G3BDQ, resurrected the design in *Ham Radio Today* (June 1985). It has also won the support of several members of the West Kent Amateur Radio Society, as reported in their *Update* newsletter of 24 January, 1986 by Alex Korda, G4FDC: Fig 6.

The feedpoint impedance of a T2FD is considered as roughly 300Ω, and the antenna can simply be fed directly with any length of Ω balanced feeder or from 50Ω coaxial cable via a 6:1 balun or with a 4:1 balun plus transmission-line transformer, Fig 7. It is claimed that a low vswr can be achieved (with suitable atud), over at least a 4:1 frequency range. Undoubtedly, with a good site and with the element sloping at about 20° to 40° to the horizontal, then the 2 to 3dB of power that may be lost in the

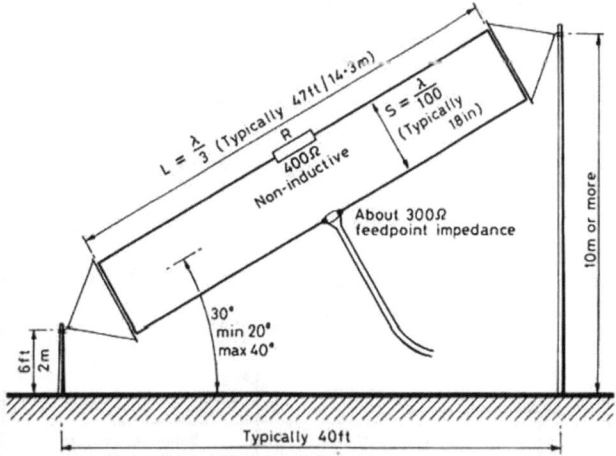

Fig 6. The controversial but often useful T2FD antenna. With a span of only about one-third of the wavelength of the lowest band of interest, it covers a frequency range of at least 4:1 and often more (3·5MHz design suitable for up to 14 or even 28Mhz)

non-inductive resistor (several resistors in parallel can give the necessary wattage) is not a serious drawback, though it always goes against the grain to develop expensive rf only to lose it all in a resistor, though there are other quite well-respected antennas where it is not unusual to have an efficiency of a similar order.

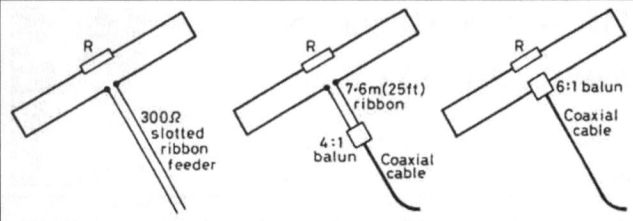

Fig 7. Some methods of feeding the T2FD antenna which has a feedpoint impedance of roughly 300Ω

Back-window VHF Transmitting Antennas

Extracted from 'Technical Topics', *Radio Communication,* September 1986

Back-window vhf transmitting antennas

From an amateur radio viewpoint, one of the most practical papers was that by Dr J D Last, GW3MZY, and B Easter of UCNW and the associated "Industrial Development Bangor Ltd" on "Broadcast reception and mobile radio communication using vehicle rear-window heater aerials". Their system is currently being used by several vehicle manufacturers as broadcast (lf/mf/vhf) receiving antennas (see *Electronics & Wireless World* February 1985, pp64–67): Figs 1 and 2. Recent work has shown, however, that the technique can also be used for two-way vhf mobile radio, and it has been tested by the Essex Police. It has also been used successfully on 145MHz. Although window-heater antennas are not intended to outperform quarter-wave roof-mounted whips, they overcome the expense of fitting, the need for holes in the bodywork, the vulnerability to car-washes and vandals, aerodynamic drag etc. They can provide entirely satisfactory broadcast receiving antennas, provided they are not too close to the "rubber" (carbon-loaded plastic) flexible glass-retaining mouldings used on many vehicles.

It has been found that the characteristics of a typical window demister heater used as a transmitting antenna can be affected by the choice of the terminal configuration by which the heater supply and rf power are connected. Compared to broadcast reception, better impedance matching is needed at the operating frequency. It is also usually necessary to achieve nominally vertical polarization. For the police radio experiments (82 to 83MHz transmit, 97 to 100MHz receive) the natural choice is to connect the two heater terminals in parallel (at rf) and to couple an unbalanced feed

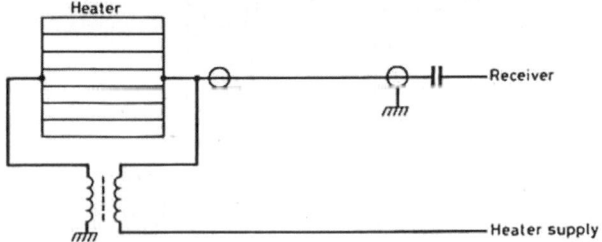

Fig 1. Basic back-window heater antenna isolated from the vehicle chassis by an isolating choke which is bifilar-wound to eliminate dc magnetization of the core. Problems arose on some vehicles due to the capacitance coupling to the "rubber" (often carbon-loaded plastic) flexible glass-retaining mouldings, but this is being overcome by increasing the physical separation

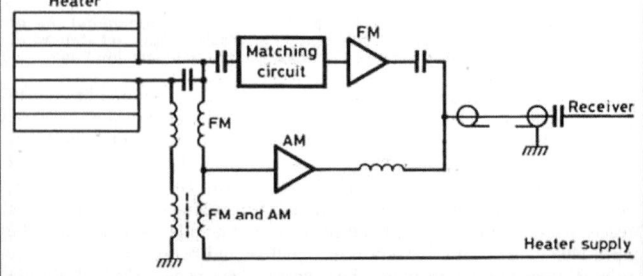

Fig 2. Arrangement for a combined lf/mf and vhf/fm antenna

between this joint and the nearby metalwork. The structure is series resonant within the required frequency range, with a Q-factor of about 30. In this case, because of the separation between transmit and receive frequencies, a single matching network is not possible and relay switching of two matching networks was needed (this would not be the case for 145MHz). A vswr of better than 1·2:1 was achieved on transmission, but it was first necessary to remove the standard tailgate wiper arm which proved to have an unfortunate resonance, replacing a part of the arm assembly with a non-conductive component. The local field from an 18W transmitter at 83MHz did not present a safety hazard to passengers in the rear seat.

The authors conclude that the performance of a heater antenna, for pure vertical polarization, is (as might be expected) inferior to that of a centrally-mounted whip antenna. However, its superior performance for horizontal polarization strongly suggests that in many situations, especially where propagation is strongly perturbed and the polarization is altered, the overall performance will often be comparable, particularly in urban areas. Performance at 145MHz is substantially similar to that achieved on the police frequencies.

the 144MHz band, but this is not considered a serious problem since it is possible to slightly redesign the antenna by scaling the dimensions. The main problem that emerged was that maximum radiation is at 22° above the horizontal, whereas it is usually desirable for a broadcast antenna to radiate most energy at 0° or even at a slight downward tilt. They retained the basic shape of the antenna but varied the place of the feedpoint, the leg distance and the place and the length of the gap.

The paper presents theoretical and experimental results of a number of variations of these dimensions, aiming at achieving maximum horizontal radiation while keeping the input impedance close to 50Ω.

Their final choice was based on that suitable for an antenna sited near a hill in the city. The actual dimensions for 101·8MHz are as follows: height 2·21m; leg distance 0·06m; height of gap (beginning) 1·10m; height of gap (ending) 1·25m; height of the feedpoints 0·37m; radius of wire 0·004m.

From an amateur viewpoint, the slight upward tilt would not be a disadvantage for some applications, but, for example, for a repeater station on a hill, the modified radiation pattern of the "msj" would be an advantage. The authors conclude: "We believe that with larger leg distance the radiation pattern will become directional in the horizontal plane." This will give some new ideas about the use of the msj as an element in directive arrays.

The 'MSJ' Antenna

Extracted from 'Technical Topics',
Radio Communication, September 1986

The "msj" antenna
Most of the antenna technology used by radio amateurs is derived from professional research and development, some of it stretching back to the early days of hf radio. It is unusual to find a design presented as suitable for professional local broadcasting or communications that stems directly from a design originally developed for use on the amateur bands.

However, in *IEEE Transactions on Broadcasting* (Vol BC-32, No 1, March 1986) E Demacopoulos and P Zimourtopoulos, of the University of Thrace, and J N Sahalos of the University of Thessaloniki, Greece, present a detailed description and analysis of a vertically-polarized "msj" antenna as developed for use at a local 101·8MHz experimental vhf/fm broadcast station. The "msj" turns out to stand for "modified slim jim" and the design is based with only minor modifications on the 144MHz "slim jim" (*j*-type *i*ntegrated *m*atching stub) antenna first described by F C Judd, G2BCX in *Practical Wireless* April 1978, pp899-901. It is pointed out that this antenna well meets the needs of broadcasters in offering omni-directional radiation concentrated in the horizontal plane, wide usable bandwidth and impedance stability.

The dimensions and geometry of the original Slim Jim (Fig 6) were first analysed theoretically using the so-called "method of moments". This showed that the antenna has an impedance of 50Ω at 155MHz and not in

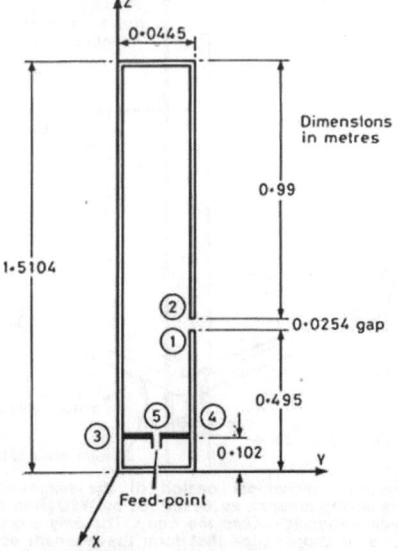

Fig 6. Dimensions of the original "Slim Jim" 145MHz antenna described by Fred Judd, G2BCX, in *Practical Wireless* in 1978 and now proposed in a slightly modified form as a Band 2 broadcast antenna

More on the T2FD

Extracted from 'Technical Topics',
Radio Communication, September 1986

More on the T2FD
The Revd John Marshall, G3RKH, draws attention to an article "More on the T2FD" which appeared in *CQ* (February 1953) reprinted in *CQ Antenna Roundup 1963*. This included a 600Ω, open-wire version of the T2FD (*TT* July 1986) and some useful general design principles:
(1) Length of each leg should be $(50,000/f \times 3·28)$ft where f is the lowest frequency of operation in kilohertz.
(2) Spacing is $(3000/f \times 3·28)$ft.
(3) Angle of slope is about 30°.
(4) Terminating resistor should be non-inductive and rated at 35 per cent of dc input power (Note that this would have been for a.m operation, and a lower value would suffice for other modes—*G3VA*).
(5) The resistor value is quite critical: 390Ω for 300Ω feeder; 500Ω for 450Ω feeder; 650Ω for 600Ω feeder.
(6) If other than a non-inductive resistor is used, an atu will be necessary.

I must admit to a continued mistrust of an antenna system in which up to about 50 per cent of the rf power fed to it ends up (on some bands) in that non-inductive resistor. With open-wire feeder and a good atu, I strongly suspect that you could radiate equally effectively without there being any resistor in place, though this could result in what would amount to a voltage-fed arrangement on some bands. It must also be admitted that radiating half of your power effectively on a convenient multiband system that can be implemented at low cost is quite likely to result in a well-satisfied operator!

Roach Pole plus
Sailboard Mast Vertical

Extracted from 'Technical Topics',
Radio Communication, September 1986

Roach pole plus sailboard mast vertical
A D Macfadyen, G3ZHZ, has been making good use of a multiband Windom (perhaps more correctly a variation of the VS1AA). This uses 300Ω ribbon feeder at roughly one-third the distance from one end (in practice a 140ft top, fed 44ft 5in from the end): Fig 7. This antenna, fed at the shack end through a 1:4 step-up balun, provides an swr of roughly 2:1 on most bands, with G3ZHZ using a transmatch to reduce the swr to near unity swr at the transmitter output. This works well on all pre-WARC

ANTENNA TOPICS

bands from 1·8 to 28MHz.

Later, after reading the various notes in *TT* on the use of roach poles, he obtained one of these plus, from the local sailboard stockist, a *free* broken sailboard mast, 4·5m long. He found this could be easily repaired, at least for his purpose, with resin and glass-fibre tape. Among the masts from which he could choose were some made of carbon fibre. Again, recalling earlier *TT* notes, these were rejected. All the masts had carbon fibre

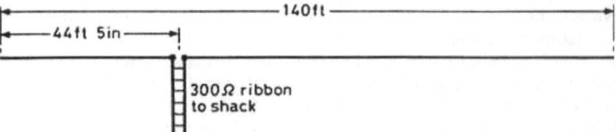

Fig 7. G3ZHZ's horizontal multi-band Windom with 300Ω transmission line

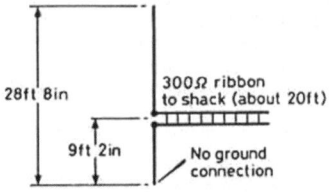

Fig 8. Vertical quarter-sized version of the 300Ω wire Windom used as a vertical dipole antenna by using a roach pole mounted atop of a repaired sailboard mast to provide an effective 33ft-high support. Resonate to 14·1MHz using gdo at shack end of feeder

reinforcement in the form of four thin strips running longitudinally along the mast. However, no problems have arisen in practice from these thin strips. The top of the sailboard mast fits neatly into the butt end of the roach pole, giving a strong self-supporting "whip" some 33ft long. G3ZHZ mounted this on tabernacles to facilitate easy raising and lowering.

After some experimentation he developed a quarter-sized version of his multiband Windom. Final dimensions, following work with a gdo and swr meter, were as shown in Fig 8. The antenna element comprises switchgear cable to BS6231, type BU, 1/1·78mm (2·5mm²). This is approximately 15swg copper wire pvc sheathed and is available from electrical wholesalers. Fed via the 4:1 balun, the swr is about 1·1:1 over most of 14MHz and about 2·5:1 on 28MHz.

G3ZHZ reports that this antenna works excellently on 14 and 28MHz. With careful adjustment of the atu, good results can be achieved on 7MHz. 21MHz is not currently in use at G3ZHZ, but there is no reason to believe that performance on that band would not be more than adequate. Unlike most verticals, no radials or elaborate ground connection are used even on 7MHz. During May/June 1986 a series of 14MHz cw skeds with ZF1JC (Cayman Islands) showed an advantage on receive of some 3 to 4 S-points over the horizontal windom. On 7MHz, once tuned up, signals are much the same on the vertical and horizontal antennas, suggesting that for those with tiny gardens or small flat roofs there is still hope of harvesting dx while growing vegetables rather than radials!

Magnetic (Small Loop) Antennas

Extracted from 'Technical Topics', *Radio Communication,* October 1986

Magnetic (small loop) antennas

The June *TT* item (pp418-9) on the use of large-diameter compact loops as transmitting antennas has resulted in a long and interesting letter from John Brown, G3EUR, who draws attention to articles in *cq-DL* (No 2/1983 and No 5/1984). The first of these, by Hans Wuertz, DL2FA, was Part 12 of a detailed series of articles on dx-antennas and their image. Part 12 dealt with loop and ferrite-loaded antennas in considerable detail, including the various ways in which they can be coupled to the 50Ω output socket of a transmitter.

I have also received from Ted Hart of W5QJR Antenna Products, PO Box 334, Melbourne, FL 32902, USA, a copy of his *Small High Efficiency Antennas—Alias The Loop* which runs to some 100pp (soft covers $11.95 plus $3.30 to cover overseas air mail). W5QJR also has an article on the loop antenna, which he insists is no "second-rate" antenna when it comes to dx operation, in *QST* June 1986.

While I have always stressed the need for extreme low-loss, low-ohmic construction, W5QJR is an unashamed enthusiast. His back cover proclaims: "At last a dream come true. The loop antenna provides high efficiency for transmitting and low noise for receiving. It provides an optimum radiation pattern for both local and dx communications. The pattern gain is second only to multi-element beam antennas. For the small city lot and for apartment dwellers, there is no other antenna that will provide equivalent performance in a small space—and it does all this when mounted at ground level."

While this is putting it a bit strong, the book does stress the practical problems that are involved with small loops of high-Q and hence narrow resonate bandwidth (although capable of being resonated over a wide frequency range). He provides an octagonal-loop design based on 0·75in copper pipe with motor driven remote tuning: Fig 1.

John Brown, G3EUR, has put together some useful notes on the fundamentals of small loops that will help put this approach in perspective. He writes: "Siemens and Telefunken have used loops and ferrite assemblies for many years, mainly for hf/df and selective reception in commercial stations where the ability to null out interfering signals arriving from a different direction to that of the wanted station is often more important than high efficiency in converting field strength into microvolts at the receiver terminals. The principles of frame and loop antennas go back many years, and were set out in the classic *Admiralty Handbook of Wireless Telegraphy* in 1927 alongside "jars" of capacitance.

A loop can be equated to a resonant tuned circuit: in the conventional full-wave "quad" the resonance results from the electrical length of the conductor; in the small single-turn loop the smaller inductance is tuned, with the aid of a capacitor, to the operating frequency. The Q can be very high, say 300 at 10MHz. Radiation into space (hence the radiation resistance) increases with loop diameter; this represents "work done" and results in a lowering of the working Q. By reducing losses in the inductor by using large-diameter copper tubing and low-loss insulation in the (high-voltage) tuning capacitor, the ratio of tuned circuit loss to radiated energy can be kept low and an efficient antenna for transmission and reception results. It should be noted that with a high-Q resonant circuit even a few watts of rf power results in high circulating currents in the loop and high voltage across the capacitor. Most loops of practical size are limited to transmitter powers of 100-300W, even when well protected from damp and stray power losses induced into nearby conductive material. The high-Q

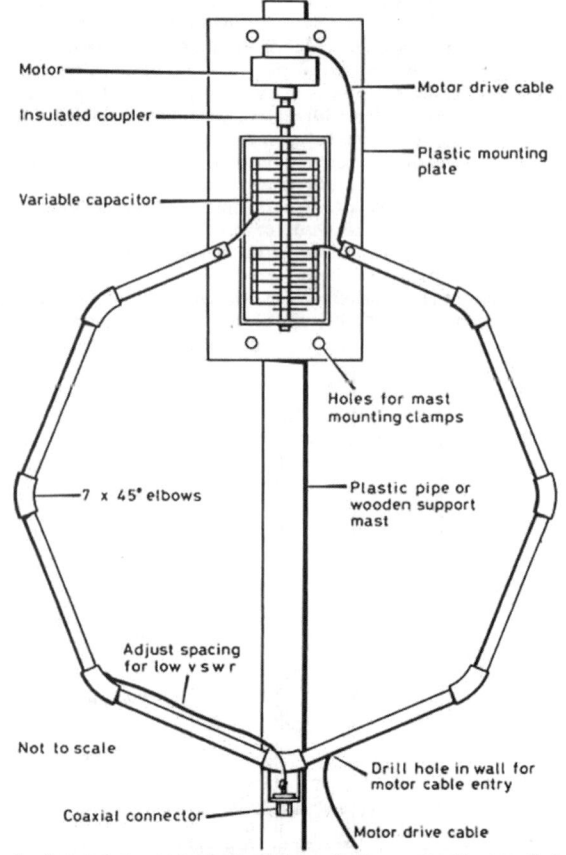

Fig 1. Suggested mechanical design of the magnetic (small loop) transmitting/receiving antenna as described by W5QJR in his book *Small High Efficiency Antennas—Alias the Loop*. The only changes are in the straight lengths of copper pipe that form the resonant octagon loop on different bands. Loops recommended by W5QJR include: (a) circumference of 8·5ft for use in 10/29MHz, approximate capacitance 125pF (10), 60 (14), 35 (18), 23 (21), 16 (24) and 9 (29); (b) circumference 20ft, capacitance 73pF (7), 29(10) and 6 (14)

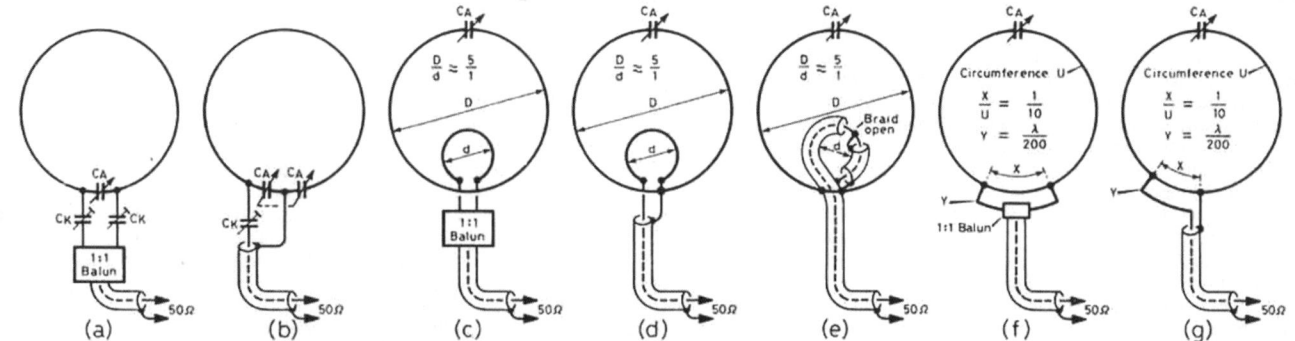

Fig 3. Matching a loop transmitting or receiving antenna to 50Ω cable as described in 1983 by DL2FA. The Faraday-loop coupling coil made from coaxial cable in (e) is considered optimum. (g) is the arrangement used by W5QJR

results in a narrow bandwidth so that *accurate* retuning is necessary even for small changes of frequency. The radiation from a small loop is essentially via the magnetic field, hence the name "magnetic antenna".

Matching the loop into a receiver or transmitter can present problems. As a receiving antenna, the system is, in effect, a bandpass filter with some form of tap or link coupling between the element and the first stage (Fig 2). For a single-peak response the coupling (as in i.f transformers) must be critical; the first-stage tuned circuit needs to be high-Q so that its losses, coupled back to the antenna, do not reduce efficiency. By comparison, matching to a transmitter is easier since this can provide a low-impedance source from a broadband solidstate amplifier via lowpass filter and wideband transformer. Such an arrangement avoids the need to retune the transmitter tank circuit when changing frequency (but the high-Q loop itself *must* be retuned).

The loop radiation pattern is similar to that of a dipole, but efficiency will usually be lower. The advantages are primarily the smaller physical size, the ability to null unwanted signals during reception and the possibility of good performance close to ground.

Fig 3, derived from DL2FA's articles, shows options for matching a loop, including the use of capacitive networks and "miniloop" inductive coupling as discussed in the June *TT*. Fig 11 (e) is probably the optimum arrangement in practice. With optimum coupling between the primary and secondary loops, highest efficiency (maximum radiation resistance) occurs when the loop resonates with the tuning capacitance approaching 0pF. At frequencies above loop resonance, the system is no longer a true magnetic antenna, and electric fields develop in the neighbourhood of the antenna. This means that the loop circumference should not exceed about $0 \cdot 4\lambda$ at the highest operating frequency.

Tuning with very small values of capacitance (about 5 to 10pF) is critical, and this usually requires a good remote tuning system. Small, geared "models" can be used, although tuning with them can prove rather slow. The power supply cable for the motor should be routed vertically from the zero point (mid-inductor).

DL2FA claims to have built and tested over 100 magnetic antennas, including ferrite types, with large area "air-cored" loops emerging as the most satisfactory. This checks with some wartime experiments made in 1943 by G3EUR with dust-core "loaded" wire antennas. Ferrite core losses tend to be significant for this application; the resulting smaller diameter loop for equivalent inductance reduces radiation (which is governed by the area enclosed within the loop). The reduced area offsets the concentration of flux via the core(s).

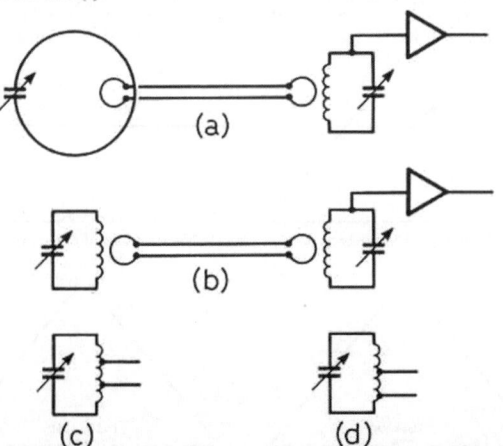

Fig 2. Coupling a resonant loop to a receiver. (a) Link coupling forming in effect a high-Q bandpass filter. (b) Electrical equivalent to (a). (c) Balanced and unbalanced tapped impedance coupling. Practical arrangements are shown in Fig 3

Among the advantages of the magnetic antenna, other than those already mentioned, is the fact that provided there are no masses of closed-loop or sheet conductors in the immediate vicinity, proximity to ground or to a typical building tends to result in lower losses than the electric field losses of a dipole or other conventional antennas. There is also, incidentally, less coupling to the human body.

The magnetic field tends to result in less mutual interference (tvi and ivt) with television receivers. Small loop receiving antennas are less susceptible to all forms of local electrical interference. As df enthusiasts will appreciate, a loop antenna can be combined with a vertical element to achieve a cardioid radiation pattern (transmit as well as receive) but both antennas need to be resonated accurately (in amplitude and phase) to obtain useful gain in a desired direction.

A major disadvantage of the magnetic loop antenna is that using two or more closely-spaced loops to increase gain and directivity results in narrower bandwidths and individual tuning, so that a multiband antenna seems to be impractical (arrays of small broadband "active" loops have been used professionally as beam receiving arrays since the 'sixties). Some work has also been done commercially in the use of multiple loops for fixed frequency operation, using phasing networks in the feeder lines to reconcile the physical spacing of the loops.

Magnetic (Loop) Antennas

Extracted from 'Technical Topics', *Radio Communication*, December 1986

Magnetic (loop) antennas

The description of magnetic (small loop) antennas (*TT*, October, pp 705-7) was intended primarily to show the practical advantages and disadvantages of the compact loop transmitting antenna formed from large-diameter copper tubing or similar materials of very low ohmic loss, necessary to achieve reasonable efficiency in spite of the very low radiation resistance. However, Dr Andrew Smith, G4OEP is rightly concerned that some of the comments could inadvertently give rise to misconceptions as to the fundamental principles governing all transmitting antennas. As he puts it:

"*TT* occasionally reminds us about the mystic fog which surrounds the vswr fetish, but it is possible now that you might be in process of creating a myth around loop antennas.

"Possibly, the term 'magnetic antenna' has become established as a generic term for loops, ferrite rods etc in which, during reception, the device generates an emf in response to the magnetic field vector component of an incident electromagnetic wave. If the term has become established, there is little one can expect to do to influence its usage. But it is less than ideal when applied to transmitting antennas, which have the dual task of creating E and H fields in strict proportion (E/H = c) if they are to act as em radiators. If a magnetic antenna creates an H field in excess of E/c then the excess magnetic field cannot result in the radiation of em energy, and so is accidental to the operation of the device as an antenna. As *TT* suggested, this can be a source of inefficiency in such aerials.

"This is fairly obvious, but should be borne in mind when discussing the operation of these antennas. The statement '... the system is no longer a true magnetic antenna, and electric fields develop in the neighbourhood of the antenna'... suggests that a purely magnetic transmitting antenna might in some way be possible. It would be unfortunate if *TT* were to be

ANTENNA TOPICS

caught in the act of perpetrating an antenna mythology!

"I also feel uneasy about the discussion of coupling a loop antenna to a receiver. Surely the idea suggested by '... the first-stage tuned circuit needs to be high-Q so that its losses, coupled back to the antenna, do not reduce efficiency' could be more accurately stated by something such as 'the source resistance of the antenna is unusually low, and so must be appropriately coupled to the first stage of the receiver'. Losses in the input circuit of a receiver must always be low in order to avoid inefficiency, but allowing the input resistance of the amplifier (and source resistance of the aerial) to lower the Q of the input filter is one way of avoiding losses! I think your point is really one about impedance matching and power transfer. "Finally, could a loop antenna radiate if it were enclosed in an electrostatic screen as most df receiving loops are?"

To the best of my knowledge, the term "magnetic antenna" originated in Germany and is widely used there. Incidentally, I was interested recently to have a 10·1MHz contact with a German amateur (DL8WR near Darmstadt) who was using a 1·4-metre diameter loop antenna mounted on his balcony—and putting excellent signals into the UK.

Folded-back Dipoles

Extracted from 'Technical Topics',
Radio Communication, December 1986

Folded-back dipoles

One of the lessons that can perhaps be learned from the work on small loop transmitting antennas, which could be expected to have a radiation resistance of less than 1Ω, is that this is not necessarily a bar to achieving a reasonably effective antenna system. This is always provided that we recognise the problems and limitations that stem from the low radiation resistance (which must not, of course, be confused with the feed-point impedance).

In *HF antennas for all locations*, Les Moxon, G6XN rightly does not recommend the use of dipoles physically shortened by folding back the ends to a central insulator, since he believes that there are more efficient ways of end loading. He shows that in the folded back arrangement significant current flows in both directions, thereby decreasing the radiation resistance by a factor of about four when compared with some other forms of end-loaded elements which he describes (pages 148–9).

Dr Constantino Feruglio, IV3VS, recognizes the force of this argument, but nevertheless believes that such a system when designed for 1·8MHz (or possibly 3·5MHz) with a top span of 40m (or 20m) can form the basis of a useful multiband antenna since, when used in conjunction with a remotely-controlled switch it can work not only on 1·8MHz but also on 3·5, 7, 14, 21 and 28MHz (and with suitable atus on 10, 18 and 24MHz —G3VA). IV3VS uses the K8ANG balanced-output atu circuit shown in the June *TT*, Fig 9(b), page 420.

With the folded-back top of Fig 4(a), IV3VS achieves good 1·8MHz contacts throughout Europe. Switched into the arrangement of Fig 4(b), the system becomes a "double Zepp" antenna for 3·5, 7, 14, 21 and 28MHz etc. Alternatively it can be switched as in Fig 4(c) to provide a 3·5MHz half-wave folded dipole with useful broad-band characteristics. Length of the balanced feeder (slotted 300Ω ribbon line or open-wire feeder) is not critical since the entire system can be resonated on virtually any frequency by means of the atu, permitting operation in the (b) configuration also on 10, 18 or 24MHz. For limited spaces, the "top" could be reduced to 20m overall in which case the folded dipole configuration would be for 7MHz and efficiency on 1·8MHz would be lower. With a two-way rather than three-way remote-controlled switch the folded-dipole configuration could be omitted. Fig 5 shows the system as used by IV3VS.

Compact Multiband Delta Loop

Extracted from 'Technical Topics',
Radio Communication, January 1987

Compact multiband delta loop

Alasdair Fraser, GM3AXX, is pleased with the performance of a compact four-band delta loop antenna that can be fed directly from coaxial cable without an atu yet fits into a small garden. Since inductive loading is required only on 10MHz the efficiency is reasonably good and the only snag would appear to be the need to pop out to the switch box when changing bands, though even that could be overcome with the aid of a high-voltage remote-controlled three-position switch.

The theory is extremely simple; a full-wave on 14MHz is approximately the same physical length as a half-wave on 7MHz or 1·5λ on 21MHz: Fig 2. Originally, when 10MHz was released, GM3AXX fitted a small loading coil to his 14MHz delta loop antenna and found this to work remarkably well. Since then he has modified the loop as shown in Fig. 3 to include also 7 and 21 MHz operation. This arrangement has been used successfully by a number of local and English amateurs who report it to be ideal for small gardens. If the 10MHz facility is not required it would be possible to use a larger loading coil for 3·5MHz operation although inevitably this would have the effect of greatly lowering the radiation resistance, increasing the Q (thus narrowing the bandwidth) and significantly lowering the efficiency on that band; 1·8MHz loading is not recommended, but might put you on

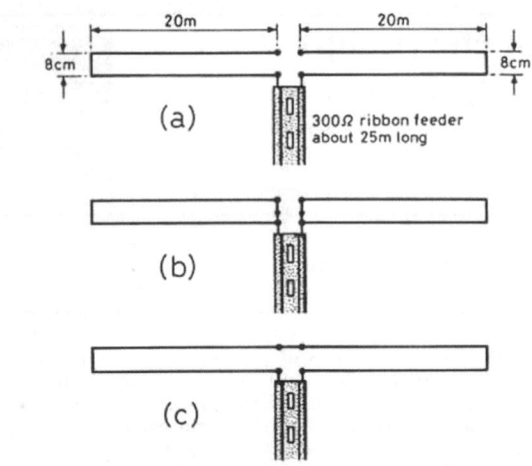

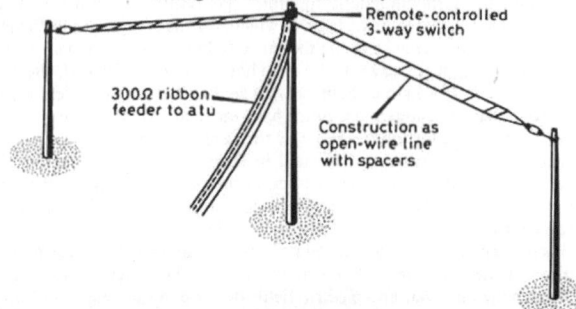

Fig 4. (a) The folded-back dipole as used on 1·8MHz by IV3VS. (b) Switched into the "double zepp" configuration (c) Switched into the "folded dipole" configuration for 3·5MHz operation

Fig 5. Implementation of IV3VS's multiband folded-back dipole antenna. As usual, performance is improved when the antenna is as high up as possible

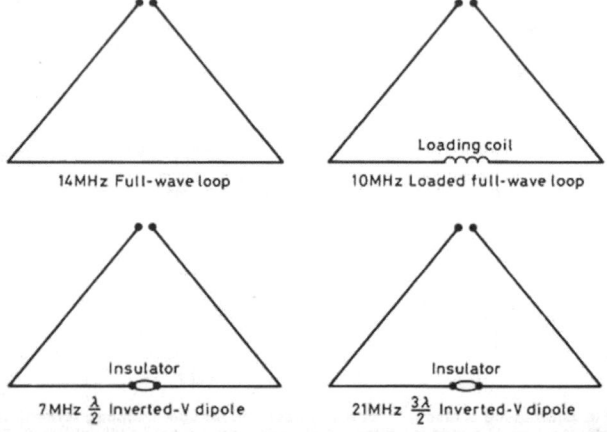

Fig 2. How a 66ft delta loop antenna can be configured for 14, 10, 7 and 21MHz to form the basis of GM3AXX's four-band antenna

the band.

GM3AXX describes construction and adjustment as follows:
(1) Make up a 14MHz delta loop using two 33ft lengths of wire. Suspend the loop at its apex about 20 to 25ft above ground. Connect coaxial cable to apex (with or without balun) and run the cable (any length) to an swr bridge/transceiver. The base corners are connected via insulators to a

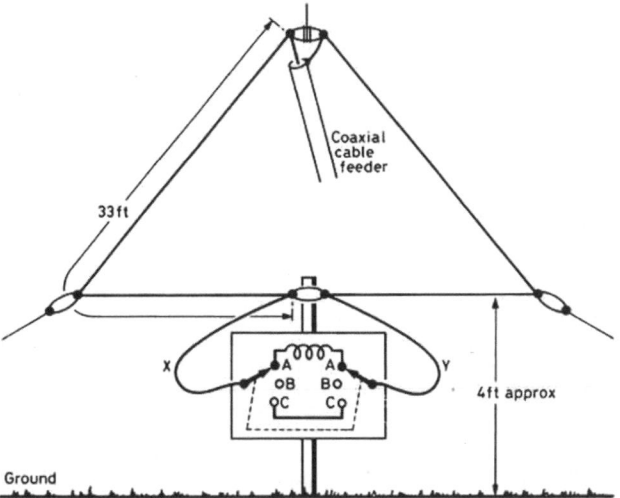

Fig 3. Practical construction of the GM3AXX's four-band antenna but note that having the base wire only 4ft above ground would breach safety recommendations except when used for very low power transmissions

convenient garden fence, etc, so that the base section is about 4ft above ground (*Note:* it needs to be higher if there is any risk of people touching wires at high rf—*G3VA*).
(2) Make up a ground post with insulator at the top and the switch box near the top. The insulator separates the two sections of the loop.
(3) With switch in position 'C' adjust lengths of stubs X, Y until loop resonates (ie shows low swr) at 14,050kHz (cw operation), 14,250kHz (ssb), or 14,200kHz (both).
(4) Then, and only then, with switch in position A, adjust the loading coil until loop resonates (low swr) at 10,125kHz. It is important that operation (3) is carried out before attempting (4). GM3AXX's coil is 20 turns on a 2in diameter former but a start should be made with 30 turns, then remove turns one at a time until the loop resonates.

The switch box should be waterproof and contains the two-pole, three-way switch (which needs to withstand high rf voltages except for really low-power operation). Switch positions are A for 10MHz, B for 7 and 21MHz and C for 14MHz.

I feel that it should be stressed that, except on very low power, the wires X and Y connected to the switch will be at high rf voltage, particularly on 7 and 21MHz, and that this needs to be taken fully into account where there is any possibility of anyone else, especially young children, having access to these wires.

The 'Claw Mark 4' Antenna

Extracted from 'Technical Topics', *Radio Communication,* January 1987

The "Claw Mark 4" antenna

TT (March 1985, pp180-1 and a brief note in February 1986, page 107) provided information on a new form of loaded folded-dipole element for use in multiband arrays that has been under development over the past two years by Les Moxon, G6XN. The innovatory design, while remaining basically the same, has progressed through various detail changes in an effort to retain the advantages while eliminating problems in achieving repeatability and equally good performance on different bands, etc.

This has led to a Mk4 version, Fig 4, and G6XN has recently outlined the background to this development. He writes: "I remarked previously (*TT* March 1985) that the Mk3 version appeared to have no vices. However I later realized that on 10·1 MHz, whereas the Mk2 elements had been undercoupled, those of the Mk3 were seriously overcoupled. The neutralizing capacitances became so large that it became virtually a driven array. As indicated in my *HF Antennas for All Locations* book this meant that tuning and matching became difficult on this band, although with patience reasonable performance could be obtained.

"For Mk4 I have reverted to the earlier Mk2 arrangement in which the bent-over ends of the multi-wire section are brought down the expanding arms. Although the elements are shorter, the radiation resistance is not reduced and the effective height is increased. Coupling is satisfactory at 10MHz and current distribution in the loop is improved at 28MHz, removing any tendency for the radiation pattern to break up as well as providing a better match to 600Ω line. Planar loading has been discarded in favour of conventional helical (inductive) loading; replacement of metal by fibreglass has allowed the helices to be wound on 1in diameter tube at the lower end of the fishing rods. The number of wires in parallel has been reduced to two, simplifying construction.

"Another development is the discovery that for three-band operation it is not essential to use resonant feeder lines. For 14/28MHz a 50Ω feeder can be connected directly through a 4:1 balun. For 21MHz it is necessary to switch in another quarter-wave impedance transformer using a relay (a typical small relay proved successful) though no linear amplifier was used on 21MHz. Coaxial feeders, however, reduce the flexibility of the 'poor man's log periodic' feature."

Developed initially as a two-element multiband antenna G6XN has also tried it as a three-element array. While performance was improved on 28MHz, it is difficult to justify the extra complexity on other bands, and G6XN continues to stress that a two-element array can often be raised higher above ground than a heavier three-element antenna. He does not recommend using the extra element.

A small version of the "Mk4 Claw" has also been tested. The two outer elements (18ft span) from the three-element array were used. Arm lengths were increased to 16ft by means of 3ft 6in alloy extensions (for 28MHz this amount of metal should not be exceeded) and spacing reduced to 8ft to improve performance on 28MHz. Although not intended for 10MHz, this proved successful despite a calculated loss of 3dB relative to full size monoband performance. Feeders were short enough (about 40ft) to permit all tuning, matching and coupling adjustments to be carried out from the operating position, the loops being resonated only roughly prior to erection. Helical loading was distributed along the lower halves of the elements in contrast to the central loading of the basic Mk4.

Constructional notes for the Claw Mk4

Reference should be made to the notes on the earlier "Claw" elements in *TT*, March 1985 and February 1986. The "example" dimensions shown in Fig 4 refer to a simulated loop laid out horizontally six feet above a lawn for investigation of current distribution, etc. The lower dipole (BGE) may be helically wound along the entire length or end-loaded as shown with short helices (10ft of wire in helix is roughly equal to 6ft straight). The stub dimensions for 600Ω line or other feeder systems could be calculated from the figures given, though these are intended only as rough guide-lines. An atu in the shack is usually all that is needed (ie *no* stubs) with 600Ω line except on 10MHz and, if long feeders are used, on 21MHz. To match on 21MHz (at ground level) feed with 600Ω line and find point of "zero" current. Insert 10pF capacitors in series with each wire at a point 3ft closer to the antenna. In two cases this met the requirements for 21MHz also (about 17pF at 5ft should give approximate match to 50 ohms via 4:1 balun). Antenna resonances checked with gdo should be in-band if feeder is shorted on the transmitter side of the capacitors.

For a two-element beam, a loop spacing of 12ft at top (lower ends at mast head) is recommended if 10MHz facility is required; otherwise 8ft spacing is sufficient. The semicircular shape shown in Fig 4 is believed to be optimum. This shape is readily achieved with glassfibre fishing rods tapering down to about ¼in diameter and suitably angled. Metal extensions at the lower ends of fishing rods may be used but a total horizontal metal dimension of one-fifth wavelength at the highest frequency band should not be exceeded. Helices may be wound on the fishing rods or on any glass-fibre struts but *not* on the metal extensions.

The use of two feeders in order to allow beam reversal from the shack (see previous notes in *TT* etc) is very strongly recommended by G6XN. It is highly desirable to make the elements and especially the electrical length of the feeders *identical* (use gdo) so that nulling for one direction holds for the other and there is no need to readjust the atu. It is easy to provide reflector tuning at the operating position. Reflectors need to be tuned only slightly lower (typically 1 per cent) than the operating frequency. Tune for signal nulls. Should the nulls not be reasonably deep, coupling needs adjusting (eg by fixed capacitors, in or out of phase) between feed lines; see Fig 4 (b). Two element arrays as described tend to provide deep nulls on most bands but with the Mk4 element G6XN obtained only about 10dB on 21MHz. In such cases the coupling needs adjusting, for example, by capacitors between points on the feeders where there is significant rf voltage. The correct phase can be determined by observing the current in the reflector relative to the driven element, or more easily by trial and error. Points such as Y-Y on the diagram are ideal for a coupling adjustment (in-phase connection to increase coupling). In practice, a single small trimmer just inside the shack sufficed to give an "infinite" null depth.

ANTENNA TOPICS

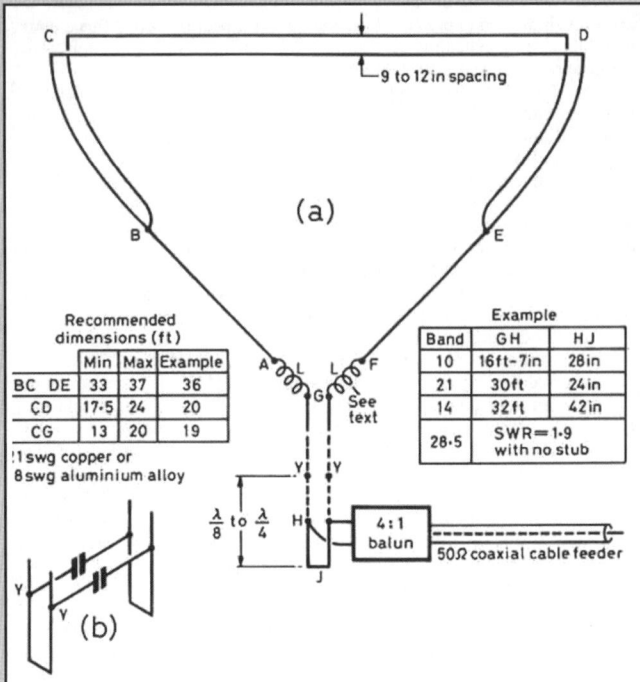

Fig 4. G6XN's improved Mark 4 element for "The Claw" multiband beam array.
(b) Use of small capacitors to vary the coupling and so to improve the depth of the nulls on some bands

Small Loop Antennas

Extracted from 'Technical Topics',
Radio Communication, March 1987

Small loop antennas
In December *TT*, Dr Andrew Smith, G4OEP, in taking exception to the term "magnetic antenna" when applied to compact transmitting loops, raised several interesting, if provocative, questions.

Tony Harwood, G4HHZ, agrees that in the *far field* of an electromagnetic field the E and H fields are in strict proportion (ie E/H is a constant, though not c in the usual sense of this being the velocity of light but 120π). However this does not apply to the *near field* of a transmitting loop where the magnetic field can predominate and perhaps justify the German term 'magnetic antenna'. He also, in answer to G4OEP's question "could a loop antenna radiate if it were enclosed in an electrostatic screen as most df receiving loops are?" says that the answer is undoubtedly "yes, it could and would". He points in confirmation to the classic text book on antennas: *Antennas theory and practice* by S Schelkunoff and the review of Lorentz's classic theory of reciprocity formulated in 1895 and derived from Clerk Maxwell's equations as described in last year's IERE's 11th Clerk Maxwell Memorial lecture by Professor A L Cullen.

The attraction of compact electrostatically screened loop receiving antennas in being much less susceptible to the electric fields of local electrical interference and, by dint of their directional properties, able to minimize co-channel interference from distant stations should not be overlooked by 1·8MHz and mf/dx enthusiasts. Following the recent items on transmitting loops two practical receiving designs have come from G3OUC and G8YZW.

Pat Painting, G3OUC writes: "For many years I have used kite-supported antennas for 1·8MHz field operation. Results have been well worth-while as far as transmission is concerned but severe problems have resulted on weak-signal reception from the pick-up of atmospheric and man-made noise. The same problem is also experienced when using my roachpole vertical antenna. At times rain-static can make it impossible to use 1·8MHz due to the receiver being swamped by noise.

"Various frame, loop and ferrite-rod active antennas have been constructed and all have worked quite well. However the shielded loop system shown in Fig 3 seems to give maximum noise reduction. All previous active antennas have picked up noise from the main station transmitting antenna if this is left connected. The shielded loop system works very well indoors and in suitable conditions provides reception of American and Russian stations; its directional properties can also be used to minimize noise and interference.

Passive 1.8MHz Shielded Loop

Extracted from 'Technical Topics',
Radio Communication, March 1987

Passive 1·8MHz shielded loop
Mike Shepherd, G8YZW similarly writes: "I listen to several nets on 1·8MHz but have to contend with the background noises from electric motors and other sources of impulse interference which tend to be too fast to permit useful reduction by means of conventional noise limiters and often with several different electric motors being received at the same time from nearby woodyard, builders, launderette and vehicle coachwork rebuilders. Some of the nets use a.m which, when the signals are weak, is badly affected by the strong electrical interference.

"The *TT* item on loops prompted me to construct a Mark 1 version based

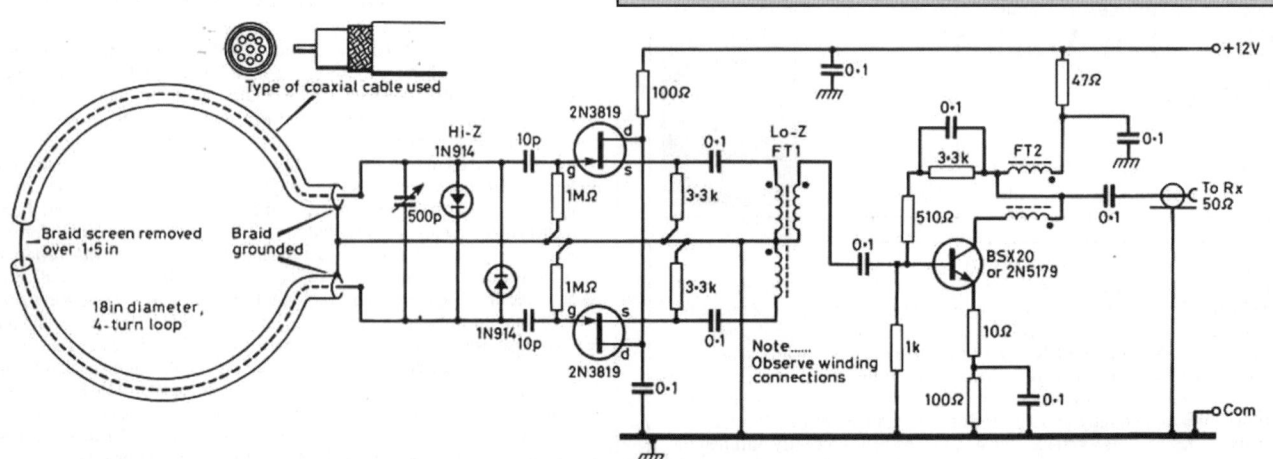

Fig 3. 1·8MHz "active" shielded loop receiving antenna used by G3OUC to minimize pick-up of local electrical impulse noise etc while providing good performance on weak signals. The 18in diameter four turn loop is formed from air spaced 75Ω coaxial cable. 1·5in of copper braid is removed at centre of cable. Loop is then taped with pvc electrical tape to secure turns. Tuned with a miniature broadcast type variable capacitor. Note that the loop is mounted vertically. For the broadband rf transformers, FT1 consists of 15t trifilar windings with 28swg enam wire on Amidon FT37-61 ferrite core. FT2 has 15t bifilar windings on similar core

on the impedance matching loop arrangement shown in Fig 3(e) page 706 of the October 1986 issue and the shielded "Indoor loop aerial for short waves" by S Mukherjee in *Electronics & Wireless World*, April 1985, pages 38 to 39, which describes receiving loops for 4–9MHz, 8–18MHz and 18–26MHz found to give more protection than a rod antenna against noise from electrical appliances. I scaled up the 4–9MHz version (700mm main loop diameter, 500pF tuning capacitor) to 1000mm main loop, 200mm coupling loop. But, possibly due to using H100 stiff coaxial cable (double screened) to provide some rigidity of the loop, found that the self-inductance and capacitance of the 10ft 4in length (including connecting ends) of the main loop required 750pF postage trimmer plus a 350pF sm fixed capacitor across the twin-gang variable capacitor (over 2000pF of which 1000pF is variable) as currently set to tune 1·85 to 2MHz. It could probably be converted to cover both 1·8 and 3·5MHz by switching in or out the extra capacitance. The 10ft version (Fig 4) results in a loop 42-inches wide. My next version will use 15–16ft of "ordinary" thick TV coaxial feeder cable to reduce the value of capacitance as well as improving performance generally.

"Tests so far show it to be far 'quieter' with relatively little loss of wanted signal strength compared with a 50ft check antenna used with an atu."

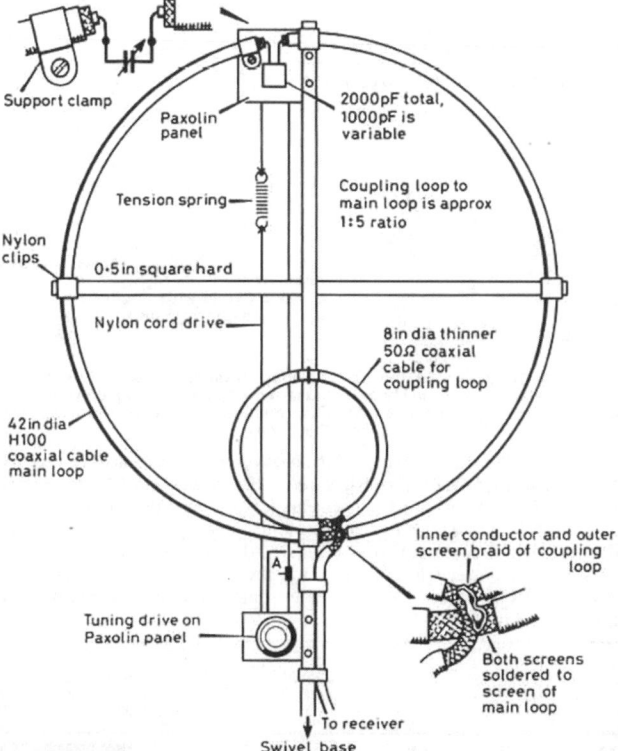

Fig 4. Prototype 1·8MHz shielded loop receiving antenna as built as a prototype by G8YZW. "Plastic" drive drum fitted to tuning capacitor. Aluminium drum to drive shaft and knob with small pulley wheel fitted close to cage to keep cord drive in line with "drums". At "A" a small calibration scale is fitted on wood shaft. Pointer fitted on inner cord with "card" scale fitted to take frequencies and/or stations for reference on removal

Short Antenna Elements

Extracted from 'Technical Topics', *Radio Communication*, April 1987

Short antenna elements
Some 25 or 30 years ago, 1·8 and 3·5MHz mobile operation sparked interest in the use of radiating elements very short in terms of wavelength. It was soon discovered that inductively-loaded elements needed to be very accurately tuned (ie high Q, narrow bandwidth); base-loaded whips left a lot to be desired; moving the loading some way up the element improved performance but made the antenna top-heavy and liable to bend over alarmingly while the car was moving. Theoretically, the optimum position for a loading coil on a whip is at a height varying from about 0·4 to, with top capacitance loading, about 0·66 of the height.

An alternative to the loading coil is the helical-wound antenna that provides inductive loading continuously throughout its length. Although this provides a useful increase in the radiation resistance, it does mean that about $0·5\lambda$ of wire is needed to achieve $0·25\lambda$ resonance. This also implies that a metal whip cannot form a low-resistance antenna element so that, unless very thick, low-gauge wire is used, the rf ohmic losses will tend to be higher. Dielectric (eg ferrite) loaded whip elements are possibly the optimum approach for transmission but this technique has received little attention from amateurs.

It will be appreciated, at least by regular *TT* readers, that theoretically a short, well-matched radiator can be just as efficient and has the same radiation pattern as a full-length monopole or dipole. Unfortunately, this cannot be fully achieved in practice since the efficiency (E_f) of an antenna is $R_r/(R_r + R_{loss})$ where R_r is the radiation resistance and R_{loss} is the *rf* ohmic resistance of the element, the loading coil, and the ohmic losses in the matching network. If there were no R_{loss}, this would reduce to unity regardless of the shortness of the radiator and consequent very low radiation resistance. The practical problem is that as the radiation resistance becomes much lower, the ohmic losses assume proportionately more significance. The radiation resistance tends to decrease as the square of its length and may well be only of the order of an ohm or so on 1·8 or 3·5MHz.

A continuously loaded element does raise the radiation resistance significantly above that of a base-loaded element, and this can be further materially improved and the bandwidth increased by the use of a capacitance hat.

Since the transfer of most UK mobile operation to vhf/uhf, interest in very short and/or compact antennas has tended to be concentrated on balcony antennas, antenna arrays that need to rotate without extending over neighbours' gardens, and transmitting loops.

Ten years ago, Ronald Gorski, W9KYZ (*QST* April 1977) wrote a basic article, "Efficient short radiators" that provided some useful notes on helically-wound short elements, using wide copper ribbon tape, in conjunction with capacitance-hats.

He investigated these techniques on model antennas at about 100MHz showing that they can result in physically short but efficient two-element Yagi arrays providing some 4dB forward gain and about 15dB front/back ratio.

The vhf model comprised a 28in length of 0·75in cpvc tubing (plastic water pipe) wound with 38 equally spaced turns of 0·5in wide copper tape (resonance 104MHz). Then he added two 5·5in diameter, six-spoke, capacitance hats (resonance became 84MHz) and fed at low impedance via a C-match network (ie capacitors not inductors).

Translated to 14MHz, bandwidth would be 500kHz with element lengths slightly over 12ft and boom 10·5ft, diameter 1·5in or more.

W9KYZ's 1977 design pointers remain valid:
1. Make the element length no shorter than physically necessary for the particular location since both bandwidth and efficiency improve with longer elements.
2. Use large capacitance hats as these reduce the length of helical conductor for a given frequency and this minimizes R_{loss}.
3. Use large formers of good dielectric quality (eg fibreglass). The larger the form diameter (eg 1·5in), the greater the length reduction for a given number of turns and the greater can be the width of the conductor, so reducing R_{loss}.
4. Solder *all* joints and seal with silicone rubber. Do *not* rely on pressure joints.
5. For a good f/b ratio of a Yagi array with a split driven element fed from coaxial cable, some form of balun transformer is needed.
6. Use of a gdo is the only practical method of securing resonance with a fixed physical length. Construction requires cut and try. Proximity to surrounding objects affects resonance and should be minimized during tuning up.

An 'Ultra Mini-beam' from VK2ABQ

Extracted from 'Technical Topics', *Radio Communication*, May 1987

An "ultra mini-beam" from VK2ABQ
For many years the various low-cost "wire" two-element antennas (and bow-tie dipoles) developed by Fred Caton, VK2ABQ/G3ONC, and

ANTENNA TOPICS

introduced initially in *TT* and *Electronics Australia*, have become well-established as a logical and technically-justifiable approach for those with small gardens and/or limited budgets. The basic VK2ABQ wire array gained the cachet of being included, with some further suggestions, in *HF Antennas for all locations* by Les Moxon, G6XN. This design maintains its

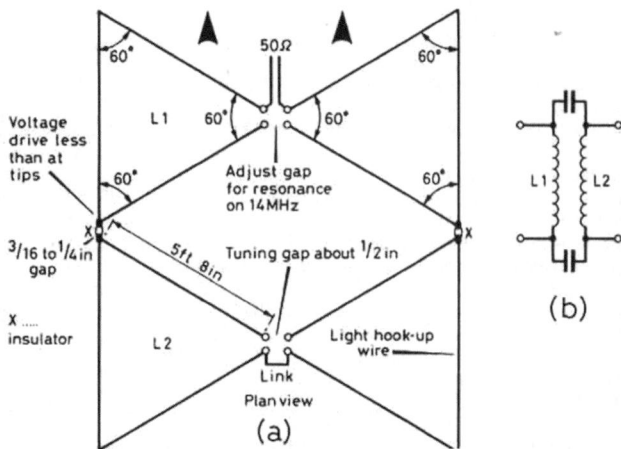

Fig 1. (a) Bird's eye view of the VK2ABQ "Ultra Mini Beam" for 14MHz. (b) Equivalent lumped circuit with inherent phase shift between L1 and L2.

popularity and, for example, turns up again in *Practical Wireless* (February 1987).

Recently VK2ABQ has sent along one of his annotated sketches outlining a new 14MHz "double triangle dipole" array (Fig 1(a)) suitable for very small gardens etc. It uses no loading coils or traps, and he believes it to be more efficient than an array with capacitively end-loaded elements. He stresses that being a fairly high-Q structure, the bandwidth is restricted and that its main attraction is that it provides a unidirectional antenna with good side rejection and some gain in spite of its small size. Size, rather than the overall performance of a full size beam, is the main attraction.

Both the dipole and the reflector consist of two open-ended loops in the form of equilateral triangles, each of the four triangles being formed from about 17ft of light hook-up wire. It provides a unidirectional cardioid radiation pattern, and can also work well on 21MHz in the form of extended dipoles, although the feedpoint impedance (about 40Ω on 14MHz) increases; presumably it could be scaled down as a 21/28MHz array.

It is necessary to adjust the loops using a grid dip oscillator, first adjusting the driven element and then making the "voltage-driven" reflector identical. Good insulation is needed, particularly at the central voltage nodes.

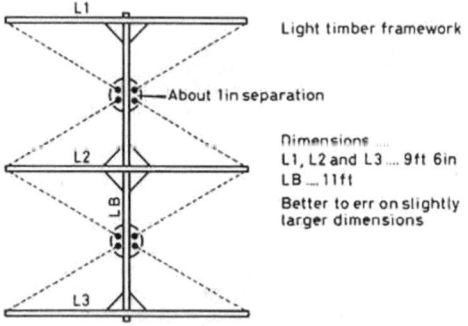

Fig 2. Light timber framework for the VK2ABQ array

VK2ABQ suggests mounting the array on a light timber frame (Fig 2). He points out that the antenna is not a close-spaced Yagi, since the reflector is voltage-driven with an inherent quarter-cycle phase shift. An equivalent lumped circuit (Fig 1(b)) may help to explain the principle. He adds that maximum gain will be achieved only when L1 and L2 are identical and in the form of equilateral triangles, although those experimentally inclined may wish to use a small stub at the reflector in lieu of the "link" shown.

I trust this is an accurate and understandable interpretation of Fred's rather cryptic notes.

Feedback on 1.8MHz Shielded Loop

Extracted from 'Technical Topics',
Radio Communication, May 1987

Feedback on 1·8MHz shielded loop

No matter how hard everyone along the publishing chain from original letter-writer to the printer tries, errors do creep into published material.

John Hawes, G4UAZ, draws attention to the vital caption of Fig 2 (*TT* June 1986, p417) giving the component values of his stable bipolar-assisted mosfet vfo. An obtrusive "k" crept unnoticed into the values of the emitter and collector resistors (R4, R5) for TR2. The value of each should have been 270Ω not 270k. G4UAZ mentions that there has been considerable interest in this vfo, suggesting that home-construction is not dead. He still has "no reason to doubt this is the 'ultimate' vfo circuit for stability". At least, until someone comes up with a "more ultimate" arrangement.

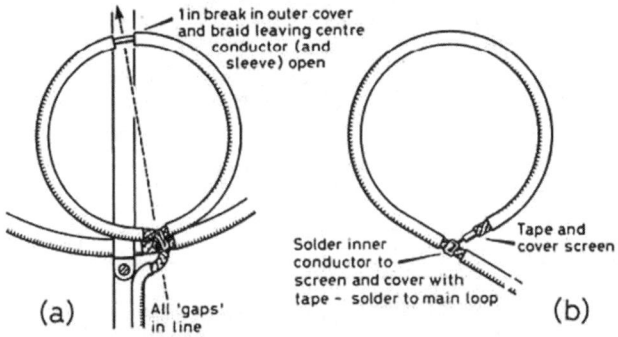

Fig 4. (a) Correction to the passive loop antenna shown in *TT* March indicating the 1in break in the outer braid of the small coupling togs opposite the feedpoint. (b) A possible alternative method of forming a Faraday type coupling loop.

More recently the 1·8MHz shielded loop receiving antenna developed by Mike Shepherd, G8YZW, from a *Wireless World* article (*TT* March, Fig 4, p181), unfortunately omitted the essential "gap" near the top of the small coupling loop where the outer covering and screening braid of the cable has to be removed over about 1in (see Fig 4(a)). Alternatively it might well prove possible to re-arrange the connections at the base of this coupling loop so that it forms a Faraday loop as used in some atus and tvi screen-breaker filters (Fig 4 (b)).

Broadbanding the Dipole

Extracted from 'Technical Topics',
Radio Communication, June 1987

Broadbanding the dipole

A perennial topic is the *Q*, and hence the effective resonant bandwidth, of an antenna. The higher the element *Q*, as in any resonant circuit, the narrower the bandwidth, the more critical the tuning, and the greater the detuning influence of nearby objects. For amateur radio, and for many professional communications applications, it is usually a significant advantage for an antenna to have a low *Q* structure. This implies either a wire at least a full wavelength long or some form of "fat" dipole which may use large diameter tubing (as for most hf and vhf arrays), wide copper or aluminium foil, or multiple wires which can range from the separate twin wires of a folded dipole to the classic multi-wires of a "caged dipole" or the various forms of discones, biconical monopoles, etc. Such structures radiate much the same power as a simple half-wave resonant wire dipole, but over a greater span of frequencies.

In practice, a simple wire dipole has a bandwidth to its −3dB points of something like ±2·5 per cent of its resonant frequency. This is adequate for most amateur bands, with the exception of the North American 3·5MHz band (3,500 to 4,000kHz) *provided* that the antenna stays accurately trimmed to mid-band frequency when elevated. Short elements inductively-loaded have very high Q; "stretched" dipoles capacitively-loaded have low Q and are much less affected by nearby wires or trees etc, but need a good deal more space.

The classic folded-dipole with twin wires of equal diameter remains an extremely useful single-band antenna. There is still considerable room for experiment in the use of different diameter conductors to provide any desired feedpoint impedance (Arch Doty, K8CFU, has just completed an extensive and very interesting study of the impedance transformation characteristics of folded monopoles which I hope to refer to soon). With equal diameters, folding a dipole raises its feedpoint impedance by a factor of four (ie nominally 300Ω for a single-element antenna).

However, many years ago it was shown that a folded dipole in which the element itself is largely formed from coaxial cable does not exhibit this "times four" factor and can be fed directly from similar cable: Fig 1(a). A variation on this antenna (but including a 1:1 balun) was patented a few years ago in the USA (R D Synder "Broadband antennae employing coaxial transmission line sections" US Patent 4,479,130 October 23, 1984) and has been marketed for professional or amateur radio use, with rather extravagent claims as to its performance, as the Synder dipole: Fig 1(b). This antenna has recently been analysed by a well-known American antenna engineer ("Evaluation of the Synder Dipole" by Robert C Hansen, *IEEE Trans on Ant & Prop*, February 1987, pages 207-10). Although Hansen is critical of the claims made for the Synder dipole and points out that the bandwidth is roughly equal to that of a dipole of the same fatness, with a lumped resonant circuit at the feedpoint terminals, or to that of a conventional folded dipole, he does show that these coaxial-type elements do not raise the impedance by the factor of four. This would seem to me to indicate that the original version (Fig 1(a)) can still be an effective single-band antenna, fed by coaxial cable without a balun, without infringing the Synder patent.

A rather different technique for increasing the bandwidth of a fat dipole element is *resistive loading*. Correctly applied, this can result in a really broadband dipole, capable of being used over virtually the entire hf spectrum. The best-known example is the so-called "Australian dipole" with 300Ω feed, due to Guertler and Collyer and described in *TT* June 1974

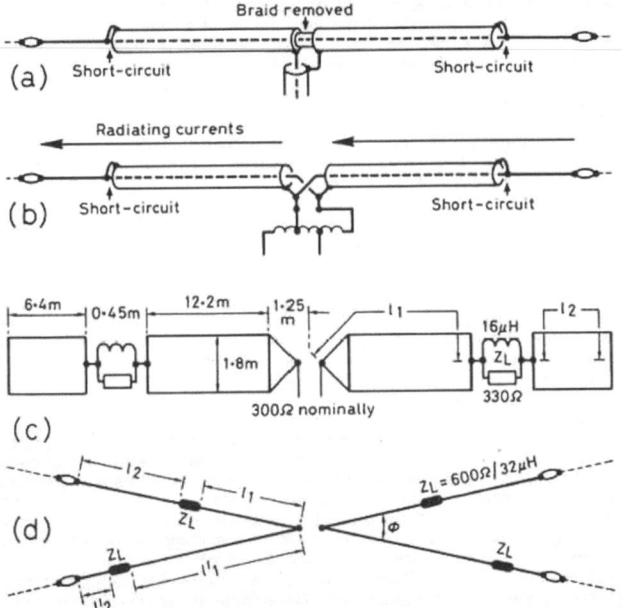

Fig 1. (a) Folded-dipole element suitable for feeding directly from coaxial cable. Overall length of the element is an electrical half-wave with the coaxial section also an electrical half-wave taking into account the reduced velocity ratio of the cable. (b) The Synder dipole with 1:1 balun. (c) The "Australian dipole" as described in *TT* June 1974 and September 1984. (d) Broadband resistive-loaded antenna reported by Austin and Fourie in *Electronics Letters* covering 3 to 30MHz with good efficiency when fed from 500Ω line

and September 1984, and in "sloper" or monopole form in *TT* September 1984: Fig 1(c). It could be argued that the T2FD antenna (*TT* July 1986) is a much earlier though less sophisticated form of a resistive-loaded antenna.

Dr Brian Austin (ZS6BKW and now also G0GSF) whose detailed computer studies of the G5RV-type antenna (*TT* May 1982 and *Rad Com* August 1985, pp 614-7, 624) attracted considerable attention, has more recently become intrigued with the possibilities of resistive loading ("Wire antennas for tactical hf communication" Part 1, *Elektron* June 1986 Part 2, July 1986). Together with A P C Fourie he has recently described an "Improved hf broadband wire antenna" (*Electronics Letters*, 12 March 1987, pp 276-7). In this he reports an inverted-V form of "fat" (diverging wires) resistive/inductive loaded dipole (Fig 1(d)) which can result in an antenna covering the entire range 3-30MHz with an swr not exceeding 2·5:1 and a radiation efficiency better than 40 per cent even at the low-frequency end (40 per cent may not seem high but in fact it is very much higher than with most broadband antennas!) when fed from 500Ω transmission line. This seems a highly promising development of the Australian dipole, and with Dr Austin now based at Liverpool University it is to be hoped that he will find time to describe some of his recent work in *Radio Communication*.

Antenna Basics

Extracted from 'Technical Topics', *Radio Communication,* July 1987

Antenna basics

In compiling *TT*, in order to provide members with information that will be fresh and interesting to the majority, it is necessary to assume that most readers will already have absorbed and understood the basics of established technology, either as the result of studying for the RAE or (more importantly) as part of their practical activities, using the basic handbooks and manuals such as the long-established *A Guide to Amateur Radio*. It would be tedious in the extreme if every *TT* item had to be based on the idea that readers had little or no practical or theoretical knowledge of radio communication engineering!

However, one becomes increasingly aware that the practice of absorbing technical information from books appears to have declined, possibly due to the pervasive influence of other media; including television, which in general does not lend itself to serious study unless accompanied by note-taking, revision and practical projects. The value of amateur radio as an enjoyable form of self-training has always pre-supposed the combination of book-study with do-it-yourself projects.

Antennas and transmission lines are prime examples of areas of radio technology where some knowledge of fundamentals beyond that required for the RAE is necessary. AC theory has never been a requirement of the RAE, yet some understanding of terms such as reactance, impedance, radiation resistance etc is vital to understanding antennas. So this month we include a very brief rundown on just a few of the basic terms that so often seem to give rise to misunderstandings. If you find such definitions tough going, this may be an indication that you need to refer back to one of the established handbooks. Familiarity with these terms is essential to understanding articles on antennas at other than the most elementary level.

Radiation

Energy is conveyed away from a conductor carrying a periodically varying current by means of the electromagnetic field which is set up in the surrounding space. This field has two components: an electric wave with vectors in the same plane as the conductor; and a magnetic wave having vectors at right-angles to the electric wave. Both sets of vectors are perpendicular to the direction in which the energy travels.

If two conductors are placed close together and carry equal "go and return" currents, the electric and magnetic fields are cancelled at all distant points by the fields due to the reverse current in the other conductor. Thus no energy is conveyed away (radiated) from the pair which constitute a transmission line; all the energy remains in the electric and magnetic fields in the space between the conductors. But if the conductors are moved apart and placed end-to-end the fields no longer cancel at distant points in space. Energy is conveyed out of the conductors by the electric and magnetic fields; and these two fields form the electromagnetic field.

When the conductors are in series or parallel resonance at the frequency of the generator—that is, of an electrical length one-half of c/f (where c is the velocity of propagation of electromagnetic waves, and f is the frequency of the generator, so that c/f is the wavelength), a standing wave of current is set up on the conductors. In these circumstances, the input impedance is purely resistive, and all the input power, apart from any rf ohmic losses, is radiated. In the series resonant form the magnitude of this resistance is called the *radiation resistance*, or perhaps more correctly as "the radiation resistance referred to the loop current I_o" so that: R_r equals P/I_o^2 where the term I_o is the maximum value of the standing wave of current on the conductors and R_r is assumed to be located at the point where I_o is flowing. Two conductors in series resonance form what is termed a "half-wave dipole". This is the fundamental form of resonant antenna comprising a single conductor with an electrical length equal to half the wavelength of the working field.

Radiation intensity

The power per unit area in the field of an antenna is termed the power density. If this power density is multiplied by the square of the radial distance from the antenna, the product is the power per unit solid angle, and is called the radiation intensity.

Free space fields

In the equatorial plane of a half-wave dipole, the field in free space is 7·02 $\sqrt{(P)}/d$ V/m, where P is the transmitted power in watts out of the dipole and d is the distance in metres. With an output of 1,000W (1kW) the field is

ANTENNA TOPICS

d is the distance in metres. With an output of 1,000W (1kW) the field is $222/d$ V/m.

Polarization
The polarization of an electromagnetic wave is defined in relation to the electric field; thus a vertically-polarized antenna is one that radiates a vertical electric field, and a horizontal magnetic field. A vertically-polarized wave will be radiated when a generator is connected between a vertical wire and earth, in which case the field strength of the wave will be due to the combined effects of the wire and its image in the surface of the ground (earth) plane. Antennas with either vertical or horizontal polarization, or at some angle between, are termed **linearly-polarized antennas**. If the antenna responds to two orthogonal field components (ie components at 90° to each other) having time phase between these components, the antenna is termed elliptically polarized. In the one particular case where the magnitudes of the two orthogonal components are equal and the phase angle is ±90°, the antenna is said to be circularly polarized.

Reciprocity
In reference to antennas, the term reciprocity means that the directivity and characteristics of an antenna are the same for receiving as for transmitting.

Gain
The gain of an antenna is the ratio of power required at the input of a reference antenna to the input of the given antenna needed to produce, in a given direction, the same field at the same distance. It is usually given in the logarithmic representation in decibels (dB). Basically the gain equals (maximum radiation intensity)/(maximum radiation intensity from a reference antenna with the same power input). Normally such gain is along the main lobe of radiation. It should be noted that the gain of an antenna may be specified in decibels with reference to an isotropic antenna (dBi), or to a half-wave loss-free dipole isolated in space and the equatorial plane of which contains the given direction (dBd), or to a perfect vertical antenna, much shorter than $\lambda/4$ placed on the surface of a perfectly conducting earthplane (dBv).

Isotropic radiator
An imaginary (hypothetical) antenna which is assumed to radiate equally in all directions. Compared with an isotropic antenna, a half-wave dipole has a gain of 1·64 times (2·15dBi); an elementary dipole (an imaginary point source much shorter than a half-wave dipole) has a gain of 1·5 times (1·76dBi); a short vertical has a gain of three times (4·76dBi); a quarter-wave monopole has a gain of 3·28 times (5·15dBi): see Table 1.

Effective radiated power (erp)
This is the power supplied to the antenna multiplied by the relative gain of the antenna in a given direction. For "omnidirectional" vertical antennas the more common term is ermp (effective rdiated monopole radiated power). The term eirp (effective isotropic radiated power) is also used.

Beamwidth
The beamwidth of a directional antenna is generally specified as the angle subtended by the major lobe between the points at which the power has fallen to one-half of its peak value. At these points, field intensity is 0·707 (−3dB) of its maximum value.

Array
A group of radiating elements spaced some distance apart and with the current in each element having a particular amplitude and phase is termed an array. An array of several dipole elements will, in some direction, produce a maximum field strength K times that of a single dipole carrying the same current at its centre as each dipole in the array. The term K is used to denote the array factor.

Front-to-back ratio
The ratio of power radiated in the forward direction of an antenna to that radiated in the opposite direction.

Endfire antenna
An endfire source has maximum radiation along the linear axis; a representive endfire array is the Yagi-Uda antenna.

Broadside array
A broadside source has maximum radiation normal to its axis. A representative broadside array is the horizontal array of dipoles as used for hf broadcasting or, say, a colinear array of dipoles.

Driven element
An element which is connected to the transmitter/receiver via a transmission line. A driven array is one in which all the elements are driven elements.

Parasitic element
An element which is not connected directly to the transmitter/receiver via a transmission line, but receives its energy by the coupling due to the proximity of other elements. In any parasitic array (eg Yagi-Uda antenna) there will be one or more parasitic elements, but at least one element must be a driven element.

Radiation resistance
An antenna has distributed inductance, capacitance and resistance. When the inductance is very much greater than resistance per unit length, the current along the radiation portion varies sinusoidally and the radiation resistance is considered as lumped at the position of maximum current. Where an antenna is less than $\lambda/4$, radiation resistance is considered as being located at the feedpoint. For a resonant half-wave dipole, the radiation resistance is at the centrepoint, and since it is purely resistive it is *in this case* the same as the antenna input impedance and feedpoint impedance. In free space the radiation resistance of a half-wave dipole is approximately 73Ω, neglecting losses and assuming that the dipole length is infinitely greater than its width. In these circumstances radiated power equals the square of the feed current times the radiation resistance.

In practice the centrepoint impedance of a half-wave dipole will be affected by its height above earth, being roughly 73Ω at $\lambda/4$, $\lambda/2$ and $3\lambda/4$ etc, but rising to about 100Ω at $3·5\lambda/10$ and falling to about 60Ω at $6·7\lambda/10$. The presence of additional parasitic or driven elements will tend to reduce the impedance significantly; a reflector placed $1·5\lambda/10$ behind a dipole will reduce its impedance to roughly 25Ω; a three-element close-spaced Yagi array may have a feedpoint impedance of only about 10Ω. The impedance of points equidistant on either side of the centrepoint of a dipole rises with the electrical distance from the centre and, theoretically, at the ends would be infinity; in practice, the ends may have resistive impedance of the order of 2,000 to 5,000Ω, the actual value depending on the losses.

In non-resonant antennas, the input impedance is the vector sum of the effective radiation resistance and the resultant reactance. $Z = \sqrt{(R^2 + X^2)}$, where R is the effective radiation resistance (ie, radiation resistance plus loss resistance) and X is the resultant reactance (ie, the difference between the inductive and capacitive reactances).

Bandwidth
The current taken by a resonant antenna, and hence the radiation, falls off as the frequency is varied away from resonance. There will be two frequencies, one above and one below resonance, at which the power will be reduced by half. The difference between these frequencies is termed the **bandwidth** of the antenna. For example, a half-wave dipole having a length/diameter ratio of 10,000 will have a bandwidth, expressed as a percentage of the resonant frequency, of the order of eight per cent. With a length/diameter ratio of 100 this increases to about 15 per cent. Bandwidth of multi-element Yagi arrays may well be less than five per cent, unless the designer has taken steps to increase this figure.

Folded dipole
A dipole antenna may be made in the form of one or more narrow loops so that, although the overall length is still an electrical half-wave, the antenna current flows through two or more paths. If the conductors are identical, equal and in-phase currents will flow, and the total radiation will be the same as from a simple dipole. But since the currents have been divided equally between the two conductors, the centre feedpoint impedance will be four times as great although the radiation resistance remains the same; thus 4 × 73Ω, nominally taken as 300Ω. As the number of wires in which the current flows increases, the feedpoint impedance increases by the square of the number.

Thus a two-wire folded dipole has four times, a three-wire dipole nine times, and a four-wire dipole 16 times the feedpoint impedance of the single wire dipole. This assumes that the currents divide equally between the wires; in practice a wide range of impedance transformations can be obtained by varying the ratio of diameters and spacings. For example, in practice a two-wire folded dipole using different diameter conductors may have a feedpoint impedance from roughly 2 to 12 times that of the single-wire dipole. It is thus possible to arrange for, say, a multi-element Yagi array with a folded driven element to match accurately a 52Ω coaxial or, preferably, a balanced transmission line.

An important characteristic of the folded dipole is that it will have a bandwidth significantly greater than that of a simple dipole.

Table 1. Maximum (theoretical) gains of lossless basic antennas

Type	Location	Max gain (dBi)	Max gain (dBd)	Direction of max gain
$\lambda/2$ dipole	Free space	2·15	0	Plane perpendicular to axis
$\lambda/4$ vertical monopole	Over perfect ground	5·15	3	On horizon
$\lambda/2$ vertical dipole	Centre $\lambda/2$ above perfect ground	8·2	6.05	On horizon
$\lambda/2$ horizontal dipole	Immediately above perfect ground	9·1	6.95	Straight up
$\lambda/2$ horizontal dipole	$\lambda/4$ above perfect ground	7·4	5.25	Straight up
$\lambda/2$ horizontal dipole	$\lambda/2$ above perfect ground	8·2	6.05	Plane perpendicular to axis, 30° above horizontal
$\lambda/2$ horizontal dipole	$3\lambda/5$ above perfect ground	9·2	7.05	Plane perpendicular to axis, 24·6° above horizontal

(Adapted from *HF Communications Data Book*, Rockwell-Collins)

Notes. In practice, the gain and direction of maximum gain of vertical antennas are affected very much more by ground losses than are horizontal antennas. A power gain of about 5 to 6dBd is usually the most that can be achieved in practice with an hf three-element close-spaced Yagi beam (theoretical 7·5 to 8·5dBd). About 4 to 5dBd (theoretical maximum 5·2dBd) can, with care, be obtained from two elements. Better overall results may often be achieved by raising a (lightweight) two-element Yagi than by increasing the number of elements at a lower height. Field strengths over a long, low-angle path when compared to an antenna at $\lambda/5$ height are roughly × 2 at $2\lambda/5$, × 3 at $3\lambda/5$, × 4 at $4\lambda/5$ and × 5 at 1λ. 1λ loops give roughly a 1dB gain over dipole elements (ie gain of two-el quad can be up to about 6dBd). At vhf, height gain in the range 3 to 10m can amount to about 5·5 to 6·5dB for each doubling of the height in rural areas, 8 to 9dB in urban areas on paths up to 50km, and about half these gains for distances exceeding 100km (source ICAP87). +1dB = × 1·4 the power, +3dB = × 2, +4dB = 2·5, 5dB = × 3·2, 6dB = × 4, 7dB = × 5, 8dB = × 6·3, 9dB = × 7·9, and 10dB = × 10.

The folded Dipole and Monopole

Extracted from 'Technical Topics',
Radio Communication, July 1987

The folded dipole and monopole

The notes above underline the very useful features of using folded elements, though this form of antenna seems to be less commonly used than a few decades ago. Like so many other important developments, the folded dipole came from the fertile brain of Dr John D Kraus, W8JK, whose work has spanned and influenced both professional and amateur radio communications over several decades.

The folded dipole provides roughly twice the bandwidth and, for a given weight of copper, only half the rf ohmic losses of a single-wire dipole. Multi-wire dipoles are, in effect, narrow loop elements and can be implemented with an overall span of λ/2 or alternatively 3λ/4 or 3λ/8 as shown in Fig 1. In each case the antenna current flows through two or more paths, and the nominal feedpoint impedance shown is that for equal wire conductors. A remote high-voltage switch can be used to provide a two-band antenna: Fig 2.

As noted below, recent interest has been centred on folded monopoles but, before reporting this work, it may be worth drawing attention to a relatively little-known 3λ/8 vertical folded antenna working against ground. Fig 3 shows this arrangement together with the total current distribution (vector sum of currents in both wires). The terminal feedpoint impedance is about 250Ω. As W8JK puts it in *Electronics Manual for Radio Engineers:* "An interesting property of this antenna is that due to the multi-wire construction, a current distribution is produced which is similar to that of a vertical top-loaded single-conductor antenna." It can also be assumed that the higher feedpoint impedance, not at the current node, means that earth losses would be less than for a conventional vertical monopole.

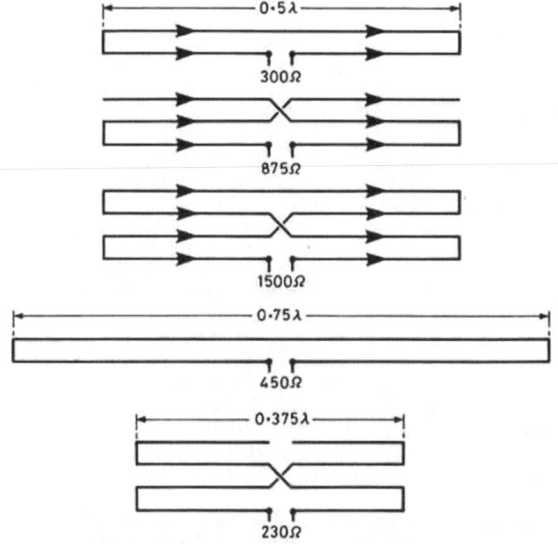

Fig 1. Basic folded twin and multi-wire dipole antennas showing nominal feedpoint impedances (resistive) when used as a single element with equal-diameter wires forming the folded elements

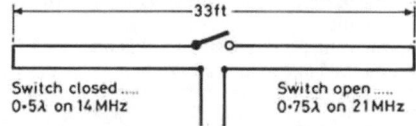

Fig 2. Two-band folded dipole for 14 and 21MHz. Could be scaled for 21/28MHz operation. Best used with open-wire transmission line and atu to accommodate feedpoint impedances of about 300Ω on 14MHz and about 450Ω on 21MHz

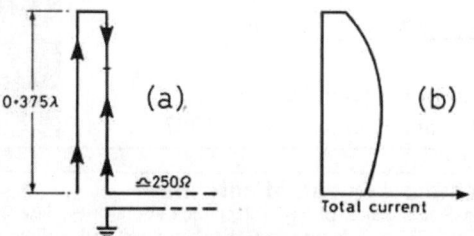

Fig 3. The 3λ/8 vertical folded antenna working against earth. Feed impedance about 250Ω. Current distribution is similar to that of a vertical top-loaded single-conductor antenna

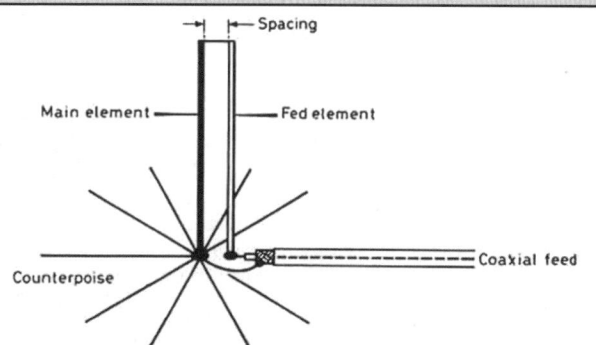

Fig 4. Form of the folded monopole antennas thoroughly investigated by K8CFU and his team. A selection of just six of the 13 variations used on 14MHz is listed in Table 2. Similar exhaustive investigations were carried out on all pre-WARC hf bands from 1·8 to 28MHz. The final detailed report has not yet been published.

Quarter-wave Folded Monopoles

Extracted from 'Technical Topics',
Radio Communication, July 1987

Quarter-wave folded monopoles

Arch Doty, K8CFU, a retired professional engineer, recently kindly sent me a long, detailed report of an extensive study made by himself; John Frey, W3ESU; and Harry Mills, K4HU, and with an input from Dr George Brown, made during 1985-6. This covers the characteristics of λ/4 folded monopole antennas used in conjunction with a 64-radial counterpoise (Fig 4). This work followed on previous investigations into the use of counterpoise and ground-screen "artificial ground" systems as originally reported in *TT* (February 1983).

The final report runs to some 48 pages and includes suggested dimensions of 50Ω and 75Ω folded-monopole antennas for the 1·8, 3·5, 7, 14, 21 and 28MHz bands (the 1·8MHz monopole calls for elements up to 115ft high!) The feedpoint impedance, by using different diameter elements, is designed to match directly into 50Ω and 75Ω coaxial cables without any requirement for an antenna tuning unit. An unexpected, but potentially important, finding was the discovery of the existence of "capacitance bottom loading".

As with the counterpoise study (which involved making some 20,000 measurements) this new study has involved taking thousands of measurements. The detailed report is not intended for publication and has resulted in a patent for land mobile antennas based on these principles. While K8CFU sent his report to prove that not all of the older amateurs are afflicted with neophobia (*TT* March 1987), I have abstracted (Table 2) just a tiny part of the massive amount of data collected by K8CFU.

It is interesting to note that early on in this investigation, the three doughty experimenters (whose combined ages come to 215 years) found that the base impedance of a groundplane monopole is much lower than the oft-published figure of 35Ω. It may be recalled that attention was drawn to this point by G6CJ in *TT* where it was shown that 19 to 21Ω is a typical range, with a few raised horizontal radials. The American team measured the base resistance of λ/4 vertical antennas over a 64-radial counterpoise at between 21 and 33·5Ω, the value decreasing with larger-diameter unipole elements.

ANTENNA TOPICS

Folded Normal-mode Helix Vertical

Extracted from 'Technical Topics',
Radio Communication, July 1987

Folded normal-mode helix vertical

Iain Morris, ZC4IM, has been using some limited spare time to investigate a novel form of folded monopole that shows considerable promise, though it still calls for the type of thorough investigation undertaken by K8CFU and his team of "Old men of the mountains". ZC4IM writes:

"I have been playing about with an antenna idea which looks very promising but I am being beaten by the fact that I have to work! I wonder if those with the time and/or test equipment could take it a stage or two further.

"It concerns the normal-mode helix short elements which, as noted in the April *TT*, have a lot of potential. They also have at least three disadvantages. The first two, restricted bandwidth and low radiation resistance, are common to all loaded antennas. The third, and the reason why the helix element has never really taken off, is the pain and strain of winding the beast, particularly if you want a tapered pitch. That's my opinion, anyway.

"One way of raising the radiation resistance of an antenna is to fold it. But a folded helix sounds as though it would be even more strain and pain to wind. That was my reaction, too, when the idea first crossed my mind. My limited technical library did not mention such a process. So, I folded a vertical helix with four radials and tuned it for 28·5MHz. The reflectometer revealed that not much power was being reflected when fed with 75Ω coaxial cable. The bandwidth between the 2:1 vswr points was 400kHz. Drooping the radials raised the vswr so they were left horizontal. A Chinese copy was made and installed at ZC4AB, the local 28MHz expert. His pet HB9CV antenna had obviously suffered during the winter, and signal reports on the folded helix were about two S-points up. The HB9CV was given a good going over and then showed about an S-point-and-a-bit up on the vertical helix; the trial continues.

"The fuss was taken out of winding the helix elements by using 300Ω ribbon shorted at the top. Just over a λ/2 of ribbon was wound single-spaced by using two lengths of ribbon and then taking one away. The former was a plastic water pipe (32·5mm pvc) and the ribbon was anchored using pvc tape. In the tuning process one of the good points of this format showed itself. Naturally enough, in pruning the ribbon I took a little too much off. It was easy just to uncoil a little of the helix and this put matters right. In fact *The ARRL Handbook* recommends a linear portion at the end to lower the *Q*. The size reduction factor was 0·4 using single spacing.

"The system clearly works. But there are at least two avenues to be explored. The first is the use of this principle for shortened verticals for the lower hf bands. At 7 and 3·5MHz, there should be an increase in radiation efficiency as it would put more power into the antenna and less into the earth resistance. A 7MHz groundplane antenna would be only about 13ft in height. It would be nice to raise this into more-open space, although the 28MHz prototype clearly did not like drooped radials so they must remain horizontal. This is a limitation because, while the radiator has shrunk, the radials remain full size. The next step might be the use of a single radial folded back on itself in a circle. (Or possibly the G6XN form of inductance and capacitively loaded counterpoise?—*G3VA*.) The radius of such a circle would be close to ⅟₁₆th wavelength and such a compact radial could probably be mounted above head height, allowing the lawn to be mowed and stopping anyone from coming into contact with points at high rf. With ribbon helix elements one might need to think of the current capabilities of the ribbon, but since the current would be shared they would be lower than the traditional loaded vertical. Certainly there was no sign of ZC4AB's antenna melting.

"The other use for such helix-wound elements might be for shortened beams, which is how this project started. Believe it or not, I was looking for a beam that would have no forward gain (I am a confirmed 1W QRP man with 90 countries worked) but a good front-to-back ratio. A folded helical dipole works and gives me the required 'no-radiation-off-the-ends and no-real-directivity-anywhere-else' characteristics so I never progressed to an array. I can now work Africa and Japan without attracting the attention of large numbers of strong-signal European stations!

"There are still a number of questions. Can the turns be touching? Could I run two or three different-length ribbons in parallel, just like the old three vertical wires taped to one bamboo? I have a modern version of this on the aforementioned pvc pipe on top of a lightweight aluminium mast and it works a treat. If such a three-band vertical was erected at any height, the horizontal radial system might be three concentric circles. Variation of radiation resistance with spacing and/or diameter could do with looking at. There's plenty of scope for further experimentation."

Two-element HF Beams

Extracted from 'Technical Topics',
Radio Communication, August 1987

Two-element hf beams

Attention is drawn to the long, chapter-length article by Les Moxon, G6XN, "Two-element hf beams" in *Ham Radio* (May 1987, pp 8–12, 14, 17, 19, 21–2, 25–7, 29–32) introduced as follows:

"Physically small beam antennas that represent the least compromise in gain and directivity have been discussed in the literature. Large antennas, for those for whom size is no problem, have received widespread coverage ... Yet the topic of medium-sized antennas—which includes the majority of amateur beams—remains an area of uncertainty, about which many have sought, without success, for more information. The quad-versus-Yagi controversy continues unabated; conflicting claims are made for what might appear to be bewildering variety of different beams; and an imperfect grasp of essentials has turned an inherently simple situation into one of needless complexity, with two-element beams deprived of their rightful status."

TT on a number of occasions has espoused G6XN's belief that it is better to have a lightweight two-element array at a good height than a heavier three-element array nearer the ground; and that the maximum theoretical gain of a two-element array (often dismissed in many texts as 3dB) rises with close-spacing to above 5dBd, only about 1db less than what is likely to be achieved in practice with a 3-element array.

In *Ham Radio* G6XN shows that for two elements the directive pattern—and therefore the gain—depend only upon the phase shift ratio $0/0_0$ and are independent of the size, shape or spacing of elements, provided the dimensions are not excessive. This, he points out, is in flat contradiction of widely-published figures: "Those figures derived mathematically for parasitic arrays show gain and directivity to be *critically* dependent upon spacing and whether an element is tuned as a director or reflector ... although the calculations are correct they happen to be the wrong ones! ... normally performance is sacrificed if the elements are straight ... this is the worst possible shape because it minimizes coupling, consequently precluding the possibility of the presence of equal currents except with very close spacing of the order of 0·05λ."

G6XN outlines a number of designs of two-element horizontal beams with reduced length and enhanced coupling, as well as the application of enhanced coupling to conventionally-shaped beams. A number of his recommended designs should already be familiar to readers of his *HF Antennas for all locations* book and his later "Claw-type" designs, VK5HA planar loading techniques etc as described in *TT*, though with some further developments such as a form of vertical VK2ABQ array suitable for mounting on fence posts.

G6XN concludes by pointing out that his 16-page article is intended to provide guidance, rather than blueprints, for the construction of antennas tailored to suit individual needs. "The Claw designs will be useful even if the best mast available is only a garden post, and I hope that some who have decided that beams are 'not for them' will have second thoughts ... Claw elements are particularly suitable for use as top-loaded verticals for the lower-frequency bands."

For *TT* items on some of the recent G6XN designs see *TT* August 1983, April 1984, March 1985 and January 1987.

The Rhombic - Queen of Antennas

Extracted from 'Technical Topics',
Radio Communication, August 1987

The rhombic—Queen of antennas

In the 'thirties, E Bruce, of Bell Telephone Laboratories, described (*Proc IRE*, August 1931 and January 1935) a then novel highly-directive, long-wire hf antenna in the form of a rhombus (a squashed square): Fig 7. Terminated correctly at the far end, this high-gain antenna provides unidirectional characteristics; unterminated it works as a bidirectional array shooting both forwards and backwards. Within a few years, the rhombic antenna became firmly established for fixed point-to-point commercial and military strategic communications as well as for signals-intelligence interception. Despite limited sidelobe suppression, hf gains of about 8 to over 15dBd could be achieved with broadband characteristics that could extend over several octaves, and gave very desirable low vertical angle performance even when suspended from four relatively low masts (low in terms of professional communications). It rapidly came to dominate the hf point-to-point scene.

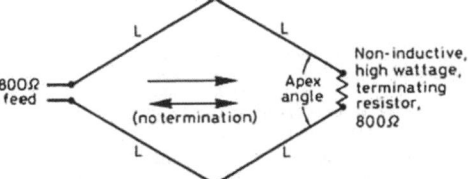

Fig 7. The classic rhombic antenna array providing a unidirectional beam when terminated or bidirectional when there is no terminating resistor. L is normally at least one-wavelength long at the lowest operating frequency

The foreword to a book *Rhombic Antenna Design* by A E Harper of BTL (published by Van Nostrand in 1941) recalled that "When there was built in 1929 at Lawrenceville, New Jersey, a radio telephone station for initiating overseas short-wave service, the most pictured feature of the new establishment was a gigantic wire fence or net, a mile long, stretched across the landscape on a row of 185ft towers. This comprised the transmitting antenna complement for the three telephone circuits to Europe.

"A year ago the nets were taken down, the towers dismantled and sold for junk. Near them had arisen a number of telephone poles carrying at odd-looking angles a few almost invisible wires ... the most spectacular conquest of the rhombic antenna."

Unfortunately for amateur radio, there were two major drawbacks to the rhombic: it needed a lot of space and the directivity could not be easily changed. The result was that amateurs developed instead the compact rotary close-spaced Yagi and W8JK arrays despite the usually lower gain. But amateurs who have ever had access to rhombics for professional applications tend always to cherish a dream that one day they may retire into the countryside and acquire, or get permission to erect poles in, a large flat field and have envied those Australians, ARRL headquarters staff etc with space to erect hf rhombics.

Curiously, few amateurs have shown much interest in using long-wire or rhombic antennas for vhf or uhf where they can be fitted into a suburban garden or even a loft-space, and where an "antenna-farm" of several rhombics pointing in different directions is by no means out of the question.

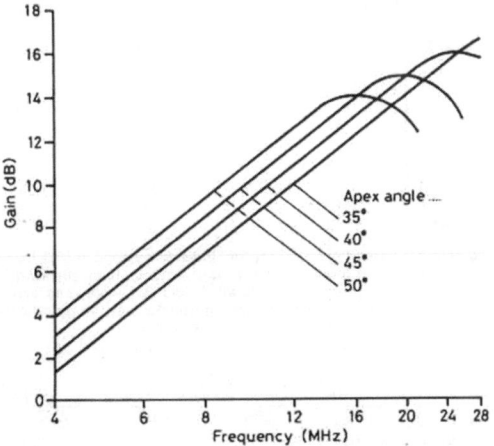

Fig 8. Calculated free-space gain for rhombic in which L is 100m for various apex angles, showing that bandwidth of the array can be used as a design parameter. Note that gain above ground is up to 6dB greater at some elevation angles

Years ago G6CJ demonstrated table-top rhombics working in the microwave region.

Joe Ellis, VK4GL *(Amateur Radio (VK)*, March 1986, pp 10-11) is fortunate enough to be a farmer with access to a rather rough field, about 300 by 140ft, sufficient for an hf rhombic. He notes that "the rhombic antenna is the ultimate in simple wire arrays, where maximum gain is required in a given direction. Many amateurs have aspired to a rhombic only to be deterred by space considerations. To be effective, this antenna needs to be big (in terms of wavelength). Apart from space the requirements are simple: some poles, lots of wire, and a good antenna tuner ... my rhombic is near and over the tops of trees at an average height of 45ft, which is too low. Nevertheless it works superbly ... if I could discover how to turn the farm around, I would dispense with my Yagi antennas."

With a history dating back more than 50 years, it might be supposed that there is little need for more research and development of this antenna. So it was interesting to find in the ICAP87 *IEE Conference Book No 274* (pp 79-80) a paper by A G P Boswell, of the Marconi Research Centre, on "Wideband rhombic antennas for hf" in which the design of rhombics is approached on the basis of achieving performance over a desired frequency range, using modern electromagnetic-computing design techniques. The parameters are the leg length (L) and the apex angle at the feeder/terminating ends; lesser design parameters are the wire diameter, the terminating impedance and the height above ground which affects the elevation angle of the beam.

It is noted that with single-wire rhombics, the characteristic impedance (feed and terminating) is often assumed to be 600Ω but in practice is usually about 800Ω. The paper shows that varying the apex angle results in sub-optimum gain but changes the bandwidth of the antenna. This is illustrated in Table 1. From this it can be seen that a rhombic covering 4 to 16MHz could be constructed with an apex angle of 48° and a leg length of 107m to provide a 10dB gain (4dB free-space gain) at the lowest frequency of 4MHz. With the same apex angle, an antenna with legs 20m long would be usable up to beyond 56MHz whereas if the apex angle was reduced to about 38° the bandwidth would extend to beyond 70MHz band. Conversely it should be possible to achieve 10dB gain at 50MHz on a rhombic covering the 50, 70 and 144MHz bands with legs only about 6.8m long and an apex angle of around 50°. Fig 8 from the ICAP paper shows the calculated free-space gain for a rhombic with 100m legs for various apex angles plotted against frequency, showing how gain increases with frequency up to a fairly clearly defined maximum frequency and then falls off quite rapidly. In practice gain is further increased by 6dB by the presence of the earth plane, as for all practical antennas, to a degree depending upon earth conductivity and the required elevation angle of the main lobe. Theoretically, gain rises at 6dB/octave above an arbitrarily chosen minimum gain of 10dB over ground.

A G P Boswell notes that rhombics fail at the high frequency end of their operating range when the individual radiation patterns of the four radiating wires align themselves so closely with the directions of the wires that the azimuth radiation pattern of the antenna splits into two. This effect is more marked with the wider-angle designs, which also show rather worse sidelobe suppression at the higher frequency.

In his *HF antennas for all locations*, Les Moxon, G6XN, sets out the attractions and the drawbacks of large arrays such as rhombics, and shows that the theoretical gain of a terminated rhombic with the appropriate apex angle increases from about 5dBd with legs one-wavelength long to about 12dB for 5λ legs. He also notes that "with some manipulation of ropes, terminating resistors and feed points, a rhombic can be switched to provide a choice of four directions with a good chance of being able to put a useful sidelobe in most of the other directions that may be needed." The natural level for the pair of first sidelobes is -6dB so that this can still provide a powerful dx signal.

Table 1. Bandwidth of rhombic antennas versus apex angle

Apex angle	f_{max}/f_{min}	L/λ for 10dB gain at f_{min}
36°	5·3	1·82
38°	5·1	1·73
40°	4·9	1·67
42°	4·7	1·60
44°	4·5	1·53
46°	4·3	1·48
48°	4·0	1·42
50°	3·7	1·36

Note: Minimum operating frequency is arbitrarily defined as the frequency at which the free-space gain is 4dB (ie the gain over ground is up to 10dB). Maximum operating frequency is defined as the frequency of maximum gain.

(Source: A G P Boswell, ICAP87)

Resistive-loaded Broadband Antennas

Extracted from 'Technical Topics', *Radio Communication,* September 1987

Resistive-loaded broadband antennas

TT (June 1987, p406) in discussing techniques for broadbanding dipole antennas, made brief reference to the recent work of Dr Brian Austin (G0GSF/ZS6BKW) and Andre Fourie on resistive-loaded antennas, including a new high-efficiency design covering the entire hf band 3 to 30MHz: Fig 2. This uses parallel inductive/resistive loading in much the same way as the "Australian dipole" but as an inverted-V type of "fat dipole" with diverging

ANTENNA TOPICS

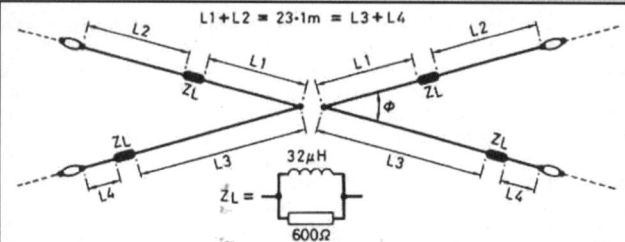

Fig 2. The 3 to 30MHz broadband resistive-loaded inverted-V antenna developed by Dr Brian Austin (G0GSF/ZS6BKW) and Andre Fourie, providing high radiation efficiency and low swr at frequencies down to 3MHz. Feedpoint impedance about 500Ω

wires that would, incidentally, be easier to implement than the Australian dipole with its 1·8m spreaders. However, I omitted to include any information on the actual dimensions of this antenna.

G0GSF, noting the omission, writes: "The homebrew community will be pulling their hair out now that you have whetted their appetites by quoting its performance characteristics without giving the key dimensions! They are as follows:

$$L1 + L2 = L3 + L4 = 23 \cdot 1m$$
$$L1 = 13 \cdot 5m \text{ (hence } L2 = 9 \cdot 6m)$$
$$L3 = 17m \text{ (hence } L4 = 6 \cdot 1m)$$

"Whereas the included angle ϕ does not markedly affect the vswr, the characteristic impedance of the feedline is dependent upon it to some extent. When $\phi = 5°$, Z_o (opt) = 500Ω, whereas $\phi = 0°$ requires Z_o (opt) = 400Ω. The change is so slight that it is probably not really worth worrying about in practice."

With an overall element span of $2 \times 23 \cdot 1 = 46 \cdot 2m$, it could prove difficult to fit such a useful antenna into a back garden, though the inverted-V bow-tie form of construction allows the centre support to be on a roof in order to make use of both front and back gardens.

In my June TT comments I noted that the T2FD was an early form of an antenna loaded resistively to increase bandwidth. Although some amateurs consider that (with a suitable atu) the T2FD does form an effective multi-band design, it was noted many years ago that the T2FD originally stemmed from a US Navy design intended only to broaden the bandwidth of a dipole by a relatively modest degree. Dr Austin comments:

"We certainly did examine the so-called T2FD configuration: both with the computer and experimentally (at least in measuring vswr). Our conclusions were that it is not an effective broadband configuration, and your term 'aperiodic multi-band' is probably far more accurate. Its vswr is certainly very peaky and nowhere near as flat as one American manufacturer would have his customers believe. This was confirmed by both the measured results and the computer prediction. However, when one examines radiation efficiency as well (as we clearly must) then its performance — or lack of it! — becomes really evident. At the 3MHz end it performs about as well as a resistor, rising thereafter in a series of sawtooth-like oscillations to about 70 per cent at 18MHz, but with deep notches down to about 20 per cent around 12 and 24MHz. These figures apply to an antenna 27·4m long and 0·46m between conductors, with nominally an 800Ω load, as would be given by the equations quoted in TT September 1986 for a low-frequency cut-off of 1·8MHz. Scaling dimensions to operate from 3·5MHz would produce the more usual T2FD geometry. This research brought to light a number of important aspects and some of these will be published soon."

'Coco' - the Coaxial Colinear Array

Extracted from 'Technical Topics',
Radio Communication, September 1987

"Coco"—the coaxial colinear array

Some 15 years ago, TT (September and November 1972) drew attention to the way in which coaxial colinear ("coco") antenna arrays (Fig 3) were being used professionally; not only for the comparatively well-known vertical vhf antennas having an omnidirectional horizontal radiation pattern and narrow vertical radiation pattern, but also as a transportable 26-element horizontally-polarised centre-fed array on 49·8MHz (Fig 4) described in *IEEE Trans on Ant & Prop* July 1972, pp513–6. The November 1972 TT included an example of a more conventional 144MHz vertical coco design by W6PIV (Fig 5), and a note from Dud Charman, G6CJ, who recalled that the famous tv pioneer Alan Blumlein of EMI had tried, unsuccessfully, to make such a system work as early as 1935. Although 144MHz designs regularly turn up in amateur radio magazines, there is in my mind a question-mark over this approach. One could not guarantee 100 per cent success.

Recently, however, a detailed theoretical model together with computer simulations of its current distribution and measured performance characteristics have been published for 24- and 26-element coco antennas at 50MHz and for six- and eight-element coco antennas at 915MHz in a short paper by Thiery J Judasz (University of Colorado) and Warner L Ecklund and Ben B Balsey (US National Oceanic and Atmospheric Administration) in *IEEE Trans on Ant & Prop* (March 1987, pp327–31). Warner Ecklund was one of the authors of the 1972 paper noted above.

The paper recalls that large coco antenna arrays along the lines outlined in 1972 have been used successfully for many years. The mesosphere-stratosphere-troposphere radar at Poker Flat, Arkansas, has an antenna made of 256 separate coco antennas constructed from coaxial cable. The Jicamarc radar observatory in Peru has a 50MHz array of 1,536 separate coco antennas, in this case constructed from aluminium tubing. Commercial vertically-polarised coco communication antennas—for example, for two-way mobile radio—are available in the range 400 to 520MHz. Yet, in spite of its relatively wide usage, no thorough theoretical description has previously been published.

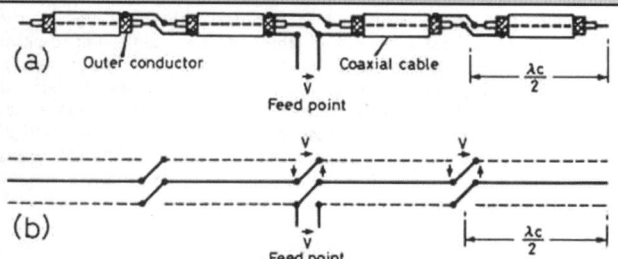

Fig 3. Basic geometry of the "coco" (coaxial colinear) antenna formed from a series of electrical quarter-wave sections of coaxial cable taking into account the velocity factor of the cable

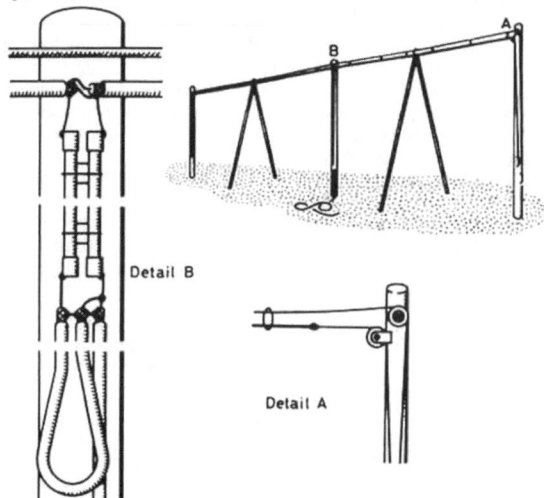

Fig 4. The 26-element portable coco array for 50MHz described in 1972 for mounting on three poles. The nylon messenger line and polyethylene slip rings used to connect to the antenna are shown in detail A and B shows feed arrangement consisting of balun and quarter-wave matching transformer. All electrical connections should be waterproofed

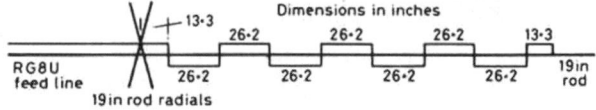

Fig 5. The vertical 144MHz colinear antenna shown horizontally

The IEEE paper includes a first-order mathematical "model" that would be of interest mainly to professional antenna engineers rather than radio amateurs. Nevertheless, the fact that computed and measured radiation patterns of the various coco arrays are in close agreement does at least give more confidence in this design approach. It is also interesting to note that a modification akin to that found in the W6PIV design (Fig 5) was found beneficial. To quote the paper:

"A modification of the 26-element 50MHz antenna yields a much smoother current and phase distribution. In this instance, the last element on both ends of the array has been replaced by a shorted section ($\lambda c/4$ in length) followed by a section of cable ($\lambda air/4$ in length) as discussed by Wheeler in 1956 and by Branner and Williams of RSRE in 1981. For short antennas, both model and measurements show that the final section should be somewhat shorter than $\lambda air/4$ (0·21 λ air) for a modified eight-element antenna at 915MHz... the result of the end treatment is to sharply reduce the sidelobe levels."

1980 - 1989

Antennas - Theory or Practice?

Extracted from 'Technical Topics',
Radio Communication, November 1987

Antennas—theory or practice?
There is an old joke about the newly-licensed amateur who complained that he had standing waves on his antenna. But before joining in the laughter at his expense, one should not forget that there is an important class of antennas which does not (or should not) have any standing-waves on their radiating element—the so-called travelling-wave or transmission-line antennas, including the terminated long-wire, vee-beams and rhombics.

In *HF communications—a systems approach,* Dr Nicholas Maslin provides a grouping of antennas into three main classes to which I have attempted to add some examples from amateur practice:

(1) Self-resonant antennas. In this class fall all types that are based on the half-wave dipole or quarter-wave monopole. While basically single-band systems, there is also a class of multi-band antennas arranged to resonate at a number of frequencies, such as the G5RV, the W3DZZ trap-dipole, multi-wire dipoles etc.

(2) Resonated antennas. These comprise the antennas that use an antenna tuning or matching unit to transform widely varying input impedances to a specific value such as 50Ω, and can be used over a number of bands provided that the atu is adjusted correctly at the different frequencies; examples include Marconi antennas, centre-fed doublets, whip antennas, random-length wires etc.

(3) Broadband antennas. These include antennas designed to present an impedance which remains near-constant over a wide band of frequencies, and are often of the travelling-wave type. Examples include fat dipoles (caged, fan and bow-tie), Beverage and terminated long-wires, rhombics, log-periodics and some Yagi and monopole antennas using special techniques such as discones etc.

The amateur approach to antennas has always tended to be largely pragmatic, often drawing on professional designs but then making modifications and changes until satisfied with the performance by using a gdo, noise bridge etc to make final adjustments rather than attempting to analyse the design mathematically. There is a lot to be said for amateur pragmatism which avoids the complex mathematical procedures that arise from the need to take into account the many variations in siting, element/wire diameter in terms of length/diameter ratios, earth conductivity, effect of nearby objects.

But there is the danger that myths can be created by the absence of objective measurements. It is usually enormously difficult for an amateur to measure, except in the crudest terms, the efficiency or the precise radiation pattern (particularly the vertical radiation pattern) of his or her antenna. Put up a new hf antenna during a spell of good propagation conditions and even the most inefficient "piece of wet string" will span the world. Again, the logarithmic nature of the decibel makes it largely pointless to strive for small increases in efficiency; remember that a terminated rhombic antenna, hailed in the August *TT* as the "queen of antennas" has a maximum "efficiency" of around 50 per cent, compared with the near 100 per cent of a good dipole, with almost half of the transmitter power dissipated in the 800Ω terminating resistor. In the case of the rhombic this matters not at all because that power, had it not been "wasted" in the resistor would have been radiated in the opposite direction to the target area. For sky-wave contacts, it is usually only the tiny fraction of the total power that is radiated at the appropriate vertical elevation in the right direction that travels to the distant station.

In practice some antennas of extremely low efficiency have to be tolerated. Dr Maslin points out that with some of the electrically-small hf antennas used on aircraft, the radiation efficiency at 2MHz can approach −50dB; that is to say, only 10mW radiated from an antenna fed from a 100W output transmitter.

The author of the ICAP87 paper on rhombics, featured in the August *TT,* A G P Boswell of the Marconi Research Centre, is, in *alter ego,* G3NOQ. He writes: "I was pleased to see the *TT* references to my ICAP paper and interested in your suggestions for using these antennas for the low-vhf amateur bands. This had not occured to me, but I would expect them to be equally good at frequencies above 30MHz. At really high frequencies they might benefit from an earth mat to reduce the effects of resistive losses in the ground under the antenna, but I have not done any work to determine at what frequency this effect becomes significant.

"The gain figures I quoted are related to an isotropic radiator and the gain shown in Fig 8 (free space) should be reduced by 2dB to give values relative to a dipole (dBd).

"The usual resistive termination at the unfed end of a rhombic can be replaced by a short-circuit. This does not affect the forward radiation but adds an equal lobe in the reverse direction, although the impedance match might suffer a bit. Another common technique is to run a feeder to both ends of the antenna so that either end can be fed, the other being resistively terminated."

The Groundplane Dissected

Extracted from 'Technical Topics',
Radio Communication, November 1987

The groundplane dissected
Professional engineers have always been far more concerned than amateurs in detailed analyses of the electrical characteristics of antennas. Computer software based, for example, on the "Method of Moments" has opened new possibilities and is encouraging antenna specialists to take a new look at some long-established designs. One antenna that has come under new scrutiny is the humble groundplane.

In a series of *TT* items in 1981 and 1983 an attempt was made to sort out some of the factors affecting the performance of the popular elevated "groundplane" with wire radials and the vertical quarter-wave monopole, with the real earth often assisted by buried radials forming the groundplane (Fig 3). *TT* also told the story (July 1981, page 626) of how Dr George Brown of RCA first used an elevated groundplane antenna with just two wire radials for American police radio operating between about 30 to 45MHz in the

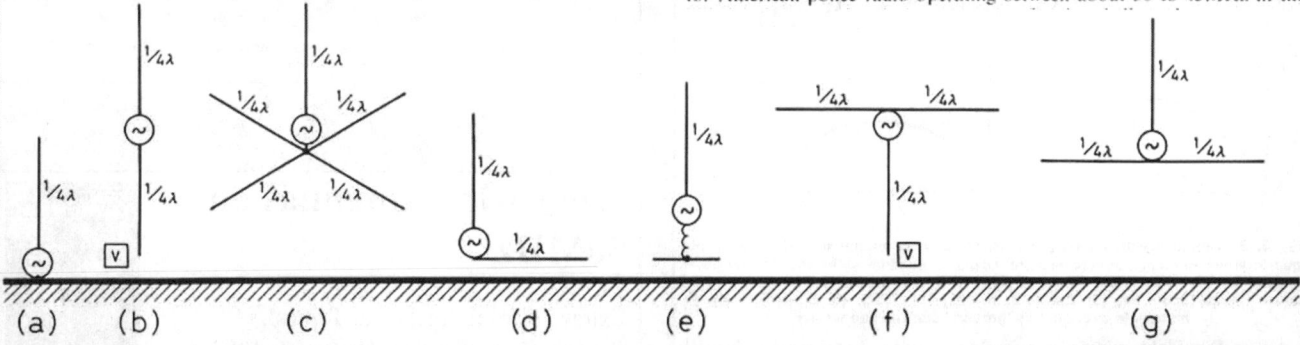

Fig 3. The family of verticals. (a) Standard monopole (unipole) antenna fed against earth. Any significant resistance in the earth connection will dissipate a substantial amount of the transmitter power so that good earthing systems (stakes, radials, mats etc) are most important. (b) The λ/2 vertical dipole requires no direct earth connection but has both high and low angle lobes of radiation. As for all vertical antennas the earth conductivity is important because of the large induced currents. Without very extensive earth mats only limited improvement is likely from any buried radials etc. The antenna can be voltage-fed at V with the current feed-point short-circuited. (c) Conventional four radial ground plane (radials usually slope downwards to facilitate impedance matching). The artificial earth formed by the four radials does not prevent large currents being induced in the real earth. (d) The "bent" dipole (ie single-radial ground plane) results in mixed polarisation and is unlikely to provide true omnidirectional horizontal radiation pattern. Nevertheless it can form an effective general purpose antenna, particularly if the earth conductivity is good. (e) G6XN's inductively loaded counterpoise form of monopole/dipole (March 1981). In practice the "coil" can be in the form of distributed inductance. (f) G3VA's 1970 "inverted ground plane" or "λ/4 T" raises the current maximum in cluttered sites. It can be voltage-fed at V if the current feed-point is short-circuited. (g) The "original" two radial ground plane as developed by Dr George Brown of RCA (additional radials added later to meet customers' wishes!)

ANTENNA TOPICS

'thirties. It was only when customers refused to believe that an antenna having two quarter-wave radials looking like a half-wave horizontal dipole could provide an omnidirectional radiation pattern that he simply added two more radials on the classic principle that the customer is always right. Later, for hf, amateurs found they could obtain a better match to a coaxial feeder by drooping the radials downwards, with the added convenience that these could be extended beyond the insulators to form additional guy wires.

While there is no doubt in my mind that the practical development of the elevated ground-plane antenna in the form we know it was one of the many fundamental contributions to antenna development made by Dr George Brown, and that it was from the RCA work that it reached radio amateurs, Alois Krische, DJØTR/OE8AK (letter in *Ham Radio*, June 1987, page 6) has traced an earlier description of this antenna in a series of patents taken out by Dr Maurice Ponté of CSF (French patent No 764,473 of 1933, US patent No 2,026,652 applied for in 1933, UK patent No 414,296 applied for in 1934) covering all the significant features such as elevated feedpoint, coaxial feeder and radials. Alois Krische points out that this does not diminish the role of Dr George Brown as a great American inventor and antenna specialist.

A check of the Patent Office summary of 414,296 confirms that part of a patent for "Aerials: directive wireless signalling" indisputably includes the outline of a groundplane antenna and the note: "To reduce losses in the feedline to a short-wave aerial mounted at a considerable height above the ground, a conductor which may be shaped as a disc or square, or as a series of radiating wires, is mounted at the foot of the aerial and connected to one of the feedlines". A diagram shows a current distribution with both element and groundplane a quarter-wavelength. And if you are wondering how an "omni-directional" gpa could form part of a directive system, the answer is that a series of vertical reflectors were mounted at the extremity of part of the solid ground-plane which was rotatable!

Melvin M Weiner of The Mitre Corporation (an American research organisation that specialises in R&D for the US Services) in "Monopole element at the center of a circular groundplane whose radius is small or comparable to a wavelength" (*IEEE Trans on Ant & Prop* May 1987, pp488 to 495) takes an in-depth look at elevated monopole antennas above circular thin-copper groundplanes. To quote the abstract: "The input impedance and directive gain of a monopole antenna at the centre of a circular groundplane in free space are summarised for arbitrary element length and element radius with groundplane radii of zero to more than two wavelengths. Numerical results are obtained by utilising various models and are compared with measurements. The models include a groundplane of zero extent, the integral equation method, method of moments, combined with the geometric theory of diffraction (gtd)."

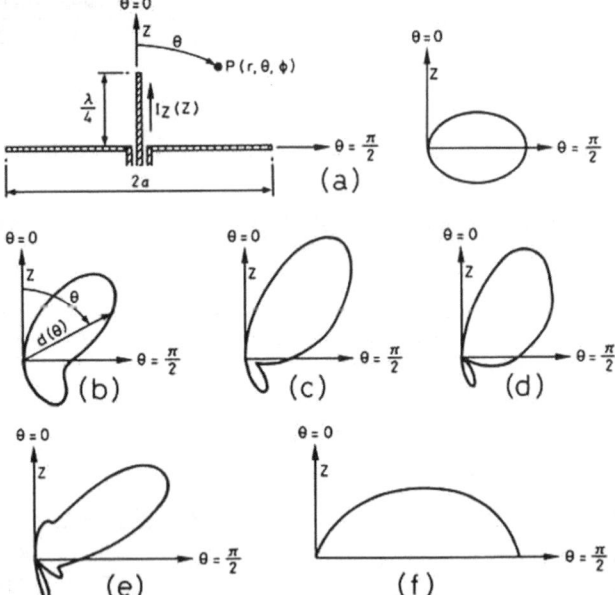

Fig 4. Elevation directive gain patterns, for any azimuthal direction, of a thin quarterwave element mounted on a ground plane of radius *a*. The patterns are polar graphs on the same linear scale. (a) $2\pi a = 0$ ie wire radial(s) in free space. (b) $2\pi a/\lambda = 3$, (c) $2\pi a/\lambda = 4$, (d) $2\pi a/\lambda = 5$, (e) $2\pi a/\lambda = \sqrt{(42)}$, (f) $2\pi a/\lambda =$ infinity (ie monopole over perfect "ground" such as sea water)

Such a formidable paper may seem far removed from amateur radio, and certainly much of it is far beyond my understanding, but it has the merit of including not only computer modelling but direct comparisons with practical antennas between 30 and 254MHz, using a circular copper ground plane of 4ft radius. And by a groundplane of "zero-extent" I assume that what is meant is a quarter-wave element with one or more thin-wire radials. It thus helps to settle those 1981-3 debates about such matters as the input impedance of a groundplane antenna (theoretically 19·43Ω).

Many published texts continue to give the impedance (radiation resistance) at the base of both grounded monopoles and elevated ground-plane antennas having a few insulated wire radials as about 35–36Ω (half of the 70–73Ω of a half-wave dipole, half-wave above ground), and shows how the diameter of a solid ground plane affects the vertical radiation pattern: Fig 4.

While the figure of 35Ω is roughly correct for the ideal monopole mounted on a perfectly conducting earth, or earth assisted by a large number of buried radials, this is **not** the case for the elevated gpa, as Dud Charman, G6CJ pointed out in *TT*, many years ago. He reported having measured the radiation resistance of an elevated resistance as "less than 20Ω" (the figure given in *Radio Communication Handbook*). To provide a good match to 50Ω coaxial cable it is necessary to use either a folded radiating element (*TT*, July 1987) or to slope the radials downwards by about 40°. G6CJ gave the simple formula $R = 18(1 + \sin\theta)^2$ as a useful guide. If θ is 90° the antenna becomes a vertical half-wave dipole, with an R of 72Ω; the solution for 50Ω gives θ as 42°.

Linear Loading of Short Elements

Extracted from 'Technical Topics', *Radio Communication,* November 1987

Linear loading of short elements

A note from Dr Constantino Feruglio, IV3VS expresses satisfaction with the technique of "linear loading" elements for a 1·8MHz dipole antenna with an overall span of 54m. He based his design on the notes by Bill Orr, W6SAI in his *Antenna Handbook* which in turn drew upon the Hy-Gain linear loaded elements for their 7MHz beam. He simply multiplied the dimensions shown in Fig 5 by four. W6SAI points out that loading coils, unless of exceptionally high-Q construction, add considerable rf ohmic resistance loss. While the Hy-gain elements are made of aluminium tubing with the folded portions of 12 gauge hard-drawn copper wire, the version built by IV3VS for 1·8MHz uses only copper wire of 2·5mm diameter. Feed impedance will be affected by the folding and also, of course, by the height above ground which on 1·8MHz is likely to be only a small fraction of a wavelength. This is no problem if a balanced feeder (open wire, slotted 300Ω ribbon etc) is used with a suitable atu. IV3VS points out that if switched into the arrangement of Fig 4(b) of *TT*, December 1986, ("folded back dipoles") the system becomes a random "double zepp" working well on 3·5, 7, 14, 21 and 28MHz. But in the version shown here it will work without switching on the same bands. He adds: "Even shortening the span to 40m and increasing the folded lower portion, the antenna will still work satisfactorily on 1·8MHz." My own feeling is that with open-wire balanced feeder one could dispense with the linear loading altogether provided that the atu can cope with the impedances which will then be governed by the overall length of element plus feeder wire, in a conventional "doublet" arrangement.

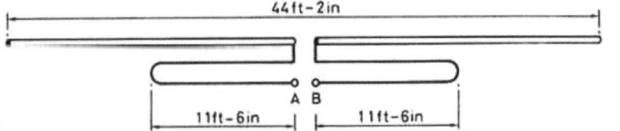

Fig 5. "Linear loading" of a short half-wave element as used in 7MHz array (W6SAI's Antenna Handbook)

Long-wire Antennas on 50MHz

Extracted from 'Technical Topics', *Radio Communication,* December 1987

Long-wire antennas on 50MHz

In the August *TT* I wrote: "Curiously, few amateurs have shown much interest in using long-wire or rhombic antennas for vhf or uhf where they can be fitted into a surburban garden or even a loft-space...". Mike Parkin, G8NDJ is an exception and confirms that a simple long-wire antenna can put out a potent signal on 50MHz. He writes: "Having built a 50/144MHz transverting system.

I was naturally keen to test it out. I did not have a 50MHz antenna so I decided to try my long-wire antenna used for listening on the hf spectrum. Rather to my surprise the antenna loaded after using a length of 75Ω coaxial cable as a matching transformer. The system worked well and I was constantly asked by the amateurs contacted for the details. It was sugested that I send along the information for possible publication.

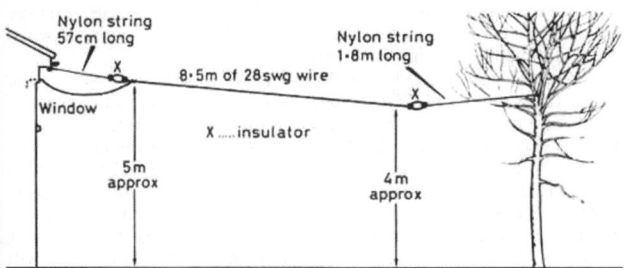

Fig 8. Basic 50MHz "long-wire" antenna used by G8NDJ

"Basically the antenna is 8·5m of 28swg copper wire suspended between the house and a tree at the bottom of the garden using insulators and nylon cord. At the house end is attached 1·8m of copper wire to act as feeder between the 75Ω matching transformer and the horizontal span of the antenna. There is 9cm of this inside the house, the rest (1.71m) attached (by soldering) to the antenna and passed through the wooden window frame.

"Initally the coaxial cable was 4m long and I chopped it back 5–10cm at a time until the swr meter reading dropped to near unity. In practice 3.9m of cable resulted in a match of 1·1:1.

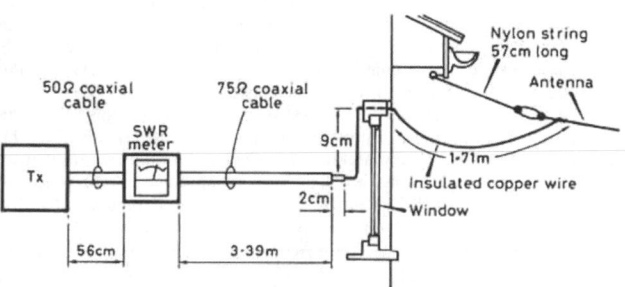

Fig 9. Details of matching arrangement used by G8NDJ

"I have been very pleased with the performance. Local contacts fall off beyond about 20 miles but it has resulted in cross-band contacts (via Sporadic-E?) with Norway, Spain, Switzerland, Italy, Germany and Portugal in a few weeks of operation. It provides a simple and cheap antenna and one that would be well suited to portable operation."

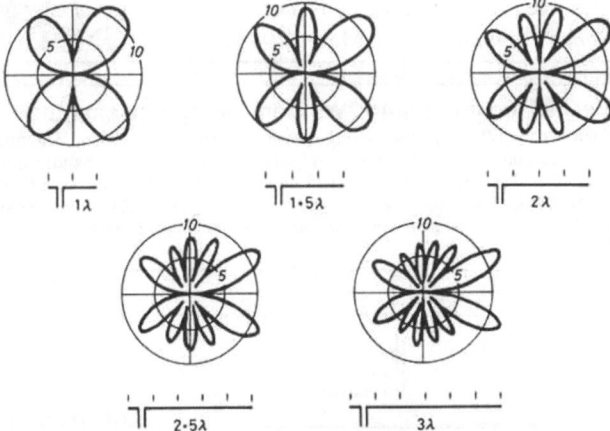

Fig 10. Horizontal radiation patterns of "long-wire" antennas fed at one-quarter wavelength from one end. Note increasing asymmetry with length of resonant long wire antennas

The ususal way of feeding a vhf long-wire with coaxial cable is simply to connect the coaxial cable to a resonant long-wire, a quarter-wave in from one end. The possibility of using "stretched" long-wire antennas using capacitors at the appropriate intervals should not be overlooked.

G6XN's End-fed Windom

Extracted from 'Technical Topics', *Radio Communication,* February 1988

G6XN's end-fed Windom

Almost 60 years ago (*QST* September 1929), L Windom, W8GZ, described the use of a single-wire feeder for a half-wave dipole antenna. This soon became known worldwide as a "Windom antenna" although (as John D Kraus, W8JK, has pointed out) the principle of the single-wire feeder was originally conceived and developed by Bill Everitt and John Byrne at Ohio State University.

In effect, the single-wire feeder, when matched correctly to the correct point along the dipole element, is itself a transmission-line antenna so that some energy must always be radiated from such a feeder, unlike a twin-wire or coaxial transmission line. The traditional method of adjusting the tapping point is to aim at there being no standing waves on the feeder wire (in the early days by running a neon along the line). Nevertheless, even when correctly adjusted, a single-wire feeder always radiates some energy and is to some extent a lossy feeder and a source of moderate rf fields when brought into the shack.

Les Moxon, G6XN, in a recent letter, admits that in his book, *HF antennas for all locations* (RSGB), he gives the Windom antenna a rough time, including it in the section "feeder systems to be avoided" and emphasising its losses. However, this assumed a long feeder line, and he points our that for a feeder length of around λ/2 it can be shown that the power radiated from it is the same as from a dipole carrying, at its centre, the same relatively low current. It is thus equivalent to a loss of only 0·6dB; this would rise to a much more significant 3dB loss by radiation only for a very long straight single-wire feeder.

"In addition there is the earth loss which comes to 0·18dB for a quarter-wave 'artifical earth' which has the advantage of being easy to calculate, but could probably be eliminated (at least at the lower frequencies where it can be long enough to be out in the clear) by using a shorter wire or counterpoise with inductive loading.

"I have applied the idea to a full-wave inverted-V for 7MHz, erected as a temporary substitute for a beam lost in the October hurricane. This has yet to be evaluated for 7MHz dx but works as well as can be expected of a long-wire antenna on 14MHz where the swr is about 3·0, though on 7MHz it is less than 1·2! Perhaps more to the point, I set up a 'scale model' at 29MHz, comparing a half-wave dipole centre-fed (75Ω twin feeder) with the same dipole end-fed with about 1·5λ of single wire. Assuming a loss of 0·35dB in the twin feeder, the total loss for the single-wire feeder plus artificial earth came to 2dB (ie 1·65dB down) which seems reasonable but emphasises the need to keep the single-wire feeder lengths as short as possible (for 3·5MHz even a half-wavelength would represent a very long feeder!).

"Replacement of the centre feed by end-feeding, Zepp-fashion but with a G6CJ balancing stub, gave identical results but only after going to some length to reduce stub losses (heavy gauge and widespacing). Removal of the balancing stub then caused a loss of only 1dB, in line with experience that the conventional Zepp feed *sometimes* seem to work well enough."

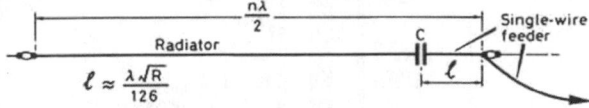

Fig 11. G6XN's end-fed Windom antenna with single-wire feeder. λ is wavelength in feet. R is radiation resistance (referred to a current loop). A value of 500Ω is assumed for the impedance of the single-wire feeder. Reactance of capacitor C is 1/λ. C approximately equal to 70λ/l.
Values found in practice:
At 7MHz, l = 12ft for n = 2 (C = 27pF)
At 29MHz, l = 2ft for n = 1 (C variable and not measured but estimated to be about 5pF).
Principle of operation: From a point of maximum rf voltage on the antenna one moves a short distance outwards to find an impedance (from a Smith Chart) equal to R + jx, where R matches the single wire feeder, X being tuned by the capacitor. Since l is short and current in it small, its virtual removal from the radiator has negligible effect on field strength

G6XN has developed further thoughts on Zepp antennas and or radials but these must be held over. So back to the end-fed Windom: Fig 11. G6XN writes: "The important thing is that it provides a much simpler method of end feeding, without the complication of the G6CJ balancing stub, the unpredictable losses of the conventional Zepp arrangement, or the mechanical and weatherproofing problems of remote tuners for voltage-fed antennas. Were it not for these problems, end-feeding would tend to be more attactive than centre feeding for non-rotatable antennas,

ANTENNA TOPICS

since the ends are more likely to be within reach of or close to the shack. In addition the centre of the element no longer has to support the weight of the feeder.

"The matching principle used for the single-wire feed had previously been used in a two-wire version for matching the 'Claw' antenna at ground level (near the mast) on 10MHz, and for matching each of a pair of inverted-V elements at 7MHz. I have never come across it elsewhere and find it extremely useful; however, since it is more or less what the Smith Chart tells one to do, I can hardly claim it to be original.

"The single-wire feeder should be particularly useful for inverted groundplanes (see for example *TT* November 1987, Fig 3(f), p836). It may also be of interest to note that if R increases as f^2 and is small enough, one would have an ideal multiband system with nearly the same value of capacitance needed, in the same place, on the fundamental and all harmonics until l approaches one-eighth-wave. There is a tendency for this and, though it does not quite happen in practice, the fact that capacitors for different bands are nearly co-located and in many cases accessible does lead to interesting possibilities for multiband operation, without the loss of efficiency and the 'rf in the shack' problems sometimes associated with random-length wire antennas; but one is restricted by the need to keep the feeder short in terms of wavelength."

Groundplanes of Zero Extent

Extracted from 'Technical Topics',
Radio Communication, March 1988

Groundplanes of zero extent

In *TT* November 1987, pp836-7, in "The groundplane dissected", it was reported that in his analysis of the groundplane antenna, Melvin M Weiner (The Mitre Corporation) referred to a groundplane of "zero-extent" without explaining what this implied. The term was unfamiliar to me, and I assumed wrongly that the author meant a quarter-wave monopole element with one or more thin wire radials, as opposed to the solid groundplanes of the other groundplane antennas analysed in his paper.

However, Dr Brian Austin, G0GSF, of the University of Liverpool, has followed up the references listed in Weiner's paper and has obtained, for the university library, a copy of the book *Monopole Elements on Circular Elements on Circular Ground Planes* by M M Weiner, S P Cruze, Li Cho-Chou and W J Wilson (Artech House, 1987). This devotes a

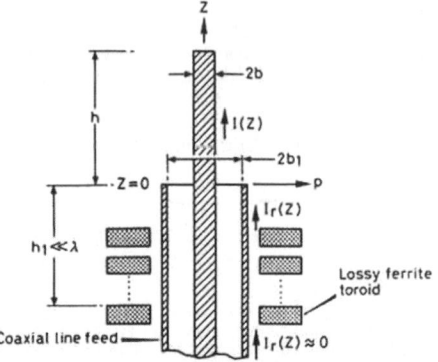

Fig 13. Zero-extent groundplane antenna as described by Melvin Weiner (Mitre Corporation)

special section to the concept of a groundplane of zero extent. It turns out to be precisely that: a quarter-wave elevated monopole with *no* radials. Such an antenna could be of practical value for some amateur radio as well as professional applications, as well as throwing fresh light on the role of radials. G0GSF writes:

"This antenna is effectively an electrically thin monopole element with no groundplane nor any semblance of one, even in the form of radials. What is interesting of course is how one feeds such a configuration, and Fig 13 from the book contains the answer. The use of the lossy ferrite toroids around the coaxial cable, providing a choke against the outer-braid current, does the trick. This is, in effect, the form of balun proposed by Walter Maxwell, W2DU, in *QST* March 1983.

"Weiner's experimental results (Table 2 in the IEEE paper) do not show this configuration though, so it leaves unanswered the question to some extent. What it does seem to suggest is that the usual horizontal radials are in effect playing no part other than acting as a shield which prevents (decreases?) the flow of current on the outer-braid of the coaxial feeder cable. Tilting the radials downwards through an angle does indeed (as G6CJ has shown) increase the feed point resistance. But is this effect though not just because more current can now flow on the braid because of a decrease in shielding effectiveness of the tilted radials, thereby bringing the 'other half' of the dipole into play? There is clearly scope for some careful measurements in this area!"

The W2DU ferrite-bead choke balun (*QST* March 1983) referred to above was described in *TT* February 1984, pp134-5, and does appear to differ from the zero-extent groundplane in one important respect. The *TT* item noted that the choke balun "is obtained by placing numbers of ferrite beads or sleeves around the final length of coaxial feedline. By using the added lengths of small diameter cable of the same impedance as the main feeder, numbers of ferrite beads having an inner diameter of 0·197in and length of 0·190in can be threaded on to the extra cable to produce 'a superb, compact, wide-band balun'. Note that such a balun does not transform the impedance and so may not be directly substituted for a 4:1 ratio balun."

W2DU described a 1·8 to 30MHz choke balun, only 12in long including connector, using 50 No 73 ferrite beads (Amidon FB-73-2401 or Fair-Rite 2673002401-0, μ 2,500 to 4,000) over 50Ω Teflon-dielectric RG303/U cable (or RG-141/U with the fabric covering removed). For 30 to 250MHz, use 25 No 43 beads (Amidon FB-43-2401, Fair-Rite No 2643002401, μ 950 to 3,000).

The ferrite beads used by W2DU form primarily an rf choke, blocking the flow of rf currents down the outer braid of the feeder, as an alternative to coiling into a few turns the final length of the coaxial feeder (for 14 to 30MHz several turns of cable of about 8in diameter should suffice). On the other hand, the Weiner groundplane requires the use of *lossy* ferrite, as used in tvi filters, to absorb the power on the outer of the cable braid. To quote the book: "For sufficiently lossy ferrite toroids along the outside of the coaxial line, the current on the exterior of the coaxial line's outer conductor may be neglected."

What is by no means clear, at least to me, is whether this technique means that the feedpoint impedance of the monopole is raised to the extent of permitting direct matching of a 50Ω feedline. There is obviously work to be done in evaluating this form of antenna, which could be likened to the once-popular "sleeve dipole" without the sleeve but with a considerable amount of power wasted in those lossy toroids.

Coaxial-fed Multiband 'Windom' Long-wire

Extracted from 'Technical Topics',
Radio Communication, March 1988

Coaxial fed multiband "Windom" long-wire antenna

Gian Moda, I7SWX, sends along details of a simple multiband antenna that works on all bands from 3·5 to 28MHz, including WARC bands other than 10·1MHz: Fig 15. It is in effect an adaptation of the twin-wire form of the 300Ω Windom antenna but fed with 75Ω coaxial cable by means of a 4:1 balun. He has used this antenna for nearly 10 years with powers up

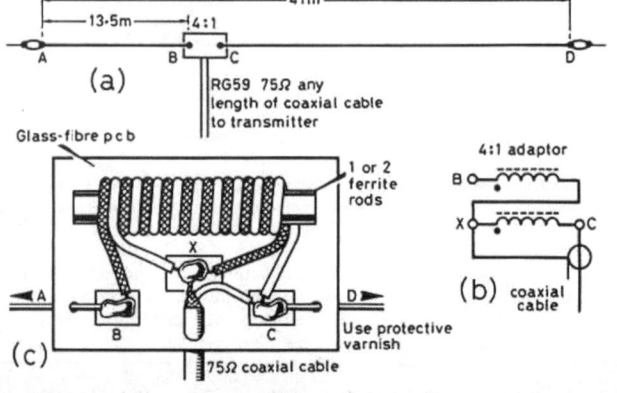

Fig 15. I7SWX's multiband antenna and 75/300Ω balun transformer

a 4:1 balun. He has used this antenna for nearly 10 years with powers up to 200W rf, and finds the swr at the transmitter is quite low, not more than 2:1 at the band edges. The 4:1 transformer is made of pvc wire (eg black and red wire used for connecting loudspeakers to hi-fi amplifiers) connected as shown. It does not saturate, I7SWX reports.

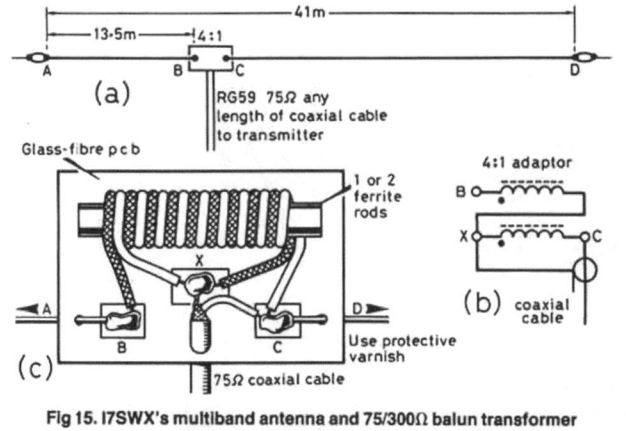

Fig 15. I7SWX's multiband antenna and 75/300Ω balun transformer

Small Antenna Elements

Extracted from 'Technical Topics', *Radio Communication,* May 1988

Small antenna elements

While the vhf/uhf operator seldom needs to worry about the size of his dipole elements, this is by no means the case on hf, and even more so on our single mf band (1·8MHz). The restricted size of the average British garden and the limited scope for antennas for the flat-dweller has encouraged the use of electrically-short antennas: elements brought into half-wave or quarter-wave resonance by means of coils, capacitance hats or the various forms of linear loading, including the simple dropping down of the ends of a dipole element, zig-zag or meander or helical elements etc. Over the years, *TT* has included many novel forms of small antennas, many developed initially for professional applications.

Recently, skimming through a library copy of *Small Antennas* by K Fujimote, A Henderson, K Hirasawa and J R James (Research Studies Press), I was relieved to find that the majority of the loading techniques in this high-cost book have been featured in *TT*, though by no means all have subsequently received the attention that they perhaps deserve.

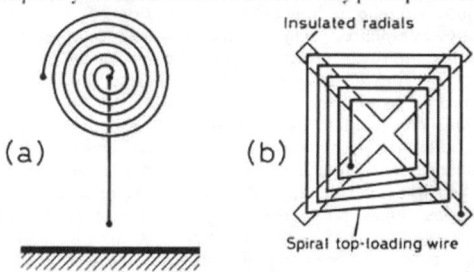

Fig 4. (a) Basic configuration of the spiral top-loaded antenna (stla) designed initially for use at vlf but later investigated by the Canadian Broadcasting Corporation and shown to be effective at mf and hf. (b) Practical implementation as used by CBC

The long-established "T" and "inverted-L" form of top-loading, although requiring two supports, remains among the most effective vertically-polarised antenna where there is not sufficient height for a full quarter-wave monopole. Less recognised is the spiral top-loaded antenna (stla) which was described in *TT* November 1974, pp764-5: Fig 4. This is a more effective form of loading, provided that the turns are far enough apart, than the more usual top-loading coil plus capacitance hat of equivalent area. Another little-used arrangement is the folded umbrella arrangement (*TT* July 1974) which allows a mast radiator of only 0·1λ (or more) to be fed directly from coaxial cable: Fig 5.

The use of short linear or helical dipole elements with capacitance hats, however, is now quite widely used. Both Doug Harris, GW3NDR and Dr Constantino Feruglio, IV3VS, have recently reported good results from the use of this class of antenna.

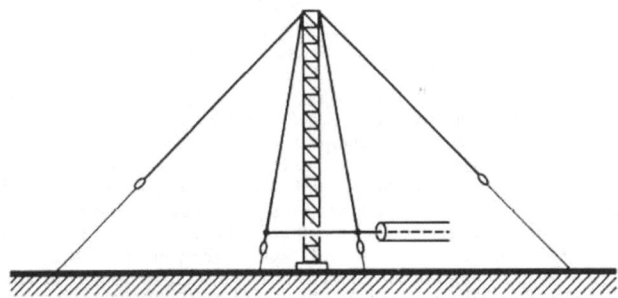

Fig 5. The folded umbrella antenna configuration which allows mast radiators of one-tenth-wavelength or more to be fed directly from low-impedance coaxial feeder cable as developed for mf broadcasting

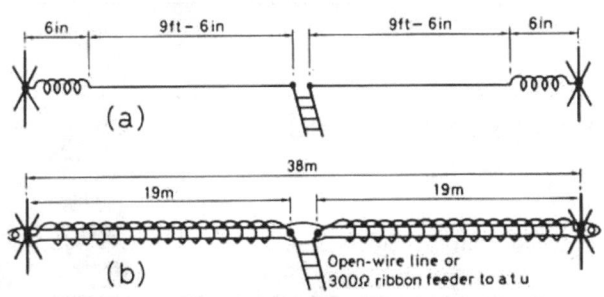

Fig 6. Shortened dipole antennas. (a) GW3NDR's 14MHz dipole with 20ft span using aluminium tubing with loading coils and capacitance hats. (b) IV3VS's multiband dipole for 1·8 to 30MHz using helically-wound wire element wound on nylon rope with capacitance hats that serve also as corona dischargers

GW3NDR, with a span limited to about 20ft, uses the arrangement shown in Fig 6(a) on 14MHz with excellent results, the element being mounted 30ft above ground on a chimney. He writes: "The end-loading coils are wound with 18swg on 0·75in plastic waste water pipe. The capacitance hats were made from copper-plated mild-steel welding rods (from Halfords). The loading coils have spaced turns (about single wire diameter spacing) and consist of about twice the length of wire of the portion of the element missing from a full-size dipole (in this case each coil comprises about 13ft of wire). The antenna was checked with a gdo at ground level, and adjusted by means of the coils so that the antenna was roughly resonant on 14MHz. Because it is fed with open-wire feeders this is not critical. Using aluminium tube the antenna is very light and easily mounted on a single pole or support. I feed it with a Z-match atu and find it will work also on 21MHz. The results seem comparable to a full-sized dipole. It is easy to make, cheap and requires little adjustment. The hardest part is making the open-wire feeders."

IV3VS noted relevant references in *TT* November 1974; *QST* June 1971, and the Teletron Slinky Dipole (*QST* February 1974) as well as some references to helically-wound dipoles in the 1986 *ARRL Handbook*. He built a helically-wound dipole using nylon rope (diameter 10mm). Each arm is 19m long wound with 80m 1·6mm-diameter enamelled copper wire (total of 160m of wire). The turns are about 7/8mm spaced. The ends of the helical diple have capacitance hats, which prevent corona

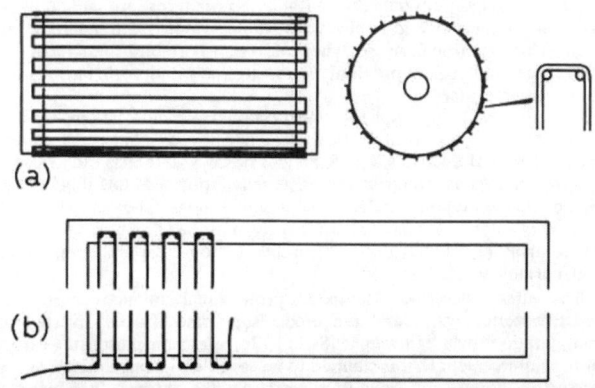

Fig 7. Non-inductive end loading for very short end-fed 1·8MHz antennas. (a) Coil-like construction suitable for external use. (b) A flat frame may be more suitable for indoor/attic antennas. As described by G2QM in 1958

ANTENNA TOPICS

effect (three wire spokes, each wire 1m long) and which also lengthen the antenna electrically. The antenna is fed directly using 300Ω ribbon feeder and atu. This works well from 1·8 ro 28MHz (some peculiar radiation patterns). IV3VS considers this a really good multiband compromise for those without space for a full 1·8MHz dipole.

It is not effective to end-load an antenna element with a close-wound coil unless this connects into a capacitance hat. However, as for the stla it *is* possible to end-load with a wire having relatively little mutual inductance between the turns. As long ago as 1958, Dr M J Heavyside, G2QM ("Aerials for confined spaces", *RSGB Bulletin* January 1958, pp318-9) showed how a loading "coil" comprising 37 wires each 3ft long (114ft in all) could be "wound" between two circular end pieces spaced 3ft apart, using insulated pegs, and winding as shown in Fig 7(a). With this amount of loading, a 14ft length of antenna wire, fed as a quarter-wave Marconi antenna, was claimed to radiate well on 1·8MHz. G2QM also used an end-loaded indoor antenna in his attic, for which he found a flat 3ft square frame, suitably insulated, more convenient. Then, with a 15ft wire and 8W input to his transmitter, he could work around the UK on 1·8MHz, even reaching Paris and attracting a letter of complaint from the GPO saying he was causing interference to marine traffic at a Danish coast station!

Antennas for Medium-haul Paths

Extracted from 'Technical Topics', *Radio Communication*, June 1988

Antennas for medium-haul paths

The changing role of hf for professional and military communications, with the emphasis now increasingly on its use for medium-distance links of under 2500km, has resulted in new thinking in relation to mobile, transportable and fixed antennas. The traditional whip is not suitable where maximum high-elevation radiation is required; adaptive frequency control and frequency-hoppers have similarly caused more emphasis to be given to broadband rather than sharply resonant systems. Mobility demands antennas that are easily erected.

Sky-wave radiation from a dipole only a few feet above ground is often far more suitable for distances of a few hundred miles than a 10m whip. Some broadcast antennas, particularly those for "tropical" broadcasting, have long recognised the need for antennas radiating skywards. Indeed this was once vividly described in a two-part article by Paul Sollom, G3BGL/VS7PS, "Skybeams, Moonbeams and Howitzers" (*RSGB Bulletin*, July, August 1952) where he reported his experimental work for a broadcast service from Ceylon (Sri Lanka) to Southern India with a target area some 300 to 700 miles distant. Even broadcasters aiming at world coverage are now concentrating more on "single-hop" coverage by making use of relay bases dotted around the globe, backed up by transmitters with powers climbing up to megawatt levels.

The April IEE HF Conference included a paper "Numerical modelling and design of loaded broadband wire antennas" by Dr Brian Austin (G0GSF) and Andre Fourie, describing in detail the broadband resistive-loaded antenna noted in *TT* (September 1987, p662) and also mentioned briefly in *Electronics & Wireless World* and *Ham Radio*. In the IEE paper, it is pointed out that "Radiation patterns are generally of secondary importance in applications where low-gain wire antennas are used. This is particularly so when the (transportable) antenna is frequently erected in close proximity to the ground with its orientation often somewhat irregular".

A term now being applied in professional communications is "nvis links", standing for "near-vertical incidence skywave links". A conference paper by B S Collins & B R Phillips of C&S Antennas Ltd gives the options for nvis as: compact loop antennas; horizontal low dipoles; fan dipoles; loaded dipoles; delta (half-rhombic) loops. The "most satisfactory" nvis antenna for fixed stations is given as the (sloping) log-periodic dipole array (1pda) but this is regarded as "too large and complex for transportable use."

The authors describe a new C&S professional antenna comprising a resistive-loaded broadband fan dipole supported (in the inverted-vee configuration) by a lightweight (8·2kg) 12m telescopic mast using carbon fibre reinforcement that is claimed to be capable of being erected by one person in 10min, and able to support an 8kg antenna in a wind of 100km/h. The antenna (Fig 3) is a three-wire fan dipole intended for use at any frequency between about 4MHz and about 15MHz, presenting an average and reasonably constant impedance of 450Ω. No details are given of the resistive loading devices positioned towards the ends of the dipole arms but these presumably are basically similar to those of the Australian dipole and the improved Austin/Fourie design.

The paper notes that: "the absolute gain of the antenna was compared at the lower end of its working band (ie about 5MHz) with that of a half-wave dipole mounted 0·25λ over good flat ground, confirming that

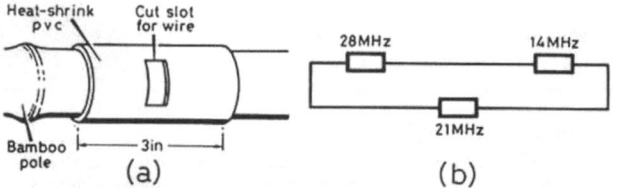

Fig 3. Practical resistive-loaded transportable fan dipole antenna with broad-band feed impedance of about 450 ohms between about 4 and 15MHz as developed for commercial and military applications by C&S Antennas Ltd (*IEE Conference Publication No 284*)

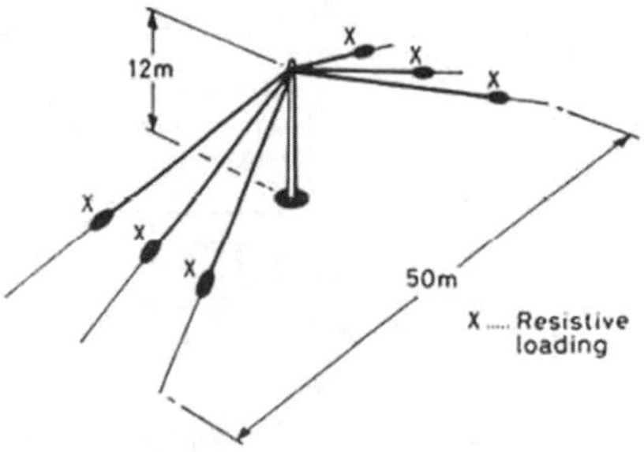

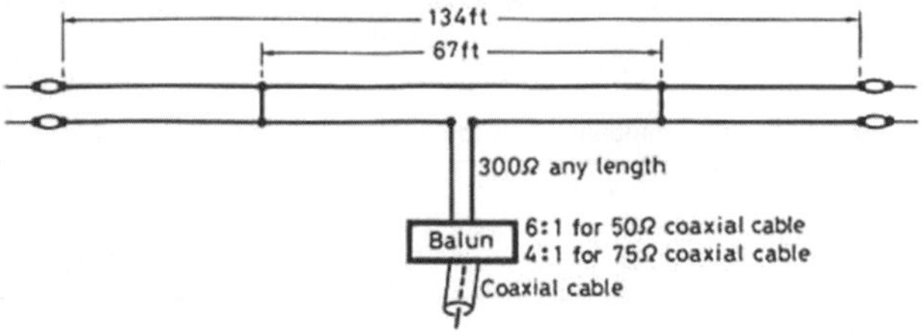

Fig 4. Dual (harmonic) band dipole. As shown it acts as folded half-wave dipole on 7MHz and as a T-matched dipole on 3·5MHz but dimensions can be scaled for 7/14 or 14/28MHz (VK1PM reported in W6SAI's *Ham Radio Techniques*)

Fig 5. Construction hints for quad antennas: (a) pvc heat shrink tubing as wire support. Glue wire to quad arm with pvc cement. Two-wire wraps will hold it securely after the glue has dried. Stagger the quad wire supports on each side of the arm to distribute the stress more equally; (b) it can be better to use two smaller booms spaced about 1ft apart as supports. The wire supports shown in (a) are staggered on quad arms to distribute wire stress.

the target of -4dBi was met. At 5MHz, a 1200km ssb voice link was set up in a clear channel using a 1kW transmitter, but was still operable when the transmitter power was reduced to 7W." The antenna uses kevlar-covered conductors fitted with stainless-steel snap-hooks and fasteners. The antenna kit weighs 16kg including the mast and it has been erected single-handed in 15min.

It could be argued that hf amateurs traditionally seek long-distance rather than nvis links. Yet in practice, for the majority of us, inspection of the log-book will tend to show most hf contacts on 3·5, 7, 10, even 14 and 21MHz are, in practice, single-hop medium-distance contacts for which nvis-type antennas can provide very strong signals. Of course, the real dx-fanatic will turn his nose up at such a heresy and insist on calling dx-only on a flat band!

For those who want to increase low-angle radiation from vertically polarised antennas, right down to the horizon, another hf conference paper "Launching of hf surface waves" was by a team at the University of Birmingham who are concerned with developing hf surface-wave radar. This discusses a technique for obtaining a 3-6dB improvement in hf signal strength at ground level, when used with a coast-located vertically-polarised dipole already equipped with extensive radials filling in the space between the antenna and the sea-plane. The new technique consists of using a very large number of vertical monopole rods connected to the ground mat to provide "inductive ground loading" and thus forming a "two-layered ground". An interesting technique but, since the number of vertical rods appears to be over 500 in the trial installation, not one likely to be copied by many amateurs, although there are interesting possibilities in surface-wave rather than just ground-wave propagation over sea paths.

On the other hand, one can imagine quite a lot of locations where the dual-band (harmonic bands) antenna shown in Fig 4 could be used. This system was spotted in *Ham Radio* (March 1988) and apparently stems from Ron May, VK1PM. With the dimensions shown the antenna is for 3·5 and 7MHz, but it could be scaled down for 7/14MHz or 14/28MHz. The central 67ft portion forms a 7MHz folded dipole with the end pieces acting as decoupled quarter-wave linear traps. On 3·5MHz it functions as a half-wave dipole with T-match feed. There is of course no technical reason why the 300Ω feeder should not be brought down to a suitable atu with balanced output in the shack to avoid the need for a balun to match to co-axial feeder.

Also in *Ham Radio Techniques* (April 1988) Bill Orr, W6SAI points out that the rising sun-spot count means that it is time again to think seriously about 28MHz antennas. He writes:

"It's not hard to build a quad, but it is difficult to construct one that will stay up in bad weather. They are floppy affairs at best, and you must put a lot of thought into the physical arrangement of the antenna.

"Lloyd Hosor, W9YCB, has some interesting ideas on quad construction. He says the best quad arms are made of 'Calcutta bamboo' with pvc heat shrink tubing slid over the bamboo between the joints. The end of the arm is also sealed with a short piece of heat shrink. An acceptable alternative for the quad arm is a fibreglass (grp) drapery pole. Lloyd has found a lot of these at garage sales.

"The poles should not be drilled for the quad wire after they've been protected with heat-shrink tubing. Instead, cut a piece of pvc lengthwise to fit the pole. Cut a slot in the tubing to hold the wire and glue it to the quad arm with pvc cement. Two-wire wraps will hold it securely after the glue has dried (Fig 5(a))

"Lloyd staggers the quad wire supports on each side of the arm to distribute the stress more equally (Fig 5 (b)). He uses two smaller booms spaced about one foot apart as supports because a single boom for a four element quad will not stand the gaff in bad weather."

John Levesley, G0HJL passes along what he refers to as "just a minor but I hope helpful tip to those operators who, like me, use a tapped coil vertical hf multiband antenna (or conceivably tap a 'sloper' to change its centre resonant frequency). It is well-known that it is convenient to mark the tap points on the coil for future quick retuning of an antenna such as my Hi-Gain 18V-2. With this particular antenna care is also needed to ensure that the feeder clamp is secured outwards at 90° to the coil, otherwise there is a possibility that the close spacing of the coils will allow the feeder clamp to connect with the sections of the coil above and/or below the feed point required. The answer to both problems has proved to be the little plastic pegs sold to hang Christmas Cards from. These mark the tap points clearly and permanently, and even have ridges on the outer surface which help lock the peg between the turns of the coil. An additional benefit is that they force the coil open that extra millimetre at the tap points, preventing unwanted taps above or below the feeder clamp."

End-feeding and the Zepp

Extracted from 'Technical Topics', *Radio Communication*, July 1988

END-FEEDING AND THE ZEPP

In introducing the novel concept of an end-fed Windom (*TT*, February 1988, pp111-2) Les Moxon, G6XN, pointed out that "were it not for the problems, end-feeding would tend to be more attractive than centre feeding for non-rotatable antennas since the ends are more likely to be within reach of, or close to, the shack. In addition the centre of the element no longer has to support the weight of the feeder."

The end-fed Windom antenna provides a useful, if partial solution to this problem but is essentially confined to a specific band, for which both the capacitor and its position need to conform to the values and dimensions suggested by G6XN. Although, presumably, the antenna would function to some degree on other bands as a simple "random-length" long-wire antenna when tuned against earth or a counterpoise by means of a suitable pi-network matching unit. Alternatively, the 40m (134ft) long-wire is an effective end-fed antenna capable of working well on virtually any frequency, but is not without its problems. With an atu close to the operating position, the amount of rf floating around the shack is bound to be high. The antenna will also be susceptible to picking up electrical interference radiated from the mains, and at higher frequencies there will be pronounced nulls and lobes in directions governed by the site rather than the direction of the desired dx. Nevertheless, it is a simple, low-cost solution that has proved useful over a number of years at G3VA with the far end supported by trees.

But my first transmitting antenna, in common with many other amateurs of the day, was the then popular zepp with 66ft top and 32 or 16ft tuned feeders. This was in 1938-39. Again in 1946-47, a zepp antenna helped me achieve post-war DXCC Nr 321 worldwide, so I have always retained an interest in this type of antenna, even after it fell out of favour in the early 1950s.

The zepp, as noted in *TT*, January 1986, dates back to a German patent of 1908: **Fig 5(a)**. It was extremely popular for amateur operation in the 'twenties and 'thirties, before the availability of co-axial cable feeders, as a convenient end-fed arrangement, seemingly well suited to operation on harmonically-related bands. It was not until 1956 that serious doubts were cast on the efficiency of this form of antenna. Then, in discussing the use of baluns, Dud Charman, G6CJ (*RSGB Bulletin*, December 1955) noted that "simple connection of a resonant antenna to one side of a tuned line will not work – it is necessary to add the transformer winding in the form of the stub to tell the line it is balanced. *This is one reason why the old zepp antenna was so uncertain in its behaviour.*'

In his 1982 *HF antennas for all locations*, Les Moxon, G6XN, really put the boot in, explaining why, in his opinion "Despite its time-honoured status this (traditional form of end-fed zepp) is very uncertain in its behaviour. Put bluntly it usually **does not work** and the reason is the same one that we have met before in a different guise. In going from a balanced to an unbalanced system or *vice-versa*, a balun is essential. Without one, there is no guarantee that the antenna will work better than a random length of wire. Nor, to be fair, any certainty that it will *not* work, but the zepp feed has been found particularly uncooperative in this respect." A suitable balun stub, as suggested by

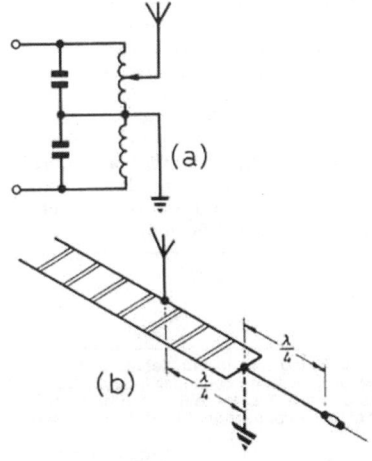

Fig 6. The unbalanced-antenna/balanced-line stub as suggested by G6CJ in 1955 together with its equivalent circuit

G6CJ, and endorsed by G6XN, is shown in **Fig 6**. However, the need to employ this stub, which may not be readily accessible, makes it more difficult to exploit efficiently the multiband properties inherent in this system.

G6XN added: "The reader may well be wondering how it is that if the zepp feed does not work it managed to avoid suspicion of its 'bona-fides' for so many years, being ousted from popularity mainly by the swing of fashion, which currently favours low-impedance coaxial lines. . . . It has, in fact, been found by the author that in two cases the balancing stub was not essential, but in each of these cases the wires were spaced about 7in (18cm) and only some 2-3ft (0·6-0·9m) from the ground. Even so the system did seem to be less critical, particularly in respect of balance in the main feeder, when the stub was in use." In this section of *HFafal* G6XN emphasised that

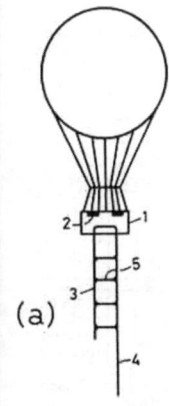

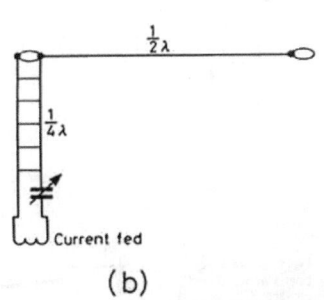

Fig 5. (a) The original zeppelin antenna stems from a 1909 patent by Dr Hans Beggerow intended for suspension from a balloon or airship to reduce the risk of explosion caused by high rf voltage near the balloon. (b) Form of zepp antenna as widely used by amateurs up to the 1950s

ANTENNA TOPICS

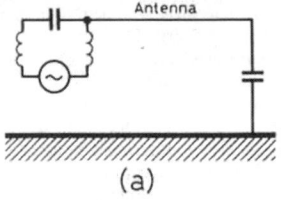 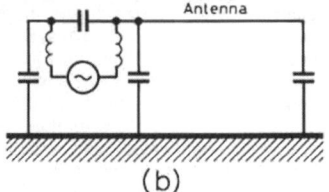

Fig 7. (a) How G6XN illustrates the problem posed by the conventional zepp arrangement. (b) Improved results without a G6CJ stub appear to be possible where the resonant feeder wires are well spaced and close to the ground: the equivalent circuit

there is an urgent need for the end-feeding of some types of antenna, particularly vertical dipoles or inverted ground-planes which are often difficult for mechanical reasons to feed anywhere other than at their base.

It is thus not surprising that G6XN took another look at zepp feeding while working on his end-fed Windom. To add to the notes in the February TT, G6XN wrote: "My experience is that the conventional zepp feed *sometimes* seems to work well enough. In this, and the one other case in my experience that leaves no margin for doubt, the feeders were widely spaced and close to ground so that the field at the ground produced by one conductor would not be completely cancelled by the other (ie the equivalent circuit is not as in **Fig 7(a)** but as in **Fig 7(b)**). In other words, there is capacitance from each wire to ground as well as between the wires, thus completing the circuit.

"I am sure that this is not the full story. With the dipole centre-fed, the zepp stubb (improved version) could be connected without noticeable loss, though the current flowing in them was large and there was no way it could be reduced. With a stub end-impedance possibly as high as 0.3MΩ, an out-of-balance capacitance of 0.03pF would be enough to energise it. To energise the antenna (say 5000Ω end-impedance) from the stub requires a lot more out-of-balance – but enough to cause significant feeder radiation? Even more doubtful, but it could be a useful field for further study, though I fear not by me. At my age, life is too short for tidying up all the loose ends, and one tends to have other priorities!"

Intrigued by these remarks and convinced that there is a real need for a reliable, reproducible form of multiband end-fed antenna, I temporarily lowered the long-wire antenna and replaced it with a 21MHz zepp that bore more relationship to the original zepp designs than to either of the ones suggested by G6CJ or G6XN. I used some transmitter-type 300-ohm cable with the wires spaced about 0.75in (18mm) apart as the "open" feeder, in conjunction with a pi-network matching unit which provided balanced output. I struck the exceptionally good hf conditions at the end of April and had little difficulty in making plenty of contacts, including some reasonable dx. But I soon became uncertain. Was the antenna really functioning as a half-wave element or as a random-length long-wire antenna? I soon reverted to the end-fed long-wire of which a significant proportion runs through the roof space. So there still remains a real problem to solve in developing a genuine transmission-line, end-fed antenna that can be relied upon to work every time! But how do you prove an antenna is working as a zepp rather than as an inefficient long-wire with lots of power wasted in high circulating currents?

Unidirectional Receiving Loop

Extracted from 'Technical Topics', *Radio Communication*, July1988

UNIDIRECTIONAL LOOP RECEIVING ANTENNA

The two simple loop receiving antennas developed by Mike Villard and George Hagn (plus a contribution by George's 13 year old daughter!) were designed primarily to meet the needs of those listening to high-power hf broadcast stations, particularly in areas still beset by ground-wave or sky-wave jamming.

The most novel is a co-planar twin loop (ctl) antenna which could well have useful applications for amateur-band reception or possibly for d/f hunts. It was developed to meet the following goals: (1) no active elements; (2) reasonable sensitivity (by broadcast-reception standards); (3) simplicity of construction; (4) use of commonly available materials; (5) ease of operation; and (6) satisfactory performance indoors if possible (in practice this can be achieved, although the 'direction' of signals indicated by the position of the loop may not be accurate).

The ctl comprises two loops, both loaded to resonance, with the inner loop made of a flat, foil element: see **Fig 8**. A third inner 'coupling' loop may be provided to permit a co-axial cable feed to a receiver located away from the loop.

The ctl exhibits unidirectional properties and, when correctly adjusted, shows a pronounced null on sky-wave as well as ground-wave signals. W6QYT describes this (*IEE Conference Publication No 284*, pages 141 to 144) as follows:

"In contrast with the conventional loop whose null is perpendicular to the plane of the structure, the ctl null is in the plane of the loop(s). Because of symmetry, when this is the case, both loops respond very similarly to variations in the angle of the elevation of the incoming signal over an appreciable range of angles."

W6QYT calls the inner loop, the R (receiver) loop and the outer loop is designated I (independent) loop. He explains: "To generate a unidirectional null, the side of the loops opposite to the tuning capacitors is pointed towards the distant station. When I-loop tuning is correct, current flowing in that loop generates a local H-field whose phase is opposite to that of

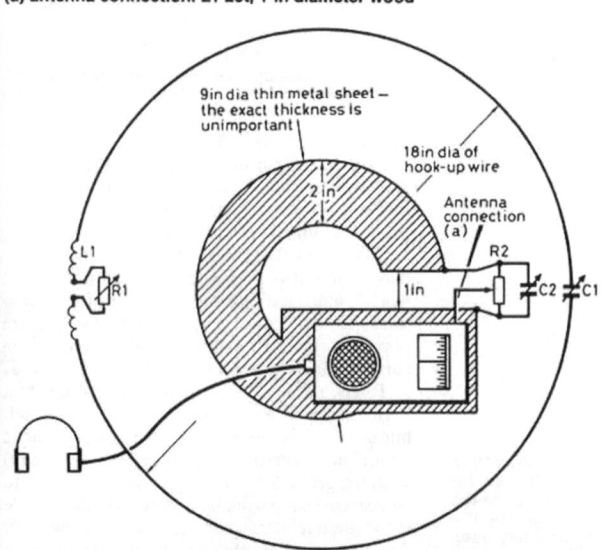

Fig 8. Wiring and layout details of the Stanford Research Institute co-planar loop antenna described by W6QYT at the IEE's hf conference. Notes: (a) antenna connection. L1 23t, 1-in diameter wood core, No 18 GA insulated wire. C1 5-20pF. C2 350 to 600pF (eg medium-wave tuning capacitor) R1 250-ohm composition resistor for Q adjustment R2 [...] attenuator to overcome agc action during initial tuneup. Receiver Panasonic RF9, Sony ICF4901 or similar

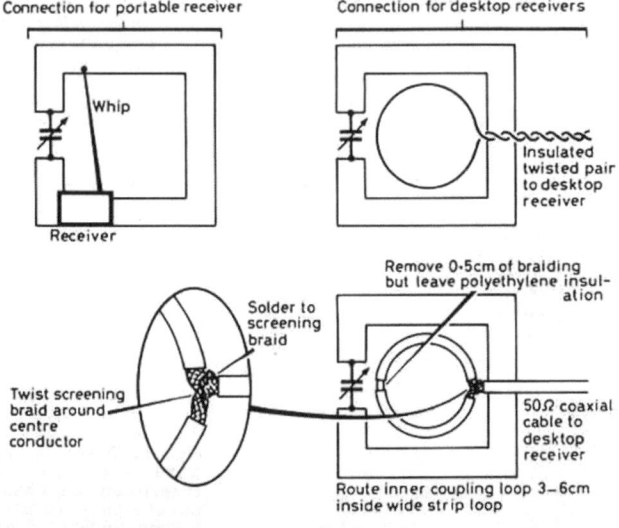

Fig 9. Different types of feeds for the SRI horizontal loop antenna

the H-field of the incoming signal. The magnitude of this local field may be adjusted by altering the Q of the I-loop by means of a variable resistor when the Q is higher than necessary for the purpose. When the local H-field magnitude and phase are such as to cancel exactly the ambient H-field, the R-loop (located inside the I-loop and designed to respond *only* to H-fields) finds itself in a null region, or 'shadow' and the receiver registers a greatly reduced output. In this situation, the effective coupling between loops is very small. If the signal direction changes (or the direction of the loops is changed relative to the signal), the phase, and to some extent the amplitude, of current in the I-loop changes. The cancellation is then no longer complete, and the signal reappears in the output of the R-loop".

He has found that "on average, a readily-attainable front-to-back ratio for the ctl in the case of skywave signals seems to be around 20dB. This is sufficient to attenuate co-channel interference in typical situations to an extent which gives the listener the choice of two independent programmes (on the same frequency), instead of an unacceptable mixture. The antenna also rejects ground-wave interference". Results are presented of antenna patterns relating to signals from 15MHz broadcast stations.

The alternative SRI horizontal loop antenna (hla) is a very simple single-turn, resonant loop constructed of a wide strip of metal or foil and brought to resonance by means of a variable capacitor. It can be implemented in any one of several versions (see **Fig 9**). It will effectively null out ground-wave interference in much the same way as the more usual vertical-plane loop. Nulls are unlikely to be observed on incoming sky-wave signals but it could be used by amateurs to reduce local electrical interference, where this is radiated directly from information-technology, industrial, scientific or medical signals, or ground-wave signals from a nearby transmitter.

course, applicable to amateur antennas, particularly for 1·8, 3·5 and 7MHz, and their report was published in detail in *QST*.

A recent *IEEE Trans on Broadcasting* paper by a team comprising American university and broadcast engineers, using a 'Method of Moments' computer program, seems to bear out the measurements made by K8CFU team although no reference is made to their pioneering work. The paper concludes: "Studies of vertical monopole antennas, using the NEC-GS computer code, indicate that a radiator elevated several metres above ground and having only four elevated horizontal radials can outperform a ground-mounted antenna with 120 buried radials, over any type of soil. Field measurements are planned for the purpose of verifying these computer predictions. If the NEC output is correct, then the construction, cost and complexity of vertical monopole antenna systems can be reduced significantly. At the same time, the elevated-radial antenna provides increased groundwave field intensity while attenuating skywave radiation."

In effect, they suggest that the elevated ground-plane antenna, as widely used on hf/vhf, represents a superior approach to using a grounded monopole with an extensive system of buried radials, at frequencies down to below 1MHz.

Short Loaded Harmonic Dipoles

Extracted from 'Technical Topics', *Radio Communication*, November 1988

SHORT LOADED HARMONIC DIPOLES-

Gerald Stancey, G3MCK draws attention to an article 'Multi-band antennas using loading coils' by William J Lattin, W4JRW which appeared in *QST*, April 1961 (pp43, 148, 150). Although this was more than a quarter of a century ago, the information remains valid, fresh to many, and possibly of interest to those amateurs who have not the space available to put up resonant half-wave dipoles yet wish to use a co-ax feeder without requiring the use of an atu.

W4JRW recalled a Bureau of Standards Circular C74 *(Radio Instruments and Measurements)* first published in 1924 which showed that while the use of loading coils decreases the natural resonant frequency of antennas, it means that the harmonic frequencies are no longer integral multiples of the fundamental, as in the case of the conventional unloaded resonant antenna. An inductively loaded antenna also represents a higher Q system, decreasing the operational bandwidth over which an swr of, say, less than 2:1 can be achieved.

In his article, W4JRW showed that with careful placement of two 120µH loading coils (low-loss construction, close-wound with No 18 Nyclad wire on bakelite tubing ⅞in outside diameter, 14in long) it is possible to achieve a low swr on both the (American) 3·5 and 7MHz bands, with an overall span of around 80ft, without the use of 'tuned' traps.

For European operation, there is the problem that the optimum results achieved by W4JRW represented resonant frequencies more suited to the extended American (Region 2) bands (3·5-4·0MHz and 7·0-7·3MHz) than our restricted (Region 1) bands. However it would seem that with some experimentation, and parameters

approximately as in Fig 1 (a), it should be possible to achieve a satisfactorily low swr over the Region 1 bands.

W4JRW stresses that: "There are no capacitors to break down as in traps and the 120µH coils have been used with a kilowatt transmitter input with no difficulty." He also adds: "We have not found any exact formulae to determine the relationship between the lengths of wire, loading coils and the two (resonant) frequencies. The antennas are very simple to adjust with a grid-dip meter coupled to a single-turn loop connected to the feed terminals, as quite small changes in the wire lengths result in appreciable

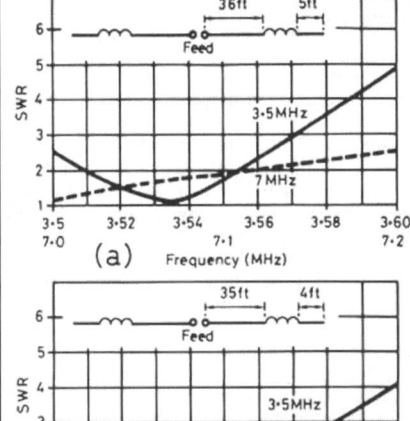

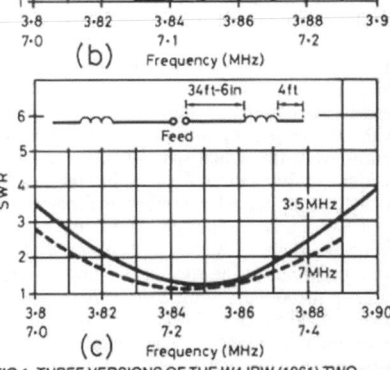

FIG 1. THREE VERSIONS OF THE W4JRW (1961) TWO-BAND LOADED DIPOLES USING TWO 120µH LOADING COILS (SEE TEXT), ILLUSTRATING THE EFFECT OF SMALL VARIATIONS IN THE DIMENSIONS.

in resonant frequencies.

"This principle can be extended: that is, by using two sets of coils, operation on three frequencies is possible, on four frequencies with three sets of coils, and so on. However these get very complicated to adjust, since the second set of loading coils changes operation of the first set somewhat, and the adjustment process gets rather tedious.

Elevated Radials Vindicated

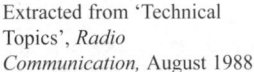 

Extracted from 'Technical Topics', *Radio Communication*, August 1988

— ELEVATED RADIALS VINDICATED —

TT has referred on several occasions to the sterling work done in 1980-81 by Arch Doty, K8CFU, John Frey, W3ESU and Harry Mills, K4HU (retired professional engineers) in investigating the characteristics of electrically-short vertical antennas using elevated counterpoise and insulated radials, and comparing them with those of antennas using large numbers of buried radials, as customary for mf broadcast antennas ever since the classic paper "Ground systems as a factor in antenna efficiency" by the late Dr George Brown and his RCA colleagues R F Lewis and J Epstein (*Proc IRE*, June 1937, pp753-787). The K8CFU team made literally thousands of measurements which strongly suggested that, for equal efficiency, a counterpoise comprising insulated radials elevated a few feet above ground would require fewer radial wires than the 120-150 buried radials normally mandated for US medium-wave transmitters by the FCC. Their findings were, of

Multiband Non-Loaded Dipole

Extracted from 'Technical Topics', *Radio Communication*, November 1988

MULTIBAND NON-LOADED DIPOLE

Where an atu is used with open-wire transmission line it becomes possible to resonate a

ANTENNA TOPICS

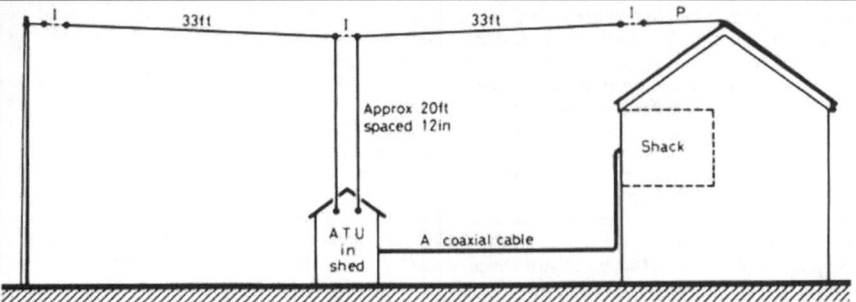

FIG 2. G2DXK'S MULTIBAND DIPOLE ANTENNA. I REPRESENTS INSULATORS COMPRISING 12IN LENGTHS OF NYLON LINE. P IS LENGTH OF POLYPROPYLENE CORD THROWN OVER ROOF AND ANCHORED TO EAVES.

centre-fed dipole antenna system on virtually any frequency. Lorin Knight, G2DXK admits that the principle used in his all-band hf antenna is nothing new, but the method of construction and the location of the atu should be of interest to those amateurs who do not wish to have open-wire feeders extending all the way into the domestic environment. He writes:

"Instead of the traditional 14swg hard-drawn copper wire, I use a black pvc-covered stranded wire (14 × 0·2mm, overall diameter 1·5mm). This wire has one-fifth the weight, is considerably cheaper, is easier to handle, is almost invisible when up in the air – and is not noticeably inferior in performance. Instead of the traditional glass or porcelain insulators I use 12-inch lengths of 1·5mm diameter monofil nylon line – also lighter, cheaper and practically invisible.

"The feeder wires drop down to two standoff insulators mounted 12 inches apart on my garden shed which, very conveniently, stands right under the centre of the antenna: Fig 2. The wires are cut so that they are under slight tension and they maintain a nominal spacing of 12 inches without the use of any spreaders. In a very strong wind the actual spacing half-way up the feeder can fluctuate ± 2" or so, but this appears to have negligible effect on the performance.

"I have an atu in the shed and a coaxial cable feed from there to the house. (This means that I have to go out to the shed every time I want to tune up the antenna for a different band but as I do not change bands all that often this is no great hardship.) The atu is homemade and has a separate plug-in coil assembly for each band from 3·5 to 28MHz (see Fig 3). Each coil assembly has written on it the relevant capacitor settings so that band-changing is a fairly simple operation.

"It will be noted that on 3·5MHz the active part of the antenna is only a quarter-wave long, but this does not prevent it from loading up and operating very satisfactorily. On 7MHz the antenna is a simple half-wave dipole; on 14MHz it acts as two half-waves in phase, giving some gain in the broadside direction. On the other bands it has multiple-lobe polar diagrams."

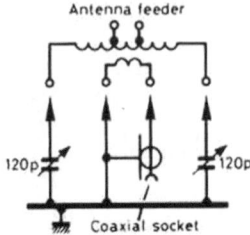

FIG 3. THE ATU USED WITH THE MULTIBAND DIPOLE IS SITED IMMEDIATELY UNDER THE CENTRE OF THE DIPOLE.

Elevated Vertical Antennas

Extracted from 'Technical Topics', *Radio Communication*, December 1988

ELEVATED VERTICAL ANTENNAS

An item in the August TT "Elevated radials vindicated" (p599) made reference to a paper in *IEE Transactions on Broadcasting* (March 1988, pp75-77), "AM broadcast antennas with elevated radial ground systems" by Al Christman and Roger Radcliff of Ohio University. This reported computer modelling studies that have indicated that a lower-cost elevated vertical monopole antenna with four elevated horizontal radials can be expected to produce more ground-wave (low-angle) field strength than a conventional (broadcast) grounded monopole with 120 buried radials. I pointed out that this goes a long way to confirm, at least theoretically, the important practical work of Arch Doty, K8CFU and his colleagues, based on thousands of field measurements, first reported in *TT* (February, 1983, p131) and in more detail in *QST* (February 1983, pp20-25) and *CQ* (April 1984, pp24-42).

It transpires that Al Christman is KB8I and an expanded version of the *IEE Trans* paper, with emphasis on amateur-radio applications, appears under his name in *QST* (August 1988, pp35-42) as 'Elevated vertical antenna systems'. In this he writes:

FIG 7(a) THE BASIC FOUR-RADIAL, ELEVATED VERTICAL-MONOPOLE (GROUND-PLANE) ANTENNA DESIGN AS SUBJECTED TO COMPUTER INVESTIGATION BY KB8I (QST). (b) ELEVATION-PLAN RADIATION PATTERN WITH ANTENNA ISOLATED FROM SUPPORT MAST WITH FEED-POINT HEIGHT OF 15 FEET (COMPUTER SIMULATION, GROUND CONDUCTIVITY NOT STATED).

"In agreement with the findings of Arch Doty, K8CFU, I believe that the use of elevated, rather than buried, radials provides superior performance, because it allows the collection of electromagnetic energy in the form of *displacement currents*, rather than forcing *conduction currents* to flow through lossy earth.

"I will be doing field studies to verify the computer predictions. . . . If the information gathered from (the) NEC-GSD software is correct, the construction, cost and complexity of effective vertical-monopole antenna systems can be greatly reduced over that of comparable buried-radial systems now widely in use. At the same time, ease of installation and low-angle gain will be increased. The elevated-radial technique appears to be equally valid in the medium-frequency broadcast band and at the lower end of the hf range, so perhaps the ground-plane vertical is 'the antenna for all bands'!

"My studies on vertical monopole antennas (eg Fig 7) using the NEC-GSD computer code indicate that a radiator elevated 10 to 20 feet above ground and having only four elevated horizontal radials can outperform a ground-mounted monopole with 120 buried radials. At 3·8MHz an elevation of about 15 feet is adequate for average soil, while a lower height is satisfactory for shorter wavelengths. Higher elevation above ground is necessary over soil with poorer electrical characteristics and at lower operating frequencies."

G3SBI's Six-band Vertical

Extracted from 'Technical Topics', *Radio Communication*, March 1989

G3SBI's SIX-BAND VERTICAL ANTENNA

The 30ft vertical whip antenna with remote, automatically-tuned matching network has been widely used in professional HF land and maritime mobile communications but tends to be too costly an approach for widespread use by amateurs.

However, Colin Horrabin, G3SBI has developed an ingenious lightweight vertical antenna that can be used on 1·8, 3·5, 7, 14, 21 and 28MHz, providing on each band a nominal 50ohm base feedpoint impedance and functioning on each band without any remote switching or matching from a 50-ohm coaxial transmission line. Colin hopes later to prepare a detailed constructional article but feels that his unusual method of feeding the antenna on 14 and 28MHz, and the consequent enhanced 28MHz performance, should prove of general interest. His method of using stubs appears to be novel. His antenna was initially developed using a one-tenth scale model enabling current distributions and feedpoint impedance to be measured.

Fig 9 shows the complete antenna and Fig 10 the current distribution on 14 and 28MHz. G3SBI writes:

"On 14MHz the current distribution is similar to a 200° (electrical degrees) vertical; on 21MHz it resembles that of an 'elevated-feed' vertical one-wavelength high; over good earth this provides a main lobe at an elevation of only 10° above the horizon.

"To set-up the stubs initially, the 14MHz stub is adjusted for minimum SWR (Note that the length is such that a 90° bend is required as in Fig 9). The tapping point is moved up and down the element until an SWR better than about 1·3:1 is achieved.

The same method is used with the 28MHz stub; but in this case a length of nylon rope is attached temporarily by means of PVC tape so that the length of the stub can be adjusted from ground level with minimum SWR centred on 28·5MHz.

"The 14MHz stub wire should not be more than 2-in from the vertical element since at any greater distance it will affect the resonance on 21MHz where the antenna functions as a ¾-wave monopole. It may prove necessary to readjust the length of the 14MHz stub slightly after adjusting the 28MHz stub."

G3SBI has recently expanded his original notes to give some further explanation of the feed mechanism for 14 and 28MHz: "The tapping point for the stubs on the 2-in OD aluminium mast-element determines the minimum SWR that can be achieved; the length of the stub determines at what frequency within the band this occurs. In my case the actual tapping points were within six inches of those predicted from my one-tenth scale model to obtain an SWR of less than 1·5:1.

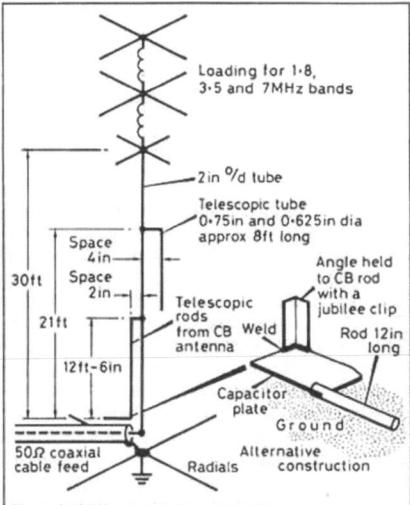

Fig 9. G3SBI's six-band vertical HF antenna.

Fig 10. Current distribution of the G3SBI antenna on 14 and 28MHz.

"What did surprise me was that, with base feed, the current distribution on 28MHz, where the vertical height is roughly 1λ, is similar to that of the 1λ elevated-feed vertical derived from a Marconi D/F system described many years ago in TT and included in most editions of *Amateur Radio Techniques* though now out of print.

"My back garden is 36ft by 24ft and the results seem particularly good on 28MHz although the antenna has been used to work South America (LU) and Australia (VK6) on 3·5MHz. I am convinced that this feed method would be of use to anyone with a conventional 33ft vertical at the bottom of their garden, since no remote L-network is required to match the element to coaxial cable."

Elevated Verticals

Extracted from 'Technical Topics', *Radio Communication*, April 1989

ELEVATED VERTICALS

In April 1958, in introducing the first *TT*, I wrote: "All we can hope to do (in this new feature) is to survey a few ideas from the technical press; a few hints and tips that have come to our notice; with perhaps an occasional comment thrown in for good measure". *TT* has always aimed at encouraging a spirit of experimentation and novelty rather than purely the continuation of established systems, providing a technical and ideas forum in which nothing is guaranteed, everything subject to trial and error; heresy given priority over technical dogma as seen in the light of the ways in which amateur radio is evolving, for better or for worse. A recognition that most of what we do is rooted in the past but also that physicists today are having to learn to cope with entirely new theories of 'chaos' – those inexplicable situations where even the most fundamental laws are broken or thrown into confusion.

There are two extremely difficult tasks an amateur can set him or herself: (1) To invent something entirely new; and (2) to persuade others that long-established practice, as described in the standard handbooks, may not always be the optimum or even the correct solution. This applies particularly in those areas of radio physics where it is virtually impossible for an amateur to plot or quantify exactly what is happening. Notable examples are radio propagation and antennas, where very large numbers of variables affect the performance. For instance, one cannot easily measure vertical radiation patterns.

An important area in which our ideas may need to change is in the design of elevated vertical antennas, even though the "ground-plane" has a history dating back over 50 years and is currently used successfully by many thousands of amateurs.

It has been noted previously in *TT* that there is still confusion between the true vertical monopole, with its 'infinite' ground plane, the real Earth, often assisted by a large number of buried earth radials or an earth mat, and the elevated ground plane with quarter-wave horizontal or sloping wire radials or rods as a 'non-radiating' artificial earth plane.

In 1981 I revealed, possibly for the first time, that the late Dr George Brown of RCA, who developed the ground-plane antenna in the mid-1930s for 30-40MHz police communications, had told me that his original system had just two radials and that this

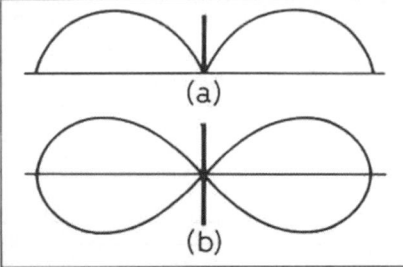

Fig 1. (a) Vertical radiation pattern of a quarter-wave monopole above an infinitely ground plane of perfect conductivity – this can be approached in maritime mobile operation. (b) VRP of half-wave dipole in free space.

was later altered to four radials for purely commercial reasons. Similarly, Les Moxon, G6XN has strongly advocated the use of a single short (inductively loaded) counterpoise (radial). If one thinks of the antenna as a *bent dipole*, it becomes evident that the antenna will radiate efficiently with just *one* elevated radial (counterpoise) but in this case there will be a tendency for the outgoing wave to have mixed horizontal/vertical polarisation with its maximum lobe at a relatively high angle to the horizon: nevertheless a perfectly satisfactory arrangement as a general purpose antenna. For DX operation with the desirable low angle of vertical radiation, the trick is to find some method of reducing the radiation from the wire forming the horizontal side of the 'dipole'.

Some years ago Canadian engineers W V Tilson and A H Secord in 'The radiation patterns of ground rod antennas' (*Electronics & Communications*, August 1967, pp27-30) showed that the VRP of ground rod antennas varies markedly with changes in element lengths and the degree to which RF currents can be kept off the outer braid of coaxial feed lines. Only in a limited number of cases does it provide its lobe directed towards the horizon to resemble the radiation pattern of a quarter-wave monopole above an infinitely perfectly conducting ground plane, or that of a vertical half-wave dipole in free space, Figs 1 and 2. Professional engineers tend to assume that the lobe of an elevated ground-plane antenna must always be tilted upwards. Tilson and Secord concluded: "It is clear that one cannot merely say that ground rod antenna patterns tilt up and leave it at that. The pattern depends on both the length of monopole and ground rods, and also on how well the currents can be kept off the feed cable. Secondly, when the

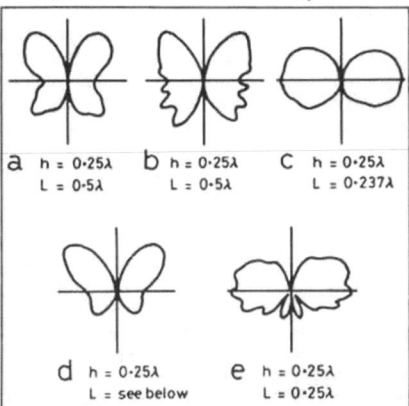

Fig 2. Some typical VRPs of ground rod antennas showing the effect of radial lengths (L) and of chokes on the feedline: (a) with chokes, (b) without chokes, (c) with chokes, (d) circular ground plane of radius 0.03 with chokes, (e) without chokes. (Tilson & Secord, 1967)

monopole radiator is a half-wavelength, the pattern resembles a typical dipole pattern even with no ground rods or chokes present on the feed cable. When a quarter-wave monopole is used with no chokes, suitable patterns may be obtained with ground rod lengths near three-eighths of a wavelength."

TT (March 1981) reported that Les Moxon, G6XN had developed an effective short (loaded) 'counterpoise' technique and this is explained in more detail in his *HF Antennas for all Locations* (RSGB 1982). G6XN was careful not to claim originality since military manuals often show pack sets working into a dipole in which one arm is run just above the ground while *TT* had earlier included notes on using trap verticals by converting them into vertical dipoles and had also shown how loaded 'counterpoises' can be used to remove unwanted RF-voltages from otherwise 'hot' metalwork or chassis in upstair shacks.

At about the same time, Arch Doty, K8CFU and colleagues carried out hundreds of measurements that showed that a few elevated 'radials' perform as well as or better than the 120 or more buried radials traditionally used for medium-wave broadcasting and often advocated for 1.8 and 3.5MHz DX operation despite the cost and effort required in such construction. As noted in *TT*, August 1988 and

ANTENNA TOPICS

December 1988, K8CFU's laborious field measurements have been confirmed as the result of computer studies by a team of professional engineers including Al Christman, KB8I (*QST*, August 1988, pp33-42). Both studies have been based on the use of four or more elevated radials. There has also been some interest in the concept of a 'zero-extent' ground-plane antenna using lossy ferrite chokes to absorb energy fed back down the outer of the coaxial feeder (*TT*, March 1988 and November 1987).

But it would seem that the penny has yet to drop. Amateurs the world over continue to spend time, money and energy in improving earth systems for vertical monopoles, vertical arrays and erecting multi-radial systems for their ground-plane antennas. To quote from a recent letter from G6XN, parts of which it is hoped to cover later: "Despite proof of the efficiency and major practical advantages, my advocacy of short radials clearly stood no chance since, as you have related, even the inventor of ground-plane was unable to get away with two radials but had to bow to commercial pressure. To suggest shorter radials and, beyond that, the possible use of only a single radial, provided it is *short* enough, is clearly heresy of the worst kind. It still seems to be universally accepted that a radial length of a quarter-wave is necessary; moreover from *TT* and elsewhere it appears that an enormous amount of effort continues to be misdirected at 'improving' earthed and radial systems which inflict a maximum of inconvenience and inhibit the use of vertical elements for beam arrays. Furthermore multiple quarter-wave radials offer no advantages but instead involve the major disadvantage that the rapid change of impedance close to resonance can cause problems of electrical equalisation of the radials. Short radials are superior also for multiband operation although grounded verticals have the edge in this respect, provided that the extra radiation loss due to ground losses is acceptable.

"Searching for ways to put my case over more effectively, I felt there was a need for more information on bandwidth and other limiting factors including the effect of the height of radials (shortened or not) above ground. A few simple experiments led to what, relative to my limited resources, became a massive research programme digging deeply into fundamental questions. The results have included a few surprises as well as establishing that *over a very wide range there is no significant difference between short and long radials in respect of any important aspect of performance*. This applies regardless of height although the so-called ground-plane, at extremely low height, turns into a completely different kind of antenna, ie, a *genuine* ground plane (monopole), whereas in the normal case, ie, height of radials more than a foot or two, it is a *dipole*. The fact that it is basically a dipole is implicit given that it works in free space where monopoles cannot exist. As I see it the practical distinction between dipole and monopole depends on whether current flows from one pole to the other of the source as it would in free space, or whether it does so at least in part via the ground."

I hope to return to G6XN's letter on another occasion but for the present reproduce his summary of main conclusions relating to "unsymmetrical dipoles":

(1) Ground plane antennas with radials at normal heights are dipoles not monopoles.

(2) Over a wide range there is virtually no difference between short radials with a shared loading coil and quarter-wave radials in respect of any aspect of performance. Bandwidth is reduced by excessive shortening, typically 30% reduction for two 0.08-wave radials or four 0.06-wave radials.

(3) Ground losses for quarter-wave vertical antennas operating with a set of radials and fed at the base are virtually zero at 14MHz for heights more than 4ft and only just over 0.5dB for a height of 2ft. There are no losses in the case of parasitic beam elements of this type.

(4) Variation of such losses with frequency is likely to be negligible but this has not yet been determined.

(5) For a base-fed element the maximum loss resistance for radial heights less than 4inches is in the region of 35ohms for two radials and can probably be halved with four radials. Comparable losses were observed with buried radials (poor soil).

(6) Horizontal dipoles may also be loaded asymmetrically, for example a quarter-wave radiator can be fed against the equivalent of a pair of short-loaded radials or even a single short resonant helix. Loading does not affect the current distribution or the height at which ground loss disappears, even if carried to extremes.

(7) Horizontal antennas, whether loaded or not, have negligible ground losses above a height of about 0.16-wave.

(8) Comparisons of ground loss information from several sources suggest that it is much less variable than the DX signal performance of vertical antennas and not directly related to it. There is no connection between DC resistance and RF resistance of earths, nor would one expect any, although this point has seldom if ever been discussed in print.

Capacitive Loading & NEC

Extracted from 'Technical Topics', *Radio Communication*, April 1989

MININEC LOOK AT CAPACITIVE LOADING

TT has referred on several occasions to the increasing use of computer software to analyse the characteristics of antennas without any requirement actually to construct either a full-scale or a model antenna. One of the best-known techniques is the so-called 'Method of Moments' using various NEC (Numerical Electromagnetic Code) programs. The original NEC programs tend to be rather costly for purely amateur use but, as with the various programs for propagation prediction, simplified versions are being developed. For example, the US Naval Postgraduate School in California has written MININEC for use with readily available personal computers and able to analyse basic wire antennas. While there is no doubt that such computer techniques are providing a valuable new tool for the antenna engineer, there is always the danger of writing off antennas that in the real world may have practical advantages not catered for by the software. One *must* treat computer simulations with caution.

Almost 28 years ago, 'Dud' Charman, G6CJ introduced to radio amateurs the principles and potential applications of dipoles, monopoles and ground planes, and long-wire antennas with their elements 'stretched' by the insertion of capacitance loading at intervals along their length ("Loaded wire aerials" F J H Charman, *RSGB Bulletin*, July 1961 and see also most editions of *Amateur Radio Techniques*). He showed that the capacitors could conveniently be formed using 80ohm flat-twin feeder line for the element cut to form overlapping sections. Later designs in American and Australian publications have tended to use conventional capacitors.

Because most of us have locations of restricted length, there has always been more interest, at least on HF, in antennas of compressed rather than stretched size. Capacitive loading has never attracted a great deal of attention, and when it has, some of the claims made for it have been rather extravagant (compare with those made for the T2FD antenna). In one small respect, the *G6CJ/ART* information is misleading in suggesting that a terminated stretched long-wire has only a single main lobe; in practice the radiation pattern has the usual split lobes of its non-stretched equivalent.

G6CJ showed that a dipole stretched by a factor of two, ie, a half-wave dipole 'stretched' to the span of a full-wave element, has only a modest gain of about 1dB, a similar broadside radiation pattern with slightly reduced beamwidth (56° instead of 78°) and a central resistive feedpoint of about 200ohms rather than the nominal 70ohms of a conventional dipole. It needs a lot of stretching to obtain substantial gain: see Table 1. But as noted in 1961 there are other advantages. A unique feature of stretched antennas is that they can be placed quite close to an unstretched wire without the radiation pattern being distorted by mutual coupling. For example, a 14MHz 'stretched' dipole could be hung directly beneath a conventional 7MHz dipole with both elements providing the radiation pattern of a half-wave dipole. The higher feedpoint can also be beneficial for monopole, Marconi or ground-plane vertical antennas, though stretching does unfortunately call for a very high mast if advantage is to be taken of the much lower ground losses for earthed monopoles, resulting from their higher impedance feed point.

A recent article 'The capacitively loaded dipole antenna – some new findings' by Dick Turrin, W2IMU in the Australian *Amateur Radio* (November 1988) presents the results of analysing a stretched antenna using a MININEC-3 program on an AT&T 6300 PC. He investigated the 7MHz capacitively loaded dipole shown in Fig 4(a) with

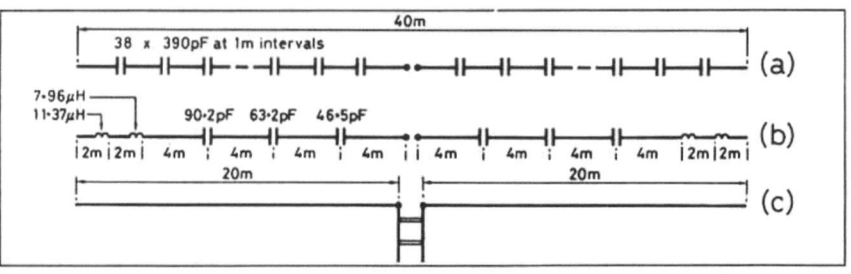

n-factor	C(pF)	No of Sections	½ dipole length (ft)	Input Z Ω	Beam-width	Gain (dBd)
1	—	2×1	33	70	78°	0
2	68	2×6	66	200	56°	1
3	50	2×9	99	400	42°	2·1
4	43	2×12	132	550	32°	3·1

For other bands change C and section length proportional to wavelength eg for 21MHz reduce values by two-thirds. *G6CJ, 1961.*

Fig 14. (a) Capacitively loaded 7MHz half-wave dipole as computer-analysed by W2IMU. (b) Combination of inductive and capacitive loading to give rather more broadside gain. (c) Double Zepp (two half-waves in phase, voltage fed with open-wire feeders).

Table 1. Basic information on 14MHz dipoles Capacitive loading at 5ft 6in intervals.

the following results: The broadside radiation pattern gain was +3.0dBi instead of the +2.1dBi of a standard dipole, giving a gain of 0.84dB with reference to a dipole, a little less than the 1dB of Table 1. Feed-point impedance came out at about 200ohms, the same as given by G6CJ. Bandwidth between the 2:1 VSWR points is about 6.65 to 7.45MHz compared with 6.8 to 7.2MHz for the conventional dipole; a useful but not exceptional improvement. Higher order resonances occur at 12.6, 19.5 and 26.5MHz.

W2IMU comments critically on the factor-two stretched dipole: "This cannot be regarded as a high-performance antenna nor can it be considered an ultra-broadband antenna. In the author's opinion, the physical size and difficulties of including capacitors along a wire antenna do not justify the predicted increase in performance". He notes that in contrast the gain from a 'double Zepp' (two half-waves in phase) is +3.69dBi, about 0.7dB more than the stretched wire of similar overall span and about 1.5dB more than a conventional dipole of half the length.

Clearly if 'gain' is the only consideration, there would be little justification in still regarding capacitive loading as a useful weapon in the antenna armoury. At least in some circumstances, it could prove unwise to write-off entirely capacitive loading, where the capacitors are formed by overlapping, purely on the basis of a MININEC run which largely confirms the earlier performance figures of G6CJ. It seems to me that what W2IMU has done is to underline the credibility of the MININEC program. As he points out: "The MININEC program permits a fairly straightforward and rapid analysis of complex wire antennas using readily available personal computers, a facility which, ten years ago, was virtually impossible".

His computer has also shown that because of the resulting improved current distribution, an antenna using mixed inductance/capacitance loading with four inductors and six capacitors as in Fig 4(b) would achieve a broadside gain of 3.51dBi, virtually the same as the double Zepp, and a feedpoint impedance very close to 300ohms resistive, making such an arrangement convenient to feed with the low-cost 300-ohm ribbon feeder widely used for TV reception in the USA.

More on Elevated Verticals

Extracted from 'Technical Topics', *Radio Communication*, May 1989

MORE ON ELEVATED VERTICALS

The April *TT* introduced the important concept, put forward by Les Moxon, G6XN, that the popular elevated ground-plane antenna should be regarded as basically a *dipole* rather than a quarter-wave monopole antenna. Some readers may have been tempted to say: "So what. As long as it works with my rig, I couldn't care less that the boffins say it's a dipole!"

But it *does* matter. For years the reputable sources of technical information, such as the *ARRL Antenna Handbook*, have described the radials of a ground-plane antenna (GPA) as 'simulating' a solid (circular) plate, and thus resembling a grounded monopole, adding that four radials are sufficient to achieve this effect but implying that the more radials the better. It was not until 1981 that I was able to reveal,

following a pleasant lunch with the late Dr George Brown and his wife Elizabeth, that the GPA, as originally conceived in the 1930s, used only two radials, later increased to four in order to make it more marketable for American police radio communications. Some years before this, I had successfully tried out and described in *TT* an 'inverted ground-plane' in the form of a T-antenna or single-element 'Bobtail antenna' with two quarter-wave horizontal radials: **Fig 6**. I still believe this is a useful antenna for those wishing to use vertical polarisation, have two supports and are prepared to use an outdoor antenna matching network to provide a high-impedance, voltage feed. It has the advantage of raising the high-current section of the radiating element well above surrounding fences, shrubs etc which can

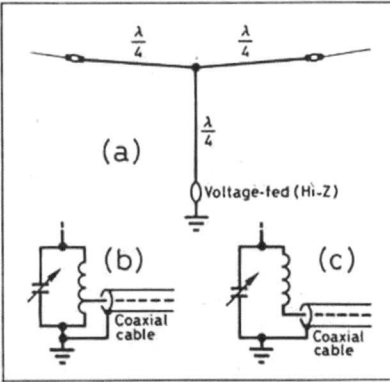

Fig 6. The 'inverted ground plane' antenna using two horizontal radials. (b) and (c) show two possible matching networks for voltage feeding at the base of the quarter-wave radiating element.

absorb an appreciable amount of the RF energy from ground-mounted verticals.

As explained last month, G6XN takes the further step of advocating the use of a single *short* loaded radial, otherwise counterpoise, an arrangement that must seem illogical if you still regard the GPA as a monopole with a simulated earth plane.

In *Ham Radio* (October 1988), Bill Orr W6SAI retold my account of how the RCA ground-plane antenna came to have four radials and my 1981 conclusion that "a two-radial ground plane certainly serves the purpose the inventor had in mind!". In the March 1989 issue, W6SAI returns to this subject on the basis of letters received from readers. He writes:

"A letter from Don Norman, AF8B says that experiments he ran in 1982 on an elevated 147MHz ground-plane showed two radials were a considerable improvement over one, three radials were a considerable improvement over two. He said his tests also showed conclusively that the radials served to decouple the feedline from the antenna. Don's opinion is that HF multiband verticals planted in backyards around the world would probably perform much better if they were placed on rooftops and equipped with two radials for each band."

Certainly, as mentioned last month, the degree to which RF currents can be kept off the feedline is an important factor in determining the vertical radiation pattern of a GPA no matter how many radials are used. Nevertheless it should be possible to minimise such current by the use of chokes, including a coiled length of the coaxial feeder, stub filters etc or ferrite absorbing toroids as in the zero-extent GPA described in *TT*, November 1987, rather than depending on multiple radials.

Another *Ham Radio* reader, Bill Bringler, K5CSJ ran the ground-plane programme on his computer using MININEC (see April *TT*) and compared the field patterns of two and four radial configurations for a GPA with base 25ft above 'average' earth and with the radials sloping down to 15ft elevation at their ends: "At a vertical radiation angle of 10°, the horizontal pattern of the two-radial design was omni-directional within a fraction of a decibel. In the vertical plane, the angle of the main lobe above the horizon was less than 20°." This corresponded to the pattern of the equivalent four-radial design. K5CSJ concluded that there was no significant difference in operation between the two antennas. He also did a computer-run to compare a ground-mounted monopole vertical against the elevated two-radial design and found it about 1·5dB worse at an elevation angle of 10°. His conclusion was that "A two-radial ground plane, when elevated, works just fine!"

'New' Antenna

Extracted from 'Technical Topics', *Radio Communication*, August 1989

'NEW' ANTENNA?

With a century of antenna development behind us, it takes some courage to claim to have developed an antenna system that depends on

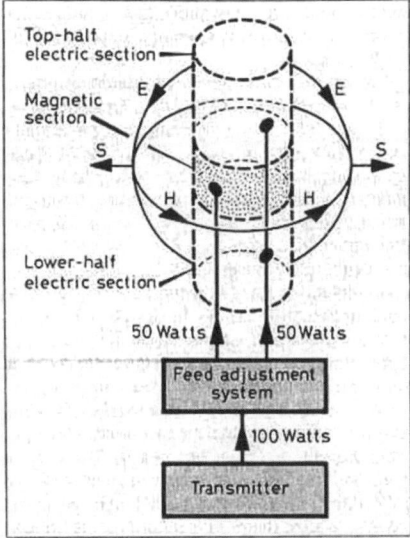

Fig 6. Basic configuration of the GM3HAT/GM3DTI controversial 'crossed-field antenna'. Does it really work by direct synthesis of the Poynting Vector cross product?

doing something "for the very first time in the history of radio-communications". Indeed, anyone making such a claim has to expect that it will be received with a degree of scepticism, particularly when the system is claimed to overcome most of the disadvantages traditionally associated with electrically-short antennas.

Maurice Hately, GM3HAT and F M Kabbary, GM3TDI have certainly stirred things up by describing their new "crossed-field antenna (CFA)" as exploiting "for the very first time, radio waves that have been efficiently generated by direct synthesis of the Poynting Vector cross product, by using separately stimulated electric and magnetic fields cutting at right angles." In effect they claim

ANTENNA TOPICS

that reversing the form of Maxwell's original equations has led to the realisation and development of a revolutionairy new antenna system **(Fig 6)** for which they have applied for patents in a number of countries and are marketing through Hately Antenna Technology, the firm associated with GM3HAT's dipole of delight!.

An article (with B G Stewart) "Maxwell's equations and the crossed-field antenna" appeared in the March issue of *Electronics & Wireless World* that I for one found virtually impossible to understand and which has since been savaged by a number of antenna specialists including Dr A G P Boswell, G3NOQ, who points out: 'The value or otherwise of the CFA could be very quickly established by an experiment conducted by any generally-accepted method. The radiated field produced at some large distance from the antenna should be measured and related to the RF power being fed to the antenna terminals. The *IEEE Standard Test Procedure for Antennas* (IEEE Std 149-179) offers one such procedure by which the authors could (maybe) silence their critics immediately. Can they explain why this has not been done? Until it is, the verdict on the CFA must remain 'not proven'." Others have suggested the article was an April Fool article published a month too soon! My own ill-informed opinion is that it rather proves that if you can feed RF to any lump of metal in the sky it will radiate effectively on HF in good conditions. It may well be advisable to wait for the results of a carefully controlled test before accepting that GM3HAT and GM3TDI are really generating radiowaves in a unique and revolutionary manner, despite their claim that many prototypes smaller than 1m in height and 0.4m in diameter have been tested and have radiated any frequency from 1.8 to 30MHz at powers up to 400W with the only adjustment necessary to change the wavelength generated is a change of proportional feed voltage and phase to the two field-stimulating electrodes. Wonderful, if it really works as claimed and in the manner claimed! Meanwhile they have certainly blinded me with science and Maxwell's equations.

Gary Milton, G0CUQ provides a cautionary tale for owners of FT-747GX HF transceivers and possibly also relating to some other equipments. On the rear of the FT747 is a socket which provides 13.8V for powering keyers etc. The manual points out that it is intended only for supplying loads of a few hundred mA. G0CUG was unlucky enough to fit a homebrew connector to this socket which proved to have a short-circuit between the power rail and 0V. This resulted in excessive current which burnt the 13.8V supply track off the PCB. Too late he realised that this supply is not separately fused. He warns readers to check carefully any connectors, accessories etc for short-circuits before plugging into the rear panel socket. It could save them a nasty repair bill.

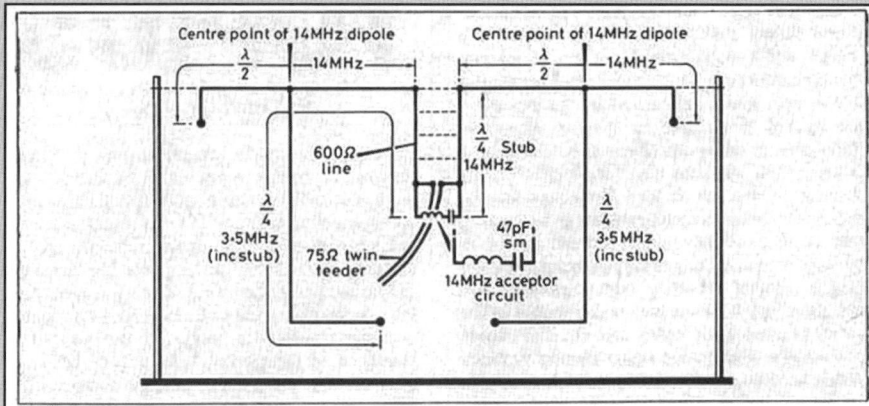

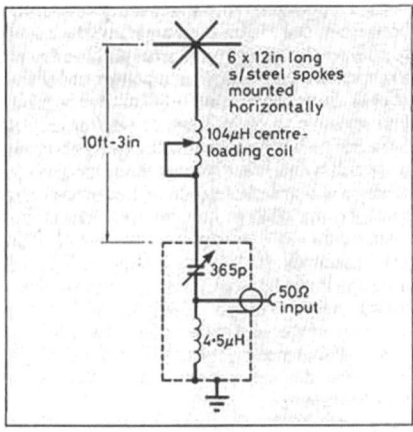

Fig 2. (top) G8GS's dual-band (3.5 and 14MHz) antenna.

Fig 3; G0CBM reduces the need for multiple loading-coil taps by adding a variable capacitor to peak for resonance while maintaining near-unity VSWR. Dimensions of his 3.5MHz mobile antenna for guidance only.

of narrow bandwith HF mobile antennas from Charles Wilkie, G0CBM.

G8GS writes: "After improving signals to VK/ZL on the long path by using a four-element wire beam comprising two colinear horizontal dipoles, each with a director, it was desired to incorporate a 3.5MHz facility into the system. This has been done and the arrangement works successfully on both bands. The method is shown in simple outline in **Fig 2**, utilising the voltage node points, switching being achieved with a 14MHz acceptor circuit fitted into the bottom of the quarter-wave stub. The array is compact, measuring approximately 52ft in length, the mast height being 30ft. No deterioration of the out-going 14MHz signals has been detected." The illustration does not show the 14MHz director wires.

G0CBM required an efficient mobile antenna for 3.5MHz and recognised that the key to efficiency with electrically-short (high Q) antennas is achieving accurate resonance when changing frequency. He writes: "The usual way of achieving resonance of mobile antennas is by means of a tapped loading coil, thus resonance occurs as a series of steps through the band with maximum efficiency only when the operating frequency coincides with the resonance of a tapping point. On the lower HF bands, bandwidth is often only about 10kHz or less, and would entail the use of some 30 taps on the loading coil. I found that by placing a variable capacitor at the base of the antenna, resonance could be achieved at any point in the band. Matching the antenna to a 50-ohm output of a transmitter is achieved by inserting a 4.5µH inductor between the variable capacitor and ground. In practice, I have found that the twin requirements of resonance and unity VSWR can be achieved with only three taps and a 365pF variable capacitor. In operation I simply peak the variable capacitor for maximum signal on a field strength meter. Dimensions shown in **Fig 3** are for guidance only."

John Heys, G3BDQ reports some very successful DX operation using a three-band (14, 21 and 28MHz) and a two-band (3.5 and 7MHz) inverted ground-plane antennas (see *TT*, May 1989 and many earlier references) based on the standard multi-band dipole principle of parallel wires of suitable resonant lengths. His triband unit (fed at the top of the three vertical radiators by means of tuned 300 ohm BOFA ribbon feeder) has the 14MHz wire inductively loaded 3.5MHz radiator with the bottom ends of both 3.5 and 7MHz radiators folded back so that the total support height is only 34ft (lower part 2ft above ground). This is end-fed to a single wire radiation feeder to an ATU which then also allows the antenna to be tuned up as form of long-wire antenna for any band. G3BDQ hopes to publish an article on them before long.

Antenna Topics

Extracted from 'Technical Topics', *Radio Communication*, October 1989

ANTENNA TOPICS

From a number of antenna ideas recently received from readers, this month's selection includes an ingenious 3.5/1.4MHz wire antenna from C W Farrell, G8GS and a method of ensuring resonance

Elements Fatigued

Extracted from 'Technical Topics', *Radio Communication*, November 1989

ELEMENTS FATIGUED BY FLUTTERING

An article by Dick Weber, K5IU 'Vibration induced Yagi fatigue failures' *Ham Radio*, August 1989) reminded me of one of the most traumatic events of the years I spent with the IBA. About 5pm on the evening of March 19, 1969, the news broke that one of the two IBA 1265 ft masts (the tallest masts in the UK) had suddenly collapsed. This was the TV mast at Emley Moor, Yorkshire and its collapse, fortunately without causing injuries or deaths, threatened the entire project aimed at introducing 625-line UHF colour on the ITV network by November of that year. Fortunately the engineers were able to erect a temporary mast, brought from Sweden, and this enabled the colour service to begin on time; meanwhile the present Emley Moor concrete tower was built in quick time.

Naturally, there followed a lengthy inquest on why the cylindrical steel guyed mast, erected in 1966, should have collapsed on a cold but not particularly windy evening (wind speed at the time only about 19 mph). Some pundits claimed it was due to the effect of unequal ice loading on the guys, but the inquiry discounted this hypothesis and came to the conclusion that the mast had been excited into a resonant mode of violent oscillation by 'vortex shedding' induced by the moderate wind speed. It fell to my lot later to try to put together a layman's guide to vortex shedding when the IBA fought (and won) an action against the prime contractors, arguing that the effects of such vortex-shedding induced oscillation should have been foreseen by the designers. To prevent a repetition of this collapse in the remaining two masts of this type (1265 ft at Belmont, Lincolnshire and 1015 ft at Winter Hill, near Bolton) the IBA installed suspended counterweights inside the masts — over twenty years later both are still standing.

In his *Ham Radio* article, K5IU writes: "Yagi element failures can be attributed to two basic causes. The first type of failure occurs when an element isn't strong enough to hold up when forces are applied. These forces may be caused by a thick layer of ice, high winds, or a combination of the two. Under the stress of these forces the element either bends or breaks off, with signs of bending in the area of the break.

"The second type of failure takes place after an element has been fluttering, or vibrating, in a relatively low wind stream. The break caused by this kind of failure is quite different. There's no sign of bending in the area of the break; it's a jagged line through the element. Boom fluttering (although not as common as element fluttering) can also lead to this type of failure.

"Because there's no sign of bending you'll know that the stress levels in the material are relatively low, yet failure occurs. What causes the element to flutter in the wind? What causes the break although the stress levels are well below those required to bend the tube? And what methods will minimise this type of failure?"

In answering these questions at some length, K5IU stresses that an antenna element will have high-Q mechanical (as well as electrical) resonances that can be excited into large displacement oscillations by quite small exciting forces. Medium speed winds, at well under 35 mph, when they strike an elongated cylindrical object create vortices or swirls of air; if these are shed from the object in a regular, orderly manner related to a natural resonance of the object, they constitute an exciting force. A commonly cited example is the pronounced low-frequency hum that comes from overhead telephone wires when the wind blows at a specific speed.

Unfortunately, when aluminium is flexed at levels below its yield-stress, while no permanent bend results, the damage accumulates and if the flexing is repeated sufficiently often there will be a fatigue failure. In effect metal fatigue is the weakened condition induced in metal parts of machines, vehicles or structures by repeated stresses or loadings, ultimately resulting in fracture under a stress much weaker than that necessary to cause fracture in a single application (*Britannica Encyclopedia* definition). Metal fatigue was noted in the 19th century but only came to public (and engineering) attention in 1954 with the failure of the pressure cabins and consequent crashes of the early Comet airliners (the first jet airliner), although this problem in aircraft had been previously forecast with surprising accuracy by Neville Shute, engineer turned novelist, in his book *No Highway*.

What then can be done to minimise fatigue failures in antenna elements? The basic approach is to try and limit the amplitude of the stresses during fluttering by damping the Q of the mechanical resonances. K5IU notes that the following ideas have been suggested:

(1) Filling the inside of tubular elements with the type of foam intended for sealing and insulating cracks and holes in buildings.

(2) Modifying the shape of the element so that orderly vortices cannot be shed. A practical technique is to wrap a wire in a helix around the element; wire diameter about 0.09 times that of the element with the turns of he helix spaced about five times the diameter (K5IU recommends this method).

(3) By attempting to move the mechanical resonances of the element out of the range of vortex shedding. Some amateurs have fitted damping ropes inside the elements (K5IU doubts the value of this). A small weight (eg 3oz) fastened to the tip of an element can alter its resonant frequency appreciably.

Many years ago, I reported in *TT* (and subsequently in many editions of *ART*) a technique used to overcome metal fatigue fluttering of Yagi and log-periodic HF arrays at Washington State Unversity originally published in *Electronic Design* (2 August, 1966) for use in locations where there are persistent winds and the risk of elements being flexed continuously over long periods.

As shown in **Fig 2**, flat rubber sheets, or sheets fashioned by splitting a length of rubber garden hose, can be used as energy absorbers (dampers). The mechanical (as well as the electrical) impedance of any rod-like element is high at its free end(s), regardless of the number of modes along the elements. This means that placing an energy-absorbent device at the ends can reduce the amplitude of the oscillations and minimise the chance of metal-fatigue breakage (although possibly slightly increasing the bending stresses in gale-force winds).

For the 1966 approach a short section of lightweight garden hose, split lengthwise every 90° is held in place on the end of the element by a hose clamp: **Fig 2**. A more efficient and durable protection can be made from a sheet of flat rubber

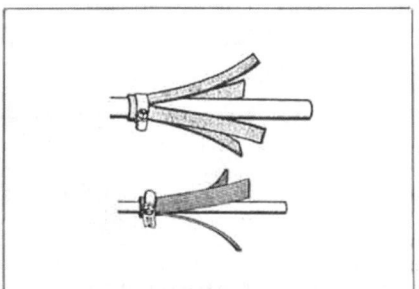

Fig 2. Energy absorbers fitted at the ends of antenna elements to reduce flutter-type oscillation due to vortex shedding.

or pliable plastic material ⅛in to ¼in thick by 5-6in long. If this is made just wide enough to wrap once round the element, the damping will be matched to the size of the element. This material is cut lengthwise to make four tabs. Ideally, such devices would be more effective if clamped at the very end of the elements, but in practice they are positioned so that the free end of the tabs are about 2in from the ends to prevent changes in the electrical length of impedance of the elements.

This system was used at a site exposed to the Pacific coastal breezes. Fitted to elements with diameters ranging from ⅜in to 1in, no breakages occurred over three years. Previously, breakages had been frequent. It occurs to me that if the energy-absorbers are made of plastics, it would be advisable to ensure that they are as UV-resistant as possible, or replaced occasionally.

For coping with the different problem of gale-force wind stresses, reference should be made to the two-part article 'Wind Loading' by David Reynolds, G3ZPF (*RadCom*, April/May 1988).

1980 - 1989

DX Antennas for 3.5MHz

Extracted from 'Technical Topics', *Radio Communication*, November 1989

DX ANTENNAS FOR 3.5MHz

Earlier this year, Martin MacGregor, G4EZG gave a talk to a local club on the options and considerations surrounding the design of DX antennas for the lower HF bands (eg 3.5MHz) for sites of different sizes and terrains (sloping, low-lying, high-plateau etc). In this he was at pains to emphasise the concept of antenna directivity and radiation versus height and ground effects.

He has sent along some of his notes and relevant diagrams; unfortunately it is not possible to include in *TT* more than a very brief digest of some of his material but even so this should help clear the minds of those who wonder why their antennas work well on the higher HF bands and for medium-distance contacts on all bands, but leave much to be desired when striving to work DX on 3.5MHz or 1.8HMz.

He notes that it is well understood that, at least theoretically, horizontal dipoles at heights of 0.25λ or less have little or no horizontal directivity (ie are virtually omni-directional) and very little radiation at the lower vertical angles (say 10-30°) desirable for DX working under normal propagation conditions: Fig 7. At 3.5MHz, 0.25λ is roughly 66ft so that the basic horizontal dipole is of limited value to the majority of amateurs who cannot aspire to antenna supports higher than about 60ft. As previously noted in *TT* the effective height of an antenna is usually several feet more than its actual height above ground; this is particularly true at the lower frequencies where the ground behaves rather as a lossy conductor, changing to a dielectric at higher frequencies. Additionally, a 'real' (imperfect) earth has the effect of filling in the nulls between the theoretical vertical and horizontal radiation lobes.

As confirmed by experiments by DJ2NN some years ago an optimum cost-effective height for 14-28MHz arrays is about 18.5m and 60ft has become a median height for amateur HF towers. This height can be shown to be suitable for DX operation on all bands down to and including 7MHz although theoretically unsuitable for 3.5MHz DX (*unless used to support an inverted-vee dipole with its vertically-polarized component — G3VA*). Empirically this is not the case: dipoles and their variants at 60ft do show DX capabilities under those propagation conditions that favour high-angle openings. Even so, comparatively small height increases above 60ft can dramatically improve their DX performance.

Directivity (effective gain) of an antenna has an important if secondary effect on the vertical radiation pattern of an antenna, and this has a particularly important, if secondary, effect at low antenna heights in reducing the strength of unwanted incoming high-angle signals. In general, a Yagi or other array concentrates the vertical radiation lobe to much the same extent as its horizontal (HRP) directivity.

While a 3.5MHz array at 60ft, or possibly a little less, can give acceptable results it cannot challenge the superiority of an efficiently installed and well-sited vertically-polarized array in an area of reasonably good ground conductivity. (*Hence the popularity of inverted-vees, slopers and top-loaded tower antennas — G3VA*).

G4EZG adds: "Large 3.5MHz arrays apart, in my experience the best DX antenna of moderate dimensions for use with a 60ft tower, is the apex-

ANTENNA TOPICS

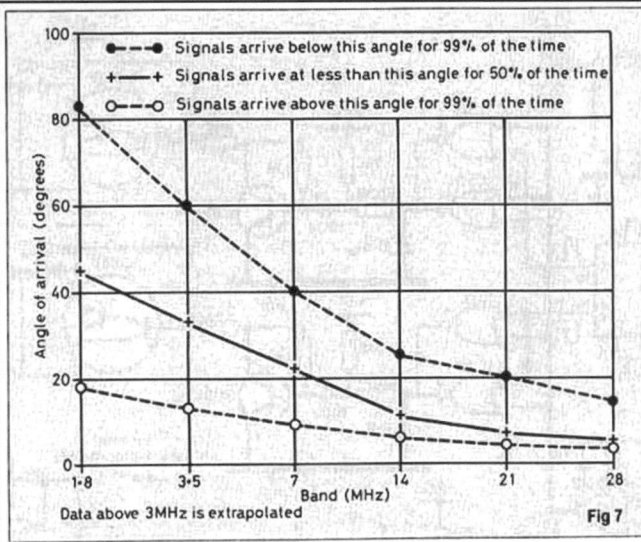

Fig 7. Verticle arrival angles of sky-wave signals, 3.5-30MHz.

Fig 8. 3.5MHz delta-loop antenna system preferred by G4EZG (a) Apex fed for high-angle radiation. (b) Bottom-corner fed for low-angle (DX) radiation. With a system of pulleys, G4EZG was able to move the feed point between these positions.

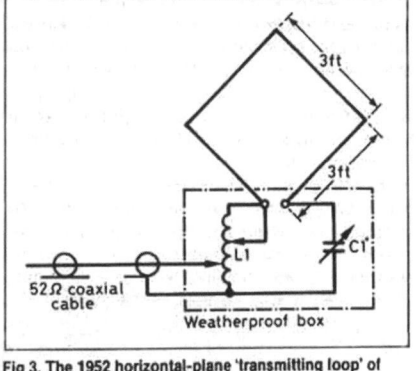

Fig 3. The 1952 horizontal-plane 'transmitting loop' of W4LW was simply connected in series with a conventionally tuned circuit. For a loop with 3ft sides at 7MHz, L1 had an inductance of 2.5µH and C1 a maximum capacitance of about 150pF (high-voltage spacing).

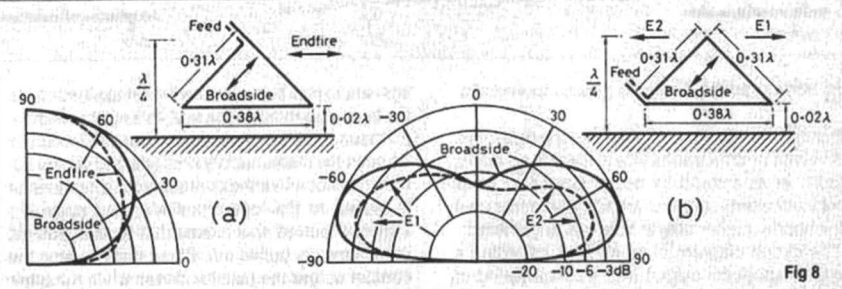

up, bottom-corner-fed Delta loop: **Fig 8** (b). The best *local* antenna is the same but apex-up, apex-fed: **Fig 8** (a). My antenna was constructed from 2.5mm², PVC, stranded wire, fed with an 0.5λ (electrical length) of RG62A/U (93-ohm) coaxial cable. this gave a good match to the loop feed-impedance of roughly 100 ohms, and most rigs will happily load this arrangement. It obviates the need for a 0.25λ (72-ohm) matching section to a 52-ohm cable. The absence of a matching section and the use of large-diameter wire resulted in a very broad-band system.

"By placing pulleys at each of the three corners I could physically move the feed point around one side of the loop to change the vertical radiation angle to suit conditions for DX and local operation. The difference such adjustments made had to be heard to be believed! It would have been interesting to motorize this operation to see what could be achieved with remote fine-tuning of the feed-point position."

For those who cannot aspire to a 60ft antenna-support, the system could be scaled down for 7 or 10MHz and 30ft height.

An Early Transmit Loop

Extracted from 'Technical Topics', *Radio Communication*, December 1989

AN EARLY TRANSMITTING LOOP

Gerald Stancey, G3MCK was not taken by the idea of Richard Silberstein, W0YBF of putting a secret antenna under the floorboards (*RadCom*, September 1989) and my own concern at the idea was that no mention was made of the possible radiation hazard to anyone in the room immediately above (or below) the antenna. On the other hand the compact transmitting loop of high-conductivity copper tubing, out-of-doors if QRO, is establishing itself as an effective antenna for those with restricted sites.

G3MCK continues to find much of interest in the back copies of amateur journals, often unearthing items which attracted little attention when originally published. In this process he has come across an article 'Ham-band transmitting loops' by Richard Hay, W4LW (*QST*, September 1952, pp14, 118) that pre-dates by 15 years the US Army Loop of 1967 to which most recent loop ideas can be traced back. G3MCK writes: "This loop antenna appears to have the dimensions of a modern 'magnetic loop' but is not fed like one nor used in the vertical plane. However it seems certain to radiate better than something under the floorboards! At the worst it supports the theory that anything fed with RF will radiate!"

W4LW's horizontal square loop suitable for balcony mounting had 3ft sides and was connected directly in series with a conventional tank circuit (**Fig 3**). He reported that it gave him 7MHz CW contacts up to 2500 miles when fed with 40Watts of RF, with 'reliable' contacts up to 1000 miles. He wrote: "The possibilities of this system have not been explored fully. However, two facts have been established: it works, and it is a wonderful subject for conversation during QSOs!"

W4LW's loop used No 12 wire for both the loop and for L1 but he pointed out "an improvement could probably be effected by the use of heavier wire or even copper tubing." In 1952, SWR meters were still uncommon and he described an adjustment technique that did not depend on their use. He wrote: Adjustment is as follows: (a) Substitute a 52-ohm dummy load for the antenna system and adjust transmitter for proper loading. (b) Remove dummy load and replace the loop antenna assembly. (c) Set the tap for the coax connection at about 3 turns and tune C1 to resonance at the transmitter frequency. (If necessary, reduce inductance of L1 by shorting turns with the second tap.). (d) Vary the position of the coax tap (retuning C1 each time) until proper loading is indicated. The position of the coax tap is a fairly critical adjustment and must be set to the nearest ¼-turn for best results. An SWR indicator would be very helpful, although it *can* be done by 'cut and try'... It would be desirable to make the loop as large as possible, with corresponding reduction in L1. The ultimate would be to reduce L1 to just enough inductance to match the coax line impedance; the larger the loop, the greater the (desirable) radiation resistance and the wider the band of frequencies that can be covered without re-adjusting." The square loop with 2-ft sides had a bandwidth on 7MHz of about 20kHz. W4LW reported "An unexpected by-product of this system is freedom from TVI and, on reception, marked reduction in local QRN with interference from the line output oscillator of a neighbour's TV set disappearing entirely."

The inclusion of the loop within the lumped inductance tuned circuit must inevitably increase the resistive losses compared with the present use of a small inductively coupled matching loop. However, there are circumstances in which W4LW's horizontal loop might be useful, if makeshift, arrangement.

1990-1999

Mesny - A French Pioneer

Extracted from 'Technical Topics', *Radio Communication*, February 1990

MESNY — A FRENCH PIONEER

H R Mesny, GJ3LFJ, noted with interest the references (*TT*, June 1989, p33 and November 1989, p38) to the 1920s push-pull oscillator of his namesake "(R) Mesny." In the June *TT*, I mentioned that neither G8FEQ nor I had traced anything further of his work, though in my case I had forgotten that in *TT*, January 1977 I included a diagram of the Chireix-Mesny HF beam antenna that was developed in France as an early alternative to the original Marconi-Franklin beam arrays made up of large numbers of 'uniform' vertical dipoles. At that time I noted: "In the Chireix-Mesny array the ½λ dipoles are disposed in the form of saw-teeth, rather like a series of 2λ quad elements. This has the advantage over the Franklin

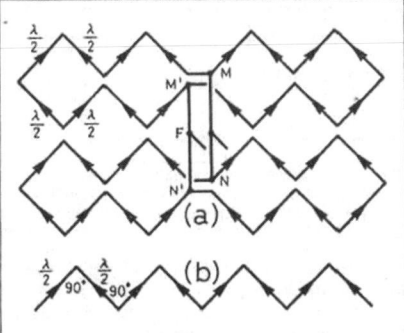

Fig 12(a). Large Chireix-Mesny array of half-wave dipoles arranged in saw-tooth configuration and providing vertically-polarized signals with broadside directivity. Might have application as fixed beam on VHF/UHF.
(b). Simplified Chireix-Mesny array which can be end-fed: such 'zig-zag' arrays have been used at VHF/UHF for TV broadcasting.

array that each dipole element may be driven directly by the one preceding it. Fig 12(a) shows a large Chireix-Mesny array which would require vast space for HF but might be well worth investigating for VHF or UHF. From the point of view of the radiated field, such a sawtooth network is equivalent to an array of parallel dipoles. Fig 12(b) forms the basis of the 'zig-zag' antennas used at VHF/UHF for television broadcasting."

GJ3LFJ traced a reference to the Chireix-Mesny beam in *The Radio Engineers Handbook* by Henney. He recalls that some years ago the late Max Tourniquet de Brandt, F5HJ mentioned that Mesny was still well remembered and respected in France for the work he did as an engineer in the French Army. He was responsible, with others, for introducing radio communication in the French forces before and during the First World War.

I can now add a further reference. Elizabeth Antebi, in her massive *The Electronic Epoch* (Van Nostrand Reinhold, 1982) in discussing the parallel development of radar in many countries writes:

"In France, Henri Gutton and Pierret began to experiment with (very) short waves; and Maurice Ponté, who had been working with Gutton, Sylvain Berline and Hugon at the CSF Laboratory, since 1930, began his work on the magnetron. In 1931, Mesny and David, technical consultants for the French Military Signals Department, noted that a disturbance was created in communications whenever an aircraft passed through the zone between the transmitting and receiving stations. At the beginning of 1934, the first equipment using returning radio wave echoes to locate a moving obstacle was produced..."

Without detracting from the value of the breakthrough made by J T Randall and H A H Boot in demonstrating the first high-power 10cm cavity magnetron at Birmingham University in early 1940, and the important role of the French team, we should also be proud of the part played in this work by Eric Megaw, MBE, DSc, GI6MU/G6MU, a former RSGB Council Member and contributor to the old *T&R Bulletin*. He worked on magnetrons at the GEC Research Laboratories in the 1930s, liaised with Henri Gutton and was the man chiefly responsible for turning the experimental Birmingham magnetron (which worked directly on its vacuum pump) into a production device. He had an E1188 cavity magnetron designed and made in collaboration with Birmingham working by 16 May 1940 producing 500W CW or pulse at 10cm. Previously, in collaboration with HM Signal School, he had been able to obtain 1.5kW pulse output from a segmented magnetron at 37cm. A most notable British professional scientist who was also a keen amateur.

Steerable 7MHz DX Antenna

Extracted from 'Technical Topics', *Radio Communication*, April 1990

STEERABLE 7MHz DX ANTENNA

Tony Preedy, G3LNP notes that anybody who still has an unguyed 18-metre tower supporting an HF rotary beam (and a garden that can accommodate a circular radius of some 4.6m) still standing after the winter's persistent gales can easily provide themselves with an effective steerable 7MHz DX antenna: see **Figs 1 and 2**.

He writes: 'A figure-of-eight horizontal radiation pattern with a theoretical gain of about 5.5dB over a quarter-wave (monopole) radiator is achieved by driving two vertical wires in antiphase. The central metal tower does not greatly influence the radiation pattern since the net current induced from the two wires is theoretically zero. Similarly the horizontal feed sections are dimensioned such that they have no net radiation perpendicular to their axis. Radiation is therefore only end-fire and at low angles of elevation.

'The method of driving the wires in antiphase by using a balanced ATU as shown eliminates any need for a counterpoise or ground radials. The

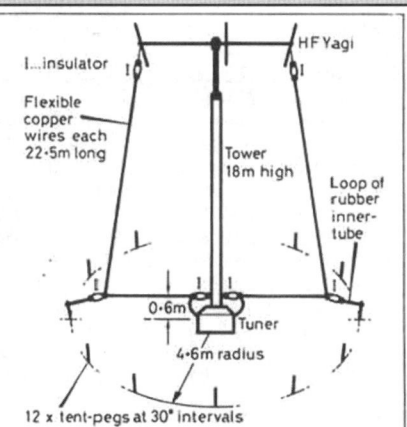

Fig 1. Construction details of G3LNP's steerable 7MHz DX antenna providing roughly 5dB bi-directional (figure-of-eight) gain and good low-angle characteristics with some 30dB rejection of signals from the sides.

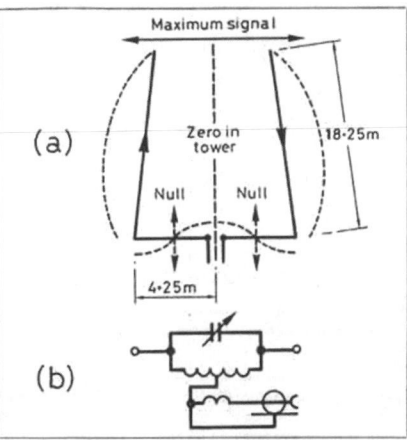

Fig 2(a) Dimensions and current distribution of the G3LNP antenna for optimum directional performance. (b) Tuner as built in waterproof plastic carton. Coil 26 turns, 16 swg, 5cm diameter, 15cm long. Link 3 turns insulated wire. High-voltage 50pF variable capacitor.

tuner, assembled in a plastic ice-cream carton, was adjusted for minimum VSWR at the centre of the band only.

'Construction is straightforward, as illustrated, but unfortunately rotating the beam is a three-stage operation which involves first unhooking the ground attachments, rotating the HF Yagi and then re-attaching the wires to the appropriate pair of tent pegs.

"Performance has been impressive in spite of poor local ground conductivity. DX stations were typically 3 'S-points' stronger compared with a horizontal dipole; Western European stations about 5 'S-points' weaker; side rejection at least 30dB."

ANTENNA TOPICS

24MHz Dual-loop Chireix-Mesny

Extracted from 'Technical Topics', *Radio Communication*, June 1990

Army Low-profile Loop

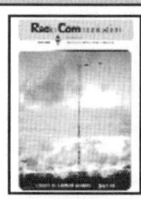

Extracted from 'Technical Topics', *Radio Communication*, July 1990

24MHz DUAL-LOOP HALF-SIZE CHIREIX-MESNY

In view of recent items on the classic Chireix-Mesny antenna (*TT*, February and April) with its arrays of half-wave dipoles arranged in squares (each square 2-λ perimeter), I was interested to note in 'Ham Radio Techniques' by Bill Orr, W6SAI (*Ham Radio*, January 1990) a 24MHz antenna described as a 'dual quad-loop antenna' but which could equally well be considered as a half-size Chireix-Mesny array using ¼-λ rather than ½-λ sides: **Fig 3**. Such a design would be effective also on even harmonic bands, eg a 24.9MHz double-loop would probably work well on 50MHz.

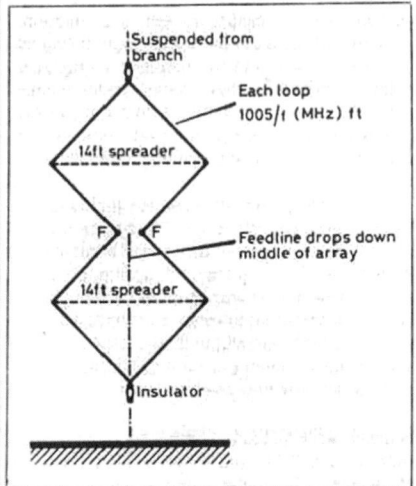

Fig 3. K4BLT's dual-loop 24.9MHz antenna. This is in effect a half-size Chireix-Mesny array on 24.9MHz and should work as a full-size array on 50MHz.

W6SAI writes: 'A single vertical quad-loop makes an effective antenna. It has the radiation pattern of a dipole and provides an additional gain of approximately 1.2dB. The quad loop has a very broadband response and a feedpoint impedance of about 120 ohms. Place two of these loops in phase and feed them at the common point, and you have Jeff O'Connell's K4BLT dual-quad loop antenna. Jeff's antenna is cut for the 12-metre (24.9MHz) band. It's suspended from a branch of a pine tree. Two oak spreaders, 1¼-in square and 14ft long form the diamonds. The pattern is bidirectional and the gain is estimated to be about 3.5dBd. Polarisation is horizontal.

'The antenna is fed at the centre with a coaxial line. The feedpoint impedance is very close to 50 ohms. The line is wound into an RF choke at the feedpoint. The choke consists of four turns of coaxial 5-in in diameter. This helps keep RF off the outer shield. Bring the line down the middle of the array, as shown.'

ARMY LOW-PROFILE LOOP ANTENNA

Quite a few compact transmitting (magnetic) loop antennas can be heard these days on the amateur bands putting out respectable signals for their small size. This approach has also been taken up recently by the Royal Signals in the form of a dismantable, rectangular loop designed and manufactured by British Aerospace (Dynamics) Ltd at Filton, Bristol.

At an IEE Colloquium, David Griffiths and Alan Baker of BAe described how this loop has been designed to provide both high-angle, near vertical incident skywave (NVIS) and effective ground-wave propagation for two-way communications between mobile sites (vehicles, helicopters etc) at ranges up to 300km (with minimum or no 'skip zone') on frequencies between 1.5 and 12MHz. Traditionally, military tactical HF communications have depended on 3-4m vertical whips which give good ground wave signals up to about 30km but very little NVIS radiation. This has meant that for ranges over about 30km it has usually been necessary to erect a low horizontal dipole; for the lower night-time frequencies resonant half-wave dipoles need a large site; short non-resonant dipoles can be used but require more complex matching units that often need considerable operator experience to achieve good results. Again, dipoles cannot be fitted to mobile platforms. A transmitting loop can overcome these problems provided that careful attention is given to the fundamental problem of the extremely low radiation resistance of any compact loop.

In their colloquium paper 'A low profile loop antenna for communications using NVIS', the authors outline the basic considerations and component selection necessary to reduce loss-resistances to a minimum; describe a capacitive-type (automatic) tuning/matching network; and the result of trials of a 2m x 1m (rectangular) loop and tuner unit fitted to a Land Rover and coupled to a standard 50W HF transceiver. The tests with this loop showed once again that it is virtually impossible to design a single loop that is effective over more than about an octave range of frequencies (eg 7/10/14MHz amateur bands). This has led to the design of a loop formed from lengths of 1¼in diameter aluminium tubes) with slide-fit joints that can be assembled either as a 2m x 1m rectangular loop usable from 2 to 10MHz (but with low-efficiency below about 5MHz) or a bigger 'night-frequency' loop (3m x 2m) for use between about 1.5 to 5MHz: see **Fig 3**.

Calculated values of the voltages across and currents through the tuner network capacitors (**Fig 4**) underline the demanding specification that must be met by these components. With 200W input to the 2m x 1m at 2MHz the peak voltage across the series capacitor (120pF) will be about 3.8kV while the shunt capacitor (1300pF) has to carry an RF current of 62 amps! With this type of all-weather loop, gas filled or vacuum capacitors become virtually essential for professional applications.

While I am not convinced that amateurs would be wise to take the British Aerospace approach (the I1ARZ approach in the February 1989 *Rad Com* seems more suitable), it is nevertheless interesting to study the results of the trials etc.

With the original 2m x 1m loop, trials during the day showed that the loop achieved much the same performance as existing tactical antenna systems. However, adequate night-time performance was not achievable because of the need to use low frequencies to facilitate ionospheric reflection of NVIS waves.

It was concluded that: "the gain could be improved only by increasing the size of the loop, at the expense of mobility. Discussion with typical

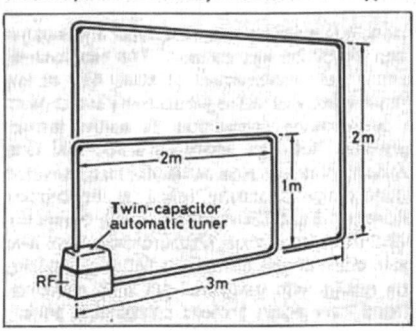

Fig 3. The British Aerospace 1.5 — 12MHz transmitting loop antenna using 1¼in diameter aluminium tubing that can be fitted together to form 2m x 1m or 3m x 2m loops etc.

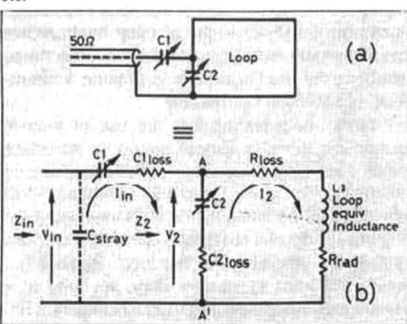

Fig 4. (a) Practical matching/tuning unit with series and shunt capacitors used as the basis of the automatic tuning unit. (b) Equivalent circuit emphasising the importance of using low-loss components.

users indicated this was acceptable and a larger loop 3m by 2m was devised." The new system, with a gain improvement of about 5dB at low frequencies, was tested exhaustively and showed a performance comparable to earlier tactical antennas "with the added attraction that loop elements of various sizes can readily be constructed to maximise directivity (gain) at frequencies between 1.5 and 12MHz which readily covers the NVIS frequency range. Measurements have also been made of ground-wave radiation comparing the results with traditional 4m whip elements. These have again showed comparable performance."

A final conclusion is that "the use of gas filled variable capacitors in the matching unit will permit high-power transmitters to be used in any weather conditions. The work on loop impedance fluctuations with changes of local environment has shown that the introduction of pre-determined positions for the capacitors to provide a 'silent-tune' capability is not feasible."

I cannot help feeling that the use of slide-fit aluminium tubes is almost bound to introduce much loss-resistance after a time; nor would amateurs often strive to achieve maximum NVIS radiation. At the meeting, the authors discounted any possibility of a radiation hazard to the users, even when very close to the loop. Personally I would not want to sit very close for long to a vehicle loop when powered from 50 to 200W of RF! Nevertheless this loop does prove once again that small loops can radiate well provided always that the resistive losses do not greatly exceed the radiation resistance.

1990 - 1999

The 'Counterpoise' Revisited

Extracted from 'Technical Topics', *Radio Communication*, July 1990

More Chireix-Mesny Zig Zag

Extracted from 'Technical Topics', *Radio Communication*, July 1990

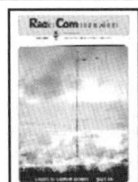

THE 'COUNTERPOISE' REVISITED

For many years the word counterpoise virtually vanished from the vocabularies of amateur radio antenna designers. The once-popular technique of using a single or multiple wire in lieu of a direct earth (ground) connection to bring a Marconi-type (non-resonant) wire antenna into resonance largely disappeared from both amateur and professional practice except in the form of the radials of elevated ground-plane antennas. Radials, in fact, like counterpoises convert a monopole form of antenna to dipole form, though this is not always recognised by users.

One exception to the disappearance of counterpoises is the W3EDP 84ft wire with its 17ft counterpoise (6ft on 14MHz) which seems to have been undergoing something of a revival since the *TT* references to it as the 'ageless W3EDP' in January and April, 1985: **Fig 5**. Last year, Byron Goodman, W1DX (ex-W6CAL, -W1JPE) brought to my attention the very first description of the 'W3EDP' as 'An unorthodox antenna' by Yardley Beers, W0JF (but then W3AWH) in *QST*, March 1936, pp32-33. This describes how H J Siegel (then W3EDP) had used over 1,000ft of wire in experimenting with various standard antennas. Finally he hung a 100ft roll of wire to his mast and carefully tabulated the results he achieved on 7MHz using this as an end-fed wire antenna: 'Four feet of wire was then cut off and this process repeated several times. When all his tabulations were complete, a length of 84ft seemed to stand out as best ... Not liking entirely the idea of an end-fed single wire antenna, W3EDP set about to find a counterpoise for the best results with his 84ft antenna. Going through a pruning process similar to that with the antenna itself produced a counterpoise length of 17ft as the one working best in combination with the antenna. This combination seemed to work excellently on 160, 80, 40 and 10m, but on 20m a counterpoise length of 6½ft seemed to outshine all others. (Note there was no 15m band in the 1930s).

My own feeling and practice is not to regard 84ft as a 'magic' length but rather to use virtually any long length of end-fed wire and then to find a counterpoise length that results in most

Fig 5 (below). The 'unorthodox' multiband antenna that emerged from the experiments by W3EDP in 1936: an 84ft end-fed antenna with 17ft or (on 14MHz) 6½ft counterpoise.
Fig 6 (right). The simple antenna systems that were suggested for use with the Polish 'clandestine' receiver-transmitter type AP5 which covered 2 to 16MHz. Connections A and P for the 6L6 transmitter are shown in Fig 9.

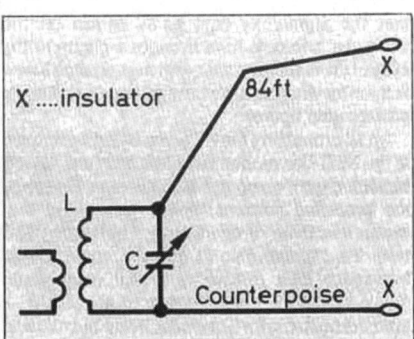

MORE ON CHIREIX-MESNY / ZIG-ZAG ANTENNAS

Antennas seem to follow a cyclic pattern of interest: forgotten, hardly mentioned for years and then a period of sharply mounting interest. In

RF current flowing into the antenna when the whole system is brought into resonance with the aid of an antenna tuner. I continue to be surprised at the difference in current on some bands between a counterpoise and the shortest direct earth connection possible from my upstairs 'shack'.

Undoubtedly, the 'end-fed' Marconi antenna with counterpoise remains a useful multiband antenna for those locations where it is inconvenient to erect a centre-fed dipole with open-wire feeders (with the dipole section not necessarily resonant). This may often be the case when operating from a temporary or upstairs shack where it is usually impossible to provide a true low-impedance earth connection. Even if the 'earth' is an excellent low-resistance connection from buried rods, an 11ft lead from this represents a quarter-wavelength at 21MHz so that from the transmitter ATU end it 'looks' like a top-fed (high-impedance) monopole — quite the opposite to what is required. A much better way of delivering current into the antenna will often be to insulate the 11ft wire from true earth and use it as a single-wire counterpoise. A quarter-wave counterpoise also has the effect of removing 'hot spots' from the transmitter chassis.

Recently, Keith Edwards, G3XUO mentioned to me that he had found a suggestion of using a counterpoise antenna in the instruction sheet relating to the wartime Polish clandestine radio type AP5 (see below): he has a model in good working order. Although the text of this leaflet is in Polish, it includes three diagrams of suitable wire antenna systems for use between 2 to 16MHz: **Fig 6**. He had tried out the counterpoise arrangement with his AP5 (about 7-8 watts output) and had been surprised at how effective it proved on the amateur bands.

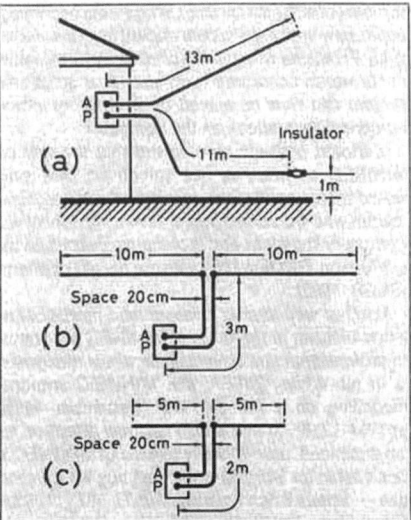

the February *TT*, I included diagrams of the Chireix-Mesny array of half-wave dipoles (developed by French engineers in the 1920s) and the associated simplified zig-zag form: my first mention of this basic but seldom mentioned array technique since 1977. This encouraged G3ESP to recall (*TT*, April) how a relatively compact 500MHz Chireix-Mesny array had been used by the Germans in the second world war. Next, came the May issue of *Television* (IPC) with an article 'An experimental Band IV (470-585MHz) zig-zag aerial' described by Percy Lamb: **Fig 12**.

This describes his experience with what he calls a 'double zig-zag' but what is in effect a classic Chireix-Mesny array mounted in front of a mesh reflector and providing a horizontally-polarised, broad-band receiving antenna with a measured gain of about 14dBi. The gain comes from the narrow vertical radiation pattern, akin to that of stacked dipoles. Directivity is thus sharp in the vertical plane but broad in the horizontal plane. Although designed for Band IV, sensitivity and gain is maintained well up into Band V. Percy Lamb concludes: "The performance could probably have been improved by using ⅜in aluminium strip instead of the ⅛in solid rod. The reflector's efficiency would probably have been enhanced by using ½in spacing instead of the 1in mesh. In addition a more precise matching to the feeder cable would appear to be desirable. Even without these refinements however the zig-zag configuration offers interesting possibilities when a wideband design with low horizontal directivity is to be combined with high directivity in the vertical plane." For UHF television reception the sharp vertical radiation pattern should reduce 'aircraft flutter,' a useful feature for viewers living close to air lanes.

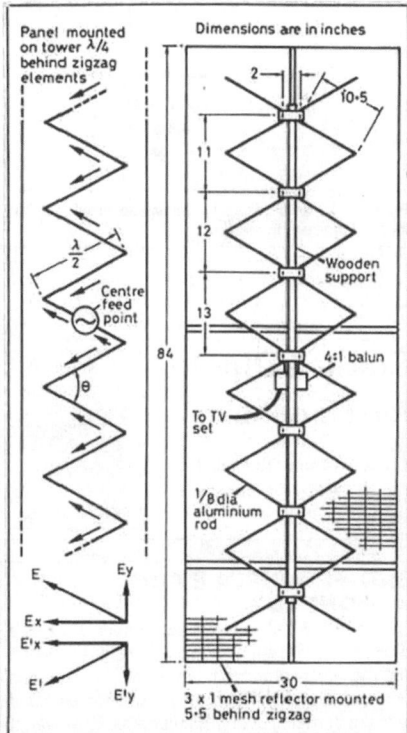

Fig 12. (a) Principles of the zig-zag antenna array. RF power fed to mid point produces horizontally polarised radiation from a vertically mounted panel since the vertical vectors cancel while the horizontal vectors add. (b) The experimental Band IV 'double zig-zag' (ie Chireix-Mesny TV receiving antenna with reflecting screen as described by Percy Lamb in Television (May 1990).

Clearly, if such an array is mounted horizontally rather than vertically, the result would be low directivity in the vertical plane and high horizontal directivity, with vertical polarisation.

ANTENNA TOPICS

An 80m Delta Loop on 1.8MHz

Extracted from 'Technical Topics', *Radio Communication*, August 1990

FEEDING AN 80-metre DELTA LOOP ON 1.8MHz

The 1-λ delta loop has become a very popular HF antenna and provides a useful multiband loop, particularly if fed with open-wire line. In practice it is seldom possible to erect such a system with a 1-λ loop on 1.8MHz as this would require something like a 500ft loop perimeter. Even a 3.5MHz 1-λ loop (268ft) needs a fair space and high supports. Roy C Koeppe, K6XK in *QST*'s 'Hinks & Kinks' (April 1990) indicates a satisfactory way of feeding an 80 metre loop on 1.8MHz, an approach that could also be adopted for scaled down loops to permit operation on a lower band: **Fig 8**. K6XK writes: "C1 tunes the antenna to act as a three-quarter-wave resonator and allows the SWR at the feed point to be no more than 1.1 across the 160 metre band."

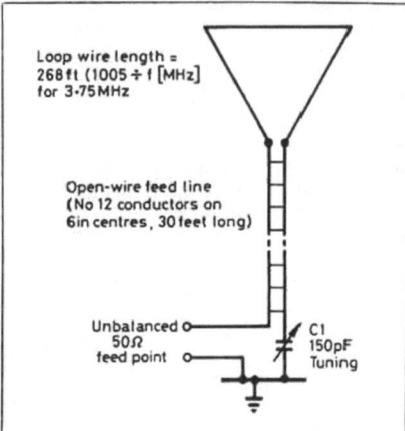

Fig 8. K6XK's arrangement for feeding an 80 metre delta loop antenna on 160 metres.

End-fed Dipole for Handhelds

Extracted from 'Technical Topics', *Radio Communication*, September 1990

END-FED DIPOLE FOR HANDHELDS

The short ¼λ helically-wound 'rubber duck' is a most convenient antenna for hand-helds (provided that the power radiated close to the user's eyes is kept low) since such units are not usually expected to make contacts over difficult paths. However, it is not a particularly efficient type of antenna. One reason for this is that the 'ground plane' is dependent to a large extent on the capacitance of the hand-held transceiver to earth via the 'lossy' body of the user. An antenna that does not depend on an 'earth' connection should prove both more efficient and more consistent.

In *Radio-ZS* (February 1990), Chris Turner, ZS6GM, reviews favourably the AEA 'Hot Rod' 144MHz half-wave antenna: **Fig 5**. In tests with ZS6BTD via the local repeater, he reports achieving a very clear improvement in performance compared with a 'rubber ducky'. Laboratory tests showed that the feed impedance varied only over the range 40-65Ω compared with the 45-350Ω of a rubber duck helical where the feed impedance depended on how close the transceiver was to the body. He concludes: "It is my opinion that AEA has succeeded in overcoming the matching problems associated with end feeding a ½λ monopole. The result is a highly efficient portable antenna which performs well under laboratory conditions and in the field. If it were not for the 1m length I would have no hesitation in using this antenna permanently. For anyone who uses a handheld and needs to communicate from an area of poor signal strength, this antenna is certainly the answer."

Unfortunately for home constructors, it is not clear from this review of a commercial product what type of matching section AEA have included to transform the '50Ω' transceiver output to the 1000-1500Ω of an end-fed rod dipole. I recall that some multi-element UHF TV receiving antennas have been marketed with end-fed elements.

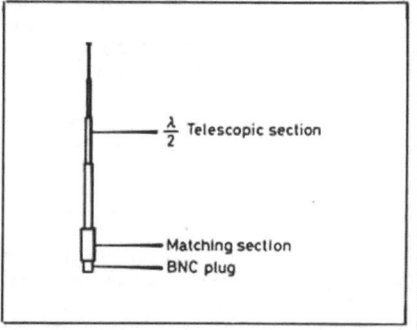

Fig 5. The AEA 'Hot Rod' λ/2 end-fed dipole antenna for 144MHz as reviewed by ZS6GM.

8JK Revisted and New BRD-Zapper

Extracted from 'Technical Topics', *Radio Communication*, September 1990

THE 8JK REVISITED AND THE NEW BRD-ZAPPER

The major breakthrough in the design of amateur rotary beams came in 1937 from Professor John D Kraus, W8JK (my apologies for giving him last month the callsign W8XK, that of the old Pittsburgh HF broadcast station, later KDKA). Both his work on the first close-spaced 'flat-top' bidirectional driven arrays (often implemented as fixed beams), and that of Walter Van Roberts, W3CHO, shortly afterwards on the first close-spaced, two-element Yagi-Uda unidirectional parasitic array, were based on recognizing the significance of the work of Dr George Brown (RCA) on vertical monopole arrays for medium-wave broadcasting. Until then it had always been assumed that a Yagi parasitic reflector should be ¼λ behind the driven element, requiring a boom length, at least on 14MHz, that virtually ruled out flat-topped arrays, although a few amateurs had built Yagi rotary beams based on vertical elements spaced ¼λ apart.

By the time that UK amateur operation was closed down on 1 September 1939, knowledge of the family of 8JK bidirectional arrays and close-spaced Yagi arrays had crossed the Atlantic (see for example brief references in the first edition of

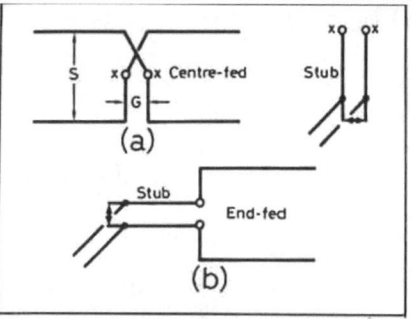

Fig 6. Basic single-section W8JK flat-top antennas. In 1981 Dr Kraus pointed out that the centre-fed arrangement with a typical spacing, S, of about λ/8 on the lowest frequency used, L can range from less than λ/2 to more than 1.5λ, permitting its use over a continuous frequency range of 3:1. With L equal to 7.3m (centre gap G forms part of the measurement) and S equal to 2.6m, the bidirectional gains are: 14MHz 5.7dBi; 21MHz 6.7dBi; 28MHz 7.7dBi; 50MHz 8.2dBi. Values for 18 and 24MHz bands can be interpolated. The end-fed version should provide roughly similar results if correctly tuned.

the RSGB's *The Amateur Radio Handbook* (1938) but were still rare. It was not until the early post-war period that the three-element Yagi array began to establish itself worldwide. Due to their unidirectional properties, Yagi arrays became, and remain, far more popular than the 8JK driven bidirectional arrays, although these have some important advantages, including multiband operation with a single set of two elements: **Fig 6**.

In *QST* October 1981 (see *TT*, November 1982) Dr Kraus restated the very real attractions of the centre-fed design when it comes to multiband use, showing that a compact single-array with 7.3m elements can cover 14, 18, 21, 24, 28 and 50MHz bands. Among the plus points he listed in 1981 were: (1) continuous frequency span of more than 3 to 1 (with suitable matching/tuning arrangements); (2) no traps or loading coils; (3) no critical dimensions, as the entire antenna and feed system can be resonated; (4) it can be used horizontally or vertically for optimum radiation angle; (5) it is ideal for finding round-the-world (long path) openings; (6) it has theoretically zero radiation off the ends of the elements; (7) it can be fed with low-loss, inexpensive twin line (or very-low-loss cut-away 300Ω line or open-wire line); and (8) a compact array can cover many bands including the non-harmonically related bands. Minus points are that the bidirectional pattern does not give protection against continental European signals when the array is pointed towards North America; the forward gain is lower than with a good monoband Yagi array; and the low radiation resistance does not make it a good system to install indoors in the presence of metal structures etc (but in practice some amateurs have found the 8JK most satisfactory as a fixed indoor array). The end-fed form is particularly easy to install in, for example, a roof space or as an outdoor antenna supported from a mast or tree using two light wooden spreaders.

For those who require unidirectional patterns, it is possible to convert the 8JK into this form by using the fact, shown in Dr Brown's classic paper, that when two driven elements are fed 135° out-of-phase with equal amplitudes of RF power, a cardioid radiation pattern results, giving forward gain and a deep rejection null in the reverse direction. Exploitation of this principle has led to such antennas as the ZL-Special, the HB9CV and G8PO antennas as described in *TT*, October 1981.

The ZL-Special was so named and described in print by Fred Judd, G2BCX, (*Shortwave Magazine* July 1950, pp337-9) where he commented on its origins: "Data on the aerial came to the writer from New Zealand, hence the name ZL-Special. Little is known of its origin save that it was designed in the

USA just prior to the war, for commercial purposes. (This is probably a reference to the work of Dr Brown on MP broadcast antennas – G3VA). Since the war it has been modified and developed for amateur use by W5LHI, W0GZR and ZL3MH. Further tests and measurements made by the writer may be of interest."

The 'G8PO Special', as described by J E Ironmonger, G8PO, in the *RSGB Bulletin* (November 1947), provides a 'reversible' unidirectional fixed beam, originally developed as a result of a 'mistake' in cutting feeder lengths when erecting an 8JK. It uses two feeders of different length, ie arranged so that either feeder can be $1/8\lambda$ longer than the other by having two sockets into which the transmitter feed-line is connected: see **Fig 7**.

The same basic approach is also used in the antenna developed by Rudolf Baumgartner, HB9CV, which in recent years has become a popular 144MHz portable antenna, with unidirectional characteristics.

Now Rod Newkirk, W9BRD, has come up with an antenna that combines the relatively little-used 8JK end-fed arrangement with the 135° out-of-phase approach. This has been implemented as an indoor 21MHz fixed wire-beam pushing signals into Europe from the Chicago area with less interference from the western States than with the basic 88JK end-fed array **(Fig 8)** from which the 'BRD Zapper (*QST* June 1990, pp28-29: 'The 'BRD Zapper: A Quick, Cheap and Easy "ZL Special" Antenna') was developed with the same basic dimensions.

Instead of feeding the elements 180° out of phase, they are driven 135° out of phase by feeding the stub $\lambda/16$ from the stub's shorted end so that the feed path to one element is $1/8\lambda$ (45°) longer or shorter than the other, which, after the stub's 180° phase reversal, produces the required (180-45 = 135°) phase shift. W9BRD points out: "You can find the proper feed point on the stub by 'sniffing' signals of known origin along *one side* of the stub with the insulated centre conductor of some coax hooked to a receiver. (Start looking for this point by measuring $\lambda/16$ up from the bottom.) Directivity is reversed by selecting the opposite side of the twin-lead stub... Pattern distortion through incidental radiation and pickup must be minimized. The coupler must be built in the most compact form possible, mounted right at the stub, and isolated to keep the feed line from distorting the pattern. Such isolation is done at W9BRD via a home-brew coaxial choke made of 30 turns of the antenna's RG58 feed line wound on a ferrite rod just before the matching network: see **Fig 9(b)**. The single wire run from matching network to antenna had better be no more than an inch or two. Here, I'm borrowing on the single-wire-feed theme by Windom. Since any circuitry above the choke will be hot with RF a bulky matching unit will not do... System Q is lower with wider spacings but gain is maximum with the elements spaced $1/8\lambda$."

Horizontal Loop (Real & Mininec)

Extracted from 'Technical Topics', *Radio Communication*, September 1990

HORIZONTAL LOOP ANTENNAS (REAL AND WITH MININEC)

Although the 1λ wire loop antenna (square or triangular (delta)) has long been established both as a single-element antenna or, with a parasitic reflector loop, as the respected two-element quad beam, it is usual practice to have the loop in the vertical plane, providing either horizontally or vertically polarized signals according to how it is fed. A loop antenna mounted in the horizontal plane is still something of a rarity despite having been discovered by serendipity (the happy accident) over 20 years ago by the late Peter Pennell, G2PL, who for many years was a prominent DXer.

A *TT* item in July 1968 (later included in many editions of *ART*) described how, during some severe gales, he took the precaution of lowering his three-band quad, mounted on a tilt-over mast, so that the quad elements were in effect firing straight upwards, with the reflector loop touching the ground in places. *TT* continued: "Under these conditions, he found the performance of the aerial to be superior to that of a resonated vertical on all three bands (typically receiving S9 from VK on 14, S7 from W6 on 21 and 28MHz). The feeder SWR was little different from that in the usual vertical position... The 28MHz driven element was about 7ft above ground and that of the 14MHz element about 12ft... Tests at G2PL suggest that the angle of radiation compares with a dipole a half-wave above ground, and he feels it would be a simple matter to erect such a system using four (short) vertical posts." Personally, I would not expect a low, horizontal loop to have much low-angle radiation, although entirely suitable for NVIS (near vertical incident skywave) short-range working.

A few years later (June 1972 *TT* and digested in later editions of *ART*) S M de Wet, ZS6AKA, reported on a series of "experiments with multiband loop aerials" including loops 1λ and $2/3\lambda$ (with stub matching), rectangular and triangular loops in both vertical and horizontal planes and with the horizontal loops at heights of about 35-40ft: **Fig 1**. He pointed out (as G6XN had done earlier) that a 1λ loop (unlike a $1/2\lambda$ dipole or $1/2\lambda$ loop) provides a low-impedance (resistive) feed-point not only at *f* but at all harmonics of *f*. His 1λ (3.5MHz) loop had an input impedance of about 100Ω at 3.5MHz, rising to roughly 200Ω at 28MHz, with intermediate impedances at 7, 14 and 21MHz.

General observations made at the time by ZS6AKA seem worth recalling: "(1) the loop tuned much more broadly than a dipole; (2) the voltages along the loop were much lower than a dipole; (3) although the loop requires a minimum of three supports, the extra support was usually easy to

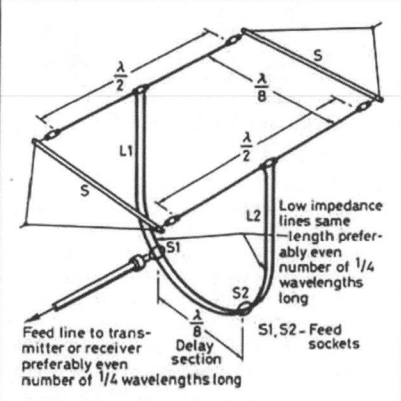

Fig 7. G8PO reversible unidirectional 14MHz array as described in 1947. Direction depends on whether transmitter feed is connected at S1 or S2. Note the delay line section is twisted once to provide the 135° out-of-phase drive.

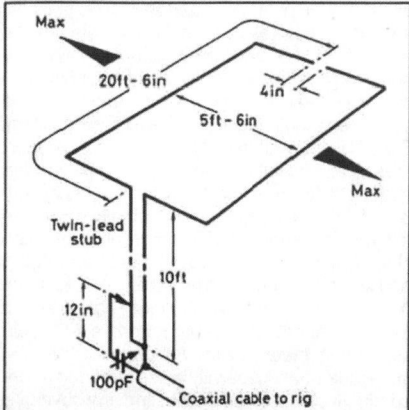

Fig 8. W9BRD's W8JK gamma-fed wire beam for 21MHz made to fit the dimensions of the bedroom it occupies. Dimensions are not critical for the elements but they should be close to $\lambda/2$ (total each), with the stub about $\lambda/4$ or multiples. Phasing point is fairly critical and should be selected as described.

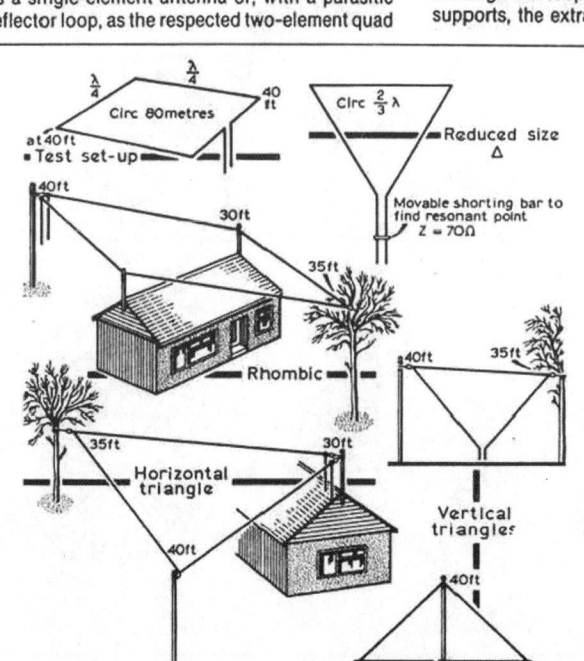

Fig 1. Some of the loop antennas tested by ZS6AKA in the early 1970s. No unbalanced line currents were detected with either twin or coaxial feeder despite the absence of a balun transformer.

ANTENNA TOPICS

find in practice — the best results were obtained with the loop horizontal, but it did not greatly affect results with the loop horizontally slanted or even vertical; (4) when the input is balanced, the furthest mid-point may be earthed; (5) when the loop is fashioned in rhombic shape it does in fact become a rhombic directional aerial at the higher frequencies with a low input impedance; (6) if the shape of the loop is changed from circular to square, triangle, rectangle and the like, the radiation resistance decreases as the enclosed area decreases — this means that a shape may be found which has an input impedance of approximately 50Ω; and (7) there are many shapes and mounting configurations which remain to be explored."

ZS6AKA noted that on lower frequencies the loop (as with a low dipole) provides omnidirectional radiation, but breaks up into a series of lobes at higher frequencies.

That was back in 1972. Coming up to date, Doug DeMaw, W1FB, provides 'A closer look at horizontal loop antennas' (*QST* May 1990, pp28, 29, 35) providing E- and H-plane radiation pattern diagrams for a large multiband loop antenna, computer-generated by Harold Johnson, W4ZCB, using an IBM computer with MININEC software (see July *TT*). W1FB's loop (**Fig 2**) is in the form of a square with 132ft 2¾in sides at a height of 50ft, and the radiation patterns are at 1.9, 3.84, 7.16, 14.2, 21.2 and 28.5MHz; **Fig 3**. If moved up a band, the patterns should hold approximately correct for a scaled-down loop with 66ft sides at a height of 25ft. The patterns resemble those noted by ZS6AKA.

With this large multiband loop, W1FB found that "the system produces 14, 21 and 28MHz performance that is on par with, and sometimes better than, that of my commercial triband Yagi at 55ft." He concludes his article as follows: "The point is that, if you have space for one, you can use a horizontal loop as a multiband antenna. You need not tailor it for 160m. A 75 or 40m full-wave loop will usually fit into a city lot. The higher you erect it above ground, the better its performance will be. But, don't give up the notion of a loop if you can't get it high above ground. Height extends the useful working distance of a loop, but many loops at low heights still permit good DX results at the higher end of the HF spectrum. The improvement in noise rejection during receive may be sufficiently rewarding to justify putting up a large piece of wire, especially if you live in a noisy neighbourhood.

"One word of caution: Wire that has thick polyvinyl insulation (such as No 14 (American) electrical wire) causes the antenna resonance to be somewhat lower than the formula dictates. Apparently the propagation factor of the wire, when used in a closed loop, causes this phenomenon."

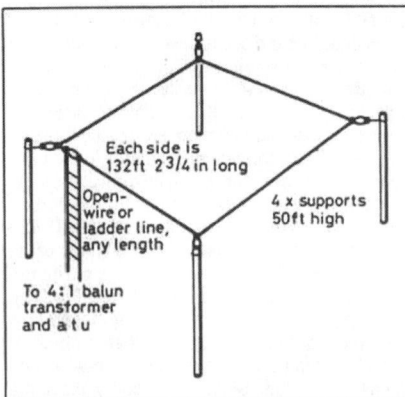

Fig 2. The 1.9MHz/multiband horizontal loop at 50ft as used by W1FB.

Fig 3. E- and H-plane radiation patterns for the loop of Fig 2 derived by W4ZCB using MININEC computer-simulation for 1.9, 3.84, 7.16, 14.2, 21.2 and 28.5MHz.

The Bi-square Array Reappears

Extracted from 'Technical Topics', *Radio Communication*, October 1990

THE BI-SQUARE ARRAY REAPPEARS

RECENT *TECHNICAL TOPICS* ITEMS have described various forms of antennas using closed loops. But there is another approach in which the loop is open rather than closed, formed from two full-wave sections bent to form a square with an insulator at the top junction, voltage-fed at the base with (600 ohm) open-wire or (450 ohm) ladder line (**Fig 4**). C Drayton Cooper, N4LBJ (*HAM RADIO*, May 1990) shows that this old favourite, dropped from most recent handbooks, known as a bi-square array, "works wonders on the new 17m band".

Such an antenna is usually hung from a single, high support to give vertical polarization. With a suitable ATU providing balanced output to the transmission line, the whole system can be resonated on several bands. N4LBJ finds his 18MHz bi-square works quite well also on 14 and 21MHz, though gain and directivity will differ somewhat to that on its design frequency. Because current flow reverses at the half-wave points, elements A and A' are in phase: similarly B and B' are in phase. The antenna thus operates as four collinear elements in phase yielding about 4 to 5dBd gain on its design frequency with broadside directivity. It was originally derived in this form as a variant of the once-popular Lazy-H fixed array (I once had a Lazy-H on 28MHz and was delighted with the results). N4LBJ hung his bi-square with two 53ft lengths of wire for a full wavelength at 18.1MHz from a 65ft self-supporting metal tower. Although in the past such antennas generally used wooden (non-conductive) masts, he did not find any obviously detrimental effects. Amateurs without such high supports could probably accommodate a bi-square cut for 28 or 50MHz.

There can be little doubt that the greater use now being made of the 18 and 24MHz "WARC" bands is leading to a revival of interest in anten-

1990 - 1999

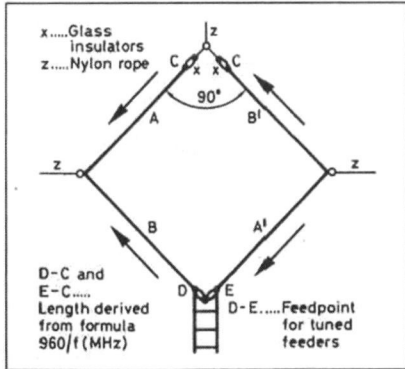

Fig 4. 18MHz bi-square array used by N4LBJ capable of reasonable performance on 14 and 28MHz bands. N4LBJ considers it performs best when feedpoint is about a quarter to a half wavelength above ground but adequate performance possible at lower heights, down to about 3 to 5ft above ground. Note that since the array is voltage fed, care should be taken with medium or high power that this does not represent a hazard to people or animals.

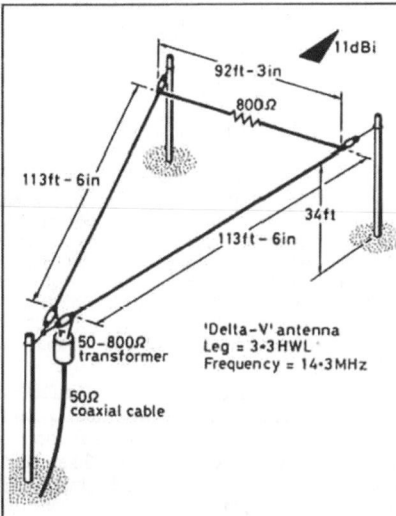

Fig 5. KL7ISA's broadband Delta-V antenna optimised for 14MHz band. Requires a triangular (pie-shaped) area 104ft by 93ft base.

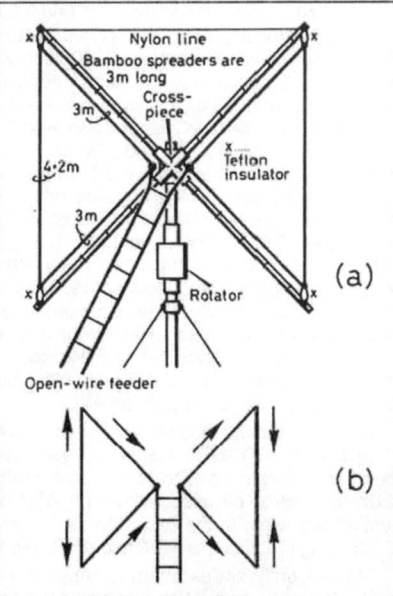

Fig 6. Multi-band V-dipole for 14, 18, 21, 24 and 28MHz bands as used by PA3BNT.

nas capable of working over more than a single band - for example the W8JK and 'BRD Zapper described last month. Another article in *HAM RADIO* (May 1990) by Robert Wilson KL7ISA covers "Non-resonant delta and V-beam Antennas" including a design optimized for 14MHz that can be contained in an area 104ft by 93ft or so (**Fig 5**). He also introduces the concept of a tie wire between the ends of the V wires, including the terminating resistor (he forms a single 800 ohm non-inductive resistor by parallelling fifty 39K, 2W carbon resistors soldered between two parallel copper wires). This will cope with an average output power of some 200W since half the power will be radiated before reaching the resistor. SSB only can be used at slightly higher powers but excessive average power will quickly result in a permanent change to the value of the resistors.

A low-cost form of multiband V-dipole which can be used with open-wire feeder and suitable ATU on 14, 18, 21, 24 and 30MHz stems from Maarten v.d. Velde, PA3BNT and appears in 'Reflecties door PA0SE' (*Electron*, August 1990) (**Fig 6**). This broad band wire dipole uses a framework made from four 3m bamboo spreaders with a centre cross-piece. It could be used as a fixed or rotary antenna.

Square and Delta Loops

Extracted from 'Technical Topics', *Radio Communication*, November 1990

SQUARE AND DELTA LOOP ANTENNAS

TT SEPTEMBER described some of the useful, multiband properties of closed square loop antennas with sides of 0.25λ mounted in horizontal or vertical plane. It seems worth adding some follow-up comments applicable to HF, VHF and UHF designs.

A basically similar antenna to that described by W1FB (*TT*, September Fig 2) is discussed in 'The full-wave 80-metre loop antenna - revisited' by Paul D Carr, N4PC in *CQ*, August 1990. He uses a 272ft perimeter ('almost square') horizontal loop suspended at about 50ft from pine trees. He concludes: "There are only three antennas for any amateur - the one you had, the one you have presently, and the one you plan to build. This antenna has helped to postpone the one I plan to build."

N4PC reminds us that the virtues of horizontal loops were described by Dave Fisher, W0MHS in 'The Loop Skywire', *QST*, November 1985, an article sub-headed 'Looking for an all-band HF antenna that is easy to construct, costs nearly nothing and works great DX? Try this one!'. W0MHS suggested that: "There is one wire antenna that performs exceptionally well on the HF bands, but relatively few amateurs know about it or use it.... what one user has described as the 'best kept secret in the amateur circle'.... Since 1957, I have used this antenna (**Fig 4**) in many locations with great success every time." He dismisses the idea, held by some, that the horizontal loop is basically a high-angle radiator. In fact, the vertical angle of radiation, like that of other horizontally polarized antennas, depends on the height of the loop and even a 25ft high loop should prove effective as a DX antenna above 14MHz. It is worth looking at the vertical radiation patterns shown in the September *TT*, Fig 3.

W0MHS used a co-axial cable rather than open-wire transmission line, providing some useful constructional hints and showing also how the antenna could be used effectively on the 1.8MHz band as a top-loaded vertical antenna: **Fig 5**.

Dr Mike King, G3MY is another advocate of closed loops. He writes: "Over the years I have used nothing but closed loops on the HF bands, having a great liking for the low-Q characteristics of this type of antenna. This interest started in 1963 while on holiday in Cornwall. I was using an end-fed 3/4 wave antenna tuned against a 1/4 wave counterpoise and realised that the end of the bent wire and of the counterpoise were in phase, so I decided to see what would happen if I joined the ends together. I will say only that on my return home that triangular loop went up, supported by two trees and the house. It stayed up for more than twenty years.

"More recently, I developed what I call the HOVER loop which I described in *Sprat* (issue Nr 54, Spring 1988). I hope that **Fig 6** makes the format and feed method clear. Suffice to say that it has been used effectively on all bands from 1.8MHz to 28MHz and has given me 85 countries in 6 continents using QRP (3W or less).

"Hover" comes from HOrizontal/VERtical, and the *Sprat* description makes its operation a little clearer:

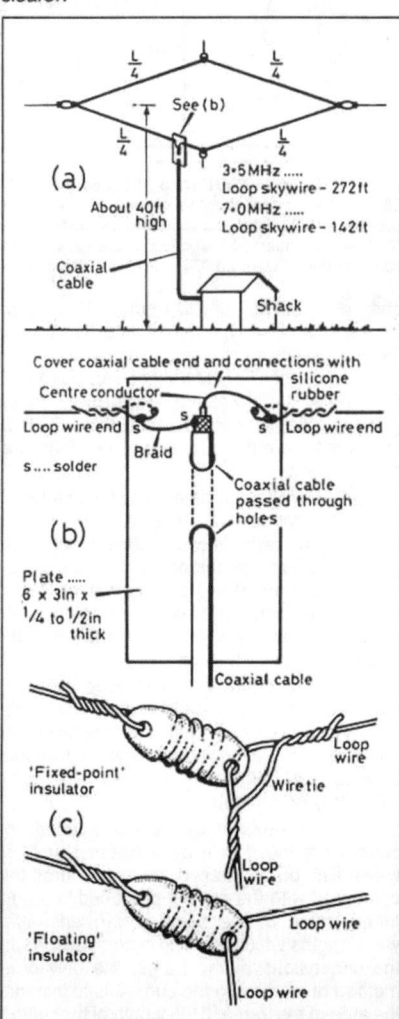

Fig 4. The W0MHS "Loop Skywire" horizontal loop antenna as described in *QST*, November 1985.

ANTENNA TOPICS

The HOVER loop is basically a full-wave wire loop antenna cut to the usual loop formula L = 1005/f where f is the frequency in MHz and L the length in ft. The physical form is an inverted V with the apex at 60ft. Each leg of the V is about 60ft long with an apex angle of about 110°. The rest of the length comprises a low horizontal V at some 12 to 15ft above the ground. The feedpoint is at the apex of the inverted V. The feeder comprises two equal lengths of low-loss UHF TV coax cable, giving a screened balanced 150Ω feedpoint. Measurements have shown that the loop has a feedpoint resistance of about 110

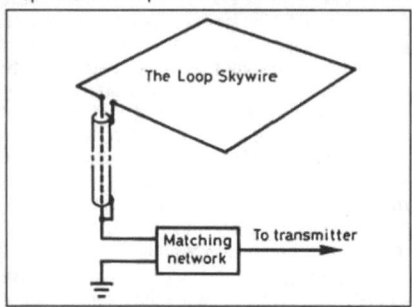

Fig 5. Feed arrangement for the loop as a top-loaded vertical antenna on lower frequency band.

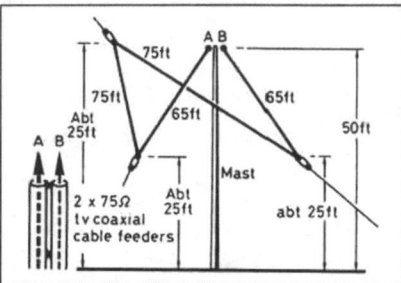

Fig 6. G3MY's 'HOVER' loop effective on 1.8 to 28MHz. Two equal lengths of 75Ω coaxial cable provide a 150Ω balanced screened feed to the apex (A-B) of the inverted-V section of the loop. Use a balun at the ATU, or an ATU with balanced output.

ohms on 3.5MHz, rising to around 220-250Ω on 28MHz. If a valve-type power amplifier is used, the two feeders can be brought into a simple 1:1 balun on the back of the transceiver, and the pi-network will then match it satisfactorily. When using a solid-state PA, I use a small QRP Z-match to tune out the reactance on higher frequency bands.

On 1.8MHz it is possible to use the antenna in one of two modes: (1) As a 'fat' quarter-wave against earth with the two feeders in parallel to give a 37.5-ohm feeder; or (2) The lines can be tuned at the bottom end to give a voltage feed to the two free ends of a half-wave antenna. Although this puts a high SWR on the line, the losses do not seem excessive.

Large single-turn resonate loop antennas mounted in the vertical plane have a long history. Some interesting work was reported in the 1930s by L S Palmer and D Taylor (University College, Hull) in *Proc IRE*, January 1934, pp93-114. They noted that:

"When a frame or loop aerial is tuned, the current produced in it by a passing wireless wave will be increased many hundred-fold compared with the current produced in an untuned frame of the same dimensions. With wavelengths which are long in comparison with the dimensions of the frame, the only other method of increasing the current is to increase the area of the frame. If the length of the wave is of the same order as the dimensions of the frame then it is found that the current, even in a tuned frame may be still further increased by many hundredfold not by increasing the area of the frame, but by critically adjusting the ratio of the frame dimensions to the wavelength. In a previous communication this process was described (Palmer & Moneyball, *Proc IRE*, August 1932, pp1345-67) and a theory outlined which accounted for the experimental values of the critical ratios of frame-height/wave-length (H/λ) and frame-width/wavelength (W/λ) for which the received current became abnormally large."

In effect, this adjustment resulted in the two vertical wires being in phase resulting in a directive antenna in the plane of the frame. The 1934 paper extended the work to transmitting loop antennas, using a VHF transmitter on about 5-6 metres with an adjustable framework that allowed rectangular loops of differing aspect ratios to be investigated. To quote again from the paper:

"For the particular case of radiation along the earth's surface in the plane of the frame, both of the (above) equations are satisfied simultaneously only by a frame of dimensions H = 0.40λ and W = 1.0λ and for no other dimensions (less than 1λ) will the radiation be as great for the same applied electromotive force. If the transmitting frame receivers reflected waves from the ground there will be another set of critical dimensions, namely H = W = 0.47λ for which the radiation (or re-radiation in this case) will be a maximum."

Off-centre-fed Dipoles

Extracted from 'Technical Topics', *Radio Communication*, December 1990

OFF-CENTRE-FED MULTI-BAND DIPOLES

THE ORIGINAL SINGLE-WIRE transmission line 'Windom' dipole, originally developed at Ohio State University (but named after Loren Windom, W8GZ, who described it in *QST* back in 1929) was, like a conventional centre-fed half-wave dipole, intended to be a single-band antenna, **Fig 3 (a)**. It was the late Jim MacIntosh, VS1AA (later GM3IAA), who found that a one-third-wave tapping point (ie one-sixth-wave from its centre point) can match well on several harmonically related bands. This tapping point gives a resistive feed impedance of roughly 300 ohms. The VS1AA was described in the *T&R Bulletin*, November 1936 although often described as a 'Windom' antenna: **Fig 3 (b)**.

As Les Moxon, G6XN, has pointed out, any single-wire transmission line, even when correctly matched, radiates some RF energy which will affect the radiation patterns. This does not, however, imply that a Windom or VS1AA, if correctly set up, is not capable of giving excellent results.

The dislike of single-wire feeder radiation, with its increased possibility of RFI problems, led in the late 1940s to the use of 300 ohm balanced line as a non-radiating feeder to a VS1AA/Windom 'one-third' tapped element: **Fig 3 (c)**. This antenna was described in *QST* and the *Radio Amateurs Handbook* and was subsequently included in an early *TT* (July 1958 and all editions of *ART*). With a 136ft top, fed 44ft from one

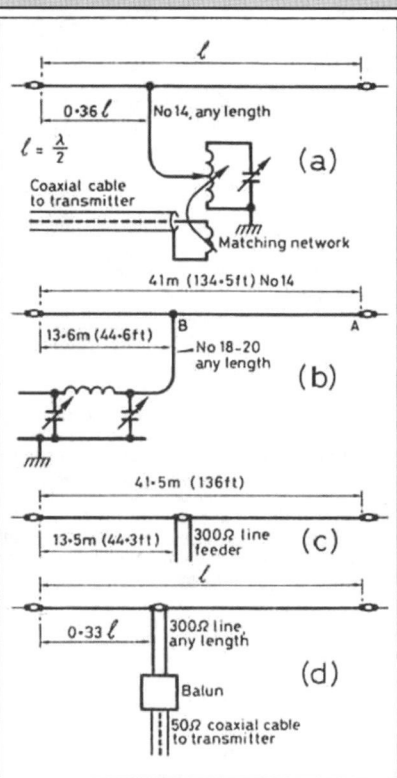

Fig 3 Basic off-centre-fed dipoles. (a) The original 'Windom' half-wave dipole as developed at Ohio State University over 60 years ago. (b) The multiband VS1AA introduced the concept of 'one-third' tap for multiband operation. (c) The twin-feeder (300 ohm) version became popular in the late 1940s. (d) Later still, a 6:1 balun was introduced to permit the use of 50 ohm coaxial feeder for direct connection to the transmitter.

end, this could be used on 3.5, 7, 14 and 28MHz from an ATU providing balanced output. It could also be modified to include 21MHz by adding two shorted-quarter-wave stubs at 76ft and 38ft from the feed point. Later the use of a balun was introduced: **Fig 3 (d)**.

As noted by Tom Sorbie, GM3MXN, in *Sprat*, Autumn 1990, a modified form of the four-band off-centre-fed dipole was described by DJ2KT in *QRV* (December 1971) and has since become widely used, particularly in Germany, under the name 'FD4 Windom'. This substituted 75Ω or 50Ω coaxial cable for the balanced 300Ω line but with a 4:1 or 6:1 balun at the one third feedpoint. This means that it can be used on modern transceivers with 50Ω unbalanced sockets without an ATU on 3.5, 7, 14 and 28MHz. **Fig 4** shows the FD4 antenna used for QRP operating by GM3MXN, who is well satisfied with the results, and also his ferrite-rod balun based on a well-known G6XN design (see for example 'Balanced to unbalanced transformers' by Dr Ian White, G3SEK, *RadCom*, December 1989, pp39-42). GM3MXN simply used twin-coloured grey and black wire wound together six turns on a scrap ferrite rod. He finds that his FD4 provides also an acceptable match on 18 and 24MHz but for 10.1 and 21MHz he needs an ATU.

A year after the appearance of the FD4, F Spillner, DJ2KY (*QRV*, August 1972) showed how the multi-wire dipole technique enables the 21MHz band to be used without an ATU by adding two wires to the basic FD4, 4.5m and 2.52m long (*TT*, October 1972 and *ART*): **Fig 5**.

More recently, as described in an Appendix to a detailed discussion of Windom-type antennas 'The off-centre-fed dipole revisited: a broad-band, multiband antenna' by Dr John Belrose,

VE2CV, and Peter Bouliane, VE3KLO (*QST*, August 1990, pp28-32) - Hubert Scholle, DJ7SH and Rolf Steins, DL1BBC (*CQ-DL*, September 1983) have shown that a 'double Windom' based on the FD4 can be extended to cover all eight HF bands without an ATU, or, if the space is available, expanded to cover also 1.8MHz. **Fig 6 (a)** shows the eight-band design while **Fig 6 (b)** gives SWR measurements made by DJ7SH and DL1BBC indicating very low SWR on all bands except possibly 7MHz. However, the 7MHz figures are perfectly acceptable unless your solid-state rig starts cutting back power output at about 1.5:1 SWR. The longer nine-band version is shown in **Fig 7**.

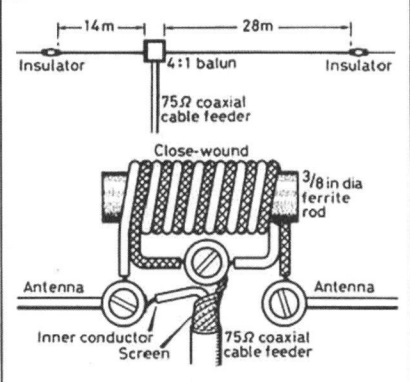

Fig 4. Since the 1970s, the four-band 'FD4 Windom' has been popular, particularly in Germany, with the balun up at the feed point. Shown also the simple 4:1 balun used by GM3MXN for low-power operation. The FD4 does not match on 21MHz (*Sprat*).

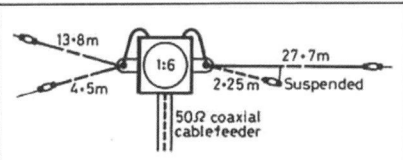

Fig 5. DJ2KY's five-band version of the FD4 introduced the concept of the double-Windom. Note 300 ohm line could be used without a balun.

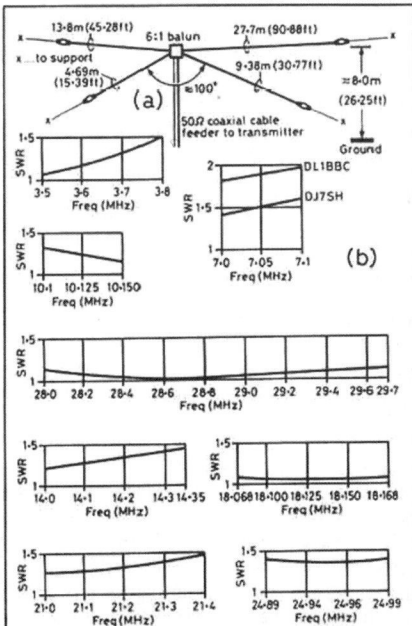

Fig 6. (a) The eight-band "double-Windom" with (b) SWR measurements made by DJ7SH and DL1BBC.

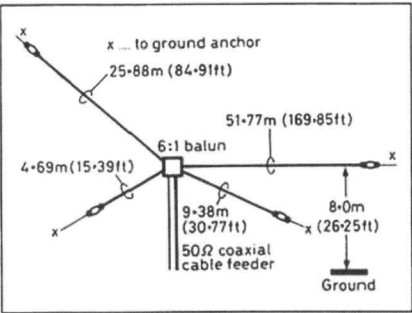

Fig 7. The extended nine-band version covering all bands from 1.8MHz to 28MHz.

End-feds for Handhelds

Extracted from 'Technical Topics', *Radio Communication*, January 1991

HOME-BREW END-FED ANTENNAS FOR HANDHELDS

TT, SEPTEMBER 1990 p31, DREW attention to a South African review of the AEA 'Hot Rod' 144MHz, end-fed, half-wave antenna which plugs into hand-held transceivers in place of the usual short helically-wound 'rubber-duck' antenna. ZS6GM reported a very noticeable improvement in performance, although his review gave no information on the matching section used by AEA to permit end feeding from the transceiver socket (it has been pointed out to me that some CB antennas are end-fed dipoles).

The item has resulted in useful comment from Hans-Joachim Brandt, DJ1ZB, who sent along a copy of a 1985 article he wrote for the German magazine *Funk* describing a home-brew half-wave 144MHz dipole that gave markedly superior results to rubber-duck antennas. He writes:

"In the February 1985 issue of *Funk* I presented a concept for home-brewing a 144MHz end-fed half-wave antenna with an LC matching section in a small plastic box, a telescopic antenna of rather random length

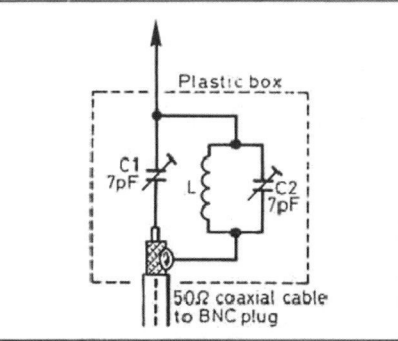

Fig 1. DJ1ZB's end-fed 144MHz antenna using a telescopic rod (80cm to 133cm) with matching network enclosed in plastic box (57mm x 28mm x 28mm). When the box is fitted with a flange-type BNC plug the antenna can be plugged directly into a hand-held transceiver or mounted separately and connected to the transceiver by length of 50Ω low-loss cable.

(80cm to 133cm) and a flange BNC plug (or similar): **Fig 1**. The trimmers were 7pF air-dielectric made by Tronser. Starting values for the coil are 5 turns, inner diameter 5mm, total length 8mm. The coil may be varied if the setting of capacitor C2 is at an extreme end (when the section is being aligned using a VHF SWR meter). The plastic box is superior to a metal box in two aspects: it is easier to isolate the telescopic antenna; and there is no difference in tuning with the box open or closed.

"Simple comparisons between a rubber duck and this telescopic antenna were conducted from the flat roof of a city building in Munich. With the rubber duck and 2.5W, the Austrian repeaters OE2XSL and OE7XKI could just be opened, but the German repeater DB0XF north of Munich could not be opened. With the telescopic antenna, all three repeaters could be opened easily with the low power option of 0.3W of this hand-held, indicating an improvement of at least (10log 2.5/0.3) equal to 9dB.

"Other comparisons were done as follows: An aluminium plate 20cm by 20cm was placed as a ground-plane on the roof of a car having a sliding opening in the roof, with the test antenna mounted on this. The feeder cable was routed into the interior of the car to the handheld receiver via a variable step attenuator. Either a fixed S-meter reading or the closing of the squelch was used as the input voltage reference. With each antenna, the attenuator was adjusted so that this condition was met. With a telescopic length of 90cm an improvement over the rubber-duck of 7 - 11dB was noted; with a length of 116cm the improvement was 11 to 15dB.

"Another type of matching section for this type of antenna employs a parallel resonant circuit, with a tap on the coil for the 50 ohm input (as often used on HF for voltage-fed antennas - G3VA). Such an antenna is being marketed in Germany by Bensch. This saves the use of a second high-grade trimmer but I would guess that the matching transformation cannot be as accurate as when using two continuously variable trimmers. I am also using this type of matching section for an 'under the roof' fixed vertical antenna for local FM working. In this case two quarter-wave radials are used as a counterpoise (see *Sprat*, Autumn 1981 'QRP via repeaters')."

DJ1ZB also mentions that his matching section arrangement with the two trimmers appears in the latest edition (11th edition) of *Antennenbuch* by K Rothammel, Y21BK, the most popular antenna book in the German language. Y21BK died a few years ago, but his widow hopes to recruit a group of competent antenna specialists to continue to update this most useful book. A copy of the first edition (1961) is still in use at G3VA, the many illustrations and tables overcoming the language barrier!

Rubber-duck antennas can, of course, be replaced by home-made quarter-wave systems without the use of matching networks. J M Osborne, G3HMO, writes: "I recently acquired a dual-band handheld (IC24FT) with the usual rubber-duck antenna. I had decided to use this for mobile operation during my summer holiday but two days before leaving had got only as far as reading the literature on mobile antennas. The shortage of time forced

ANTENNA TOPICS

an empirical, but in the event entirely satisfactory, KISS solution.

"I extracted a telescopic antenna from a scrap transistor radio and fixed it to a piece of plastic channelling. An odd length of coaxial cable (about 2m long) with a BNC connector was also secured to the plastic, the inner being connected to the telescopic rod and the outer to a screw through the plastic channelling. The whole was fixed with insulating tape to the integral roof rack (Passat estate) so as to earth the coax outer to the roof rack via the screw. The lead was brought through a rear door to the handheld on a front seat through an SWR/power meter. The telescopic rod length was then adjusted for best compromise SWR on both 70cm and 2m bands (about 1.3:1 SWR on both). This proved to be with about a 54cm extension of the rod (roughly quarter-wave on 2m and 3/4-wave on 70cm). No coils were used for loading or matching and the antenna connected to the handheld via the meter or direct.

"My excuse for bringing this simple system to your attention is that the results were most satisfactory. From South Devon, I worked stations from Dorset to Cornwall (and in France) via a Brittany repeater on 144MHz during a lift, and routinely simplex as well as many other repeaters en route. On 70cm, results were equally good; during my return trip, I raised G0AKN (Twickenham) via the Farnham (UHF) repeater to give my ETA while on a high spot on Salisbury Plain (about 36 miles from the repeater). The handheld was producing about 5 watts on the power meter when running off the cigar lighter 12V supply.

"Once the optimum setting had been ascertained, the segments of the antenna were taped to fix the length. Mechanical performance was (unexpectedly) good. Once the contraption was dislodged by a branch in a Devon lane, but a spare reel of tape quickly restored it. Three months later the system still functions normally."

1.8MHz Helical Vertical Dipole

Extracted from 'Technical Topics', *Radio Communication*, January 1991

1.8MHZ HELICAL VERTICAL DIPOLE

NOT MANY OF US COULD contemplate putting up a vertical resonate half-wave dipole for 1.8MHz since, if unloaded, it would call for at least a 250ft mast. However with a helically wound element (normal mode) the total height can be brought down to well under 20ft, though of course at the cost of lower radiation efficiency and more critical tuning.

In the Australian magazine *Amateur Radio* (October 1990), N Chivers, VK2YO described experiments with such an antenna, using wire wound on two 2m fibreglass rods (wooden curtain rod could be used): **Fig 3**. Each rod has a PL259 coaxial plug at one end which screws into a coax 'Tee' piece so that the lower rod hangs vertically under the higher rod, and is mechanically rigid. The top rod is fitted with a hook to hang it from a convenient support which could be a rope stretched between two points.

VK2YO describes construction as follows: "Wind enough wire onto one of the rods at the opposite end to the PL259 plug so that when it is coupled to a GDO it shows self resonance at about 3.6MHz. This took 132m of 26SWG enamelled wire scrounged from an old power transformer primary. The wire is close-wound over 1.2m of rod, then the winding is tapered to connect with the PL259 connector at the other end. Repeat this process for the other rod. The wire on the upper rod is connected to the centre pin of the PL259 plug, while that on the lower rod connects to the outer collar of its PL259 plug.

"With the two rods assembled with the inter-connecting coax 'Tee' and supported horizontally on three chair backs, a socket with one turn was screwed on to the plug section of the tee connector. A GDO coupled to this loop dipped at 1.79MHz but when the antenna was raised vertically with the lower rod about 1m above ground, the resonant frequency went up to 1.86MHz. Squashing up the turns a bit lowered this to about 1.83MHz a popular frequency in Australia. The turns were then fixed with a coating of araldite.

"When coupled directly to a TS680S transceiver with 50Ω coax, results on reception were satisfactory but on transmit the VSWR was high and the built-in protection circuit reduced the power output."

With an impedance bridge, the antenna was found to null broadly about 20Ω at 1.86MHz indicating the need for some form of impedance matching. VK2YO put together the arrangement shown in Fig 3, winding 100 turns of 18SWG wire, tapped every 5 turns onto a piece of orange 20mm diameter electrical conduit, with a wide-spaced 20-150pF variable capacitor of second world war vintage.

This combination tunes from about 1.75 to 1.95MHz. By trial and error, moving the taps up and down the coil and adjusting the capacitor, a low VSWR could be achieved. The interconnecting cable between antenna and tuner should be kept as short as possible to minimise radiation from the outer skin of the coax-cable braid (unbalanced feed to balanced antenna). VK2YO adds: "Do not connect the transceiver to the tuner or the tuner to the load (antenna) via a coax switch, since the braid side will be common to all connected antennas and connected to earth for lightning protection. This antenna floats above ground and is independent of ground. If the station transceiver is separately RF grounded, then the tuned circuit should be fed by a link coupling wound over the centre of the tapped coil with a series capacitor (eg 10-100pF ceramic-based mica capacitor) in one leg of the link winding of about 20 turns 18 SWG."

VK2YO finds this modest 1.8MHz vertically-polarised antenna works as well as or better than his end-fed wire about 80m long, usually one S-point up on transmit.

The Lazy Man's Multibander

Extracted from 'Technical Topics', *Radio Communication*, January 1991

THE LAZY MAN'S MULTIBANDER

GEORGE CRIPPS, , G3DWW, WRITES: "For some time I have obtained very good results from a 66ft inverted-L antenna used as a quarter-wave on 3.5MHz and fed directly from 50Ω coaxial cable. The need then arose for operation on 7MHz in daylight and 3.5MHz at night. A second 33ft length of wire was then strung under the first spaced from it with plastic insulators of the type used for open-wire line (about 6in). This worked well. It was then realised that the 33ft wire would also provide a low-impedance feed-point on 21MHz as a three-quarter-wave antenna. Later still a 16ft 6in wire was hung vertically downwards from the horizontal wire to form the arrangement shown in **Fig 4**. The final result performs well on 3.5, 7, 14 and 21 MHz with a low SWR on each band and permitting direct feed from the 50Ω cable. The vertical portion of the antenna is at the bottom of my garden, about 48ft from the house and away from the zone of domestic electrical interference noises."

While clearly G3DWW is satisfied with his multibander, it needs perhaps to be said that the low SWR (if really low) does not necessarily imply high-efficiency. His diagram does not indicate a direct earth connection at the antenna end of the coax cable (which I would expect to see) so presumably there is an RF earth provided at the transceiver end of the feeder. Since one would expect the feed-point impedance of a quarter-wave wire to be only about 19-20Ω resistive, it is possible that

Fig 3. VK2YO's 1.8MHz helical-type vertical antenna can be suspended from a height of less than 20ft and operates independently of an RF earth connection.

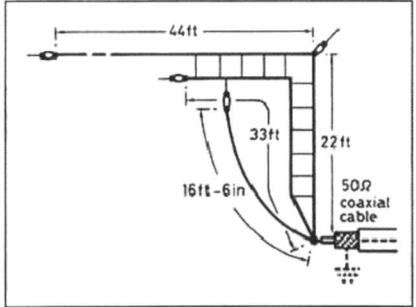

Fig 4. G3DWW's 'Lazy Man's Multibander' antenna for 3.5/7/14/21MHz.

the 'earth' is contributing extra RF resistance to achieve a match somewhere near-unity and that considerable RF current is flowing back down the outer braid of the cable (unless perhaps G3DWW buries the cable in its passage down the garden, in which case one would expect an SWR of at least 2:1). Such an SWR would be perfectly satisfactory from a radiation-efficiency point of view but might cause the transceiver to reduce power. A unity SWR might be more worrying since it would suggest power wastage. As W2DU pointed out many years ago: "A low SWR is *not* evidence that an antenna system is working efficiently. On the contrary, a lower than normal SWR over a significant bandwidth is reason to suspect that a dipole or vertical antenna is being affected by resistance losses. These may arise from poor connections, poor earthing systems, lossy cable or other causes."

Loop Radiation Patterns

Extracted from 'Technical Topics', *Radio Communication*, February 1991

THOSE LOOP RADIATION PATTERNS

THE SEPTEMBER *TT* ITEM 'Horizontal loop antennas (real and with MININEC)' included as Fig 3 elevation and azimuth-plane radiation patterns of a multiband 1.9MHz (4 x 132ft) horizontal square loop antenna at a height of 50ft. These patterns were generated by W4ZCB using an IBM computer with MININEC-variant software and used by Doug DeMaw, W1FB, in 'A closer look at horizontal loop antennas' (*QST*, May 1990). Unfortunately, they show how easy it is to use valid computer-software to come up with incorrect results.

James W Healy, NJ2L (a staff member of ARRL), in *QST*, September 1990, with the assistance of KI6WX, VE2CV and W7EL shows that the patterns and gains in the May article were wrong. This was due to an axis-of-symmetry discrepancy. It is apparent that the patterns reproduced in the September *TT* were based on an incorrect axis, brought about by the fact that the MININEC variant used by W4ZCB assumes an axis shown by the line CD in **Fig 1**, whereas the axis of the corner-fed antenna described by W1FB is in fact A-B.

Fig 2 shows KI6WX's NEC3-generated patterns which differ substantially from those shown in September. NJ2L writes:

"The elevation angles at which the azimuth-plane patterns in the May *QST* (September *TT*) were plotted (30° at and below 7MHz, 15° at the higher frequencies) were probably chosen because those were the signal-arrival angles of most interest to the author. The patterns of Fig 2 are shown at the same elevation angles, not at the elevation-plane gain peaks.

"The gains shown in Fig 2 are in decibels relative to an isotropic source (dBi) in free space whereas the earlier patterns show gains relative to a half-wave dipole in free space. Comparing antennas to that of a dipole in free space can be misleading.

MININEC says that the gain of a half-wave dipole in free space is 2.14dBi (0dBd) but at 50 feet above average ground, NEC3 shows that the gain of that same dipole is 6.26dBi (4.12dBd). How can a dipole have 4.12dB gain over a dipole? Easy - the reference antenna is in free space, but the dipole over ground is subject to ground reflections that increase its gain (in this case) by 4.12dB. The same 1.9MHz dipole antenna 50ft above average ground has a whopping 10.4dBi gain at 28MHz - only 4dB less than the 1.9MHz loop's gain at 28MHz. In general, it's less potentially confusing to compare antenna gains to that of an isotropic source in free space".

It may be recalled that in the July *TT*, G3SEK drew attention to what he felt to be a potentially misleading use of ground reflection gain in MININEC diagrams/leaflets associated with a recently introduced compact HF

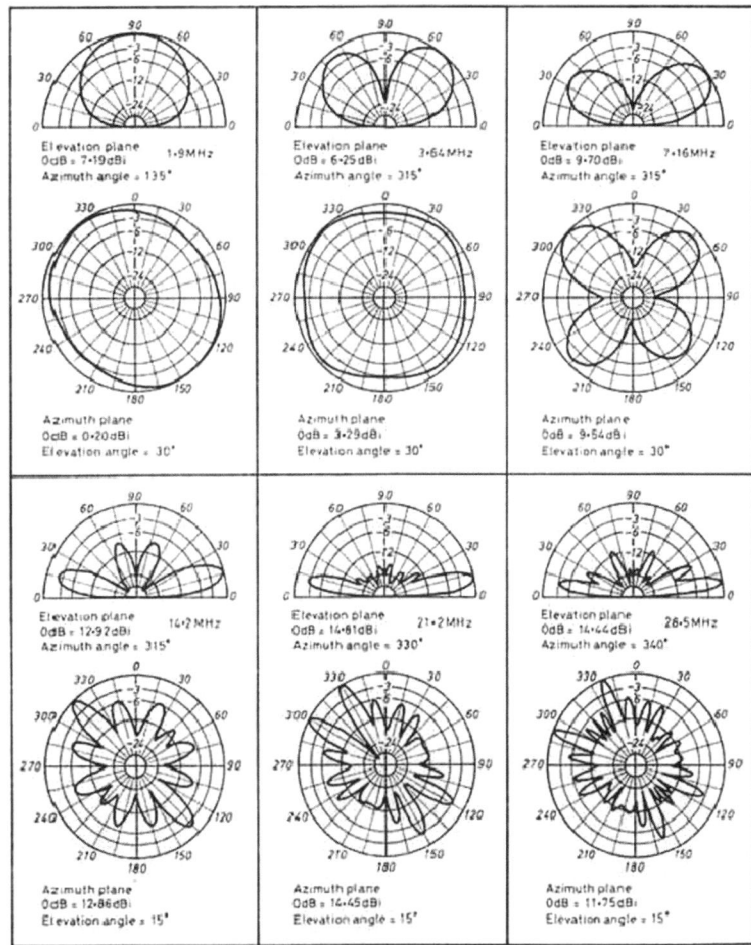

Fig 2: Recalculated radiation patterns of the large horizontal loop antenna using the correct axis of symmetry in conjunction with NEC3 software.

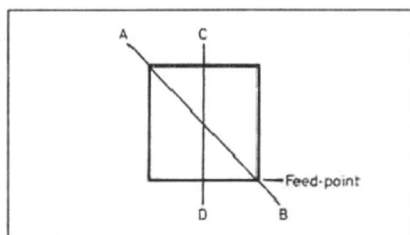

Fig 1: Top view of the horizontal loop described in QST, May and *TT*, September. Line AB represents the true axis of symmetry. CD is the axis that was incorrectly used in calculating the patterns published at the time.

ANTENNA TOPICS

beam with 11dBd claimed gain. It seems only fair to mention that I subsequently received (indignant) letters from the designers of that antenna who pointed out, *inter alia*, that the need for amateurs to be aware of the differences between an isotropic reference, a dipole reference, free space and above real ground. As G3SEK made clear in his letter, no criticism of the actual antenna was intended but he was surely right to draw attention to this important distinction in the way antennas may be described.

Ground gain has been well understood for many years by professional antenna engineers but this is not necessarily the case for many amateurs. It can be substantial. To quote data from the *HF Communications Data Book* published by Rockwell International (Collins Radio), the maximum gains of theoretical lossless elementary antennas, together with the direction of maximum gain, are as follows:

- Short dipole in free space: 1.76dBi in plane perpendicular to axis.
- Half-wave dipole in free space: 2.15dBi in plane perpendicular to axis.
- Vertical short monopole over perfect ground: 4.76dBi on horizon.
- Vertical quarter-wave monopole over perfect ground: 5.15dBi on horizon.
- Horizontal half-wave dipoles:
  (a) Infinitesimal height above perfect ground: 9.1dBi straight up.
  (b) Quarter-wave above perfect ground: 7.4dBi straight up.
  (c) Half-wave above perfect ground: 8.2dBi in plane perpendicular to axis 30 deg above horizontal.
  (d) Sixth-tenths-wave above perfect ground: 9.2dBi in plane perpendicular to axis 24.6 deg above horizontal.
- Vertical half-wave dipole, half-wave (to centre of antenna) above perfect ground: 8.2dBi on horizon.

In practice, unfortunately, no antennas are lossless (particularly monopoles) nor, except at sea, will the ground be even nearly perfect!

Reverting to the question of the performance of horizontal loop antennas, after the September *TT*, I received letters from Gus Taylor, G8PG, and Roy Hill, GM0IJF, both of whom have for some time been very pleased with the results achieved with multiband horizontal loops at very modest heights.

G8PG has used a rectangular loop (**Fig 3**), about 20ft high, for about six years, feeding it with only about 3 watts of RF with which, on CW, he has worked more than 100 countries, including to his surprise spanning the Atlantic on 3.5MHz and all continents except Oceania on 7MHz. His loop is non-resonant, lower and smaller than those usually recommended. He writes: "I believe that to get the best out of these loops one should make it as big (and as high) as local conditions allow, and feed it via tuned, open-wire line by means of a suitable coupler such as the Z-match with balanced output shown in Fig 12.77 of the fifth edition of the *Radio Communication Handbook*. He wrote up his antenna in *Short-Wave Magazine* (February 1985) and mentions that other QRP enthusiasts have been very satisfied with the results achieved using various horizontal and (smaller) vertical loops. Recently he has been testing an indoor 8ft-square version about 17ft high, with good results on all bands from 10.1MHz upwards and short-skip contacts on 7MHz. He hopes to enlarge on this indoor version in *Sprat*.

GM0IJF has been similarly pleasantly surprised with the DX performance of large loops only 4, 6 or 8m high, one of which was around the eaves of his bungalow. He feeds the loop with 300Ω slotted ribbon feeder with a Z-match coupler. Unlike the majority of such loops, he feeds in the middle of one span rather than at the corner.

Weather-resistant Wire Arrays

Extracted from 'Technical Topics', *Radio Communication*, March 1991

WEATHER-RESISTANT ARRAYS

AGAIN THIS WINTER, MOST PARTS of the UK have suffered from frequent high winds and gales that have not proved kind to HF antennas. Some tips for achieving longer life for wire-type arrays such as quads, VK2ABQ or G3LBQ antennas have been given by Paul T Atkins, K2OZ, with editorial additions in *QST*, (November 1989, p39). K2OZ has succeeded in keeping his quad antenna up and working for about 25 years, following modifications when it began to deteriorate after about 10 years - no mean feat! He writes:

"Sad experience has been my teacher. My first quad required periodic patching because of ice and wind-related flexing. Typically element wire breakage occurred at the element corners where they are supported by the spreaders. Adding a two-wire strengthener, as in **Fig 4(a)**, at each corner solved this problem. Teflon insulated wire is a better choice than stranded bare wire for the elements which suffer from oxidation (elements turning green). The spreaders were tied together (**Fig 4(b)**) with 50-pound monofilament (nylon) fishing line which deteriorates in sunlight from UV radiation and was replaced by more durable cord (Editorial note: Nylon cord, especially that treated to improve UV resistance, is much better than monofilament fishing line for outdoor use; *Dacron* cord is even better. Because it deteriorates rapidly in UV light, avoid using polypropylene lines in sunlit locations - *QST*).

"My quad used tapped-coil inductive reflector tuning. I replaced the Miniductor coils with home-made, 1" ID coils wound with No 12 tinned bus wire (winding each coil on a 1" dia temporary form then removing it from the form and slipping it into position on its respective quad insulator). In the belief that tapped coils, whether unused turns are left open or short-circuited, introduce loss, I tuned the quad reflectors by adjusting the coil turn spacing as necessary. Following these modifications, I have not had to repair my quad for almost 15 years."

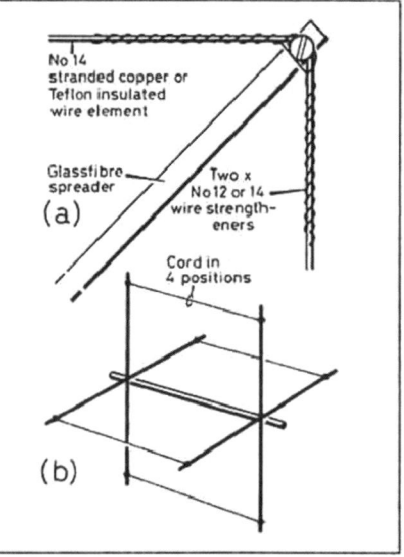

Fig 4: K2OZ's survivable quad modifications, applicable also to other wire-element arrays.

Some additional information is given in the *QST* caption. This points out that Teflon-insulated No 14 stranded copper wire is a better choice than bare stranded copper but care is needed not to nick the wire strands when removing its insulation for soldering (if possible use a thermal stripper). Each corner strengthener consists of two pieces of No 12 or 14 bus wire some 14 to 16" long. After cleaning the element wire until it is bright and solderable, twist on one strengthener wire *in the other direction*. Using resin-cored solder and a soldering iron hot enough to heat the work thoroughly, solder the three wires together. Complete the job by cleaning the joint to remove whatever resin remains. The finished strengthener can be wrapped with tape as required.

50.1MHz Yagi Dimensions

Extracted from 'Technical Topics', *Radio Communication*, March 1991

50.1MHZ YAGI DIMENSIONS

RON FISHER, VK3OM, AND Ron Cook, VK3AFW, in their *Random Radiators* column (*Amateur Radio* VK, October 1990) provide a useful table to facilitate the construction of DL6WU-type optimised Yagi antennas com-

1990 - 1999

TABLE 1 - 50.1MHz Yagi Design Data

Element lengths are for constant diameter tubing. Both incremental and progressive spacing dimensions are given.

Element	Spacing Incremental	Spacing Progressive	Element lengths			
			6mm	9mm	12mm	16mm
Reflector	0	0	3002	2980	2964	2949
Radiator	1436	1436	2920	2880	2851	2823
1st Dir	449	1885	2774	2741	2716	2689
2nd Dir	1077	2962	2753	2718	2692	2664
3rd Dir	1287	4249	2733	2697	2669	2640
4th Dir	1496	5745	2715	2677	2649	2618
5th Dir	1675	7420	2698	2659	2630	2598
6th Dir	1795	9215	2682	2642	2612	2580
7th Dir	1884	11099	2667	2627	2596	2562

dimensions in mm

piled by VK3AUU: **Table 1** This provides a selection of element lengths and spacings related to the diameter of tubular (non-tapering) elements. For intermediate diameters it should be possible to find dimensions by interpolation.

Fig 9 shows the suggested matching arrangements for the driven folded-dipole element with the two rods spaced about 75mm apart. The balun transformer is based on an electrical half-wave length of coaxial cable, typically about 1976mm long for 50.1MHz. If the elements pass through a metal boom they should be lengthened by two-thirds of the diameter of the boom.

As a nine-element array, the power gain should be about 11dBd, considerably more than most of the arrays used on 50MHz. Even with four directors, it should provide up to about 8dBd gain, but the matching may suffer and some adjustment in the optimum spacing of the first director is likely to be required.

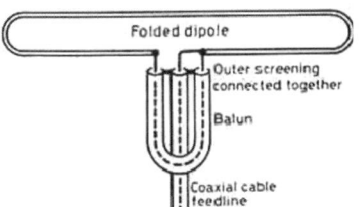

Fig 9: Matching system for DL6WU-type Yagi. For 50.1MHz the dimensions of elements/spacings are given in Table 1. For the driven folded dipole, the elements can be spaced 75mm apart. The balun is made from an electrical half-wavelength of cable (typically 1976mm at 50.1MHz but dependent on velocity factor of the cable).

Analysing GP & Sleeve Antennas

Extracted from 'Technical Topics', *Radio Communication*, April 1991

ANALYSING GROUND-PLANE AND SLEEVE ANTENNAS

TT, NOVEMBER 1987, pp836-837 included an item 'The groundplane dissected' that referred to the computer (NEC) study by Melvin Weiner of a "Monopole element at the centre of a circular ground plane whose radius is small or comparable to a wavelength" (*IEE Trans on Ant & Prop*, May 1987). This indicated the vertical radiation patterns of quarter-wave elements with varying forms of circular (radial) ground planes, introducing the novel concept of a GPA with a ground-plane of zero-extent.

The zero-extent concept was followed-up by Dr Brian Austin, G0GSF, who ran it to earth (no pun intended) in the book *Monopole Elements on Circular Ground Planes* by M M Weiner *et al* (Artech House, 1987). This resulted in *TT* (March 1988) reproducing a diagram of the Weiner form of zero-extent GPA, showing the use of lossy ferrite toroids (beads) around the coaxial feeder cable, providing a choke against the flow of outer-braid current. This description, unfortunately, left unanswered the question of the return current, and I received no further comments on this potentially interesting form of antenna until recently Peter Chadwick, G3RZP, mentioned the Artech book as a source of reference.

The GPA, particularly for VHF, remains of considerable interest not only to radio amateurs (for whom it provides one of the most popular simple antennas on HF) but also for professional users. This interest is reflected in 'Sleevve Antenna with Ground Wires' by Mitsuo Taguchi *et al* (*IEEE Trans Ant & Prop*, January 1991, pp 1-7). This presents a detailed mathematical and experimental analysis of a sleeve antenna, a monopole antenna with ground wires (ie the GPA with wire radials) and a sleeve antenna with ground wires.

Among the information presented in this paper is some useful information on the input impedance of a GPA with the radials at different sloping angles (**Fig 1**). The authors note that the input impedance depends on the length of the ground wires (radials) and their inclination, making it easy to match the antenna to a 50Ω feeder by adjusting these parameters, adding: "Since the input resistance of this antenna with inclined ground wires decreases considerably for some feeder lengths, the mismatch of impedance with the feeder and degradation of radiation characteristics arise."

The sleeve antenna is much less popular with amateurs than the GPA although long featured in the handbooks. It normally consists of a monopole with a quarter-wave extension surrounding the feeder cable; the idea of adding radials to the sleeve, as described in the IEEE paper, is new to me, but it is concluded that a sleeve antenna with ground wires combines the advantages of both a sleeve antenna and a Brown GPA: "The input impedance of the sleeve antenna with ground wires can be easily changed by adjusting the length, inclination angle, and position of the ground wires. The directivity is not sensitive to these parameters when the lengths of the ground wires are less than 0.2λ.

"The input impedance is 50Ω and the actual gain is about 2.1dBi when the length of the sleeve is 0.2λ, the length and inclination angle of the ground wires are 0.1λ and $0°$, and the distance of the ground wires from the feed point is 0.025λ. The current induced on the feeder of the sleeve antenna can be reduced at the design frequency of the *sperrtopf*."

The experimental UHF (340MHz) model antennas used by the Japanese authors in-

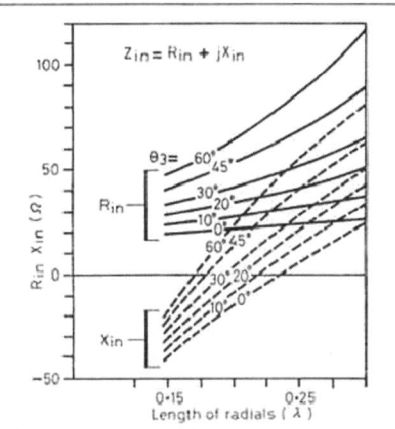

Fig 1: Calculated input impedance of a quarter-wave ground-wave type antenna with varying lengths of radials for different downward inclinations.

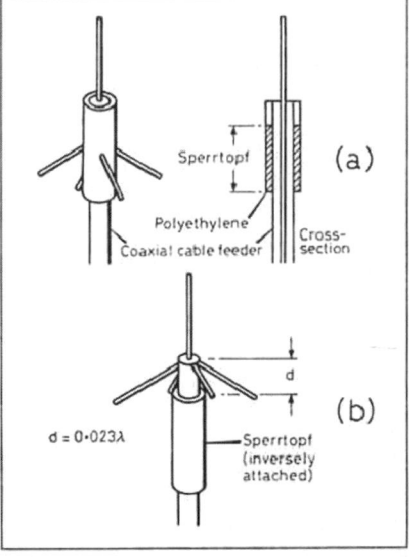

Fig 2: Test antennas as used by Mitsui Taguchi *et al*. (a) Sleeve antenna with ground wires (radials). (b) Monopole with ground wires (i.e. GPA). the *sperrtopf* appears to be a form of coaxial stub arranged to suppress RF currents on the outer-braid of the coaxial cable feeders.

273

ANTENNA TOPICS

clude a 'quarter-wave *sperrtopf*, to suppress or reduce the RF current feeding back down the outer braid of the coaxial feeder cable. This appears to be some form of tuned, coaxial stub forming, in effect, an RF choke on the outer braid. Unfortunately, no details of the construction of such a *sperrtopf* is given in the paper, but the reader is given a reference to the Japanese-published book *VHF Antennas* by H Uchida and Y Mushiake, Tokyo 1955, p192. Of the sleeve antenna without ground wires, it is considered difficult to match this antenna to a 50Ω feeder, so that it "is usually constructed with a matching circuit such as a coaxial impedance transformer." **Fig 2** shows details of the 340MHz test antennas.

Of the quarter-wave monopole with ground wires in the horizontal direction, it is concluded that the input resistance is near 20Ω even if the length of the ground wires is increased up to 0.3λ: "It increases as the ground wires are inclined below horizontal and their lengths are increased. The input reactance varies towards inductive as the lengths of the ground wires are increased.

The so-called Brown antenna (ie the ground-plane antenna as originally described in the 1930s by Dr George Brown of RCA - G3VA), which is a monopole antenna with quarter-wavelength horizontal ground wires, has a directive gain of 1.61dBi. The gain increases slightly as the ground wires are inclined in the downward direction. When the angle of inclination is 60°, the gain increases to 2.11dBi, which is about the same gain as a half-wave dipole.

The antenna can be matched with a 50Ω feeder if the ground wires are about 0.17λ long and are directed 60° downwards. The gain is then improved by about 0.5dB compared with the horizontally directed quarter-wavelength ground wires. However, the current induced on the surface of the feeder is not small compared with the current on the antenna. Without a *sperrtopf*, the input resistance seems to depend on the length of the feeder, and is smaller than the value calculated by neglecting the effect of feeder if the ground wires are inclined downwards. This creates an impedance mismatch and results in performance degradation." I wonder if any reader can provide fuller details of the (clearly useful) *sperrtopf*?

antenna, the real earth provides the missing quarter-wave section. I also emphasised that the loss-resistance of such an earth not only reduced radiation efficiency but could also result in a misleadingly low VSWR on the feeder.

In the follow-up letter, G3DWW agreed with my comments but added that in fact he does have a good RF earth connection at the antenna end of the feeder, though he omitted this in his diagram. His earth comprises a spike about 2ft from the end of the coaxial cable, paralleled to three 4ft earth spikes at the end of 20ft radials buried about 2in under his lawn. One radial runs directly under the horizontal run of the antenna.

Even so, he has measured the DC earth resistance as roughly 20Ω, which he assumes could be limiting the radiation efficiency to roughly 50% - a quite reasonable and practical figure for such a simple multiband antenna. This assumes that the RF loss resistance is the same as the DC resistance, an assumption that is probably pessimistic in view of the presence of the radials; in practice the efficiency may be appreciably higher than he suggests. Incidentally, it is yet another indication that the use of elevated quarter-wave-resonated radials (possibly much reduced in size by the use of inductive loading as suggested by G6XN, or by the adaption of DL1VU's 'sardine tin opener' folding technique as a counterpoise rather than a top-loading system; see G4LQI's *Eurotek* column in the February *RadCom*, p45) is likely to prove superior to the use of earth spikes alone. It may, however, still be advisable to earth the system to reduce damage from nearby lightning strikes.

In practice, a DC earth resistance of 25Ω probably represents a better than average figure for amateur radio earthing in typical residential areas. A useful item on 'improved grounding techniques' appears in the new column by Bill Orr, W6SAI 'Radio Fundamentals; things to learn, projects to build and gear to use' which started in *CQ*, December 1990, p85. This is based on an article in the American military-communications magazine *Signal* (March 1988), brought to W6SAI's notice by George Riddle, W6FMZ.

Signal reported earth measurements made by the US Army Materials Systems Analysis Activity outfit in various parts of the USA. They found that measurements using a single 6ft earth rod (of the type used by the US military for over 50 years) ranged from 13Ω in moist soil at Fort Story, Virginia, to over 7000Ω at Fort Lewis, Washington. The US military regards 10Ω as the upper limit of acceptability, presumably requiring the use of multiple earth rods for virtually all installations.

The W6SAI item continues: "Continued testing on various grounding schemes led to the surface-wire-ground (SWG) technique. The early SWG consisted of a number of 6in-long stakes used to secure a 100ft-long, 1/8in dia, cable to the earth in a straight line. In the final design, the wire length is reduced to 70ft, the wire being grounded along its length by 15 stakes, each 10in long. The wire is looped around the equipment, and three heavy connecting wires ground the equipment to the SWG as in **Fig 5**.

"The short ground stake is a tapered, star-shaped design (**Fig 5(b)**) that provides enhanced soil contact and can easily be inserted into or removed from the ground.

"The SWG has been tested against a conventional 6ft ground rod in a number of locations in the continental United States, Alaska and Germany. In all cases, the SWG offered improved performance, with values ranging from 2:1 to 10:1 better than the ground rod."

Low-resistance Earthing

Extracted from 'Technical Topics', *Radio Communication*, April 1991

LOW-RESISTANCE EARTHING

IN COMMENTING ON THE 'lazy man's multibander' HF antenna contributed by George Cripps, G3DWW, (*TT*, January 1991), I expressed surprise at the absence, in the diagram he sent along, of an earthing point at the antenna end of the coaxial feeder cable. In this type of quarter-wave inverted-L type of

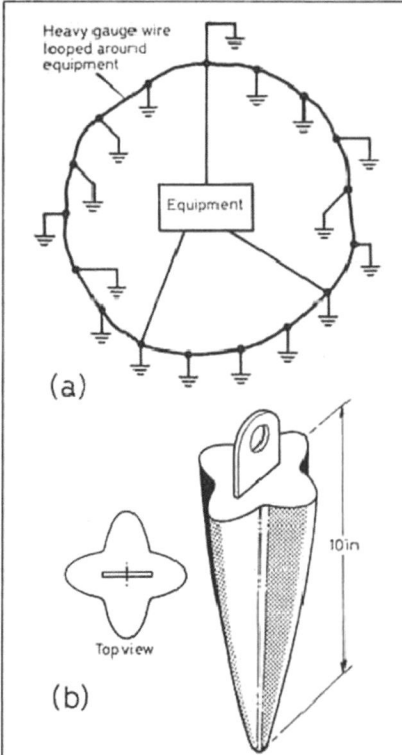

Fig 5: Surface-wire-ground (SWG) system as used by US Army. The SWG wire is looped around the equipment and earthed at 15 to 18 points, using the 10in ground stakes of cruciform shape with connecting bolt at top as shown in (b).

Tips & Topics: Corrosion

Extracted from 'Technical Topics', *Radio Communication*, April 1991

TIPS & TOPICS

Prevention of Corrosion in Antennas

Contact between copper and aluminium, for example in an antenna, can result in corrosion and, therefore, a poor electrical connection. According to Karel Barton (*Protection against atmospheric corrosion*, published by John Wiley, 1976), "contact between copper and aluminium should be avoided at all costs!". However, the author goes on to say that stainless steel causes no trouble. I suggest that a stainless steel washer between the copper cable and the aluminium of an antenna element may well reduce the likelihood of corrosion, especially if used with a stain-

less steel bolt. It is wise to add other precautions such as the application of grease, lanolin (my favourite) or RTV silicone rubber. If RTV silicone rubber, use the type that does **not** give off acetic acid (vinegar-type) fumes.
- *Dick Biddulph, G8DPS.*

End Feeding a Windom, etc

Extracted from 'Technical Topics', *Radio Communication,* May 1991

END FEEDING A WINDOM AND RELATED TOPICS

LES MOXON, G6XN, IN *TT*, February 1989, pp111-112, introduced the radical concept of end-feeding a Windom-type antenna by inserting a specific capacitive reactance a given length along a resonant wire element, preferably keeping reasonably short the length of the single-wire feeder connected to the end of the antenna: Fig 1.

He has now provided an up-date on this concept, including showing a means of end-feeding the element from co-axial cable with counterpoise, showing also the potential of this approach for other antennas, including arrays.

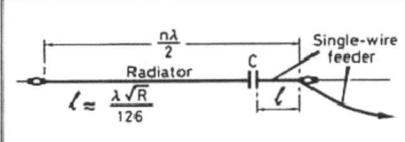

Fig 1: G6XN's end-fed Windom antenna with single-wire feeder as described in *TT*, February 1989). λ is wavelength in feet. R is radiation resistance (referred to a current loop). A value of 500Ω is assumed for the impedance of the single-wire feeder. Reactance of capacitor C is $1/\lambda C$ approximately equal to $70\lambda/l$. Values found in practice:
At 7MHz, l = 12ft for n = 2 (C = 27pF).
At 29MHz, l = 2ft for n = 1 (C variable and not measured but estimated to be about 5pF).

Principle of operation: From a point of maximum RF voltage on the antenna, one moves a short distance outwards to find an impedance (from a Smith Chart) equal to R + jx, where R matches the single wire feeder, X being tuned by the capacitor. Since l is short and current in it small, its virtual removal from the radiator has negligible effect on field strength.

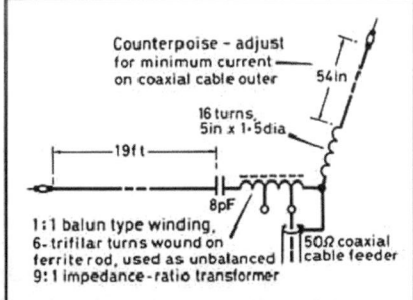

Fig 2: The G6XN Windom with 'zero-length' single wire feeder arranged for end-feeding from coaxial cable feeder with short resonant counterpoise.

G6XN writes: "As described in February 1989, the end-fed Windom has the same defects as the ordinary Windom, ie radiation from the feeder and losses in the ground return path, but nevertheless derives interest from the defects of *other* forms of end-fed antennas (despite their convenience at typical sites). Suppose, however, that we shorten the single-wire feeder so that the matching unit (complete with the artificial ground) gets dragged up towards the antenna followed by the 50Ω-ohm line connecting it to the transmitter (akin to the FD4 form of Windom described in the December *TT* - G3VA).

"Let's go all the way. We now have an antenna end-fed with a co-axial cable feeder as in Fig 2. The single-wire line, shrunk to zero length, cannot radiate. My work on ground planes provides proof that the antenna current will return directly to the counterpoise (except at very low heights) instead of via the ground. (Nor should the co-axial cable radiate unlike the situation with an off-centre-fed antenna - G3VA).

"Incidentally we can do anything we like with the antenna proper, subject to the conditions outlined in February 1989, without any change to the (matching) transformer since its impedance ratio is given by Z_0(wire)/Z_0(cable), ie about 11:1 with R not involved. We can shorten the antenna by loading its further half capacitively or inductively, it can be any number of half-waves (minus a little bit) long, or you could replace it with one of the 'inverted ground planes' (resonant T-antennas) described on many occasions in *TT* and *Amateur Radio Techniques.*

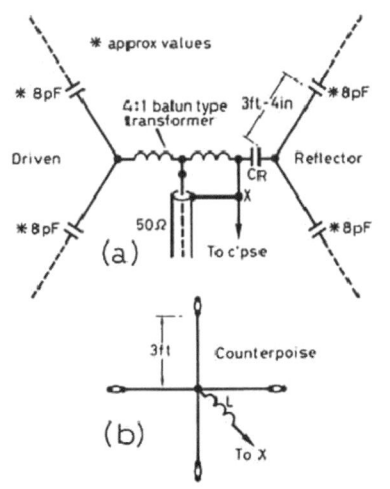

Fig 3: (a) Single-pole-mounted, switchable four-quadrant directional 21MHz array modified for end-fed Windom-type feed. CR tunes reflector by resonating with the single-wire feeders (which in the reflector case are "inductive connections to ground" so the inductance has to be removed.
(b) Counterpoise details. Four radials (each 3ft long) are used for reasons of symmetry. L is 8 turns, 2.75-in diameter, 6-in long, wound over fishing rod extension.

"Different again, and possibly much more important, is the *nearly* zero-length version which can be used to push points of high RF voltage away from places where they are causing problems such as inside the shack, or on switch contacts. This opens the way to what I believe to be a major breakthrough in the design of directionally switched arrays based on vertical dipoles (eg Fig 162, p333 of *Amateur Radio Techniques*; 7th edition out-of-print, or Fig 13.9b of my book *HF Antennas for all Locations*). These arrays, in which four dipoles are held up by a single pole, have attracted a lot of interest in spite of the difficulty of switching them remotely. One or two people have succeeded in this, but hitherto it has not been easy. By inserting capacitors at 0.075λ from the bottom ends of the dipoles they can become 'single-wire, end-fed' elements in pairs as in Fig 3(a) which shows some details of a 21MHz array I have just completed. This achieves four-quadrant directional switching by means of a pair of 'ordinary' double-pole reversing relays. Thin wire elements are used (20SWG) held up by a 17ft fishing rod with its base 4ft off the ground.

"Earlier experiments, at 14MHz, disclosed an important new aspect of this type of array: the very wide bandwidth which results from the use of two widely-spaced wires in parallel. Hitherto, this characteristic had been masked by the very *narrow* bandwidth of the Zepp-type feed, especially when using the (essential) G6CJ balancing stub. The change in SWR over a 2% band was barely detectable, and in one case the null depth exceeded 30dB over more than 100kHz without retuning. Less useful was the discovery of a small horizontally-polarised *low-angle* mode associated with *low* antenna heights. If one considers the top and bottom halves of the antenna separately, there is a small horizontal component resulting from the phase-difference between reflector and driven elements; this has a figure-of-8 pattern at right angles to the main beam. The 'top' and 'bottom' contributions should cancel each other out, but if the height and the angle of radiation are low enough the 'bottom' is less effective than the 'top' so cancellation is incomplete.

"Unfortunately at my present QTH, because of sandy soil and lots of trees, vertical antennas are very poor low-angle radiators (though quite useful at medium angles). The upshot of this was that in tests with VK5MS, towards the end of a path-opening, the horizontal mode actually took over! These 14MHz tests were discontinued when a faulty relay coincided with realisation of the need for a less cluttered environment. Not being able to expand the environment, I am contracting the antenna by changing to 21MHz instead!

"The result does little for popular beliefs about vertically-polarized antennas. On the other hand, in a good location they can give consistently good DX results with very modest structures *which do not need planning consent* !"

In a postscript to his report, G6XN adds some further relevant information: "I have found it impossible to design broadband (several octave) transformers for 550-600Ω impedance despite the ease of doing so for 200Ω. The trouble is self-capacitance, but for monoband operation all one needs to do is partly withdraw the core from the winding so that a GDO indicates resonance (with the transformer isolated) or if everything else is correct one can tune it for minimum SWR when *in situ.*

"Earlier references to this type of array have pointed out that the four wires of the beam can be arranged in either a 2- or 3- element configuration, but 3-elements can no longer be recommended as one loses the broadband feature, and there is an overcou-

ANTENNA TOPICS

pling problem with 2-elements which is cured by the new feed system (another plus). Attempts to apply this to the 3-element case proved a dismal failure in line with experience with a 3-element Claw antenna, emphasising the general problem of having 'too many variables', whereas *given a proper understanding* of the principles, optimisation is easy with two elements. One has to concede an advantage of 1.5-2dB (half an average S-point) to three elements but only if one has a long boom and can get it up equally high! (NB 'trapped tribanders' are a different case)."

Off-centre-fed Windoms

Extracted from 'Technical Topics', *Radio Communication*, May 1991

MORE ON OFF-CENTRE-FED (WINDOM) ANTENNAS

FURTHER TO THE ABOVE, G6XN writes to clear up a potentially misleading comment that I made in the discussion about the family of off-centre-fed (Windom/VS1AA) antennas in *TT*, December 1990. He points out that "far from being non-radiating, the two-wire (300Ω) feeder, especially as shown in Fig 3(d) of the December issue, can be quite efficient as a radiator of vertically-polarised signals, which may well account for its apparent success."

The reason is that, for a twin-wire feeder line to be non-radiating, the voltages and current need to be balanced throughout its length, a condition that does not apply when the feedpoint to a dipole element is not balanced about its centre.

G6XN writes: "Using my 'square-counting' method (see 'Radiation from a conductor' *HF Antennas for all locations*, p9). I have calculated that for a feeder length of one half-wave, total radiation from the antenna will have identical vertical and horizontal components. This, admittedly, ignores any change in impedance (Z) at the feed-point, which could change the balance between vertical/horizontal components, but seems unlikely in practice to make much difference."

To explain his conclusions, G6XN has sketched the current distribution starting from each end of the dipole element where current is zero: **Fig 4**. He writes: "There is (current) balance at the feedpoint, but below this (in the feeder) the maximum current in the righthand wire nearly coincides with minimum in the other. For the arrangement of December's Fig 3(d) a likely consequence, apart from radiation from the 300Ω line, could be lots of current on the outer of the braid of the co-axial cable section, but this will depend on other factors as well."

It must be stressed that the radiation of a vertically-polarized component, resulting in mixed-polarization is not necessarily a bad thing, as users of inverted-L type antennas have long found. Indeed it can be an advantage for HF ionospheric propagation, not only because of the potentially low-angle radiation (over good ground) of the vertical component but also in reducing fading (polarization diversity) so perhaps we should not worry overmuch (and possibly in some cases even welcome) the radiation from the feeder in this form of Windom-type antenna.

In fact, Bill Wright, G0FAH reports finding a 66ft (half-size) version of the Fig 3(d) type of multiband Windom/VS1AA a useful antenna that can be arranged to be used, without an ATU, on 21MHz as well as on 7, 14 and 28MHz simply by using a resonant length of 300Ω ribbon feeder and then swapping on 21MHz a different ratio balun transformer.

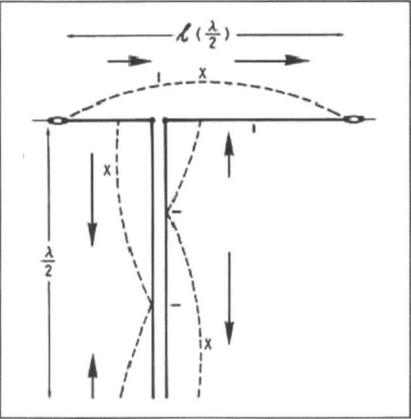

Fig 4: Using his 'square-counting' procedure (760 squares for both horizontal and vertical portions) G6XN considers that with the one-third off-centre-fed Windom/VS1AA of the dimensions shown, vertically-polarized radiation from the 300Ω twin-wire feeder would be about equal to that from the horizontal element.

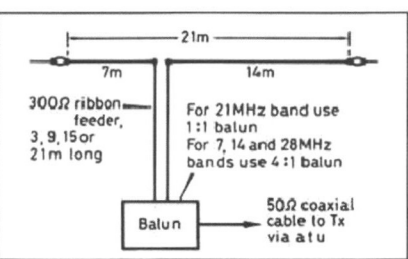

Fig 5: G0FAH's multi-band Windom/VS1AA antenna which on 21MHz uses the 300Ω ladder feeder as a quarter-wave impedance transformer to provide a match to the coaxial cable with a 1:1 balun, but is used on 7, 14 and 28MHz with a step-down balun. Without an ATU it should be possible to obtain a VSWR of 2:1 or better on each of the four bands, although a simple non-critical tuner (eg T or L network) can be used to adjust the VSWR to unity. Adjusting the feeder length a few centimetres may be required for optimum match on 21MHz. Best results were obtained using toroid-type coax baluns as described in *RadCom* March 1982, using two TVI ferrite rings taped together and then wound with RG58 cable. G0FAH advises coating the ribbon feeder with car polish to waterproof it since this reduces VSWR changes in wet weather.

G0FAH writes: "I have, like many experimenters, tried all manner of bits of wire in the search for that elusive 'all-band' antenna, but feel we need to consider just what we mean by 'all-band'. Given that most of what we call 'wire antennas' (ie ignoring quad-type and VK2ABQ-type arrays) are non-rotatable and, for the lower HF frequencies well under a half-wave above ground, we seldom have much control over where signals from it will be directed. 'Gain' is only worthwhile if it happens to be directed towards the distant station which we wish to contact. We do, however, have some control over how well the antenna system matches our transmitters and make it easier to do away with the need for an ATU - or at least not have to put up with critical ATU adjustments in order to meet the requirements of fussy black-boxes as well as operating convenience.

"Thus virtually all multiband wire antennas concentrate more on attempting to achieve a good 50Ω match on as many bands as possible, taking 'pot-luck' on the question of radiation lobes. My version of the Windom is no different in this respect. It presents a good match on four bands, and with the use of a wide-range ATU could be made to function on at least some of the other HF bands.

"As shown in **Fig 5**, it is a 'half-size' Windom of the December Fig 3(d) type, fed one-third from the end with balanced 300Ω slotted feeder. With a 4:1 balun this can be transformed to 75Ω unbalanced co-axial cable, providing a reasonable match on 7, 14 and 28MHz regardless of the length of the 300Ω line.

"On 21MHz the 'top' is three half-waves long and the feedpoint is at the junction of two of these half-waves, in other words a high-impedance point which can be transformed down to a low-impedance by making the feeder an odd number of electrical quarter-wavelengths. With slotted ribbon feeder having a velocity factor of about 0.85 this means the feeder can be 3, 9, 15 or 21m long, using a 1:1 balun on 21MHz.

"I put up this antenna using 9m of feeder and measured 2:1 or less VSWR on each band, swapping baluns when changing to the 21MHz band. A simple L-network ATU was used to get spot-on matching without restricting the good bandwidth. A useful solution to the multiband problem, although as a true experimenter since superseded with a bi-directional Lazy-H 21MHz antenna giving some 5.5dB gain towards the USA (though also to Italy)."

More on Sperrtopfs

Extracted from 'Technical Topics', *Radio Communication*, July 1991

MORE ON SPERRTOPF COAXIAL SLEEVES

FURTHER EXPLANATIONS HAVE come in confirming the explanation given by G4LQI of the term 'sperrtopf' as a 'blocking-pot', with an amateur radio 'Sperrtopf vertical' marketed for amateur radio use by Antenna Andes. Charles James, G0ILF, also points out that the 'FD4 Windom' is as well-known in Germany as the G5RV is in the UK. Peter Nolte, GW7IZG/DC6BN adds that sperrtopf coaxial sleeve antennas have been produced in Germany for many years as commercial VHF/UHF antennas by such firms as Kathrein

Rosenheim and the well-known Rohde & Schwarz.

He explains that in commercial/military communications wide-band characteristics of antennas are essential, with the ratio of length to diameter an important factor. For some sperrtopf VHF antennas in the region of 150MHz some of the elements are 35mm diameter and some about 50mm. Two designs from Rohde & Schwarz (HKO12 and HKO14), both wideband antennas, have the sperrtopf part of the assembly really looking like inverted pots, in contrast to narrower-band versions (about 10MHz bandwidth) which have about 35mm diameter. The R&S designs HK001, 012 and 014 feature additionally a kind of inverted basket in order to reduce further the unwanted re-radiation from the feeder cable. Another feature of some designs is the slightly raised elevation angle of the main radiation for ground-to-air operations, whereas normally radiation from such antennas is in the horizontal plane.

Professor Guenter Beuche, DL6AB, adds further details of this barrier-pot form of RF choke, emphasising that there is nothing magic behind the 'sperrtopf' which could just as well be called a 'sleeve' and is widely used as a form of balun to facilitate feeding a balanced load with coaxial cable, with the normal arrangement as in **Fig 4**. As used in Fig 2 of the April *TT* (with details of connections shown in (a)) the sole purpose is to suppress RF current on the outer-braid of the coaxial feed-line. Filling with suitable dielectric material, as mentioned, helps to shorten the length of the electrical quarter-wave sperrtopf used in this way.

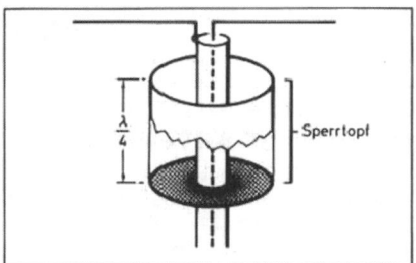

Fig 4: The Sperrtopf (barrier-pot) sleeve used to reduce outer-braid current when feeding a balanced element from unbalanced feedline.

Fig 5: Sketch of the AEA IsoPole VHF/UHF omni-directional base station antenna using two modified Sperrtopf-type 'decouplers'.

He also refers to the 'IsoPole' omni-directional VHF/UHF base station antennas (**Fig 5**) manufactured in the USA by AEA who claim "exceptional decoupling results in simple tuning and a significant reduction in TVI potential" by the use of "decoupling cones offering great efficiency over obsolete radials which radiate in the horizontal plane." They also claim a low SWR across the entire American two-metre band 144 - 148MHz. DL6AB writes: "Although I have not done any analysis of the IsoPole antenna it looks like an application of two Sperrtopf (used inversely) and called by AEA 'decoupling cones' to produce the same effects as the arrangements described by Taguchi (*TT*, April) although with a different mechanical arrangement."

Zapper II and Zapper III

Extracted from 'Technical Topics', *Radio Communication*, July 1991

ZAPPER II AND ZAPPER III ANTENNAS

ROD NEWKIRK, W9BRD was particularly pleased to find the *TT* references to his 'BRD Zapper antenna, the unidirectional version of a single-section, end-fed W8JK array (*TT*, September 1990, pp31-32). He sends along two variations, one of which obviates need for the home-built matching circuit.

He writes: "The simplified approach to phased antenna directivity suggests variations. For example, need for a dedicated matching circuit at the stub can be avoided by using two Zapper arrays in phase (**Fig 3(a)**) for an acceptable match to balanced 300Ω line. A standard balanced-output matching unit can then be used at the transmitter. Directivity reversal must be done at the stubs. Added collinear gain, up to about 3dB, can be realized by spacing the Zappers apart, as limited by the combined stub lengths.

"A vertical version provides switchable unidirectivity in four directions (**Fig 3(b)**). This version requires the single-tap feed approach detailed in the original article (*QST*, June 1990 for full details), a dedicated T-match being recommended. The selectable patterns are cardioidal, broad in the front quadrant, with a sharp rear null. A high-grade rotary switch at the stubs-juncture selects any one of four lobe/null directions. (The sharpness and depth of the target-frequency null suggests VHF benefits for clashing repeaters, etc). Note that while Zapper/W8JK configurations are fundamentally simple, optimum results depend heavily on proper symmetry and accurate resonance (high-Q). *Ergo*, each half of a double Zapper should be physically identical and identically resonant. Directivity switching then has little effect on matcher settings for unity SWR".

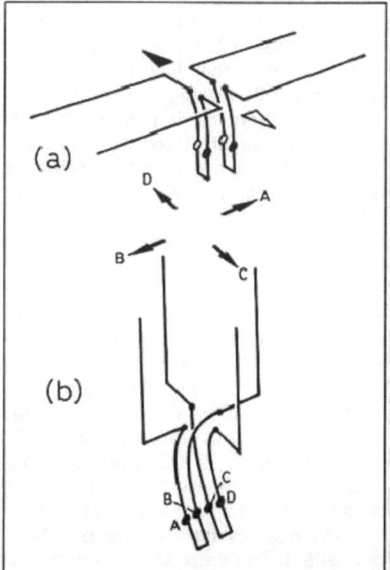

Fig 3: (a) The Zapper II antenna by W9BRD uses two unidirectional Zapper/W8JK arrays. (b) The Zapper III antenna with four vertical elements can provide switched directivity in each of the four quadrants.

Collinears for VHF/UHF Mobile

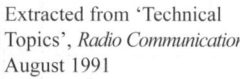

Extracted from 'Technical Topics', *Radio Communication*, August 1991

COLINEAR ANTENNAS FOR VHF/UHF MOBILE OPERATION

WHAT APPEARS TO BE A realistic use of the moment method (program not specified) to investigate the performance to be expected from a colinear monopole anna (CMPA) as a 900MHz mobile radiotelephone antenna, or as a dual-band antenna permitting also the reception of Band II (85 - 108MHz) FM broadcasting, is presented in *Electronic Letters* (6 June 1991, pp1103-4) by H Nakano *et al* of Hosei University, Tokyo.

This indicates how the gain of a conventional quarter-wave mobile antenna above an infinite ground plane (in practice a vehicle roof) having a gain of around 1dB can be improved by using two linear wire sections (L_F 0.23λ and L_S 0.5λ) connected by a coil with a diameter of $\frac{1}{16}$thλ, a pitch angle of P1 7° and a coil wire length of 0.5λ : **Fig 1**. All dimensions are for a λ equivalent to 900MHz. At this frequency, **Fig 1(a)** shows the calculated current distribution along the antenna. The wire radii of both antenna sections and the coil is taken as 1mm.

The Japanese authors write: "It is found that the current amplitude and phase on the first element are close to those on the second

ANTENNA TOPICS

element. Because the contributions of both the antenna elements in the far field add constructively, the radiation pattern becomes narrower than that in the conventional monopole antenna, as shown in **Fig 2(b)**. The gain is increased by 3.3dB compared with a conventional monopole antenna. The input impedance is calculated to be 69 - j32Ω."

The Japanese also discuss a double-band version of the CMPA with a further section connected to the top of the 900MHz colinear antenna via a (900MHz) trap coil, with the length of the third section arranged to resonate the antenna in the FM broadcast band (input impedance at 85MHz 21 - j4Ω).

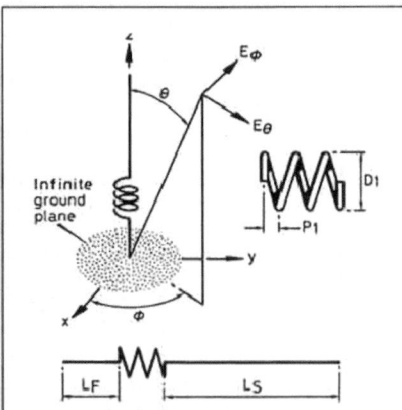

Fig 1: Configuration of the 900MHz colinear monopole antenna (CMPA) with loading coil (180° phase change) analysed by H Nakano *et al* in the IEE's *Electronics Letters*.

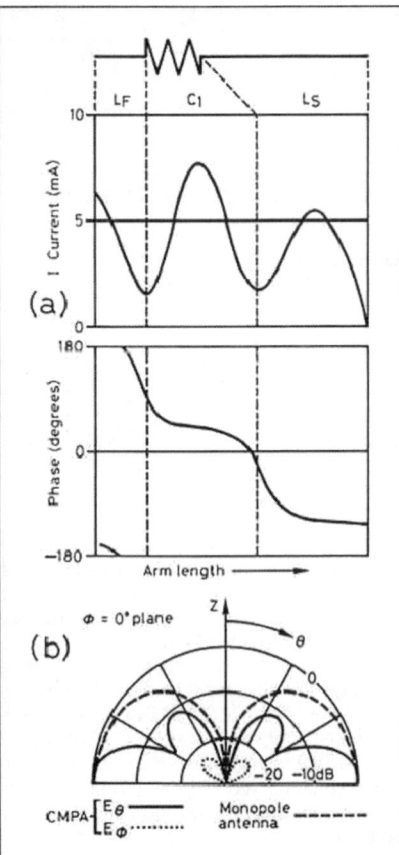

Fig 2: Current distribution and vertical radiation pattern of the 900MHz CMPA. (a) Current distribution. (b) Radiation pattern.

Consideration is also given to the use of a CMPA with four quarter-wave ground wires (radials) rather than an infinite ground plane: "The absolute gain at 900MHz is calculated to be 3.6dB which is significantly higher than a value of 1.4dB obtained by a quarter-wave monopole antenna with ground wires."

Capacitive Bottom-loading

Extracted from 'Technical Topics', *Radio Communication*, August 1991

CAPACITIVE BOTTOM-LOADING OF ANTENNAS

THAT REDOUBTABLE TROIKA OF retired engineers - Arch Doty, K8CFU, John Frey, W3ESU, and Harry Mills, K4HU - did much a few years ago to revive the interest of broadcast antenna engineers, as well as amateurs, in the use of elevated radials and counterpoises rather than extensive and costly buried radials and earth systems (by making thousands of measurements rather than using computer software). They have more recently turned their attention to the use of capacitive bottom loading in order to tune approximately-quarter-wave vertical elements to resonance over a quite wide frequency band, without changing the dimensions of the element, by varying the capacitance of the bottom loading. They have constructed many test antennas at 450MHz and also tried out the system at 144 and 28MHz using quarter-wave folded monopole elements (see *TT*, July 1987); at 450MHz constructed from printed circuit board.

They presented a paper on this subject at the Radio Club of America Technical Symposium in November 1987 of which some parts were published in the July 1990 issue of *Mobile Radio Technology* under the title 'Capacitive bottom-loading tunes mobile antennas'. This emphasised that the technique eliminated the need to change element length for different frequencies or vehicles. K8CFU has sent some selected pages from this article from which the following notes are derived.

"Loading vertical antennas to reduce their physical height is not a new idea. Verticals often are loaded inductively, as with 'top-loading coils' and 'base-loading coils' and capacitively with 'top hats'. The idea of capacitive bottom-loading, although mentioned by K Henny *Principles of Radio*, p462 (John Wiley, 1938) as early as 1938, apparently has not been tested or applied extensively. The authors conducted a series of tests to better define and quantify the capacitive bottom-loading effect. The emphasis in these tests was to determine what range of frequencies could be attained with a fixed height of vertical element by varying the value of the capacitive bottom-loading.

"In deriving the test programme, it was considered that the capacitive bottom-loading effect may be described as follows: As the frequency of operation is raised, an antenna of fixed length looks at its base feedpoint as an increasing resistance in series with a decreasing capacitance. The resulting inductive reactance at the feedpoint must be tuned out, which necessitates the use of capacitive reactance, which is provided by a capacitor. . . . In the tests, a sufficiently accurate impedance bridge was not available, so VSWR data were taken instead. The data and subsequent tests show:

(1) The resonant frequency of a quarter-wavelength vertical antenna used with a counterpoise varies as the size of the ground system (or plate in the design tested) under the counterpoise (in the 450MHz unit this comprises a circular 'wheel' with many wire spokes), the larger the ground system, the lower the resonant frequency.

(2) The resonant frequency of a vertical antenna used with a counterpoise varies with the distance between the counterpoise and the ground. The greater the distance, the higher the resonant frequency.

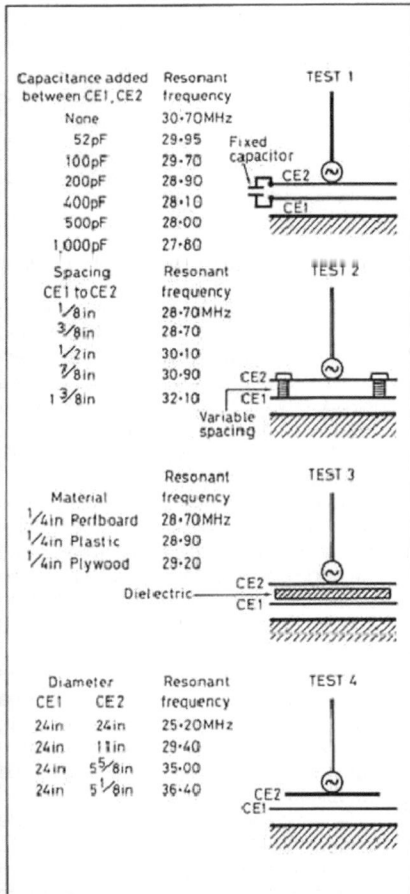

Fig 4: The 28MHz version of the capacitive bottom-loaded antenna showing how its resonant frequency can be changed by bottom-loading without varying the length of the vertical element. The arrangement resulting from Test 4, varying the diameter of CE2, provided an antenna tunable from 25.2 to 36.4MHz.

"In other words, the capacitance between counterpoise and ground acts to capacitively bottom-load the vertical element. In these tests, capacitance was added between the feedpoint and the ground system to supply the required capacitive reactance. By varying the value of this reactance, the frequency at which the base impedance of the antenna is purely resistive, ie its resonant frequency, was varied."

Extensive tests of vertical antennas using this principle have been made on amateur bands from 3.5MHz to 450MHz, including fixed as well as mobile applications. K8CFU has also made some 800MHz versions for use with his (American) cellular telephone: "Each of the antennas boost simple construction because they have fixed, rather than adjustable, whips."

Some test results of various methods of 'tuning' 28MHz antennas are shown in **Fig 4**. It is stated that the 28MHz antenna (presumably the Test 4 version) was tested extensively and found to be tunable from 25.9 to 31.5MHz without changing the height of the vertical element: "On-the-air performance on the amateur 10-metre band was excellent."

Earths, Counterpoises and Radials

Extracted from 'Technical Topics', *Radio Communication*, August 1991

EARTHS, COUNTERPOISES AND RADIALS

THE ITEM "LOW RESISTANCE EARTHING" (*TT*, April) outlined the American military "surface-wire-ground" (SWG) system using a series of short, cruciform-shaped stakes as a means of providing a lower DC earth resistance than the traditional 6ft earth rod. It also referred briefly to the important difference between DC earth resistance (important where the system is used as a *protective earth*) and the RF return-current efficiency when the earth is used to provide the missing half of a monopole or Marconi-type antenna, where RF loss resistance can dramatically reduce radiation efficiency.

As emphasised on many occasions in *TT*, there is growing evidence that elevated radials or even a single quarter-wave counterpoise (which may be physically shortened by inductance loading etc) tend to provide better radiation efficiency (ie lower RF ohmic loss) than all but the most elaborate buried earths, which for broadcast applications may consist of 120 or even 150 buried wires in addition to earth stakes.

The detailed measurements some years ago by Arch Doty, K8CFU, and his friends provided a very strong case for using elevated wire(s) and this has since been further strengthened by NEC-software computer studies reported in *TT*.

As a result of the April item, Allan Taylor, G3JMO, has commented in some detail on the question of 'earths' used as an integral part of vertical monopole antennas. He writes: "Although the SWG system apparently bettered the results of earthing by a 6ft rod in terms of DC resistance compared with 6ft rods, I am very suspicious of its use as part of an antenna system based on my own experiences with the vertical antennas used consistently for over 30 years.

"To judge from results of earthing experiments in my own locality (Redcar, Cleveland), I do not think a series of 10in ground rods would achieve very much, in fact any length of rod is nearly useless in ground which will not carry earth currents - and that goes for most of it. The short-ground-rod philosophy appears to be based on the assumption that earth currents travel near the surface which gets the rain (but dries out easily) whereas formerly it was considered that any ground rod less than three-feet long was of very little use. This can suggest only that the subject of earthing is still uncertain, at least in respect of RF ohmic losses.

"It is well recognized that if a vertical radiator of about a quarter-wavelength is to radiate effectively then its efficiency depends upon the earth creating the antenna's 'mirror image' of the quarter-wave element. Provided that the 'return' earth currents flow back to the feeder, then the antenna radiates, but in practice low earth-conductivity means that such current does not flow readily and the antenna radiates poorly with low efficiency. Indeed, in some circumstances the earth forms virtually a dummy load on the end of the feedline, absorbing most of the transmitter output, particularly where the antenna element is mismatched or mistuned.

"There is thus often a large difference in radiation efficiency between a vertical antenna tuned against ground and one tuned with a counterpoise or radial, either as a 'ground-plane-antenna (GPA)' elevated above ground, or with radial(s) at about ground level. I suspect that the improved results of the American SWG system, if they relate to antenna earth rather than protective earths, may be due more to the counterpoise effect of the circular ring of cables than to the actual short earth rods. Indeed, if the 10in rods are as inefficient at linking the wire to the ground as I suspect they are, the wire may well be acting more as a counterpoise than as a 'true' earth. The improved (ie lower) DC resistance compared to 6ft spikes reported by the Americans may, from the figures quoted, still be far too high in areas of poor earth conductivity, to form an efficient antenna 'mirror image' earth.

"In my experience, most antennas work far better isolated from true earth even by a foot or so, rather than being connected directly to earth as part of the antenna system. If a 'true earth' cannot equal or excel the efficiency of a simple counterpoise, which can be isolated from ground and tuned as part of the antenna system, why bother to use ground in the first place?

"However, this does not include the coaxial feeder; by burying the cable a few inches underground, this will kill off the outer-braid common-mode current and may reduce the pick-up of local electrical interference close to the house (recognising that vertical elements are in any case prone to pick-up more interference than horizontal elements)."

G3JMO discusses other possibilities including the use of balun impedance matching transformers with the feeder earthed at both ends but this is a rather different question to that of SWG earths. He does however point out that the cruciform rods used for SWG look familiar, as he uses MetPosts from a garden centre as guy anchors and finds them very effective in holding the guys of his 30ft vertical; but being painted he would *not* recommend them as short earth rods!

L E Newnham, G6NZ, points out that much information on earths, and the configuration of earth rods (but for protective rather than RF earthing systems) can be found in such books as: *Earth Resistances* by Dr G E Tagg (Newnes, pp258) and *Earth Conduction Effects in Transmission Systems* by Erling D Sunde (Dover Publications, New York, pp370 (rather more mathematical)). I tried to find these in some professional libraries but without success.

Compact Loops for Transmitting

Extracted from 'Technical Topics', *Radio Communication*, October 1991

MORE ON COMPACT LOOP TRANSMITTING ANTENNAS

INTEREST CONTINUES IN the use of compact loop antennas for transmission, for reception and for direction-finding. This month there is space only to consider the development of HF transmitting loops ('magnetic antennas') along the lines described by Roberto Craighero, I1ARZ, in *Radio Communication* (14 MHz and above, Feb 89, pp38-42; 1.8, 3.5 and 7MHz, Feb 1991, pp38-40) and in the various references quoted in his articles, including many *TT* items since 1967 [see also 'Loop Antennas - Facts, not fiction', *RadCom* last month and this, and this month's *Eurotek* - Ed]. Their use has become well established, with few disappointments provided always that the basic design criteria are followed.

Dick Kelsall, G4FM, has rearranged the equations given by Ted Hart, W5QJR, in the 1988 edition of *The ARRL Antenna Book*. He writes: "Quite a number of amateurs are now using small loop antennas basically along the lines originally developed in the 1960s for the US military and finding them of value, particularly if they have a restricted QTH. The equations given by W5QJR provide a most helpful insight into the design of these loops. A little rearrangement makes them easier to use

	14MHz	7MHz
Radiation resistance	0.78Ω	0.048Ω
Loss resistance		
(22mm tube)	0.17Ω	0.012Ω
Efficiency	97.8%	80%
Inductance	4.7 µH	4.7 µH
Reactance	413Ω	206.6Ω
Tuning Capacitance	27.5pF	110pF
Q	435	3443

The last three values are readily calculated from the preceding ones.

ANTENNA TOPICS

and to decide on the best size for the bands required.

"In designing a loop it is convenient to think in terms of circumference (S) only and to express the enclosed area of a loop (A) in terms of S: $A = S^2 / (4\Pi)$. Further it helps to use "S x F" (circumference x frequency) as the variable when plotting radiation resistance (R_r), loss resistance (R_l) and efficiency. Since wavelength (metres) x frequency (MHz) = 300, one can see from the graphs (**Fig 6**) where the practical limits to loop circumference lie (0.125 to 0.25λ). Working in feet, 300 becomes the familiar number of 984.

"For example, a loop to cover 7 to 14MHz would need to have a circumference of about 0.125 λ on 7MHz and 0.25λ on 14MHz. Thus 14 x S = 246 for the quarter-wave on 14MHz, giving S = 17.6ft, ie a loop diameter of 5.6ft." From the graphs, **Table 1** can be produced.

Several novel features are to be found in the loop antennas initially designed by Zygmund Chowaniec, G3PTN, and subsequently also constructed, in a slightly different form, by G H Lucas, G3TWE. Both loops are intended primarily for efficient operation on 7MHz, but function with lower efficiency on 3.5MHz (G3TWE also mentions 10MHz).

G3PTN writes: "I started two years ago with a loop for the higher end of the HF spectrum, made along orthodox lines. My conclusion was that there is not much to be gained in performance in comparison with a good dipole antenna if you have space for this. (A point emphasised in I1ARZ's 1989 article - *G3VA*). However, the situation is different on the lower HF spectrum where there are a number of benefits, size being but one.

"For optimum efficiency, the circumference should be about 5 or 10% less than a quarter-wave at the required frequency. To construct a loop from 25mm or 30mm copper tubing presents a number of problems since, unless the tubing can be formed into a circle, it is likely to be made into a square, hexagon or octagon, introducing joint resistance with consequent lowering of the Q.

"I decided to use coaxial cable, rather than tubing, but instead of using a single loop I constructed two loops in parallel, along the lines of a folded dipole, spaced 3in apart. My cable is standard ¼in (RG8U) coax, 32ft per loop, forming an 8ft square (using quad-like spreaders and a centre pole). This loop is designed for maximum efficiency on 7MHz.

"According to computer calculations, such spaced cables offer a performance roughly similar to that of 3in-diameter tubing. Predicted and measured bandwidths agree.

"Mechanically, it is rather difficult to mount a tuning capacitor at the top of a loop. Current distribution in the loop is approximately uniform but nevertheless there is maximum current opposite the high-voltage open gap across which the tuning capacitor is connected. It is thus advantageous, both mechanically and electrically, to have the capacitor at the base of the loop and the coupling loop at the top, the reverse of the orthodox arrangement. In practice, such an arrangement appears to give improved performance for a given height of the loop over ground. No adverse effect was apparent from the capacitor being at the lower end.

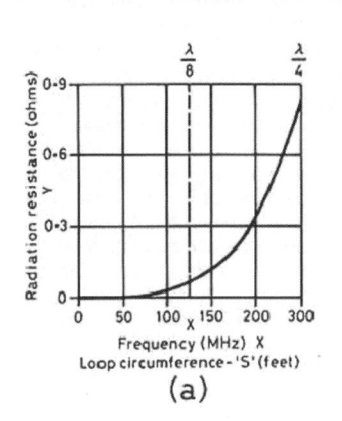

(a)

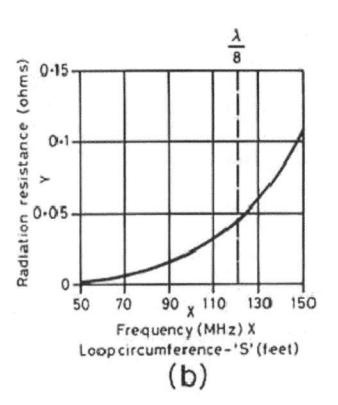

(b)

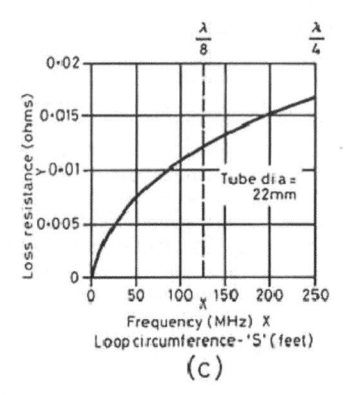

(c)

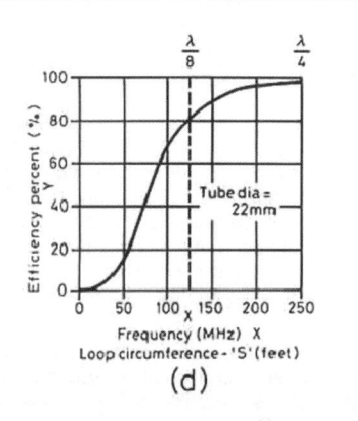

(d)

Fig 6: A useful series of graphs by G4FM to aid the design of compact loop transmitting antennas. (a) Radiation resistance; (b) Radiation resistance (expanded for low frequency x circumference products); (c) Loss resistance (25mm tubing); (d) Efficiency; (e) Inductance.

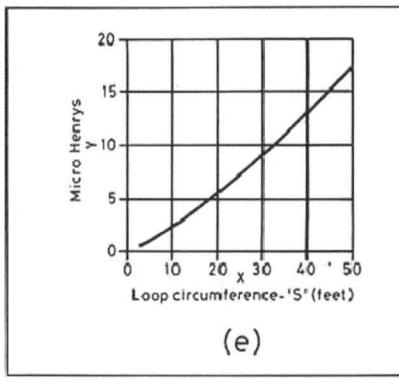

(e)

"It appears to be common practice for the coupling loop to be half-shielded rather than a true Faraday shield. The reason may be that this can make it easier to obtain a unity SWR. It is accepted that there is a definite relationship between the conductor sizes of the link coupling and of the antenna loop, a factor of five or ten or so. If the link is made of RG8 cable with 25mm tubing, this will result in a shielded-half of a ratio 25:1. A loop made on the lines as above produced at best a 1.4:1 SWR. A loop constructed of RG8 cable, using outer as a conductor, produced immediately 1:1 SWR. A Faraday shield was made using aluminium foil all the way round, reducing the pick-up of local electrical interference etc with the SWR remaining 1:1."

G3PTN's notes are rather cryptic and it seems useful to add comments made by G H Lucas, G3TWE, even though to some extent these duplicate the statements of G3PTN. G3TWE writes:

"To re-cap, the basic design criteria for a compact loop antenna:

(a) Ohmic resistance must be minimum;

(b) Area enclosed must be maximum, hence a circular loop gives better performance than an equivalent square;

(c) The Q must be maximum even though this will result in very low bandwidth at the lower frequencies; any attempt to earth the main loop at the current node will degrade the Q;

(d) The tuning capacitor *must* be of the highest quality, with wide spacing and preferably split-stator. This is expensive, if bought new, but costs can be re-couped in the construction of the main loop; my 3.5/7/10MHz loop cost £85, the cost of the capacitor and its motorised drive;

(e) The diameter of the conductor of the main loop must be as large as possible, preferably about 50mm copper tubing with no soldered connections or joints, where only a single loop is to be used.

"The problem presented by (e) can be overcome by using two 10m lengths of good coaxial cable, inners and outers strapped together in parallel and spaced by about 4in.

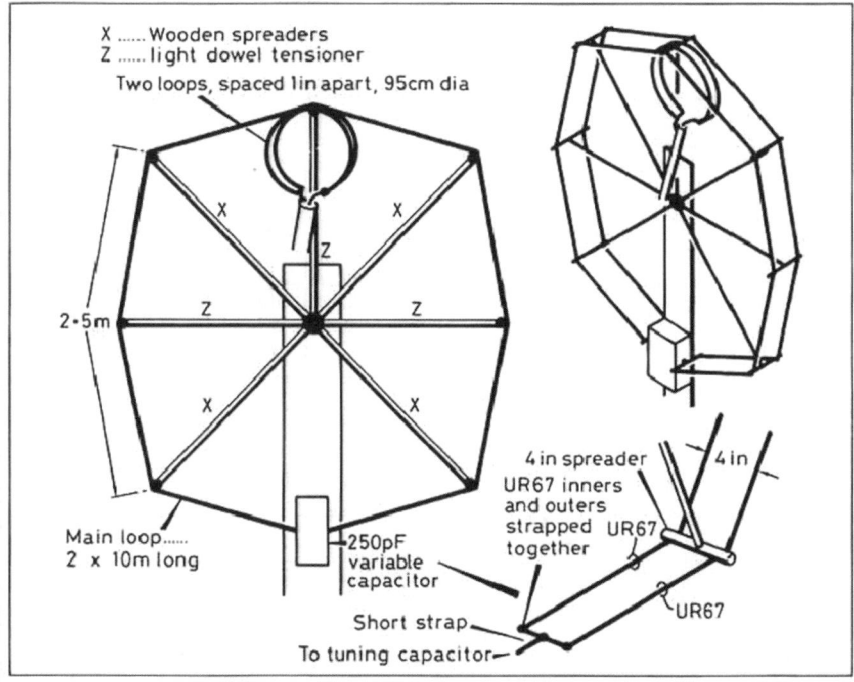

Fig 7: G3TWE's version of the two-coaxial-cable loop antenna originally developed by G3PTN.

This, to RF, will look like 50mm or more copper tubing. G3PTN uses RG8U, I use UR67, the conductors being braced by diagonal spreaders to form a square, and then tensioned further by light-weight spreaders to push the complete assembly into the form of an octagon, thus nearly satisfying (b) above: see **Fig 7**.

"The capacitor assembly in its box weighs about 2kg. It seems poor engineering practice to have this waving about at the top. As with the G3PTN original, the whole antenna is turned upside-down: the capacitor at the bottom, the coupling loop at the top. It must be remembered that there maybe up to 5kV of RF at the tuning capacitor - the antenna should be sited or protected so that there is no likelihood of any person (particularly children) or pets etc coming in to contact with high RF voltages.

"The diameter of the coupling loop is not critical; anything between 10 to 20% of the diameter of the main loop should be satisfactory. What is critical is the ratio of the size of the materials used in the loops (compare to the principles of gamma matching for Yagi arrays). Anyone who is unable to obtain a better SWR than about 1.3:1 with an accurately tuned loop is probably using the wrong gauge of conductor in the coupling loop. My coupling loop is again fabricated from two turns of the same UR67 cable used in the main loop, inners and outers strapped and spaced about 1in. This spacing may be varied to adjust the SWR for optimum on the highest frequency band, the lower bands will then follow.

"The loop will work with normal inductive coupling and it is unnecessary to go to the complication of using Faraday or half-Faraday coupling until development work is completed. SWR and transmitter performance will not be affected. However, there is considerable advantage to be gained in terms of static and electrical noise level in the receive-mode by using a full Faraday screen on the coupling loop. G3PTN has achieved this by threading the coupling loop through a length of garden hose and wrapping the whole issue in aluminium foil.

"Mounting: If the loop is to be mounted horizontally then it should be well up in the air - preferably a half-wave above ground. In most cases, however, such a loop will be mounted in the vertical plane and can be just a few feet above ground. My loop has its bottom about 1m off the ground, with the top about 4m high, partly concealed in fruit trees and mounted on the side of a garden shed. As with any high-Q antenna the loop should be in the clear as far as is possible. There is an advantage in elevating the assembly off the ground.

"Despite the satisfactory performance of this type of loop antenna, I still feel that it would be outperformed by a really good half-wave dipole in the clear, by one or two S points. But where real-estate is limited and a low visual impact is considered essential, a well-engineered loop is capable of surprisingly good results."

Counterpoises & Elevated Radials

Extracted from 'Technical Topics', *Radio Communication*, November 1991

COUNTERPOISES AND ELEVATED RADIALS

THE AUGUST ITEM 'Earths, counterpoises and radials' emphasised that there is growing evidence (I am tempted to write 'proof') that buried earths, even when there are a large number of buried radials or several deeply-sunk earth rods, should be avoided wherever possible as part of an antenna system. The remarks on this topic from Allan Taylor, G3JMO, in his criticism of the American 'surface wire ground' (SWG, *TT* April 1991), rang a bell for Arch Doty, K8CFU, who has done so much to re-awaken us to the advantages of the nearly forgotten 'counterpoise' approach. He writes: "Several years ago some of the data we collected on earth conductivity was published by the IEEE and in *QST* but was largely ignored (I suppose only real antenna nuts can be expected to show much interest in the topic of earth conductivity!). The data based on my daily measurements showed clearly that even in areas of relatively good earth conductivity this varies significantly over a period of months: **Fig 3**. If short ground rods are used, as with the US Army SWG system, it is obvious that, if used as part of the antenna system, the return ground currents (which vary with earth conductivity and on which the efficiency of the antenna will depend), will be unpredictable, to say the least. I feel that G3JMO's conclusions are right on the mark!"

G3JMO, himself, in a follow-up letter, traces the concept of using the earth as part of an antenna system back to the era of very long wave communications (wavelengths of thousands of metres) as used by Marconi in the first decades of the Century: "From there it was natural that amateurs should carry on this practice for '200 metres and down' since it is not easily recognised that the shorter the wavelength, the less efficient and less appropriate becomes the use of the Earth as part of a radio transmission system. To some extent amateurs were lead astray in carrying on long-wave practice down into the short-wave region.

"If radio had developed directly from the dipole-like 'antenna' structures of Hertz who in the pre-Marconi era experimented with spark equipment on very short wavelengths, it is possible that the concept of using the Earth as part of a tuned antenna (eg Marconi Antenna or verticals at ground level) would never have caught on.

"That a number of amateurs in the 1920s appear to have recognised the value of antenna systems not directly connected to earth can be seen from George Jessop's all-too-short but fascinating *Bright Sparks of Wireless* (RSGB) where references to the then popular and clearly effective 'counterpoise' approach appear on pages 15, 26, 27 and 37 - not bad considering the relatively few stations described. It would seem that amateurs in general have, over the years, been using very-long-wave techniques for short-wave radio and paying the price in terms of efficiency and unpredictability."

The early stations referred to as using counterpoises in G6JP's book were those of H W Pope, PZX (later G3HT); E J Simmonds, 2OD (one of the most active and successful pioneers of the short waves in the early twenties); the receiving station of W R Wade of Clifton for the 1921 Transatlantic Tests (although in this case the counterpoise was buried); and that of Jack Partridge, 2KF who was the first British amateur to make two-way contact with the USA on 200 metres and who used "a five-wire counterpoise mounted some 7ft above the ground with an antenna of the L-type with three wires 60ft long in parallel at a

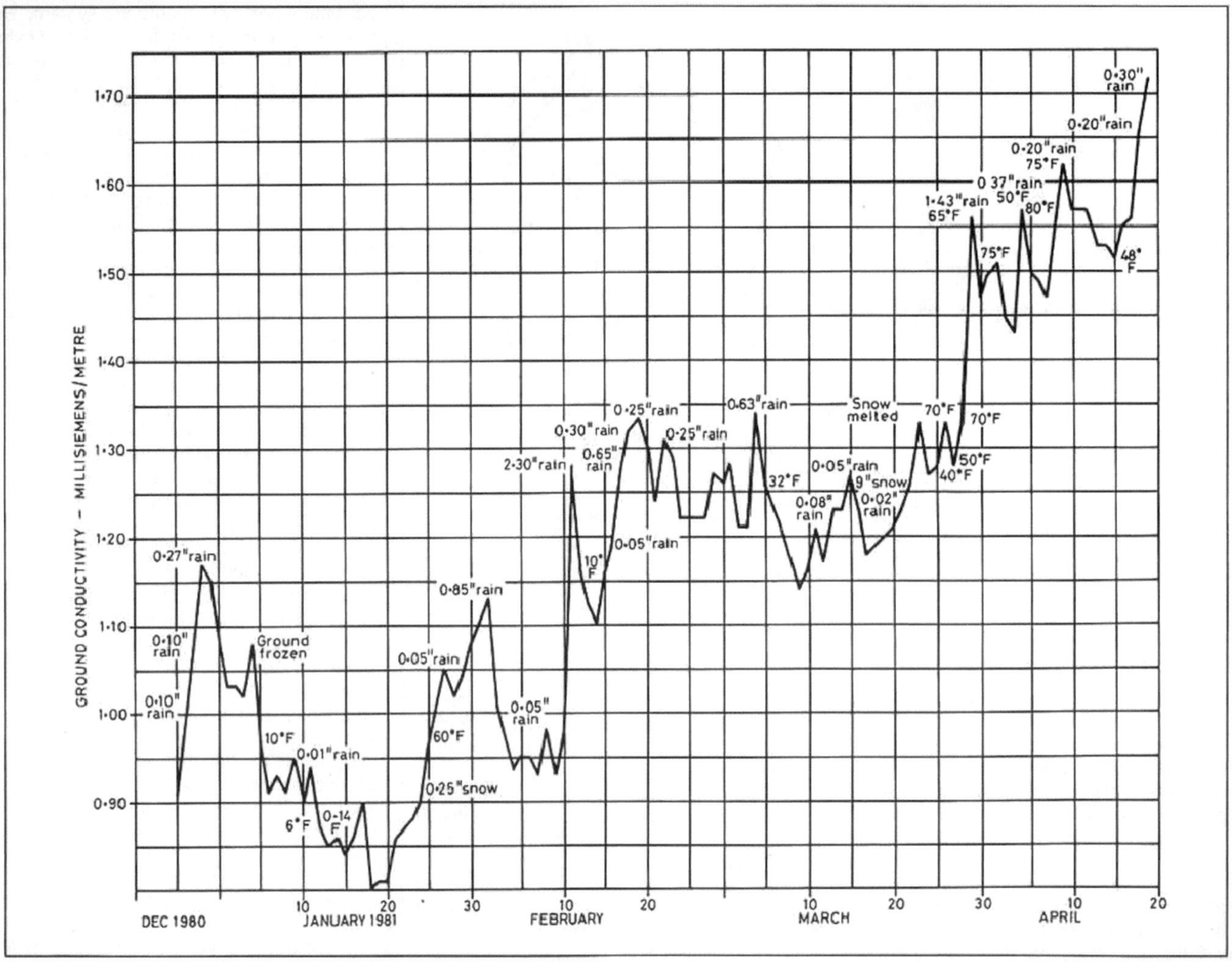

ANTENNA TOPICS

Fig 3: Ground conductivity measured over some four months during 1980-81 at K8CFU's test site at Fletcher, North Carolina shows that conductivity varies significantly under different weather conditions.

height of 50ft."

The single-wire counterpoise remained popular in the 1930s and I recall using one for Top Band in 1938 and also putting one up at Helmond, Holland in 1944 for use with a Whaddon Mk III transmitter. The popularity of a large number of buried radials stems from Dr George Brown's classic study of *medium-wave* broadcast antennas in the 1930s.

Balanced Active Receiving Loops

Extracted from 'Technical Topics', *Radio Communication*, November 1991

BALANCED ACTIVE RECEIVING LOOPS

J A LAMBERT, G3FMZ, in a full-length article 'A directional active loop receiving antenna system' in *RadCom*, November 1982, pp944-949 described in detail the development by C&S Antennas Ltd of a novel form of resistance-loaded compact receiving loop antenna with an associated 2 - 30MHz wideband matching pre-amplifier. This provided a cardioid (heart-shaped) horizontal radiation pattern rather than the usual figure-of-eight pattern. Such loops were then (and possibly still are) being marketed for use at professional receiving stations, usually with a number of loops forming an endfire or broadside directional array suitable for permanent, temporary or portable use. G3FNZ provided constructional details of an experimental loop with an 0.5W carbon non-inductive resistor (value between 47 and 100 Ohms) connected across the top of the loop with the matching amplifier across the base junction: **Fig 4**.

Dick Rollema, PA0SE had his attention drawn by PA0EZ to a contribution to the IEE's *Electronics Letters* (18 July 1991, pp1320-21) by P V Brennan and Y Valverde of University College, London. This shows how the C&S type of unbalanced loop can be changed into balanced form by using two resistors and a balanced feed arrangement, maintaining the cardioid pattern but not suffering from the problems associated with the requirement of an unbalanced antenna for a solid ground connection, which becomes particularly important in the lower HF spectrum.

To quote their introductory remarks: "An antenna with a cardioid radiation pattern can be produced by taking an electrically smaller circular loop and introducing an imbalancing resistance in the top of the loop, as shown in **Fig 5**. This is the basis of a commercially produced antenna for HF reception purposes which includes a low noise amplifier mounted at the base of the loop.

"The antenna, being electrically small, has a very low radiation efficiency, but this is of little concern in HF reception applications, because the system is usually limited by external noise . . . . The antenna relies on a ground plane connection to one side of the loop, without which a figure-of-eight would be obtained, and this can often be difficult to achieve in the HF band. A stake may be driven into the ground for this purpose or the trailing coaxial cable may be used as a pseudo-ground plane; in both cases it is found that the antenna pattern varies quite considerably depending on the quality of the ground connection and/or the position of the coaxial cable. For this reason, it is attractive to consider a balanced version of the antenna that does not require a ground connection".

Of interest also is that they describe a scaled down prototype antenna of this type suitable for use between 40 and 600MHz, presenting measurements made between 150 and 200MHz which shows that a good performance may be obtained without the need for a ground connection or careful placing of the feed cable. It would thus appear that this technique might be useful, for example, for 144MHz D/F.

Their prototype antenna (**Fig 6(a)**) consists of a printed rectangular loop, of 3mm track width, with a 180° hybrid for the balun and an MMIC amplifier mounted within the loop. The resistor values required for a good cardioid pattern were found not to be critical and were in the same range as for the original unbalanced antenna. The antenna was measured in a relatively small anechoic chamber, using a dipole as the source antenna. **Fig 6(b)** shows the radiation pattern (linear scale) at 200MHz, with a front-to-back ratio of some 17dB and the field pattern dropping "quite convincingly" to -6dB at +/- 90° from the main beam direction.

Incidentally, Dick Rollema, PA0SE questions the mathematics (not given in the *TT* digest) of the Canadian VHF D/F loop with half of the coaxial-cable screening braid removed (*TT*, June 1991 p29) which is claimed

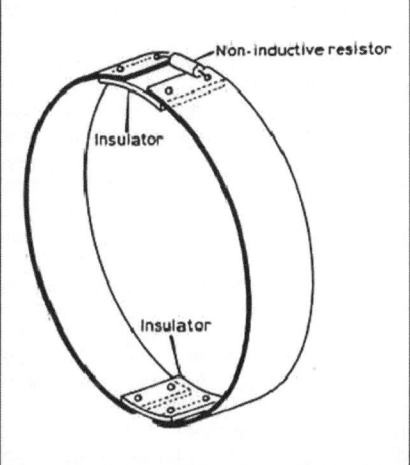

Fig 4: The experimental 3 - 30MHz HF unbalanced active-antenna described (with associated matching pre-amplifier) by G3FNZ in *RadCom* November 1982. The 1m-diameter loop is made from a 150mm-wide strip of 16SWG aluminium, cut into two parts and then rejoined using two blocks of insulating material. The amplifier is mounted and connected across the lower insulator, with a 47 to 100-Ohm non-inductive resistor across the top insulator. Cardioid horizontal radiation pattern.

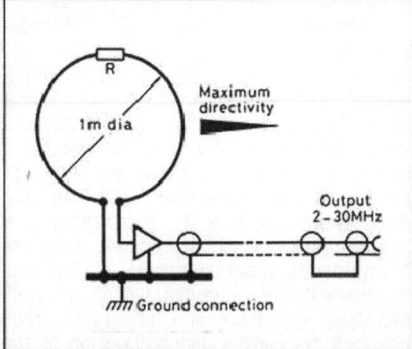

Fig 5: Unbalanced HF active loop receiving antenna system as originally described by G3FNZ of C&S Antennas Ltd.

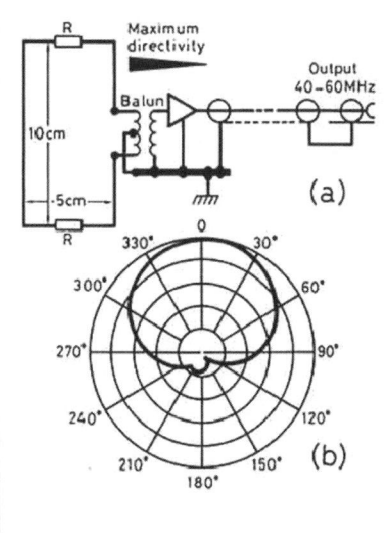

Fig 6: (a) Balanced form of the prototype active VHF/UHF loop antenna as a scaled down version intended for HF reception. (b) Radiation pattern of the prototype at 200MHz showing operation without the need for an earth or ground-plane.

to give a cardioid pattern with a single deep null. He points out that in their paper it is assumed that there is uniform current distribution on the loop; however since this is a 'half-wave' in circumference this cannot be the case, although it would apply to electrically very small loops. I am not clear whether this error in any way affects practical results and it would be interesting to learn whether anyone has any comments based on a practical test. In fact the authors seem to have tried to put together possible theoretical explanations to fit their practical results, so possibly this theoretical error is of little practical consequence.

Horizontal Loops + 1.8MHz

Extracted from 'Technical Topics', *Radio Communication*, December 1991

HORIZONTAL LOOPS PLUS 1.8MHZ

WHILE THE 'SUNSPOT MAXIMUM' year of 1989 was, on the whole, rather disappointing in not yielding exceptionally good HF propagation periods, this has not been true of 1991 when the rich mixture of sunspots, geomagnetic activity and solar flares has seen periods when it has been possible to enjoy worldwide contacts with low-power or 'pieces of string' antennas or even both! This means that one may have to discount slightly some claims for antennas put up during 1991.

Nevertheless, there seems little doubt that the large horizontal loop has now established itself as a reliable performer on all bands from 3.5 to 28MHz (and probably also on 50MHz). *TT*, September 1990 and February 1991 presented some of the attractions of the large loop for multiband operation, even when suspended from supports considerably lower than the 50ft masts used by W1FB. As illustrated again in the September 1990 survey, the attractions of large wire loops in either the horizontal or (quad type) vertical planes were outlined by S M de Wet, ZS6AKA, as long ago as June, 1972 (and even earlier by G2PL when he reported excellent results using a quad antenna with its reflector element resting on the ground). Today, at last, this type of antenna is enjoying considerable popularity even among those with only limited-size gardens.

Mike Hollebon, G4HOL, is particularly enthusiastic. He writes: "Following the *TT* items on horizontal loop antennas I put one up early this year (1991). A whole new world of DX has opened up for me. Using the familiar 1005/F formula, I cut mine for 3.55MHz, with resonances at approximately 7.1, 14.2, 21.3 and 28.4MHz.

"In switching checks on 3.5MHz in conjunction with my well-trusted 0.25λ sloper (66ft support) the loop was consistently some 9dB better - a tremendous boost for my 50W FT7B transceiver. The DX rolls in on 28/21/14MHz and I flabbergast 3.5/7MHz operators when I tell them I have only a FT-7B. My loop is an irregular four-sided affair fed at one corner with 300-ohm slotted-ribbon feeder. I can tune it nicely from 3.5 to 28MHz with my Nevada TM1000 ATU. As it is only 21ft above ground level, I am patiently waiting for the supporting trees to grow..."

A new twist to the use of a modified horizontal loop has come from Jean M Bourdereau, F1LCl, (Champniers, France) who has investigated methods of using his horizontal loop as a top-fed grounded Marconi antenna on 1.8MHz well suited to his attic shack, and with some affinity to the G3BDQ 'Steeple' antenna (or the earlier G8ON 1.8MHz antenna), making it a 'top-fed, top-cap antenna for top-band'.

His ideas took shape in 1990 but he has since upgraded the system and also completed an analysis with ELNEC software. His QTH, with a useful sized garden, is in a small village but near the Angouleme airfield so that a low profile approach is an advantage. He realised that he could take advantage of ZS6AKA's observation that "when the input is balanced, the furthest mid-point may be earthed" (originally adopted to form a static leakage path in thunderstorm-prone South Africa). F1LCI saw that earthing the loop and shorting the balanced feeder would transform the loop antenna into a top-fed inverted-L antenna with, in effect, capacitance loading by the two sides of the loop, providing a vertically-polarized component for DX operation on 1.8 and 3.5MHz etc.

He writes: "My loop is one full wavelength for 3.5MHz, and rectangular (18 by 24m) to fit my garden. Its mean height is 12m (varying between 8 and 14m). The higher (further) end is now grounded and supported by a fishing rod and telescopic mast, placed on a large aluminium plate (1m squared), to which are connected 20 radials and the neighbours' fences (**Fig 3**). The opposite end is connected to open-wire twin-line running 10m to the house roughly horizontally. It comes into the attic where there is a relay which provides

ANTENNA TOPICS

the option of two transmission lines to my rig (my shack is in another part of the attic). The relay gives the options of: (a) open wire line and inductive coupler in the shack for 3.5/28MHz, which gives a horizontal loop antenna, grounded against static; and (b) the relay short-circuits the outdoor open-wire line and connects it to coaxial cable, providing the 'vertical mode' for the lower frequency bands. A 2nd 'matchbox' (SPC) tuner is in the shack, but could be moved close to the relay.

"Results: Immunity to static with no more sparks in the inductive coupler due to the permanent grounding of the antenna. In the horizontal mode, grounding the loop at a current maximum does not effect performance and pattern (as stated by ZS6AKA and verified with ELNEC). In the vertical mode, which I prefer to consider as a 'top-fed Marconi' rather than a 'half loop' à la VE2CV, since the size is not right for a half-loop and one leg is in the house. There are some points in common with G3BDQ's 'steeple antenna' (*RadCom*, August 1986, pp556-568, 575) which I tried without as much success, as this design.

"Vertical-mode operation is of no interest above 14MHz. On 10MHz it permits filling in some notches in the horizontal-mode pattern. On 7 and 3.5MHz the vertical mode has less high-elevation gain but noise is stronger; again the major lobes are 90° apart. On 1.8MHz the horizontal loop is practically unusable for transmitting. But the ground connection and shorting the feeders (ie vertical mode) makes it function like a top-loaded vertical. The horizontal pattern is quasi-circular, the vertical one seems closer to a pure vertical than a conventional inverted-L, as if the two paths in the loop tend to cancel some radiation from the cap."

F1LCI has provided much information and comments on the ELNEC computer analysis of this antenna but this would require considerable space to reproduce. He does however also provide some constructional tips, as well as mentioning that one of his projects will be to try adding some short counterpoise wires.

On construction, he writes: "Fishing rod (fibreglass cheaper than carbon fibre): choose a non-telescopic one and discard the last segment. Flexibility provides resistance to French gales provided that three levels of nylon cord guys are used. With the loop stretched, the end will stay lightly bent. Inside, use the biggest wire available (eg piece of hi-fi 'esoteric' loudspeaker cable - very expensive - or similar less costly wire).

"Loop: no precise dimensions but the two arms must be equal. One approach is to take a 100m reel and fold it; solder the mid-point to the vertical, with the remainder (after forming the loop) used for the open-wire line (any spacing). The whole system can easily be erected by one man, provided the wires do not get entangled in branches. Make connections between copper wire and aluminium with stainless steel bolts and washers."

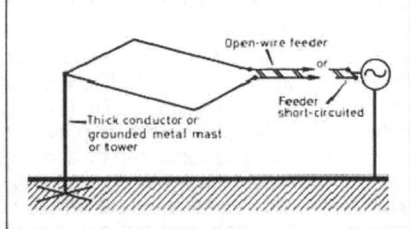

Fig 3: The 84-metre multiband horizontal loop used by F1LCI from his attic shack. It can be switched to form a vertical-mode top-fed Marconi antenna for 1.8MHz DX working.

Optimisation of Yagi Arrays

Extracted from 'Technical Topics', *Radio Communication*, December 1991

GAIN OPTIMIZATION OF YAGI ARRAYS.

OVER THE YEARS, AMATEURS have built some very large and complex antennas, but I cannot help feeling that the recent efforts of a troika of veteran Californian amateurs (combined ages total 178 years) would take some beating. Jack Hachten, Bud Ansley and Dan Bathker (W6TSW, W6VPH and K6BLG) have drawn on their professional expertise and Method of Moments software in building a gain-optimised 13-element, divided-boom, Yagi array for 14MHz, in an area 10 by 100 metres, with the elements 25 metres above ground. This is briefly described in 'A Modern Giant Yagi' (*IEEE Antennas & Propagation Magazine*, June 1991, pp19-21).

The structure, using MININEC, has thirteen widely-spaced elements mounted on six towers as a fixed beam. It is located in Southern California with a boresight 15 degrees East of True North, a great-circle heading to cover selected portions of Europe and Asia. The azimuth beamwidth is slightly less than +/- 15° to the 3dB points. First used in February 1991, it very quickly became evident that the performance in both transmission and reception equalled or exceeded all expectations. The elements are arranged for a considered balance between forward gain, side-lobe level, impedance level, bandwidth, structural wind survival and construction economies, with emphasis on forward gain. Using Brian Beezley's, K6STI, MN-software some 15,000 machine-aided EM design iterations were made, although it is emphasised also that 'indispensable human judgement, experience and strategy remained necessary ingredients'. But without such (PC-implemented) method-of-moments analysis and weighted, multi-parameter optimization, such a project would not likely to be initiated. The wire and optimization codes have enabled such a large undertaking to be approached with high confidence.

According to the authors, the 100m (divided boom) antenna operates at a centre frequency of 14.150MHz. The design provides a comfortably-high feed-point resistance (30Ω) with an impedance bandwidth (VSWR = 1.5) somewhat more than 2%. In free space, the predicted directivity is +15.8dBi. The predicted directivity is fully +21.5dBi at a favourably-low elevation angle, when arrayed over low conductivity (in fact, good dielectric) ground. The actual power gain is 0.1dB less at the feed point, due to calculated element dissipations, and 0.5dB less again, due to the loss in the 55m of cable between the feed point and the transmitter/receiver. Each element is built with heavy-wall aluminium tubing, starting in the centre with 32mm diameter, stepped twice, and ending with 19mm diameter at the tips. Each of the six, 75mm-diameter boom segments (on the six towers) measures 9m. To assure EM field purity in the six-tower environment, the topmost tower guys are dielectric. A conductor-free zone of a half-wavelength (minimum) radius is thus provided for the intended horizontal polarization.

This monster has been tested in comparison with an adjacent, well-constructed and widely-spaced five-element rotary Yagi, having a similar high feed-point resistance and overall efficiency - an antenna that I guess most of us would be more than content with!

As somebody who continues to believe in KISS and simple, negligible-cost wire antennas (tree and house supported), I nevertheless believe that a remarkable project such as this Californian monster antenna has a valuable role to play. This is emphasised in the accompanying editorial by W Ross Stone, editor of the *IEEE A&P Magazine*: "I once designed and built a professional one-kilometre long, 32-element, vertically-pointed array of crossed Yagi antennas. In doing so, I came to understand just how crazy I really was. It is thus with true awe that I present to you the article on a 100 metre Yagi.... (This) is important for two reasons. First, it provides unequivocal proof of the power of the Yagi design - as well as of the knowledge, the design tools, and the engineering expertise of the authors. Second, it is a testament that the amateur radio roots of our profession are alive, flourishing and continuing to set examples (or, at least, landmarks!) for us."

In the same issue of the *IEEE A&P Magazine*, David K Cheng (Syracuse University) reviews his work in the 1960s on 'Gain Optimization for Yagi-Uda Arrays' (pp42-45) that shows clearly why it has taken some 60 years really to come to grips with this deceptive simple-looking antenna. He writes: "Although the geometrical arrangement of a Yagi-Uda array appears simple, it's optimization is a different problem, mainly because there are many interdependent variables .... Since all the elements are electromagnetically coupled, the adjustment of any one of these variables changes the current distributions on all the elements. The optimization process cannot follow a one-variable-at-a-time procedure; all variables must be adjusted at the same time."

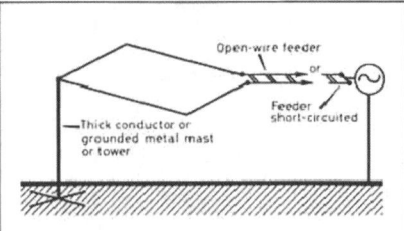

Fig 3: The 84-metre multiband horizontal loop used by F1LCI from his attic shack. It can be switched to form a vertical-mode top-fed Marconi antenna for 1.8MHz DX working.

He notes that: "Many early studies of Yagi-Uda arrays made the basic assumption that the current distributions along all the array elements were sinusoidal. This assumption is not true, and the deviations from sinusoidal current distributions are critical in the calculations of the conditions for optimum gain...."

He concludes: "The evolution of the research work that my former students and I carried out.... went through several stages, and we overcame a number of difficulties. With both spacing and length perturbations, we were able to find the optimized array analytically in a systematic way - some examples having gain increases of nearly 80%. The effects of finite dipole radius and mutual coupling were included in the theoretical treatment. Yagi-Uda arrays are used extensively in practice; but manufacturers have not been pressed to offer arrays with an optimum gain, because most users have scant idea of what gain or directivity is. It is hoped that our work will eventually have an impact on the design of Yagi-Uda arrays.

"We have, in fact, more recently looked further into the problem of increasing the gain of Yagi-Uda arrays, based upon an observation by Landstorfer, that properly-shaped wire antennas (**Fig 5**) longer than a wavelength, could yield a higher directivity than straight dipoles (see *TT*, December 1982). By assuming a sinusoidal distribution that did not change with the shape or the radius of the dipole, he obtained a dipole geometry for maximum directivity by a piecewise-linear approximation. He also found by experimentation that a 3-element Yagi-Uda array of shaped wires, each 1.5λ long, could be adjusted to yield a maximum gain of 11.5dBi (**Fig 6**). We managed to put Landstorfer's results on a firm analytical basis, by applying the method for function minimisation. We found the optimum shapes (bent like bows), as well as the positions of the array elements, both of which depend on the radius of the wire dipoles. The calculated current distributions on the shaped dipoles differ markedly from sinusoids (*Electronics* Letters, September 1982 pp816-818 and *IEEE Trans Ant & Prop*, May 1983)."

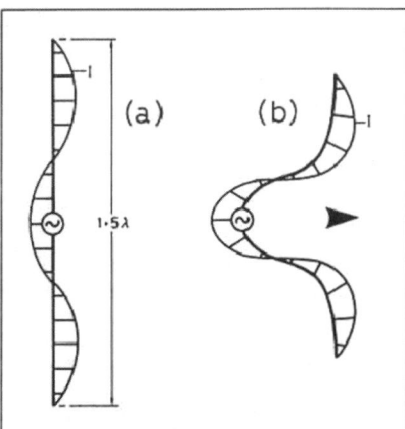

Fig 5: The current distribution on (a) a straight 1.5λ dipole where the phase reversal reduces radiation normal to the axis of the dipole; (b) A 1.5λ dipole with a gain-optimized shape producing maximum radiation in the forward direction (F M Landstorfer, 1982).

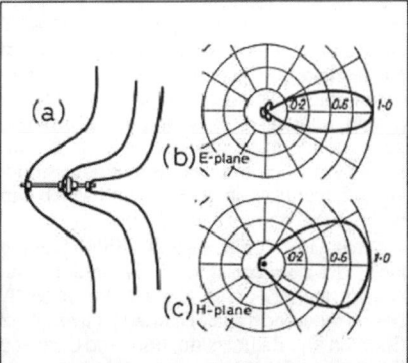

Fig 6: A Yagi array using three Landstorfer gain-optimized 1.5λ elements. A VHF array of this type provided a gain of 11.5dBi, sidelobe attenuation better than 20dB, and a front-to-back ratio of 26dB.

Indoor VK2ABQ-type 28MHz Beam

Extracted from 'Technical Topics', *Radio Communication*, January 1992

AN INDOOR 'VK2ABQ-TYPE' 28MHZ BEAM

IT IS VIRTUALLY impossible to predict how well or how badly an indoor transmitting antenna will behave among so many lossy materials: electrical wiring, water tanks and radiators and general domestic metalwork. Roof-space and attic-room antennas usually work reasonably well, rooms lower in a building or in tower-block apartment can vary from just acceptable to downright poor, compared with a similar antenna erected outside the house. For VHF operation, an antenna - foil or wire - taped to a window can give excellent results in the directions away from the building but tend to be pretty poor in the opposite directions where the building and contents will tend to attenuate signals by some 10dB or so - more in a reinforced concrete structure. Nevertheless, DX operation on HF is often possible. *TT* (September 1990, pp31-32 and July 1991, p26) gave brief information on W9BRD's 'Zapper' antennas (a form of unidirectional W8JK driven array) which he finds effective for working into Europe from the Chicago area.

Tony Baker, G3JSF, has found early retirement an incentive to get back on the bands with his TS520 transceiver after an interval of some eight years. One result is that he has devised a novel form of a single-band VK2ABQ compact array that gives his signal some gain and directivity, while fulfilling his belief in low-cost KISS philosophy and the value of lateral thinking.

In effect, he uses a fixed VK2ABQ-type of square wire structure arranged so that he can direct signals towards any one of the four quadrants simply by changing the feed point and inserting a 'jumper' wire across the opposite gap. As shown in **Fig 1**, the antenna comprises four quarter-wave lengths of wire - AB, BC, CD and DA - arranged with gaps at the points A, B, C and D. The array can be fed at any of the four points, A, B, C and D from 75Ω cable terminated with a couple of crocodile (alligator) clips. If fed at A, a jumper wire (about 2") similarly with crocodile clips is connected across gap C. Then to change direction in steps of 90°, the feedpoint and jumper are changed as required.

G3JSF writes: "I am currently using crocodile clips on the feeder and on the jumper wire. By using coax with no balun and then reversing the 'inner' and 'outer' connections at the feed-point, some slewing of the main lobe can be achieved. Direction of fire can be changed in about 30 seconds. My Monimatch SWR meter indicates an almost perfect match to 75Ω cable, flat from 28.3 to 28.7MHz. Standard DIY connecting strip is used to fix this beam horizontally to the ceiling of the room next to the shack, fixing the corners also with the same connector strip. This allows a good mechanical/electrical connection as the feed point is changed. Used with a home-brewed ATU and low-pass filter there is a complete absence of any TV/radio/telephone breakthrough and I find that I can put out a signal on 28MHz with around 90% success rate on the first call.

"Results have included RS58-9 from the Falklands, Brazil, etc. 59+ East Coast USA, 55-8 West Coast, RS58 Japan, 52 New Zealand, 59++ short skip. When not in use, the coaxial cable is simply coiled up and put away. If white PVC covered wire is used for the elements together with the clear connecting blocks for fixing, the beam itself is unobtrusive. The beam also provides a great talking point with my contacts!"

Clearly such a 28MHz beam could be put up in quite a small room sized some 9ft by 9ft. A 21MHz version would often be possible, although a 14MHz version would need a fair-sized room or a roof-space with easy access. But with different sites, different buildings, there can be no guarantee of achieving the same DX results as G3JSF. It can also prove difficult to clear EMC problems when using indoor antennas. But it should not cost more than a few pounds to give the idea a try-out should you be unable to put up an outside antenna giving the required directivity.

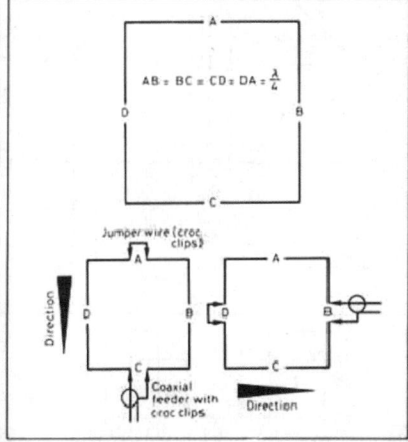

Fig 1: (a) Basic form of the indoor VK2ABQ-type antenna developed by G3JSF. (b) Showing how the directivity is changed by changing the feeder point and the jumper wire to form a driven element and reflector.

ANTENNA TOPICS

A 144MHz Unipole

Extracted from 'Technical Topics', *Radio Communication*, January 1992

A 144MHZ UNIPOLE ANTENNA

THE CONVENTIONAL quarter-wave 144MHz vertically-polarized rod antenna for repeater/mobile operation with horizontal radials (or metal ground plate) has a feedpoint impedance of under 20Ω. This can be raised either by sloping the radials downwards or by lengthening the element slightly so that it is no longer an electrical quarter-wave. Another rather more elegant solution is the 'unipole' (folded-monopole element) which has the added advantage of increasing the bandwidth of the antenna.

Constructional details of a 144MHz unipole antenna are given by Des Greenham, VK3CO in the WIA's *Amateur Radio* (October 1991, p14). He writes:

"Performance of this antenna (**Fig 2(a)**) has been found to be marginally better than a normal quarter-wave vertical, and the impedance match (SWR) is certainly better with a broader frequency range. The construction is simple using readily available components along with some 'junk box' bits. The main component is a standard CB-type 'mirror mount' bracket used to mount whips on the heavy-duty mirrors of trucks, and is readily available from CB shops: those with workshop facilities, however, could easily fabricate a suitable bracket from 3/16" aluminium plate along with suitable 1/4" U-bolts.

"A standard PL259 flange type chassis socket is mounted on the bracket using four machine screws, reaming the hole slightly if necessary. This requires the use of a small file and some muscle. Place a solder tag under one of the mounting screws to terminate one end of the antenna. The radials are made from aluminium tubing of any diameter between 1/4" and 1/2" (scrap from old TV antennas is suitable). The radials are attached to the bracket with pop rivets, self-tapping screws, or small 1/8" diameter machine screws. Radials need to be mounted solidly as they are likely to be used as birdperches.

"The antenna proper can be made from any available suitable material such as aluminium, wire or brass. Salvaged copper wire should have a diameter of at least 1.5mm, thinner wires will be too fragile. Perhaps the best solution is to use 1/8" bronze welding rods, available in various lengths. If one length is not enough to form the folded element, a soldered joint can be easily made at the top bend. Bronze solders well and a good connection can be made to the PL259 socket and earth tag secured under the mounting screw. A good clean with steel wool will make for easier soldering. Don't forget to waterproof the exposed end of the coax cable at the antenna to prevent water entering the cable and ruining it. Finally mount the antenna on a mast at the maximum possible height and in the clear (eg chimney mounted mast).

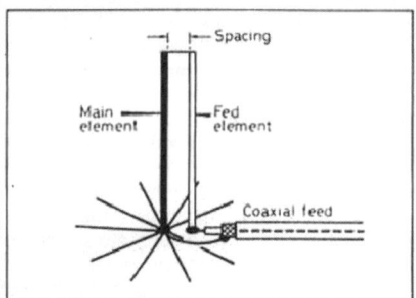

Fig 3: Basic form of the folded-monopole (unipole) antenna. Step-up ratio of feedpoint impedance compared with single quarter-wave element is approximately 4:1 for equal-diameter conductors in fed and main element.

If in the clear, such an antenna should give good 'omnidirectional' performance, but remember it is intended for working stations using vertical polarisation. *TT* July 1987, p497 and August 1991 gave more information on the fundamentals of folded monopoles, including the work of Arch Doty, K8CFU, and his colleagues on their use for HF, VHF and UHF, as well as their technique of bottom-loading. One of the advantages of the folded element is that by using different diameter wires or rods in the main and fed element it is possible to design into the antenna almost any required feed-point impedance for 50 or 75Ω cables etc. **Fig 3** shows the basic structure. VK3CO uses the conventional four radials but as *TT* has pointed out in the past, it should be possible to obtain virtually the same performance using only three or even two radials.

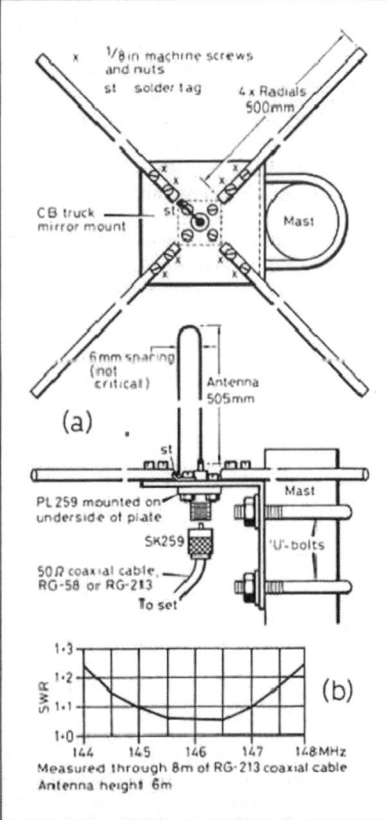

Fig 2: (a) Constructional details of the VK3CO 144MHz unipole antenna. Note that dimensions of element and radials are centred on 146MHz to suit Australian 144-148MHz band. For the UK it would be better to make them slightly longer to resonate at 145MHz.

Meander Antennas

Extracted from 'Technical Topics', *Radio Communication*, February 1992

RESONANT MEANDER ANTENNAS

SPACE RESTRICTIONS in the average domestic environment have always resulted in amateur radio interest in methods of shortening the overall span of resonant HF antennas, as well as finding ways of the efficiency of loaded vertical whips: loading coils, capacitance hats, L- and T-antennas, ends dropping down, (**Fig 1(a)**) or bent sideways as in the VK2ABQ type of compact array. It is becoming increasingly difficult to think of a configuration that somebody has not already thought of and tried, often as long ago as the 1920s or 1930s. Even planar (linear) loading elements can be traced back some 60-plus years to the Franklin Uniform Antenna, although in this case used for phasing rather than loading 1.5-lambda dipole elements or 0.75-lambda monopoles.

TT, November 1984, p965, presented two relatively novel methods of shortening the overall span of half-wave dipoles without significant loss of efficiency or directivity: the zig-zag element and the meander-line element: **Fig 1(b) and (c)**. These came from a paper 'Shortening Ratios of Modified Dipole Antennas' by a team of Japanese engineers at Hosei University, Tokyo (*IEEE Trans on Ant & Prop*, April 1984, pp385-6). It was noted that a meander-line element can use up to about 0.7-lambda of wire to achieve 0.5-lambda resonance but can result in shortening the span by 30% compared with a conventional dipole and with a radiation resistance still as high as 43 ohms.

Soon afterwards (*TT*, March 1985, p190), Les Moxon, G6XN showed how a form of planar loading, attributed to VK5HA and using a string of one-turn loops as in **Fig 2(a)**, could be used to fold a half-wave dipole element into about one third of its normal length at the cost of only some 15-20% increase in total wire length. G6XN who used this technique in some of his 'Claw' antennas commented: "This is a big improvement over a helix (loading coil) or another alternative such as a form of 'meander' system shown recently in *TT* (see above) as means of reducing the overall span of dipole and which can be implemented as in **Fig 2(b)**".

While G6XN believes that VK5HA loading loops are near optimum, a detailed discussion of meander-type loading has recently been presented by Jalil Rashed (University of Seestan and Baluchistan, Iran) and Chen-To Tai (University of Michigan, USA) in 'A New Class of Resonant Antennas' (*IEEE Trans on Ant & Prop*, September 1991, pp1428-30). The abstract of this paper is as follows: "A

ELEVATED RADIALS VERSUS BURIED EARTHS

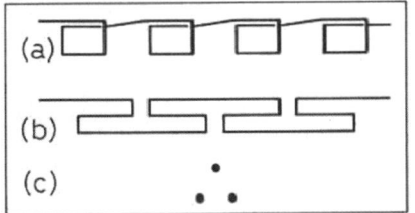

Fig 2: (a) VK5HA-type planar loading as recommended by G6XN in 1985. This involves a string of one turn loops which may be implemented using three cords as in (c) with appropriate spacers. With three loops each side of centre, he was able to fold a half-wave dipole into about one-third of its normal length, at the cost of an increase of only some 15-20% in total wire length, a big improvement in size reduction compared with a helix or meander elements as shown in (b).

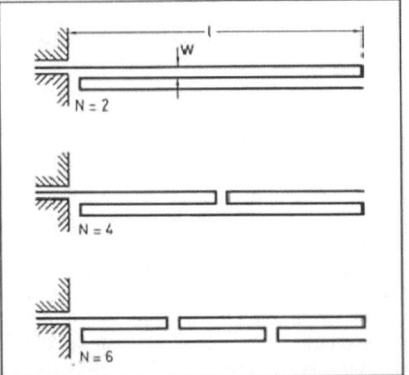

Fig 3: Some special cases of meander antennas (shown in monopole form) discussed by Rashed and Tai. N = 2 corresponds to half a meander section while N = 4 constitutes a complete section. See also Table 1.

'USING ELEVATED RADIALS with ground-mounted towers' by Al Christman (KB8I and Grove City College) and Roger Radcliff (Ohio University) in *IEEE Trans on Broadcasting*, September 1991, pp77-82) reflects the continuing saga of the move to use a few elevated radials as a counterpoise in order to replace the extensive 120 (or more) buried radials which, for many years, have been standard for medium-wave broadcast installations. An earlier paper by KB8I on his computer studies was digested in *TT*, August 1988. For this further paper, computer-modelling studies (backed up by some full-scale experiments) were used to investigate several different methods of attaching radials to ground-mounted (insulated) towers, along with variations in radial height, radial length etc. Limited full-scale outdoor tests on several of these configurations have been carried out by William Culpepper, a consulting radio engineer. The preliminary results show good agreement between the measured data and the computer predictions although it is stated that Mr Culpepper plans to present the measured data separately soon.

The computer predictions, as with the earlier modelling, indicate that 'it is possible to use four elevated radials together with a conventional ground-mounted, base-insulated tower for MF broadcasting purposes, and achieve the same level of performance which is normally obtained from a classic 120-buried-radial system.'

Such an approach would clearly be most suitable for use by amateurs on the 1.8, 3.5 and 7MHz bands for verticals; on the higher frequency bands it is already conventionally adopted in the form of the popular ground-plane antenna (GPA).

The paper is based on MF broadcast systems with quarter-wave towers 75m or 84m in height, insulated at the base with the following elevated radials: radials with 45° sloping ends, at heights of 5m and 10m; radials with steeply-sloping ends at heights of 5m and 10m; and an elevated feed method (fed at 5m and 10m) with the radials horizontal over their full length. The four radials are similarly about 75m (quarter-wave) in length. There appears to be relatively little difference in performance between the different systems (**Fig 7**) but it is recognized that much more experimental verification work needs to be done.

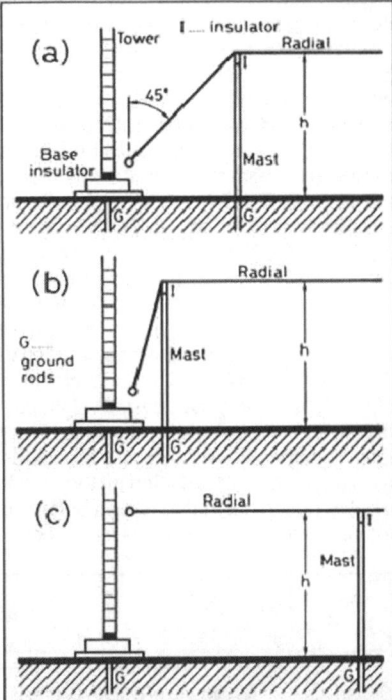

Fig 7: Elevated radial systems investigated by KB8I using computer-modelling to simulate a typical base-insulated broadcast quarter-wave tower antenna. Each of these configurations was modelled for radial heights of 5m and 10m above ground.

new class of wire antennas called meander antennas is introduced as possible elements for size reduction. Efficiency is affected only by the ohmic losses in the wire, and cross-polarization is negligible.

"An increase in the number of meander sections introduces less size reduction in return for an improved bandwidth. These antennas can be used to reduce the size of the existing wire antennas such as Yagi-Uda antennas and log-periodic dipole arrays".

In view of the Japanese 1984 paper it seems a little strong to claim meander-type elements such as a new class of resonant antenna, particularly when implemented in the form that has been used for some years for 7MHz quad antennas under the term 'planar loading'. However the recent paper does provide new insights in to these forms of element shortening. It is noted that, in general, any attempt to reduce the physical size of a monopole (ie half a dipole) while preserving the same resonant frequency ends up with deficiencies such as bandwidth deterioration, pattern distortion and reduction in efficiency. The authors present theoretical and experimental data (UHF model antennas) on some special cases of meander antennas, as shown (in monopole form) in **Fig 3** and **Table 1**. N is in effect the number of meander sections, with N = 2 corresponding to half a meander section while N = 4 constitutes a complete section. In general the lower the N, the greater is the reduction property but at the cost of a lower resonant radiation resistance and bandwidth. The authors write:

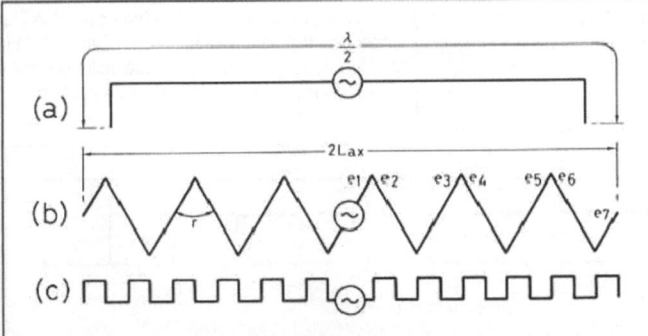

Fig 1: Significant shortening of the overall span of a half-wave dipole element can be achieved without significant loss of efficiency or directivity. (a) Ends dropped down or bent inwards. (b) Zig-zag element where e1 = e7 =0.0208λ and e2 = e3 ... = e6 = 0.0416λ. (c) Meander-line element as discussed by Japanese engineers in 1984.

ANTENNA TOPICS

50-ohm 'Quad Loop' Antenna

Extracted from 'Technical Topics', *Radio Communication*, February 1992

7MHz Dipole on 21MHz

Extracted from 'Technical Topics', *Radio Communication*, March 1992

50-OHM "QUAD-LOOP" ANTENNA

THE ONE-LAMBDA square-loop, mounted either in the vertical or horizontal plane, is a deservedly popular form of antenna. However, with a feed-point impedance of roughly 120-ohms it can present SWR problems when fed directly from 50 or 75-ohm feeder unless a quarter-wave matching transformer is interposed between feeder and element (eg an electrical quarter-wavelength of 75-ohm cable between 50-ohm feeder and the 120-ohm feed point). Bill Orr, W6SAI, in his *Radio FUNdamentals* column in *CQ* (November 1991, pp56-57) shows how by changing the shape away from a square into a rectangle it is possible to achieve a feed-point impedance very close to 50-ohm [or with less elongation of the square close to 75 ohms - G3VA]: **Fig 4**. A horizontal loop of this type retains the figure-of-eight pattern of a dipole but with some extra directivity resulting in slightly more broadside gain (at the cost of radiation off the ends). W6SAI points out that feeding a balanced element from unbalanced coax may benefit from slipping some ferrite-beads on the line at the feedpoint or by using a balun. But he adds that "The experimenter will hook the coax directly to the quad loop, see how it works, and then determine if he has to go to the bother of adding a balun or beads on the line".

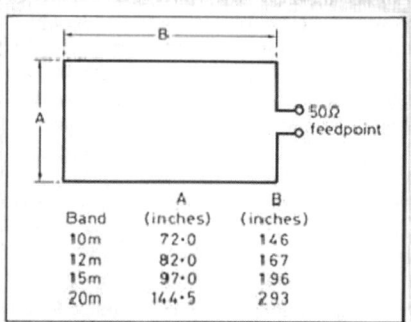

Fig 4: W6SAI's suggested oblong quad loop antenna providing a feedpoint of 50-ohms resistive, a roughly figure-of-eight dipole-type radiation pattern but with some extra directivity and gain.

THE 7MHZ DIPOLE ON 21MHZ

IT HAS LONG BEEN accepted that a 7MHz half-wave dipole may be used as a 1.5-wave dipole on the 21MHz band. This approach can often work satisfactorily, even without an ATU, particularly with older valve-type rigs that are happy to 'see' a moderately high SWR. Remember that unless an HF coaxial feeder is very long, a reasonably high SWR does not represent significant lost power. But with modern solid-state rigs that may begin to throttle back the power with an SWR above about 1.5 or 2.0:1, so the 7MHz antenna can prove unsatisfactory in practice.

Bob Raffaele, W2XM in 'Hints and Kinks' (*QST*, December 1991) points out that 'end effect' causes a half-wave dipole resonant at 7.1MHz to resonate as a 1.5λ dipole at about 22MHz and not 21.3MHz: **Fig 1**. Furthermore the feed-point impedance of a resonant 1.5λ dipole tends to be higher than that of a half-wave dipole. His suggestions include using a compromise antenna length of 67ft and feeding the antenna via a coaxial feeder that includes a 21MHz quarter-wave matching section between the antenna element and its 50Ω feed line; this 21MHz impedance transformer should have little effect at 7MHz. He uses 7ft 7in of RG-59 cable as the Q-section. Since different cables of a common impedance vary in capacitance per unit length, the length of the matching section may have to be changed slightly. With this compromise arrangement W2XM provides a lower SWR at the low end of 7MHz and the high end of 21MHz.

In an editorial comment, WJ1Z notes that at a height of 25ft (about 0.2λ) above ground, a flat-top half-wave 7.1MHz dipole exhibits a radiation resistance of around 65Ω. A 50Ω feed line connected to such an antenna should exhibit an SWR of about 1.3:1. Operated as a 1.5λ dipole, the same antenna (0.5λ high at 21MHz) exhibits a radiation resistance of about 110Ω at resonance, resulting in an SWR of about 2.2:1 when fed with 50Ω cable. Resonance is at about 22MHz, so that the SWR may be unacceptable (without an ATU) when operating at the low-end of the 21MHz band, unless some compromise solution, such as that suggested by W2XM is adopted.

"By means of a sleeve, one is able to match the antenna to any desirable impedance level. Unlike most of the size reduction techniques such as lumped loading and the use of dielectric materials, the efficiency of the meander geometry is comparable to that of a conventional monopole. Since meander dipoles have a resonant length less than half a wavelength, and the separation W is negligibly small, they have essentially a figure-of-eight pattern and unlike many size reduction schemes, the undesirable radiation for horizontal portions is negligible . . . . Meander antennas can be used in the existing wire antennas; especially large arrays with long elements. As an example, a log-periodic dipole array (LPDA) is compared with its meander version (LPMDA). A 35% reduction in element size is obtained with an average loss of 2.5dB in the gain of the antenna over a 5:3 band: J. Rashed-Mohassel 'A Miniaturised Log-periodic Dipole Array' presented at ICAP89 (IEE Conference Publication No 301, part 1 - *Antennas* pp403-406). A whip antenna with partial meandering in the base of the whip is another example with the advantage of higher efficiency in comparison to lumped loading . . . . The meander geometry can be applied equally to other existing wire antennas such as Yagi-Uda arrays".

Antenna type	N	Resonant frequency (MHz)	Band-width (%)	Efficiency (%)	Calculated Radiation Resistance (ohms)
Monopole	-	545	9.5	99.1	36.5
Meander	2	922	3.0	96.7	13.5
	6	1050	7.0	97.8	17.0
	10	1110	7.5	97.9	19.0
	14	1180	8.0*	98.0	21.5

*Approximation from extrapolation

TABLE 1: Experimental data based on model antennas made from a 13.5cm length of wire (diameter 0.8mm). The height of the meander antennas (ie l shown horizontally) is 4.5cm with a small separation W less than 0.3cm (W/l = 0.06).

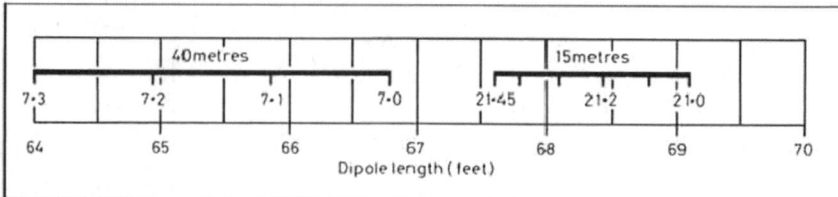

Fig 1: The resonant frequency of a harmonic antenna as a function of length in feet. Calculated from the formula $492(n - 0.05)/f$ where f is frequency in MHz and n is the number of half-waves in the antenna, so that n is 1 for a half-wave dipole and 3 for a 1.5-wave dipole. For example, a dipole resonant at 7.1MHz is not resonant at 21.3MHz but at nearer 22MHz. The radiation resistance of a typical horizontal 7MHz antenna at a typical height will also differ significantly as a 1.5-wave dipole at 22MHz.

Broadband Radials

Extracted from 'Technical Topics', *Radio Communication*, April 1992

BROADBAND RADIALS

THE AVAILABILITY OF FIVE amateur HF bands between 14.0 and 29.7MHz, including bands without any harmonic relationship, provides an incentive to develop broadband antennas capable of efficient operation over at least an octave of spectrum. A well established method of increasing the effective bandwidth of any antenna element is to increase the diameter/length ratio, as for example in the once popular caged dipole.

One practical form of broadband antenna exploiting this technique is the vertical biconical monopole, despite its rather complex structure. Way back in the *RSGB Bulletin* (now *Radio Communication*) of May 1966, pp305-306, an amateur example of a biconical antenna, originally described by W5WEU/4 in *CQ*, January 1966, was presented in *TT* together with details of a professional antenna of this type as used at a number of Royal Navy HF coast stations (described by H P Mason of the Admiralty Surface Weapon Establishment (now Admiralty Research Establishment) at a 1963 IEEE HF Convention) and implemented in three forms: for 2-5MHz, 4-11MHz and 10-26MHz. The W5WEU and ASWE designs are shown in the 7th editon of *Amateur Radio Techniques*, p277.

It was then emphasised that, as for any monopole antenna, it is necessary to use the best possible ground plane. For the ASWE designs, 36 buried radials about one quarter-wave long at the lowest frequency were used. Interestingly, I find that I then added the comment: "What I have never yet found is any detailed comparison between the effectiveness of a ground radial system and that of the three or four-wire up-in-the-air technique which we associate with 'ground-plane' antennas - and how much the ground conductivity below such sloping ground-plane systems affects low angle radiation". That was in 1966 and since then both these topics have been well aired (and answered) with some assurance!

It is now widely accepted (and in increasing evidence for amateur 1.8MHz practice) that a few elevated radials can be every bit as effective as a massive buried earth system (although the very low angle radiation will be much attenuated in either case in areas of poor ground conductivity extending out to some 50 wavelengths). But when used with a broadband radiating element it is clearly desirable that elevated radials should also be broadband in order to achieve equal efficiency and a similar radiation pattern over the full frequency range.

What appears to be an effective means of implementing such an approach appears in the Russian *Radio* No 12, 1991, page 19, in a short article by UT5YB in conjunction with a biconical monopole antenna originally described by UW4HW in *Radio* No 9, 1981: see **Fig 5**.

If my guesses at the Russian text are correct, then UT5YB claims that fed with 75Ω coax feeder, the antenna shows an SWR of only about 1.05 to 1.2 throughout the band 14 to 30MHz. Each of the radials is similar to the vertical element, 5.1m (5100mm) long.

Another Compact VK2ABQ

Extracted from 'Technical Topics', *Radio Communication*, May 1992

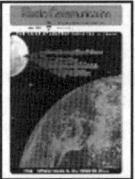

ANOTHER COMPACT VK2ABQ 14MHZ ANTENNA

IT IS NOW ALMOST 20 years since *TT* presented the original VK2ABQ three-band (14/21/28MHz) wire beam antenna, first published as a short letter in *Electronics Australia*. Since then, Fred Caton, VK2ABQ (formerly G3ONC) has followed this with a number of other ideas, submitted directly to *TT*, including several modified forms of his original design which has become well-established (see ART7) and which has been endorsed by Les Moxon, G6XN in his book *HF Antennas for All Locations* (available from RSGB sales). I must admit that I sometimes wonder what professional antenna specialists such as VE2CV would make of the jottings which Fred sends along to explain his ideas.

A recent letter is no exception and I can only hope that I have understood at least the gist of this new design which dispenses with the open-wire phasing line used in the original VK2ABQ design, and has the driven element fed directly from a coax feed-line. The dimensions shown are for 14MHz, and should be divided by two for 28MHz. A 14MHz antenna can be used on 21MHz as an extended-element array, but the feedpoint impedance will rise and become reactive, so that an ATU will be necessary.

In effect, **Fig 1** shows a KISS recipe for a simple 14MHz two-element array. The unidirectional 135° phase shift is achieved using equal-length elements without a phasing line but with critical coupling.

Take a 71ft length of lightweight plastic-coated wire (bare/enamelled copper wire would need to be rather longer). First check for resonance with the wire fitted on the wooden frame, using a GDO. Then fold the 71ft wire into four, and touch the plastic with a hot soldering iron to identify where the sides are to be cut. The frame can be constructed from four 11ft 6in dowels ($^5/_8$in diameter) or garden canes, mounted on a square piece of board with about 15in sides (as in the original VK2ABQ designs). In placing the wire on the framework, make sure the two current-focus sections are placed an eighth-wave apart (2.5m on 14MHz) with the voltage-tips adjustable to 4in gaps in order to provide the quarter-cycle (90°) phase-shift between L1 and L2. The 90° critical coupling between L1 and L2 plus the 45° current loop spacing gives the required 135° phase-shift between the two elements resulting in an effective unidirectional two-element array with a satisfying front-to-back ratio, useful forward gain and sharp side nulls. VK2ABQ stresses that the gaps between the elements are critical in achieving critical coupling, in his case he found 3.75in optimum.

Fig 1(b) shows the piece of flat plastic material used as an insulator at the element feed point. The 0.25in coax cable is then routed down through the hole in the centreboard. Seal and 'gunk' the feedpoint, using for example *black* bitumen paint or similar. A nylon cord is loosely connected as a stabilizer between the feed-point insulator and the centre rear of the L2 current loop. VK2ABQ likens the array to an old-style critically-coupled IF transformer with lumped-components, but opened-up to tickle the ether and provide a simple, cheap, compact but effective two-element beam. To adjust the coupling, a simple current sampling gimmick can be used as in **Fig 2(a)**. Provided that the loop of the device is very small in terms of wavelength, it will not respond to the electric (voltage) field. **Fig 2(b)** shows a similar device but with a meter to increase sensitivity. With the antenna at shoulder height, and with the aid of a helper, the gaps at the voltage tips can be adjusted for equal current in both elements, indicating a 90° phase shift. Overcoupling will be indicated by more power in the reflector element, undercoupling by more power in the driven element. When power is shared equally, the coupling will be providing the correct 90° phase-shift. It should be appreciated that a VK2ABQ-type array is basically a form of driven array rather than a Yagi parasitic-reflector array.

Adjustments may be carried out with one person standing in the middle of the shoulder-high array using the current sampler, and with a few watts of 14.05MHz RF fed to the antenna. The helper then adjusts the spacing at the voltage tips, but moves *well away* from the

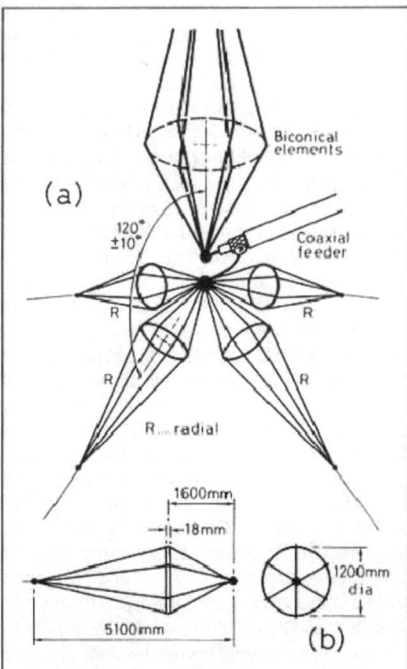

Fig 5: UT5YB's use of broadband radials in conjunction with a biconical vertical antenna covering 14-30MHz continuously with low SWR on the coax feedline.

ANTENNA TOPICS

voltage tips after adjusting the spacing to instructions. Any large object near the voltage tips will nullify the adjustments.

Finally, VK2ABQ endorses the value of a tip that appeared many years ago in *TT* and elsewhere, and is applicable to all dipole-type antennas with low-impedance feeder. A 20KΩ carbon resistor soldered across the element feedpoint has no effect on the operation of the antenna but allows an ohmmeter check to be made in the shack as a warning against a broken feedline. VK2ABQ has used such a resistor (well covered in 'gunk') for some 25 years.

Incidentally, at the age of 74 years, Fred no longer feels able to correspond with readers seeking further advice on his antennas. He hopes that the information provided here will enable readers to achieve satisfactory results.

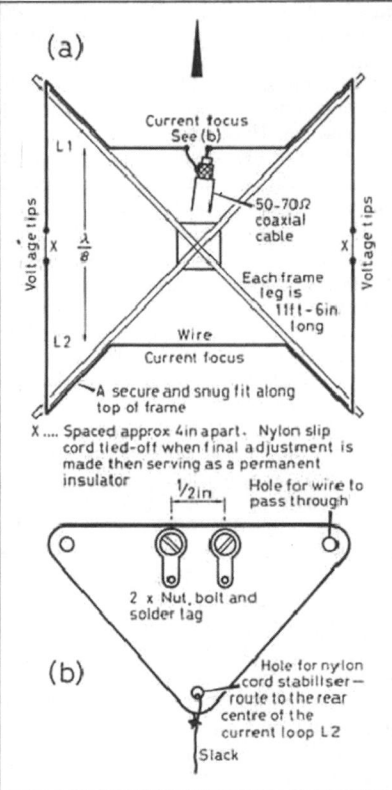

Fig 1(a): The VK2ABQ KISS 14MHz array. (b) Feedpoint insulator with nylon cord stabiliser.

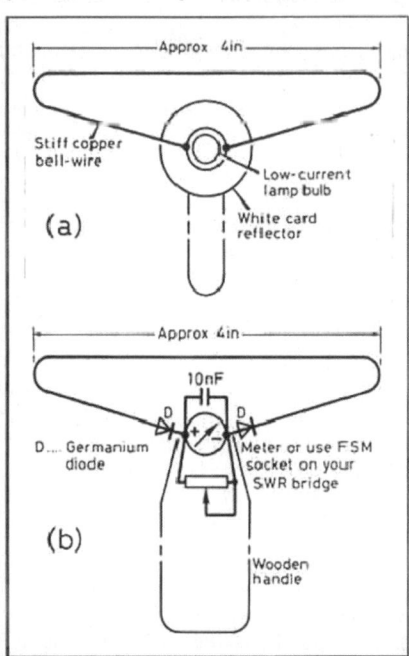

Fig 2(a): Simple current sampler. (b) More sensitive current sampler.

Antenna Gain and Efficiency

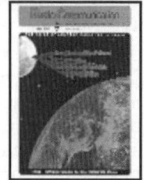

Extracted from 'Technical Topics', *Radio Communication*, May 1992

ANTENNA GAIN AND EFFICIENCY

JOHN BELROSE, VE2CV, as a professional antenna engineer, is clearly concerned at the looseness and inexactitude of much of the terminology and information that appears in the amateur radio periodicals (including, I must confess, those in *TT*). For example he was disturbed to read the suggestion by G4HOL (*TT*, December 1991) that "his horizontal loop at 3.5MHz has 9dB more gain than his quarter-wave sloper". VE2CV comments: "Great. Should he throw out his sloper? Maybe not? When on 3.5MHz I switch from my dipole to my half-delta loop, which has an overhead null, the signals received from stations a few hundred kilometres away decrease by up to three S-units (15dB); whereas the signals from DX stations a long way away, on the west coast of Canada, increase by up to three S-units, depending on propagation conditions (angle of arrival of the skywave signal). No wonder amateurs do not understand antennas. They read so much conflicting information."

In pleading *mea culpa* I would suggest that this is an age-old problem not made easier by the fact that the whole subject of antenna gains and losses offers enormous scope for sophistry, semantics and what is known in the trade as 'specmanship' - ie why say your antenna has a gain of 6dB when with some subtle redefinition you can say the gain is 12dB? For those of us who are not professional engineers, antennas are not easy to understand even in purely pragmatic terms! Think of the signal leaving the antenna and spraying out in many directions, possibly boosted by ground reflection according to polarization. Then consider the tiny percentage of the original power that actually tickles the receiving antenna, as found only by accurate ray-tracing of the signal over the specific path concerned and the actual height of the reflecting layers. It then becomes evident that the performance of an antenna may bear little relationship to a single definition of gain without reference to the lobe patterns of both horizontal and vertical radiation. The development of computer-modelling based on NEC codes has made it easier for professional-amateurs and some others to assess antenna performance without actually engaging in practical trials - but most of us still depend on subjective assessments.

Tony Henk, G4XVF, has shown clearly that the overall efficiency of small transmitting loop antennas in terms of the amount of power actually radiated compared with the output power of the transmitter is usually quite low with more energy being lost in the matching components including the capacitors than in the actual loop element.

Rightly, he warns against spending a lot of money on a remotely tuned loop if you have sufficient space to erect a more conventional transmitting antenna. But the small loop can be a useful addition to the amateur antenna armoury. I seem to be bombarded with enthusiastic letters and information from amateurs who have developed or used such loops (I will try to find space to include some of this information before too long). And for those who would wish to experiment with low-cost loops, a reminder that the idea can be tried out without remote tuning or expensive high-voltage capacitors using 'capacitors' formed from parallel rods (as in a *CQ* design from the Dec 1991 and Jan 1992 issues) or from lengths of coaxial cable etc. Certainly, many of those who have built small magnetic loop antennas have been pleasantly surprised how well they work, even though they tend to be inherently 'low-efficiency' antennas. They bestow a number of useful characteristics both for medium and long-distance operation.

John Brodzky, G3HQX, uses both a small loop and a full-wave (3.5MHz) more-or-less horizontal loop antenna formed by conversion from a long-wire antenna by continuing it back up his garden, across the house and back to where it started, fed at one corner with 300-ohm ribbon and through a 4:1 balun to his ATU. He considers the large loop is "the best wire antenna that I have ever used". It works well on all bands up to 28MHz. On 3.5MHz the low height means that it radiates at a high vertical angle primarily suitable for medium-distance contacts but able to get across the Atlantic at times. Above 14MHz he works anything he can hear. But he was not satisfied with the performance on 7MHz after hearing UK stations working JA and ZL stations that he could not even hear. He was attracted by the idea of introducing some further vertically polarized components into his signal and studied the F1CLI antenna but he decided that it would not suit his location. Instead he hit on the idea of bringing down near the ground a point that was removed from the feed-point by 3λ/4. He felt that the two arms of a V (see **Fig 3**) formed by this alteration would now be at about 45° and carrying currents in phase, with a current maximum at the top of each arm. In making this change the overall length of the loop had to be increased by 12ft and the feed-point moved down one of the legs to get the bottom of the V to come to the bottom centre of his garden. The increased length has shifted the loop resonance to the CW end of 3.5MHz and at 7MHz it is also at the preferred frequency. The overall length of the loop is now 286ft.

I am not sure what computer-modelling (or VE2CV) would make of this arrangement - and one may have to discount the unusually good HF propagation conditions early this year - but G3HQX reports that since he made the changes he finds that on 7MHz most mornings he can work ZL, JA, VE (including VE7) and plenty of Ws (including West Coast W6s). He bases his operating times on 'gray-line' propagation as described in the book *Low-band DXing* by ON4UN (available from RSGB) using his computer to predict sunrise and sunset times at the home QTH and those of the areas of interest. It is unlikely that others will wish to duplicate an arrangement designed to fit a particular location, but it is interesting to note that good 7MHz DX is possible with a large loop having a height varying between 12ft and 24ft.

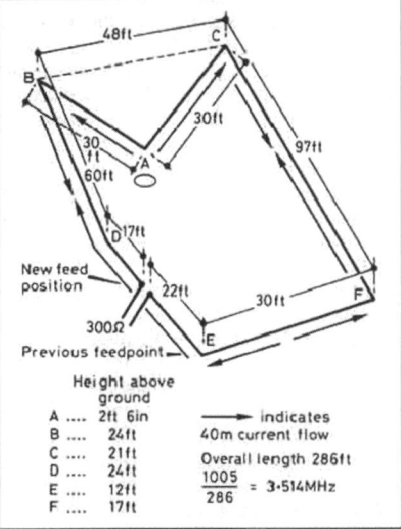

Fig 3: The large multiband loop antenna as modified by G3HQX to improve DX performance on 7MHz by adding the V-shaped section.

VE2CV on the F1LCI Antenna

Extracted from 'Technical Topics', *Radio Communication*, May 1992

VE2CV'S COMMENTS ON THE F1LCI ANTENNA

IN *TT*, DECEMBER 1992, Jean Bourdereau, G1LCI, showed how he had effectively adapted an 84-metre horizontal loop antenna to provide 1.8MHz DX operation by grounding the far-end (centre-point) of the loop via a thick conductor (or grounded metal mast) and by connecting the open-wire loop feeders together at the attic transmitter end to form what was termed a top-fed grounded Marconi antenna on 1.8MHz. On other bands, by restoring the balanced feed, the operation of the antenna as a multiband horizontal loop was not affected: **Fig 4**.

The item has resulted in correspondence between Dr John Belrose, VE2CV (well-known as a professional antenna specialist who acts as an ARRL Technical Adviser) and F1LCI. VE2CV was intrigued by the idea of a single antenna that could be switched between: (1) a horizontal rectangular loop and (2) what is technically more accurately described as a form of vertical electromagnetic ground-plane loop (akin to the VE2CV half-delta loop as described in *QST* etc).

His own interests centre more on the 3.5MHz band than 1.8MHz. He writes: "Since both short and long distance communication is possible on this band, one would like to have more than one antenna with a switch to choose between antennas matched to the distance or azimuthal direction requirement. For near-vertical-incidence-skywave (NVIS) signals, out to several hundred kilometres, we want an antenna that favours high-angle skywaves, such as a dipole or horizontal loop at a height of about a quarter-wave (or less - *G3VA*). For distant stations, we want an antenna that has a vertical-plane pattern that favours low-angle skywaves; a null for NVIS signals is useful in order to reject nearby strong interfering signals, man-made radio noise and radio noise from nearby to medium-distance thunderstorms."

Consequently, VE2CV computer-modelled (ELNEC) the F1LCI antenna with reference to 3.5 and 7MHz as well as for its intended 1.8MHz. He comments as follows:

(1) The description of the antenna as (a) 'horizontal mode' and (b) 'vertical mode' is somewhat a misnomer. Both arrangements when used for the higher frequency bands are electrically large, and both polarizations (horizontal and vertical) are radiated by each arrangement. The change of pattern with frequency for the EMGP arrangement is particularly complicated.

(2) With the shorted-feed line, the antenna is *not* 'a top fed Marconi antenna' (the same applies to G3BDQ's 'steeple antenna'). It is a kind of electromagnetic ground plane (EMGP) loop; a rectangular half-loop top-corner-fed, excepting that there are two top wires, and this makes the difference between this EMGP loop and thin-wire half-loop. The grounded metal mast or tower at the far end of the horizontal loop and the 'ground wire' to the transceiver chassis-ground both carry current and are connected to real earth. It is thus an EMGP loop no matter how you look at it.

If you insulate the end of the horizontal loop from the grounded mast or ground wire, the antenna truly becomes a top-fed Marconi antenna or inverted-L. This is a perfectly good antenna and the lack of success with it on 1.8MHz reported by F1LCI is undoubtedly because the transceiver 'ground wire' which forms the vertical element of the inverted-L is inside the house.

(3) According to ELNEC, the EMGP loop is resonant at about 1.72MHz. Its radiation pattern for 1.9MHz is not unlike that for a

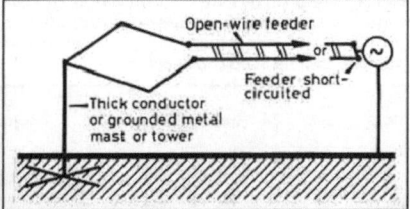

Fig 4: The F1LCI antenna as described in the December 1991 *TT* with option of a short-circuited feeder for 1.8MHz operation.

thin wire half-quad, diamond or delta loop. That is the direction of fire is broadside to the plane containing the loop, and the radiated field is almost entirely vertically polarized. However, this is clearly not the case for 3.5MHz.

(4) At 3.75MHz the pattern is quite different, not unlike that for a horizontal dipole or a full-wave horizontal loop, except that the input impedance is not particularly easy to tune or match. The field radiated is analogous to two dipoles fed in phase - a broadside pattern horizontally polarized. The azimuthal pattern resembles that of a broadside array.

(5) The radiation patterns for 7.15MHz are more complicated. At this frequency the sides of the loop are approximately a full-wave long and therefore there is a null in the broadside direction for horizontal polarization. The azimuthal pattern is a complicated mixture of the two polarizations. According to ELNEC the impedance is not particularly attractive for matching purposes.

VE2CV summarises that the EMGP loop is a good antenna for 1.9MHz (the band for which F1LCI intended it - *G3VA*), but he is not impressed with either impedance or pattern when used as an EMGP loop on other bands. He feels that it is not a suitable candidate to complement his own 3.5MHz antenna system. But notwithstanding these comments, he recognizes that the system is, in principle, a neat idea. He adds some further suggestions:

"One problem with large horizontal loops is that as frequency increases the antenna's azimuthal pattern breaks down into many lobes, which in my view is undesirable. The ability to switch between two different arrangements could give the ability to hear a station that might otherwise have been missed in a pattern null. The following remarks refer to the method of feed and the function of the 'ground wire' to the attic-located transceiver. When the open-wire transmission line is fed in the balanced mode, this ground connection is unimportant since little current will flow on the wire. It might even be better to let the transceiver chassis-ground float, from the viewpoint of the antenna's response to local man-made radio noise. The horizontal loop is grounded at the far end, and it is sometimes better that antenna systems which are physically large have only one earth-ground, so that a noise current will not flow between two earth-grounds.

"When the open-wire feeder is shorted at the end, and the antenna is fed as a form of EMGP loop, the equipment ground becomes very important. This wire will carry a radiating current, and unfortunately the wire will usually be inside the house as at F1LCI. In this case the transceiver will certainly not be at RF ground. It would be preferable to modify the method of feed. The EMGP should be tuned to 1.9MHz by means of a series capacitor and this tuned loop fed by a current balun. The loop would connect to one of the balanced terminals of the balun and the 'ground wire' to the other balanced terminal of the balun, which could be a W2DU type of current balun. This comprises a short length of transmission line with ferrite beads to kill current flow on the

ANTENNA TOPICS

outside of the shield of the ferrite-loaded transmission line. The transceiver ground-wire should connect to the 'shield' of the W2DU transmission line balun on the balanced side, and the transceiver chassis ground should be connected to the 'shield' on the unbalanced side. This avoids forcing the balun to work in the phase reversal mode, and connecting the balun this way means that the transceiver chassis ground will be tied to DC (and 50Hz) ground, but leaving the chassis ground floating with reference to RF ground. There will be little or no RF voltage on the chassis ground of the equipment. The 'ground wire' should be insulated since it will have RF voltage on it, and currents can be coupled into the electrical wiring of the house, and into water pipes if a water heating system is used. This ground should be a heavy wire running down the outside of the house, and tied to a good earth system."

The Extended Double Zepp

Extracted from 'Technical Topics', *Radio Communication*, June 1992

THE EXTENDED DOUBLE ZEPP ANTENNA

THE UNEXPECTEDLY RAPID decline in solar activity during March would seem to foreshadow some years during which 14, 18 and 21MHz rather than 24, 28 and 50MHz will be of major interest for long-distance daytime working, with 1.8, 3.5, 7 and 10MHz increasingly useful during the hours of twilight and darkness - though it is much to be hoped that 28 and 50MHz will continue to be well occupied for medium-distance Sporadic E, extended local operation etc.

Recent *TT* items have underlined the usefulness of such multiband wire antennas as the large horizontal loop, but there are many locations where loops tend to be difficult if not impossible to fit into narrow gardens, even where these are long enough to accommodate a single span of say 70 to 100ft. In such circumstances, as past *TT* items have frequently emphasised, a centre-fed dipole fed with open-wire feeders and a flexible ATU with balanced output will work well on any band, whether or not the top span is resonant. Admittedly, the horizontal radiation pattern will differ on the various bands, splitting into multi-lobe patterns on the higher frequencies.

A well-established, but seldom used, configuration of this general type is a centre-fed antenna designed as an extended double-zepp antenna for a favourite band (providing a broadside gain of an extra 3dB over a half-wave dipole) but eminently usable on other bands with various radiation patterns and gains.

A timely reminder of the usefulness of the EDZ appears in *QST* (Feb 1992) as a *Hints & Kinks* item from Bob Baird, W7CSD, supported by editorial addenda. W7CSD writes:

"Although the extended double zepp (EDZ) antenna (**Fig 1**) has been in just every antenna handbook since the year one, hams seldom use it. Its overall length is 1.28λ and it is bidirectional broadside. Fed with open-wire line and a balanced antenna tuner, an EDZ also makes a fine multiband antenna. Let's look at an EDZ for 18MHz. We can calculate the overall length in feet as (984 x 1.28)/f(MHz) from which an 18.15MHz EDZ works out to be 69.4ft long. At this frequency the EDZ exhibits 3dBd gain in a figure-of-eight pattern with two major and four minor lobes. It still performs usefully when operated on several bands lower in frequency. At 14MHz, an 18MHz EDZ acts as two slightly long half-waves in phase, exhibiting between 1.6 and 2dBd gain. At 7MHz, it is a slightly long half-wave dipole. All these modes are directional broadside if the EDZ is positioned at least a half-wave high at 7MHz. At 21MHz, it exhibits a four-leaf-clover pattern, with minor lobes broadside; at 28 and 24MHz, it is close to two full waves in phase and produces a pattern similar to that at 21MHz. It can even be used as a short 3.5MHz dipole - not bad for a 70ft piece of wire! .... There's nothing magic about the EDZ. It's a tried-and-true dipole that offers useful gain at its design frequency and good multiband performance."

W7CSD does not mention the 10.1MHz band but a good performance could be expected from an 18MHz EDZ. On 1.8MHz it could be used either as a very short dipole or with the open-wire feeder strapped together as a T-antenna fed against earth (or a counterpoise), with a high T-antenna providing vertically-polarized radiation.

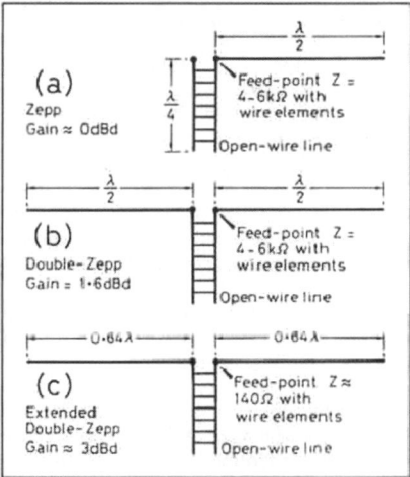

Fig 1: Evolution of the extended double zepp antenna. (a) Classic zepp antenna, originally developed for use in the Zeppelin airships but now considered uncertain in behaviour due to the unbalanced connection of the element to the resonant balanced transmission line. (b) Double zepp (two half-waves in phase) provides a broadside gain of 1.6dBd. (c) By extending the dipole element lengths to 0.64-wave, the gain is raised to 3dBd with two major and four minor lobes. It is termed an extended double zepp (EDZ) antenna.

Two-band Quad-loop

Extracted from 'Technical Topics', *Radio Communication*, July 1992

TWO-BAND QUAD-LOOP ANTENNA

LES MOXON, G6XN has shown (*HF Antennas for all Locations*) how a quad-loop element can form a multiband antenna by the use of stubs, etc. Many years ago there was included in *TT* and later *ART* a more conventional dual-band quad-loop antenna for 14 and 21MHz with a 75Ω coaxial feeder connected directly across a common feed-point of two resonant, one-wavelength loops. Originally published in *73* (Sept 1965), W6WAW claimed that this had proved effective in spite of the fact that the theoretical feed-point impedance of a loop element is approximately 125Ω.

Al Akers, ZS2U, (*Radio-ZS*, Feb 1992, pp5 and 8) uses a basically similar arrangement as a lightweight quad-loop antenna for 14 and 21MHz portable operation from the Ciskei, but with a ingenious matching network designed to provide a good match between a 50Ω cable and the 125Ω element impedance: **Figs 1 and 2**. His antenna is claimed to be easy to erect, dismantle and transport and uses garden canes for spreaders with an aluminium centre piece and aluminium mast, with no traps, etc to catch and damage among bushes and trees.

ZS2U writes: Fig 1(a) shows the antenna. L1 is the 28MHz loop and is 10.9m in length. The centre plate A is shown in Fig 1(b) with U-clamps used to fasten it to the mast (not shown are four saddles which fasten the pipes to the plate, also a centre piece which serves to hold these pipes and to block off their ends. The support arms are garden canes (2m long) and are epoxied onto lengths of 16mm outside-diameter aluminium tubing which make up the extra length needed. These pipes plug into the pipes on the mounting plate.

B is an ABS box, 15 x 8 x 5cm usually available from local electrical emporiums. It is used to house the acceptor-rejector circuits and L-match networks. The box is fastened to a 32mm PVC waterpipe about 80mm longer than the box and slotted for about 50mm. The pipe slides onto the mast and a hose clamp round the slotted section serves to clamp it to the mast.

In Fig 2, L1, C1, C2 and L2, L3, C3 form the two acceptor-rejector circuits. L4 and C4 is the L matching network for the 21MHz loop and C5 and L5 is the L matching network for the 14MHz loop. The upper acceptor-rejector circuit forms a series-resonant circuit on 21MHz (very low impedance) and a parallel-resonant circuit on 28MHz (very high impedance). The lower circuit functions similarly providing very low impedance on 28MHz and very high impedance on 21MHz.

ZS2U adds that he used silver mica capacitors, two in parallel in each case to make up the required value, and that these are standing up as well to the 50W output from his

1990 - 1999

FT7B transceiver. The coils were air-wound with 14SWG copper wire, 22mm in diameter and 4mm-per-turn spacing. He used 3 turns for L2 and L3, 4 turns for L1 and L5 and 5 turns for L4. Adjustments were made by varying the coils in length, most of them requiring some spreading: "Orientate the coils so as to minimise inductive coupling between them. Start with L1 and C1 only. Resonate on 21MHz, then connect C2 and resonate on 28MHz. C3 and L3 are resonated on 28MHz, then L2 connected and adjusted to resonate on 21MHz. Wire up the whole unit and test. Probably minor adjustments will need to be made to the L matches. I used an SO239 socket at the bottom of the box for feedline attachment". ZS2U concludes his article as follows: "You may think, as I did, that this antenna will be difficult to make and adjust and, with all the coils etc, would be rather inefficient. I found that it was not difficult to adjust and it has proved itself in operation. It is a useful antenna where space is limited and has the advantage that it is directional".

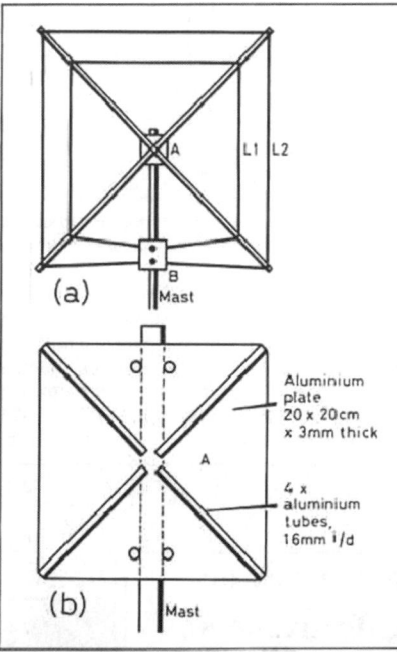

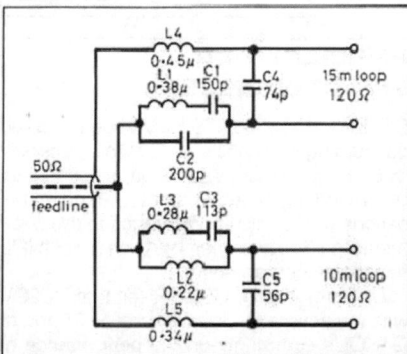

Fig 2: Acceptor-rejector matching networks providing good matching between a single 50Ω feedline and the separate 21 and 28MHz quad-loops.

Antenna Roundup

Extracted from 'Technical Topics', *Radio Communication*, July 1992

ANTENNA ROUND-UP

ONE OF THE MORE POWERFUL forms of broadside, vertically-polarized antennas suitable for amateur HF operation (although very little used) is the Bobtail Curtain: **Fig 4**. Its low-angle radiation provides a hefty gain on DX. The broadside horizontal directivity is only moderate, an advantage for a fixed, suspended wire array. Some relatively high-angle, horizontally polarized radiation will, in practice, result from imperfect cancellation of radiation from the top horizontal span (as with a T-antenna, most of the radiation from the two halves of this section cancel out). Perhaps the most obvious disadvantages are that it is basically a single-band array, requires a matching network at the base of the central vertical wire to provide a voltage (high impedance) feed and a site that can accommodate a full-wave span at a height of just over a quarter-wave.

In the NRRL journal *Amator Radio* (4/92), LA5UF has a short note on a simple variation which, although no longer a true Bobtail, should provide a simple DX antenna that can be fed directly from 50Ω co-axial cable, providing a mixture of horizontally and vertically polarized radiation: **Fig 5**

Dave Plumridge, G3KMG, has some useful thoughts on feeder radiation and RF current measurement. He writes: "Recent comments on baluns and the controlled feeder radiation antenna have made me realise that nowhere have I noticed (handbooks included) any information on how to measure or even check the magnitude of current on the outer braid of a coaxial line. The last time I can recall antenna current being mentioned was many years ago in *TT* when a device involving a spring-type of clothes-peg with two half toroids which could be clipped round a coax cable to form a current transformer with diode rectifier and meter was described (Despite a lengthy search I cannot trace the issue in which this appeared - *G3VA*). (But see 'Remote Reading RF Ammeter', *RadCom* June and July 92 - *Ed*.)

"I needed to check a loaded 7MHz dipole made for a local blind amateur to use as an indoor antenna. On testing it in my attic I was plagued by RF feedback. I wanted to confirm whether it was just the close proximity of the antenna or outer braid radiation from the feeder. To check the RF on the feeder I made a current transformer with one of the large 'braid breaker' ferrite toroids of the type available from the RSGB (see *Book Case* pages - *Ed*). This consisted simply of 20 turns of wire wound on the toroid, a 47Ω load resistor with a simple diode detector (the *QST* detector shown in the April *TT* would allow accurate measurements!). The large toroid allows coax plugs to pass through without any need for disconnection or a split clothes peg toroid. The device was calibrated by coupling to the inner of the coax feeding the station power meter and dummy load and noting the voltage at various power levels. A bit of maths gave the RF current for a given detected voltage.

"Application of this meter to the dipole feeder showed the presence of a large current on the outer braid. A balun choke made by coiling the coax at the feed point into six turns at about 10in diameter reduced the current significantly and eliminated the RFI problems. Out of interest, a further 'coil balun' a few feet away from the feed point reduced the current on the outer braid to a negligible level. Such an RF current meter can thus give a quantifiable measure as to the effectiveness of a balun. On a controlled feeder radiation antenna the ratios of 'antenna' to 'feeder' currents could be quantified to check theory with practice.

"When my parallel dipoles, fed via an ATU with 75Ω twin feeder, seemed to be playing up badly on 21MHz only, a check with the current meter showed a large unbalanced current on this band with next to nothing on the other bands. Lowering the antenna showed there was a break in the 21MHz dipole near the feed point.

"A further application came with a desire to try a ground-plane antenna on 21MHz. Remembering the suggestion in *TT* that the requirement for 'four' radials is something of a modern myth with the inventor, the late George Brown, originally being satisfied with only two, I used only two radials, making the installation much less messy with fewer wires hanging about. Apart from the SWR and performance being fine, the current meter showed negligible current on the outer braid - so who needs four or even three radials?"

John Heys, G3BDQ tried the flattened-loop antenna noted in the February *TT*, p37 using the dimensions given by W6SAI but found they did not give unity SWR on the design frequency and found that on 21MHz

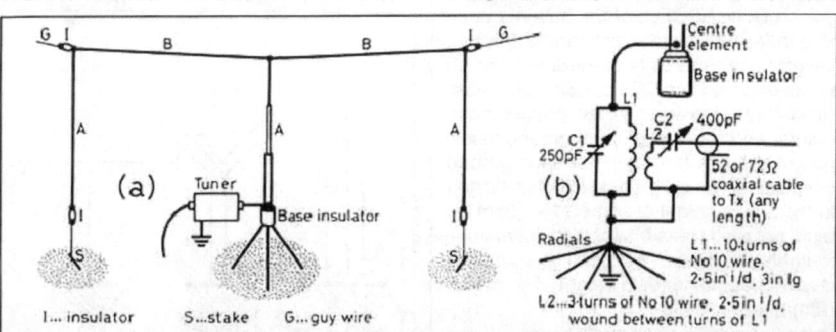

Fig 4: (a) The Bobtail-curtain antenna as described in many Handbooks. This design comes from VE1TG (*Ham Radio*, July 1969) as reproduced in *ART7*. Dimensions for 14MHz A 16.5ft, B 33ft (7MHz A 33ft, B 66ft). (b) Tuner used by VE1TG on 7MHz. For 14MHz L1 and C1 about half the values shown, C2 about the same.

ANTENNA TOPICS

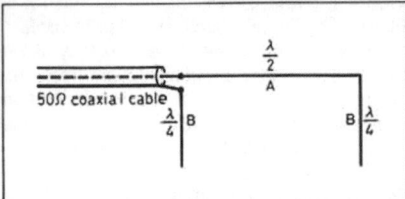

Fig 5: The simple DX-antenna described by LA5UF in *Amator Radio*. A = 75/f (MHz) in metres, B = 150/f.

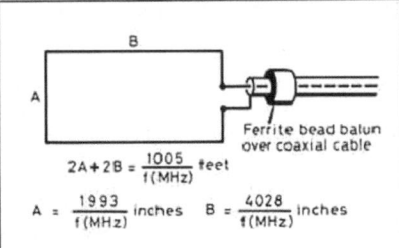

$2A + 2B = \dfrac{1005}{f(MHz)}$ feet

$A = \dfrac{1993}{f(MHz)}$ inches $B = \dfrac{4028}{f(MHz)}$ inches

Fig 6: Elongated quad-loop antenna as implemented by G3BDQ.

his formula gave a loop that resonated at 20.5MHz. Much trimming eventually gave unity SWR at 21.2MHz. G3BDQ considers that the total wire length should be that used for a normal quad-loop element:

1005/f(MHz) ft with the side lengths chosen as shown in **Fig 6**. He finds that this gives a perfect match and an antenna that has worked 'really well' when with the lower side some 10ft from the ground.

It would appear that G3BDQ has his quad-loop in the vertical plane. The design is equally suitable as a horizontal loop and this may account for the lower resonant frequency found by him due to proximity of the lower element to ground.

The Folded-tee Antenna

Extracted from 'Technical Topics', *Radio Communication*, August 1992

THE FOLDED-TEE ANTENNA

IN *TT*, JULY 1987 and again in August 1991, some details were given of the investigation by Arch Doty, K8CFU, of the advantages of the quarter-wave folded monopole antenna, including the possibility of feeding such antennas directly from 50Ω coaxial cable feeders (or 75Ω cable with different diameter conductors) and the reduction of ground losses brought about by the higher feedpoint impedance. But, as noted then, a 1.8MHz monopole requires a height of some 115ft (35m) - a height not really feasible for the vast majority of amateurs. Even for 3.5MHz a quarter-wave monopole needs a height of some 66ft (20m) or so.

Anthony Preedy, A45ZZ/G3LNP, a professional broadcast-antenna engineer writing from the Sultanate of Oman, has come up with an effective way of reducing the height of folded monopoles with an original design - the 'folded-Tee antenna'. This design was first proposed for use in Saudi Arabia to enable MF transmitters to be tuned rapidly to various frequencies but would seem to offer significant advantages for amateur operation on 1.8MHz and the lower HF bands. Tony Preedy writes:

"DX operation on the lower bands usually calls for a vertical antenna. The height of a self-resonant quarter-wave or half-wave antenna for 1.8MHz is generally beyond the facilities available to most amateurs.

"An 'L' or 'T' configuration is the usual solution to this problem. The 'T' is preferred because, otherwise wasteful high angle (horizontally-polarized) radiation is conserved by cancellation between each half of the horizontal section. But a single wire 'T' for 1.8MHz with a 'reasonable' height of, say, 15m will have a feed resistance of only about 10Ω and requires a matching network if coaxial feeder is to be used. A tuned network will considerably reduce the effective bandwidth of the antenna.

"**Fig 1** shows how a 'folded-Tee' antenna can be derived from the quarter-wave folded monopole as described in the standard handbooks or *TT*, July 1987. This is a special form of 'T' antenna developed for MF broadcasting, and largely retains the significant advantages of the folded monopole which are bandwidth, a static discharge path to earth and a moderate feed resistance.

"With similar diameter conductors, the feed resistance of the folded-Tee is four times that of a simple 'T' and varies as the square of the height as shown in **Fig 2**. A match to 50Ω coaxial feeder requires a height of approximately only one-tenth of a wavelength, although this is dependent to some extent on earth loss resistance. Earth resistance should be minimised for optimum efficiency as with any vertical antenna driven against ground.

"Adjustment is simple and this feature made the antenna attractive for MF broadcasting during the 1991 Middle East conflict. Determine the height which provides 50Ω feed resistance, then trim the top lengths symmetrically at the centre for resonance.

"Dimensions for a 1.85MHz antenna are shown in **Fig 3**. This requires supports a little over 15m high and should cover the whole band with low VSWR without the need for base matching networks. The dimensions can be scaled for other bands with final top lengths trimmed for minimum VSWR".

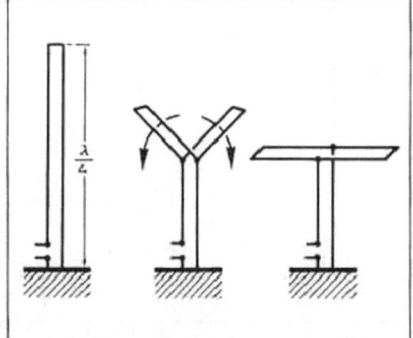

Fig 1: The derivation of the G3LNP/A45ZZ folded vertical quarter-wave monopole antenna.

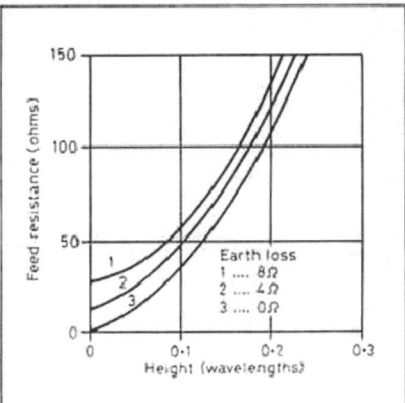

Fig 2: Resonant feed-point resistance versus height for the folded 'T' antenna.

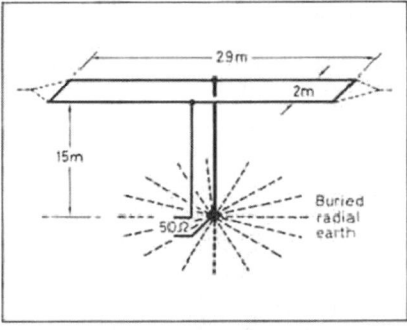

Fig 3: Dimensions for a 1.85MHz folded 'T' antenna. Dimensions can be scaled for higher-frequency bands.

It is interesting to note that a folded-Tee antenna for 7MHz DX with support heights of one-tenth wavelength would have a height of only about 4 to 4.5m. It should prove effective in any location having reasonable earth conductivity, or alternatively could be used with elevated resonant radials or counterpoises.

Efficiency or Effectiveness?

Extracted from 'Technical Topics', *Radio Communication*, August 1992

EFFICIENCY OR EFFECTIVENESS?

SEVERAL COMMENTS HAVE been received concerning the criticisms levelled generally by Dr John Belrose, VE2CV, at the looseness of terminology found in amateur-radio publications with particular reference to the comments in *TT* (December 1991) on the G4HOL horizontal loop antenna.

Dr Brian Austin, G0GSF, felt that VE2CV was too severe in his criticisms of *TT* and of G4HOL's comments on the performance of his loop on 3.5MHz but also brings out the important difference between antenna 'efficiency' and antenna 'effectiveness'. He writes:

"G4HOL didn't say in *TT* that his new loop had 9dB more gain than his sloper but simply that it 'was consistently some 9dB better'. That surely is completely fair comment since that is what he observed on the signals and over the period of time concerned. At no stage was gain actually mentioned.

"I certainly agree with VE2CV when he says that there are probably more erroneous statements made and written about antennas than any other aspect of amateur radio but in my experience *TT* has not been guilty of many, if at all.

"One example of loose terminology which I see and hear often involves the concept of efficiency. Frequently one will hear amateurs comparing antennas on the basis of their 'efficiency' when, in fact, they don't mean efficiency at all. If they had said 'effectiveness', I would have been entirely satisfied since effectiveness can be a subjective assessment of an antenna's performance. It is not a characteristic that is defined mathematically, unlike 'efficiency' which is. AJ Henk, G4XVF, in his articles about electrically small loops (*RadCom*, Sept/Oct 1991) made the distinction between efficiency and effectiveness very clearly, but maybe it needs restating in completely general terms lest anyone thinks that only such small antennas can be inefficient.

"Mathematically the gain, G, of an antenna and its directivity, D, are related by the radiation efficiency or just the efficiency, e, thus $G = eD$. As in all cases where efficiency is involved in engineering we mean the ratio of output power to input power, usually expressed as a percentage. Since the output power from an antenna is a measure of how well it radiates, we would expect the radiation efficiency to involve the radiation resistance R_{rad}, and the overall loss resistance, R_{loss}, of the antenna. Hence:

$$e = R_{rad}/(R_{rad} + R_{loss}) \times 100 \text{ per cent}$$

"For most antennas that amateurs use in a fixed installation, the radiation efficiency will be very close to 100%, in which case gain and directivity can be used interchangeably. However, mobile whips with sizeable loading coils and any other antenna containing significant amounts of lumped loading may well be rather inefficient: the so called Australian Dipole and the T2FD which have become popular again because of their broadband performance by trading efficiency for bandwidth. In both cases their radiation efficiencies, which vary with frequency, are typically less than 50 per cent and considerably less than that at the low end of the HF band".

If I have understood G0GSF correctly (and to save protests from users of Australian dipoles and T2FD antennas which use resistive loading) he is emphasising that antennas which have only low or moderate efficiency can yet prove quite effective in certain applications. For example, the small loop in those situations where an antenna of dimensions comparable to half-wavelength is impracticable; or the Australian dipole where multiband operation matching adjustments are more important than radiating every watt of transmitter output - 50 per cent efficiency, after all, represents a drop of only 3dB, or less than one S-point. After all, it is only the power radiated towards the target area, at the right elevation angle for the propagation conditions at that moment, which governs the signal strength.

Fishing for Antennas

Extracted from 'Technical Topics', *Radio Communication*, September 1992

FISHING FOR ANTENNAS WITH MONOFILAMENT LINE

AS NOTED RECENTLY IN *TT*, a whole battery of weapons can be used to shoot a thin line over a high branch of a tree: bow-and-arrow; catapult-sling (Nov 1991); even a blow-pipe (July 1992). They form an alternative to the usually less-effective method of attaching a weight to the line and throwing it over a suitable branch.

A less warlike approach is suggested by Bill Glung, KC3XO (*QST*'s 'Hints and Kinks'): "If you are a proficient fisherman with the ability to cast a line, a fishing rod and heavy sinker is an excellent way to throw a line where you need it. I pulled a nylon line over with the fishing line, then a rope with the nylon line - result a newly erected 3.5 and 7MHz sloper antenna."

Sounds easy - but Norman Bonnet, G0NNA/DL, warns that any method involving monofilament fishing line can result in a nasty tangle unless care is taken. He writes:

"Monofilament fishing line is a truly wondrous material *but* it needs a little forethought in use:

(1) You need to buy the strength of line you want. 50kg line will give a truly strong support but will bring its own problems. A better weight is in the range 5 - 15kg depending on what you are going to heave or pull.

(2) Take the length you want and (exactly as for copper wire) put one end in the vice and stretch the line. This helps to defeat the desire of fishing lines to form themselves instantly into coils. The working strain of the line is marked on it so there should be no breakages as can happen with copper wire.

(3) *Wearing a strong pair of gloves* start at the vice end and run the whole length of line through your fingers to remove finally any remaining coils.

(4) Normal 'Boy Scout knots' are of little use with fishing line as there is too little friction for them to hold. It is better to use a knot as shown in **Fig 2** which has never lost me a salmon or trout!

(5) While buying your line at a tackle shop, you can also buy very neat beachcasting weights.

(6) Small cut-off pieces of fishing line are deadly to small animals and birds, so ensure that you remove all such pieces which should then be destroyed.

(7) When throwing (or casting) the line do not lay it on the grass and hope it won't snag the grass or small twigs. Instead, lay it on a large sheet of plastic and then coil it in as concentric a circle as you can manage.

(8) Do not be tempted into thinking that fishing line is inert. You will find it has a mind of its own and will try to form itself into a bird's nest. If this happens, years of fly-fishing have taught me not to attempt to unravel it, but to replace and destroy it painlessly indoors.

"Use the above tips and problems should disappear!"

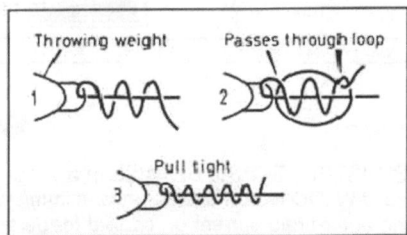

Fig 2: G0NNA's recommended knot for fixing sinker to monofilament fishing line.

7MHz Halfwaves on 21MHz

Extracted from 'Technical Topics', *Radio Communication*, September 1992

MORE ON USING 7MHZ HALF-WAVE DIPOLES ON 21MHZ

ROBIN MOSELEY, WA3T, WITH REFERENCE to the March item 'The 7MHz dipole on 21MHz' points out that there are two methods of forcing a dipole antenna to be simultaneously resonant at any two desired frequencies: one in the 7MHz band and the other in the 21MHz. He writes: "One solution is to use capacitive loading as described by NJ2L in *QST*, June 1991. Another is to use a small amount of inductive loading, positioned approximately at the centre of each of the 'outside' halfwaves of the 21MHz 1.5-wave dipole. The inductors should be positioned near the maximum-current points in the 21MHz dipole. When operating at 7MHz they carry only half the maximum current. Taking this and the frequency difference into account, the inductors present about six times more

ANTENNA TOPICS

loading effect on 21MHz than they do on 7MHz. Thus they increase the electrical length correspondingly more on 21MHz.

"In a practical antenna, the two design and adjustment variables are the inductance of the loading coils, and the overall length of the dipole. Rather than worry too much about putting the inductors at the exact maximum-current points for 21MHz, I suggest they be positioned 20ft from the centre, and the final length adjustment made in the outer section without changing the position of the inductors.

"A good value for the inductors is 0.5μH, corresponding to four turns on a 1.5in plastic tube, spaced over about 1.3in. A good starting point for the overall length is 66.5ft.

"For an antenna height of 30ft, MININEC predicts a 21MHz resonant impedance of 82Ω, giving an SWR of 1.65 on a 50Ω line. A 75Ω quarter-wave section could be used (as suggested by W2XM in the March item) to reduce this mismatch to about 1.3. The 'ideal' antenna impedance when this arrangement is used would be 112Ω, but the good news is that over-compensation at resonance will widen the SWR bandwidth, somewhat offsetting the inevitably narrower bandwidth of a long antenna. Note that these inductors are not 'traps' merely slight loading to adjust the electrical length. The bandwidth of the antenna is not significantly affected by their presence."

W2DU-type Current Balun

Extracted from 'Technical Topics', *Radio Communication*, September 1992

Earths, Losses and Verticals

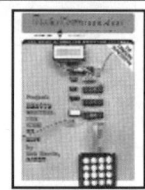

Extracted from 'Technical Topics', *Radio Communication*, October 1992

EARTHS, LOSSES AND VERTICAL ANTENNAS

RECENTLY, I WAS CHECKING ON the early history of the BBC's original 'Empire Service' that was launched from Daventry almost exactly 60 years ago, in November 1932. It was interesting to find that the quite complex series of vertically-polarized directional antenna arrays, plus some omnidirectional Franklin Uniform vertically polarized antennas for the 49, 31, 25, 19 and 16m bands, had proved unsatisfactory. They provided weaker than expected signals into the various target zones from the two 10kW STC transmitters, and as a result the BBC engineers began a series of experiments with horizontally-polarized dipoles. These were initially strung from the 500ft masts used for the original 1600m Daventry long-wave station opened in 1925. This has since been relocated to Droitwich.

As described in Edward Pawley's *Engineering History of the BBC, 1922-72*: "Early in 1933 it became clear from reports from listeners that the Daventry transmissions were not being received as well as might be expected and poor performance of the transmitting aerials appeared to be a likely cause. A series of experiments with different types of aerial was undertaken, the first step being to suspend simple horizontal dipoles from the 500ft masts carrying the Daventry long-wave aerial and to compare their performance with that of the existing low vertical aerials. The first test was made in May 1933 to compare directly a high horizontal half-wave dipole (10 wavelengths above the ground) dimensioned for an operating frequency of 11.86MHz - with one of the low vertically-polarized non-directional aerials.

"The results of this comparative test were quite definite and showed the high aerial to give a gain of 5 to 10dB in the strength of the signals received in Buenos Aires and Bermuda. In December 1933 a high horizontal half-wave dipole dimensioned for 9.7MHz was compared with a low vertical four-element aerial operating on the same wavelength and oriented on India. The high dipole was found to give equal strength signals in Ceylon (Sri Lanka), on the centre line of the directional transmission, although the theoretical gain of the four-element aerial was 9dB above that of the non-directional dipole. At this time it was not known whether the superiority of the horizontal aerial was due to its polarisation or to its height above ground."

Pawley describes how further tests were made between October 1934 and March 1935 with eleven different antennas on 12MHz, using 350ft towers, in order to determine the choice between horizontally and vertically polarized antennas and to discover the minimum mast height for optimum reception with a given transmitter power. The conclusion reached was that, at least at Daventry, horizontally-polarized antennas were better than vertical, that it would be unnecessary to have more than four horizontal radiators stacked vertically at half-wave intervals, and that the lowest element should be not less than one-wavelength above ground.

Since then, to the best of my knowledge, HF broadcast antennas have been horizontally polarized for sky-wave transmission whereas medium- and long-wave broadcast

W2DU-TYPE CURRENT BALUN

CONSTRUCTIONAL DETAILS of a wideband W2DU-type choke-balun for minimising outer-braid current on coaxial feeders connected to dipole-type balanced elements over the range 2 to 30MHz are given in "Reflecties door", PA0SE, (*Electron*, April 1992, p189) reproduced from "Le Balun W2DU" by Maurice Limes, F6ELM (*Radio-REF*, October 1991): Fig 7. The 50 ferrite beads are Amidon type FB-73-2401 (outer diameter 9.7mm, inner diameter 5mm, length 4.8mm, permeability about 2500) and are slipped over a length of RG141 (50ohm) coaxial cable using two spirals of Teflon thread to secure them. This is then sealed (waterproofed) into a length of PVC tubing with an inner diameter of 16mm, using a rubberized adhesive filler given as Dow Corning Silastic 7338 (or UK equivalent). Impedance of this choke balun is stated to be more than 800Ω throughout the range 2 to 30MHz, peaking to about 1500Ω between 7 and 10MHz.

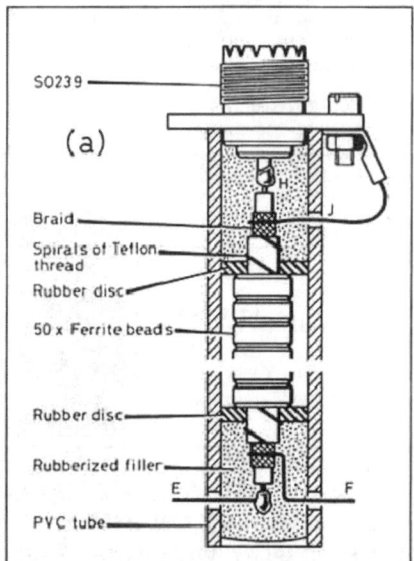

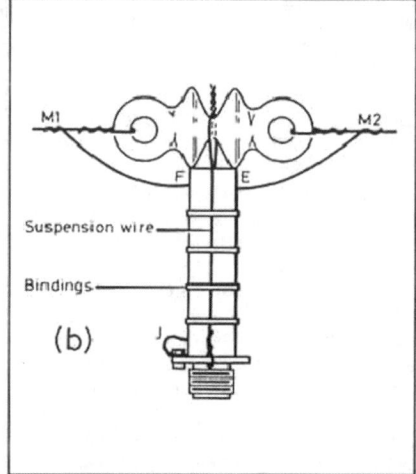

Fig 7: (a) Mechanical details of the W2DU-type wideband choke balun as constructed by F6EIM. (b) The balun suspended to feed a dipole-type wire element.

heavily in terms of convenience, was compared experimentally with the Zepp feed form shown in Fig 8(c), with and without a G6CJ-type balancing stub. Apart from establishing the credentials of the new method, the results were highly instructive. Differences in field strengths were small provided the current on the outer of the coaxial cable was sufficiently low, a condition achievable in the case of the Zepp by using *either* the stub *or* the more convenient linear trap. As this was a one-off experiment it should not be assumed to apply in other cases without further checking, but it would appear that the absence of any path to ground ensures that the same current has to flow in both feeder wires. In the case of Fig 8(b) the trap was needed only in the event of maladjustment of L. Bandwidth was adequate for coverage of the 21MHz band even in the case of the Zepp feed.

"If vertical polarization is favoured and two supports are available the inverted ground-plane antenna of Fig 8(b) can be recommended. This can also be used as a horizontal half-wave dipole or a top-loaded ground-plane antenna at half the frequency."

Les also mentions that at long last the ARRL have accepted his 20Ω figure for the radiation resistance of a ground-plane antenna, as this has now been backed by their own computer study. The recognition that, as he has often pointed out, the GPA is a form of dipole and not a form of monopole antenna has a devastating effect on a large number of sacred cows but, adds G6XN "it may be more than a coincidence that the large numbers of radials demanded by some authors ties in very closely with the mesh size requirements specified by Proctor 'Input impedance of horizontal dipole aerials at low heights above the ground' (*Proc IEEE*, part 3, May 1950) - a very important reference since it is possible to extrapolate from **Fig 9** etc to get an idea of ground losses in horizontal wires generally. Vertical wires do not induce significant losses. The reference also shows effect of ground screens."

My 1970s version of the inverted ground-plane antenna was derived as a single-element version of the Bobtail array mentioned and illustrated in the July *TT* (p39). This has encouraged Bill Wheeler, G3BFC, to comment as follows: "When *TT* first referred to the

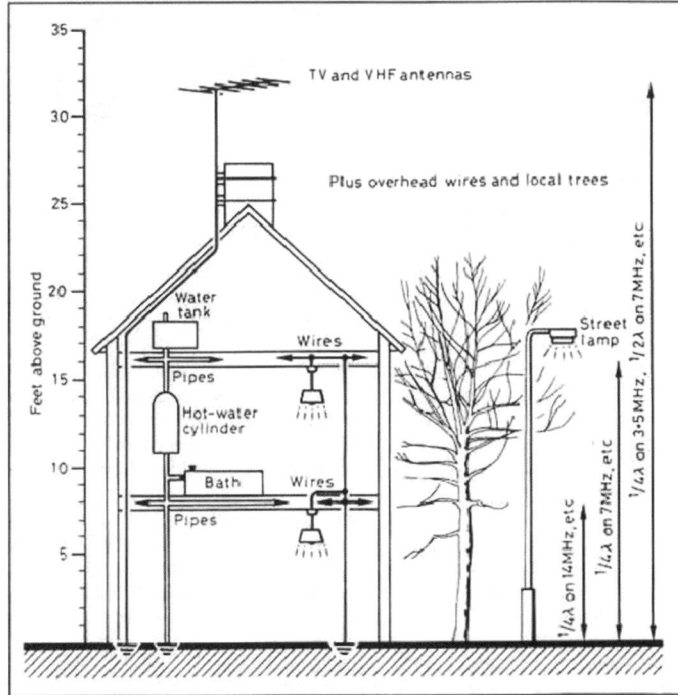

Fig 7: The possibility of unwanted resonances of metal conduits, pipes etc in a typical residential environment as suggested in *TT*, January 1985, by G3BLK. The houses can also have broadband resonances. Energy induced will be re-radiated by a lossless 'element' but will be absorbed by 'lossy' conductors, including the earth, building, tree trunks, etc.

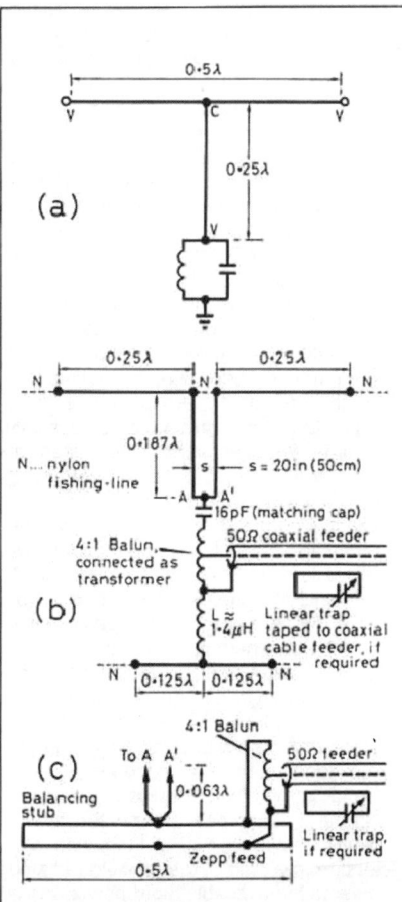

Fig 8: (a) Basic inverted ground-plane (also known as Vertical-Tee) antenna. (b) G6XN's recommended method of end-feeding from coaxial-cable. (c) Zepp form of feed as tested by G6XN.

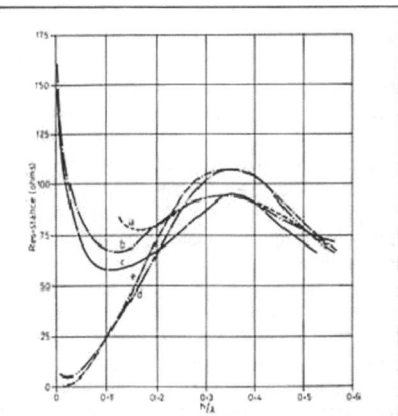

Fig 9: Measured input impedance of a resonant horizontal half-wave dipole above ground where h is height above ground. (a) Calculated for soil permittivity of 6. (b) Dry ground. (c) Wet ground. (d) Conducting mat (large, fine-mesh copper mat representing perfectly conducting ground for comparison purposes). (e) Calculated for infinite permittivity. Results quoted are for an open site covered with short grass and having a gravel subsoil, of which a sample measured a value of six after a long spell of fine weather. Above the dielectric ground there is a large increase in the radiation resistance of the antenna as it approaches ground-level. Close to the ground the radiation resistance is about double that of a similar antenna in free space. (Source: Proctor, *Proc IEE*, Part 3, May 1950)

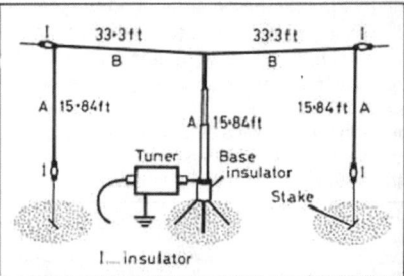

Fig 10: Bobtail curtain for 14MHz as originally used by G3BFC at 9Y4BFC in 1970.

Bobtail in 1970, I was living in Trinidad and operating 9Y4BFC. I constructed the antenna as shown in **Fig 10** using four radials and a tuned LC circuit. It performed well over the 4500-mile path to the UK in the evenings on 14MHz. Later, back in the UK, I returned to the Bobtail using the same approach as at 9Y4BFC. My near neighbour, Bill Sykes, G2HCG, suggested that I omit the radials and LC and replace them with a tuned closed stub - this worked well. Then along came 'Controlled feeder radiation' (CFR) by G2HCG in *RadCom*, May 1990 and July 1991. So my Bobtail was made simpler still using CFR in accordance with the July, 1991 article again with good performance. However, size was then reduced to two vertical elements instead of three, but with each carrying equal current rather than the original version in which the two outer of the three elements carried half the current of the centre element.

"Fig 5 of the July, 1992 *TT* showed a two vertical element form of Bobtail directly fed at the top with 52Ω co-axial cable although I consider the dimensions given in this account should be read in reverse. I have found a 28MHz version seems to work well when compared with a three-element monoband beam (not as well since the comparison is hardly a fair one).

ANTENNA TOPICS

"To sum up, of the various Bobtail-type configurations I have tried, the two element version using a tuned toroid as described in the two *RadCom* articles by Bill Sykes (the founder and Chairman for many years of Jaybeam Ltd) is well worth considering."

It seems to me that the G3BFC version with the 'reversed' dimensions changes the arrangement from a broadside array to an endfire system, though both approaches seem logical enough.

While on the subject of vertically-polarized antennas, it seems worth noting a comment from C W ('Mick') Cragg, G2HDU, about my comment in the August *TT* that a folded monopole has lower earth losses than a simple monopole (not claimed by Tony Preedy, G3LNP, for his 'folded-tee' antenna). He writes: "This has been stated many times, and in many places, but I have never seen an acceptable proof. It seems to be taken for granted, but a little thought will show that in fact the earth current is the same as with a simple monopole, so that for a given earthing system the loss is the same. There is no question that the feed point impedance is higher since only half the current flows in each side of the folded monopole. However, both of these half currents flow in the earth so that the total earth current is the same as with a simple monopole. I would be interested to learn whether the antenna pundits agree."

While one could use two separate earths for a folded monopole putting the earth currents in 'parallel', this would be unusual and G2HCG appears to have a valid point, although there seems evidence that in practice the efficiency (as well as the effectiveness) of the folded version may be significantly higher.

Earths and Marconis

Extracted from 'Technical Topics', *Radio Communication*, December 1992

EARTHS AND MARCONI ANTENNAS

IT IS NOTICEABLE THAT every time the topic of earths and earthing as part of a vertical monopole or Marconi-type antenna crops up in *TT*, it produces correspondence from those who hold diverse views. It sometimes seems that the subject can be as controversial as that of the antenna itself! John Heys, G3BDQ, for example, crosses swords with Dennis Unwin, G0FMT, in connection with his in-built earthing system for his quarter-wave Marconi antenna (*TT*, October). While personally I am not persuaded to start digging or laying an earth mat by G3BDQ's suggestions (surely with a resonant quarter-wave Marconi or monopole vertical the feed impedance is assumed by convention to be directly related to the radiation resistance and the more RF current that you can push into the antenna for a given transmitter power

continued on page 299

GP Antennas Close to Earth

Extracted from 'Technical Topics', *Radio Communication*, November 1992

GROUND PLANE ANTENNAS CLOSE TO EARTH

A RECENT *TT* ITEM from Les Moxon, G6XN, has emphasised that the usual form of elevated ground plane antenna with two, three or four quarter-wave wire radials, as normally found in the Amateur Service, needs to be considered as a form of dipole rather than a vertical monopole antenna. As he pointed out "this has a devastating effect on a large number of sacred cows".

However, antennas for the lower frequency bands - including medium-wave broadcast antennas and antennas for 1.8 and 3.5MHz - consist of a vertical radiating element and a large number of wire radials buried in close proximity to the surface of the earth or elevated just a few feet above earth. These radials which form the 'ground plane' may or may not be resonant lengths. Such antennas are normally analysed as 'monopole' antennas.

Dr Brian Austin, G0GSF, has drawn attention to "a particularly interesting set of computed results" that has been published in *Electronics Letters*, 30 July 1992, pp1550-51. This is 'Radiation efficiency and input impedance of monopole elements with radial-wire ground planes in proximity to earth' by M M Weiner, S Zamoscianyk and G J Burke of The MITRE Corporation and Lawrence Livermore National Laboratory. A number of earlier *TT* items have reported briefly on earlier publications by Dr Weiner on aspects of ground-plane antennas.

The results have been computed using the NEC-GS program (an optimisation for radial-wire ground planes of NEC-3) based on an antenna geometry consisting of a vertical monopole element, of length h and radius b, on a groundscreen consisting of N equally-spaced radial wires, of length a and radius b_w, at a depth of z_o below a flat lossy Earth surface of defined dielectric constant and conductivity. The monopole element and the radial wires are assumed to have infinite conductivity.

Results are presented in **Fig 5(a), (b) and (c)** for parameters with fixed values of quarter-wave height, b and b_w equal to 0.00001 wavelength, Earth dielectric constant of 15 and frequency-dependent conductivity, for a varying number of wire radials at a height of 0.0001 wavelength (ie a 'negative depth') above lossy Earth. The radiation efficiency, input resistance and input reactance are plotted in the graphs shown in Fig 5. Radiation efficiency is the ratio of the far-field radiated power to the available input power and is a measure of the power loss in the particular characteristics chosen to represent the lossy earth since the monopole element and radial wires are assumed to have infinite conductivity.

While clearly one needs to interpret these results with care - and I hesitate to give my own interpretation - they appear to show that radiation efficiency with radials a few feet above ground is virtually independent of the number of radials, at least for ground screens of normal size. This seems a further justification of the work initiated over a decade ago by Arch Doty, K8CFU, which showed, from hundreds of actual measurements, that a few elevated wire radials were as efficient as the standard broadcast practice of using 120 buried radials. The input resistance seems curiously high and presumably reflects earth losses.

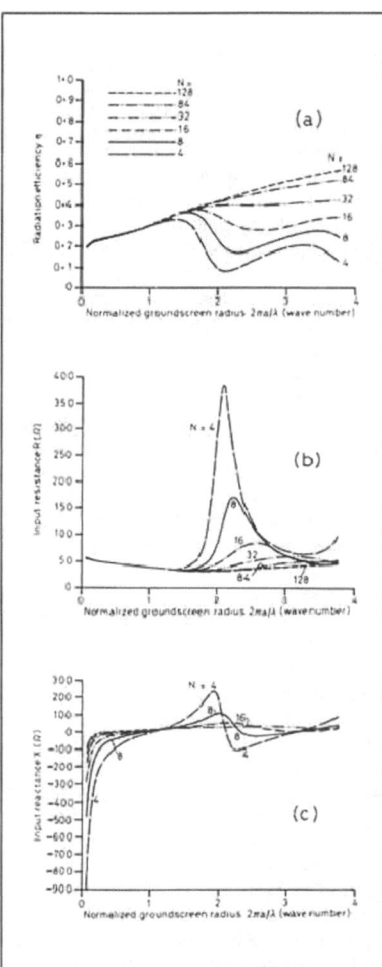

Fig 5: Computerized results shown by M M Weiner et al in *Electronics Letters* in connection with the radiation efficiency and input impedance of monopole elements with radial-wire ground planes in proximity to earth. (a) radiation efficiency; (b) input resistance; and (c) input reactance for varying numbers (N) of wire radials at a height of 0.0001-wavelength above a 'lossy' Earth of specified dielectric constant and conductivity.

continued from page 298

then the more efficient the antenna), it seems only fair to reproduce G3BDQ's remarks:

"I must cross swords with G0FMT. He is wrong in assuming that efficiency is directly related to feed impedance on a quarter-wave wire. You can juggle about with feed impedance in many ways (usually by lengthening or shortening the wire) but this will have little effect upon the efficiency of the system. The only way to increase the efficiency is to raise the radiation resistance of the antenna and/or reduce the earth resistance.

"This latter factor is the thing we can do ourselves. Running wires around the house, along the floor or putting in earth rods is almost a waste of time and effort. Salt water all around the antenna for a considerable distance, a copper sheet of enormous dimensions represent the ultimate . . . . earth rods are 'no-go' and buried wires unless very long and very numerous are not very good either. I find that an effective compromise is a comprehensive 'earth mat' of galvanised 'chicken wire'. this must cover a considerable area all around the antenna. As my 'mat' was increased the efficiency of my antenna was raised dramatically. I certainly did not try to equate efficiency with feed impedance.

"An earthing system must have a very low resistance return for the earth current back to the antenna base. The late Dr George Brown (*Proc IRE*, February 1935) states: 'In the operation of the usual transmitting antenna, the conduction current in the antenna diminishes as we proceed upward along the antenna. This is explained by displacement currents which are assumed to flow in the antenna, through space to the conducting plane below. This conducting plane completes the circuit by forming the return path to the base of the antenna. If this plane is not a perfect conductor, some power must be expended in returning the current to the base of the antenna'."

While one would not quarrel with the general tenor of the later comments, it does seem to me that they at odds with the now widely held view that, for example, a monopole antenna with a few radials elevated a few feet above ground and forming a counterpoise has been shown to be as effective as the usual form of broadcast antenna earth with 120 buried radials. Les Moxon, G6XN (*HF antennas for all locations*) shows clearly (page 4) that "high efficiency can be achieved with very short radials or counterpoises . . . ." The important thing is to make sure that the currents flowing to and from the feed line are maximised. In the old days, before we worried about SWR and power meters, an RF ammeter in the antenna wire or the earth wire formed a valuable guide to antenna radiation. If altering the earthing or counterpoise system increases the current then one could safely assume that the radiation efficiency had been increased. While a large earth mat made from chicken wire *does* form an effective earth it is not the only approach that yields high radiation efficiency. One method may well be the in-built system used by G0FMT that could save a lot of back-breaking digging.

ZS6BKW/G0GSF Multiband Dipole

Extracted from 'Technical Topics', *Radio Communication*, January 1993

MORE ON THE ZS6BKW/ G0GSF MULTIBAND DIPOLE

JUST OVER A DECADE AGO, *TT*, May 1982, pp412-3, presented an item 'Potential of the G5RV antenna' which brought to the notice of amateurs the computer-aided work of Dr Brian Austin (ZS6BKW and more recently G0GSF). He showed how the dimensions of the multiband dipole antenna popularised by Louis Varney, G5RV, some forty years ago could be modified to extend its performance to the 18 and 24MHz bands. A few years later, Dr Austin provided a full-length description (*RadCom*, Aug 1985, pp614-617, 624) of this antenna. Computer aided work showed how such an antenna could be dimensioned so that, even without an ATU, an effective match could be obtained on most bands from 7 to 28MHz. With the aid of an ASMU (ATU), operation on 3.5, 10 and 21MHz was possible.

Surprisingly, relatively few UK amateurs seem to have taken advantage of this modified design which eliminates the disadvantages of traps, multiple wire elements etc, yet still provides a coaxial feed into the shack. Also, it can be used as a readily transportable wire antenna for field events, expeditions etc. It has, however, been attracting increasing attention overseas, and also for non-amateur communications.

Fig 6 as given in the Danish journal *OZ* (10/92) and initially in Rothammel's *Antennabuch*, shows **(a)** the standard 'G5RV' antenna together with two modified versions, **(b)** as proposed by W5ANB in *QST*, Nov 1981, for 7, 14 and 28MHz, and **(c)** the ZS6BKW/G0GSF arrangement discussed below. **Fig 6(d)** shows one form of ATU that can be used with any of these antennas on bands where the VSWR without a tuner is more than about 2:1. The Danish article by Rick Meilstrup, OZ5RM, gives results of measurements made on the original G5RV antenna now being marketed by DeeComm, although normally a wire antenna can be constructed at lower cost than a packaged product.

In the New Zealand journal *Break-in*, May 1992, Rick Hill, ZL1OK presents some SWR measurements made on what he describes as "a very useful cheap antenna that thrashes the pants off a G5RV . . . . The main disadvantages are the lack of 15m band coverage, the 10m resonance is rather high in the band and the antenna is de-tuned somewhat by heavy rain."

ZL1OK writes that his antenna has a feedpoint impedance close to 50Ω on five bands - "operation on all or part of the 40, 20, 17, 12 and 10 metre bands is quite practical using a solid-state rig with no tuner. I have built several versions of this antenna. Results have been good with the antenna in the inverted vee configuration with the apex 12m above the ground. He gives measurements made on a lightweight version using slotted low-loss TV ribbon (300Ω) for the matching section and 0.55mm² hookup wire for the 'top'. It is possible to optimize SWR for your favourite portion of your favourite band by adjusting the dipole length, but this may result in the 'loss' (without an ATU) of one of the other bands."

A recent IEE colloquium on 'Multi-band Antennas' was concerned primarily with antennas for the microwave and millimetre wave bands, but provided also a forum for Brian Austin, G0GSF, to describe his version of the G5RV type antenna as a solution to the problems of tactical HF one-hop communications. He emphasised that ionospheric propagation mechanisms used at HF involve diurnal, seasonal and sunspot cycle variations that make multi-frequency operation obligatory if 24-hour contact is required over any given path.

"This requirement places quite considerable constraints on the antenna systems used and would suggest that either a multiplicity of antennas or a single broadband configuration is required . . . . If operational requirements (eg tactical situation or non-permanent installations) preclude the use of large broadband antennas then a viable alternative is the multiband antenna.

"A configuration which achieves multiband performance, at high radiation efficiency, was first used in the 1930s, then popularised for

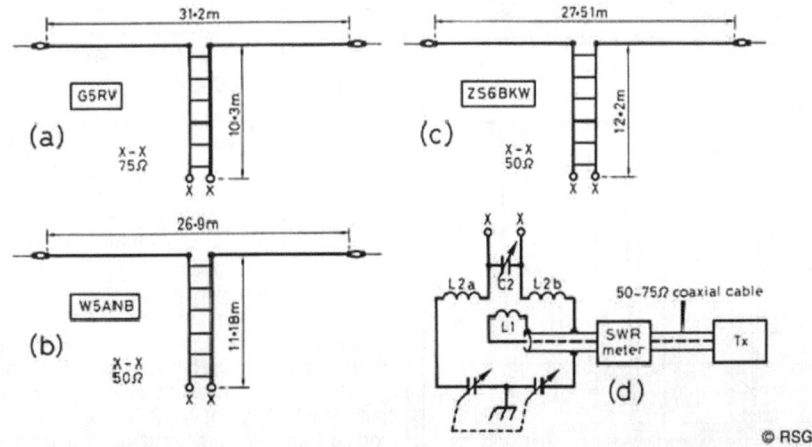

Fig 6: Three versions of multiband dipoles providing low SWR on the coaxial cable feeder on a number of HF bands. (a) The original 'G5RV'; (b) version proposed by W5ANB; (c) the ZS6BKW/G0GSF antenna discussed in the text and (d) a suitable ATU for all versions for use on bands not providing low SWR.

ANTENNA TOPICS

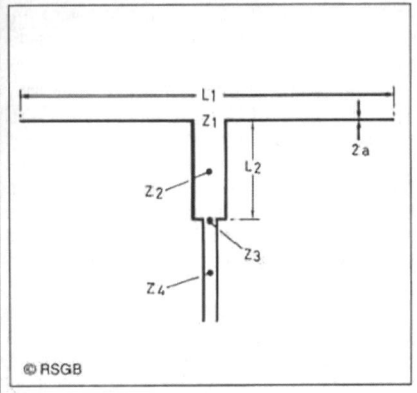

Fig 7: Basics of the multiband wire antenna.

radio amateurs by Louis Varney, G5RV, (*RSGB Bulletin*, Vol 34, No 7, 1958, pp19-20) and more recently optimized in terms of its VSWR performance (B A Austin, 'An HF multiband wire antenna for single-hop point-to-point applications', *J.IERE*, Vol 57, No 4, 1987, pp167-173).

"The antenna is shown in **Fig 7**. The transmission line section L2 acts as a series-section impedance transformer whose function is to transform Z1, the driving-point impedance of L1, into a suitable value Z3 which will match the characteristic impedance Z4 of the system transmission line to the terminal equipment. The performance criterion used is the VSWR on that cable (usually coaxial with Z4 equal to 50Ω). An acceptable match exists when VSWR is equal to or less than 2:1 . . . . In general, the relationship between L1, L2 and Z2 when the VSWR with respect to Z4 is shown in **Fig 8**."

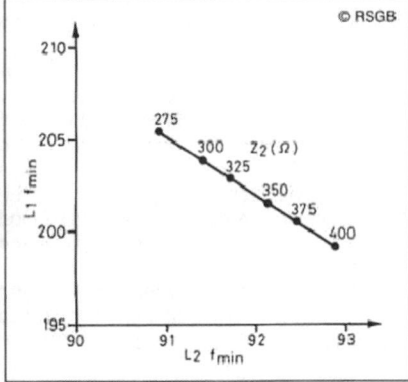

Fig 8: 'Design line' for the multiband antenna.

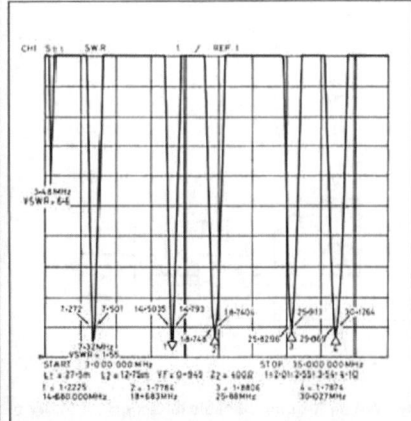

Fig 9: VSWR vs frequency for multiband antenna.

In the IEE colloquium digest No 1992/181, Dr Austin presents two relatively simple manual methods to analyse the performance of this antenna (see also the *J.IERE* reference given above). He shows that where Z2 is greater than 275Ω and less than 450Ω an acceptable impedance match will occur at a number of frequencies in the HF range. The optimum value of Z2 lies between 325-400Ω. Within this range the matching performance of the antenna is basically independent of Z2, and a simple design equation for the antenna is L1 (f_{min}) = 473.44 - 2.95 L2 (f_{min}) where f_{min} is the lowest frequency at which the antenna is to operate, constrained by the requirement that $\pi L1/\lambda$ is greater than 1.

For any given values of f_{min} and Z2, there are specific lengths L1 and L2 which will satisfy the matching criterion. The frequencies at which this match occurs are related by the following series which varies slightly for different values of Z2: f/f_{min} = 1: 1.99: 2.53: 3.49: 4.07: 5.62: 7.18.

Dr Austin has designed and tested a number of these antennas in various practical situations. Fig 9 shows the VSWR for an antenna providing resonant frequencies just outside amateur bands with L1 27.5m, L2 12.75m, Z2 400Ω (velocity factor 0.95) and Z4 50Ω. With these dimensions five bands of frequencies in the HF band, between 3 and 30MHz, yielded VSWRs less than 2:1 with f_{min} equal to 7.32MHz and the matching series 1: 2.01: 2.55: 3,54: 4.10. A ferrite sleeve balun, consisting of 40 ferrite beads (type 73 material, permeability 2500) was used at the intersection between the balanced line L2 and the coaxial cable Z4. Its effect on the measured impedance Z3 and hence on the VSWR was minimal. He concludes: "It would appear, therefore, that the use of a balun is not justified in this application."

Roof-space Dual Band Loop

Extracted from 'Technical Topics', *Radio Communication*, February 1993

ROOF-SPACE DUAL BAND MAGNETIC LOOP

SOME MONTHS AGO, FOLLOWING the publication of a number of items on magnetic loop antennas (both in *TT* and as full-length *RadCom* articles), I began to feel that the subject deserved a rest. What more could be written - it had been shown that such antennas were capable of achieving good results, particularly on the lower frequency HF bands, for amateurs without sufficient space or high enough supports to allow the erection of an antenna providing the higher radiation resistance that makes for good efficiency at low cost. It did seem, at least to me, that the models that had appeared on the market were costly compared with a simple wire dipole, while home-constructed models called for good quality tuning capacitors welded to

GI2FHN has constructed this dual loop in his roof space.

an extremely low-resistance loop, with the complication of accurate remotely controlled motor tuning. Nevertheless, well made compact transmitting loops do work surprisingly well and represent a valid approach for those without space. From a number of contacts made with stations using small loops, it does appear that they compare well with, for example, trapped verticals mounted on the ground.

Roberto Craighero, I1ARZ, with much personal experience of using loops, writes: "I confirm once more that the radiation efficiency of a short loop antenna having a circumference slightly less than 0.25-wave approaches the efficiency of a half-wave dipole a half-wave above ground. It is clear that having sufficient space to erect a dipole at such a height provides a more convenient antenna than a compact loop. However, it is clear that most amateurs wishing to work the lower frequency bands find it difficult to erect long dipoles at the required height. In such cases the compact loop is certainly better than a dipole at a very low height in terms of wavelength.

"But I wish to stress once again that to obtain good results with a compact loop, the materials employed must be of good quality. An excellent split-stator capacitor must be used to tune the loop. Welding must be accurate to keep ohmic losses to a minimum.

"In my experience a ground plane improves the overall efficiency of a compact loop even if not directly connected to the antenna. An 80cm loop mounted over the roof of my car, but not connected to the car body, showed a significant improvement due to the ground plane provided by the roof of the car. With my large square loop for the lower frequency bands, I could notice an improvement when the surface of the flat roof is wet following rain. [But is rain water electrically conductive? *G3VA*].

"I can confirm DK5CZ's remarks (*Eurotek*, Oct 1991, p39) that the high loop currents tend to heat and thereby distort the thin metal in vacuum capacitors and consequently detune the loop. With my large low-frequency loop which has a vacuum capacitor, I find that on SSB (about 60W PEP) with its low power factor there is no need to retune the antenna. But when I use CW with its greater power factor, there is a need to retune the loop from time to time.

I1ARZ also drew attention to a loop described by Sergio Clauser, IV3RLL, in *Radio Rivista*, 7/91, using a length of low-loss UHF Heliax cable. This has an external diameter of 41mm after removing the internal nylon spiral and inner conductor to provide a very light but solid copper conductor of large diameter that can be bent into a circle by hand. Such bending is possible since this type of cable has copper tubing with a special knurling that permits bending and increases the electrical surface of the antenna by about 20%. Such cable is very expensive but it is sometimes possible to acquire short end-of-reel lengths at much reduced cost since short lengths have low commercial value. I1ARZ also mentions the use of 3in elliptical waveguide.

Eric Sandys, GI2FHN, has been making good use of a multiband form of magnetic loop that borrows a dual tuning technique from the Z-match tuner: **Figs 1 and 2**. He writes:

"On 14, 18, 21, 24 and 28MHz, L1 is tuned by C1A and C1B in series. As L3 is high impedance at these frequencies, it can be ignored. On 3.5 and 7MHz, L3 is tuned by C1A placed in parallel with C1B through L1. The coupling links L2 and L4 are connected in parallel and RF is fed in through a 1:1 choke balun. The sizes of the coupling links were selected to give the lowest SWR which is better than 1.5:1 on all bands. If coverage of the 10MHz band is required, L4 needs to be reduced slightly in size.

"The same diameter coaxial cable is used for the loops and coupling links. Note that the connections between the two coupling links should not be transposed. A should go to C and B to D. Failure to observe these points can result in degradation of the SWR.

"The loop is housed in the roof space using a timber framework to provide the necessary support. All functions are carried out from a control box (Fig 9) at the operating position. Changing bands is made easy by using a Wheatstone bridge to give a visual indication on M1 of the travel of C1. The variable arm R1 is gear driven from the shaft connecting the motor and reduction gearing to C1.

"Direction of rotation is controlled by S1, a DPDT switch (centre-off). Fine tuning is provided by a speed control R2. A current probe enables exact resonance to be established at the operating frequency.

"Results have exceeded all expectations and the arrangement can be recommended for anyone who does not have space for a fullsize outside antenna."

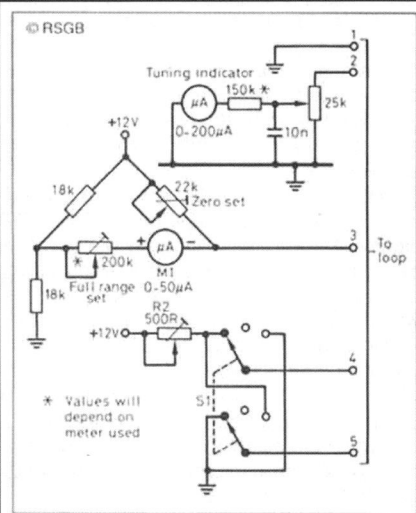

Fig 2: Control unit for tuning the loop antenna.

The loop's tuning unit with slow-motion drives.

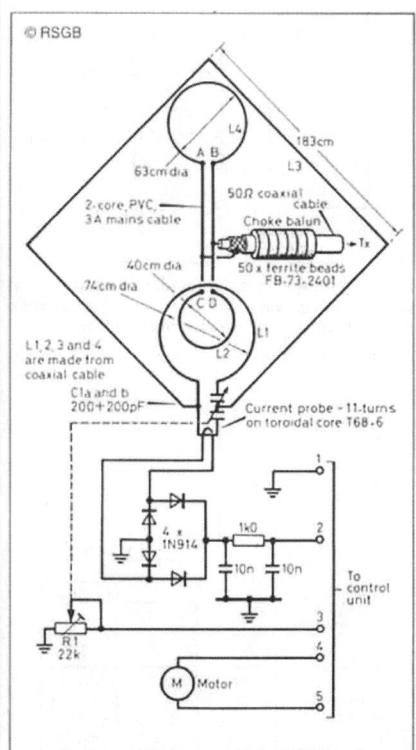

Fig 1: GI2FHN's dual magnetic loop antenna covering 3.5 to 28MHz erected in the roof-space.

More on the G5RV/ZS6BKW

Extracted from 'Technical Topics', *Radio Communication*, February 1993

MORE ON THE G5RV/ZS6BKW ANTENNAS

THE JANUARY *TT* drew attention to the growing interest overseas in the ZS6BKW/G0GSF antenna developed from the G5RV but offering a reasonable match (without ATU) on five bands: 7, 14, 18, 24 and 28MHz. It is interesting to note that Bill Orr, W6SAI, in his *Radio FUNdamentals* column in *CQ* (November 1992) also presents information on both versions under the heading 'The G5RV antenna revisited - again'.

In addition, he traces some early history, writing: "To go back a bit, the G5RV antenna is an offspring of a 3-band antenna (80-40-20 metres) designed by Art Collins (ex-W9CXX) and L M Croft and described in detail by Croft in the December 1935 issue of *Signal* magazine, the house publication of the old Collins Radio Company . . . . The idea behind the antenna was sound, but the execution was a failure because the antenna used a 300Ω section made of two 82.5ft lengths of aluminium tubing hanging from the centre of the 103ft flat top. The weight of the installation made it heavy and impractical. Signal gain of this antenna was about 1dBd.

"In the early 1950s the antenna reappeared in modified form in England, redesigned and popularized by Louis Varney, G5RV. The Varney antenna functions as a 1.5-wave antenna on 14MHz with a feedpoint impedance slightly over 100Ω. The matching section of heavy tubing is replaced by a 450Ω open-wire half-wave line. This light-weight (Matching section) transformer closely matched the antenna feedpoint impedance to an 80Ω transmission line on 20 metres . . . . it was quickly found that the G5RV would function quite well on other bands if an antenna tuning unit was used at the transmitter. No one worried much about SWR in those days . . . ."

Curiously enough, the highly-respected Walt Maxwell, W2DU, in his book *Reflections - Transmission lines and antennas* (ARRL, 1990) commits one of his very few errors in dismissing as "one of the myths and confusion concerning the G5RV" that it can yield a low SWR [admittedly not 1:1 but below 2:1 - *G3VA*] on bands other than 14MHz. He states categorically that "there is no length of open-wire line of any characteristic impedance Zc that will transform the antenna impedance Za to an impedance that is even close to presenting a match to 50 or 75Ω coax, except on 20 metres". May I humbly suggest to W2DU that before the next edition is published, he should carefully read the various papers by G0GSF mentioned in the January *TT*.

ANTENNA TOPICS

Antenna Lore Mk2

Extracted from 'Technical Topics', *Radio Communication*, March 1993

ANTENNA LORE MK2

THE DECEMBER *TT* ITEM on 'Persistent SWR myths' attracted several supportive comments and it does appear that the whole subject of antennas and feeders is still for many of us surrounded with an air of mystery. *QST* (November 1992) has recently published a five-page article by Kenneth Macleish, W7TX 'Why an antenna radiates' providing what is described as "a searching look at the mysterious process by which our antennas hurl energy from here to there". As a starter it challenges the reader to answer "true" or "false" to four statements:

(1) In a centre-fed, half-wave dipole, electrons surge back and forth from one side of the antenna to the other.
(2) It is possible for a perfect insulator to radiate.
(3) Unlike ohmic resistance, 'radiation resistance' has significance only at the feed point of an antenna or antenna system.
(4) The ground around a transmitting antenna radiates.

W7TX puts the answers in a footnote at the end of his article but, to save any embarrassment, the first and third are false; the second and fourth are true. I won't ask how many you got right! Fortunately, it is not necessary to know exactly how an antenna works to make or use one, but it helps when it doesn't seem to work in the expected manner!

Antenna Follow-ups

Extracted from 'Technical Topics', *Radio Communication*, April 1993

Dennis Unwin, G0FMT, believes (as I do) that G3BDQ (*TT*, December) misread the original item on the earthing of his 1.8MHz Marconi antenna and failed to appreciate that the changes were only to the earth or counterpoise and not to the length of the antenna itself. G0FMT stresses that he was using feed impedance solely to indicate the effectiveness of the earthing system without making any changes in the antenna itself. He still considers this a reasonable way to proceed but adds:

"Your remarks about the use of RF ammeters induced me to make one and connect it in the antenna lead. I soon discovered that you have to be very careful to adjust the ATU following every change in the earthing system, and also to standardise the output level. I was unable to duplicate all my earlier measurements (*TT*, October) since the wire counterpoise has been removed, but the five earth stakes and the underfloor system could still be compared. The current (in arbitrary units) using the five earth stakes was 5.43 and the current using the underfloor system alone was 5.99.

This appears to confirm the finding based on impedance measurements that the efficiency of the underfloor earth was slightly better than the earth stakes, the current using both together was 7.66. If we compare this with the five earth stakes alone, clearly the aerial current has substantially increased. Since we are measuring current, the im

5.43) = 2.99dB, indicating that the radiated power had almost doubled. My previous estimate based on impedance measurements was that efficiency had increased from 33% to 60%. It is power this time, so 10 log (60/33) = 2.6dB, a remarkably close agreement between two very different measurement techniques. It does also highlight the value of the 'old-fashioned' RF current meter in settling antenna arguments."

For my part I have always used RF current to optimise tuning up 'long-wire' and some other antennas, using torch bulbs shunted with a loop of wire as a crude and inexpensive form of 'current meter'.

This approach has always served me well in finding the correct inductance and correct capacitance and showing the significant difference when using various lengths of 'counterpoise' as an upstairs 'earth'.

Multi-band & All-band HF Dipoles

Extracted from 'Technical Topics', *Radio Communication*, April 1993

MULTI-BAND AND ALL-BAND HF DIPOLES

AS A PRE-WW2 AMATEUR, I soon became acquainted with the idea of open-wire feeders for resonant elements (both end-fed and so-called centre-fed Zepp) and also low-impedance feeders (often twisted electric flex before coaxial cable became readily available). But I was not really aware of using open-wire transmission lines to non-resonant elements.

Exactly 50 years ago, I arrived at a radio station at Upper Weald, near Stony Stratford, from where we keyed transmitters about a mile away at Calverton. It was something of a surprise to find that fixed-length dipole (doublet) transmitting antennas with open-wire feeders were used on all frequencies between about 3 and 10MHz with the aid of ATUs - probably based on the original balanced form of Collins Universal Coupler (pi-network): eg **Fig 4**.

In recent years, particularly since the arrival of the WARC non-harmonic bands, the attractions of open-wire feeders (or the slightly more lossy 300Ω ribbon feeders) have become ever more evident. It is convenient, though not essential, where the ATU sees a reasonably low (current fed) impedance rather than a voltage feed. It is for this reason that multiband dipoles based on the G5RV/ZS6ABW principle have special appeal.

The February *TT* quoted Bill Orr's belief that the G5RV is an offspring of the 1935 three-band antenna originated by Art Collins, ex-W9CXX, and L M Croft. However, I had forgotten that a few months earlier, Dean Manley, KH6B, writing from the Hawaiian Islands, had sent me details of the Collins antenna as reprinted in *Electric Radio* of April 1991 by Bill Stewart, K6HV. The reprint included the original data as shown on a Collins Radio Company drawing of March 1935. K6HV pointed out:

"I think Varney came up with the idea not knowing of Art's work." Art Collins's design brought the 300Ω transmission line all the way to the transmitter, whereas a feature of Louis Varney's design has always been the connection of the shortish 300ohm section to any length of (70Ω) coaxial cable.

From the original Collins Radio drawing it is clear that the antenna (**Fig 5**) came in three versions. 'A' had an element (L) length of 99ft, with 82.5ft of line, intended for 14.0-14.4MHz, 7.0-7.3MHz and 3.7-4.0MHz. 'B' with 133ft top, 48.5ft line for 14.0-14.4MHz, 7.0-7.3MHz and 3.7-4.0MHz and 'C' 266ft top, 48.5ft line for 14.0-14.4MHz, 7.0-7.3MHz, 3.5-4.0MHz and 1.7-2.0MHz. It does seem however that L M Croft in his *Signal* article also recommended 103ft for L, very close to the full-size G5RV.

The Collins work sheet shows L comprising No 10 B&S hard drawn enamelled copper

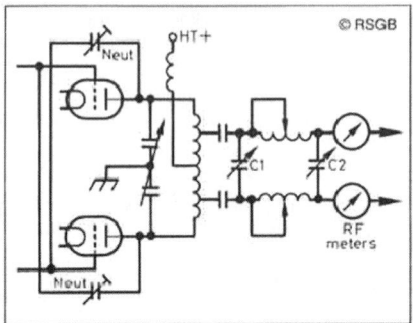

Fig 4: One form of the original Collins Universal Coupler that provided balanced output over a wide range of resistive or reactive impedances.

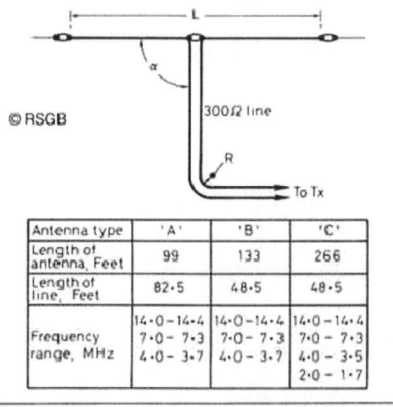

Fig 5: The Collins multi-band dipole antenna of 1935.

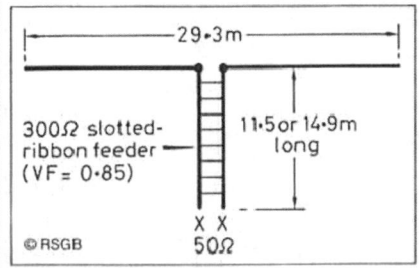

Fig 6: The 1992 G0FAH all-band dipole antenna.

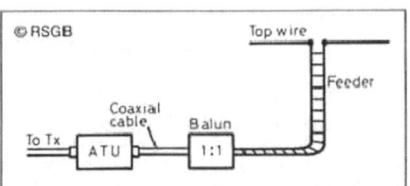

Fig 7: Use a simple current balun and L-network ATU where an SWR of less than 2:1 is needed for solid-state transmitters or for 1.8MHz.

with six inch insulators at ends and centre, supported 40ft or more above ground. The transmission line, as mentioned in the February *TT*, was formed from 0.25 inch copper or aluminium tubes spaced 1.5in by means of isolantite (a ceramic material) or impregnated maple blocks at intervals of 20in with bends (R) not less than 1ft radius.

Bill Wright, G0FAH, has drawn my attention to his 'All-band dipole' published in *Sprat*, Spring 1992, as "One antenna for every band - almost!": **Fig 6**. This antenna draws on the work of ZS6AKW/G0GSF in using computer modelling to optimise the number of bands on which the impedance seen at the transmitter is reasonably close to 50Ω and can be connected to coax cable via a simple 1:1 current balun.

The problem of covering 10MHz and 21MHz is solved by changing the length of the 300Ω feeder from 11.5m to 8.8m. With a good ATU it will also work on 1.8MHz either 'as is' or as a top loaded vertical.

With a 'top' length of 29.3m and 11.5m of 300Ω slotted ribbon (velocity factor 0.85) the computer results were:

Frequency (Mhz)	Resistance (ohms)	Reactance (ohms)	SWR into 50ohms
3.56	6.7	-4	7.6
7.03	35	+28	2.1
14.06	40	-3	1.2
18.07	39	+69	4.3
24.90	98	-31	1.9
28.06	46	+81	3.5
With Feeder Length 8.8m			
10.1	27	+234	1.8*
21.06	24	-4	2.0
With Feeder Length 14.9m			
10.1	52	-422	1.0*
21.06	24	+3	2.0

* Negative reactance is capacitive (positive is inductive) in series with the resistive part of the impedance. To get a good match on the 10.1MHz band it is necessary only to tune out the series reactance - with 8.8m feeder a 130pF capacitor put in each leg of the feeder right at the base (with 14.9m feeder inductors of 3.3µH in each leg).

Efficiency should remain good with any SWR below about 10, although for solid-state transceivers this can be reduced by a 1:1 balun followed by a simple L network ATU: **Fig 7**. The current choke balun can be formed by coiling up a length of the coax, or a ferrite or steel wool. Alternatively, the one-coil Z-match ATU could be used without a balun.

Howarth Jones, GW3TMP, who, after experimenting with fitting ferrite sleeved baluns to G5RV antennas over several years, eventually marketed his 'choke balun' under the name Ferromagnetics, queries the comments by G0GSF (*TT*, January) that fitting such baluns is not justified since "Its effect on the measured impedance Z3 and hence on the VSWR was minimal."

GW3TMP writes: "I would have been very surprised if there had been any effect on the measured impedance or the VSWR. The insertion of the balun at the junction of L2 and Z4 will have no effect on line impedance or VSWR but it has a marked effect on the current balance on the output side of the balun as measured in the balanced line L2. The other significant difference is in the current flow on the coaxial screen outer on line Z4. If this is measured before and after insertion of the balun, using a current probe, it will be found that without it there will be quite a large amount of current flowing on the braid outer on some bands. The ferrite sleeved balun will stop this happening. It is this outer braid current that causes most problems with TVI or RFI etc. Many of my customers have solved their EMC problems by fitting sleeve baluns . . . ."

PA0SE Comudipole

Extracted from 'Technical Topics', *Radio Communication*, May 1993

THE PA0SE COMUDIPOLE MULTIBAND HF ANTENNA

RECENT *TT* ITEMS have underlined the value of simple multiband dipole-type HF antennas including the G5RV and the derivatives based on the work of G0GSF/ZS6AKW. Also the use of open-wire feeders with a non-resonant 'top' in conjunction with a flexible ATU providing balanced output over a wide range of resistive and reactive impedances. Although as mentioned in the March *TT*, this latter type of 'doublet' antenna was quite widely used more than 50 years ago, Lew McCoy, W1ICP, in *CQ* Magazine has recently resurrected this form of antenna using a horizontal or inverted-Vee radiator of random length. This is preferably not less than about 40% of the lowest wavelength for which it is to be used and is centre fed with open-wire line. He has even rechristened this classic antenna a 'McCoy Dipole'!

Dick Rollema, PA0SE, notes that it is not always convenient or practicable to bring the open wire feeders into the shack. Instead, he has drawn inspiration from a paper presented by Dr Mike Underhill, G3LHZ, (wearing a Philips Research Laboratories hat) at an IERE Conference 'Radio Receivers and Associated Systems' at Leeds University in July 1981. His long paper 'Widerange antenna matching networks' (*IERE Conference proceedings No 50*, pages 101-135) was briefly summarised in *TT*, September 1981, pp818-819).

As pointed out many years ago: "When an antenna element presents to the transmission line an impedance other than its characteristic impedance, the impedance offered to the transmitter at the input end of the line may be quite different from either the characteristic impedance of the line or (unless the line is an exact multiple of an electrical half wavelength) the impedance at the antenna junction. The impedance represented by the line then depends on the length of the feeder (which acts as an impedance transformer). In such cases unless a suitable matching network is interposed between transmitter and transmission line, the impedance may be of a value (in the form R + jX) with which the transmitter output circuit cannot cope. But, if the reactance is cancelled out and the impedance falls within the values suitable for the transmitter output circuit, (now invariably 50Ω since the demise of the pi-network tank circuit), then the antenna system is matched and all the real power delivered by the transmitter (other than the usually modest losses in the transmission line and resistive losses in the antenna) will be radiated. It is the job of the ATU both to balance out the reactive element and to make the resistive impedance suitable for the transmitter output. The prob-

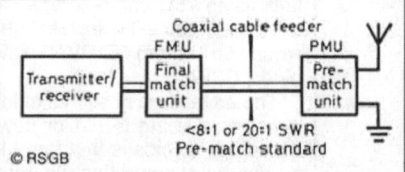

Fig 1: The two-stage tuning and wide range matching philosophy advocated by G3LKZ in 1981.

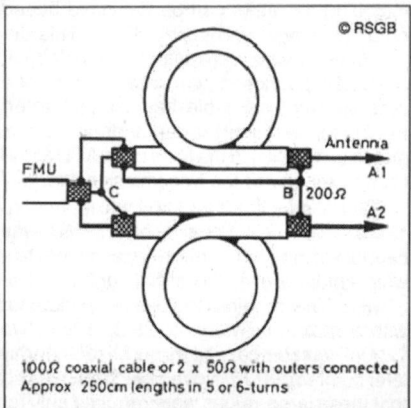

Fig 2: A pre-match unit (PMU) in the form of a 50-200Ω coaxial wideband balun transformer as described in the 1981 IERE paper by Dr Mike Underhill, G3LKZ.

ANTENNA TOPICS

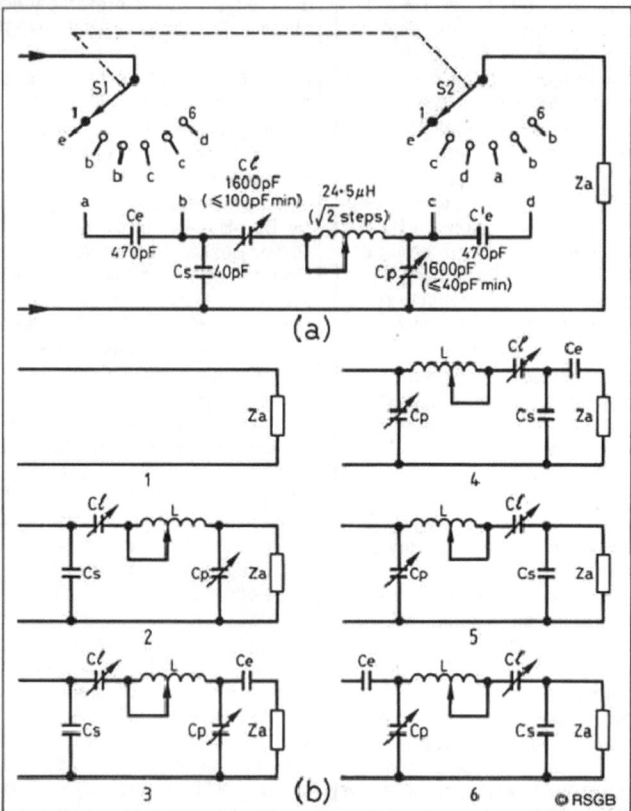

Fig 3: (a) The flexible final-match unit (FMU) with component values modified by G3LKZ to cover 1.8-30MHz rather than the full military specification of 1.5-30MHz. (b) The network configurations of the matching unit in the various switching positions.

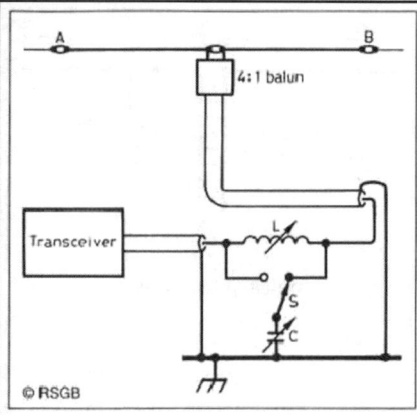

Fig 4: PA0SE's Comudipole (coaxial cable fed multiband dipole). The length AB can be of any value, but preferably not less than about 40% of the wavelength on the lowest frequency band to be used. L can be a roller-coaster or a coil with multiple switched taps. C can be one of the old style three-gang (3 x 500pF) receiver capacitors with the three sections in parallel (the PMU reduces the need for a special high voltage capacitor). If a proper match cannot be obtained with S in one position, the other position should be tried.

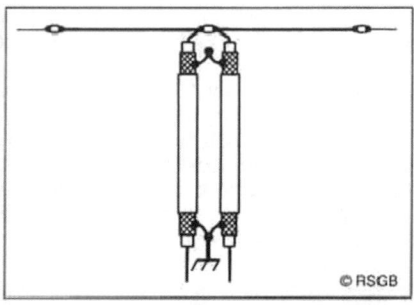

Fig 5: An alternative method of feeding a multiband dipole with parallel coaxial cables used to provide a balanced transmission line less affected by nearby metal objects than open wire line. Radiator should be at least 40% of the wavelength of the lowest frequency to be used. The cables can have any characteristic impedance and in principle can be of any length, but experience has shown that it is advisable that they should be somewhat longer than a quarter-wave of the lowest frequency to be used (ie about 17m for 3.5MHz with cables having a velocity factor of about 0.66). In practice this form of multiband dipole has not been found by PA2ABV as satisfactory as the single coax-fed Comudipole.

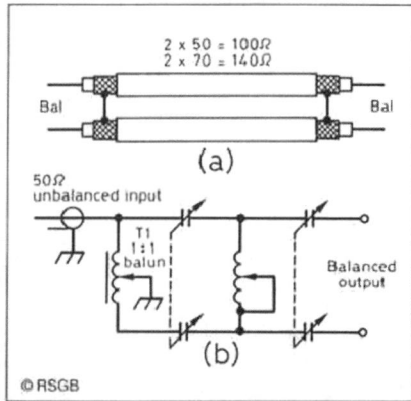

Fig 6: (a) Showing how two coaxial cable lengths can be used as a balanced transmission line. (b) Flexible ATU providing balanced output from 50Ω unbalanced input in such a manner that losses in a 1:1 ferrite balun tend to be minimised. Choke 1:1 baluns would be preferable.

lem with designing a flexible ATU is that ideally it needs to cope with a very large range of impedances, both very low and very high, and transform them to around the 50Ω suitable for most modern transmitters. Basically only one capacitor and one inductance are required to do this, but amateurs soon discover that to cover many bands and many possible impedances a very large value, high voltage variable capacitor is needed and preferably a very large and expensive variable (roller coaster) inductance. In practice, most ATUs represent configurations that help to reduce these components to reasonably manageable proportions.

At Leeds in 1981, G3LHZ showed that practical and versatile wide range antenna matching networks can be designed based on a 'two-stage' philosophy: **Fig 1**. This depends on having a pre-match unit (PMU) at the antenna junction (which can consist of a wideband coaxial-cable balun transformer: **Fig 2**) in order to limit the demands on the final match unit (FMU) in the form of an ATU at the transmitter end of the transmission line.

G3LHZ described an FMU which, in conjunction with the 4:1 coaxial balun PMU, was capable of matching a military transmitter to a whip antenna over the entire range of 1.5-30MHz. This required the use of an inductor with a maximum value of 28.3μH and two 2200pF variable capacitors but Mike Underhill later pointed out (*TT*, November 1981, p1034) that these large values were required only for the lowest frequencies between 1.5-1.8MHz, and that for the lowest amateur frequencies (ie 1.8MHz), these values could be reduced to 24.5μH and 1600pF, or less, if the antenna was only intended to cover 3.5MHz upwards: **Fig 3(a)** shows the 1.8-30MHz FMU which can be switched to provide the network configurations shown in **Fig 3(b)**.

PA0SE has adopted G3LHZ's two-stage PMU/FMU approach for his 'comudipole' (coaxial cable fed multiband dipole) but with a simplified FMU. He writes: "G3LHZ again suggests a radiator of approximately a half-wavelength or slightly less on the lowest frequency band to be used. Matching to the transmitter takes place in two stages; by a PMU between the centre of the antenna and the coaxial cable transmission line and an FMU between the cable and the transmitter. The PMU is a 4:1 balun made of coaxial cable, similar to one I used for feeding the two loops of my seven-band 'Optiquad' (see Eurotek in the August 1992 *RadCom*). [This is basically similar to that used by G2LHZ and shown in Fig 2 but Eurotek gave constructional details using 75Ω cable scraps left over from cable-TV installations wound on 110mm OD PVC waste pipe - *G3VA*].

The advantage of such a balun over those using ferrite or powdered-iron toroids is that there is no danger of saturating the core, resulting in losses and harmonic

"The rather complicated FMU unit devised by G3LHZ can for amateur bands be replaced by a simple L-network with a switch (S) to change from matching to high or to low impedances as shown in **Fig 4** which shows the complete comudipole antenna system."

PA0SE adds: "Following publication of the system in *Electron* (December 1992) this form of multiband dipole is now being used successfully in The Netherlands by several amateurs. One is Ton Verberne, PA2ABV, who lives on the second floor of a five-storey apartment building. On the roof he has an inverted-Vee dipole of about 2 x 19m and a 4:1 coaxial balun as described in Eurotek, August 1992, but with the connection between the flange of the coax socket and the boom of the quad deleted. From there some 30m of RG-213 coax leads to the shack where an L-network takes care of matching to the transceiver. In practice PA2ABV can match perfectly on all nine amateur bands from 3.5MHz-50MHz. Even on l.8MHz a match is possible but efficiency is low. On all bands 28-3.5MHz results are excellent (and much better than the previously used double-coax balanced feed system shown in **Fig 5**).

Further information on the use of twin coaxial cables to form balanced line is shown in **Fig 6**.

Beverage & his 'Wave' Antenna

Extracted from 'Technical Topics', *Radio Communication*, June 1993

BEVERAGE AND HIS 'WAVE ANTENNA'

THE DEATH LAST JANUARY of Harold H Beverage, one-time W2BML, at the age of 99 years, has taken from us one more of those immortal pioneers of radio communications who were willing to admit that their interest in radio engineering stemmed from amateur radio. Harry Beverage began as an amateur-radio enthusiast, yet he rose to the highest ranks of the professionals. Honoured in 1957 by The American Institute of Electrical Engineers "for his pioneering and outstanding achievements in the conception and application of principles basic to progress in national and world-wide radio communications".

Beverage not only invented diversity reception – for long a key feature in point-to-point communications – but also the 'Wave Antenna' that for almost 70 years has generally been called the 'Beverage antenna'. It was so described in *QST* in 1922 by Paul Godley (W)2XE who met Beverage on the liner *Acquitania* en route to the UK. Godley came to Britain on behalf of ARRL for the transatlantic tests in the winter of 1922/23. Beverage in cooperation with Chester Rice and Edward Kellog (who were later responsible for the moving-coil loudspeaker) presented detailed information in a 50-plus page paper 'The Wave Antenna – A New Type of Highly Directive Antenna' in the *Journal of the AIEE* spread over six issues (March 1923, pp258-269, April pp372-381, May pp510-519, June pp636-644 and July pp728-738).

In *TT*, October 1970, pp686-7, I wrote: "Top-band DX enthusiasts will probably need no reminding of the Beverage antenna which has recently been used on both sides of the Atlantic for the reception of 1.8MHz signals . . . . The antenna was developed in the early 'twenties for the reception of commercial transocean stations operating on the very low frequencies [in the region of 15,000 metres]. In its simplest form it consists of a very long straight wire, extending up to several miles in length, mounted on quite low poles, and correctly terminated at the far end to earth so as to prevent reflections (**Fig 1(a)**) – not exactly an antenna for the amateur with only a short garden.

"But a check with the original description has brought to light several features which are seldom mentioned. For instance, the normal system on VLF was to use two wires with a reflecting transformer at the far end and the terminating impedance at the receiving end, making it possible accurately to null out [off-beam] interference [the same principle as the Jones, the W1ETC and the VK5LR noise-cancelling systems described in *TT*, March 1993].

"Then again, although one normally thinks of the Beverage as being many wavelengths long, this was always impossible at VLF, and the paper suggests that pronounced directional effects can be achieved with an electrical length of one-half to one-wave-length –

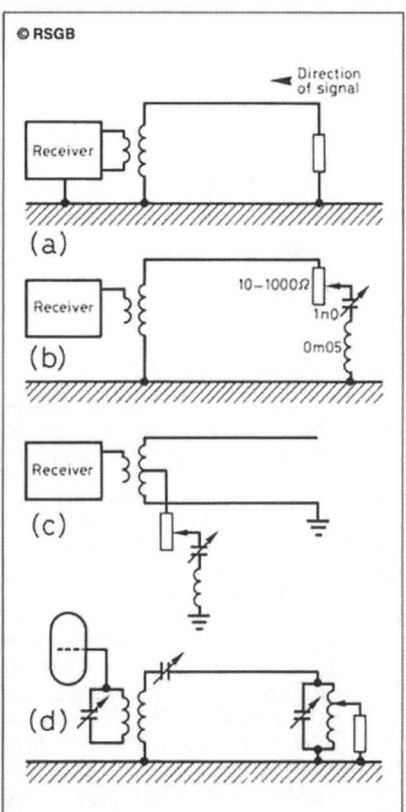

Fig 1: Some of the many possible variations of the Beverage or 'Wave Antenna'. (a) The basic arrangement as used by a number of amateurs on 1.8MHz for long-distance reception. (b) an arrangement suggested by Harold Beverage in 1923 for 'short waves' (ie wavelengths less than about 450 metres). (c) Is a variation of (b) enabling the termination to be at the receiving site. (d) This was an arrangement illustrated in the 1931 edition of the 'Admiralty Handbook of Wireless Telegraphy'.

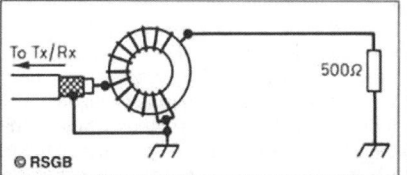

Fig 2: An all-band 'terminated long-wire' Beverage antenna used in the 1970s by Richard White, G3SRO, and suitable for transmission as well as reception. It was about 400ft long, 40ft high. At the far end terminated with a non-inductive high-wattage 500Ω resistor earthed via a vertical down-lead to an 8ft aluminium stake via a vertical down-lead. The transmitter fed the antenna via a ferrite toroidal step-up transformer using a toroid of about 1.5in diameter, with 3 turns input and 7 turns to the antenna, bifilar wound and space. It should have a worst SWR on any band 3.5-28MHz of only about 1.8:1. Unlike a low antenna this has two main lobes and by directing it towards central America G3SRO got good coverage of North and South America.

putting a different order of magnitude on the real estate needed on HF! The Beverage is related to the vee-beam and rhombic antennas, and is not limited to low frequencies . . . . The 1923 paper showed how the electrical length of the antenna could be reduced by 'stretching' the wire by inserting a series of capacitors at intervals along its length [the basis of G6CJ's 'Loaded wire dipoles' described in the *RSGB Bulletin*, July 1961 [and since then in *TT*, *ART* and other RSGB publications].

"One of the famous early Beverage antennas was that erected by Paul Godley at Ardrossan in Scotland during the vital amateur transatlantic tests of 1922 when his 400-metre long wire collected signals from a number of American amateurs between about 200 to 300 metres. I can recall using a wartime Beverage antenna [at Hanslope Park in late 1941] about 0.5-mile long, on frequencies of the order of 3.5 to 9MHz where it proved a very effective antenna [for receiving an Abwehr network of stations in Norway].

"So far as signal collecting properties are concerned, there is little point in stringing this type of antenna higher than is required for ordinary security and to pass over obstructions. One of the organisations [BBC Monitoring Service near Reading] currently using Beverage antennas for the reception of overseas MF broadcasting stations has recently [late 1960s] been carrying out theoretical studies on optimum lengths and heights to see if any improvement could be obtained by raising the present antennas (from 1000ft to 2500ft long and about 10ft high) to a height of about 30ft. Generally, these studies indicate that the first effect of raising height is to degrade sidelobe performance: the only real advantage in raising height would seem to be where extremely long antennas are possible, since additional height lowers the rate of attenuation. It is also shown that by connecting two Beverage antennas in parallel it is possible to slew the directivity over a useful angle. The [BBC Research] study suggests that these antennas are useful for the reception of signals arriving at angles of 5° to the horizon". I have added text within square brackets – G3VA.

As a result of Harold Beverage's work, RCA built six VLF transmitting stations on the Atlantic coast of the USA, some using high-frequency alternators, plus one receiving sta-

ANTENNA TOPICS

tion at Riverhead, Long Island. Here a Beverage antenna some six miles long erected between Eastport and Riverhead was used to prove the system. Terminated, very long, wire antennas can also make excellent unidirectional transmitting antennas but in this case it is usually necessary to raise the height which reduces ground absorption but degrades the sharp directivity into two lobes. **Fig 2** shows a transmitting type 400ft all-band unidirectional terminated long-wire for HF operation reported some years ago in *TT* (*ART7* p305) by Richard White, G3SRO.

Further background information on the Beverage antenna is given by Peter Lankshear in a four-page article 'The Vintage Beverage' (*Electronics Australia*, April 1993, pp98-101). This shows that Beverage began development of his directional antenna in 1917 at the suggestion of Dr E F W Alexanderson, chief engineer of General Electric (USA) to safeguard wartime traffic across the Atlantic from the possibility of German jamming. Beverage always acknowledged that he drew on the earlier work on directional antennas by Marconi (1906) and the 'Ground Aerial' developed in Germany by F Kieblitz in 1911 who had found that he could obtain good directional signals at the centre of a length of wire supported about one metre above ground and earthed at its extremities. The first Wave Antenna was erected at New Brunswick (New Jersey) near the high-power US Navy station NFF equipped with an Alexanderson alternator.

'Invisible' and Indoor Antennas

Extracted from 'Technical Topics', *Radio Communication*, August 1993

"INVISIBLE" AND INDOOR ANTENNAS

A GROWING PROBLEM in many countries is the imposition by local authorities, landlords, estate managers, etc of restrictions on the erection of any type of outside antenna. Where such restrictions do not cover TV antennas, it is possible for amateurs to use these as, in effect, random length HF antennas with the outer-braid of the coaxial feeder cable connected to an ATU. Efficiency of such antennas is likely to be reduced by the proximity of the cable to the building but nevertheless they usually provide plenty of contacts.

A more efficient, and well-tested, technique is to use a fixed outdoor long-wire antenna using very thin enamelled wire (24 or 26 gauge) supported by nylon kite string. Such an antenna will be almost impossible to spot from a distance. Provided that it is between fixed supports that do not sway with the wind, such an antenna can last a reasonably long time, unless broken by an unwary bird for whom such antennas can be a hazard – and vice versa. Another echo from war-time clandestine radio is to use an aluminium-wire 'clothesline' or to conceal a wire in a cord clothesline or indeed in any rope that does not seem clearly out of place.

A more challenging situation arises when there are restrictions against any sort of antenna and no supports for an 'invisible' antenna. Albert Parker, N4AQ, in *QST*, May 1993, p65 tells how when he moved to a retirement community in Florida in 1991 he faced and overcame this difficulty. He writes: "I was eager to get on the air and began looking around for an inconspicuous antenna. It couldn't be just any antenna; I needed one with multiband capability . . . . but not one that would send the clear message (of traps) when displayed in public – "Ham Antenna Here!"

His solution was to purchase a Hustler 4-BTV four-band trap vertical antenna which he felt he could squeeze inside a 2-inch PVC pipe. At his first attempt he found the hose clamps on the traps were too large: "Knowing nothing about plumbing and even less about PVC pipes, I was very discouraged. I journeyed to another hardware store and found another 2-inch section of PVC and again tried to insert the trap. To my delight, it fitted perfectly!

"This was thin-wall PVC whereas the first one I had tried was heavy-duty PVC I

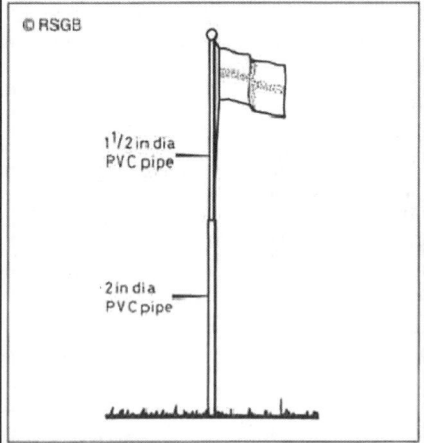

Fig 5: Sketch of N4AQ's disguised flagpole antenna in which a Hustler 4-BTV trap vertical is concealed in 2-inch PVC pipe as described in *QST* (May 1993).

purchased a 14ft section of thin-wall PVC along with a 12ft section of 1.5 inch PVC. I assembled the Hustler and cut the 2 inch PVC to fit over the lower part of the antenna, ending about two inches above the 20-metre trap. At that point I used a reducer to couple to the 1.5 inch PVC that I had slipped over the thinner top section that remained. When I finished, the entire antenna was enclosed in PVC! I had to leave off the 7MHz capacitance hat but later found no trouble operating on that band without it.

N4AQ drove a 1.5in thick wall pipe about 4ft into the ground to serve as base, trimming the length to keep the feed point about 4in above ground. A 5ft section of copper pipe was driven into the soil to serve as a ground connection (burying radial wires might have attracted attention). Buried 50Ω coax cable was used to feed the antenna with about 10 turns of coax cable near the base to act as an RF choke [probably not necessary with a buried cable – *G3VA*] and another 10 turns

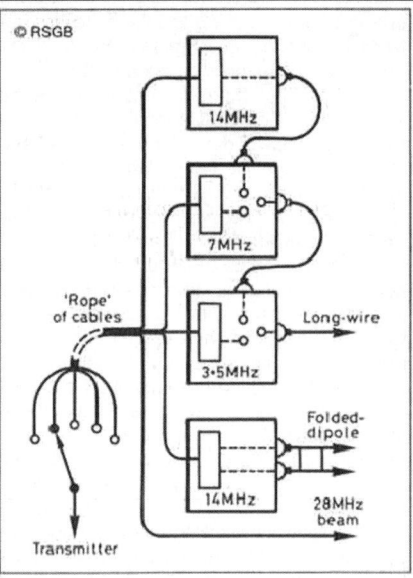

Fig 6: Layout of the feeder cables and switching relays used in 1950 by the late G2EC for his 'quick put up and take down antennas' on the roof of a seven-storey Mayfair building in 1950 after his earlier more visible antennas had been declared architecturally unsightly. Although he declared the antennas "fell far short of the ideal" they enabled him to obtain the leading G score of 130,442 points in the 1949 ARRL DX Contest.

near the MFJ989C ATU. The antenna, **Fig 5**, loads his Collins KWM-380 transceiver well on the four bands from 7 to 28MHz providing good CW and SSB reports even if not really capable of competing with high-gain antennas.

N4AQ adds: "Finishing touches consisted of adding a used toilet-tank-float ball on top of the pole as an ornament, and a three-inch bolt near the top to mount a pulley. The base is hidden by flowers which I water often to enhance my ground conductivity! My neighbours see the Stars and Stripes flying proudly day after day, unaware that the flagpole is really a multiband antenna."

The use of aluminium flag-poles as vertical 'whip' antennas was a well-known arrangement for Diplomatic HF installations in embassies etc in the days when most countries used HF for diplomatic traffic, but the idea of enclosing a multi-band trap vertical in a plastic pipe is new to me.

How one well-known amateur overcame similar problems while living in a sixth-floor flat in Mayfair was described over forty years ago by G2EC in 'Aerial Systems for the Flat Dweller!' (*RSGB Bulletin*, August 1950, pp55-56). G2EC was, of course, the unique call (the only British two-letter call with an 'E') of the late Major-General Eric Cole, CB, CBE, Director of Telecommunications at the War Office, 1956-61, and President of RSGB in 1961, who died last December at the age of 86 years. For reasons that will become obvious, no name was attached to his article.

In 1950 he wrote: "Some eighteen months ago, after much argument with higher authority, the aerial systems, erected with much painstaking effort on the roof of the building, were declared architecturally unsightly and 'were to be removed forthwith'. Courses open were thus: (a) Give up Amateur Radio; (b) Change location; (c) Use 'invisible' wires; or (d) Use systems which could be erected and dismantled at short notice for use during darkness hours or when censorious eyes were absent.

"The latter, course (d), was chosen and though it has been irritating to have to move out of a warm room and grope around a roof 80ft high in stygian blackness, sometimes in wind and snow, before being able to put the transmitter on the air, it has proved on the whole very well worth while."

The final system he adopted, based on a 'put up and take down quickly' principle included a long-wire (132ft) antenna for use on 3.5, 7 or 14MHz, end-fed by one of the three 72Ω coaxial cables through suitable impedance matches with matching unit remotely selectable from the operating position; a half-wave, three-wire folded dipole for 14MHz to cover the nulls of the long-wire; and a three-element rotary beam for 28MHz (the 21MHz band was not available until 1952). G2EC reported: "These were so arranged that after considerable practice, all three could be erected and put into operation from their normal completely prone positions lying flat on the roof of the building in a total time at night of eleven minutes away from the operating shack. Times were slightly quicker in daylight!"

The roof of the seven-storey building was some 150ft long and 50ft wide at its widest point and with lift and water outhouses on the top. To feed RF from the transmitter, **Fig 6**, a rope of 73Ω and relay switching cables, terminated at the operating position in a five-way coaxial switch, was led out through the shack window juxtaposed to a black, though otherwise friendly drain pipe, and thence to the roof; the resulting cable run was virtually invisible from the street below.

G2EC described in detail the construction of the antennas on 12ft poles and (for the beam) a 12ft steel mast all arranged so that they could be quickly heaved up and fitted into prepared bases. He wrote: "It looks so simple in print, but in complete darkness, single-handed, possibly in a half-gale with a 70ft unfenced drop to the street a few feet away, the writer recommends manipulating 28lb at the end of a 12ft pole to upset even the most well-behaved human circulating organs, at least until confidence is gained . . . . The aerials fall far short of the ideal, but nevertheless, observing the local strictures, they permitted G2EC to continue to enjoy the 'vice' of Amateur Radio without causing affront. After all 'What the eye never sees, the heart never grieves over'".

Another exploit of G2EC while SU1EC in the 'thirties is recalled in an obituary note in *The Journal of the Royal Signals Institution*: "In 1934, while serving in Egypt, he participated in a three-car expedition through the Western Desert and the Libyan Sand Sea, a round trip of some 1500 miles. Radio contact was maintained with Egypt Signals using a transmitter and receiver constructed by Eric Cole, proving that 'long distance' communications [from a vehicle] were possible, later becoming routine practice for units such as the Long Range Desert Group". The writer also notes that during WW2, while serving with Joint Combined Operations, G2EC designed the Wireless Hand Cart – nicknamed the 'Radio Pram' which was used during the Normandy landings.

Reverting to the topic of invisible antennas, there are unfortunately many flat dwellers who have no access to a large flat roof, or even a balcony, and must perforce make do with either an indoor antenna or a thin wire lowered out of a window or, for example, coupling their RF into a metal drainpipe or metal windows etc.

The effectiveness of an indoor antenna depends on many factors that cannot be readily predicted or measured. For example a wire antenna erected in a roof-space of a conventional building can often prove almost as good as one outside at a similar height; on the other hand an antenna in a room in a steel-framed building is unlikely to perform well. 144MHz VHF single-element quad antennas can be taped to a window and will radiate well in the direction faced by the window. A number of designs for simple indoor antennas were given in *TT*, July 1983 as shown in **Figs 8 to 10**. The three random-length Marconi antennas for HF are taken from the manual for the paramilitary/clandestine Mk 123 transmitter-receiver. Rather better results could be expected from a compact 'magnetic loop' antenna since there would be less absorption by nearby objects. I would not advise the use of any form of room antenna for high-power operation, but with say 20-40 watts CW there should be no difficulty in achieving plenty of contacts. This assumes you can overcome the potential problems of RFI, often due to leakage into the electricity wiring etc.

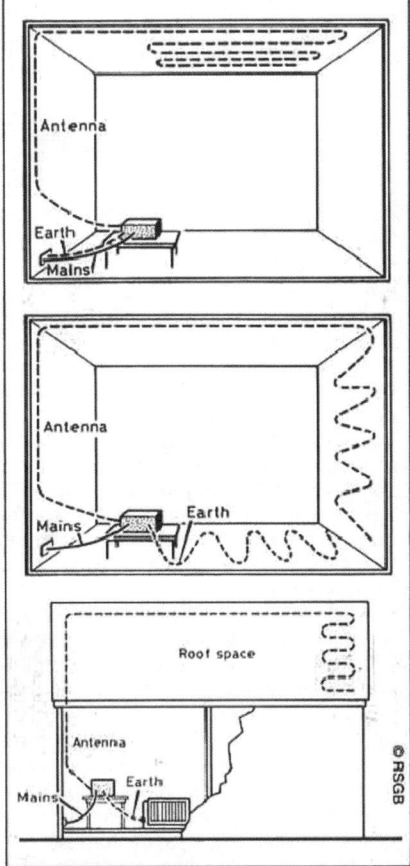

Fig 10: Random-length Marconi HF antennas as suggested in the manual for the Mark 123 paramilitary transmitter-receiver. (a) Preferably in a room high in the building and using a 'mains earth'. (b) Alternative arrangement using a wire counterpoise on the floor. (c) Antenna in roof space with central-heating radiator used as 'earth'. For transceivers intended for fixed 50Ω feed an ATU suitable for end-fed antennas would be required.

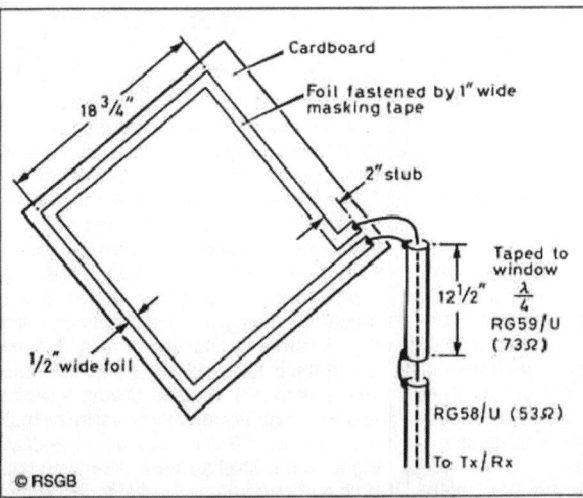

Fig 8: A 144MHz single-element quad antenna suitable for use on windows and made from household aluminium foil mounted on cardboard.

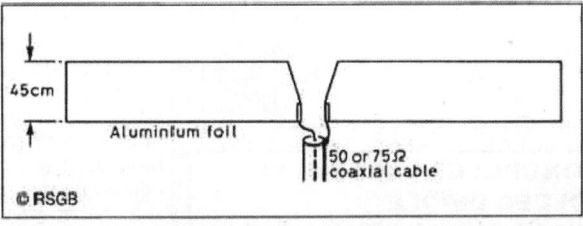

Fig 9: An indoor broadband 'fat dipole' antenna using aluminium ('kitchen') foil for use in lofts or for mounting on indoor walls. Suggested lengths for 3.5MHz are two by 12m; 7MHz two by 6.2m; 10.1MHz two by 4.4m; 14MHz two by 3.4m.

ANTENNA TOPICS

Metal Fatigue and Antenna Elements

Extracted from 'Technical Topics', *Radio Communication*, December 1993

METAL FATIGUE & ANTENNA ELEMENTS

ON A NUMBER OF occasions, *TT* has noted that tubular antenna elements often fail after they have been fluttering, or vibrating, over a long period even in a relatively low wind speed, and has suggested that this is due to a combination of metal fatigue and vortex shedding. Medium speed winds, at well under 35MPH, when they strike an elongated cylindrical object create vortices or swirls of air; if these are shed from the object in a regular, orderly manner related to a natural resonance of the object, they constitute an exciting force. A commonly cited example is the pronounced low-frequency hum that comes from overhead telephone wires when the wind blows at a specific speed.

As explained in *TT*, November 1989, p30, when aluminium is flexed at levels below its yield-stress, while no permanent bend results, the damage accumulates and if the flexing is repeated sufficiently often there will be a fatigue failure. In effect metal fatigue is the weakened condition induced in metal parts of machines, vehicles or structures by repeated stresses or loadings, ultimately resulting in a fracture under a stress much weaker than that necessary to cause fracture in a single application.

It was suggested by K5IU that antenna-element fatigue failures can be minimised in a number of ways, including filling the inside of tubular elements with the type of foam intended for sealing and insulating cracks and holes in buildings, or by fitting energy absorbers at the ends of the antenna elements to reduce flutter-type oscillation.

Energy absorbers, of a type suggested many years ago, can be made from a sheet of flat rubber or pliable plastic material 1/8th to 1/4-in thick by 5-6in long, If this is made just wide enough to wrap once round the element, the damping will be matched to the size of the element. This material is cut lengthwise to make four taps and positioned so that the free end of the tabs are about 2in from the ends to prevent changes in the electrical length or impedance of the elements: **Fig 9**. Roger Bunney, for many years the DX-TV columnist in *Television*, noticed the earlier reference to fatigue failures in *ART7* and comments as follows: "Some years ago I was involved in a partnership with South West Aerials and made a number of aerials for Band I (41-68MHz) TV-DX enthusiasts. The problem of flutter metal fatigue was noticed and quickly rectified. At these frequencies, resonance tends to occur on very warm still days and can cause a loud buzzing/rasping noise. I found

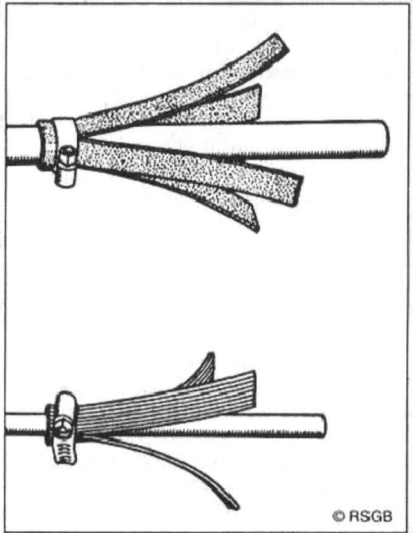

Fig 9: Energy absorbers fitted at the ends of antenna elements to reduce flutter-type oscillation brought about by vortex shedding at specific, low wind speeds.

that climbing a mast to examine a 50MHz element will show the points of resonance: on a reflector cut to Channel E2, there are usually two points of vibration in each element (ie the two elements comprising the one reflector) one very close to the boom and another near the extreme end. Touching the point of vibration can be very uncomfortable, almost painful.

"In all my aerials only the reflector would display this resonance. Elements made of seamed alloy generally do not display this problem which occurs primarily in seamless tubing. We always used hard-drawn seamless tubing for maximum strength so as to avoid bending or damaging the elements during erection. The solution was simply to insert about 12-in of sash cord into each element. this will damp the resonance and prevent vibration. If the elements are plugged then normal sash can be used; otherwise use waxed sash to prevent water soaking up and producing a heavy weight that will cause the ends of the element to sag. Elements should be plugged, in any case, as a precaution against wind whistle! Another TV-aerial firm of yesteryear, Telerection of Weymouth used to make numerous Band 1 arrays, filled their elements with sawdust – this tends to soak up water but the general principle is the same."

On the topic of antenna metalwork, a rather different tip comes from Peter J Cott, G3BDV. He suggests that when the household needs a new rotating 'washing line', have a good look at the old one before it is thrown away. In his case he found that by turning it upside down, it became an instant antenna support for experimental purposes. But don't be tempted to use one that has not been discarded or this could provoke domestic discord!

Monopole Loaded with Folded Dipole

Extracted from 'Technical Topics', *Radio Communication*, January 1994

MONOPOLE LOADED WITH FOLDED DIPOLE

ON A NUMBER OF OCCASIONS in the past, *TT* has discussed antennas loaded with resistances in order to widen the effective bandwidth. an interesting and novel derivative of this approach is described by Dr Edward E Altshuler (Hanscom AFB) in 'A monopole antenna loaded with a modified folded dipole' (*IEEE Trans Ant & Prop*, July 1993, pp 871-876). This notes that a travelling-wave distribution of current can be produced on a linear antenna by inserting a resistance of approximately 240Ω one-quarter wavelength from its end to form an antenna which is very broadband and has much weaker mutual coupling than a conventional linear antenna. A travelling-wave antenna or section of an antenna is where the current and voltage remains substantially the same along its length as in the terminated rhombic or terminated long-wire antenna. Travelling-wave antennas may also have directional properties useful for special applications, such as Beverage-type antennas. Dr Altshuler points out that the main disadvantage of the resistance-loaded travelling-wave antenna is that it is only about 50 per cent efficient because part of the input power is absorbed by the resistor [unless the element(s) are very long so that most of the energy is radiated before it reaches the resistive termination – *G3VA*]. He points out that it is possible to replace the resistor with a resonant antenna having a radiation resistance approximately equal to the matching resistor, ie in this case about 240Ω. the input section still has a travelling-wave distribution of current up to the inserted element, but the power previously dissipated in the resistor will now be radiated, although since the impedance of the folded element is more frequency sensitive than that of the resistor, the antenna will not be so broadband as with purely resistive loading.

This new form of loaded antenna may be implemented either as a loaded dipole or a loaded monopole over a ground plane. The article describes a model monopole antenna (1.2GHz) in which the folded section is a modified folded dipole; by adjusting the length of this element, a radiation resistance of about 240Ω can be obtained.

The horizontally polarized patterns are similar to those of a horizontal dipole over a ground plane, and vertically polarized patterns in a plane orthogonal to the folded element are similar to those of a monopole over a ground plane. Dr Altshuler presents input impedance, current distribution and radiation patterns as computed using the Nu-

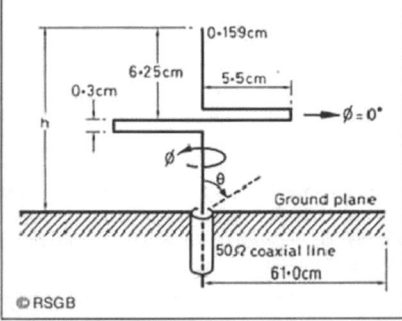

Fig 9: Monopole antenna loaded with a modified folded dipole resulting in the lower segment having a travelling-wave distribution of current so that it can be of virtually any length. A similar (even more broadband) effect can be achieved by inserting a non-inductive 240Ω resistor (of suitable wattage) in place of the folded dipole, but this will reduce radiated power by up to 50%. Dimensions are for the 1.2GHz antenna were measured in a model antenna range. Such antennas can be implemented as monopoles or dipoles etc.

merical Electromagnetics Code (NEC); input impedance and radiation patterns were also measured in a model antenna range. Results are obtained for half-lengths varying from 0.35 to 2.0 wavelengths at a frequency of 1.2GHz on a monopole antenna loaded with a modified folded dipole as shown in **Fig 9**.

The Comudipole is Revisited

Extracted from 'Technical Topics', *Radio Communication*, February 1994

THE COMUDIPOLE IS REVISITED

JOHN HEYS, G3BDQ, ADDS a suggestion concerning the PA0SE 'Comudipole' multi-band antenna (*TT*, May): "The technique of having a 'pre-ATU' matcher is one I have found useful, especially on 1.8 and 3.5MHz when using end-fed wires presenting an unworkable impedance/reactance into a conventional ATU.

"I feel, however, that the PA0SE design as shown presents a practical problem: weight and sag. The balun as described will have appreciable weight (500cm of coax plus former and hardware) with the coax downlead, even when using RG58 or similar, will add to this. Were I to make a similar antenna, I would have a vertical section using open wire, 300Ω slotted line, or the new, excellent 450Ω slotted line which would descend down to a wood pole about 10ft (or less) high, at the top of which would be the balun. Onwards would be the coax (even heavy UR67) which could be run along the ground to the operating position. An added bonus to this scheme would be that the open-wire part of the downlead would in effect increase the total length of the antenna, making it effective on 3.5MHz even were the top (A-B) only 60 or 70% of the half-wave dipole length for the lowest frequency

TOROIDAL HELIX ANTENNAS

I GATHER THAT THE articles by Roger Jennison, G2AJV, on his compact single and twin toroidal antennas (*RadCom*, April and May, 1994) were mistakenly considered by some readers to be an elaborate April Fool joke rather than a practical approach to mobile and space-limited applications. It therefore seems worth pointing out that alternative forms of toroidal helix antennas (without the top and bottom plates) were outlined in *TT* in October 1983, pp889-890. This was the result of Alec Clelland, DJ0FL/G3UUQ drawing attention to the 70-page European Patent Application EP 0 043 591 AI made by James Corum of West Virginia, who, from the examples described, appeared to hold an amateur licence. [K1AON – *Ed*]

In his application, James Corum claimed that various implementations of the basic principle "possess greater radiation resistance and radiation efficiency than loop antennas of similar size". He also claimed that such elements "radiate controllable mixtures of vertically, horizontally and el-

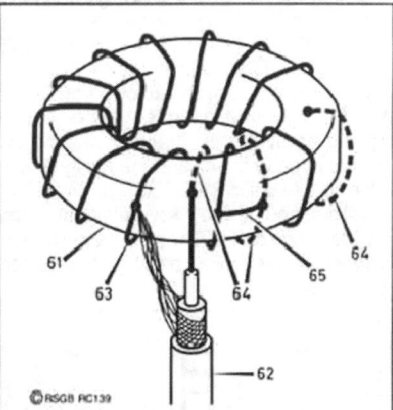

Fig 7: One of the several forms of toroidal helix antennas described by James F Corum in his patent application. Isometric representation of the antenna (61) and transmission line (62). The main conductor (63) is continuous. In addition there is a shorter inductor (64) helically wound around the toroidal support between some of the turns of the main conductor (63). A sliding tap (65) connects the two conductors 63, 64. One side of the transmission line is connected to one end of the shorter conductor (64) and the other side attached to the main winding 63. The sliding tap (65) is moved to provide proper impedance matching. This point is found empirically at the operating frequency by moving the sliding tap to the optimum position.

liptically polarized electromagnetic waves, and possess radiation patterns different from those produced by small loop antennas, and can be used to form both driven and parasitic arrays." It was pointed out that although such elements are similar in form to a toroidal inductor, they are essentially not perfect toroidal inductors which would have zero radiation efficiency.

Examples given in the Patent Application (including those outlined in **Figs 7 and 8**) covered frequencies as low as 200kHz and as high as 450MHz. The inventor admitted that "one does not get something for nothing. The price one pays with the toroidal helix is that it is a narrowband (high-Q) structure and inherently not a broadband device . . . . [but] these antennas by virtue of their construction possess a greater radiation resistance than known antennas of similar electrical size not having the slow-wave winding features . . . . the helix permits the formation of a resonant antenna current standing-wave in a region of electrically small dimensions, and it permits the controlled variation of antenna currents, resonant frequency, impedance, polarization and antenna pattern."

I cannot recall the 1983 *TT* item attracting any great attention and we owe a debt to G2AJV for further developing this interesting antenna concept and showing its practical value for such applications as mobile operation. His articles clearly deserve to attract further work.

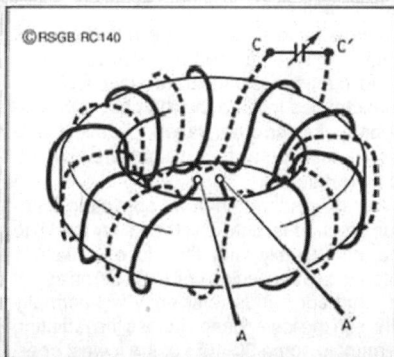

Fig 8: Use of a variable capacitor to vary the resonant frequency of a toroidal helix antenna without changing the number of turns. The antenna comprises two helices, one fed at points AA' and the other at CC'. The variable capacitor is connected across feedpoints CC'.

ANTENNA TOPICS

band." G3BDQ adds: "The high SWR on the coax (up to 20:1) means that for powers above about 100W it would be advisable to use good quality UR67 or similar to avoid the flash over that could occur with 'thin' cables." **Fig 3**.

I might also add that the weight problem with the balun situated as specified by PA0SE might also be overcome with the antenna erected as a symmetrical inverted-vee with central support.

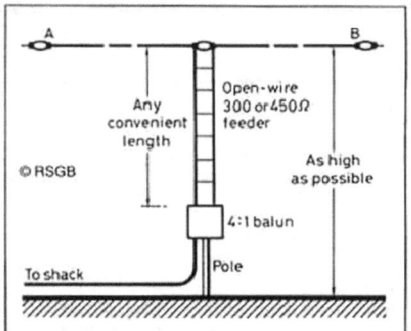

Fig 3: G3BDQ suggests that supporting the pre-match-unit (balun) of PA0SE's 'Comudipole' multiband HF antenna (*TT*, May) on a low pole with an open-wire section would minimize sag and weight problems and permit effective use of smaller A-B top spans.

Multiband or All-band for HF

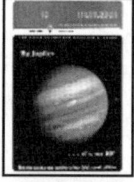

Extracted from 'Technical Topics', *Radio Communication*, June 1994

MULTIBAND OR ALL-BAND HF ANTENNAS?

THE AVAILABILITY OF THE 'WARC' bands not harmonically related to the 'traditional' amateur bands has led to increased interest in HF antennas that work well on all bands between 3.5 and 30MHz. However it has also apparently led to some confusion between such terms as 'broadband', 'all-band' and 'multiband' each of which refers to a particular class of antenna.

A broadband antenna is one that will present roughly the same feed impedance over a broad, continuous band of frequencies. Notable examples include the rhombic, terminated long-wire and other travelling-wave antennas. Directivity may be substantially unaffected by frequency.

An 'all-band' antenna as applied to amateur practice is one which can be made to operate (usually with the aid of a flexible antenna system tuning unit (ASTU)) on any of the amateur bands (efficiency will normally fall off on the lower bands unless the radiating element is some 30-40% of the lowest operating wavelength). Radiation pattern will normally differ on different bands unless, for example, this is determined by an additional element as with the W8JK centre-fed driven array.

A 'multiband' antenna implies an antenna that will work well on two or more of the amateur bands, but not necessarily on all bands. A simple example is a 7MHz half-wave dipole which provides a near match on 21MHz but would normally not be used on the intervening 10 and 14MHz bands except possibly with the aid of a flexible ASTU and a reasonably short coax feeder capable of withstanding a high SWR.

These thoughts have been stimulated by an article 'On centre-fed multiband dipoles' by Dr John Belrose, VE2CV, and Peter Bouliane, VE3KLO, (*QST*, March 1994, pp34-36) with its provocative sub-title 'Is the G5RV really an all-band antenna?'. VE2CV notes the several references made in *TT* to the G5RV and to the modified version developed by Dr Brian Austin, ZS6BKW/G0GSF, using computer-aided design which can provide (without ASTU) an SWR of around 2:1 or less at five frequencies close to amateur bands, but which should always be considered a 'multiband' rather than an 'all-band' antenna.

The Canadian authors have long been worried by some of the claims made (not by G5RV or G0GSF themselves) for this form of antenna. They point out: "Many amateurs regard this antenna with its so-called special feed-line arrangement as a panacea, particularly when it is used in a drooping dipole (inverted-vee) configuration. There is, however, nothing magical or superior about the antenna. It is merely a centre-fed dipole with a particular feed-line arrangement, which the newcomer to amateur radio may or may not want to duplicate. In fact, the performance of a multiband drooping dipole can be inferior to a dipole at the same apex height.

As pointed out many times in *TT*, the non-resonate centre-fed dipole (doublet) fed with open-wire (or ladder-line) feeder of any convenient length connected directly to a wide-range, flexible ASTU with balanced-output as in **Fig 2(a)** can provide an effective all-band antenna without the special feed arrangements of the G5RV, G0GSF antennas **Fig 2(b)** or PA0SE's 'Comudipole' etc. A variation of the Comudipole as praised by Jorge Dorvier, EA4EO, is shown in **Fig 3**. All three of these systems provide the attractiveness of a coax feeder into the shack and the ability of being able to use a G5RV/G0GSF antenna on at least one and possibly several bands without a wide-range ASTU. The justification for these variants is convenience rather than superior performance.

What seems to have got under the skin of the Canadian authors are the exaggerated claims for the various variants of the doublet-antenna using special feed arrangements: "In our view, the correct feed-line length for a multiband dipole is that required to go from the output terminals of the antenna tuner to the antenna terminals, because – regardless of the length of the feed line – both the antenna and the feed line are made resonant by the tuner. Our recommendation, based on personal experience, is to use open-wire line for the total length of the required feeder. This will result in lower losses. An additional advantage in using a full-length feed-line is that any necessary balun can be inside the station, easing evaluation of its performance, or you can use a balanced tuner."

J H Gazard, VK5JG, in 'Tuned Feeders and Multiband Antennas' (*Amateur Radio*, April 1994, pp8-9) provides his experiences of both centre- and off-centre-fed antennas with tuned feeders. He concludes: "As a result of studying the operation of tuned feeders and making these and other tests my ideas of tuned feeder have changed and I have become aware of some facts that I have never seen in handbooks. These are that if the length of the antenna plus the length of each feeder wire is greater than a half-wavelength at the frequency concerned almost any combination of antenna length, feeder length, and feed point will function as a workable antenna . . .".

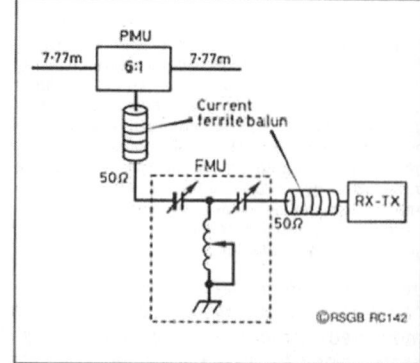

Fig 3: The EA4FO version of the Comudipole antenna. Note that the system works well without the toroidal ferrite current baluns. EA4FO uses 30m of RG-8 between the PMU and the FMU with no problems. Results have been excellent with an 8W transceiver. Between the FMU and the transceiver there is an SWR meter (not shown).

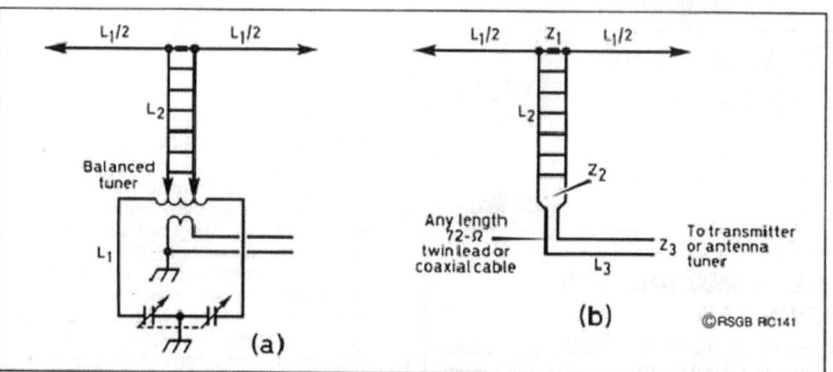

Fig 2: (a) Multiband or all-band dipole fed directly with open-wire line. The line is matched at the transmitter end with a balanced tuner. It is convenient (but not essential) if the length of the open-wire feeder is preferably an odd multiple of a quarter wavelength on the band in which the top element represents a resonant dipole in order to provide a low-impedance at the ASTU. (b) The basic arrangement of the G5RV or ZS6BKW variation, suitable for use (without an ASTU) on only some bands.

'KISS' VK2ABQ 14MHz Beam

Extracted from 'Technical Topics', *Radio Communication*, August 1994

'KISS' VK2ABQ 14MHZ BEAM ANTENNA

VERSIONS OF THE 1973 VK2ABQ three-band two-element parasitic wire array (ART 7 etc) continue to attract interest: see for example 'Antenna Workshop' by Peter Dodd, G3LDO (*Practical Wireless*, June 1994, pp42-43) in which he traces an earlier but basically similarly shaped single-band version to W1QP/W8CPC in *QST*, October 1937. More recently, Fred Caton, VK2ABQ (formerly G3ONC) has described several even simpler and/or smaller single-band arrays, including a KISS array in *TT*, May 1992, p37. (But note that he has pointed out that the gaps between the elements given as 4-inches should have been 4-mm or about 0.25-in).

VK2ABQ has now sent along details of a simple array that does not use the 'square' folding with crossed X-type bamboo spreaders, but retains the small gaps between driven and parasitic elements. This can be erected as shown in **Fig 10** as a single-mast, inverted-vee type structure or (for a fixed array) as a conventionally suspended array using a cantenery rope in lieu of the mast.

What VK2ABQ calls the phase adjustment gaps are adjusted for equal power in the two half-wave elements, as discussed in the earlier May 1992 item. He has, however, provided details of an improved 'current sampler' giving better position stability and greater sensitivity and, in his letter, provides some further hints on construction and adjustment but I find these a little confusing, and hope that the information given above and in the May 1992 *TT* will at least prove a starting point for investigating this simple directional antenna.

VK2ABQ acknowledges that modelling of this antenna was first done on 144MHz by VK3KZ in Melbourne who built a 7MHz version which proved very effective on long-haul DX to Europe etc. VK2ABQ claims that his antenna outperforms a much larger standard 2-element Yagi array and has a forward gain of the order of 5dB and a front/back ratio of over 30dB.

I suspect that other users may find the forward power gain of such an array to be rather less impressive when compared to the theoretically possible gain for a close-spaced two-element Yagi array of 5.2dB. Nevertheless, it should provide a useful power gain and a good front-to-back ratio.

In *TT*, October 1983, attention was drawn to the use by the IBA (now NTL) of a medium-wave vertical monopole antenna with a sloping twin-wire reflector. This approach gave a single-mast array with vertical polarization, providing roughly 3dB forward gain and an f/b ratio of from 5-15dB and better than 20dB in laboratory studies.

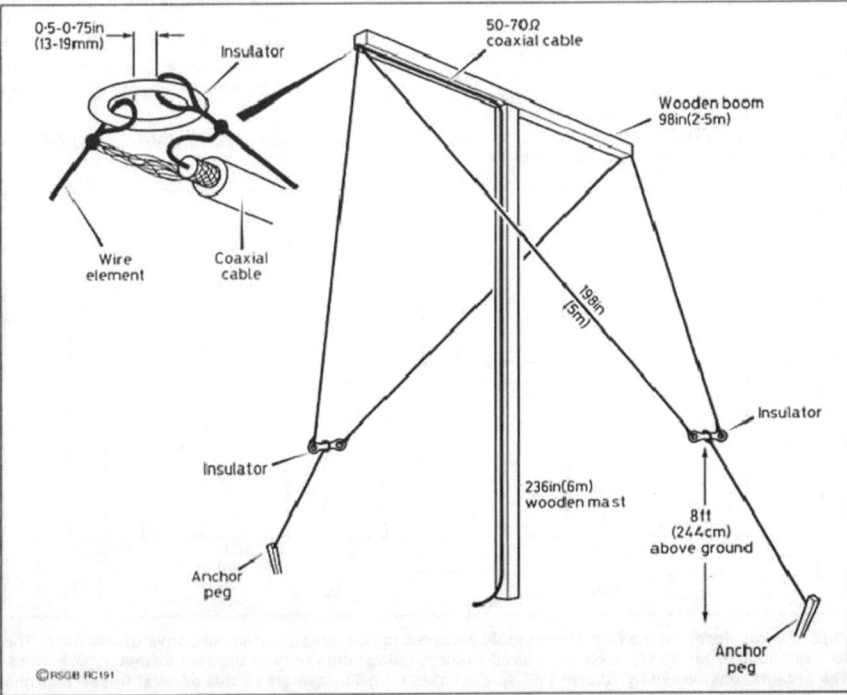

Fig 10: 2-element 14MHz 'KISS-type' beam antenna in inverted-vee form with the end 16-feet above ground level. It can be rotated at ground level by moving the ground pegs. Note that the two-dimensional representation shows the 90-deg angles as acute angles.

Multi-wire Dipoles and Monopoles

Extracted from 'Technical Topics', *Radio Communication*, October 1994

MULTI-WIRE DIPOLE AND MONOPOLE ANTENNAS

AN INTERESTING LETTER from Dr David Pearson, GM3TLA, draws attention to various forms of multi-wire folded dipoles that are often overlooked, including the possibilities

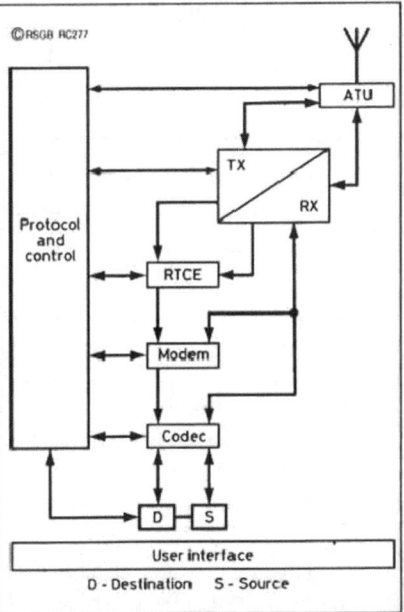

Fig 4: Professional low-cost 'suitcase' portable HF terminal using a 100-watt amateur transceiver and adaptive Piccolo-type MFSK digital transmission with real-time-channel-evaluation to control bit-rate (M Darnell, B Honary, R Enright & I Martin, *IEE Conference Publication No 392*).

they present for dipoles with short-spans and their use as two- or multi-band antennas. This has arisen from his use as a receiving antenna of the four-wire, three-eights wave, folded dipole which was described originally by Dr John D Kraus, W8JK, in the late 1930s and which is briefly described in several editions of *Amateur Radio Techniques* (ART7, pp 296-7) and *TT, July 1987* (see also *Technical Topics Scrapbook, 1985-89*, pp179-180).

GM3TLA notes that his antenna, with a three-eighths-wave span on 21MHz uses 20 metres of wire and also resonates on 7MHz, although the radiation resistance is probably too low to make this a really efficient 7MHz transmitting antenna – but it might be worth trying. Several other, too-often forgotten, types of folded dipoles and folded monopoles were described by W8JK. **Fig 5** shows some of these folded antennas and the approximate resistive feed impedance with wires of equal diameter when erected about a half-wave above ground.

It should not be forgotten, however, that a folded element used in a beam array will have a reduced input resistance which can, for example, provide a good match to 50 or 75Ω coax feeder. Similarly a wide variety of input

ANTENNA TOPICS

resistances can be obtained by using wires of unequal diameter, a technique originally described by W Van Roberts, W3CHO in *RCA Review*, June 1947 and in the UK in an article by H A M Clark, G6OT (*RSGB Bulletin*, October 1947 with an abac for finding the input resistance for unequal wire/rod diameters etc). As for a single-wire half-wave dipole the height of a folded antenna above ground has an important effect on its terminal resistance and reactance, as does also mutual coupling to nearby objects or array elements.

While the three-eights-wave folded dipole means that a 14MHz antenna can be erected with the span normally required for 21MHz, GM3TLA raises the question that this type of multiple folding might possibly provide a way of building a dipole with one half wavelength of wire with an overall span of only one-eighth wave which could be erected in a highly restricted space. I suspect that such an antenna would require critical adjustment of the element to resonance. W8JK in his *Electronics* article (reproduced in the *Electronics Manual for Radio Engineers*) points out that the length of an antenna becomes more critical as the number of wires is increased beyond two, reducing rather than as might be expected increasing the effective bandwidth.

The original dipoles investigated by W8JK were for the pre-war 14MHz band (14.0 to 14.4MHz) and were constructed with No 12 (B&S gauge) with the overall spacing (d) of the order of 0.015 wavelength or less. Thus his two-wire 14MHz dipole was 34ft long and had a wire spacing of one foot.

In his article, W8JK referred to the work of N E Lindenblad for the original television (sound) transmitting antenna on the Empire State Building (*RCA Review*, April 1939). W8JK stressed that "The transmission line terminals of all the types described [in Electronics] are located at a current loop point. Lindenblad has recently described a folded antenna, which might be called a two-wire quarter-wave doublet, in which the terminals are located at a current node."

As I had never previously followed up this reference to a quarter-wave folded doublet, it seemed worth seeking out, in the IEE Library, the April 1939 issue of *RCA Review*. I found that the first VHF TV-sound antenna (modern TV antennas are broad-band and carry both vision and sound, usually on UHF for four channels) on the Empire State Building consisted of a loop antenna made up from four folded dipoles bent into circular segments.

To quote Lindenblad: "Among the dimensions of folded radiators which, at a given frequency, result in resistive input impedance, only the two smallest dimensions are of any interest in this case. At the larger of these dimensions the distance between the folding points of the radiator is approximately a half wave: **Fig 5(a)**. The folding points coincide with maximum potential and the currents in the parallel conductors flow in the same direction.

"The distance between the folding points at

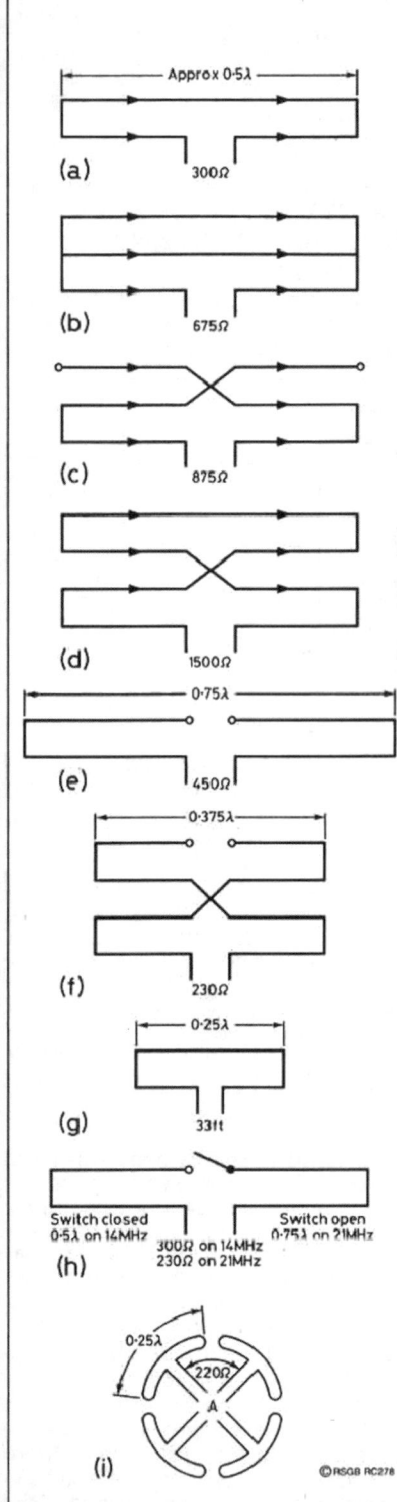

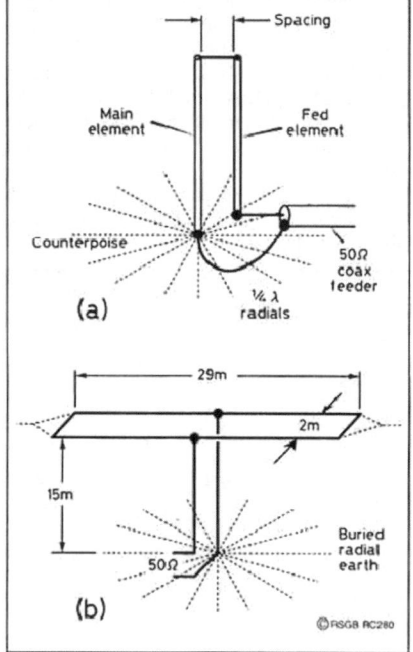

Fig 7: (a) Form of folded monopole investigated in detail by K8CFU in the mid 1980s. Provisional dimensions for 14.2MHz antenna are listed in Table 1. (b) Dimensions of a 1.85MHz folded-T antenna as described by G3LNP in 1992. Dimensions can be scaled for higher-frequency bands.

Fig 5: Various forms of folded dipole antennas. (a) and (b) physical span 0.49-wave. (c) 0.46 wave. (d) 0.47-wave. (e) 0.71-wave; (f) 0.38-wave. (g) basic quarter-wave, folded dipole, voltage-fed. (h) Practical two-band 14 and 21MHz antenna with switch closed on 14MHz. (i) The original Empire State Building TV-sound VHF ring antenna using four quarter-wave dipoles to form circular omni-directional ring. The mutual coupling reduces the feed impedance of each segment to about 220Ω, with four twin feeders parallelled at A and coupled to 55Ω coax cable via a balun. The folded parts are of equal length mounted one above the other but shown in two-dimension form in the diagram.

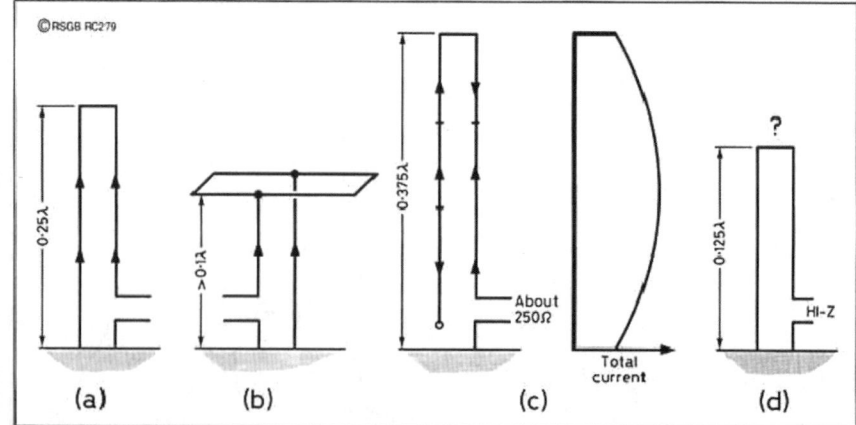

Fig 6: Various forms of the folded monopole antenna. (a) λ/4 folded vertical of conventional form. The feed impedance can be adjusted to required value by using wires/rods of different diameter. (b) Folded-Tee antenna developed by G3LNP (*TT*, August 1992). (c) Three-eights-wave vertical folded antenna working against earth with feed impedance about 250Ω. Current distribution is similar to that of a vertical top-loaded single-conductor antenna with maximum radiation a λ/4 above earth. (d) Possible form of a λ/8 wave monopole which might be worth trying but will have a low radiation resistance that will reduce efficiency.

1990 - 1999

Base impedance	Height	Main el dia	Fed el di	Spacing
50Ω	15.1ft	0.25in	1.75in	3.0in
			2.75in	4.0in
			4.0in	6.0in
75Ω	15.1ft	0.25in	1.25in	14.25in
			1.75in	16.25in
			2.75in	22.5in

Table 1.

the smaller dimension is only about a quarter of a wave: **Fig 5(g)**. The input terminals are at maximum potential and the currents in the parallel conductors flow in opposite directions. A ring antenna of this later type need only be about half the size of that required by the first type, reduces the possibility of undesirable mutual effects between the sound and the vision antennas and reduces the mechanical problems. For these reasons, the small-type folded dipole was chosen."

For a λ/4 folded dipole the terminal resistance would be very high, implying a voltage-fed system – possibly from a resonant open-wire feeder (preferably about one-quarter or three-quarters wave long to provide a current fed system from a balanced ATU output). In the case of the four λ/4 radiators in the RCA ring antenna, by properly spacing adjacent folding points, it was found possible to influence the characteristics of the radiator so that the input impedance of each radiator in the combination was reduced to 220Ω, permitting parallel connection of the four short open-wire balanced 220Ω lines via a balance converter [1:1 balun] to a 55Ω coaxial line without impedance transformation: **Fig 5(i)**.

For amateur operation with a quarter-wave dipole, it would presumably be possible to use 300Ω line as a resonant line on the fundamental frequency but as a flat line on the harmonic frequency at which it would be a conventional half-wave dipole.

There might also be a possibility of an effective one-eighth-wave high folded monopole. Dr Kraus pointed out the advantages of a three-eighths wave vertical antenna working against ground including the lower ground loss due to the higher feed resistance: **Fig 6(c)**. Whether a one-eighth wave vertical monopole without top loading (**Fig 6(d)**), would be effective is questionable but might form an interesting experimental project. The radiation resistance would be low. **Fig 7** shows two practical implementations of folded monopoles.

144MHz J-pole and Slim Jim

Extracted from 'Technical Topics', *Radio Communication*, December 1994

144MHZ J-POLE & SLIM JIM ANTENNAS

BACK IN 1978 the late Fred Judd, G2BCX, described in *Practical Wireless*, a low-cost 144MHz vertical antenna based on the classic J-Pole antenna (**Fig 3(a)**) but with a folded element structure along with the integrated matching stub (**Fig 3(b)**). He named this antenna the 'Slim Jim'.

Later, in *TT*, September 1986 (see also *Technical Topics Scrapbook 1985-89*, pp124-5) I noted that a Modified Slim Jim (MSJ) antenna had been described and analysed in *IEEE Transactions on Broadcasting* (March, 1986) by Greek university authors as a suitable antenna for 101.8MHz VHF/FM local sound radio. Computer analysis of the G2BCX design (**Fig 3(b)**) had shown that this provided a 50Ω resistive match at 155MHz rather than the intended 145Mhz, with maximum radiation at about 22° above horizontal. VHF broadcast antennas (and amateur repeaters etc) should ideally radiate most energy at 0° or even slightly tilted downwards since the transmitters are normally located at a high site, serving adjacent lower areas. The Greek MSJ dimensions for 101.8MHz were thus not an exact scaling of those shown in **Fig 3(b)**. The dimensions used were: height 2.21m; leg distance 0.06m; height of gap (beginning) 1.10m; height of gap (ending) 1.25m; height of the feedpoints 0.37m; radius of wire 0.004m. These dimensions could be scaled for 145MHz.

The principle, if not the origination, of the Slim Jim has crossed the Atlantic. In 'More Bang for the Buck - How to build a really cheap but good antenna for 2 metres', Lew Mccoy, W1ICP (*CQ*, July 1994, pp50-51) recounts how, while attending a meeting of the Quarter Century Wireless Association in Palm Springs, he came across a group of local amateurs building Slim-Jim type antennas using ordinary 300Ω twin-wire feeder: "They had had very good luck with the antenna". W1ICP took a note of the dimensions they were using (**Fig 4(a)**) but found it difficult to get a good match for 50Ω; Their suggestion was to wrap a small piece of aluminium foil around the twin lead and then slide it up and down to achieve a match." In the outcome, W1ICP reverted to a design closer to the classic J-pole antenna but retaining the

The Multee Folded Dipole

Extracted from 'Technical Topics', *Radio Communication*, November 1994

THE MULTEE QUARTER-WAVE FOLDED DIPOLE

RECENTLY IN DISCUSSING folded dipole antennas, I mentioned that I had not come across the concept of a quarter-wave folded dipole with high-impedance feed until following up a reference to the original American TV-sound antenna erected on the Empire State Building in the late 1930s. Memory is fallible - I now realise that the dual-band W6BCX Multee (**Fig 11**), described in *TT* over 30 years ago and reproduced in all editions of *Amateur Radio Techniques* (but in which an error has crept in giving the feed impedance of the λ/4 element as 600Ω instead of up to 6000Ω although this does not affect the dimensions or matching) has the top radiator (as used on the higher of the two bands) in the form of a λ/4 folded dipole, fed from 50Ω coaxial cable by means of the vertical section which forms a linear impedance transformer on the higher band while acting as a top-loaded vertical radiator on the lower band.

This antenna, described in various editions of *The Radio Handbook*, is claimed to form a compact antenna which can be used 'with excellent results on 1.8/3.5MHz (with 52ft vertical section and 70ft span) and 3.5/7MHz (with 28ft vertical section and 35ft span). The 'feedline' should be held as vertical as possible, since it radiates vertically polarized signals on the lower (fundamental) frequency. A good 'earth' system, preferably of buried or elevated radials, is desirable for the lower-frequency band but of little importance on the higher band with horizontally-polarized radiation from the λ/4 'top'.

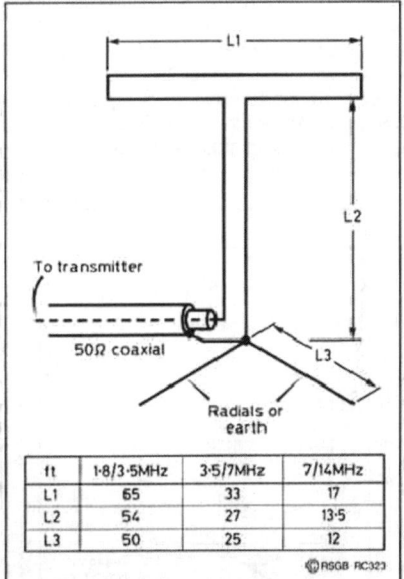

ft	1·8/3·5MHz	3·5/7MHz	7/14MHz
L1	65	33	17
L2	54	27	13·5
L3	50	25	12

Fig 11: The Multee two-band antenna using L1 as a λ/4 Ω folded dipole on the higher band, with the high feed-impedance (up to 6000Ω) provided by L2 acting as a linear transformer (λ/2 times velocity factor).

313

ANTENNA TOPICS

use of twin-wire line for the element, although using 450Ω ladder line rather than the solid 300ohm type: **Fig 4(b)**. He used an ELNEC program for the wire lengths, and then found that he could reproduce similar results (less than 1.5:1 SWR across the American band of 144-148MHz). In the USA the cost of such ladder line is less than 20 cents a foot and, since only 5ft is required, the cost is less than the dollar (buck) of his title.

He writes: "The antenna undoubtedly has good gain as compared to a quarter-wave ground plane and immeasurably more gain than a rubber duck. It is simple to hang one end of the antenna up on a support as high as possible. Also, it would be a good traveller's antenna because it can be coiled up and easily stored in luggage. The antenna connections could be coated with waterproofing material and installed outside. Still another method would be to slip the antenna inside a length of 1 inch PVC and mount the PVC up in the air. There are scores of possibilities . . I think it's pretty hard to beat one dollar or less for a fine-performing antenna."

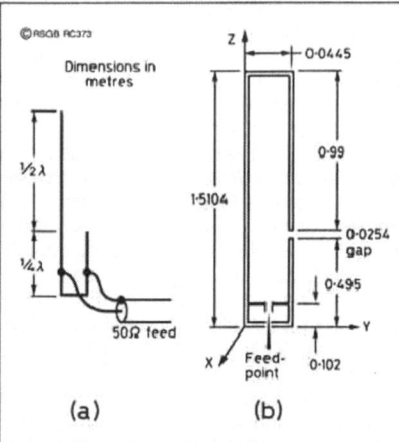

Fig 3: (a) The classic J-Pole antenna provides a vertical half-wave radiating element with quarter-wave matching stub: it rather resembles an inverted form of the original Zepp antenna as patented by Dr Hans Beggerow in 1909 as an antenna for balloons or airships. (b) Dimensions of the original 'Slim Jim' 145MHz antennas described by G2BCX in *Practical Wireless* in 1978, although later computed as resonating about 155MHz.

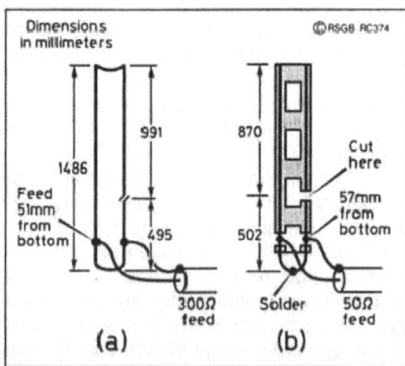

Fig 4: (a) The 300Ω twin-lead Slim Jim antenna as used by a group of Californian amateurs, although W1ICP found it difficult to obtain a good match. (b) The easily reproduced J-pole antenna made from 450Ω ladder line by W1ICP: Flat across 144-148MHz (SWR less than 1.5:1). Found to work very well with hand-held transceivers etc as a fixed or traveller's antenna.

Near-to-earth Antennas

Extracted from 'Technical Topics', *Radio Communication*, February 1995

NEAR-TO-EARTH ANTENNAS

ON A NUMBER OF OCCASIONS attention has been drawn to the value of NVIS (Near Vertical Incidence Skywave) propagation for medium-distance contacts on such bands as 3.5, 7 and 10MHz as a means of largely overcoming the problem of the skip ('dead') zone. By directing the bulk of radiation at a high vertical angle at frequencies around the critical frequency, reliable working at distances up to a few hundred miles, without a skip zone, can usually be achieved. For military applications, this requirement has encouraged the use of compact transmitting loops or very low dipoles not more than about 10ft above ground (*TT* noted many years ago the marketing by Racal of a low dipole for this application). Conventional vehicle whip antennas, on the other hand, have a pronounced null in the vertical direction.

Traditionally, amateurs plan their antennas to provide maximum low-angle radiation and so enhance long-distance working, or use vertically-polarized antennas to maximise ground-wave propagation. As William McLeod, VK3MI puts it in 'Low Radiators and High Ground Planes' (*Amateur Radio*, November 1994, pp10-14): the accepted amateur criteria for horizontal HF radiators has traditionally been 'as high as possible' not only to take advantage of ground reflection but also to clear obstructions, particularly metal conductors and sizeable buildings. Yet, on the lower HF bands, for most suburban and portable locations these conditions of height and space are virtually impossible. Furthermore, in the real world, the ground reflector is anything but perfectly conducting and should be regarded as a lossy dielectric.

VK3MI points out that for 7MHz a height of 10m is a bare quarter-wave above ground; on 3.5MHz only an eighth-wave. This raises the question whether in practice it is worth striving even for this height. What sort of performance can be expected from horizontal antennas only a metre or two above ground? VK3MI summarises the factors involved with low horizontal radiators as follows:

- For low practical heights the radiation resistance at the centre of a resonant dipole remains within the 2:1 VSWR range for the usual coaxial cable feeder so matching procedures are minimal, more so when an electrical half-wave of cable is used to transfer the centre impedance directly to the transmitter: see **Fig 1**.
- Whereas the resonant length of a dipole remote from ground is mainly determined by the length-to-diameter ratio of the conductor, when the ground becomes an increasing part of the dielectric the length is determined by the height to diameter ratio: see Tables 1 and 2. Due to the wide spread of dielectric constant no simple formula can determine this ratio.
- The losses increase as height decreases towards ground level but do not become prohibitive until very low levels are reached; for a 7MHz dipole above common clay this can be as low as λ/40 (1m). [In desert conditions, an antenna can be laid directly on the sand, or even buried a few inches below the surface and yet still radiate reasonably well - G3VA].
- The 'cone' of radiation directed vertically, then reflected back from the ionosphere, can produce non-direction communication with no 'skip distance' to some 400-500km. This is NVIS transmission and is the mode supporting most of those semi-local nets on the 3.5MHz and 7MHz bands. There is usually some fading but for SSB reception the long AGC time-constant of the receiver will alleviate this.
- Two or three hop transmission can occur where the intermediate reflection points fall at sea so some long-distance working is possible in these favoured directions without low-angle transmission lobes. Land reflection points include greater losses which soon become excessive.

VK3MI in his Amateur Radio article provides detailed test results and tabulated data, including **Tables 1** and **2**. He sums up his results as showing that: "In general, the resonant horizontal dipole is an effective radiator at very low height from ground, particularly for NVIS transmission, or where a 'concealed' antenna is required. Losses increase seriously below λ/30 and the high impedance ends of the elements should have at least this amount of separation from ground or metallic earthed objects, towers and poles - but λ/30 is only 1.5m for the 7MHz band.

"Kevlar, Black Dacron, Polypropylene Baler Twine and Nylon Rope are all suitable insulating supports with far less end effects than the single egg-shaped strain insulator wired back to a steel tower which has been commonly used. Supports of this nature have been measured with 6 to 15pF coupling to the earthed object and Table 2 can be used to estimate the end effects of this type of support.

"With the elements double-insulated inside the popular 12mm polypropylene garden irrigation piping erected at 1.5m on the post side of a suburban wooden fence a very effective

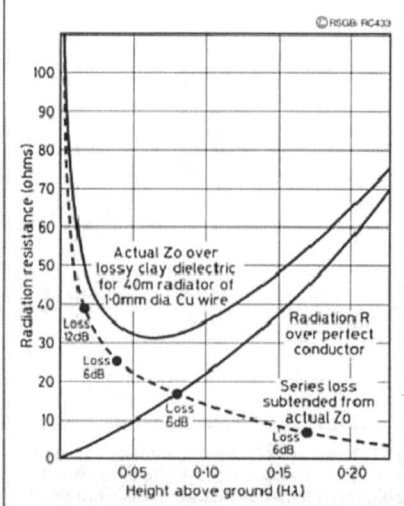

Fig 1: Radiation resistance of a half-wave dipole less than a quarter-wave above ground.

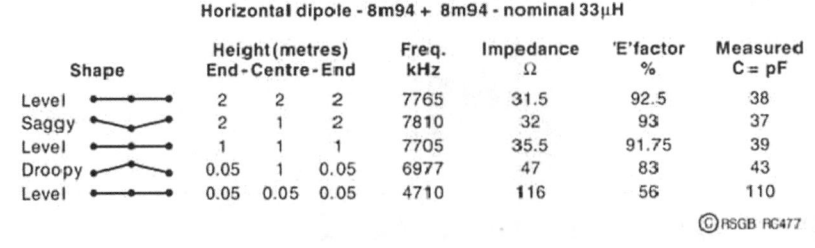

Table 1: Effects of shape, close to clay ground for Dipole of 1mm dia. PVC covered wire - (hot, dry weather - green grass).

Shape	Height (metres) End-Centre-End			Freq. kHz	Impedance Ω	'E' factor %	Measured C = pF
Level	2	2	2	7765	31.5	92.5	38
Saggy	2	1	2	7810	32	93	37
Level	1	1	1	7705	35.5	91.75	39
Droopy	0.05	1	0.05	6977	47	83	43
Level	0.05	0.05	0.05	4710	116	56	110

Level horizontal dipole - 8m94 + 8m94 - nominal 33µH

Height	Freq. kHz	Impedance Ω	'E' factor %	Measured C = pF	Resonant C = pF
2m0	7767	31R5	92.5	38	12.5
1m5	7745	32R	92.3	37	=
1m	7727	35R5	92	38	=
0m5	7550	45	90	40	=
0m2	7135	61	83	46	15
0m1	6400	70	76	87	=
0m05 (50mm)	4710	116	56	110	35

Table 2: Effects of height above clay ground for Dipole of 1mm dia. PVC insulated copper wire - (hot, dry weather - green grass).

concealed radiator should result. For portable use a couple of 4m bamboo poles for end supports and a saggy dipole radiator require no apology as to effectiveness for NVIS transmission but directivity, if any, depends on local obstructions and reflectors."

Apart from considerations of possible RF health hazards with high-power operation if the radiator is close to a living area (most current guidelines stipulate a minimum safe height of 30-35ft for high-power HF operation) there are other safety aspects that need to be considered. VK3MI writes: "Safety is an important consideration for both low radiators and for elevated ground planes. One part is physical in that any wires below 3m can be regarded as a trap for man and beast, including horses and wandering cattle. Even in daylight a thin wire can disappear against some backgrounds and at night is a very serious hazard. Therefore a protective, non-metallic guard-rail or fence is necessary, not just a coloured streamer tied in the middle of the hazard.

"Another aspect of safety is electrical as even at low power a nasty sting and RF burn can occur which, for non-technical people or for climbing children, can produce an emotional reaction far in excess of the initial injury. At medium power, around 100 watts, these effects can become severe and for higher powers the effect of corona and irradiation must also be considered. The use of unprotected low installations is not recommended for high powers and even for low power the radiator should be double insulated by enclosure in plastic pipe or conduit."

In his article, VK3MI also describes how by erecting an antenna above the double-pitched metal roof of a building about 20m long and some 6 to 8m wide, it is possible to obtain low-angle radiation: a system he dubs a 'Woolshed Reflector'. He also provides information on elevated ground-plane antennas and vehicle whip antennas.

New Look at the Multee Antenna

Extracted from 'Technical Topics', *Radio Communication*, February 1995

A NEW LOOK AT THE MULTEE ANTENNA

IN CONNECTION WITH the quarter-wave folded dipole antenna, I included in the November 1944 *TT* (p62) an outline of the two-band Multee antenna originally devised by W6BCX and which has appeared for many years in editions of the *Radio Handbook*. However the dimensions given in Fig 11 were those given in *TT*, May 1965 and appear to have been taken from an article in *73* or *CQ*, although the rather different dimensions given in the text for a 1.8/3.5MHz version are as

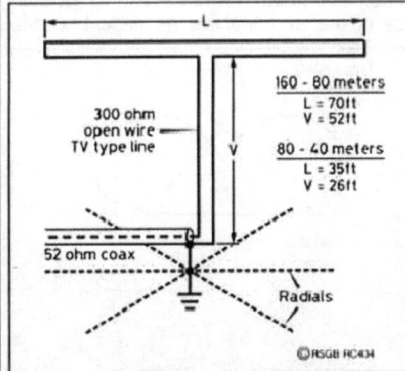

Fig 5: The Multee two-band antenna with dimensions as shown in *The Radio Handbook*.

given in the *Radio Handbook*. The version reproduced in *TT* suggested open-wire line and not 300ohm ribbon with its lower velocity ratio for both the vertical and horizontal sections whereas recent editions of the *Radio Handbook* (including the 1992 edition) suggest that 300ohm open-wire TV-type line can be used. **Fig 5** shows the Handbook dimensions.

Dr John S (Jack) Belrose, VE2CV has sent some pertinent comments on this antenna. He writes:

"I wonder whether anyone has fabricated a Multee - in my view it is certainly not a resonant antenna, but it does have interesting radiation characteristics. I can computer-model antennas, including folded antennas, provided that open wire is used.

"The purpose of my letter is to question the dimensions given in *TT*. You have suggested making the antenna out of 300W twin lead. [Actually the November *TT* referred to 300ohm *open wire* - G3VA]. This is not a good suggestion, since whatever the frequency (low-band or high-band) there is a large standing wave on the antenna. Also re-dimensioning the antenna raises the question of dimensioning the length of a radiator (which is independent of velocity factor) and dimensioning a transmission line (where the velocity factor is important).

"A folded dipole is a (sort of) complex radiator, since it carries both transmission line currents (out of phase currents) and radiating currents (the in-phase currents) on the two conductors. The velocity factors for these two modes are quite different when using 300Ω ribbon.

Let us consider a 3.75MHz half-wave folded dipole made with 300Ω twin-lead. The resonant dipole length for a half-wave radiator is about 123.2ft (37.55m), [half-wavelength times antenna factor] with an arm length 61.6ft or 18.77m. Whereas for the transmission line mode the length for a quarter wavelength is 53.86ft (16.43m quarter-wavelength times velocity factor). Therefore, for the antenna to function properly (better impedance match) you have to include shorting straps at the shorter dimension locations: see **Fig 6** for a folded dipole made from 300ohm ribbon as described in many editions of the *Radio Handbook*.

[The need for such shorting straps with folded-dipoles using 300ohm ribbon was described many years ago in *TT*, and an example appears in *ART7*, p265, derived from *The Radio Handbook* and which, incidentally, was used as a 14MHz antenna for many years at G3VA].

VE2CV continues: "All this raises the question: how to dimension the Multee when changing from open-wire line to 300ohm (ribbon or ladder) twin-lead? This begs the question concerning the original dimensions (dimension L2 is not a high-band half-wave times velocity factor). Furthermore, you cannot consider that the two-conductor transmission line forming the vertical element of the antenna acts like a linear (impedance) transformer, when it is fed in an unbalanced way (ie fed on one leg only).

"I have rather carefully modelled the 160/80-metre Multee, having the original dimensions for open-wire line, using a version of NEC-2. I modelled the antenna using 600ohm

ANTENNA TOPICS

Waterproofing Dipole Tees

Extracted from 'Technical Topics', *Radio Communication*, February 1995

WATERPROOFING DIPOLE TEES

THE PROBLEM OF providing effective waterproofing of the connection between a coaxial-cable feeder and an antenna element has been raised a number of times in *TT* and elsewhere but it seems worth emphasising that this is a perennial problem. As Dr J A Share, G3OKA puts it: "One of the curses of the British climate is the rain and the resulting tendency of rainwater finding its way into small openings and ruining any electrical contact with which it comes into contact. Over the past thirty years countless lengths of coax cable have been destroyed by rain water penetrating dipole-centre connections." [A major problem is that, particularly with air-spaced and semi-air-spaced cables, a single entry-point can ruin many metres of costly cable - G3VA].

G3OKA continues: "Some six years ago a simple waterproofing idea was noted in the *ARRL Handbook* in connection with a lightweight portable dipole design. This used a plumbers plastic Tee, three rubber bungs, DIY sealant, waterproof adhesive and some scrap fibreglass circuit board. Since adopting this practice and despite the rigours of six winters and summers, I have experienced no repetition of water penetration and the design (**Fig 4**) seems worthy of greater exploitation.

"The Plumbers Tee can be purchased from DIY stores (22mm ideal size) and suitable rubber bungs are available from stores selling home wine-making materials. A tube of black waterproof glue is recommended but clear Bostick would no doubt suffice. Superglue can be used but this makes it impossible subsequently to take the connection apart. Only a small amount of silicone sealant is required (left over from some other DIY project?). Since the full strain of the antenna is taken on the centre insulator, 3.2mm fibreglass PCB is recommended, but alternatively two pieces of standard 1.6mm board could be superglued together, but in this case it is essential to roughen the surfaces to be joined, otherwise the pieces will not adhere.

"Hold the Tee in a vice, force in the bungs and drill the holes with a hand drill, using sharp bits somewhat smaller than the required hole sizes. If done slowly and carefully the bungs will be a tight fit onto the coax/antenna-wire. Cut the centre insulator so that it is about 6mm less than the distance between the inside ends of the bungs; drill holes for the connections; and remove the unwanted copper from the centre of the insulator using a rough file or by tinning the entire area and then lifting off the copper using a sharp knife while the solder is molten.

"Fit bung (3) onto the coax and feed the coax into the tee so that it exists at one of the wire holes; feed the antenna wire through bung (1) and then through the Tee. Feed the second antenna wire through bung (2) and assemble the centre insulator. Ensure the solder joints are of high quality because it is difficult to resolder once the centre is fully assembled. It takes a little dexterity to push the insulator back into the tee, rather akin to a ship in a bottle.

"Apply Waterproof Bostick to the antenna wires close to the centre insulator and also to the inside of the Tee where bungs are going to be fitted. Slide the bungs into place and leave until the adhesive is cured. Fill the Tee-piece with the silicone sealant leaving space to fit the final bung. Curing time varies according to the sealant but at least 24 hours should be allowed. The final step is to coat the coax with more waterproof Bostick and glue the last bung into position.

"In practice, the whole assembly is light yet strong, and has withstood the wind-loading on a W3DZZ trap-dipole at 40ft in a location only a few hundred metres from the Irish Sea for the past six years without failure or water penetration.

Fig 4: Detail drawing of the waterproof dipole Centre Tee.

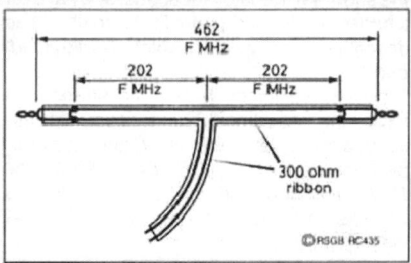

Fig 6: Single-band folded dipole formed from 300ohm ribbon feeder with shorting straps to compensate for the velocity factor of the cable as suggested for many years in The Radio Handbook.

open-wire line (neither MININEC nor NEC can model transmission lines, particularly shorted (folded) lines, if the spacing between conductors is too small). I have assumed that the antenna is used with four insulated radials, 15.24m (50ft) long, as in the November *TT*. The height of the radials for my model is one metre, but this is not a critical dimension. I have assumed average ground characteristics ($\sigma = 3$mS/m, $\varepsilon = 13$).

The antenna is in the X-Z plane, the radials in the 45° planes. The input impedance, according to NEC-2 is $16 - j247\Omega$ at 3.75MHz and $72 - j1059\Omega$ at 1.9MHz (remember that the impedance of the open wire line for the model is 600ohm, not 300Ω). However it is clear that the antenna is not resonant in either the 1.8MHz or 3.5MHz bands.

"**Figs 7** and **8** show the computed radiation patterns. Indeed, the radiation characteristics of the antenna are as described, viz dominantly vertically polarized in the 1.8MHz band; for the 3.5MHz band the polarization is horizontal in the plane orthogonal to the horizontal element, and vertically polarized in the plane of the antenna. The asymmetry of the pattern in the plane of the antenna is interesting. The antenna's impedance will depend on the characteristic impedance of the transmis-

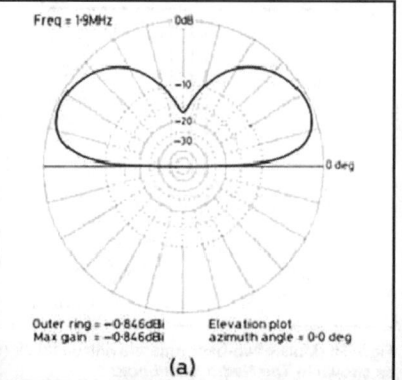

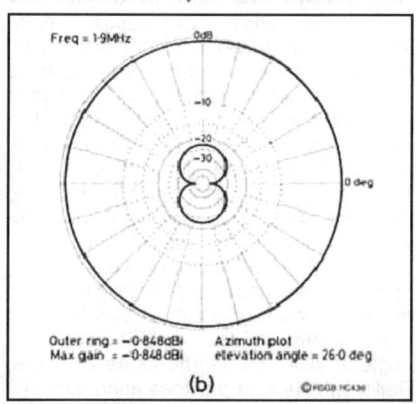

Fig 7: VE2CV's computed radiation patterns for the Multee antenna at 1.9MHz.

sion line used, the dimensions of the antenna, the length and height of the insulated radials, and to some extent on the characteristics of the ground beneath the antenna. A low-loss coaxial feeder must be used together with a good antenna system tuning unit (ASTU)."

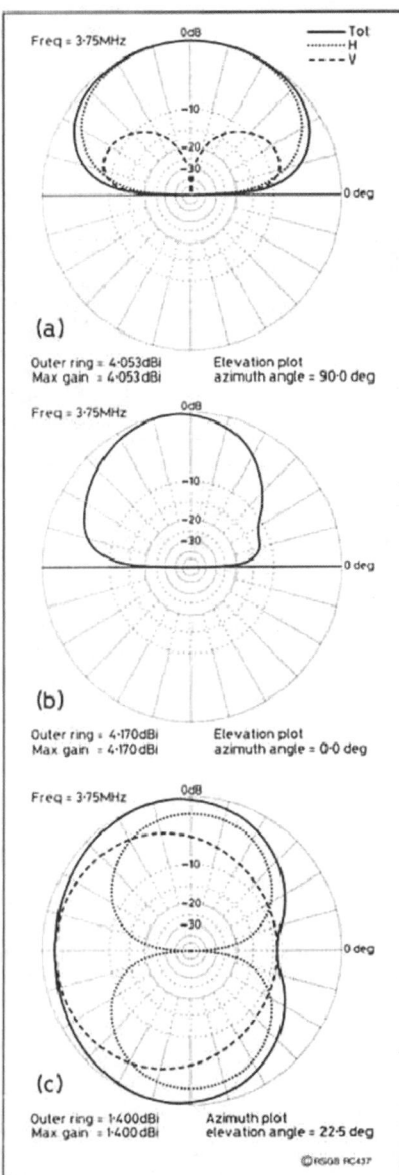

Fig 8: VE2CV's computed radiation patterns for the Multee antenna at 3.75MHz.

Quarter Wave Marconi

Extracted from 'Technical Topics', *Radio Communication*, February 1995

QUARTER WAVE MARCONI ANTENNA

AN OLD BUT STILL useful compact antenna idea for the lower-frequency bands is revived in *CQ*, June 1994. This is the λ/4 grounded

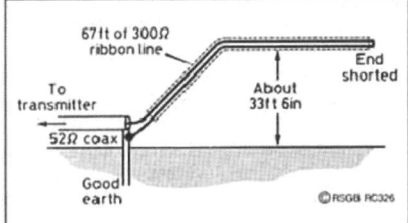

Fig 9: λ/4 ground Marconi antenna for 3.5MHz using 57ft of 300- or 450-ohm ribbon line. A good earth system (preferably including radials or elevated counterpoise) is needed for good performance.

Marconi antenna fed from coaxial cable using 300Ω or 450Ω ribbon feeder (or open line): Fig 9. For 3.5MHz some 67ft of cable is used and the length can be halved for 7MHz or doubled for 1.8MHz (preferable at double the height of the horizontal span). A good earth or radials system is essential. At low power, it is believed that a length of coaxial cable could be used short-circuited at the far end.

Slim Jim & ELNEC

Extracted from 'Technical Topics', *Radio Communication*, March 1995

SLIM JIM & ELNEC

TT, DECEMBER 1994, pp62-63 and Fig 3(b) gave the dimensions of the original G2BCX 'Slim Jim' 144MHz antenna but noted that in 1986 Greek university authors had made a computer analysis of the design and found that these dimensions resulted in a 50Ω resistive match at 155MHz rather than 145MHz and with maximum radiation at an undesirable 22° above the horizon; modified dimensions for a 101.8MHz broadcast antenna were given.

This resulted in an interesting letter from Bernard Spencer, G3SMW which, inter alia, shows that despite the many benefits that have stemmed from the development of user-friendly versions of 'method of moments' (NEC) antenna evaluation software, some care is still needed in setting up the 'model' for analysis. While professional antennas can usually be erected in the clear, most of our antennas are surrounded by conductive objects which affect radiation patterns etc. G3SMW writes: "I put the Slim Jim configuration of your Fig 3(b) in my ELNEC program, and sure enough got a main-lobe elevation of some 22°, and a best match on 50Ω at about 155MHz. I also got a similar elevation at 145MHz for the same antenna dimensions.

"While the Fig 3(b) configuration (without a feeder) is the obvious way to put this antenna into ELNEC, I was puzzled by the main-lobe elevation, having over the years made and tested Slim Jims and other vertical antennas without finding in practice this large elevation angle.

"So I then, in the ELNEC program, dangled a piece of wire from the bottom right-hand corner of Fig 3(b) to simulate a coaxial feeder. This had a marked effect on the main-lobe elevation. In general it made the lobe much nearer the horizontal, whether connected to the antenna at the corner, or not connected (with a small gap). Naturally the effect varied somewhat with the length of the dangling wire, being greatest for a half wavelength. With this, and for some other lengths, the main lobe given by ELNEC was within about 5° above or below the horizontal.

"This was not an exhaustive investigation, but perhaps shows that the G2BCX Slim Jim usually proves satisfactory in practice when fed as usual by vertical coaxial feeder, although admittedly this does have any bearing on the matter of the best match being at 155MHz is that it may be advisable to scale the dimensions from the Greek antenna as suggested in *TT*.

"From both my amateur and professional studies of the nasty VRPs of many vertically polarised VHF antennas, I believe that these do not arise simply from currents on the outside of the coax braid due to its connection to the antenna but also (as shown by my ELNEC run with a gap) by currents induced on the feeder from the dipole element above. This implies that no single choke-balun or gap would prevent them. I hope to investigate this further, as this represents a nasty problem with many vertical antennas."

More on 144MHz Ribbon J-pole

Extracted from 'Technical Topics', *Radio Communication*, May 1995

MORE ON THE 144MHZ RIBBON J-POLE ANTENNA

THE DECEMBER 1994 *TT* item on J-Pole and Slim-Jim antennas continues to attract comment and suggestions. Dr John Belrose, VE2CV, has been using various versions of the ribbon J-antenna since about 1979. He helped to develop this versatile and useful antenna which makes a very effective roll-up and put-in-your-pocket antenna, particularly for hand-held rigs.

"It can be used as a back-up antenna if a standard whip or rubber duck antenna is broken or mislaid. It can provide improved performance over a vehicular mounted half-wave whip if it is elevated above ground level,

ANTENNA TOPICS

by suspending it from the branch of a tree. The gain over a rubber-duck antenna can be greater than 7dB."

However, VE2CV takes issue with W1ICP (whose article I quoted in *TT*) and also with J Reynante, KD6GLF, whose article appeared in *QST*, September 1994. Regarding the comments from W1ICP which appeared in *TT*, VE2CV points out that while a ribbon J-Pole antenna can certainly be slipped inside a PVC pipe to form a more permanent base station antenna it then requires redimensioning by a significant factor.

KD6GLF proposed its use as a dual-band (146/435MHz) antenna. VE2CV comments that while ribbon J-antenna dimensions for two metres may have a low or acceptable SWR on the 70cm band, the radiator length for the UHF band is 1½-wavelength so that the major lobe is no longer directed at the horizon; in fact the lobe towards the horizon is a minor lobe: see **Fig 4**.

VE2CV writes: "The J-antenna is a half-wave length radiator, fed and matched by a shorted stub one quarter-wavelength long. The feeder transmission line is tapped onto the stub at an appropriate point to match its impedance. If coaxial cable is used to feed the antenna, a balanced-to-unbalanced (current balun) transformer should be used to minimise the current flow on the outside of the cable shield, which contributes to the radiated field.

"A flexible 2-metre J-antenna can be made out of 300Ω twinlead: see the photo (overpage). The length of the radiating part of the antenna is about 0.95 times a free-space half-wavelength (where 0.95 is the experimentally determined antenna factor). The length of the quarter-wave stub is about 0.83 times a free space quarter wavelength (the factor 0.83 corresponds to the velocity factor for Beldon Type 8230 twinlead). The tap point for a 144MHz J-antenna was determined experimentally to be about 0.0136 times the wavelength.

"In most designs, including my early versions, no balun was used and current flow on the outside of the cable shield affected the radiating properties and impedance (hence dimensions experimentally determined) of the antenna. The effect was noticeable particularly on receive. A variation of the received signal strength could be observed as one ran one's hand along the coaxial cable when receiving a distant station.

"The improved design of **Fig 5** uses a choke balun. This is formed by coiling up a few turns of the feedline which, in effect, inserts an RF choke in the outer conductor (shield) of the coaxial feedline. For the frequency range 144-148MHz, six turns of the feed line coiled into a 2.5cm diameter coil provides an inductor with more than enough impedance to minimise feed-line radiation. It was found by experiment that the optimum location for this stub is one quarter of a wavelength from the tap point. The addition of this coaxial choke coil not only isolates the antenna from its feeder, it broadens the bandwidth, and increases the effective gain of the antenna. The SWR versus frequency response is shown in **Fig 6** (note that for the

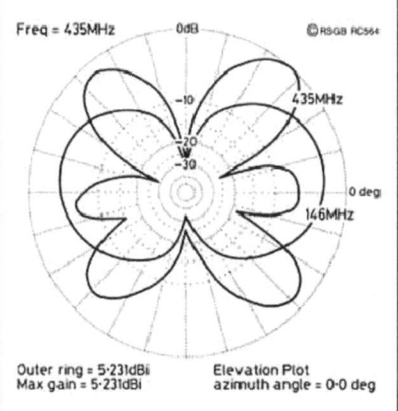

Fig 4: Vertical radiation pattern of a 2-metre Ribbon-J antenna as found with ELNEC by VE2CV at 146 and 435MHz. This shows that while such an antenna could have an acceptable SWR at 435MHz, the horizontal lobe is a minor lobe.

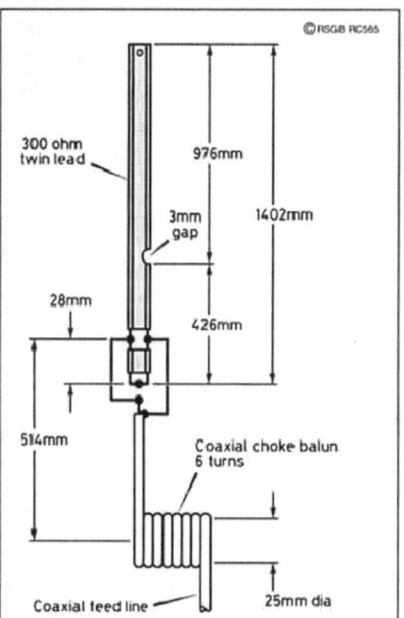

Fig 5: Constructional details of the improved two-metre Ribbon-J antenna as developed by VE2CV.

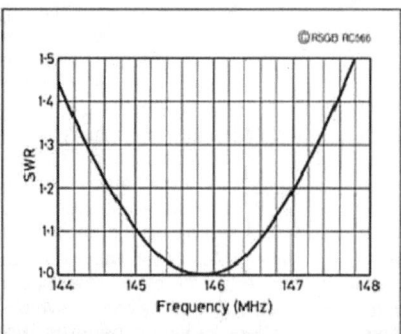

Fig 6. SWR performance of the VE2CV Ribbon-J antenna over the North American two-metre band

VE2CV's two-metre Ribbon-J antenna showing the current balun formed by coiling a small length of the coaxial feedline.

smaller European two-metre band - 144-146MHz - it would be better but not essential to aim for minimum SWR at 145 rather than 146MHz - G3VA).

"Since the antenna is not self-supporting it can be hung from a tree branch, from the ceiling of a hotel room or suspended from a non-metallic mast or rod. But it should not lie against the supporting device, even if this is non-conducting. It should certainly not be slipped inside a PVC pipe without redimensioning it."

Close-coupled Resonator Multibander

Extracted from 'Technical Topics', *Radio Communication*, June 1995

CLOSELY-COUPLED RESONATORS FORM MULTIBAND ANTENNA

IN THE NOVEMBER 1994 issue of *RF Design*, editor Gary Breed, K9AY, provides design and construction information for an HF or VHF antenna that operates effectively on two, three, four or more different frequencies. The approach permits multi-band operation without the use of reactive decoupling networks or tuned stubs or traps etc. It also has the advantage of providing control over the feedpoint resistance and reactance at each frequency.

He has a patent pending (application July 1994) for "a method for constructing multiple-frequency dipole or monopole antenna elements using closely-coupled resonators" and is investigating applications including VHF/UHF cellular and mobile bands, HF broad-

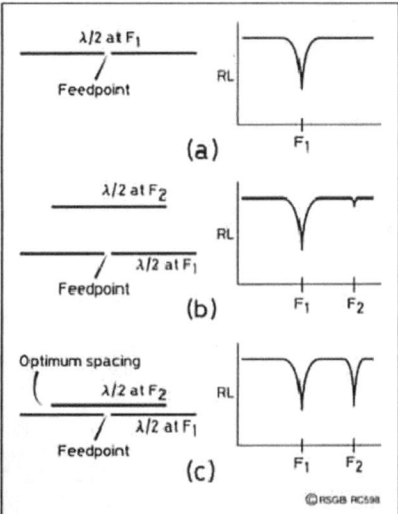

Fig 2: Principles of the close-coupled multiband antenna. (a) Shows a simple half-wave dipole element and its typical return-loss sweep; (b) shows the effect of an additional conductor, resonant at a higher frequency (F2), placed in the vicinity of the F1 driven dipole; and (c) shows how an effective antenna for both F1 and F2 emerges when the spacing of the second conductor is such that coupling is optimum. (Source *RF Design*)

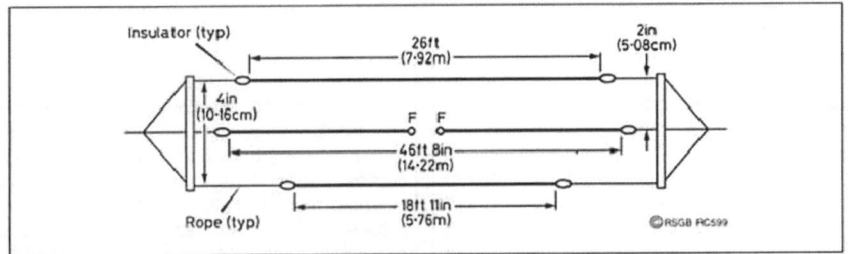

Fig 3. K9AY's experimental tri-band antenna for the 10, 18 and 24MHz band using the close-coupled (open-sleeve) approach. Dimensions are for an antenna made from No 12 AWG wire at a height of 45ft. Insulated spacers are required to keep the wires in alignment. Extra closely coupled wires could be added radially around the driven element for 14 and 21MHz but there will be a practical limit to the number of bands due to the growing complexity of interactions and structure.

casting and amateur radio. However, it seems doubtful whether practical use of this technique is original. For instance, C B Sibley, G0LMC, reminded me that in the days of VHF television in the UK, one of the main antenna manufacturers patented and marketed a combined Band I and Band III antenna. This appeared to follow the same basic principle in which only the lowest frequency resonant dipole element is fed directly with the other dipole element being closely spaced from this element.

Similarly, Bill Orr, W6SAI, in reporting on K9AY's article (*CQ*, February, 1995) suggests that the principle was the subject of some six US patents issued between 1946 and 1950 and, as in the UK, was used for TV antennas and some log-periodic designs and is described as the 'Open Sleeve Dipole' in the 17th edition of *The ARRL Antenna Book*. But, without entering too deeply into any arguments about patents, we should all be grateful to K9AY for bringing this system more fully into the public domain and, especially, for providing computer analysis and practical details of an antenna for the 10, 18 and 24MHz bands.

K9AY introduces the Coupled-Resonator (C-R) principle as follows: "It is well known that conductors in close proximity exhibit strong mutual coupling. A design technique called the C-R principle has been developed which uses this coupling to great advantage. The C-R principle defines the conditions for optimum coupling, creating a system with multiple resonant frequencies, driven at a single feedpoint. Such a multiple-resonant structure consists of a driven dipole or monopole at the lowest frequency of operation, with additional resonant conductors surrounding it, placed at the appropriate distances.

"**Fig 2** demonstrates the C-R principle in its simplest form, a two-frequency system. A half-wave driven dipole is resonant at F1 and driven at the centre. A typical return loss sweep for such a dipole is depicted in (a). In (b) an additional conductor, half-wave resonant at an arbitrarily-chosen higher frequency, F2, is placed nearby. Some degree of coupling will exist between this conductor and the driven dipole, and the return loss sweep of the dipole shows a 'bump' at the resonant frequency of the second conductor.

"The main premise of the coupled-resonator principle is that there is an optimum spacing distance where the coupling results in a matched condition at F2 as in Fig 2 (c). The return loss remains good at F1 and, therefore, the system is matched at both frequencies."

K9AY shows that the same principle can be applied to monopole as well as dipole elements and can be expanded to three, four, five or more frequencies by adding additional resonators and placing them radially around the fed dipole or monopole. A practical upper limit is reached when the complexity of multiple interactions obscures the desired coupling, but systems up to seven frequencies have been successfully modelled.

He points out that the variables involved in the design of C-R antennas are: conductor diameter, conductor spacing, feedpoint impedance, and the ratio of frequencies. The feedpoint impedance at each additional frequency can be controlled by adjustment of resonator spacing and length.

The five-page *RF Design* article provides information on the design equations, radiation characteristics, advantages and limitations and also details of a practical C-R antenna. K9AY states: "Various antennas were constructed to verify the accuracy of the computer models, and to assure that the concept was valid. The first versions of these antennas were designed for HF amateur radio bands, where they could be evaluated 'on the air' and compared with other antennas of known performance . . . this arrangement allowed extensive experimentation in conjunction with enjoyment of the hobby.

"**Fig 3** shows the dimensions of a three-frequency dipole constructed from No 12 AWG wire. The driven dipole is resonant at 10.1MHz, with additional resonators for 18.1 and 24.9MHz . . . Choosing 50 ohms as the design impedance for F2 and F3, the required spacing was determined to be approximately 1.75in (4.5cm) for each resonator. After modelling the design in ELNEC the spacing was increased to 2.0in (5cm), primarily to compensate for installation above real ground at a design height of 45ft (13.7m) . . . Return loss is greater than 20dB at the three design frequencies, exceeding 30dB at the highest two frequencies (those added by coupled-resonators); see **Fig 4**. 30dB corresponds to a VSWR of 1.06:1. Bandwidth tends to be reduced slightly at the higher frequency resonances.

"On-air performance of the three-band antenna proved to be indistinguishable from that of separate dipoles for each band. The radiated performance, the feedpoint impedance, and the variations in impedance with installation height above ground also served to confirm the validity of the MININEC-based ELNEC model."

Here & There: Inverted GP

Extracted from 'Technical Topics', *Radio Communication*, June 1995

It has been noted several times in *TT*, that the inverted ground plane (vertical-T) antenna can readily be adapted to provide either horizontal or vertical polarization. 'Reflecties door PAOSE' (*Electron*, March 1995, p91) draws attention to an interesting way of providing alternative feed inputs for such an arrangement stemming from Ingo Huettie, DJ6YC: **Fig 8**. It would be feasible to provide remote switching by means of a coaxial relay or (for HF) a less expensive relay. With the dimensions shown, the system is intended for

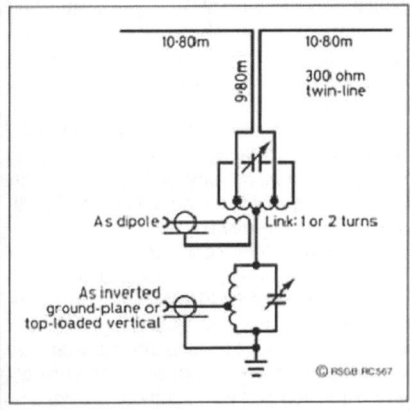

Fig 8: How an inverted Ground Plane (Vertical-T) antenna can be arranged to function alternatively as a horizontal dipole by using two matching networks which may be permanently connected. The coaxial feedline is then plugged into the appropriate socket. Dimensions shown are for 7MHz but could be scaled for other bands.

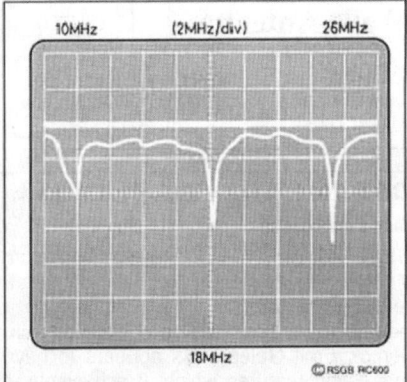

Fig 4: Return loss sweep of the triband antenna. The scales are 2MHz/division horizontal (centred on 18MHz) and 10dB/div vertical.

ANTENNA TOPICS

Vehicle Antennas for HF NVIS

Extracted from 'Technical Topics', *Radio Communication*, August 1995

VEHICLE ANTENNAS FOR HF NVIS

THOUGH COVERING all types of communications systems, the recently published book *Naval Shipboard Communications Systems* by John C Kim and Eugen I Muehldorf of TRW Inc (Prentice Hall PTR, 1995) points out that "over the past few years HF radios staged a comeback as an alternative means of shipboard long-haul communications, since HF communications feature portability, versatility of location, and long-distance connectivity. In addition, users became aware of problems associated with satellite communications due to high costs and congested satellite channels. Newly automated and micro-processor-controlled (HF) radios now offer capabilities previously not available for automatic HF link establishment (ALE)".

A standard form of US Navy HF antenna is the 10-metre Fibreglass whip antenna but such antennas have a null in the vertical direction, and for near vertical incidence skywave (NVIS) medium-distance operation a form of this antenna, known as a 'Towel Bar' antenna, comprises a whip bent over to run 14in above a metal deck.

As mentioned previously in *TT*, NVIS HF systems, which minimise the 'dead zone' (skip zone) by maximising radiation vertically upwards, are of increasing interest for all forms of military and some civilian communications systems. A paper 'Novel antenna configurations for vehicle-borne NVIS applications' by K P Murray and Dr Brian Austin (G0GSF), University of Liverpool, was presented last April at the IEE's Antennas and Propagation Conference (ICAP95) in Eindhoven and is published in *IEE Conference Publication No 407* (Vol 1, pp415-418).

This again emphasises that "HF (3-30MHz) propagation still has an important role to play in certain communication scenarios. Of particular importance is the so-called Near Vertical Incidence Skywave (NVIS) mode of propagation where the ionosphere is utilised for relatively short-range communication . . . Of particular importance is the ability to communicate beyond the line of sight (BLOS) but within the normal HF skip-zone associated with the usual vertical whip antenna. The only way to achieve this, without the use of artificial relay facilities, is skywave propagation with a high angle of incidence to the ionosphere. However, this presents particularly demanding constraints on the antenna designer, especially when the terminals are mounted in vehicles.

"Firstly, in order to ensure signal return, frequencies close to the prevailing critical frequency must be employed. The electrical size of the vehicle is generally below the first fundamental resonance. Hence, the input impedance characteristic is generally categorised by a small resistive component with a relatively large reactance. Secondly, the usual vertical whip antenna is inherently unsuitable because of the pronounced null (greater than 20dB) in its radiation pattern towards the zenith."

The paper analyses two types of tilted whips and a vertically mounted (magnetic) loop using the Moment Method (NEC). In the first simulation, a typical 4.8m whip antenna was mounted at the rear corner of the vehicle roof and was tilted forward and backwards along

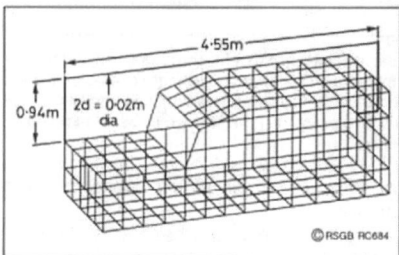

Fig 1: The vehicle wire grid model with loop antenna used for computer simulation by the Moments Method at the University of Liverpool.

its longest dimension. The best performance was seen with the whip tilted backwards away from the vehicle at a substantial angle. At tilt angles less than 50° from the vertical, performance remains similar to that of the vertical whip. This introduces severe practical constraints in terms of the antenna's robustness. (And for civilian vehicles would hardly be popular with other road users! - G3VA).

The authors conclude that for NVIS systems "a better antenna was found to be the vertically mounted loop (simulated as in **Fig 1**) . . . A variety of configurations is possible using either single and multiple feed-points. On the basis of robustness, the percentage of radiated power at elevations greater than 45° and the power lost due to coupling into lossy ground, the loop is clearly a superior antenna to the whip. A possible disadvantage, though not considered here, is the lower loop input resistance and the associated feed-system efficiency".

This ICAP95 paper is concerned with computer simulation rather than practical hardware and one wonders how the preferred multiple feedpoints could be implemented.

Ken Hirschberg, K6HPX, in the 'Technical Correspondence' section of *QST* (March 1995, pp72-73) reports on his use of a ferrite toriod core as a current transformer to feed a compact transmitting loop (**Fig 2**). He views this as a preferred alternative to coupling by a one-turn link (transformer), a tap, or by a capacitive divider that can also be used to resonate the loop.

He writes: "The central feedpoint of the loop (directly opposite the resonating capacitor) is passed through the toroid, making the loop itself a one-turn secondary of the transformer. In this particular set-up, the coaxial feed line was used as the primary by passing it through the core, then soldering (terminating) its centre conductor to its shield through a small hole cut into the cable jacket (ie a Faraday link - G3VA). This forms a shielded link, which serves to reduce the capacitive coupling between the feed line and the loop.

"Based on limited experimentation, I have discovered that (at least at the moderate power level of 100 watts) this means of coupling is physically smaller, does not have to be adjusted for use on different bands, and can be made rigid and weatherproof (eg by encapsulation) for mobile operation. The toroid transformer provided the same apparent coupling as that observed with an ordinary link or balun, each of which encompassed an area about 20% of the size of the main loop's area. For these experiments, the loop I used was an 11 by 4.5ft rectangle made from 1in diameter copper water pipe, with a coaxial capacitor or vacuum variable capacitor; the toroid was made of two Amidon FT-240-61 cores.

"I operated the loop on 1.8, 3.5 and 7MHz bands with an SWR of near 1:1 easily obtained at resonance without the use of an antenna tuner. The antenna - designed for mobile NVIS use - exhibited the expected high-Q properties, and a quite narrow bandwidth. The loop is mounted in the vertical plane, with its feed just above the metal roof of the van. On-the-air results are outstanding, with S9+ reports on 3.5MHz over western North America in the early morning".

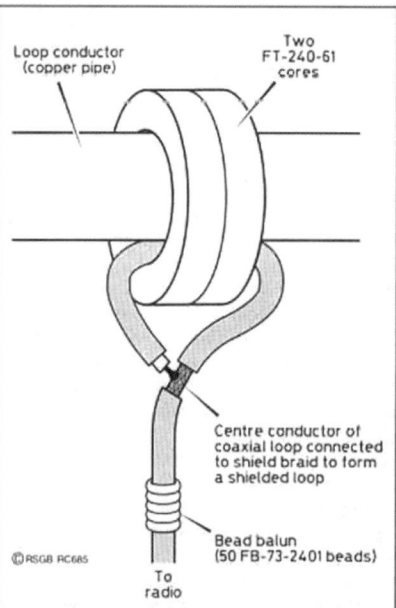

Fig 2: Feedpoint detail as used by K6HP for a mobile (magnetic) loop antenna on the 1.8, 3.5 and 7MHz bands.

Coaxial Travelling Wave Antenna

Extracted from 'Technical Topics', *Radio Communication*, August 1995

COAXIAL TRAVELLING WAVE ANTENNA?

SEVERAL ARTICLES IN the Australian *Amateur Radio* since 1992 have drawn attention to a form of antenna based on a patent granted in 1927 to a Romanian inventor, Emil Geles. This appears to have interesting features which, if achievable in practice, could offer significant advantages as a broadband 'travelling wave' antenna, for example, as a vertical antenna without the usual significant RF ohmic earth losses. It needs to be used with a suitable antenna tuner or balun providing balanced output from a coaxial cable feedline. However, although successfully exploited by several Australian amateurs, it still calls for a degree of experimentation.

The latest article, by Leo Weller, VK3YX (*Amateur Radio*, June 1995, pp 4-6) acknowledges that his work was initiated by an article written by George Thatcher, VK2EHN, in the September 1993 issue, and after re-reading the earlier note by Clive Cook, VK4CC, which drew attention to the UK patent issued in 1927 to Emil Geles of Bucharest. Although VK4CC did not give the Patent Number, it was possible to trace the full patent specification at the National Science Reference Library in High Holborn, London. It proved to be UK patent No 260,005 (UK Application Date October 19, 1926, accepted March 24, 1927).

In summary, this covered a closed-circuit antenna comprising a central wire surrounded by a tubular conductive (metal) structure (**Fig 6**).

"The central wire may be completely separated from, or connected directly to, the top of the tube; or it may be capacity coupled with the tube as shown in **Fig 6 (b)**. The outer tube screens all radiation from the inner wire. The system functions practically as an ordinary open aerial with small ohmic losses. No earth or counterpoise is required."

In more detail, the patent states: "This invention relates to an improved aerial for the transmission of electromagnetic waves such as used in wireless telegraphy or telephony.

"It is stated in various text books on wireless telegraph that the radiation of a closed circuit aerial is nil. This is not strictly true and the proof is that in certain cases use is made of frame aerials for transmitting purposes. On the other hand, it has been shown, and can be verified experimentally, that the radiation of an aerial increases with the surface of the aerial . . . It is also known that the penetration of high frequency currents either from the outside to the inside or vice versa through the walls of a metallic screen is very small.

"Aerials for transmitting and receiving purposes are broadly known in which a vertical wire or inner tube is enclosed in an outer vertical tube from which the said wire or inner tube is insulated and connected to earth or a counter-poise. The invention consists of a transmitting aerial constituted by a vertical tube wherein is enclosed a vertical wire with which the said vertical tube forms a radiating closed circuit without earth connection or counter-poise . . ."

"The field produced by the wire is completely stopped by the tube which acts as a screen. Consequently, it can no longer destroy the field produced by the outer surface of the tube which is free to radiate exactly as an open aerial. The aerial may be excited by connecting the lower ends of the tube and of the inner wire to the transmitting apparatus, for instance through the intermediacy of a transformer as shown in Fig 6. The losses of such an aerial are reduced to the ohmic losses which are exceedingly small and to the losses produced by eddy currents".

It was claimed that the main advantage of such antennas is that no earth connection or counter-poise is employed and that, consequently, neither a large earth area nor a great number of poles which are required for a high power transmitting antenna is required. It is claimed that this would be of special advantage "for use on aeroplanes".

It does appear that a coaxial antenna of this type, together with a black box tuner, was marketed in Australia some years ago (CTW Antenna Coupler), the CTW standing for 'coaxial travelling wave'. If, in fact, this structure does represent a true form of travelling wave antenna (ie an antenna with constant current along the radiating element rather than a resonant standing wave), then clearly this would represent a further valuable feature. Experimental systems by both VK2EHN and VK3YX seem to bear this out, with VK3YX warning that the antenna should not be of a length resonant in any amateur band.

In effect, it appears to be a low impedance closed-circuit antenna of a form rather like an extended transmitting loop antenna but without the complication of the high-Q tuning associated with compact loop antennas. Provided that the losses in the tuner/balun can be kept low, there seems no reason why this type of antenna should not be reasonably efficient both for transmission and reception, and should avoid the major problem of conventional monopoles of the high RF ohmic ground losses and the inconvenience of elevated ground-plane radials.

VK3YX's practical realisation of this form of antenna is outlined in **Fig 7**, with details in **Fig 8 (a), (b)** and **(c)**. His antenna is constructed from three equal lengths of imperial aluminium tubing of total length 12m. As the three lengths are of different diameters (1.75/1.5/1.25in), its characteristic impedance as a 'coaxial cable' is not constant, but this does not seem important. In the centre of the tubing, kept in place by triangular spacers as in Fig 8(a), is a PVC covered wire of 5mm diameter, or 47/03.

VK3YX emphasises that "with so little information available it is an experimenter's delight. Nevertheless, looking through my notes, more than 80 different baluns have been

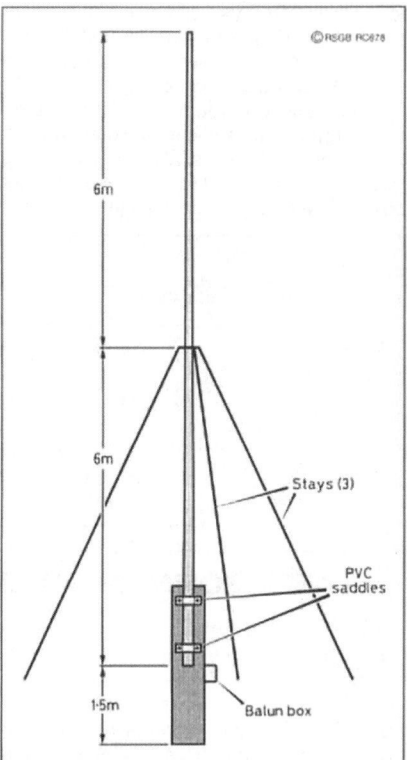

Fig 7: The coaxial travelling wave antenna as implemented by VK3YX based on three lengths of aluminium tubing of total length of 12m, mounted with insulated saddles to an insulated mast stub.

wound with an endless number of readings. Although this was time consuming the result is most gratifying".

He concludes: "It is unlikely that, in the first experiment, maximum performance can be achieved. Much more work will be needed to arrive at fully understanding this system, and the real design considerations. I would like to collect data from other experimenters by letter, telephone or amateur radio regarding their experience with this project". (His address is 46 Peperell Avenue, Syndal, VIC 3150, Australia).

VK3YX lists a number of observations, stressing that "with an antenna so different from all accepted theories and practices, one does not know what to expect and every observation is a discovery for which one tries to find an explanation: (1) I noticed no reverse TV interference, which has plagued me for years. (2) No TVI and I could remove all suppressors, braid-breakers and the like from my own TV set. (3) No earth wire or radials . . . every attempt to use them reduced receive sensitivity. (4) Easy and smooth tuning with a Z match antenna tuner . . . SWR of 1.1 right across the band, even on 21MHz. (5) Good signal to noise ratio which compared favourably with a 3.5MHz dipole with open feeders. (6) Sensitivity on receive and field strength on transmit increases step by step on each higher frequency amateur band. (7) No high voltage spots. Even at 50 watts, a sensitive neon bulb did not glow. Touching the antenna with the hand pushes the SWR meter off the scale. (8) High current. I measured 0.5A at 5 watts on all bands, except the 7MHz band, including 1.8MHz and all WARC bands. (9) The 7MHz band needs more power to achieve 0.5A and tuning is different. This does not affect per-

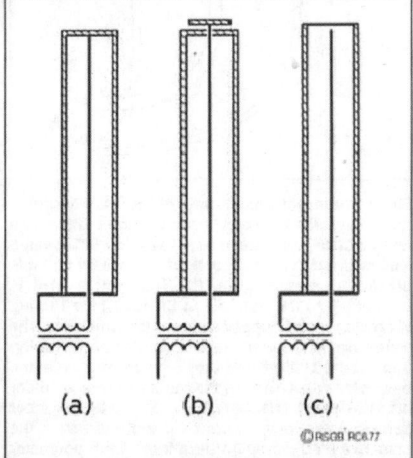

Fig 6: Coaxial closed-circuit antenna principle from UK Patent 260,005 of 1927. (a) Internal wire connected at top to metal tubes as with VK3YX's antenna. (b) Wire coupled capacitive to top of tube. (c) Wire left isolated from tube.

ANTENNA TOPICS

formance. (10) Three turns of heavy, insulated wire around the tubing and short circuited reduced receive sensitivity. This is the reason for the PVC saddles and clamps..."

It seems important to note that the RF feed to this form of 'closed-circuit' antenna must be balanced. There is also an interesting possibility that, at least for low power, it might be possible simply to use a length of conventional coaxial cable - short circuited at the far end - rather than the home made variety with a wire enclosed within a metal tube used by the Australian experimenters. I tried this on receive, using the ATUs that I use for my large looped wire antenna mentioned in June's *TT* and certainly it seemed to receive signals quite well. It seems as though the 1927 idea is worth reviving and developing further, whether or not it forms a genuine 'travelling wave' antenna. It could presumably be used as a horizontal or sloping antenna.

It should be stressed that this form of untuned closed-circuit (loop) antenna requires a low RF ohmic resistance approach akin to that of a compact (magnetic) tuned transmitting loop. Otherwise, there is the likelihood of low transmit efficiency due to RF power losses in both the antenna structure and the tuner or balun transformer needed to provide a low-impedance balanced-output. It must be noted that there will be high RF currents flowing even at relatively low power. As with a conventional frame or loop antenna, the very low radiation resistance may be of minor consequence on receive but could greatly reduce efficiency on transmit. This is presented as an interesting experimental project rather than a fully-proven design. Good performance on transmission cannot be guaranteed!

New Form of Helical Beam

Extracted from 'Technical Topics', *Radio Communication*, August 1995

NEW FORM OF HELICAL-BEAM ANTENNA

DR JOHN D KRAUS, W8JK, has long been recognised by amateurs and professionals as one of the world's leading antenna specialists. He is highly regarded both for the many designs he has pioneered - including the 8JK which in 1936 was the first array to make use of close-spaced driven elements; the first folded dipoles; the first corner reflector; the first axial-mode helical antennas - and for his classic textbook *Antennas*, first published in 1950.

In *IEEE Antennas & Propagation* Magazine (April 1995, p45) he contributes a short article, 'A Helical-Beam Antenna Without a Ground Plane', in which he writes: "The helical-beam antenna (also known as axial-mode helix), which I devised in 1946, was fed via a ground plane. This arrangement has proven very satisfactory for many applications. Now, almost 50 years later, I present a version in which the ground plane is replaced by one or more loops. This design is well suited for pole mounting, as shown in **Fig 9**. It has less wind resistance, and presents a much-cleaner appearance, while providing equivalent performance to a helix with ground plane.

"The inner conductor of the coaxial line feeding the antenna is connected to the end of the helix, and the outer conductor to the base of an adjacent loop. A second (buffer) loop may be situated 1/3 to 1/2 wavelength from the feed point. This loop may or may not be continuous. A third loop, one wavelength or less from the feedpoint, is optional. The helix and all loops are approximately one wavelength in circumference at the centre frequency of operation. A typical pattern is shown in **Fig 10**".

Dr Kraus stresses that the new version retains the broadband and non-critical nature of the ground-plane helix to a marked degree. In the 'Microwaves' chapter of the current *Radio Communication Handbook* (p9.57), it is noted, in describing an axial-helix antenna (with ground-plane) for 1.3GHz, that such antennas "are useful both as test antennas and also as a general-purpose, medium-gain antennas of wide bandwidth. An eight-turn antenna will have about 10dB gain over an approximately 2:1 frequency range".

The new form of 10-turn, pole-mounted antenna with a centre frequency of 1680MHz and a turn spacing of 0.27-wavelength, as described by Dr Kraus, is stated to have a gain of about 15dBi.

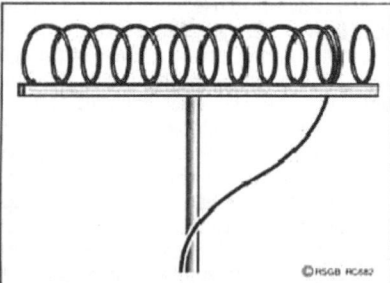

Fig 9: A ten-turn pole-mounted helical-beam antenna, using loops instead of the conventional ground plane. The turn spacing is 0.27-wavelength, and the gain is about 15dBi.

Fig 10: Radiation pattern of the experimental 10-turn antenna shown in Fig 9 at its centre frequency of 1680MHz. Half-power beamdwidth is 34°.

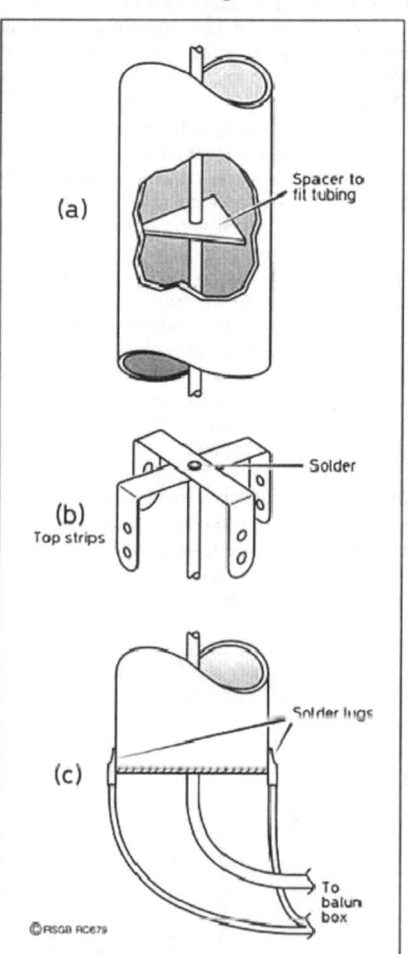

Fig 8: Constructional details of VK3YX's antenna. (a) Triangular perspex spacers 2mm thick and spaced 30cm apart are used to keep the PVC covered wire centred in the tubes, held in place by suitable plastic to plastic glue. (b) The centre wire is connected to the outside on the top of the tubing, via two crossed copper strips. After soldering, the strips are bent down over the outside of the tubing and secured with 8 self-tapping screws. (c) On the base of the antenna, on the outside, are two solder lugs 180° apart. These are fastened with 6mm copper screws, washers and nuts. Note that half way up the mast is a PVC clamp holding three 6mm polyester stays.

1990 - 1999

1.3GHz Conical & Parabolic Reflectors

Extracted from 'Technical Topics', *Radio Communication*, October 1995

1.3GHZ CONICAL AND PARABOLIC REFLECTORS

MANY YEARS AGO, I noticed in *TT* (still in *ART7* pp316-7) that for the UHF and microwave operator the ultimate in high-gain antennas has for long been the parabolic dish reflector, the larger the better. But for the home constructor a true paraboloid is not an easy shape to come to terms with. The main difficulty is that the paraboloid is a doubly-curved surface: if constructed from flat sheets of material, part of the material needs to be either stretched or compressed or both.

An effective alternative was brought to attention by Fred Brown, W6HPH (then also G5AWI). He showed in a 1966 issue of the *VHF'er* and later in *TT* that conical reflectors, constructed very easily from flat sheets of material (hardware cloth in his case) could provide an extremely useful substitute. A conical reflector can give considerably more gain than would a corner reflector antenna yet it is just as easy to build.

A shallow cone has the advantage of being a singly-curved surface and can be made from flat circular sheet by removing or overlapping a segment of the material. Performance depends on the fact it is not really vital for the surface of a parabolic reflector to be a true paraboloid. W6HPH pointed out that it is usually accepted that there can be departures of up to one-sixteenth of the wavelength at any point on the surface without suffering any significant deterioration of gain and directivity.

While one-sixteenth of a microwavelength may not sound much, in practice it permits quite drastic changes in the overall shape. Up to a certain size, in terms of wavelength, it can be two shallow cones, one inside the other: **Fig 3**. A two-cone reflector can be satisfactory up to a diameter of 13.86-wavelengths in certain conditions. This means that for 1296MHz one could build a reflector of some 10ft diameter, or even 31.5ft at 432MHz without having to worry about double-curved surfaces, and yet obtain virtually as much gain and directivity as with a true paraboloid.

A single conical reflector is satisfactory up to 3.46-wavelengths. W6HPH provided details of a 1296MHz single conical reflector antenna with a gain of about 16dB: **Fig 4**. He

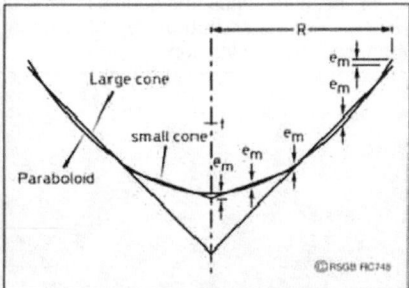

Fig 3: Principle of the polyconic reflector showing the small departures (m) from the true paraboloid.

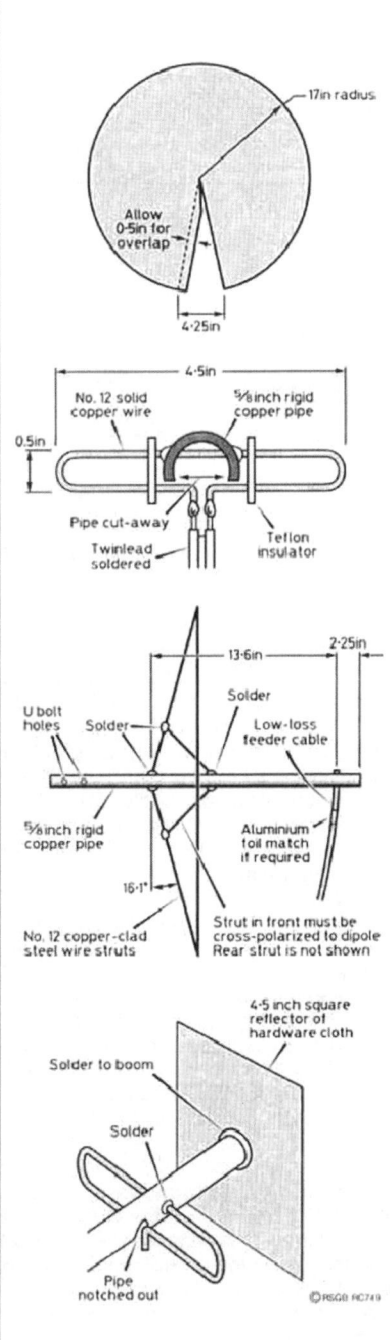

Fig 4: Details of the 1296MHz single conical reflector antenna as designed by W6HPH providing about 16dB gain.

claimed this could be constructed in a few hours for a cost (in 1966) of about $1.50. The cone has a radius of 17in. Both the cone and the small 4.5in square reflector for the folded dipole element were made from 0.5in mesh hardware cloth.

I was reminded of W6HPH's suggestions by an article 'High-Performance Antenna for 24cm' by John Cronk, GW3MEO (*Electronics World + Wireless World*, August 1995, pp 699-700). He introduced his design as having fewer critical dimensions than most other configurations, and capable of being easily customised. It comprises a lightweight parabolic-shaped plane reflector which is illuminated with a horizontally polarised dipole and reflector feed.

Gain is given as about 15dBd (ie about 17dBi) representing a power increase of almost 32 times. Bandwidth is more than ample even for amateur-television. Wind resistance is lower than for expanded aluminium mesh.

The mesh reflector was fashioned from a 3ft by 2ft sheet of wire mesh called Handy mesh obtained from a local hardware store. The mesh consists of half-inch squares formed by 22swg tinned wire. The sheet was cut in half to form a strip 60in long with the overlapped section strengthened by binding some of the coincident wires with 22swg tinned copper wire and then soldering. The mesh is then fixed to an aluminium square former which is shaped as a parabola.

For full details on building GW3MEO's antenna see the original article in *EW + WW*. The design includes a balun feed etc and is considerably more complex than the W6HPH design. But it seems worthwhile to show how he obtains a parabola profile, without resorting to mathematics, by using a pin and string: **Fig 5**.

GW3MEO explains this as follows: "First draw line AB, and then at its centre draw line PFX, at right angles to AB. Next either draw line Xy parallel to AB, or use a long rule or tape parallel to AB, this must be marked off with regular divisions - X1, X2 etc. Now fix one end of a piece of string at point F using a pin. Take the string around another pin at P1, and then up to the point X1, and mark this length with a knot. Now plot the curve by moving the knot to X2, and keeping the string at right angles to XY, prick a mark at P2, and so on, until half the curve is marked out. Repeat for the other half of the curve. Draw a line smoothly through the pin pricks to show the shape of the reflector surface."

The curve is later transferred to a homemade bending device using hardwood blocks and a vice to avoid crumpling the tubular reflector former which comprises 60in of 0.5in square aluminium tube stock, as commonly used for TV yagi antenna booms: **Fig 6**.

Since this is a planar reflector with a parabolic profile, the problem of the double curve is avoided. GW3MEO gives the acceptable tolerance of one-tenth of a wavelength (2.5cm at 1.3GHz), a looser tolerance than W6HPH's one-sixteenth wavelength. It would be interesting to compare the two designs in terms of performance, cost and time of construction.

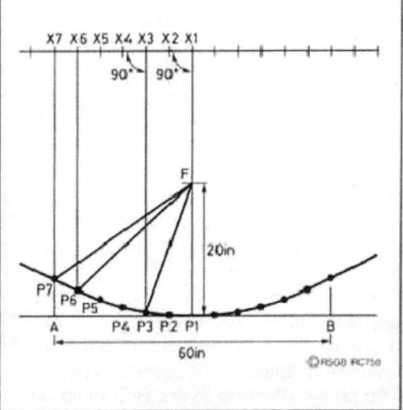

Fig 5: How GW3MEO produces his antenna's parabolic profile drawn without resorting to mathematics by using a pin and string.

ANTENNA TOPICS

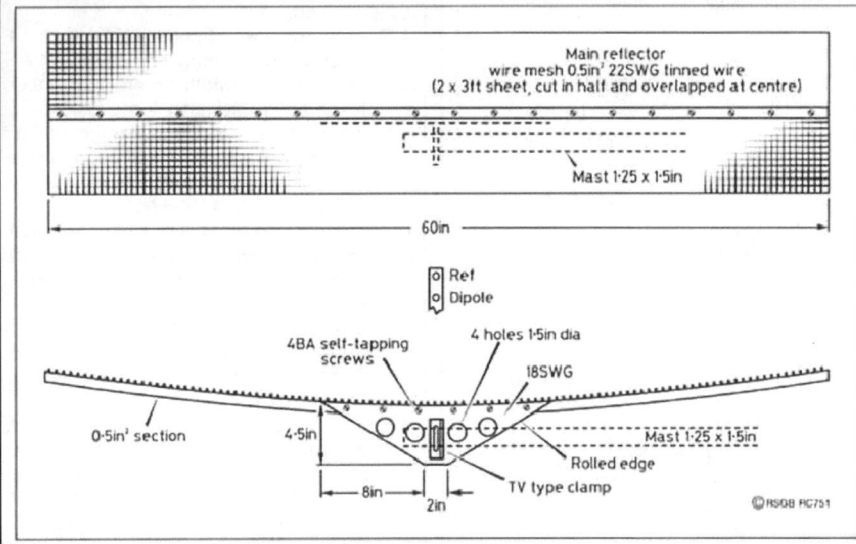

Fig 6: Reflector detail of the GW3MEO antenna. Mesh is a commercially-available type comprising half-inch squares formed from 22SWG tinned wire.

Antenna System Efficiency

Extracted from 'Technical Topics', *Radio Communication*, October 1995

ANTENNA SYSTEM EFFICIENCY

LEW MCCOY, W1ICP, in 'Antenna Efficiency - What is it?' (*CQ*, April 1995, pp 14, 17, 18) reminds us that antenna efficiency is not a question of gain, radiation patters or directivity but is nevertheless an important factor that is too often overlooked.

He stresses that the most efficient antenna, which can radiate about 97% of the power fed to it, is the basic half-wave resonant dipole. Compare this with some mobile and aircraft antennas which at about 2MHz may radiate only some 10mW for every 100 watts of transmitter power.

W1ICP is primarily concerned with the RF ohmic losses in antenna elements, but it should not be forgotten that wasted power may also be a feature of the ATU matching network and the transmission line (feeder). As a simple illustration, he points out that a beam antenna with a 3dBd gain but an efficiency of about 50%. This will radiate in the favoured direction only the same power as a dipole with an efficiency of near 100% and considerably less power in other directions (although the directivity of the beam may still be advantageous for reception and in vertical angle of radiation).

But why should a beam tend to be less efficient than a half-wave dipole? W1ICP notes that the power that is fed into the antenna is spent or dissipated in two ways. The power used up in the RF ohmic resistance is spent in heating up the wire in the antenna, or the traps, bad connections, ground losses, etc. Only the remaining power is spent in the "radiation resistance" of the antenna - in other words, launched into space. Whereas the radiation resistance of a half-wave dipole at a height of a half-wavelength above ground is approximately 73Ω, a close-spaced Yagi array will have a much lower radiation resistance (which is why some form of matching is required between a coax feeder and the driven element). Thus in a Yagi antenna the ratio between radiation resistance and RF ohmic resistance will normally be lower than for a dipole. To quote W1ICP:

"Let's look at beams. We must first consider the impedance. Many newcomers get hung up when they assume that the impedance of all beams is of the order of 50Ω. This is because the antenna is fed with 50Ω cable and produces a match of nearly 1:1 SWR. But remember that nearly all Yagi-type beams have some sort of 'matching' device in order to transform the real impedance up to 50Ω... A monoband three-element beam using close-spaced elements, say one-tenth spacing, will have the rather low overall impedance of about 4 to 5Ω...

"A beam with 5-10Ω impedance is certainly going to have ohmic losses as an important factor ... telescoping element connections, possible boom losses the matching network itself, and so on. With a 10Ω impedance made up of, say, 5Ω radiation-resistance and 5Ω RF ohmic resistance, then we are looking at 50% efficiency."

W1ICP stresses that aluminium elements are good conductors but, depending on the atmosphere, can get corroded and 'scummy'. If this happens, ohmic losses can rocket, and performance and efficiency can go to pot. *TT* (July and September 1993) included notes on fighting antenna corrosion with specific reference to electrolytic action between dissimilar metals and the 'fretting corrosion' that occurs whenever there is a small repetitive or cyclical motion at a metal-to-metal joint or seam, in the presence of moisture.

W1ICP lives in an area that has one of the few remaining really clean atmospheres - 6400ft up in the Rockies - yet he still had joint corrosion of the aluminium elements of his log-periodic type antenna. The elements and joints had developed a scum covering which certainly would increase ohmic losses. He advises: "If your beam has been up a long time, take it down and clean and polish all connections. It will pay off. There is no magic in antennas - just good common sense."

Salty and industrial atmospheres can result very quickly in deterioration of sliding joints in antenna elements. Moisture ingress into coaxial feeder cables and baluns significantly increases losses and lower overall efficiency. Loading coils used with electrically short elements need to be of excellent high-Q construction if they are not to seriously reduce efficiency.

The need for extreme precautions to reduce losses in small transmitting 'magnetic-loop' antennas is well recognised, but serious doubts remain as to the overall efficiency of small loop systems since the losses in the matching networks are seldom taken into account.

A few years ago, Tony Henk, G4XVF, in a two-part article 'Loop Antennas - Facts not Fiction' (*RadCom*, September, October 1991) showed clearly that the overall efficiency of small transmitting loop antennas, in terms of the amount of power actually radiated compared with the output power of the transmitter, is usually quite low, with more energy being lost in the matching components, including the capacitors, than in the actual loop element.

The radiation resistance of a 1.8MHz mobile whip, like that of a small loop antenna, will be only a small fraction of an ohm and there will usually be significant ground losses in using the vehicle as a ground plane. Again, high-Q construction of the loading coil is necessary, although the overall efficiency will be very low.

W1ICP notes that, on the other hand, quad-type (wire) elements with one-wave or longer elements have relatively high impedance, largely comprising radiation resistance, resulting in efficiencies in the order of 90% or more; a significant advantage over the typical tri-band Yagi.

For many years, I have used at G3VA a long-wire antenna (of indeterminate length, initially about 42m, partly indoors) fed against quarter-wave counterpoises to overcome the problem of the long earth lead to an upstairs shack. While this performed satisfactorily, I recently attached and brought back into the shack sufficient wire to form an irregular narrow loop fed from a couple of balanced pi-network tuners (one for 14 to 28MHz, the other covering 3.5 and 7MHz). This overcomes the question of the ground losses of unbalanced antennas and seems to work at least as well as and probably rather better than the long-wire version.

1990 - 1999

Coupled Resonator Antennas

Extracted from 'Technical Topics', *Radio Communication*, October 1995

BACKGROUND TO COUPLED-RESONATOR ANTENNAS

TT, JUNE 1995, pp67-69 described the construction of multiband antennas using several closely-coupled dipole elements each cut for a particular band based on a detailed article by Gary Breed, K9AY, in *RF Design* (November 1994).

I noted that similar ideas had been patented and used some years ago for combined Band I/Band III television antennas and added: "Without entering too deeply into any arguments about patents, we should all be grateful to K9AY for bringing this system more fully into the public domain..... and for providing practical details of an antenna for the 10, 18 and 24MHz bands."

Shortly after publication I received a letter from K9AY who is the Editor of *RF Design* explaining the background to his designs and to his patent application.

He wrote: "One of the most remarkable insights gained while investigating this type of antenna is how few people know about it. It has both advantages and drawbacks, as does any multiband technique, but if you don't know it's there, you can't give it consideration!

"The main purpose of this letter is to clarify what portion of my work I consider original. I make no claim to have 'discovered' the principle of one conductor imposing its resonance on another.

"This concept was discovered in the 1940s, and has appeared in many products, including the TV receiving antennas noted by G0LMC. The *RF Design* article was not meant to describe my patent application, but rather to introduce the couple-resonator principle to the readers. By using the simplest examples of two and three frequency antenna configurations, I meant only to illustrate the principle on a territorial level, not to suggest that I was the sole originator of that work.

"I also intentionally avoided using the term 'sleeve' or 'open sleeve' to describe this type of antenna, although these terms have been used by others. Past antenna developments using these names are clearly members of the coupled-resonator antenna family. But I wanted to emphasise the generality of the concept and chose to use a more broadly descriptive label.

"The work I have done that has been accepted as original is the mathematical characterisation of the principle. I have derived the equation given in the *RF Design* article, which establishes the required spacing distance between the driven conductor and an additional coupled-resonator.

"To recap, the basic relationship is:

$$\frac{\text{Log}(d)}{\text{Log}(D/4)} = 0.54 \quad \text{or} \quad d = 10^{[0.54 \log(D/4)]}$$

where d is the required spacing in wavelengths at the coupled-resonator frequency, and D is the element diameter (assuming elements of equal diameter) also in wavelengths at the coupled-resonator frequency. This relationship is the situation where the impedance seen at the coupled-resonator frequency is equal to that of a dipole in free space (approximately 72Ω). It ignores the effect of the impedance that the driven dipole has at this frequency. I have developed a correction factor for obtaining other impedances, and another factor for small frequency differences, where the impedance of the driven element becomes a significant contributor. The driven element also has a significant effect when it is 3/2-wave resonant.

"These factors are noted in the *RF Design* article. My patent application covers a family of antenna elements obtained by using the design equation.

"Finally, readers attempting to duplicate my 10/18/24MHz example antenna must remember that the required spacing is a function of conductor diameter - the 2in (5.07cm) spacing is valid only for No 12 AWG wire! Use the design equation or an antenna modelling program to determine spacings for other wire sizes.

"I am pleased to have received many constructive comments from antenna experts, and lots of interest from the amateur community. Although I didn't discover this antenna type, I'll gladly take credit for 'uncovering' it once again, and adding to our understanding of its behaviour! Thanks again for introducing it to *RadCom* readers."

Another Look at Coaxial Antennas

Extracted from 'Technical Topics', *Radio Communication*, November 1995

ANOTHER LOOK AT COAXIAL ANTENNAS

THE AUGUST 1995 *TT* item 'Coaxial Travelling Wave Antenna?', based on the implementation by Australian amateurs of the 1927 patent of Emil Geles, has attracted comment from a number of readers. Several share my own view that it is difficult to see how this structure can provide for transmission an efficient form of non-resonant broadband travelling wave antenna, despite its apparently successful use as such by VK3YX and VK2EHN, especially when powered from a truly balanced feed. The point is made that there must be common-mode current on the outer surface of the tubular mast.

Nic Hamilton, G4XTG, pointed out: "Unless the radius of the tube is large, the field produced by the (inner) wire is completely stopped by the opposite field produced by the balancing current flowing inside the tube. So, as the patent says, the radiation is due to the current flow on the outside of the tube, which is not balanced by the current on the wire. So far, so good. But where does this unbalanced current come from? The balun (a current type) is there to make certain that the currents at its terminals are equal. If this in fact happened, there would be no radiation.

"The unbalanced current on the outside of the tube must be provided by the balun. This may be why VK3YX found it necessary to experiment with some 80 different baluns. It would seem that the antenna will only work well if the balun doesn't! The unbalanced current flows from the outer of the feeder coax, through the balun, and on to the outside of the tube.

"I believe that a better system for this type of antenna would be to dispense with the balun, and to connect the outer of the feed coax to the inner wire of the 'radiating' element, and the inner of the feed coax to the tube of the 'radiating' element. This type of feed is well known; the most recent reference is 'A Modular Coaxial Collinear Antenna' by B

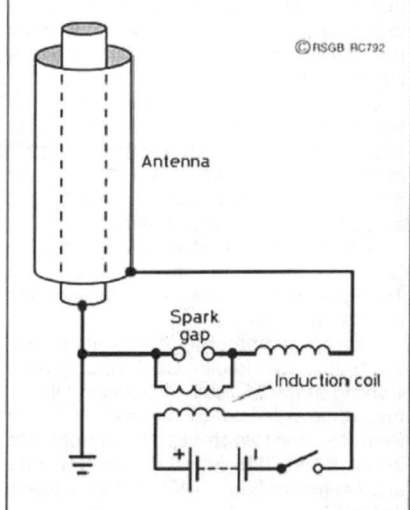

Fig 8: Basic form of Marconi's 1901 concentric cylinder antenna used as a spark transmitting antenna.

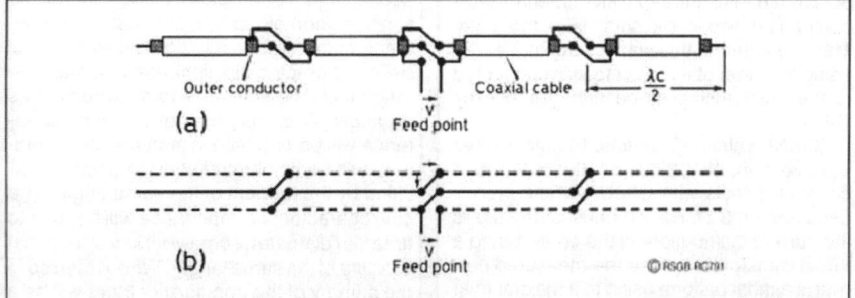

Fig 7: Basic geometry of the 'coco' (coaxial collinear) antenna formed from a series of electrical quarter-wave sections of cable incorporating cable velocity factor and transposing the inner and outer connections.

ANTENNA TOPICS

Lagoun and L Bertel (IEE Conference on HF Radio Systems and Techniques, July 1994, *IEE Conference Publication No 392*, pp234-238)". (This type of coaxial collinear antenna has been noted several times in *TT*, for example the Coco array in *TT*, September 1987, pp662-3 or *Technical Topics Scrapbook*, 1985-89, pp191-2, see **Fig 7** - G3VA).

G4TXG points out that there will be a practical difficulty with this type of feed; the efficiency of the antenna will be higher with the result that the bandwidth will be reduced. It is likely that TVI will return with a vengeance, as it is more or less bound to do with an antenna that uses the outer of the feeder as a radiator.

He also believes that the logical conclusion with this type of antenna would be to reconfigure it as a quarter-wave vertical with a good ground-plane or elevated radials. He is convinced that in the arrangement used by VK3YX it does not work in the manner intended by its Romanian inventor.

Dr Brian Austin, G0GSF, is similarly puzzled at the description of the system as a broadband travelling-wave independent of frequency. But he also reminds us that the basic idea of using a coaxial (ie concentric cylinder) antenna dates back much further than 1927. W J Baker in *A History of the Marconi Company* writes that Marconi took out patent No 5387 on 21 March, 1900 for a transmitting antenna consisting of two concentric cylinders, the outside one forming the radiator and the inside one earthed: **Fig 8**. The receiving antenna was similar. It is claimed that this "provided a fair degree of syntony"; that is to say it helped to "tune" the spark transmitter fairly sharply with an antenna of limited height.

G0GSF, who has been researching the use of radio communication during the Boer War, also draws attention (**Fig 9**) to Marconi's mobile wireless station of 1901 - intended for army use - with what appears to be a hinged concentric cylinder antenna mounted above a steam Thornycroft vehicle (the antenna lay flat on the roof of the vehicle during travel). The equipment was rejected by the army and transferred to the navy.

To bring the story of coaxial antennas up to the 1970s, John Pegler, OBE, G3ENI, while working in the Ministry of Defence (Navy), tried some experiments on a basically similar form of antenna which was officially recorded in October 1976 to protect the government's interest (under Section 4692) of the Patents Act 1949.

This comprised a coaxial structure a quarter-wave or less long exhibiting an inductive reactance at the base, which is matched to 50Ω by means of the capacitive potentiometer comprising two capacitors. Like the early Marconi antenna this was fed against earth, using the inner of the coax feeder connected to the outer tubing as described above by G4TXG.

G3ENI writes: "From time to time, I have used versions on 7, 3.5 and 1.8MHz and have conducted tests with G3ZUN who currently uses one on 3.5MHz. An unusual feature is the current distribution on the outer. Using a toroid transformer probe the measured current is almost uniform rising to a maximum at the end which seems to indicate a tendency to be a travelling wave."

G3ENI's draft patent specification of 1976 describes the system (**Fig 10**) as a "radio aerial and impedance matching system" with the object of providing a short antenna system of robust construction for reception and transmission of radio signals. "Another object of this invention is to provide an easily adjusted feeder to aerial impedance matching device which makes use of the inherent characteristics of the aerial in its operation. A further object is to provide a low-loss high-efficiency feeder to aerial impedance matching device which avoids the losses in coils often used for this purpose. An embodiment includes an arrangement for exciting with radio frequency energy a part of the structure of a ship, aircraft, armoured vehicle or other metallic structures and to provide a simple means of tuning the aerial to resonance over several decades of frequency.

"Basically the invention consists of an aerial which is substantially shorter than 90° of electrical length and which consists of an inner rod or wire of high conductivity metal which is coaxially surrounded by a tube of high conductivity metal, and separated by a dielectric. In the case when the aerial is erected vertically, the inner rod and outer tube are electrically connected at their top ends . . ." A further explanation of the coax antenna has come from G4LU and will appear later.

More on Coaxial Antennas

Extracted from 'Technical Topics', *Radio Communication*, December 1995

MORE ON COAXIAL ANTENNAS

COMMENTS HAVE CONTINUED to come in about August's *TT* item 'Coaxial travelling wave antenna?' (see also November's *TT*). Stan Brown, G4LU, writes: "I would suggest that the so called 'coaxial travelling wave antenna' is anything but that. It seems to me to be just a coaxial stub almost in parallel with the feed point of a vertical antenna, *viz* the outer surface of the tube. I say 'almost in parallel' because the coaxial stub is connected across the whole of the transformer secondary winding whereas the vertical antenna is connected between one end and the secondary's virtual earth point. Taking the simplest form of Fig 6(a) (August), the reactance of the short-circuited coaxial stub will be its characteristic impedance times the tangent of its electrical length expressed as an angle. The reactance of the vertical antenna will be opposite in sign and its magnitude will be its characteristic impedance divided by the tangent of the same angle. The stub characteristic impedance will be, due to its larger diameter, somewhat lower than that of a wire of the same length. When referred to the primary of the transformer there will be a cancellation of reactances which in effect will enhance the bandwidth of the antenna over that obtained from a simple vertical.

"However, the tangent of an angle and its inverse have a 'see-saw' relationship. When one is infinite, the other is zero and vice-versa; but in mid-range, when the angle is about 45° (or its odd multiples) they are about equal. Thus cancellation of the reactances will take place only over a small range of angles of mid-value; but at the extremes, when the angle is a multiple of 90°, the reactances will diverge considerably in magnitude. Hence the statement that the antenna will not work if it is resonant (nor anti-resonant). At these latter points the SWR will go haywire so one has to trade off the inferior performance of a short vertical antenna against the improved bandwidth over what one would normally obtain."

G4LU continues: "The radiation resistance of the antenna will be that of a short vertical and lower than one could expect with a longer wire antenna. Consequently, the transformer must be designed to suit the lower value or alternatively designed to be compatible with the ATU in use.

"It is interesting to note, from the dimensions quoted, that the tangent of the angle corresponding with the electrical length is between 0.5 and 1.6 for the 1.8, 3.5, 14 and 28MHz bands; whereas it is above 4.5 at 7MHz, which probably explains the quoted performance difference on that band. The other variants in Fig 6 (August) are modified versions of the stub and provide different values of reactance at its input, but the same analysis will apply.

"Since the antenna is essentially a vertical antenna, albeit with reactance compensation at its feed point (which adds nothing to its radiation properties), I cannot see why its performance should not be enhanced if it were mounted above an earth plane (ie earth mat or radials)."

Elevated Radials vs Buried Earths

Extracted from 'Technical Topics', *Radio Communication*, January 1996

ELEVATED RADIALS VERSUS BURIED EARTHS

THE AVAILABILITY OF computer programs based on the Method of Moments formulated by R P Harrington in the late 1960s - including progressively 'easier to use' and more accurate MININEC software developed with Amateur Radio applications in mind - is unquestionably playing an ever greater role in the design of antenna systems. While early programs ignored the presence of real earth, this is no longer the case, and there are now even programs that can calculate elevation patterns over sloping ground: See 'The effects of local terrain on HF launch angles' by R Dean Straw, N6BV, of ARRL staff (*QEX*, July 1995, pp3-15) which introduces the YTAD (Yagi Terrain Analysis, with Diffraction) program.

N6BV states that YTAD.ZIP is available,

free, on Internet by anonymous FTP from ftp.cs.buffalo.educ in the /pub/ham-radio/qex directory. He adds: "What I'd like in return is validation data for the results computed by YTAD for your QTH. I don't expect you to hire a helicopter and a team of dedicated scientists to generate validation data, but for those of you with access to stacked antennas, the methodology shown in Fig 15 (of the *QEX* article) may be useful . . . using a well calibrated receiver S-meter." For anyone interested is using YTAD it would be necessary to read N6BV's *QEX* article.

For those of us who remain computer illiterates, it is satisfying to note that while programs such as ELNEC and the later EZNEC are proving powerful design tools, many of the most valuable antenna system ideas have stemmed from old-fashioned back of envelope ideas or measurements based on trial and error, even if later honed by the MININEC programs.

An excellent example of an important development of this type is the current interest in the use on the lower HF bands of elevated radials with electrically-short vertical antennas rather than striving for the 120-buried radials that for so long were held up by broadcasters and amateurs as a necessity for an efficient system on MF and lower HF bands.

The 120-buried radial system stemmed from the classic 1930s MF work of Dr George Brown and his RCA colleagues R F Lewis and J Epstein (*Proc IRE*, June 1937, pp753-787). 120 radials were subsequently adopted by FCC as a standard requirement for MF broadcast channels. The RCA work, however, was specifically concerned with 'buried earths' although it seems to have for many years been assumed that their results ruled out the use of multiple elevated radials (counterpoises and ground screens). Few amateurs could hope to implement a 120-buried radial system, but 1.8 and 3.5MHz enthusiasts were encouraged post-war to bury as many wires as possible.

George Brown, it needs to be stressed, was not averse to elevated, artificial ground screens. He was, in fact, the inventor of the HF/VHF artificial ground-plane antenna. He once confessed to me over lunch that his original version used only two radials, but to satisfy early police-radio customers this was increased to four radials without significantly increasing radiation efficiency.

It was not until the early 1980s that the buried earth screen concept was challenged by three retired professional engineers who were also radio amateurs: Arch Doty, K8CFU, John Frey, W3ESU, and Harry Mills, K4HU. K8CFU kindly sent me a copy of a paper he had presented in the US to an IEEE meeting entitled 'Characteristics of the Counterpoise and the Elevated Ground Screen' based on literally *thousands* of measurements. I was delighted to include some notes on this work in *TT* (February 1983) and a longer version of their paper 'Efficient Ground Systems for Vertical Antennas', appeared in *QST*, (February 1983 pp20-25).

As I wrote in *TT* (February 1983): "A privately-funded research project of such a magnitude, undertaken by three elderly engineers with an aggregate age of 203 years, setting out and succeeding in showing that a good deal of what has appeared in the professional antenna literature during the past 60 years on this subject is in error, or at least seriously flawed, is remarkable. That the project succeeds in pinpointing how the errors occurred and in resurrecting the importance of the counterpoise is even more remarkable!"

I continued: "This ambitious project has unearthed (if I dare use that word) several important new facts; in particular it shows that the currents flowing in buried radials of the conventional type are not, as usually postulated, uniform, but depend upon ground conductivity in the immediate vicinity of the individual wires. It indicates that there can be unexpectedly large variations in surface ground conductivity within the area covered by the ground system of a typical vertical antenna." The *QST* article showed average conductivity varying with seasonal rainfall etc by a factor of over 2:1 in a matter of months: see **Fig 6**. Ground conductivity along different radials may vary by a factor of as much as 7.5:1 within a distance of 10ft at the site in North Carolina.

In *TT* I wrote: "But the tests further show that the distribution of return currents collected by wires elevated by 6 to 8ft is distinctly different from that found in buried radials. Lossy ground between the antenna and the radials reduces their efficiency in providing return currents. All the initial indications are that elevated ground systems (whether counterpoise or elevated but earthed ground screens), used with electrically-short vertical antennas *require substantially fewer radials than needed by a buried wire system of equal efficiency*'. A conclusion calculated to upset conventional thinking of the past 40 years! This does not mean that buried radials do not make good earth systems, but it does suggest that elevated wires are more efficient (and much cheaper and simpler to install)." **Fig 7** shows some typical elevated ground screens as used by K8CFU.

This outstanding amateur-professional research did not immediately make much impression on professional (or amateur) users of vertical antennas. But in the 1990s, a number

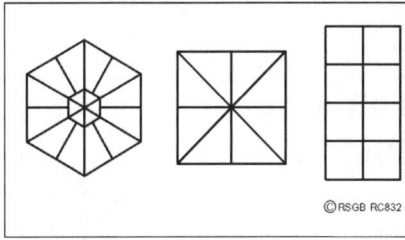

Fig 7: Typical multi-wire counterpoise or elevated ground screen mounted below a vertical antenna as investigated by Arch Doty, K8CFU, and his colleagues. They showed clearly that such systems are more efficient than buried systems of comparable size. (*TT*, Feb 83)

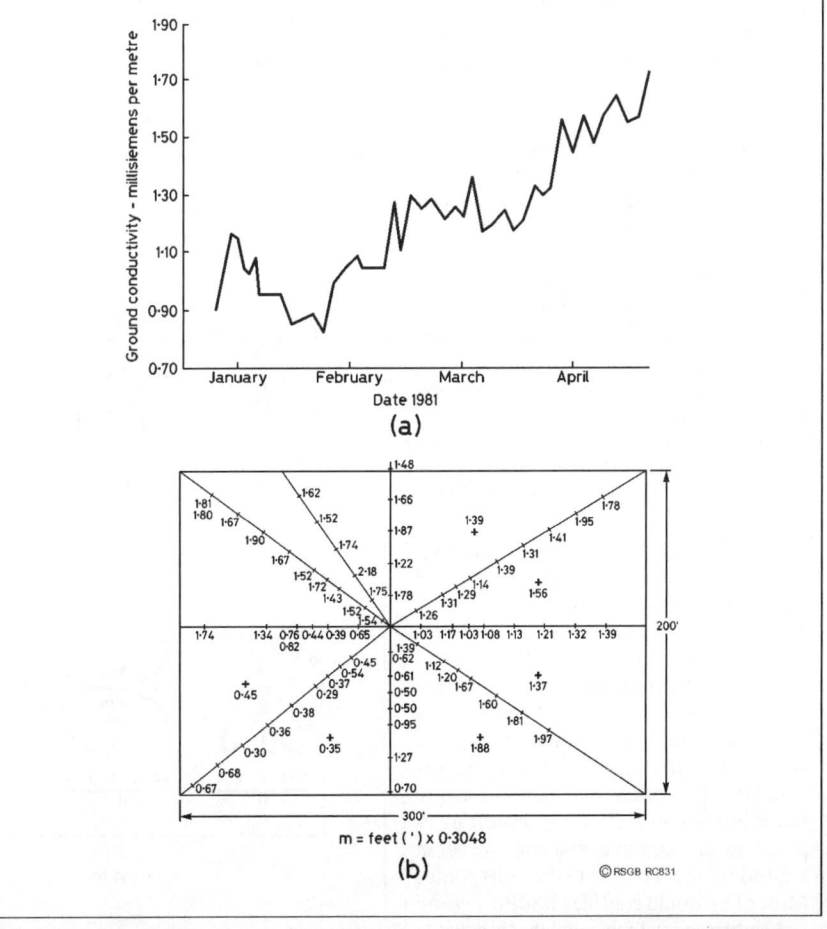

Fig 6: a) Ground conductivity at one fixed location in K8CFU's test site at Fletcher, North Carolina. Measurements were taken daily during the first four months of 1981; (b) Ground conductivity along different radials at the test site. Note there are differences of as much as 7.5:1 within a distance of 10ft. (*QST*)

ANTENNA TOPICS

of articles, based on NEC-type calculations, have been appearing - for example 'Using Elevated Radials with Ground Mounted Towers' by Al Christian, KB8I (*IEE Trans on Broadcasting*, September 1991, pp77-82, see a summary in *TT*, February 1992, p38). This predicted that "it is possible to use four elevated radials together with a conventional ground-mounted, base-insulated tower for MF broadcasting purposes, and achieve the same level of performance which is normally obtained from a classic 120-buried-radial system".

I noted than that "such an approach would clearly be most suitable for use by amateurs on the 1.8, 3.5 and 7MHz bands for verticals; on the higher frequency bands it is already conventionally adopted in the form of the popular ground-plane antenna (GPA)".

Regretfully, as far as I am aware, none of the subsequent articles on elevated ground screens has acknowledged the breakthrough investigation by Arch Doty and his colleagues, and to my mind computer simulations take more for granted (for example uniform ground conductivity) than was found during the field measurements made by K8CFU *et al*.

Nevertheless, a useful addition to the amateur literature based on computer simulations is a recent article 'Short Vertical Antennas and Ground Systems' by Ralph Holland, VK1BRH (*Amateur Radio*, October 1995 pp9-13). He presents a number of graphs based on the NEC-81 code which can model antennas in proximity to lossy ground. NEC-81 is a PC version of NEC-2.

His introduction states: "There has been a number of articles discussing the merits or otherwise of various types of ground systems. The analysis of such systems is complicated by the facts that practical ground system parameters are difficult to quantify, antennas are situated in less than ideal locations, and literature that may provide insight into what is happening often does not present the information in a practical or applicable form. Often the reader is left to extrapolate beyond the bounds of presented data and arrive at the incorrect conclusion. Some folklore has been generated as a result of these types of difficulty; one such lore is 'the higher the better' which is an over-generalisation if said without qualification."

While I have an uneasy feeling that his simulations leave some questions hanging in the air, he provides some conclusions and points to remember that seem to be essentially correct: "It is obvious that the simulated antenna efficiency declines dramatically when the groundplane displacement (that is height above ground) approaches zero. With three or more radials the radial length is more important to the overall efficiency than the number of radials, with a few exceptions.

"An interesting side-effect is that under certain conditions a vertical antenna with one radial was substantially more efficient than

Full-wave Dipoles

Extracted from 'Technical Topics', *Radio Communication*, January 1996

FULL-WAVE DIPOLES

THE RADIATION patterns of half-wave and full-wave dipoles have long been well understood including the difference between those fed at the centre and voltage fed at both ends. The full wave dipole, if fed at the ends or centre, needs to be high-impedance voltage fed but can be current fed one quarter wave from either end. When centre fed the full wave dipole becomes, in effect two collinear half-waves with a sharpened up radiation pattern; when fed a quarter-wave from one end or voltage fed at one end, it provides the clover leaf four lobes pattern. **Fig 8** shows the radiation patterns of these arrangements.

But what is the radiation resistance (which will also be the feed impedance) of the current-fed arrangement shown in Fig 8 (d)?

An 'Analysis of the Radiation Resistance and Gain of a Full Wave Dipole' by S H Idris and C M Hadzer appeared in the *IEEE Antenna & Propagation Magazine* (October 1994 pp45-47) This notes that "the full wave dipole antenna is very seldom used in communication systems, and yet this type of antenna offers a very high gain". The authors show that the radiation resistance is 194Ω (in free space). The gain of a centre fed collinear pair Fig 8 (c) is 3.94dB compared to an isotropic antenna (ie about 1.8dBd) with a 42° lobe to the -3dB points. Most of us would consider 1.8dBd a useful rather than a very high gain but it is equal to a 50% increase in transmitter power.

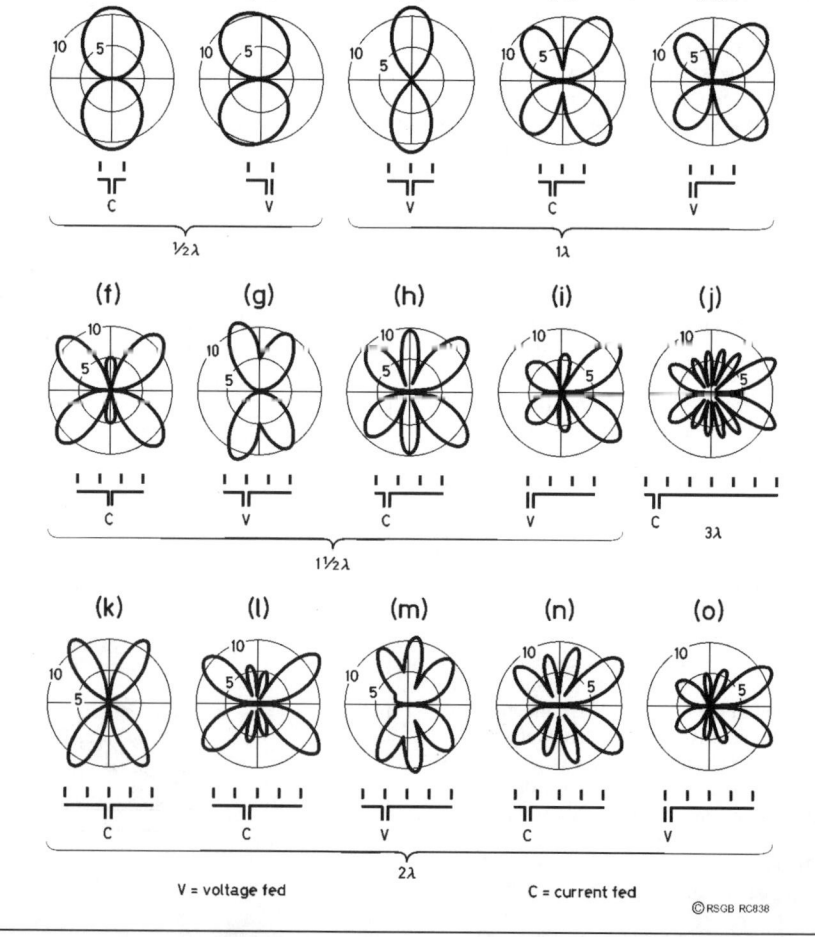

Fig 8: Horizontal radiation patterns of various dipole antennas showing the effect of the current and voltage feedpoints. Originally based on model antenna range measurements by D C Cleckner.

one with any other number; such a hybrid antenna has been studied and applied in marine and land-based systems: see for example 'HF Antennas for all Locations' by Les Moxon, G6XN, (2nd edition page 183). Among the points to remember listed by VK1BRH are:

1) Short radiating elements have a low base resistance, a relatively low radiation resistance and consequently lower efficiency; nevertheless short elements can still be quite efficient. The shorter radiators require shorter radials at lower heights. Remember that short radiators have high RF voltages at the base.

2) There is an optimal height for an elevated groundplane; typically this is about $0.05\text{-}\lambda$. Do not place radials on or below the ground unless there is space for some 120 radials and the site has good ground conductivity; (with poor ground conductivity it is useful regularly to water the ground! (Preferable with salty water if this does not harm the garden).

3) Efficiency curves are tolerant in regard to the height of the groundplane; displacements can be as little as $0.005\text{-}\lambda$ and in some cases efficiency peaks around $0.01\text{-}\lambda$. [Note that safety requirements mean that elevated garden radials should be at least 7 - 8ft (over 2m) high - *G3VA*]

4) Large numbers of radials are not required for elevated groundplane systems. Three of four is sufficient. Doubling the number does not double the efficiency.

5) Substantially better results can be obtained by siting an antenna near swamps, lakes or in close proximity to the sea.

VK1BRH emphasises that simulated results are only as good as the computer program. However he considers that NEC-81 is good at modelling linear antennas close to lossy ground. It has been validated numerous times but, even so, it has failed even more times due to inappropriate use.

G5IJ Push-pull-fed Twin Line
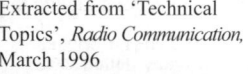

Extracted from 'Technical Topics', *Radio Communication*, March 1996

G5IJ PUSH-PUSH-FED TWIN LINE ANTENNA

COMMENTS CONTINUE to arrive on the coaxial antenna in its various forms (*TT*, August, November & December 1995) including interesting letters from Kenneth Parker, G3PKR, and also J A Mullin, DA1MU, who encloses copies of 'Unipole Antennas - Theory and Practical Applications' by Ron Nott, K5YNR, etc from the *ARRL Antenna Compendium Vol 2*.

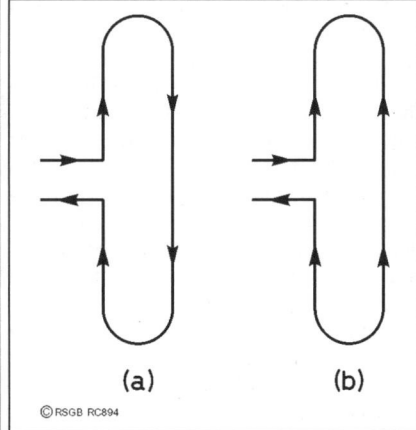

Fig 5: The current modes on a folded dipole antenna. (a) Transmission line mode. (b) Antenna (radiating) mode.

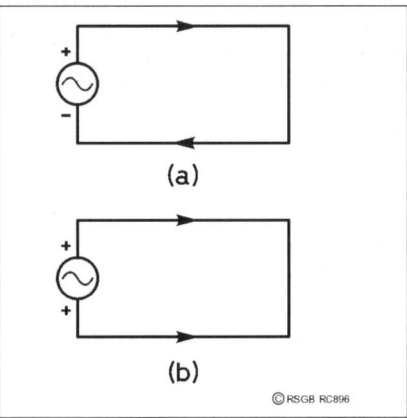

Fig 6: Mode excitation and current for a voltage V applied to the terminals of a folded dipole. Superimposition of these modes gives the complete folded dipole model. (a) Transmission line mode; (b) Antenna mode.

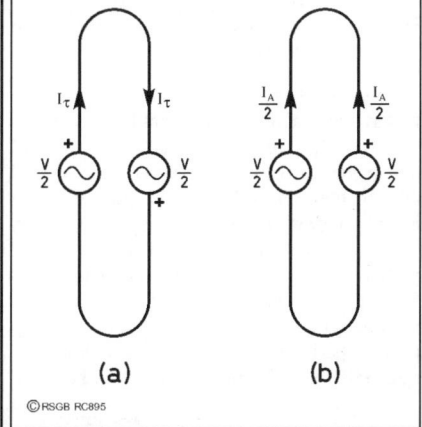

Fig 7: With half of a folded dipole (folded monopole) a voltage generator drives the system as a transmission-line mode. (b) Radiation mode calls for push-push drive (in effect turning the element into a fat element).

However, this month it seems time to move on to what could to be an interesting development in the implementation of 'folded monopole' and transmission-line antennas. This seems to offer the possibility of providing a novel and practical form of a multiband, twin-wire antenna fed in 'push-push' mode at one end from 50Ω coaxial cable via a toroidal transformer when using a simple ATU between the transmitter and the coax feeder cable. It would appear to offer reduced dependence on ground losses in the earth image and on higher bands and may just possibly be acting as a travelling-wave 'launcher' rather than a twin-wire form of Marconi antenna.

The new push-push antenna drive system is the brainchild of Ivan James, G5IJ, who for many years before his retirement was an eminent television engineer with EMI, following wartime membership of the radar development team led by Alan Dower Blumlein. The team worked on the AI Mk VI and later on H2S (during which Blumlein and some other members of the EMI team lost their lives when the field trial aircraft crashed in South Wales in 1942).

First, I have a confession to make. When G5IJ originally sent me details of his push-push antenna driving system, I began to prepare an item for *TT* but found it difficult to conceive how the G5IJ system could work efficiently as a multiband transmitting antenna independently of earth radials or counterpoise or terminating resistors. I wrote to him of the problem I was having in coming to grips with his material. He promptly offered to lend me the antenna to try. For various reasons, the tests had to be postponed for several weeks, but finally I have been able very briefly to try it out on 3.5, 7 and 14MHz bands (and check that it would load satisfactorily on 21MHz although the band was virtually dead). It functioned on all three bands, particularly well on 7MHz with strong lobe(s) into Eastern Europe. At my location, the twin wire runs roughly from west to east with the free end pointing eastwards. I must stress that while these tests show that the drive system is certainly capable of delivering RF power into the twin wires from the coax line, it would need many more checks than I have been able to make to determine exactly how the antenna functions on the various bands and the radiation patterns etc.

G5IJ has provided further information and explanations that answer some of the points I raised. But I should perhaps emphasise that it

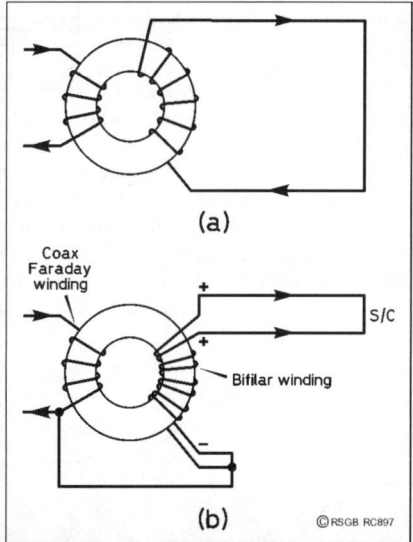

Fig 8: Substituting a transformer-coupled arrangement for case (a) can be met by a single-wound secondary winding. For case (b) the antenna mode can be met by using a bifiliar winding arranged to provide equal outputs to the two wires. (b) is the system used for the G5IJ antenna.

ANTENNA TOPICS

seems unlikely the antenna really functions as a broadband travelling wave antenna on the higher frequency bands. All one can say for sure is that it puts out a potent signal with a degree of directivity on 7MHz. I tend to think of it as a form of half a fan dipole or a conical broadband monopole. I now have no doubts that push-push drive of twin wires works - and works well - although I am still uncertain of the part played by the earth on bands in which the wires are not one half-wave long or multiples thereof. I can see no reason why his antenna should not be duplicated to provide practical antenna system while still offering plenty of scope for further experimentation and development. To my mind, the main advantage is end feeding multiband twin wires from a length of low-impedance coax able via an ATU in the shack - a configuration that suits many practical locations, but not one to be used without a good ATV or with unprotected solid-state PAs!

To return to G5IJ's letter: "When I read the *TT* items in the August and November [1995] issues of *RadCom*, I was reminded of some experiments I did in 1988 and have been refreshing my memory in regard to monopole antenna and small gardens.

"I wanted to operate on 3.5MHz from my upstairs bedroom, the window of which is 72ft from the back fence. If I were to use a Marconi quarter-wave antenna with a 66ft wire a problem would be the long earth lead. The grounded folded monopole antenna using 67ft of 300Ω ribbon line, which has appeared in all editions of *Amateur Radio Techniques* (eg, 7th edition, p266) stemming from an early edition of *The Radio Handbook* showed promise, but I did not feel that the feed arrangement was optimum. I wondered whether a closely wound toroidal transformer would be a better method with the object of raising the radiation resistance and reducing earth currents.

"But first I felt it was necessary to understand how the basic folded dipole operates. An excellent exposition of the theory appears in *Antenna Theory and Design* by Stutzman & Thiele (John Wiley & Sons, 1981, pp205 - 212).

"To quote the book: 'The folded dipole antenna is basically a half-wave dipole parallel with another dipole, the latter being endfed from the main dipole, raising the drive impedance from the usual 75Ω to 300Ω. As shown in Figs 5 and 6 there are two current modes in a folded dipole: (a) the transmission line mode; and (b) the antenna (or radiating) mode'.

"If a folded dipole is cut in half it can be seen that to form a folded monopole a generator is required to voltage drive the system: **Fig 7 (a)** shows the transmission line mode; **Fig 7 (b)** shows the radiating mode. With a transformer-coupled arrangement this becomes: **Fig 8(a)** and for the radiating mode **Fig 8(b)**. It is important to note that the short-circuited end (s/c) can be open-circuited, if required. Also note that the transmitting (drive) terminals can be short-circuited without virtually affecting the operation, since both terminals (+ +) are at equal potential at any instant in time.

"Put in an alternative way, the transmission line mode needs a push-pull generator and the radiating mode favours a push-push generator.

"To the best of my knowledge all previous proposals for feeding twin, multiple, or coaxial systems (such as the Emil Geles 1927 patent or the earlier Marconi Patent No 260,005) or the arrangement shown in **Fig 9** from ART use push-pull drive, balanced or unbalanced to ground. That must be why they may be relatively inefficient as non-resonant radiators or else confined to

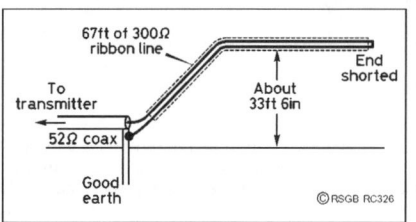

Fig 9: Quarter-wave grounded Marconi antenna for 3.5MHz using 67ft of 300Ω or 450Ω ribbon line. A good earth system (preferably including multiple radials or elevated counterpoise or ground screen) is needed for good performance.

resonant operation with the standing wave-patterns producing narrow-band effects.

"My early experiments in 1988 were carried out in the upstairs bedroom with the slotted 300Ω cable coming through the upper opening in the window. Because maximum radiation was thus taking place within the room, the system was very prone to line time-base interference, etc, and also caused RFI problems with audio equipment. As a result I gave up these experiments and ended up with a half-size G5RV and EL40/EL40X traps. I began to write a patent specification covering the bifilar push-push monopole driving system but did not pursue this.

"However, I did make measurements of input resistance versus frequency with a Palomar Engineering R-X bridge which showed how flat the curve is over the European 3.5MHz band (3.5 to 3.8MHz) compared with the usual 100kHz or so bandwidth of a standard dipole. The measurements applied to a horizontal 300Ω slotted feeder, 19m in length and probably about 20ft high.

"After reading the *TT* items on coaxial transmission line antennas, my interest in the push-push system revived and just recently I have plotted a set of measurements (**Fig 10**) using the original toroid transformer (BM1) and using about 20m of (UR43) see **Fig 11** Faraday-screened coupling coil. Unfortunately, the height of the horizontal twin-wire element varied from 10ft to 6ft to 15ft. From 3.8MHz to 3.6MHz the resistance averaged 25 to 30Ω and rose to 50Ω at 3.5MHz.

The toroid Amidon T200/2 core was wound with bifilar winding (40 turns with inductance about 18uH at 3.78MHz). The 20swg length of wire was folded into two parallel lengths and then twisted loosely into about 2in twists in a hand drill, and finally wound around the toroid as evenly as possible. The coaxial winding was wired as a Faraday screen (to reduce capacitance efforts). It was a 1.5m length of UR43 which gave 18 turns in the toroid. Tests with a trifilar closely coupled set of windings shows that little capacitance effects should be apparent since all three windings at each toroidal turn have equal potentials.

"Incidentally, the closely-coupled bifilar winding was used by Alan Blumlein in his first patent in bridge measurements; and led to the so-called 'in-situ bridge' and the wartime capacitance altimeter.

"The suppression of the transmission line mode by the use of the bifilar circuit seems to produce remarkable results compared with the standard push-pull arrangements, and I feel the message should be spread to stimulate further experimental verification. My rough experiments so far indicate not only that the SWR ratios over the bands remain reasonable, but also operation at multiple frequency bands, and even sub-frequency bands, is effective.

"With a Lowe HF225 receiver and with the

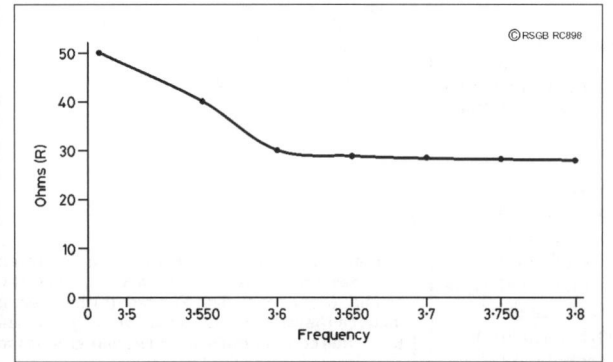

Fig 10: Measurements made by G5IJ in November 1995 using his original BM-1 transmitter on 3.5 - 3.8 MHz. Antenna 20m of heavy-duty slotted 300Ω line 6 to 15ft above ground. Bifilar winding on Amidon T200/2 (120μH per 100 turns) Output 50Ω, third winding using 50Ω coaxial cable arranged as faraday screen.

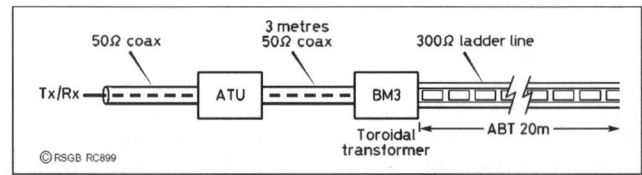

Fig 11: The G5IJ twin-wire antenna system as tried at G3VA from upstairs shack with part of the ladder line and the toroidal transformer indoors.

system connected to the 50Ω input socket, signals are effectively received all the way from 30kHz to 90MHz. With the increasing use of 'black boxes' and smaller gardens, the scheme should encourage antenna experimentation at relatively little expense. There seems endless possibilities for the optimisation of the transformer and its applications."

G5IJ prepared the above notes towards the end of November 1995 but subsequently (early December) sent a series of measurements made with his R-X noise bridge with a new BM3 toroidal transformer: see **Table 1**. BM3 comprises an Amidon T200/2 toroid (120uH per 100 turns). Bifilar winding 27 turns (8.5uH) 4.40m length of UR43 50Ω coax used as Faraday screen taking 1.30m of the cable leaving about 3m to reach outside the window. The inner end of coax is soldered to braid of coax and also connected to common end of the bifilar winding. The antenna was 20m of 300Ω heavy duty twin slotted feeder (Westlake) weight 1lb 4oz (575 grams) stranded wire only 6 - 10ft high.

Although as shown in Table 1, it was originally impossible to get a balance on 24.800MHz (R = 50, XL =>7.5); by connecting a 350pF mica capacitor across the coax at entry to the noise bridge (to cancel out the inductive reactance of the antenna) it proved possible to get a balance of R = 18Ω, Xc 0.8Ω on 24.930MHz. During these tests the toroid was inside the window with the 3m of feeder cable.

To calculate the knob in actual ohms positive or negative reactance is rather difficult, depending on frequency (see *QST*, May 1988). The Xc (XL) capacitor has a maximum capacitance of 140pF and is divided into 7 divisions from the 0 (in 20pF sectors). It would seem, at least with the particular dimensions of this specific antenna, that the coax feeder must be fed through an ATU to balance out the reactances. Whether this could be overcome by a little tweaking of lengths etc is one of the many still unknowns. G5IJ hopes that these notes will encourage others to explore the possibilities offered by push-push drive systems but the results are not guaranteed.

Travelling Wave Antennas

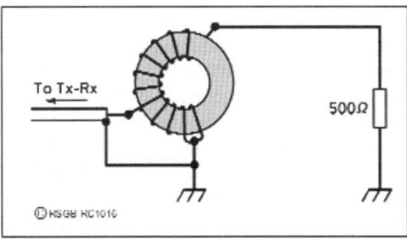

Extracted from 'Technical Topics', *Radio Communication*, June 1996

TRAVELLING WAVE BROADBAND ANTENNAS

THE TOPIC OF travelling wave antennas seems to have cropped up several times recently in *TT* but it is clear that there is some misunderstanding of the ways in which this concept is normally applied to long wire HF antennas.

As noted by Robert S Elliott in his book *Antenna Theory and Design* (Prentice-Hall, 1981), one of the simplest travelling wave antennas is the long horizontal wire at a distance *h* above the earth, fed at one end against ground and usually terminated at the other end in a matched load formed from a non-inductive high-wattage resistor. If *h* is not negligible compared to a wavelength, the wire and its ground image do not behave like a two-wire transmission line, but rather comprise an efficient radiating system.

Whereas with a matched low-loss transmission line the RF current (and voltage) remain near constant, the travelling wave of current proceeding outwards along the wire of a long-wire antenna is attenuated due to the radiation, and thus the power absorbed in the matched load may be reduced to an acceptable level by making the wire long enough. Indeed, the leakage (ie radiation) may be sufficient to obviate the need for a terminating load. The net current distribution on the wire is then not a standing wave, but is essentially an outward travelling damped wave.

The Bruce inverted vee antenna is a vertically polarised form of travelling wave antenna. Other TW antennas are the sloping vee, the vee-beam and the rhombic, regarded for many years as the Queen of all directional antennas for those with sufficient space. However it should be noted that the very long, very low, Beverage directional receiving antenna works on a different principle and cannot readily be used as an efficient transmitting antenna. It should not be forgotten that long-wire, vee and rhombic travelling wave antennas can also be used very effectively at VHF or even UHF where space requirements for such high-gain fixed beams are far more modest than on HF.

One of the major advantages of travelling wave antennas is that their impedance remains virtually the same over a wide frequency range, enabling them to be used as truly broadband antennas without the need for a variable ATU.

Fig 4: G3SRO's terminated long wire antenna with ferrite broadband matching transformer as described in 1972.

With an impedance of somewhere between about 400-800Ω, they also lend themselves to the use of a fixed ferrite-toroid matching transformer fed from 50Ω coaxial cable. Of course, like all truly broadband antennas, care must be taken that the output from the transmitter does not contain significant spuriae which would be radiated along with the fundamental. The longer the wire, in terms of wavelengths, the sharper the main lobes, the lower the angle of elevation, and the less power wasted in the terminating resistor.

Many years ago, Richard White, G3SRO, described for *TT* a terminated long-wire travelling wave antenna suitable for use on all frequencies from 3.5 to 30MHz (this could today be extended to 50MHz) that does not require an ATU (at least for matching purposes) yet is capable of giving a satisfactorily low SWR across all HF bands (including WARC bands). He was fortunate in being able to run out some 400ft (122m) of wire at a height of 40ft (12.2m). At the far end this is terminated with a non-inductive high-wattage 500Ω resistor earthed

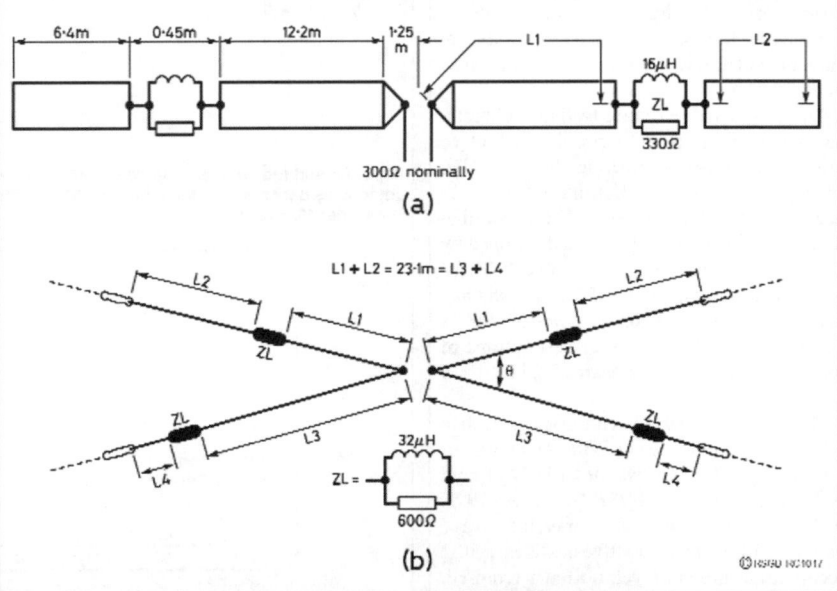

Fig 5: (a) The broadband 'Australian Dipole' antenna originally described by R J F Guertier and G E Collyer in 1973 for use between 2.3 to 30MHz (see *TT*, June 1974) but shortened for use from 3.5MHz. **(b)** The resistive loaded broadband inverted vee 'fat dipole' as developed in South Africa by Dr Brian Austin, G0GSF/ZS6BKW, and Andre Fourie for use over the entire HF spectrum 3 to 30MHz. The key dimensions (*TT*, September 1987) are L1 + L2 = L3 + L4 = 23.1m; L1 = 13.5m (hence L2 = 9.6m); L3 = 17m (hence L4 = 6.1m). While the included angle does not markedly affect the VSWR, the impedance of the feedline is affected to some extent. For a 5° angle optimum feedline impedance is 500Ω, but as this angle is reduced the impedance decreases to about 400Ω

ANTENNA TOPICS

inductive high-wattage 500Ω resistor earthed to an 8ft aluminium stake via a vertical down lead (see **Fig 4** and also *ART7*, p305). The transmitter feeds the antenna via a ferrite toroidal step-up transformer using a toroid of about 1.5in or more diameter. The transmitter feed goes to a three turn winding and the antenna to seven turns bifilar wound and spaced. This gave a worst SWR on any band of only about 1.8:1. In practice, the antenna provides the two main lobes to be expected from the theory of terminated long wire antennas, with the lobes showing up well on 14MHz and above. By directing the run of the antenna towards central America, he achieved good coverage of North and South America.

In 'The Travelling-wave Linear Antenna' (*IRE Trans on Antennas & Propagation*, July 1961), Dr Edward Altshuler showed that an essentially travelling-wave distribution of current can be produced on a linear (ie resonant) antenna by inserting a resistance of suitable magnitude one-quarter wavelength from the far end of the antenna. He showed that this resulted in an input impedance that remains essentially constant as a function of antenna length, whereas that of a conventional antenna varies considerably, with the input impedance of the antenna varying only slightly over a 2:1 frequency band. He also compared the directional properties of a travelling wave dipole and a conventional dipole and showed that a minor lobe does not appear in the radiation pattern of the TW dipole until it is much longer than the conventional dipole. Although the use of a resonant quarter-wave (artificial earth) wire beyond the resistor reduces somewhat the broadband characteristics, such an antenna can still be used effectively over a 2:1 frequency range.

An early form of an antenna with a loading resistance to increase bandwidth was the T2FD folded dipole antenna, although this was described originally (by the US Navy) only as increasing the bandwidth by a moderate amount, and involved considerable power loss in the resistor.

Dr Altshuler's resistance loading technique has since been used to provide effective broadband antennas covering the entire HF spectrum. Examples, which have been published in *TT*, include the so called 'Australian dipole' and an improved version developed by Dr Brian Austin, G0GSF: see **Fig 5**. These antennas were described in *TT*, June 1987 and September 1987 (see also *Technical Topics Scrapbook, 1985-90*). Earlier descriptions of the 'Australian dipole' appeared *TT*, June 1974 and September 1984.

A somewhat more conventional approach to 'Broadband Transmitting Wire Antennas for 160 through 10 metres' was described by Floyd A Koontz, WA2WVL (*QST*, November 1995, pp22-24). This noted that "a travelling wave antenna offers some attractive qualities: a 50Ω feedpoint at ground level, no tuner required, horizontal and vertical radiation components, no radials, nothing in the air but wire, and flexible size and height requirements. In his recommended two-mast configuration (**Fig 6**) he uses two broadband toroidal transformers to match to the 50Ω transmitter coax-line and to a 50Ω non-inductive termination to the 450Ω

impedance of the TW antenna (high wattage non-inductive resistors are more likely to be available at 50Ω (dummy antenna resistors) than at 450Ω). The *QST* article provides tabulated information on the impedance and SWR for a typical TW antenna (50 x 50Ω) together with calculated efficiency versus various antenna dimensions. Winding details of a 50 to 450Ω impedance transformer wound on an Amidon FT-240-61 core with a trifilar winding of nine turns of no 18 Teflon-insulated stranded wire are shown in **Fig 7**. (Such transformers would also be suitable for use with the G3SRO terminated long-wire antenna described above).

A commercially-available form of broadband travelling wave HF antenna that has proved popular among amateurs in North America is the 'vertical half rhombic (VHR)' antenna made by Barker & Williamson as Model AC-1.8-30 (for use between 1.8 and 30MHz). Dr Brian Austin, G0GSF, has drawn my attention to an article 'Practical Characteri-

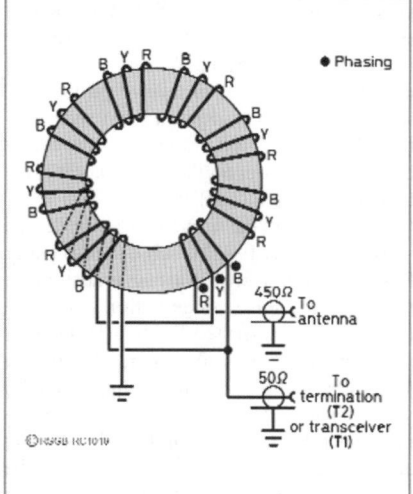

Fig 7: Winding details of the 50 to 450Ω (1:9) impedance broadband toroidal transformers as used by WA2WUL but which should also prove suitable for other TW antennas such as that used by G3SRO or the vertical half rhombic (VHR) design. It is advisable to use different coloured insulated wires to facilitate identification of the windings (eg Blue, Yellow, Red). Core is Amidon (FT-240-61) with each winding 9 turns of No 18 AWG Teflon insulated stranded wire.

sation of a High Frequency Vertical Half Rhombic' by Mike Fanning (Motorola) and W Perry Wheless Jr (University of Alabama) in the *Newsletter of the Applied Computational Electromagnetics Society*, Vol 10, No 1, March 1995, pp41-50. This provides selected radiation pattern characteristics of the AC-1.8-30 antenna above finite ground investigated both experimentally and numerically using both NEC-81 with a PC and NEC3 running on an IBM 3090 mainframe computer.

While the prime aim of this paper is to compare and contrast the accuracy and reliability of NEC2 and NEC3 radiation pattern predictions for HF wire antennas in close proximity to finite ground, and with ground stakes extending into the earth, it serves also to draw attention to the VHR antenna which could be built rather than bought.

The authors note that the popularity of the HF rhombic is restricted in practice by the large area required: "A logical alternative to the individual who does not have the necessary

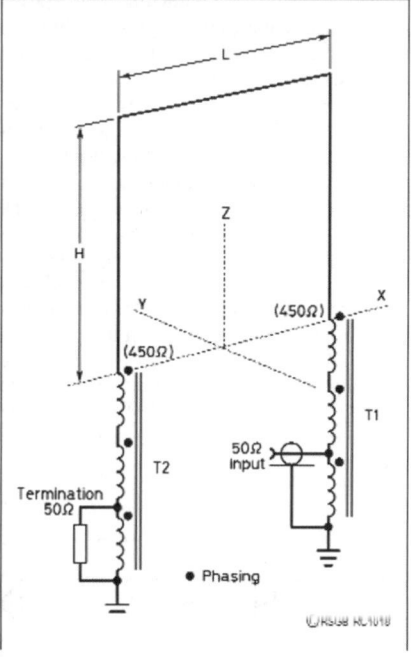

Fig 0. An end fed, end terminated travelling wave antenna as described in detail by WA2WVL in the November 1995 QST.

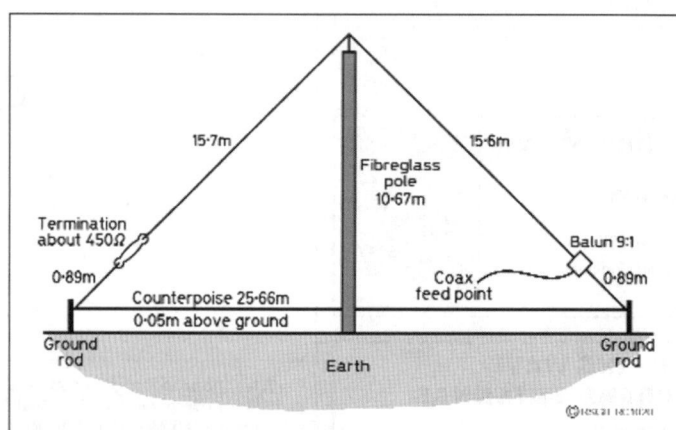

Fig 8: Configuration of the Barker & Williamson Model AC-1.8-30 vertical half rhombic antenna as used by Mike Fanning and W Perry Wheless to compare computed and experimentally determined radiation characteristics. The VHR forms a broadband TW antenna for use between 1.8 and 30MHz.

room to construct a full horizontal rhombic antenna is to reduce the area required for installation by cutting the rhombic in half and rotating the assembly into the vertical plane. In this case, it is possible to reduce the overall surface area drastically, as the antenna can be placed so that the legs are terminated at ground level in a relatively small installation space. The remaining interior angle of the rhombus is mounted vertically away from the ground as high as practically possible. The distant ends of the antenna are grounded and tied together by a single counterpoise wire, and the whole structure is fed through a 9:1 balun.

"This configuration is commonly known as a vertical half rhombic (VHR), although an alternative description would be a 'balanced-feed, loaded pyramid' [It could also be considered a form of the original Bruce inverted vee antenna - *G3VA*], the VHR chosen for this study is the Barker & Williamson model AC-1.8-30 which is designed primarily for broadband amateur use in confined areas. The configuration is depicted in **Fig 8**. Antenna wire is stranded Nr 14 AWG, and the centre support for this study was a 10.7m fibreglass pole." [Non-conductive supports as high as possible are advisable for Bruce and VHR antennas. The terminating resistor is presumably again about 450Ω, non-inductive - *G3VA*].

Rhombic Loops & Hula Hoops

Extracted from 'Technical Topics', *Radio Communication*, August 1996

RHOMBIC LOOP & HULA HOOP ANTENNAS

SOME INTERESTING new concepts in antenna systems - which are capable of radiating circularly polarised waves and could well prove suitable for amateur UHF, VHF and possibly even HF applications - have been described by a team of Japanese antenna engineers at the Japanese National Defense Academy and the University of Tsukuba, Japan.

The original disclosure by H Morishita and K Hirasawa, 'Wideband Circularly-Polarised Loop Antenna', was at the 1994 IEEE Antennas & Propagation Conference (I have not seen this paper). A subsequent paper 'A Dual Rhombic Loop Antenna for Circular Polarisation', with additional authors T Hzuka and T Nagco, appears in the IEE Conference Publication No 407 (pp500 - 503); and the most recent development 'Circularly Polarised Rhombic Hula Hoop Antennas' by H Morishita, K Hirasawa and T Nagco is published in the IEE's *Electronic Letters*, (23 May 1996, pp946 - 947).

Basically, the concept uses rhombic loop element(s) with a perimeter of only about 1.3λ at the centre frequency (ie only a little larger than the usual 1.0 lambda quad element). The antenna, it is claimed, "can have a travelling-wave type current distribution, which has approximately a constant amplitude and a linearly changing phase. This current distribution is realised by making one point open (ie a small gap) or loading an infinitely large impedance on the proper position of the loop."

The experimental models described in the Japanese papers are based on 1.5GHz with the four sides of the rhombus only about 60 to 68mm long (ie perimeter of about 250mm) and with a bandwidth of roughly 20%.

The 1995 IEE conference paper extended the basic idea of a single rhombus loop in a plane parallel to and above a perfectly conducting ground plane to a dual rhombus system: see **Fig 1**. In this version, two types of single feed dual rhombic loop antennas for circular polarisation are proposed: **Fig 2**. The antenna consists of single or dual rhombic loops of the same size located above a theoretically infinite perfectly conducting ground plane. For the dual system, it is shown that by adjusting the perimeter, the rhombus vertex angle, and the gap position on the loop, the axial ratio 2dB bandwidth is more than 20% for both types of feed and the gain of about 10dBi for the parallel feed and 11dBi for the series feed (about 3dB more than for the single rhombus). In addition, the possibility of controlling the input impedance is found by selecting the gap position, the rhombus vertex angle and the feed type.

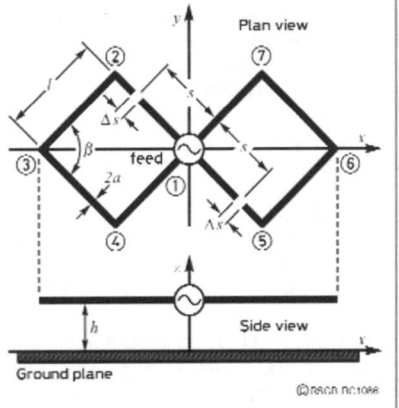

Fig 1: Dual rhombic loop antenna as described by Japanese engineers at a 1995 IEE conference.

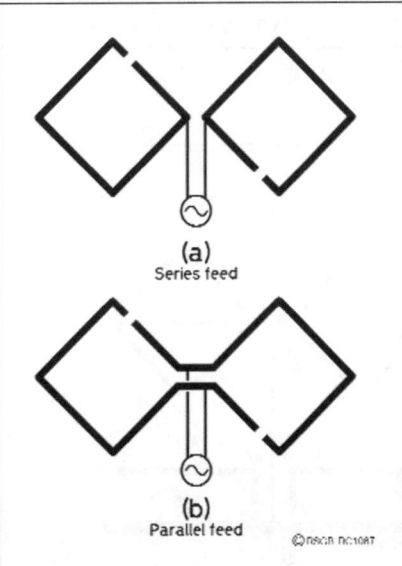

Fig 2: (a) Series feed and (b) parallel feed for the dual rhombic loop antenna.

I must admit that on first reading, I could not see how a horizontal rhombic loop and its ground plane image could radiate circular polarised waves, since there appeared to be no vertical component. The penny dropped (at least in my opinion) when I realised that there would inevitably be current flowing down the outer braid of the coaxial feedline between the ground plane and loop element.

This factor seems to have led the Japanese research engineers to develop an alternative form of the antenna utilising the 'hula hoop' principle (more correctly known as a Directional Discontinuities Ring Radiator or DDRR). The antenna was originally described for operation from 2 to 4MHz with the ring only 2.8 electrical degrees high by J M Boyer, W6UYH, of Northrop Ventura in *Electronics*, January 11, 1963 (see briefly in *ART7*, p272). This was later extended in 1965 to half-wave closed loops by Italian engineers (see *ART7*, p288).

These antennas (**Fig 3**) were designed to provide primarily vertical polarization from an electrically very short vertical section. Boyer pointed out that (with a perfect ground plane) a height of 2ft for the circular ring section could provide equivalent results to a quarter-wave vertical monopole, a saving of 30 times in height, but requiring real estate for the horizontal loop. The snags are that the system requires a highly conductive ground plane, for example when erected on the metal deck of a large vessel (or with the 120 radials of an MF broadcast station), with low resistive losses and a very high Q (comparable to a small transmitting loop) that requires retuning for even small changes of frequency. It is possible that the 120 radials could be replaced by an elevated counterpoise system, or on UHF by a metal plate of reasonable dimensions.

The Italian half-wave closed loop version (although requiring more real estate) has a bandwidth some 10 times that of the original hula hoop DDRR when the ring has a vertical height/wavelength ratio of about 5%. Although there was interest among American amateurs of the original Boyer version, and a dipole version was also published in one of the amateur magazines, I cannot recall the *TT* or *ART* item on the Italian modified system (originally published in *Electronic Letters*) ever attracting amateur radio interest.

In their recent contribution to *Electronics Letters*, the Japanese team write in their introduction: "It is well known that hula hoop antenna is a variant of an inverted-L antenna and radiates a linearly polarised wave with vertical and horizontal components. Single feed rhombic loop antennas radiating a circularly polarised wave... can have a travelling wave type current distribution on the loop, which has approximately a constant amplitude and linearly changing phase... This current distribution is realised by making a gap at the proper position of the loop and by selecting the loop length."

They show that rhombic hula hoop antennas (RHHA), in either one or two rhombic loop configuration, radiate circularly polarised waves. As shown in **Fig 4**, the antennas are composed of a rhombic loop terminated in a gap. The main difference between the RHHA and their earlier rhombic loop antenna is in the

ANTENNA TOPICS

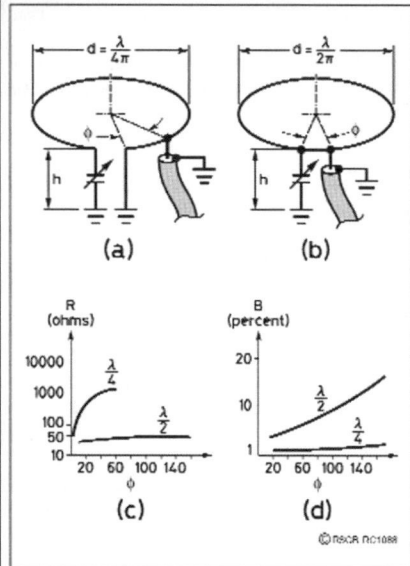

Fig 3: (a) Quarter-wave hula hoop DDRR antenna. (b) Half-wave closed loop DDRR antenna. (c) Resonance impedance versus feed-point angle. (d) Bandwidth versus feed-point angle.

Feeding F5LCP's Loop + 1.8MHz

Extracted from 'Technical Topics', *Radio Communication*, August 1996

FEEDING F5LCI'S LOOP + 1.8MHZ ANTENNA

TT (DECEMBER 1991, p28) presented details of how Jean-Marc Bourdereau, F5LCI (then F1LCI), uses a large 84m horizontal loop for HF operation on 3.5MHz and above. He then utilises the fact that the far end is at zero RF voltage and can be earthed as protection against static electricity and also to form an inverted L-antenna for 1.8MHz with a large vertically polarised component, the loop providing top capacitance loading.

Fig 5 shows the antenna as given in December 1991. His loop is one full wavelength long for 3.5MHz, rectangular in shape (18 by 24m) to fit his garden. The mean height is 12m (varying between 8 and 14m), balanced, open-line fed from his attic shack for the HF bands, but with short-circuited feeders for 1.8MHz. Dr John Belrose, VE2CV, (*TT*, May 1992, pp38 - 39) subsequently commented at some length on this arrangement, showing that with both feeder arrangements, there would be some vertical and horizontal polarisation, and that the RF power absorbed from the long earth lead from the attic could not be ignored. However, he expressed the opinion that the system, which he termed a vertical electromagnetic ground-plane loop (EMGP) antenna, should prove a good 1.8MHz antenna, though he was less impressed by its calculated characteristics on the HF bands in the balanced feed configuration.

I must admit that, despite VE2CV's misgivings, I use a large horizontal loop, of about 80m length (exact length uncertain). This is formed out of an existing long wire antenna by bringing back a second wire to a balanced pi-network ATU, resulting in a most irregular shape and with the wires at differing heights. I find it provides a reasonably useful antenna on all the

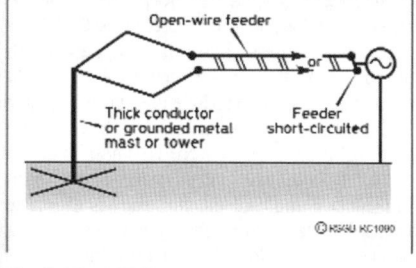

Fig 5: The F5LCI antenna as described in the December 1991 *TT* with the option of a short-circuit feeder for mainly vertical polarisation on 1.8MHz.

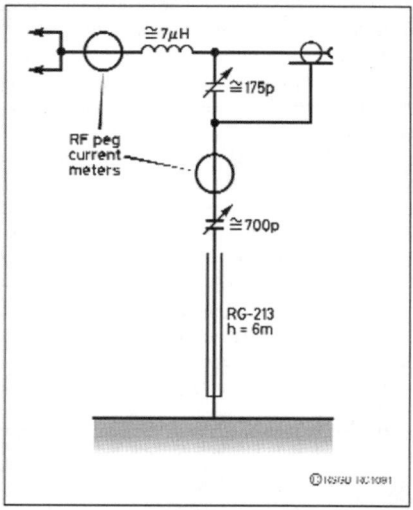

Fig 6: F5LCI's modified feed arrangements to reduce RF losses and radiation from the earth lead.

provides a reasonably useful antenna on all the HF bands I use and is not dependent on the long earth wire to the upstairs shack or the counterpoise wire previously used with the standard long wire configuration.

Recently, F5LCI had written further on using his 84m horizontal loop on 1.8MHz: "The 84m horizontal loop, although only a half-wave loop on 1.8MHz, was eventually found usable on 160m; its high input impedance is somewhat transformed down by the open wire line forming a linear transformer so matching is easier. Its radiation pattern, according to EZNEC, is almost spherical. Reception is very quiet. Short-skip (NVIS) contacts are more comfortable than with the shorted feeder configuration.

"Feeding of the vertical set-up ('mode') has been modified: Fig 6. The major drawback of the earlier system was radiation from the 'earth wire'. A Faraday screen (coaxial cable shorted at ground level) did not bring any improvement (noise pickup probably still coming from other parts of the system). I decided the reactance of the ground wire had to be cancelled. No direct measurement (with a GR bridge) proved consistent so a gross estimate was calculated from the straight-wire impedance formula. A magnitude-order of the neutralising series capacitor was then calculated. After many attempts to find a satisfactory way of tuning it, two methods were used: (a) finding a null on a portable receiver connected to this 'antenna'; and (2) the ever useful simple shunt flashlight bulb or, better, and RF current meter (peg type). I was delighted to find a marked increase in the wanted antenna current indicated on a

feed configurations. The RHHAs are fed by a coaxial cable, of which the inner conductor is conductor is connected to the ground plane, whereas for the rhombic loop both the outer and inner conductor of the cable is connected to the horizontal loop(s) as shown in Fig 4.

Two RHHA antennas were investigated, a single and a dual rhombic with the loops having the same parameters: Beta = 90-°, Delta s – 0.016λ, a – 0.008λ and h – 0.21λ, where λ is the wavelength at the centre frequency of the antenna. The perimeter of the loop is chosen to be L – 1.29 λ for the single loop and 1.20 λ for the double-loop hula hoop antenna. No information is provided on the ground plane other than that indicated in Fig 4.

Calculated (Method of Moments) and measured data are presented on current distribution, frequency characteristics and radiation patterns, and the letter concludes: "Two types of rhombic hula hoop antennas are proposed to radiate a circularly polarised wave and their radiation characteristics are investigated. It is found that the axial ratio bandwidth (2dB) of approximately 10% and the gain of approximately 10dBi are obtained by selecting the loop configuration."

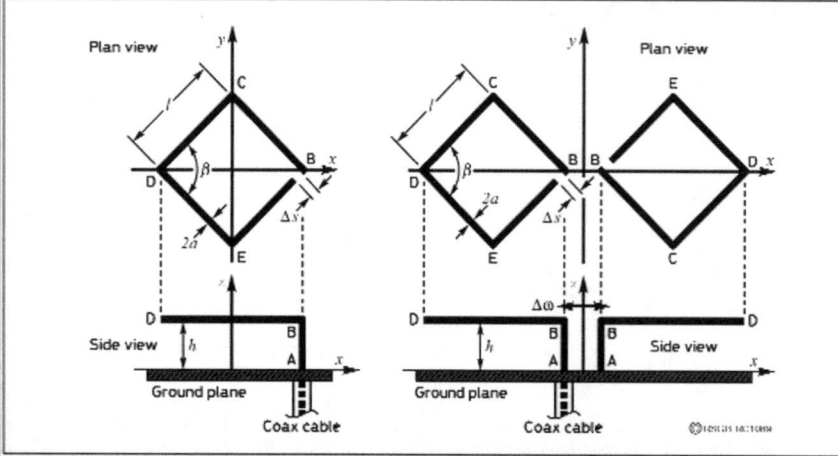

Fig 4: Rhombic hula hoop antennas (RHHAs). (a) Single RHHA; (b) dual-RHHA.

second RF peg meter. This seemed proof of the validity of the setting of the 700pF capacitor.

"Next I measured, with the help of an Autek RF-1 meter, the impedance of the antenna. This led to my replacing the standard T-match ATU with a simple L network in order to minimise losses (TT program by N6BV or ARRL). I found that the SWR was still different on the shack side of the coax, and RF found its way to the PC keyboard. It seems likely that the only remaining cause is RF pickup from the antenna on the braid. A coil choke and a ferrite sleeve balun are used, although these are large on 1.8MHz!

"In short, radiation is now believed to be almost entirely confined to the vertical down wire from the middle of the loop, with the loop playing the role of a top-loading hat (its own radiation some 25dB lower)."

One cannot help feeling that F5LCI's 1.8MHz antenna has a striking similarity to some aspects of the Japanese UHF rhombic hula hoop antenna! But I am not sure whether he or VE2CV would agree with this suggestion.

SWR on Centre-loaded Whips

Extracted from 'Technical Topics', *Radio Communication*, September 1996

REDUCING SWR ON CENTRE-LOADED MOBILE WHIPS

DR JOHN (JACK) Belrose, VE2CV, whose experience of mobile HF antennas now covers some 50 years and whose first article on the subject appeared in a 1953 *QST*, recently purchased a Pro-Am 3.5MHz mobile antenna. He was reminded of the review of this series of antennas by RSGB HQ staff in the August 1995 *RadCom*, pages 44 and 80.

On re-reading the text he noted the comment "additional information on how to use shunt capacitor matching to obtain a lower SWR than shown in Fig 1 (PHF-20) and Fig 2 (PHF-80) would have been useful." [Figures in the August 1995 issue].

VE2CV writes: "That is easy. I have copied the pertinent page from my 1953 *QST* article [see below]. Fig 2 of the RSGB review gave an SWR at resonance of 1.9. I measured my pro-Am PHF-80 and obtained an SWR of 2. For an SWR of 2 at resonance the antenna's impedance is about 25Ω. To match 25Ω to 50Ω, the shunt capacitor C at say 3750kHz is 849pF. For the required series inductance lengthen the whip just a bit, looking for resonance. I put an 820pF silver mica capacitor (20% tolerance) across the base of my Pro Am and the SWR was as close to unity as I could measure."

Extract from *QST*, September 1953 p.34, section on '*Tuning and Matching Centre-loaded Whips*':

A method of matching the antennas to the transmitter will now be considered, and a method outlined by which the antenna can be tuned using a GDO and an SWR detector (equipment normally owned by the average amateur).

First, let us consider what matching involves. If we consider the 16ft [3.81MHz] antenna just discussed, the input impedance at resonance was a pure resistance equal to 29.7Ω. We must transform this low value to 50Ω so that the antenna can be fed with standard coaxial cable (RG-8/U or RG-58/U). This can be done with an L-section matching unit as shown in **Fig 10**.

Here,

$$2\pi f L = \sqrt{(R_1(R_2 - R_1))}$$
$$1/(2\pi f C) = R_2 \sqrt{(R_1/(R_2 - R_1))}$$

Substituting values,

$$2\pi f L = 24.5\Omega$$
$$1/(2\pi f C) = 60.6\Omega \text{ or } C = 690pF$$

Now the inductance, L, can be artificially obtained by adding just a small amount more inductance to Lo, the centre-loading coil, than needed for resonance, thus making the antenna input impedance inductive. An exact match to 50Ω can be obtained by adjusting the capacitor, C, and the centre-loading inductance, Lo.

The formula given by VE2CV is also applicable to the general design of L/C single-frequency impedance transformation as used for ASTUs etc.

Monopole Loaded with a Loop

Extracted from 'Technical Topics', *Radio Communication*, October 1996

MONOPOLE LOADED WITH A LOOP

ON SEVERAL OCCASIONS recently I have referred to the work of Dr Edward Altshuler, an eminent American antenna engineer currently working at the Rome Laboratory of the Hanscom Air Force Base. In 1961 he showed that a travelling-wave distribution of current can be produced on a linear antenna by inserting a resistance of about 240Ω one-quarter wavelength from its end ('The Travelling Wave Linear Antenna' *IEEE Trans Ant & Prop*, July 1961, pp324-329). Such an antenna can have the lower section virtually of any length and provides reasonably broadband characteristics. In 1993 he further showed that the main disadvantage of a relatively short resistance-loaded system - that such an antenna is only about 50% efficient because of the power dissipated in the resistor - can be overcome by replacing the resistor with a resonant antenna having a radiation resistance approximately equal to a 240Ω resistor (see *TT*, January 1994, p44). He showed that with a modified folded dipole replacing the 240Ω loading resistor, virtually the full power will be radiated with mixed horizontal and vertical polarisation. **Fig 1**, reprinted from the January 1994 item, shows his 1.2GHz antenna which could be constructed using stiff wire. The system would work also on HF although construction would be rather more demanding in support structures.

Dr Altshuler returns to this form of antenna in a recent paper 'A Monopole Loaded with a Loop Antenna' (*IEEE Trans Ant & Prop*, June 1996, pp787-791). The main objective is to obtain an antenna with hemispherical coverage which is circularly polarised. Both series and parallel-fed circular and square loops (**Fig 2**) were investigated both by NEC computer simulations and by actual measurements at 1.6GHz. He found that these very simple, low-cost antennas can operate effectively over the entire band 1.4 to 2.0GHz. It was shown that circular polarisation could be obtained over most of the hemisphere with both types of series-fed loops; the parallel-fed loop insertions produced more directional circularly polarised patterns.

Loop perimeters of approximately one wavelength produced the best results. Increasing the height of the monopole (and the corresponding distance of the loop over the ground plane) enhanced the low elevation angle radiation but nulls also appeared. When the monopole was 0.75λ (and the loop 0.5λ above the ground plane) there was, as expected, a deep null in the zenith direction. Optimum results were obtained when the loop was approximately 0.25λ above the ground plane . . . The antennas were constructed from 18AWG copper wire which has a diameter of about 1.0mm. However, for the wire to hold its desired shape, it had to be stretched; this process reduced the wire diameter slightly.

Dr Altshuler points out that as long as the receiving antenna has the same sense of polarisation as the transmitter, then a maximum polarisation loss of 3dB occurs when the receiver is linearly polarised. But if a circularly-polarized receiving antenna has the opposite sense of polarisation to a circularly polarised signal from the transmitter then the polarisation loss becomes very high.

His conclusions were that "all loaded monopoles operated satisfactorily over the frequency band from 1.4 to 2.0GHz. The agreement between computed and measured results was very good considering the computational model and the actual antenna were not exactly alike. Whereas this type of antenna can produce circular polarisation over most of the hemisphere and over a broad bandwidth without the use of phasing networks, it may prove to be a very low cost alternative for systems such as IRIDIUM [the planned low-earth-orbiting satellites for use with handheld radiophones - *G3VA*] and the Global Positioning System. Finally, the null that is usually present over a limited range of azimuth angles may be useful for some applications. For example,

ANTENNA TOPICS

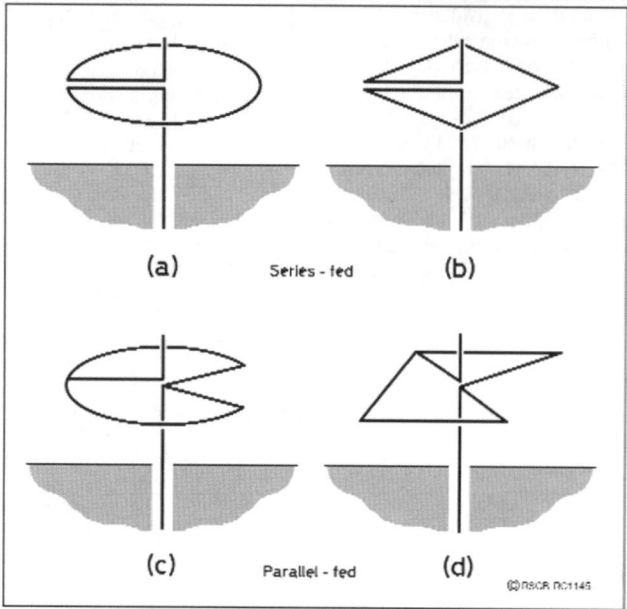

Fig 2: Altshuler-type monopoles loaded by circular or square loops, series- or parallel-fed.

there is concern that radiation from a handset held to one's head may be dangerous. This antenna can easily be designed so that the null is in the direction of the head, thus minimising the radiation in that direction".

Tuneable HF Loop Antenna

Extracted from 'Technical Topics', *Radio Communication*, November 1996

TUNEABLE HF LOOP ANTENNA

CHRIS TOWNS, G8BKE, draws attention to an 'Ideas for Design' item in *Electronics Design* (July 22 1996, p112). M J Salvati describes a 'High-frequency Loop Antenna' pointing out that tuned loop active receiving antennas have tended to be confined to low and medium frequencies primarily due to the difficult requirements associated with the active circuitry: "Good performance in the 5 - 30MHz range requires an amplifier with extremely high input impedance and low noise that can drive 75Ω loads at high signal levels at frequencies to 30MHz. Combining dual FET source-followers and the new Maxim 436 wideband transconductance amplifier can produce just such an amplifier: [see Fig 8 - G3VA]."

He adds: "A balanced configuration is used for the tuned loop to preserve the symmetry of the figure-of-eight polar antenna pattern. As a result of using FET source followers, only the 1 Megohm gate resistors load the tuned circuit, so tuning is very sharp and resistance to off-frequency interference is very high. The FETs drive the differential inputs of the MAX436 which amplifies the balanced signal and converts it to a single-end output."

Voltage gain is switch selectable (8dB or 20dB) into a 75Ω load. Maximum undistorted output is 1500mV across 75Ω. The 470Ω resistors prevent gate damage from accumulated static charge when handling the loops to change the frequency range. A three-turn, 15in diameter loop made from No 8 aluminium ground wire spaced ½in between turns) will cover from 4.4 to 16MHz with a dual 10 - 330pF variable capacitor. A single loop using a 48in long strip of 1⅛in wide sheet aluminium should cover from 13 to about 55MHz although performance falls off beyond about 40MHz.

If the site has very strong AC fields, adding 100pF input capacitors can reduce hum pickup, otherwise they are not needed. The only adjustment is to zero (balance) the output by means of the 330Ω trimpot.

Elevated vs Buried Radials

Extracted from 'Technical Topics', *Radio Communication*, December 1996

MORE SIMULATIONS OF ELEVATED VERSUS BURIED RADIALS

IN A DETAILED look at the question of elevated radials versus buried earths (*TT*, January 1996, pp69-71) I referred to work on this topic by Ralph Holland, VK1BRH, suggesting, *inter alia*, that there is an optimal height for an elevated groundplane, typically about 0.05λ and that large numbers of radials are not required with three or four being sufficient. In a follow-up note in the March *TT*, I mentioned that N6BV had reported that Al Christman, KB8I, had also uncovered further intriguing aspects of this work.

These findings are probably those disclosed in the article 'AM broadcast antennas with elevated radials: varying the number of radials and their height above ground' by Al Christman and Roger Radcliff (*IEEE Trans on Broadcasting*, March 1996, pp10-13). This covers much the same ground as the work of VK1BRH but with computer simulation for a quarter-wave monopole at a frequency of 1.0MHz. The American paper concludes:

"Computer-modelling exercises indicate that it is possible to construct an elevated-radial vertical monopole which is mounted too close to the ground to ever achieve performance equivalent to that of a conventional 120-buried-radial antenna.

"Generally, the necessary ground clearance increases as the soil conductivity decreases. However, once sufficient height over

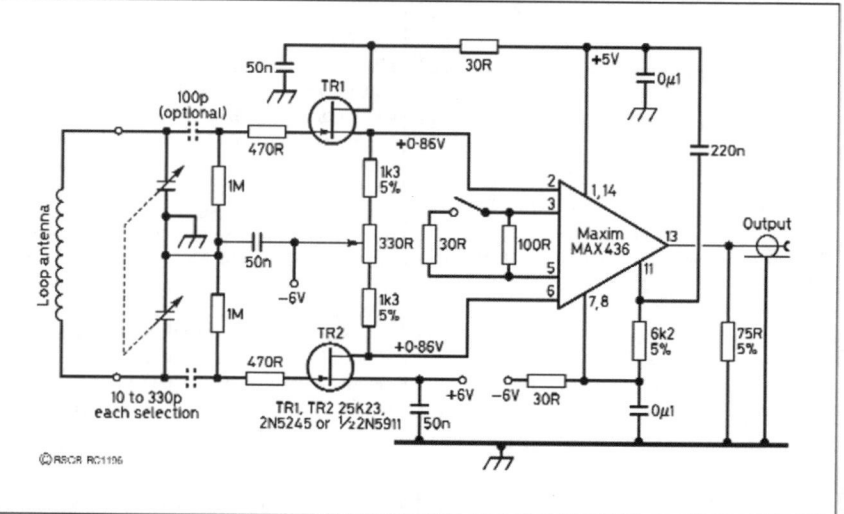

Fig 8: Balanced HF tuneable 'active' loop antenna using dual FET source-followers with Maxim 436 transconductance amplifier to create a high-impedance, low-noise amplifier that makes it possible to use effectively loop antennas throughout the HF spectrum.

ground has been attained, it is also possible to use *too many* elevated radials, causing an actual diminution in the radiated field strength. A study was conducted in which three different soil types have been examined, along with numerous combinations of elevation height, feed methodology, and number of radials. Interestingly, it appears that using 8 radials in an isolated-feed configuration at a height of 10m above ground produces a competitive antenna for all of the soil types reviewed herein."

A height of 10m at a frequency of 1MHz (300m) is 0.033λ, quite close to VK1ABH's 0.05λ for one type of soil. The three sets of ground constants used by KB8I were: very poor soil (conductivity 0.0005 S/m, relative permittivity 4); average soil (conductivity 0.004S/m; relative permittivity 15); and very good soil (conductivity 0.03 S/m, relative permittivity 40).

It is noted that with 120 buried radials, the electrical character of the soil can cause the radiated field to vary by a factor of two or more. Improving the quality of the soil leads to an increase in the magnitude of both the field intensity and the input impedance.

Half-Rhombic Antennas

Extracted from 'Technical Topics', *Radio Communication*, December 1996

HALF-RHOMBIC ANTENNAS

JUNE'S *TT* (p72) drew attention to the Barker & Williamson vertical half-rhombic attention with 450Ω resistor loading, a 10.7m Fibreglass pole and a low 25.66m counterpoise as a broadband travelling-wave antenna for use between 1.8 and 30MHz. I pointed out that this type of antenna is closely related to the original Bruce terminated inverted-vee antenna.

The Bruce antenna was for many years described in the amateur radio handbooks as an effective vertically polarised directive antenna. However, for optimum performance it was said to require a very high (non-conductive) mast and a very good earth connection in an area of good earth conductivity. The use of this antenna with a counterpoise to form a half-rhombic or 'balanced-feed, loaded pyramid' antenna, although less well-known, also dates back many years.

Recently, by chance, I stumbled on a detailed 50-year-old article by Capt John H Mullaney, W4HGU, entitled 'The half-rhombic antenna - a directive system for VHF' in *QST* January 1946, which stressed: "At lower frequencies the half-rhombic antenna is impractical for amateur use because of the required height of support.

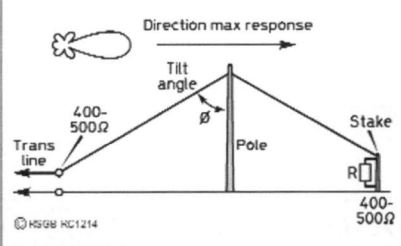

Fig 3: The inverted-rhombic (half-rhombic) antenna with counterpoise. Directivity is in the direction of the terminated end. Although originally developed (by Bruce) for HF, for which a very high (non-conductive) mast is required to obtain significant gain, this broadband travelling-wave antenna can provide a most effective fixed antenna for the 50 and 70MHz bands. The terminating resistor should be non-inductive and have a power rating up to half the RF power delivered to the antenna. For SSB an appreciably lower wattage rating (dependent on the duty cycle) can be used. For reception only a receiver-type resistor need be used if non-inductive.

However, at VHF it provides a relatively simple means of obtaining high directivity and gain with vertical polarisation."

W4HGU discusses the design and performance of half-rhombic antennas (**Fig 3**) at about 41MHz and a compromise design for use on military frequencies between 27 to 38.9MHz. But clearly this type of antenna would prove effective on 50, 70 and possibly 144MHz. **Table 1** provides basic design data for half-rhombic antennas. He points out that for a design frequency of 41MHz, an optimum-performance half-rhombic with 2λ per leg, requires a tilt angle of about 50°, a pole height of 31.2ft and a counterpoise length of 72ft, and would have a half-power beamwidth of 72°: **Fig 4**. With 6λ

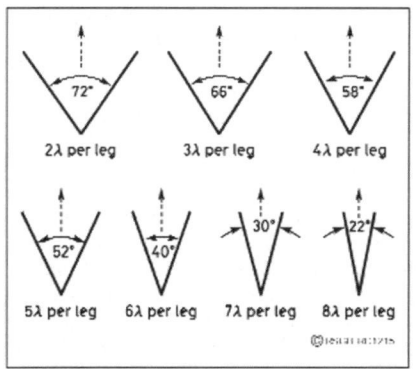

Fig 4: Approximate beam widths for the half power point for half-rhombic antennas of various leg dimensions.

λ per leg	Tilt angle θ°	Pole height in λ	Counterpoise length in λ
1	30	0.87	1
2	49	1.3	3
3	57	1.6	5
4	62	1.9	7
5	65	2.1	9
6	67	2.3	11
7	68	2.6	13
8	70	2.7	15

Table 1: Half-rhombic design data.

per leg beam-width is cut to about 40°. At VHF, gains as high as 15dB can be achieved, although with compromise designs around 10dB is more likely. A half-rhombic designed for 50MHz should be usable from about 28MHz to over 70MHz.

W4HGU states: "The terminating resistor plays a dual function in the operation of a half-rhombic antenna. Upon it depends the unidirectivity of the antenna and the absence of any resonant effect. When a half-rhombic antenna is properly terminated it will offer a constant input impedance. This allows it to be

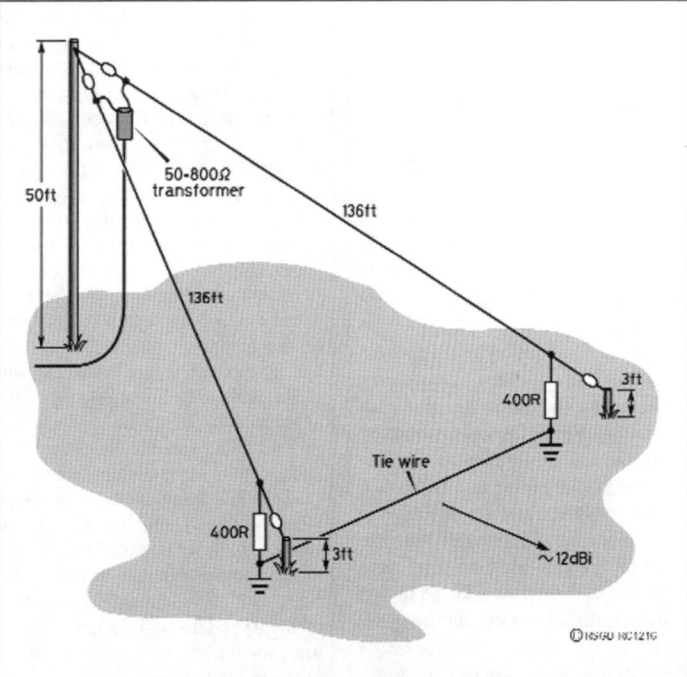

Fig 5: The terminated sloping vee beam antenna.

ANTENNA TOPICS

operated over a wide band of frequencies without the necessity for readjusting the coupling at the transmitter. The resistor should be a non-inductive type and it may have a resistance between 400 and 700Ω without adversely affecting its terminating properties. It must be rated to handle approximately one-half the transmitter input power to the antenna. When using a half-rhombic for reception only, the resistor power rating is not important. The terminating resistor should be mechanically suitable for outdoor installation. Common practice dictates that it should be placed in a weatherproof box for protection from the elements.

"It should be noted that the terminating resistor affects neither the strength of the signal nor the field distribution in the forward direction. Its primary function is to decrease the radiation and reception from the back or reverse direction when it is connected. The power is wasted only in the sense that it is not radiated in the reverse direction... In other words, the terminating resistor is the factor responsible for making a half rhombic a unidirectional antenna. In cases where interference is negligible it is possible to remove or short-out the resistor and make the antenna bi-directional..."

While on this topic, it seems worth including brief details of a couple of other 'sloping' antennas. **Fig 5** shows one form of the unidirectional travelling-wave terminated vee-beam antenna intended for 14MHz (2λ legs) but usable from 3.5MHz to over 30MHz. The recommended pole height is shown as 50ft and should be at least 10m.

The low tie wire between the ends improves performance particularly in areas of relatively poor earth conductivity. This particular design comes from a survey of 'Some useful wire antennas for HF - Part 2' by Rob Gurr, VK5RG (*Amateur Radio*, April 1996) but originated in the unfortunately defunct *Ham Radio*, May 1990, p49). But note that the end wires are only a couple of feet above ground and thus represent both a physical and electrical hazard unless some form of protection is provided to prevent contact by humans or animals.

In 'An optimised sloper for 80 metres' (*Amateur Radio*, August 1996) Felix Scerri, VK4FUG, advocates the use of a sloper with an elevated radial: **Fig 6**. He claims that the use of an elevated radial is the key to success. He writes: "It was staggering to note during tests, the effect on both transmit and receive of varying the height of the radial. With the radial resting on the ground the results were very poor. When raised 1.5 to 2.4m (5 to 8ft) above ground, the difference was amazing." It would seem a wise precaution to clear heads etc with the radial at least 2.4m or 2.5m high.

He adds: "Direct coax feed can be used, but a tuner is probably necessary, as the feed resistance will probably be significantly less than 50Ω. Open wire line with a 4:1 balun is an option."

Dipoles with Counterpoises

Extracted from 'Technical Topics', *Radio Communication*, January 1997

DIPOLES WITH COUNTERPOISES

ONE OF THE advantages of a dipole-type antenna over a monopole is that it does not require a loss-inducing earth connection. However, it should be remembered that all antennas that are situated close to the ground are affected by that ground to some extent. This point is stressed by Ralph Holland, VK1BRH, in his article 'Horizontal half-wave dipole above a counterpoise' (*Amateur Radio*, November 1996, pp12-13).

He points out: "The most obvious effect is that the ground forces the antenna's radiation pattern to appear in the half-space above the ground. This is illustrated by comparing the radiation around a monopole fed against ground to that of a dipole in free-space. The monopole has twice the power in the hemisphere of symmetry for the dipole in free-space. The nature of this reflection of energy above the ground is governed by the polarisation of the antenna and the ground effectiveness. The dielectric constant and conductivity of the ground determines how well or how badly the ground acts as a conductor and hence as a reflector.

"A less obvious effect is that the ground absorbs energy from the antenna; this energy is wasted in the intrinsic resistance of the ground."

VK1BRH goes on to show how - particularly on the lower frequency bands where a horizontal dipole is likely to be less than a quarter-wave above the earth - the placement of an artificial ground screen, or elevated counterpoise, can decrease the ground losses and enhance the performance of a horizontal antenna. He shows how the enhancement can be investigated either by NEC-type computer simulation or by comparative measurements of the feedpoint resistance before and after adding a counterpoise under the antenna.

He used NEC-2 computer specifications for antenna systems at 1.825MHz over average ground with a relative dielectric constant of 13 and a conductivity of 5 millisiemens per metre (13, 5). The simulations were performed for ideal (loss-less) antenna elements with a diameter of 1.2mm. He uses the term "displacement" for the distance between the counterpoise (which is the antenna system's lowest element) and ground. "Separation" is the term used for the distance between the driven-element and the counterpoise.

Fig 1 illustrates the efficiency of a horizontal half-wave dipole at various heights (displacements) above ground. In general, the efficiency improves as the dipole is raised higher. **Fig 2** illustrates the efficiency for various counterpoise system and a dipole above ground. Note that there is a knee in the counterpoise curves. This indicates that there is an optimum displacement. Be careful in interpreting the graphs because increasing the separation suffers from the law of diminishing returns. The efficiency of a counterpoise system must be compared with that of a dipole at the same equivalent height, ie the counterpoise displacement plus the driven element separation. Nevertheless, Fig 2 shows that under some conditions, a counterpoise improves the efficiency of a horizontal antenna system.

VK1BRH concludes that "the placement of a counterpoise below a horizontal antenna can improve the antenna efficiency by a reasonable amount. The effect under a horizontal antenna is similar to the effect of elevated ground-planes for vertical antennas. You can measure this effect by observing an increase in field strength or by observing the lowering of the feedpoint resistance when adding the counterpoise. At 1.8MHz, with 13, 5 ground parameters, the effect peaks with counterpoise displacements of about 0.02-λ above ground. Increasing the antenna system efficiency with a counterpoise increases the gain at all angles, effectively lowering the effective vertical radiation angles."

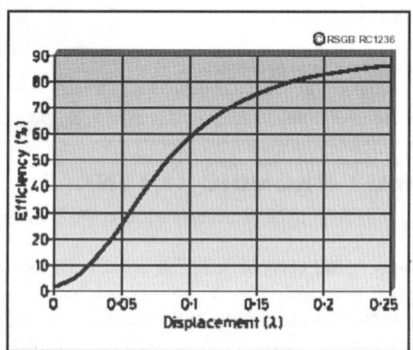

Fig 1: Efficiency of a half-wave dipole above average ground (13, 5 = dielectric constant of 13, conductivity of 5 millisiemens per metre).

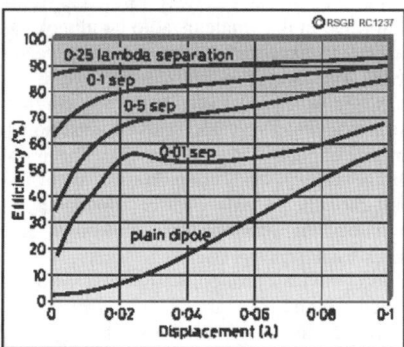

Fig 2: Efficiency of a half-wave dipole separated from a counterpoise for various displacements above real ground.

Improved Multiband Dipole

Extracted from 'Technical Topics', *Radio Communication*, February 1997

IMPROVED MULTIBAND TRAP DIPOLE

FOR SOME 40 or so years, the multiband two-trap dipole (as originally developed and popularised by W3DZZ and G8KW) has been recognised as one of the most useful and effective HF multiband wire antennas. Advantages include reduced span, instantaneous band switching and a standard dipole radiation pattern achieved at the cost of a fairly modest power loss in the traps, and having to support the weight of the traps. An alternative form of trapped dipole uses a series of resonant traps, one pair for each (except one) of the bands covered.

As noted, for example in *TT*, March 1984 pp220-221, the original and most popular version used only two 7.1MHz traps but when correctly dimensioned and implemented can provide a reasonably low-impedance centre feedpoint on 3.5 / 7 / 14 / 21 / 28MHz with an

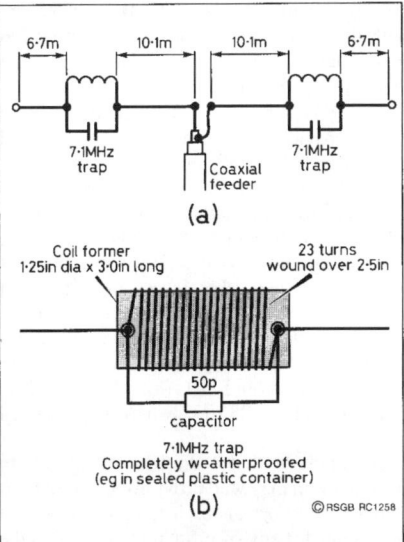

Fig 1: The original W3DZZ multiband trap dipole using only two 7.1MHz traps yet providing a low-impedance centre feedpoint on 3.5 / 7 / 14 / 21 / 28MHz with an SWR not greater than about 3:1. The 50pF capacitor must be a high-voltage type capable of withstanding high RF voltages. The whole system should be symmetrical about the feedpoint, with the top span either horizontal or in inverted-vee form but not as a continuously sloping wire. For use with solid-state transmitters an ATU is advisable on at least some bands where the SWR is greater than about 2:1.

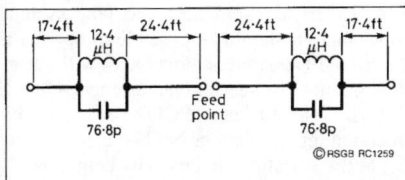

Fig 2: W8NX's basic design for his improved 3.5, 7, 18 and 28MHz trap dipole.

SWR of not much more than about 2.5:1 on at least some parts of each band. To achieve such results it is important that the traps are correctly positioned in the element and have the correct LC ratio. **Fig 1** shows an acceptable W3DZZ design requiring the use of very-high-voltage 50pF capacitors in the traps and excellent weatherproofing. The whole system should be symmetrical about the feedpoint, with the top span either horizontal or in inverted-V form but not as a continuously-sloping wire.

Some 12 years ago, Robert Sommer, N4UU, (*QST*, December 1984 - see also comments by Geoff Roberts, G3ENY in *TT*, May 1986, p338) showed that the use of coaxial cable to form the traps has the unique advantage of providing an in-built high-voltage capacitor as well as other useful features.

N4UU noted that there is an optimum way to use the cable to form an inductor, the whole acting as a parallel resonant circuit: "The trick is to use the shortest length of cable (minimum capacitance) which can be closewound (maximum inductance) on a former of such a diameter to make a coil of correct inductance having a length-to-diameter ratio to give a good value of Q."

G3ENY pointed out that this is not easy or simple to achieve using cut-and-try methods since it requires the use of a computer to solve, by an iterative loop, the cubic equation which ties together the LC ratio and diameter variables to obtain resonance. However, G3ENY provided two near optimum designs of trap for 7010kHz (probably more suitable for European bands than 7.1MHz), one using standard coaxial cable (RG58/U) and the other miniature coaxial cable: **Table 1**. He noted that since there is only a limited range of PVC pipe sizes available from builder's merchants, the constructor would be well advised to choose a diameter which gives a length-to-diameter ratio of about 0.6 certainly less than one (a square coil).

Al Buxton, W8NX, in 'An improved multiband trap dipole antenna' (*QST*, July 1996, pp32-34) introduces a new trap design and a change in trap location: **Fig 2**. His design features double-coaxial-cable-wound traps (**Fig 3**) having a higher quality (Q) factor (**Fig 4**) than earlier coax-cable traps, and hence providing a useful reduction of power loss in the

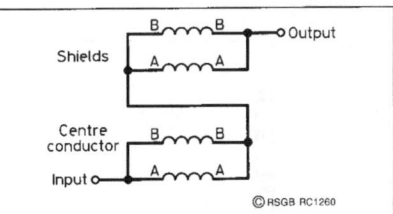

Fig 3: Diagram showing the connections of a double-coaxial-cable trap providing integral capacitance.

	RG-58/U	RG-174/U
Length of coaxial cable	61.6in	52.7in
Diameter of former	2.125in	1.6in
Number of turns	7.8	9.8
Length of former	2.5in	2in
Coil Inductance	3.35µH	3.78µH

Table 1: 7.01MHz traps based on coaxial cable.

traps. The traps also provide a fourfold increase in power-handling capability over that of the earlier single wound coax traps.

The new design is for operation on the American 3.5 - 4.0MHz and 7.0 - 7.3MHz bands plus the 18 and 28MHz bands. At his location, with a 50-to-75Ω transformer and a 75Ω feed line, in an inverted vee configuration with the apex at 40ft above ground, the SWR performance achieved by W8NX is shown in **Fig 5**, showing that no ATU would be needed on 7MHz, on part of the 3.5MHz band and on part of the 28MHz band (SWR less than 2:1) but advisable with solid-state transmitters on 18MHz and for extending low SWR coverage of the 28MHz and 3.5MHz bands.

Fig 6 shows how the traps are made. Each trap requiring no external high-voltage capacitor consists of 6.88 double turns of seven-foot lengths of RG-59 (Belden 8241) coaxial cable wound on a 5.33in length of 3.5in outer diameter (schedule 50) PVC pipe (three-inch inner-diameter). Check that the form is actually 3.5in OD as the trap frequency (5.16MHz ±25kHz) is sensitive to the diameter of the former. Use a high-quality 1:1 balun; the apex should be at least 35ft high, the ends at least 15ft high. Feed the antenna with either 50 or 75Ω cable, the higher value being preferred to lower the feed-line SWR on 18 and 28MHz.

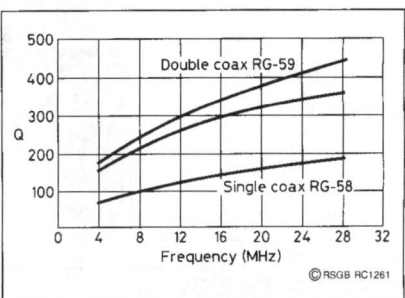

Fig 4: Quality factor (Q) versus frequency of coax traps.

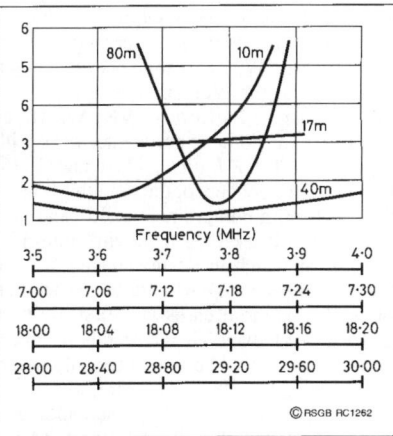

Fig 5: W8NX's SWR plot of his improved trap dipole for the 3.5/7/18/28MHz bands based on the design shown in Fig 1.

W8NX suggests that trap loss on 3.5MHz is 1.66dB but only 0.04dB on 7MHz, 0.001dB on 18MHz and 0dB on 28MHz. He provides further detailed constructional information on the traps but it is hoped that the brief outline given here will at least allow experimentation with his 'improved' system.

ANTENNA TOPICS

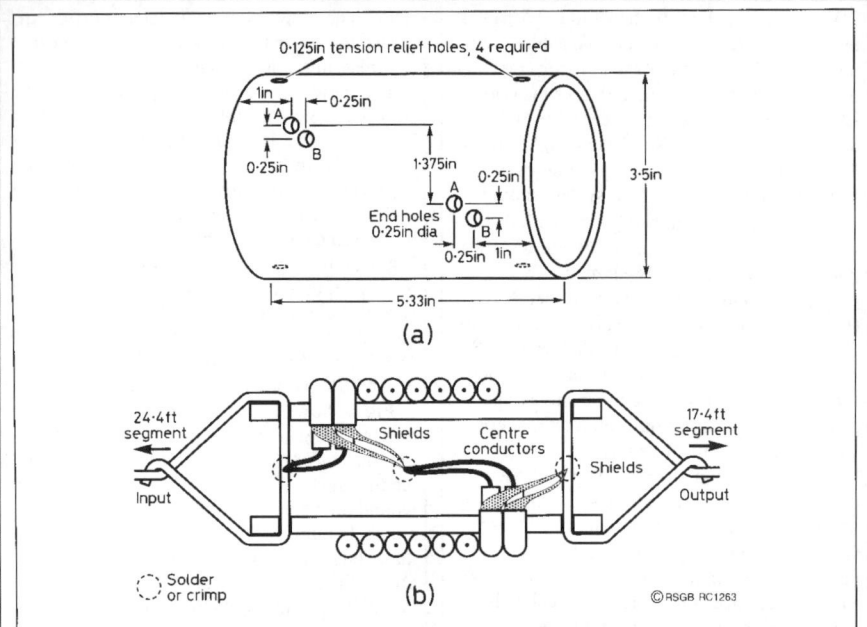

Fig 6: Constructional details of the W8NX double coaxial traps. (a) Position of holes in the trap coil former. (b) Cross-sectional view of a double-coax trap.

Feeding the OCFD

Extracted from 'Technical Topics', *Radio Communication*, March 1997

FEEDING THE OCFD

THE OFF-CENTRE-fed-dipole (OCFD) began life in the late 1920s as a single-wire-fed, half-wave dipole antenna developed by Bill Everitt and John Byrne at Ohio State University. First described in *QST* (September 1929) by L Windom, W9GZ, it soon became known world-wide as the Windom antenna.

Later, Jim MacIntosh, VS1AA (later GM3IAA), in 'Some experimental work with aerials' (*The T & R Bulletin*, November 1936) introduced the concept of the 'one-third' feed-point to form a compromise multi-band version. This still used a single-wire 'transmission-line' in which an essential feature was the use of a thinner-gauge wire for the feeder than for the element. In all cases where a single-wire feeder is used, even when correctly matched, there will inevitably be some vertically-polarised radiation from the feeder wire, which may or may not (TVI) be desirable. It should also be remembered that the VS1AA one-third tap antenna was developed before the allocation of the 21MHz band and cannot be expected to work as a matched antenna on that frequency.

From across the Atlantic in the 1950s came the concept of using 300Ω twin transmission line while still retaining the 'one-third' feedpoint. Alternatively, it was possible to use coaxial cable feeder with a suitable balun transformer at the element feed-point.

Richard Formato, K1POO, in 'Feeding the off-centre dipole' (*Electronics World*, November 1996, pp853-854) suggests - following a theoretical study - that while it is widely acknowledged that the best place for the OCFD feed point remains the one-third distance from

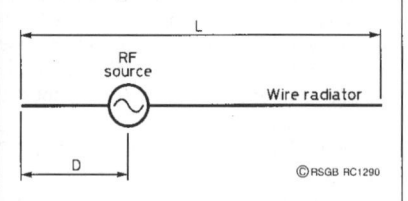

Fig 9: For off-centre-fed-dipoles it is usual to make D one-third of L, but K1POO argues that this may not be the best arrangement for four-band operation including 21MHz.

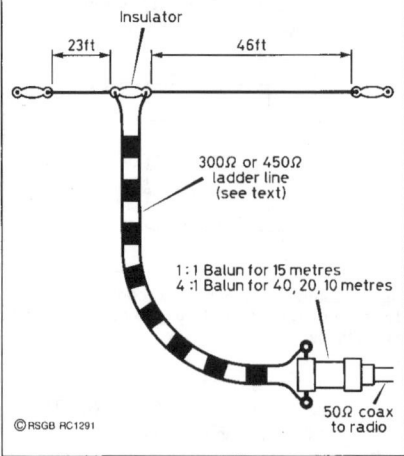

Fig 10: The OCFD four-band (7, 14, 21, 28MHz) antenna as described by G0FAH in *QST* using the ladder-line feeder as a quarter-wave impedance transformer by making this an odd multiple (electrical) of quarter waves. It is necessary to change baluns for 21MHz.

one end (as originally recommended by VS1AA/GM3IAA) - **Fig 9** - this should not be regarded as a universal rule.

He points out that the OCFD is an attractive multi-band antenna "because it is simple, inexpensive, and requires no antenna tuner [at least on some of some bands - *G3VA*]. Improving its performance simply by moving the feed point makes the antenna even more attractive."

He based his computer studies on a wire element 21.03m (69ft) long, 0.2053cm diameter (No 12 AWG) - dimensions taken from a February 1996 *QST* article by Bill Wright, G0FAH, entitled 'Four bands, Off Centre' (7, 14, 21, 28MHz bands). The G0FAH design (**Fig 10**) uses the one-third point with (preferably) 300Ω ladder line which forms an impedance matching transformer on 21MHz by making the ladder line an electrical multiple of a quarter-wave. eg 55 or 111ft of 450Ω line. At the transmitter end, the ladder line is matched to 50Ω by the use of a 4:1 balun on 7, 14 and 28MHz and a 1:1 balun on 21MHz.

K1POO computed the band-centre travelling-wave ratios of the G0FAH design computed on the four bands at the antenna input terminals for a feed-point impedance of 200Ω located at 6.98m (one third) from one end: **Fig 11(a)**. He then computed the SWR when the feed point is located 8.65m from one end: **Fig 11(b)**. While the SWRs on 7, 14 and 28MHz are slightly higher, that on 21MHz is very low with the result that all four bands can be fed from 50Ω coax with a single 4:1 balun at the element feed-point.

K1POO then shows that changing D to 3.65m provides excellent results on 7, 14 and 21MHz with the SWR on 7MHz only slightly above 2, and the SWR on the 14 and 21MHz bands below 2; the highest SWR is on 28MHz where it is approximately 2.4: **Fig 11(c)** showing the computed values. He points out that since balun and cable losses increase with frequency, the SWRs measured in practice at the transmitter end of 50Ω cable with a 4:1 balun at the element feed-point should be lower than those given in Fig 11(c), with the reduction greatest on 28MHz where it is needed most.

He concludes that feeding the antenna 3.65m from one end may well provide the best overall four-band performance. He notes however that in practice for any specific implementation the OCFD, like any other resonant antenna, must be "tweaked" for optimum SWR. "This is accomplished by adjusting the feed point location. Other antennas, nearby metallic objects, and the earth are typical factors that influence antenna performance. Since these factors are not included in the computer model, they must be dealt with empirically by adjusting the antenna on-site. The 8.65m and 3.65m points should provide a starting point... Depending on total antenna length L, height above ground, earth electrical parameters and feed system impedance, it should be possible to operate a single OCFD on four or more bands without an antenna tuner or special feed arrangement."

It will be noted that K1POO bases his results on computer simulations but his results - subject to the variations imposed by height, earth constants and nearby objects etc - are unlikely to be much in error. On the other hand, it is

1990 - 1999

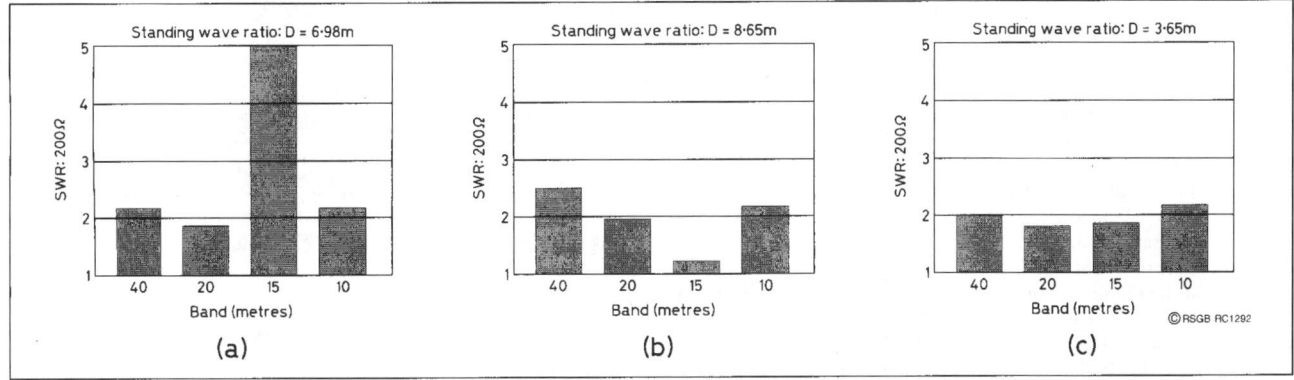

Fig 11: K1POO's computed standing wave ratios on 40, 20, 15 and 10 metres mid-band for a 21.03m (69ft) element (L). No 12AWG wire for a feed system impedance of 200ohms (the antenna was assumed not to be tuned to resonance) for three different feed points (D). (a) D = 6.98m (one-third L). (b) D = 8.65m. (c) D = 3.65m. K1POO suggests that with (b) or (c) it should be possible to tweak the antenna to provide an SWR of less than 2:1 on all four bands using only a single 4:1 balun at the feed-point with coaxial cable feeder without requiring an ATU.

worth stressing once more that this is not true of all published computer-simulations.

Alan Taylor, G3JMO, for example, is rather dubious about the conclusions (based on computer simulations with NEC-2) reached by Ralph Holland, VK1BRH, (*TT*, January 1997, p61) that putting a counterpoise below a horizontal antenna (on the lower HF and 1.8MHz bands) is likely to improve the antenna efficiency by a reasonable amount and lower the effective vertical radiation angle.

G3JMO writes: "I have tried this out (mainly on 1.8MHz) but with inconclusive results. The counterpoise, like any parasitic element can be tuned to either accept or reject energy from the radiating element, in this case above it. One way to tune it is by placing a tuned circuit in the middle, or even one end of it.

"When the counterpoise accepts energy from the radiating element, the skyward is reduced and the local radiation about the counterpoise is increased. As this is nearer the ground, the ground absorbs more energy and the overall result is a lowering of signal strength reports received from my local stations.

"When the counterpoise is tuned to reject energy, giving very low radiation levels near the counterpoise, this increased the skywave radiation as it would if the antenna itself was lowered near the ground. However, I did find the local stations again reported lower signal strengths. One way to increase the high angle radiation from a horizontal dipole, to increase signal strength in the near field, is to lower it nearer the ground, providing the ground is a reasonable reflector.

"I was sufficiently discouraged from proceeding further. In summary I suggest that a counterpoise below an antenna does have a pronounced effect on the radiation from the antenna, dependent on the tuning of the counterpoise, and needs to be investigated further."

Resonant Feedline Dipoles

Extracted from 'Technical Topics', *Radio Communication*, June 1997

RESONANT FEEDLINE DIPOLES

THERE ARE MANY locations where an end-fed antenna can be more convenient than a centre or off-centre fed system. The end-fed 40m (132ft) long-wire antenna or even the 84ft W3EDP (see *RadCom*, August 1996 article by G3LCK) take a lot of beating as multiband antennas provided that they are fed with a suitable ATU against a good earth or a quarter-wave or appropriate counterpoise. The main snag is that these antennas bring high RF voltages or currents into the shack, with possible health hazards and/or RFI problems when using high power.

James E Taylor, W2OZH, offers an alternative (single-band) solution in the form of the RFD (resonant feed-line dipole) antenna. His original presentation 'RFD-1 and RFD-2: Resonant Feed-Line Dipoles' (*QST*, August 1991, pp24-27) was sub-headed 'This unique design offers simplicity and general utility. In short, these are "reel" great antennas for the HF bands'. The play on the words "real/reel" reflects the ability to roll up the antenna for portability.

He developed his antenna while seeking a universal solution under the following ground rules. (1) No separate antenna tuner would be required; (2) the antenna could be deployed with no more difficulty than stringing up a length of coax; and (3) the antenna could be easily stored and unwound from a cord reel without a tangle of cable and wire.

In effect, his RFD antennas are based on the traditional vertical linear coaxial sleeve antenna in which a vertical dipole is constructed from a quarter-wave whip and a quarter wavelength of shielding braid with the coaxial feedline passing through the braid (sleeve). But instead of fitting an extra sleeve he takes advantage of the fact that the inner and outer surfaces of coaxial cable can carry separate RF currents. He uses the inner of a section of the coax braid as the feed-line but the outer of the braid as the sleeve. The problem then becomes letting the common-mode RF on the outer of the braid 'know' when to stop flowing down the coax and reflecting back towards the centre to form a radiating half-element.

One method is to use a coaxial choke balun (T) as shown in **Fig 3** comprising 13 turns of cable coil on a cord reel (13 turns, 6-in diameter) as shown. The remainder of the feed-line is then used as an electrical half-wavelength, resulting in a 50Ω match at the choke balun and at the transceiver output.

In his letter on 'Alternative end fed antennas', W2OZH writes: "Briefly, the basic RFD antenna offers a method of achieving an end-fed resonant dipole antenna which is well matched to a 50Ω feedline. Fig 3 shows the construction, schematically, for a frequency of

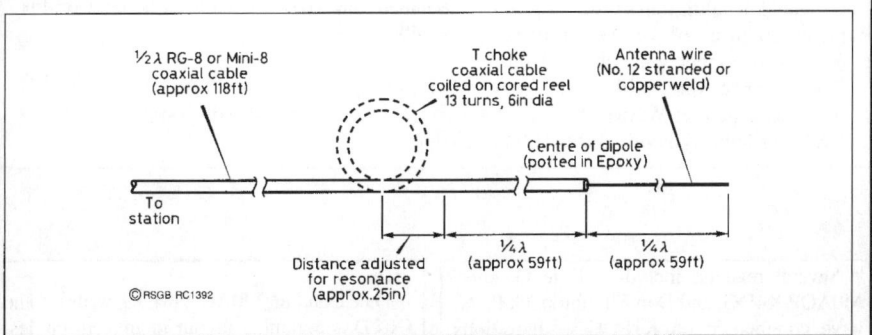

Fig 3: The W2OZH resonant Feed-Line dipole (RFD-1) as implemented for a nominal frequency of 3.95MHz requiring the use of 118ft length of RG-8x (minifoam) coaxial cable; 59ft length of No 12 (AWG) stranded or Copperweld wire; PL-259 male coaxial cable connector; 10in diameter cord reel; 3in length of ½in OD PVC pipe (for centre insulator) and sufficient epoxy potting compound to fill the pipe.

341

ANTENNA TOPICS

about 3.95MHz (in the American 3.5MHz band). Other frequencies can be simply computed from the equation for simple dipole antennas.

"Mechanically, the joining of the two halves is accomplished by use of SO-239 coaxial sockets mounted in a suitable insulating cylindrical tube (I found the apothecary pill bottles 1¼in diameter and 2½in long, with the locking top to be very satisfactory). Mating PL-259 coaxial plugs are placed at the input ends of the two halves of the dipole radiator. The 13-turn T-choke coil was wound on a cord reel or other 6in diameter tube or reel. During adjustments the winding of this coil can be slightly re-spaced to achieve the 1:1 SWR at resonance."

RFD-2 was a two-band antenna covering 7 and 3.5MHz without severing the coaxial cable (but with a second T-choke when set up for 7MHz). The *QST* article also provided scaling of the T-choke for other (American) bands: 160m, 1.90MHz 19 turns; 40m 7.26MHz 9 turns; 30m 10.12MHz 8 turns; 20m 14.29MHz 7 turns; 17m 18.14MHz 6 turns; 15m 21.38MHz 6 turns; 12m 24.96MHz 5 turns; 10m 28.65MHz 5 turns.

Later, W2OZH authored 'The Improved Resonant Feed-Line Dipole' (*73 Amateur Radio Today*, July 1994, p44-ff) of which he has provided the following brief summary:

"The improved RFD retains essentially the same electrical and mechanical features as the original version with one notable exception - the somewhat cumbersome 6in diameter T-choke has been replaced by two compact toroidal coils which, in concert, act to provide the desired high impedance at the input-end of the dipole. Details and arrangement of these coils, which are wound on Amidon cores, are shown in **Fig 4**. They are mounted in a (Radio Shack) plastic box 6 by 3-3/16 by 1-7/8 inches.

"The above brief notes should be sufficient to start experimenters with either of these interesting and effective antennas. The original articles give many more details including calculated design figures for other amateur bands."

K1POO OCFD Antenna

Extracted from 'Technical Topics', *Radio Communication*, July 1997

K1POO OCFD ANTENNA

TT (MARCH 1997, pp72 and 77) presented details of two variations on off-centre-fed-dipole (OCFD) antennas which Richard Formato, K1POO, has suggested as improved alternatives to the classical 'one-third' feed point for Windom-type multiband antennas fed by coaxial cable or twin feeder. The item included computed SWR information but emphasised that final adjustments were likely to be necessary to take into account variations imposed by height, earth constants, nearby objects etc.

Multiband OCFD Antenna

Extracted from 'Technical Topics', *Radio Communication*, June 1997

MULTIBAND OCFD ANTENNA

THE MARCH *TT* item 'Feeding the OCFD' stimulated Peter Pickering, G3ORP, chairman of the Maidstone YMCA Amateur Radio Society, to pass on details of an OCFD antenna which has been used by a number of amateurs in the Kent area for the past 30 years, developed from basic theory in the days before the emergence of NEC computer programs. He writes:

"The antenna (**Fig 5**) was developed as an 'idiot-proof' system to present a 50Ω load to a rig on most bands. It is currently used at the society station GX3TRF for operation from 1.8 to 28MHz (feeder strapped on the 1.8 and 10MHz bands as a Tee-antenna). A good outdoor earth system is used for lightning and EMC protection. We have called it 'a coax-fed Windom'. A smaller version (**Fig 6**) for 7MHz and non-WARC bands was also in use for a few years.

"The antenna could be fed with any length of 75Ω (RG213) or 93Ω (RG62) coax, but the system shown in Fig 50 gives a very low SWR on the none-WARC bands. The 93Ω line (Section E) is for improved matching on the 7MHz band (quarter-wave transformer). The 50Ω line (Section D) acts as a 1:1 transformer on most bands except 3.5MHz where it forms a quarter-wave transformer. Capacitor Cx is adjusted for resonance (lowest SWR) on your most-used frequency in the 3.5MHz band. Select-on-test within the range 200 to 470pF. I used a series/parallel combination of four heavy duty mica capacitors mounted on a glass fibre tag-board; it does not affect resonance on the other bands. On the CW-only end of 3.5MHz the capacitor can be 470pF or even replaced by a link.

"The 4:1 balun transformer T1 comprises 10 turns of 14AWG (16SWG) enamelled copper wire on an Amidon T200-2 core covered with a thin layer of PTFE plumbers' tape. Use an ATU on the WARC bands. On the non-WARC bands, the match can be near perfect with feeder balance and SWR particularly good on the 21 and 28MHz bands."

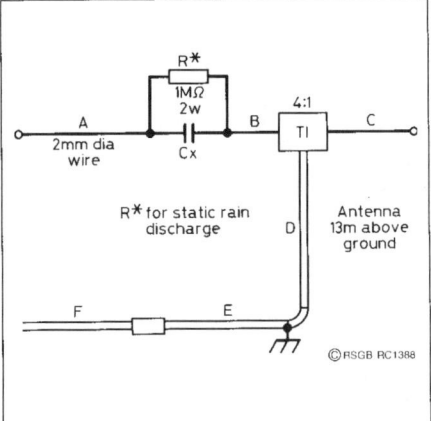

Fig 5: The 'Kent Windom' multiband off-centre-fed-dipole as used at GX3TRF and by amateurs in the Maidstone area of Kent. Dimensions as reported by G3ORP: Antenna formed from 12AWG aluminium wire: Section A = 20.8m; Section B = 3.048m; C = 17.754m. A + B + C = 41.6m. Coaxial cable D = 13.94m of RD213 (50Ω); E = 8.87m of RG62 (95Ω); F any length of 50Ω cable to rig. The antenna can be used as a Tee by strapping the feeder at the junction of coax sections D and E (useful on 1.8 and 10MHz bands).

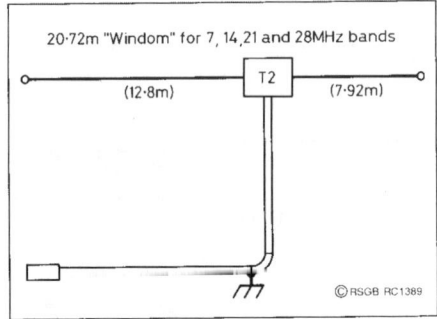

Fig 6: The 'Baby Kent Windom' for 7, 14, 21 and 28MHz bands. Do not run feeder parallel or close to antenna (drop it vertically at right angles to the element. T2 is 6:1 for 50Ω feeder and 4:1 for 75 or 93Ω feeder, wound on T200-2 core). Feeder balance and SWR are likely to be best on the 28MHz band.

Several readers, including Dale Gaudier, M0AOP/K4DG, and Don Elkington, G0PAN, have commented on K1POO's suggestions with particular respect to the difference between computer modelling and practical results in typical amateur locations, resulting from the limitations of some NEC-type programs.

Dale Gaudier, M0AOP/K4DG, writes: "The OCFD is regaining favour in amateur circles. With the advent of antenna modelling programs for personal computers, optimising an OCFD for four-band operation (40, 20, 15 and 10 metres) has become possible.

"The preferred design by K1POO, as reported in the March *TT*, comprised an overall length of 21.03m (68ft 5.5in) with the feedpoint located 17.4% (3.65m ie 11ft 10.5in) from one end: see March Fig 9 and Fig 11(c). The design has a nominal feed-point impedance of 200Ω so that it must be driven through a 4:1 balun to give a good match to a standard 50Ω coaxial feed-line.

"First, I modelled his design using the EZNEC Version 1.0 by Roy Lewallen, W7EL. Using K1POO's design criteria the free space SWR curves were a good match to those set forth in *TT* and Fig 11(c).

"I then built an antenna based on the 3.65m feed-point model. The dipole was constructed conventionally of 16SWG (1.628mm diameter) stranded copper wire mounted approximately 10m above ground. A 4:1 balun was inserted at the feed-point with RG-8X 50Ω coax used for the feed-line: **Fig 1**.

"The resonance and SWR of the antenna were then tested using an SWR analyser attached to the feed-line: see **Table 1**.

"Clearly the SWR minimum and the 2:1 SWR range for the 28MHz band were higher than desirable for an antenna whose purpose is to minimise the need for an ATU. However, the real puzzle was the lack of resonance anywhere near the 7MHz band! The SWR minimum around 8.5MHz was neither pronounced nor very deep, and certainly not what was predicted by computer modelling.

Band (MHz)	Frequency of Minimum SWR (Resonance) (MHz)	2:1 SWR Range (MHz)
7	approx 8.500	(SWR >> 3)
14	14.170	13.250-15.500
21	21.580	20.420-22.350
28	29.690	28.550-30.480

Table 1: Resonant frequencies and 2:1 SWR bandwidth of the OCFD

Band	Minima (MHz)	SWR at Minima	2:1 SWR Range (MHz)
7	7.000	1.1	6.850-7.220
14	14.100	1.2	13.520-14.420
21	21.220	1.1	20.420-22.340
28	28.340	1.4	27.460-29.050

Table 2: Measurements with the RF choke formed from coiling the RG-8X coaxial feed-line close to the feed-point and balun. Note: The 7MHz band minimum and SWR range can be raised by removing part of a turn of the RF choke.

Frequency (MHz)	R (ohms)	X (ohms)
7.05	314	+ 30
14.175	123	-23
21.225	99	-13
28.4	184	- 9

Table 3: Performance of the K1POO's improved OCFD antenna using NEC/NEC2D with true ground parameters and the dimensions given the impedance at the antenna input to the 450Ω twin feeder (21.262m electrical length) at 30ft height.

Reference point	Distance from feed point to cross arm (inches)	Cross-arm length (inches)
A	27.5	30.5
B	50	42.5
C	77	12.0

Table 4: Dimensions of 1.3GHz dual-rhomboid antenna of Fig 3.

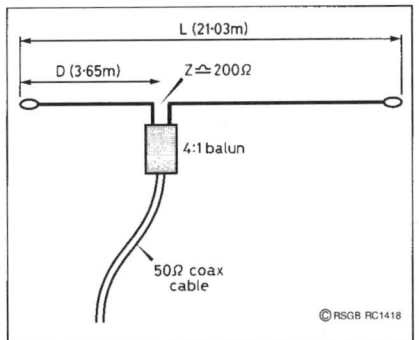

Fig 1: The K1POO-type Off Centre Fed Dipole design criteria for operation on 7, 14, 21 and 28MHz, as computer-simulated for free-space conditions. A practical version some 10m above ground failed to show a 7MHz resonance until an RF choke formed from five turns of the RG-8X coax with a diameter of 24cm was included close to the feed-point. With this addition, SWR ratios of not more than 1.5:1 were measured on all four bands.

"I tried pruning the two legs of the dipole: this only caused the 8.5MHz minimum to shift somewhat. Pruning did not produce an acceptable (<2:1 SWR) minimum anywhere in the 7MHz band; it also caused the SWR to worsen for the 14, 21 and 28MHz bands minima.

"It then occurred to me that the effects I was observing might be due to unequal currents flowing at the feed-point (possibly due to the asymmetrical design of the OCFD). I then made a simple RF choke by coiling several turns of the RG-8X feed-line close to the feed-point and balun. After some initial adjustments of the choke diameter and number of turns, I had my 7MHz band resonance! The coil comprised 5½ turns of RG-8X with a diameter of 24cm (9.5 inches). **Table 2** shows the results with the RF choke fitted.

M0AOP/K4DG concludes: "As apparent from Table 2, the OCFD design of K1POO is surprisingly broadbanded and, with a little adjustment, capable of covering virtually all of the 7, 14, 21 and 28MHz bands at 2:1 SWR or less without involving the use of an ATU. However, it appears that an RF choke - the need for which is not apparent from computer modelling - is necessary for this design to work on its fundamental frequency".

Don Elkington, G0PAN, has a special interest in computer modelling of antennas. He is critical of the findings of Ralph Holland, VK1BRH, in modelling horizontal dipoles above counterpoises (*TT*, January 1997, p61). He comments: "This added nothing to what has been well known for some time, ie how antenna height and ground affect feed and radiation characteristics. Had the modelling looked at the extent of ground screen required to achieve particular results it would perhaps have added something.

"To do this VK1BRH would have needed to use NEC2D, not plain NEC2, in order to model a sufficiently fine ground mesh (Result = bigger the screen, more reflection, lower the feed impedance).

"You referenced some time ago in *TT*, the work of R F Proctor in the Ministry of Supply (Signals Research & Development Establishment) which was VHF related, but which relied upon the classic work of Sommerfield and Renner.

In connection with K1POO's improved OCFD antenna (*TT*, March) using NEC/NEC2D with true ground parameters and the dimensions, **Table 3** shows the given impedance at the antenna input to the 450Ω twin feeder (21.262m electrical length) at 30ft height.

"NEC2/NEC2D can model any nearby conductive structure, as well as feedlines, networks, loads and conductor specifications. The following are some general notes on NEC modelling that need to be taken into account.

"The NEC code employs the Sommerfield and Renner approach to evaluating the effect of near ground on antenna characteristics. For those who want it, their 28-page paper was published in three issues of *Wireless Engineer* (1942) including the detailed mathematics. The issues are available at the British Library.

"The Lawrence Livermore National Laboratories (LLNL) in the USA incorporated their findings into NEC2/3/4 which now also covers modelling of antennas in insulated/buried media rather than plain air. LLNL also did work on ground penetrating imaging radar and the permitivity/permeability of various materials such as buried reinforced concrete. Numerical modelling topics can be found on the Internet at http://www.llnl.gov with other leading edge material such as Planetary Defence.

"NEC2D code allows larger models to be run than NEC with drawings of a variety of structures entered via digitisers.

"Nevertheless, I would raise a fundamental question about the modelling of amateur antennas at low heights: 'How do you know the nature of the ground below your antenna?' This will be frequency dependant and needs to be measured somehow. DC and 50Hz based techniques are probably wrong and errors will be significant."

UHF Dual-Rhomboid

Extracted from 'Technical Topics', *Radio Communication*, July 1997

UHF DUAL-RHOMBOID ANTENNA

ON MANY OCCASIONS, *TT* has drawn attention to the attractions of high-gain rhombic and long-wire vee antennas when scaled down to the more modest dimensions required on VHF/UHF. On HF, the fixed rhombic antenna long-ago earned the title of 'Queen of Antennas' but its size rules out its use by all but a tiny minority of amateurs. On UHF the dimensions are such that even a rotary rhombic-type beam becomes a practical proposition.

Recently, Terry Brown, G4TZB, was intrigued by a photograph published in the December 1996 *QST* of a dual-rhomboid antenna built by Dayton Johnson, W0OZI, for 1255MHz amateur television with a gain approaching

ANTENNA TOPICS

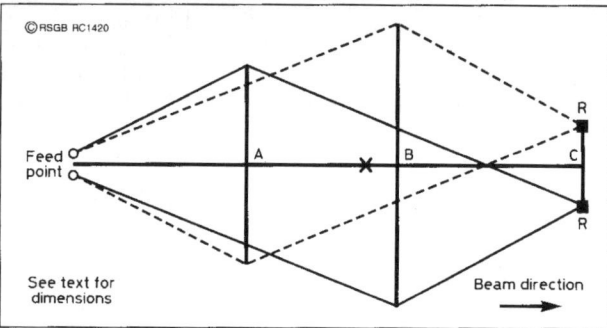

Fig 3: The 1.3GHz dual-rhomboid antenna which provides some 20dB gain with a boom about 8λ long. The longer sides of each rhomboid are 6λ and the shorter sides 3.5-λ. R marks the position of the 600Ω non-inductive termination resistors. See text for the non-critical dimensions of this broadband antenna.

20dBi. G4IZB was one of a number of amateurs who got in touch with W0OZI to find out more about his antenna which it transpires was based on a 20-year-old article by Bill Parker, W8DMR, 'Dual Rhombic for VHF-UHF' (*73 Magazine*, August 1977).

In view of the considerable interest, W0OZI provided detailed information on the antenna not only to G4IZB but also to Emil Pocock, W3EP, for his *QST* (March 1997) column 'The world above 50MHz'. The following brief notes are based on both sources.

W3EP writes: "The rhomboid (a parallelogram with no right angles and adjacent sides of unequal length) is not new to antenna design. It is a variation of the rhombic, which has been used for many decades to achieve high-gain, primarily on the HF bands. The dual-rhomboid achieves even higher gain than a traditional rhombic by combining two antennas in such a way that useful sidelobes are reinforced, while those in unwanted directions are cancelled... The configuration of wires and supports that constitutes the dual-rhomboid looks confusing at first glance, but a close inspection shows that the antenna is simply two identical wire rhomboids in the same plane, with one flipped over. The rhomboids are fed in parallel and terminated at their opposite ends with 600 to 800Ω non-inductive resistors."

W3EP gives the essential dimensions for the 1296MHz dual-rhomboid shown in **Fig 3**. He states that this provides about 20dBd gain with a total boom length of just under 6ft 6in and other dimensions as listed in **Table 4**. The longer sides of each rhomboid are six wavelengths; the shorter sides 3.5 wavelengths. A major bonus for this type of antenna is its broadband characteristics making dimensions relatively non-critical and the possibility of it being used on more than one band.

For a 432MHz version all dimensions should be multiplied by three, requiring a boom length of just under 20ft, making it easier on this band to implement the antenna as a fixed-beam rather than a rotary system. This would certainly be the case on 144MHz. For 1.3GHz about 30ft of wire is required, preferably not thinner than No 12 AWG. The boom and cross-pieces must be non-metallic with W0OZI recommending clear fir, protected by paint or other proactive coating. Wires should be insulated from each other where they cross over. W0OZI used five plexiglass insulators with 6-32 bolt nut terminators at either end to interface wires to terminating loads and his input balun.

The two 600Ω non-inductive terminating resistors (R) should be capable of dissipating at least one-quarter of the power input to the antenna. For example, five 2W carbon-composition resistors in parallel would be sufficient for 40W continuous power supplied to the antenna, or some 80W SSB or CW. If the wires are left open, without terminating resistors, the antenna becomes bi-directional which may be preferable for fixed VHF/UHF antennas. The element can be mounted in either a horizontal or vertical plane depending on the required polarisation. The centre of gravity is between points A and B (closer to B) with the exact point governed by the constructional techniques but easily found by balancing the completed element.

Since the input impedance to each rhomboid is about 600Ω, with the two in parallel, the antenna can be fed directly from 300Ω balanced twin ladder-line with a suitable ATU or 4:1 balun into 50Ω coaxial line for connection to the transmitter. Alternatively, a common half-wave balun made from 75Ω coaxial line at the antenna feed-point can transform the 300Ω balanced load of the antenna to 75Ω unbalanced line to permit 75Ω coaxial feed-line to be used. W0OZI used an effective quarter-wave sleeve balun using 3/8th inch diameter brass tubing.

Experimental Helical Vertical

Extracted from 'Technical Topics', *Radio Communication*, August 1997

EXPERIMENTS WITH A HELICAL-WOUND VERTICAL

EVER SINCE THE early 1930s, it has been accepted that vertical HF antennas are likely to prove variable in performance, significantly affected by site factors. These include the local earth constants, the efficiency of the earthing system (buried earth mats, radials or counterpoise), and the proximity of surrounding objects to which there may be strong mutual coupling, resulting in absorption or re-radiation. All this implies that not only may the overall results vary greatly when a given type of vertical antenna is used at different sites, but also that virtually any resonant antenna, vertically or horizontally polarised, usually requires careful tweaking if it is to achieve its full potential.

One recalls the controversy that in the 1950s surrounded the short 'Joystick' helically wound antenna, made and sold in fairly large numbers in the UK by G3VFA. Some of those who purchased the antenna swore by it; many others swore at it.

Things have moved on since then. Antenna manufacturers, on the whole, strive to design, produce and market reliable products, even if at times they tend to over-emphasise the SWR performance or gain or the results likely to be achieved without further tweaking.

An interesting recent design is the Chelcom CA HFV1 helically wound vertical antenna. This has two fibreglass sections (each 2.74m in length) plus two alternative whip sections (to adjust the resonant frequency) which can provide a 3.5MHz resonant quarter-wave antenna with an overall height of just 7m (23 ft). No tuning unit is required for part of the 3.5MHz band and it is claimed that the antenna can be used on other HF bands provided a suitable ASTU is employed. A favourable two-page review of this antenna by John Heys, G3BDQ, appeared in *Practical Wireless* (April 1997, pp21-22).

John Brodzky, G3HQX, writes: "I have for some time been using a Chelcom 3.5MHz vertical antenna Model HFV1. This is helically wound and comes in two 10ft sections that screw together. There are also 23in and 51in rods, either of which is intended to be installed at the top as a whip for use at the HF or LF end of the band.

"My experiences have not worked out quite as expected. My findings agree neither with the *PW* review nor with the specification sheet provided by Lowe who market this antenna in the UK. Lowe show a response across the 3.5MHz band of around 3:1 with a minimum of about 1.25:1 at 3640kHz. G3BDQ suggests an SWR of 4:1 at 3500kHz reducing to 1:1 at 3800kHz, he also gives SWR figures for 10, 14, 21, 24 and 28MHz bands. Chelcom consider it a single-band (3.5MHz) antenna, although Lowe suggest it is good also for 14 and 28MHz.

"When I first had the antenna, I found that at my site both whips were too long. Instead I used an 11.5in rod and achieved good results using just four radials. I have since installed eight radials ranging from 68ft to 44ft and plan to install at least two more.

"I did not find it possible to obtain a good match on 14MHz and decided to try using a close-coupled resonator as described for wire dipoles by Gary Breed, K9AY, (*TT*, June 1995, pp67-69 and October 1995, p78). Rather to my surprise it worked, although the 14MHz resonator needed to be just under 12ft long, rather than the 16ft that I had expected. I used some aluminium rods which were on hand, varying from 0.75in to

1990 - 1999

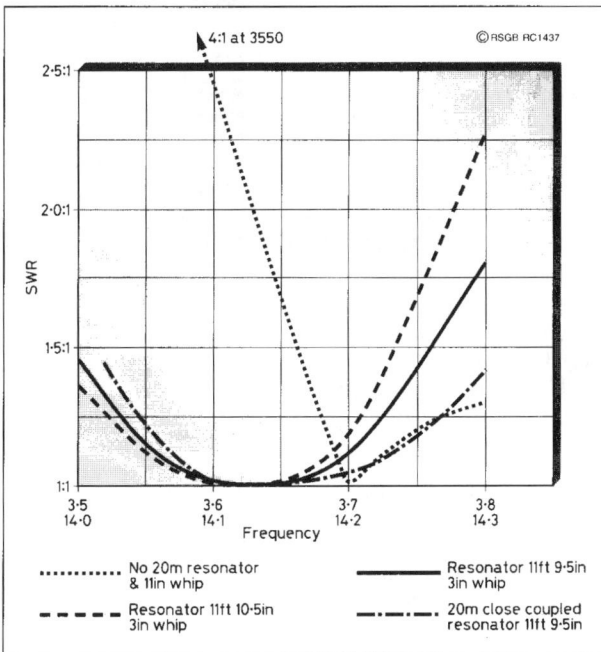

Fig 5: SWR measurements by G3HQX on his HFV1 helical wound vertical antenna showing effect of adding a close-coupled 14MHz resonator.

0.5in diameter and spaced them from the HFV1 using empty 35mm film canisters, secured using plastic adhesive tape. There is no electrical connection to the 'resonator'.

"I have now been using this modified 3.5/14MHz antenna for about six months. I find it works well on both bands. On 3.5MHz SSB I worked VK, ZL, four VE districts, for W districts, JA, PY, LU, TI, VP2, YN; all W call areas except 7 and 3.5MHz CW. On 14MHz there is not much that I hear that I cannot work.

"But, for me, the bonus is that I achieve a low SWR right across both bands: see **Fig 5**. It appears that the introduction of the close-coupled 'resonator' has loaded the vertical in such a way that the system has become much lower-Q and hence has a markedly greater resonant bandwidth. On 14MHz, I have been using a 11ft 10.5in 'resonator', recently reduced by one inch to improve the SWR at the HF end of the European 3.5 to 3.8MHz band.

"I feed the antenna with a 50m length of 50Ω coaxial cable; this is slightly more than I need so I have coiled up the surplus at the base of the antenna, forming a coil of nine turns of approximately 14 - 15in diameter. This is presumably acting as a form of choke balun (or rather unun).

"The SWR readings were taken at the base of the antenna, using a simple L-section matching device at the transmitter to ensure maximum power transfer.

"It all seems too good to be true, but it certainly works. Whether it would be exactly reproducible at other sites must be left to others to find out. Meanwhile, I hope to continue experimenting with this rewarding system."

[The close-up rod appears to lower the Q of the HFV1 rather than form a resonator in the K9AY sense - *G3VA*.]

Drooping (Inv-V) G5RV Analysed

Extracted from 'Technical Topics', *Radio Communication*, August 1997

VE2CV ANALYSES THE DROOPING (INV-V) G5RV

FOR SOME 50 years a popular multiband antenna has been the G5RV system developed by Louis Varney, G5RV, in the immediate post-war era. After enjoying widespread use in Europe, in recent years it has also come to the fore as a simple wire antenna in North America. The original full-size 31.1m centre-fed dipole version was developed before the 21MHz band was released to amateurs and it has normally been essential to use an ASTU on that band, and preferably on other bands. A few years ago, Dr Brian Austin, G0GSF/ZS6AKW, presented an improved version - made possible by computer simulations - taking 21MHz into account (see, for example, *TT*, January 1993).

On the other side of the Atlantic, Dr John (Jack) Belrose, VE2CV, has, over several years, criticised some aspects of the G5RV particularly when used in the drooping dipole (inverted vee) configuration (see for example *ARRL Antenna Compendium Volume 4*). This has tended to upset some amateurs who have told VE2CV "the G5RV is a great antenna and you should not be critical of it". In reply, VE2CV admits that he has commented at times adversely on the method of feed and the difficulty of achieving resonance in several amateur bands. But his main criticism is concerned with its use in the drooping dipole configuration.

In response to a recent enquiry from Bob Ackman, VE6RI, Dr Belrose replied: "Yes, I have modelled this dipole in the drooping dipole configuration over a larger range of variable (droop and frequency) than in my *Antenna Compendium Vol 4* article . . . In **Table 1**, the reference angle A is the included angle between the arms of the dipole. The bracketed () number following the maximum gain figure (in dBi taking into account the ground image) is the elevation angle for maximum gain (take-off angle). The antenna is modelled for an apex at 15.24m (50ft) over average ground. The computer code is NEC-2, considered to be the industry standard for simple wire antennas. For 'grounded' antennas one has to use NEC-4.

"The dipole gain is a maximum for the horizontal configuration (A=180°) but maximum gain is not necessarily in the broadside direction for frequencies at or above 14MHz. The azimuthal pattern becomes lobed. In the drooping configuration, the gain is reduced, and for A=90° the performance is particularly poor on the 14MHz band, *the band on which G5RV wanted his antenna to work best*. This is because not only is the gain lower, but the elevation angle for maximum gain is increased, and increased significantly. On the higher bands, most amateurs want to work DX and seek a low take off angle. The take off angle for the horizontal configuration changes with frequency in about the right way. That is unless you (like me) wants to work coast-to-coast on the 3.5MHz band.

"If I calculate the gain as a function of frequency at the corresponding take off angle for the horizontal configuration, the gain in the drooping configuration is poor. The gain difference (drooping compared with horizontal) increases with increase in frequency and decrease in A as referenced in the square-bracketed numbers in Table 1.

"I fail to understand the popularity of the multi-band inverted-V. For years our Handbooks stated that the optimum angle A was between 90° and 110°, but now it is stated that A should be greater than 90° (optimum angle is 180°).

"But all this relates to horizontal and drooping dipoles supported by a tree limb or wooden mast, and fed with a balanced transmission line. The G5RV type of feed - balanced feeder with connecting coax usually without a balun since baluns do not perform very well when

Freq (MHz)	A = 180°	A = 130°	A = 115°	A = 90°
3.75	5.97 (90)	5.13 (90) [5.13]	4.66 (90) [4.66]	3.65 (90) [3.65]
7.15	6.7 (39)	5.7 (48) [5.49]	5.2 (51) [4.88]	4.11 (55) [3.61]
10.15	9.74 (27)	7.4 (35) [6.98]	6.33 (38) [5.67]	4.23 (43) [3.1]
14.15	8.21 (19)	5.26 (21) [5.21]	7.11 (49) [3.16]	6.26 (64) [0.68]
21.15	10.11 (13)	7.97 (17) [7.37]	6.59 (18) [5.71]	2.44 (11) [2.26]
29.0	10.25 (9)	7.87 (11) [7.8]	6.83 (12) [6.15]	3.44 (12) [2.86]

Table 1: Gain dBi (and take-off angle) for a 31.1m multiband dipole versus drooping angle (A).

ANTENNA TOPICS

working into a mismatched load - can result in the conducting tower, or the coax itself (current on the outer surface of the shield) becoming at some frequencies an important part of the antenna system.

"In my files, I have a letter from an amateur reporting that when a balun was added to his drooping G5RV system, the ability to work DX on 14MHz went the way of the birds. Clearly, for this amateur, his metal support tower and/or coax was acting as part of the antenna system. I can include a tower, and the effect of an unbalanced coaxial feeder in my modelling, but this is all very geometry sensitive, and dependent also on how effectively the tower/and or coax is 'grounded'. The effects of re-radiation may be small, but only providing there are no resonances in the grounded conductors associated with the antenna system, in which case re-radiation can be dominant."

It seems possible that these criticisms of the inverted-vee configuration would apply to the G0GSF/ZS6AKW versions and indeed to other drooping dipole antennas, although clearly this configuration has the advantage of requiring only one high support mast.

Tetrahedral Dipole Antenna

Extracted from 'Technical Topics', *Radio Communication*, September 1997

TETRAHEDRAL DIPOLE ANTENNA

THESE DAYS THE bulk of effort by the professional antenna engineers is directed towards satellite, UHF, microwave and gigahertz antennas. Conversely, relatively little attention is given to HF with the exception of improved near-vertical-incidence-systems for mobile units. Therefore, it was with something like relief that I came across a paper presented last April at the '10th International Conference on Antennas & Propagation' (ICAP97 - *IEE Conference Publication No 436*, pp 1.428 - 1.430) describing a novel HF antenna that could have promise for amateur as well as professional applications.

This is the 'Tetrahedral Antenna', invented by Alan Boswell and Barry Peters of the GEC-Marconi Research Centre (UK Patent GB 230.2990 granted February 1997). Basically, it is a development of the centre-fed biconical dipole, but using a spaceframe made from 12 metal tubes with good RF conductivity (copper or aluminium alloy etc) in the form of two regular tetrahedrons mounted one above the other with their apexes separated by an insulated platform into which three tubes are fixed on each side: see **Fig 1**. The self-supporting framework is held in place either by insulated rods or by insulated halyards (**Fig 2**) made from non-stretchable plastic rope etc.

A tetrahedron is a pyramid with four trian-

The Bent Dipole

Extracted from 'Technical Topics', *Radio Communication*, August 1997

THE BENT DIPOLE

THE HORIZONTAL RESONANT half-wave dipole centre-fed from coaxial cable remains probably the most popular HF wire antenna. It is capable of providing near 100 per cent radiation efficiency, is relatively easy to adjust and if erected in the clear and with the feeder descending vertically can be relied upon to work well without an ATU or balun. But in these days of small gardens, it may prove difficult to provide a half-wave span even on 14MHz, more often on 10 or 7MHz, and normally on 3.5 or 1.8MHz.

Nizar Mullani, K0NM, ('The Bent Dipole' *QST*, May 1997, pp56-57) uses NEC-2 computer simulation to show that surprisingly little radiation efficiency is lost, and matching to 50Ω coax may be improved, when the ends are bent down by up to about 40% of its length; even when half the dipole element is bent down, radiation may be reduced by only about 0.6dB providing that the horizontal portion is at a reasonable height above ground: see **Figs 6** and **7**. The radiation pattern is also relatively little affected, although the vertical take-off angle may be raised and the SWR bandwidth reduced a little.

As K0NM puts it: "Don't be afraid to bend your dipole antennas if you're cramped for space."

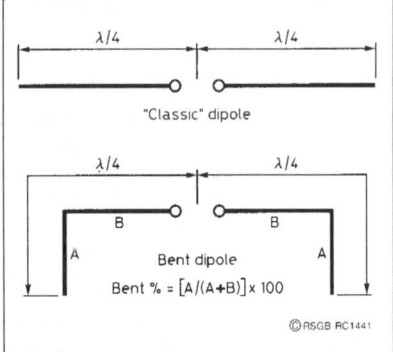

Fig 6: Comparison of a half-wave dipole with a level horizontal span and a bent dipole. The total length of the bent dipole is one-half wavelength and the percentage of bend is defined by the ratio of A divided by A+B.

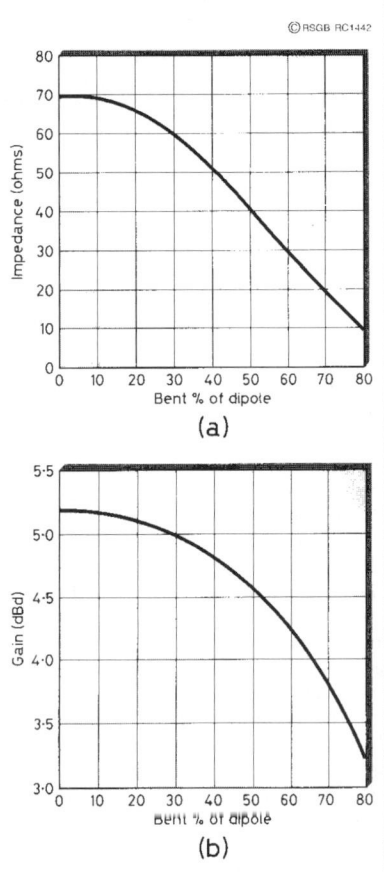

Fig 7: (a) Bent dipole feed-point impedance as a function of the percentage of bend, assuming a height of one-half wave above ground. There will be some variation of feed-point impedance at other heights. (b) Gain of the bent dipole (including ground image) as a function of the percentage of bending. 50 per cent bending reduces the span to 50 per cent of a dipole without bending.

gular faces; a regular tetrahedron has all four faces in the form of equilateral triangles. The tetrahedrons are substituted for the cones of the biconical antenna. By making all edges conductive, the dimensions of the dipole are further reduced. In the Marconi prototype all four tubes are 2.9m in length, and the resonant frequency is approximately 22.5MHz. The height of each tetrahedron is just over 2.1m, making the overall height approximately 4.2m,

roughly similar to that of a 22.5MHz quarter-wave monopole. The structure can be stood on insulating spacers (E) raising the low base a few inches above ground. It was also tried raised about 0.5m above ground in which case the frequency of minimum return loss (ie resonant frequency) rose to 26.1MHz, an increase of 16%. Constructional methods can be varied to reflect whether the antenna is to be fixed or needs to be readily dismantled for

1990 - 1999

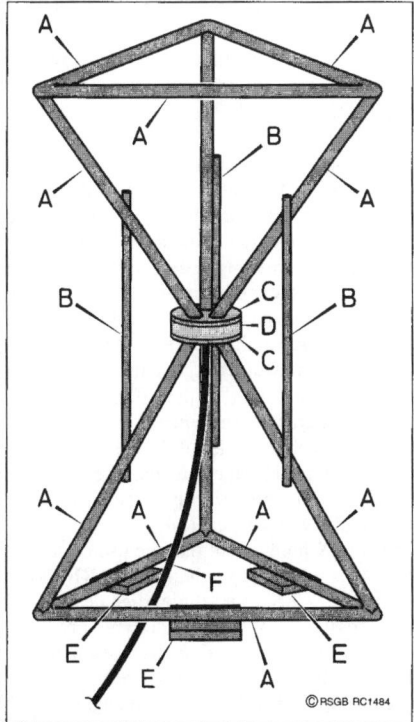

Fig 1: Initial implementation of the GEC-Marconi Tetrahedral vertical antenna - a novel form of the classic centre-fed biconical - to provide a self-supporting dipole antenna with good bandwidth characteristics, permitting operation on several amateur bands and not requiring an earth connection. The height of the 'dipole' is roughly the equivalent of a quarter-wave monopole antenna. A = 12 metal (eg alloy or copper) tubes of equal length (2.9m in the Marconi prototype) forming two skeletal regular tetrahedrons. B = 3 rigid insulated supports holding the structure in shape. C-D-C central sandwich of two metal plates (C) separated by insulated layer (D). E = 3 support blocks insulating the element from earth (about 0.1m height). F = coaxial feeder (preferably 75 ohms impedance).

easy transportation and erection on site.

The prototype antenna was made with two small conductive plates at the centre of which the six tubes are attached (for example, by means of a flattened end to the tubes as in **Fig 3**), with three to each plate with the plates separated by an insulated centre to form a 'sandwich' (C-D-C in Fig 1 or see the enlarged drawing of Fig 3). A coaxial connector may be mounted on the lower plate with its inner conductor connected via braiding to the

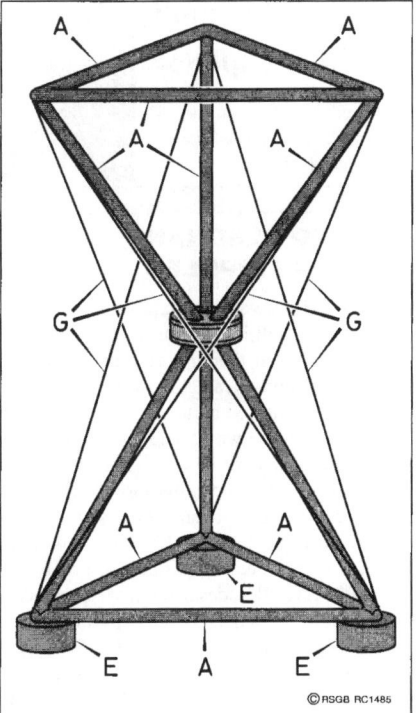

Fig 2: Second implementation (on which the IEE paper was based) in which the rigid supports are replaced with six halyards (G) of insulated, non-stretchable rope etc). 0.1m support blocks (E) are now at the corners.

upper plate as shown. The coax feeder is attached and should hang vertically downwards and then run horizontally along the ground. In this way, any currents induced in the outer surface of the coax will decay rapidly in the horizontal run.

The tetrahedral dipole antenna has a bandwidth of around 35% for an SWR of less than 2:1 (return loss more than 9.54dB) when fed with 75Ω coax-cable (less with 50Ω cable) compared with roughly 10% or less for typical vertical dipoles or monopoles of equivalent element diameter: see **Fig 4**. At 22.5MHz the measured input impedance of the Marconi prototype was

68-j14Ω with the antenna in the normal position, and 42-j32Ω when raised 0.5m above ground.

It should thus be possible to use this antenna on all bands from 14 to 24MHz with the simplest of ATUs or a broadband 50-to-75 **ohm** matching transformer at the transceiver end of the feeder. By adding a series inductance of 1μH, the resonant frequency of the prototype was lowered to 15.5MHz with a 9.5dB return-loss bandwidth of 2.7MHz: see **Fig 79**. The broad bandwidth of the antenna means that dimensions are far less critical than for a conventional dipole.

The motive for developing this antenna was to provide an easily transportable and erectable self-supporting (no mast) antenna for HF radars sited on beaches, but it is also suitable for communications. Some readers may have recognised that Alan Boswell holds the amateur callsign G3NOQ. In his IEE paper he reports that "the antenna was used for two-way contacts with several countries on all amateur bands from 7 to 24MHz".

It will be appreciated that, as with any non-expired patented design, it would not be possible for an amateur radio version of the tetrahedral antenna to be marketed commercially without a licence from GEC-Marconi. But this does not prevent any amateur from building and testing such antennas on an experimental basis.

In his paper, Alan Boswell provides an illuminating comparison between vertical dipoles and monopoles, applicable to all such antennas and not merely his tetrahedral design. Although the conventional vertical dipole does not depend on a low-loss earth connection or ground plane, it requires double the height of a ground-mounted monopole. The tetrahedral antenna provides the combined advantages of the monopole (small height) and the dipole (no wires in the ground).

Tubes at the base and at the top can be joined in various ways, for example by welding for a fixed structure, by flattened ends joined by nuts and bolts or by plumbers joints etc.

Ground losses occur for both dipoles and monopoles, but overall the dipole is superior to the extent that it is possible to dispense

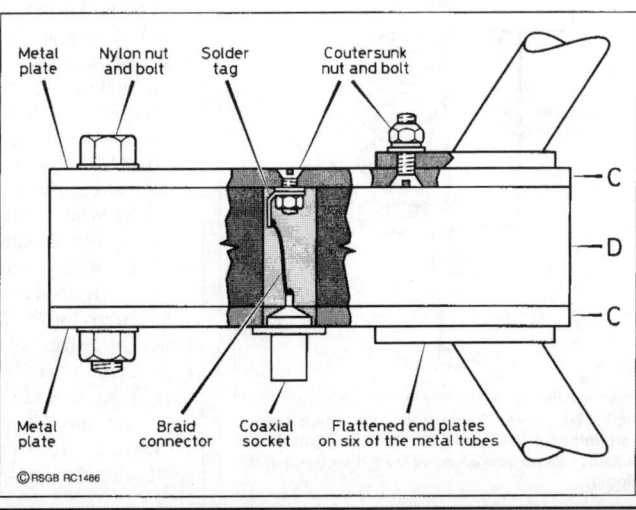

Fig 3: Detail of a section of the centre 'sandwich' showing how the antenna is fed and how six of the tubes are fastened to the metal plates (C) with flattened ends and countersunk nuts and bolts.

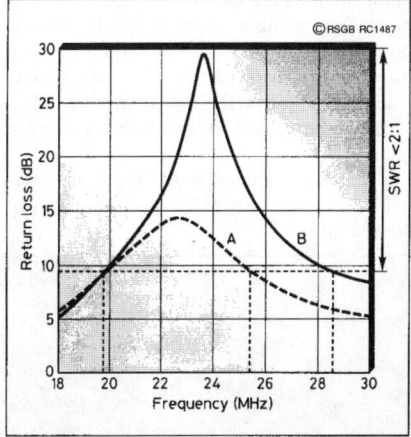

Fig 4: Measured return loss of the antenna with A 50Ω and B 75Ω coaxial cable. A return loss greater than 9.54dB represents an SWR of less than 2:1.

347

ANTENNA TOPICS

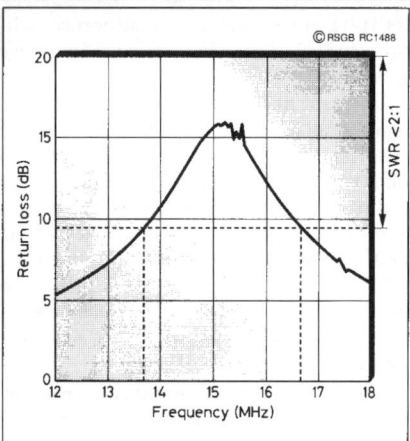

Fig 5: Measured return loss of the antenna with series coil (1uH) lowering resonant frequency but decreasing bandwidth.

altogether with an earth mat although in the absence of good ground conductivity it may still be an advantage to use an earth mat or buried radials in order to improve the low-angle radiation. The absence of a direct earth connection may result in a small loss of gain, but a monopole would undoubtedly suffer a severe loss of gain without an effective earth mat. Radiation efficiency of the antenna itself has been shown to be approximately 100% although there will inevitably be some ground losses and possible absorption in nearby structures etc.

It should be noted that as with any vertical dipole close to ground, there will be high RF voltages at the base as well as potentially strong RF radiation (although this will be less than with a ground mounted monopole). Care should always be taken to ensure that there is no danger to children, adults or pets.

This antenna should function effectively when mounted on the ground via short insulating supports, and form an effective low-angle non-critical DX radiator for 18, 21 and 24MHz and give reasonable results on the 14 and 28MHz bands. However, results would be further improved if mounted at a height (possibly with slightly longer sides to the tetrahedrons to lower the resonant frequency). One way of achieving this would be to mount the antenna securely on a flat roof or similar high platform; the skeletal framework which could be made from lightweight alloy tubes should minimise wind resistance. It would be relatively easy to carry the tubes and the central 'sandwich' up to a flat roof or elevated platform in dismantled form and then assemble them.

The patent notes that the tetrahedral antenna can form part of an antenna array (eg phased array).

End-fed Resonant Feedline Dipoles

Extracted from 'Technical Topics', *Radio Communication*, September 1997

END-FED RESONANT FEEDLINE DIPOLES

ONE OF THE rewarding features of *TT* is that some items stimulate further comments and suggestions from readers; at times it seems that the column is able to draw upon the collective memories as well as the practical experiences of the world-wide amateur-radio community. Two examples of such follow-up comments can be cited this month. Roberto Craighero, I1ARZ, exercises his excellent memory to add to the June 1977, p63-64, item on 'Resonant feedline dipoles'; and Chas Reynolds, GW3JPT, describes his experiences with double-wound coaxial traps (see 'Improved multiband trap dipole' *TT*, February 1997, pp70-71).

I1ARZ felt there was something vaguely familiar about the resonant feedline dipole based on the *QST* (July 1996) article by Al

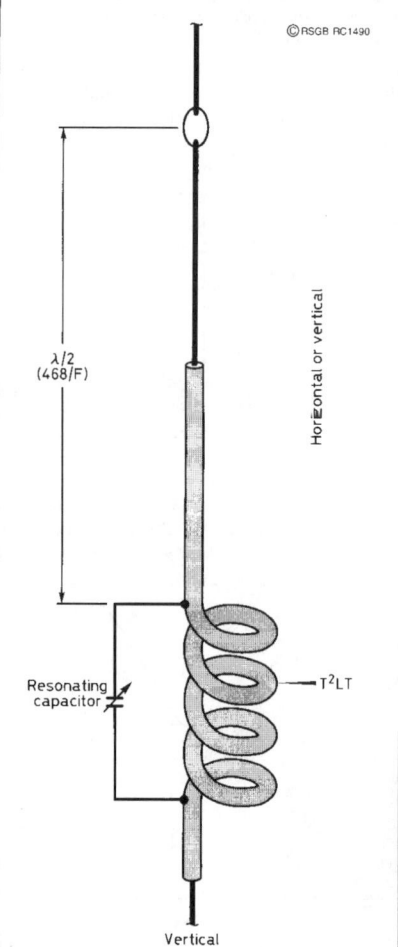

Fig 7: The end-fed dipole antenna in which a tuned transmission line trap (T2LT) is inserted in the coaxial cable a quarter-wave from the centre of the dipole.

Burton, W8NX. A check of his collection of *73 Magazine* confirmed that an article 'New dipole feeder – tuned feeders, yet!' by A F Stahler, AA6AX, appeared in the June 1978 issue making use of his earlier article on what he termed the 'T2LT' (Tuned Transmission Line Trap): **Figs 7** and **8**.

In his case, the line trap was tuned to resonance (high Q) with the aid of a variable capacitor across the coaxial coil formed by coiling up a few turns in the feeder cable: see Fig 7. The number of turns should be kept low by using a large capacitance. The higher the Q the more efficient the dipole (but the narrower the useful bandwidth). Again, the technique is to use the outer braid of the cable beyond the trap as a quarter-wave element while the inner conductor and the inner of the braid provides the current feed for the antenna. The length of the feeder before the trap should, at least theoretically, not be critical.

AA6AX pointed out that the use of such a high-Q resonant trap rather than an RF choke (as in the W8NX and the earlier designs of end-fed dipoles of this general type) provides superior performance since it copes with the considerable difference between the end impedance of half-wave dipoles fed against real rather than ideal earth.

In practice, AA6AX used his system as an end-fed 14MHz vertical dipole for QRP operation (2W HW-7 transceiver) and from the photographs appears to have used a fairly conventional variable capacitor. Presumably, for QRO operation this would need to have the vanes spaced more widely to avoid RF arcing. As a vertical dipole this antenna does not depend on radials or an earth mat, making it a good choice for portable operation.

GW3JPT as 'Beacon Traps' of Welshpool (see *Product News*, April 1996, p57) has been supplying amateurs with pairs of high-quality 7MHz traps together with a rain-proof dipole centre-piece to enable amateurs to build their own W3DZZ/G8KW multiband trap dipoles.

He writes: "I was very interested in the details given in *TT* of the double-wound coaxial traps. Over the years I have made various versions of dipole traps, and finally - a couple of years ago - settled on the form of construction illustrated in the 1996 New Products item. The coaxial coil is fully enclosed and the connections brought out via stainless steel bolts. There is also an extra hole for use with loopback and the shape was designed so that water did not collect in the end and gave extra thickness for fixings.

"Having studied the details given in *TT* I made up two double-wound coils with RG58 for 5.16MHz and put up the antenna as an inverted-vee. The results proved much as detailed by W8NX. The traps used a larger size pipe but were constructed in much the same way as that shown in the February Fig 6.

"I then decided to make up a pair of double-wound traps for 7.00MHz using RG58 and the larger pipe size. Again, as for the 5.16MHz traps, they showed a big improvement of 'Q' over single-wound traps. The 3:1 SWR readings were only 50kHz apart with an SWR of 1:1 in the centre. This compares with 150kHz apart with the single wound coils. **Table 1**

Freq	SWR	Freq	SWR	Freq	SWR	Freq	SWR	Freq	SWR
3.5	3.1	7.0	2.1	14-15	3.1	20.5	1.2	28.0	2.5
3.55	1.7	7.05	1.2			21.0	1.7	29.0	1.7
3.6	1.1	7.1	1.2			21.45	2.5	30.0	2.1
3.65	1.5	7.3	3.1			21.9	3.1		
3.7	1.6								
3.75	2.5								
3.8	3.1								

Table 1: SWR readings on horizontal dipole using double-wound 7.0MHz coaxial traps. Frequency in MHz.

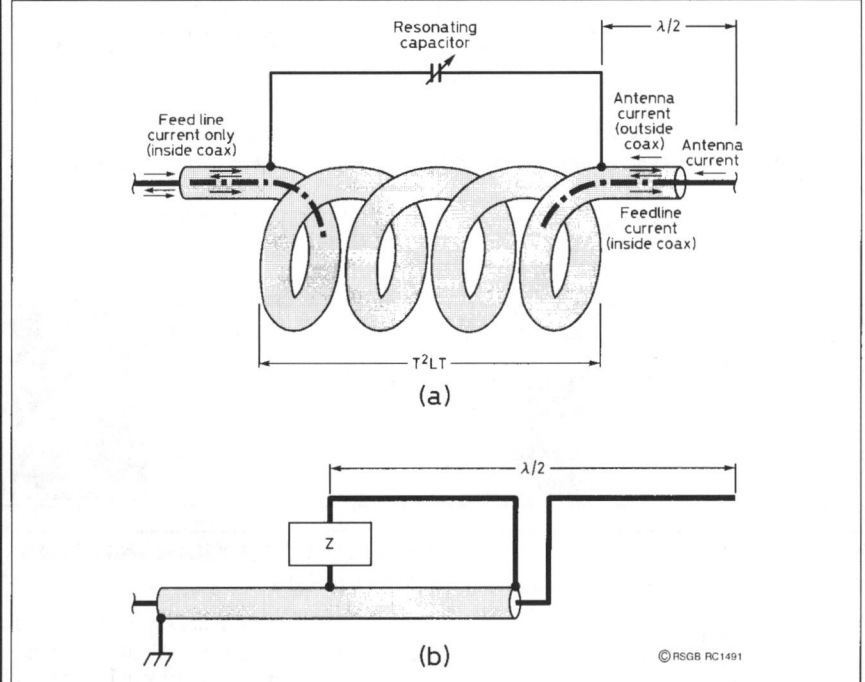

Fig 8: (A) Current distribution in the T2LT trap with a standing-wave formed on the outer-braid of the coax while the inner of the braid carries the low-impedance drive current. (B) Equivalent configuration.

apart with the single wound coils. **Table 1** shows the SWR readings taken on a horizontal trap dipole with an SWR Analyser."

Two for the Price of One

Extracted from 'Technical Topics', *Radio Communication*, October 1997

TWO FOR THE PRICE OF ONE

JOHN BRODZKY, G3HQX, has added some further notes to his "experiments with a helical-wound vertical" (*TT*, August 1997, p78) in which he showed how he had been able to obtain improved SWR bandwidth on both 3.5MHz and 14MHz for a Chelcom HFV1 helical wound vertical monopole antenna by adding a second 'resonator' 12ft rod element closely spaced (although not electrically connected). He points out that, "the main difference between the K9AY approach and my experience seems to be that the driven element in my case could be considered as a long inductance, and hence the amount of coupling

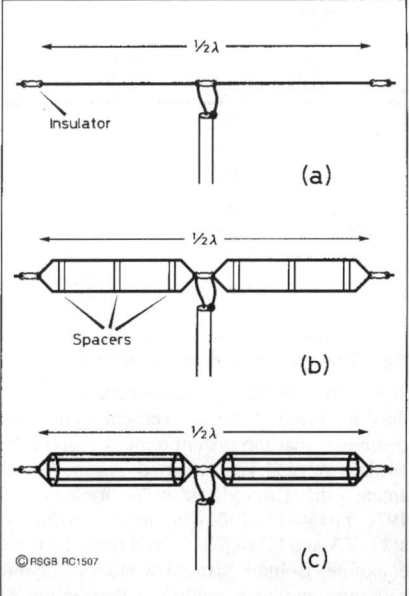

Fig 3: (a) Conventional single-wire half-wave dipole antenna. (b) Use of twin wires increases bandwidth. (c) Multiple-wire 'caged dipole' that can result in broadband operation over about an octave.

between it and the added element could be expected to be considerably greater. I have measured the capacitance between the two elements as some 120pF.

"I would speculate that under these conditions, the resonant frequencies of both 'elements' are modified and could account for the very short length of the 14MHz 'resonator'. My guess is that both the resonant frequency and the Q of each element are altered by the mutual coupling.

"That the added element has a direct influence on the main helically-wound element was demonstrated when I reduced the 'resonator' length by one inch to 11ft 9½ in. The SWR at 3800kHz increased from 1.35:1 to 1.45:1, thus shifting its response upwards in frequency, when measured at the base of the antenna. Using a rather insensitive GDO, I have attempted to find the resonant frequency of the added element although the close coupling to the main element makes this difficult. I do obtain a shallow dip around 27.89MHz."

It would seem worth recalling that the bandwidth of a conventional half-wave is related to the diameter of the wire or rod and can be increased by using twin closely spaced wires. This is usually done in the form of the 'folded dipole' with the feed impedance of one wire increased to about 300Ω. But in years past, before the development of the folded dipole by Dr Kraus, W8JK, it was quite common to break and centre feed two or more wires: see **Fig 3**. In its multiple wire form, it became the 'caged dipole' or the 'biconical dipole' or 'conical monopole'.

With valve transmitters there was little advantage to be obtained by reducing the SWR much less than 5:1 (see 'Persistent SWR Myths' based on the writings of Walter Maxwell, W2DU, *TT*, December 1992, pp31-32). So, a single wire dipole would work satisfactorily across any of the European HF amateur bands, and the twin-wire dipole fell into disuse. It is important to remember that the usual formula for resonance length is intended for use with elements having length/diameter ratio of over 1000. The resonant length of 'fat dipoles' is significantly less but the low-SWR bandwidth greater. It was the coming of the solid-state power amplifier with the need to guard against excessive SWRs, that brought about protection circuits that often begin to reduce transmitter power automatically when the SWR at its output socket rises to more than about 1.5:1. Rather surprisingly, the twin-wire dipole has not been resurrected except to a limited degree in such forms as the broadband, resistance-loaded 'Australian dipole'.

However, as the experiences of G3HQX and also Steve Ford, WB8IMY, ('Two for the price of one' *QST*, July 1997, pp56-57) show, the presence of a second closely coupled non-resonant element, whether electrically connected or not, can result in improved bandwidth.

The prime aim of WB8IMY was to add a 50MHz capability to an existing 14MHz wire-dipole antenna by using the well-tested arrangement of simply adding a 50MHz element connected to the same feed-point as the 14MHz wire: **Fig 4**. Before adding the new

ANTENNA TOPICS

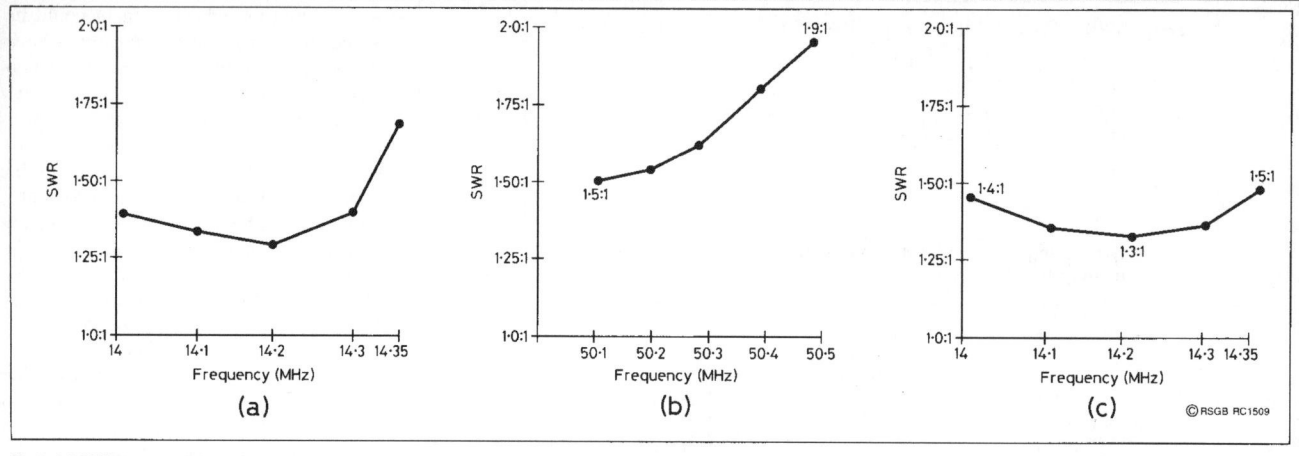

Fig 5: (a) SWR curve of the 14MHz dipole before the 50MHz addition. (b) Final SWR curve on 50MHz after trimming. (c) Improved 14MHz SWR curve after addition of the 50MHz element.

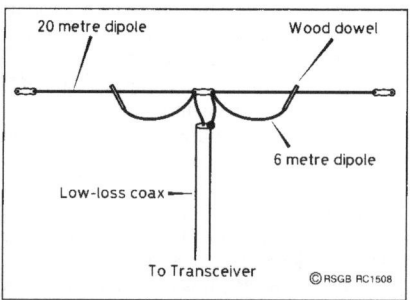

Fig 4: WB8IMY's combined 14 and 50MHz dipole.

element, WB8IMY plotted the SWR of his existing 14MHz wire: **Fig 5**. After adding and resonating the new element to 50.1MHz, the SWR plot on 14MHz was significantly improved: Fig 5(b). The SWR on the 50MHz was also satisfactory: Fig 5(c).

WB8IMY provides some pertinent constructional advice: "Never, ever, cut a wire dipole to the exact length the formula dictates. That's the first step on the road to Looneyville. The purpose of the formula is to get you in the ballpark... that adage should be carved in granite. Always cut your wires with a generous surplus of length to anticipate the trimming that must surely come later. With that in mind, I added about 12 inches to my calculation (6 additional inches for each wire)... The next challenge was keeping the 6 and 20 metre dipoles separated from each other. I needed something mechanically sturdy that could stand up to a stiff nor'easter. It also had to be aesthetically pleasing... I opted for thin wood dowels (each about one foot in length) treated with preservative. I passed the antenna wires twice through small holes drilled in each end. You might use strips of plastic or what is at hand or a multiple-spacer scheme to keep the 50MHz dipole parallel to the wire above it. Using extremely stiff wire would probably help."

Here & There: Carolina Windom

Extracted from 'Technical Topics', *Radio Communication*, October 1997

HERE & THERE

JOHN BRODZKY, G3HQX, draws attention to a novel form of 3.5MHz OCFD antenna, known as the 'Carolina Windom' which is apparently being quite widely used for DX operation. **Fig 9** shows the basic outline, a half-wave horizontal wire fed off-centre through a 4:1 balun from a 23ft vertical section of 75Ω coaxial cable, which is then isolated by a choke wound on a ferrite rod or ring from the 50Ω coaxial transmission line. G3HQX believes that the DX capability of this antenna arises

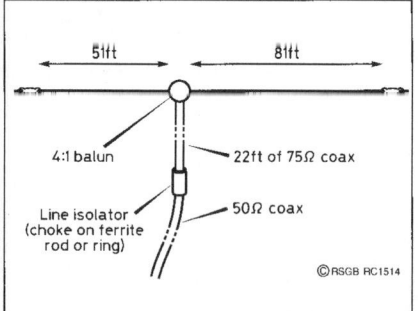

Fig 9: The 'Carolina Windom' antenna for 3.5MHz.

largely from vertically-polarised radiation from the outer braid of the 23ft vertical section. He comments that the system reminds him of the 14MHz vertical-Tee (inverted, ground-plane) antenna that I introduced in *TT* back in July 1970, pp450-451 following its successful use at G3VA and G3HQX, derived from the more elaborate 'Bobtail' array. I wonder if anyone can refer me to a published description of exactly how this antenna functions and who and where it was originated? 'Carolina Window' antennas are marketed in the UK by Haydon Communications.

Tuned Loops for Transmitting

Extracted from 'Technical Topics', *Radio Communication*, November 1997

TUNED LOOP TRANSMITTING ANTENNAS

IT IS EXACTLY 30 years since *TT* reported (November 1967, pp732-733) the development at the US Army Limited War Laboratory of an efficient 2-5MHz octagonally-shaped (eight 5ft tubes) transmitting loop antenna for use in the jungles of Vietnam. This was claimed as "usually doing as good a job as a full-length half-wave dipole 40ft above ground".

It was this development, soon taken up by amateurs, military and diplomatic HF users throughout the world, on which all the many subsequent compact transmitting loops have been based. It was emphasised that in order to overcome the extremely low radiation resistance of electrically small loops it was essential to reduce the RF ohmic resistance to a very low figure and to minimise losses in coupling RF into the loop. For HF diplomatic links, commercial models using copper tubing of up to about 6in diameter were used, with vacuum-type tuning capacitors. Amateur designs were soon increasingly based on the use of a small matching loop.

Most descriptions of loop antennas repeated the claim that, if well constructed, performance at the higher end of the frequency range could approach that of a half-wave dipole well above ground. It was not until 1991 that Tony Henk, G4XVF, FIEE in a clearly expressed two-part article 'Loop Antennas - Facts not Fiction' (*Radio Communication*, September/October, 1991) threw well-reasoned doubt on the basic efficiency of small loop antennas. Efficiency is difficult to measure accurately but G4XVF based his study on calculating Q from the measured bandwidth of a small loop whose inductance could be calculated. He concluded that radiation efficiency as a percentage was often in single figures (significantly below 10 per cent) whereas that of a resonant and well matched half-wave dipole approaches 100 per cent.

But there has continued to be difficulty in relating theoretical efficiency calculations, as exemplified by G4XVF, with the on-air results achieved by some amateurs using either home-brew loops or, more recently, the loops offered for amateur use by a number of manufacturers. Four models from three manufacturers were reviewed by Peter Hart, G3SJX in 'Loop Antennas for the HF bands' (*Radio Communication*, July 1994, pp41-44). He concluded: "I was really quite surprised at how effective these small loops could be. Being roughly equivalent in performance to a dipole or a multiband vertical, effective performance on the HF bands is still feasible when space for other antennas is not possible."

A most interesting new proposal about how small tuned loop transmitting antennas work is put forward in a paper 'Magnetic Loop or Small Folded Dipole' by Professor Mike Underhill, G3LHZ and M J Blewett, G4VRN of the University of Surrey (*IEE Conference Publication No 411*, pp216-225). The paper, presented at the 'HF Radio Systems and Techniques' IEE conference in July 1997, is based on theoretical and practical studies primarily centred on the Model AMA-3 compact loop antenna made by the UK firm Advanced Antennas and Ancillaries (one of the loops reviewed by G3SJX in 1994).

In their introduction the authors write: "The single turn tuned loop antenna is a remarkably effective small transmitting antenna... Effective performance can be obtained for loops with diameters down to as little as two per cent of the wavelength. For the HF band of 1.5 to 30MHz two per cent corresponds to loop diameters of 4m down to 20cm. For deployment in the confined space allowed to many, if not most, of the users of the HF band such a small size is of great importance... The main disadvantages are its narrow fractional bandwidth and, when used for transmitting, the high RF voltages which occur across the tuning capacitor. Both disadvantages are a consequence of the intrinsically high Q of this and any small antenna.

"A further important feature is that a tuned loop antenna can have a frequency tuning range of up to 3 to 1, depending primarily on the minimum-to-maximum capacitance ratio of the tuning capacitor. Furthermore, the on-tune match resistance is remarkably constant over the whole of the tuning range provided that the antenna is not used in an electromagnetically confined space...

"Most of the evidence for the 'effective' performance of the tuned loop is anecdotal and qualitative, not quantitative... Theoretical predictions remain pessimistic with respect to the performance actually being achieved by users, but it is not easy to find evidence adequate to be able to prove whether

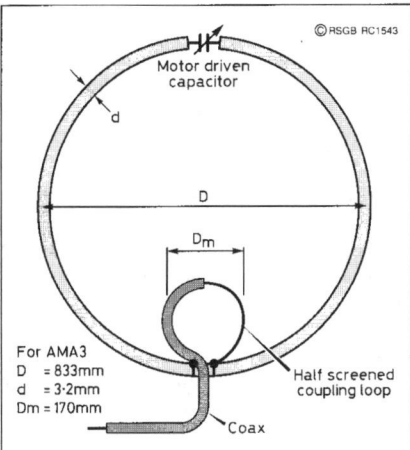

Fig 2: Representative tuned loop antenna with dimensions of the AMA3 model.

there is a real discrepancy between theory and practice...

"The main purpose of this paper is to propose an additional and different mode of operation for the loop antenna and to give some initial evidence that this 'small folded dipole' mode is usually the dominant mode. The dipole mode has a polarisation and radiation pattern which differs significantly from the normal loop mode. However, as will be seen, this difference can in practice be expected to be less apparent in the confined environment of typical deployment and operation."

The AMA3 antenna is intended for use over a range of 14 to 28MHz and has a diameter of 833mm and 16mm tube radius: **Fig 2**. At 14.0MHz the loop resonates with a capacitance of about 73pF and is shown by the authors to have an inductance of some 1.79μH. At 14MHz the radiation resistance is calculated to be only 0.0439Ω, increasing with the fourth power of the frequency, becoming 0.7024Ω at 28MHz. They conclude that for this antenna the loop-mode of radiation cannot contribute significantly to radiation at 14MHz, although at 28MHz some significant loop-mode radiation could be expected.

How, then, can the AMA3 loop antenna work quite well, as it undoubtedly does, on 14MHz? The authors propose that a dipole-mode rather than a loop-mode of radiation is

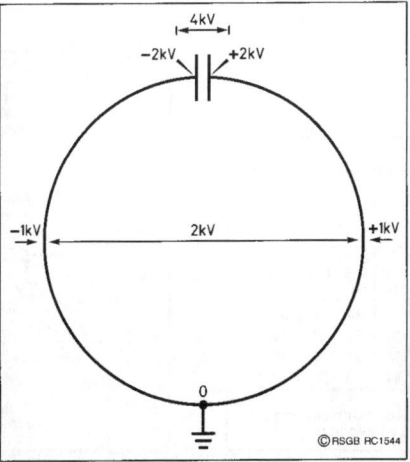

Fig 3: Voltage on the tuned loop antenna.

usually dominant for small tuned-loop antennas. They believe that the antenna works, in effect, largely as a very small folded dipole. "The dipole mode is assumed to be excited by the voltage which appears across the capacitor when power is transformer-coupled into the tuned loop from the source connected to the subsidiary loop." See **Fig 3** for a typical voltage distribution on a tuned loop.

They calculate that in the loop-dipole mode, the radiation resistance at 14MHz becomes 0.484Ω (some 12 times that for the loop mode) and at 28MHz 1.94Ω (nearly three times that for the loop mode). The paper provides a detailed if somewhat confusing explanation of these findings, together with information on their attempt in practice to determine the actual radiation mode, and to determine antenna efficiency. They admit that, "it is not easy to determine antenna efficiency with any accuracy".

Using a network analyser with the AMA3 loop in a screened room, the authors obtained a Q value of 790 at 14MHz, giving a worst case dipole-mode efficiency of 68% (corresponding to a reduction of only 1.7dB on an antenna radiating with an efficiency of 100%). They add: "This predicted value is probably pessimistic. Some evidence is that the AMA3 antenna does not get perceptibly warm to the touch even after prolonged operation with 400 watts PEP of peak SSB speech power."

The paper discusses in some detail the practical difficulties of using SWR/bandwidth measurements to determine the Q and/or efficiency of an antenna. "In principle this is a very good method for measuring the Q of a tuned loop antenna. In practice, because the antenna has a high Q, any matching unit losses markedly degrade the measurement accuracy. In fact, none of the commercially available AMUs were found to be sufficiently low loss. The main problem would appear to be contact resistance in the variable capacitors. On receive, or for the low powers used in network analysers, 'roller coaster' mechanically variable inductors are unusable. Contact resistances were found to be highly variable and a few watts of power obviously are needed to 'microweld' the contact points into a low resistance condition. The best variable capacitors are those which have, or have been modified to have, flexible wire connections directly to the rotor. A further difficulty with the SWR method for measuring Q is that the 'on tune' SWR should be better than 1.02:1 for results to be obtained to about 3% accuracy and repeatability."

It is pointed out that

ANTENNA TOPICS

the L-network AMU originally described by G3LHZ in 1981 and which has been shown in *TT* several times (most recently *TT*, May 1993, pp54-55) is suitable for this purpose.

They conclude: "The tuned loop antenna does not appear to operate significantly in its loop mode. The small folded dipole mode proposed gives much better agreement between theory and measured results. It provides an explanation of why the loop antenna performs so well in practice . . . The radiation resistance of the loop antenna is sensitive to the environment but no more so than for a full size dipole or monopole. The tuning point is almost unaffected by environmental changes . . .

"Because the dipole mode in practice always is the dominant mode and never the loop mode, it is proposed that the term 'magnetic loop' antenna should not be used. The term 'small folded dipole' is a better term to use. However, the term 'tuned loop' antenna is more generic. It would remain correct if new modes of loop or dipole excitation prove to be possible with new, as yet, unexplored tuned loop arrangements."

It is possible here only to outline this interesting contribution (with its detailed mathematical support) to compact transmitting tuned-loop antenna theory and practice. In putting forward the suggestion that these antennas radiate primarily as small folded dipoles rather than in the magnetic-loop mode, G3LHZ and G4VRN appear to have shown for the first time how it is feasible for a well-constructed and well-matched loop really to compare well with a full-size half-wave dipole - a position from which it was to a marked extent toppled in 1991 by G4XVF.

I drew the paper to the attention of G4XVF who points out that it is not an easy paper to follow, contains many typographical and some fundamental errors and generally bears the hallmarks of a conference paper designed to impress rather than elucidate.

But to my mind, the important thing is whether or not the basic proposal of significant dipole-mode radiation from a tuned loop is fact or fiction. Hopefully that will become clear in time.

Antennas - Here and There

Extracted from 'Technical Topics', *Radio Communication*, November 1997

ANTENNAS - HERE & THERE

MANY YEARS ago, the late H S Chadwick, G8ON (father of RSGB Council member and past president Peter Chadwick, G3RZP) developed a 1.8MHz voltage-fed (end fed) half-wave antenna which could be fitted into a restricted space. It had an 84ft horizontal span at a height of some 40ft but with an all-important vertical 30ft section in the maximum current section. It did not require an earth connection but included a loading coil to bring the wire to half-wave resonance: see **Fig 4**. *ART7* (pp299-300) provides some further details. It tends to be most effective in sites having poor earth conductivity.

Another 1.8MHz limited-space antenna as used successfully by S92SS appears in the 'Radio Fundamentals' column by Bill Orr, W6SAI, in *CQ*, August 1997, pp85-86. A quarter-wave of wire includes a vertical, current-carrying section of about 37ft with the remainder of the wire folded around: see **Fig 5**. S92SS also found that with voltage feed the antenna works well on 7MHz. To break the ground return path to the transmitter, he wound as many turns as practical of the RG-58 feedline on a ferrite toroid salvaged from a TV set flyback transformer.

During the development of his limited space antenna, S92SS made use of a simple and inexpensive RF current detector: **Fig 6**. He used a rectangular split-toroid which could be clipped around the conductor under test and the loop with a small pilot bulb. While using low power to prevent burning out the bulb, he was able to check that current at the feed-point divided reasonably between four radials.

'A short, two-band vertical for 160 and 80 metres' is described by Paul Carr, N4PC, in *CQ* (April 1997 pp20, 22-23) including remote switching for the antenna tuner located at the base of the antenna: see **Figs 7** and **8**. N4PC used only an 8ft ground rod but is convinced that results would be further improved by adding a large number of buried radials [or a few elevated radials - *G3VA*].

Stewart Cameron, GM4UTP, was very interested in the GEC-Marconi 'Tetrahedral Antenna' (*TT*, September 1997, pp69-70). He writes: "So much so that I scaled it down and built it as a 144MHz antenna.

"Results were: Frequency coverage 142 to 161MHz to the 2.5:1 SWR points, with unity SWR at the centre.

"Then as an experiment I removed the six horizontal elements shown as A in the September *TT*, the antenna becoming more like a conventional VHF biconical dipole. Frequency coverage increased to 130 and 170MHz with the SWR reducing to 1.7 at these limits, making it a very useful

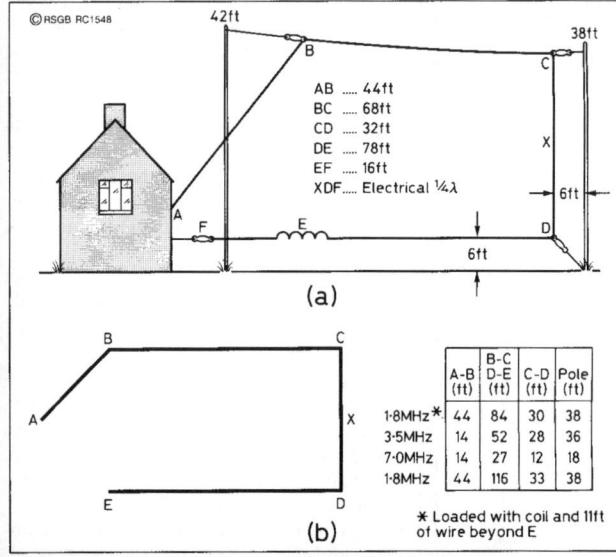

Fig 4: The original G8ON antenna providing some vertically polarised radiation from relatively low antennas, primarily for use on 1.8MHz.

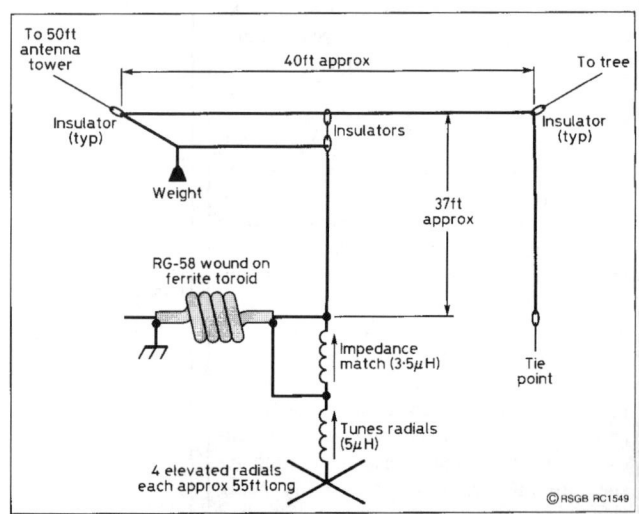

Fig 5: The 1.8MHz 'DX' antenna as used at S92SS. Inductance values are approximate.

1990 - 1999

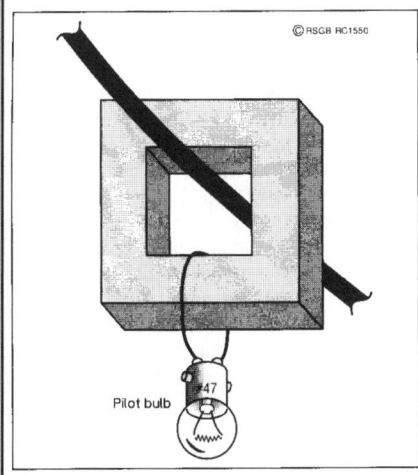

Fig 6: A low-cost RF current detector using ex-TV split ferrite core. Keep power low to avoid burning out the bulb.

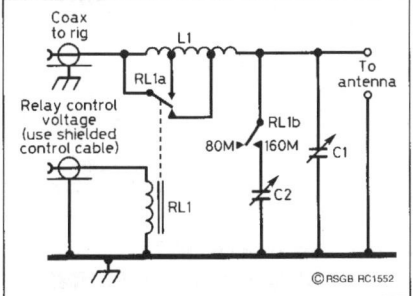

Fig 8: Remote two-band switchable antenna tuner as used by N4PC. L1 10-in long Nr 14 AWG wire, 2½-in diameter, 6 turns per inch (original used Air Dux 2006T). C1, C2 200pF, 4.5kV rating for high power, 2kV for low power. RL1 DPDT relay with 10A contacts.

was that for transmission the radiation efficiency was reduced by about 50% with almost half the RF power absorbed in the resistor. [A much earlier use of resistive loading to increase bandwidth at some loss of radiation efficiency was the T2FD (Terminated Tilted Folded Dipole) antenna developed by the US Navy. Another impedance loaded antenna is the 'Australian Dipole' which has similarly been described in *TT*, most recently in June 1987, and in *TT Scrapbook*, p171 - *G3VA*]. K1POO has developed computer software to optimise the design of impedance loaded wideband antennas of reasonable efficiency and this is being offered through *Electronics World*.

antenna for both the 144MHz amateur band and the 156MHz maritime mobile band."

Richard Formato, K1POO, in 'Design Wideband Antennas' (*Electronics World*, October 1997, pp825-829) provides detailed guidelines on adding impedance loading - resistance and reactance - to antennas in order to create wideband antennas. He gives a design example for continuous coverage from 6 to 150MHz without resorting to tuning and matching. He points out that in 1961, E E Altshuler pioneered resistance loading of antennas by building a centre-fed dipole whose input impedance was, for practical purposes, flat over a 2:1 frequency range by inserting a single 240Ω resistor in each arm a quarter-wavelength from the end. The snag

Antenna Efficiency

Extracted from 'Technical Topics', *Radio Communication*, November 1997

ANTENNA EFFICIENCY

FROM TIME TO time, Lew McCoy, W1ICP, reminds us that antenna efficiency is not a question of gain, radiation patterns or directivity but is nevertheless an important factor that is too often overlooked. *In Antenna 'Efficiency' - What is it?* (*CQ*, April 1995, pp14, 17 and 18) and *Antenna Efficiency One More Time* (*CQ*, February 1997, pp18, 19), he stresses that the most efficient antenna, which can radiate about 97% of the power fed to it, is the basic half-wave resonant dipole. Compare this with some mobile and aircraft antennas which at about 2MHz may radiated only

about 10mW for every 100 watts output of transmitter power.

W1ICP is primarily concerned with the RF ohmic losses in antenna elements, but remember that wasted power may also be a feature of any matching unit and the feeder.

As a simple example, he points out that a beam antenna with a 3dBd gain, but an efficiency of 50%, will radiate in the favoured direction only the same power as a dipole having a near 100% efficiency and considerably less power in other directions [the directivity of the beam may, however, be advantageous for combating the reception of unwanted signals and in its low vertical angle of radiation - *G3VA*].

But why should a beam be less efficient as a radiator than a half-wave dipole? And tend to be even less efficient within a few months (or even weeks) of being erected?

W1ICP stresses that the power that is fed into an antenna element is spent or dissipated in two ways. The RF ohmic resistance of the wire or tubing (greater than the DC ohmic resistance due to skin effect) results in power being dissipated in heating up the element or any traps, earth losses, rusty connections etc. Only the remaining power is spent in the 'radiation resistance' of the antenna - in other words launched into space. Efficiency depends on how much greater is the radiation resistance than the loss resistance.

Whereas the radiation resistance of a half-wave dipole a half-wave above earth is about 73Ω, that of a close-spaced Yagi array may be as low as 4 or 5Ω (which is why some form of matching is required between a coax feeder and the driven element). The ratio between radiation resistance and RF ohmic resistance will almost always be much lower than for a dipole.

As W1ICP puts it: "A beam with 5 - 10Ω impedance is certainly going to have RF ohmic losses as an important factor . . . telescoping element connections, possible boom losses, the matching network itself, and so on. With a 10Ω impedance made up of, say, 5Ω radiation-resistance and 5Ω RF ohmic resistance, then we are looking at 50% efficiency. Although aluminium tubular elements are good

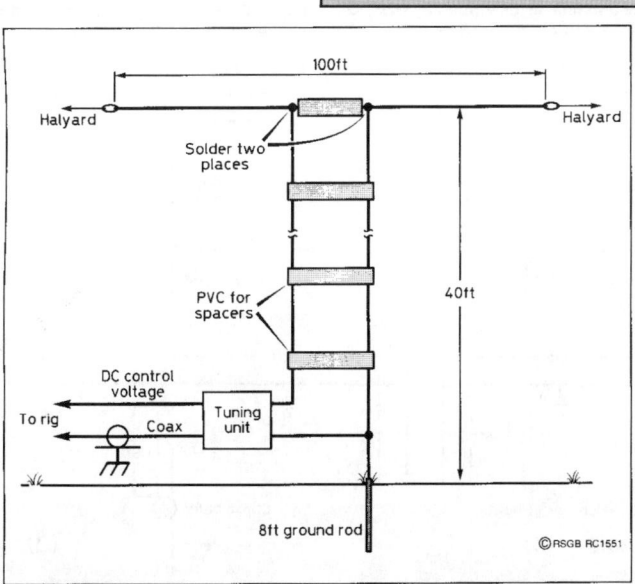

Fig 7: Details of the 1.8 and 3.5MHz vertical antenna as described by N4PC.

ANTENNA TOPICS

though aluminium tubular elements are good conductors, depending on the atmosphere, can get corroded and 'scummy'. If this happens, ohmic losses can skyrocket, and performance and efficiency can go to pot: "If your beam has been up a long time, take it down and clean and polish all connections."

Salty and industrial atmospheres can result very quickly in deterioration of sliding joints in antenna elements; moisture ingress into coaxial feeder cables and baluns etc may significantly increase losses and lower overall efficiency. Traps and loading coils used with electrically short elements need to be of excellent high-Q construction if they are not to reduce efficiency seriously.

W1ICP notes that delta-loop or two-element quad-type (wire) antennas with one-wave or longer elements have relatively high impedance largely comprising radiation resistance, resulting in efficiencies of the order of 90% or more, a significant advantage over a typical tri-band Yagi.

For all types of antennas, VHF as well as HF, he stresses always solder any antenna connections, particularly wire antennas: "Don't be lazy and just twist leads of wire together. It only takes days for unsoldered connections to corrode and resistance to sky rocket."

Nearer home, Mike Gibbings, G3FDW, has been endeavouring to find effective ways of measuring the true power gain of beam antennas that take account of their efficiency - something which is seldom attempted by manufacturers or by those using NEC programs. He proposes that instead of dBd, a new unit is required - dBby or gain in decibels in your own back yard.

He noted the case of a local amateur with a three-element tribander of well-known make: "One day in the depth of winter the beam was seen to be covered with a thick coating of ice, after using the beam for an hour, the ice had all melted from the six traps, whereas the sub-zero weather still held the rest of the beam in its icy grip. As the transmitter was running only 100 watts he was surprised. As there had been no change in the SWR it was evident that traps could lose in heat a considerable amount of input power ... The moral of this tale is that a prudent amateur does not spend hard cash to put a dummy load on the top of his mast. As G6XN has pointed out, a two-element beam may give more dBd (and dBby) gain, certainly more dBd per dollar, than a three element beam at twice the price."

Carolina Windom & IGP Antenna

Extracted from 'Technical Topics', *Radio Communication*, December 1997

CAROLINA WINDOM & SWITCHED POLARISATION WITH IGP ANTENNA

THE NOTE IN THE OCTOBER *TT* querying the origins of the Carolina Windom brought me a plethora of information from Roy Price, GW3SYL; Geoff Dyson, M0AOG; Tony Morton, G0MDZ; and Ted Younge, G3IVH. M0AOG also provided a copy of an article by Mike Lee, G3VYF, from the *Short Wave International Frequency Handbook* covering Windoms generally as well as the Carolina type. This included a reference to a comprehensive article on the standard form of multiband windoms: 'The Off-Centre-Fed Dipole Revisited: a Broadband, Multiband Antenna' by Dr John Belrose, VE2CV, and Peter Bouliane, VE3KLO (*QST*, August 1990, pp28-34). Peter Waters, G3OJV, of Waters & Stanton PLC added further information and also pointed out his firm was the original importer of - and continues to market - this antenna, made in the States by Radio Works Inc. Several writers have pointed out that it is designed not only for 3.5MHz but, with a suitable ATU, can function effectively on all bands from 3.5 to 28MHz. The antenna was illustrated in the October *TT* but, for convenience, is shown again in **Fig 3**.

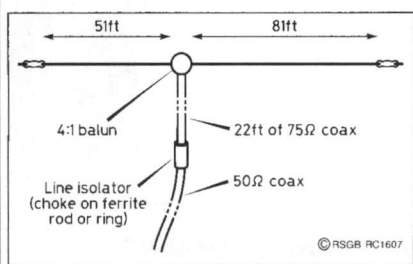

Fig 3: The multi-band (3.5-28MHz) Carolina Windom antenna, manufactured by Radio Works Inc of Virginia and marketed in the UK by Waters & Stanton PLC, and Haydon Communications.

The Carolina Windom was developed by Jim Wilkie, WY4R; Edgar Lambert, WA4LVB; and Joe Wright, W4UEB, then optimised by Jim Thompson, W4THU, and copyrighted. In 1989 a licence was granted to The Radio Works Inc of Portsmouth, Virginia, USA. It was developed as a multiband antenna, radiating both horizontally and vertically polarised signals. The 22ft vertical section provides vertical polarisation, part of the transmitter power being reflected down the outer braid of the feeder.

Although claimed to provide pragmatically a gain of up to 10dBd, this claim is clearly based primarily on the modification by the vertical element of the overall vertical radia-

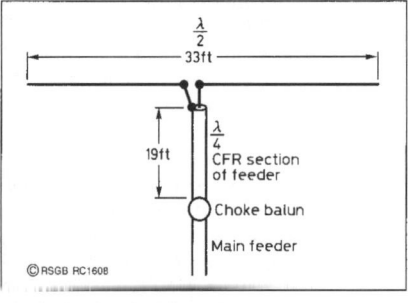

Fig 4: A 14.2MHz CFR (Controlled Feeder Radiation) half-wave dipole antenna, as described by G2HCG in the May 1990 *Radio Communication*.

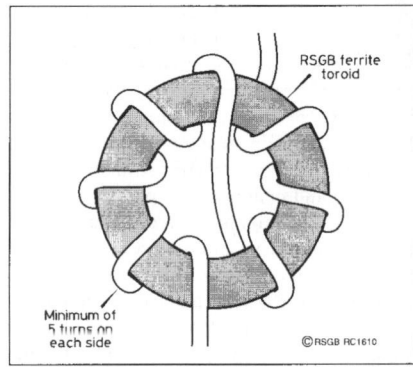

Fig 6: G2HCG's suggested method of winding a choke balun on a large toroid.

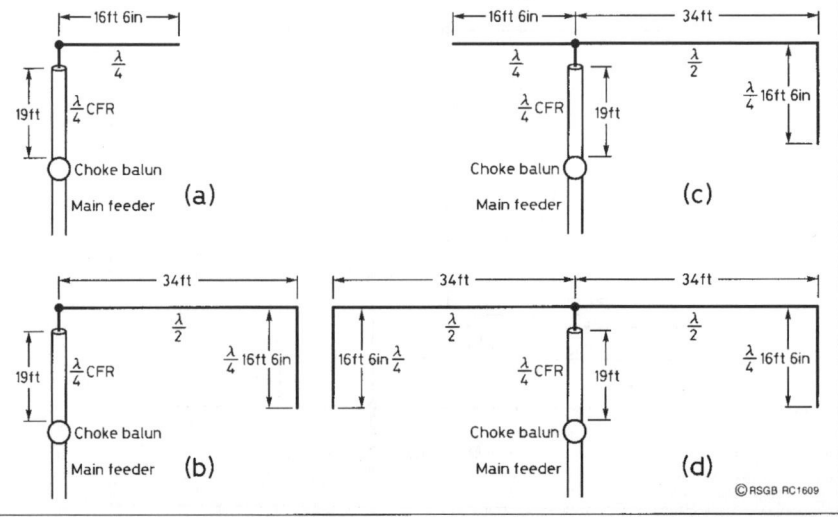

Fig 5: G2HCG's suggested variations for CFR. (a) isotropic, (b & c) half-square, (d) Bobtail.

1990 - 1999

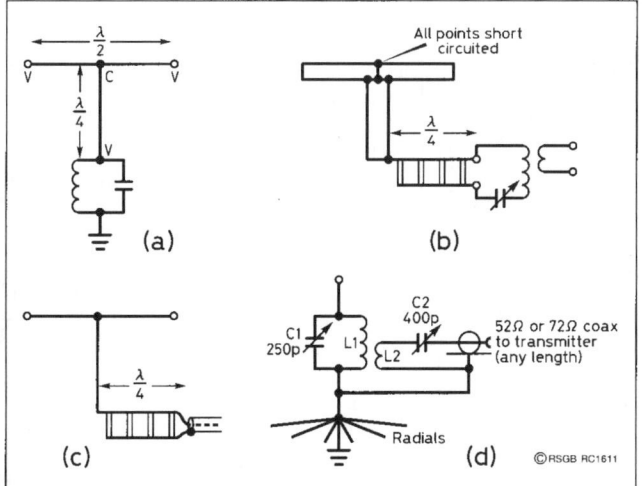

Fig 7: The basic single-band IGP (Inverted Ground Plane) or vertical T antenna, as first described by G3VA in 1970. Virtually all radiation is vertically polarised. Readily converted from a conventional dipole or folded dipole. Voltage fed at the base.

Broadband HF Kite Antennas

Extracted from 'Technical Topics', *Radio Communication*, February 1998

BROADBAND HF IMPEDANCE-LOADED KITE ANTENNAS

"NEW DESIGNS OF ultra wide-band communication antennas using a genetic algorithm" by Zwi Altman, Raj Mittra and Alona Boag (*IEEE Trans Ant & Prop*, October 1997, pp1494-1501) describes a two-step design technique that can result in vertically polarised kite antennas capable of effective, low vertical angle operation over ultra wide low VSWR bandwidths of 4 to 30MHz (four-arm) or even 2 to 30MHz (eight-arm). The four-arm version (**Fig 3**) requires 12 impedance-loading 'tanks' (resistance loaded traps), and the eight-arm version 24.

Although basically a design paper, it provides worked examples of the impedance loading tanks and matching networks for both versions. The loads enhance the antenna characteristics to yield high gain and low VSWR by modifying the current distribution, and can

tion pattern rather than conventional forward HRP power gain, with low-angle radiation from the 22ft vertical radiator boosting the DX capabilities of the antenna. The sales literature makes what must appear extravagant claims, but users generally appear to have found the antenna a satisfactory performer with some suggesting that as an OCFD it is a world beater. Well, perhaps.

As pointed out by G3HQX, there is some resemblance to my 1970 Inverted Ground Plane (Vertical-T) antenna, but whereas the IGP is intended to radiate almost entirely vertically polarised signals the Carolina Windom is designed to radiate primarily horizontally polarised signals but with a significant vertically-polarised component. As pointed out by G3OJV, and in the article by G3VYF, the American design is a good example of the 'Controlled Feeder Radiation (CFR)' technique described by B Sykes, G2HCG in *Radio Communication*, (May 1990, pp40-41).

G2HCG discovered that the polar diagram of an antenna can be modified and often improved by controlling the radiation from its feeder. He placed a choke balun some distance down the feeder line of a dipole element fed from an unbalanced coax feeder: **Fig 4**.

G2HCG provided several other examples of Controlled Feeder Radiation (CFR) antennas based on variations of the IGP, half-square and bobtail antennas etc: **Fig 5**. In these cases the outer braid of the final length of coax feeder was not connected to the element. **Fig 6** shows how G2HCG recommended winding a choke balun on a large toroid.

As noted in *ART7* (p315). "In first describing the Vertical-T or Inverted Ground Plane antenna, **Fig 7**, I wrote "The ease with which a dipole antenna can be converted to a vertical-T suggests that it should be relatively easy to develop an antenna which could be switched from horizontal to vertical polarisation and vice versa." In *CQ* (June 1972), Ken Glanzer, K7GCO, followed-up this suggestion and described "The 10°/90° antenna for 75 to 40 metres": the two angles referring to the predominant vertical radiation angle - 90° with the fairly low horizontally polarised dipole and 10° with the antenna in its Vertical-T configuration: **Fig 8**.

"The twin open-wire feed is used as such for horizontal polarisation, but switched so that both wires go to the same side of the matching coil to form the voltage-fed quarter-wave top-loaded vertical. In his implementation of this arrangement, K7CGO incorporated remote switching and remote (selsyn) tuning of the matching unit, in his belief that it is very useful to be able to switch rapidly between the two polarisations to take advantage of propagation quirks, noting that there may even be occasions when it is better to switch to a different polarisation for reception to that used for transmission."

While the IGP and the K7GCO versions were designed as single band resonant antennas, either version can be used over a wide range of frequencies, provided that suitable impedance matching networks are located at the base of the vertical section. MF broadcast stations radiate efficiently with T-antennas significantly less than a quarter-wave high.

The manuals for the Carolina Windom stress that the vertical section *must* be kept well away from metallic objects such as towers, masts, gutters, metal roofing, etc. If a tower is used to support the antenna, a 10ft length of 2-inch PVC pipe may be used to hold it away from the metalwork. The vertical radiator section and the line isolator should both be more than 15ft from the tower. With the IGP-type arrangement and with the vertical section centred between two supports, it should be relatively easy to provide sufficient clearance from metal objects.

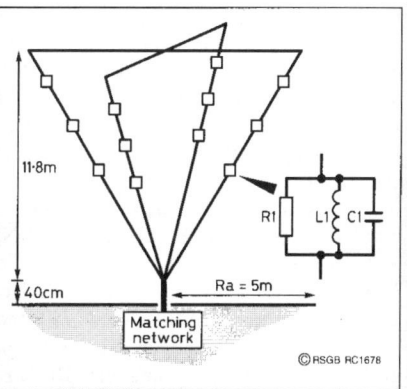

Fig 3: Broadband four-arm loaded kite antenna, mounted over an infinite, perfectly conducting ground plane.

force it to radiate nearer to the horizon in the elevation plane with an almost omnidirectional pattern in the azimuth plane.

Note that "kite" refers to the shape of these antennas. They are not intended to be carried aloft by kites.

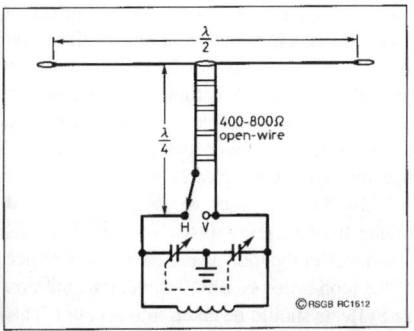

Fig 8: K7GCO antenna which can be switched to function as either a conventional half-wave dipole (open feeders) or as an Inverted Ground Plane (vertical T). Although described as an antenna for the 3.5 & 7MHz bands, with suitable matching it can be used on any of the higher bands as a doublet or T-antenna.

355

ANTENNA TOPICS

Transmit Loops Controversy

Extracted from 'Technical Topics', *Radio Communication*, February 1998

TUNED TRANSMITTING LOOPS CONTROVERSY

THE NOVEMBER, 1997 *TT* item reporting the belief of Professor Mike Underhill, G3LHZ and M J Blewen, G4VRN that the compact tuned transmitting loops tend to function primarily as small folded dipoles rather than as magnetic loops has certainly attracted serious attention, indeed it would be possible to fill *TT* for several months with the many thoughtful comments received. On one point, virtually all agree: these compact antennas are surprisingly effective no matter whether their total radiation efficiency is or is not as low as was suggested by Tony Henk, G4VXF in 1991.

While the majority of those who wrote to me - including Jack Hollingworth, ZF1HJ; Dr John (Jack) Belrose, VE2CV; B Edginton, G0CWT; Jimmy Bolton, G3HBN - remain rather sceptical of the dipole-mode hypothesis, there has also been some disbelief in the validity of the 1991 article of Tony Henk, G4VXF. I would stress that G4VXF's findings as relating to the magnetic loop mode are not disputed in any way by G3LHZ. I understand that most of those who commented directly to G3LHZ supported his view that dipole-mode radiation from the loops may be the dominant mode.

But first a word of explanation about the "AMA-3" loop, used by G3LHZ/G4VRN, and also reviewed by G3SJX in 1994. These loops were, as stated, manufactured in the UK by Advanced Antennas and Ancilliaries (no longer trading), apparently based on a design by Dipl-Ing Christain Kaeferlein, DC5CZ, (Weinbergstrasse 5, Darmstadt D 64285, Germany), whose firm has, since 1983, manufactured a range of Abstimmbare Magnetische Antennen (AMA) loop antennas, including the AMA-3. The mathematical/electrical design of the German AMA-3 loops was based on the work of Hans Wuertz, DL2FA (summarised in *TT*, October 1986 and *TT Scrapbook 1985-89*, P127-8). Detailed information on the original AMA loops, still in production, has been published by DL5CZ in German and English. **Fig 4** shows the basic design of the AMA loops. **Fig 5** shows two AMA loops on a single pole.

ZF1HJ is representative of the sceptics. To quote briefly from a long, well reasoned letter: "There is no doubt that claims for the efficiency of magnetic loop antennas by both manufacturers and writers of construction articles are often greatly exaggerated. They appear to result from a calculation of radiation resistance derived from physical dimensions

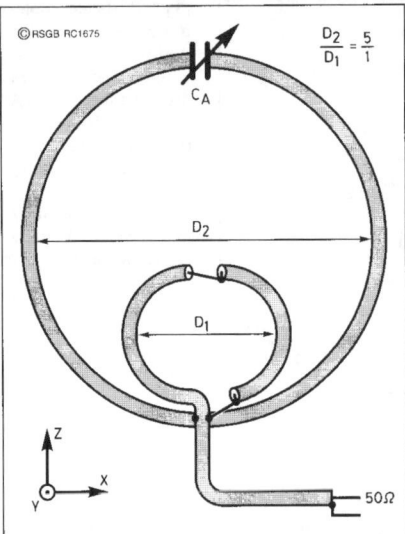

Fig 4: Basic design of the DL5CZ "Abstimmbare Magnetische Antennen" (AMA) tuned transmitting loop antennas with coupling loops, as manufactured in Germany since 1983. Currently there are some 24 models, grouped in four diameter sizes (0.6m, 1.3m, 1.7m and 3.4m).

and an estimate of resistive losses only in the loop itself, based on its dimensions and material, perhaps with a fudge factor worked-in to allow for skin effect. As my friend G4VXF pointed out in his excellent article, there are other significant sources of loss which result in much lower than anticipated efficiencies.

"Nevertheless, I do not share Tony's pessimism. Like others, in practice I have found these antennas, even when mounted close to the ground, perform almost as well as a dipole at a much greater height. I have (at least until now) considered the explanation to lie in there being a substantial lobe in the vertical plane at a relatively low angle to the horizon, so that the loop, despite its low efficiency, radiates more power than a dipole at the low angles required for DX communication." (On the other hand, the attraction of loops for military applications is the strong vertical radiation required for short/medium range NVIS working - G3VA).

VE2CV has also found from personal experience that loops can be an excellent choice for HF camp/portable/mobile operation. Nevertheless he believes that "the proposed dipole-mode for compact loops is in fact fiction . . . It is surprising how well compact loops work, even on bands where the efficiency is very poor (HF can be very forgiving)." With access to genuine AMA loops of 0.8, 1.7 and 3.4 metre diameters, he has carried out both rigorous measurements and NEC-4 (EZNEC pro version with the NEC-4D machine) studies on the AMA-11 loop at 3.852MHz, showing efficiencies of 4.7% and 5.5% respectively."

VE2CV concludes: "A small compact loop behaves like a loop. The method of tuning and matching, resonating by a capacitor, and magnetically coupling power to the loop by means of a small coupling loop, is an efficient way to resonate and match the loop. To keep conductor losses low, the diameter of the loop's conductor must be large. The conductor diameter of the DK5CZ AMA loops is 32mm, the loop being made from a formed (almost a perfect circle) aluminium tube."

Due to space considerations I drastically condensed the information from ZF1HJ and VE2CV. My apologies to these - and the other correspondents - if I have misrepresented or omitted their views.

I passed the detailed (critical) comments made by G4XVF and VE2CV to G3LHZ, who, although very much bound up with his professional academic work, has provided additional notes in support of his dominant dipole-mode hypothesis. One of the contentions raised by G4VXF related to the space in the IEE Conference Paper given over to the calculation of inductance. He points out that this is well covered in NBS Technical Note C74. Using this, G4XVF calculated the loop inductance as 1.748µH without introducing a fiddle factor, as against the measured value of 1.77µH. G3LHZ has not yet had a chance to study C74, but he has checked the most quoted NBS inductance formula for a single-turn loop, which appears in some editions of the ITT *"Reference Data for Radio Engineers"*:

$$L = a/100 \, (7.353 \log_{10} 16a/d - 6.386) \, \mu H$$

where 'a' = mean radius of ring in inches, 'd' = diameter of wire in inches, and $a/d > 2.5$

G3LHZ comments "There is no doubt that this is a very good formula, giving excellent predicted results at low frequencies. Out of curiosity I have manipulated and changed the units of the formula for direct comparison with the formulas given in my paper. Interestingly, all formulas can be encompassed within exactly the same expression. The only difference is a single constant k (a fiddle factor?) which differentiates between the formulas... Theory derived from direct solutions of Maxwell's equations for wires gives k=1. The NBS loop inductance formula corresponds to k = 2.166. Our paper calculated k as equal to 2.09, but suggested it could be rounded down to 2.0. Since 2.09 is nearer to 2.166, I am happy for others to accept a rounding up to 2.166 on the basis of the NBS measurements. The effect on the calculated inductance values is a little over 1%. The real mystery is why there is a two to one difference between theory and practice. It implies that the effective diameter of the wire or tube is doubled over its real diameter. Further investigation is clearly necessary!

"Also in our paper we suggested that at higher frequencies, approaching the first self-resonance of the loop where the circumference of the loop becomes a half-wave, transmission line effects should be taken into account. This can be achieved with all the above inductance formulas by multiplying by the factor $(\tan y)/y$, where y equals $\pi^2 D/\lambda$. This give inductance values which are 27% higher at half the resonant frequency, +5.5% at a quarter wave, and

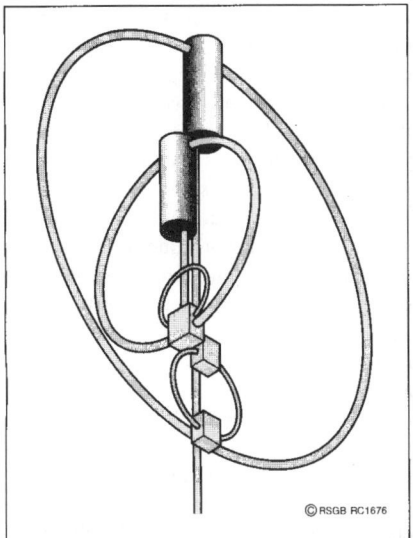

Fig 10: How a combination of 1.7m and 0.8m AMA loops can be mounted on a single pole.

+1.3% at one-eighth-wave. (At 14.3MHz for an 0.833m diameter loop, the increase of 5.5% should be applied)."

G3LHZ then turns to the $64k question of whether dipole-mode radiation is fact or fiction. He writes:

"Judging by letters and phone calls received or passed on, the dipole-mode proposal has raised a lot of interest. There would appear to be slightly more believers than sceptics. The case I would make for the dipole-mode now includes the following points, intended to counter the negative comments so far received.

1) Q values measured by SWR and antenna-bandwidth methods are much lower than predicted by the traditional loop radiation formulas.
2) There is a large increase in Q, typically by two to three times, if the loop antenna is placed in a large, reasonably low-loss tin box (three different screened rooms have been tried). This is Wheeler's Cap method for measuring the ratio of radiation resistance to antenna loss resistance.
3) The loop antenna does not get hot (enough), even with 400W supplied to the antenna at the lowest frequency of operation.
4) There is a strong, horizontally-polarised field, radiated from a vertical loop. 3ft long fluorescent tubes remain ignited to at least two loop diameters distant from the loop (with 100-400W) but only if deployed horizontally. This component is retained (dominantly) in the far field.
5) The SWR and match resistance at the minor loop input remains approximately constant for up to a three to one frequency range on a given loop antenna. The traditional loop formulas would predict a nine to one change in antenna input resistance over this range, provided antenna losses are kept small.
6) The patterns predicted by the NEC simulation code as given in VE2CV's 1993 *QST* article are exactly those given by the assumption that either the current around the loop is exactly uniform or that any out-of-balance currents do not radiate. These patterns do not show any dipole-mode radiation. B Edginton, G0CWT has supplied loop measurements showing a two to one ratio in currents (I think he used thermocouple-type RF ammeters, although this is for somewhat larger loop sizes). G4VRN is checking this for smaller loop sizes, and we also intend measuring the relative phases at the two sides of the loop. Using a simple, ferrite rod current transformer, first indications are that the currents are exactly as one would expect at the ends of a shorted-transmission line of length equal to half-loop circumference. At 14MHz a ratio of 0.95:1 and at 28MHz a ratio of 0.75:1 were measured."

G3LHZ concludes: "It is a pity that NEC fails to model the tuned loop correctly. This is because it fails to predict or take account of any imbalance in current around the loop. While for most applications NEC is enormously successful, like all simulations it is only as good as its internal assumptions, no matter what arithmetical precision it has.

"For the time being, I rest my case for the dipole mode of tuned loops on the above six points, but I am sure we have not heard the last word on this subject. For example, I intend to make measurements of the far field phase and will try to relate this to the loop current phase. This should give further information on the exact mechanism of radiation for this or any thick or thin wire antenna."

Antennas VRPs, HRPs and Gain

Extracted from 'Technical Topics', *Radio Communication*, March 1998

ANTENNAS VRPs, HRPs AND GAIN

THE NOVEMBER 1997 *TT* discussed the question of the lower radiation efficiency of most HF Yagi antennas, compared with simple half-wave dipoles. This was based on points made by Lew McCoy, W1ICP, who, as a simple example, pointed out that a beam antenna with a 3dBd gain but an efficiency of 50%, will radiate in the favoured direction only the same power as a dipole having a near 100% efficiency - and considerably less power in other directions. However, I added the comment: "The directivity of the beam may, however, be advantageous for combating the reception of unwanted signals and in its low vertical angle of radiation."

Gerald Stancey, G3MCK sought clarification of the comment that one of the advantages of a beam (Yagi) over a dipole is its lower angle of radiation: "This statement is often heard, but I would welcome a definitive confirmation. In the 14th edition of the *ARRL Antenna Handbook* there is a diagram which shows the calculated vertical radiation pattern (VRP) of a Yagi 1.25 wavelengths above ground. The lowest major lobe occurs at exactly the same angle as that given by a dipole at the same height. Could you provide a definitive statement on this?"

To answer this question adequately involves some appreciation of the fundamentals of antenna operation. In particular, it is essential to remember that the radiation is three-dimensional, rather than as shown in single-plane drawings.

We need to think in terms of solid geometry, with solid angles. Radiation from a short length of wire is in the form of a 'doughnut' or 'toroid' threaded on the wire, rather than only two-dimensional. Similarly, it is important to remember that a directional antenna, regardless of type, concentrates radiation in both the vertical and horizontal planes; eg a long-boom VHF/UHF Yagi, with many elements, radiates in a solid angle along the axis of the boom. For amateur satellites, moonbounce, etc, a long-boom Yagi needs to be directed in both azimuth and elevation.

The following notes draw in part upon the *HF Communications Data Book*, published in the 1970s by Rockwell International.

The power gain in decibels of an antenna in a specified direction is the ratio, expressed in decibels, of the radiation intensity of the antenna in that direction, compared to the intensity produced by some reference antenna, when equal powers are delivered to the two antennas. Radiation intensity is defined as the power radiated per unit solid angle from the antenna. Note that polar diagrams of directive, horizontally polarised antennas, show the radiation pattern at the optimum elevation, rather than parallel to the ground.

The presence and conductivity of the ground beneath, and for many wavelengths around the antenna, profoundly affects the performance of an antenna: (1) antenna efficiency is reduced due to the finite conductivity of the ground; and (2) radiation in the vertical plane is modified. As noted in many standard texts, the vertical radiation pattern of either horizontally or vertically polarised antennas is determined by the directional properties of the antenna and by the additive and subtractive

ANTENNA TOPICS

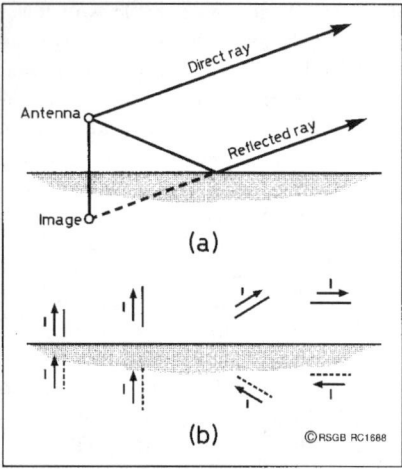

Fig 1 (a): Image antenna and ground effect, resulting in a direct and reflected ray. However, the effect of ground losses is more severe with vertical polarisation, where additional ground losses occur in the vicinity of the ground reflection. The relationship between the direct and reflected wave in any direction depends on the height of the antenna above ground, plus the electrical properties of the ground. The vertical plane pattern can be determined by substituting an image antenna for the earth. (b) To simulate perfect ground, the image antenna is fed with a current of the same amplitude as the actual antenna. The correct phase is indicated by the relative directions of the current arrows. The image concept is useful in antenna modelling for determining the patterns of antennas fed against ground. At some radiation angles, the direct and reflected waves reach the same point in space in phase, the resultant field strength then being the sum of the two. With horizontally polarised antennas at least a quarter-wave above ground, total radiation will closely approach that with perfect ground. (Source: *HF Communications Data Book*).

interference between the direct waves and reflected waves. That is, the waves that are radiated from the antenna at angles below the horizon are reflected from the ground: **Fig 1(a)**.

At some radiation angles, the direct and reflected waves reach the same point in space in phase, and the resultant field strength is the sum of the two. Under perfect ground conditions (usually approached with horizontally polarised antennas at least a quarter-wave above ground), the ground-reflected wave from the 'image antenna', **Fig 1(b)**, is equal in amplitude to the direct wave, giving a gain of 6dB at these angles.

Table 1 was originally published in *TT*, July 1987. It shows the maximum gain of lossless elementary antennas with reference to an isotropic source and to a dipole. In practice, gains for horizontal antennas are normally specified relative to a half-wave dipole at the same height above ground as the antenna's phase centre. Gains of vertical antennas are normally specified with respect to a quarter-wave monopole with either 100% efficiency or with 60 quarter-wave radials, which is close to 100% efficiency.

In practice, the gain and direction of maximum gain of vertical antennas are affected very much more by ground conductivity than horizontal antennas. The elevated $\lambda/4$ ground plane antenna with sloping $\lambda/4$ radials is more akin to a $\lambda/2$ vertical dipole than a $\lambda/4$ vertical monopole. A power gain of about 5 to 6dBd is usually the maximum that can be achieved in practice for an HF three-element close-spaced Yagi beam (theoretical 7.5 to 8dBd). About 4 to 5dBd (theoretical maximum 5.2dBd) can, with care, be obtained from two close-spaced elements. Better overall results may often be achieved by raising a lightweight 2-element Yagi, rather than by increasing the number of elements at a lower height. Field strengths over a long, low-angle path, when compared to an antenna at $\lambda/5$, are roughly x2 at $2\lambda/5$, x3 at $3\lambda/5$, x4 at $4\lambda/5$ and x5 at 1λ. 1λ loops give roughly a 1dB gain over dipole elements (ie the gain of a 2-element quad can be up to about 6dBd). At a VHF, height gain in the 3 to 10m range can amount to about 5.5 to 6.5dB for each doubling of the height in rural areas (8 to 9dB in urban areas) on paths up to 50km, and half these gains for distances exceeding 100km. For consistent HF DX, one needs to radiate and receive signals at vertical angles to ground of about 8 to 15°, although, in chordal hop (grey line) conditions, contacts may sometimes be made with antennas radiating at relatively high angles.

When it comes to a directional, horizontal antenna above an earth of finite conductivity, it becomes very difficult to determine the actual vertical radiation pattern, since - as noted above - this will depend both on its directivity and its height above ground. In most cases there will be a major lobe and one or more minor lobes at greater angles. In general terms, the greater the gain of the antenna, the greater will be the reduction in the angle of the major lobe, although the height above ground remains the dominant factor. Note that this does not apply only to Yagi antennas, but to all antennas exhibiting directivity. Long-wires, vees and rhombics will all have lower vertical angles than simple dipoles at equivalent heights. The greater the directivity, the greater the effect on the vertical angle of the major lobe.

With broadband antennas, such as rhombics, the vertical angle of maximum radiation will vary with frequency, since the height of the antenna varies in terms of wavelength. Even with the aid of computers, the calculation of vertical plane radiation patterns of antennas over finitely conducting earth is tedious, and such calculations are extremely difficult to validate. For professional HF antennas, one of the few practical methods is to fly an aircraft around the antenna at various heights. One must be very cautious in relying on NEC-type computer programs, since the amateur has no way of checking the results.

A 1940s book on rhombic antennas includes VRPs for a high-gain rhombic at a height of 16m above perfectly conducting ground. At 4.7MHz (64m), where the rhombic is a quarter-wave above ground, the main lobe peaks at about 40°, whereas, if it were a dipole a quarter-wave above ground, the main lobe would be directly upwards (90°). At 9.4MHz (32m), where the height is a half-wave above ground, the rhombic lobe peaks at about 25° compared with 30° for the corresponding dipole (see Table 1). At 18.8MHz (16m), with a height of one wavelength, the rhombic main lobe is down to about 11°. The directivity clearly influences the VRP at all heights, but the height is the main determining factor on how low an angle can be achieved. It is thus entirely possible for a rather low Yagi to have a greater vertical angle of radiation than a dipole at a good height. Incidentally, Table 1 shows that a lower angle of radiation is achieved by a dipole at 0.6λ, than the usually quoted 0.5λ.

Thus, any horizontally polarised antenna exhibiting directivity, will inherently have a lower vertical angle of optimum radiation than a dipole. However, since we are dealing with solid angles, this does not mean that the power gain of an antenna, as shown by conventional radiation patterns, can then be increased by the VRP directivity. The power gain of a two-element Yagi thus remains about 4dB, even though, over a specific DX path, it may provide, under some propagation condition, signals very many decibels above that provided by a low dipole. On the other hand, a dipole may out perform the Yagi over short, NVIS paths.

Type	Location	Max gain (dBi)	Max gain (dBd)	Direction of max gain
$\lambda/2$ dipole	Free space	2.15	0	Plane perpendicular to axis
$\lambda/4$ vertical monopole	Over perfect ground	5.15	3	On horizon
$\lambda/2$ vertical dipole	Centre at $\lambda/2$ above perfect ground	8.2	6.05	On horizon
$\lambda/2$ horizontal dipole	Immediately above perfect ground	9.1	6.95	Straight up
$\lambda/2$ horizontal dipole	$\lambda/4$ above perfect ground	7.4	5.25	Straight up
$\lambda/2$ horizontal dipole	$\lambda/2$ above perfect ground	8.2	6.05	Plane perpendicular to axis, 30° above horizontal
$\lambda/2$ horizontal dipole	$3\lambda/5$ above perfect ground	9.2	7.05	Plane perpendicular to axis, 24.6° above horizontal

Table 1: Maximum (theoretical) gain of lossless basic antennas.

'Magic' Fractal Antennas

Extracted from 'Technical Topics', *Radio Communication*, April 1998

'MAGIC' FRACTAL ANTENNAS?

BOTH JOE KESSEL, G7RWH, and I found 'Aerial Magic' by Mike May (*New Scientist*, 31 January 1998, pp28-30) of more than passing interest. It claims: "Your mobile phone, the gas meter under the stairs and the vending machine down the hall may soon sport the world's smallest, weirdest antennas." Professor Nathan ('Chip') Cohen is presented as the inventor of a new family of 'fractal antennas' which may come to be used in everything from mobile phones to huge receiving arrays. The idea emerged from an experience in 1988 when Cohen wanted to use his ham radio equipment at a flat in the centre of Boston, where the landlords stipulated no outside antennas.

Instead of using a difficult-to-disguise conventional antenna, Chip Cohen cut a sheet of aluminium foil into the shape of a mathematical pattern known as an inverse Koch curve, and stuck it onto a sheet of A4-sized paper: "Cohen connected the foil to his radio receiver, to see if it might serve as a covert antenna if he mounted it outdoors. To his surprise, the fractal foil pattern worked well and Cohen was able to continue his hobby without arousing suspicion [no indication is given of the frequency band(s) concerned - G3VA].

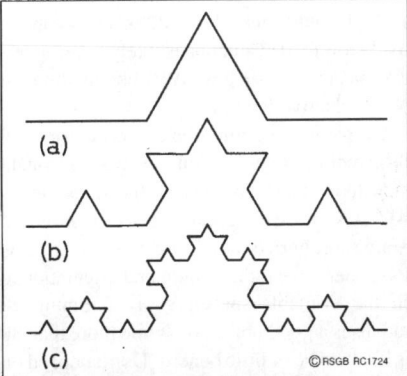

Fig 1: Construction of a von Koch 'snowflake' fractal, formed from the basic curve of (a), with successive iterations shown in (b) and (c). As stages are added, the total length of the curve tends to infinity, although the curve is confined to a finite space.

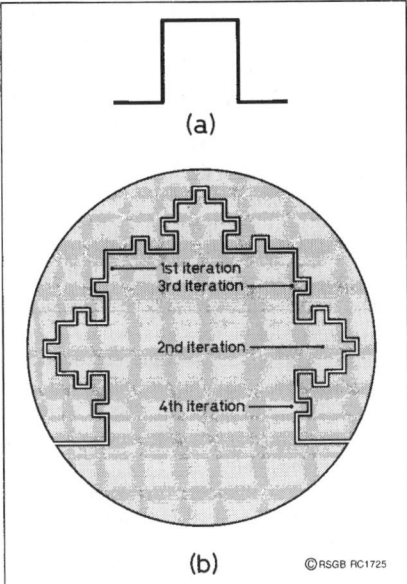

Fig 2: Illustration of a fractal antenna that could be built into a military helmet, as described in the *New Scientist* article, built up from the iteration of the basic curve (a).

"Today, Cohen's experiment has made him a pioneer in the new field of fractal antenna design. It turns out that fractal antennas have many advantages over their conventional counterparts. For a start, they are smaller - a fractal antenna for a mobile phone can be made the size and shape of a 35mm photographic slide and can be built into the casing . . . fractal antennas are also better at picking up signals and can receive them over a wider range of frequencies. But . . . physicists are being left behind. Nobody is exactly sure why fractals make good antennas. Now the race is on to find out."

It seems, according to the article, that a fractal pattern antenna provides the 3-4dB gain of two half-wave elements in phase, but it is by no means clear how this relates to its useable bandwidth and what this amounts to.

Although the article describes in general terms what constitutes a fractal pattern, it does not attempt to provide precise details of the dimensions, impedances, etc, of a practical fractal antenna. Nor, in a quick library search, could I discover any further information on fractal antennas. My dictionary does not even list 'fractal'. I did, however, find out that fractal geometric structures are of particular interest to computer scientists, because of their use in computer graphics to depict landscape and vegetation in a very natural way. There is also apparently a strong connection between fractal geometry and the trendy chaos theory. Fractal geometric structures include the so-called snowflake curve, devised by Swedish mathematician Helge von Kohn in 1904 (**Fig 1**). Fractal patterns exhibit a 'self-similarity' when the distance at which they are viewed is changed. They consist of many repetitions (iterations) of a basic shape.

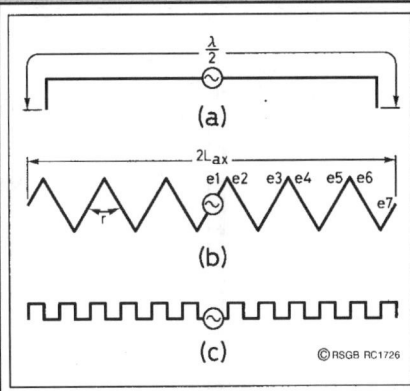

Fig 3: Significant shortening of the overall span of a conventional half-wave dipole element can be achieved without significant loss of efficiency or directivity. (a) Ends dropped downwards or bent inwards. (b) Zigzag element, where $e1 = e7 = 0.0208\lambda$ and $e2 = e3 \ldots e6 = 0.0416\lambda$. (c) Meander-line element as noted in *TT* of February 1992.

The inverse Koch curve used by 'Chip' Cohen for his covert amateur radio antenna was apparently a fractal, comprising a series of triangles stacked up on top of each other like a pagoda, but his UHF micropatch fractal antennas seem to be variations of the Koch snowflake curve: **Fig 2**.

There is of course nothing new about using elements bent into regular shapes in order to reduce overall length, as in the 'Meander' and 'zigzag' antennas (see for example *TT*, February 1992, from which **Fig 3** is taken).

Semi-elevated Ground-planes

Extracted from 'Technical Topics', *Radio Communication*, April 1998

SEMI-ELEVATED GROUND-PLANE ANTENNAS

I HAVE COMMENTED a number of times (most recently in *TT*, January 1996, pp69-71) on the professional interest of broadcast engineers in the revival of the 'counterpoise' elevated radial as an alternative to the standard 120-wire buried earth that stemmed from Dr George Brown's classic MF work in the 1930s.

It was Arch Doty, K8CFU, and his elderly friends who, in the early 1980s, challenged the buried radial concept on the basis of extensive measurements. This led to computer simulations by Al Christian, KN8I, prompting several American broadcast stations to try us-

ANTENNA TOPICS

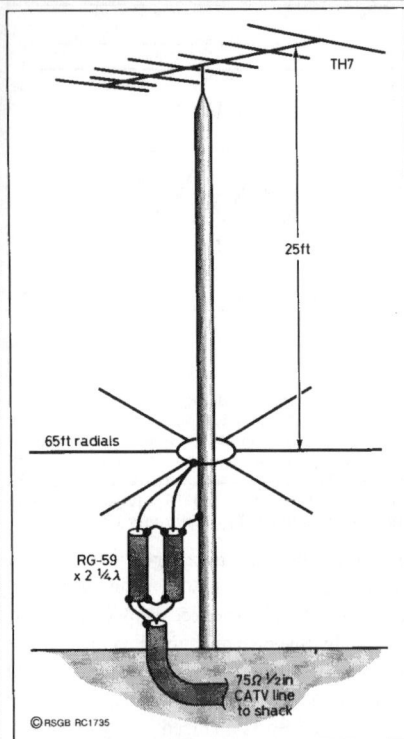

Fig 12: A 3.5MHz top-loaded 'reverse-fed' elevated ground plane type antenna, with earthed tower and top-loading provided by the TH-7 Yagi antenna for higher frequency bands, as illustrated in VE2CV's ICAP paper, and based on the article by Russell in *QST* (June, 1994). Note that the tower at the feed point shown, carrying the TH7 triband Yagi antenna, is resonant on the band of interest.

ing four elevated radials (instead of 60-120 buried radials each ¼-½λ long), with mixed results. Some professionals now swear by elevated radials; others swear at them.

Two well-respected writers have faced up to this controversy, and both seem to have come to much the same conclusion: elevated radials *must* each be resonant electrical quarter-wavelengths if they are to equal or even improve on the extensive ground screens provided by large numbers of buried radials. This may come as no great surprise to the many users of elevated HF/VHF ground-plane antennas with sloping or horizontal radials, but was by no means clear from the earlier work, with even George Brown postulating radials of up to 0.5λ.

Dr John S (Jack) Belrose, VE2CV, presented a paper 'Vertical Monopoles with Elevated Radials: An Update' at the 10th International Conference on Antennas and Propagation (ICAP) held in April 1997 (IEE Conference Publication No 436, pp1.190-195). His conclusions provide a useful summary of his findings, based on computer studies and practical experience:

"Elevated radial ground systems can be used effectively for many applications: (1) to realise achievable gain for ground plane type antennas over real ground with only a few radials; (2) to provide versatility, eg control of radiation pattern, and (3) for numerical modelling purposes, to simulate connection to ground. To realise achievable gain and not change the resonant frequency of the antenna system, the radials must be resonant. While this conclu-

sion has been discovered during the course of our study, in retrospect it should have been anticipated at the outset. The magnitude of the difference (antenna gain and impedance), however, is particularly striking when there is a significant difference between the electrical and physical length of the radial wires, such as a radial wire system at a very low height."

VE2CV also concludes that phased array directional systems can employ elevated resonant radials, thus simplifying the installation of ground mounted antenna systems that employ great numbers of buried radial wires.

Inter alia he notes that radio amateurs have used elevated radials in a sort of reverse-feed arrangement as a method to feed a grounded tower (Russell, 'Simple, Effective, Elevated Ground-Plane Antennas' *QST*, June 1994, pp45-46). VE2CV wrote: "The radials are attached to a ring, centred on the tower at the point of feed, but insulated from the tower. The feed, using coaxial cable, is between the tower and the ring, with the shield of the coax connected to a tower leg: see **Fig 12**. The legs of the tower should be strapped together at this point. The radiator is the part of the tower above the radial system. Evaluation by impedance measurement and over-the-air QSOing support the view that this method of feeding a grounded tower works very well indeed. This method should be modelled (using NEC-4) and evaluated by full-scale field strength measurement. Elimination of the base insulator for guyed towers is a distinct advantage."

W A (Bill) McLeod, VK3MI points out that "Over many years the counterpoise has remained non-dimensional in most texts. So in a follow-up to my previous work on 'Near to Earth Antennas' (*TT*, February 1995, based on VK3MI's 'Low Radiators and High Ground Planes', *Amateur Radio*, November 1994, pp10-14) I wrote 'The Semi-Elevated Ground Plane - GIRFU style' (*Amateur Radio*, July 1997, pp13-15): 'I believe that this corrects the traditional view that the length of a counterpoise is not important. This is based on full-size antenna tests, not modelled, and the computer simulation of similar systems by VK1BRH (see 'Dipoles with Counterpoise', *TT*, January 1997) generally confirms my results.'

"My new article presents a procedure for tuning the counterpoise to the electrical equivalent of the radiator, for a low-loss balanced system with respect to the feed point. The displacement height above ground is a matter of judgement of the affordable losses, based on the results presented in 'Near to Earth Antennas'. The unexpected result was the necessity to isolate the system from actual earth, but, in retrospect, it is quite logical to isolate the return circuit from the lossy earth capacitance."

In case you are wondering what 'GIRFU' in the title of his article stands for, the answer is 'Get-It-Right-First-Up'. VK3MI gives a nine-point procedure for ensuring that an unbalanced antenna system resonates in both dimensions. For general information on VK3MI's 'saggy' approach to elevated radials, in which the ends are raised higher above ground than

the base of the vertical element, it may prove useful to refer to the January 1996 item. **Fig 13** shows a 10.1MHz antenna with two 'saggy' wire radials. Note the difference in physical length of the radials to the vertical element, a difference which would be even greater if the entire radial was at the lower level.

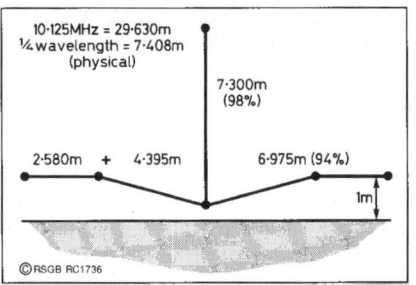

Fig 13: VK3MI's suggested antenna for 10.1MHz, with 'saggy' radials.

Short Vertical Antennas

Extracted from 'Technical Topics', *Radio Communication*, June 1998

SHORT VERTICAL ANTENNAS AND THEIR RADIALS

ALTHOUGH AT PRESENT, with sunspot cycle 23 increasingly making good progress (the daily sunspot number reached 192 on 9 April, with a Solar Flux of 141 on 11 April, a Kiel A of 25 on 11 April, with the solar flux exceeding 100 throughout the first half of April, resulting in a number of 28MHz openings) it may seem perverse to discuss how a reasonably efficient 1.8MHz antenna can be fitted into a postage-stamp-sized garden or backyard. However, Thomas Kuehl, AC7A, in 'Build efficient, short vertical antennas' (*QST*, March 1998, pp39-44) provides useful advice on both inductively and capacitively loaded vertical antennas based on 44ft, 1.5in diameter tubular masts intended for a segment of the 1.8MHz band centred on 1825kHz. A capacitively top-loaded antenna is likely to provide a significantly wider low-SWR bandwidth than with inductive loading.

Of paramount importance for those with little real-estate, where quarter-wave resonant elevated radials are out of the question, is AC7A's advice on 'grounds'. His advice is that more short buried radials are better than a few long ones: "Set radial length and orientation to fit the available space. As a minimum, 20 radials is a good objective, while more than 80 is likely to be of little benefit. Don't depend on ground rods, they are an ineffective earth return in many locations."

More on Fractal Antennas

Extracted from 'Technical Topics', *Radio Communication*, June 1998

MORE ON FRACTAL ANTENNAS

ALTHOUGH APPARENTLY some readers thought the item 'Magic Fractal Antennas?' in the April *TT* was an April Fool joke, I am grateful to Peter Chadwick, G3RZP, (and subsequently VP8AEM) for drawing my attention to the series of articles by (Professor) Nathan ('Chip') Cohen, N1IR, in *Communications Quarterly*. These articles, which I have located in the RSGB Library at Potters Bar, provide in considerable detail (totalling over 50 large pages) background information on antennas having their elements shaped in fractal geometric forms as dipoles, folded dipoles and loop antennas. Many of the looped designs are based on various iterations of the Minkowski Island (MI) fractal, starting (MI0) from a quad (square) element. The basic Minkowski fractal, with four iterations, forms the basis of the military helmet antenna shown in Fig 2 of the April *TT* (p59); see also **Fig 4** for M0, M1 and M2 geometry. Among the fractal antennas illustrated are an MI3 antenna for 144MHz, about 8in per side and a MI2 for 50MHz about 30in per side. **Fig 5(a)** shows the geometry of a first iteration Minkowski Island (MI1) and **Fig 5(b)** a second iteration, MI2.

In 'Fractal Antennas: Part 1 - Introduction and the Fractal Quad' (*Communications Quarterly*, Summer 1995, pp7-22), N1IR provides a good introduction to the geometry of antenna elements, pointing out that although antenna design has become a mature field, there is still room for a new approach that uses fractal geometry to produce very small antennas of high efficiency and with some other useful attributes. He presents a design for very small area single-element cubical quads, along with their comparative results. He makes it clear that although work on fractal antennas has

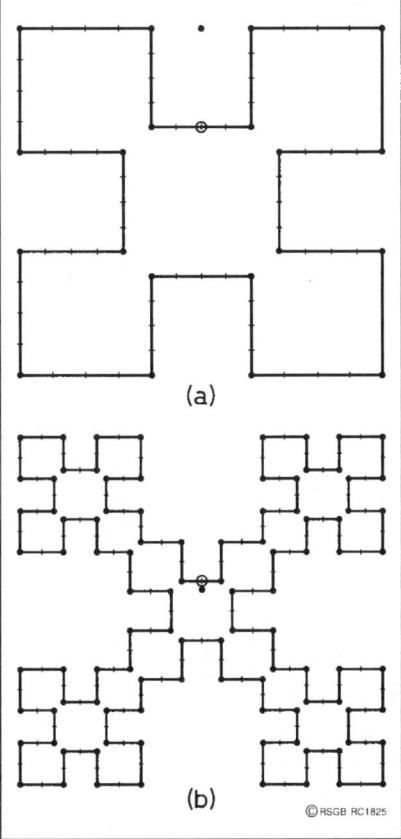

Fig 5: (a) First iteration Minkowski Island (MI1) fractal developed from the quad square element and used in several N1IR designs. (b) Second Iteration Minkowski Island (MI2) has also been used by N1IR.

blossomed recently, they are not entirely a new idea. One of the original forms of microwave log periodic microwave antennas, as built over 40 years ago by DuHamel and Isbell, was a toothed spiral fractal.

Then, in a decade of work some 15-20 years ago, Prof F M Landstorfer and R R Sacher at the Technical University of Munich, investigated the use of bent antenna elements in order to develop an optimum shape. This work was noted several times in *TT*. For example 'Optimum-shaped antennas' December 1982, pp1054-5, from which **Fig 6** and **Fig 7** are

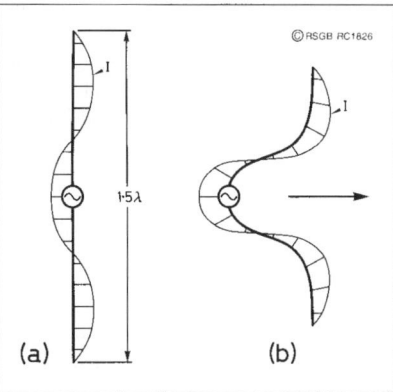

Fig 6: Showing the current distribution on (a) a straight 1.5λ dipole where the phase reversal reduces radiation normal to the axis of the dipole; and (b) with a Landstorfer gain-optimized shape, which causes radiation to increase significantly in the forward direction as a single-element 'beam'.

reproduced. See also 'Directivity of optimum-shaped antennas' (February 1983, pp131-2). Although the Landstorfer element was not a fractal, nevertheless his work showed that the conventional straight element was not necessarily the optimum approach.

'Fractal Antennas: Part 2 - A discussion of relevant, but disparate qualities' (*Communications Quarterly*, Summer 1996, pp53-71) came a year after Part 1. But before then a further article by N1IR on fractal antennas had appeared: 'Fractal and Shaped Dipoles - Some simple fractal dipoles, their benefits and limitations' (*Communications Quarterly*, Spring 1996, pp25-36). Then, together with Robert G Holfeld, N1IR, presented 'Fractal loops and the small loop approximation - Exploring fractal resonances' (*Communications Quarterly*, Winter 1996, pp77-81).

After attempting to digest, at least in outline, this mass of information, I remain rather uncertain as to its present practical value to amateur constructors. Clearly, as with the Landstorfer designs, it would not be easy to implement multi-iteration fractal elements on HF, where the space condensation would be most valuable. On 144MHz, fractal designs could be implemented using aluminium foil pasted on a dielectric, as in N1IR's original 144MHz an-

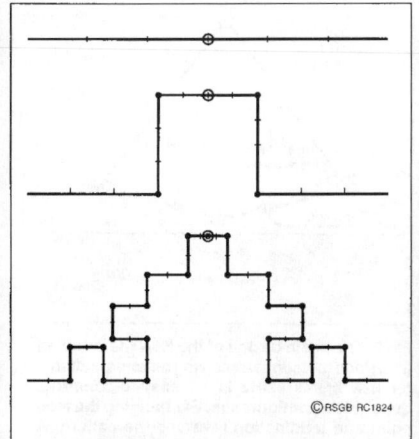

Fig 4: The Minkowski (box) fractal for iterations 0 (straight line), 1 and (bottom) 2.

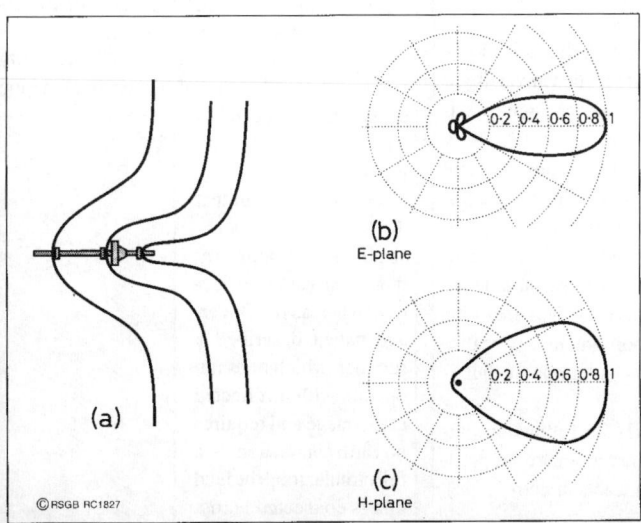

Fig 7: A Yagi array using three gain-optimised elements each approximately 1.5λ long. A VHF array of this type, reported in 1982 by Dr Landstorfer, provided a forward gain of 11.5dBi, sidelobe attenuation better than 20dB and a front-to-back ratio of 26dB.

ANTENNA TOPICS

tenna (which he reveals was eventually spotted and cut down by his landlord). N1IR has also implemented VHF fractal loop-type antennas using heavy gauge wire for 50 and 144MHz, and these should not prove too difficult to implement and mount.

N1IR shows clearly that this approach appears to be quite practical at VHF or UHF, offering several resonances and capable of providing resonant feedpoints with little reactance. I suspect that a practical difficulty would arise for an experimenter in dimensioning the more complex fractal antennas so that the major resonance fell in the desired amateur band without a fair amount of trial and error. Nevertheless it is clearly an important field for experimentation and may possibly come to represent the 'magic' breakthrough suggested in the *New Scientist* article on which the April *TT* item was based.

After writing the above item, further references to published articles on fractal antennas have been sent in by readers, including the use of fractal radials for vertical antennas (*73 Amateur Radio Today*, September 1996, pp34-35) from PA3CQQ.

Fractals Again

Extracted from 'Technical Topics', *Radio Communication*, August 1998

FRACTALS AGAIN

JOHN HARBOTTLE, RS96257, points out that further information on fractal antennas (see *TT*, April and June 1998) can be found on a number of web sites. A check by RSGB HQ shows the following were still to be found during June:

http://www.mbvlab.wpafb.af.mil/rkutter/thesis

http://www.mbvlab.wpafb.af.mil/rkuttere/thesis/thesis2.html

This provides the undergraduate Honours Thesis of Richard E Kutter at the University of Dayton, Department of Electrical Engineers. It includes some useful introductory notes: "Why fractals? Fractals are perhaps the most efficient way of increasing the perimeter of an area. It is well known that the perimeter of a loop antenna is the most important factor in determining its resonant frequency. A fractal antenna with a given perimeter takes up less area than a comparable square loop antenna (I realise this is a rather simplistic assumption, but is does work - to a point!).

Why a fractal antenna? (The following comparisons are made against a square loop antenna, assuming the user wants directive gain).

Advantages:
- Smaller cross-sectional area.
- No impedance matching network required.
- Multiple resonances.
- Higher gain in some cases.

Disadvantages:
- Lower resonant bandwidth than loop antenna.
- Creation is more difficult.
- Lower gain in some cases.

The Terminated Receiving Loop

Extracted from 'Technical Topics', *Radio Communication*, August 1998

THE TERMINATED RECEIVING LOOP

GARY BREED, K9AY, in the September, 1997 *QST* (pp43-46) presented an article that offered a novel solution to the amateur with limited space seeking a compact, low-band directional receiving antenna. He described an easy to construct antenna having a polar diagram that could be remotely switched to the four quadrants of the compass, yet capable of being fitted into a 30ft diameter (10m) circle. He called this 'the K9AY terminated loop', and acknowledged that it had been developed from the much larger EWE antenna developed by Floyd Koontz, WA2WVL (*QST*, February 1995), which required an 80ft diameter circle.

Subsequent comments in *QST*'s Technical Correspondence column (April 1998, pp77-78) by Bill Bridges, W6FA, revealed that the origin of the terminated loop can be traced back to HH Beverage (W2BML) of RCA and his US patent 2,247,743 of July 1941. W6FA emphasised that the terminated loop is not a wave antenna with which the name of Beverage is more usually associated and which was developed by him in the early 1920s. The only commercial application of his terminated loop appears to have been as a VHF television receiving antenna.

W6FA points out that the K9AY design is basically a half loop, requiring an earth connection, whereas the Beverage patent described a full loop which does not operate with a reflected earth image and requires no earth connection. In a full circular loop the feed line is connected across a break in the loop, with a terminating resistor connected across another break in the circle diametrically opposite the feed line.

Fig 2 shows the basic design of a single K9AY type terminated half loop receiving antenna in an easy-to-construct quasi-delta loop configuration. In this form the antenna is unidirectional, in the sense that it receives best signals from the left hand side of the page, with a sharp null at an elevated angle in the opposite direction. If the feed point and termination resistor are exchanged the pattern is reversed, receiving signals better from the right hand side.

In practice, K9AY developed a four direction system by using two of these loops hung from a single support and installed at right angles to one another. A relay controlled switching system, located at the base of the loop (**Fig 3**) enables a single terminating load and matching transformer to be switched to each loop in each configuration. Later, K9AY provided modified circuits of his switching system (*QST*, May 1998, p73) to overcome some hum problems reported by users: **Fig 4** and **Fig 5**.

A single or double terminated loop system could clearly have useful applications from LF to VHF, either as a fixed directional antenna, switchable bi-directional antenna, or as the K9AY dual loop system switchable to any of four quadrants.

To quote K9AY: "The terminated loop is physically and electrically quite simple. It consists of a wire loop of any convenient shape (diamond, delta, etc), hung from a single support and with a ground rod at the bottom. A 9:1 impedance matching transformer connects from one end of the loop to ground, a terminating resistor connects the other end of the loop to ground. This antenna is directional, favouring signals arriving from the feed point end, rejecting by several S-points any signals arriving from the end connected to the terminating

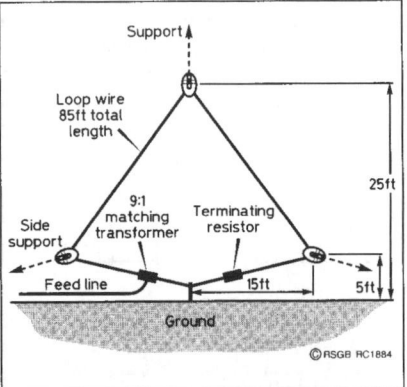

Fig 2: The basic design of the K9AY terminated (half) loop directional receiving antenna, suitable for use below 4MHz in an easy-to-construct quasi-delta configuration. Exchanging the feed point and termination reverses the pattern. A four direction system uses two similar loops installed at right angles to each other with a relay controlled switching system.

resistor... A very small terminated loop maintains its directional pattern. As the loop's size gets smaller, however, the desired signal strength is also reduced."

K9AY suggests that the value of the terminating resistor should lie between 390 and 560Ω, with 390Ω about optimum on 1.8MHz, 560Ω optimum for 3.5MHz and 470Ω "pretty good" on both bands. For amateur two-way operation with a separate transmitting antenna, the resistor should be rated at least 1 watt (K9AY uses a 2 watt carbon resistor), in case some of the transmitter power ends up on the loop. "The matching transformer is a 9:1 impedance, 3:1 turns-ratio type that should be familiar to many readers.

It is claimed that with an optimum value of terminating resistor, the rejection null can be as deep as 40dB at 20 to 55° elevation, depending on the shape of the loop and local ground conditions. Unless the loop is short and wide or tall and skinny, the null will be at 30 to 40° elevation and very useful for rejecting medium distance signals, although such a loop would not be suitable for DF applications on ground wave signals. The circumference of the loops (essentially half loops reflected in the ground) should not exceed a quarter wavelength at the highest frequency band on which they are to be used. With full loops, without the ground connection, circumference should be less than a half-wavelength.

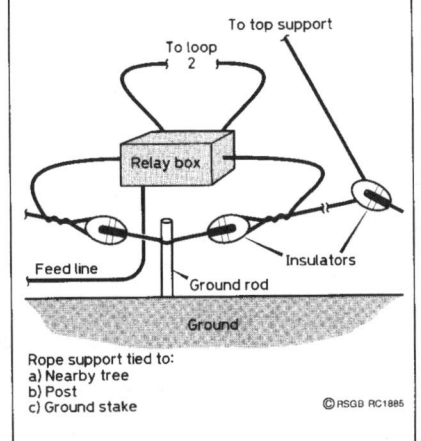

Fig 3: How the relay-control box, which also contains the matching transformer and terminating resistor, is located at the base of the K9AY terminated loop.

K9AY points out that the terminated loop antenna is an excellent antenna for weak AM broadcast reception and, if scaled in size, can be used for HF broadcast or amateur reception. For reception from a fixed area, a single loop without remote switching could be used.

3.5/7MHz Folded Umbrella

Extracted from 'Technical Topics', *Radio Communication*, November 1998

G3DWW'S 3.5/7MHz FOLDED UMBRELLA ANTENNA

WAY BACK IN July 1974, pp445-446, *TT* noted that while the use of guy wires to provide top loading for short vertical antennas in the form of 'umbrella' antennas was well known, an article by S U Nolan 'Developments in MF radiator systems' in the Marconi journal *Sound & Vision Broadcasting*, Vol 15, No 1, Spring 1974, described a useful looking variation in the form of a 'folded umbrella' antenna.

S U Nolan pointed out that many of the developments in MF antennas had been concerned with giving the users more for their money, both for broadcasting and maritime radio applications at 500kHz. He noted that typical low power umbrella antennas consist of a mast radiator with a number of wires (typically nine) attached to the top and radiating downwards at an angle of about 45° to the horizon.

The main limitations which arise from using any vertical radiator which is short in terms of wavelength are efficiency and bandwidth. Acceptable values of 90% efficiency and 10kHz bandwidth with an SWR less than 1.2 can be achieved with a mast height of only one-tenth of a wavelength at frequencies down to about 500kHz.

The July 1974 item continued: "It is claimed that a further simplification results from 'folding' the vertical element, to raise the impedance at the base to that of a coaxial feeder, so allowing the antenna to be fed directly without any matching network at the bottom of the mast, and also *allowing the mast itself to be grounded for lightning protection* (stress added by G3DWW).

"The way this is done is to form a cage of wires running parallel to the mast and with all wires directly connected to the top of the mast and connected together at the base, but insulated from ground and the mast: **Fig 2**.

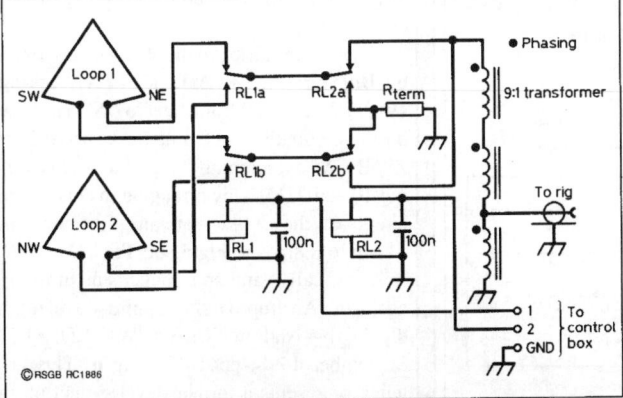

Fig 4: Circuit details of the relay box at the base of the antenna. The relays switch between the two loops and also reverse the lead point and termination resistor connections. This diagram is from the later K9AY note, with his original system modified to avoid hum pick up from the relay power being fed over the coaxial feeder. K1 and K2 are 12V DC, DPDT relays. For the value of the termination resistor R, see text.

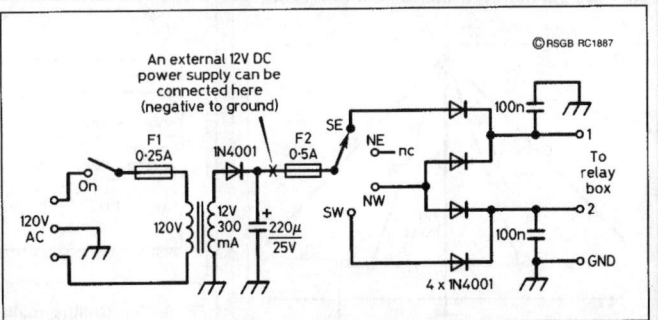

Fig 5: Circuit details of the control box located in the shack. This is the modified arrangement designed by K9AY to overcome hum pick-up from the relay power being fed over the coaxial feed line.

ANTENNA TOPICS

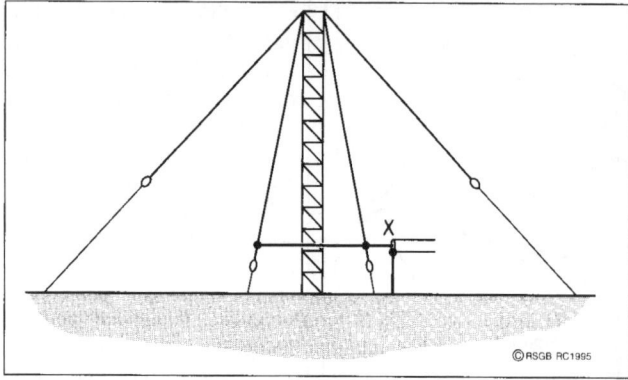

Fig 2: The folded umbrella antenna, which allows mast-radiators of as little as one-tenth-wavelength to be fed directly from low impedance coaxial feeder, as described in 1974.

The antenna is made self-resonant, that is to say the inductance of the mast and cage of wires in parallel must tune with the 'guy wire' top capacitance... The input impedance at the base of the mast will be purely resistive and about 15Ω. This can be raised to the impedance of the coaxial feeder by the folding process and by adjusting the number of wires in the cage... The folded umbrella antenna looks quite a useful approach for 1.8 and 3.5MHz, although to be most effective it needs either good ground conductivity or an effective earthing mat of radials."

In the 24 years since the item was published, I cannot recall any reaction from readers until a letter arrived recently from George Cripps, G3DWW: "I have recently been using a form of 'Folded Umbrella' antenna based on the [1974] item in *TT*. In my case the mast is a 21ft, 1in-diameter ex-WD copper plated tubular mast and the triangular section resonated around 7MHz (**Fig 3**). It was fed from a TS520 transceiver via 50ft of 50Ω coaxial cable. Without an ATU, the SWR was 1.1 on 7MHz, 1.6:1 on 3.7MHz and 2.1:1 on 14MHz. With an ATU, all three bands show 1:1 SWR.

"I have not tried the antenna on 1.8MHz, but the performance on 7 and 3.5MHz has been very satisfactory, particularly at around the 300-mile range. On reception it is a good deal quieter than a T-antenna similarly used." I feel a little doubtful whether G3DWW's antenna is in practice a mast radiator radiating primarily vertically polarised signals, as with the Marconi design, but nevertheless it looks useful.

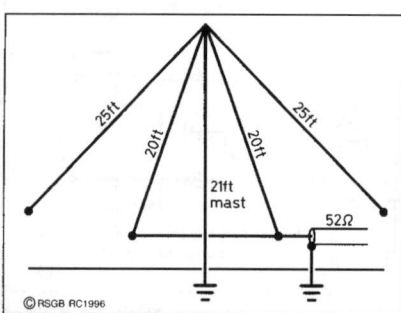

Fig 3: G3DWW's 7MHz version of the folded umbrella antenna.

1/3 Lambda Dipole

Extracted from 'Technical Topics', *Radio Communication*, December 1998

1/3 LAMBDA DIPOLE

THE CONCEPT OF a multi-band doublet antenna fed with a length of open wire, 450Ω ladder-line or 300Ω twin transmission line, with dimensions such that the end of the balanced feeder provides an impedance of roughly 50Ω (say 25-100Ω) and can thus be connected to a reasonably short length of 50Ω or 75Ω coaxial cable that is brought into the shack, has a long-established role in amateur radio. There was the Collins Radio three-band multi-band dipole of 1935 (**Fig 3** and see *TT*, April 1993) in which the open-wire feeder was brought into the shack. Then, in the late 1940s,

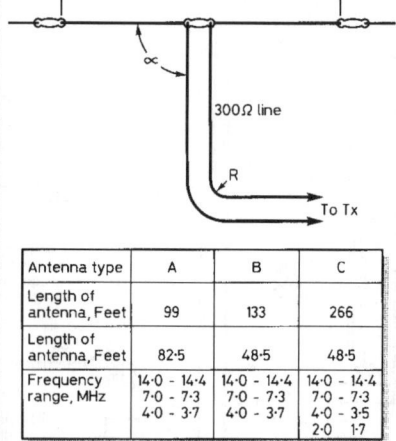

Fig 3: The Collins multi-band dipole antenna of 1935, in which the 300Ω line was brought into the shack and matched to the transmitter through a balanced pi-network tuner, to provide equal RF current in both feeder wires.

Frequency (MHz)	Resistance (Ohms)	Reactance (Ohms)	SWR into 50ohm
3.56	6.7	-4	7.6
7.03	35	+28	2.1
14.06	40	-3	1.2
18.07	39	+69	4.3
24.90	98	+81	1.9
28.06	46	-31	3.5
With feeder length 8.8m			
10.1	27	+234	1.8*
21.06	24	-4	2.0
With feeder length 14.9m			
10.1	52	-422	1.0*
21.06	24	+3	2.0

Negative reactance is capacitive (positive is inductive) in series with the resistive part of the impedance.
*On 10.1MHz a 130pF capacitor in each leg of the feeder will tune out the reactance. With the 14.9m feeder, 3.3μH inductors should be used instead.

Table 1: G0FAH all-band HF antenna.

came the subsequently well-known 'G5RV', developed independently by Louis Varney, and incorporating the non-critical length of 75Ω coax feeder.

The 'G5RV' - **Fig 4(a)** - remains one of the most-popular multiband 'wire' antennas. This is despite it having been designed in the late 1940s, ie before the 21MHz band was available to amateurs, and long before the 10, 18 and 24MHz bands. It will work on all HF bands, provided that it is used with a flexible ATU, although on some bands the SWR on the coaxial cable will be very high.

In the early 1980s, as a result of an early use of computer-modelling, Dr Brian Austin, ZS6BKW/G0GSF, modified the dimensions of the G5RV to provide an antenna that could be used with 50Ω coax without an ATU on three bands - 7, 14 and 28MHz - and with a simple one also on 3.5, 10 and 21MHz (*TT*, May 1982, with a full length article by G0GSF in *RadCom*, August 1985): **Fig 4(b)**. Another modification to the G5RV was proposed by W5ANB in *QST*, November 1981: **Fig 4(c)**. A five band version (7, 14, 18, 24, 21MHz) that is claimed to operate without an ATU has been described by Rick Hill, ZL1OK (*Break-in*, May 1992), although I do not have any further details.

In 1992, an 'all-band dipole' was described by Bill Wright, G0FAH, in *SPRAT*, Spring 1992, *TT*, June 1992, and later in *QST*. He drew on the computer-modelling work of G0GSF/ZS6BKW, overcoming the problem of covering 10 and 21MHz by arranging to change the length of the 300Ω matching section from 11.5m to 8.8m: see **Fig 5** and **Table 1**.

A basically similar arrangement turns up again in 'An improved one-third-wavelength dipole' by Andrew Griffith, W4ULD (*QST*, September 1998, pp41-45): **Fig 6**. This antenna represents a further development of an antenna he described in *QST*, September 1993, but now includes a remote matching network (**Fig 7**) for better performance on 3.5MHz. With the network remotely switched (from the

1990 - 1999

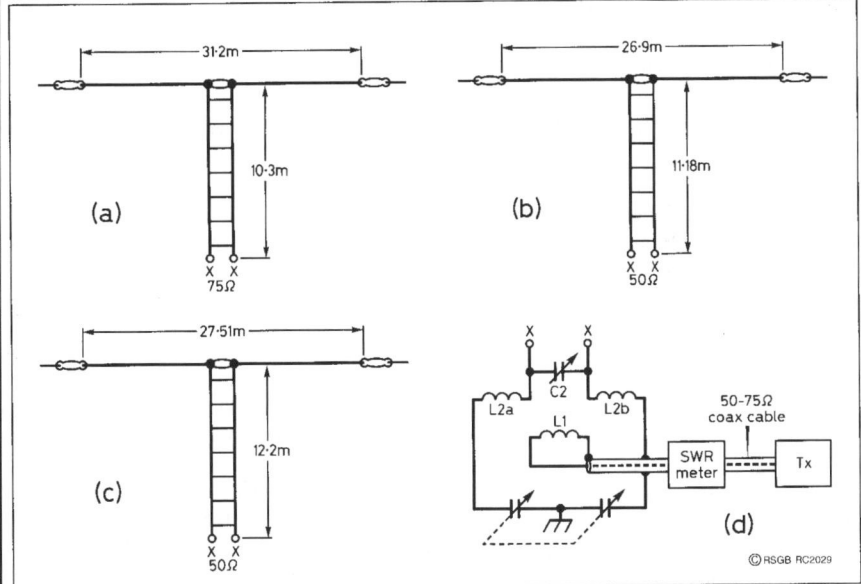

Fig 4: Three versions of multi-band dipole antennas designed to enable 50Ω coaxial cable to be connected to the end of the balanced line and brought into the shack. (a) The original 1940s 'G5RV', with 102ft (31.2m) top. (b) The computer-based 'ZS6BKW', developed in South Africa by Dr Brian Austin, G0GSF/ZS6BKW, which can provide five low-VSWR frequencies in the HF spectrum. (c) A version developed by W5ANB. (d) A suitable ATU for use on those bands where there is appreciable VSWR on the coax section.

shack), the antenna functions on 7, 14, 17.5, 24.5 and 28MHz with an SWR of less than 3:1, and less than 2:1 on most. The 1:1 balun used by W4ULD is a commercial unit capable of handling powers in excess of a kilowatt, but for his earlier implementation (powers up to 200 watts) his balun was made by stringing 10 FB-77-5621 beads close together on a length of RG-8X coax.

C1, C2, C3 and C4 matching network capacitors, which carry high RF currents or voltages when using the American legal power limits, are all home-made from readily available materials (construction details calling for some skill are given in the *QST* article). My own feeling is that if one wished to avoid the complications of the remote matching network, the 40ft of ladder line could be brought into the shack and then used with a flexible ATU providing a balanced output and manually adjusted for the band in use. With the dimensions shown, the ladder line should be current fed on most bands. The one-third lambda approach should prove an effective doublet antenna although, as for all the other G5RV variations and long-wire antennas, the horizontal radiation pattern will not be the same on all bands (not necessarily a disadvantage when chasing countries).

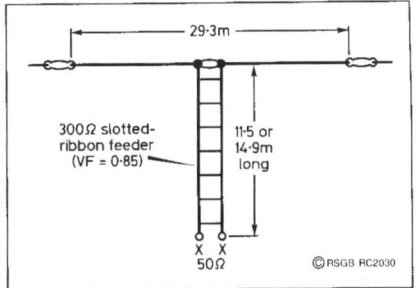

Fig 5: The G0FAH 'all-band' dipole, which can be used on all bands including the WARC bands from 1.8 to 30MHz, derived from the computer-modelling work of G0GSF in which the length of the balanced feeder section is changed on some bands. The SWR presented to the transmitter can be reduced by using the ATU shown in Fig 101(d).

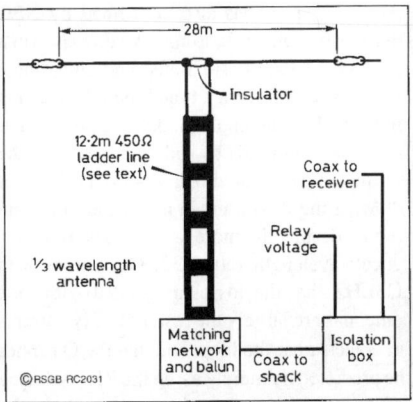

Fig 6: W4ULD's 'improved one-third-lambda dipole', with a remote switched matching network for improved performance on 3.5MHz.

WARC Bands & Cubical Quads

Extracted from 'Technical Topics', *Radio Communication*, December 1998

WARC BANDS ON CUBICAL QUADS

BOB COX, G3PLP, has found a solution to the problems that can arise when attempting to add 24 and 28MHz to a two-element cubical quad antenna designed for the 18 and 21MHz bands.

He writes:

"I built my first quad antenna in 1977 and have been using them ever since. My present two-element quad antenna uses the classical fibreglass spreaders and wire arrangement, with some metalwork to support and locate the gamma matches for each band. Recently, with the increasing sunspot activity, I decided to add 24 and 28MHz, taking the dimensions from the magnificent book on cubical quads by Bill Orr, W6SAI.

"As for the existing array, each driven element was provided with its own feed, switched at the mast, with its own gamma match. The result was a four-band quad for 18/21/24/28MHz. However, tests soon showed that something was very wrong. The front-to-back ratio on 21MHz, better than 20dB before the addition of the higher bands, had fallen to no better than 10dB, seemingly also with some loss of forward gain. Checking the antenna on all four bands showed that the new 28MHz section appeared to be working perfectly, but this was not the case on the other three bands, even though the gamma matches were adjusted close to unity SWR on each band.

"It then became obvious what the problem was. When operating on 28MHz, all four reflector loops were larger than the driven element - fine! But on 24MHz, the driven element could 'see' not only its own reflector, some 3.5% bigger, but also the 28MHz reflector loop, resonant in the region 26-27MHz and apparently acting as a director on the 24MHz band. Similar situations exist on 21 and 18MHz. Thus on all three-lower-frequency bands the array no longer comprised a driven element and an effective reflector, but instead a driven element plus opposing reflector and director loops.

"To verify that this really was the case, I decided to mount relays on the 21/24/28MHz reflectors (the 18MHz loop acts as a reflector on all bands and does not therefore require switching). The relays were in the normally closed position, with the relay coils RF by-passed. Switching was then arranged as follows:

On 28MHz	All loops closed
On 24MHz	28MHz reflector open-circuited
On 21MHz	28 and 24MHz reflectors open circuited
On 18MHz	28, 24 and 21MHz reflectors open-circuited.

"Eureka! All was now well again. Ground wave tests with a local station (G3AQM) about 7 miles distant confirmed this, with my 21MHz quad now having its front-to-back ratio of better than 20dB restored.

"I note that Bill Orr's book recognises some degradation in F/B ratio on tri-band quads (14/21/28MHz). Clearly the introduction of WARC bands, with the much closer frequency separation between bands, exacerbates this effect.

365

ANTENNA TOPICS

N1R on his Fractals

Extracted from 'Technical Topics', *Radio Communication*, January 1999

N1IR, ON HIS FRACTALS

AN UNEXPECTED letter has arrived from Professor Nathan 'Chip' Cohen, N1IR, who has done so much pioneering work on 'fractal antennas' (see *TT* April and June, 1998), and whose attention had been drawn to the April item while in contact with G3BDQ. N1IR was using his 28MHz fractal quad-yagi antenna. He writes: "Given the sensational nature of the *New Scientist* ['Aerial Magic'] article, I thought *TT* did a very good job in presenting a sane perspective on this... There is, of course, no magic. But there are advantages when compared to other loading and/or band-broadening methods. The 4dBd dipole (Cohen dipole) mentioned, for example, is not for an electrically small antenna, but one that has a fractal stub at its centre, giving it echelon/colinear phasing. A Landstorfer dipole [see the June item] also shares this attribute, but is larger. I have found it convenient to look at meander and Landstorfer structures as the first 'pass' at a fractal.

"The main advantage of the fractal is that it provides ultra wide bandwidth (UWB) capabilities at the higher frequencies, where the fractally bent wire (for example) is very large electrically. This is of limited interest to the ham community - emphasis on shrinkage seems to be the issue. Here the fractal gives a small antenna with very high efficiency. Naturally, this is at the expense of bandwidth, and the Q increases for the lowest resonance. Upper resonances are usually *not* harmonic, and often merge from the 'fractal loading' effect. It is also noteworthy that the fractal generator and iteration allows one to 'tune' the antenna as desired, for multiband operation for instance.

"Readers may wish to look at the web site *www.fractenna.com* In addition to the ham page, a 'white paper' should be posted in the New Year."

N1R on his Fractals

Extracted from 'Technical Topics', *Radio Communication*, January 1999

SMALL LOOP TRANSMITTING 'MAGNETIC' ANTENNAS

IT IS NOW a year since *TT* reported the view expressed by Professor Mike Underhill, G3LHZ, and M J Blewitt, G4VRN, at the IEE 1997 conference on 'HF radio systems and techniques' that a "small folded dipole mode was usually the dominant mode". This represented a serious attempt to reconcile the anecdotal evidence that the performance of these small loop antennas appeared better than suggested by conventional theory (for example, as investigated by Tony Henk, G4XVF, in 1991). See **Fig 1** for various methods of matching small loops to 50Ω cable.

These views attracted mostly adverse comment from a number of readers, with ripostes from G3LHZ. I would like to report that this controversy has been settled one way or another; however, both sides continue to stick to their original opinions, presenting additional evidence. The matter is far from settled, though tending to move into exotic areas that have only limited bearing on the practical use of small mag-loop antennas by amateurs.

However, in some respects, both factions are coming to agree on certain aspects. There is convincing evidence that significant dipole-mode radiation does occur, increasing as the circumference of the loop approaches a quarter-wave, though it seems unlikely that in practice this is the dominant mode claimed by G3LHZ. There is also evidence that this dipole-mode radiation is taken into account in the NEC 'Method of Moments' software. The work at the University of Surrey also shows that Q factor made by measuring the bandwidth is significantly affected by coupling into the environment, ie by creating eddy currents in nearby structures.

From the viewpoint of the user, the eddy current losses account quite significantly for the differences in efficiency of the antenna calculated from RF-resistance losses in the loop and the overall radiation efficiency of the antenna. The eddy current losses contribute to the radiation resistance, thus, to some extent, they account for the relatively low heating of the loop as found by G4VRN and other users. Measurements made by G4VRN suggest at least 30% of the total radiated power may be absorbed by the environment and then either dissipated as losses, or re-radiated, causing distortion of the tuned loop antenna pattern. It would thus seem that the siting of a small loop antenna affects it performance and that it is wrong, as sometimes stated, that this is little affected by height and surrounding structures. It does not however invalidate G4XVF's finding that the effective overall radiation efficiency of a small loop, as found from far-field measurements, is relatively low (usually under 10%) compared with a dipole at a reasonable height.

The most significant new contribution to the debate comes from John Crabtree, writing from South Edina, MN, USA (e-mail: crabtreejr@aol.com). Here I quote briefly from his letter:

"I have read the item on the loop antenna debate with interest, and offer another perspective on the central issue, whether or not significant dipole radiation from a tuned loop is fact or fiction.

"The different current modes in loops have been extensively analysed in 'Antennas and Waves: A Modern Approach' by Prof Ronald W P King and Charles W Harrison jr, MIT Press, about 1969. Chapter 9 on 'The Loop Antenna: Currents, Impedances, Fields' includes a section 'The Small Loop: Electromagnetic Field' (pp577-581) which is particularly relevant. [Those seeking to consult this erudite book must be warned that it is highly mathematical, virtually double-Dutch to me, and I depend below on John Crabtree's interpretation - G3VA.]

"The section starts with the comment 'In numerous applications the loop antenna is electrically quite small... However, it is not always true - as often assumed - that all higher-mode currents may be neglected.' King goes on to develop a model of the parallel loop impedances for the loop and dipole modes (page 581).

"On page 578 King shows a graph of the ratio of the amplitude of the far field of a circular loop maintained by currents in the dipole mode to that maintained by currents in the circulating mode. The graph is approximately linear, with the maximum amplitude of the fields being the same when the loop circumferences/wavelength is approximately 0.4. I conclude that there can be significant dipole mode radiation from a small loop."

John Crabtree also shows that King makes it clear that the dipole mode plays a significant (but not dominant) role in the moderately small loop. He also draws attention to 'A note on the radiation resistance of loop antennas with short circumferences' by Peter Bertram, DJ2ZS (*Communications Quarterly*, Summer 1997, pp99-100). DJ2ZS modelled a loop antenna using EZNEC and obtained results in very good agreement with those of King... I conclude, rightly or wrongly, that NEC takes imbalanced currents into account. This is a point disputed by G3LHZ, who believes that NEC fails to predict the tuned loop correctly."

Alan Boswell, G3NOQ, a professional antenna engineer, has also confirmed by NEC that out-of-balance loop currents do exist when an AMA-3 loop is simulated and give dipole mode radiation from a tuned loop. His results indicate that the dipole mode becomes weaker than the loop mode by -6db per octave as the frequency is lowered below 40MHz. Even at 40MHz the dipole mode is not the dominant mode, despite the more favourable circumference/wavelength ratio. G3NOQ agrees with G3LHZ that the losses associated with loop antennas are largely the result of eddy currents in objects near the loop, and that the Q cannot be predicted by merely using the RF resistance of the conductor as the loss resistance in the equivalent circuit. DJ2ZS accepts that a mag-loop antenna works slightly better than pre-

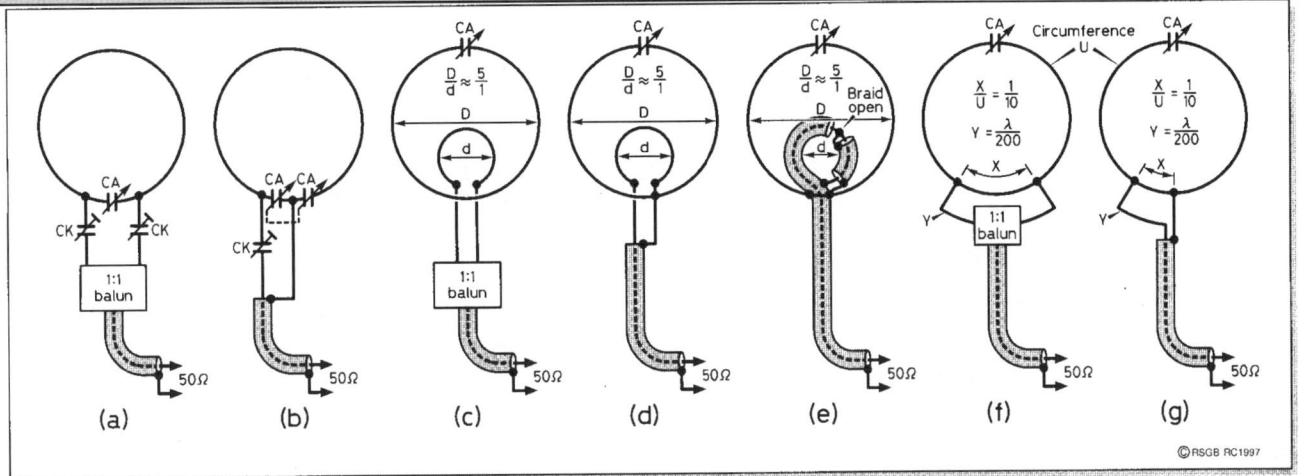

Fig 1: Methods of matching a tuned single-turn transmitting or receiving mag-loop antenna to 50Ω cable, as described in 1983 by DL2FA, whose work inspired the AMA range of loop antennas.

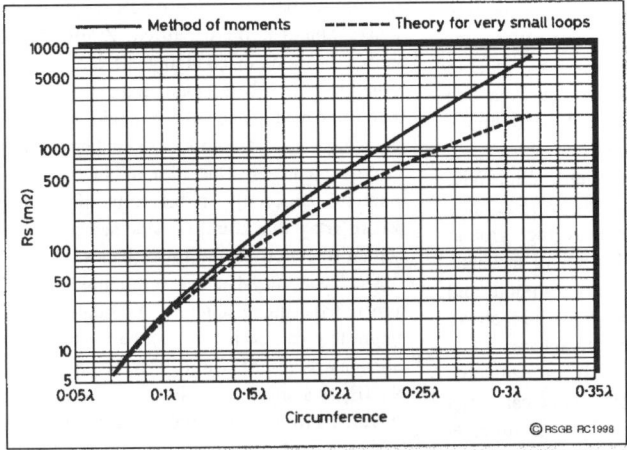

Fig 2: Radiation resistance of small loop antennas (assuming loss-less conductors) as calculated by DJ2ZS: Theory vs. Method of Moments.

dicted from the basic formulae that take no account of displacement currents: **Fig 2**.

John Crabtree concludes that there is significant dipole radiation from small loops, but is sceptical of G3LHZ's claim that on any tuneable frequency the dominant mode is that of a small folded dipole.

All this points to the validity of G4XVF's 1991 finding, supported by his far-field measurements, that the total effective radiation efficiency of small loops is very low (usually under 10%) and that the good results achieved by many users only underline the tolerance on HF of antennas with low overall efficiency. Tolerance to low efficiency is strained when using very low power. As many enthusiasts have found, QRP performs well with a good dipole, as can a mag-loop with reasonable transmitter power. A loop cannot be recommended for QRP unless made mandatory by space considerations, etc.

It should be appreciated that there is a limit to the space that can be devoted to this subject in *TT*, and that the above notes represents only a small portion of the comments received.

Bobtail, Half-square & Lazy-U

Extracted from 'Technical Topics', *Radio Communication*, April 1999

BOBTAIL, HALF-SQUARE AND LAZY-U ANTENNAS

WITH IMPROVING conditions on the higher HF bands but continued interest in chasing DX on the lower HF bands, the search for wire antennas that perform well at relatively low vertical radiation angles continues to exercise many enthusiasts worldwide. For those with plenty of space and supports at least a quarter-wave high, a single-band broadside antenna that has been shown to be a particularly effective low angle radiator (at least over good ground) is the Bobtail Curtain. This was included in many editions of *The Radio Handbook* (see also *ART* or *TT* July 1970). **Fig 2** and **Fig 3** show a version described by VE1TG with dimensions for the 3.5, 7 and 14MHz bands (dimensions for the 10, 18, 24 or 18MHz bands could be readily calculated from basic formulae). It should be appreciated that this antenna provides predominantly vertically polarized signals and over ground of good conductivity is capable of very low angle radiation. In its simplest single-element form, the Bobtail antenna reduces to the inverted ground plane (vertical-Tee) - a useful omnidirectional antenna: **Fig 4**.

Another loosely related configuration is the 7MHz low-angle directional parasitic array (a vertically-polarized wire squashed Yagi) developed by G6XN that provides good performance with relatively low supports: **Fig 5**. In this antenna the horizontal wires provide end-loading of the shortened vertical elements.

In all of the above configurations, the bulk of horizontally-polarized radiation is balanced out. This does not apply to the 'half-square' antenna, although this, in my view wrongly, is sometimes referred to as a bobtail antenna. The half-square antenna (**Fig 6**) however deserves consideration in its own right. This is the basis of 'A visit to the Half-square Antenna' by Hannes Coetzee, ZS6BZP (*Communications Quarterly,* Spring 1998, pp83-90). In 1997, ZS6BZP began experi-

ANTENNA TOPICS

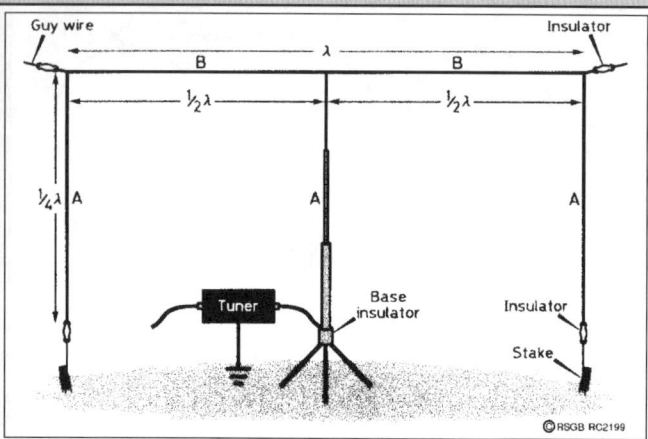

Fig 2: The classic Bobtail-curtain antenna with dimensions suggested by VE1TG.

Dimension	3.5MHz	7MHz	14MHz
A	66ft	33ft	16.5ft
B	132ft	66ft	33ft

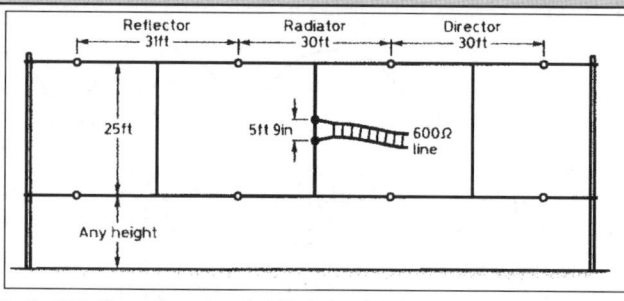

Fig 5: 7MHz three-element vertical Yagi array (wire) with element lengths much reduced by loading with the horizontal sections. Originally developed by Les Moxon, G6XN, in connection with experiments on extremely low-angle DX with low-power. It provided highly-reliable communication with Australia.

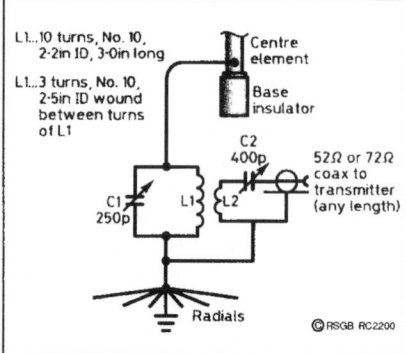

Fig 3: VE1TG's tuner for his 7MHz Bobtail-curtain array. For 14MHz L1 and C1 should be about half the values shown. C2 about the same. L1 10 turns of No 10 enamelled copper wire wound on former of inner diameter 2.5in over a length of about 3in. L2 3 turns wound between turns of L1 at the earthy end. Radiates predominantly vertically polarized signals.

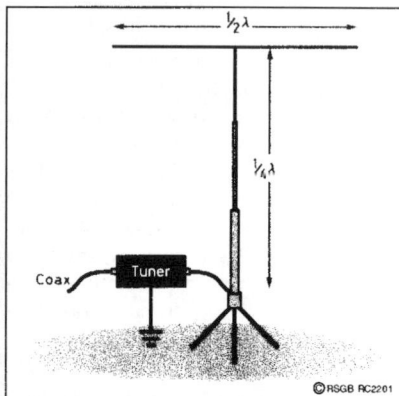

Fig 4: How the Bobtail can be reduced to form an omnidirectional inverted ground-plane antenna (Vertical-Tee)

menting with a 14MHz version, based on a 7MHz half-square antenna described by W8HXR in *73* in May 1985. He used two 6m (later increased to 9m) masts. As a comparison antenna he used the modified form of G5RV developed by Dr Brian Austin, ZS6BKW/G0GSF, which has been described several times in *TT* and in a full-length article in *RadCom* (August, 1985), at a height of 12 metres. To the disappointment of ZS6BZP, on-air tests showed the G5RV dipole consistently out-performing the 14MHz half-square antenna: "After many comparative tests, I had to accept defeat. The half-square antenna had been thoroughly beaten by a multiband dipole. I had to find the reason why!"

Together with Danie Brynard, ZS6AWK, and his copy of EZNEC2 by W7EL, they simulated both antennas over average ground at a height of 12m. The bottom of the half-square verticals were 7m above ground, and the radiation at an elevation of 11° above horizon was calculated for both antennas. The simulated half-square gave 3dBi per main lobe, whereas the improved G5RV gain came top with 7dBi in the main lobe. ZS6BZP suggests that the reason for the higher gain of the G5RV antenna can, to an extent, be found in the fact that its legs are considerably longer than those of a 14MHz dipole, with results on higher frequencies producing even more respectable gains.

He notes that the half-square antenna was intended for use on 7MHz, delivering a bi-directional pattern with a simulated gain of 1.78dBi and nulls in the direction of the antenna nearly 13dB deep; a very useful per-

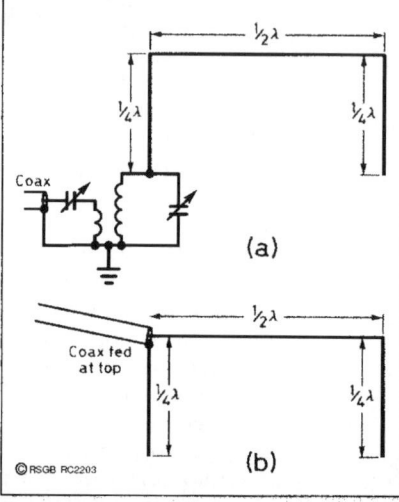

Fig 6: The basic Half-Square antenna. (a) voltage fed; (b) current fed. Mixed polarization.

formance. In comparison, the improved G5RV resulted in a figure-of-eight pattern with a maximum gain of 1 to 1.16dBi, a realistic figure for a 11° elevation angle for a dipole at close to a quarter-wavelength above ground, an improvement of some 0.5dB on the half-square antenna. In his article ZS6BZP describes methods of changing the direction of radiation from a half-square and also suggests that improved performance could result in changing it to a Phased Lazy-U antenna using Lazy-U elements. This idea might be worth pursuing, especially in the form of a four-square array that could provide selectable radiation direction on the lower bands.

The basic Lazy-U antenna resembles an upturned half-square antenna, although with a height that can be less than a half-wave. This antenna was described in 1992 by Henry Elwell, N4UH, as a short vertically polarized antenna in which, provided the total element length is a half-wave or multiple thereof with equal horizontal sections, the radiation from the horizontal sections is largely cancelled out: Fig 7.

ZS6BZP concludes: "Despite all the claims in the amateur press over the years, the half-square antenna is not the ultimate solution to all your needs. At 14MHz and higher, a tri-bander (or even a G5RV dipole) at the same height, outperforms the half-square by a fair margin. At 7MHz and lower, the half-square antenna has distinct advantages over a small beam or dipole used at less than a third of a wavelength above ground. The directivity and off-axes nulls also count in its favour. The antenna is also simple to construct."

It should be noted that with all the above antennas there will be high RF voltages at the base of the elements and care should be taken to ensure the safety of people and animals.

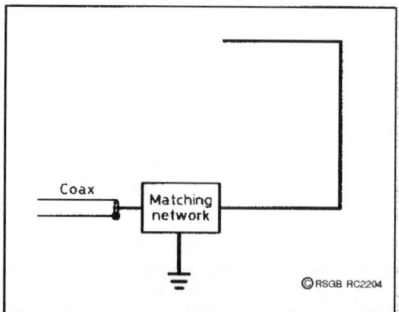

Fig 7: The basic Lazy-U antenna element. Produces predominantly vertically polarized signals.

Camp/Mobile Antennas

Extracted from 'Technical Topics', *Radio Communication*, April 1999

CAMP/MOBILE ANTENNAS

FOR 50 YEARS, Dr John (Jack) Belrose, VE2CV, has been using HF antennas from remote sites, including camping parks and the like. Initially he used simple, easily erectable dipole antennas, including the single-wire fed Windom wire dipole. Later he devised a centre-fed dipole with the element wound up on bobbins so that the system could provide a resonant half-wave dipole on any frequency (or band) of interest. More recently he used a coax-fed, off-centre-fed dipole, again with the wire elements wound on bobbins and suitable for 3.5, 7 and 14MHz bands (41.5m long, fed 13.8m from one end with a home brew 4:1 ferrite bead over coax current balun).

While such dipoles could be supported from one tree with a sloping element, their length could be a nuisance, as they usually had to stretch over neighbouring sites or roads. In 1993, he evaluated a number of DK5CZ's AMA tunable loop antennas, and has used the AMA6 (6.7 to 25MHz) as a camp antenna for a number of years. Vehicle-mounted loops have been proposed for NVIS operation, although they are rather daunting for all but the keenest amateurs. The traditional HF antenna used with land vehicles is a vertical whip - relatively poor for NVIS propagation - although VE2CV considers that the coil-loaded monopole is more easily transported than a loop because it breaks down into sections and can be used as a camp or mobile antenna from 1.8 to 30MHz. ('A tunable all-bands HF camp/mobile antenna' by VE2CV and Larry Parker, VE3EDY, *Communications Quarterly,* Fall 1998, pp47-57). He points out that from a campsite it is better to go up, than up and out.

The article describes in detail a TABA (Tunable All-Bands Antenna) system for mobile/transportable applications. Sufficient details are provided to enable amateurs with the necessary tools and machine shop skills to construct it, together with measured data to determine efficiency of the antenna for the 3.5MHz band plus computer-calculated performance on this and several other bands.

It is stressed that for any vehicle-mounted, electrically short, base-loaded HF antenna, the loading coil is a key component, as high-Q and remote tuning ability are highly desirable requirements: "The inductance required for the lower bands (1.8/3.5MHz) can be near the self-resonant frequency for the coil, so a coil with a space between the turns must be used to reduce its self-capacitance and increase its self-resonant frequency. For typical mobile antennas, a separate coil is used for each band, with no ability to retune. An alternative system was originally devised by D K Johnson, W6AAQ, and a version described by Lodewijk Stuyt, PA3BTN, and Hans Spits, PD0NCF, (*Electron*, March 1997, pp98-103, Dutch text). A translation of the Dutch article 'The 'Screwdriver' Rapid QRV Antenna' translated and edited by Erwin David, G4LQI, appears in the February 1999 issue of *RadCom*, pp16-19. This describes the construction of a continuously tuneable W6AAQ-type 'DK3' 3.5-30MHz mobile or portable antenna with, for fixed operation, a radial earth mat.

In Canada, two versions based on the W6AAQ design, independently of the Dutch work, of this form of tunable whip antenna (one for 1.8MHz and above, the other for 3.5MHz and above) were fabricated by VE3EDY. Their radiation characteristics were determined by VE2CV, and their on-air performance extensively evaluated by both. Coil length is 55.9cm (22in) for 3.5MHz, 81.3cm (32in) for 1.8MHz. A 1.5m stainless steel whip is installed for mobile use and a sectionized 4.9m whip used on camp sites etc, although the full-length 4.9m antenna can be used on a stationary vehicle which then, in effect, forms the earth mat.

The W6AAQ ingenious remotely-tunable loading coil system clearly requires some care and expertise in mechanical construction and is well illustrated in the February *RadCom*. For the Canadian versions, the lower section of the antenna is a 5cm (2in) diameter stainless steel pipe. The Canadians do not use the toroidal impedance-matching transformer advocated by W6AAQ and the Dutch authors. They claim that no other antenna system tuning unit is needed.

Much of the Canadian article is devoted to a discussion of the radiation characteristics and efficiency, including comparisons with an AMA8 loop and with a low dipole, both for NVIS medium-distances and for long-haul working, showing the effect of the vehicle body on the radiation characteristics: **Fig 10**. Among their concluding remarks, they stress: "The important features of the TABA (and the compact loop)

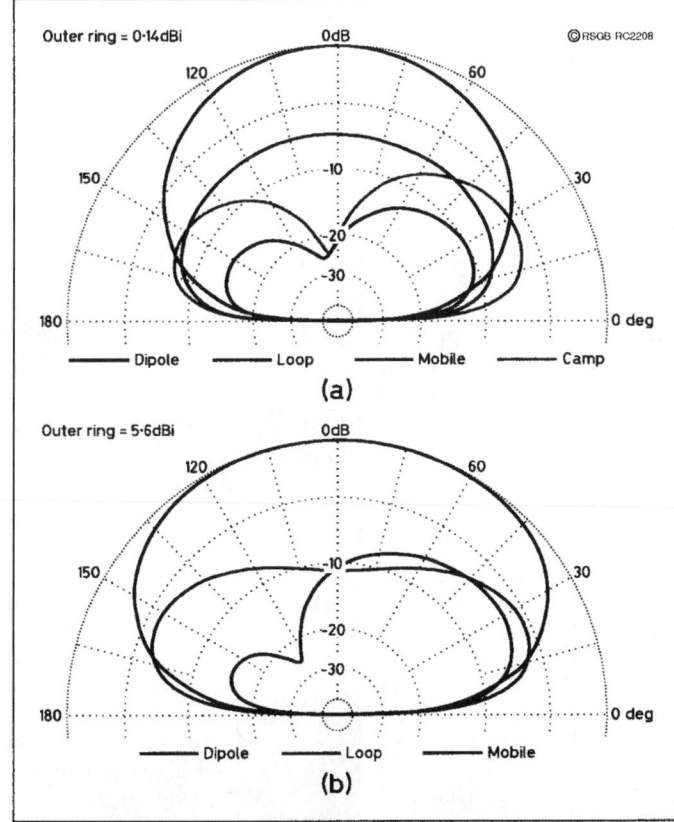

Fig 10: (a) Predicted vertical radiation pattern performance of VE2CV's 3.5MHz camp and mobile installations, compared with a dipole at low height and a vertical 1.6m compact loop (AMA8). (b) Predicted performance of the mobile antenna on 14MHz compared with the loop and dipole with an apex height and droop as for the 3.5MHz dipole.

ANTENNA TOPICS

is the ability to tune for a minimum SWR on the frequency of choice. This is particularly important for 3.5 and 1.8MHz, where their bandwidth is narrow. The TABA is not confined to the amateur bands but can be used on any frequency in the HF spectrum."

Fig 1: The multi-band clothesline folded dipole described in 1998 by VA3ERY.

Clothesline Antennas

Extracted from 'Technical Topics', *Radio Communication*, May 1999

CLOTHESLINE ANTENNAS

A TRADITIONAL FORM of covert antenna consists of a clothesline threaded with a thin, concealed wire, but in *TT*, March 1999, pp62, (shown again here as **Fig 1**) we reproduced a novel form of multi-band folded clothesline (washing-line) dipole in which the position of the 300Ω feedpoint could be adjusted by means of low-cost plastic pulleys normally intended for outdoor clotheslines of upstairs apartments etc. This came from a collection of HF antenna ideas in the Dutch VERON journal *Electron*, collated by PE1PVB and ascribed to VA3ERY, although the original source was not given by PE1PVB. This resulted in a letter from Roberto Craighero, I1ARZ, who provided the original *QST* article by VA3ERY and also revealed an earlier Italian endorsement of this ingenious approach. He wrote:

"The article on which PE1PVB drew was 'The Clothesline Antenna' subtitled 'Dry your laundry or work DX - Could this be the first dual-purpose antenna?' by Robert Victor, VA3ERY (*QST*, July 1998, pp56-58). I was impressed and decided to translate it into Italian for possible publication in the ARI journal *Radio Rivista*. It duly appeared in the February 1999 issue (pp43-44). Following publication I received a letter from Goffredo Navacci, I0TWA, who pointed out that a similar form of clothesline antenna had been developed and used by him since 1995, with publication in the Italian magazine *Radio Kit* (March 1995)."

I1ARZ enclosed copies of the relevant articles, which make it clear that while VA3ERY genuinely believed that he was the first to describe such an antenna, he recognised that: "Every once in a while, you run across an idea that seems so simple, so obvious, you can't believe it hasn't been done before. Surely (you say to yourself) you're not the first person in the universe to have thought of this... As far as I'm concerned, *I've* invented the Clothesline antenna. Still, I'm not going to be surprised if someone shows me that it's been done before! But even if this antenna design has been around since hydrogen, it may still be new to you. And even if you have seen something similar to the Clothesline, this design may be worth a second look. For hams in a variety of situations, this could be just what the doctor ordered to cure your DX dilemma."

VE3ERY waxed enthusiastically on the usefulness of this approach for the many amateurs operating from flats, condominiums or apartments. He claimed that his 132ft span version (as reproduced again as Fig 1) "works all the HF bands, and it gets great results. It doesn't need a tuner because it's dead-on resonant on the 80, 40, 20, 15 and 10 metre bands. A tiny tweak will bring in 12 and 17 metres too. It's remarkably easy to build. There are no traps, no stubs, no loading coils, no variable or fixed capacitors, no screws, no clamps, and you don't have to drill anything. This antenna is so simple to put up, it hurts. It consists of little more than a piece of wire, a centre insulator, some feed-line and a couple of $2 hardware-store fittings."

VA3ERY advises that for covering the 17 and 12 metre bands, you should cut the original length for resonance just a little up from the bottom of the 80 metre band, at 3615MHz. The fifth harmonic is then smack on 17 metres. Cut it to 3.55MHz and the seventh harmonic is on 12 metres. In practice, because of the folded dipole form of element, exact resonance will be much less critical than with a single thin wire element. VA3ERY reported that "On every band I tuned for, the SWR was well below 1.5:1 without a tuner."

The 1995

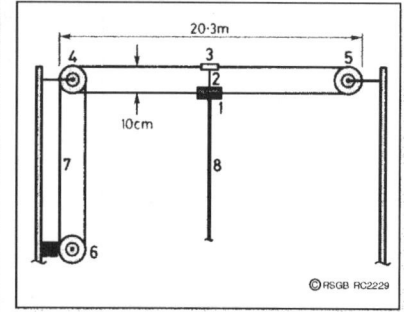

Fig 2: The multi-band clothesline folded dipole antenna as conceived and described in 1995 by I0TWA. (1) balun (see text). (2) Nylon cord. (3) PVC tube. (4), (5) and (6) plastic washing-line pulleys. (7) Nylon cord. (8) Coaxial cable feeder.

I0TWA design, although basically similar, differed in some practical details: **Fig 2**. Instead of using a non-critical length of 300Ω feeder, he put the balun (6:1 for 50Ω coax, 4:1 for 75Ω coax) at the element feed point. He also used three plastic pulleys, with a nylon cord permitting the lower pulley to be mounted so that the feed point could be adjusted from ground level, rather than by leaning out of the apartment window. I0TWA suggested that a folded element with a span of 20.3m would resonate on approximately 7050kHz, 14100kHz, 21,150kHz and 28200kHz. With the longer span of 39.6m it will have a fundamental resonance at 3600kHz, second harmonic 7200kHz, third 10,800kHz, fourth 14,400kHz, fifth 18,000, sixth 21,600kHz, seventh 25,200kHz and eighth 28,800kHz - all reasonably close with the wide bandwidth of a folded element to the amateur HF bands. For each band the feed point should be adjusted by means of the pulleys to approximately a quarter wavelength from the near end and then 'fine tuned' for minimum SWR.

All-in-all, it seems that the clothesline antenna, whether you go for the Canadian or the Italian job, is a useful addition to the stable of multi-band HF antennas.

Tuned Loops & VHF/UHF Loops

Extracted from 'Technical Topics', *Radio Communication*, May 1999

TUNED LOOPS & VHF/UHF LOOPS

I HAD THOUGHT that the February *TT* item (pp77-78) on compact HF tuned loop transmitting antennas would put this topic to rest at least for a time. However, the item had been written before receiving a letter from Dr Jack Belrose, VE2CV. His letter, originally directed to John Crabtree, went a long way to explaining the reason why the measured bandwidth of a compact loop is significantly larger than would be expected from calculating the Q of the loop on the basis of the ohmic losses. He feels that the prime reason for this difference arises from the differ-

1990 - 1999

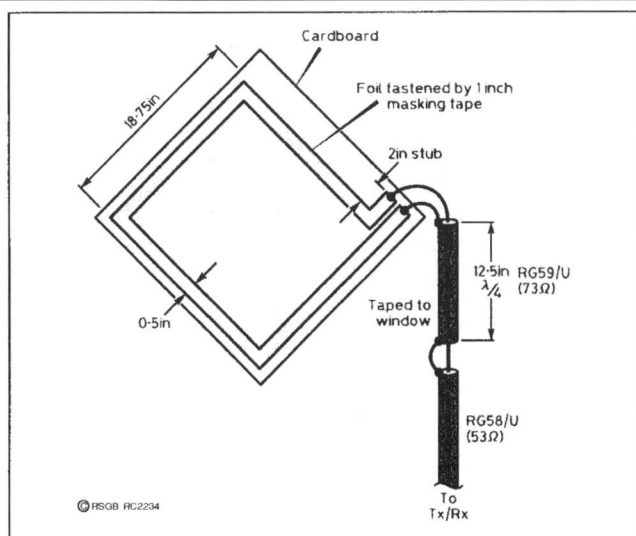

G8BTH's 50MHz (left) and 144MHz loop antennas, formed from copper strip mounted above ground planes.

Fig 7: Window-pane single-element quad for 144MHz operation, using household aluminium foil mounted on cardboard. As originally described by W8AP in 1971.

ence between the unloaded (theoretical) antenna bandwidth and the loaded operational bandwidth - and that discussion of eddy current losses in the February item is largely a red herring.

To quote very briefly from his long letter: "G3LHZ has noted that the Q values measured by SWR and antenna bandwidth methods are much lower than predicted by the traditional loop radiation formula. But this is to be expected. . . When we measure bandwidth by measuring SWR, we must remember to take into account the effect of the output impedance of the RF power amplifier, since for maximum power transfer the output or source impedance is the complex conjugate of the antenna's impedance (reference Belrose, VE2CV, Maxwell, W2DU and Rauch, W8JI, *Communications Quarterly*, Fall 1997, pp25-40) - and while not representing a loss, the source impedance (for narrowband antenna systems) increases the bandwidth of the antenna system. The operational bandwidth can theoretically be double the antenna bandwidth, but in practice the realized operational bandwidth is somewhat less (in my experience the increase in bandwidth is by a factor somewhat > 1.5 . . . For AMA-2 the measured operational bandwidth is greater than the antenna's bandwidth by a factor of about 1.7. The operational Q is lower than the antenna Q by this same factor."

It needs to be emphasised that the relatively low overall radiation efficiency of small transmitting 'magnetic' loop antennas arises from their electrically small dimensions, and that a large loop (for example a quad element) is a highly efficient radiator. On VHF/UHF a resonant or near-resonant loop antenna can provide a compact and attractive system. A useful form of indoor 144MHz antenna, comprising a quad element formed from household aluminium strip, stuck to a card and mounted on a window pane, has been described before in *TT*: **Fig 7**. Construction is roughly as follows: Cut a piece of aluminium foil to the outside dimensions, and a piece of cardboard of the same size. With 1in masking tape, fasten the foil and cardboard sheets together on the window. Cut the inside of the foil out with a razor, taking care not to go through the cardboard and scratch the window. Then tape the inside edge of the foil to the cardboard, leaving the 2in slit free of tape. The quarter-wave matching transformer reduces the feedpoint of about 100Ω to match the 50Ω coax feeder. The antenna, when arranged as shown, results in vertically polarized signals; if it is moved around through 90° so that the feed point is at the bottom of the square, the signals will be horizontally polarized. Mount on a window broadly facing the most desired direction; the window glass will give little attenuation and results outwards should be much the same as an outdoor quad element antenna mounted at the same height. This form of construction could also be used to experiment with fractal designs. There is plenty of room for further exploitation of loops on VHF/UHF.

Colin Harlow, G8BTK, writes: "For many years I have experimented with various forms and types of antennas for VHF and UHF. This interest more than paid off, as some eight years ago we moved into a small flat with no possibility of an outdoor or loft antenna. Accordingly I have constructed, for various applications, many types, shapes and sizes of antennas suitable for use indoors.

"My main 50MHz antenna is a 20in loop of 9.5in wide cooper strip over a 48in square ground plane, mounted on a microphone stand. The loop is horizontally positioned over the ground plane. I have worked more than 30 counties and over 150 squares covering from North Africa to North Norway, Stornaway, etc, using a genuine 9 watts SSB from an FT680R.

"For 144MHz, a 6in diameter loop of 3.5in wide copper strip is used, with a tube 19.5in long and 3in diameter of wire mesh in addition. Also in use are some resonant 'delta-type' loops for 50 and 144MHz and flat resonant 'discs' for 144MHz and 70cm. These antennas may be mounted for either horizontal or vertical polarization. Some of these are shown in the photo opposite.

"I feel that small loops for the VHF/UHF bands could help many people who, like myself, have no hope of erecting antennas other than indoors - in my case at the end of my bedroom!"

Fractal & Log Periodics

Extracted from 'Technical Topics', *Radio Communication*, June 1999

FRACTAL & LOG PERIODICS UPDATE

FRACTAL ANTENNAS have figured prominently in recent *TT*s (April and June 1998, and January 1999) and I note that by the time these notes appear a poster paper 'Printed fractal antennas' will have been presented at this year's 'IEE Conference on Antennas & Propagation' (University of York, 31 March to 1 April) by R J Langley and R Breden of the University of Kent, showing that investigation into these antennas has spread across the Atlantic.

Meanwhile, Professor 'Chip' Cohen, N1IR, of Boston University, who has done so much to develop fractal antennas, writes: "Research continues to be heated at the fractal front. Although most hams have an especial interest in the shrinking ability of fractals as antennas, another salient aspect has been resolved which

ANTENNA TOPICS

is most likely to affect much antenna use in the future.

"Dr Hohlfeld and I have just published an article in the journal *Fractals*, effectively revisiting the notion of what makes a log periodic frequency independent, that is, having the same gain, impedance, and pattern over a large wavelength range. I had previously shown that very broad bandwidths are ascribable to all fractals, but many were confused why there was changing gain over the very broad bandwidth.

"The new surprise is not that log periodics are fractal (a point I first published in the 1995 *Communications Quarterly* article) but that everyone missed, for over 42 years, the true motivator of this important antenna behavior. We find that Maxwell's equations require that an antenna has symmetry about a point of origin and self-similarity (of fractals), in order to be frequency independent. Log periodics become strictly a subclass of the overall family of frequency independent - fractal - antennas. Commensurately, not all fractal antennas will be frequency independent. The origin symmetry is just as vital, an 'A and B' situation.

"What this leaves us with is a huge variety of potentially useful frequency independent antennas - which are not log periodic. We have a new era of antenna development ahead of us for frequency independence - and a new independence from log periodic construction constraints."

It was the introduction of the non-harmonically related WARC bands at 18 and 24MHz that gave amateurs a special interest in frequency-independent antenna arrays and induced a number to tackle the by no means insignificant problems of constructing large periodic arrays, with their need for many elements in order to obtain forward gains comparable to those provided by far fewer Yagi elements. If it proves in practice that new forms of fractal antennas can provide similar frequency independence with or without significant forward gain but without so many constructional constraints, then indeed the new work by N1IR and his colleagues would seem to open up most interesting possibilities.

Here & There: Loops

Extracted from 'Technical Topics', *Radio Communication*, July 1999

HERE & THERE

IN WHAT I HAD hoped would be a wind-up item on compact tuned transmitting loops [*TT*, May 1999, pp 60-61], I quoted Dr Belrose, VE2CV, as writing "we must remember to take into account the effect of the output impedance of the RF power amplifier, since for maximum power transfer the output or source impedance is the complex conjugate of the antenna's impedance (reference Belrose, VE2CV; Maxwell, W2DU; and Rauch, W8JI; *Communications Quarterly*, Fall 1997, pp25-48)." At the time, I had a feeling that this statement would be disputed and sure enough Bob Pearson, G4FHU, and Dr Andrew Smith, G4OEP, have expressed the opinion that VE2CV has mis-applied the maximum power transfer theorem, thus perhaps unknowingly re-opening one of the long-lasting disputes that have persisted

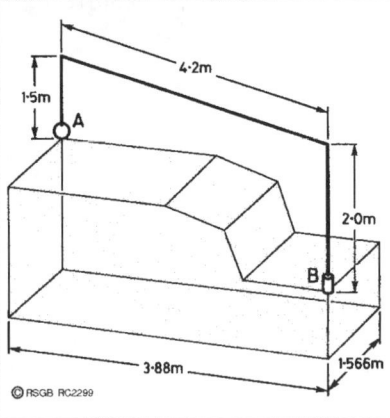

Fig 3: Configuration of the vehicle-mounted loop antenna for NVIS operation, developed and evaluated at Liverpool University by G0GSF *et al*. Generic Algorithm/NEC-2 simulation shows that optimum results were achieved when a capacitor is positioned at point B with a single RF source at point A.

for years among the leading technical boffins of our hobby as to the validity of the conjugate matching theory when applied to power amplifiers. The contrary view was first brought to my notice by one of my former IBA colleagues, Tony Harwood, G4HHZ. It eventually led to the ARRL removing references to conjugate load impedance matching from the *ARRL Handbook* and declining to publish articles by Dr Belrose and others protesting at their action. All I will do here is refer readers to the long (23-page) article in *Communications Quarterly* sited above, and in which such eminent engineer-authors as VE2CV, W2DU and W8JI argue strongly and in great detail for their belief in the validity of conjugate matching as applied to matching antennas to RF power amplifiers. This is a controversy into which I have no intention of entering at this time!

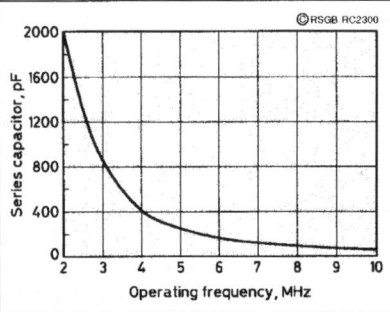

Fig 4: Capacitor values for optimum radiation toward zenith at frequencies from 2 to 10MHz. At 10MHz the percentage of power radiated towards the zenith increased from under 20% with a single source to about 35% with either dual, in-phase sources or with a single source plus series capacitor.

FOR THOSE interested in the use of military-type vehicle transmitting loops as developed at Liverpool University under Dr Brian Austin, G0GSF (see for example: 'The Application of Characteristic-Mode Techniques to Vehicle-Mounted NVIS Antennas' by Brian A Austin and Kevin P Murray, *IEEE Antennas and Propagation Magazine*, Vol 40, No 1, February 1998), attention is drawn to a further contribution 'Genetic algorithm optimisation of vehicle-mounted loop antenna for NVIS' by B A Austin and Wen-Chung Liu (*Electronics Letters*, Vol 35, No4, 18th February 1999) in which a series capacitor with one rather than the two feedpoints in the earlier model is used to restore the uniform current distribution as the frequency approaches first resonance, as is likely for day-time operation and typical loop dimensions. This ensures the radiation of as much energy as possible towards the zenith, highly desirable for NVIS operation: **Figs 3, 4**.

An overview of 'Short-haul Communications Using NVIS HF Radio' by S J Burgess and N E Evans (*Electronics & Communication Engineering Journal*, April 1999, pp95-104) includes an assessment of results using a 6793kHz NVIS simplex link over a 42km path to a monitoring receiver at the University of Ulster's Jordanstown campus. The paper provides advice on the use of typical horizontal wire antennas at low heights, as widely used by amateurs on 3.5 and 7MHz, and various amateur radio publications are listed in an extensive list of references, perhaps not surprising since Dr Noel Evans is presumably GI4BDR.

Efficient Short Meanders

Extracted from 'Technical Topics', *Radio Communication*, August 1999

EFFICIENT SHORT MEANDER ANTENNAS

IF YOU WERE asked to put up a 14MHz resonant dipole antenna with an overall span of just 3ft (1m) with a 2:1 SWR bandwidth of over 5 per cent of the centre frequency and a measured radiation efficiency of some 80 per cent, or a 21MHz monopole some 17in high over a 3ft by 4ft ground plane with a measured impedance of some 22Ω, you would probably regard such a request as asking for the moon. Such performance would seem to fly in the face of the classical theory of electrically short antenna elements. The trick, it seems, is to make the elements physically long but folded repeatedly into a short span, with for example a construction resembling the old caged dipole but with the short sections in series rather than parallel. This technique is described by Thomas J

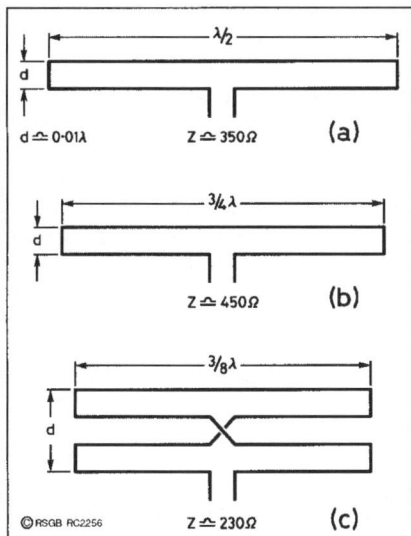

Fig 1: Three of the many folded-dipole antennas developed by Dr Kraus, W8JK, in the 1940s. (a) The conventional half-wave folded dipole with a resistive input impedance of about 300-350Ω. (b) The longer three-quarter-wave dipole; and (c) the shorter three-eighth-wave folded dipole.

Warnagiris and Thomas J Minardo of the Southwest Research Institute, San Antonio, Texas in 'Performance of a Meandered Line as an Electrically Small Transmitting Antenna' (*IEEE Trans on Antennas and Propagation*, December 1998, pp 1797-1801). The techniques they describe would seem to open the way for the erection of LF/MF/HF antennas at sites where space will not support a conventional resonant antenna without incurring the restricted bandwidth and low efficiency normally associated with compact high-Q antennas such as magnetic loops.

The idea of multiple folding of elements is not new. Dr Kraus, W8JK, long ago described a three-eighth wave folded dipole and monopole, and these were included in *TT* back in May, 1971: see **Fig 1** and **Fig 2**. There was also an ingenious *Radio Handbook* system based on the 3/8-wave folded element that could be switched to form an antenna resonant at half the frequency, eg for 7MHz and 3.5MHz, fed with 600Ω open line: **Fig 3**. But, even earlier, there had stuck

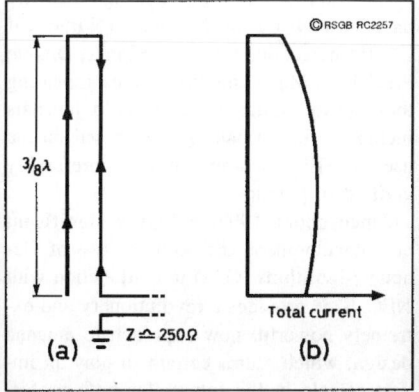

Fig 2: The three-eighth-wave folded monopole fed against ground. The resistive input impedance of about 250Ω is much higher than the conventional quarter-wave monopole.

in my memory an article I had read a few months after receiving my G3VA licence: 'Improving the Performance of Short Aerials' by M J Heavyside, G2QM (*The T&R Bulletin*, January 1939, p4). This described an antenna for the (then) 1.7MHz band, comprising 15ft of wire fed from a Collins pi-network tuner and going up to an attic. This, as might be expected, gave a relatively poor performance. But G2QM then added at the end of the 15ft wire some 120ft of 18SWG cotton-covered wire "wound in a zig-zag fashion on nails spaced six inches apart, driven into two beams situated five feet apart". This form of non-inductive 'loading' greatly improved results with his 7 watts (DC input) of AM phone. Reports increased from 3 to 5 S points, compared with the 15ft wire alone. Two other local amateurs, G6KU and G8CB, carried out tests with similar antennas and both reported gains in signal strength, particularly on reception. G2QM wrote: "When the 100ft outside aerial was compared with the loaded roof-space aerial, the signal-to-noise ratio of the indoor aerial was found to be so much better that it is now being used in preference to the outdoor one." He also tried the antenna on 3.7MHz, reducing the length of the zig-zag wire to 60ft: "Results on this band were found to be just as good, especially as regards reception."

Unhappily, all British amateur licences were withdrawn on 1 September 1939, before I and possibly others had much opportunity of trying out G2QM's ideas, and by 1946 they had been put on the back-burner. It is only in recent years that there has been increasing interest in the use of such meander line elements to reduce the overall span of resonant dipole antennas, reflected several times in *TT*.

The recent *IEEE Trans Ant & Prop* paper takes meandered elements a step further. The introduction reads: "At its operating frequency, an electrically small antenna is much shorter than a quarter wavelength. It has been occasionally pointed out that such an antenna, free of dissipation, could take from a radio wave and deliver to a load an amount of power independent of the size of the antenna. But the characteristics expected of an electrically small antenna are low-radiation resistance and large reactance and, therefore, very small instantaneous bandwidth with respect to the impedance of normal radio equipment. It's the matching of the antenna impedance to the radio equipment that can significantly affect the overall system performance. This is especially important for transmitting antennas, since a good impedance match is essential for maximum power transfer and hence efficient radiation."

The abstract of this interesting paper, apparently with amateur radio involvement, emphasises: "For antennas to radiate at maximum efficiency, their dimensions must be of the same order as the radiated wavelength. At frequencies below 30MHz, antennas with efficient radiation are often too large for mobile and portable applications. Smaller antennas can be made to radiate efficiently by use of matching networks. For convenience and ease of adjustment, these networks are usually placed between the transmitter and the antenna input, but it has been found that for best radiation efficiency, matching network elements should be placed at points on the antenna structure. Unfortunately, such matching networks must be tuned for each transmitting frequency, and when mounted on the antenna, they cannot easily be tuned. A meander element antenna was found to present some electrical and mechanical properties allowing convenient placement of tuning elements when configured as an electrically small transmit-

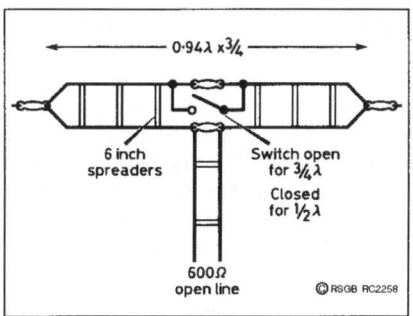

Fig 3: An adaptation of the Kraus three-quarter-wave dipole, which can be switched to operate on twice the frequency. For example with L = 98ft, the antenna is resonant on 14MHz with the switch closed and on 7MHz with the switch open.

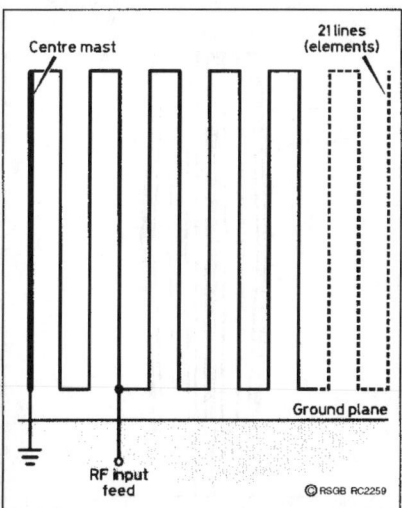

Fig 4: Electrical configuration of a very short multi-element meander monopole antenna with a height of only 17.25in with the 21 elements connected as a continuous single wire.

ting antenna. Some simplified design guidelines were derived from experimental data."

One technique for increasing the terminal resistance (maximum current point) and, therefore radiation efficiency, is antenna folding. This technique is beneficial to radiation resistance without decreasing antenna band-

ANTENNA TOPICS

width. It was shown in 1958 that capacitive top loading and folding may be combined to produce a small broad-band antenna with high-radiation resistance.

The authors emphasise that the important factor provided by a folded structure is that the cancellation of opposite polarity currents from the various elements generally results in a higher average impedance along the folded element as the number of folds increases: "What apparently has not been heavily investigated is the effect on radiation resistance of electrically small antennas of many folds. A meander antenna is an extension of the basic folded antenna to include a large number of folded elements in various linear patterns." They point out that an interesting property of meander antennas is the number of resonant modes beyond the lowest resonant frequency [It could be argued that meander antennas are closely related to fractal antennas - *G3VA*].

Fig 4 shows the electrical configuration of a prototype 20.1MHz meander monopole antenna much shorter than a quarter-wave high investigated at the Southwest Research Institute. Mechanical implementation of this antenna is outlined in **Fig 5**. The input impedance of this 17.5in high antenna with 21 elements of No26 AWG wire was tested over a 3ft by 4ft ground plane. Measured imped-

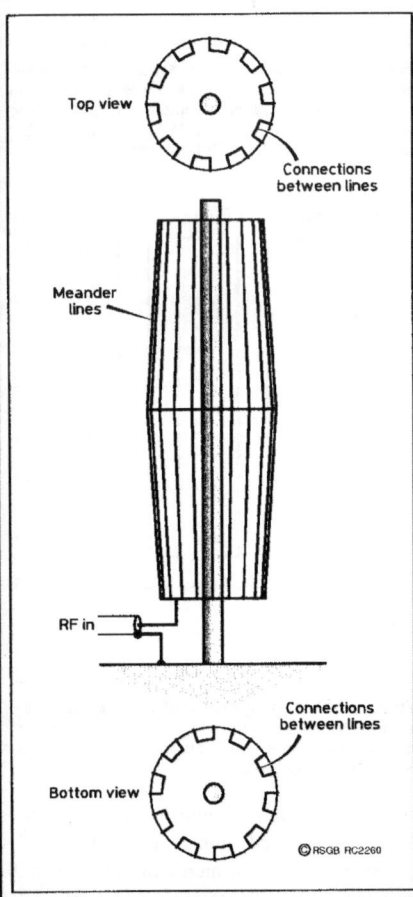

Fig 5: Typical mechanical structure of a meander monopole. The discs and central spacer ring or disc should be made from material offering good RF insulation.

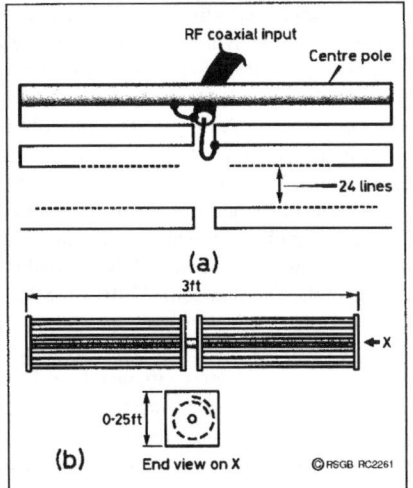

Fig 6: A 14.2MHz meander dipole with a span of only 3ft.

ance at first resonance (20.1MHz) was 21.9Ω, much higher than would be expected from an 0.03λ monopole. The bottom fold feed points were usually at points 10-20% of the total antenna length and produced a 2:1 VSWR bandwidth of about 2-4% of centre frequency (about twice as wide as bandwidths reported for reactively loaded monopoles 0.06λ long).

Another prototype antenna investigated was a 14.2MHz dipole with an overall span of only 3ft. A 2:1 VSWR bandwidth was measured over 6.5% of the centre frequency: **Fig 6**. When tested for radiation efficiency using the Wheeler method, this antenna exhibited a radiation efficiency of 80%, much higher than would be expected for a loaded 0.05λ dipole.

The authors write: "Although meandered antenna structures have been investigated by others, there have been no known attempts to construct practical meandered antennas for tuneable applications. SwRI has developed several basic meander structures that lend themselves to switch tuning by the low-loss connection or disconnection of elements at various points on the antenna to optimise performance. Practical RF switches can be solid-state devices such as PIN diodes, FETs, or even mechanical switches. The grounded mast of a meander monopole antenna can be a high-strength conductive mast that can be directly connected to the ground plane, offering also some protection from lightning strikes. Wide spacing between the elements and high RF voltage points allows transmission of high-power without arcing. . . Dipole configurations can be constructed consisting of two monopole meandered structures end-to-end, fed through a balun or unbalanced at their common point."

The *IEEE Trans* paper notes that more work is needed to characterise the many possible meander antenna variants. It would seem to me the one possibility could be a 1.8MHz antenna with possibly a 30ft (10m) metal support pole with a circular RF insulated disc at the top and then a series of zigzag wires down to insulated stakes, rather in the form of an umbrella antenna but with the guy-like wires forming a single resonant mast plus wire, rather than forming a capacitive top-cap. The total wire-plus-metal mast length would be best determined by trial and error, and would need to be rather longer than an electrical quarter-wave due to its folded form. There would also seem to be the possibility of using this approach for a 136kHz Marconi-type antenna (a resonant antenna would presumably require over 500m of wire!) In this case, the higher the support pole and the more folded elements the better - but it could prove more efficient than most of the antennas now in use on this interesting and antenna-challenging band. At the other extreme, the meander antenna has possibilities for mobile or transportable operation on 1.8MHz, 3.5MHz or on the HF bands in restricted spaces.

Yagis Using Genetic Algorithms

Extracted from 'Technical Topics', *Radio Communication*, September 1999

YAGI ANTENNAS USING GENETIC ALGORITHMS

FOR OVER at least a decade it has been widely recognised by both professional and amateur antenna designers that a major design-aid has resulted from widespread use of the Numerical Electromagnetics Code (NEC) based on Harrison's Method of Moments (MoM), permitting computer analysis of projected designs while still in the planning stage. NEC determines the current distributions on each wire of a selected antenna design and from these, the radiation characteristics. NEC has been progressively refined with recent software packages, usually based on NEC2 or NEC-2D (Numerical Electro-magnetics Code, Version 2, Double Precision). Many antenna designs appearing these days in the amateur radio journals include radiation patterns etc, based on the use of NEC software on PCs, preferably verified in practice.

Since about 1997, a highly significant new development has been the use of Genetic Algorithms (GAs) in conjunction with NEC. This provides a revolutionary and extremely powerful new approach to antenna design, which seems certain to play an important role in the future, for both professional and amateur designs, including, particularly, multi-element Yagi arrays. The following notes are based largely on three recent papers: Two articles by Dr Richard Formato [WW1RF, former K1POO] in *Electronics World* 'Genes and Yagis' (August 1998, pp646-648) and 'Improving VHF Yagis' (June 1999, pp505-509); and a conference paper 'An Optimized Shaped Yagi-Uda Array Using The Genetic Algorithm' by Dr Brian A Austin [G0GSF/ZS6BKW] and Wen-Chung Liu, both of the University of Liverpool (National Conference on Antennas and Propagation, 30 March - 1 April 1999, IEE Conference Publication No 461, pp245-247).

The aim here is primarily to show how GAs can improve antennas, even for those of us who are computer illiterates, rather than to attempt to explain how or why GAs work and how to use them. WW1RF looks at this question in the first article by comparing four 12-element Yagi antennas designed using genetic algorithms. In effect, this is done by the computer searching a 'decision space', which is defined by specifying minimum and maximum values for each antenna parameter. He stresses that only antennas falling within these limits are allowable solutions to the optimum solution, a characteristic of GAs that gives an antenna designer exceptional flexibility.

The process is introduced in the Liverpool paper as follows: "Until recently, traditional techniques used the Method of Moments (MoM) to determine the current distributions on each wire of a selected antenna configuration and, from these, the radiation characteristics were calculated and compared with a target specification. The procedure is iterative and both experience and some appropriate candidate configurations are usually required to ensure success. By contrast, the GA is based on the processes of natural selection and the 'survival of the fittest' in an

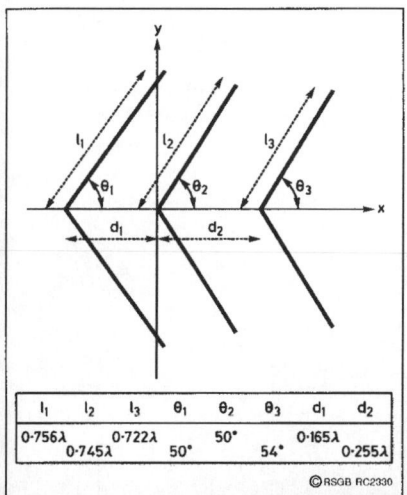

Fig 5: The optimised Vee-shaped Yagi-Uda antenna (L2 driven element) designed at the University of Liverpool by Brian Austin, G0GSF and Wen-Chung Liu, using the Genetic Algorithm. Computed gain of 12.1dBi. The linear elements of about 1.5λ do not present the constructional problems presented by curved elements of earlier 'optimum' designs, yet provide higher gain and directivity.

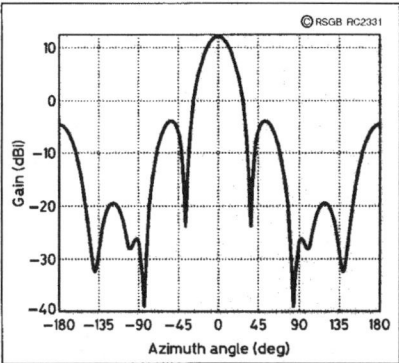

Fig 6: Radiation pattern of the optimized Vee-shaped Yagi-Uda using linear elements.

evolutionary system, which leads iteratively to the desired specification with minimal foresight or pre-conditioning on the part of the designer. In using the GA, all design parameters are encoded into a string of binary bits known, unsurprisingly, as a chromosome, while each parameter is represented by several bits - the genes. The genes are the basic building blocks of the GA and map directly to the associated real, physical properties of the antenna. The immense power of the technique is its ability to satisfy a performance criterion without any a prior knowledge of candidate configurations, and the facility for finding the global optimum result."

The paper shows how a simple three-element Vee-shaped antenna with the elements roughly 1.5λ can achieve markedly better directivity than the elaborate element-curvature used for the Liang/Cheng (1983) or the Landstorfer (1977) antennas. The Landstorfer design with its curved 1.5λ elements has been described a number of times in *TT* (most recently June 1998, p59, Fig 7) in which it has been noted that a VHF antenna of this type, reported in 1982 by Dr Landstorfer, provided a forward gain of 11.5dBi, sidelobe attenuation better than 20dB and a front-to-back ratio of 26dB.

The Liverpool work with the GA produced an optimized array which would be relatively simple and straightforward to construct, at least for 50MHz and above (or possibly below 50MHz in the form of a fixed array). As shown in **Fig 5**, the GA-optimized array comprised three, linear elements with included angles of the order of 100°, in marked contrast to the elaborate element curvature that was found necessary in the Liang (11.8dBi) and Landstorfer (11.5dBi) arrays.

Fig 6 shows a plot of the gain against the azimuth angle of the Liverpool array, showing a maximum gain of 12.1dBi - some 0.6dB better than the Landstorfer design and 0.3dB better than that of Liang. The half-power beamwidth meets the specified 30°; the front-to-back ratio 16.6dB and front-to-side ratio 15.9dB. The computed input impedance is given as 20.4+j19.9Ω.

WW1RF's 'Genes and Yagis' article compares four 12-element Yagis designed using GA. He points out that each element in a Yagi-Uda array has three design parameters: length, spacing, and radius. The minimum/maximum range of each parameter can be set on an element-by-element basis, although the usual approach is to restrict all elements in the same way. For the four arrays described the range of elements (in terms of wavelength) were reflector 0.35 - 0.65; driven element 0.35-0.60; and directors 0.3-0.6; element spacing 0.05-0.5, limiting the longest boom to 5.5λ. For the first three designs, element radius was constant at 0.003369λ. His fourth design allowed the driven-element radii to range from 0.001 to 0.0075λ. His first array was a sub-optimum design to illustrate that a GA does not produce a single 'best' design, but instead produces a group of designs, with each design ranked from best to worst. This feature, he claims, may be very useful, since even sub-optimal designs may be attractive in some instances.

His second design (**Fig 7** and **Table 1**) provided a maximum gain of 15.26dBi with an F/B ratio of 20.5dB and an input impedance of 19.8+j0.4Ω. Incidentally, his fourth design with slightly lower gain (14.53dBi) had an input impedance of 48.8-j0.1Ω, resulting in an SWR of only 1.02 when fed with 50Ω cable. Number 3 was gain maximised (15.86dBi) but had an input impedance of 5.3+j179.3Ω, making it unsuitable for use with a coaxial feeder.

In his later article 'Improving VHF Yagis', WW1RF uses GA to design a 12-element VHF Yagi antenna suitable for use with a 300Ω open-wire transmission line. He emphasises that high-impedance Yagis can improve VHF antenna system performance, because of the much lower attenuation of open-wire line (typically 0.25dB/100ft at 144MHz). The widely used RG-8 foam-dielectric coaxial cable has a loss of about 2.1dB/100ft). He writes: "The easiest way to take advantage of the extremely low attenuation of open wire line is to design a good Yagi with a high input impedance. One approach is to use a half-wave folded dipole as the driven element. Another is to increase the input impedance of the usual centre-fed linear dipole driven element by proper place-

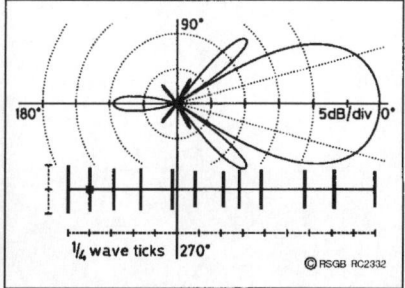

Fig 7: One of the four VHF 12-element antennas developed by Dr Formato, WW1RF, using the genetic algorithm. See text and Table 1.

ANTENNA TOPICS

ment of the array's parasitic elements. His design matches 300Ω line. The positions, lengths and spacings of the 'directors' are certainly unconventional: **Fig 8**. For full details refer to *EW*, June 1999.

Yagi Genetic Optimizer version 2 used by WW1RF is a freeware program, available on the web (Ray Anderson, WB6TPU's 'NEC Archive' web site, URL: http://www.qsl.net/wb6tpu). This uses NEC-2D, also available on the web or directly from the Applied Computational Electromagnetics Society (ACES) Attn; Dr Richard W Adler, ACES Executive Officer, ECDE Dept., Code ECAB, Naval Postgraduate School, 833 Dyer Road, Room 437, Monterey, CA 93943-5121, USA.

One thing seems certain, genetic algorithms are going to play an important role in future antenna designs and may result in some unexpected variations on traditional designs. And at least genetically-modified antennas present no new health or environmental hazards!

Element	Length	Spacing
1 (reflector)	0.5006	0.0000
2 (driven element)	0.4549	0.2388
3 (first director)	0.4388	0.2671
4 (2nd dir.)	0.4318	0.3006
5 (3rd dir.)	0.4141	0.3641
6 (4th dir.)	0.3624	0.2582
7 (5th dir.)	0.3718	0.3218
8 (6th dir.)	0.4012	0.1806
9 (7th dir.)	0.4200	0.2424
10 (8th dir.)	0.4035	0.4876
11 (9th dir.)	0.4176	0.3218
12 (10th dir.)	0.3471	0.4559

Table 1: WW1RF's 2nd design. Dimensions in terms of wavelength.

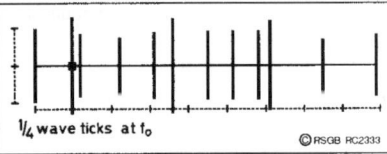

Fig 8: The 'high-impedance' VHF 12-element antenna developed by Dr Formato, WW1RF, using the genetic algorithm and described in *Electronics World*, June 1999. The 300Ω input impedance enables the array to be fed from low-loss open-wire line.

Index

A

Absorbing elements 190, 197, 202
Active aerials *(see Receive aerials)*
AX-special multiband aerial 105

B

Backfire 10, 12, 76, 226
Baluns in reverse 84
Bandwidth, increasing *(see also Broadband)* . 227
Basics 84, 226, 239, 245, 302
Beverage *(see Receive aerials)*
Beam *(see also Quad, Rhombic and Yagi)*
    Compact. 85
    Two-element HF 242
    With Multi-band element 143
Birdcage aerial *(See G4ZU)*
Bi-square array 266
Bobtail curtain 35, 293, 297, 367
Bow-tie 92, 118
BRD-zapper 264, 277
Broadband 2, 9, 13
    Australian sloper. 211
    Biconical. 14, 225
    Conical. 94
    Dipoles 50, 61, 199, 238
    Discone 94
    Double bazooka dipole. 109, 112, 116
    Fractal *(see Fractal antennas)*
    Impedance loaded kite antennas. 355
    Log periodic. 59, 174, 214, 216, 371
    Loops. 203
    Radials. 289
    Resistive loaded 243
    Travelling wave dipole
        . . . . *(see Travelling wave antennas)*
Bruce array 16
Butterfly monoband beam 133, 197

C

Capacitive loading *(see Loading, capacitive)*
Chireix-Mesny 117, 261, 262, 263
Choke balun 296
Circularly polarized antennas 210, 213
Claw antenna 215, 235
Close coupled resonators 318, 325
Coaxial antennas
    (see also Travelling wave antennas),128, 325, 326
Colinear array coaxial *(see also Verticals)*
. . . . 67, 69, 244, 277
Compact beams *(see Mini)*
Composite T, all band 98, 101

Computer modelling 256, 265, 317, 336
Comudipole *(see Dipole)*
Controlled current distribution 179
Controlled feeder radiation 354
Counterpoise *(see Earthing)*
Corrosion 272, 275
Crossed field antenna 257

D

DDRR (Hula-hoop)
    . . . . 5, 6, 7, 13, 23, 24, 25, 58, 68, 155, 333
Delta loop *(see Loops)*
Dipole
    7MHz, using on 21MHz. 288, 295
    All-band. 56, 61, 155, 163
    Aluminium foil. 49
    Balanced and coaxial cable 147
    Balcony 192
    Bent 346
    Bi-band 146
    Broadband *(see Broadband)*
    Capacitively loaded. 26
    Capactively tuned. 83
    Centre-fed, the flexible 214
    Comudipole, PA0SE 303, 309
    Condensed rotary. 5
    End-fed for handhelds. 264, 269
    Flexible. 161
    Folded 81, 234, 241, 311, 313, 370
    Full-wave, ... 7, 328
    Harmonic, short loaded. 253
    Helical *(see Helical antennas)*
    Hibernating, VK2ABQ. 201
    Inverted V *(see Inverted-V)*
    Multiband 8, 31, 88, 148, 152, 205, 353, 299,
    . . . . 301, 302, 310, 339
    Of delight 219, 221
    Off-centre-fed (OCFD) multiband 268, 340, 342, 350
    One and a half wavelength 63
    One third Lambda. 364
    Resonant feedline. 341, 348
    Shortened 53, 199, 213
    Short-span 3.5MHz. 62
    Sleeve 131, 134
    Stacked, folded, 28MHz 62
    Switched. 162
    Tetrahedral. 346
    Trapped, WARC bands. 221
    Unidirectional 71
    Versus loops. 227
    Vertical *(see Vertical, dipoles)*
    With counterpoise. 338

v

ANTENNA TOPICS

Diversity 115
DL7AB multiband 5
Double-delta
    HF 122
    VHF and UHF 28
Double tuning fork beam 102
Doublet, centre-fed 221
Driven array, unidirectional 173
DX antenna
    For 1.8MHz 352
    For 3.5MHz 259
    For 7MHz 261

E

Earthing, radials and counterpoises 2, 10, 21,
          46, 87, 136, 169, 170, 186, 187, 224,
        253, 254, 255, 263, 274, 279, 281, 287,
        289, 296, 298, 302, 326, 336, 338, 360
Earth, supergain or attenuator 114
Echelon or Model C 48
Efficiency *(see Gain)*
Elevated feed *(see Verticals)*
Elements of non-uniform cross-section ... 223
End-fed *(see also Long wire antennas and Dipole)*
    And the Zepp *(see Zepp)*
    Multiband 52
    Three-eighths wave 52
    W3EDP 213, 218
    Windom *(see Windom)*

F

Feeder
    300-ohm, matching a beam to 54
    Ribbon *(see Ribbon)*
Feed points and radiation patterns 56
Fractal antennas 359, 361, 362, 365, 371
Franklin Uniform 27

G

G0GSF dipole *(see Dipole, multiband)*
G2PL special *(see Quad, German)*
G4ABS multiband for limited spaces 79
G4ZU
    Birdcage aerial 2, 6, 11, 75
    Ferrite bead five-band 4
G5RV *(see also Dipole, multiband)* ... 178, 180, 345
G6CJ special 70
G6XN multiband elements 103, 106
G8GS two-band antenna 258
G8ON multiband aerial 58, 193, 194, 352
G8PO unidirectional array 265
Gain 184, 290, 294, 324, 353, 357
Gamma deived stub match 90
Ground *(see Earthing)*
Ground-plane *(see Verticals, and Earthing)*
Guidance, practical 147

H

Half-square aerial 89, 178
HB9CV portable beam 103
Height of antennas 217
Helical antennas 105, 270, 322, 343
Helicone 21
Helix
    Normal mode 197, 242
    Toroidal *(see Toroidal antenna)*
Hula-hoop *(see DDRR)*

I

Impedance, feedpoint 108
Indoor antennas 191, 221, 285, 300, 306
Insulation 190
Inverted-L *(See Verticals)*
Inverted-V 2, 110, 111, 115, 117
Invisible 209, 306

J

J-pole 231, 313, 317

K

KISS 193

L

Lazy Quad *(see Quad)*
LF *(see Long wave antennas)*
L-network for voltage fed aerials 39
Loading 249
    Capacitive 26, 82, 179, 256, 278
    Dielectric 93
    Ferrite 145
    Helical *(see Helical antennas)*
    Inductive 88
    Linear 247, 286
    Resistive *(see Broadband)*
    Spiral 93
    With folded dipole 308
    With loop 336
Log periodic *(see Broadband)*
Long wave antennas 224
Long wire antennas *(see also End-fed)*
    All-band terminated 70
    Some hints 69
    Upstairs operation, and 55
    VHF, on 116, 246
Loops *(see also Quad)*
    Active *(see Receive aerials)*
    And dipoles 222, 227
    Broadband *(see Broadband)*
    Delta 28, 32, 42, 75, 77, 158,
          171, 180, 220, 221, 234, 265, 267
    Feeding 79, 84, 265
    Groundplane 195
    Half-delta 200
    Horizontal 186, 188, 265, 283, 291, 334

Loft mounted. 42, 300
Long. 205
Medium sized 122, 140
Mobile 28
Multiband 63, 72, 74, 193.197, 212
Polygonal 163
Radiation patterns. 271
Receiving *(see **Receiving aerials**)*
Thin wire 24
Transmitting 19, 22, 23, 47, 162, 172,
. . . . 209, 228, 232, 233, 260, 262,
. . . . 279, 351, 356, 366, 370, 372
Vertically polarized 78
VHF 98, 307
Low angle, 7MHz, G6XN 34
Low profile antennas for 1.8 and 3.5MHz. 157, 160

M

Making antennas work 153
Marconi *(see also **Verticals**)*
Earths and 298
Grounded 3
Quarter-wave 317
U-shaped, 1.8MHz 54
Maria Maluca multiband 6
Matching technique, dual band 108
Meander antennas *(see also **Fractal antennas**)*
. . . . 286, 372
Medium haul paths, antennas for
(see Radiation angle)
Mesny *(see **Chireix-Mesny**)*
Metal fatigue 25, 258, 308
Microwave aerials 21, 82, 175, 323
Mini-antenna, 3.5MHz, ZL1AYN 27
Mini-beam ideas 118, 129
Mobile aerials 28, 53, 65, 230, 237, 258,
. . . . 320, 335, 369, 372
Monopole, variable length 33
MSJ antenna *(see **J-pole**)*
Multibander, lazy man's 270
Multiband or allband for HF? 310
Multiwire elements 311

N

NVIS *(see **Radiation angles, vertical**)*

O

One-third multiband 4
Optimum-shaped antennas 184, 188, 190, 209

P

Polarisation
Circular *(see **Circularly polarized antennas**)*
DX, for 16
Gains and losses 44
Changing 67, 100
Vertical on HF. 165
Push-push-fed twin line antenna, G5IJ 329

Q

Quad 13
50-ohm. 288
Compact for 14 and 21MHz 130
Cubical. 30
Delta loop *(see **Loops**, Delta)*
Element, phantom stub. 151
Feeding 79, 84
For WARC bands 365
German 183
Horizontally elongated. 204
IP, G3LHZ. 113
Lazy. 26
Levy 58, 61
Low cost mini 95
Loop. 293
Miniaturized elements. 107
Multiband 72
Reflectors, tuning 80
Simple, window-pane 59
Switch rotatable 134, 136, 137, 138, 140, 142, 144
Three-band single element 72
Versus Yagi 145
Quadplane. 200

R

Radials *(see **Earthing**)*
Radiation angles, vertical. 36, 45, 65, 99, 100,
. . . . 250, 259, 315, 320
Radiation patterns 177, 271
Receive aerials
Active 18, 22, 23, 30, 32, 108, 109,
. . . . 166, 229, 282, 336
Beverage 39, 177, 305
Loops 66, 108, 119, 121, 236, 238,
. . . . 252, 282, 336, 362
Low noise, 1.8/3.5MHz 126
Superdirective arrays 139
Reflectors
Conical and parabolic. 323
Under dipoles. 49
Trigonal 219
Resonance, trimming aerials for 107
Resonant lengths 177
Rhombic 111, 126, 158, 162, 177, 242, 333
Half 337
Rhomboid, dual for UHF. 343
Ribbon feeder
Aerials from 1, 3
Simple aerials using 1
Wet weather. 60
RMCS compact VHF antenna 124

S

Series-phase antenna. 120
Simple antenna, DX and the 159, 180
Size, reducing the. 127
Skeleton slot. 29

ANTENNA TOPICS

Sleeve dipole *(see Dipole)*
Slim Jim *(see J-pole)*
Sloper 209, 211
    Yagi 200
    Zig-zag 127
Slotted cylinder, stretching and 175
Slowing the wave 206
Sperrtopfs *(see Dipoles, sleeve and Verticals, sleeve)*
Stretched VHF/UHF antennas 167, 168
Stubs, multiband aerials using 3, 31, 32
Supports, elastic 101

T

T2FD 1, 31,. 230, 231
Titfer antenna, G4BWE 123
Top band with ATU 229
Toroidal antenna 198, 309
Transmission lines, matching with 51, 57
Trapped aerials
    Two-band 11
    Multi-band vertical 33
Travelling-wave antennas 89, 185, 321
Trees
    As aerials 97
    As supports 208, 295
Trimming antennas 164
Turnstile for 144MHz 160

U

Unobtrusive antennas 191

V

Vee beam
    Sloping 47, 82
Verticals *(see also Earthing)*
    5/8-wave 220
    200-ohm 216
    All-band 37, 130, 132
    Base-fed 42
    Colinear, 144MHz 148, 277
    Dipoles 76, 207, 220
    Directional arrays 102, 165
    Elevated 254, 255, 257, 359
    Elevated feed 15, 17, 178
    Folded 241, 286
    Ground-plane 8, 10, 12,13, 38, 100, 169,
            170, 175, 176, 179, 189, 190, 195,
            202, 203, 210, 245, 273, 298
    Half-wave 4
    Helical *(see Helical antennas)*
    High angle, super-gain 65
    IGP, T and M antennas 196
    Impedance of 201
    Inverted ground-plane 34, 72, 94, 189, 196, 319, 354
    Inverted-L 43, 123
    Losses 296
    Multee 313, 315
    Multiband 33, 40, 70
    No radial *(see Verticals, sleeve)*
    PA0RCH short, for 1.8MHz 87, 93
    PA0RCH twin 112, 116
    Phased 39, 64, 156
    Short 181, 182, 187, 249, 360
    Six-band, G3SBI 254
    Sleeve 166, 248, 273, 276
    Spiral top loaded 93
    T antenna 131, 196, 294
    Thoughts on 170
    Triband 33, 45
    Two-band trap 11
    Umbrella, folded 90, 363
    Using roach pole and sailboard mast ... 231
    Zepp 4
Very low 99, 100
VHF/UHF antennas 7, 23, 24, 25, 28, 55, 58, 67,
        70, 83, 97, 98, 103, 111, 115, 116,
        123, 124, 125, 127, 134, 148, 155,
        158, 160,162, 167, 168, 182, 219,
        221, 230, 231, 246, 264, 269, 272,
        277, 286, 307, 313, 317, 343, 370
VK2ABQ
    Another compact 14MHz antenna 289, 311
    Mini-beam 118, 119, 136, 171
    Pseudo quad 96
    Triband beam 86, 91, 92, 114, 151, 153, 154
    Ultra mini beam 237
VS1AA *(see Windom)*

W

W3EDP *(see End-fed)*
W6BCX Multee 9
W8JK 57, 66, 172, 183, 264
Walkie-talkie aerials 24
Waterproofing *(see also Corrosion)* 316
Windom 1, 5, 68, 231, 247, 248, 275, 276
    Carolina 350, 354
Wires in parallel 216

Y

Yagi 12, 55, 124, 125, 127, 134, 137,
        145, 152, 165, 182, 201, 208,
        213, 219, 272, 284, 374

Z

Z-beam, 9M2CP 50
Zapper *(see BRD-zapper)*
Zepp 4, 212, 222, 251, 292
Zip-cord antennas 146
ZL special 17, 264
ZS6BKW dipole *(see Dipoles, multiband)*